Fodor's

ESSENTIAL
GREAT
BRITAIN

D0094739

Excerpted from *Essential England* and *Essential Scotland*.

WELCOME TO GREAT BRITAIN

Great Britain packs spectacular landscapes, as well as rich history, into the compact borders of England, Wales, and Scotland. From the southern coast up to the Highlands, its lush countryside and jagged mountains may surprise you. In London and other urban centers, explore iconic sights and great museums—and also discover cutting-edge cultural scenes that tweak tradition. Beyond the cities, ancient castles and pretty villages entice. Britain's iconic products and customs—from pubs to tartans—may travel the globe, but there's nothing like experiencing them firsthand.

TOP REASONS TO GO

★ **Hip Cities:** London's celebrated landmarks, Edinburgh's innovative festivals, and more.

★ **History:** Sites from Stonehenge to Stirling Castle bring the nation's past to life.

★ **Pubs:** For a pint or a chat, a visit to one of "Britain's living rooms" is essential.

★ **Landscapes:** Wooded hills, sparkling lakes, rugged mountains, wide-open moors.

★ **Idyllic Towns:** Cozy cottages with flower beds, pastel-painted seaside charmers.

★ **Great Walks:** In England's Lake District, Scotland's Highlands, and along the Welsh coast.

20 ULTIMATE EXPERIENCES

Great Britain offers terrific experiences that should be on every traveler's list. Here are Fodor's top picks for a memorable trip.

1 Oxford and Cambridge

England is home to these two prestigious universities, where you'll find centuries of history among ancient buildings and museums. Tour the accompanying towns via punting boats on local waterways. *(Ch. 6, 10)*

2 London

London is the beating heart of England, a world-class city whose museums, palaces, and iconic sights define the country for many. *(Ch. 2)*

3 Isle of Skye

With the misty Cuillin Mountains and rocky shores, Skye has few rivals among Scotland's islands for sheer loveliness. Links to Bonnie Prince Charlie add further allure. *(Ch. 19)*

4 Seafood

From salmon to oysters, enjoy the delicious fish and seafood from Britain's rivers, lakes, and the sea. Fried fish-and-chips are the ultimate British comfort food. *(Ch. 5, 17)*

5 Yorkshire

The stunning natural landscape of Yorkshire's moors and dales inspired the Brontës, and continues to attract hikers, cyclists, and nature-lovers. *(Ch. 11)*

6 Loch Lomond

Clear water and access to Edinburgh and Glasgow make Loch Lomond a coveted retreat. The Trossachs are the essence of the Highlands. *(Ch. 16)*

7 Glasgow

An urban renaissance has brought great shopping and nightlife to complement the city's rich architectural heritage and museums like the Kelvingrove. *(Ch. 14)*

8 The Cotswolds

Full of quaint English villages, the Cotswolds is one of the prettiest regions of the country, thanks to the stone cottages, famed gardens, and rural charm. *(Ch. 7)*

9 Castles

Castles dating from the medieval period to Victorian times are among Britain's glories, including Windsor in England, Dunnottar in Scotland, and Conwy in Wales. *(Ch. 17)*

10 Stratford-Upon-Avon

The birthplace of William Shakespeare offers plenty for fans of the Bard, including performances of his plays at the Royal Shakespeare Company. *(Ch. 7)*

11 Afternoon Tea

For a quintessential British ritual, enjoy a pot of tea served in bone china alongside finger sandwiches, fruit scones, and cakes. *(Ch. 2)*

12 Cardiff

As the capital of Wales, Cardiff is lively and charming, with plenty of castles, museums, and pubs to explore. *(Ch. 12)*

13 Golf

The home of golf, Scotland claims some of the world's most challenging holes but has courses for all levels, many in beautiful settings. *(Ch. 13–19)*

14 Snowdonia National Park

Experience the Welsh countryside at its most gorgeous and dramatic at Snowdonia National Park, home to the country's highest mountain. Hiking opportunities abound. *(Ch. 12)*

15 Glencoe

The wild beauty of Glencoe's craggy peaks and deep valley provided the background for a tragic massacre in 1692. Today the area is popular for outdoor activities. *(Ch. 19)*

16 Whisky Tours

From Speyside to Islay, whisky distilleries offer tours and tastings of Scotland's signature drink. Their often-spectacular settings are an added bonus. *(Ch. 13–19)*

17 Cathedrals

The cathedrals of Salisbury, Westminster, Canterbury, and York Minster, among others, are an essential part of England's urban landscapes and history. *(Ch. 2-11)*

18 Historic Pubs

The history of Britain's taverns and pubs is the history of the country itself. Grab a pint or a gin cocktail, and get to know how the locals live. *(Ch. 2)*

19 Edinburgh

Scotland's capital charms with its Royal Mile and Old Town, and events such as the Edinburgh International Festival and the Fringe keep areas like the Grassmarket lively. *(Ch. 13)*

20 Stonehenge

Awe-inspiring and mystical, Stonehenge is one of the most famous prehistoric sites in England, as well as one of history's most enduring mysteries. *(Ch. 4)*

Fodor's ESSENTIAL GREAT BRITAIN

Editorial: Douglas Stallings, *Editorial Director*; Margaret Kelly, Jacinta O'Halloran, *Senior Editors*; Kayla Becker, Alexis Kelly, Amanda Sadlowski, *Editors*; Teddy Minford, *Content Editor*; Rachael Roth, *Content Manager*

Design: Tina Malaney, *Design and Production Director*; Jessica Gonzalez, *Production Designer*

Photography: Jill Krueger, *Senior Photo Editor*

Maps: Rebecca Baer, *Senior Map Editor*; Mark Stroud (Moon Street Cartography), *Cartographers*

Production: Jennifer DePrima, *Editorial Production Manager*; Carrie Parker, *Senior Production Editor*; Elyse Rozelle, *Production Editor*

Business & Operations: Chuck Hoover, *Chief Marketing Officer*; Joy Lai, *Vice President and General Manager*; Stephen Horowitz, *Director of Business Development and Revenue Operations*; Tara McCrillis, *Director of Publishing Operations*

Public Relations and Marketing: Joe Ewaskiw, *Manager*; Esther Su, *Marketing Manager*

Writers: Robert Andrews, Nick Bruno, Jo Caird, Rhonda Carrier, Sally Coffey, Robin Gauldie, Michael Gonzalez, Kate Hughes, Sophie Ibbotson, Jack Jewers, Eilidh McCabe, James O'Neill, Toby Orton, Joseph Reaney, Rachael Rowe, Ellin Stein, Victoria Trott, Alex Wijeratna

Editors: Amanda Sadlowski (lead editor), Linda Cabasin, Debbie Harmsen, Salwa Jabado, Alexis Kelly, Denise Leto

Production Editor: Elyse Rozelle

2nd edition

ISBN 978–1–64097–082–3

ISSN 2373–9169

Library of Congress Control Number 2018950372

SPECIAL SALES

This book is available at special discounts for bulk purchases for sales promotions or premiums. For more information, e-mail SpecialMarkets@fodors.com.

PRINTED IN THE UNITED STATES OF AMERICA

10 9 8 7 6 5 4 3 2 1

CONTENTS

CONTENTS

CONTENTS

MAPS

CONTENTS

ABOUT THIS GUIDE

Fodor's Recommendations

Everything in this guide is worth doing—we don't cover what isn't—but exceptional sights, hotels, and restaurants are recognized with additional accolades. Fodor's Choice ★ indicates our top recommendations. Care to nominate a new place? Visit Fodors.com/contact-us.

Trip Costs

We list prices wherever possible to help you budget well. Hotel and restaurant price categories from **$** to **$$$$** are noted alongside each recommendation. For hotels, we include the lowest cost of a standard double room in high season. For restaurants, we cite the average price of a main course at dinner or, if dinner isn't served, at lunch. For attractions, we always list adult admission fees; discounts are usually available for children, students, and senior citizens.

Hotels

Our local writers vet every hotel to recommend the best overnights in each price category, from budget to expensive. Unless otherwise specified, you can expect private bath, phone, and TV in your room. *For expanded hotel reviews, visit Fodors.com.*

Top Picks
★ Fodor's Choice

Listings
✉ Address
✉ Branch address
☎ Telephone
📠 Fax
🌐 Website
✉ E-mail
🎫 Admission fee
🕒 Open/closed times
[M] Subway
✥ Directions or Map coordinates

Hotels & Restaurants
🏨 Hotel
🛏 Number of rooms
🍽 Meal plans
🍴 Restaurant
✍ Reservations
👔 Dress code
💳 No credit cards
[$] Price

Other
⇨ See also
☞ Take note
⛳ Golf facilities

Restaurants

Unless we state otherwise, restaurants are open for lunch and dinner daily. We mention dress code only when there's a specific requirement and reservations only when they're essential or not accepted. *For expanded restaurant reviews, visit Fodors.com.*

Credit Cards

The hotels and restaurants in this guide typically accept credit cards. If not, we'll say so.

EUGENE FODOR

Hungarian-born Eugene Fodor (1905–91) began his travel career as an interpreter on a French cruise ship. The experience inspired him to write *On the Continent* (1936), the first guidebook to receive annual updates and discuss a country's way of life as well as its sights. Fodor later joined the U.S. Army and worked for the OSS in World War II. After the war, he kept up his intelligence work while expanding his guidebook series. During the Cold War, many guides were written by fellow agents who understood the value of insider information. Today's guides continue Fodor's legacy by providing travelers with timely coverage, insider tips, and cultural context.

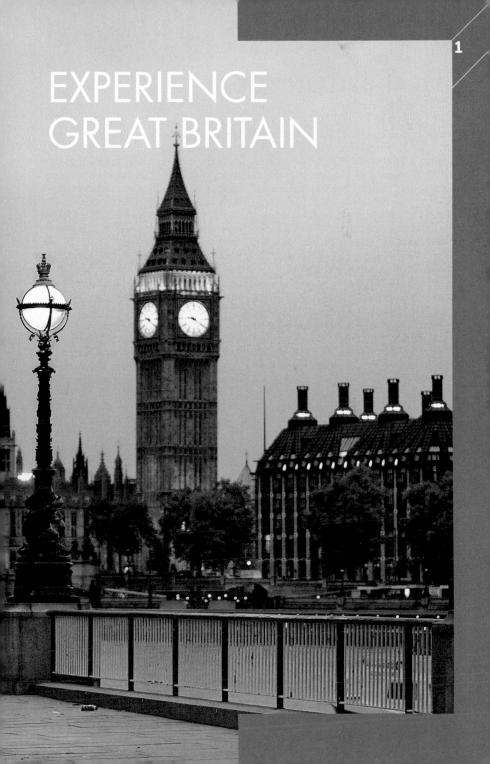

EXPERIENCE
GREAT BRITAIN

GREAT BRITAIN TODAY

Great Britain and the United Kingdom—what's the difference? Historically the United Kingdom (or U.K.) has consisted of the countries of England, Scotland, Wales, and Northern Ireland; the Channel Islands; and the Isle of Man. Great Britain, meanwhile, is the landmass occupied by England, Scotland, and Wales. Despite this precise definition, "Britain" is often used as a synonym of the U.K., and "the British" refer to all its citizens.

In a 2014 referendum, the Scottish people narrowly voted to remain as part of the U.K. However, a subsequent U.K-wide vote in 2016 to leave the European Union (popularly termed "Brexit"), supported by a majority of voters in England and Wales, but only a minority in Scotland and Northern Ireland, has led to further debates about the future of the union. Currently, the official exit is set to occur in March 2019, but much discussion is still necessary before the move finally happens.

It is important to note that neither Scotland nor Wales have ever been part of England, or vice versa, and each has their own unique heritage and culture. Get that wrong at your own peril—you haven't seen angry until you've seen a Scot referred to as English. That being said, all three countries (and the rest of the U.K.) still pledge loyalty to the British Royal Family, and, despite each having selected devolved powers, are generally governed by the Parliament of the United Kingdom centered in London.

The Royal Family

Essentially a figurehead monarchy with a symbolic political role, the Royal Family and each member of its four generations continue to exercise the public's fascination, both at home and abroad. Although taxpayer cost for supporting the family is estimated at £45 million (more than $61 million), many consider the tourists they bring worth the cost (tourism numbers have been helped along in recent years with the success of television shows like *The Crown* and *Victoria*). The Queen, now the world's longest reigning monarch, celebrated her Sapphire Jubilee (65 years on the throne) in February 2017 and still maintains a full working schedule, although her husband, Prince Philip, recently retired from public life at the age of 96.

Prince Charles remains in the wings; his sons, the Princes William and Harry, have both given up their jobs to concentrate on royal duties and are permanently based in London. The younger royals have gained popularity with the people through their support of mental health and conservation issues and, in the case of Prince Harry, creating the Invictus Games for ill or wounded servicemen and -women. Their personal lives have also generated buzz, with William's 2011 wedding to Kate Middleton (now known publicly as Catherine, Duchess of Cambridge) and the births of their first two children, future king Prince George and Princess Charlotte, celebrated by the public. Prince Harry's wedding to American actress Meghan Markle in May 2018 and the April 2018 birth of third child Prince Louis to the Duke and Duchess of Cambridge have also increased public interest.

Politics

Since the general election of 2015, the United Kingdom's government has been in the hands of the Conservative Party. But the unexpected result of a June 2016 referendum, in which the country voted to leave the European Union (a decision known commonly as Brexit), led to the resignation of prime minister David Cameron, who was replaced by Theresa May. Her decision to call a snap election in April 2017 was supposed to strengthen her party's power and thereby ease the many issues in navigating Brexit, but the plan backfired. The result was a loss of an overall parliamentary majority by the Conservatives, a yield of 30 seats to the Labour Party (led by progressive hero Jeremy Corbyn), and a reliance on the support of parliament members from the Northern Ireland Democratic Unionist Party. In addition, the United Kingdom Independence Party (UKIP), a strong advocate of Brexit, lost public support and its only seat in parliament. However, Theresa May has continued to survive the machinations of Brexit, numerous cabinet resignations, tragic terrorist attacks in London and Manchester, the horrific Grenfell Tower fire disaster, and a crisis in the National Health Service (NHS). However, all these issues continue to be on the forefront of English minds and will be for the next several years.

London

Dynamic, complex, and cosmopolitan, London is undoubtedly a success story. Economically vibrant, it is Europe's financial hub—although whether it will maintain this position post-Brexit remains to be seen. London also holds the nation's greatest concentration of arts, contains some of its most iconic attractions, and boasts its most vibrant restaurant and theater scenes. Consequently, it's also the U.K.'s top tourist draw, with ongoing debates about how to increase the capacity of its airports to meet visitor demand. However, London's extraordinary success has often come at the expense of the rest of the country, with many cities and towns still struggling with austerity measures imposed after the financial crash of 2008. Nor is London's preeminence always good news for Londoners, many of whom have been priced out of a skyrocketing property market by investors and foreign buyers (London is, by quite some distance, the most expensive British city to live in). London is in a category of its own—for better or worse.

Scotland

At first glance, visitors to Scotland who have already been to its southern neighbor England will find much that is familiar. After all, the two countries have had a common history since their crowns were united in 1603 and their parliaments merged a hundred years later. Scotland's distinctiveness soon becomes apparent, however, as does the country's fiery pride in its own identity. It may only have 5.3 million people (to England's 53 million), but in modern history Scotland has had an extraordinary global influence in everything from art and literature to science and engineering. Today, it continues to have some big ideas about where it's headed socially, culturally, and economically.

This self-confidence is immediately evident in its thriving arts scene, with arts festivals proliferating and such companies as the National Theatre of Scotland continuing to enjoy international success. And it's just as evident when talking to locals, who will proudly proclaim their landscapes, their castles, and their food and drink to be the best in the world. One visit to Scotland and it's clear to see: this confidence is very well placed.

WHAT'S WHERE

1 London. Not only Britain's financial and governmental center but also one of the world's great cities, London has mammoth museums, posh palaces, double-decker buses, and iconic sights.

2 Canterbury and the Southeast. This compact green and pleasant region within day-trip distance of London takes in Canterbury and its cathedral, funky seaside Brighton, Dover's white cliffs, and gorgeous castles.

3 Stonehenge and the South. Hampshire, Dorset, and Wiltshire have quintessential English countryside. Explore the stone circles at Stonehenge and Avebury, take in Winchester and Salisbury, and discover Highclere Castle.

4 Cornwall and the West Country. Somerset, Devon, and Cornwall are sunnier and warmer than the rest of the country. Of the cities, Bristol is the largest and most vibrant; Wells and Exeter are attractive and compact.

5 Oxford and the Thames Valley. London's commuter belt takes in Windsor, where the Queen spends most weekends. Then there are the spires of Oxford, peaceful river towns such as Henley and Marlow, and stately homes like Blenheim Palace.

6 Bath, the Cotswolds, and Stratford-upon-Avon. The grand Georgian town of Bath is one of England's highlights with its Roman baths. Nearby, the Cotswolds region is justly famous for tranquil, stone-built villages. Stratford-upon-Avon is the place to see Shakespeare's birthplace and watch his plays.

7 Manchester, Liverpool, and the Peak District. Liverpool rides the Beatles' coattails but, like Manchester, has transformed its warehouses and docks into sleek hotels, restaurants, and shops. The surrounding Peak District has great opportunities for walking and visiting stately homes.

8 The Lake District. A popular national park, this is a startlingly beautiful area of craggy hills, wild moorland, stone cottages, and glittering silvery lakes. Among the literary high points are the homes of Wordsworth and Beatrix Potter.

9 Cambridge and East Anglia. The biggest lure in this green, flat, low-key region is Cambridge, with its medieval halls of learning. The countryside is dominated by time-warp towns such as Lavenham and coastal spots like Aldeburgh.

WHAT'S WHERE

10 **Yorkshire and the Northeast.** This wilder part of England has great appeal for lovers of the outdoors, but the ancient walled city of York is also a center of attention. In the Northeast, medieval Durham, Hadrian's Wall, and coastal castles are highlights.

11 **Wales.** Clinging to the western edge of England, Wales is green and ruggedly beautiful, with mountains, magnificent coastline, and stunning castles.

12 **Edinburgh.** Scotland's captivating capital is the country's most popular city, famous for its high-perched castle, Old Town and 18th-century New Town, and the most celebrated arts festival in the world, the International Festival.

13 **Glasgow.** The country's largest city has evolved from prosperous Victorian hub to depressed urban center to thriving modern city with a strong artistic, architectural, and culinary reputation.

14 **The Borders and the Southwest.** Scotland's southern gateway from England, the Borders, with its moors and gentle hills and river valleys, is rustic but historically rich.

15 **The Central Highlands, Fife, and Angus.** Convenient to both Edinburgh and Glasgow, this area encompasses some of Scotland's most beautiful terrain, including Loch Lomond and the Trossachs. In Fife, St. Andrews has world-famous golf courses.

16 **Aberdeen and the Northeast.** Malt-whisky buffs can use the prosperous port city of Aberdeen as a base for exploring the region's distilleries, including those on the Malt Whisky Trail. Aberdeen also makes a good starting point for touring Royal Deeside, with castles like Balmoral.

17 **Argyll and the Isles.** Remote and picturesque, this less visited region of the southwestern coastline has excellent gardens, religious sites, and distilleries.

18 **Inverness, Skye, and the Northern Highlands.** An awe-inspiring valley laced with rivers defines the Great Glen. Inverness, capital of the Highlands, is near Loch Ness. The beautiful Isle of Skye is a highlight for visitors, and the north's rugged highlands have wild moors.

NEED TO KNOW

Scotland

GREAT BRITAIN

Wales

England

London

AT A GLANCE

Capital: London

Population: 65,640,000

Currency: Pound

Money: ATMs are common; credit cards accepted widely

Language: English

Country Code: 44

Emergencies: 999

Driving: On the left

Electricity: 220-240v/50 cycles; electrical plugs have two or three square prongs

Time: Five hours ahead of New York

Documents: Six months with valid passport

Mobile Phones: GSM (900 and 1800 bands)

Major Mobile Companies: EE, 3, Vodafone, O2

WEBSITES

Official U.K. Tourism site: ⊕ www.visitbritain.com

The National Trust: ⊕ www.nationaltrust.org.uk

GETTING AROUND

✈ **Air Travel:** The major airports are London Heathrow, London Gatwick, Manchester, Edinburgh, and Birmingham.

🚌 **Bus Travel:** An extensive network of long-distance buses offers such luxuries as sleeper seats on some routes.

🚗 **Car Travel:** Rent a car to explore at your own pace, but never in London. Gas can be expensive; also be sure to check regulations if you park in a town.

🚆 **Train Travel:** There are fast train links between major cities and slower trains to smaller towns. Fares can be high, particularly if booked at the last minute.

PLAN YOUR BUDGET

	HOTEL ROOM	MEAL	ATTRACTIONS
Low Budget	£100	£15	Tate Modern, free
Mid Budget	£200	£30	Tower of London ticket, £21.45
High Budget	£300	£100	West End Theatre premium ticket, £100

WAYS TO SAVE

Go for a fixed-price lunch. Many restaurants offer good prix-fixe lunch deals (Indian restaurants especially).

Book a Wolsey Lodge. If you're touring the country-side, Wolsey Lodges offer bed-and-breakfast rooms in comfortable private homes, some historic or with beautiful grounds, at reasonable prices. ⊕ www.wolseylodges.com

Buy a Visitor Oyster Card for London. This is the easiest and cheapest way to pay for public transport around the capital, as well as train services to and from Gatwick Airport. ⊕ www.visitorshop.tfl.gov.uk

Go to a free museum. Many London museums—including the British Museum, the V&A, and the National Gallery—are free to visit, though donations are appreciated. Expect a charge for temporary exhibitions.

PLAN YOUR TIME

Hassle Factor	Low. Flights to London are frequent, and links for onward travel are good.
3 days	You can see some of London's historic sights and perhaps take a day trip out to Windsor Castle or Oxford.
1 week	Combine a short trip to London with a one-day trip to Stonehenge and then travel on to Salisbury Cathedral and the grand estates of Stourhead and Longleat, or else head south to Jane Austen's house, the New Forest, and the Jurassic Coast.
2 weeks	This gives you time for a stop in London plus excursions farther north to the beautiful Lake District, the wild moors of Brontë Country in Yorkshire, and even Scotland.

WHEN TO GO

High Season: You'll find good weather, sports events, and a busy music festival calendar from June through August. This is also the most expensive and popular time to visit Britain, though the natives tend to desert London in August.

Low Season: Rain and cold make winter the best time for airfares and hotel deals—and to escape the crowds. However, London is mobbed with Christmas shoppers in December.

Value Season: September has the most settled weather, plus saner airfares and the buzz of the new season's cultural events. The weather is still good in October, though temperatures start to drop in November. Late April and May is a great time to visit: fewer crowds, lower prices, and a glorious display of flowers. In March and early April, weather can be changeable and rainy.

BIG EVENTS

May: Meet leading writers at the huge Hay Festival in Wales's lovely Brecon Beacon National Park. ⊕ www.hayfestival.com.

July: Wimbledon starts at the beginning of the month and runs for 14 days. ⊕ www.wimbledon.com.

August: A galaxy of arts luminaries perform at the Edinburgh International Festival and Edinburgh Festival Fringe. ⊕ www.edinburghfestivals.co.uk.

September: The Open House Weekend is a rare chance to set foot inside many of London's most beautiful buildings for free. ⊕ www.londonopenhouse.org.

READ THIS

■ **London: The Biography,** Peter Ackroyd. A magisterial history of the city.

■ **The English: A Portrait of a People,** Jeremy Paxman. Longtime news anchor wryly examines his compatriots.

■ **Notes from a Small Island,** Bill Bryson. An American's look at his adopted home.

WATCH THIS

■ **Notting Hill.** A rose-color view of London.

■ **Local Hero.** A close-knit Scottish community tries to fend off developers.

■ **Tamara Drewe.** Comic modern reworking of Hardy's Far from the Madding Crowd.

EAT THIS

■ **Roast lamb with mint sauce**: a traditional Sunday lunch

■ **"Full English" breakfast**: eggs, back bacon, sausages, mushrooms, grilled tomatoes, and toast

■ **Shepherd's pie**: minced lamb with vegetables under a mashed potato crust

■ **Cheese**: Cheddar, Blue Stilton, and Wensleydale are especially prized

■ **Fish-and-chips**: cod or haddock fried in a beer-batter crust with thick-cut fries

FLAVORS OF GREAT BRITAIN

The New Food Scene

Great Britain has never lacked a treasure store of nature's bounty: green pastures, fruitful orchards, and the encompassing sea. Over the past few decades, dowdy images of British cooking have been consigned to history. Today, a new focus on the land and a culinary confidence and expertise are exemplified by the popularity and influence of celebrity chefs such as Rick Stein, Heston Blumenthal, Gordon Ramsay, Jamie Oliver, and Mary Berry. And television programs on home baking like *The Great British Bake-off* have proved phenomenally popular.

The famous chefs and bakers are only one indicator of change: all over the country, artisanal food producers and talented cooks are indulging their passion for high-quality, locally sourced ingredients. Whether restaurants are riding the green wave or just following good food sense, they are trying their best to buy from local suppliers; many proudly advertise their support.

Food festivals, farmers' markets, and farm shops have sprung up in cities and towns across the country. Alongside the infiltration of supermarkets, much opposed by some people, comes a more discriminating attitude to food supplies. Outdoors-reared cows, sheep, and pigs; freshly caught fish; and seasonal fruits and vegetables provide a bedrock upon which traditional recipes are tempered with cosmopolitan influences. The contemporary British menu takes the best of Mediterranean and Asian cuisines and reinterprets them with new enthusiasm.

Natural Bounty

Craft beers and cask ales. The interest in the provenance of food extends to beer, with a recent boom in microbreweries developing craft beers and real ales: beer that's unfiltered and unpasteurized, and that contains live brewer's yeast. Generally served by the pint (19.2 fluid ounces) from kegs, bottles, or casks, local brews range from easy-sipping pale ales to rich, dark stouts and porters.

Dairy produce. The stalwart Cheddar, Cheshire, Double Gloucester, and Stilton cheeses are complemented by traditional and experimental cheeses from small, local producers. Some cheeses come wrapped in nettles or vine leaves, others stuffed with apricots, cranberries, or herbs. British dairies also produce delicious sheep and goat cheeses, yogurts, and ice creams.

Game. In the fall and winter, pheasant, grouse, partridge, and venison are prominent on restaurant menus, served either roasted, in rich casseroles, or in pies. Duck (particularly the Gressingham and Aylesbury breeds) and rabbit are available all year round.

Meat. Peacefully grazing cattle, including Aberdeen Angus, Herefordshire, and Welsh Black varieties, are an iconic symbol of the countryside. When hung and dry-aged for up to 28 days, British beef is at its most flavorsome. Spring lamb is succulent, and salt-marsh lamb from Wales and the Lake District, fed on wild grasses and herbs, makes for a unique taste. Outdoors-reared and rare breeds of pig, such as Gloucester Old Spot, often provide the breakfast bacon.

Seafood. The traditional trio of cod, haddock, and plaice is still in evidence, but declining fishing stocks have brought other varieties to prominence. Hake, bream, freshwater trout, wild salmon, sardines, pilchards, and mackerel are on the restaurant table, along with crab, mussels, and oysters. The east and Cornish coasts are favored fishing grounds in England.

Some of the most coveted fish and seafood in the world live in the rivers and lakes, as well as off the coasts, of Scotland. Smoked fish (most notably, haddock, salmon, and trout) is the national specialty—so much so that the process of both hot and cold smoking has developed to a fine art. Scots often eat smoked fish for breakfast and lunch, and as an appetizer with their evening meal. The fish is commonly served with a squeeze of lemon and a sprinkle of cracked pepper, and accompanied by thin slices of hearty bread or oat crackers. Places like Arbroath as well as the isles of North Uist and Skye have won international praise for their delicious, locally smoked haddock, salmon, and trout.

Whiskies

"Uisge-beatha," translated from Scottish Gaelic, means "water of life," and in Scotland it most certainly is. Whisky helps weave together the country's essence, capturing the aromas of earth, water, and air in a single sip.

Whiskies differ greatly between single malts and blends. This has to do with the ingredients, specialized distillation processes, and type of oak cask. Whisky is made predominantly from malted barley that, in the case of blended whiskies, can be combined with grains and cereals like wheat or corn. Malts or single malts can come only from malted barley.

The five main whisky regions in Scotland produce distinctive tastes, though there are variations even within a region: the Lowlands (lighter in taste), Speyside (sweet, with flower scents), the Highlands (fragrant, smooth, and smoky), Campbeltown (full-bodied and slightly salty), and Islay (strong peat flavor). Do sample these unique flavors; distillery tours are a good place to begin.

Traditional Dishes

Good international fare is available, and you shouldn't miss the Indian food in England. But do try some classics.

Black pudding. This dish, most commonly associated with Scotland but also a local favorite in the English regions of Lancashire, Yorkshire, and the Midlands, consists of onions, pork fat, oatmeal, herbs, and spices blended with the blood from a pig (or, on occasion, from a sheep or goat). At its best, this dish has a delicate, crumbly texture and can be served at breakfast or as a starter to a meal.

Fish-and-chips. This number-one seaside favorite not only turns up in every coastal resort, but in fish-and-chip shops and restaurants throughout the land. Fish, usually cod, haddock, or plaice, is deep-fried in a crispy batter and served with thick-cut french fries (chips) and, if eaten out, wrapped up in paper. The liberal sprinkling of salt and vinegar as well as "mushy" (mashed) peas are optional.

Haggis. Food in Scotland is steeped in history, and a rich story lies behind many traditional dishes. Once the food of peasants, haggis—a mixture of sheep's heart, lungs, and liver cooked with onions, oats, and spices, and then boiled in a sheep's stomach—has made a big comeback in more formal Scottish restaurants. If the dish's ingredients turn you off, there's often an equally flavorful vegetarian option. You'll find "neeps and tatties" alongside haggis; the three are inseparable. Neeps are yellow turnips, potatoes are the tatties, and both are boiled and then mashed.

Meat pies and pasties. Pies and pasties make a filling lunch. Perhaps the most popular is steak-and-kidney pie, combining chunks of lean beef and kidneys mixed with braised onions and mushrooms in a thick gravy, topped with a light puff- or short-pastry crust. Other combinations are chicken with mushrooms or leek and beef slow-cooked in ale (often Guinness). Cornish pasties are filled with beef, potato, rutabaga, and onions, all enveloped in a circle of pastry folded in half.

Sausages. "Bangers and mash" are sausages, commonly made with pork, beef, or lamb, served with mashed potatoes and onion gravy. Lincolnshire sausage consists of pork flavored with sage. Cumberland sausage comes in a long coil and has a peppery taste.

Shepherd's and cottage pie. These classic pub dishes have a lightly browned mashed-potato topping over stewed minced meat and onions in a rich gravy. Shepherd's pie uses lamb, cottage pie beef.

Tempting Baked Goods

The British love their cakes, biscuits, breads, and pies. There's always something sweet and most likely crumbly to indulge in, whether after a meal or with a nice cup of tea. Bakeries are the perfect places to sample fresh goodies. Some of the local favorites range from conventional butter-based shortbreads and Victoria sponge (a light sponge cake filled with softly whipped cream and jam, and sprinkled with castor sugar) to mince pies (small pies filled with brandy, stewed dried fruits, and nuts), and fluffy fruit scones. Treacle tarts, gingerbread, butterscotch apple pie, and oatcakes (more a savory cracker than a sweet cake) with local cheese are also popular as late-morning or early afternoon temptations.

Meals Not to Be Missed

Full English breakfast. The "full English" is a three-course affair. Starting with orange juice, cereals, porridge, yogurt, or stewed fruit, it's followed by any combination of sausages, eggs, bacon, tomatoes, mushrooms, black pudding, baked beans, and fried bread. The feast finishes with toast and marmalade and tea or coffee. Alternatives to the fry-up are kippers, smoked haddock, or boiled or poached eggs. Many cafés and pubs serve an all-day breakfast.

Ploughman's lunch. Crusty bread, English cheese (perhaps farmhouse Cheddar, blue Stilton, crumbly Cheshire, or waxy red Leicester), and tangy pickles with a side-salad garnish make up a delicious light lunch, found in all good pubs.

Roast dinners. On Sunday, the traditional roast dinner is still popular. The meat, either beef, pork, lamb, or chicken, is served with roast potatoes, carrots, seasonal green vegetables, and Yorkshire pudding, a savory batter baked in the oven until crisp, and then topped with a rich, dark, meaty gravy. Horseradish sauce and English mustard are on hand for beef; a mint sauce accompanies lamb; and an apple sauce enhances pork.

Afternoon tea. Tea, ideally served in a country garden on a summer afternoon, ranks high on the list of Britain's must-do experiences. You may simply have a scone with your tea, or you can opt for a more ample feast: dainty sandwiches with the crusts cut off; scones with jam and clotted cream; and an array of homemade cakes. You can also choose from a variety of teas; Earl Grey is an afternoon favorite that you can take with either milk or lemon.

BEST FESTIVALS AND EVENTS

Spring

St. David's Day. Leeks and daffodils are ubiquitous on Wales' national day on March 1, with carnivals and processions in Cardiff and other places.

RHS Chelsea Flower Show. This five-day floral extravaganza in May is also a society event, held in London's upmarket Chelsea neighborhood. ⊕ *www.rhs.org.uk/chelsea.*

Shakespeare Birthday Celebrations. In late April, the Bard is celebrated with full pageantry and drama in his hometown of Stratford-upon-Avon. ⊕ *www.shakespearescelebrations.com.*

Summer

Edinburgh Festival. Taking over Scotland's capital every August, this cultural cornucopia is an amalgam of festivals running concurrently. Most prominent are the **Edinburgh International Festival**, featuring everything from opera to cutting-edge theater, and the rowdier **Edinburgh Fringe**, which highlights comedy and cabaret. ⊕ *www.eif.co.uk* and ⊕ *www.edfringe.com.*

Eisteddfod. The **International Musical Eisteddfod** is a gathering of choirs and dancers from around the world in the Welsh town of Llangollen in July. The **National Eisteddfod of Wales** in August focuses on Welsh culture, alternating between venues in north and south Wales. ⊕ *www.international-eisteddfod.co.uk* and ⊕ *www.eisteddfod.org.uk.*

Glastonbury Festival. Iconic and idiosyncratic, this not-quite-annual music event sprawls across Somerset farmland and features hundreds of big-name bands over three days in late June or early July. ⊕ *www.glastonburyfestivals.co.uk.*

Highland Games. This annual shindig takes place in Highland locations between May and September, and includes hammer-throwing, caber-tossing, and traditional dancing. ⊕ *www.shga.co.uk.*

Notting Hill Carnival. West London's Caribbean community takes to the streets at the end of August, with spectacular floats, costumes, and steel bands.

The Proms. The main venue for this distinguished July–September series of classical music concerts is in London's Royal Albert Hall. ⊕ *www.bbc.co.uk/proms.*

Royal Henley Regatta. High society lines the banks of the Thames River to cheer on rowers from around the world during this five-day event in early July. ⊕ *www.hrr.co.uk.*

Trooping the Colour. Queen Elizabeth's official birthday is marked in majestic style in mid-June in London's Horse Guard Parade. ⊕ *www.royal.uk/trooping-colour.*

Fall

Guy Fawkes Day. A foiled attempt in 1605 to blow up Parliament is remembered every November 5, when fireworks are set off all over the country. Lewes and York stage some of the biggest festivities.

Winter

Burns Night. Ceremonial dinners are held throughout Scotland to celebrate poet Robert Burns on his birthday, January 25.

Celtic Connections. During the last two weeks of January, musicians gather in Glasgow to play Celtic-inspired music. ⊕ *www.celticconnections.com.*

Hogmanay. Scotland's ancient, still-thriving New Year's bash extends over three days, with celebrations that are especially exuberant in Edinburgh. ⊕ *www.edinburghshogmanay.com.*

PLAYING GOLF IN SCOTLAND

There are some 550 golf courses in Scotland and only 5.3 million residents, so the country has probably the highest ratio of courses to people anywhere in the world. If you're visiting Scotland, you'll probably want to play the "famous names" sometime in your career.

So by all means play the championship courses such as the Old Course at St. Andrews, but remember they *are* championship courses. You may enjoy the game itself much more at a less challenging course. Remember, too, that everyone else wants to play the big names, so booking can be a problem at peak times in summer. Reserving three to four months ahead is not too far for the famous courses, although it's possible to get a time up to a month (or even a week) in advance if you are relaxed about your timing. If you're staying in a hotel attached to a course, get the concierge to book a tee time for you.

Happily, golf has always had a peculiar classlessness in Scotland. It's a game for everyone, and for centuries Scottish towns and cities have maintained courses for the enjoyment of their citizens. Admittedly, a few clubs have always been noted for their exclusive air, and some newer golf courses are losing touch with the game's inclusive origins, but these are exceptions to the tradition of recreation for all. Golf here is usually a democratic game, played by ordinary folk as well as the wealthy.

Tips About Playing

Golf courses are everywhere in Scotland. Most courses welcome visitors with a minimum of formalities, and some at a surprisingly low cost. Other courses are very expensive, but a lot of great golf can be played for between about £30 to £100 a round. Online booking at many courses has made arranging a golf tour easier, too.

Be aware of the topography of a course. Scotland is where the distinction between "links" and "parkland" courses was first made. Links courses are by the sea and are subject to the attendant sea breezes—some quite bracing—and mists, which can make them trickier to play. The natural topography of sand dunes and long, coarse grasses can add to the challenge. A parkland course is in a wooded area and its terrain is more obviously landscaped. A "moorland" course is found in an upland area.

Here are three pieces of advice, particularly for North Americans: (1) in Scotland the game is usually played fairly quickly, so don't dawdle if others are waiting; (2) caddy carts are hand-pulled carts for your clubs and driven golf carts are rarely available; and (3) when they say "rough," they really mean "rough."

Unless specified otherwise, hours are generally sunrise to sundown, which in June can be as late as 10 pm. Note that some courses advertise the SSS, "standard scratch score," instead of par (which may be different). This is the score a scratch golfer could achieve under perfect conditions. Rental clubs, balls, and other gear are generally available from clubhouses, except at the most basic municipal courses. Don't get caught by the dress codes enforced at many establishments: in general, untailored shorts, round-neck shirts, jeans, and sneakers are frowned upon.

The prestigious courses may ask for evidence of your golf skills by way of a handicap certificate; check in advance and carry this with you.

Costs and Courses

Many courses lower their rates before and after peak season—at the end of September, for example. It's worth asking about this. ■TIP→ Some areas offer regional golf passes that save you money. Check with the local tourist board.

For a complete list of courses, contact local tourist offices or VisitScotland's official and comprehensive golf website, ⊕ *golf.visitscotland.com.* It has information about the country's golf courses, special golf trails, regional passes, special events, and tour operators, as well as on conveniently located accommodations. U.K. Golf Guide (⊕ *www.uk-golfguide. com*) has user-generated reviews. *For information about regional courses, also see individual chapters.*

Best Bets Around Scotland

If your idea of heaven is teeing off on a windswept links, then Scotland is for you. Dramatic courses, many of them set on sandy dunes alongside the ocean, are just one of the types you'll encounter. Highland courses that take you through the heather and moorland courses surrounded by craggy mountains have their own challenges.

Boat of Garten Golf Club, Inverness-shire. With the Cairn Gorm Mountain as a backdrop, this beautiful course has rugged terrain that requires even seasoned players to bring their A game. As an added bonus, a steam railway runs alongside the course.

Carnoustie Golf Links, Angus. Challenging golfers for nearly 500 years, Carnoustie is on many golfers' must-do list. The iconic Championship Course has tested many of the world's top players, while the Burnside and Buddon courses attract budding Players and Watsons.

Castle Stuart Golf Links, Inverness-shire. A more recent addition to Scotland's world-class courses offers cliff-top hazards, sprawling bunkers, and rolling fairways overlooking the Moray Firth.

Cruden Bay Golf Club, Aberdeenshire. This challenging and enjoyable links course was built by the Great North of Scotland Railway Company in 1894. Its remote location beside a set of towering dunes makes it irresistible.

Dunbar Golf Club, East Lothian. This classic and challenging links course has dramatic weather and scenery, with a backdrop of the Firth of Forth, Bass Rock, and a lighthouse.

Gleneagles, Perthshire. Host of the 2014 Ryder Cup championship, Gleneagles has three 18-hole courses that challenge the pros and a 9-hole course that provides a more laid-back game. It's also home to the PGA National Golf Academy.

Machrihanish Golf Club, Argyll. A dramatic location on the Mull of Kintyre and some exciting match play make these links well worth a journey.

Royal Dornoch Golf Club, Sutherland. Extending across a coastal shelf, Royal Dornoch has fast greens, pristine beaches, and mountain views. In spring yellow gorse sets the green hills ablaze.

St. Andrews Links, Fife. To approach the iconic 18th hole in the place where the game was invented remains the holy grail of golfers worldwide.

Western Gailes Golf Club, near Glasgow. This splendid links course is a final qualifying course for the British Open. Sculpted by Mother Nature, it's the country's finest natural links course.

GREAT ITINERARIES

HIGHLIGHTS OF ENGLAND: 12 DAYS

Day 1: London

The capital is just the jumping-off point for this trip, so choose a few highlights that grab your interest. If it's the Changing of the Guard at Buckingham Palace, check the time to be sure you catch the pageantry. If Westminster Abbey appeals to your sense of history, arrive as early as you can. Pick a museum (many are free, so you needn't linger if you don't want to), whether it's the National Gallery in Trafalgar Square, the British Museum in Bloomsbury, or the Tate Modern on the South Bank. Stroll Hyde Park or take a boat ride on the Thames before you find a pub or Indian restaurant for dinner. End with a play; the experience of theatergoing may be as interesting as whatever work you see.

Day 2: Windsor

Resplendent with centuries of treasures, Windsor Castle is favored by the Queen, and has been by rulers for centuries. Tour it to appreciate the history and wealth of the monarchy. The State Apartments are open if the Queen isn't in residence, and 10 kings and queens are buried in magnificent St. George's Chapel. Time permitting, take a walk in the adjacent Great Park. If you can splurge for a luxurious stay (versus making Windsor a day trip from London), head up the valley to Cliveden, the Thames Valley's most spectacular hotel.

Logistics: Trains from Paddington and Waterloo stations leave about twice hourly and take less than one hour. Green Line buses depart from the Colonnades opposite London's Victoria Coach Station.

Day 3: Salisbury and Stourhead

Visible for miles around, Salisbury Cathedral's soaring spire is an unforgettable image of rural England. See the Magna Carta in the cathedral's Chapter House as you explore this marvel of medieval engineering, and walk the town path to get the view John Constable painted. Pay an afternoon visit to Stourhead to experience the finest example of the naturalistic 18th-century landscaping for which England is famous; the grand Palladian mansion here is a bonus.

Logistics: For trains to Salisbury from Windsor and Eton Riverside, head back to London's Waterloo to catch a train on the West of England line.

Day 4: Bath and Stonehenge

Bath's immaculately preserved, golden-stone Georgian architecture helps you recapture the late 18th century. Take time to stroll; don't miss the Royal Crescent (you can explore the period interior of No. 1), and sip the Pump Room's (some say vile-tasting) water as Jane Austen's characters might have. The Roman baths are an amazing remnant of the ancient empire, and today you can do as the Romans did as you relax in the warm mineral waters at the Thermae Bath Spa. There's plenty to do in Bath (museums, shopping, theater), but you might make an excursion to Stonehenge (by car or tour bus). Entry is by timed ticket, so make sure to book in advance to guarantee seeing this most popular and enigmatic site. It's usually at its least crowded early or late in the day.

Logistics: Trains and buses leave hourly from Salisbury to Bath.

Site Text 5.5/6/40

Day 5: The Cotswolds

Antiques-shop in fairy-tale Stow-on-the-Wold and feed the ducks at the brook in Lower Slaughter for a taste of the mellow stone villages and dreamy green landscapes for which the area is beloved. Choose a rainy or off-season day to visit Broadway or risk jams of tourist traffic. Another great experience is a walk on the Cotswold Way or any local path.

Logistics: Drive to make the best of the beautiful scenery. Alternatively, opt for a guided tour bus.

Day 6: Oxford and Blenheim Palace

Join a guided tour of Oxford's glorious quadrangles, chapels, and gardens to get the best access to these centuries-old academic treasures. This leaves time for a jaunt to Blenheim, a unique combination of baroque opulence (inside and out) and naturalistic parkland, the work of the great 18th-century landscape designer Capability Brown. For classic Oxford experiences, rent a punt or join students and go pub crawling around town.

Logistics: Hourly trains depart from Bath for Oxford. Buses frequently depart from Oxford's Gloucester Green for Blenheim Palace.

Day 7: Stratford-upon-Avon

Skip this stop if you don't care about you-know-who. Fans of Shakespeare can see his birthplace and Anne Hathaway's Cottage (walking there is a delight), and then finish with a memorable performance at the Royal Shakespeare Company's magnificently renovated main stage. Start the day early and be prepared for crowds.

Logistics: From Oxford, trains involve one or two changes; there is a less frequent Stagecoach bus service.

Day 8: Shrewsbury to Chester

Head north to see the half-timber buildings of Shrewsbury, one of the best preserved of England's Tudor towns. Strolling is the best way to experience it. In Chester the architecture is more or less the same (though not always authentic), but the Rows, a series of two-story shops with medieval crypts beneath, and the fine city walls are sights you can't pass by. You can walk part or all of the city walls for views of the town and surrounding area.

Logistics: For Shrewsbury, change trains at Birmingham. The train ride to Chester is less than an hour.

Days 9 and 10: The Lake District

In the area extending north beyond Kendal and Windermere, explore the English lakes and beautiful surrounding mountains on foot in the Lake District National Park. This area is jam-packed with hikers in summer and on weekends, so rent a car to seek out the more isolated routes. Take a cruise on Windermere or Coniston Water, or rent a boat for another classic Lakeland experience. If you have time for one Wordsworth-linked site, head to Dove Cottage; you can even have afternoon tea there.

Logistics: Take the train to Oxenholme with a change at Warrington Bank Quay. At Oxenholme you can switch to Windermere.

Day 11: York

This historic cathedral city is crammed with 15th- and 16th-century buildings, but don't miss York Minster, with its stunning stained glass, and the medieval streets of the Shambles. Take your pick of the city's museums or go shopping; have tea at Betty's or unwind at a pub. A walk along the top of the city walls is fun, too.

Logistics: By train from Oxenholme, switch at Manchester Piccadilly, or from Carlisle change at Newcastle or Leeds.

Day 12: Cambridge

Spend the afternoon touring King's College Chapel and the Backs—gardens and sprawling meadows—and refining your punting skills on the River Cam. The excellent Fitzwilliam Museum, full of art and antiquities, is another option, as is the Polar Museum. To relax, join the students for a pint at a pub.

Logistics: For train service, switch at Peterborough. Trains leave Cambridge for London frequently.

TIPS

■ Train travelers should keep in mind that regional "Rovers" and "Rangers" offer unlimited train travel in one-day, three-day, or weeklong increments. See ⊕ *www. nationalrail.co.uk* for details. Also check out BritRail passes, which must be purchased before your trip.

■ Buses are time-consuming, but more scenic and cheaper than train travel. National Express offers discounts including fun fares—fares to and from London to various cities (including Cambridge) for as low as £5 if booked more than 24 hours in advance. Or check out low-cost Megabus.

■ To cut the tour short, consider skipping Chester and Shrewsbury and proceed to the Lake District from Stratford-upon-Avon on day eight. Likewise, you can consider passing up a visit to Cambridge if you opt for Oxford. You can add the time to your London stay or another place you want to linger.

■ It's easy to visit Stonehenge from Salisbury, as well as from Bath, whether you have a car or want a guided excursion.

■ Buy theater tickets well in advance for Stratford-upon-Avon.

GREAT ITINERARIES

HIGHLIGHTS OF SCOTLAND IN 10 DAYS

Scotland isn't large, but its most famous cities and most iconic landscapes take time to explore. This itinerary packs in many national icons: Edinburgh's enormous charm and Glasgow's excellent museums; a castle or two; lochs, mountains, and an island. It's a busy pace, but you'll still be able to fit in a whisky distillery visit and even a round of golf. You can do parts of this trip by public transportation, but beyond the cities, a car allows more flexibility.

Days 1 and 2: Edinburgh

The capital of Scotland is loaded with iconic sights in its Old Town and New Town. Visit **Edinburgh Castle** and the **National Gallery of Scotland,** and take tours of the **National Museum of Scotland** and the modern **Scottish Parliament** building. Walk along Old Town's **Royal Mile** and New Town's **George Street** for some fresh air and retail therapy. Later on, seek out a traditional pub with live music.

Logistics: Fly into Edinburgh Airport if you're flying via London. If you're flying directly into Glasgow from overseas, make your way from Glasgow Airport to Queen Street Station via taxi or bus. It takes an hour to travel from Glasgow to Edinburgh by car or bus, about 45 minutes to an hour by train. Explore on foot or by public transportation.

Day 3: Stirling to St. Andrews

Rent a car in Edinburgh and drive to the historic city of **Stirling.** Spend the day visiting **Stirling Castle** and the **National Wallace Monument.** If you're eager to tour a distillery, make time for a stop at the **Famous Grouse Experience** at the Glenturret Distillery in **Crieff.** For your overnight stay,

drive to the seaside town of St. Andrews, famous for golf.

Logistics: It's 35 miles or a one-hour drive to Stirling from Edinburgh, and 50 miles and 90 minutes from Stirling to St. Andrews. You can easily take a train or bus to these destinations.

Day 4: St. Andrews to Aviemore

Spend the morning exploring **St. Andrews,** known for its castle and the country's oldest university as well as its golf courses. If you've booked well in advance, play a round of golf. After lunch, drive to **Aviemore.** Along the way, stretch your legs at one of Scotland's notable sights, **Blair Castle** (just off the A9 and 10 miles north of **Pitlochry**). Head to Aviemore, gateway to the Cairngorm Mountains and Britain's largest national park, for two nights. The town is a center for outdoor activities and has many choices for accommodations, dining, and shopping, but you can also consider the more attractive surrounding villages and towns such as **Kingussie** for your stay.

Logistics: It's 120 miles from St. Andrews to Aviemore via the A9, a drive that will take 2½ hours. You can also take a train or bus.

Day 5: The Cairngorms

For anyone who enjoys outdoor pursuits or dramatic scenery, the arctic plateau of the Cairngorms is a must. Hiking, biking, and climbing are options (Glenmore Lodge is a renowned outdoor-sports center), but so is visiting attractions such as the **Cairngorm Reindeer Centre** and **Highland Folk Museum.**

Day 6: The Isle of Skye

Leave Aviemore early and head to Inverness, which has a busy center suited for a wander. **Inverness Castle** and the **Inverness Museum and Art Gallery** are worth

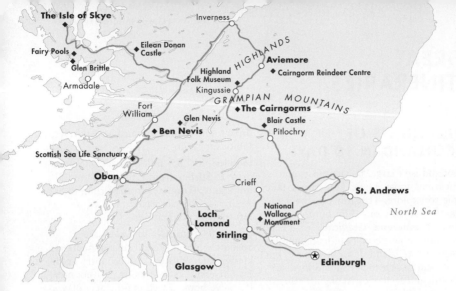

seeing. The drive southwest to Skye is peaceful, full of raw landscapes and big, open horizons. Stop at **Eilean Donan Castle** on the way. Set on an island among three lochs, the castle is the stuff postcards are made of from the outside, although the interiors are comically underwhelming. Explore Skye: **Glen Brittle** is the perfect place to enjoy mountain scenery including the crystal-clear **Fairy Pools** at the foot of the Black Cuillins; and **Armadale** is a good place to go crafts shopping. End up in Portree for dinner and the night.

Logistics: It's 30 miles (a 40-minute drive) via the A9 from Aviemore to Inverness, and then it's 80 miles (a two-hour drive) from Inverness to Skye. Public transportation is possible but a car is best.

Day 7: Oban via Ben Nevis

Leave Skye no later than 9 am and head for **Fort William**. The town isn't worth stopping for, but the view of Britain's highest mountain, the 4,406-foot Ben Nevis, is. If time permits, take a hike in **Glen Nevis**. Continue on to **Oban,** a traditional Scottish resort town on the water, to overnight. Outside Oban, stop by the **Scottish Sea Life Sanctuary**. At night, feast on fish-and-chips in a local pub.

Logistics: It's nearly 100 miles from Skye to Oban; the drive is 3½ hours without stopping. Public transportation is challenging.

Days 8 and 9: Loch Lomond and Glasgow

Enjoy a waterfront stroll in Oban. Mid-morning, set off for **Glasgow** via **Loch Lomond**. Arrive in Glasgow in time for dinner; take in a play or concert, or just relax in a pub on the first of your two nights in this rejuvenated city. Spend the next day visiting the sights: **Kelvingrove Art Gallery and Museum,** Charles Rennie Mackintosh's iconic buildings, and the **Riverside Museum** are a few highlights.

Logistics: It's 127 miles (a three-hour drive) from Oban to Glasgow via Balloch. Traveling by train is a possibility, but you won't be able to go via Balloch. Return your rental car in Glasgow.

Day 10: Glasgow and Home

On your final day, stow your suitcases at your hotel and hit Buchanan and Sauchiehall streets for some of Britain's best shopping. Clothes, whisky, and tartan items are good things to look for.

Logistics: It's less than 10 miles (15 minutes) by taxi to Glasgow's international airport in Paisley but more than 30 miles (40 minutes) to the international airport in Prestwick.

2

LONDON

Visit Fodors.com for advice, updates, and bookings

WELCOME TO LONDON

TOP REASONS TO GO

★ **The abbey and the cathedral:** That Gothic splendor, Westminster Abbey, soars above the final resting place of several of Britain's most distinguished figures. To the east is St. Paul's, the beautiful English baroque cathedral.

★ **Buckingham Palace:** Although not the prettiest royal residence, this is the public face of the monarchy and the place to watch the culmination of the Changing the Guard ceremony.

★ **Tower of London:** Parts of this complex date back 11 centuries. The tower has been a prison, an armory, and a mint—now it houses the Crown Jewels.

★ **Majestic museums:** Discover the Old Masters at the National Gallery, the cutting-edge works at Tate Modern, and the historical artifacts of the British Museum.

★ **A city of villages:** Each of London's dozens of neighborhoods has its own personality. Parks, shops, pubs: walk around and discover them for yourself.

1 **Westminster and St. James's.** Embrace your inner tourist. Take pictures of the mounted Horse Guards, and drink in the Old Masters at the National Gallery. It's well worth braving the crowds to visit historic Westminster Abbey.

2 **Soho and Covent Garden.** More sophisticated than seedy these days, the heart of London puts Theatreland, strip joints, Chinatown, and notable restaurants side by side.

3 **Bloomsbury and Holborn.** The University of London dominates the city's historical intellectual center, Bloomsbury. Allow for long visits to the incomparable British Museum.

4 **The City.** London's Wall Street might be the oldest part of the capital, but thanks to the futuristic skyscrapers and a sleek Millennium Bridge, it looks like the newest. There's plenty for period architecture buffs as well, like St. Paul's Cathedral and the Tower of London.

5 **East London.** Once known for its slums immortalized by Charles Dickens and Jack the Ripper, today the area is home to London's contemporary art scene, along with Brick

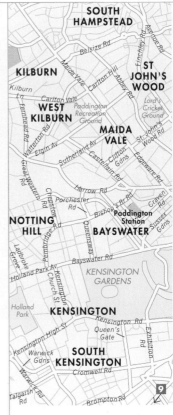

Lane's curry houses and Spitalfields Market.

6 **South of the Thames.** The National Theatre, Old Vic, Royal Festival Hall, BFI Southbank, Shakespeare's Globe, and Tate Modern make this area a cultural hub. Get a bird's-eye view of the whole city from the Shard or the London Eye.

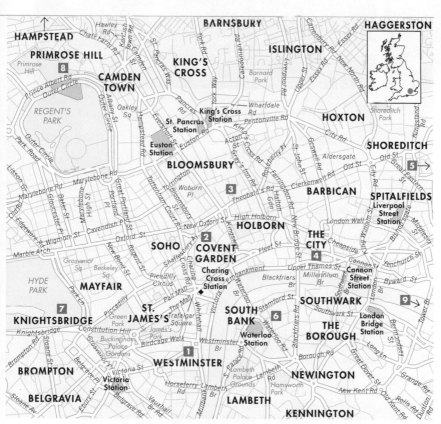

7 Kensington, Knights-bridge, Notthing Hill, and Mayfair. Kensington's museums are filled with treasures, with the Science Museum and the Natural History Museum offering the most fun for children. Shopaholics should head for Bond Street and Sloane Street while Notting Hill is a trendsetting hub of boutiques and eateries.

8 Regent's Park and Hampstead. London becomes noticeably calmer and greener as you head north from Euston Road. Come here to experience just how laid-back moneyed Londoners can be.

9 Up and Down the Thames. Maritime Green-wich boasts masterpieces by Wren and Inigo Jones. Other river excursions take you to Kew Gardens and Hampton Court Palace.

Updated by Jo Caird, Jack Jewers, James O'Neill, Toby Orton, Ellin Stein, and Alex Wijeratna

If London's only attraction were its famous landmarks, it would still be unmissable. But London is so much more. Though its long history is evident at every turn, it's also one of the world's most modern and vibrant cities.

London beckons with great museums, royal pageantry, and historically significant buildings. Unique Georgian terraces perch next to cutting-edge modern skyscrapers, and parks and squares provide unexpected oases of greenery amid the dense urban landscape. Modern central London still largely follows its winding medieval street pattern. Even Londoners armed with the indispensable *London A–Z* street finder or equivalent app can get lost in their own city.

As well as visiting landmarks like St. Paul's Cathedral and the Tower of London, set aside time for random wandering; the city repays every moment spent exploring its backstreets and mews on foot. Go to lesser-known but thoroughly rewarding sites such as Kensington Palace and the unique home of 19th-century architect Sir John Soane, which houses his outstanding collection of antiquities and art.

Today the city's art, style, fashion, and restaurant scenes make headlines around the world. London's chefs have become internationally influential, its fashion designers and art stars set global trends, its nightlife continues to produce exciting new acts, and its theater remains celebrated for superb classical and innovative productions.

Then there's that greatest living link with the past—the Royal Family. Don't let fear of looking like a tourist stop you from enjoying the pageantry of the Changing the Guard at Buckingham Palace, one of the greatest free shows in the world.

As the eminent 18th-century man of letters Samuel Johnson said, "When a man is tired of London, he is tired of life, for there is in London all that life can afford." Armed with energy and curiosity, you can discover its riches.

PLANNER

WHEN TO GO

The heaviest tourist season runs April through September, with another peak around Christmas. Late spring is the time to see the Royal Parks and gardens at their freshest; fall brings autumnal beauty and fewer people. Summer gives the best chance of good weather, although the crowds are intense. Winter can be dismal—it's dark by 5—but all the theaters, concerts, and exhibitions go full-speed ahead, and Christmas lights bring a major touch of festive magic. Weather-wise, winter is cold and wet with occasional light snow and spring is colorful and fair. June through August can range from a total washout to a long hot summer and anything in between. Autumn ranges from warm to cool to mild. It's impossible to forecast London weather, but you can be certain that it will not be what you expect.

GETTING HERE AND AROUND

AIR TRAVEL

Most international flights to London arrive at either Heathrow Airport (LHR), 15 miles west of London, or at Gatwick Airport (LGW), 27 miles south of the capital. Most flights from the United States go to Heathrow, which is divided into five terminals, with Terminals 3–5 handling transatlantic flights. Gatwick is London's second gateway. It has grown from a European airport into an airport that also serves dozens of U.S. destinations. A third airport, Stansted (STN), is 35 miles northeast of the city; it handles European and domestic traffic. Three smaller airports, Luton (LTN), 30 miles north of town, Southend (SEN), 40 miles to the east, and business-oriented London City (in East London E16), mainly handle flights to Europe.

BIKE TRAVEL

Nicknamed "Boris bikes" after the former mayor and dedicated cyclist Boris Johnson, a 24-hour bike-rental program called Santander Cycles enables Londoners to pick up a bicycle at one of more than 750 docking stations and return it at another. The first 30 minutes are free, then it's £2 for every 30-minute period thereafter. There is also a £2-per-day access charge. You pay at the docking station, using credit or debit cards only (cash is not accepted)—simply follow the instructions on the touch screen and away you go.

BUS TRAVEL

In central London, Transport for London (TfL) buses are traditionally bright red double- and single-deckers. Not all buses run the full length of their route at all times, so check with the driver. In central London you must purchase tickets from machines at bus stops along the routes before you board. The main bus stops have a red TfL symbol on a white background. When the word "Request" is written across the sign, you must flag the bus down. Buses are a good way to see the town, but don't take one if you're in a hurry. Buses are supposed to swing by most stops every five or six minutes, but in reality you often end up waiting a bit longer, although those in the city center are quite reliable.

All London buses are now cash-free, which means you must buy your ticket *before* you board the bus. There are a number of ways to do this. One-day paper bus passes are available at Underground and rail stations as well as London Transport Visitor Centres and cost £5. An easier, and cheaper, option is to pay by prepaid Oyster card or "contactless" bank card. Visitor Oyster cards must be purchased before you arrive; they cost £3 but a day's bus travel is capped at £5. Normal Oyster cards, which cost £5, are available from ticket desks at all major airports or at any Tube station and are transferable if you have money left over. Contactless cards are the future of London travel: you touch a compatible debit or credit card on a bus or Tube-station's reader, and the fare is automatically debited from your bank account.

One alternative is to buy a one- or seven-day Travelcard, which is good for both Tube and bus travel. Travelcards can be bought at Tube stations, travel information centers, and some newsagents. However, note that seven-day Travelcards bought in London *must be loaded onto an Oyster card*. Although using a Travelcard may save you some money, it might be easier to just add additional money to your Oyster card as needed, since there are machines at all Tube stations and at lots of London newsagents. A seven-day paper Travelcard can only be purchased in advance, online.

Night buses, denoted by an "N" before their route numbers, run from midnight to 5 am on a more restricted route than day buses. However, some night bus routes should be approached with caution and the top deck avoided. All night buses run by request stop, so flag them down if you're waiting, or push the button if you want to alight.

Buses, or "coaches," as privately operated bus services are known here, operate mainly from London's Victoria Coach Station to more than 1,200 major towns and cities.

Contact Transport for London. ☎ *0343/222–1234* ⊕ *www.tfl.gov.uk.*

CAR TRAVEL
The major approach roads to London are six-lane motorways. Motorways (from Heathrow, M4; from Gatwick, M23 to M25, then M3; Stansted, M11) are usually the faster option for getting in and out of town, although rush-hour traffic is horrendous. Stay tuned to local radio stations for updates.

The simple advice about driving in London is: don't. If you must drive, remember to drive on the left and stick to the speed limit (30 mph on some city streets, in the process of changing to 20 mph in several boroughs).

To encourage public-transit use and reduce traffic congestion, the city charges drivers of most vehicles entering central London £12 on weekdays from 7 am to 6 pm (excluding public holidays). Traffic signs designate the entrance to congestion-charge zones, and cameras read car license plates and send the information to a database. Drivers who don't pay up by midnight of the next charging day are penalized £130 (reduced to £65 if paid within 14 days).

2

TAXI TRAVEL

Taxis are expensive, but if you're with several people they can be practical. Hotels and main tourist areas have taxi ranks; you can also hail taxis on the street. If the yellow "For Hire" sign is lighted on top, the taxi is available. Fares start at £3, and there are per-minute charges. Taxi fares increase between 10 pm and 5 am, and a £2 surcharge is applied to telephone bookings. You don't have to tip taxi drivers, but it's advised; 10% of the fare is the norm, and most passengers round up to the nearest pound.

Like with most major cities, ride-sharing apps like Uber have become popular over the last few years (Uber's biggest competitor in the States, Lyft, has yet to arrive in London) despite legal action that temporarily halted service in late 2017.

TRAIN TRAVEL

London has eight major train stations, each serving a different area of the country, and all are accessible by Underground or bus. Various private companies operate trains, but National Rail Enquiries acts as a central rail information number.

Contact National Rail Enquiries. ☎ *0345/748–4950* ⊕ *www.nationalrail.co.uk.*

UNDERGROUND (TUBE) TRAVEL

London's extensive Underground train system (Tube) has color-coded routes, clear signage, and many connections. Trains run out into the suburbs, and all stations are marked with the London Underground circular symbol. (Do not be confused by similar-looking signs reading "subway," which is British for "pedestrian underpass.") There is also an Overground network serving the farther reaches of Inner London. Some lines have multiple branches (Central, District, Northern, Metropolitan, and Piccadilly), so be sure to note which branch is needed for your particular destination. Do this by noting the end destination on the lighted sign on the platform, which also tells you how long you'll have to wait until the train arrives. Compare that with the end destination of the branch you want. When the two match, that's your train.

London is divided into six concentric zones (ask at Underground ticket booths for a map and booklet, which give details of the ticket options), so be sure to buy a ticket for the correct zone or you may be liable for an on-the-spot fine of £80. Oyster cards are "smart cards" that can be charged with a cash value and then used for discounted travel throughout the city. A Visitor Oyster card, which you must buy before arriving in the United Kingdom, costs £3. Normal Oyster cards cost £5 and you can open an Oyster account online or pick up an Oyster card at any London Underground Station, and then prepay any amount you wish for your expected travel while in the city.

Passengers using Oyster cards pay lower rates. For one-way Tube fares paid in cash, a flat £5 price per journey now applies across all central zones (1–2), whether you're traveling 1 stop or 12. However, the corresponding Oyster card fare is £3. One-day Travelcards used to be good value for money but now, costing from £13 per card, they're a much less attractive option. If you're planning several trips in one day, it's much cheaper to buy an Oyster card: because of the system's daily "cap," you can make as many journeys as you want in Zones 1–2 for just £7 (or, in Zones 1–3 for £8). If you're going to be in town for several days, a seven-day Travelcard gives you the same value as an Oyster card (£33 for Zones 1–2, £61 for Zones 1–6). Oyster card Tube fares start at £2 and go up depending on the number of zones you're covering, the time of day, and whether you're traveling into Zone 1.

Although Oyster cards sound like the way of the future, they will soon be a thing of the past. Moves are underway to gradually phase out Oyster cards and to encourage passengers to move to a system of direct payments using their bank debit or credit cards instead. In practice, this means swiping a "contactless" bank card instead of your Oyster card at ticket barriers. The cheaper fares available to Oyster card holders are the same as those who pay by contactless cards.

Tube trains now run for 24 hours a day on weekends on five major lines: Piccadilly, Victoria, Northern, Central, and Jubilee. On all other lines the usual timetable still applies, with trains running from just after 5 am Monday to Saturday, and with the last services leaving central London between midnight and 12:30 am. On Sunday, trains start an hour later and finish about an hour earlier. The frequency of trains depends on the route and the time of day, but normally you should not have to wait more than 10 minutes in central areas.

TOUR OPTIONS
BOAT TOURS

Year-round, but more frequently from April to October, tour boats cruise the Thames, offering a singular view of the London skyline. Most leave from Westminster Pier, Charing Cross Pier, and Tower Pier. Boats on downstream routes pass by the Tower of London, Greenwich, and the Thames Barrier. Upstream destinations include Kew, Richmond, and Hampton Court (mainly in summer). Depending upon the destination, river trips may last from one to four hours.

London's tranquil side can be experienced on narrow boats that cruise the city's two canals, the Grand Union and the Regent's Canal; most vessels operate on the latter, which runs between Little Venice in the west (nearest Tube: Warwick Avenue, on the Bakerloo Line) and Camden Lock (about 200 yards north of the Camden Town Tube station). Fares start at £14 for 1½-hour round-trip cruises.

FAMILY
Fodor's Choice
★
City Cruises. In nice weather, an open top-deck ride from Westminster, the London Eye, or Tower Piers to the ancient royal romping ground of Greenwich along the Thames River is one of the best ways to get acquainted with the city. You'll pass sights like Tower Bridge, the Tower of London, and St. Paul's Cathedral, all with a chirpy Cockney boatman running commentary. Lunch, Afternoon Tea, and nighttime cruises are also available. ⊠ *Cherry Garden Pier, Cherry Garden St.* ☎ *020/7740–0400* ⊕ *www.citycruises.com* ⊠ *From £10.25.*

FAMILY
Fodor's Choice
★
London Duck Tours. Hop aboard one of the garish yellow, vintage amphibious trucks (originally used during World War II), and get ready to sputter past a stack of sights including 10 Downing Street and Westminster Abbey. Once at the spy agency MI6 building, you'll take like a duck to water and gently amble up the Thames to the Houses of Parliament.

Other tours focus on James Bond and the D-Day Landings. ✉ *55 York Rd.* ☎ *020/7928–3132* ⊕ *www.londonducktours.co.uk* ✆ *From £27.*

BUS TOURS

Guided sightseeing tours on hop-on, hop-off double-decker buses—open-top in summer—cover the main central sights. Many companies run daily bus tours that depart, usually between 8:30 and 9 am, from central points. Best Value and other outfits conduct guided tours in traditional coach buses. Tickets can be bought from the driver and are good all day. Prices vary according to the type of tour.

FAMILY
Fodor'sChoice
★

The Original London Sightseeing Tour. Like its double-decker competitors, the Original London Sightseeing Tour offers various hop-on, hop-off open-top tours of the city, but its most popular feature is its 48-hour pass that includes loops of the main historic sites, The City, Westminster, and the South Kensington museum districts. They also throw in free tickets for a Thames boat cruise, plus Jack the Ripper, Changing of the Guard, and Rock 'n' Roll walking tours. ✉ *London* ☎ *020/8877–1722* ⊕ *www.theoriginaltour.com* ✆ *From £29.*

WALKING TOURS

One of the best ways to get to know London is on foot, and there are many guided and themed walking tours, which cover everything from Jack the Ripper's East End to Dickens's West End.

FAMILY
Fodor'sChoice
★

London Food Lovers. Combine walking, talking, and eating (but not at the same time) on these fabulous multistop trails, featuring interesting restaurants and London cultural history. There are four half-day Soho-focused food tours complete with 10 stops, as well as two shorter three-hour evening options that include 5 stops, like the Jack the Ripper Happy Hour tasting tour, which focuses on gin, bagels, and locally brewed craft ales. ☎ *0777/409–9306* ⊕ *www.londonfoodlovers.com* ✆ *From £60.*

FAMILY
Fodor'sChoice
★

London Walks. With London's oldest established walking tours, there's no need to book ahead; instead, just turn up at the meeting point at the allotted hour and pay £10 for a first-rate, guided two-hour walk with themes like Secret London, Literary London, Harry Potter film locations, Haunted London, and much more. Top crime historian and leading Ripper authority Donald Rumbelow often leads the 7:30 pm Jack the Ripper walk in Whitechapel. ☎ *020/7624–3978* ⊕ *www.walks. com* ✆ *From £10.*

VISITOR INFORMATION

You can get good information at the Travel Information Centres at Victoria Station and St. Pancras International train station. These are helpful if you're looking for brochures for London sights and if you need a hotel. Travel Information Centres can also be found at the Euston and Liverpool Street train stations, Heathrow Airport, St. Paul's Cathedral churchyard, and Piccadilly Circus, as well as in Greenwich and some other Outer London locations.

Information Visit London. ⊕ *www.visitlondon.com.*

EXPLORING LONDON

Westminster and The City contain many of Britain's most historically significant buildings: the Tower of London, St. Paul's Cathedral, Westminster Abbey, the Houses of Parliament, and Buckingham Palace. Within a few-minutes' walk of Buckingham Palace lie St. James's and Mayfair, neighboring quarters of elegant town houses built for the nobility during the 17th and early 18th centuries and now notable for shopping opportunities.

Hyde Park and Kensington Gardens, originally Henry VIII's hunting ground, create an oasis of greenery in congested west London. Just south of the parks is South Kensington's museum district, with the Natural History Museum, the Science Museum, and the Victoria & Albert Museum. Another cultural center is the South Bank and Southwark: the concert halls of the South Bank Centre, the National Theatre, Tate Modern, and the reconstructed Shakespeare's Globe. Farther downstream is Maritime Greenwich, home of the meridian and a World Heritage Site, with its gorgeous Wren and Inigo Jones landmarks.

WESTMINSTER AND ST. JAMES'S

This is postcard London at its best. Crammed with historic churches, grand state buildings, and major art collections, the area unites politics, high culture, and religion. (Oh, and the Queen lives here, too.) World-class monuments such as Buckingham Palace, the Houses of Parliament, Westminster Abbey, and the National Gallery sit alongside lesser-known but lovingly curated museums redolent of British history. If you only have time to visit one part of London, this is it. This is concentrated sightseeing, so pace yourself. For much of the year a large portion of Royal London is floodlighted at night, adding to the theatricality of the experience.

GETTING HERE

Trafalgar Square—easy to access and in the center of the action—is a good place to start. Take the Tube to Embankment (District, Circle, Bakerloo, and Northern lines) and walk north until you cross the Strand, or exit to Northumberland Avenue at Charing Cross (Bakerloo and Northern lines). Buses are another great option, as almost all roads lead to Trafalgar Square.

Fodor'sChoice **Buckingham Palace.** When the Queen heads off to Scotland on her annual
★   summer holiday (you can tell because the Union Jack flies above the palace instead of the Royal Standard), the 19 State Rooms of her official residence, which was begun in 1702, plus the sprawling palace gardens, open up to visitors. However, the north wing's private apartments always remain behind closed doors. With fabulous gilt moldings and walls adorned with masterpieces by Rembrandt, Rubens, and other Old Masters, the State Rooms are the grandest of the palace's 775 rooms. Admission is by timed ticket with entry every 15 minutes throughout the day. Allow up to two hours. ■TIP→ Get there by 10:30 to grab a spot in the best viewing section for the ceremonial Changing the Guard—one of London's best free shows—that happens daily at 11

A classic photo op: don't miss the cavalry from the Queen's Life Guard at Buckingham Palace.

from May until the end of July (varies according to troop deployment requirements) and on alternate days for the rest of the year, weather permitting. ⊠ *Buckingham Palace Rd., St. James's* ☎ *020/7766–7300* ⊕ *www.royalcollection.org.uk/visit* 💷 *£24 (£33 including garden highlights tour)* 🕑 *Closed Oct.–July except on selected dates* Ⓜ *Victoria, St. James's Park, Green Park.*

FAMILY
Fodor'sChoice
★

Churchill War Rooms. It was from this small warren of underground rooms—beneath the vast government buildings of the Treasury—that Winston Churchill and his team directed troops in World War II. Designed to be bombproof, the whole complex has been preserved almost exactly as it was when the last light was turned off at the end of the war. Every clock shows almost 5 pm, and the furniture, fittings, and paraphernalia of a busy, round-the-clock war office are still in situ, down to the colored map pins.

During air raids, the leading government ministers met here, and the Cabinet Room is arranged as if a meeting were about to convene. In the Map Room, the Allied campaign is charted on wall-to-wall maps with a rash of pinholes showing the movements of convoys. In the hub of the room, a bank of differently colored phones known as the "Beauty Chorus" linked the War Rooms to control rooms around the nation. The Prime Minister's Room holds the desk from which Churchill made his morale-boosting broadcasts; the Telephone Room (a converted broom cupboard) has his hotline to FDR. You can also see the restored rooms that the PM used for dining and sleeping. Telephonists (switchboard operators) and clerks who worked 16-hour shifts slept in lesser quarters in unenviable conditions.

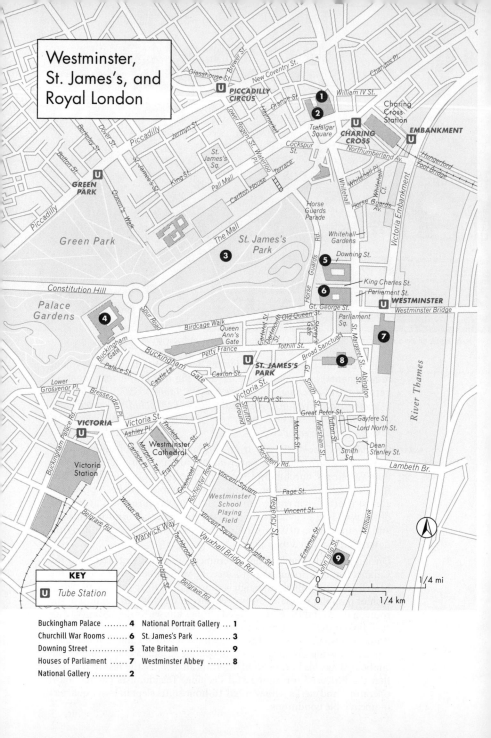

Westminster, St. James's, and Royal London

KEY

U Tube Station

An excellent addition to the War Rooms is the Churchill Museum, a tribute to the great wartime leader himself. ⊠ *Clive Steps, King Charles St., Westminster* ☎ *020/7416–5000* ⊕ *www.iwm.org.uk/visits/churchill-war-rooms* ⊠ *£21* Ⓜ *Westminster.*

Downing Street. Were it not for the wrought-iron gates and armed guards that block the entrance, you'd probably miss this otherwise unassuming Georgian side street off Whitehall—but this is the location of the famous **No. 10**, London's modest equivalent of the White House. The Georgian entrance to the mid-17th century mansion is deceptive; it's actually a huge complex of discreetly linked buildings. Since 1732 it has been the official home and office of the prime minister—the last private resident was the magnificently named Mr. Chicken (the current prime minister actually lives in the private apartments above No. 11, traditionally the residence of the Chancellor of the Exchequer, the head of the Treasury). There are no public tours, but the famous black front door to No. 10 is clearly visible from Whitehall. Keep your eyes peeled for Larry the cat, whose official title is Chief Mouser to the Cabinet Office. Just south of Downing Street, in the middle of Whitehall, is the **Cenotaph,** a stark white monolith built to commemorate the 1918 armistice. On Remembrance Day (the Sunday nearest November 11), it's strewn with red poppy wreaths to honor the dead of both world wars and all British and Commonwealth soldiers killed in action since; the first wreath is always laid by the Queen. A hundred yards farther, toward Parliament, is the **Monument to the Women of World War II.** The prominent black marble sculpture uses a string of empty uniforms to symbolize the vital service of women in then-traditionally male jobs during the war, as well as in frontline roles, such as medics and auxiliary officers. ⊠ *Whitehall* Ⓜ *Westminster.*

Houses of Parliament. The Palace of Westminster, as the complex is called, was first established on this site by Edward the Confessor in the 11th century. William II built a new palace in 1097, and this became the seat of English power. Fire destroyed most of the palace in 1834; the current complex dates largely from the mid-19th century. The Clock Tower— renamed Elizabeth Tower in 2012—dates from 1858 and contains the 13-ton bell known as Big Ben. The Visitors' Galleries of the House of Commons are particularly popular during the Prime Minister's Questions at 12 pm every Wednesday when Parliament is sitting (tickets are free, but noncitizens can only line up and hope for no-shows). Westminster Hall, with its remarkable hammer-beam roof, was the work of William the Conqueror's son William Rufus and is one of the largest remaining Norman halls. ⊠ *St. Stephen's Entrance, St. Margaret St., Westminster* ☎ *0207/219–4114 for public tours* ⊕ *www.parliament.uk/visiting* ⊠ *Free; tours £28, audio tours £20.50* ☉ *Closed Sun.* Ⓜ *Westminster.*

National Gallery. Standing proudly on the north side of Trafalgar Square is truly one of the world's supreme art museums, with more than 2,300 masterpieces on show. The collection includes masterpieces by Michelangelo, Leonardo, Turner, Monet, van Gogh, Picasso, and more—all for free (however, you pay for any special exhibitions). Watch out for outstanding temporary exhibitions, too. While you could allow a handful of paintings to fill your visit, there are hundreds of other paintings to see, enough to fill a full day, including important works by Van Eyck, Holbein, Velázquez, Caravaggio, and Seurat. One-hour free, guided tours start at the Sainsbury Wing every day at 11:30 and 2:30. If you are eager for even more insight into the art, pick up a themed audio guide. Special audio tours include "sounds of the gallery," which are soundscapes to accompany the paintings. ⊠ *Trafalgar Sq., Westminster* ☎ *020/7747–2885* ⊕ *www. nationalgallery.org.uk* ✉ *Free; special exhibitions £7–£22; audio guide £5* Ⓜ *Charing Cross, Embankment, Leicester Sq.*

FAMILY
Fodor'sChoice
★

National Portrait Gallery. The National Portrait Gallery was founded in 1856 with a single aim: to gather together portraits of famous (and infamous) Britons throughout history. More than 150 years and 200,000 portraits later, it is an essential stop for all history and literature buffs. If you visit with kids, ask at the desk about the excellent Family Trails, which make exploring the galleries with children much more fun. Galleries are arranged clearly and chronologically, from Tudor Times to the present. The huge permanent collections include portraits of all the British monarchs, Shakespeare, the Brontë sisters, and Jane Austen. Temporary exhibitions can be explored on the first three floors, particularly in the Wolfson and Porter galleries, on the ground floor. ■TIP➔ On the top floor, the Portrait Restaurant has one of the best views in London—a panoramic vista of Nelson's Column and the backdrop along Whitehall to the Houses of Parliament. ⊠ *St. Martin's Pl., Westminster* ☎ *020/7306–0055* ⊕ *www.npg.org.uk* ✉ *Free; special exhibitions £6–£18; audiovisual guide £3; family audio guides £6 for 5 people* Ⓜ *Charing Cross, Leicester Sq.*

FAMILY
Fodor'sChoice
★

St. James's Park. There is a story that, many years ago, a royal once inquired of a courtier how much it would cost to close St. James's Park to the public. "Only your crown, ma'am" came the reply. Bordered by three palaces—Buckingham, St. James', and the governmental complex of the Palace of Westminster—this is one of London's loveliest public parks. It's also the oldest; the former marshland was acquired by Henry VIII in 1532 as a nursery for his deer. Later, James I drained the land and installed an aviary, which gave Birdcage Walk its name, and a zoo (complete with crocodiles, camels, and an elephant). When Charles II returned from exile in France, where he had been hugely impressed by the splendor of the gardens at the Palace of Versailles, he transformed the park into formal gardens, with avenues, fruit orchards, and a canal. Lawns were grazed by goats, sheep, and deer, and in the 18th century the park became a different kind of hunting ground, for wealthy lotharios looking to pick up nighttime escorts. A century later, John Nash redesigned the landscape in a more naturalistic, romantic style, and if you gaze down the lake toward Buckingham Palace, you could easily believe yourself to be on a country estate.

A large population of waterfowl—including pelicans, geese, ducks, and swans (which belong to the Queen)—breed on and around Duck Island at the east end of the lake. The pelicans are fed at 2:30 daily. From March to October, the deck chairs (charge levied) come out, crammed with office workers at midday, eating lunch while being serenaded by music from the bandstands. One of the best times to stroll the leafy walkways is after dark, with Westminster Abbey and the Houses of Parliament rising above the floodlit lake. ⊠ *The Mall or Horse Guards approach or Birdcage Walk, St. James's* ⊕ *www.royalparks.org.uk* Ⓜ *St. James's Park, Westminster.*

FAMILY **Tate Britain.** First opened in 1897, and funded by the sugar magnate Sir Henry Tate, this stately neoclassical institution is a great place to explore British art from 1500 to the present. The museum includes the Linbury Galleries on the lower floors, which stage temporary exhibitions, and a permanent collection on the upper floors. And what a collection it is—classic works by John Constable, Thomas Gainsborough, Rachel Whiteread, Francis Bacon, Duncan Grant, Barbara Hepworth, and Vanessa Bell, and an outstanding display from J. M. W. Turner in the Clore Gallery. Sumptuous Pre-Raphaelite pieces are a major draw, while the Contemporary British Art galleries bring you face to face with Damien Hirst's *Away from the Flock* and other recent conceptions. There's a good little café, and the excellent Rex Whistler Restaurant has been something of an institution since it first opened in 1927. ■ TIP→ **The Tate Boat (£8.30 one-way) offers a direct trip to the Tate Modern every 40 minutes.** ⊠ *Millbank, Westminster* ☎ *020/7887–8888* ⊕ *www.tate.org.uk/britain* ⊠ *Free; special exhibitions £13–£22; audio guide £4.50* Ⓜ *Pimlico.*

Fodor's Choice **Westminster Abbey.** Steeped in hundreds of years of rich and occasionally bloody history, Westminster Abbey is one of England's most iconic buildings, most of which dates from the 1240s. It has hosted 38 coronations and no fewer than 16 royal weddings, but it is equally well known for its permanent residents, from kings to writers, who are buried here—and many more who are memorialized. Highlights include the world's largest rose window, the Coronation Chair (dating to 1301), Grave of the Unknown Warrior, and the Poet's Corner. The adjoining medieval Chapter House is adorned with 14th-century frescoes and a magnificent 13th-century tiled floor. The **College Garden** of medicinal herbs is a delightful diversion. Exact hours are long and complex (and can change), so it's important to check before setting out. ⚠ Beware: Lines can be long during peak hours. ⊠ *Broad Sanctuary, Westminster* ☎ *020/7222–5152* ⊕ *www.westminster-abbey.org* ⊠ *£22* ⊙ *Closed Sun., except for worship* Ⓜ *Westminster, St. James's Park.*

SOHO AND COVENT GARDEN

Soho has long been the media and nightlife center of London, its narrow, winding streets unabashedly devoted to pleasure. Wardour Street bisects the neighborhood. Many interesting boutiques and some of London's best-value restaurants can be found to the west, especially around Foubert's Place and on Brewer and Lexington streets. Nightlife central lies to the east—including London's gay mecca and Old Compton Street. Beyond that is the city's densest collection of theaters, on Shaftesbury Avenue, with London's compact Chinatown just past it. A bit of erudition surfaces to the east on Charing Cross Road, still with a couple of the secondhand bookshops it was once known for, and on tiny Cecil Court, a pedestrianized passage lined with small antiquarian booksellers.

To the east of Charing Cross Road you'll find Covent Garden, once a wholesale fruit and vegetable market and now more of a shopping mall. Although boutiques and outposts of high-end chains line the surrounding streets, many Londoners come to Covent Garden for two notable arts venues: the Royal Opera House and the Donmar Warehouse, one of London's best and most innovative theaters. To the south, the Strand leads to the huge, stately piazza of Somerset House, home to the many masterpieces on view at the Courtauld Gallery, a fine small art museum.

GETTING HERE

Almost all Tube lines cross the Covent Garden and Soho areas, so it's easy to hop off for a dinner or show in this lively part of London. For Soho, take any train to Piccadilly Circus, Leicester Square, Oxford Circus, or Tottenham Court Road. For Covent Garden, get off at the Covent Garden Station on the Piccadilly Line. It might be easier to exit the Tube at Leicester Square or Holborn and walk. Thirty buses connect to the Covent Garden area from all over London.

Covent Garden Piazza. Once home to London's main flower market, where *My Fair Lady's* Eliza Doolittle peddled her blooms, the square around which Covent Garden pivots is known as the Piazza. In the center, the fine old market building now houses stalls and shops selling expensive clothing, plus several restaurants and cafés, and knickknack stores that are good for gifts. One particular gem is Benjamin Pollock's Toyshop at No. 44 in the market. Established in the 1880s, it sells delightful toy theaters. The superior **Apple Market** has good crafts stalls on most days, too. On the south side of the Piazza, the indoor **Jubilee Market,** with its stalls of clothing, army-surplus gear, and more crafts and knickknacks, feels a bit like a flea market. In summer it may seem that everyone in the huge crowds around you in the Piazza is a fellow tourist, but there's still plenty of office life in the area. Londoners who shop here tend to head for Neal Street and the area to the north of Covent Garden Tube station, rather than the market itself. In the Piazza, street performers—from global musicians to jugglers and mimes—play to the crowds, as they have done since the first English Punch and Judy Show, staged here in the 17th century. ⊠ *Covent Garden* ⊕ *www.coventgarden.london* Ⓜ *Covent Garden.*

FAMILY
Fodor's Choice
★

London Transport Museum. Housed in the old flower market at the southeast corner of Covent Garden, this stimulating museum is filled with impressive vehicle, poster, and photograph collections. As you watch the crowds drive a Tube-train simulation and gawk at the steam locomotives and horse-drawn trams (and the piles of detritus that remained behind), it's unclear who's enjoying it more: children or adults. Best of all, the kid-friendly museum (under 18 admitted free, and there's a play area) has a multilevel approach to education, including information for the youngest visitor and the most advanced transit aficionado alike. Food and drink are available at the Upper Deck café, and the shop has lots of good options for gift-buying. ■TIP➔ Tickets are valid for unlimited entry for 12 months. ⊠ *Covent Garden Piazza, Covent Garden* ☎ *020/7379–6344* ⊕ *www.ltmuseum.co.uk* 🎫 *£17.50* Ⓜ *Covent Garden, Leicester Sq.*

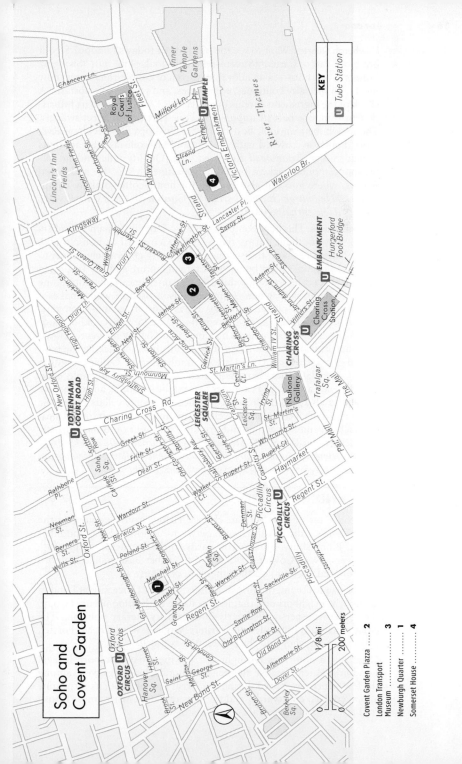

Soho and Covent Garden

KEY

U Tube Station

Covent Garden Piazza **2**
London Transport
  Museum **3**
Newburgh Quarter **1**
Somerset House **4**

Fodor's Choice ★   **Newburgh Quarter.** Want to see the hip style of today's London? Find it one block east of Carnaby Street—where the look of the '60s "Swinging London" was born—in an adorable warren of cobblestone streets now lined with specialty boutiques, edgy stores, and young indie upstarts. A check of the ingredients reveals one part '60s London, one part futuristic fetishism, one part steampunk, and one part British street swagger. The new-bohemian look best flourishes in shops like Peckham Rye, a tiny boutique crowded with rockers and fashionistas who adore its grunge–meets- *Brideshead Revisited* vibe. Quality independent coffee shops abound—take a break at Department of Coffee and Social Affairs, where you can also browse for home coffee-making equipment. ⊠ *Newburgh St., Foubert's Pl., Ganton St., and Carnaby St., Soho* ⊕ *www.carnaby.co.uk.*

FAMILY **Fodor's** Choice ★   **Somerset House.** This huge complex—the work of Sir William Chambers (1723–96), and built during the reign of George III to house offices of the Navy—has been transformed from dusty government offices to one of the capital's most buzzing centers of culture and the arts, often hosting several interesting exhibitions at one time. The cobblestone Italianate courtyard, where Admiral Nelson used to walk, makes a great setting for 55 playful fountains and is transformed into a romantic ice rink in winter; the grand space is the venue for music and outdoor movie screenings in summer. The **Courtauld Gallery** (currently closed for renovations) occupies most of the north building, facing the busy Strand. Across the courtyard are the Embankment Galleries, with a vibrant calendar of design, fashion, architecture, and photography exhibitions. The East Wing has another fine exhibition space, and events are sometimes also held in the atmospherically gloomy cellars below the Fountain Court. Fernandez & Wells is a great spot for an informal meal or snack. In summer eating and drinking spills out onto the large terrace next to the Thames. ⊠ *Strand, Covent Garden* ☎ *020/7845–4600* ⊕ *www.somersethouse.org.uk* ⊠ *Embankment Galleries price varies, other areas free* Ⓜ *Charing Cross, Waterloo, Blackfriars.*

BLOOMSBURY AND HOLBORN

The character of London can change visibly from one area to the next. There's a distinct difference between fun-loving Soho and intellectual Bloomsbury, a mere 100 yards to the northeast, or between the diversions of Covent Garden and the sober businesslike Holborn (pronounced *hoe*-bun) on the other side of Kingsway.

The British Museum, the British Library, and the University of London anchor the neighborhood that lent its name to the Bloomsbury Group, the clique who personified early-20th-century literary bohemia. The circle's mainstays included the writers Virginia Woolf, E. M. Forster, and Lytton Strachey and the painter Vanessa Bell.

Originally a notorious red-light district, these days Holborn is legal London's center. Because the neighborhood's buildings were among the few structures spared during the Great Fire of 1666, its serpentine alleys, cobbled courtyards, and the Inns of Court, where most British trial lawyers still have offices, ooze history.

The massive, glass-roofed Great Court in the British Museum has a couple of cafés.

GETTING HERE

You can easily get to where you need to be on foot in Bloomsbury, and the Russell Square Tube stop on the Piccadilly Line leaves you right at the corner of Russell Square. The best Tube stops for Holborn are on the Central and Piccadilly lines and Chancery Lane on the Central Line. Tottenham Court Road on the Northern and Central lines and Russell Square (Piccadilly Line) are best for the British Museum.

FAMILY **British Library.** With a collection totaling more than 150 million items, plus 3 million new additions every year, the British Library is a world-class repository of knowledge. Its greatest treasures are on view to the general public: the Magna Carta, the Codex Sinaiticus (an ancient bible containing the oldest complete copy of the New Testament), Jane Austen's writings, and Shakespeare's First Folio. Musical manuscripts by G.F. Handel as well as the Beatles are on display in the Sir John Ritblat Gallery. ⊠ *96 Euston Rd., Bloomsbury* ☎ *0330/333–1144* ⊕ *www.bl.uk* ☎ *Free, donations appreciated; charge for special exhibitions* Ⓜ *Euston, Euston Sq., King's Cross St. Pancras.*

FAMILY
Fodor's Choice
★
British Museum. With a facade like a great temple, this celebrated treasure house, filled with plunder of incalculable value and beauty from around the globe, occupies an imposing neoclassical building in the heart of Bloomsbury. Inside are some of the greatest relics of humankind: the Parthenon Sculptures (Elgin Marbles), the Rosetta Stone, the Sutton Hoo Treasure, Egyptian mummies, a colossal statue of Ramesses II, fragments of the Seven Wonders of the Ancient World—almost everything, it seems, but the original Ten Commandments. The museum's focal point is the **Great Court**, a brilliant modern design with a vast

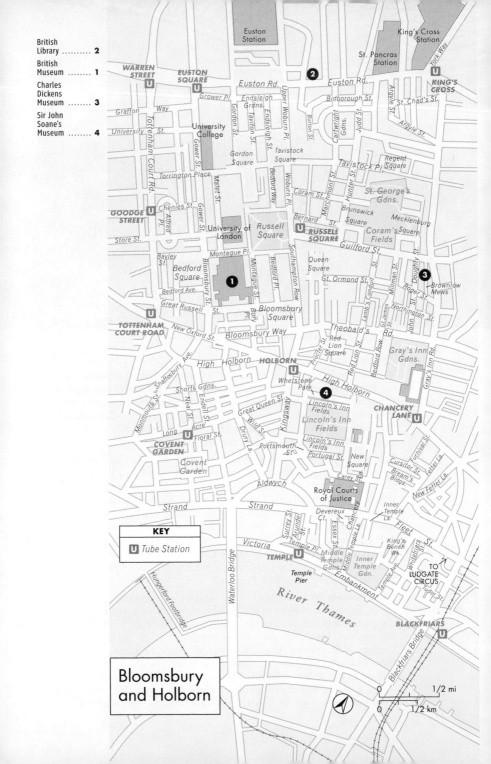

British
Library **2**

British
Museum **1**

Charles
Dickens
Museum **3**

Sir John
Soane's
Museum **4**

KEY

U *Tube Station*

Bloomsbury
and Holborn

glass roof atop the museum's covered courtyard. The elegant **Reading Room** has a blue-and-gold dome and hosts temporary exhibitions. ■ **TIP→** Free tours cover the highlights in an economical 30 or 40 minutes. ⊠ *Great Russell St., Bloomsbury* 🕾 *020/7323–8000* ⊕ *www.britishmuseum.org* ✉ *Free; donations encouraged* Ⓜ *Russell Sq., Holborn, Tottenham Court Rd.*

Charles Dickens Museum. This is one of the few London houses Charles Dickens (1812–70) inhabited that is still standing, and it's the place where the master wrote *Oliver Twist* and *Nicholas Nickleby* and finished *The Pickwick Papers*. The house looks exactly as it would have in Dickens's day, complete with first editions, letters, and a tall clerk's desk (Dickens wrote standing up). The museum also houses a shop and a garden café. ⊠ *48 Doughty St., Bloomsbury* 🕾 *020/7405–2127* ⊕ *www.dickensmuseum.com* ✉ *£9.50* ۞ *Closed Mon.* Ⓜ *Chancery La., Russell Sq.*

Fodor's Choice
★ **Sir John Soane's Museum.** Sir John (1753–1837), architect of the Bank of England, bequeathed his eccentric house to the nation on one condition: that nothing be changed. It's a house full of surprises. In the Picture Room, two of Hogarth's famous *Rake's Progress* paintings swing away to reveal secret gallery recesses where you can find works by Canaletto and Turner. Everywhere, mirrors play tricks with light and space, and split-level floors worthy of a fairground fun house disorient you. Restoration work has opened up Soane's private apartments to the public, but they can be viewed only as part of a first-come, first-served tour at 1:15 pm and 2 pm, daily. ⊠ *13 Lincoln's Inn Fields, Bloomsbury* 🕾 *020/7405–2107* ⊕ *www.soane.org* ✉ *Free; guided tours £12.50* ۞ *Closed Mon. and Tues.* Ⓜ *Holborn.*

THE CITY

The City, as opposed to the city, is the capital's economic engine room. But the "Square Mile" captures attention for more than its role as London's Wall Street. Wren's masterpiece, the English baroque St. Paul's Cathedral, still stuns, as does the medieval Tower of London (full name: Her Majesty's Royal Palace and Fortress), which has served many functions during its more than 1,000-year history. Off the main roads, The City's winding lanes and courtyards are rich in historic churches and pubs.

The City has twice nearly been destroyed, first by the Great Fire of 1666—after which Sir Christopher Wren was put in charge of a total reconstruction that resulted in St. Paul's Cathedral and 49 lovely parish churches—and later by German bombing raids during World War II. Following the raids the area was rebuilt over time, but with no grand plan. Consequently, The City is a mishmash of the old, the new, the innovative, the distinguished, and the flagrantly awful. A walk across the Millennium Bridge from Tate Modern to St. Paul's offers a superb view of the river and the cathedral that presides over it.

GETTING HERE

The Underground serves The City at several stops. St Paul's and Bank, on the Central Line, and Mansion House, Cannon Street, and Monument, on the District and Circle lines, deliver visitors to its center. Liverpool Street and Aldgate border The City's eastern edge, and Chancery Lane and Farringdon lie to the west. Barbican and Moorgate provide easy access to the theaters and galleries of the Barbican, and Blackfriars, to the south, leads to Ludgate Circus and Fleet Street.

FAMILY

Fodor'sChoice

★

Museum of London. If there's one place to absorb the history of London, from 450,000 BC to the present day, it's here. There are 7,000 objects to wonder at in all, including Oliver Cromwell's death mask, Queen Victoria's crinolines, Selfridges's art deco elevators, and an original door from the infamous Newgate Prison. The collection devoted to Roman London contains some extraordinary gems, including an astonishingly well-preserved floor mosaic uncovered just a few streets away. Innovative interactive displays abound, and there's also a fine schedule of temporary exhibitions. Don't miss the extraordinary Bronze Age and Roman artifacts unearthed during construction of the new Crossrail underground railway. ⊠ *150 London Wall, City of London* ☎ *020/7001–9844* ⊕ *www.museumoflondon.org.uk* ⊠ *Free* Ⓜ *Barbican, St. Paul's.*

Fodor'sChoice

★

St. Paul's Cathedral. For centuries this iconic structure has represented London's spirit of survival and renewal, and it remains a breathtaking structure, inside and out. The structure is Sir Christopher Wren's masterpiece, completed in 1710 after 35 years of building, and, much later, miraculously spared (mostly) by World War II bombs. It was actually Wren's third plan for the cathedral that was accepted, though he added the distinctive dome later. Up 163 spiral steps is the **Whispering Gallery**, with its incredible acoustic phenomenon; you whisper something to the wall on one side, and a second later it transmits clearly to the other side, 107 feet away. From the upper galleries you can walk outside for a spectacular panorama of London. As in Westminster Abbey, prominent people are buried inside the cathedral, including Wren himself, as well as the poet John Donne, the Duke of Wellington, and Admiral Lord Nelson. Free, 90-minute guided tours take place Monday to Saturday at 10, 11, 1, and 2; book a place at the welcome desk (on the day of only). ⊠ *St. Paul's Churchyard, City of London* ☎ *020/7246–8350, 020/7246–8357 for Triforium tours* ⊕ *www.stpauls.co.uk* ⊠ *£18* ⊙ *Closed Sun. except for services* Ⓜ *St. Paul's.*

Tower Bridge. Despite its medieval appearance, Britain's most iconic bridge was actually built at the tail end of the Victorian age, first opening to traffic in 1894. Constructed of steel, then clothed in Portland stone, the Horace Jones masterpiece was built in the Gothic style that was highly popular at the time (and it nicely complements the Tower of London, next door). The bridge is famous for its enormous bascules— the 1,200-ton "arms" that open to allow large ships to glide beneath. This still happens a few times per month (the website lists upcoming times), but when river traffic was dense, the bascules were raised about five times a day. The **Tower Bridge Exhibition** is a family-friendly tour where you can discover how the bridge actually works before heading

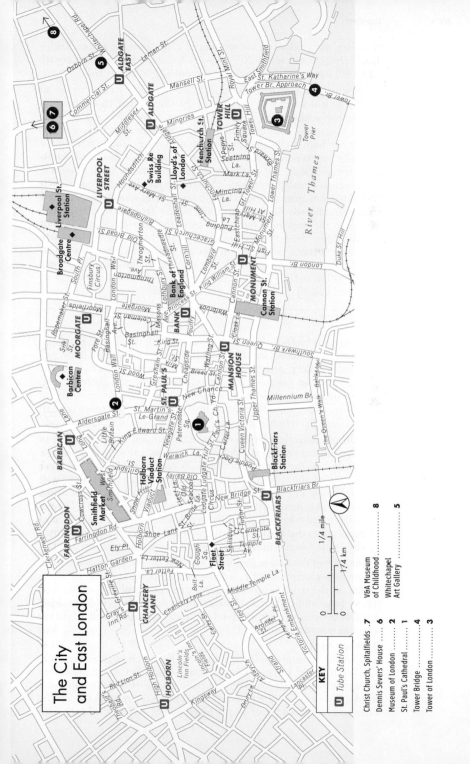

The City
and East London

KEY

🚇 *Tube Station*

out onto the walkways for wonderful city views. ✉ *Tower Bridge Rd., City of London* ☎ *020/7403–3761* ⊕ *www.towerbridge.org.uk* 🎫 *£9.80; joint admission with Monument £12* Ⓜ *Tower Hill.*

FAMILY **Tower of London.** Nowhere else does London's history come to life so Fodor'sChoice vividly as it does in this minicity of 20 towers that have housed a ★ palace, barracks, the Royal Mint, archives, an armory, and even the Royal Menagerie. Conceived in 1078 by William the Conqueror, the Tower has been a place of imprisonment, torture, and execution for the realm's most notorious traitors, and a few innocents as well. Allow at least three hours for exploring, and take time to stroll along the battlements. Highlights include the **Crown Jewels**, the **White Tower** (the oldest structure here, which includes the Armouries), the Medieval Palace, and **Bloody Tower**. Free tours by the Yeoman Warders, better known as the Beefeaters (who also mind the Tower's ravens), depart every half hour from the main entrance. ■ **TIP→ Buy tickets in advance whenever possible; write several months in advance to get free tickets to the 700-year-old Ceremony of the Keys (the nightly locking of main gates).** ✉ *Tower Hill, City of London* ☎ *020/3166–6000* ⊕ *www.hrp. org.uk* 🎫 *£26.80 (£22.70 online)* Ⓜ *Tower Hill.*

EAST LONDON

Made famous by Dickens and infamous by Jack the Ripper, East London is one of London's most enduringly evocative neighborhoods, rich in popular history, architectural gems, and artists' studios. Since the early 1990s, hip gallerists, designers, and new-media entrepreneurs have colonized its handsome Georgian buildings and converted industrial lofts. Today, the collection of neighborhoods that makes up East London lays claim to being the city's most trendsetting neighborhoods.

The British equivalent of Brooklyn, East London is a patchwork of districts encompassing struggling artists, ethnic enclaves, upscale professionals, and the digerati, occasionally teetering, like its New York equivalent, on the edge of self-parody. The vast area ranges from gentrified districts like Spitalfields—where bankers and successful artists live in desirable renovated Georgian town houses—to parts of Hackney where seemingly derelict, graffiti-covered industrial buildings are hives of exciting creative activity. As with all neighborhoods in transition, it can be a little rough around the edges, so stick to busier streets at night.

At the start of the new millennium, Hoxton, an enclave of Shoreditch, became the glossy hub of London's buzzing contemporary art scene, which accelerated the gentrification process. Some artists, such as Tracey Emin and Gilbert & George, long-term residents of Spitalfields' handsome Georgian terraces (and successful enough to still afford the area), have remained.

GETTING HERE
The London Overground, with stops at Shoreditch High Street, Hoxton, Whitechapel, Dalston Kingsland, and Hackney Central, is the easiest way to reach East London. Alternatively, the best Tube stations to use are Old Street on the Northern Line, Bethnal Green on the Central Line, and Liverpool Street on the Metropolitan and Circle lines.

Fodor's Choice
★

Christ Church, Spitalfields. This is the 1729 masterpiece of Sir Christopher Wren's associate Nicholas Hawksmoor, one of his six London churches and an example of English baroque at its finest. It was commissioned as part of Parliament's 1711 "Fifty New Churches" Act, passed in response to the influx of immigrants with the idea of providing for the religious needs of the "godless thousands"—and to help ensure they joined the Church of England, as opposed to such nonconformist denominations as the Protestant Huguenots. (It must have worked; you can still see gravestones with epitaphs in French in the crypt.) As the local silk industry declined, the church fell into disrepair, and by 1958 the structure was crumbling, with the looming prospect of demolition. But after 25 years—longer than it took to build the church—and a huge local fund-raising effort, the structure was meticulously restored and is a joy to behold, from the colonnaded Doric portico and tall spire to its soaring, heavily ornamented plaster ceiling. Its excellent acoustics make it a superb concert venue. Tours that take you "backstage" to the many hidden rooms and passages, from the tower to the vaults, are offered by appointment. There's also a café in the crypt. ⊠ *Commercial St., Spitalfields* ☎ *020/7377–2440* ⊕ *www.ccspitalfields.org* ☜ *Free, tours £6* ☉ *Closed Sat.* Ⓜ *Overground: Shoreditch High St.*

Fodor's Choice
★

Dennis Severs' House. The remarkable interiors of this extraordinary time machine of a house are the creation of Dennis Severs (1948–99), a performer-designer-scholar from Escondido, California, who dedicated his life to restoring this Georgian terraced house. More than that, he created "still-life dramas" using sight, sound, and smell to evoke the world of a fictitious family of Huguenot silk weavers, the Jervises, who might have inhabited the house between 1728 and 1914. Each of the 10 rooms has a distinctive compelling atmosphere that encourages visitors to become lost in another time, deploying evocative design details like rose-laden Victorian wallpaper, Jacobean paneling, Georgian wing-back chairs, baroque carved ornaments, rich "Catholic" wall colors downstairs, and more sedate "Protestant" shades upstairs. The Silent Night candlelight tour offered Monday, Wednesday, and Friday evenings, a stroll through the rooms with no talking allowed, is the most theatrical and memorable way to experience the house. The Exclusive Silent Night visits, which conclude with champagne or mulled wine by the fire and a chat with the curators, are available one night per month (more frequently near the Christmas holiday), and private group visits can also be arranged. ⊠ *18 Folgate St., Shoreditch* ☎ *020/7247–4013* ⊕ *www.dennissevershouse.co.uk* ☜ *£10 Sun. and Mon., £15 Mon., Wed., and Fri. evenings* ☉ *Closed Tues., Thurs., and Sat.* Ⓜ *Overground: Shoreditch High St.*

FAMILY
Fodor's Choice
★

V&A Museum of Childhood. A treat for children of all ages, this East London outpost of the Victoria & Albert Museum—in an iron, glass, and brown-brick building transported here from South Kensington in 1868—houses one of the world's biggest toy collections. One highlight (among many) is the large Dolls' Houses collection, with interiors from 1673 up to the present. You'll find everything from board games and puzzles to teddy bears and train sets. The collection is organized into galleries: Moving Toys, which includes everything from rocking horses to Xboxes; Creativity, which encompasses dolls, puppets, chemistry sets, play kitchens, construction toys, and musical instruments; and Childhood, with areas devoted to babies, an exhibit of children's clothes from the mid-1600s to the present, and toys inspired by adult pursuits, such as toy soldiers, toy guns, and toy hospitals. Don't miss the magnificent 18th-century commedia dell'arte puppet theater, thought to have been made in Venice. There are special activities for the under-fives. The shop has replica toys that make great presents. ⊠ *Cambridge Heath Rd., Bethnal Green* ☎ *020/8983–5200* ⊕ *www.museumofchildhood.org.uk* ⊠ *Free* Ⓜ *Bethnal Green.*

Fodor's Choice ★ **Whitechapel Art Gallery.** Founded in 1901, this internationally renowned gallery mounts exhibitions that rediscover overlooked masters and showcase tomorrow's legends. Painter and leading exponent of abstract expressionism Jackson Pollock was exhibited here in the 1950s as was pop artist Robert Rauschenberg in the 1960s; the 1970s saw a young David Hockney's first solo show. The exhibitions continue to be on the cutting edge of contemporary art. The gallery also hosts talks, film screenings, workshops, and other events; tours of local galleries take place on the first Thursday of every month. Pick up a free East London art map to help you plan your visit to the area. ⊠ *77–82 Whitechapel High St., Whitechapel* ☎ *020/7522–7888* ⊕ *www.whitechapelgallery. org* ⊠ *Free–£15* ⊗ *Closed Mon.* Ⓜ *Aldgate East.*

SOUTH OF THE THAMES

Culture, history, markets—the South Bank has them all. Installed in a converted 1930s power station, Tate Modern is the star attraction, with the eye-catching Millennium Bridge connecting it to The City across the river. Near the National Theatre and the concert halls of the South Bank Centre, the London Eye observation wheel gives you a bird's-eye view of the city.

Traditionally, Southwark was a rough area known for its inns, prisons, bear-baiting arenas, and theaters. The Globe, which housed the company Shakespeare wrote for and performed with, was one of several here. It has been reconstructed on the original site, so you can experience watching the Bard's plays as the Elizabethans would have. Be sure to take a stroll along Queen's Walk, the embankment along the Thames from Southwark to Blackfriars Bridge, taking in Tate Modern along the way.

GETTING HERE

For the South Bank, use Embankment on the District, Circle, Northern, and Bakerloo lines. From here you can walk across the Queens Jubilee footbridges. Another option is Waterloo—on the Northern, Jubilee, and Bakerloo lines—from where it's a five-minute walk to the Royal Festival Hall (slightly longer from the Jubilee Line Station). London Bridge on the Northern and Jubilee lines is a five-minute walk from Borough Market and Southwark Cathedral.

FAMILY
Fodor's Choice ★ **IWM London.** Despite its name, the cultural venue formerly known as the Imperial War Museum (one of five IWM branches around the country) does not glorify either Empire or bloodshed but emphasizes

understanding through conveying the impact of 20th- and 21st-century warfare on citizens and soldiers alike. A dramatic six-story atrium at the main entrance encloses an impressive amount of hardware—including a Battle of Britain Spitfire, a German V2 rocket, the remains of a car blown up in post-invasion Iraq, tanks, guns, and submarines—along with accompanying interactive material and a café. The First World War galleries explore the wartime experience on both the home and fighting fronts, with the most comprehensive collection on the subject in the world—some 1,300 objects ranging from uniforms, equipment, and weapons to letters and diaries. Three permanent exhibitions in the Second World War galleries shed light on that conflict: an extensive and haunting Holocaust exhibition; *A Family In Wartime,* which documents the story of one London family living through the Blitz; and *Turning Points 1934–1945,* which relates key moments in the conflict to objects on display. *Peace and Security 1945–2015* looks at more contemporary hostilities, including the Cold War, Iraq, Afghanistan, and Kosovo. Other galleries are devoted to works relating to conflicts from World War I to the present day by painters, poets, documentary filmmakers, and photographers. James Bond fans won't want to miss the intriguing Secret War Gallery, which charts the work of secret agents. ⊠ *Lambeth Rd., South Bank* ☎ *020/7416–5000* ⊕ *www.iwm.org.uk* ⊠ *Free (charge for special exhibitions)* Ⓜ *Lambeth North.*

FAMILY
Fodor's Choice
★
London Eye. To mark the start of the new millennium, architects David Marks and Julia Barfield devised an instant icon that allows Londoners and visitors alike to see the city from a completely new perspective. The giant Ferris wheel was the largest cantilevered observation wheel ever built at the time, and remains one of the city's tallest structures. The 25-minute slow-motion ride inside one of the enclosed passenger capsules is so smooth you'd hardly know you were suspended over the Thames. On a clear day you can see up to 25 miles, with a bird's-eye view of London's most famous landmarks as you circle 360 degrees. For an extra £9, you can save even more time with a Fast Track flight (check in 15 minutes before your "departure"). ■TIP➔ **Buy your ticket online to avoid the long lines and get a 15% discount.** ⊠ *Jubilee Gardens, South Bank* ☎ *0871/781–3000* ⊕ *www.londoneye.com* ⊠ *From £24.30; cruise package from £31 (bookable online only)* Ⓜ *Waterloo.*

FAMILY
Fodor's Choice
★
Shakespeare's Globe. This spectacular theater is a replica of Shakespeare's open-roof, wood-and-thatch Globe Playhouse (built in 1599 and burned down in 1613), where most of the Bard's greatest works premiered. American actor and director Sam Wanamaker worked ceaselessly for several decades to raise funds for the theater's reconstruction 200 yards from its original site, using authentic materials and techniques, a dream that was realized in 1997. "Groundlings"—patrons with £5 standing-only tickets—are not allowed to sit during the performance. Fortunately, you can reserve an actual seat on any one of the theater's three levels, but you will want to rent a cushion for £2 (or bring your own) to soften the backless wooden benches. **Shakespeare's Globe Exhibition,** a museum under the theater (the entry is adjacent), provides background material on the Elizabethan theater and the construction of the modern-day Globe. Admission to the museum

The South Bank

KEY

U Tube Station

Tower of London

River Thames

Tower of London

Tower Hill

Fenchurch St. Station

TOWER HILL U

Fenchurch St.

Tower Br.

Tower Bridge Rd.

Morgan's Ln.

Battle Bridge Ln.

Tooley St.

Bermondsey St.

Cornhill

Gracechurch St.

Lombard St.

EastCheap

MONUMENT U

CANNON STREET U

BANK U

King William St.

Cannon St.

Queen St.

Crook La.

Cannon St. Station

MANSION HOUSE U

Upper Thames St.

BLACKFRIARS U

St. Paul's

Blackfriars Br.

London Bridge Station

LONDON BRIDGE U

St-Thomas St.

London Br.

Clink St.

5

Southwark Br.

4

Millennium Bridge (Footbridge)

Bankside

3

Holland St.

Sumner St.

Southwark St.

Hopton St.

High St.

Long Lane

Gt. Dover St.

BOROUGH U

Borough Rd.

Great Suffolk St.

Peacock St.

Webber St.

Southwark Br. Rd.

London Rd.

Blackfriars Rd.

Union St.

SOUTHWARK U

Hatfields

The Cut

Upper Ground

Coin St.

Stamford St.

Cornwall Rd.

Roupell St.

Waterloo Rd.

Waterloo Station

WATERLOO U

LAMBETH NORTH U

Baylis Rd.

St. George's Rd.

1

South Bank Centre

Hayward Gallery

Waterloo Br.

Hungerford Bridge (Footbridge)

EMBANKMENT U

Charing Cross Station

Trafalgar Square

Whitehall

Victoria Embankment

River Thames

The Queen's Walk

Jubilee Gdns.

Belvedere Rd.

York Rd.

Chicheley St.

2

6

WESTMINSTER U

Houses of Parliament

Westminster Br.

Lambeth Palace Rd.

Hercules Rd.

Royal St.

Lambeth Rd.

Lambeth Palace

6 of 800

1/4 mi

1/4 km

0

0

also includes a tour of the theater. ⊠ *21 New Globe Walk, Bankside* ☎ *020/7902–1500 general info, 020/7401–9919 box office* ⊕ *www. shakespearesglobe.com* ⊑ *Exhibition and Globe Theatre tour £17; Bankside tour £12.50; Wanamaker Playhouse tour £13.50 (all £2 off with valid performance ticket); Globe performances £5 (standing), £22–£47 (seated); Wanamaker performances £10 (standing), £15–£62 (seated)* ⊙ *No Globe performances mid-Oct.–mid-Apr.; no Wanamaker Playhouse performances mid-Apr.–mid.-Oct.* Ⓜ *London Bridge; Mansion House, then cross Southwark Bridge.*

Southwark Cathedral. Pronounced "Suth-uck," this is the oldest Gothic church in London, parts of it dating back to the 12th century. It remains off-the-beaten track, despite being the site of some remarkable memorials and a concert program that offers free half-hour organ recitals at 1:10 pm every Monday (except in August and December) and classical music at 3:15 pm every Tuesday (except in December). Originally the priory church of St. Mary Overie (as in "over the water," on the South Bank), it became a palace church under Henry VIII (when it became known as St Saviour's) until some merchant parishioners bought it from James I in 1611. It was only promoted to cathedral status in 1905. Look for the vivid 15th-century roof bosses (small ornamental wood carvings), the gaudily renovated 1408 tomb of John Gower, Richard II's poet laureate and a friend of Chaucer's, and for the Harvard Chapel, where John Harvard, a local butcher's son who went on to found the American university, was baptized. Another notable buried here (between the choir stalls) is Edmond Shakespeare, brother of William. Forty-five minute tours are offered on Wednesday at 2 pm, Friday at 11 am, and Sunday at 1 pm (£4.50). ⊠ *London Bridge, Bankside* ☎ *020/7367–6700* ⊕ *cathedral.southwark.anglican.org* ⊑ *Free (suggested donation £4)* Ⓜ *London Bridge.*

Fodor's Choice ★ **Tate Modern.** This spectacular renovation of a mid-20th-century power station is one of the most-visited museums of modern art in the world. Its great permanent collection, which starts in 1900 and ranges from Modern masters like Matisse to the most cutting-edge contemporary artists, is arranged thematically (from In the Studio and Artist and Society to Materials and Society and Media Networks). Its blockbuster temporary exhibitions have showcased the work of such disparate artists as Gaugin, Roy Lichtenstein, and Gerhard Richter. The vast **Turbine Hall** is a dramatic entrance point used to showcase big audacious installations that tend to generate a lot of publicity. Past highlights include Olafur Eliasson's massive glowing sun and Carsten Holler's huge metal slides. ⊠ *Bankside* ☎ *020/7887–8888* ⊕ *www.tate.org.uk/ modern* ⊑ *Free (charge for special exhibitions)* Ⓜ *Southwark, Blackfriars, St. Paul's.*

The View from the Shard. At 800 feet, this addition to the London skyline currently offers the highest vantage point in Western Europe. Designed by the noted architect Renzo Piano, it has attracted both admiration and disdain. While the building itself is generally highly regarded, many felt it would have been better sited in Canary Wharf (or perhaps Dubai), as it spoils views of St. Paul's Cathedral from traditional vantage points such as Hampstead's Parliament Hill. No matter how you feel about the building, there's no denying that it offers a spectacular 360-degree view over London (extending 40 miles on a clear day) from viewing platforms on level 69, and the open-air skydeck on level 72—almost twice as high as any other viewpoint in the city. Digital telescopes provide information about 200 points of interest. There's a weather guarantee that lets you return on a more clement day if visibility is seriously impeded, and various themed events like silent discos or early morning yoga classes are offered at an extra charge. Admission is by timed ticket only. If you find the price as eye-wateringly high as the viewing platforms, there's a less dramatic but still very impressive (and free) view from the lobby of the Shangri-La hotel on the 35th floor, or, in the evenings, the hotel's chic Gong bar on the 52nd floor (over-18s only). ⊠ *Railway Approach, Borough* ☎ *0344/499–7222* ⊕ *www. theviewfromtheshard.com* ⊠ *From £30.95* Ⓜ *London Bridge.*

KENSINGTON, KNIGHTSBRIDGE, NOTTING HILL, AND MAYFAIR

The Royal Borough of Kensington & Chelsea (or "K&C" as the locals call it) is London at its richest, and not just in the moneyed sense. South Kensington has a concentration of great museums near Cromwell Road, while within Kensington Gardens is historic Kensington Palace, home to royal family members including Queen Victoria, Princess Diana, and now Prince William, Duke of Cambridge and Catherine, Duchess of Cambridge along with Prince Harry and Meghan Markle. Knightsbridge has become a playground for the international wealthy.

Hyde Park and Kensington Gardens together form by far the biggest of central London's royal parks. As the property of the Crown, which still owns them, they were spared from being devoured by London's inexorable westward development that began in the late 18th century.

With world-famous department stores, boutiques selling the biggest names in international luxury, and expensive jewelers, Mayfair is London's wealthiest enclave and reflects the taste of those who can afford the best and are prepared to pay for it.

Formerly the center of London's West Indian community, today Notting Hill is teeming with trendy restaurants, cool bars, and buzzing street markets. Every weekend, the hordes descend on Portobello Road to go bargain-hunting at one of the world's great antique markets.

GETTING HERE

Several useful Tube stations are nearby: Knightsbridge and Hyde Park Corner on the Piccadilly Line will take you to Knightsbridge, Belgravia, and Hyde Park; South Kensington and Gloucester Road on the District, Circle, and Piccadilly lines are convenient stops for the South Kensington museums and Kensington Palace; Bond Street (Central Line) and Green Park (Piccadilly and Victoria lines), both on the Jubilee Line, serve Mayfair. For Portobello Market and around, the best Tube stops are Ladbroke Grove and Westbourne Park (Hammersmith and City Line).

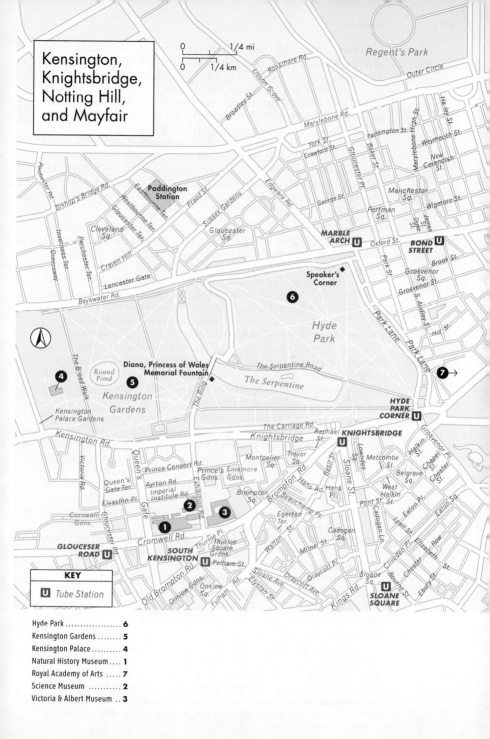

Kensington, Knightsbridge, Notting Hill, and Mayfair

0 ___ 1/4 mi
0 ___ 1/4 km

Regent's Park

Outer Circle

Rossmore Rd.

Broadley St.

Lisson Grove

Marylebone Rd.

York St.

Crawford St.

Paddington St.

Marylebone High St.

Weymouth St.

New Cavendish St.

Harley St.

Baker St.

Gloucester Pl.

George St.

Manchester Sq.

Portman Sq.

James St.
Duke St.

Wigmore St.

MARBLE ARCH 🅄

Oxford St.

BOND STREET 🅄

Brook St.

Grosvenor Sq.

Grosvenor St.

S. Audley St.

Speaker's Corner ◆

6

Hill St.

Park St.

Park Lane

Hyde Park

Paddington Station

Eastbourne Ter.

Bishop's Bridge Rd.

Westbourne Ter.

Praed St.

Sussex Gardens

Gloucester Sq.

Edgware Rd.

Cleveland Sq.

Porchester Ter.

Craven Hill

Lancaster Gate

Bayswater Rd.

Poschester Rd.

Inverness Ter.

Queensway

Westbourne Ter.

4

The Broad Walk

Kensington Palace Gardens

Round Pond

Diana, Princess of Wales Memorial Fountain

5

Kensington Gardens

The Ring

The Serpentine Road

The Serpentine

The Carriage Rd.

7 →

HYDE PARK CORNER 🅄

Kensington Rd.

Victoria Rd.

Kensington Rd.

Queen's Gate Ter.

Prince Consort Rd.

Ayrton Rd.

Prince's Gdns.

Imperial Institute Rd.

Ensmore Gdns.

Montpelier Sq.

Trevor Sq.

Brompton Rd.

KNIGHTSBRIDGE

Raphael St.

KNIGHTSBRIDGE 🅄

Basil St.

Sloane St.

Lowndes Sq.

Metcombe St.

Belgrave Sq.

West Halkin St.

Halkin St.

Grosvenor Pl.

Chapel St.

Chester St.

2

3

Brompton Sq.

Hans Rd.

Hans Pl.

Beauchamp Pl.

Pont St.

Cadogan Ln.

Eaton Pl.

Eaton Sq.

Elvaston Pl.

Egerton Ter.

Cadogan Sq.

Lyall St.

Eaton Row

Elizabeth St.

Chester St.

Cornwall Gdns.

1

Cromwell Rd.

Thurloe Pl.

Thurloe Square Gdns.

Walton St.

Milner St.

Draycott Pl.

Sloane Ave.

Cliveden Pl.

Bourne St.

Ebury St.

GLOUCESER ROAD 🅄

SOUTH KENSINGTON 🅄

Pelham St.

Old Brompton Rd.

Sloane Ave.

Draycott Ave.

Sloane Sq.

SLOANE SQUARE 🅄

Onslow Gdns.

Onslow Sq.

Fulham Rd.

Elystan St.

Kings Rd.

Chester Sq.

KEY

🅄 Tube Station

FAMILY   **Hyde Park.** Along with the smaller St. James's and Green parks to the
Fodor's Choice   east, the 350-acre Hyde Park started as Henry VIII's hunting grounds.
★   Along its south side runs Rotten Row, once Henry's royal path to the hunt—the name is a corruption of *Route du Roi* (route of the king). It's still used by the Household Cavalry, who live at the Hyde Park Barracks to the left. Hyde Park is wonderful for strolling, cycling, or just relaxing by the Serpentine, the long body of water near its southern border. On the south side, by the 1930s **Serpentine Lido,** is the site of the **Diana Princess of Wales Memorial Fountain,** which is a good spot to refuel at the café. On Sunday close to Marble Arch you'll find the uniquely British tribute to free speech, Speakers' Corner. ⊠ *Hyde Park* ☎ *030/0061–2114* ⊕ *www.royalparks.org.uk* ⌖ *Free* Ⓜ *Hyde Park Corner, Knightsbridge, Lancaster Gate, Marble Arch.*

FAMILY   **Kensington Gardens.** Laid out in 1689 by William III, who commissioned
Fodor's Choice   Sir Christopher Wren to build Kensington Palace, the gardens are a
★   formal counterpart to neighboring Hyde Park. Just to the north of the palace itself is the Dutch-style **Sunken Garden.** Nearby, the 1912 bronze statue *Peter Pan* commemorates the boy in J. M. Barrie's story who lived on an island in the Serpentine and who never grew up. Kids will enjoy the magical **Diana Princess of Wales Memorial Playground,** whose design was also inspired by Barrie's book. The **Elfin Oak** is a 900-year-old tree trunk that was carved with scores of tiny elves, fairies, and other fanciful creations in the 1920s. The **Italian Gardens** (1860) comprise several ornamental ponds and fountains, while the **Round Pond** attracts model-boat enthusiasts. ⊠ *Kensington* ☎ *030/0061–2000* ⊕ *www.royalparks.org.uk* ⌖ *Free* Ⓜ *High Street Kensington, Lancaster Gate, Queensway, South Kensington.*

FAMILY   **Kensington Palace.** Neither as imposing as Buckingham Palace nor as charming as Hampton Court, Kensington Palace is something of a Royal Family commune, with various close relatives of the queen occupying large apartments in the private part of the palace. Bought in 1689 by Queen Mary and King William III, it was converted into a palace by Sir Christopher Wren and Nicholas Hawksmoor, and royals have been in residence ever since. Princess Diana lived here with her sons after her divorce, and this is where Prince William now lives with his wife, Catherine, Duchess of Cambridge and their children. The State Apartments are open to the public, with both permanent and temporary exhibitions. Look for the King's Staircase, with its panoramic trompe-l'oeil painting, and the King's Gallery, with royal artworks surrounded by rich red damask walls, intricate gilding, and a beautiful painted ceiling. Outside, the grounds are almost as lovely as the palace itself. ⊠ *The Broad Walk, Kensington Gardens, Kensington* ☎ *0207/482–7799 for advance booking in U.K., 0203/166–6000* ⊕ *www.hrp.org.uk* ⌖ *£23* Ⓜ *Queensway, High St. Kensington.*

FAMILY   **Natural History Museum.** The ornate terra-cotta facade of this enormous
Fodor's Choice   Victorian museum is embellished with relief panels depicting living crea-
★   tures to the left of the entrance and extinct ones to the right (although some species have subsequently changed categories). Most are represented inside the museum, which contains more than 70 million different specimens. Only a small percentage is on public display, but you

These ice-skaters outside the Natural History Museum in South Kensington are making the best of London's winter.

could still spend a day here and not come close to seeing everything. A giant diplodocus skeleton dominates the vaulted, cathedral-like entrance hall, affording you perhaps the most irresistible photo op in the building. The **Darwin Centre** houses some of the millions of items the museum itself doesn't have room to display. If you want to see some of the other thousands of specimens on the shelves, you must book a behind-the-scenes **Spirit Collection** tour on the day (space is limited). ⊠ *Cromwell Rd., South Kensington* ☎ *0207/942–5000* ⊕ *www.nhm. ac.uk* ✉ *Free (some fees for special exhibitions)* Ⓜ *S. Kensington.*

Fodor's Choice
★

Royal Academy of Arts. Burlington House was built in 1664, with later Palladian additions for the 3rd Earl of Burlington in 1720. The piazza in front dates from 1873, when the Renaissance-style buildings around the courtyard were designed by Banks and Barry to house a gaggle of noble scientific societies, including the Royal Society of Chemistry and the Royal Astronomical Society.

The house itself is home to the Royal Academy of Arts and an ambitious redevelopment for the academy's 250th anniversary in 2018 has meant that even more of its 46,000 treasures are now on display. The statue of the academy's first president, Sir Joshua Reynolds, palette in hand, stands prominently in the piazza. Free tours show off part of the collection and the excellent temporary exhibitions. Every June through August, the RA puts on its Summer Exhibition, a huge and eclectic collection of art by living Royal Academicians and many other contemporary artists. ⊠ *Burlington House, Piccadilly, Mayfair* ☎ *020/7300–8000* ⊕ *www.royalacademy.org.uk* ✉ *£12–£18* Ⓜ *Piccadilly Circus, Green Park.*

FAMILY **Science Museum.** With attractions ranging from painlessly educational
Fodor'sChoice exhibits, like an interactive gallery where kids can perform their own
★ hands-on scientific experiments to an exhibition on the fight against
superbugs, the Science Museum brings the subject alive for visitors of
all ages. One of the three great South Kensington museums, it stands
next to the Natural History Museum in a more modern, plainer building. Highlights include the Launch Pad gallery, which demonstrates
basic laws of physics; *Puffing Billy*, the oldest steam locomotive in the
world; and the actual Apollo 10 capsule. The six floors are devoted to
subjects as diverse as the history of flight, space exploration, jet flight
simulators, the large Hadron collider, 3-D printing, and the history of
robots over the last 400 years. The museum also contains a 450-seat
IMAX theater and a motion simulator ride. ⊠ *Exhibition Rd., South
Kensington* ☎ *0870/870–4868* ⊕ *www.sciencemuseum.org.uk* ✉ *Free
(charge for special exhibitions, IMAX, Wonderlab, and simulator rides)*
Ⓜ *South Kensington.*

Fodor'sChoice **Victoria & Albert Museum.** Known to all as the V&A, this huge museum
★ is devoted to the applied arts of all disciplines, all periods, and all
nationalities. First opened as the South Kensington Museum in 1857,
it was renamed in 1899 in honor of Queen Victoria's late husband and
has since grown to become one of the country's best-loved cultural
institutions. Many collections at the V&A are presented not by period
but by category—textiles, sculpture, jewelry, and so on. Nowhere is
the benefit of this more apparent than in the **Fashion Gallery**, known
for its high-profile temporary exhibitions. There are galleries devoted
to Britain, Japan, China, Korea, and the Islamic Middle East. More
recently installed areas include the Ceramics gallery and the Medieval
and Renaissance galleries, which have the largest collection of works
from the period outside of Italy. The **Europe Gallery** (Rooms 1–7) brings
together more than 1,100 objects from 1600 to 1800. ⊠ *Cromwell Rd.,
South Kensington* ☎ *020/7942–2000* ⊕ *www.vam.ac.uk* ✉ *Free (charge
for some special exhibitions, from £5)* Ⓜ *South Kensington.*

REGENT'S PARK AND HAMPSTEAD

Regent's Park, Primrose Hill, and Hampstead are three of London's
prettiest and most civilized neighborhoods. The city becomes noticeably
peaceable as you wind your way up from Marylebone Road through
Regent's Park, with its elegant Nash terraces, to the well-tended lawns
of Primrose Hill and the handsome Georgian streets of Hampstead.

GETTING HERE

To get to Hampstead by Tube, take the Northern Line (the Edgware
branch) to Hampstead or Golders Green Station, or take the London
Overground to Hampstead Heath Station. To get to Regent's Park, take
the Bakerloo Line to Regent's Park Tube station or, for the Zoo, the
Camden Town stop on the Northern Line. St. John's Wood has its own
stop on the Jubilee Line.

FAMILY **Hampstead Heath.** For generations, Londoners have headed to Hamp-
Fodor'sChoice stead Heath to escape the dirt and noise of the city. A unique expanse
★ of *rus in urbe* ("country in the city"), its 791 acres encompass a variety

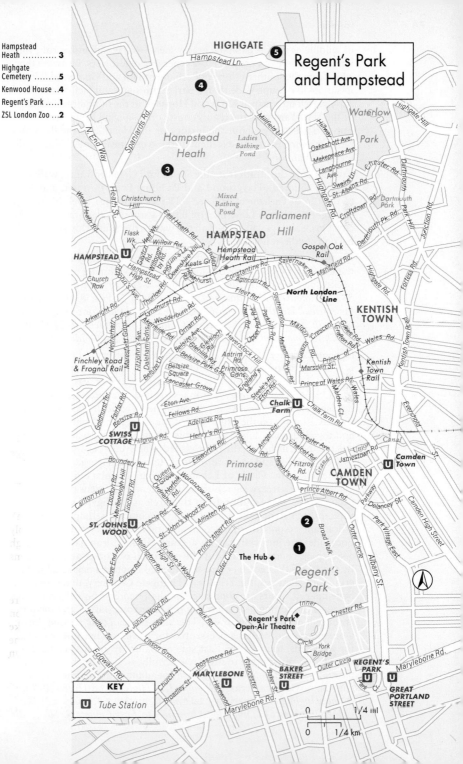

Regent's Park and Hampstead

HIGHGATE

5

4

Hampstead Ln.

Waterlow
Park

Highgate Hill

Hampstead
Heath

Ladies
Bathing
Pond

Hillway

Oakeshott Ave.

Makepeace Ave.

Langbourne
Ave.

Swains La.

St. Albans Rd.

Chester Rd.

Dartmouth

N. End Way

Spaniards Rd.

Christchurch
Hill

3

Mixed
Bathing
Pond

Parliament
Hill

Gospel Oak
Rail

Highgate Rd.

Dartmouth
Park

Croftdown

Dartmouth Pk. Rd.

Dartmouth
Park Hill

Junction Rd.

West Heath Rd.

Heath St.

Flask
Wk.

Willow Rd.

East Heath Rd.

HAMPSTEAD

Hampstead
Heath Rail

Savernake Rd.

Mansfield Rd.

Forress Rd.

HAMPSTEAD U

Church
Row

Gayton Rd.

Willoughby Rd.

Downshire Hill

S. End Rd.

Keats Grove

Flask Wk.

Keats Grove

Constantine Rd.

Agincourt Rd.

**North London
Line**

Gayton Rd.

Hampstead
High St.

St. John's Ave.

Thurlow Rd.

Downshire Hill

Rosslyn Hill

Pilgrim's La.

Pond St.

Fleet Rd.

Southampton Rd.

Maiden Rd.

Gaisford Rd.

Crofton Rd.

**KENTISH
TOWN**

Kentish Town Rd.

Arkwright Rd.

Netherhall Gdns.

Wedderburn Rd.

Lyndhurst Rd.

Akenside Rd.

Lower Rd.

Parkhill Rd.

Upper Park Rd.

Maiden Crescent

Queen's

Wales Rd.

Wales Rd.

Finchley Road
& Frognal Rail

Maresfield Gdns.

Fitzjohn's Ave.

Belsize Ave.

Glenloch Rd.

Belsize Grove

Belsize Park Gdns.

Ornan Rd.

Antrim
Rd.

Haverstock Hill

Primrose
Gdns.

Prince of
Wales Rd.

Marsden St.

Kentish
Town
Rail

Daleham Gdns.

Belsize La.

Belsize
Square

Lancaster Grove

England's

Steele's Rd.

Eton Rd.

Prince of Wales Rd.

Maiden Ct.

Wales

Evereholt

Eton Ave.

Fellows Rd.

Adelaide Rd.

Henry's Rd.

Primrose Hill Rd.

Eton Rd.

**Chalk
Farm** U

Chalk Farm Rd.

**SWISS
COTTAGE** U

Hilgrove Rd.

Boundary Rd.

Queen's
Grove

Ordnance Hill

Norfolk
Rd.

Worcronzow Rd.

Elsworthy Rd.

**Primrose
Hill**

Ainger Rd.

Regent's Rd.

Gloucester Ave.

Chalcot Rd.

Fitzroy
Rd.

Gloucester Ave.

Jamestown Rd.

Union

Grand

Canal

**Camden
Town** U

**CAMDEN
TOWN**

Camden High Street

Carlton Hill

Loudoun Rd.

Marlborough Hill

Finchley Rd.

Prince Albert Rd.

Parkway

Delancey St.

Park Village East

**ST. JOHN'S
WOOD** U

Acacia Rd.

St. John's Wood Ter.

Allitsen Rd.

Prince Albert Rd.

2

Broad Walk

Outer Circle

Albany St.

Grove End Rd.

Circus Rd.

St. John's Wood
High St.

Wellington Rd.

Queen's
Grove

Park Rd.

Outer Circle

The Hub ◆

1

*Regent's
Park*

Inner

Chester Rd.

Hamilton Ter.

St. John's Wood Rd.

Lodge Rd.

Prince Albert Rd.

Regent's Park
Open-Air Theatre ◆

Circle

York
Bridge

**REGENT'S
PARK** U

Edgware Rd.

Lisson Grove

Rossmore Rd.

MARYLEBONE U

Gloucester Pl.

Baker St.

**BAKER
STREET** U

Outer Circle

Park

Marylebone Rd.

**GREAT
PORTLAND
STREET**

Church St.

Broadley St.

Harewood

Baker Rd.

Marylebone Rd.

KEY

U   *Tube Station*

0   1/4 mil

0   1/4 km

of wildlife as well as habitats: grassy meadows, woodland, scrub, wetlands, and some of Europe's most venerable oak forests. Be aware that, aside from the southern slope of Parliament Hill and Golders Hill Park, it is more like countryside than a park, with signs and facilities in short supply. Pick up a map at Kenwood House or at the "Enquiries" window of the Staff Yard near the tennis courts off Highgate Road, where you can also get details about the history of the Heath and the flora and fauna growing there. An excellent alfresco café near the Athletics Field serves Italian food.

Coming onto the Heath from the South End Green entrance, walk east past the children's **Playground** and **Paddling Pool,** turn left, and head to the top of **Parliament Hill.** At 321 feet above sea level, it's one of the highest points in London. You'll find a stunning panorama over the city. On clear days you can see all the way to the South Downs, the hills beyond southern London.

If you keep heading east from the playground instead, you'll come to the **Lido,** an Olympic-size outdoor unheated swimming pool that gets packed on all-too-rare hot summer days. ⊠ *Hampstead* ☎ *020/7332–3322* ⊕ *www.cityoflondon.gov.uk/hampstead* ⊠ *Free* Ⓜ *Overground: Hampstead Heath for west of Heath or Gospel Oak for south and east of Heath and Lido; Northern Line: Golders Green, then Bus 210 or 268 to Whitestone Pond for north and west of Heath and Golders Hill Park.*

Highgate Cemetery. Highgate is not the oldest cemetery in London, but it is probably the best known, both for its roster of famous "inhabitants" and the quality of its funerary architecture. After it was consecrated in 1839, Victorians came from miles around to appreciate the ornate headstones, the impressive tombs, and the view. Such was its popularity that 19 acres on the other side of the road were acquired in 1850, and this additional East Cemetery is the final resting place of numerous notables, including the most visited, Karl Marx (1818–83), as well as George Eliot and, a more recent internment, George Michael. At the summit is the **Circle of Lebanon,** a ring of vaults built around an ancient cypress tree, a legacy of the 17th-century gardens that formerly occupied the site. Leading from the circle is the **Egyptian Avenue,** a subterranean stone tunnel lined with catacombs, itself approached by a dramatic colonnade that screens the main cemetery from the road. Both sides are impressive, with a grand (locked) iron gate leading to a sweeping courtyard built for the approach of horses and carriages. By the 1970s the cemetery had become unkempt and neglected until a group of volunteers, the Friends of Highgate Cemetery, undertook the huge upkeep. Tours are conducted by the Friends, who will show you the most interesting graves among the numerous statues and memorials once hidden by overgrowth. The West side can only be seen during a one-hour tour. Booking is essential for weekdays but not permitted for weekends; tours of the East side on Saturday are first-come, first-served. You're expected to dress respectfully, so skip the shorts and the baseball cap; children under eight are not admitted and neither are dogs, tripods, or video cameras. ⊠ *Swains La., Highgate* ☎ *020/8340–1834* ⊕ *www.highgatecemetery.org* ⊠ *East Cemetery £4, tours £8; West Cemetery tours £12, includes admission to East Cemetery. No credit* *cards* Ⓜ *Archway, then Bus 210, 271, or 143 to Waterlow Park; Belsize Park, then Bus C11 to Brookfield Park.*

Fodor's Choice ★ **Kenwood House.** This largely Palladian villa offers an escape to a gracious country house with a magnificent collection of Old Masters and beautiful grounds, all within a short Tube ride from central London. Originally built in 1616, Kenwood was expanded by Robert Adam starting in 1767 and later by George Saunders in 1795. Adam refaced most of the exterior and added the splendid library, which, with its vaulted ceiling and Corinthian columns, is the highlight of the house's design. A major renovation restored four rooms to reflect Adam's intentions as closely as possible, incorporating the furniture he designed for them and his original color schemes. Kenwood is also home to the **Iveagh Bequest,** a world-class collection of some 60 paintings that includes masterworks like Rembrandt's *Portrait of the Artist* and Vermeer's *The Guitar Player,* along with major works by Reynolds, Van Dyck, Hals, Gainsborough, Turner, and more. The grounds, designed by Humphrey Repton and bordered by Hampstead Heath, are equally elegant and serene, with lawns sloping down to a little lake crossed by a trompe-l'oeil bridge. All in all, it's the perfect home for an 18th-century gentleman. In summer, the grounds host a series of popular and classical concerts, culminating in fireworks on the last night. The Brew House café, occupying part of the old coach house, has outdoor tables in the courtyard and a terraced garden. ⊠ *Hampstead La., Highgate* ☎ *0870/333–1181* ⊕ *www.english-heritage.org.uk/visit/places/kenwood* 🎫 *Free, house and estate tour £16.30* Ⓜ *Golders Green or Archway, then Bus 210. Overground: Gospel Oak.*

FAMILY **Fodor's Choice** ★ **Regent's Park.** The formal cultivated Regent's Park, more country-house grounds than municipal amenity, began life in 1812, when John Nash was commissioned by the Prince Regent (later George IV) to create a master plan for the former royal hunting ground. Nash's original plan included a summer palace for the prince and 56 villas for friends, none of which were realized except for 8 villas (only 2 survive). However, the grand neoclassical terraced houses on the south, east, and west edges of the park were built by Nash and reflect the scope of his ambitions. Queen Mary's Gardens, which has some 30,000 roses and is a favorite spot for weddings, was created in the 1930s. Today the 395-acre park, with the largest outdoor sports area in central London, draws the athletically inclined from around the city.

At the center of the park is the **Queen Mary's Gardens,** a fragrant 17-acre circle containing more than 400 varieties of roses. Just to the east of the Gardens is the **Regent's Park Open-Air Theatre** and the **Boating Lake,** which you can explore by renting a pedalo (paddleboat) or rowboat. Heading east from the rose gardens along Chester Road past the **Broad Walk** will bring you to Nash's iconic white-stucco **Cumberland Terrace,** with its central Ionic columns surmounted by a triangular Wedgwood-blue pediment. At the north end of the Broad Walk you'll find the **London Zoo,** while to the northwest of the central circle is **The Hub** (☎ *0300/061–2323*), a state-of-the-art community sports center that has changing rooms, exercise classes, and a café with 360-degree views of the surrounding sports fields, used for soccer, rugby, cricket, field hockey, and softball contests. There are also tennis courts toward the park's southeast (Baker Street) entrance, and the park is a favorite north–south route for cyclists. ⊠ *Chester Rd., Regent's Park* ☏ *0300/061–2300* ⊕ *www.royalparks.org.uk* ⧉ *Free* Ⓜ *Baker St., Regent's Park, Great Portland St.*

FAMILY
Fodor's Choice
★

ZSL London Zoo. With an emphasis on education, wildlife conservation, and the breeding of endangered species, London Zoo offers visitors the chance to see tigers, gorillas, meerkats, and more in something resembling a natural environment rather than a cage. Operated by the nonprofit Zoological Society of London, the zoo was begun with the Royal animals collection, moved here from the Tower of London in 1828; the zoo itself did not open to the public until 1847. Big attractions include Land of the Lions, a walk-through re-creation of an Indian forest where you can see three resident Asiatic lions relaxing at close range; Gorilla Kingdom, which provides a similar re-created habitat (in this case an African rain forest) for its colony of six Western Lowland Gorillas; and the Attenborough Komodo Dragon House, renamed to honor the renowned naturalist. The zoo also offers the chance to get up close and personal with 15 ring-tailed lemurs. The huge B.U.G.S. pavilion (Biodiversity Underpinning Global Survival) is a self-sustaining, contained ecosystem for 140 less-cuddly species, including invertebrates such as spiders and millipedes, plus some reptiles and fish. Rainforest Life is an indoor tropical rain forest (complete with humidity) inhabited by the likes of armadillos, monkeys, and sloths. A special nighttime section offers glimpses of nocturnal creatures like slow lorises and bats. The Animal Adventures Children's Zoo allows kids to closely observe coatis, as well as to interact with llamas, donkeys, small pigs, sheep, and goats. Two of the most popular attractions are Penguin Beach, especially at feeding time (1:30 and 4:30), and meerkat snack time (11:15), where you can see the sociable animals keeping watch over their own sandy territory.

If you're feeling flush, try to nab one of the six daily "Meet the Penguins" VIP tickets (1:45 pm) that offer a 20-minute guided close encounter with the locals (£54); there are similar VIP encounters with giraffes, meerkats, and rain forest monkeys. Other zoo highlights include Butterfly Paradise and Tiger Territory, an enclosure for four beautiful endangered Sumatran tigers (including two cubs born at the zoo). Adults-only Zoo Nights held Friday nights in June offer street food, alcoholic drinks, and entertainment. You can also experience the zoo after-hours by booking an overnight stay in one of the cozy cabins near (not *in*) the lion enclosure. Check the website or the information board out front for free events, including creature close encounters and "ask the keeper" sessions. ⊠ *Outer Circle, Regent's Park* ☏ *0844/225–1826* ⊕ *www.zsl.org* ⧉ *From £27.04* Ⓜ *Camden Town, then Bus 274.*

UP AND DOWN THE THAMES

Downstream—meaning seaward, or east—from central London, Greenwich will require a day to explore, especially if you have any interest in maritime history or technology. Upstream to the west are the royal palaces and grand houses that were built as country residences with

A TRIP TO ABBEY ROAD

The black-and-white crosswalk (known as a "zebra crossing") near the Abbey Road Studios at No. 3, where the Beatles recorded their entire output from "Love Me Do" onward, is a place of pilgrimage for Beatles' fans from around the world, many of them teenagers born long after the band split up. They converge here to re-create the cover of the Beatles' 1969 *Abbey Road* album, posing on the crossing despite the onrushing traffic. ■TIP→ Be careful if you're going to attempt this; traffic on Abbey

Road is busy. One of the best ways to explore landmarks in the Beatles' story is to take one of the excellent walking tours offered by **Original London Walks** (☎ *020/7624–3978* ⊕ *www.walks.com*). Try **The Beatles In-My-Life Walk** (Saturday and Tuesday at 11 am outside Maryle-bone Underground) or **The Beatles Magical Mystery Tour** (Wednesday at 2 pm and Thursday except for December and January and Sunday at 11 am, at Underground Exit 1, Tottenham Court Road).

easy access to London by river. Hampton Court Palace, with its famous maze, is the most notable.

GREENWICH
8 miles east of central London.

Greenwich makes an ideal day out from central London. Maritime Greenwich is a UNESCO World Heritage Site and includes Inigo Jones's Queens House, the first Palladian building in England; the Old Royal Observatory, home of the Greenwich Meridian that is the baseline for the world's time zones and the dividing line between the two hemispheres (you can stand astride it with one foot in either one); and the National Maritime Museum, which tells the story of how Britain came to rule the waves. Landlubbers, meanwhile, can explore the surrounding Royal Park, laid out in the 1660s and thus the oldest of the royal parks, or central Greenwich with its attractive 19th-century houses.

The monorail-like Docklands Light Railway (DLR) will take you to Cutty Sark Station from Canary Wharf and Bank Tube stations in The City. Or take the DLR to Island Gardens and walk the old Victorian Foot Tunnel under the river. However, the most appropriate way to travel is—time and weather permitting—by water via River Bus.

FAMILY
Fodor's Choice
★
National Maritime Museum. From the time of Henry VIII until the 1940s, Britain was the world's preeminent naval power, and the collections here trace half a millennia of that seafaring history. The story is as much about trade as it is warfare: *Atlantic: Slavery, Trade, Empire* gallery explores how trade in goods (and people) irrevocably changed the world, while *Traders: The East India Company and Asia* focuses on how the epoch-defining company shaped trade with Asia for 250 years. One gallery is devoted to Admiral Lord Nelson, Britain's most famous naval commander, and among the exhibits is the uniform he was wearing, complete with bloodstains, when he died at the Battle of Trafalgar in 1805. Temporary exhibitions here are usually fascinating—those in recent years have included personal accounts of the First

Among the botanical splendors of Kew Gardens is the Waterlily House.

World War at sea. Borrow a tablet computer from the front desk and take it to the giant map of the world in the courtyard at the center of the museum; here, a high-tech, interactive app opens up hidden stories and games as you walk between continents. The Ahoy! gallery is filled with interactive fun for kids, where they can learn about polar exploration, pirates, and more. The adjacent **Queen's House** is home to the museum's art collection, the largest collection of maritime art in the world, including works by William Hogarth, Canaletto, and Joshua Reynolds. Permission for its construction was granted by Queen Anne only on condition that the river vista from the house be preserved, and there are few more majestic views in London than Inigo Jones's awe-inspiring symmetry. ✉ *Romney Rd., Greenwich* ☎ *020/8312–6608* ⊕ *www.rmg.co.uk/national-maritime-museum* ✐ *Free; tours £10; fee for special exhibitions* Ⓜ *DLR: Greenwich.*

FAMILY
Fodor'sChoice
★
Royal Observatory. Greenwich is on the prime meridian at 0° longitude, and the ultimate standard for time around the world has been set here since 1884, when Britain was the world's maritime superpower.

The observatory is actually split into two sites, a short walk apart—one devoted to astronomy, the other to the study of time. The enchanting **Peter Harrison Planetarium** is London's only planetarium, its bronze-clad turret glinting in the sun. Shows on black holes and how to interpret the night sky are enthralling and enlightening. Even better for kids are the high-technology rooms of the **Astronomy Centre,** where space exploration is brought to life through cutting-edge interactive programs and fascinating exhibits—including the chance to touch a 4.5-billion-year-old meteorite.

Across the way is **Flamsteed House,** designed by Christopher Wren in 1675 for John Flamsteed, the first Astronomer Royal. A climb to the top of the house reveals a **28-inch telescope,** built in 1893 and now housed inside an onion-shape fiberglass dome. It doesn't compare with the range of modern optical telescopes, but it's still the largest in the United Kingdom. Regular viewing evenings reveal startlingly detailed views of the lunar surface. In the **Time Galleries,** linger over the superb workmanship of John Harrison (1693–1776), whose famous **Maritime Clocks** won him the Longitude Prize for solving the problem of accurate timekeeping at sea, which paved the way for modern navigation. ⊠ *Romney Rd., Greenwich* ☎ *020/8858–4422* ⊕ *www.rmg. co.uk/royal-observatory* ⊡ *Astronomy Centre free, Flamsteed House and Meridian Line courtyard £10, planetarium shows £8; combined "Astro Ticket" £15.50; combined ticket with Cutty Sark £20* Ⓜ *DLR: Greenwich.*

RICHMOND
20 miles southwest of central London.

Named after the (long-vanished) palace Henry VII started here in 1500, Richmond is still a welcoming suburb with a small-town feel. It's also home to Hampton Court Palace, one of the country's grandest royal palaces.

FAMILY

Fodor's Choice

★

Hampton Court Palace. The beloved seat of Henry VIII's court, sprawled elegantly beside the languid waters of the Thames, Hampton Court is steeped in more history than virtually any other royal building in England. Begun in 1515 by Cardinal Wolsey to curry favor with the young Henry, the Tudor palace actually conceals a larger 17th-century baroque building partly designed by Christopher Wren. George II moved the royal household closer to London in the early 18th century. Wander through the State Apartments before taking in the strikingly azure ceiling of the Chapel Royal. Well-handled reconstructions of Tudor life take place all year. Latter-day masters of the palace, the joint rulers William and Mary (reigned 1689–1702), were responsible for the beautiful King's and Queen's Apartments and the elaborate baroque of the Georgian Rooms. Don't miss the famous hedge maze and the Lower Orangery Garden, which shows off thousands of exotic species that William and Mary gathered from around the globe. ⊠ *Hampton Court Rd., East Molesey* ☎ *020/3166–6000* ⊕ *www.hrp.org.uk/ hamptoncourtpalace* ⊡ *£22.70 palace, maze, and gardens; £4.40 maze only; £7 maze and gardens* Ⓜ *Richmond, then Bus R68. National Rail: Hampton Court, 35 mins from Waterloo (most trains require change at Surbiton).*

KEW
6 miles southwest of central London.

A leafy suburb, Kew offers little to see except for its two big attractions: the lovely Kew Palace and the Royal Botanic Gardens—anchored in the landscape for several miles around by a towering, mock-Chinese pagoda.

FAMILY

Fodor's Choice

★

Kew Gardens. Enter the Royal Botanic Gardens, as Kew Gardens are officially known, and you are enveloped by blazes of color, extraordinary blooms, hidden trails, and lovely old follies. Beautiful though it all is, Kew's charms are secondary to its true purpose as a major center for serious research; over 200 academics are consistently hard at work here on projects spanning 110 countries. First opened to the public in 1840, this 326-acre site has been supported by royalty and nurtured by landscapers, botanists, and architects since the 1720s. Today the gardens, now a UNESCO World Heritage Site, hold more than 30,000 species of plants, from every corner of the globe. Although the plant houses make Kew worth visiting even in the depths of winter (there's also a seasonal garden), the flower beds are, of course, best enjoyed in the fullness of spring and summer.

Architect Sir William Chambers built a series of temples and follies, of which the crazy 10-story **Pagoda**, visible for miles around, is the star. The Princess of Wales conservatory houses 10 climate zones, and the Xstrata Treetop Walkway takes you 59 feet up into the air. Two great 19th-century greenhouses—the **Palm House** and the **Temperate House**—are filled with exotic blooms, and many of the plants have been there since the final glass panel was fixed into place, including the largest greenhouse plant in the world, a Chilean wine palm planted in 1846 (and so big that you have to climb the spiral staircase to the roof to get a proper view of it). ⊠ *Kew Rd. at Lichfield Rd., for Victoria Gate entrance, Kew* ☎ *020/8332–5000* ⊕ *www.kew.org* ✆ *£17, Explorer bus £5, Discovery tour £5* Ⓜ *Kew Gardens. National Rail: Kew Gardens, Kew Bridge.*

WHERE TO EAT

For many years English food was a joke, especially to England's near neighbors, the French. But the days of steamed suet puddings and overboiled brussels sprouts are long gone. For a good two decades London's restaurant scene has been booming, with world-class chefs—Jamie Oliver, Gordon Ramsay, Heston Blumenthal, and Jason Atherton among them—pioneering concepts that quickly spread overseas. Whether you're looking for bistros that rival their Parisian counterparts, five-star fine dining establishments, fantastic fried-chicken and burger joints (American diner food is a current trend), gastro-pubs serving "Modern British," or places serving Peruvian–Japanese fusion, gourmet Indian, or nouveau greasy spoon, you'll be spoiled for choice. And that's just as well because you'll be spending, on average, 25% of your travel budget on dining out.

The British now take pride in the best of authentic homegrown food—local, seasonal, regional, and foraged are the buzzwords of the day. But beyond reinterpretations of native dishes, London's dining revolution is built on its incredible ethnic diversity, with virtually every international cuisine represented. *Restaurant reviews have been shortened. For full information, visit Fodors.com.*

2

PRICES AND SAVING MONEY

In pricey London a modest meal for two can easily cost £40, and the £110-a-head meal is not unknown. Damage-control strategies include making lunch your main meal—the top places have bargain midday menus—going for early- or late-evening deals, or sharing an à la carte entrée and ordering an extra appetizer. Seek out fixed-price menus, and watch for hidden extras on the menu—that is, bread or vegetables charged separately.

WHAT IT COSTS IN POUNDS				
	$	$$	$$$	$$$$
At Dinner	under £16	£17–£23	£24–£31	over £31

Prices are the average cost of a main course at dinner or, if dinner is not served, at lunch.

Use the coordinate (✣ B2) at the end of each listing to locate a site on the corresponding map.

WESTMINSTER AND ST. JAMES'S

ST. JAMES'S

$$$ MODERN EUROPEAN FAMILY

🍴 **Le Caprice.** Celebrity hot spot Le Caprice commands the deepest loyalty of any restaurant in London. It must be the 38-odd-year history of famous diners (think Liz Taylor, Joan Collins, Lady Di, and Victoria Beckham), the pitch-perfect service, and the long-standing menu that sits somewhere between Euro peasant and trendy fashion plate. **Known for:** celebrity sightings galore; classic fish-and-chips with minted pea puree; live jazz on Sunday night. [$] *Average main: £26* ✉ *Arlington House, 20 Arlington St., St. James's* ☎ *020/7629–2239* 🌐 *www.le-caprice.co.uk* [M] *Green Park* ✣ *D4.*

$$$$ BRITISH FAMILY

🍴 **The Ritz Restaurant.** London's most opulent dining salon here at the Ritz would impress even Marie Antoinette with its sumptuous Gilded Age Rocco Revival trompe-l'oeil frescoes, tasseled silk drapery, and towering marble columns. Sit at the late Baroness Thatcher's favorite seat overlooking Green Park (Table 1) and luxuriate in unreconstructed British haute cuisine such as Bresse chicken with black Périgord truffles or beef Wellington carved table-side. **Known for:** luxurious dining made for the British elite; possibly London's best beef Wellington; legendary traditional Afternoon Tea. [$] *Average main: £42* ✉ *The Ritz, 150 Piccadilly, St. James's* ☎ *020/7300–2370 for reservations only* 🌐 *www.theritzlondon.com* 👔 *Jacket and tie* [M] *Green Park* ✣ *D3.*

$$$$ BRITISH

🍴 **Wiltons.** Lords, Ladies, and aristocrats blow the family bank at this Edwardian bastion of traditional English fine dining on Jermyn Street (the place first opened on the Haymarket as a shellfish stall in 1742). Posh patrons tend to order half a dozen Beau Brummell oysters, followed by grilled Dover sole, Blythburgh pork from the carving trolley, or fabulous native game, such as roast partridge, grouse, or teal. **Known for:** traditional English dining focused on shellfish and game; waiter service that would put Jeeves to shame; Bordeaux-heavy wine menu.

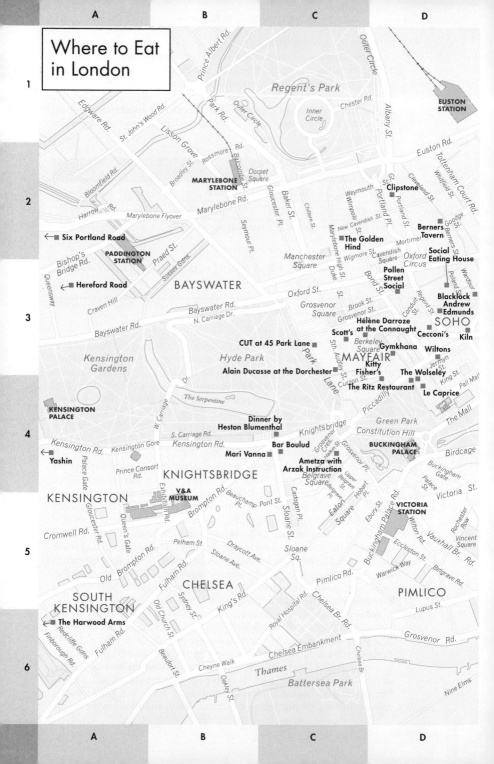

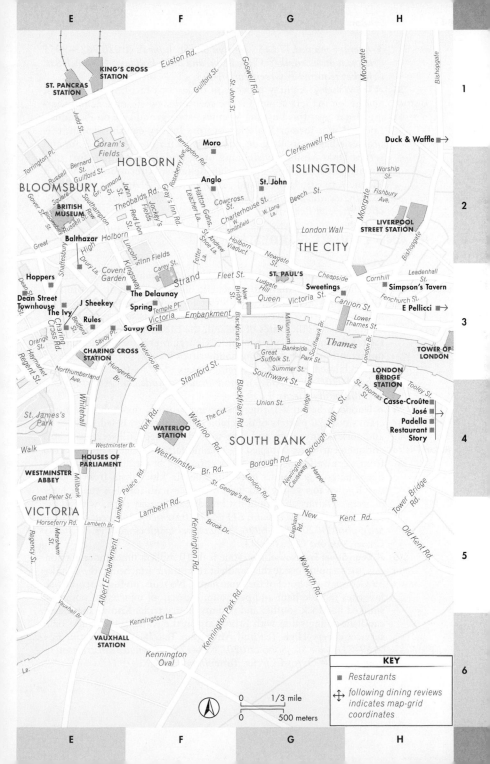

[$] *Average main: £37* ✉ *55 Jermyn St., St. James's* ☎ *020/7629–9955* 🌐 *www.wiltons.co.uk* 🕓 *Closed Sun. and bank holidays. No lunch Sat.* 👔 *Jacket required* [M] *Green Park* ✥ *D3.*

$$ AUSTRIAN FAMILY 🍴 **The Wolseley.** A glitzy procession of famous faces, media moguls, and hedge-funders comes for the spectacle, swish service, and soaring elegance at this bustling Viennese-style grand café on Piccadilly. Located in a former Wolseley Motors luxury-car showroom, this brasserie begins its long decadent days with breakfast at 7 am and serves Dual Monarchy delights until midnight. **Known for:** old-country Austrian and Hungarian delights; Afternoon Tea with a Viennese twist; classic grand café ambience. [$] *Average main: £22* ✉ *160 Piccadilly, St. James's* ☎ *020/7499–6996* 🌐 *www.thewolseley.com* [M] *Green Park* ✥ *D4.*

SOHO AND COVENT GARDEN

SOHO

$$ MEDITERRANEAN 🍴 **Andrew Edmunds.** Candlelit at night, with a haunting vibe, Andrew Edmunds is a permanently packed, old-school dining institution. Tucked away behind Carnaby Street in an 18th-century Soho town house, it's a cozy favorite whose unpretentious and keenly priced dishes draw on the tastes of Ireland, the Mediterranean, and Middle East. **Known for:** deeply romantic, Georgian-era town-house setting; unpretentious daily changing handwritten menus; bargains galore on the acclaimed wine list. [$] *Average main: £19* ✉ *46 Lexington St., Soho* ☎ *020/7437–5708* 🌐 *www.andrewedmunds.com* [M] *Oxford Circus, Piccadilly Circus* ✥ *D3.*

$ STEAKHOUSE FAMILY Fodor'sChoice ★ 🍴 **Blacklock.** Set in a former basement brothel, this Soho meatopia cranks out £20 platters of delectable char-grilled grass-fed lamb, beef, and pork skinny chops and juice-soaked flat bread, all served on retro antique pearlware. Supplied by organic farm butchers Philip Warren from Cornwall, Blacklock's killer chops are beautifully seared on an open charcoal grill under heavy antique Blacklock irons from Tennessee. **Known for:** young and bubbly service with top '80s tunes; huge platters of skinny chops and flat bread; £18 Sunday roasts with all the trimmings. [$] *Average main: £11* ✉ *The Basement, 24 Great Windmill St., Soho* ☎ *020/3441–6996* 🌐 *www.theblacklock.com* [M] *Piccadilly Circus, Oxford Circus* ✥ *D3.*

$$$ BRITISH FAMILY 🍴 **Dean Street Townhouse.** Everyone feels 10 million times more glamorous just stepping inside this candlelit restaurant attached to the swanky 39 Georgian-era hotel of the same name. No frills, no fuss retro-British favorites include ham-and-pea soup, old-school mince and potatoes, smoked haddock soufflé, and yummy sherry trifle. **Known for:** classy candlelit dining salon with British art on the walls; superprofessional service; cheery High Tea and Afternoon Tea. [$] *Average main: £24* ✉ *69–71 Dean St., Soho* ☎ *020/7434–1775* 🌐 *www.deanstreettownhouse.com* [M] *Oxford Circus, Tottenham Court Rd.* ✥ *D3.*

$ SRI LANKAN FAMILY Fodor's Choice ★

🍴 **Hoppers.** Curry fiends have gone mad for the cheap egg hopper pancakes (a Sri Lankan specialty) and paper-thin griddled dosas at this highly spiced, no-reservations Frith Street snuggery. Diners gorge on chilli mutton rolls, curried duck hearts, and piles of steamed string hoppers dipped in spicy broth, coconut chutney, or onion and Maldives fish flakes relish. **Known for:** crispy egg hopper pancakes with coconut sambol; authentic Colombo-style cabin atmosphere; signature black pork kari curry. [$] *Average main: £8* ✉ *49 Frith St., Soho* 🌐 *www.hopperslondon.com* [M] *Tottenham Court Rd., Oxford Circus* ✣ *E2.*

$ THAI Fodor's Choice ★

🍴 **Kiln.** Earthy northern Thai cuisine bursts out of the charcoal-fired kiln at this BBQ-focused wonderland in Soho. Overlook the open kitchen and you'll see sizzling cumin-dusted hogget skewers and charcoal-grilled chicken thigh bites, along with other village-style dishes that show influences from Laos, Myanmar, and the Yunnan province of China. **Known for:** open kitchen counter setup with charcoal grill and hot clay pots; awesome array of specially grown Thai, Burmese, and other Asian herbs and spices; popular cumin-dusted fatty hogget skewers. [$] *Average main: £9* ✉ *58 Brewer St., Soho* 🌐 *www.kilnsoho.com* [M] *Oxford Circus, Piccadilly Circus* ✣ *D3.*

$$$ FRENCH FAMILY

🍴 **Social Eating House.** At Jason Atherton's underrated but brilliant French bistronomie Soho hangout, witty dishes like smoked duck's ham (made from cured duck's breast) and Scotch egg-and-chips are served alongside classics like the "CLT," consisting of white crabmeat, lettuce, and roast heritage tomato. The moodily lit bare-brick ground-floor salon is tricked out with dark parquet floors, antique mirrored ceilings, and red leather banquettes. **Known for:** vintage cocktails in the speakeasy lounge; affordable set lunches and extravagant tasting menus at the chef's table; signature boil-in-the-bag British wild mushrooms on toast. [$] *Average main: £26* ✉ *58 Poland St., Soho* ☎ *020/7993–3251* 🌐 *www.socialeatinghouse.com* ⏲ *Closed Sun.* [M] *Oxford Circus, Tottenham Court Rd.* ✣ *D3.*

COVENT GARDEN

$$ BRASSERIE FAMILY

🍴 **Balthazar.** British restaurateur Keith McNally re-creates his famed New York Parisian brasserie at this corner spot off Covent Garden. The decor creates an enchanting backdrop to enjoy a classic French brasserie menu of few surprises, including flavor-packed dishes like macaroni and Gruyère cheese or ox cheek bourguignon. **Known for:** Parisian-style grand café; handy prix-fixe, brunch, and Afternoon Tea menus; classic French plats du jour. [$] *Average main: £23* ✉ *4–7 Russell St., Covent Garden* ☎ *020/3301–1155* 🌐 *www.balthazarlondon.com* [M] *Covent Garden, Charing Cross* ✣ *E3.*

$$$ BRITISH FAMILY Fodor's Choice ★

🍴 **The Ivy.** London's onetime most famous celebrity haunt and West End landmark is still so popular it receives over a thousand calls a day. Established as an Italian café in 1917, today it's where London's wealthiest dine on haddock and chips, Thai-baked sea bass, and good ole English classics like shepherd's pie and sticky toffee pudding. **Known for:** celebrity-filled history; famed house staples like grilled calf's liver; great people-watching. [$] *Average main: £25* ✉ *1–5 West St., Covent Garden* ☎ *020/7836–4751* 🌐 *www.the-ivy.co.uk* [M] *Covent Garden* ✣ *E3.*

$$$$ ✕**J Sheekey.** This timelessly chic 1896 seafood haven is a discreet
SEAFOOD   alternative to the more celebrity-focused eateries in the neighborhood.
Sheekey charms with an inviting menu of snappingly fresh Atlantic
prawns, pickled Arctic herrings, scallop, shrimp, and salmon burgers,
or the famous Sheekey fish pie. **Known for:** low-key celebrity hideaway;
old-school seafood menu; glamorous art deco oyster bar. Ⓢ *Average
main: £27* ✉ *28–35 St. Martin's Ct., Covent Garden* ☎ *020/7240–2565*
⊕ *www.j-sheekey.co.uk* Ⓜ *Leicester Sq.* ✛ *E3.*

$$$ ✕**Rules.** Opened by Thomas Rule in 1798, London's oldest restaurant is
BRITISH   still arguably its most beautiful. Resembling a High Victoriana bordello,
FAMILY   here you can dig into classic traditional British fare like jugged hare,
Fodor's Choice   steak-and-kidney pie, or roast beef and Yorkshire pudding. **Known for:**
★   the oldest restaurant in London; fancy, high-class game-focused menu;
famous diners from Charles Dickens to the Prince of Wales. Ⓢ *Aver-
age main: £30* ✉ *35 Maiden La., Covent Garden* ☎ *020/7836–5314*
⊕ *www.rules.co.uk* 🍴 *Jacket required* Ⓜ *Covent Garden* ✛ *E3.*

$$$ ✕**Savoy Grill.** You can feel the history at this 1889 art deco hotel-dining
BRITISH   powerhouse, which has wined and dined everyone from Oscar Wilde
FAMILY   and Winston Churchill to Liz Taylor and Marilyn Monroe. Nowadays
it caters to businesspeople and wealthy West End tourists who come
for the Grill's famed table-side serving trolley, which might trundle up
laden with hulking great roasts like beef Wellington, Suffolk rack of
pork, or saddle of lamb. **Known for:** ravishing old-school dining salon;
beef Wellington from the daily carvery trolley service; signature glazed
omelet Arnold Bennett. Ⓢ *Average main: £31* ✉ *The Savoy, 100 Strand,
Covent Garden* ☎ *020/7592–1600 for reservations only* ⊕ *www.gor-
donramsay.com/savoy-grill* Ⓜ *Charing Cross, Covent Garden* ✛ *E3.*

$$$ ✕**Spring.** Australian chef Skye Gyngell worships the four seasons at
ITALIAN   her wildflower-filled dining salon in majestic Somerset House off the
FAMILY   Strand. Housed in the former Inland Revenue's neoclassical 1856 New
Fodor's Choice   Wing, Spring offers healthy root-to-stem, produce-driven Italian dishes.
★   **Known for:** homemade bread, butter, and ice cream; highly seasonal,
sustainable, and ingredient-driven dishes; biodynamic Fern Verrow sal-
ads. Ⓢ *Average main: £30* ✉ *Somerset House, New Wing, Lancaster
Pl., Covent Garden* ✛ *Turn right on entering courtyard at Somerset
House from the Strand* ☎ *020/3011–0115* ⊕ *www.springrestaurant.
co.uk* ☾ *No dinner Sun.* Ⓜ *Holborn, Charing Cross* ✛ *F3.*

BLOOMSBURY AND HOLBORN

$$$ ✕**Berners Tavern.** All the cool cats swing by this grand brasserie at Ian
MODERN BRITISH   Schrager's insanely trendy London Edition hotel near Tottenham Court
FAMILY   Road. Enter the monumental Edwardian dining salon, where you might
swoon over a light lunch of ironbark pumpkin risotto or an evening
dinner of Creedy Carver duck. **Known for:** knockout dining salon;
cool back-lit cocktail bar; slow-roast Herdwick lamb with Wye Valley
asparagus. Ⓢ *Average main: £28* ✉ *The London Edition, 10 Berners
St., Fitzrovia* ☎ *020/7908–7979* ⊕ *www.bernerstavern.com* Ⓜ *Oxford
Circus, Tottenham Court Rd.* ✛ *D2.*

$$$ ✕ **Clipstone.** Exceptionally inventive dishes elevate this hipster casual
FRENCH   joint to the top rank of London's mid-range gastro titans. With a focus
Fodor'sChoice   on in-house curing, pickling, smoked meats, and heritage vegetables,
★   expect a cavalcade of crudos, unlikely combinations, and classic gas-
tronomy specialties. **Known for:** classic French dishes in a minimalist
setting; lots of house-made, pickled, fermented, or cured extras; sooth-
ing blanquette de veau (veal ragout) and sweetbreads. $ *Average main:
£27* ⊠ *5 Clipstone St., Fitzrovia* ☎ *020/7637–0871* ⊕ *www.clipston-
erestaurant.co.uk* ۞ *Closed Sun.* Ⓜ *Great Portland St.* ✛ *D2.*

$$$ ✕ **The Delaunay.** It's all *fin de siècle* Vienna at this evocative art deco–style
AUSTRIAN   grand café on the Aldwych near Covent Garden. Dishes on the majestic
FAMILY   60-item menu would do the Austro-Hungarian Empire proud—think
Fodor'sChoice   Wiener schnitzel, Hungarian goulash, beef Stroganoff, and wonder-
★   ful *würstchen* (frankfurters and hot dogs), served with sauerkraut and
onions. **Known for:** elegant old-world Austro-Hungarian haunt; proper
Holstein schnitzel and frankfurters; affordable set lunches. $ *Average
main: £24* ⊠ *55 Aldwych, Holborn* ☎ *020/7499–8558* ⊕ *www.thede-
launay.com* Ⓜ *Covent Garden, Holborn* ✛ *F3.*

THE CITY

$$ ✕ **Anglo.** Modern British bistronomy takes a giant leap forward at chef-
MODERN BRITISH   patron Mark Jarvis's tasting menu mecca in the historic Hatton Gar-
den jewelery quarter in Farringdon. Feast on the Brit-sourced seasonal
foodie creations here, which are offered à la carte or as seven-or eight-
course tasting menus at dinner. **Known for:** well-priced tasting menus
for lunch and dinner; signature grated cheese and onion on malt toast;
wacky desserts like lemon curd and horseradish. $ *Average main: £19*
⊠ *30 St Cross St., Clerkenwell* ☎ *020/7430–1503* ⊕ *www.anglorestau-
rant.com* ۞ *Closed Sun. No lunch Mon.* Ⓜ *Farringdon* ✛ *F2.*

$$ ✕ **Duck & Waffle.** Zoom up to the 40th floor of the Heron Tower and
MODERN BRITISH   head straight for the cult signature dish of confit duck leg, Belgium
FAMILY   waffle, fried duck egg, and mustard maple syrup for a taste of foodie
bliss. Open 24/7, with spectacular panoramas of The City, you might
satisfy the munchies with a foie gras breakfast, served all day, alongside
streaky bacon and homemade Nutella or an Elvis PB&J waffle with
banana brûlée. **Known for:** rare-to-London 24-hour service; awe-inspiring panoramas of London's skyline; eponymous duck-and-waffle dish.
$ *Average main: £19* ⊠ *Heron Tower, 110 Bishopsgate, City of London*
☎ *020/3640–7310* ⊕ *www.duckandwaffle.com* Ⓜ *Liverpool St.* ✛ *H1.*

$$$ ✕ **Moro.** Up from The City, you'll find Exmouth Market, a cluster of
MEDITERRANEAN   cute indie boutiques, bookstores, vinyl shops, hardware stores, artisan
FAMILY   bakeries, and more fine indie-spirited restaurants like this one. Lovingly
nurtured for over a decade by husband-and-wife chefs Sam and Sam
Clark, the menu includes a mélange of Spanish, Moroccan, and Moor-
ish North African flavors. **Known for:** loud and buzzy dining room
with booming acoustics; expressive Moorish delights; house yogurt
cake. $ *Average main: £24* ⊠ *34–36 Exmouth Market, Clerkenwell*
☎ *020/7833–8336* ⊕ *www.moro.co.uk* ۞ *No dinner Sun.* Ⓜ *Far-
ringdon, Angel* ✛ *F2.*

$ BRITISH FAMILY 🍴 **Simpson's Tavern.** The City's oldest tavern and chop house was founded in 1757 and undoubtedly is every bit as raucous now as the day it opened. Approached via a cobbled alleyway, it draws diners who revel in the old boarding school surroundings and are eager to down oodles of claret and English tavern-style grub. **Known for:** lots of history, with past diners from diarist Samuel Pepys to Charles Dickens; signature stewed cheese on toast; charming but old-fashioned service. [$] *Average main: £10* ✉ *Ball Court, 38½ Cornhill, City of London* ☎ *020/7626–9985* 🌐 *www.simpsonstavern.co.uk* 🕓 *Closed weekends. No dinner* [M] *Bank* ✥ *H3.*

$$ MODERN BRITISH FAMILY Fodor's Choice ★ 🍴 **St. John.** Global foodie fanatics join Clerkenwell locals for the pioneering nose-to-tail cuisine at this Puritan-esque converted smokehouse near Smithfield Market. Here the chef uses all scraps of a carcass—from tongue and cheeks to tail and trotters—so brace for radically stark signatures like bone marrow and parsley salad. **Known for:** ground zero of influential Modern British nose-to-tail dining; great wine list; pig's-skin appetizer. [$] *Average main: £23* ✉ *26 St. John St., Clerkenwell* ☎ *020/7251–0848* 🌐 *www.stjohnrestaurant.com* 🕓 *No dinner Sun.* [M] *Farringdon, Barbican* ✥ *G2.*

$$$ SEAFOOD 🍴 **Sweetings.** Established in 1889 not far from St. Paul's Cathedral, little seems to have changed since the height of the British Empire at this quirky eatery. Although there are some things Sweetings doesn't do (dinner, reservations, coffee, or weekends), it does, mercifully, do great seafood. **Known for:** fresh Billingsgate fish served at raised linen-covered counters; tankards of "Black Velvet" Guinness and champagne; popular potted shrimp and Dover sole. [$] *Average main: £30* ✉ *39 Queen Victoria St., City of London* ☎ *020/7248–3062* 🌐 *www.sweetingsrestaurant.co.uk* 🕓 *Closed weekends. No dinner* [M] *Mansion House* ✥ *G3.*

EAST LONDON

$ CAFÉ FAMILY 🍴 **E Pellicci.** It's all Cockney banter and full English breakfasts at this tiny family-run café and one-time gangsters' lair near the East End's Brick Lane and Columbia Road markets. This rowdy hole-in-the-wall serves the greasy fry-ups Londoners still adore: copious scrambled eggs, bacon, sausages, baked beans, toast, tomatoes, fried mushrooms, black pudding, cabbage 'n' mash, and scorching hot tea. **Known for:** full cast of East End Cockney characters; copious full English breakfasts and builders' brew tea; cash-only cheap dishes. [$] *Average main: £8* ✉ *332 Bethnal Green Rd., Bethnal Green* ☎ *020/7739–4873* 🌐 *www.epellicci.com* 💳 *No credit cards* 🕓 *Closed Sun.* [M] *Bethnal Green* ✥ *H3.*

SOUTH OF THE THAMES

$$ BISTRO FAMILY Fodor's Choice ★ 🍴 **Casse-Croûte.** French tunes play in the background at this jaunty French bistro on Bermondsey Street near the Shard. The daily changing blackboard offers a limited three options per course menu of exceptional Gallic bistro classics and riffs—from *côte de boeuf* to glazed stuffed pig's trotters with mash. **Known for:** authentic Parisian-style neighborhood bistro; stuffed pig's trotters and côte de boeuf with French beans; delicious pastries with Chantilly cream. [$] *Average main: £20* ✉ *109*

CLOSE UP

Afternoon Tea in London

So, what is Afternoon Tea, exactly? Well, it means real loose-leaf tea—Earl Grey, English Breakfast, Ceylon, Darjeeling, or Assam—brewed in a fine bone china or porcelain pot, and served with fine bone cups and saucers, milk or lemon, and silver spoons, taken between noon and 6 pm. Tea goers dress smartly (though not ostentatiously), and conversation by tradition should avoid politics and religion. Here are some top places in town to head:

Hands-down, the superglam **Savoy** on the Strand offers one of the most beautiful settings for tea. The Thames Foyer, a symphony of grays and golds centered around a winter garden wrought-iron gazebo, is just the place for the house pianist to accompany you as you enjoy the award-winning house teas along with finger sandwiches, homemade scones, and *yumptious* pastries.

Setting the standard in its English Tea Room for some of London's best-known traditional teas, **Brown's Hotel**, at 33 Albermarle Street—charmingly set in a classic Mayfair town house—offers Afternoon Tea for £55 or, if you wish to splash out, Champagne Tea for £65.

Moving west, you can sit looking out onto fab lawns amid mini potted orange trees at **The Orangery** in Prince William and Kate's London pad, Kensington Palace, inside resplendent Kensington Gardens. Afternoon Tea is £28 and a suitably Royal Afternoon Tea (with a glass of Laurent-Perrier) is £38.

Alternatively, add spice to your Afternoon Tea by trying a popular Moroccan-style Afternoon Tea at the souk-chic tearoom at **Momo** off Regent Street, where you'll enjoy sweet mint tea in colorful glass cups plus scones with fig jam, Maghrebian pastries, Moroccan chicken wraps, and honey-and-nut-rich Berber-style crêpes.

Finally, for frilly trompe l'oeil grandeur, few can compete with Afternoon Tea at **The Ritz** on Piccadilly. It's served in the impressive Palm Court, replete with marble tables, Louis XVI chaises, resplendent bouquets, and musical accompaniment: a true taste of Edwardian London in the 21st century. Afternoon Tea is £54 and Champagne Tea £81. Reserve a few months ahead and remember to wear a jacket and tie.

Bermondsey St., Bermondsey ☎ *020/7407–2140* 🌐 *www.cassecroute.co.uk* 🕒 *No dinner Sun.* [M] *London Bridge* ✣ *H4.*

$$ TAPAS 🍴 **José.** Revered Spanish chef José Pizarro packs in diners at this tapas-and-sherry treasure trove on Bermondsey Street, just south of the Shard. With just 30 seats and no reservations, you'll be hard-pressed to find a spot after 6 pm, but it's worth the wait: the Spanish tapas dishes here are superb. **Known for:** notoriously long waits and large crowds; wondrous green padron peppers and Ibérico pork fillet; unique sherry menu. [$] *Average main: £18* ✉ *104 Bermondsey St., Southwark* ☎ *020/7403–4902* 🌐 *www.josepizarro.com/jose-tapas-bar* [M] *Borough, London Bridge* ✣ *H4.*

$ ITALIAN FAMILY Fodor's Choice ★

🍴 **Padella.** Sit at the galley kitchen counter at London's top pasta bar in Borough Market, and watch as the chefs toss and serve endless hot pans of authentic handmade Italian pasta. Seriously epic and amazingly cheap pasta dishes include egg-free Parmesan and black pepper-rich *pici cacio e pepe*from Tuscany, or devilishly addictive ricotta ravioli with a slick of sage butter. **Known for:** supercheap handmade Italian pasta; papardelle with eight-hour beef-shin ragù; fast-moving lines and no reservations. [$] *Average main: £7* ✉ *6 Southwark St., Borough* 🌐 *www.padella.co* [M] *Borough, London Bridge* ✥ *H4.*

$$$$ MODERN BRITISH

🍴 **Restaurant Story.** British chef-patron Tom Sellers storms the ramparts at this set-menu gastro mecca, with his conceptual take on intensively flavored, ingredient-led New British and New Nordic cuisine. Housed in a modish Scandinavian-inspired dining space, expect clever touches like edible nasturtium flowers or a surprise beef-dripping candle that melts into a silver candle holder, which you mop up with heritage grain sourdough throughout the meal. **Known for:** intricate and unhurried set meal extravaganzas; global foodie destination; signature beef dripping candle. [$] *Average main: £34* ✉ *199 Tooley St., Bermondsey* ☎ *020/7183–2117* 🌐 *www.restaurantstory.co.uk* ⏲ *Closed Sun. No lunch Mon.* [M] *London Bridge* ✥ *H4.*

KENSINGTON, KNIGHTSBRIDGE, NOTTING HILL, AND MAYFAIR

KENSINGTON

$$$ JAPANESE

🍴 **Yashin.** At this top London sushi bar off Kensington High Street, you can watch Japanese head chef and cofounder Yasuhiro Mineno tease, slice, tweak, and blowtorch his way to the freshest, funkiest, most colorful, and exquisite sushi, sashimi, salads, and carpaccio that you're likely to find this side of the East China Sea. Tofu-topped miso cappuccino comes in a Victorian cup and saucer, while delectable sushi spreads might mesmerize with ponzu-spiked salmon or Japanese sea bream with rice cracker dust. **Known for:** exquisite sushi and sashimi with the odd twist; 5- to 15-piece chef-decides omakase sets; superaffordable five-piece salmon sushi lunch. [$] *Average main: £28* ✉ *1A Argyll Rd., Kensington* ☎ *020/7938–1536* 🌐 *www.yashinsushi.com* [M] *High St. Kensington* ✥ *A4.*

CHELSEA AND KNIGHTSBRIDGE

$$$ SPANISH FAMILY

🍴 **Ametsa with Arzak Instruction.** At this modernist romp, lovers of all things Spain can bask in a fantasia of New Basque cuisine. Here diners enjoy the passionate service and marvel at high-spec riffs on traditional Basque dishes, like slow-cooked hen's eggs flecked with paprika-rich chistorra sausage, wild ceps, and chorizo, or lobster updated with a white cassava powder. **Known for:** modernist New Basque molecular gastronomy; stunning wavelike ceiling feature, with 7,000 spice-filled glass vials; jaw-dropping Fractal mead dessert. [$] *Average main: £29* ✉ *Halkin Hotel, 5 Halkin St., Knightsbridge* ☎ *020/7333–1234* 🌐 *www.comohotels.com/thehalkin/dining/ametsa* ⏲ *Closed Sun. No lunch Mon.* [M] *Hyde Park Corner, Knightsbridge* ✥ *C4.*

2

$$ ✕ **Bar Boulud.** United States–based French superchef Daniel Boulud
BRASSERIE combines the best of French high-end brasserie fare with a dash of
FAMILY superior Yankee gourmet burgers and fries at this popular hangout in
the Mandarin Oriental. The knockout grazing menu has something for
everyone, and the professional but informal waitstaff give out a con-
vivial vibe. **Known for:** awesome beef, BBQ pork, and foie gras burg-
ers; highly affordable set meals from noon until 6:30; global five-star
hotel crowd. $ *Average main: £23* ✉ *Mandarin Oriental Hyde Park, 66
Knightsbridge, Knightsbridge* ☎ *020/7201–3899 for reservations only*
⊕ *www.barboulud.com/london* Ⓜ *Knightsbridge* ✛ *C4.*

$$$$ ✕ **Dinner by Heston Blumenthal.** Splendidly revived old English gastron-
BRITISH omy dishes executed with ultramodern precision is the *schtick* here
FAMILY at chef Ashley Palmer-Watts's wildly popular eatery at the Mandarin
Fodor'sChoice Oriental. As you take in views of Hyde Park, slice into options like the
★ Meat Fruit appetizer (circa 1500), a ball of ultrasmooth chicken liver
parfait in a mandarin jelly. **Known for:** one of London's top destination
dining spots overlooking Hyde Park; unique historically accurate dishes
that span England's history; Sauternes-soaked brioche and pineapple
tipsy cake for dessert. $ *Average main: £34* ✉ *Mandarin Oriental Hyde
Park, 66 Knightsbridge, Knightsbridge* ☎ *020/7201–3833* ⊕ *www.din-
nerbyheston.com* Ⓜ *Knightsbridge* ✛ *C4.*

$$$ ✕ **The Harwood Arms.** British game doesn't get much finer than at this game-
MODERN BRITISH lover's paradise (and London's only Michelin-star gastro-pub). Sample a
FAMILY catalog of awesome Sunday roasts or game like the popular carve-your-
own whole roast lamb, pork, or beef joints with gravy and all the trim-
mings. **Known for:** standout Michelin-star grub in a gastro-pub setting;
seasonal game from the pub's own hunting estate; Berkshire fallow deer.
$ *Average main: £26* ✉ *27 Walham Grove, Chelsea* ☎ *020/7386–1847*
⊕ *www.harwoodarms.com* ◷ *No lunch Mon.* Ⓜ *Fulham Broadway* ✛ *A6.*

$$$ ✕ **Mari Vanna.** All of London's Russian expatriates squeeze into this fan-
RUSSIAN tasy dining salon in Knightsbridge, which overflows with a maximalist
decor of vintage chandeliers, Tiffany lamps, *tchotchkes, cheburashkas,*
and a Russian *pechka* stove. Snap into character with a horseradish
vodka shot, then carb-up on pierogi sea bass savories, Siberian *pelmeni*
(dumpling) soup, or smoked salmon blinis. **Known for:** fantastically
kitsch prerevolution Russian dining room; tasty borscht, blinis, and
beef Stroganoff; sweet crepes for dessert. $ *Average main: £28* ✉ *The
Wellington Court, 116 Knightsbridge, Knightsbridge* ☎ *020/7225–3122*
⊕ *www.marivanna.ru/london* Ⓜ *Knightsbridge* ✛ *C4.*

NOTTING HILL

$ ✕ **Hereford Road.** A Bayswater favorite with the well-connected Notting
MODERN BRITISH Hill set, Hereford Road is renowned for its pared-down, pomp-free, and
FAMILY ingredient-driven seasonal British fare, with an emphasis on well-sourced
regional British produce. Work your way through uncluttered combos like
steamed mussels with cider and thyme, lemon sole with sea dulse, or Eng-
lish rice pudding with a dollop of strawberry jam. **Known for:** pared-back
Modern British nose-to-tail dining; deceptively simple-sounding dishes like
duck livers with watercress; famously affordable two- and three-course set
lunches. $ *Average main: £15* ✉ *3 Hereford Rd., Bayswater* ☎ *020/7727–
1144* ⊕ *www.herefordroad.org* Ⓜ *Bayswater, Queensway* ✛ *A3.*

$$ FRENCH FAMILY Fodor's Choice ★ 🍴 **Six Portland Road.** The ultimate neighborhood restaurant in west London's wealthy Holland Park section draws diners with its brilliant-but-understated French classics, relaxed service, and interesting, largely French Caves de Pyrene–sourced wines. Dive in for plump Cornish mussels with white wine sauce or perfectly matched Atlantic cod with creamed leeks, shrimps, and sea aster. **Known for:** intimate seating; unpretentious but pitch perfect service; winning boutique wine list. [$] *Average main: £18* ✉ *6 Portland Rd., Notting Hill* ☎ *020/7229–3130* 🌐 *www.sixportlandroad.com* 🕒 *Closed Mon. No dinner Sun.* [M] *Holland Park* ✥ *A2.*

MAYFAIR

$$$$ FRENCH FAMILY Fodor's Choice ★ 🍴 **Alain Ducasse at the Dorchester.** One of only two three-Michelin-starred restaurants in the city, Alain Ducasse at the Dorchester achieves the pinnacle of classical French haute cuisine in a surprisingly fun, lively, and unstuffy salon. Diners feast on a blizzard of beautifully choreographed dishes including classic rum baba with Chantilly cream, sliced open and served in a silver domed tureen. **Known for:** impeccable five-star service; surprisingly unstarchy vibe; signature sauté lobster with chicken quenelles. [$] *Average main: £45* ✉ *The Dorchester, Park Lane, Mayfair* ☎ *020/7629–8866 for reservations only* 🌐 *www.alainducasse-dorchester.com* 🕒 *Closed Sun. and Mon. No lunch Sat.* [M] *Marble Arch, Green Park* ✥ *C3.*

$$$ MODERN ITALIAN 🍴 **Cecconi's.** Revel with the A-listers in the glamorous buzz at this upscale Italian brasserie wedged between Cork Street, Savile Row, and the Royal Academy of Arts. Perfect for a pit stop during a West End shopping spree or after browsing the nearby Mayfair galleries and auction houses, diners spill out onto pavement tables for breakfast, brunch, and *cicchetti* (Italian tapas), and return later in the day for something more substantial. **Known for:** favorite of nearby Vogue House staff and Sotheby's clientele; popular veal Milanese; all-day jet-setter hangout. [$] *Average main: £29* ✉ *5A Burlington Gardens, Mayfair* ☎ *020/7434–1500* 🌐 *www.cecconis.co.uk* [M] *Green Park, Piccadilly Circus* ✥ *D3.*

$$$$ STEAKHOUSE FAMILY 🍴 **CUT at 45 Park Lane.** Austrian-born star chef Wolfgang Puck amps up the stakes at this ultraexpensive steak house on Park Lane. Set against a luxe backdrop of Damien Hirst artwork and globe lights, carnivores go crazy for the pricey prime cuts from England, Australia, Japan, and the United States. **Known for:** rare Kagoshima Wagyu beef steaks; celebrity chef hot spot; art gallerylike interior. [$] *Average main: £48* ✉ *45 Park La., Mayfair* ☎ *020/7493–4545 for reservations only* 🌐 *www.dorchestercollection.com* [M] *Marble Arch, Hyde Park Corner* ✥ *C3.*

$ SEAFOOD FAMILY 🍴 **The Golden Hind.** You'll land some of the best fish-and-chips in town at this British chippy in a retro 1914 art deco café. Marylebone locals and satisfied tourists alike hunker down for the neatly prepared and decidedly nongreasy deep-fried or steamed battered cod, haddock, and plaice, the classic hand-cut Maris Piper chips, and the traditional mushy peas and homemade tartare sauce. **Known for:** some of the city's best deep-fried battered cod and chips; hard-to-find traditional mushy peas; huge portions. [$] *Average main: £10* ✉ *71A-73 Marylebone La., Marylebone* ☎ *020/7486–3644* 🌐 *www.goldenhindrestaurant.com* 🕒 *Closed Sun. No lunch Sat.* [M] *Bond St.* ✥ *C2.*

$$$ MODERN INDIAN FAMILY Fodor's Choice ★

🍴 **Gymkhana.** The last days of the Raj are invoked here at one of London's finest Indian curry emporiums, where top choices include dosas with fennel-rich Chettinad duck or the famed suckling pig vindaloo. Diners admire the whirring ceiling fans, rattan chairs, and other decor inspired by the Colonial-era gymkhana sporting clubs of yesteryear. **Known for:** unusual game curries; Indian punches in the basement private dining booths; signature kid goat methi keema. [$] *Average main: £28* ✉ *42 Albemarle St., Mayfair* ☎ *020/3011–5900* 🌐 *www.gymkhanalondon.com* 🕒 *Closed Sun.* [M] *Green Park* ✣ *D3.*

2

$$$$ FRENCH FAMILY

🍴 **Hélène Darroze at the Connaught.** The city's wealthy flock to French virtuoso Hélène Darroze's restaurant at the Connaught for her dazzling regional French haute cuisine, served up in a stylish Edwardian wood-paneled dining salon. Taking inspiration from Les Landes in southwestern France, Darroze sallies forth with a procession of magnificent dishes, like Robert Dupérier foie gras with fig and port or Limousin sweetbreads with Jerusalem artichokes. **Known for:** sumptuous dining salon; classy French haute dishes; relatively affordable three-course set lunch. [$] *Average main: £38* ✉ *The Connaught, Carlos Pl., Mayfair* ☎ *020/3147–7200 for reservations only* 🌐 *www.the-connaught.co.uk* 👔 *Jacket required* [M] *Green Park* ✣ *C3.*

$$$ MODERN BRITISH

🍴 **Kitty Fisher's.** Named after an infamous 18th-century courtesan, Kitty Fisher's is situated in a tiny, creaky Georgian town house in Mayfair's Shepherd Market. Crammed with antique prints, portraits, and silver candelabras, here you can sample some of the finest wood-grill and smokehouse fare around. **Known for:** cozy and candlelit townhouse setting; signature wood-grilled old Galician beef with scorched onions; high-end showbiz and politico diners. [$] *Average main: £24* ✉ *10 Shepherd Market, Mayfair* ☎ *020/3302–1661* 🌐 *www.kittyfishers.com* 🕒 *Closed Sun.* [M] *Green Park* ✣ *D3.*

$$$$ MODERN EUROPEAN

🍴 **Pollen Street Social.** Gastro god Jason Atherton may not man the stoves here anymore, but his flagship in a cute Dickensian alleyway off Regent Street still knocks the London dining scene for a loop. Fans can enjoy refined small and large dishes ranging from a full English breakfast appetizer to sublime Scottish ox cheek with 50-day Black Angus rib eye. **Known for:** Michelin-star riffs on classic British dishes; dedicated dessert bar; Lake District roast lamb with shallots and mint sauce. [$] *Average main: £35* ✉ *8–10 Pollen St., Mayfair* ☎ *020/7290–7600* 🌐 *www.pollenstreetsocial.com* 🕒 *Closed Sun.* [M] *Oxford Circus, Piccadilly Circus* ✣ *D3.*

$$$$ SEAFOOD FAMILY

🍴 **Scott's.** Imposing doormen in bowler hats greet visitors with a wee nod at this ever-fashionable seafood haven on Mount Street in Mayfair. Originally founded in 1851 in the Haymarket, and a former haunt of James Bond author Ian Fleming (he apparently enjoyed the potted shrimps), Scott's draws the wealthiest of London, who enjoy the fresh Lindisfarne oysters, Dover sole, and tasty shrimp burgers. **Known for:** possibly London's most magnificent crustacean bar; huge platters of fresh fruits de mer; extravagant prices. [$] *Average main: £37* ✉ *20 Mount St., Mayfair* ☎ *020/7495–7309 for reservations only* 🌐 *www.scotts-restaurant.com* [M] *Green Park, Bond St.* ✣ *C3.*

WHERE TO STAY

If your invitation from Queen Elizabeth still hasn't shown up in the mail, no worries—London's grande-dame hotels are the next best thing—and possibly better. If your budget won't stretch to five-star luxury, don't worry. There are plenty of comfortable, clean, friendly options available for a relatively reasonable price. The key word is relatively. In recent years London has seen a welcome growth in the value-for-money sector, but overall, accommodations here still remain on the costly side.

If money is no object, London has some of the world's most luxurious hotels. Even these high-end places have deals, and you can sometimes find a bargain, particularly during January and February. Meanwhile, several mid-range hotels have dropped their average prices, which has made some desirable options more affordable. Large business-oriented hotels frequently offer weekend packages as well. Those on a budget should check out the stylish and supercheap hotels that have shaken up the lodging scene of late. The downside is that these places tend to be a little out of the way, but you may find this a price worth paying. Another attractive alternative includes hotels in the Premier and Millennium chains, which offer sleek, modern rooms, many up-to-date conveniences, and discount prices that sometimes fall below £100 a night.

You should confirm *exactly* what your room costs before checking in. The usual practice in all but the less expensive hotels is for quoted prices to cover room alone; breakfast, whether Continental or "full English" (i.e. cooked), costs extra. Also check whether the quoted rate includes V.A.T. (sales tax), which is a hefty 20%. Most expensive hotels include it in the initial quote, but some middle-of-the-range and budget places may not. *Hotel reviews have been shortened. For full information, visit Fodors.com.*

WHAT IT COSTS IN POUNDS			
$	$$	$$$	$$$$
Hotels	under £125	£125–£250	£250–£400	over £400

Hotel prices are the lowest cost of a standard double room in high season, including 20% V.A.T.

Use the coordinate (✛ B2) at the end of each listing to locate a site on the corresponding map.

WESTMINSTER AND ST. JAMES'S

WESTMINSTER

$$$$
HOTEL
Fodor's Choice
★

The Corinthia. The London outpost of the exclusive Corinthia chain is design heaven-on-earth, with levels of service that make anyone feel like a VIP. **Pros:** so much luxury and elegance you'll feel like royalty; exceptional spa with indoor pool; excellent fine dining options. **Cons:** prices jump to the stratosphere once the least expensive rooms sell out;

not many special offers; not all room prices include breakfast. $ *Rooms from: £500* ✉ *Whitehall Pl., Westminster* ☎ *020/7930–8181* ⊕ *www.corinthia.com* ➾ *294 rooms* ⦿ *No meals* Ⓜ *Embankment* ✛ *G4.*

$$ ⚏ **DoubleTree by Hilton Hotel London Westminster.** Spectacular views of the
HOTEL   river, Big Ben, and the London Eye fill the floor-to-ceiling windows in
FAMILY   this rather stark, steel-and-glass building steps from the Tate Britain,
and a plethora of techy perks await inside. **Pros:** amazing views; flat-screen TVs and other high-tech gadgetry; can be surprisingly affordable for the location. **Cons:** small bedrooms; tiny bathrooms; TV has to be operated through a computer (confusing if you're not used to it). $ *Rooms from: £175* ✉ *30 John Islip St., Westminster* ☎ *020/7630–1000* ⊕ *www.doubletreewestminsterhotel.com* ➾ *460 rooms* ⦿ *Some meals* Ⓜ *Westminster, Pimlico* ✛ *F5.*

$$$$ ⚏ **Hotel 41.** With faultless service, sumptuous designer furnishings, and
HOTEL   a sense of fun to boot, this impeccable hotel breathes new life into the
Fodor'sChoice   cliché "thinks of everything," yet the epithet is really quite apt. **Pros:**
★   impeccable service; beautiful and stylish; Buckingham Palace is on your
doorstep. **Cons:** unusual design is not for everyone; expensive; the private bar can feel stuffy. $ *Rooms from: £431* ✉ *41 Buckingham Palace Rd., Westminster* ☎ *020/7300–0041* ⊕ *www.41hotel.com* ➾ *32 rooms* ⦿ *Free Breakfast* Ⓜ *Victoria* ✛ *E5.*

$$ ⚏ **Lime Tree Hotel.** In a central neighborhood where hotels veer from
HOTEL   wildly overpriced at one extreme to grimy bolt-holes at the other, the
Lime Tree gets the boutique style just about right—and at a surprisingly reasonable cost for the neighborhood. **Pros:** lovely and helpful hosts; great location; rooms are decent size. **Cons:** cheaper rooms are small; some are up several flights of stairs and there's no elevator; lack of amenities. $ *Rooms from: £195* ✉ *135–137 Ebury St., Westminster* ☎ *020/7730–8191* ⊕ *www.limetreehotel.co.uk* ➾ *25 rooms* ⦿ *Free Breakfast* Ⓜ *Victoria, Sloane Sq.* ✛ *E5.*

$$ ⚏ **Windermere Hotel.** This sweet and rather elegant old hotel, on the
HOTEL   premises of London's first B&B (1881), is a decent, well-situated
FAMILY   option. **Pros:** good location close to Victoria Station; free Wi-Fi; good
amenities for an old hotel of this size, including air-conditioning and an elevator. **Cons:** rooms and bathrooms are tiny; traditional decor might not suit all tastes; many major attractions are a 20-minute walk away. $ *Rooms from: £153* ✉ *142–144 Warwick Way, Westminster* ☎ *020/7834–5163* ⊕ *www.windermere-hotel.co.uk* ➾ *19 rooms* ⦿ *Free Breakfast* Ⓜ *Victoria* ✛ *E6.*

ST. JAMES'S

$$$$ ⚏ **The Stafford London.** This is a rare find: a posh hotel that's equal parts
HOTEL   elegance and friendliness, and located in one of the few peaceful spots
Fodor'sChoice   in the area, down a small lane behind Piccadilly. **Pros:** great staff; home
★   to one of London's original "American Bars"; quiet location. **Cons:**
traditional style is not to all tastes; perks in the more expensive rooms could be more generous (free airport transfer, but one-way only; free clothes pressing, but only one item per day); some rooms can feel small. $ *Rooms from: £460* ✉ *16–18 St. James's Pl., St. James's* ☎ *020/7493–0111* ⊕ *www.thestaffordlondon.com* ➾ *106 rooms* ⦿ *Free Breakfast* Ⓜ *Green Park* ✛ *E4.*

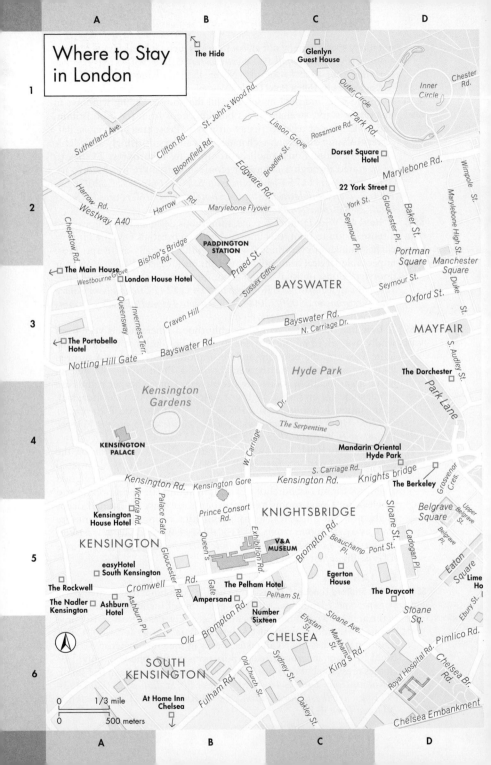

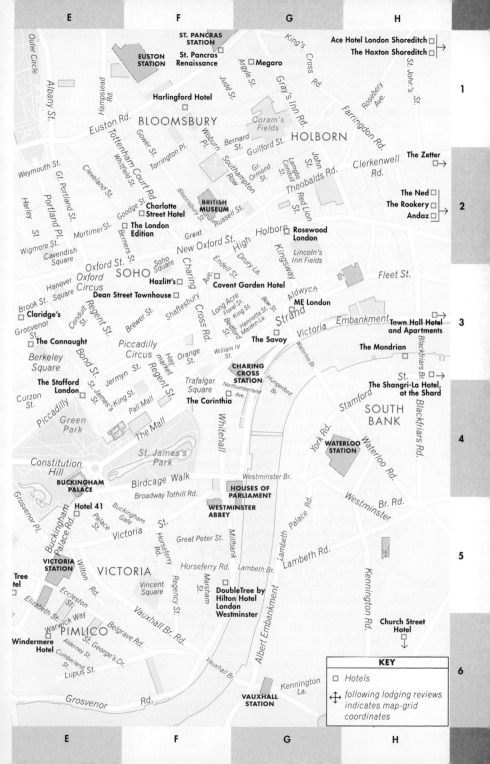

SOHO AND COVENT GARDEN

SOHO

$$$
HOTEL
Fodor's Choice
★
⛆ **Dean Street Townhouse.** Discreet and unpretentious—and right in the heart of Soho—this oh-so-stylish place has a bohemian vibe and an excellent Modern British restaurant, hung with pieces by renowned artists like Peter Blake and Tracy Emin. **Pros:** ultracool vibe; resembles an upper-class pied-à-terre; great location in the heart of Soho. **Cons:** some rooms are extremely small; rooms at the front of the building can be noisy, especially on weekends; the crowd can often feel cooler-than-thou. ⓢ *Rooms from: £315* ✉ *69–71 Dean St., Soho* ☎ *020/7434–1775* ⊕ *www.deanstreettownhouse.com* ⤴ *39 rooms* ❑ *Free Breakfast* Ⓜ *Leicester Sq., Tottenham Court Rd.* ✛ *F3.*

$$$
HOTEL
Fodor's Choice
★
⛆ **Hazlitt's.** This disarmingly friendly place, full of personality, robust antiques, and claw-foot tubs, occupies three connected early 18th-century houses, one of which was the last home of essayist William Hazlitt (1778–1830). **Pros:** great for lovers of art and antiques; historic atmosphere with lots of small sitting rooms and wooden staircases; truly beautiful and relaxed. **Cons:** no in-house restaurant; breakfast costs extra; no elevators. ⓢ *Rooms from: £251* ✉ *6 Frith St., Soho* ☎ *020/7434–1771* ⊕ *www.hazlittshotel.com* ⤴ *30 rooms* ❑ *No meals* Ⓜ *Tottenham Court Rd.* ✛ *F3.*

COVENT GARDEN

$$$
HOTEL
Fodor's Choice
★
⛆ **Covent Garden Hotel.** It's little wonder this is now the London home-away-from-home for off-duty celebrities, actors, and style mavens, with its Covent Garden location and guest rooms that are design-magazine stylish, using mix-and-match couture fabrics to stunning effect. **Pros:** great for star-spotting; supertrendy; basement cinema for movie buffs. **Cons:** you can feel you don't matter if you're not famous; location in Covent Garden can be a bit boisterous; only some rooms come with balcony views. ⓢ *Rooms from: £315* ✉ *10 Monmouth St., Covent Garden* ☎ *020/7806–1000, 800/553–6674 in U.S.* ⊕ *www.firmdalehotels.com/hotels/london/covent-garden-hotel* ⤴ *58 rooms* ❑ *No meals* Ⓜ *Covent Garden* ✛ *F3.*

$$$
HOTEL
Fodor's Choice
★
⛆ **ME London.** A shiny fortress of luxury, the ME brings a splash of modern cool to a rather stuffy patch of the Strand. **Pros:** sleek and fashionable; full of high-tech comforts; stunning views from rooftop bar. **Cons:** design can sometimes verge on form over function; very small closets and in-room storage areas; the rooftop bar can get uncomfortably busy. ⓢ *Rooms from: £280* ✉ *336 The Strand, Covent Garden* ☎ *0808/234–1953* ⊕ *www.melia.com* ⤴ *157 rooms* ❑ *Free Breakfast* Ⓜ *Covent Garden* ✛ *G3.*

$$$$
HOTEL
Fodor's Choice
★
⛆ **The Savoy.** One of London's most iconic hotels maintains its status at the top with winning attributes of impeccable service, stunning decor, and a desirable location on the Strand. **Pros:** one of the top hotels in Europe; iconic pedigree; Thames-side location. **Cons:** everything comes with a price tag; street noise is surprisingly problematic, particularly on lower floors; street can be too busy for some. ⓢ *Rooms from: £504* ✉ *The Strand, Covent Garden* ☎ *020/7836–4343, 800/257–7544 in U.S.* ⊕ *www.fairmont.com/savoy-london* ⤴ *268 rooms* ❑ *Free Breakfast* Ⓜ *Covent Garden, Charing Cross* ✛ *G3.*

BLOOMSBURY AND HOLBORN

BLOOMSBURY

$$$
HOTEL
Fodor's Choice
★

Charlotte Street Hotel. Tradition and modern flair are fused together in this superstylish retreat, a short walk from Oxford Street. **Pros:** elegant and luxurious; great attention to detail; decent chance at finding a good deal. **Cons:** the popular bar can be noisy; reservations essential for the restaurant; some rooms are small considering the price. $ *Rooms from: £306 ⊠ 15–17 Charlotte St., Bloomsbury ☎ 020/7806–2000, 800/553–6674 in U.S. ⊕ www.firmdalehotels.com ⇌ 52 rooms* ⦷ *No meals* Ⓜ *Goodge St. ✛ F2.*

$$
HOTEL

Harlingford Hotel. The most contemporary of the hotels around Bloomsbury's Cartwright Gardens offers sleek, quiet, and comfortable bedrooms and perfectly appointed public rooms. **Pros:** good location; friendly staff; private garden. **Cons:** rooms are small; no air-conditioning; no elevator. $ *Rooms from: £140 ⊠ 61–63 Cartwright Gardens, Bloomsbury ☎ 020/7387–1551 ⊕ www.harlingfordhotel.com ⇌ 43 rooms* ⦷ *Free Breakfast* Ⓜ *Russell Sq. ✛ F1.*

$$
HOTEL

Megaro. Directly across the street from St. Pancras International station, the snazzy, well-designed, modern rooms here surround guests with startlingly contemporary style and amenities that include powerful showers and espresso machines. **Pros:** comfortable beds; great location for Eurostar travelers; short hop on Tube to city center. **Cons:** neighborhood isn't interesting; standard rooms are small; interiors may be a bit stark for some. $ *Rooms from: £210 ⊠ Belgrove St., King's Cross ☎ 020/7843–2222 ⊕ www.hotelmegaro.co.uk ⇌ 57 rooms* ⦷ *Free Breakfast* Ⓜ *King's Cross St. Pancras ✛ G1.*

$$$
HOTEL
Fodor's Choice
★

St. Pancras Renaissance. This stunningly restored Victorian landmark—replete with gingerbread turrets and castlelike ornaments—started as a love letter to the golden age of railways, and now it's one of London's most sophisticated places to stay. **Pros:** unique and beautiful; faultless service; close to the train station. **Cons:** very crowded bar and restaurant; streets outside are busy 24/7; some cheaper rooms don't include free Wi-Fi. $ *Rooms from: £255 ⊠ Euston Rd., King's Cross ☎ 020/7841–3540 ⊕ www.marriott.com/hotels/travel/lonpr-st-pancras-renaissance-hotel-london ⇌ 245 rooms* ⦷ *Free Breakfast* Ⓜ *King's Cross St. Pancras. National Rail: Kings Cross, St. Pancras ✛ F1.*

HOLBORN

$$$$
HOTEL

Rosewood London. So striking it was featured in the movie *Howards End*, this landmark structure (built by the Pearl Assurance Company in 1914) now houses a beautiful hotel with a clubby atmosphere, subtly elegant India Jane fabrics, and huge comfortable beds. **Pros:** gorgeous romantic space; excellent restaurant; great spa. **Cons:** luxury comes at a price; the area can be quiet on weekends; the rooms can't quite match the splendor of the public areas. $ *Rooms from: £450 ⊠ 252 High Holborn, Holborn ☎ 020/7781–8888, 888/767–3966 in U.S. ⊕ www.rosewoodhotels.com/en/london ⇌ 306 rooms* ⦷ *Free Breakfast* Ⓜ *Holborn ✛ G2.*

FITZROVIA

$$$ HOTEL Fodor's Choice ★ **The London Edition.** Style and image are the draw at the London Edition Hotel, where Michelin-starred chefs and hip bars complement the boutique property's sleek, contemporary design. **Pros:** very trendy; great bars; beautifully designed bedrooms. **Cons:** rooms may feel small to some; lobby can get crowded with trendsetters descending upon the bars and nightclub; can at times feel more like an events space than a hotel. [$] *Rooms from: £358* ✉ *10 Berners St., Fitzrovia* ☎ *020/7781–0000* 🌐 *edition-hotels.marriott.com/london* 🛏 *173 rooms* 🍴 *Free Breakfast* [M] *Oxford Circus* ✣ *F2.*

THE CITY

$$ HOTEL Fodor's Choice ★ **The Ned.** Bursting with eye-catching art deco design and achingly hip interiors, the Ned is as close to the glamour of the 1920s Jazz Age as you'll find in contemporary London. **Pros:** amazing variety of bars and restaurants, all of high quality; rooftop pool with views of St. Paul's Cathedral; beautiful interiors in all rooms. **Cons:** location in The City means public spaces get very busy after work; neighborhood is deserted on weekends; also doubles as a private members' clubs, so the vibe can get snooty. [$] *Rooms from: £180* ✉ *27 Poultry, City of London* ☎ *020/3828–2000* 🌐 *www.thened.com* 🛏 *252 rooms* 🍴 *Free Breakfast* [M] *Bank* ✣ *H2.*

$$ HOTEL Fodor's Choice ★ **The Rookery.** A stylish period masterpiece in the heart of laid-back Clerkenwell, the Rookery is a luxury boutique hotel with a hefty dollop of *Downton Abbey* charm. **Pros:** helpful staff; free Wi-Fi; good deals in the off-season. **Cons:** breakfast costs extra; Tube ride to tourist sites; no restaurant in the hotel. [$] *Rooms from: £210* ✉ *12 Peter's La., at Cowcross St., City of London* ☎ *020/7336–0931* 🌐 *www.rookeryhotel.com* 🛏 *33 rooms* 🍴 *No meals* [M] *Farringdon* ✣ *H2.*

$$ HOTEL Fodor's Choice ★ **The Zetter.** The five-story atrium, art deco staircase, and slick European restaurant hint at the delights to come in this converted warehouse—a breath of fresh air with its playful color schemes, elegant wallpapers, and wonderful views of The City from the higher floors. **Pros:** huge amounts of character; big rooms; free Wi-Fi. **Cons:** rooms with good views cost more; the contemporary style won't appeal to everyone; the property's best bar is across the street at the Zetter Townhouse. [$] *Rooms from: £221* ✉ *86–88 Clerkenwell Rd., Clerkenwell* ☎ *020/7324–4444* 🌐 *www.thezetter.com* 🛏 *59 rooms* 🍴 *Free Breakfast* [M] *Farringdon* ✣ *H2.*

EAST LONDON

$$ HOTEL **Ace Hotel London Shoreditch.** The first European outlet of the superhip Ace hotel chain fits right into the scenery in achingly cool Shoreditch, surrounded by galleries and on-trend boutiques every bit as style conscious as its own creatively minimalist interiors. **Pros:** extremely fashionable; large and comfortable bedrooms; great bar. **Cons:** not everyone will enjoy being surrounded by hipsters; street noise can be a problem; frustrating online booking system. [$] *Rooms from: £175* ✉ *100*

Shoreditch High St., Shoreditch ☎ 020/7613–9800 🌐 www.acehotel.com 🛏 258 rooms 🍴 Free Breakfast [M] Shoreditch High St. ✣ H1.

$$ HOTEL 🏨 **Andaz.** Swanky and upscale, this hotel sports a modern masculine design, and novel check-in procedure—instead of standing at a desk, guests sit in a lounge while a staff member with a tablet takes their information. **Pros:** nice attention to detail; no standing in line to check in; "healthy minibars" are stocked with nuts, fruit, and yogurt. **Cons:** sparse interior design is not for all; rates rise significantly for midweek stays; busy, sometimes hectic neighborhood. *[$] Rooms from: £175 ✉ 40 Liverpool St., East End ☎ 020/7961–1234, 800/492–8804 in U.S. 🌐 www.andaz.hyatt.com 🛏 269 rooms 🍴 Free Breakfast [M] Liverpool St. ✣ H2.*

$$ HOTEL Fodor's Choice ★ 🏨 **The Hoxton Shoreditch.** The design throughout this trendy East London lodging is contemporary—but not so modern as to be absurd; in keeping with a claim to combine a country-lodge lifestyle with true urban living, a fire crackles in the lobby. **Pros:** cool vibe; neighborhood known for funky galleries and boutiques; huge weekend discounts. **Cons:** price skyrockets during the week; away from major tourist sights; cheapest rooms are called "shoeboxes" for a reason. *[$] Rooms from: £149 ✉ 81 Great Eastern St., East End ☎ 020/7550–1000 🌐 www.thehoxton.com/london/shoreditch/hotels 🛏 210 rooms 🍴 Free Breakfast [M] Shoreditch High St. ✣ H1.*

$$ HOTEL 🏨 **Town Hall Hotel and Apartments.** An art deco town hall, abandoned in the early 1980s and turned into a chic hotel 30 years later, is now a lively and stylish place, with the best of the building's elegant original features intact. **Pros:** beautifully designed; lovely staff; big discounts on weekends. **Cons:** the area is far from the major sights; a 15-minute Tube ride from central London; some rooms choose style over function. *[$] Rooms from: £185 ✉ Patriot Sq., Bethnal Green, East End ☎ 020/7871–0460 🌐 www.townhallhotel.com 🛏 90 rooms 🍴 Free Breakfast [M] Bethnal Green ✣ H3.*

SOUTH OF THE THAMES

$ HOTEL Fodor's Choice ★ 🏨 **Church Street Hotel.** Like rays of sunshine in gritty south London, the rooms at this Camberwell hotel are decorated in rich bold tones, and authentic Central American touches like elaborately painted crucifixes, tiles handmade in Guadalajara, and homemade iron bed frames. **Pros:** unique and arty; great breakfasts; closer to central London than it might appear. **Cons:** would suit adventurous young people more than families; a mile from a Tube station (though bus connections are handier); some rooms have shared bathrooms. *[$] Rooms from: £90 ✉ 29–33 Camberwell Church St., Camberwell, South East London ☎ 020/7703–5984 🌐 www.churchstreethotel.com 🛏 31 rooms 🍴 Free Breakfast [M] Oval St. ✣ H6.*

$$$ HOTEL Fodor's Choice ★ 🏨 **The Mondrian.** A quirky yet sophisticated addition to the burgeoning South Bank, the Mondrian is a fun callback to the area's docklands history. **Pros:** excellent bars and restaurants; beautiful river views; short riverside walk to Tate Modern and Shakespeare's Globe. **Cons:** riverview rooms are pricey (of course); public areas, outside the lobby and bars, are a little bland; standard rooms are small. *[$] Rooms from: £256*

✉ *Sea Containers House, 20 Upper Ground, Southwark* ☎ *020/3747–1000* 🌐 *www.morganshotelgroup.com/mondrian/mondrian-london* 🛏 *359 rooms* 🍴 *Free Breakfast* [M] *Blackfriars, Southwark* ✥ *H3.*

$$$$ HOTEL Fodor's Choice ★ 🏨 **The Shangri-La Hotel, at The Shard.** With its floor-to-ceiling windows, the city's highest cocktail bar and infinity pool, and unrivaled views of the London skyline from 1,016 feet above the South Bank of the Thames, the Shangri-La has become one of London's most chic addresses. **Pros:** matchless views; excellent service; superb restaurants and cocktail bar. **Cons:** a design flaw allows some guests to see into their neighbor's rooms at night; decor may feel cold to some; restaurant, bar, and elevator often overcrowded due to popularity of the view. [$] *Rooms from: £468* ✉ *31 St. Thomas St., South Bank* ☎ *0207/234–8000* 🌐 *www.the-shard.com/shangri-la* 🛏 *202 rooms* 🍴 *No meals* [M] *London Bridge Station* ✥ *H3.*

KENSINGTON, KNIGHTSBRIDGE, NOTTING HILL, AND MAYFAIR

KENSINGTON

$$ HOTEL Fodor's Choice ★ 🏨 **Ampersand.** A sense of style emanates from every surface of this sumptuous hotel in the heart of Kensington, and the playful vintage vibe lends the property a refreshingly down-to-earth feel in a neighborhood that can feel stodgy. **Pros:** flawless design; great service; good restaurant. **Cons:** ground-floor rooms can be noisy; breakfast is not included in the price of a room; the area swarms with tourists visiting the museums on weekends. [$] *Rooms from: £216* ✉ *10 Harrington Rd., Kensington* ☎ *020/7589–5895* 🌐 *www.ampersandhotel.com* 🛏 *111 rooms* 🍴 *No meals* [M] *Gloucester Rd.* ✥ *B5.*

$$ HOTEL 🏨 **Ashburn Hotel.** A short walk from Gloucester Road Tube station and within walking distance of Harrods and the Kensington museums, the Ashburn is one of the better "boutique" hotels in this part of town. **Pros:** friendly atmosphere; free Wi-Fi; different turndown gift every night. **Cons:** summer prices sometimes hike the cost; some rooms on the small side; immediate vicinity lacks a little life. [$] *Rooms from: £144* ✉ *111 Cromwell Rd., Kensington* ☎ *020/7244–1999* 🌐 *www.ashburn-hotel.co.uk* 🛏 *38 rooms* 🍴 *Free Breakfast* [M] *Gloucester Rd.* ✥ *A5.*

$ HOTEL 🏨 **easyHotel South Kensington.** London's original "pod hotel" has tiny rooms with a double bed, private shower room, and little else—each brightly decorated in the easyGroup's trademark orange and white (to match their budget airline easyJet). **Pros:** amazing rates; safe and decent enough space; good location. **Cons:** not for the claustrophobic—rooms are truly tiny and most have no windows; six floors and no elevator; Wi-Fi is not included in the price of rooms. [$] *Rooms from: £42* ✉ *14 Lexham Gardens, Kensington* ☎ *07951/440134* 🌐 *www.easyhotel.com* 🛏 *34 rooms* 🍴 *No meals* [M] *Gloucester Rd.* ✥ *A5.*

$ HOTEL 🏨 **Kensington House Hotel.** A short stroll from High Street Kensington and Kensington Gardens, this refurbished 19th-century town house has streamlined contemporary rooms with large windows letting in plenty of light and comfortable beds with luxurious fabrics and soft comforters. **Pros:** attractive design; relaxing setting; free Wi-Fi. **Cons:**

rooms are on the small side; bathrooms are minuscule; room decor might feel quite plain to some. $ Rooms from: £120 ✉ 15–16 Prince of Wales Terr., Kensington ☎ 020/7937–2345 ⊕ www.kenhouse.com ⟳ 41 rooms ¡⊙¡ Free Breakfast Ⓜ High Street Kensington ✛ A5.

$$
HOTEL
⚉ The Nadler Kensington. Known as an "aparthotel," this creamy white Georgian town house offers a useful compromise between full-service hotel and the freedom of self-catering in the form of comfortable rooms with a stylish modern look and tiny kitchenettes. **Pros:** handy mini-kitchens; free Wi-Fi; televisions can stream content from your tablet or phone. **Cons:** basic rooms are small; breakfast is served to the room only; 15-minute Tube ride to central London. $ Rooms from: £130 ✉ 25 Courtfield Gardens, South Kensington ☎ 020/7244–2255 ⊕ www. nadlerhotels.com ⟳ 65 rooms ¡⊙¡ No meals Ⓜ Earl's Ct. ✛ A5.

$$$
HOTEL
Fodor's Choice
★
⚉ Number Sixteen. Rooms at this lovely luxury guesthouse, just around the corner from the Victoria & Albert Museum, look like they come from the pages of *Architectural Digest,* and the delightful garden is an added bonus. **Pros:** just the right level of helpful service; interiors are gorgeous; the afternoon tea is excellent. **Cons:** no restaurant; small elevator; the intimate nature of the small boutique hotel won't appeal to everyone. $ Rooms from: £288 ✉ 16 Sumner Pl., South Kensington ☎ 020/7589–5232, 888/559–5508 in U.S. ⊕ www.firmdale.com ⟳ 41 rooms ¡⊙¡ Free Breakfast Ⓜ South Kensington ✛ B5.

$$
HOTEL
⚉ The Pelham Hotel. One of the first and most stylish of London's famed "boutique" hotels, this still-chic choice is but a short stroll away from the Natural History, Science, and Victoria & Albert museums. **Pros:** great location for museum-hopping; elegant interior design; lovely staff. **Cons:** taller guests will find themselves cursing the top-floor rooms with sloping ceilings; some rooms are on the small side given the price; some suites are only accessible via the stairs. $ Rooms from: £200 ✉ 15 Cromwell Pl., South Kensington ☎ 020/7589–8288, 888/757–5587 in U.S. ⊕ www.pelhamhotel.co.uk ⟳ 52 rooms ¡⊙¡ Free Breakfast Ⓜ South Kensington ✛ B5.

$
HOTEL
⚉ The Rockwell. Despite being on the notoriously traffic-clogged Cromwell Road, this excellent little place is one of the best boutique hotels in this part of London—and windows have good soundproofing. **Pros:** large bedrooms; stylish surroundings; helpful staff. **Cons:** on a busy road; 20-minute Tube ride to central London; street noise is a potential problem. $ Rooms from: £108 ✉ 181 Cromwell Rd., South Kensington ☎ 020/7244–2000 ⊕ www.therockwell.com ⟳ 40 rooms ¡⊙¡ Free Breakfast Ⓜ Earl's Ct. ✛ A5.

CHELSEA

$$
B&B/INN
FAMILY
⚉ At Home Inn Chelsea. King's Road and the rest of superrich Chelsea is just a short stroll from this delightfully informal B&B, and you'd be hard pressed to find a better room in this neighborhood for the price. **Pros:** picturesque top floor terrace; short Tube ride to tourist sites; can be booked as a whole apartment. **Cons:** only accessible via the owners' own apartment's main entrance; few extras; only two guest rooms available. $ Rooms from: £125 ✉ 5 Park Walk, Chelsea ☎ 07790/844–008 ⊕ www.athomeinnchelsea.com ⟳ 2 rooms ¡⊙¡ Free Breakfast Ⓜ Fulham Broadway ✛ B6.

$$$
HOTEL
FAMILY
Fodor'sChoice
★

⛶ **The Draycott.** This elegant yet homey boutique hotel near Sloane Square is the stuff London dreams are made on—if your dream is to live like a pleasantly old-fashioned, impeccably mannered, effortlessly stylish Chelsea lady or gentleman. **Pros:** lovely traditional town house; great service; discreet and peaceful. **Cons:** no restaurant or bar; single rooms are very small; elevator is tiny. $ *Rooms from: £286* ⊠ *26 Cadogan Gardens, Chelsea* ☎ *020/7730–0236* ⊕ *www.draycotthotel.com* ⇆ *35 rooms* ⏽⃝⃞ *Free Breakfast* Ⓜ *Sloane Sq.* ✛ *D5.*

KNIGHTSBRIDGE

$$$$
HOTEL
FAMILY
Fodor'sChoice
★

⛶ **The Berkeley.** Convenient for Knightsbridge shopping, the very elegant Berkeley is known for its renowned restaurants and luxuries that culminate—literally—in a splendid penthouse swimming pool. **Pros:** lavish and elegant; attentive service; great drinking and dining options. **Cons:** you'll need your best designer clothes to fit in; even the cheapest rooms are expensive; while beautiful, the style is very traditional. $ *Rooms from: £440* ⊠ *Wilton Pl., Knightsbridge* ☎ *020/7235–6000, 800/637–2869 in U.S.* ⊕ *www.the-berkeley.co.uk* ⇆ *190 rooms* ⏽⃝⃞ *Free Breakfast* Ⓜ *Knightsbridge* ✛ *D4.*

$$$
HOTEL
Fodor'sChoice
★

⛶ **Egerton House.** A sensationally soigné and chic space that feels like your own private London home, this hotel has some truly luxuriant design touches, including guest rooms lavishly decorated with rich fabrics and a knockout white-on-gold dining room. **Pros:** lovely staff; magnificent interiors; striking art. **Cons:** some style touches are a little too froufrou; sensory overload from the decor of some rooms; the traditional elegance won't appeal to everyone. $ *Rooms from: £290* ⊠ *17–19 Egerton Terr., Knightsbridge* ☎ *020/7589–2412, 877/955–1515 in U.S.* ⊕ *www.redcarnationhotels.com* ⇆ *29 rooms* ⏽⃝⃞ *Free Breakfast* Ⓜ *Knightsbridge, South Kensington* ✛ *C5.*

$$$$
HOTEL
Fodor'sChoice
★

⛶ **Mandarin Oriental Hyde Park.** Built in 1880, the Mandarin Oriental welcomes you with one of the most exuberantly Victorian facades in town, then fast-forwards you to high-trend modern London, thanks to striking and luxurious guest rooms filled with high-tech gadgets. **Pros:** great shopping at your doorstep; amazing views of Hyde Park; excellent service. **Cons:** nothing comes cheap; you must dress up for dinner (and lunch and breakfast); located on a traffic-clogged stretch of Knightsbridge. $ *Rooms from: £720* ⊠ *66 Knightsbridge, Knightsbridge* ☎ *020/7235–2000* ⊕ *www.mandarinoriental.com/london* ⇆ *181 rooms* ⏽⃝⃞ *Free Breakfast* Ⓜ *Knightsbridge* ✛ *D4.*

NOTTING HILL AND BAYSWATER

$$
B&B/INN
Fodor'sChoice
★

⛶ **The Main House.** A stay in this delightfully welcoming B&B feels more like sleeping over at a friend's house than a stay in a hotel—albeit a particularly wealthy and well-connected friend. **Pros:** unique and unusual place; charming and helpful owners; room prices decrease for longer stays. **Cons:** three-night minimum stay is restrictive; few in-house services; no single night stays. $ *Rooms from: £150* ⊠ *6 Colvile Rd., Notting Hill* ☎ *020/7221–9691* ⊕ *www.themainhouse.com* ⇆ *4 rooms* ⏽⃝⃞ *Free Breakfast* Ⓜ *Notting Hill Gate* ✛ *A3.*

$
HOTEL

⛶ **London House Hotel.** Set in a row of white Georgian town houses, this excellent budget option in hit-or-miss Bayswater is friendly, well run, and spotlessly clean. **Pros:** friendly and efficient; emphasis on value; good location. **Cons:** basement rooms lack sunlight; smallest rooms are tiny; the area isn't quite as vibrant as neighboring Notting Hill. [$] *Rooms from: £110* ✉ *81 Kensington Garden Sq., Bayswater* ☎ *020/7243–1810* 🌐 *www.londonhousehotels.com* 🛏 *103 rooms* 🍴 *Free Breakfast* [M] *Queensway, Bayswater* ✥ *A3.*

$$ HOTEL **The Portobello Hotel.** One of London's quirkiest hotels, the little Portobello (formed from two adjoining Victorian houses) has attracted scores of celebrities to its small but stylish rooms over the years, and the decor reflects these hip credentials with joyous abandon. **Pros:** stylish and unique; pets are allowed; guests have use of nearby gym and pool. **Cons:** all but the priciest rooms are quite small; may be too eccentric for some; a 25-minute Tube ride into central London. [$] *Rooms from: £205* ✉ *22 Stanley Gardens, Notting Hill* ☎ *020/7727–2777* 🌐 *www.portobello-hotel.com* 🛏 *21 rooms* 🍴 *Free Breakfast* [M] *Notting Hill Gate* ✥ *A3.*

MAYFAIR

$$$$ HOTEL FAMILY Fodor's Choice ★ **Claridge's.** The well-heeled have been meeting—and eating—at Claridge's for generations, and the tradition continues in the original art deco public spaces of this superglamorous London institution. **Pros:** see-and-be-seen dining and drinking; serious luxury everywhere—this is an old-money hotel; famed history. **Cons:** better pack your designer wardrobe if you want to fit in with the locals; all that luxury means an expensive price tag; to protect the privacy of guests, photographs are prohibited in some areas. [$] *Rooms from: £550* ✉ *Brook St., Mayfair* ☎ *020/7629–8860, 866/599–6991 in U.S.* 🌐 *www.claridges.co.uk* 🛏 *203 rooms* 🍴 *Free Breakfast* [M] *Bond St.* ✥ *E3.*

$$$$ HOTEL FAMILY Fodor's Choice ★ **The Connaught.** A huge favorite of the "we wouldn't dream of staying anywhere else" monied set since its opening in 1917, the Connaught has many dazzlingly modern compliments to its famously historic delights. **Pros:** legendary hotel; great for star-spotting; Michelin-starred dining. **Cons:** history comes at a price; bathrooms are small; the superior king room is small for the price. [$] *Rooms from: £600* ✉ *Carlos Pl., Mayfair* ☎ *020/7499–7070, 866/599–6991 in U.S.* 🌐 *www.the-connaught.co.uk* 🛏 *121 rooms* 🍴 *Free Breakfast* [M] *Bond St.* ✥ *E3.*

$$$$ HOTEL Fodor's Choice ★ **The Dorchester.** Few hotels this opulent manage to be as personable as the Dorchester, which opened in 1939 and boasts a prime Park Lane location with unparalleled glamour; gold leaf and marble adorn the public spaces, and guest quarters are awash in English country house–meets–art deco style. **Pros:** historic luxury in 1930s building; lovely views of Hyde Park; excellent spa. **Cons:** traditional look is not to all tastes; prices are sky-high; some rooms are disappointingly small. [$] *Rooms from: £592* ✉ *53 Park La., Mayfair* ☎ *020/7629–8888* 🌐 *www.thedorchester.com* 🛏 *250 rooms* 🍴 *Free Breakfast* [M] *Marble Arch, Hyde Park Corner* ✥ *D4.*

$$$ HOTEL Fodor's Choice ★ **Dorset Square Hotel.** This fashionable boutique hotel occupies a charming old town house in one of London's most upscale neighborhoods. **Pros:** ideal location; lovely design; good afternoon tea. **Cons:** some rooms are small; no bathtub in some rooms; no gym. [$] *Rooms from: £252* ✉ *39 Dorset Sq., Marylebone* ☎ *020/7723–7874* 🌐 *www.firmdalehotels.com* 🛏 *38 rooms* 🍴 *No meals* [M] *Baker St.* ✥ *D2.*

$$ ⊡ **22 York Street.** This lovely Georgian town house has a cozy family
B&B/INN feel, with polished pine floors and fetching antiques decorating the
homey, individually furnished guest rooms. **Pros:** live out your London
town-house fantasy; flexible check-in times; good location for shop-
pers. **Cons:** if you take away the great location, you're paying a lot for
a B&B; not everyone enjoys socializing with strangers over breakfast;
some guests won't enjoy the lack of anonymity. $ *Rooms from: £150*
⊠ *22 York St., Mayfair* ☎ *020/7224–2990* ⊕ *www.22yorkstreet.co.uk*
↪ *10 rooms* ⦿ *Free Breakfast* Ⓜ *Baker St.* ✛ *D2.*

REGENT'S PARK AND HAMPSTEAD

$ ⊡ **Glenlyn Guest House.** An excellent option for travelers who don't mind
B&B/INN being a long Tube ride away from the action, this converted Victorian
town house offers a high standard of accommodation a few miles north
of Hampstead. **Pros:** comfortable and friendly; you get more for your
money than you would in central London; five-minute walk to Tube
station. **Cons:** you have to factor in the cost and inconvenience of a half-
hour Tube ride to central London; no in-house restaurant; room decor
is simple yet uninspiring. $ *Rooms from: £81* ⊠ *6 Woodside Park Rd.,
Hampstead* ☎ *020/8445–0440* ⊕ *www.glenlynhotel.com* ↪ *24 rooms*
⦿ *Free Breakfast* Ⓜ *Woodside Park* ✛ *C1.*

$ ⊡ **The Hide.** This cozy, chic little hideaway is exceptional value for
HOTEL money and exceeds virtually anything you could hope to find in central
London for the price; the downside is that the half-hour Tube ride to
and from town can be exhausting after a long day of sightseeing. **Pros:**
excellent value; great service; free Wi-Fi. **Cons:** far from the center;
somewhat dull neighborhood; no restaurant on-site. $ *Rooms from:
£105* ⊠ *230 Hendon Way, Hendon, Hampstead* ☎ *020/8203–1670*
⊕ *www.thehidelondon.com* ↪ *23 rooms* ⦿ *Free Breakfast* Ⓜ *Hendon
Central* ✛ *B1.*

NIGHTLIFE AND PERFORMING ARTS

London is a must-go destination for both nightlife enthusiasts and cul-
ture vultures. Whether you prefer a refined evening at the opera or
ballet, funky rhythm and blues in a Soho club, hardcore techno in East
London, a pint and gourmet pizza at a local gastro-pub, or cocktails
and sushi at a chic Mayfair bar, Great Britain's capital has entertain-
ment to suit all tastes. Admission prices are not always low, but when
you consider how much a London hotel room costs, the city's arts and
nightlife diversions seem like a bargain.

NIGHTLIFE

There isn't *one* London nightlife scene—there are many. As long as there
are audiences for obscure indie bands, cabaret comedy, or the latest
trend in dance music, someone will create a venue to satisfy the need.
The result? London is more than ever party central.

WESTMINSTER AND ST. JAMES'S

BARS

FAMILY

Fodor'sChoice

★

American Bar. Festooned with a chin-dropping array of old club ties, vintage signed celebrity photographs, sporting mementos, model airplanes and baseball caps, this sensational hotel cocktail bar has superb martinis and manhattans. The name dates from the 1930s, when hotel bars in London started to cater to growing numbers of Americans crossing the Atlantic in ocean liners, and in the 1970s, when a customer left a small carved wooden eagle, the collection of paraphernalia was started. ⊠ *The Stafford, 16–18 St. James's Pl., St. James's* 🕾 *020/7493–0111* ⊕ *www. thestaffordlondon.com* Ⓜ *Green Park.*

FAMILY

Fodor'sChoice

★

Gordon's Wine Bar. Nab a rickety candlelit table in the atmospheric, 1890s low-slung brick vaulted cellar interior of what claims to be the oldest wine bar in London, or fight for standing room in the long pedestrian-only alley garden that runs alongside it. Either way, the mood is always cheery as a diverse crowd sips on more than 60 different wines, ports, and sherries. Tempting cheese and meat plates are great for sharing. ⊠ *47 Villiers St., Westminster* 🕾 *020/7930–1408* ⊕ *gordonswinebar. com* Ⓜ *Charing Cross, Embankment.*

SOHO AND COVENT GARDEN

BARS

FAMILY

The Dog and Duck. A beautiful example of a late 19th-century London pub, the Dog and Duck has a well-preserved Heritage-listed interior furnished with glazed tiles, mirrors, and polished wood, though it's often so packed that it's hard to get a good look. There's a decent selection of real ales at the bar and a restaurant serving outstanding ale-battered fish-and-chips. The cozy upstairs dining room is named for writer George Orwell, who frequented this spot. ⊠ *18 Bateman St., Soho* 🕾 *020/7494–0697* ⊕ *www.nicholsonspubs.co.uk* Ⓜ *Tottenham Court Rd.*

Experimental Cocktail Club. It's easy to miss the unmarked shabby chic black door with a scuffed wash of red paint on Chinatown's hectic main drag Gerrard Street, but once you finally find it and make your way past the hard-to-please doorman, you'll be in a secret three-floor speakeasy-style cocktail bar that is also one of London's coolest bars. With a lively crowd, creative cocktails, subtle lighting, and a DJ spinning smooth sounds, the vibe is laid-back, sexy, Parisian cool. ⊠ *13A Gerrard St., Chinatown* ✦ *Look for unmarked scuffed black and red door* ⊕ *www.experimentalcocktailclublondon.com* ◳ *£5 cover charge after 11 pm* Ⓜ *Leicester Sq., Piccadilly Circus.*

Heaven. With the best light show on any London dance floor, Heaven is unpretentious, loud, and huge, with a labyrinth of rooms, bars, and live-music parlors. Thursday through Saturday nights it's all about the G-A-Y club and comedy nights. Check in advance about live performances—they can take place any night of the week. If you go to just one gay club in London, Heaven should be it. ⊠ *Under the Arches, Villiers St., Covent Garden* 🕾 *020/7930–2020 24-hr ticket line* ⊕ *www.heavennightclub-london.com* ◳ *£15–£26* Ⓜ *Charing Cross, Embankment.*

FAMILY **Terroirs.** Specializing in low-intervention "natural wines" (organic, unfiltered, and sustainably produced with minimal added ingredients), Terroirs wine bar has an unusually careful selection of 260 wines from small French and Italian artisan winemakers. These are served, along with delicious, relatively simple wine-friendly dishes—charcuterie, tapas, cheese, and more substantial French-inspired dishes—at a bar and bare oak tables surrounded by whitewashed walls and wooden floors. ⊠ *5 William IV St., Covent Garden* ☏ *020/7036–0660* ⊕ *www. terroirswinebar.com* Ⓜ *Charing Cross.*

COMEDY AND CABARET

Fodor'sChoice **The Comedy Store.** Before heading off to prime time, some of the United
★ Kingdom's funniest stand-ups cut their teeth here, at what's considered the birthplace of alternative comedy. Comedy Store Players, a team with six comedians doing improvisation with audience suggestions, entertain on Wednesday and Sunday; the Cutting Edge steps in with a topical take every Tuesday; and Thursday, Friday, and Saturday have the best stand-up acts. There's also a bar with food. You must be over 18 to enter. ⊠ *1A Oxendon St., Soho* ☏ *020/7024–2060 for tickets and booking* ⊕ *www.thecomedystore.co.uk* ⊠ *£16–£25* Ⓜ *Piccadilly Circus, Leicester Sq.*

LIVE MUSIC

Pizza Express Jazz Club. One of the United Kingdom's most ubiquitous pizza chains also runs a leading Soho jazz venue. The dimly lighted restaurant hosts both established and emerging top-quality international jazz acts every night, with food available in the downstairs venue (as opposed to the upstairs restaurant) around 90 minutes before stage time. The Italian-style thin-crust pizzas are about what you'd expect from a major chain. ⊠ *10 Dean St., Soho* ☏ *020/7439–4962 for the jazz club, 020/7437–9595 for restaurant* ⊕ *www.pizzaexpresslive.com* ⊠ *£16–£38* Ⓜ *Tottenham Court Rd.*

BLOOMSBURY AND HOLBORN

BARS

FAMILY **The Lamb.** Charles Dickens and his contemporaries drank here, but today's enthusiastic clientele make sure this intimate and eternally popular pub avoids the pitfalls of feeling too old-timey. One interesting feature: for private chats at the bar, you can close a delicate etched-glass "snob screen" to the bar staff, opening it only when you fancy another pint. ⊠ *94 Lamb's Conduit St., Bloomsbury* ☏ *020/7405–0713* ⊕ *www. thelamblondon.com* Ⓜ *Russell Sq.*

FAMILY **Princess Louise.** This fine popular pub is an exquisite museum piece of a Victorian interior, with glazed tiles and intricately engraved glass screens that divide the bar area into cozy little annexes. It's not all show, either. There's a good selection of excellent-value Yorkshire real ales from Samuel Smith's brewery. ⊠ *208 High Holborn, Holborn* ☏ *020/7405–8816* ⊕ *www.princesslouisepub.co.uk* Ⓜ *Holborn.*

THE CITY
BARS

FAMILY

Fodor'sChoice

★

The Blackfriar. A step from Blackfriars Tube station, this spectacular pub has an Arts and Crafts interior that is entertainingly, satirically ecclesiastical, with inlaid mother-of-pearl, wood carvings, stained glass, and marble pillars all over the place. Under finely lettered temperance tracts on view just below the reliefs of monks, fairies, and friars, there is a nice group of ales on tap from independent brewers. The 20th-century poet Sir John Betjeman once led a successful campaign to save the pub from demolition. ⊠ *174 Queen Victoria St., City of London* ☎ *020/7236–5474* ⊕ *www.nicholsonspubs.co.uk* Ⓜ *Blackfriars.*

FAMILY

Fodor'sChoice

★

Jerusalem Tavern. Loved by Londoners and owned by the well-respected St. Peter's Brewery in Suffolk, the Jerusalem Tavern is one-of-a-kind: small, historic, atmospheric, and endearingly eccentric. Antique Delft-style tiles meld with wood and concrete in a converted watchmaker and jeweler's shop dating back to the 18th century. The beer, both bottled and on tap, is some of the best available anywhere in London. It's often busy, especially after work. ⊠ *55 Britton St., Clerkenwell* ☎ *020/7490–4281* ⊕ *www.stpetersbrewery.co.uk/london-pub* Ⓜ *Farringdon.*

FAMILY

Ye Olde Cheshire Cheese. Yes, this pub on Fleet Street is full of tourists, but it deserves a visit for more than its popularity. It's extremely historic, dating to 1667, the year after the Great Fire of London. The most frequented pub of Dr. Johnson's and Charles Dickens's many locals, it has sawdust-covered floors, low wood-beam ceilings, and the 14th-century crypt of Whitefriars' Carmelite monastery under the cellar bar. Food is served in the Chop Room—one of London's earliest steak houses. ⊠ *145 Fleet St., City of London* ☎ *020/7353–6170* ◎ *Closed Sun. from 4* Ⓜ *Blackfriars.*

EAST LONDON
BARS

Callooh Callay. Cocktails are tasty, well-executed classics, and there's also a selection of unique instant-classics at this eccentric Hoxton bar where the bells and whistles are left to the decor. There's a secret hidden bar accessed Narnia-like through a wardrobe and an upstairs rock-themed 'Palace of Humbug' bar where VLPs (Very Lovely People) can hide away. ⊠ *65 Rivington St., Hoxton* ☎ *020/7739–4781* ⊕ *www.calloohcallaybar.com* Ⓜ *Old St.*

FAMILY

The Ten Bells. Although the number of bells in its name has varied between 8 and 12, depending on how many bells were used by neighboring Christ Church, Spitalfields, this pub retains it original mid-Victorian interior and original tiles, including a frieze depicting the area's French Huguenot silk weaving tradition on the north wall and particularly fine floral tiling on two others. Urban legend says that Jack the Ripper's third victim, Annie Chapman, had a drink here before meeting her gory end. The pub is also depicted in Alan Moore's acclaimed graphic novel *From Hell.* ⊠ *84 Commercial St., Spitalfields* ☎ *020/7247–7532* ⊕ *www.tenbells.com* Ⓜ *Liverpool St.*

DANCE CLUBS

Fodor's Choice
★
Cafe Oto. A relaxed café by day, and London's leading venue for experimental music by night, Cafe Oto is a Dalston institution. Its programming of free jazz, avant-garde electronica, and much more is enough of a draw that it regularly sells out, with music fans steaming up the windows and spilling out onto the pavement and road outside to smoke during breaks. Healthy Japanese food is served in the daytime, before customers are kicked out at 5:30 pm to make way for sound checks. It's open as a bar (no cover) on nights when no concerts are taking place. ⊠ *18–22 Ashwin St., Dalston* ⊕ *www.cafeoto.co.uk* ⊠ *Café free, concerts free–£30* Ⓜ *Overground: Dalston Junction.*

SOUTH OF THE THAMES

BARS

Fodor's Choice
★
Aqua Shard. This classy bar on level 31 of the Shard, London's most iconic skyscraper and the tallest building in the United Kingdom (fourth in Europe), is worth a visit for the phenomenal views alone. The cocktail list is pretty special, too—big on fruit purées and unusual bitters. No reservations are taken in the bar, so be prepared to wait during busy periods. ⊠ *The Shard, 31 St. Thomas St., Level 31, London Bridge* ☎ *020/3011–1256* ⊕ *www.aquashard.co.uk* Ⓜ *London Bridge.*

FAMILY **Three Eight Four.** Epitomizing a new breed of Brixton bar, Three Eight Four mixes up inventive cocktails. The menu changes seasonally but always involves boutique spirits and unusual mixing techniques—try the Nightshade, which comes with a pipette that you use to add the final ingredient (crème de cassis) yourself. Bare lightbulbs and brick walls seem to be the style of choice for lots of cool London bars these days, but this place manages it with particular panache. A delectable selection of small dishes is also available. ⊠ *384 Coldharbour La., Brixton* ☎ *020/3417–7309* ⊕ *www.threeeightfour.com* Ⓜ *Brixton.*

KENSINGTON, KNIGHTSBRIDGE, NOTTING HILL, AND MAYFAIR

BARS

The Blue Bar at the Berkeley Hotel. With low-slung dusty-blue walls and Edwardian plasterwork, this black onyx hotel bar at the Berkeley is ever so slightly sexy. Immaculate service, an excellent seasonal cocktail list and a trendy David Collins design make this an ideal spot for a romantic tête-à-tête, complete with jazzy music in the background. ⊠ *The Berkeley, Wilton Pl., Knightsbridge* ☎ *020/7235–6000* ⊕ *www. the-berkeley.co.uk* Ⓜ *Knightsbridge, Hyde Park Corner.*

Claridge's Bar. This elegant Mayfair meeting place remains unpretentious even when it brims with beautiful people. The bar has an art deco heritage made hip by the sophisticated touch of designer David Collins. A library of rare champagnes and brandies as well as a delicious choice of traditional and exotic cocktails—try the Flapper or the Black Pearl—will occupy your taste buds. Request a glass of vintage Cristal in the darkly moody leather-walled 36-seat Fumoir. ⊠ *Claridge's, 55 Brook St., Mayfair* ☎ *020/7629–8860* ⊕ *www.claridges.co.uk* Ⓜ *Bond St.*

FAMILY **The Nag's Head.** The landlord of this idiosyncratic little mews pub in Belgravia runs a tight ship, and no cell phones are allowed. The lovingly collected artifacts (including antique penny arcade games) that decorate every inch of the place, high-quality beer, and old-fashioned pub grub should provide more than enough distraction. ✉ *53 Kinnerton St., Belgravia* ☎ *020/7235–1135* Ⓜ *Knightsbridge, Hyde Park Corner.*

LIVE MUSIC

FAMILY

Fodor's Choice

★

606 Club. This Chelsea jazz club has been doing things speakeasy-style since long before it became a nightlife trend in London. Buzz the door and you'll find a basement venue showcasing mainstream and contemporary jazz by well-known U.K.-based musicians. You must eat a meal in order to consume alcohol, so allow for an extra £30. Reservations are advisable. Lunchtime jazz takes place on select Sundays; call ahead. ✉ *90 Lots Rd., Chelsea* ☎ *020/7352–5953* ⊕ *www.606club. co.uk* 🖃 *£10–£12 music charge added to bill* Ⓜ *Fulham Broadway. Overground: Imperial Wharf.*

PERFORMING ARTS

Whether you prefer your art classical or contemporary, you'll find that London's vibrant cultural scene has as much to offer as any in the world. The Royal Opera House hosts world-class productions of opera and ballet, the reconstructed Shakespeare's Globe re-creates seeing the Bard's work as its original audience would have, and the National Theatre, the Royal Court, and several other subsidized theaters produce challenging new plays and reimagined classics.

To find out what's showing now, the free weekly magazine *Time Out* (issued every Tuesday in print and online at ⊕ *www.timeout.com*) is invaluable. The free *Evening Standard* carries listings, many of which are also available online at ⊕ *www.standard.co.uk*. *Metro*, London's other widely available free newspaper, is also worth checking out.

PERFORMING ARTS CENTERS

FAMILY

Barbican Centre. Opened in 1982, the Barbican is an enormous Brutalist concrete maze that Londoners either love or hate—but its importance to the cultural life of the capital is beyond dispute. At the largest performing arts center in Europe, you could listen to Elgar, see 1960s photography, and catch German animation with live accompaniment, all in one day. The main concert hall, known for its acoustics, is most famous as the home of the London Symphony Orchestra. The Barbican is also a frequent host to the BBC Symphony Orchestra. Architecture tours take place several times a week. ✉ *Silk St., City of London* ☎ *020/7638–8891* ⊕ *www.barbican.org.uk* 🖃 *Art exhibits free–£14.50, cinema £6–£14, theater and music £10–£85, tours £12.50* Ⓜ *Barbican.*

FAMILY

Fodor's Choice

★

Southbank Centre. The public has never really warmed to the Southbank Centre's hulking concrete buildings (beloved by architecture aficionados), products of the Brutalist style popular when the center was built in the 1950s and '60s—but all the same, the masses flock to the concerts, recitals, festivals, and exhibitions held here, Europe's largest arts center. The **Royal Festival Hall** is truly a People's Palace, with seats for 2,900 and a schedule that ranges from major symphony orchestras to pop stars. The smaller **Queen Elizabeth Hall** is more classically oriented. It contains the **Purcell Room**, which hosts lectures and

2

The Royal Opera House is simply dazzling inside and out, including at night.

chamber performances. For art, head to the **Hayward Gallery**, which hosts shows on top contemporary artists such as Anthony Gormley and Cy Twombly. The Queen Elizabeth Hall and Hayward Gallery reopened in early 2018 following a major renovation and are looking and sounding better than ever. The center's riverside street level has a terrific assortment of restaurants and bars, though you'll need to head to The Cut, just south of here, for independent eateries. ⊠ *Belvedere Rd., South Bank* 🕾 *020/3879–9555* ⊕ *www.southbankcentre.co.uk* 🎟 *Free–£120* Ⓜ *Waterloo, Embankment.*

CLASSICAL MUSIC

Fodor's Choice
★

Royal Albert Hall. Opened in 1871, this splendid iron-and-glass-domed auditorium hosts everything from pop and classical headliners to Cirque du Soleil, awards ceremonies, and sumo wrestling championships, but it is best known for the annual July–September BBC Promenade Concerts. Bargain-price standing-room (or promenading or sitting-on-the-floor) tickets for "the Proms" are sold on the night of the concert. The circular 5,272-seat auditorium has a terra-cotta exterior surmounted by a mosaic frieze depicting figures engaged in cultural pursuits. The hall is open most days for daytime guided tours and Tuesday through Sunday for afternoon tea. ⊠ *Kensington Gore, Kensington* 🕾 *0207/589–8212* ⊕ *www.royalalberthall.com* 🎟 *£6– £90; tours £13.25* Ⓜ *South Kensington.*

FAMILY
Fodor's Choice
★

Wigmore Hall. London's most beautiful venue for chamber music also happens to boast near-perfect acoustics. The hall has a rich history, including hosting the premieres of a number of works by the British composer Benjamin Britten, and today attracts leading ensembles from all over the world. The varied program contains lunchtime and Sunday morning concerts, plus workshops and concerts for babies and toddlers. ⊠ *36 Wigmore St., Marylebone* ☎ *020/7935-2141* ⊕ *www.wigmorehall.org.uk* 🎫 *£18–£50* Ⓜ *Bond St.*

DANCE

The Place. The Robin Howard Dance Theatre at The Place is London's only theater dedicated to contemporary dance, and with tickets often under £20 (performances by student dancers, for example, cost just £15), it's good value, too. The "Resolution" festival in January and February is the United Kingdom's biggest platform event for new choreographers. ⊠ *17 Duke's Rd., Bloomsbury* ☎ *020/7121-1100* ⊕ *www. theplace.org.uk* 🎫 *£10–£25* Ⓜ *Euston.*

FAMILY **Sadler's Wells.** Head to this gleaming building, which opened in 1998
Fodor'sChoice and is the seventh on the site in its 300-year history, to see perfor-
★ mances by leading classical and contemporary dance companies. Matthew Bourne's New Adventures is in residence, and the little Lilian Baylis Studio hosts avant-garde work. ⊠ *Rosebery Ave., Islington* ☎ *020/7863-8000* ⊕ *www.sadlerswells.com* 🎫 *£12–£45* Ⓜ *Angel.*

FILM

FAMILY **BFI Southbank.** With the best repertory programming in London, the three movie theaters and studio here are effectively a national film center run by the British Film Institute. More than 1,000 titles are screened each year, with art-house, foreign, silent, overlooked, classic, noir, and short films favored over recent Hollywood blockbusters. The center also has a gallery, bookshop, and "mediatheque" where visitors can watch film and television from the National Archive for free (closed Monday). This is one of the venues for the BFI London Film Festival; throughout the year there are minifestivals, seminars, and guest speakers. ■TIP➜ The BFI Bar & Kitchen, toward the back of the building, is a great secret spot for a drink. ⊠ *Belvedere Rd., South Bank* ☎ *020/7928-3232* ⊕ *www.bfi.org.uk* 🎫 *£10–£17* Ⓜ *Waterloo.*

OPERA

Fodor'sChoice **Royal Opera House.** Along with Milan's La Scala, New York's Metropoli-
★ tan, and the Palais Garnier in Paris, this is one of the world's great opera houses. The resident troupe has mounted spectacular productions in the past, while recent productions have tended toward more contemporary operas. Whatever the style of the performance, the extravagant theater delivers a full dose of opulence. The famed Royal Ballet performs classical and contemporary repertoire here, too, and smaller scale works of both opera and dance are presented in the Linbury Studio Theatre and Clore Studio Upstairs. A small allocation of tickets for each performance of main stage productions for the week ahead—even those that are sold out—goes on sale online at 1 pm every Friday. ■TIP➜ If you wish to see the hall but are not able to procure a ticket, you can join a backstage tour or one of the less frequent tours of the auditorium; they book up several weeks in advance. BP Big Screens is the ROH's summer series of live relays of its opera and ballet productions; screenings are free and take place outdoors in public spaces all over the country, including Trafalgar

Square. ✉ *Bow St., Covent Garden* 🕾 *020/7304–4000* ⊕ *www.roh.org. uk* 🎟 *Performances £4–£280; tours £10–£15* Ⓜ *Covent Garden.*

THEATER

Almeida Theatre. This Off West End venue, helmed by director Rupert Goold, premiers excellent new plays and exciting twists on the classics, often featuring high-profile actors. There's a good café and a licensed bar that serves "sharing dishes," as well as tasty main courses. ✉ *Almeida St., Islington* 🕾 *020/7359–4404* ⊕ *www.almeida.co.uk* 🎟 *£10– £40* Ⓜ *Angel, Highbury & Islington.*

Fodor's Choice ★ **Battersea Arts Centre** (*BAC*). Battersea Arts Centre has a reputation for producing innovative new work as well as hosting top alternative stand-up comics. Performances take place in quirky spaces all over this atmospheric former town hall. Check out Scratch events, low-tech theater where the audience provides feedback on works-in-progress. Entry for Scratch events is pay-what-you-can (minimum £3). The bar, which serves snacks and sharing plates, is open all day. ✉ *176 Lavender Hill, Battersea* 🕾 *020/7223–2223* ⊕ *www.bac.org.uk* 🎟 *Pay what you can (£3 suggested)–£30* Ⓜ *National Rail: Clapham Junction.*

FAMILY Kiln Theatre. Committed to representing the cultural diversity of its community, the Kiln (known as the Tricycle until its reopening after a major refurbishment in 2018) shows the best in black, Irish, Jewish, Asian, and South African drama, and also promotes new work. There is a movie theater, too: expect top-quality new European and international cinema, including films from the United States, occasionally screened at film festivals the theater organizes. Discounted movie tickets are available on Monday. ✉ *269 Kilburn High Rd., Kilburn* 🕾 *020/7328–1000* ⊕ *www. kilntheatre.com* 🎟 *Theater £10–£33, movies £5–£12* Ⓜ *Kilburn.*

FAMILY Little Angel Theatre. Innovative puppetry performances for children and adults have been taking place in this adorable former temperance hall since 1961. ✉ *14 Dagmar Passage, Islington* 🕾 *020/7226–1787* ⊕ *www. littleangeltheatre.com* 🎟 *£5–£15* Ⓜ *Angel, Highbury & Islington.*

FAMILY Fodor's Choice ★ **National Theatre.** When this theater designed by Sir Denys Lasdun opened in 1976, Londoners weren't all so keen on the low-slung Brutalist block. Prince Charles described it as "a clever way of building a nuclear power station in the middle of London without anyone objecting." But whatever its merits or demerits, the National Theatre's interior spaces are worth a visit. Interspersed with the three theaters—the 1,150-seat Olivier, the 890-seat Lyttelton, and the 450-seat Dorfman—is a multilayered foyer with exhibitions, bars, restaurants, and free entertainment. Musicals, classics, and plays are performed by top-flight professionals, and they sometimes give talks as well. Backstage, costume, and architecture tours are available. The Clore Learning Centre offers courses and events on all aspects of theater making, and you can watch staff at work in the backstage workshops from the Sherling High-Level Walkway. Each weekend in August, the River Stage Festival presents live music, dance, workshops, and DJ sets in the area in front of the theater. ✉ *Belvedere Rd., South Bank* 🕾 *020/7452–3000* ⊕ *www.nationaltheatre.org.uk* 🎟 *£15–£72, tours £11–£12.50* Ⓜ *Waterloo.*

FAMILY
Fodor's Choice
★

Open Air Theatre. Works by Shakespeare have been performed here every summer (from mid-May to mid-September) since 1932, with casts including luminaries such as Vivien Leigh, Dame Judi Dench, and Damien Lewis. Today the theater also mounts productions of classic plays, musicals, and shows for family audiences among its four annual productions. *A Midsummer Night's Dream* is the one to catch, if it's on—never has that enchanted Greek wood been better evoked, especially when enhanced by genuine birdsong and a rising moon. There's a covered restaurant for pretheater dining, an informal café, and, of course, a bar. You also can order picnic hampers in advance. The park can get chilly, so bring a blanket. Performances proceed rain or shine (umbrellas aren't allowed) with refunds only in case of a very heavy downpour. ✉ *Inner Circle, Regent's Park* ☎ *0844/826–4242* ⊕ *www. openairtheatre.com* 🎟 *£25–£59* Ⓜ *Baker St., Regent's Park.*

Royal Court Theatre. Britain's undisputed epicenter of new theatrical works, the Court continues to produce gritty British and international drama. Don't miss the best deal in town: four 10-pence standing tickets go on sale one hour before each performance (of sold-out shows), and £12 tickets are available on Monday. Backstage and building tours take place at 11:30 am on the first or second Saturday of the month. ✉ *Sloane Sq., Chelsea* ☎ *020/7565–5000* ⊕ *www.royalcourttheatre. com* 🎟 *£12–£49; tours £9* Ⓜ *Sloane Sq.*

Young Vic. At this Waterloo theater, big names perform alongside young talent, often in daring innovative productions of classic plays that appeal to a more diverse audience than is traditionally found on the London scene. Good food is served all day at the bustling bar. ✉ *66 The Cut, Waterloo, South Bank* ☎ *020/7922–2922* ⊕ *www.youngvic. org* 🎟 *£10–£40* Ⓜ *Southwark, Waterloo.*

SHOPPING

The keyword of London shopping has always been "individuality," whether expressed in the superb custom tailoring of Savile Row, the nonconformist punk roots of quintessential British designer Vivienne Westwood, or the unique small stores that purvey the owner's private passion, whether paper theaters, toy soldiers, or buttons. This tradition is under threat from the influx of chains—global luxury, domestic mid-market, and international youth—but the distinctively British mix of quality and originality, tradition and character, remains.

If there's anything that unites London's designers, it's a commitment to creativity and originality, underpinned by a strong sense of heritage. This combination of posh and rock-n-roll sensibilities is exemplified by designers like Sarah Burton—the late Alexander McQueen's successor at his eponymous label and designer of the Duchess of Cambridge's wedding dress—Stella McCartney, the creative milliner Philip Treacy, and the imaginative shoemakers United Nude. If anything, London is even better known for its vibrant street fashion found at the stalls at Portobello, Camden, and Spitalfields markets.

LONDON'S SPECTATOR SPORTS

Sport in the capital comes into its own when it's watched, rather than participated in. You'll most easily witness London's fervent sporting passions in front of a screen in a pub with a pint in hand. And those passions run deep.

FOOTBALL

London's top teams—Chelsea, Arsenal, Tottenham Hotspur—are world-class (especially the first two) and often progress in the European Champions League. It's unlikely you'll be able to get tickets for anything except the least popular Premier League games during the August–May season, despite absurdly high ticket prices—as much as £41 for a standard, walk-up, match-day seat at Chelsea, and a whopping £126 for the match-day tickets at Arsenal.

TENNIS

Wimbledon Lawn Tennis Championships. The All England Club's Wimbledon Lawn Tennis Championships are famous for Centre Court, strawberries and cream, a gentle spot of rain, and a nostalgic old-school insistence on players wearing white. Thankfully, the rain has been banished on Centre Court by the nifty retractable roof, but whether you can get tickets for Centre Court all comes down to the luck of the draw—there's a ballot system for advance purchase (see website for more details). ⊠ *The All England Lawn Tennis Club, Church Rd.* ☎ *020/8971–2473 for general inquiries* ⊕ *www.wimbledon.com.*

London's shopping districts are spread all over the city, so pace yourself and take in only one or two areas in a day. Or visit one of the grand department stores such as Selfridges, Liberty, or Harvey Nichols, where you can find a wide assortment of designers, from mass to class, all under one roof.

WESTMINSTER AND ST. JAMES'S

ANTIQUES

The Armoury of St. James's. Besides fine toy soldiers in lead or tin representing conflicts ranging from the Crusades through World War II with prices starting at £15 and going into four figures, the shop has regimental brooches and drums, historic orders and medals, royal memorabilia, and military antiques. ⊠ *17 Piccadilly Arcade, St. James's* ☎ *020/7493–5082* ⊕ *www.armoury.co.uk* ⊘ *Closed Sun.* Ⓜ *Piccadilly Circus.*

BEAUTY

Floris. What did Queen Victoria, Mary Shelley, and Marilyn Monroe have in common? They all used products from Floris, one of the most beautiful shops in London, with gleaming glass-and-Spanish-mahogany showcases salvaged from the Great Exhibition of 1851. In addition to scents for both men and women (including the current queen), Floris has been making its own shaving products—plus combs, brushes, and fragrances—since 1730 (and is still owned by the same family), reflecting its origins as a barbershop. Other gift possibilities include goose-down powder puffs, a famous rose-scented mouthwash, and beautifully packaged soaps and bath essences. There's another branch in Belgravia. ✉ *89 Jermyn St., St. James's* ☎ *0330/134–0180* ⊕ *www.florislondon. com* Ⓜ *Piccadilly Circus, Green Park.*

BOOKS

Fodor's Choice
★ **Hatchards.** This is the United Kingdom's oldest bookshop, open since 1797 and beloved by writers themselves—customers have included Oscar Wilde, Rudyard Kipling, and Lord Byron. Despite its wood-paneled, "gentleman's library" atmosphere and eclectic selection of books, Hatchards is owned by the large Waterstone's chain. Nevertheless, the shop still retains its period charm, aided by the staff's old-fashioned helpfulness and expertise. Look for the substantial number of books signed by notable contemporary authors on the well-stocked shelves. There's another branch in the St. Pancras International train station. ✉ *187 Piccadilly, St. James's* ☎ *020/7439–9921* ⊕ *www.hatchards. co.uk* Ⓜ *Piccadilly Circus.*

CLOTHING

Turnbull & Asser. The Jermyn Street store sells luxurious jackets, cashmere sweaters, suits, ties, pajamas, ready-to-wear shirts, and accessories perfect for the billionaire who has everything. The brand is best known for its superb custom-made shirts—worn by Prince Charles and every James Bond to appear in film, to name a few. These can be ordered at the nearby Bury Street or Davies Street branches, which are devoted to bespoke wear (Note: Bury and Davies are two separate stores). At least 15 separate measurements are taken, and the cloth, woven to the company's specifications, comes in 1,000 different patterns—the cottons feel as good as silk. The first order must be for a minimum of six shirts, which start at £195 each. ✉ *71–72 Jermyn St., St. James's* ☎ *020/7808– 3000* ⊕ *www.turnbullandasser.co.uk* ☾ *Closed Sun.* Ⓜ *Green Park.*

FOOD

Fodor's Choice
★ **Berry Bros. & Rudd.** Nothing matches Berry Bros. & Rudd for rare offerings and a unique shopping experience. A family-run wine business since 1698 (Lord Byron was a customer), BBR stores more than 4,000 vintage bottles and casks in vaulted cellars that are more than 300 years old. The in-house wine school offers educational tasting sessions, while the dedicated spirits room also has an excellent selection of whiskeys, cognacs, rums, and more. The shop has a quirky charm, and the staff are extremely knowledgeable—and not snooty if you're on a budget. ✉ *63 Pall Mall, St. James's* ☎ *800/280–2440* ⊕ *www.bbr.com* ☾ *Closed Sun.* Ⓜ *Green Park.*

Fortnum & Mason. Although F&M is jokingly known as "the Queen's grocer" and the impeccably mannered staff still wear traditional tailcoats, its celebrated food hall stocks gifts for all budgets, including irresistibly packaged luxury foods stamped with the gold "By Appointment" crest for under £5. Try the teas, preserves (including the unusual rose-petal jelly), condiments, or Gentleman's Relish (anchovy paste). The store's famous hampers are always a welcome gift. The gleaming food hall spans two floors and incorporates a sleek wine bar, with the rest of the store devoted to upscale housewares, men's and women's accessories and toiletries, a dedicated candle room, and a jewelry department

Choices, choices: there are plenty of prints—and much else—at the Portobello Road Market.

featuring exclusive designs by breakthrough talent. If you start to flag, take a break in the tea salon, the Gallery café offering tastes of the Food Hall, the contemporary 45 Jermyn Street restaurant (the three-course set menu is good value), or an indulgent ice-cream parlor, where you can find decadent treats like a banana split or a less-traditional gin-and-cucumber float. There's another branch at St. Pancras International train station. ⊠ *181 Piccadilly, St. James's* ☎ *020/7734–8040* ⊕ *www. fortnumandmason.com* Ⓜ *Green Park, Piccadilly Circus.*

SOHO AND COVENT GARDEN

ACCESSORIES

Fodor's Choice
★
Peckham Rye. On the small cobblestone streets leading off Carnaby Street, among other little specialty shops, the family-run Peckham Rye sells heritage-style men's accessories: handmade silk and twill ties, bow ties, and scarves, all using traditional patterns drawn from the archives going back to 1799. Embodying the Ralph Lauren aesthetic even more than Ralph Lauren, the socks, striped shirts, and handkerchiefs attract modern-day dandies like Mark Ronson and David Beckham. Bespoke tailoring for men is also offered. ⊠ *11 Newburgh St., Soho* ☎ *0207/734–5181* ⊕ *www.peckhamrye.com* Ⓜ *Oxford St.*

BOOKS

Fodor's Choice
★
Foyles. Founded in 1903 by the Foyle brothers after they failed the Civil Service exam, this family-owned bookstore is in a 1930s art deco building, once the home of the renowned art college Central Saint Martins. One of London's best sources for textbooks and the United Kingdom's largest retailer of foreign language books, with more than 200,000

titles on its four miles of bookshelves, Foyles also stocks everything from popular fiction to military history, sheet music, medical tomes, graphic novels, and handsome, illustrated fine arts books. It also offers the store-within-a-store Ray's Jazz (one of London's better outlets for music) and a cool café. Foyles has branches in the Southbank Centre, the Westfield shopping center in Stratford, l and Waterloo Station. ⊠ *107 Charing Cross Rd., Soho* ☏ *0207/437–5660* ⊕ *www.foyles.co.uk* Ⓜ *Tottenham Court Rd.*

CLOTHING

Covent Garden Market. This popular destination includes three separate market areas: the Apple Market, the East Colonnade Market, and the Jubilee Market. In the covered area originally designed by Inigo Jones and known as the Apple Market, 40 stalls sell handcrafted jewelry, prints, clothes (such as hand-painted dancewear), ceramics, and crafts Tuesday through Sunday, while Mondays are given over to antiques, curios, and collectables. The East Colonnade Market has stalls with mostly handmade specialty items that include handmade soaps and jewelry, as well as housewares, accessories, and magic tricks. The Jubilee Market, in Jubilee Hall toward Southampton Street, tends toward the more pedestrian (kitschy T-shirts, unremarkable household goods, and the like) Tuesday through Friday, but has vintage collectibles and antiques on Monday and worthwhile handmade goods on weekends. Largely aimed at the tourist trade in the past, Covent Garden Market continues its ascent, introducing a more sophisticated image (and correspondingly high prices) with the opening of upscale restaurants and chains in the surrounding arcades, including the world's largest Apple Store and a Disney store; beauty outlets for Chanel, Bobbi Brown, and Dior; and boutiques for brands like Tumi, Mulberry and N. Peal. ■ TIP→ Don't miss the magicians, musicians, and escape artists who perform in the open-air piazza; the performances are free (though contributions are welcome). ⊠ *The Piazza, off Wellington St., Covent Garden* ⊕ *www.coventgarden.london* Ⓜ *Covent Garden.*

Paul Smith. British classics with an irreverent twist define Paul Smith's collections for women, men, and children. Beautifully tailored suits for men and women take hallmarks of traditional British style and turn them on their heads with humor and color, combining exceptional fabrics with flamboyant linings or unusual detailing. Gift ideas abound— wallets, scarves, phone cases, and distinctive belts and socks—all in Smith's signature rainbow stripes. There are several branches throughout London, in Notting Hill, Soho, Marylebone, Southwark and Canary Wharf, plus a Mayfair shop that includes vintage furniture. ⊠ *40–44 Floral St., Covent Garden* ☏ *020/7379–7133* ⊕ *www.paulsmith.co.uk* Ⓜ *Covent Garden.*

DEPARTMENT STORES

Fodor'sChoice
★

Liberty. The wonderful black-and-white mock-Tudor facade, created from the timbers of two Royal Navy ships, reflects this store's origins in the late-19th-century Arts and Crafts movement. Leading designers were recruited to create the classic art nouveau Liberty prints that are still a centerpiece of the brand, gracing everything from cushions and silk kimonos to embossed leather bags and photo albums. Inside, Liberty is a labyrinth of nooks and crannies stuffed with thoughtfully chosen merchandise, including niche beauty, perfume, footwear, and housewares lines such as Soho Home, which features furniture and textiles from the membership clubs. Clothes for both men and women focus on high quality and high fashion, with labels like Roland Mouret and Tomas Maier. The store regularly commissions new prints from contemporary designers, and sells both these and its classic patterns by the yard. If you're not so handy with a needle, an interior design service will create soft furnishings for you. There's also a florist, a hair salon, a traditional men's barber, branded beauty treatment rooms, a brow bar, a piercing studio, and a foot spa. ⊠ *Regent St., Soho* ☎ *020/7734–1234* ⊕ *www.liberty.co.uk* Ⓜ *Oxford Circus.*

TOYS

FAMILY

Fodor's Choice

★

Benjamin Pollock's Toyshop. This landmark shop still carries on the tradition of its founder, who sold miniature theater stages made from richly detailed paper from the late 19th century until his death in 1937. Among his admirers was Robert Louis Stevenson, who wrote, "If you love art, folly, or the bright eyes of children, speed to Pollock's." Today the antique model theaters are expensive, but there are plenty of magical reproductions for less than £10. There's also an extensive selection of new but nostalgic puppets, marionettes, teddy bears, spinning tops, jack-in-the-boxes, and similar traditional children's toys from the days before batteries were required (or toys were even run on them). ⊠ *44 The Market Bldg., Covent Garden* ☎ *020/7379–7866* ⊕ *www.pollocks-coventgarden.co.uk* Ⓜ *Covent Garden.*

BLOOMSBURY AND HOLBORN

ACCESSORIES

Fodor's Choice

★

James Smith & Sons Ltd. This has to be the world's ultimate umbrella shop (it is definitely Europe's oldest), and a must for anyone interested in real Victorian London. The family-owned shop has been in this location on a corner of New Oxford Street since 1857 and sells every kind of umbrella, parasol, cane, and walking stick imaginable (including some containing a small flask or a corkscrew, or that fold out into a seat). The interior is unchanged since the 19th century; you will feel as if you have stepped back in time. Umbrellas range from about £40 for a folding umbrella to more than £265 for a classic man's umbrella with a carved animal-head handle and thousands for bespoke items. If the umbrella prices are too steep, there are smaller accessories like a horn shoehorn or letter opener that make perfect gifts. ⊠ *Hazelwood House, 53 New Oxford St., Bloomsbury* ☎ *020/7836–4731* ⊕ *www.james-smith.co.uk* ۞ *Closed Sun.* Ⓜ *Tottenham Court Rd., Holborn.*

ANTIQUES

London Silver Vaults. Originally built in 1876 as Britain's first safe deposit building, with basement strong rooms for storing household valuables like jewelry, silver, and documents, this extraordinary underground space has been converted to more than 30 small units housing silver (plus a few jewelry) dealers, the majority of which are family businesses.

Products range from 16th-century items to contemporary pieces (with everything in between), and from the spectacularly over-the-top costing thousands to smaller items—like teaspoons, candlesticks, or a set of Victorian cake forks—at £25. ⊠ *53-64 Chancery La., Holborn* ☎ *020/7242–3844* ⊕ *www.silvervaultslondon.com* ⊗ *Closed Sun.* Ⓜ *Chancery La.*

EAST LONDON

CLOTHING

FodorsChoice
★
Hostem. Drawing style-conscious customers from nearby tech start-ups, Hostem is for the man who wants to be well dressed without looking like he's trying too hard, with a mixture of casual luxury, streetwear, and fashion-forward edge from tastemaker favorites including John Alexander Skelton, Casey Casey, and Geoffrey B. Small. The womenswear area offers pieces by designers like Prada and Amy Revier. There's also a bespoke service for clothing and exquisite men's shoes by cobbler Sebastain Tarek. It's achingly hip (clothes hang from a wooden "monolithic site specific sculpture"), but in superb taste. The store also operates a three-bedroom guesthouse (a converted Georgian town house in Whitechapel), where you can buy the crockery, bed linens, glassware, and more at the end of your stay. ⊠ *28 Old Nichol St., Shoreditch* ☎ *020/7739–9733* ⊕ *www.hostem.co.uk* Ⓜ *Overground: Shoreditch High St.*

Rokit. Magazine and music stylists love these two premises along Brick Lane that carry everything from handbags and ball gowns to jeans, military garb, and Western wear. The ever-changing stock spans the 1930s to the 1990s. There are also branches in Camden and Covent Garden. ⊠ *101 and 107 Brick La., Spitalfields* ☎ *020/7375–3864* ⊕ *www.rokit.co.uk* Ⓜ *Overground: Shoreditch High St.*

HOUSEHOLD GOODS

FodorsChoice
★
Labour & Wait. Although mundane items like colanders and clothespins may not sound like ideal souvenirs, this shop (something of a hipster heaven selling both new and vintage items) will make you reconsider. The owners are on a mission to revive retro, functional British household goods, such as enamel kitchenware, genuine feather dusters, bread bins, bottle brushes, and traditional Welsh blankets. ⊠ *85 Redchurch St., Shoreditch* ☎ *020/7729–6253* ⊕ *www.labourandwait.co.uk* ⊗ *Closed Mon.* Ⓜ *Overground: Shoreditch High St.*

MUSIC

Rough Trade East. Although many London record stores are struggling, this veteran indie-music specialist in the Old Truman Brewery seems to have gotten the formula right. The spacious surroundings are as much a hangout as a shop, complete with a stage for live gigs and a café. There's another branch on Talbot Road in Notting Hill. ⊠ *Dray Walk, Old Truman Brewery, 91 Brick La., Spitalfields* ☎ *020/7392–7788* ⊕ *www.roughtrade.com* Ⓜ *Liverpool St. Overground: Shoreditch High St.*

STREET MARKETS

Fodor'sChoice ★ **Broadway Market.** This parade of shops in hipster-centric Hackney (north of Regent's Canal) is worth visiting for the specialty bookshops, independent boutiques, organic cafés, neighborhood restaurants, and even a traditional (but now rare) pie-and-mash shop. But wait for Saturday (9–5), when it really comes into its own with a farmers' market and more than 100 street-food and produce stalls rivaling those of south London's famed Borough Market. Artisanal breads, cheeses, pastries, organic meats, waffles, fruit and vegetables, seafood, and international food offerings: this is foodie heaven. There are also stalls selling vintage clothes, crafts, jewelry, and more. ⊠ *Broadway Market, Hackney* ☎ *0787/246–3409* ⊕ *www.broadwaymarket.co.uk* ⊗ *Market closed. Mon.–Sat.* Ⓜ *London Fields.*

Fodor'sChoice ★ **Columbia Road Flower Market.** London's premier flower market is about as pretty and photogenic as they come, with more than 50 stalls selling flowers, shrubs, bulbs, and trees—everything from bedding plants to 10-foot banana trees—as well as garden tools, pots, and accessories at competitive prices. The stallholders' patter is part of the fun. It's on Sunday only, and it's all over by 2 pm. Columbia Road itself is lined with 60 interesting independent shops purveying art, fashion, furnishings, and the local cafés are superb. ⊠ *Columbia Rd., Hoxton* ⊕ *www. columbiaroad.info* ⊗ *Market closed Mon.–Sat.* Ⓜ *Old St. Overground: Hoxton.*

Old Spitalfields Market. Once the East End's wholesale fruit and vegetable market and now restored to its original architectural splendor, this fine example of a Victorian market hall is at the center of the area's gentrified revival. The original building is largely occupied by shops (mostly upscale brands like Rag & Bone, Lululemon, and Superga, but some independents like trendy homeware-and-fashion purveyor The Mercantile), with traders' stalls in the courtyard. A modern shopping precinct under a Norman Foster–designed glass canopy adjoins the old building and holds approximately 70 traders' stalls. You may have to wade through a certain number of stalls selling cheap imports and tacky T-shirts to find the good stuff, which includes vintage and new clothing, handmade rugs and jewelry, hand-carved toy trains, vintage maps, unique baby clothes, rare vinyl, and cakes. Thursday is particularly good for antiques; Friday for a biweekly record fair; while weekends offer a little of everything. The new The Kitchens, 10 central dining venues showcasing small, independent chefs and restaurants, provide fresh takes on Nordic, Mexican, Japanese, and other world cuisines. There are also indie street food stalls and some superior chain outlets. ⊠ *16 Horner Sq., Brushfield St., Spitalfields* ☎ *020/7375–2963* ⊕ *www. oldspitalfieldsmarket.com* ⊗ *Stalls closed Mon.–Wed.* Ⓜ *Liverpool St. Overground: Shoreditch High St.*

THE SOUTH BANK

STREET MARKETS

Fodor'sChoice **Borough Market.** There's been a market in Borough since Roman times.
★ This latest incarnation, spread under the arches and railroad tracks leading to London Bridge Station, is where some of the city's best artisanal food producers set up stalls. Fresh coffees, gorgeous cheeses, chocolates, and baked goods complement the organically farmed meats, fresh fish, condiments, fruits, and vegetables.

Don't make any other lunch plans for the day; this is where celebrity chef Jamie Oliver's scallop man cooks them up fresh at Shell Seekers, and The Ginger Pig's rare-breed sausages sizzle on grills, while for the sweets lover there are chocolates, preserves, and Whirld's artisanal confectionery, as well as 18 restaurants and cafés, most above average. The Market Hall hosts workshops, tastings, and demonstrations, and also acts as a greenhouse. On Monday and Tuesday only stalls for hot food and produce are open.

On weekends, a separate, highly regarded market specializing in produce and street food operates on nearby Maltby Street. It was originally established by eight breakaway Borough Market traders. Stalls include African Volcano, purveyors of Mozambique-style hot sauces and marinades, and Raclette Brothers' superb melted cheese. ⊠ *8 Southwark St., Borough* ☎ *020/7402–1002* ⊕ *www.boroughmarket.org.uk* ☉ *Closed Sun.* Ⓜ *London Bridge.*

KENSINGTON, KNIGHTSBRIDGE, NOTTING HILL, AND MAYFAIR

ACCESSORIES

Mulberry. Staying true to its rural Somerset roots, this luxury goods company epitomizes *le style anglais,* a sophisticated take on the earth tones and practicality of English country style. Best known for highly desirable luxury handbags—such as the Lily, Chiltern, and Bayswater models—the company also produces gorgeous leather accessories, from wallets to luggage, as well as shoes and clothing for men and women. Aside from the New Bond Street flagship, there are branches in Knightsbridge, Covent Garden, Heathrow, and the Westfield Centres, along with Mulberry concessions in most of the major upscale department stores. The small store on St. Christopher's Place in Marylebone stocks accessories only. ⊠ *50 New Bond St., Mayfair* ☎ *020/7491–3900* ⊕ *www.mulberry.com* Ⓜ *Bond St.*

Fodor'sChoice **Philip Treacy.** Magnificent hats by Treacy are annual showstoppers on
★ Ladies Day at the Royal Ascot races and regularly grace the glossy magazines' party and catwalk pages. Part Mad Hatter, part Cecil Beaton, Treacy's creations always guarantee a grand entrance and are favorites with both Hollywood and actual royalty. In addition to the extravagant, haute couture hats handmade in the atelier, less flamboyant ready-to-wear hats are also for sale, as are some bags. ⊠ *69 Elizabeth St., Belgravia* ☎ *020/7730–3992* ⊕ *www.philiptreacy.co.uk* ☉ *Closed Sun.* Ⓜ *Sloane Sq.*

ANTIQUES

Alfie's Antique Market. This four-story, bohemian-chic labyrinth is London's largest indoor antiques market, housing more than 75 dealers specializing in art, lighting, glassware, textiles, jewelry, furniture, and collectibles, with a particular strength in vintage clothing and 20th-century design. Come here to pick up vintage (1900–70) clothing, accessories, and luggage from Tin Tin Collectables, antique and vintage glassware and vases at Robinson Antiques, or a spectacular mid-20th-century Italian lighting fixture at Vincenzo Caffarrella. The atmosphere may be funky, but the prices are not. There's also a rooftop café with free Wi-Fi if you need a coffee break. In addition to the market, this end of Church Street is lined with excellent antiques shops. ⊠ *13–25 Church St., Marylebone* ☎ *020/7723–6066* ⊕ *www.alfiesantiques.com* ⊙ *Closed Sun. and Mon.* Ⓜ *Marylebone.*

BOOKS AND STATIONERY

Fodor's Choice **Books for Cooks.** It may seem odd to describe a bookshop as delicious-
★ smelling, but on several days you can't but notice the aromas wafting out of the tiny café in the back of the shop—where the resident chef cooks a three-course set lunch for only £7, served from noon to 1 pm Tuesday through Friday. The dishes are drawn from recipes in the 8,000 cookbooks on the shelves. Just about every world cuisine is represented, along with a complete lineup of works by celebrity chefs. Before you come to London, visit the shop's website to sign up for a specialized cooking workshop in the upstairs demonstration kitchen. ⊠ *4 Blenheim Crescent, Notting Hill* ☎ *020/7221–1992* ⊕ *www.booksforcooks.com* ⊙ *Closed Sun. and Mon.* Ⓜ *Notting Hill Gate, Ladbroke Grove.*

Smythson of Bond Street. No hostess of any standing would consider having a leather-bound guest book made by anyone besides this elegant stationer, and the shop's social stationery and distinctive diaries with their pale-blue pages are the epitome of British good taste. These, along with other made-in-Britain leather goods including a small line of handbags, backpacks, and luggage tags, can be personalized. There are branches in Chelsea, Notting Hill, and The City, plus concessions in leading department stores. ⊠ *40 New Bond St., Mayfair* ☎ *020/3535–8009* ⊕ *www. smythson.com* Ⓜ *Bond St., Oxford Circus.*

Waterstone's. At this megabookshop (Europe's largest, with more than 8 miles of bookshelves) in a former art deco department store near Piccadilly Circus, browse for your latest purchase, attend one of the frequent meet-the-author events, or admire the view with a glass of wine at the 5th View Bar and Restaurant (open until 9); there's also a café in the basement. Waterstone's is the country's leading book chain, and it's pulled out all the stops to make its flagship as welcoming as a bookstore can be. There are several smaller branches throughout the city. ⊠ *203–206 Piccadilly, Mayfair* ☎ *0207/851–2400* ⊕ *www.waterstones.com* Ⓜ *Piccadilly Circus.*

CLOTHING

Browns. A trendsetting boutique since it opened in the 1970s, this shop occupying interconnecting town houses has been reinvigorated after a purchase by luxury e-tailer Farfetch.com. Browns focuses on well-established international luxury designers such as Vetements, Valentino, Marques Almeida, or Saint Laurent. The menswear, footwear, and accessories collections are equally well chosen. A new Shoreditch branch showcases new design talent, and if you're about to go down the aisle, check out the appointment-only bridal boutique at 12 Hinde Street in Marylebone. ⊠ *23–27 S. Molton St., Mayfair* ☎ *020/7514–0016* ⊕ *www.brownsfashion.com* Ⓜ *Bond St.*

Jigsaw. The quality of fabrics and detailing belie the reasonable prices here, where clothes are classic yet trendy and elegant without being dull—and where cuts are kind to the womanly figure. The style is epitomized by the Duchess of Cambridge, who, as Kate Middleton before her marriage, was a buyer for the company. Although there are numerous branches across London, no two stores are the same. Preteens have their own line, Jigsaw Junior. ⊠ *The Chapel, 6 Duke of York Sq., Chelsea* ☎ *020/730–4404* ⊕ *www.jigsaw-online.com* Ⓜ *Sloane Sq.*

Ozwald Boateng. The dapper menswear by Ozwald Boateng (pronounced "Bwa-teng") combines contemporary funky style with traditional Savile Row quality. His made-to-measure suits have been worn by the dandyish likes of Jamie Foxx, Mick Jagger, and Laurence Fishburne, who appreciate the sharp cuts, luxurious fabrics, and occasionally vibrant colors (even the more conservative choices have jacket linings in bright silk). ⊠ *30 Savile Row, Mayfair* ☎ *020/7437–2030* ⊕ *www.ozwaldboateng.co.uk* ⊙ *Closed Sun.* Ⓜ *Piccadilly Circus.*

Rigby & Peller. Many of London's most affluent women find their luxury lingerie (plus swimwear) here because the quality is excellent and the service impeccably knowledgeable—and perhaps because it's the Queen's favored underwear supplier and has provided maternity wear to the Duchess of Cambridge. Despite the upscale clientele, it's much friendlier than you might expect. Brands include Primadonna and Aubade as well as R&P's own line, and if the right fit eludes you, there's a made-to-measure service that starts at around £300. There are also branches in Mayfair, Chelsea, St. John's Wood, and The City. ⊠ *2 Hans Rd., Knightsbridge* ☎ *020/7225–4760* ⊕ *www.rigbyandpeller.com* Ⓜ *Knightsbridge.*

Vivienne Westwood. From her beginnings as the most shocking and outré designer around, Westwood (now Dame Vivienne) has become a standard-bearer for high-style British couture. At the Chelsea boutique where she first sold the lavish corseted ball gowns, dandified nipped-waist jackets, and tartan-meets-punk daywear that formed the core of her signature look, you can still buy ready-to-wear—mainly items from the more casual Anglomania diffusion line and the exclusive Worlds End label, which draws from her archives. The small Davies Street boutique is devoted to couture (plus bridal), while the flagship Conduit Street store carries all of the above. There's also a men's collection at 18 Conduit Street. ⊠ *44 Conduit St., Mayfair* ☎ *020/7439–1109* ⊕ *www.viviennewestwood.com* Ⓜ *Oxford Circus.*

DEPARTMENT STORES

Harrods. With an encyclopedic assortment of luxury brands, this Knightsbridge institution, currently owned by the Qatar Investment Authority, has more than 300 departments and 25 eating and drinking options, all spread over 1 million square feet on a 4½-acre site. You can even get your eyes tested or buy a foreign villa. Now populated more by window-shopping tourists and superrich visitors from abroad than by the bling-averse natives, Harrods is best approached as the world's largest, most upscale and expensive mall. Focus on the spectacular food halls, the huge ground-floor perfumery and jewelry departments, the excellent Urban Retreat spa, and Shoe Heaven, Europe's biggest shoe department. The Superbrands area houses haute couture from 12 top international designers such as Dior, Fendi, Prada, Valentino, and Chanel, while the children's department has a mini-me version for the toddler who wouldn't be seen in anything less than the likes of Burberry, Baby Dior, Chloé for Kids, and Monclerr. Be prepared to brave the crowds, especially on weekends. ⊠ *87–135 Brompton Rd., Knightsbridge* ☎ *020/7730–1234* ⊕ *www.harrods.com* Ⓜ *Knightsbridge.*

Harvey Nichols. While visiting tourists flock to Harrods, local fashionistas shop at Harvey Nichols, aka "Harvey Nicks." The womenswear and accessories departments are outstanding, featuring top designers like Tom Ford, Elie Saab, Yeezy, Lanvin, Reem Acra, and just about every fashionable name you can think of. The furniture and housewares are equally gorgeous (and pricey), although they become somewhat more affordable during the biannual sales in January and July. The Fifth Floor bar is the place to see and be seen, but if you're in search of food, the same floor also has an all-day Modern European café, a branch of Burger & Lobster, the carnivore-friendly Zelman Meats, or sushi-to-go from Yo! Sushi. To keep you looking as box-fresh as your purchases, the Beauty Lounge features a rotating menu of treatments from brands such as Elemis, La Mer, and Dermalogia, plus makeovers, LED facials, IV vitamin infusions, and blow-dry, nail, and brow bars. ⊠ *109–125 Knightsbridge, Knightsbridge* ☎ *020/7235–5000* ⊕ *www.harveynichols.com* Ⓜ *Knightsbridge.*

Fodor's Choice ★ **Selfridges.** This giant bustling store (the second largest in the United Kingdom after Harrods) gives Harvey Nichols a run for its money as London's most fashionable department store. Packed to the rafters with clothes ranging from mid-price lines to the latest catwalk names, the store continues to break ground with its innovative retail schemes, especially the ground-floor Wonder Room (for extravagant jewelry and luxury watches), a dedicated Denim Studio, a Fragrance Bar where you can create custom perfume, an array of pop-ups ranging from spaces for designers such as Jil Sander to a healthy shot bar (if you need some colloidal silver to keep you going) or a collaboration with boutique boxing club BXR. The giant accessories hall has miniboutiques dedicated to top-end designers such as Chanel, Gucci, and Vuitton while the new Corner Shop offers U.K.-themed gifts and souvenirs at all price points. There are so many zones that merge into one another—from youth-oriented Miss Selfridge to audio equipment to the large, comprehensive cosmetics department—that you practically need a map. Don't miss the Shoe Galleries, the world's largest shoe department, which is filled with more than 5,000 pairs from 120 brands, displayed like works of art under spotlights. Take a break with a glass of wine at the rooftop restaurant or pick up some tea in the Food Hall as a gift. ⊠ *400 Oxford St., Marylebone* ☎ *0800/123400* ⊕ *www.selfridges.com* Ⓜ *Bond St.*

HOUSEHOLD GOODS

The Conran Shop. This is the brainchild of Sir Terence Conran, who has been a major influence on British taste since he opened Habitat in the 1960s. Although he is no longer associated with Habitat, his Conran Shops remain bastions of similarly clean, unfussy modernist design. Housewares from furniture to lighting, stemware, and textiles—both handmade and mass-produced, by famous names and emerging designers—are housed in a building that is a modernist landmark in its own right. Both the flagship store and the branch on Marylebone High Street are bursting with great gift ideas. ⊠ *Michelin House, 81 Fulham Rd., South Kensington* ☎ *020/7589–7401* ⊕ *www.conranshop.co.uk* Ⓜ *South Kensington.*

JEWELRY

Asprey. The company's "global flagship" store displays exquisite jewelry—as well as silver and leather goods, watches, china, and crystal—in a discreet, very British setting that oozes quality, expensive good taste, and hushed comfort. If you're in the market for an immaculate 1930s cigarette case, a silver cocktail shaker, a pair of pavé diamond and sapphire earrings, or a ladylike handbag, you won't likely be disappointed. And, for the really well-heeled, there's custom service available as well (Ringo Starr had a chess set made here). This store has occupied the premises since 1847, some 66 years after Asprey was established in 1781. ⊠ *167 New Bond St., Mayfair* ☎ *020/7493–6767* ⊕ *www.asprey. com* ⊘ *Closed Sun.* Ⓜ *Green Park.*

Butler & Wilson. Specialists in bold costume jewelry and affordable glamor, Butler & Wilson attracts fans including the Duchess of Cambridge. It's added semiprecious stones to its foundation diamanté, colored rhinestone, and crystal collections. Flamboyant skull brooches or dainty floral earrings make perfect gifts. ⊠ *189 Fulham Rd., South Kensington* ☎ *020/7352–3045* ⊕ *www.butlerandwilson.co.uk* ⊘ *Closed Sun.* Ⓜ *South Kensington.*

Kabiri. A carefully curated array of exciting contemporary jewelry by emerging and established designers from around the world is packed into this small shop. There is something to suit most budgets and tastes, though understated minimalism predominates. You can score an elegant, one-of-a-kind piece here for a very reasonable price. ⊠ *94 Marylebone La., Marylebone* ☎ *020/7317–2150* ⊕ *www.kabiri.co.uk* Ⓜ *Baker St.*

MUSIC

Music & Video Exchange. This store is a music collector's treasure trove, with a constantly changing stock refreshed by customers selling and exchanging as well as buying. The ground floor focuses on rock, pop, indie, and punk, both mainstream and obscure, in a variety of formats ranging from vinyl to CD, cassette, and even minidisk. Don't miss the classical music in the basement and the soul, jazz, house, techno, reggae, and more upstairs. Like movies? There's a wide variety of Blu-ray and DVD box sets, as well as bargain classic and cult films. Keep an eye out for rarities—including first pressings and one-offs—in all departments. Similar exchanges for comics (No. 32) and books (No. 30) are on nearby Pembridge Road (also a destination for vintage clothing for men [No. 34] and women [No. 20], plus more clothing, accessories, and retro homewares [No. 28]). Note: Stock depends on what customers bring in to exchange, so you'll surely find many more DVDs with European (PAL) formatting than the North American–friendly NTSC format, but the store does get the latter occasionally. ⊠ *38 Notting Hill Gate, Notting Hill* ☎ *020/7243–8573* ⊕ *www.mgeshops.com* Ⓜ *Notting Hill Gate.*

STREET MARKETS

Portobello Market. Still considered the best all-around market in town by many fans, and certainly the most famous, Portobello Market stretches almost 2 miles, from fashionable Notting Hill to the lively cultural melting pot of North Kensington, changing character as it goes. The southern end, starting at Chepstow Villas and going to Elgin Crescent, is lined with shops and stalls, and, on Saturday, arcades selling antiques, silver, and bric-a-brac. The middle, from Elgin Crescent to Talbot, is devoted to fruit and vegetables, interspersed with excellent hot food stalls. On Friday and Saturday, the area between Talbot Road and the elevated highway (called the Westway) becomes more of a flea market, specializing in new household and mass-produced goods sold at a discount. North of the Westway up to Goldborne Road are more stalls selling even cheaper secondhand household goods and bric-a-brac. Scattered throughout but mostly concentrated under the Westway are clothing stalls selling vintage pieces and items from emerging designers, custom T-shirts, and supercool baby clothes, plus jewelry. New and established designers are also found in the boutiques of the Portobello Green Arcade.

Some say Portobello Road has become a tourist trap, but if you acknowledge that it's a circus and get into the spirit, it's a lot of fun. Perhaps you won't find many bargains, but this is such a fascinating part of town that just hanging out is a good enough excuse to come. There are some food and flower stalls throughout the week (try the Hummingbird Bakery for delicious cupcakes), but Saturday is when the market in full swing. Serious shoppers avoid the crowds and go on Friday morning. Bring cash—several vendors don't take credit cards—but also be sure to keep an eye on it. ⊠ *Portobello Rd., Notting Hill* ⊕ *www.portobelloroad.co.uk* ⊘ *Closed Sun.* Ⓜ *Notting Hill Gate.*

CANTERBURY AND
THE SOUTHEAST

Visit Fodors.com for advice, updates, and bookings

WELCOME TO CANTERBURY AND THE SOUTHEAST

TOP REASONS TO GO

★ **Bodiam, Dover, Hever, and Herstmonceux castles:** Take your pick from the most evocative castles in a region filled with them, and let these fortresses dazzle you with their fortitude and fascinate you with their histories.

★ **Brighton:** With its nightclubs, sunbathing, and funky atmosphere, this is the quintessential modern English seaside city.

★ **Canterbury Cathedral:** This massive building, a textbook of medieval architecture, inspires awe with its soaring towers and flagstone corridors.

★ **Treasure houses:** Here is one of England's richest concentrations of historic homes: among the superlatives are Petworth House, Knole, Ightham Mote, and Chartwell.

★ **Amazing gardens:** Gardens of all kinds are an English specialty, and at Sissinghurst and Wisley, as well as in the gardens of Hever Castle and Chartwell, you can easily spend an entire afternoon wandering through acres of floral exotica.

For sightseeing purposes, the Southeast can be divided into four sections. The eastern part of the region takes in the cathedral town of Canterbury, as well as the port city of Dover. The next section stretches along the southern coast from the medieval hill town of Rye to picturesque Lewes. A third area reaches from the coastal city of Brighton inward to Chichester. The fourth section takes in the spa town of Royal Tunbridge Wells and western Kent, where stately homes and castles dot the farmland. Larger towns in the area can be easily reached by train or bus from London for a day trip. To visit most castles, grand country homes, or quiet villages, though, you need to rent a car or join a tour.

1 Canterbury and Dover. Dover's distinctive chalk-white cliffs plunging hundreds of feet into the sea are just a part of this region's dramatic coastal scenery. Don't miss Canterbury's medieval town center, dominated by its massive cathedral.

2 Rye and Lewes. Medieval villages dot the hills along this stretch of Sussex coastline. The centerpiece is Rye, a pretty hill town of cobbled streets lined with timbered homes. Lewes, with its crumbling castle, is another gem.

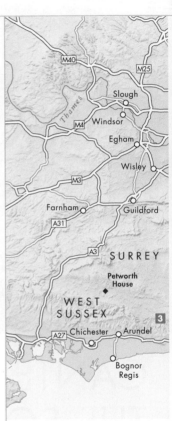

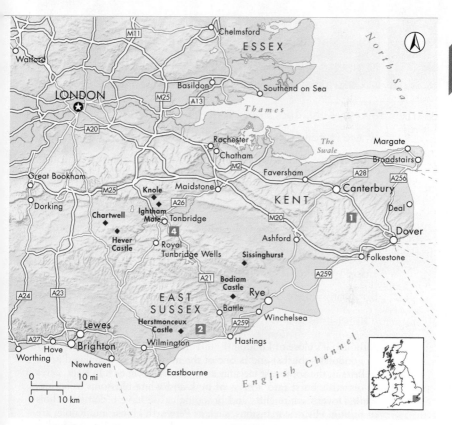

3 Brighton and the Sussex Coast. Funky, lively Brighton perfectly melds Victorian architecture with a modern vibe that includes the best shopping and dining on the coast. Outside town are beautiful old homes such as Petworth House and even a Roman villa.

4 Tunbridge Wells and Around. From Anne Boleyn's regal childhood abode at Hever Castle to the medieval manor at Ightham Mote, this area is rich with grand houses. Spend a couple of days exploring them; Tunbridge Wells is a comfortable base.

Updated by
Jack Jewers

Surrey, Kent, and Sussex form the breadbasket of England, where bucolic farmland stretches as far as the eye can see. Once a favorite destination of English nobility, this region is rich with history, visible in the great castles and stately homes that dot the countryside. Its cities are similarly historic, especially ancient Canterbury, with its spectacular cathedral and medieval streets. Along the coast, funky seaside towns have a more relaxed attitude, especially artsy Brighton, where artists and musicians use the sea as inspiration for their work.

Although it's close to London (both Surrey and Kent reach all the way to London's suburbs) and is one of the most densely populated areas of Britain, the Southeast feels far away from the big city. In Kent, acres of orchards burst into a mass of pink-and-white blossoms in spring, while Dover's white cliffs and brooding castle have become symbols of Britain. Historic mansions, such as Petworth House and Knole, are major draws for travelers, and lush gardens such as Vita Sackville-West's Sissinghurst and the Royal Horticultural Society's Wisley attract thousands to their vivid floral displays.

Because the English Channel is at its narrowest here, a great deal of British history has been forged in the Southeast. The Romans landed in this area and stayed to rule Britain for four centuries. So did the Saxons—*Sussex* means "the land of the South Saxons." The biggest invasion of them all took place here when William ("the Conqueror") of Normandy defeated the Saxons at a battle near Hastings in 1066, changing the island forever.

PLANNER

WHEN TO GO

It's best to visit in spring, summer, or early fall. Many privately owned castles and mansions are open only between April and September or October. However, the parks surrounding the stately houses are often open all year. If crowds tend to spoil your fun, avoid August, Sunday, and national holidays, particularly in Canterbury and the seaside towns.

FESTIVALS

Brighton Festival. The three-week-long Brighton Festival, one of England's biggest and liveliest arts festivals, takes place every May in venues around Brighton. The more than 600 events include drama, music, dance, and visual arts. ⊠ *Brighton* 🕾 *01273/709709* ⊕ *www.brightonfestival.org.*

Fodor's Choice **Dickensian Christmas Festival.** Rochester sponsors a Dickensian Christmas
★ Festival on the first weekend in December. Thousands of people in period dress participate in reenactments of scenes from *A Christmas Carol*. A candlelight procession, mulled wine and roasted chestnuts, and Christmas carols at the cathedral add to the celebration. There's also a summer festival that takes place in early June. Two other important Dickens festivals take place in Broadstairs, 40 miles east, every June and December. ⊠ *Rochester* 🕾 *01634/306000* ⊕ *www.rochesterdickensfestival.org.uk.*

PLANNING YOUR TIME

With the exception of Brighton, you can easily see the highlights of each of the towns in less than a day. Brighton has more to offer, and you should allot at least two days to take it all in. Consider basing yourself in one town while exploring a region. For example, you could stay in Brighton and take in Lewes on a day trip. Base yourself in Rye for a couple of days while exploring Winchelsea, Battle, Hastings, and Herstmonceux Castle. Tunbridge Wells is a great place to overnight if you plan on exploring the many stately homes and castles nearby.

GETTING HERE AND AROUND

AIR TRAVEL

Heathrow is convenient for Surrey, but Gatwick Airport is a more convenient gateway for Kent. The rail station inside Gatwick has trains to Brighton and other major towns, and you can take a taxi from Heathrow to Guildford for around £50.

BUS TRAVEL

National Express buses serve the region from London's Victoria Coach Station. Trips to Brighton and Canterbury take two hours; to Chichester, three hours. Megabus runs buses at budget prices from Victoria Coach Station to many of the same destinations as National Express and can be cheaper, although luggage limits are strict.

Bus service between towns can be useful but is often intermittent. Out in the country, don't expect buses more often than once every half hour or hour. Sometimes trains are a better option; sometimes they're much worse. Traveline is the best central place to call for bus information, and local tourist information centers can be a big help.

Contacts **Megabus.** ☎ *0900/160–0900* ⊕ *www.megabus.co.uk.* **National Express.** ☎ *0871/781–8178* ⊕ *www.nationalexpress.com.* **Traveline.** ☎ *0871/200–2233* ⊕ *www.traveline.info.*

CAR TRAVEL

Traveling by car is the best way to get to the stately homes and castles in the region. Having a car in Canterbury or Brighton, however, is a nuisance; you'll need to park and walk. Major routes radiating outward from London to the Southeast are, from west to east, M23/A23 to Brighton (52 miles); A21, passing by Royal Tunbridge Wells to Hastings (65 miles); A20/M20 to Folkestone (58 miles); and A2/M2 via Canterbury (56 miles) to Dover (71 miles).

TRAIN TRAVEL

Trains are the fastest and most efficient way to travel to major cities in the region, but they don't stop in many small towns. From London, Southeastern trains serve Sussex and Kent from Victoria and Charing Cross stations, and South West trains travel to Surrey from Waterloo Station. Getting to Brighton takes about 1 hour, to Canterbury about 1½ hours, and to Dover between 1½ and 2 hours. A Network Railcard costing £30, valid throughout the southern and southeastern regions for a year, entitles you and three companions to one-third off many off-peak fares.

Contacts **National Rail Enquiries.** ☎ *0845/748–4950* ⊕ *www.nationalrail. co.uk.* **Network Railcard.** ☎ *0345/301–1655* ⊕ *www.railcard.co.uk.*

RESTAURANTS

If you're in a seaside town, look for that great British staple, fish-and-chips. Perhaps "look" isn't the word—just follow your nose. On the coast, seafood, much of it locally caught, is a specialty. Try local smoked fish (haddock and mackerel) or the succulent local oysters. Inland, sample fresh local lamb and beef. In cities such as Brighton and Tunbridge Wells there are numerous restaurants and cafés, but out in the countryside the best options are often pubs. *Restaurant reviews have been shortened. For full information, visit Fodors.com.*

HOTELS

All around the coast, resort towns stretch along beaches, their hotels standing cheek by jowl. Of the smaller hotels and guesthouses not all remain open year-round; many do business only from mid-April to September or October. Some hotels have all-inclusive rates for a week's stay. Prices rise in July and August, when the seaside resorts can get solidly booked, especially Brighton. (On the other hand, hotels may drop rates by up to 40% off-season.) Places in Brighton may not take a booking for a single night in summer or on weekends. *Hotel reviews have been shortened. For full information, visit Fodors.com.*

WHAT IT COSTS IN POUNDS			
	$	**$$**	**$$$**	**$$$$**
Restaurants	under £15	£15–£19	£20–£25	over £25
Hotels	under £100	£100–£160	£161–£220	over £220

Restaurant prices are per person for a main course at dinner, or if dinner is not served, at lunch. Hotel prices are the lowest cost of a standard double room in high season, including 20% V.A.T.

3

VISITOR INFORMATION

Tourist boards in the main towns can help with information, and many will also book local accommodations.

Contacts Southeast England Tourist Board. ⊕ *www.visitsoutheastengland. com.*

CANTERBURY AND DOVER

The cathedral city of Canterbury is an ancient place that has attracted travelers since the 12th century. Its magnificent cathedral, the Mother Church of England, remains a powerful draw. Even in prehistoric times, this part of England was relatively well settled. Saxon settlers, Norman conquerors, and the folk who lived here in late-medieval times all left their mark. From Canterbury there's rewarding wandering to be done in the gentle Kentish countryside between the city and the busy port of Dover. Here the landscape ravishes the eye in spring with apple blossoms, and in autumn with lush fields ready for harvest. In addition to orchards and market gardens, the county contains round oast houses. These buildings with tilted, pointed roofs were once used for drying hops; now many are expensive homes.

CANTERBURY

56 miles southeast of London.

Just mention Canterbury and most people are taken back to memories of high-school English classes and Geoffrey Chaucer's *Canterbury Tales,* about medieval pilgrims making their way to Canterbury Cathedral. Judging from the tales, however, in those days Canterbury was as much a party town as it was a spiritual center.

The city has been the seat of the Primate of All England, the archbishop of Canterbury, since Pope Gregory the Great dispatched St. Augustine to convert the pagan hordes of Britain in 597. The height of Canterbury's popularity came in the 12th century, when thousands of pilgrims flocked here to see the shrine of the murdered archbishop St. Thomas à Becket. This southeastern town became one of the most visited in England, if not Europe. Buildings that served as pilgrims' inns (and that survived World War II bombing of the city) still dominate the streets of Canterbury's center, though it's tourists, not pilgrims, who flock to this city of about 40,000 people today.

Prices at city museums are higher than average, so if you plan to see more than one, ask at the tourist office if a combination ticket might be cheaper.

GETTING HERE AND AROUND

The fastest way to reach Canterbury from London is by train. Southeastern trains to Canterbury run every half hour in peak times from London's Charing Cross Station. The journey takes between 1 and 1½ hours. Canterbury has two centrally located train stations, Canterbury East Station (a five-minute walk from the cathedral square) and Canterbury West Station (a 10-minute walk from the cathedral).

National Express and Megabus buses bound for Canterbury depart several times a day from London's Victoria Coach Station. Trips to Canterbury take around two hours, and drop passengers near the train stations. If you're driving, take the A2/M2 to Canterbury from London (56 miles). Park in one of the signposted parking lots at the edge of the town center.

Canterbury has a small, walkable town center. Although the town has good local bus service, you're unlikely to need it. Most major tourist sites are on one street that changes name three times—beginning as St. George's Street and then becoming High Street and St. Peter's Street.

ESSENTIALS

Visitor Information Canterbury Visitor Centre. ⊠ *The Beaney House of Art & Knowledge, 18 High St.* ☎ *01227/862162* ⊕ *www.canterbury.co.uk.*

TOURS

Canterbury Guided Tours. Expert guides lead walking tours at 11 am daily, with an additional tour at 2 pm from April to October. Tickets cost £8. ⊠ *Arnett House, Hawks La.* ☎ *01227/459779* ⊕ *www.canterburyguidedtours.com* ⤳ *From £8.*

EXPLORING

The Beaney House of Art & Knowledge. The medieval Poor Priests' Hospital is the site of this quirky local museum, where exhibits provide an overview of the city's history and architecture from Roman times to World War II. It covers everything and everyone associated with the town, including the mysterious death of the 16th-century writer Christopher Marlowe, and the British children's book and TV characters Rupert the Bear and Bagpuss. One recent acquisition is a beautiful gold dragon pendant, made in Kent during the Anglo-Saxon era (410–1066). ⊠ *18 High St.* ☎ *01227/862162* ⊕ *www.canterburymuseums.co.uk* ⤳ *Free.*

Fodor's Choice
★

Canterbury Cathedral. The focal point of the city was the first of England's great Norman cathedrals. Nucleus of worldwide Anglicanism, the Cathedral Church of Christ Canterbury (its formal name) is a living textbook of medieval architecture. The building was begun in 1070, demolished, begun anew in 1096, and then systematically expanded over the next three centuries. When the original choir section burned to the ground in 1174, another replaced it, designed in the new Gothic style, with tall, pointed arches.

The cathedral was only a century old, and still relatively small, when Thomas Becket, the archbishop of Canterbury, was murdered here in

1170. Becket, as head of the church, had been engaged in a political struggle with his old friend Henry II. Four knights supposedly overheard Henry scream, "will no one will rid me of this troublesome priest?" (although there is no evidence that those were his actual words—the only contemporary record has him saying, "what miserable drones and traitors have I nourished and brought up in my household, who let their lord be treated with such shameful contempt by a low-born cleric?").

Thinking they were carrying out the king's wishes, the knights went immediately to Canterbury and hacked Becket to pieces in one of the side chapels. Henry, racked with guilt, went into deep mourning. Becket was canonized and Canterbury's position as the center of English Christianity was assured.

For almost 400 years Becket's tomb was one of the most extravagant shrines in Christendom, until it was destroyed by Henry VIII's troops during the Reformation. In **Trinity Chapel,** which held the shrine, you can still see a series of 13th-century stained-glass windows illustrating Becket's miracles. (The actual site of Becket's murder is down a flight of steps just to the left of the nave.) Nearby is the tomb of Edward, the Black Prince (1330–76), warrior son of Edward III and a national hero. In the corner of Trinity Chapel, a second flight of steps leads down to the enormous Norman **undercroft,** or vaulted cellar, built in the early 12th century. A row of squat pillars engraved with dancing beasts (mythical and otherwise) supports the roof.

To the north of the cathedral are the **cloisters** and a small compound of monastic buildings. The 12th-century octagonal water tower is still part of the cathedral's water supply. The Norman staircase in the northwest corner of the Green Court dates from 1167 and is a unique example of the architecture of the times. ■TIP➔ The cathedral is popular, so arrive early or late in the day to avoid the crowds. ✉ *Cathedral Precincts* ☎ *01227/762862* ⊕ *www.canterbury-cathedral.org* ✉ *£10.50; free for services and ½ hr before closing; £5 tour; £4 audio guide.*

Canterbury Roman Museum. Below ground, at the level of the remnants of Roman Canterbury, this small but informative museum tells the story of the area's distant Roman past. Highlights of the collection include a hypocaust—the Roman version of central heating—and two colorful floor mosaics dating from around the year 270, that were unearthed in the aftermaths of the bombs that fell on Canterbury during World War II. Displays of excavated objects (some of which you can hold in the **Touch the Past** area) and computer-generated reconstructions of Roman buildings and the marketplace help re-create the past. ✉ *Butchery La.* ☎ *01227/785575* ⊕ *www.canterburymuseums.co.uk* ✉ *£8.*

FAMILY **The Canterbury Tales.** Take an audiovisual tour of the sights and sounds (and smells) of 14th-century England at this cheesy but popular attraction. Verily, ye shall meet Chaucer's pilgrims and view tableaux illustrating five of his tales. In summer, costumed actors perform scenes from the town's history. ✉ *St. Margaret's St.* ☎ *01227/696002* ⊕ *www. canterburytales.org.uk* ✉ *£11* ⊙ *Closed Mon. and Tues. Nov.–Mar.*

Christchurch Gate. This huge gate, built in 1517, leads into the cathedral close. As you pass through, look up at the sculpted heads of two young

The Beaney House of Art & Knowledge **4**
Canterbury Cathedral **6**
Canterbury Roman Museum **2**
The Canterbury Tales **3**
Christchurch Gate **5**
Medieval City Walls **1**

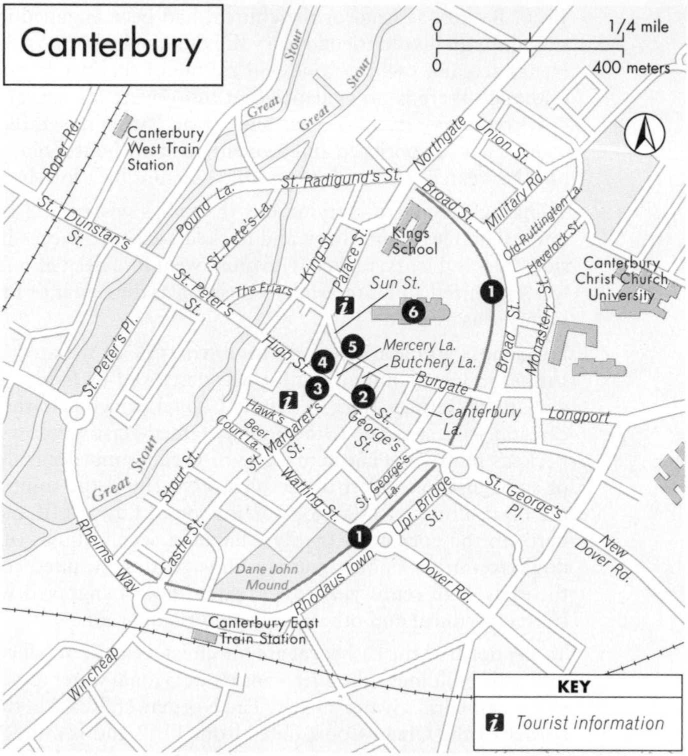

figures: Prince Arthur, elder brother of Henry VIII, and the young Catherine of Aragon, to whom Arthur was married in 1501 (when he was just 15). He died shortly afterwards, and Catherine married Henry. Jump forward 25 years, and Henry was king. But they had produced no male children, a fact Henry blamed on God's wrath that he'd married his sister-in-law. Catherine refused him a divorce, but Henry went ahead and did it anyway, creating an irrevocable breach with the Roman Catholic Church and altering the course of English history forever. ✉ *Cathedral Close.*

Medieval City Walls. For an essential Canterbury experience, follow the circuit of the 13th- and 14th-century walls, built on the line of the Roman walls. Roughly half survive; those to the east are intact, towering some 20 feet high and offering a sweeping view of the town. You can access these from a number of places, including Castle Street and Broad Street. ✉ *Canterbury.*

WHERE TO EAT

$ BRITISH

🍴 **City Fish Bar.** Long lines and lots of satisfied finger licking attest to the deserved popularity of this excellent fish-and-chips shop in the center of town, where all orders are take-out. Everything is freshly fried, the batter crisp, and the fish tasty; the fried mushrooms are also surprisingly good. **Known for:** crispy batter; chunky, hot chips; superfresh, good-quality fast food. [$] *Average main: £7* ✉ *30 St. Margaret's St.* ☎ *01227/760873.*

$$ ✕ **The Goods Shed.** Next to Canterbury West Station, this farmers' market
BRITISH restaurant with wooden tables is well known for offering fresh, seasonal
Kentish food—monkfish with parsley dumplings, locally caught fish and
smoked meats, local cider, and freshly baked bread. Whatever is freshest
that day appears on the menu, whether it's John Dory with garlic or steak
with blue cheese butter. **Known for:** fresh, local produce; great seafood;
catch of the day. $ *Average main: £19* ✉ *Station Rd.* W ☎ *01227/459153*
⊕ *www.thegoodsshed.co.uk* ⊘ *Closed Mon. No dinner Sun.*

$ ✕ **Old Brewery Tavern.** Here you can expect reliably good comfort food—
BRITISH juicy burgers, crispy fish-and-chips, or sirloin steak grilled to order. The
atmosphere is relaxed and casual, except on weekend nights when the
music gets turned up for the party crowd. **Known for:** good comfort
food; relaxed atmosphere; good-quality casual dining. $ *Average main:*
£11 ✉ *ABode Canterbury, 30–33 High St.* ☎ *01227/766266* ⊕ *www.*
abodecanterbury.co.uk/eat-drink/old-brewery-tavern-canterbury.

$ ✕ **Old Buttermarket.** A colorful, friendly old pub near the cathedral,
BRITISH the Buttermarket is a great place to grab a hearty lunch and sample
some traditional English fare with a modern inflection. You can sip a
pint of fresh English ale from the changing selection while sampling a
chicken, butter-bean, and bacon pie, or perhaps a warming bowl of
applewood-smoked macaroni and cheese. **Known for:** great selection
of ales; excellent pies; good veggie options. $ *Average main: £11* ✉ *39*
Burgate ☎ *01227/462170* ⊕ *www.nicholsonspubs.co.uk/theoldbutter-*
marketcanterbury ▭ *No credit cards.*

WHERE TO STAY

$ ▦ **ABode Canterbury.** This glossy boutique hotel inside the old city
HOTEL walls offers up-to-date style in traditional Canterbury, with good-
size rooms—modern but not minimal—classed as Comfortable,
Desirable, and Enviable. **Pros:** central location; luxurious handmade
beds; great restaurants and bars. **Cons:** one of the priciest hotels in
town; bar gets quite crowded; breakfast is extra. $ *Rooms from: £94*
✉ *30–33 High St.* ☎ *01227/766266* ⊕ *www.abodecanterbury.co.uk*
⤷ *73 rooms* ❚⊘❚ *No meals.*

$$ ▦ **Canterbury Cathedral Lodge.** There is no more peaceful place to stay in
HOTEL Canterbury then at this small and modern hotel tucked away within the
grounds of the cathedral. **Pros:** outstanding location; incredible views;
free entry to the cathedral (worth £10.50). **Cons:** no restaurant; few
services; booked up during conferences. $ *Rooms from: £120* ✉ *The*
Precincts ☎ *01227/865350* ⊕ *www.canterburycathedrallodge.org* ⤷ *35*
rooms ❚⊘❚ *Free Breakfast.*

$ ▦ **House of Agnes.** This historic B&B, which dates back 600 years and
B&B/INN was written about by Dickens, offers unique and stylish accommoda-
Fodor's Choice tions not far from Canterbury West Station. **Pros:** historic building; just
★ enough modern touches; honesty bar. **Cons:** rooms vary quite a bit in
size; no elevator; quirky designs won't be for all tastes. $ *Rooms from:*
£90 ✉ *71 St. Dunstans St.* ☎ *01227/72185* ⊕ *www.houseofagnes.co.uk*
⤷ *17 rooms* ❚⊘❚ *Free Breakfast.*

$$ ▦ **The White House.** Reputed to have been the place in which Queen
B&B/INN Victoria's head coachman came to live upon retirement, this handsome
Regency building sits on a quiet road off St. Peter's Street. **Pros:** historic

Impressive both inside and out, ancient Canterbury Cathedral dominates the town.

house; spacious rooms; family-friendly atmosphere. **Cons:** a bit outside the center; no restaurant; no elevator. $ *Rooms from: £115* ✉ *6 St. Peter's La.* ☏ *01227/761836* ⊕ *www.whitehousecanterbury.co.uk* ⇗ *7 rooms* ❑ *Free Breakfast.*

NIGHTLIFE

Alberry's Wine Bar. With late-night jazz and hip-hop and a trendy crowd, Alberry's Wine Bar is one of Canterbury's coolest nightspots. At lunchtime they serve a fine burger, too. ✉ *St. Margaret's St.* ☏ *01227/452378* ⊕ *www.alberrys.co.uk.*

Parrot. Built in 1370, the Parrot is an atmospheric old pub known for its real ale. They also do good food; Sunday lunch here is popular. ✉ *1–9 Church La.* ☏ *01227/454170* ⊕ *www.theparrotonline.com.*

Thomas Becket. A traditional English pub, with bunches of hops hanging from the ceiling and a fire crackling in the hearth on a cold winter's day, the Thomas Becket is a convivial kind of place. There is food available, but most people just come for the atmosphere. ✉ *21 Best La.* ☏ *01227/464384.*

SHOPPING

Crowthers of Canterbury. Behind the delightfully old-style red shop front, Crowthers of Canterbury carries an extensive selection of musical instruments, gifts, and other souvenirs for music lovers. ✉ *1 The Borough* ☏ *01227/763965* ⊕ *www.crowthersofcanterbury.co.uk.*

925. This shop has a great selection of handmade silver jewelry. ✉ *57 Palace St.* ☏ *01227/785699* ⊕ *www.925-silver.co.uk.*

The Saracen's Lantern. This small but delightful little curiosity shop looks like something out of a storybook. It's a lovely place to browse on a rainy afternoon. ⌧ *9 Borough* ☏ *01227/451968.*

BROADSTAIRS

17 miles east of Canterbury.

Like other Victorian seaside towns such as Margate and Ramsgate, Broadstairs was once the playground of vacationing Londoners, and grand 19th-century houses line the waterfront. In the off-season Broadstairs is peaceful, but day-trippers pack the town in July and August.

Park your car in one of the town lots, and strike out for the crescent beach or wander down the residential Victorian streets. Make your way down to the amusement pier and try your hand in one of the game arcades. You can grab fish-and-chips to go and dine on the beach.

Charles Dickens spent many summers in Broadstairs between 1837 and 1851 and wrote glowingly of its bracing freshness.

GETTING HERE AND AROUND

By car, Broadstairs is about a two-hour drive (78 miles) from London, off A256 on the southeast tip of England. Trains run from London's St. Pancras and Victoria stations to Broadstairs up to four times an hour; it's a 1½- to 2-hour trip and sometimes involves a change in Rochester. Broadstairs Station is off Broadway in the town center. National Express buses travel to Broadstairs from London several times a day; the journey takes about three hours.

EXPLORING

Bleak House. The cliff overlooking Viking Bay is dominated by this stern structure. One of Dickens's homes, it was here that he wrote *David Copperfield* and drafted the novel *Bleak House.* A devastating fire tore through the house in 2006, but it's had an extensive restoration. You can see the house by guided tour, which includes Dickens's original study. The cellars contain a small but interesting museum devoted to the shadowy history of smuggling on the south coast during the 18th and 19th centuries. ⌧ *Fort Rd.* ☏ *01843/865338* ⊕ *www.bleakhouse-broadstairs.co.uk* ⌧ *£4.*

Dickens House Museum. This house was originally the home of Mary Pearson Strong, on whom Dickens based the character of Betsey Trotwood, David Copperfield's aunt. Dickens lived here from 1837 to 1839 while writing *The Pickwick Papers* and *Oliver Twist.* Some rooms have been decorated to look as they would have in Dickens's day, and there's a reconstruction of Miss Trotwood's room as described by Dickens. ⌧ *2 Victoria Parade* ☏ *01843/861232* ⌧ *£4.50* ⊙ *Closed weekdays in Nov.*

Canterbury
and Dover

DOVER

8 miles south of Deal, 78 miles east of London.

The busy passenger port of Dover has for centuries been Britain's gateway to Europe and is known for the famous white cliffs. The town itself is, sadly, not a pretty place; the savage bombardments of World War II and the shortsightedness of postwar developers left the city center in something of a mess. Mostly Dover town is a place you go through to get to the ferry. However, there are a couple of notable exceptions, including the Roman-era legacy of a lighthouse adjoining a stout Anglo-Saxon church.

GETTING HERE AND AROUND

National Express buses depart from London's Victoria Coach Station for Dover about every 90 minutes. The journey takes between 2½ and 3 hours. Drivers from London take the M20, which makes a straight line south to Dover. The journey should take around two hours. Southeastern trains leave London's Charing Cross, Victoria, and St. Pancras stations about every 30 minutes for Dover Priory Station in Dover. The trip is between one and two hours; some services require changes in Ashford.

For the best views of the cliffs, you need a car or taxi; it's a long way to walk from town.

3

ESSENTIALS

Visitor Information Dover Visitor Information Centre. ✉ *Dover Museum, Market Sq.* ☎ *01304/201066* 🌐 *www.whitecliffscountry.org.uk.*

EXPLORING

FAMILY
Fodor's Choice ★
Dover Castle. Spectacular and with plenty to explore, Dover Castle, towering high above the ramparts of the white cliffs, is a mighty medieval castle that has served as an important strategic center over the centuries. Most of the castle, including the keep, dates to Norman times. It was begun by Henry II in 1181 but incorporates additions from almost every succeeding century. The **Great Tower** re-creates how the opulent castle would have looked in Henry's time, complete with sound effects, interactive displays, and courtly characters in medieval costume. History jumps forward the better part of a millennium (and becomes rather more sober in the telling) as you venture down into the recently opened **Secret Wartime Tunnels.** The castle played a surprisingly dramatic role in World War II, the full extent to which remained unknown for years afterward. These well-thought-out interactive galleries tell the complete story. The tunnels themselves, originally built during the Napoleonic Wars, were used as a top-secret intelligence-gathering base in the fight against Hitler. ✉ *Castle Rd.* ☎ *01304/211067* 🌐 *www.english-heritage.org.uk* 🎟 *£19.50* 🕒 *Closed weekdays mid-Nov.–mid-Feb., and Mon. and Tues. mid-Feb.–Mar.*

Roman Painted House. Believed to have been a hotel, the remains of this nearly 2,000-year-old structure were excavated in the 1970s. It includes some Roman wall paintings (mostly dedicated to Bacchus, the god of revelry), along with the remnants of an ingenious heating system. ✉ *New St.* ☎ *01304/203279* 🌐 *www.theromanpaintedhouse.co.uk* 🎟 *£4* 🕒 *Closed late Sept.–Mar.*

Fodor's Choice ★
White Cliffs. Plunging hundreds of feet into the sea, Dover's chalk-white cliffs are an inspirational site and considered an iconic symbol of England. They stay white because of the natural process of erosion. Because of this, you must be cautious when walking along the cliffs—experts recommend staying at least 20 feet from the edge. The best places to see the cliffs are at Samphire Hoe, St. Margaret's Bay, or East Cliff and Warren Country Park. Signs will direct you from the roads to scenic spots. ■ **TIP→ The visitor center at Langdon Cliffs has 5 miles of walking trails with some spectacular views.** ✉ *Dover.*

WHERE TO EAT

$$
BRITISH
🍴 **The Allotment.** This charming and slightly quirky restaurant in the center of Dover doesn't look like much from the outside, but don't be fooled—delicious, creative Modern British meals are served within. The unusual name comes from an old-fashioned British tradition of communal gardens for city dwellers: the "allotment" is a small strip of land allocated to a family with no garden who wants to grow its own vegetables. **Known for:** house special fish pie; lots of local produce; charming and quirky character. [$] *Average main: £15* ✉ *9 High St.* ☎ *01304/214467* 🌐 *www.theallotmentrestaurant.com.*

WHERE TO STAY

$$ B&B/INN **White Cliffs Hotel.** Literally in the shadow of the famous White Cliffs of Dover, this colorful little hotel is attached to a friendly pub that serves good food. **Pros:** tons of character; beautiful location; good food. **Cons:** far from central Dover; difficult to get here without a car; quite pricey for what you get. [$] *Rooms from: £110* ✉ *High St., St. Margaret's-at-Cliffe* ☎ *01304/852229* 🌐 *www.thewhitecliffs.com* 🛏 *15 rooms* 🍴 *Free Breakfast.*

RYE AND LEWES

From Dover the coast road winds west through Folkestone (a genteel resort, small port, and Channel Tunnel terminal), across Romney Marsh (famous for its sheep and, at one time, its ruthless smugglers), and on to the delightful medieval town of Rye. The region along the coast is noted for Winchelsea, the history-rich sites of Hastings, Herstmonceux, and Bodiam, and the Glyndebourne Opera House festival, based outside Lewes, a town celebrated for its architectural heritage. One of the three steam railroads in the Southeast services part of the area: the Romney, Hythe, and Dymchurch Railway.

RYE

68 miles southeast of London, 34 miles southwest of Dover.

Fodor's Choice ★ With cobbled streets and ancient timbered dwellings, Rye is an artist's dream. It was an important port town until the harbor silted up and the waters retreated more than 150 years ago; now the nearest harbor is 2 miles away. Virtually every building in the little town center is intriguingly historic. Rye is known for its many antiques stores and also for its sheer pleasantness. This place can be easily walked without a map, but the local tourist office has an interesting audio tour of the town as well as maps.

GETTING HERE AND AROUND

If you're driving to Rye, take the M20 to A2070. Trains from London's St. Pancras leave once an hour and take just over an hour, with a change in Ashford.

ESSENTIALS

Visitor Information Rye Tourist Information Centre. ✉ *The Old Sail Loft, Strand Quay* ☎ *01797/226696* 🌐 *www.ryesussex.co.uk.*

EXPLORING

FAMILY Fodor's Choice ★ **Bodiam Castle.** Immortalized in paintings, photographs, and films, Bodiam Castle (pronounced Boe-dee-um) rises out of the distance like a piece of medieval legend. From the outside it's one of Britain's most impressive castles, with turrets, battlements, a glassy moat (one of the very few still in use), and 2-foot-thick walls. However, once you cross the drawbridge to the interior there's little to see but ruins, albeit on an impressive scale. Built in 1385 to withstand a threatened French invasion, it was partly demolished during the English Civil War of 1642–46 and has been uninhabited ever since. Still, you can climb the intact towers to take in sweeping countryside views, and kids love running around the keep. The castle, 12 miles west of Rye, schedules organized activities for kids during school holidays. ✉ *Off B2244, Bodiam* ☎ *01580/830196* 🌐 *www.nationaltrust.org.uk/bodiamcastle* 🎟 *£10.*

Church of St. Mary the Virgin. At the top of the hill at the center of Rye, this classic English village church is more than 900 years old and encompasses a number of architectural styles. The turret clock dates to 1561 and still keeps excellent time. Its huge pendulum swings inside the church nave. **■TIP→ Climb the tower for amazing views of the surrounding area.** ✉ *Church Sq.* ☎ *01797/222318* 🌐 *www.ryeparish-church.org.uk* 🎟 *Free.*

Mermaid Street. One of the town's original cobbled streets, and perhaps its most quintessential view, heads steeply from the top of the hill to the former harbor. Its name supposedly came from the night a drunken sailor swore he heard a mermaid call him down to the sea (back when Rye was still a seaside town). The houses here date from between the medieval and Georgian periods; a much-photographed pair have the delightfully fanciful names "The House With Two Front Doors" and "The House Opposite." ⚠ **Be careful on your feet—the cobbles are very uneven.** ✉ *Rye.*

Ypres Tower. Down the hill past Church Square, Ypres Tower (pronounced "Wipers" by locals) was originally built as part of the town's fortifications (now all but disappeared) in 1249; it later served as a prison. A recent refurbishment has added an interesting exhibition on life here during the 1830s as a female prisoner in the "women's tower"; otherwise its local history museum holds a rather random collection of items, from smuggling bric-a-brac to shipbuilding mementos. A row of defensive cannons are fixed to the rampart overlooking the (disappointingly industrial) edge of Rye and several miles of flatland beyond. When they were installed, however, the canons pointed directly out to sea. ✉ *Gungarden* ☎ *01797/226728* 🌐 *www.ryemuseum.co.uk* 🎟 *£4.*

WHERE TO EAT

$$ SEAFOOD Fodor's Choice ★

🍴 **Webbes at the Fish Café.** One of Rye's most popular restaurants, where most of the seafood is caught nearby, occupies a brick building that dates to 1907, but the interior has been redone in a sleek, modern style. The ground-floor café has a relaxed atmosphere, and upstairs is a more formal dining room. **Known for:** top-quality seafood; local catches; great service. [$] *Average main: £15* ✉ *17 Tower St.* ☎ *01797/222226* 🌐 *www.webbesrestaurants.co.uk.*

$ CAFÉ FAMILY

🍴 **Whitehouse.** This friendly local café serves tasty baked goods, all-day breakfasts, and tapas-style light bites. Come for the Turkish eggs, poached with yogurt and dill; or if you're in the mood for something heartier, try the local Romney Marsh lamb with couscous and chickpeas. **Known for:** great coffee; healthful light bites; delicious cakes. [$] *Average main: £7* ✉ *24 High St.* ☎ *01797/224748* 🌐 *www.white-houserye.co.uk* ⏲ *No dinner.*

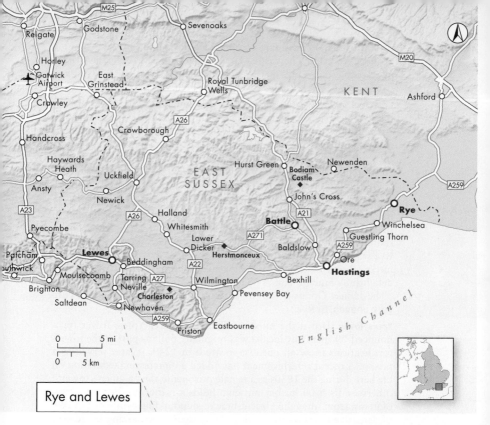

Rye and Lewes

WHERE TO STAY

$$ 🏨 **The George.** This attractive hotel on Rye's main road takes a boutique
HOTEL approach, cleverly mixing modern pieces with antiques in a sprawling
Georgian building. **Pros:** elegant room design; very central; historic
building. **Cons:** smaller rooms have tiny closets (or none at all); often
gets booked up for weddings in summer; if there's a wedding it can
be very noisy until late—and the management is bad at controlling
it. $ *Rooms from: £130* ✉ *98 High St.* ☎ *01797/222114* ⊕ *www.the-
georgeinrye.com* ➬ *24 rooms* ❐ *Free Breakfast.*

$$ 🏨 **The Mermaid Inn.** Steeped in a history of smuggling, the Mermaid is
HOTEL Rye's most historic inn; its sloping floors, oak beams, low ceilings, and
Fodor's Choice huge open hearth look like a film set, but it's all totally authentic. **Pros:**
★ dripping in atmosphere; good restaurant; 24-hour room service. **Cons:**
price is high for what's on offer; small bedrooms; allegedly haunted.
$ *Rooms from: £150* ✉ *Mermaid St.* ☎ *01797/223065* ⊕ *www.mer-
maidinn.com* ➬ *31 rooms* ❐ *Free Breakfast.*

SHOPPING

Britcher & Rivers. This traditional candy store is like something out of a
bygone age. Choose from row upon row of tall jars packed with every
imaginable type of candy, measured out into little paper bags. ✉ *89
High St.* ☎ *01797/227152.*

David Sharp Pottery. Like the distinctive ceramic name plaques that are a feature of the town? They are on offer at this sweet little shop. ⊠ *55 The Mint* ☎ *01797/222620.*

Glass Etc. A glorious collection of quality antique glass can be found in this colorful, friendly shop by the train station. ⊠ *18–22 Rope Walk* ☎ *01797/226600* ⊕ *www.decanterman.com.*

HASTINGS

3

12 miles southwest of Rye, 68 miles southeast of London.

In the 19th century Hastings became one of England's most popular spa resorts. Tall Victorian row houses painted in lemony hues still cover the cliffs around the deep blue sea, and the views from the hilltops are extraordinary. The pretty Old Town, on the east side of the city, offers a glimpse into the city's 16th-century past. Hastings has been through difficult times in recent decades, and the town developed a reputation as a rough place. It's currently trying hard to reinvent itself—a clutch of trendy new boutique bed-and-breakfasts have opened, as well as an important new art gallery—but the town center can still be quite rowdy after dark. Expect a handsome but tattered town, with a mix of traditional English seaside amusements: miniature golf, shops selling junk, fish-and-chips stands, and a rocky beach that stretches for miles.

GETTING HERE AND AROUND

If you're driving to Hastings from London, take A21. Trains travel to Hastings three or four times an hour from London's Victoria and St. Pancras stations. The journey takes between 1½ and 2 hours; some trains involve a change in Brighton or Ashford. The station, Hastings Warrior Square, is in the town center, within easy walking distance of most sights. National Express buses travel from London to Hastings about twice a day in around 3½ hours.

ESSENTIALS

Visitor Information Hastings Old Town Tourist Information Centre. ⊠ *Muriel Matters House, 2 Breeds Pl.* ☎ *01424/451111* ⊕ *www.visit1066country.com.*

EXPLORING

FAMILY **Hastings Castle.** Take a thrilling ride up the West Hill Cliff Railway from George Street precinct to the atmospheric ruins of the thousand-year-old fortress now known as Hastings Castle. It was built by William the Conqueror in 1066, before he had even won the Battle of Hastings and conquered England—making it the first Norman castle in the country. All that remains are mere fragments of the fortifications, some ancient walls, and a number of gloomy dungeons. Nevertheless, you get an excellent view of the chalky cliffs, the rocky coast, and the town below. You can buy a joint ticket that covers admission to Smuggler's Adventure and a nearby aquarium for £18 (£14 children). ⊠ *West Hill* ☎ *01424/422964* ⊡ *£5* ☉ *Closed Nov.–Mar.*

Fodor's Choice **The Jerwood Gallery.** A symbol of Hastings's slow but growing regenera-
★ tion after decades of neglect, this new exhibition space in the Old Town became one of the most talked-about new galleries outside London

when it opened in the early 2010s. The collection includes works by Walter Sickert, Stephen Lowry, and Augustus John. Temporary exhibitions change every couple of months. The glazed-tile building on the seafront was designed to reflect the row of distinctive old, blackened fishing sheds it sits alongside. ■ **TIP→ On the first Tuesday of every month the gallery stays open until 8 pm, with entry free beginning at 4.** ✉ *Rock-a-Nore Rd.* ☎ *01424/728377* 🌐 *www.jerwoodgallery.org* 🎟 *£9* 🕓 *Closed Mon. except bank holidays.*

WHERE TO EAT

$ SEAFOOD

🍴 **Blue Dolphin.** The crowds line up all day to make their way into this small fish-and-chips shop just off the seafront, down near the fish shacks. Although the decor is humble, reviewers consistently rank the battered fish and huge plates of double-cooked chips (chunky fries) as among the best in the country. **Known for:** known across Britain; beachside location; proper, traditional fish-and-chips. [$] *Average main: £6* ✉ *61 High St.* ☎ *01424/547150* 🕓 *No dinner.*

$ SEAFOOD FAMILY

🍴 **White's Seafood & Steak Bar.** Great seafood in simple, unpretentious surroundings is the order of the day at this popular place in Hastings Old Town. Fresh-as-can-be seafood, huge platters of shellfish, creamy fish pies, or delicious plates of fish-and-chips are the epitome of unfussy local flavor. **Known for:** huge seafood platters; fresh catch of the day; hot-rock cooking at your table. [$] *Average main: £14* ✉ *44-45 George St.* ☎ *01424/719846* 🌐 *www.whitesbar.co.uk.*

WHERE TO STAY

$ B&B/INN

🏨 **The Cloudesley.** No TVs and a general Zen vibe at this boutique B&B in the quieter St. Leonard's district of Hastings make it a thoroughly relaxing place to stay. **Pros:** oasis of calm; great spa treatments; impeccable eco credentials. **Cons:** chill vibe won't be for everyone; two-night minimum at certain times; 20-minute walk into Hastings. [$] *Rooms from: £95* ✉ *7 Cloudesley Rd., St. Leonards-on-Sea* ☎ *01424/722759, 07507/000148* 🌐 *www.thecloudesley.co.uk* 🛏 *5 rooms* 🍽 *Free Breakfast.*

$$ B&B/INN Fodor'sChoice ★

🏨 **Swan House.** Originally a bakery, this extraordinary 15th-century building has been beautifully converted into an elegant and welcoming B&B, where the light and airy guest rooms are decorated in neutral modern tones and retain original features such as exposed wood beams. **Pros:** beautiful, historic building; welcoming hosts; delicious breakfasts. **Cons:** some bathrooms have shower only; two-night minimum on summer weekends; gets booked up. [$] *Rooms from: £120* ✉ *1 Hill St.* ☎ *01424/430014* 🌐 *www.swanhousehastings.co.uk* 🛏 *27 rooms* 🍽 *Free Breakfast.*

BATTLE

7 miles northwest of Hastings, 61 miles southeast of London.

Battle is the actual site of the crucial Battle of Hastings, at which, on October 14, 1066, William of Normandy and his army trounced King Harold's Anglo-Saxon army. Today it's a sweet, quiet town and a favorite of history buffs.

GETTING HERE AND AROUND

Southeastern trains arrive from London's Charing Cross Station every half hour. The journey takes between 1½ and 2 hours. National Express buses travel once daily in the early evening from London's Victoria Coach Station. The trip takes around 2½ hours.

ESSENTIALS

Visitor Information Battle Information Point. ✉ *Yesterdays World, 89–90 High St.* ☎ *01797/229049* 🌐 *www.visit1066country.com.*

EXPLORING

Battle Abbey. This great Benedictine abbey was erected by William the Conqueror on the site of the Battle of Hastings—one of the most decisive turning points in English history and the last time the country was successfully invaded. A memorial stone marks the high altar, which in turn was supposedly laid on the spot where Harold II, the last Saxon king, was killed. All of this meant little to Henry VIII, who didn't spare the building from his violent dissolution of the monasteries. Today the abbey is just a ruin, but films and interactive exhibits help bring it all to life. You can also take the mile-long walk around the edge of the battlefield and see the remains of the abbey's former outbuildings. ✉ *High St.* ☎ *01424/775705* 🌐 *www.english-heritage.org.uk/battleabbey* 🎟 *£11.50* ⏲ *Closed weekdays early Nov.–mid-Feb., and Mon. and Tues. mid-Feb.–Mar.*

FAMILY
Fodor's Choice ★

Herstmonceux. A banner waving from one tower and a glassy moat crossed by what was once a drawbridge—this fairy-tale castle has everything except knights in shining armor. The redbrick structure was originally built by Sir Roger Fiennes (ancestor of actor Ralph Fiennes) in 1444, although it was altered in the Elizabethan age and again early in the 20th century after it had largely fallen to ruin. Canadian Queen's University owns the castle, so only part of it is open for guided tours, usually once or twice a day, except Saturday; call in advance to schedule a tour. (You can book a tour on the day, too, subject to availability). Highlights include the magnificent ballroom, a medieval room, and the stunning Elizabethan-era staircase. Explore the formal walled garden, lily-covered lakes, and miles of woodland—the perfect place for a picnic on a sunny afternoon. There's a hands-on science center for kids. When school isn't in session, the castle rents out its small, plain guest rooms from £40 per night. On the last weekend of August, the castle hosts a large **Medieval Festival**, complete with jousting, falconry shows, and around 100 craft stalls. The castle is 8 miles southwest of Battle. ✉ *Wartling Rd., Herstmonceux* ☎ *01323/833816* 🌐 *www.herstmonceux-castle.com* 🎟 *Castle, grounds, and science center £13; grounds only £6.50; castle tours £3* ⏲ *Closed Nov.–Feb.*

WHERE TO EAT

$$$$
MODERN FRENCH
Fodor's Choice ★

🍴 **Sundial.** A 17th-century brick farmhouse with wood-beamed ceilings and lovely views of the South Downs is home to an excellent Modern French restaurant. The imaginative three-course set menus may include turbot with citronated butter, or beef fillet with a sauce of port and shallot. **Known for:** sophisticated Modern French cooking; lovely views; fabulous desserts. [$] *Average main: £45* ✉ *Gardner St., Herstmonceux* ☎ *01323/832217* 🌐 *www.sundialrestaurant.co.uk* ⏲ *Closed Mon. No dinner Sun.*

LEWES

24 miles east of Battle, 8 miles northeast of Brighton, 54 miles south of London.

Fodor's Choice ★ The town nearest to the celebrated Glyndebourne Opera House, Lewes is so rich in history that the Council for British Archaeology has named it one of the 50 most important English towns. A walk is the best way to appreciate its steep streets and appealing jumble of building styles and materials—flint, stone, brick, tile—and the secret lanes (called "twittens") behind the castle, with their huge beeches. Here and there are smart antiques shops, good eateries, and secondhand-book dealers. Most of the buildings in the center date to the 18th and 19th centuries.

Something about this town has always attracted rebels. It was once the home of Thomas Paine (1737–1809), whose pamphlet *Common Sense* advocated that the American colonies break with Britain. It was also favored by Virginia Woolf and the Bloomsbury Group, early-20th-century countercultural artistic innovators.

Today Lewes's beauty and proximity to London mean that the counter-culture crew can't really afford to live here anymore, but its rebel soul still peeks through, particularly on Guy Fawkes Night (November 5), the anniversary of Fawkes's foiled attempt to blow up the Houses of Parliament in 1605. Flaming tar barrels are rolled down High Street and into the River Ouse; costumed processions fill the streets.

GETTING HERE AND AROUND

If you're driving to Lewes from London, take the M23 south. The journey takes around an hour and 45 minutes. Southern trains run direct to Lewes from Victoria Station about three times an hour; the journey takes an hour. There's no easy way to get to Lewes by bus; you need to take a National Express or Megabus to Brighton and change to a regional bus line.

ESSENTIALS

Visitor Information Lewes Tourist Information Centre. ⊠ *187 High St.* ☎ *01273/483448* ⊕ *www.lewes.co.uk.*

EXPLORING

FAMILY **Anne of Cleves House.** This 16th-century structure, a fragile-looking, timber-frame building, holds a small collection of Sussex ironwork and other items of local interest, such as Sussex pottery. The house was part of Anne of Cleves's divorce settlement from Henry VIII, although she never lived in it. There are medieval dress-up clothes for kids. To get to the house, walk down steep, cobbled Keere Street, past lovely Grange Gardens, to Southover High Street. ⊠ *52 Southover High St.* ☎ *01273/474610* ⊕ *www.sussexpast.co.uk/anneofcleves* ⊠ *£6.10; combined ticket with Lewes Castle £12.50.*

Fodor's Choice ★ **Charleston.** Art and life mixed at Charleston, the farmhouse Vanessa Bell—sister of Virginia Woolf—bought in 1916 and fancifully decorated, along with Duncan Grant (who lived here until 1978). The house became a refuge for the writers and artists of the Bloomsbury Group. On display are colorful ceramics and textiles of the Omega Workshop—in which Bell and Grant participated—and paintings by Picasso and

Renoir, as well as by Bell and Grant themselves. You view the house on a guided tour except on Sunday, when you can wander freely. On a handful of dates there's a special 80-minute themed tour (£13.50) that focuses on a different aspect of Charleston's history, such as the great influence French culture had on the Bloomsbury Group. There also are 30-minute family tours on certain dates. (Schedules are listed on the website.) The house isn't suitable for those with mobility problems, although reduced-price ground-floor-only tickets are available. ✉ *Off A27, 7 miles east of Lewes, Firle* ☎ *01323/811626* 🌐 *www.charleston.org.uk* 🎫 *£14.50* 🕒 *Closed late Oct.–Feb., and Mon. and Tues.*

Lewes Castle. High above the valley of the River Ouse stand the majestic ruins of Lewes Castle, begun in 1100 by one of the country's Norman conquerors and completed 300 years later. The castle's barbican holds a small museum with archaeology collections, a changing temporary exhibition gallery, and a bookshop. There are panoramic views of the town and countryside. ✉ *169 High St.* ☎ *01273/486290* 🌐 *www.sussexpast.co.uk/properties-to-discover/lewes-castle* 🎫 *£8; combined ticket with Anne of Cleves House £12.50* 🕒 *Closed Mon. in Jan.*

WHERE TO EAT

$ BRITISH 🍴 **The Limetree Kitchen.** Elegant, imaginative menus and a commitment to locally sourced produce is at the heart of this popular restaurant in the center of Lewes. Menus are heavily influenced by what's in season, with just a few, well-chosen options—tempura of Devonishire hake, or local rib-eye steak with parsley and shallot. **Known for:** excellent value fixed-price menus; seasonal menus; locally sourced produce. [$] *Average main: £11* ✉ *14 Station St.* ☎ *01273 /478636* 🌐 *www.limetreekitchen.co.uk* 🕒 *Closed Mon. and Tues.*

$ CAFÉ 🍴 **Robson's of Lewes.** Good coffee, fresh produce, and delicious pastries make this coffee shop one of the best places in Lewes to drop by for an afternoon pick-me-up. A light-filled space with wood floors and simple tables creates a pleasant, casual spot to enjoy a cup of coffee with breakfast, a scone, or a light sandwich or salad lunch. **Known for:** good coffee; light bites; good to-go options. [$] *Average main: £6* ✉ *22A High St.* ☎ *01273/480654* 🌐 *www.robsonsoflewes.co.uk* 🕒 *No dinner.*

WHERE TO STAY

$$$ B&B/INN 🏨 **Horsted Place.** On 1,100 acres, this luxurious Victorian manor house was built as a private home in 1850; it was owned by a friend of the current queen until the 1980s, and she was a regular visitor. **Pros:** historic building; amazing architecture; lovely gardens. **Cons:** too formal for some; creaky floors bother light sleepers; the English manor style doesn't come cheap. [$] *Rooms from: £200* ✉ *Horsted Pond La., Off A26, Little Horsted* ☎ *01825/750581* 🌐 *www.horstedplace.co.uk* 🛏 *20 rooms* 🍽 *Free Breakfast.*

$$ B&B/INN 🏨 **The Ram Inn.** Roaring fires, cozy rooms, and friendly locals give this 500-year-old inn its wonderful feeling of old-world authenticity. **Pros:** proper village pub atmosphere; good food; cozy, well-designed rooms. **Cons:** you need a car to get here from Lewes; those historic walls are a bit thin; rooms over the bar can be noisy. [$] *Rooms from:*

£100 ⊠ The Street, West Firle ☎ *01273/858222* ⊕ *www.raminn.co.uk* ⤴ *4 rooms* ⟅◎⟆ *Free Breakfast.*

NIGHTLIFE AND PERFORMING ARTS

NIGHTLIFE

Brewers' Arms. On High Street, this is a good pub with a friendly crowd. The half-timbered building dates from 1906, but a pub has stood on this spot since the 16th century. ⊠ *91 High St.* ☎ *01273/475524* ⊕ *www. brewersarmslewes.co.uk.*

King's Head. A traditional pub, the King's Head has a good menu with locally sourced fish and meat dishes. ⊠ *9 Southover High St.* ☎ *01273/475951* ⊕ *www.kingsheadlewes.co.uk.*

PERFORMING ARTS

Fodor's Choice ★ **Glyndebourne Opera House.** Nestled beneath the Downs, this world-famous opera house combines first-class productions, a state-of-the-art auditorium, and a beautiful setting. Tickets are *very* expensive (the cheapest start at around £85, though for many productions it's twice that, rising to around £250) and you have to book months in advance. But it's worth every penny to aficionados, who traditionally wear evening dress and bring a hamper to picnic in the grounds The main season runs from mid-May to the end of August. ■TIP→ **If you can't afford a seat, there are other ways to see the show: standing-room tickets cost £10, there are nights when adults under 30 pay just £30, and a handful of performances every year are broadcast live to U.K. cinemas.** The Glyndebourne Touring Company performs here in October, when seats are cheaper. Glyndebourne is 3 miles east of Lewes off B2192. ⊠ *New Rd., off A26, Ringmer* ☎ *01273/813813* ⊕ *www.glyndebourne.com.*

SHOPPING

Cliffe Antiques Centre. This shop carries a fine mix of vintage English prints, estate jewelry, and art at reasonable prices. ⊠ *47 Cliffe High St.* ☎ *01273/473266* ⊕ *www.cliffeantiquescentre.co.uk.*

The Fifteenth Century Bookshop. A wide collection of rare and vintage books can be found at this ancient, timber-framed building in the center of Lewes. Antique children's books are a specialty. ⊠ *99–100 High St.* ☎ *01273/474160* ⊕ *www.oldenyoungbooks.co.uk.*

Louis Potts & Co. From frivolous knickkacks to full-on formal dining sets, Louis Potts specializes in stylish bone china and glassware. ⊠ *43 Cliffe High St.* ☎ *01273/472240* ⊕ *www.louispotts.com.*

BRIGHTON AND THE SUSSEX COAST

The self-proclaimed belle of the coast, Brighton is upbeat, funky, and endlessly entertaining. Outside town the soft green downs of Sussex and Surrey hold stately homes you can visit, including Arundel Castle and Petworth House. Along the way, you'll discover the largest Roman villa in Britain, the bustling city of Guildford, and Chichester, whose cathedral is a poem in stone.

BRIGHTON

9 miles southwest of Lewes, 54 miles south of London.

Fodor's Choice ★ For more than 200 years, Brighton has been England's most interesting seaside city, and today it's more vibrant, eccentric, and cosmopolitan than ever. A rich cultural mix—Regency architecture, specialty shops, sidewalk cafés, lively arts, and a flourishing gay scene—makes it unique and unpredictable.

In 1750 physician Richard Russell published a book recommending seawater treatment for glandular diseases. The fashionable world flocked to Brighton to take Dr. Russell's "cure," and sea bathing became a popular pastime. Few places in the south of England were better for it, since Brighton's broad beach of smooth pebbles stretches as far as the eye can see. It's been popular with sunbathers ever since.

The next windfall for the town was the arrival of the Prince of Wales (later George IV). "Prinny," as he was called, created the Royal Pavilion, a mock-Asian pleasure palace that attracted London society. This triggered a wave of villa building, and today the elegant terraces of Regency houses are among the town's greatest attractions. The coming of the railway set the seal on Brighton's popularity: the *Brighton Belle* brought Londoners to the coast in an hour.

Londoners still flock to Brighton. Add them to the many local university students, and you have a trendy, young, laid-back city that does, occasionally, burst at its own seams. Property values have skyrocketed, but all visitors may notice is the good shopping and restaurants, attractive (if pebbly) beach, and wild nightlife. Brighton is also the place to go if you're looking for hotels with offbeat design and party nights.

GETTING HERE AND AROUND

Southeastern trains leave from London's Victoria and London Bridge stations several times an hour. The journey takes about an hour, and the trains stop at Gatwick Airport. Brighton-bound National Express and Megabus buses depart from London's Victoria Coach Station every half hour. The trip takes between 2½ and 3 hours. By car from London, head to Brighton on the M23/A23. The journey should take about 1½ hours.

Brighton (and the adjacent Hove) sprawls in all directions, but the part of interest to travelers is fairly compact. None of the sights is more than a 10-minute walk from the train station. You can pick up a town map at the station. City Sightseeing has a hop-on, hop-off tour bus that leaves Brighton Pier every 20 to 30 minutes. It operates May through mid-September (plus weekends, March and April) and costs £13.

ESSENTIALS

Visitor and Tour Information Brighton Visitor Information Centre. ✉ *The Brighton Centre, King's Rd.* ☎ *01273/290337* ⊕ *www.visitbrighton.com.* **City Sightseeing.** ☎ *01273/886200* ⊕ *www.city-sightseeing.com.*

EXPLORING

Brighton Beach. Brighton's most iconic landmark is its famous beach, which sweeps smoothly from one end of town to the other. In summer sunbathers, swimmers, and hawkers selling ice cream and toys pack

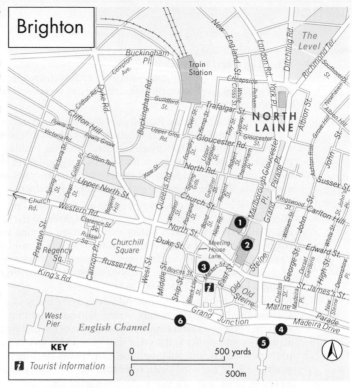

the shore; in winter people stroll at the water's stormy edge, walking their dogs and searching for seashells. The water is bracingly cold, and the beach is covered in a thick blanket of large, smooth pebbles (615 billion of them, according to the tourism office). ■TIP➜ **Bring a pair of rubber swimming shoes if you're taking a dip—the stones are hard on bare feet.** **Amenities:** food and drink; lifeguards; toilets; parking (fee); water sports. **Best for:** partiers; sunset; swimming. ⊠ *Marine Parade.*

Brighton Museum and Art Gallery. The grounds of the Royal Pavilion contain this museum, in a former stable block designed for the Prince Regent (1762–1830), son of George III. The museum has particularly interesting art nouveau and art deco collections. Look out for a tiny replica of Salvador Dalí's famous sofa in the shape of Mae West's lips. The Fashion & Style Gallery has clothes from the Regency period to the present day, and the Performance gallery has a collection of masks, puppets, and other theatrical curiosities. ⊠ *Royal Pavilion, Church St.* ☎ *0300/029–0900* ⊕ *brightonmuseums.org.uk/brighton* ▨ *£5.50* ⊗ *Closed Mon. except holidays.*

FAMILY **Brighton Pier.** Opened in 1899, the pier is an amusement park set above the sea. In the early 20th century it had a music hall and entertainment; today it has roller coasters and other carnival rides, as well as game arcades, clairvoyants, candy stores, and greasy-food stalls. In summer it's packed with children by day and (on weekends) teenagers by night. There's no fee to enter the pier, although the individual kiosks have their own charges. Alternatively, a wristband (£20 adults, £12 children) allows blanket entry, which can amount to a big savings if you're making the rounds of what's on offer. The skeletal shadow of a pier you can see off in the water is all that's left of the old West Pier. ⊠ *Madeira Dr.* ☎ *01273/609361* ⊕ *www. brightonpier.co.uk.*

FAMILY
Fodor'sChoice
★

i360. Designed by the same people who made the London Eye, this circular viewing platform ascends 531 feet into the air, allowing an incredible view of the coastline and the South Downs. On clear days you can see the Isle of Wight. The ride (or "flight" as the British Airways–sponsored company insists on calling it) lasts about 25 minutes. Booking is advisable, especially in summer; it's also 10% cheaper if you reserve online. Check out the website for special packages that include dinner. i360 stays open in all weather, other than exceptionally strong winds. It's so peaceful inside the doughnut-shaped pod, you'd never guess the storm that raged over the £43 million structure, ahead of its eventual opening in 2016. Locals worried it would ruin the character of the promenade. After you take in the sweeping view, you've got the leisurely descent back to street level to decide if you agree with them. ⊠ *Brighton Beach, Lower King's Rd.* ☎ *0337/720360* ⊕ *www.britishairwaysi360.com* ⊠ *£16.*

The Lanes. This maze of tiny alleys and passageways was once the home of fishermen and their families. Closed to vehicular traffic, the area's narrow cobbled streets are filled with interesting restaurants, boutiques, and antiques shops. Fish and seafood restaurants line the heart of the Lanes, at Market Street and Market Square. ⊠ *Bordered by West, North, East, and Prince Albert Sts.*

Fodor'sChoice
★

Royal Pavilion. The city's most remarkable building is this delightfully over-the-top domed and pinnacled fantasy. Built as a simple seaside villa in the fashionable classical style of 1787 by architect Henry Holland, the Pavilion was rebuilt between 1815 and 1822 by John Nash for the Prince Regent (later George IV). The result was an exotic, foppish Eastern design with opulent Chinese interiors. The two great set pieces are the **Music Room,** styled in the form of a Chinese pavilion, and the **Banqueting Room,** with its enormous flying-dragon "gasolier," or gaslight chandelier, a revolutionary invention in the early 19th century. The gardens, too, have been restored to Regency splendor, following John Nash's naturalistic design of 1826. For an elegant time-out, a tearoom serves snacks and light meals. ⊠ *Old Steine* ☎ *03000/290900* ⊕ *brightonmuseums.org.uk/royalpavilion* ⊠ *£14.*

WHERE TO EAT

$
CAFÉ
FAMILY
Fodor'sChoice
★

✗ **Gelato Gusto.** No seaside town would be complete without an ice-cream store, and the delicious, homemade, artisanal gelato on sale here is a real treat. Everything is made fresh daily; try the lemon-meringue-pie flavor, or maybe a scoop of the delicious sea-salt caramel. **Known for:** delicious Italian ice cream; indulgent desserts; essential part of the

CLOSE UP

Brighton and the Regent

The term "Regency" comes from the last 10 years of the reign of George III (1811–20), who was deemed unfit to rule because of his mental problems. Real power was officially given to the Prince of Wales, also known as the Prince Regent, who became King George IV and ruled until his death in 1830.

Throughout his regency, George spent grand sums indulging his flamboyant tastes in architecture and interior decorating—while failing in affairs of state.

The distinctive architecture of the Royal Pavilion is a prime, if extreme, example of the Regency style, popularized by architect John Nash (1752–1835) in the early part of the 19th century. The style is characterized by a diversity of influences—French, Greek, Italian, Persian, Japanese, Chinese, Roman, Indian—you name it. Nash was George IV's favorite architect, beloved for his interest in Indian and Asian art and for his neoclassical designs, as evidenced in his other most famous work—Regent's Park and its terraces in London.

Brighton seafront experience. $ *Average main: £6* ✉ *2 Gardner St.* ☎ *01273/673402* ⊕ *www.gelatogusto.com.*

$$$
SEAFOOD
Fodor's Choice
★

✕ **Riddle & Finns at the Lanes.** White tiles, bare metal tables, and sparkling chandeliers set the tone as soon as you walk through the door of this casually elegant restaurant. The house specialty is oysters, fresh and sustainably sourced, served with or without a tankard of black velvet (champagne and Guinness) on the side. **Known for:** romantic atmosphere; superfresh seafood; elegance in simplicity. $ *Average main: £20* ✉ *12B Meeting House La.* ☎ *01273/323008* ⊕ *www.riddleandfinns.co.uk.*

$$
VEGETARIAN

✕ **Terre à Terre.** This inspiring vegetarian restaurant is incredibly popular, so come early for a light lunch or later for a more sophisticated evening meal. Dishes have a pan-Asian influence, so you may have some "KFC" (Korean fried cauliflower) with sweet-and-sour sesame, or battered halloumi with the pleasingly tongue-twistery side of lemony Yemeni relish. **Known for:** Asian-influenced cooking; excellent vegetarian dishes; great wine list. $ *Average main: £16* ✉ *71 East St.* ☎ *01273/729051* ⊕ *www.terreaterre.co.uk.*

$
EASTERN
EUROPEAN

✕ **The Witchez.** Owned by talented graphic designers and photo artists, the Witchez Photo Design Cafe Bar is certainly a unique concept—delicious German- and Polish-influenced comfort food served in the middle of a design studio (which means you can have your passport photo taken while you wait—why not?). Never mind the weirdness of the concept; this place is a whole lot of fun, and the food is good to boot—schnitzel, pierogi, German sausage, potato dumplings—and there's also a range of pizzas. **Known for:** unique concept; tasty German and Polish dishes; great atmosphere. $ *Average main: £13* ✉ *16 Marine Parade* ☎ *01273/673652.*

WHERE TO STAY

$
B&B/INN
Fodor's Choice
★
🛏 **Brightonwave.** Chic and sleek, this hotel off the seafront but near Brighton Pier is all about relaxation. **Pros:** big, comfy beds; beautiful design; lovely hosts. **Cons:** rooms on the small side; few extras; limited parking. Ⓢ *Rooms from: £95* ✉ *10 Madeira Pl,* ☎ *01273/676794* ⊕ *www.brightonwave.com* ⌨ *8 rooms* �‖ *Free Breakfast.*

$$
HOTEL
Fodor's Choice
★
🛏 **Drakes.** It's easy to miss the low-key sign for this elegant, modern hotel tucked away amid the frilly houses on Marine Parade—but it's worth the trouble of finding, because everything is cool, calm, and sleekly designed. **Pros:** attention to detail; well-designed bathrooms; excellent restaurant. **Cons:** two-night minimum on weekends; breakfast is extra; limited parking. Ⓢ *Rooms from: £120* ✉ *43–44 Marine Parade* ☎ *01273/696934* ⊕ *www.drakesofbrighton.com* ⌨ *20 rooms* �‖ *No meals.*

$$
HOTEL
🛏 **Grand Brighton.** The city's most famous hotel, this seafront landmark is a huge, Victorian wedding cake of a building dating from 1864. **Pros:** as grand as its name; lovely sea views; luxurious spa. **Cons:** a bit impersonal; prices can rise sharply on weekends; cheaper rooms are small. Ⓢ *Rooms from: £110* ✉ *97–99 Kings Rd.* ☎ *01273/224300* ⊕ *www.grandbrighton.co.uk* ⌨ *203 rooms* �‖ *Free Breakfast.*

$
HOTEL
🛏 **Granville Hotel.** Three grand Victorian buildings facing the sea make up this hotel near Regency Square and i360. **Pros:** creative design; friendly staff; rambunctious atmosphere. **Cons:** some may find the rooms too quirky; sea-facing rooms can be noisy; some rooms are on the small side. Ⓢ *Rooms from: £88* ✉ *124 King's Rd.* ☎ *01273/326302* ⊕ *www.granvillehotel.co.uk* ⌨ *24 rooms* �‖ *Free Breakfast.*

$$
HOTEL
🛏 **Hotel du Vin.** In the Lanes area, this outpost of a snazzy boutique chain has chic, modern rooms. **Pros:** gorgeous rooms; comfortable beds; excellent restaurant. **Cons:** bar can get crowded; big price fluctuations in summer; often gets booked up. Ⓢ *Rooms from: £109* ✉ *Ship St.* ☎ *0844/364251* ⊕ *www.hotelduvin.com* ⌨ *43 rooms* �‖ *Free Breakfast.*

$$
HOTEL
🛏 **Hotel Pelirocco.** Here the imaginations of designers have been given free rein, and the result is a vicarious romp through pop culture and rock and roll. **Pros:** quirky design; laid-back atmosphere; near the beach. **Cons:** design is often form-over-function; no restaurant; to say the look is not for everyone is an understatement. Ⓢ *Rooms from: £105* ✉ *10 Regency Sq.* ☎ *01273/327055* ⊕ *www.hotelpelirocco.co.uk* ⌨ *19 rooms* �‖ *Breakfast.*

$
B&B/INN
🛏 **Nineteen Brighton.** A calm oasis, this guesthouse is filled with contemporary art and designer accessories. **Pros:** innovative design; close to the beach; three nights for the price of two. **Cons:** not on the nicest street; two-night minimum on weekends; healthy breakfasts not for those who want to indulge. Ⓢ *Rooms from: £95* ✉ *19 Broad St.* ☎ *01273/675529* ⊕ *www.nineteenbrighton.com* ⌨ *7 rooms* �‖ *Free Breakfast.*

NIGHTLIFE

Patterns. One of Brighton's foremost venues, in an art deco building east of Brighton Pier, Patterns is the latest incarnation of a string of popular nightclubs that have occupied this spot. Expect to hear live acts during the week (including a regular local slot—this being Brighton, the quality is generally quite high) and techno and house on the weekend. ✉ *10 Marine Parade* ☎ *01273/894777* ⊕ *www.patternsbrighton.com.*

The Plotting Parlour. This ultrahip nightclub on Stein Street feels like a glamorous speakeasy. Cocktails are a specialty, and the bar staff certainly know what they're doing (try the fierce chili martini). It's extremely popular with the cooler brand of local partygoer, and fabulously good fun to boot. ⊠ *6 Steine St.* ☎ *01273/621238* ⊕ *brighton.shooshh.com.*

Proud Cabaret. A mixture of vintage and avant-garde cabaret and burlesque is on offer at this stylish nightclub, with a distinct 1920s flavor. Booking is advisable. ⊠ *83 St. Georges Rd.* ☎ *01273/605789* ⊕ *www. brightoncabaret.com.*

SHOPPING

Colin Page Antiquarian Books. At the western edge of the Lanes, Colin Page stocks a wealth of antiquarian and secondhand books at all prices. ⊠ *36 Duke St., The Lanes* ☎ *01273/325954.*

Curiouser & Curiouser and The Great Frog. A two-for-one of funky jewelry stores sharing the same premises: Curiouser & Curiouser made several pieces of jewelry for the Harry Potter movies, and the shop is filled with unique handmade pieces; the Great Frog specializes in jewelry with a rock 'n' roll theme (the owners claim to be the creators of the original skull ring). ⊠ *2 Sydney St.* ☎ *01273/673120* ⊕ *www.curiousersilverjewellery.co.uk.*

The Lanes. Brighton's main shopping area is the Lanes, especially for antiques or jewelry. It also has clothing boutiques, coffee shops, and pubs. ⊠ *Brighton.*

North Laine. Across North Street from the Lanes lies the North Laine, a network of narrow streets full of little stores. They're less glossy than those in the Lanes, but are fun, funky, and exotic. ⊠ *Brighton.*

Royal Pavilion Shop. Next door to the Royal Pavilion, this shop carries well-designed toys, trinkets, books, and cards, all with a loose Regency theme. There are also high-quality fabrics, wallpapers, and ceramics based on material in the pavilion itself. ⊠ *4–5 Pavilion Bldgs.* ☎ *01273/292798.*

ARUNDEL

23 miles west of Brighton, 60 miles south of London.

The little hilltop town of Arundel is dominated by its great castle, the much-restored home of the dukes of Norfolk for more than 700 years, and an imposing neo-Gothic Roman Catholic cathedral (the duke is Britain's leading Catholic peer). The town itself is full of interesting old buildings and well worth a stroll.

GETTING HERE AND AROUND

Arundel is on the A27, about a two-hour drive south of central London. Trains from London's Victoria Station leave every half hour and take 1½ hours. No direct buses run from London, but you can take a National Express bus to Worthing or Chichester and change to a local bus to Arundel, though that journey could easily take five hours.

ESSENTIALS

Visitor Information Arundel Visitor Information Centre. ⊠ *Crown Yard, River Rd.* ☎ *01903/882419* ⊕ *www.sussexbythesea.com.*

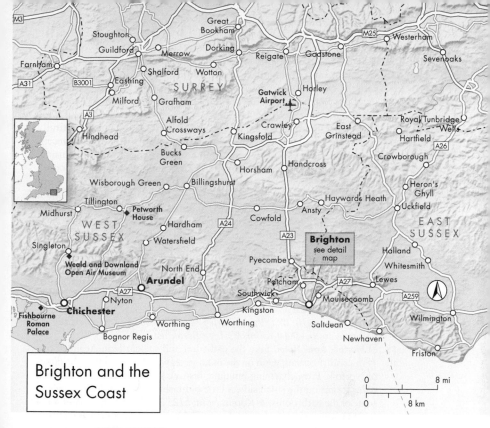

Brighton and the
Sussex Coast

EXPLORING

FAMILY
Fodor's Choice
★

Arundel Castle. You've probably already seen Arundel Castle without knowing it, at least on screen. Its striking resemblence to Windsor means that it's frequently used as a stand-in for its more famous cousin in movies and television. Begun in the 11th century, this vast castle remains rich with the history of the Fitzalan and Howard families and with paintings by Van Dyck, Gainsborough, and Reynolds. During the 18th century and in the Victorian era it was reconstructed in the fashionable Gothic style—although the keep, rising from its conical mound, is as old as the original castle (climb its 130 steps for great views of the River Arun), and the barbican and the Barons' Hall date from the 13th century. Among the treasures are the rosary beads and prayer book used by Mary, Queen of Scots, in preparing for her execution. The newly formal garden, redesigned fairly recently, is a triumph of order and beauty. Special events happen year-round, including a week of jousting, usually in late July. (Ticket prices rise slightly during event weeks). Although the castle's ceremonial entrance is at the top of High Street, you enter at the bottom, close to the parking lot. ✉ *Mill Rd.* ☎ *01903/882173* ⊕ *www.arundelcastle.org* ✑ *£22* ⊘ *Closed early-Nov.–late Mar. and Mon. except holidays.*

WHERE TO EAT

$ CAFÉ 🍴 **Berties of Arundel.** This place is a real little charmer. A lovely, old-school café in the center of Arundel, Berties serves delicious sandwiches, panini, light lunches, and homemade cakes. **Known for:** old-school vibe; excellent homemade cakes; friendly staff. [$] *Average main: £7* ✉ *31 Tarrant St.* ☎ *01903/882110.*

$$$$ BRITISH Fodor's Choice ★ 🍴 **The Town House.** This small but elegant restaurant in a beautifully converted Regency town house (look above you—the dining room ceiling is quite something) serves top-notch British and European cuisine. The fixed-price lunch and dinner menus change regularly but could include roast breast of local partridge with red-currant jelly, or trout with a chive butter sauce. **Known for:** local meats and fish; seasonal menus; beautiful dining room. [$] *Average main: £30* ✉ *65 High St.* ☎ *01903/883847* 🌐 *www.thetownhouse.co.uk.*

WHERE TO STAY

$$$$ HOTEL Fodor's Choice ★ 🏨 **Amberley Castle.** Enter under the portcullis of this genuine medieval castle, where across the moat, present-day luxury dominates. **Pros:** sleep in a real castle; lovely gardens and grounds; good afternoon tea. **Cons:** you have to dress up for dinner; a little way from Arundel town; almost have to be as rich as an actual king to stay here. [$] *Rooms from: £268* ✉ *Bury Hill, Off B2139, Amberley* ☎ *01798/831992* 🌐 *www.amberleycastle.co.uk* 🛏 *19 rooms* 🍽 *Free Breakfast.*

$$ HOTEL 🏨 **Norfolk Arms Hotel.** Like the cathedral and the castle in Arundel, this 18th-century coaching inn on the main street was built by one of the dukes of Norfolk. **Pros:** charming building; historic setting; friendly staff. **Cons:** older rooms on the small side; a little old-fashioned; bold decor choice in some of the bathrooms. [$] *Rooms from: £125* ✉ *22 High St.* ☎ *0844/855-9101* 🌐 *www.norfolkarmshotel.com* 🛏 *34 rooms* 🍽 *Free Breakfast.*

CHICHESTER

10 miles west of Arundel, 66 miles southwest of London.

The Romans founded Chichester, the capital city of West Sussex, on the low-lying plains between the wooded South Downs and the sea. The city walls and major streets follow the original Roman plan. This cathedral town, a good base for exploring the area, is a well-respected theatrical hub, with a reputation for attracting good acting talent during its summer repertory season. North of town is Petworth House, one of the region's finest stately homes.

GETTING HERE AND AROUND

From London, take A3 south and follow exit signs for Chichester. The journey takes slightly more than two hours; much of it is on smaller highways. Southern trains run to Chichester four times an hour from Victoria Station, with a travel time of between 1½ and 2 hours. Half involve a train from Brighton. Buses leave from London's Victoria Coach Station a handful of times per day and take between 3½ and 4 hours.

ESSENTIALS

Visitor Information Chichester Tourist Information Centre. ✉ *The Novium, Tower St.* ☎ *01243/775888* 🌐 *www.visitchichester.org.*

EXPLORING

Fodor's Choice ★ **Chichester Cathedral.** Standing on Roman foundations, 900-year-old Chichester Cathedral has a glass panel that reveals Roman mosaics uncovered during restorations. Other treasures include the wonderful Saxon limestone reliefs of the raising of Lazarus and Christ arriving in Bethany, both in the choir area. Among the outstanding contemporary artworks are a stained-glass window by Marc Chagall and a colorful tapestry by John Piper. Free guided tours begin every day except Sunday at 11:15 and 2:30. You can also prebook tours that concentrate on subjects including the English Civil War and the cathedral's art collection; call or go online for details. ⊠ *West St.* ☎ *01243/782595* ⊕ *www. chichestercathedral.org.uk* ☞ *Free; £4.50 suggested donation.*

Fodor's Choice ★ **Fishbourne Roman Palace.** In 1960, workers digging a water-main ditch uncovered a Roman wall; so began nine years of archaeological excavation of this site, the remains of the largest, grandest Roman villa in Britain. Intricate mosaics (including Cupid riding a dolphin) and painted walls lavishly decorate what is left of many of the 100 rooms of the palace, built in AD 1st century, possibly for local chieftain Tiberius Claudius Togidubnus. You can explore the sophisticated bathing and heating systems, along with the only example of a Roman garden in northern Europe. An extension has added many modern attributes, including a video reconstruction of how the palace might have looked. The site is ½ mile west of Chichester. ⊠ *Salthill Rd., Fishbourne* ☎ *01243/785859* ⊕ *www.sussexpast.co.uk* ☞ *£9.50* ⊘ *Closed Jan. and weekdays mid–late Dec. except Christmas.*

Fodor's Choice ★ **Pallant House Gallery.** This small but important collection of mostly modern British art includes work by Henry Moore and Graham Sutherland. It's in a modern extension to Pallant House, a mansion built for a wealthy wine merchant in 1712, and considered one of the finest surviving examples of Chichcester's Georgian past. At that time its state-of-the-art design showed the latest in complicated brickwork and superb wood carving. Appropriate antiques and porcelains furnish the faithfully restored rooms. Temporary and special exhibitions (usually around three at once) invariably find new and interesting angles to cover. ⊠ *9 N. Pallant* ☎ *01243/774557* ⊕ *www.pallant.org.uk* ☞ *Ground-floor galleries free; rest of museum £11 (£5.50 Tues.)* ⊘ *Closed Mon.*

Fodor's Choice ★ **Petworth House.** One of the National Trust's greatest treasures, Petworth is the imposing 17th-century home of Lord and Lady Egremont and holds an outstanding collection of English paintings by Gainsborough, Reynolds, and Van Dyck, as well as 19 oil paintings by J. M. W. Turner, the great proponent of romanticism who often visited Petworth and immortalized it in luminous drawings. A 13th-century chapel is all that remains of the original manor house. The celebrated landscape architect Capability Brown (1716–83) added a 700-acre deer park. Other highlights include Greek and Roman sculpture and Grinling Gibbons wood carvings, such as those in the spectacular Carved Room. Six rooms in the servants' quarters, among them the old kitchen, are also open to the public. Every winter the house undergoes extensive conservation work, but some rooms can still be seen on special tours; they take place most days, but call ahead to confirm availability. (The exception is the couple of weeks around Christmas, when the house is usually open as normal, transformed by magical festive displays). A restaurant serves light lunches. You can reach Petworth off A283; the house is 13 miles northeast of Chichester and 54 miles south of London. ⊠ *A283, Petworth* ☏ *01798/342207* ⊕ *www.nationaltrust.org.uk* ⊠ *£12; parking £4* ⊙ *Closed early Nov.–late Mar. except for tours and grounds.*

FAMILY **Weald and Downland Open Air Museum.** On the outskirts of Singleton, a secluded village 5 miles north of Chichester, is this excellent museum, a sanctuary for historical buildings dating from the 13th to 19th century. Among the 45 structures moved to 50 acres of wooded meadows are a cluster of medieval houses, a water mill, a Tudor market hall, and an ancient blacksmith's shop. ⊠ *Town La., off A286, Singleton* ☏ *01243/811363* ⊕ *www.wealddown.co.uk* ⊠ *£15.*

WHERE TO EAT

$$$ ✗ **Purchases.** This excellent bistro is popular with locals for a special-
BRITISH   occasion dinner and with the pretheater crowd, who enjoy the fixed-price early-bird menus. The food strikes a nice balance between hearty, traditional fare, and contemporary stylings. **Known for:** bargain pretheater menus; traditional cooking with a contemporary edge; beef Wellington with spinach and tarragon sauce. $ *Average main: £21* ⊠ *31 North St.* ☏ *01243/771444* ⊕ *www.purchasesrestaurant.co.uk.*

WHERE TO STAY

$$ ▥ **Chichester Harbour Hotel.** This handsome 18th-century house, known
HOTEL   for its flying (partially freestanding) staircase and colonnade, was once the residence of Admiral George Murray, one of Admiral Nelson's right-hand men. **Pros:** beautifully restored, historic building; stylish design; good location. **Cons:** street-facing rooms can be noisy; prices are a little high; gets booked up during Glorious Goodwood horse-race season. $ *Rooms from: £140* ⊠ *North St.* ☏ *01243/778000* ⊕ *www.chichester-harbour-hotel.co.uk* ⬿ *36 rooms* ⦿⦿ *Free Breakfast.*

NIGHTLIFE AND PERFORMING ARTS

Chichester Festival Theatre. The modernist Chichester Festival Theatre presents classics and modern plays from May through September and is a venue for touring companies the rest of the year. Built in 1962, it has an international reputation for innovative performances and attracts theatergoers from across the country. ⊠ *Oaklands Park, Broyle Rd.* ☏ *01243/781312* ⊕ *www.cft.org.uk.*

TUNBRIDGE WELLS AND AROUND

England is famous for its magnificent stately homes and castles, but many of them are scattered across the country, presenting a challenge for travelers. Within a 15-mile radius of Tunbridge Wells, however, in that area of hills and hidden dells known as the Weald, lies a wealth of architectural wonder in historic homes, castles, and gardens: Penshurst Place, Hever Castle, Chartwell, Knole, Ightham Mote, Leeds Castle, and lovely Sissinghurst Castle Garden.

ROYAL TUNBRIDGE WELLS

39 miles southeast of London.

Nobody much bothers with the "Royal" anymore, but Tunbridge Wells is no less regal because of it. Because of its wealth and political conservatism, this historic bedroom community has been the subject of (somewhat envious) British humor for years. Its restaurants and lodgings make it a convenient base for exploring the many homes and gardens nearby.

The city owes its prosperity to the 17th- and 18th-century passion for spas and mineral baths. In 1606 a mineral-water spring was discovered here, drawing legions of royal visitors looking for eternal health. Tunbridge Wells reached its zenith in the mid-18th century, when Richard "Beau" Nash presided over its social life. The buildings at the lower end of High Street are mostly 18th century, but as the street climbs the hill north, changing its name to Mount Pleasant Road, structures become more modern.

GETTING HERE AND AROUND

Southeastern trains leave from London's Charing Cross Station every 15 minutes. The journey to Tunbridge Wells takes just under an hour. If you're traveling by car from London, head here on the A21; travel time is about an hour.

Tunbridge Wells sprawls in all directions, but the historic center is compact. None of the sights is more than a 10-minute walk from the main train station. You can pick up a town map at the station.

ESSENTIALS

Visitor Information Royal Tunbridge Wells Tourist Information Centre. ✉ *Unit 2, The Corn Exchange, The Pantiles* ☎ *01892/515675* ⊕ *www.visittunbridgewells.com.*

EXPLORING

All Saints Church. This modest 13th-century church holds one of the glories of 20th-century church art. The building is awash with the luminous yellows and blues of 12 windows by Marc Chagall (1887–1985), commissioned as a tribute by the family of a young girl who was drowned in a sailing accident in 1963. The church is 4 miles north of Tunbridge Wells; turn off A26 before the confusingly similar-sounding town of Tonbridge and continue a mile or so east along B2017. ✉ *B2017, Tudeley* ☎ *01732/833241* 🎫 *Free; £3 donation requested.*

Church of King Charles the Martyr. Across the road from the Pantiles, this church dates from 1678, when it was dedicated to Charles I, who had been executed by Parliament in 1649. Its plain exterior belies its splendid interior, with a particularly beautiful plastered baroque ceiling. ✉ *Chapel Pl.* ☎ *01892/511745* ⊕ *www.kcmtw.org* 🎫 *Free* ☉ *Closed Sun. except for services.*

Pantiles. A good place to begin a visit is at the Pantiles, a famous promenade with colonnaded shops near the spring on one side of town. Its odd name derives from the Dutch "pan tiles" that originally paved the area. Now sandwiched between two busy main roads, the

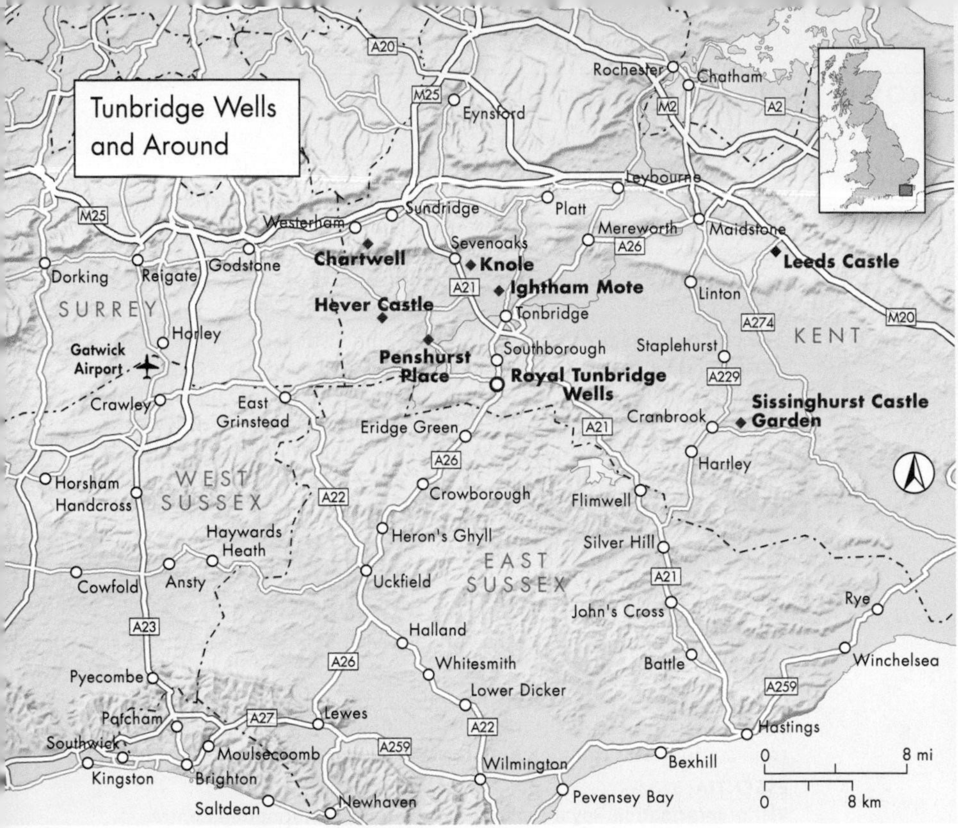

Pantiles remains an elegant, tranquil oasis, and the site of the actual well. ■ **TIP→ You can still drink the waters when a "dipper" (the traditional water dispenser) is in attendance, from Easter through September.** ✉ *Royal Tunbridge Wells.*

WHERE TO EAT

$ JAPANESE Fodor's Choice ★

🍴 **Kitsu.** Good Japanese food is often difficult to come by in England, so this tiny, unassuming restaurant seems an unlikely venue for the best sushi you're likely to find for miles. Everything is fresh and delicious, from the fragrant miso soup to the light tempura to the sushi platters that are big enough to share. **Known for:** excellent sushi; good casual dining; bring your own alcohol. [$] *Average main: £14* ✉ *82a Victoria Rd.* ☎ *01892/515510* 🌐 *www.kitsu.co.uk* 💳 *No credit cards.*

$$$$ FRENCH Fodor's Choice ★

🍴 **Thackeray's.** Once the home of Victorian novelist William Makepeace Thackeray, this mid-17th-century tile-hung house is now an elegant restaurant known for creative French cuisine. The fixed-price, three-course menu changes daily but often lists such dishes as poached monkfish tail with celeriac fondant, or beef fillet with hay-roasted carrots. **Known for:** fine dining; extravagant wine list; creative French cooking. [$] *Average main: £55* ✉ *85 London Rd.* ☎ *01892/511921* 🌐 *www.thackeraysrestaurant.co.uk* 🕓 *Closed Mon. and last wk in Dec. No dinner Sun.*

WHERE TO STAY

$$ HOTEL **Hotel du Vin.** An elegant sandstone house dating from 1762 has been transformed into a chic boutique hotel with polished wood floors and luxurious furnishings. **Pros:** historic building; luxurious linens; reliably good service. **Cons:** restaurant can get booked up; bar can be crowded; can be hard to book a room on short notice. [$] *Rooms from: £130* ✉ *Crescent Rd., near Mount Pleasant Rd.* ☎ *01892/526455* 🌐 *www.hotelduvin.com/locations/tunbridge-wells* *34 rooms* 🍴 *Free Breakfast.*

$$ HOTEL **Spa Hotel.** The country-house flavor of this 1766 Georgian mansion has been beautifully maintained by luxurious furnishings and preserved period details. **Pros:** lap-of-luxury feel; gorgeous views; traditional English style. **Cons:** breakfast is extra; very formal atmosphere; can be a bit stuffy. [$] *Rooms from: £115* ✉ *Mount Ephraim* ☎ *01892/520331* 🌐 *www.spahotel.co.uk* *70 rooms* 🍴 *No meals.*

PENSHURST PLACE

7 miles northwest of Royal Tunbridge Wells, 33 miles southeast of London.

One of the best preserved of the great medieval houses in Britain, and surrounded by stunning landscaped gardens, Penshurst Place is like an Elizabethan time machine.

GETTING HERE AND AROUND

To get to Penshurst, take the A26 north to Penshurst Road. The drive from Tunbridge Wells takes about 12 minutes. Buses 231, 233, and 237 run from Tunbridge Wells to Penshurst (no buses on Sunday).

EXPLORING

Fodor's Choice ★ **Penshurst Place.** At the center of the adorable hamlet of Penshurst stands this fine medieval manor house, hidden behind tall trees and walls. Although it has a 14th-century hall, Penshurst is mainly Elizabethan and has been the family home of the Sidneys since 1552. The most famous Sidney is the Elizabethan poet Sir Philip, author of *Arcadia*. The **Baron's Hall,** topped with a chestnut roof, is the oldest and one of the grandest halls to survive from the early Middle Ages. Family portraits, furniture, tapestries, and armor help tell the story of the house, which was first inhabited in 1341 by Sir John de Pulteney, the very wealthy four-time London mayor. On the grounds are a toy museum, a gift shop, and the enchanting 11-acre walled Italian Garden, which displays tulips and daffodils in spring and roses in summer. Take time to study the village's late-15th-century half-timber structures adorned with soaring brick chimneys. To get here from Tunbridge Wells, take the A26 and B2176. ✉ *Rogues Hill, off Leicester Square, Penshurst* ☎ *01892/870307* 🌐 *www.penshurstplace.com* 🎫 *£11.50; grounds only £9.50* ⏲ *Closed Nov.–Mar.*

WHERE TO EAT

$ BRITISH 🍴 **The Spotted Dog.** This pub first opened its doors in 1520 and in many ways hardly appears to have changed. Its big inglenook fireplace and heavy beams give it character, the views from the hilltop are lovely, and the good food (a mixture of traditional pub grub and slightly more sophisticated fare) and friendly crowd make it a pleasure to relax inside.

Known for: mixture of casual and formal dining; atmospheric old pub; pretty beer garden. $ *Average main: £13* ✉ *Smarts Hill, Penshurst* ☎ *01892/870253* ⊕ *www.spotteddogpub.co.uk.*

HEVER CASTLE

3 miles west of Penshurst, 10 miles northwest of Royal Tunbridge Wells, 30 miles southeast of London.

A fairy-tale medieval castle on the outside, and a Tudor mansion within, Hever contains layer on layer of history. It's one of the most unusual and romantic of the great English castles.

GETTING HERE AND AROUND

Hever Castle is best reached via the narrow, often one-lane B2026. From Tunbridge Wells, take A264 east then follow signs directing you north toward Hever.

EXPLORING

Fodor's Choice   **Hever Castle.** It's hard to imagine a more romantic castle than this: nestled
★   within rolling hills, all turrets and battlements, the whole encircled by a water lily–bound moat. (There are even fabulous beasts swimming in its waters, too, in the form of enormous Japanese koi carp.) Here, at her childhood home, the unfortunate Anne Boleyn, second wife of Henry VIII and mother of Elizabeth I, was courted and won by Henry. He loved her dearly for a time but had her beheaded in 1536 after she failed to give birth to a son. He then gave Boleyn's home to his fourth wife, Anne of Cleves, as a present. Famous though it was, the castle fell into disrepair in the 19th century. When American millionaire William Waldorf Astor acquired it in 1903, he needed somewhere to house his staff. His novel solution was to build a replica Tudor village, using only methods, materials, and even tools appropriate to the era. The result is more or less completely indistinguishable from the genuine Tudor parts. (Today it is mostly used for private functions.) Astor also created the stunning gardens, which today include an excellent yew maze, ponds, playgrounds, tea shops, gift shops, plant shops—you get the picture. There's a notable collection of Tudor portraits, and in summer activities are nonstop here, with jousting, falconry exhibitions, and country fairs, making this one of southern England's most rewarding castles to visit. In one of the Victorian wings, B&B rooms go for upwards of £125 per night for a basic room. ✉ *Off B2026, Hever* ☎ *01732/865224* ⊕ *www.hevercastle.co.uk* 🎫 *£16; grounds only £13.50* ⊘ *Closed Jan.–late Mar., and Mon. and Tues. late Nov.–late Dec.*

CHARTWELL

9 miles north of Hever Castle, 12 miles northwest of Royal Tunbridge Wells, 28 miles southeast of London.

Beloved of Winston Churchill, Chartwell retains a homely warmth despite its size and grandeur. Almost as lovely are the grounds, with a rose garden and magnificent views across rolling Kentish hills.

GETTING HERE AND AROUND

From Tunbridge Wells, take A21 north toward Sevenoaks, then turn east onto A25 and follow signs from there. You can travel to Chartwell by bus from the town of Sevenoaks. Take Go Coach 401, but check with the driver to make sure the bus passes near the mansion.

EXPLORING

Chartwell. A grand Victorian mansion with views over the Weald, Chartwell was the beloved private home of Sir Winston Churchill, from 1924 until his death in 1965. Virtually everything has been kept as it was when he lived here, with his pictures, books, photos, and maps. There's even a half-smoked cigar that the World War II prime minister never finished. Churchill was an amateur artist, and his paintings show a softer side of the stiff-upper-lipped statesman. Admission to the house is by timed ticket available only the day of your visit. ■TIP➜ Be sure to explore the rose gardens and take one of the walks in the nearby countryside. ⊠ *Mapleton Rd., Westerham* ☎ *01732/868381* ⊕ *www. nationaltrust.org.uk/chartwell* ☎ *£16; garden and studio only £7.50* ☉ *House closed Nov., Jan., and Feb.*

KNOLE

8 miles east of Chartwell, 11 miles north of Royal Tunbridge Wells, 27 miles southeast of London.

Perhaps the quintessential Tudor mansion, Knole is as famous for its literary connections and impressive collection of furniture and tapestries as it is for its elegant 15th- and 16th-century architecture.

GETTING HERE AND AROUND

To get to the town of Sevenoaks from Chartwell, drive north to Westerham, then pick up A25 and head east for 8 miles to A225. The route is well signposted. Southeastern trains travel from London's Charing Cross Station to Sevenoaks every few minutes and take about half an hour. Knole is a 20-minute walk from the train station.

EXPLORING

Fodor's Choice

★

Knole. The pleasant but workaday town of Sevenoaks lies in London's commuter belt, a world away from the baronial air of its premier attraction, the grand, beloved estate of the Sackville family since the 16th century. Begun in the 1400s and enlarged in 1603 by Thomas Sackville, Knole, with its sprawling complex of courtyards and outbuildings, resembles a small town. You'll need most of an afternoon to explore it thoroughly. The house is noted for its wonderful tapestries, embroidered furnishings, and an extraordinary set of 17th-century silver furniture. Most of the salons are in the pre-baroque mode, rather dark and armorial. The magnificently florid staircase was a novelty in its Elizabethan heyday. Vita Sackville-West grew up here and used it as the setting for her novel *The Edwardians,* a witty account of life among the gilded set. The gardens are beautiful to wander through (but you can only do so on Tuesdays; there is no extra charge). Encircled by a 1,000-acre park where herds of deer roam free, the house lies in the center of Sevenoaks; the incongruously low-key entrance is opposite St. Nicholas Church. ⊠ *Knole La., off A225, Sevenoaks*

☎ *01732/462100* ⊕ *www.nationaltrust.org.uk/knole* 🏠 *House £9;* *parking £4* ⊙ *House closed early Nov.–late Mar.*

IGHTHAM MOTE

7 miles southeast of Knole, 10 miles north of Royal Tunbridge Wells, 31 miles southeast of London.

Almost unique among medieval manor houses in that it still has a moat (although that has nothing to do with the name), Ightham is a captivating, unreal-looking place reached down a warren of winding country lanes.

GETTING HERE AND AROUND

The house sits 6 miles south of Sevenoaks. From Sevenoaks, follow A25 east to A227 and then follow the signs. At the village of Ivy Hatch follow signs to tiny Mote Road, which winds its way to the house. The 404 bus from Sevenoaks stops here on Thursday and Friday only; otherwise, you'll have to get off in Ivy Hatch and walk just under a mile from there. The 308 bus from Sevenoaks to Ivy Hatch runs hourly from Monday to Saturday, as does the 222 (although that may not run every day).

EXPLORING

Fodor'sChoice   **Ightham Mote.** This wonderful, higgledy-piggledy, timber-framed medi-
★   eval manor house looks like something out of a fairy tale. Even its name is a bit of an enigma—"Ightham" is pronounced "Item" (we can't quite figure that out either) and "Mote" doesn't refer to the kind of moat you get in a castle, but an old English word for meeting place. Perhaps it's also fitting, then, that finding the place takes careful navigation down tiny, winding country lanes, and then even to reach the front door you must first cross a narrow stone bridge over the moat (yes, it has one of those, too). But it's all worth the effort to see a fanciful vision right out of the Middle Ages. Built nearly 700 years ago, Ightham's magical exterior has hardly changed since the 14th century, but within you'll find that it encompasses styles of several periods, Tudor to Victorian. The Great Hall, Tudor chapel, and drawing room are all highlights. ✉ *Mote Rd., off A227, Sevenoaks* ☎ *01732/810378* ⊕ *www.national-trust.org.uk/ightham-mote* 🏠 *£9 Apr.–Oct.; £4.50 Nov.–Mar.* ⊙ *House closed Nov., Jan., and Feb.*

LEEDS CASTLE

12 miles south of Rochester, 19 miles northwest of Royal Tunbridge Wells, 40 miles southeast of London.

Every inch the grand medieval castle, Leeds is like a storybook illustration of what an English castle should look like—from the fortresslike exterior to the breathtaking rooms within.

EXPLORING

Fodor'sChoice   **Leeds Castle.** Picture what comes to mind when we say the word "castle."
★   Ramparts and battlements? Check. Moat? Check. Ancient stone walkways on which you just know a knight in shining armor might pass by at any second? Pretty much. One of England's finest castles, this storybook medieval stronghold commands two small islands on a peaceful lake.

One of England's most notable stately homes, sprawling Knole displayed the power of the Sackvilles.

Dating to the 9th century and rebuilt by the Normans in 1119, Leeds (not to be confused with the city in the north of England) became a favorite home of many medieval English queens. Henry VIII liked it so much he had it converted from a fortress into a grand palace. The interior doesn't match the glories of the much-photographed exterior, although there are fine paintings and furniture, including many pieces from the 20th-century refurbishment by the castle's last private owner, Lady Baillie. The outside attractions are more impressive and include a maze, a grotto, two adventure playgrounds, an aviary of native and exotic birds, and woodland gardens. The castle is 5 miles east of Maidstone. ■TIP→ All tickets are valid for a year, and there's a 10% discount if you buy them online. ⊠ *A20, Maidstone* ☎ *01622/765400* ⊕ *www. leeds-castle.com* 🎫 *£25.50.*

SISSINGHURST CASTLE GARDEN

10 miles south of Leeds Castle, 53 miles southeast of London.

Impeccable literary credentials go hand in hand with enchanting grounds, magnificent countryside views, and even a working kitchen garden at this beautiful home in the Sussex countryside.

GETTING HERE AND AROUND

For those without a car, take a train from London's Charing Cross Station and transfer to a bus in Staplehurst. Direct buses operate on Tuesday, Friday, and Sunday between May and August; at other times, take the bus to Sissinghurst village and walk the remaining

1¼ miles. From Leeds Castle, make your way south on B2163 and A274 through Headcorn, and then follow signs.

EXPLORING

Fodor's Choice ★ **Sissinghurst Castle Garden.** One of the most famous gardens in the world, unpretentiously beautiful and quintessentially English, Sissinghurst rests deep in the Kentish countryside. The gardens, with 10 themed "rooms," were laid out in the 1930s around the remains of part of a moated Tudor castle by writer Vita Sackville-West (one of the Sackvilles of Knole, her childhood home) and her husband, diplomat Harold Nicolson. ■ **TIP→ Climb the tower to see Sackville-West's study and to get wonderful views of the garden and surrounding fields. The view is best in June and July, when the roses are in bloom.** The stunning White Garden is filled with snow-color flowers and silver-gray foliage, while the herb and cottage gardens reveal Sackville-West's encyclopedic knowledge of plants. There are woodland and lake walks, too, making it easy to spend a half day or more here. Stop by the tea shop for lunch made with the farm's own produce. If you love it all so much you want to stay, you can—the National Trust rents the Priest's House on the property for a minimum stay of three nights; prices start at around £700 and rise to upwards of £1,600 in midsummer. See the National Trust website for details (but be warned, you'll need to book well ahead). ✉ *A262, Cranbrook* ☎ *01580/710700* 🌐 *www.nationaltrust.org.uk/sissinghurst-castle* 🎟 *£14.50.*

WHERE TO STAY

$$ B&B/INN Fodor's Choice ★ 🏨 **Sissinghurst Castle Farmhouse.** On the grounds of Sissinghurst Castle, this beautiful 1885 farmhouse was lovingly restored by the National Trust in 2009. **Pros:** beautiful location on the grounds of a historic home; elevator makes building more accessible than most older B&Bs; discounts for two or more nights. **Cons:** few amenities; need a car to get here; closed in winter. [$] *Rooms from: £150* ✉ *The Street, Sissinghurst* ☎ *01580/720992* 🌐 *www.sissinghurstcastlefarmhouse.com* 🕓 *Closed late Dec.–mid-Mar.* 🛏 *7 rooms* 🍴 *Free Breakfast.*

STONEHENGE AND THE SOUTH

WELCOME TO STONEHENGE AND THE SOUTH

TOP REASONS TO GO

★ **Salisbury Cathedral:** Crowned with England's tallest church spire, this impressive cathedral looks out to spectacular views of the surrounding countryside from the roof and spire, accessible by daily tours.

★ **Stonehenge:** The power and mystery of this Neolithic stone circle on Salisbury Plain is still spellbinding.

★ **House and garden at Stourhead:** The cultivated English landscape at its finest, with an 18th-century Palladian stately home and beautiful gardens adorned with neoclassical temples.

★ **The New Forest:** Get away from it all in the South's most extensive woodland, crisscrossed by myriad trails ideal for horseback riding, hiking, and biking.

★ **Literary trails:** Jane Austen, Thomas Hardy, John Fowles, and Ian McEwan have made this area essential for book buffs, with a concentration of sights in Chawton, Dorchester, Chesil Beach, and Lyme Regis.

In the south of England, Salisbury Plain, part of the inland county of Wiltshire, presents a sharp contrast to the sheltered villages of coastal Hampshire and Dorset, and the bustle of the port cities of Portsmouth. Culturally compelling towns like Salisbury and Winchester are great places to spend the night.

Salisbury puts you within easy reach of Stonehenge and the equally ancient stone circles at Avebury. From there you can swing south to the New Forest. Lyme Regis is the gateway to the Jurassic Coast, a fossil-filled World Heritage Site.

1 **Winchester, Portsmouth, and Around.** One of the region's most culturally and historically significant towns, Winchester lies a short distance from the genteel village of Chawton, home to Jane Austen, and the great south-coast port of Portsmouth.

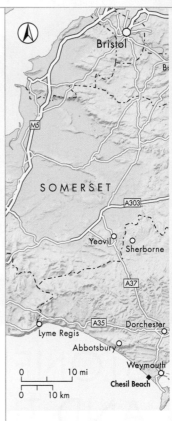

2 **Salisbury, Stonehenge, and Salisbury Plain.** Wiltshire's great cathedral city of Salisbury is close to the prehistoric monuments of Stonehenge and Avebury, as well as Wilton, a Palladian estate. Farther afield are more great estates, Stourhead and Longleat.

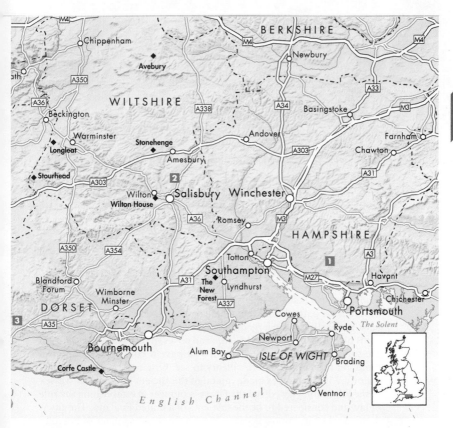

3 New Forest, Dorset, and the South Coast. The rustic, although not sparsely populated by U.S. standards, New Forest parkland stretches south of Salisbury to the coast. The route west passes ruined Corfe Castle. Also worth a stop are Sherborne, with its beautiful abbey; Dorchester, the heart of "Hardy Country"; and coastal Weymouth and Lyme Regis.

Updated by
Ellin Stein

Cathedrals, stately homes, stone circles—the South, made up of Hampshire, Dorset, and Wiltshire counties—contains a variety of notable attractions as well as several quieter pleasures. Two important cathedrals, Winchester and Salisbury (pronounced *sawls*-bree), are here, as are classic stately homes such as Longleat, Stourhead, and Wilton House—and remarkable prehistoric sites, two of which, Avebury and Stonehenge, are of world-class significance.

And these are just the tourist-brochure highlights. Anyone spending time in these parts should rent a bike or a car and set out to discover the back-road villages and larger market towns. Close to London, the green fields of Hampshire divide the cliffs and coves of the West Country from the sprawl of the suburbs. Even if you have a coastal destination in mind, hit the brakes—there's plenty to see. Originally a Roman town, historic Winchester was made capital of the ancient kingdom of Wessex in the 9th century by Alfred the Great, a pioneer in establishing the rule of law and considered to be the first king of a united England. The city is dominated by its imposing cathedral, the final resting place of notables ranging from Saxon kings to the son of William the Conqueror to Jane Austen. It's a good base for visiting Austen's home village of Chawton, as well as other locations associated with several of England's literary greats such as Thomas Hardy.

North of Hampshire and the New Forest lies the somewhat harsher terrain of Salisbury Plain, part of it owned by the British army and used for training and weapons testing. Two monuments, millennia apart, dominate the plain. One is the 404-foot-tall stone spire of Salisbury Cathedral, the subject of one of John Constable's finest paintings. Not far away is the best-known prehistoric structure in Europe, the dramatic Stonehenge. The many theories about its construction and purpose only add to its otherworldly allure.

Other subregions have their own appeal, and many are of literary or historical interest. The Dorset countryside of grass-covered chalk hills—the downs—wooded valleys, meandering rivers, and meadows, immortalized in the novels of Thomas Hardy, is interspersed with unspoiled market towns and villages. Busy beach resorts such as Lyme Regis perch next to hidden coves on the fossil-rich Jurassic Coast. Just off Hampshire is the Isle of Wight—Queen Victoria's favorite getaway—where colorful flags flutter from the many sailboats anchored at Cowes, home of the famous regatta.

The South has been quietly integral to England's history for well over 4,000 years, occupied successively by prehistoric man, the Celts, the Romans, the Saxons, the Normans, and the modern British. Though short on historic buildings due to wartime bombing, the port cities of Southampton and Portsmouth are rich in history itself; the *Mayflower* departed from the former, and the latter is home to the oldest dry dock in the world—Henry VIII's navy built its ships here. Portsmouth was also the departure point for Nelson to the Battle of Trafalgar, Allied forces to Normandy on D-Day, and British forces to the Falklands.

PLANNER

WHEN TO GO

In summer the coastal resorts of Bournemouth and Weymouth are crowded; it may be difficult to find the accommodations you want. The Isle of Wight gets its fair share of summer visitors, too, especially during the weeklong Cowes Regatta in late July or early August. Because ferries fill up to capacity, you may have to wait for the next one. The New Forest is most alluring in spring and early summer (for the foaling season) and fall (for the colorful foliage), whereas summer can be busy with walkers and campers. In all seasons, take waterproof boots for the mud and puddles. Major attractions such as Stonehenge and Longleat House attract plenty of people at all times; bypass such sights on weekends, public holidays, or school vacations. Don't plan to visit the cathedrals of Salisbury and Winchester on a Sunday, when your visit will be restricted, or during services, when it won't be appreciated by worshippers.

FESTIVALS

Salisbury International Arts Festival. Held from late May through early June, the festival has outstanding classical recitals, plays, author talks, international cinema, dance, comedy, and family events. ⊠ *87 Crane St., Salisbury* ☎ *01722/332241* ⊕ *www.salisburyfestival.co.uk.*

PLANNING YOUR TIME

The South has no obvious hub, though many people base themselves in one or both of the cathedral cities of Winchester and Salisbury and make excursions to nearby destinations. The coastal cities of Portsmouth and Southampton have their charms, but neither of these large urban centers is particularly attractive as an overnight stop. Busy Bournemouth, whose major sight is a Victorian-era museum, has quieter areas that are more conducive to relaxation. To escape the bustle, the New Forest, southwest of Southampton, has space and semi-wilderness. It's easy to take a morning or afternoon break to enjoy the available activities, whether on foot, bike, or horseback. The Isle of Wight needs more time and is worth exploring at leisure over at least a couple of days.

GETTING HERE AND AROUND

BUS TRAVEL

National Express buses at London's Victoria Coach Station on Buckingham Palace Road depart every 60–90 minutes for Bournemouth (2½ hours), Southampton (2¼ hours), and Portsmouth (2¼ hours), and every two hours for Winchester (2 hours). There are four buses daily to Salisbury (about 3 hours). Bluestar operates a comprehensive service in the Southampton and Winchester areas, as well as buses to the New Forest. Stagecoach South operates services in Portsmouth and around Hampshire. Salisbury Reds serves Salisbury; More travels to Bournemouth and Poole; First serves Portsmouth, Southampton, and Dorset locations such as Weymouth and Dorchester; and Southern Vectis covers the Isle of Wight. More, Bluestar, Salisbury Reds, and Southern Vectis sell 1-day (and 2-day, 5-day, and 15-day from Southern Vectis) passes as well as 7-, 30-, and 90-day passes for all routes. Ask about the Megarider tickets sold by Stagecoach South. Contact Traveline for all information on routes and tickets. During the school summer holidays (late July and August), the hop-on, hop-off Beach Bus runs from the Hythe Pier in Southampton to Lymington in the New Forest. Tickets are £7.

Bus Contacts Beach Bus. ☎ *01590/646600* ⊕ *www.thebeachbus.info.* **Bluestar.** ☎ *01202/338421* ⊕ *www.bluestarbus.co.uk.* **First.** ☎ *0345/602–0121* ⊕ *www.firstgroup.com.* **More.** ☎ *01202/338420* ⊕ *www.morebus.co.uk.* **National Express.** ☎ *0871/781–8181* ⊕ *www.nationalexpress.com.* **Salisbury Reds.** ☎ *01202/338420* ⊕ *www.salisburyreds.co.uk.* **Southern Vectis.** ☎ *0330/053–9182* ⊕ *www.islandbuses.info.* **Stagecoach South.** ☎ *0345/121–0190* ⊕ *www.stagecoachbus.com.* **Traveline.** ☎ *0871/200–2233* ⊕ *www.traveline.info.*

CAR TRAVEL

On the whole, the region is easily negotiable using public transportation. But for rural spots, especially the grand country estates, a car is useful. The well-developed road network includes M3 to Winchester (70 miles from London) and Southampton (77 miles); A3 to Portsmouth (77 miles); and M27 along the coast, from the New Forest and Southampton to Portsmouth. For Salisbury, take M3 to A303, then A30. A35 connects Bournemouth to Dorchester and Lyme Regis, and A350 runs north to Dorset's inland destinations.

TRAIN TRAVEL

South Western Railway serves the South from London's Waterloo Station. Travel times average 1 hour to Winchester, 1½ hours to Southampton, 2 hours to Bournemouth, and 2¾ hours to Weymouth. The trip to Salisbury takes 1½ hours, and Portsmouth about 1¾ hours. A yearlong Network Railcard, valid throughout the South and Southeast, entitles you and up to three accompanying adults to one-third off most train fares, and up to four accompanying children ages 5–15 to a 60% discount off each child fare. It costs £30. Weekend First tickets, available on weekends and public holidays, let you upgrade to first class from £5–£25, depending on the train operator.

Train Contacts National Rail Enquiries. ☏ 0845/748–4950 ⊕ www.national-rail.co.uk. **South Western Railway.** ☏ 0345/600–0650 ⊕ www.southwesttrains.co.uk.

RESTAURANTS

In summer, and especially on summer weekends, visitors can overrun the restaurants in small villages, so either book a table in advance or prepare to wait. The more popular or upscale the restaurant, the more critical a reservation is. For local specialties, try fresh-grilled river trout or sea bass poached in brine, or dine like a king on New Forest's renowned venison. Hampshire is noted for its pig and sheep farming, and you might zero in on pork and lamb dishes on local restaurant menus. The region places a strong emphasis on seasonal produce, so venison, for example, is best between September and February. *Restaurant reviews have been shortened. For full information, visit Fodors.com.*

HOTELS

Modern hotel chains are well represented, and in rural areas you can choose between elegant country-house hotels, traditional coaching inns (updated to different degrees), and modest guesthouses. Some seaside hotels don't accept one-night bookings in summer. If you plan to visit Cowes on the Isle of Wight during Cowes Week, the annual yachting jamboree in late July or early August, book well in advance. *Hotel reviews have been shortened. For full information, visit Fodors.com.*

WHAT IT COSTS IN POUNDS			
$	**$$**	**$$$**	**$$$$**
Restaurants	under £15	£15–£19	£20–£25	over £25
Hotels	under £100	£100–£160	£161–£220	over £220

Restaurant prices are the average cost of a main course at dinner, or if dinner is not served, at lunch. Hotel prices are the lowest cost of a standard double room in high season, including 20% V.A.T.

TOURS

Guild of Registered Tourist Guides. This organization maintains a directory of qualified Blue Badge guides who can meet you anywhere in the region for private tours. Tours are tailored to your particular interests or needs and generally start around £255 per full day, £158 per half day. ☏ 020/7403–1115 ⊕ www.britainsbestguides.org.

VISITOR INFORMATION

Contacts Tourism South East. ☏ 023/8062–5400 ⊕ www.tourismsoutheast.com. **Visit South West.** ☏ 01722/342860 Visit Salisbury ⊕ www.visitsouthwest.co.uk.

WINCHESTER, PORTSMOUTH, AND AROUND

From the cathedral city of Winchester, 70 miles southwest of London, you can meander southward to the coast, stopping at the bustling port of Portsmouth to explore its maritime heritage.

WINCHESTER

70 miles southwest of London, 12 miles northeast of Southampton.

Winchester is among the most historic of English cities, and as you walk the graceful streets and wander the many public gardens, a sense of the past envelops you. Although it's now merely the county seat of Hampshire, for more than four centuries Winchester served first as the capital of the ancient kingdom of Wessex and then of England. The first king of England, Egbert, was crowned here in AD 827, and the court of his successor Alfred the Great was based here until Alfred's death in 899. After the Norman Conquest in 1066, William I ("the Conqueror") had himself crowned in London, but took the precaution of repeating the ceremony in Winchester. William also commissioned the local monastery to produce the Domesday Book, a land survey begun in 1085. The city remained the center of ecclesiastical, commercial, and political power until the 13th century, when that power shifted to London. Despite its deep roots in the past, Winchester is also a thriving market town living firmly in the present, with numerous shops and restaurants on High Street.

GETTING HERE AND AROUND

On a main train line and on the M3 motorway, Winchester is easily accessible from London. The train station is a short walk from the sights; the bus station is in the center, opposite the tourist office. The one-way streets are notoriously confusing, so find a parking lot as soon as possible. The city center is very walkable, and most of the High Street is closed to vehicular traffic. A walk down High Street and Broadway brings you to St. Giles Hill, which has a panoramic view of the city.

ESSENTIALS

Visitor Information Winchester Tourist Information Centre. ⊠ *Winchester Guildhall, High St.* ☎ *01962/840500* ⊕ *www.visitwinchester.co.uk.*

EXPLORING

Fodor'sChoice
★
The Great Hall. A short walk west of the cathedral, this outstanding example of early English Gothic architecture, and one of Britain's finest surviving 13th-century halls, is all that remains of the city's original Norman castle (razed by Oliver Cromwell). It's also the site of numerous historically significant events: the English Parliament is thought to have had one of its first meetings here in 1246; Sir Walter Raleigh was tried for conspiracy against King James I in 1603; and Dame Alice Lisle was sentenced to death by the brutal Judge Jeffreys for sheltering fugitives after Monmouth's Rebellion in 1685. Hanging on the west wall is the hall's greatest artifact, a huge oak table, which, legend has it, was King Arthur's original Round Table. In fact, it was probably created around 1290 at the beginning of the reign of

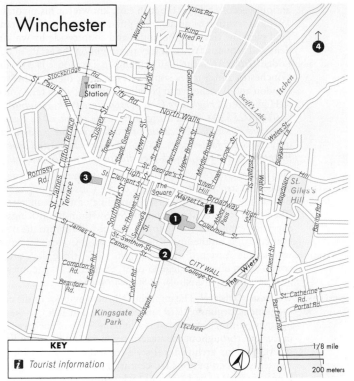

Winchester

KEY

🛈 *Tourist information*

Edward I for a tournament. It is not clear when the green and white stripes that divide the table into 24 places, each with the name of a knight of the mythical Round Table, were added, but it is certain that the Tudor Rose in the center surmounted by a portrait of King Arthur was commissioned by Henry VIII. Take time to wander through the garden—a re-creation of a medieval shady retreat, named for two queens: Eleanor of Provence and Eleanor of Castile. ⊠ *Castle Ave.* ☎ *01962/846476* ⊕ *www.hants.gov.uk/thingstodo/greathall* ⛳ *£3* ↻ *May be closed for events—check website.*

Fodor'sChoice **Highclere Castle.** Set in 1,000 acres of parkland designed by Capability
★ Brown, this is the historic home of the actual earls of Carnarvon—as opposed to the imaginary earls of Grantham that are portrayed living within it in the television drama *Downton Abbey*. Victorian Gothic rather than actual Gothic, this huge country house was designed by Sir Charles Barry, architect of the similar Houses of Parliament. Commissioned by the third earl in 1838 to transform a simpler Georgian mansion, Barry used golden Bath stone to create this fantasy castle bristling with turrets. Like its fictional counterpart, it served as a hospital during World War I. Highlights of the State Rooms include Van Dyke's equestrian portrait of Charles I in the Dining Room and the imposing library (Lord Grantham's retreat). There's also an exhibit of Egyptian

antiquities collected by the fifth earl, known for his pivotal role in the 1920s excavation of ancient Egyptian tombs, notably Tutankhamun's. Find pleasant views of the house and countryside by walking the gardens and grounds. You can stay overnight on the estate in the "London Lodge" from April through September. The house is 25 miles north of Winchester and 5 miles south of Newbury; there's train service from London and Winchester to Newbury, and taxis can take you the 5 miles to Highclere. ☒ *Highclere Castle, Highclere Park, Newbury* ✚ *Off A34* ☎ *01635/253204* ⊕ *www.highclerecastle.co.uk* ✉ *£23 castle, exhibition, and gardens; £16 castle or exhibition plus gardens; £7 gardens only* ⊙ *Closed Jan.–Easter (except for select dates) and other select days throughout the year; check website for more information.*

King's Gate. One of two surviving gateways in the city's original ancient walls, this structure to the south of the Close is thought to have been built in the 12th century as a remodeling of a Roman gate on the site. The tiny 13th-century church of St. Swithun-upon-Kingsgate, a rare surviving example of a "gateway church" (built into the walls of medieval cities), is on the upper floor. Nearby, 8 College Street is the house where Jane Austen died on July 18, 1817, three days after writing a comic poem about the legend of St. Swithun's Day (copies are usually available in the cathedral). ☒ *St. Swithun St.*

Fodor's Choice
★

Winchester Cathedral. The imposing Norman exterior of the city's greatest monument, begun in 1079 and consecrated in 1093, makes the Gothic lightness within even more breathtaking. One of the largest cathedrals in Europe, throughout the structure you will find outstanding examples of every major architectural style from the 11th to 16th century: the transepts and crypt are 11th-century Romanesque; the great nave, the longest in Europe, is 14th- and 15th-century Perpendicular Gothic, and the presbytery (behind the choir, holding the high altar) is 14th-century Decorated Gothic. Other notable features include the richly carved 14th-century choir stalls, the ornate 15th-century stone screen behind the high altar, and the largest surviving spread of 13th-century floor tiles in England. Little of the original stained glass has survived, except in the large window over the entrance. When Cromwell's troops ransacked the cathedral in the 17th century, locals hid away bits of stained glass they found on the ground so that it could later be replaced. Free tours are run year-round. The Library's Winchester Bible, one of the finest remaining 12th-century illuminated manuscripts, is temporarily on display in the North Transept. The patron saint of the cathedral is St. Swithun (died AD 862), an Anglo-Saxon bishop who is also buried here. He had requested an outdoor burial plot, but his body was transferred to the newly restored church in 971, accompanied by, legend has it, 40 days of rain. Since then, folklore says that rain on St. Swithun's Day (July 15) means 40 more days of wet weather.

Among the other well-known people buried here are William the Conqueror's son, William II ("Rufus"), mysteriously murdered in the New Forest in 1100, and Jane Austen, whose grave lies in the north aisle of the nave. The tombstone makes no mention of Austen's literary status, though a brass plaque in the wall, dating from 80 years after her death, celebrates her achievements, and modern panels provide an overview of her life and work. You can also explore the tower—with far-reaching views in fair weather—and other recesses of the building on a tour. Special services or ceremonies may mean the cathedral, the crypt, and the Treasury are closed to visits, so call ahead. Outside the cathedral, explore the Close, the area to the south of the cathedral with neat lawns, the Deanery, Dome Alley, and Cheyney Court. ✉ *The Close, Cathedral Precincts* ☎ *01962/857200* 🌐 *www.winchester-cathedral.org.uk* 🎟 *Cathedral £8; tower tour £6.*

WHERE TO EAT

$$$$ MODERN BRITISH 🍴 **The Black Rat.** This former pub is one of two Michelin-starred restaurants in town, with relatively reasonable prices. The Black Rat specializes in hearty Modern British dishes that use locally sourced, seasonal ingredients, several from the restaurant's own kitchen garden. **Known for:** imaginative flavor combinations; four huts for outdoor dining; extensive wine list. [$] *Average main: £42* ✉ *88 Chesil St.* ☎ *01962/844465* 🌐 *www.theblackrat.co.uk.*

$$$ MODERN BRITISH 🍴 **Chesil Rectory.** The timbered and gabled building may be venerable—it dates back to the mid-15th century—but the cuisine is Modern British, using locally sourced ingredients. The small but well-executed menu is particularly strong on game dishes, like pheasant with parsnip puree or duck breast and confit leg spring roll. **Known for:** historic, romantic ambience; fresh takes on British classics like the roast beef traditional Sunday lunch; good-value set-price lunches. [$] *Average main: £20* ✉ *1 Chesil St.* ☎ *01962/851555* 🌐 *www.chesilrectory.co.uk.*

$$$ SEAFOOD Fodor's Choice ★ 🍴 **Rick Stein, Winchester.** Renowned as Britain's finest seafood chef, Rick Stein chose Winchester for his first venture away from the Cornish coast. The menu is largely focused on fish and crustaceans, but carnivores and vegetarians are catered for as well. **Known for:** simply but confidently prepared classics like turbot hollandaise; exotic choices like spicy Indonesian curry with prawn and squid; good-value set menus for lunch and early evening dinner. [$] *Average main: £24* ✉ *7 High St.* ☎ *01962/353535* 🌐 *www.rickstein.com.*

WHERE TO STAY

$$$ HOTEL Fodor's Choice ★ 🏨 **Lainston House.** The 63 acres surrounding this elegant 17th-century country house retain many original features, including the walls of the kitchen garden (still in use), the apple trees in the former orchard, and a mile-long avenue of linden trees, the longest in Europe. **Pros:** beautiful setting; period detail in guest and public rooms; excellent bar and restaurant. **Cons:** lower-priced modern rooms small; country-house "shabby-chic" not to everyone's taste; restaurant service can be erratic. [$] *Rooms from: £165* ✉ *Woodman La., off B3049, Sparsholt* ☎ *01962/776088* 🌐 *www.lainstonhouse.com* 🛏 *50 rooms* 🍽 *Some meals.*

$$ B&B/INN 🏨 **Wykeham Arms.** A watering hole since 1755, this pub with rooms near the cathedral and the college wears its Britishness proudly, with photos of national heroes like Nelson and Churchill, military artifacts, and an assortment of pewter mugs hanging from the ceiling. **Pros:** quirky charm; lively bar; good food. **Cons:** rooms above bar can be noisy; not for those looking for luxury; small portions at restaurant. [$] *Rooms from: £100* ✉ *75 Kingsgate St.* ☎ *01962/853834* 🌐 *wykehamarmswinchester.co.uk* 🛏 *14 rooms* 🍽 *Free Breakfast* ☞ *No children under 14.*

4

SHOPPING

Kingsgate Books and Prints. Located on a medieval site, this atmospheric shop is filled with drawings, prints and engravings (many by local artists), rare antique county maps, and secondhand books. ⊠ *1 Kingsgate St.* ☎ *01962/864710* ⊕ *www.kingsgatebooksandprints.co.uk.*

P&G Wells. The oldest bookshop in the country (in business for more than 250 years), P&G Wells has numerous books by and about Jane Austen, who had an account here and in 1817 died almost next door. It also has the region's largest selection of children's books. ⊠ *11 College St.* ☎ *01962/852016* ⊕ *bookwells.co.uk.*

CHAWTON

16 miles northeast of Winchester.

In Chawton you can visit the home of Jane Austen (1775–1817), who lived the last eight years of her life in the village, moving to Winchester only during her final illness. The site has always drawn literary pilgrims, but with the ongoing release of successful films based on her novels, the town's popularity among visitors has grown enormously.

GETTING HERE AND AROUND

Hourly Stagecoach Bus 64 service connects Winchester and Alresford with Chawton. It's a 10-minute walk from the bus stop to Jane Austen's House. By car, take A31. Alternatively, take a 40-minute stroll along the footpath from Alton.

EXPLORING

Fodor's Choice ★ **Chawton House Library.** Located in a Elizabethan country house on a 275-acre estate (part of the South Downs National Park), this library specializes in works by English women writers from 1600 to 1830, including authors such as Mary Shelley, Mary Wollstonecraft, and Frances Burney. It also houses the Knight Collection, the private library of the family who owned the house for over 400 years. Jane Austen's brother Edward eventually inherited the property and added the walled kitchen garden, shrubberies, and parkland. ⊠ *Chawton* ☎ *01420/541010* ⊕ *www.chawtonhouse.org* ☜ *Library and gardens £8; gardens only £5.* ⊘ *Closed mid-Dec.–early Mar. and some Sat. in June and July.*

Fodor's Choice ★ **Jane Austen's House Museum.** This unassuming redbrick house is where Jane Austen wrote *Emma, Persuasion,* and *Mansfield Park,* and revised *Sense and Sensibility, Northanger Abbey,* and *Pride and Prejudice.* Now a museum, the house retains the modest but genteel atmosphere suitable to the unmarried daughter of a clergyman. In the drawing room, there's a piano similar to the one Jane would play every morning before repairing to a small writing table in the family dining parlor—leaving her sister, Cassandra, to do the household chores ("I find composition impossible with my head full of joints of mutton and doses of rhubarb," Jane wrote). In the early 19th century, the road near the house was a bustling thoroughfare, and while Jane was famous for working through interruptions, one protection against the outside world was the famous creaking door. She asked that its hinges remain unattended to so it could give her warning that someone was coming. ■ TIP→ **The museum is**

IN SEARCH OF JANE AUSTEN

Jane Austen country—verdant countryside interspersed with relatively unspoiled villages—still bears traces of the decorous early-19th-century life she described with wry wit in novels such as *Emma, Persuasion, Sense and Sensibility,* and *Pride and Prejudice.* You can almost hear the clink of teacups raised by the likes of Elinor Dashwood and Mr. Darcy. Serious Janeites will want to retrace her life in Bath (⇨ *see Chapter 7*), Chawton, Winchester, and Lyme Regis.

BATH

Bath provided the elegant backdrop for the society Austen observed with such razor sharpness. Bath was Austen's home between 1801 and 1806, and although she wrote relatively little during this time, it provided the setting for *Northanger Abbey* and *Persuasion.* The Jane Austen Centre in Bath explores her relationship to the city.

CHAWTON

About 83 miles southeast of Bath is this tiny Hampshire village, the heart of Jane Austen country. Here you will find the tastefully understated house, a former bailiff's cottage on her brother's estate, where Austen worked on three of her novels. It's now a museum that sensitively evokes her life there.

WINCHESTER

Driving southwest from Chawton, take the A31 for about 15 miles to Winchester, where you can visit Austen's austere grave within the cathedral and view an exhibit about her life; then see the commemorative plaque on No. 8 College Street, where her battle with Addison's disease ended in her death on July 18, 1817.

LYME REGIS

Lyme Regis, 110 miles southwest of Winchester, is the 18th-century seaside resort on the Devon border where Austen spent the summers of 1804 and 1805. It's home to the Cobb, the stone jetty that juts into Lyme Bay, where poor Louisa Musgrove jumps off the steps known as Granny's Teeth—a turning point in *Persuasion.*

often closed for special events, so call ahead. ✉ *Winchester Rd., signed off A31/A32 roundabout* ☎ *01420/83262* 🌐 *www.jane-austens-house-museum.org.uk* 🎟 *£8.50.*

WHERE TO STAY

$$$$ HOTEL FAMILY

🏨 **Four Seasons Hotel Hampshire.** Although deep in the peaceful British countryside, this country-house hotel on a 500-acre estate is only a half hour from Heathrow. **Pros:** peaceful location; great spa; plenty of activities. **Cons:** pricey; pool dominated by children; inconsistent dining service. [$] *Rooms from: £310* ✉ *Dogmersfield Park, Chalky La., Hook* ☎ *01252/853000* 🌐 *www.fourseasons.com/hampshire* 🛏 *133 rooms* 🍴 *No meals.*

4

PORTSMOUTH

24 miles south of Chawton, 77 miles southwest of London.

In addition to a historic harbor and revitalized waterfront, Portsmouth has the energy of a working port. At Gunwharf Quays is the soaring Spinnaker Tower, as well as shops, restaurants, bars, and a contemporary art gallery. The main attractions for many visitors are the HMS *Victory*, the well-preserved flagship from which Nelson won the Battle of Trafalgar, on view at the Portsmouth Historic Dockyard; the extraordinary record of seafaring history at the National Museum of the Royal Navy; and the D-Day Museum (Operation Overlord embarked from Portsmouth). For others, Portsmouth is primarily of interest for the ferries that set off from here to the Isle of Wight and more distant destinations.

GETTING HERE AND AROUND

The M27 motorway from Southampton and the A3 from London take you to Portsmouth. There are also frequent buses and trains that drop you off at the Hard, the main transport terminus. It's only a few steps from the Historic Dockyard and Gunwharf Quays. Regular passenger ferries cross Portsmouth Harbour from the Hard for Gosport's Royal Navy Submarine Museum. Attractions in the nearby town of Southsea are best reached by car or by buses departing from the Hard.

ESSENTIALS

Visitor Information Portsmouth Visitor Information Centre. ⊠ *D-Day Museum, Clarence Esplanade* ☎ *023/9282–6722* ⊕ *www.visitportsmouth.co.uk.*

EXPLORING

FAMILY   **D-Day Museum.** The absorbing D-Day Museum in the Southsea district tells the story of the planning and preparation for the invasion of Europe during WWII and the actual landings on D-Day—June 6, 1944—through an eclectic range of exhibits. The museum's centerpiece is the Overlord Embroidery ("Overlord" was the invasion's code name), a 272-foot-long embroidered cloth with 34 panels illustrating the history of the operation, from the Battle of Britain in 1940 to victory in Normandy in 1944. ⊠ *Clarence Esplanade* ☎ *023/9282–7261* ⊕ *www. ddaymuseum.co.uk* ⊠ *£10.*

FAMILY   **Portsmouth Historic Dockyard.** The city's most impressive attraction
Fodor'sChoice   includes an unrivaled collection of historic ships. The dockyard's
★   most recent acquisition, HMS *Warrior* (1860), was Britain's first ironclad battleship and perhaps the Royal Navy's most celebrated ship. It's currently in the process of being painstakingly restored to appear as it did when it served as the flagship of British naval hero Admiral Horatio Lord Nelson at the Battle of Trafalgar (1805). You can inspect the cramped gun decks, visit the cabin where Nelson met his officers, and stand on the spot where he was mortally wounded by a French sniper. An on-site museum houses the *Mary Rose*, the former flagship of Henry VIII's navy and the world's only 16th-century warship on display. Built in this very dockyard more than 500 years ago, the boat sank in the harbor in 1545 before being raised in 1982. Once described as "the flower of all the ships that ever

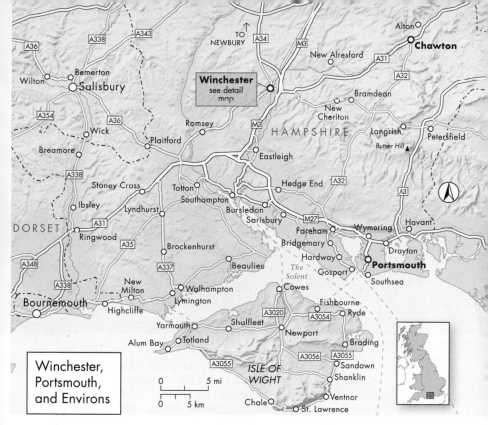

sailed," it's berthed in a special enclosure where water continuously sprays the timbers to prevent them from drying out and breaking up.

The **National Museum of the Royal Navy** has extensive exhibits about Nelson and the Battle of Trafalgar, a fine collection of painted figureheads, and galleries of paintings and mementos recalling naval history from King Alfred to the present. **Action Stations,** an interactive attraction, gives insight into life in the modern Royal Navy and tests your sea legs with tasks such as piloting boats through gales. **Boathouse 4** explores the role of smaller wooden boats in the Navy's history and challenges the adventurous to a "Mast and Rigging" experience. You should allow one or two days to tour all the attractions in the Historic Dockyard. The entrance fee includes a boat ride around the harbor, and the all-attractions ticket is valid for one year. ⊠ *Victory Gate, HM Naval Base* ☎ *023/9283–9766* ⊕ *www.historicdockyard.co.uk* ☎ *£18 each: HMS Victory, The Mary Rose, HMS Warrior, and Action Stations; Museum of the Royal Navy; £35.*

FAMILY **Royal Navy Submarine Museum.** Here you can learn about submarine history and the rigors of life below the waves with the help of family-friendly interactive games. The highlight is a tour of the only surviving World War II submarines in the United Kingdom, the HMS *Alliance* and the midget-class HMS *X24,* from the cramped living quarters to the

You can tour several different historic British ships at Portsmouth's Historic Dockyard.

engine rooms. Also on the large site is the first Royal Navy sub, Holland 1, built in 1901, and a Biber, a German WWII midget submarine. From Portsmouth Harbour, take the ferry to Gosport and walk along Millennium Promenade past the huge sundial clock. From April to October, an hourly water bus runs from the Historic Dockyard. ✉ *Haslar Jetty Rd., Gosport* ☎ *023/9251–0354* 🌐 *www.submarine-museum.co.uk* 🎫 *£13.50* 🕒 *Closed Nov.–Mar., Mon., and Tues. except bank holidays.*

Spinnaker Tower. The focal point of the lively Gunwharf Quays development of shops and bars, the Spinnaker Tower is a striking addition to Portsmouth's skyline. The slender structure evokes a mast with a billowing sail, and rises to a height of 558 feet. An elevator whisks you to three viewing platforms 330 feet high for thrilling all-around views of the harbor and up to 23 miles beyond. ✉ *Gunwharf Quays* ☎ *023/9285–7520* 🌐 *www.spinnakertower.co.uk* 🎫 *£10.50; £40.50 with Portsmouth Historic Dockyard all-attraction ticket; £23.50 with PHD single-attraction ticket.*

WHERE TO EAT

$$ MODERN BRITISH

🍴 **Abarbistro.** A relaxed, modern bistro midway between Old Portsmouth and Gunwharf Quays, this place is ideal for a snack, meal, or glass of wine from the thoughtfully chosen wine list. The changing Modern British menu specializes in seafood dishes like Keralan fish curry or battered fish-and-chips, mostly sourced from Portsmouth's fish market directly opposite. **Known for:** superfresh seafood; friendly service; extensive wine list. [$] *Average main: £16* ✉ *58 White Hart Rd.* ☎ *023/9281–1585* 🌐 *www.abarbistro.co.uk* 💳 *No credit cards.*

$$$$ BRITISH 🍴 **Montparnasse.** Modern art on taupe walls adds a contemporary touch to this relaxed restaurant, a local favorite for over 30 years. The cuisine is more Modern British–with-a-twist than classic French bistro, with dishes like slow-cooked pork belly and bream fillet with brown shrimp and lemon butter. **Known for:** nice prix-fixe menus; discreet but attentive and knowledgeable service; locally supplied ingredients. [$] *Average main: £35* ✉ *103 Palmerston Rd.* ☎ *023/9281–6754* 🌐 *www.bistro-montparnasse.co.uk* 🕒 *Closed Sun. and Mon.*

WHERE TO STAY

$ B&B/INN 🏨 **Fortitude Cottage.** With sleek modern bedrooms, this friendly B&B provides top-class waterside accommodation in two buildings in the center of Old Portsmouth, within walking distance of the Historic Dockyard via the Millennium Promenade just across the street. **Pros:** central but quiet location; helpful, friendly owners; great view from penthouse suite. **Cons:** a good amount of stairs; not all rooms have great views; some rooms on small side. [$] *Rooms from: £99* ✉ *51 Broad St.* ☎ *023/9282–3748* 🌐 *www.fortitudecottage.co.uk* 🛏 *6 rooms* 🍽 *Free Breakfast.*

$$$$ HOTEL 🏨 **No Man's Fort Hotel.** For a one-of-a-kind experience, stay in this decommissioned, iron-plated Victorian fort in the middle of the Solent, the channel between Portsmouth and the Isle of Wight. **Pros:** unique location; wonderful views from the rooftop space; game room and live entertainment. **Cons:** very pricey; only accessible by ferry, which is subject to weather conditions; being in the middle of the water is not for everyone. [$] *Rooms from: £448* ✉ *Canal Side, Gunwharf Quays* ☎ *02392/513887* 🌐 *www.amazingvenues.co.uk* 🛏 *22 rooms* 🍽 *No meals.*

SALISBURY, STONEHENGE, AND SALISBURY PLAIN

Filled with sites of cultural and historical interest, this area includes the handsome city of Salisbury, renowned for its spectacular cathedral, and the iconic prehistoric stone circles at Stonehenge and Avebury. A trio of nearby stately homes displays the ambitions and wealth of their original aristocratic inhabitants—Wilton House with its Inigo Jones–designed staterooms, Stourhead and its exquisite neoclassical gardens, and the Elizabethan splendor of Longleat. Your own transportation is essential to get to anything beyond Salisbury other than Stonehenge or Avebury.

SALISBURY

24 miles northwest of Southampton, 44 miles southeast of Bristol, 79 miles southwest of London.

The silhouette of Salisbury Cathedral's majestic spire signals your approach to this historic city long before you arrive. Although the cathedral is the principal focus of interest here, and its Cathedral Close is one of the country's most atmospheric spots (especially on a foggy night), Salisbury has much more to see, not least its largely unspoiled—and relatively traffic-free—old center. Here are stone shops and houses that over the centuries grew up in the shadow of the great church. You're never far from any of the five rivers that meet here, or from the bucolic water meadows that stretch out to the west of the cathedral and provide the best views of it. Salisbury didn't become important until the early 13th century, when the seat of the diocese was transferred here from Old Sarum, the original settlement 2 miles to the north, of which only ruins remain. In the 19th century, novelist Anthony Trollope based his tales of ecclesiastical life, notably *Barchester Towers,* on life here, although his fictional city of Barchester is really an amalgam of Salisbury and Winchester. The local tourist office organizes walks—of differing lengths for varying stamina—to guide you to the must-sees. And speaking of must-sees, prehistoric Stonehenge is less than 10 miles away and easily visited from the city.

GETTING HERE AND AROUND

Salisbury is on main bus and train routes from London and Southampton; regular buses also connect Salisbury with Winchester. The bus station is centrally located on Endless Street. Trains stop west of the center. After negotiating a ring-road system, drivers will want to park as soon as possible. The largest of the central parking lots is by Salisbury Playhouse. The city center is compact, so you won't need to use local buses for most sights. For Wilton House, take Bus Red 3 or Red 8 from Salisbury town center.

ESSENTIALS

Visitor Information Salisbury Information Centre. ⊠ *Fish Row, off Market Pl.* ☎ *01722/342860* ⊕ *www.visitwiltshire.co.uk/explore/salisbury.*

EXPLORING

Cathedral Close. Eighty acres of rolling lawns and splendid period architecture provide one of Britain's finest settings for a cathedral. The Close, the largest in the country, contains three museums: historic Mompesson House, the Salisbury Museum, and a museum devoted to the county's infantry regiments as well as the Chapter House, which houses the Magna Carta. ⊠ *65 The Close* ✛ *Bounded by West Walk, North Walk, and Exeter St.* ⊕ *www.salisburycathedral.org.uk.*

Long Bridge. For a classic view of Salisbury, head to Long Bridge and Town Path. From the main street, walk west to Mill Road, which leads you across the Queen Elizabeth Gardens. Cross the bridge and continue on Town Path through the water meadows, from which you can see the vista that inspired John Constable's 1831 *Salisbury Cathedral from the Meadows,* one of Britain's most iconic paintings, now on view in London's Tate Britain. ⊠ *Salisbury.*

Market Place. The Charter Market, one of southern England's most popular markets, fills this square on Tuesday and Saturday. Permission to hold an annual fair here was granted in 1221, and that right is still exercised for three days every October, when the Charter Fair takes place. A narrow side street links Poultry Cross to Market Place. ⊠ *Salisbury.*

Old Sarum. Massive earthwork ramparts on a bare sweep of Wiltshire countryside are all that remain of this impressive Iron Age hill fort, which was successively taken over by Romans, Saxons, and Normans (you can still see the ruins of a castle built by William the Conqueror in

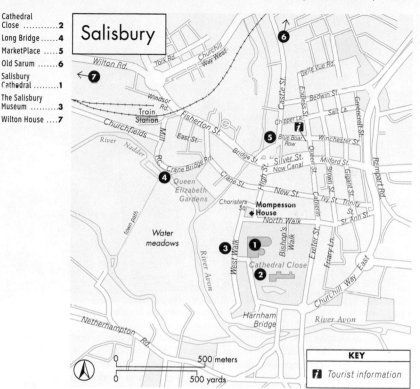

1070 within the earthworks). The site was still fortified in Tudor times, though the population had mostly decamped in the 13th century to New Sarum, or Salisbury. You can clamber over the huge banks and take in the far-reaching views to Salisbury Cathedral. ⊠ *Castle Rd.* ✛ *Off A345* ☎ *01722/335398* ⊕ *www.english-heritage.org.uk* ⊠ *£4.80.*

Fodor's Choice **Salisbury Cathedral.** Salisbury is dominated by the towering cathedral,
★ a soaring hymn in stone. It is unique among cathedrals in that it was conceived and built as a whole in the amazingly short span of 38 years (1220–58). The spire, added in 1320, is the tallest in England and a miraculous feat of medieval engineering—even though the point, 404 feet above the ground, is 2½ feet off vertical. The excellent model of the cathedral in the north nave aisle, directly in front of you as you enter, shows the building about 20 years into construction, and makes clear the ambition of Salisbury's medieval builders. For all their sophistication, the height and immense weight of the great spire have always posed structural problems. In the late 17th century Sir Christopher Wren was summoned from London to strengthen the spire, and in the mid-19th century Sir George Gilbert Scott, a leading Victorian Gothicist, undertook a major program of restoration. He also initiated a clearing out of the interior and removed some less-than-sympathetic 18th-century alterations, returning a more authentically Gothic feel.

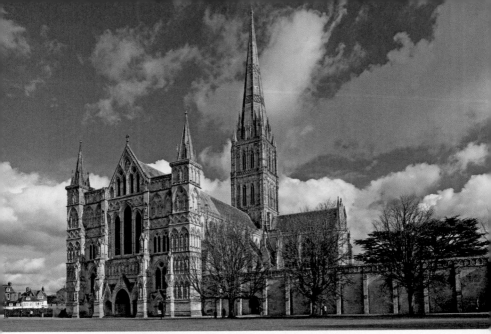

Salisbury Cathedral has a towering spire—the tallest in England—that you can tour.

Despite this, the interior seems spartan and a little gloomy, but check out the remarkable lancet windows and sculpted tombs of crusaders and other medieval notables. Next to the cathedral model in the north aisle is a medieval clock—probably the oldest working mechanism in Europe, if not the world—made in 1386.

The **cloisters** are the largest in England, and the octagonal **Chapter House** contains a marvelous 13th-century frieze showing scenes from the Old Testament. Here you can also see one of the four original copies of the **Magna Carta,** the charter of rights the English barons forced King John to accept in 1215; it was sent here for safekeeping in the 13th century. ■ TIP→ Join a free one-hour tour of the cathedral, leaving two or more times a day. For a peaceful break, the café in the cloister serves freshly baked cakes and pastries, plus hot lunches. ✉ *Cathedral Close* ☎ *01722/555120* ⊕ *www.salisburycathedral.org.uk* ✉ *Cathedral and Chapter House free, suggested donation £7.50; tower tour £12.50.*

The Salisbury Museum. Opposite the cathedral's west front, this excellent museum is in the King's House, parts of which date to the 15th century (James I stayed here in 1610 and 1613). The history of the area from prehistoric times through the Norman Conquest is explored in the Wessex gallery, which houses some of Britain's most important archaeological finds and where Stonehenge-related exhibits provide helpful background information for a visit to the famous megaliths. Also on view are collections of local costumes dating back 250 years, outstanding British ceramics, and Turner watercolors, all dwarfed by the 12-foot Salisbury Giant, a 13-century pageant figure, and his companion hobbyhorse, Hob Nob. A cozy café is in one of the oldest sections of the building. ✉ *The King's House, 65 The Close* ☎ *01722/332151* 🌐 *www.salisburymuseum.org.uk* 🎟 *£7.50 (tickets good for 1 year).*

Fodor's Choice ★ **Wilton House.** This is considered to be one of the loveliest stately homes in England and, along with its grounds, a fine example of the English Palladian style. The seat of the earls of Pembroke since Tudor times, the south wing of the current building was rebuilt in the early 17th century by Isaac de Caus, with input from Inigo Jones, Ben Jonson's stage designer and the architect of London's Banqueting House. It was completed by James Webb, again with input from Jones, Webb's uncle-by-marriage, after the recently finished south wing was ravaged by fire in 1647. Most noteworthy are the seven state rooms in the south wing, among them the Single Cube Room (built as a perfect 30-foot cube) and, one of the most extravagantly beautiful rooms in the history of interior decoration, the aptly named Double Cube Room. The name refers to its proportions (60 feet long by 30 feet wide and 30 feet high), evidence of Jones's classically inspired belief that beauty in architecture derives from harmony and balance. The room's headliner is the spectacular Van Dyck portrait of the Pembroke family. Elsewhere at Wilton House, the art collection includes several other Old Master paintings, including works by Rembrandt and members of the Brueghel family. Another exhibition is devoted to Cecil Beaton's photo portraits of 20th-century notables and the current Lord Pembroke's collection of classic cars. Also of note are the 22 acres of lovely grounds, which have sweeping lawns dotted with towering oaks; the gardens; and the Palladian bridge crossing the small River Nadder, designed by the 9th earl after the Rialto Bridge in Venice. Some public rooms may be closed on some open days—check website for more information. The town of Wilton is 3 miles west of Salisbury. Buses Red 3 and Red 8 from Salisbury depart every 10 to 15 minutes and stop outside Wilton House. ✉ *Off A36, Wilton* ☎ *01722/746728* 🌐 *www.wiltonhouse.co.uk* 🎟 *£15.50; grounds only £6.50* 🕒 *Closed Sept.–Apr., Fri., and Sat.*

4

WHERE TO EAT

$$ INDIAN Fodor's Choice ★ 🍴 **Anokaa.** For a refreshingly modern take on Indian cuisine, try this bustling restaurant a few minutes from the center. Classic recipes are taken as starting points for the artistically presented dishes, which include tandoori-seared rack of lamb, cinnamon-glazed duck breast stuffed with garlicky spinach, and black tiger prawns in a sauce of curry leaves and coconut oil. **Known for:** creative, well-executed Indian dishes; excellent service; buffet lunch. [$] *Average main: £16* ✉ *60 Fisherton St.* ☎ *01722/414142* 🌐 *www.anokaa.com.*

$$ BRITISH 🍴 **Charter 1227.** Casual and friendly but still upscale, this second-floor restaurant overlooking Market Place offers seasonal menus blending traditional British and European elements. Dishes prepared by the owner-chef include roast duck breast with artichokes and a plum and blackberry sauce, or panfried John Dory with a brioche-crumb coating in a dill-and-lime sauce. **Known for:** prix-fixe lunches and early-bird dinners; friendly service; no cocktail menu. [$] *Average main: £19* ✉ *6/7 Ox Row, Market Pl.* ☎ *01722/333118* 🌐 *www.charter1227.co.uk* 🕒 *Closed Sun. and Mon.*

$$$$ ✕ **Howard's House.** If you're after complete tranquility, head for this
MODERN BRITISH early-17th-century house on 2 acres of grounds in the Nadder Valley. The
Fodor's Choice excellent restaurant has fixed-price menus specializing in contemporary
★ English cooking using local and seasonal ingredients, such as a fillet of
wild turbot with crab consomme, or roast loin of venison. **Known for:**
excellent six-course tasting menu; relaxed and romantic atmosphere; ter-
race dining in the summer. $ *Average main: £33* ⊠ *Teffont Evias, Teffont
Evias* ✦ *Off B3089* ☎ *01722/716392* ⊕ *www.howardshousehotel.co.uk.*

WHERE TO STAY

$$ 🏨 **Cricket Field House.** Located halfway between Wilton and Salisbury,
B&B/INN this comfortable ex-gamekeeper's cottage overlooks a cricket ground
and has a large, peaceful garden of its own. **Pros:** efficient, helpful
management; well-maintained rooms; good breakfasts. **Cons:** 20-min-
ute walk from town; on a busy road; no restaurant on-site. $ *Rooms
from: £110* ⊠ *Wilton Rd.* ☎ *01722/322595* ⊕ *www.cricketfieldhouse.
co.uk* ⬅ *18 rooms* ⦿ *Free Breakfast.*

$$ 🏨 **Mercure Salisbury White Hart Hotel.** Behind the pillared portico and
HOTEL imposing 17th-century classical facade of this city center hotel (part
of the Mercure chain) are modern bedrooms (of various sizes) with a
muted cream-and-brown color scheme. **Pros:** central location; cozy public areas; comfortable rooms. **Cons:** some rooms are small; impersonal,
corporate feel; some tired design. $ *Rooms from: £130* ⊠ *1 St. John St.*
☎ *01722/312801* ⊕ *www.mercure.com* ⬅ *68 rooms* ⦿ *Free Breakfast.*

$ 🏨 **Wyndham Park Lodge.** This simple Victorian house in a quiet part
B&B/INN of town (off Castle Street) provides an excellent place to rest and a
delicious breakfast, as well as a garden. **Pros:** efficient and hospitable
owners; good breakfast; handy parking. **Cons:** spotty Wi-Fi; furnishings
a bit dated. $ *Rooms from: £85* ⊠ *51 Wyndham Rd.* ☎ *01722/416517*
⊕ *www.wyndhamparklodge.co.uk* ⬅ *4 rooms* ⦿ *Free Breakfast.*

STONEHENGE

8 miles north of Salisbury, 20 miles south of Avebury.

Almost five millennia after their construction, these stone circles on the
Salisbury Plain continue to pose fascinating questions. How were the
giant stones, some weighing as much as 45 tons, brought here, possibly
from as far away as Wales? What was the site used for? Why were the
stones aligned with the midsummer sunrise and the midwinter sunset? But
Stonehenge is more than just the megaliths; the surrounding landscape
is dotted with ancient earthworks, remains of Neolithic settlements, and
processional pathways, creating a complex of ceremonial structures that
testifies to the sophisticated belief system of these early Britons.

GETTING HERE AND AROUND

Stonehenge Tour buses leave from Salisbury's train and bus stations
every half hour from 9:30 to 2:30, and then hourly from 3 to 5, from
early June to August; hourly from 10 to 4 from April to early June and
September through October; and 10 to 2 in November through March.
Tickets cost £15 or £29 (includes Stonehenge and a visit to Old Sarum).
Other options are a taxi or a custom tour. Drivers can find the monument near the junction of A303 with A344.

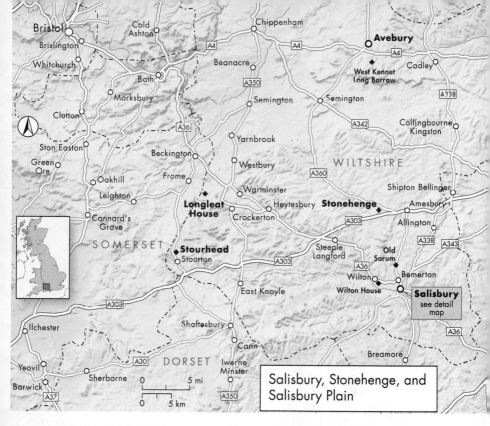

Salisbury, Stonehenge, and Salisbury Plain

EXPLORING

FAMILY
Fodor's Choice
★

Stonehenge. Mysterious and ancient, Stonehenge has baffled archaeologists, not to mention the general public, for centuries. One of England's most visited monuments and a UNESCO World Heritage Site, the circle of giant stones standing starkly against the wide sweep of Salisbury Plain still has the capacity to fascinate and move those who view it. The stone circle itself was completed in stages, beginning around 2500 BC. You can no longer walk among the stones, so bring a pair of binoculars to help make out the details on the monoliths. To fully engage your imagination, or to get that magical photo, it's worth exploring all aspects of the site, both near and far. An informative visitor center is located 1½ miles away (access to the stone circle is via a frequent shuttle). To best experience the awe and mystery of Stonehenge, visit the circle in the early morning or in the evening, when the crowds have dispersed. Visits are by timed admission slots only. ✉ *Amesbury* ✚ *Junction of A360 and Airman's Corner* ☎ *0370/333–1181, 0370/333–0605 for stone circle access* ⊕ *www.english-heritage.org.uk* ☜ *£19.30 (walk-up); £16.50 (advance).*

DID YOU KNOW?

The circle of stones at Stonehenge is impressive, but the site isn't an isolated monument. The UNESCO World Heritage Site of Stonehenge and Avebury includes more than 350 nearby burial mounds and prehistoric monuments.

AVEBURY

24 miles north of Stonehenge, 34 miles north of Salisbury, 25 miles northeast of Longleat, 27 miles east of Bath.

The village of Avebury was built much later than its famous stone circles; it has an informative museum with an outstanding collection of Bronze Age artifacts from the area around here and Stonehenge. You can also explore a cluster of other prehistoric sites nearby.

GETTING HERE AND AROUND

From Salisbury, follow A345 north to Upavon and take the A342 to Devizes; then continue 7 miles northeast on the A361. You can also take the hourly Stagecoach bus No. 49 from Swindon to Avebury (30 minutes).

EXPLORING

Alexander Keiller Museum. The Avebury Stone Circles are put into context by this collection of Neolithic and Bronze Age artifacts from the site, one of the most important prehistoric archaeological collections in Britain. The museum contains charts, photos, models, and home movies taken by its namesake, archaeologist Alexander Keiller. It has been suggested that Keiller, responsible for the excavation of Avebury in the 1930s, may have adapted the site's layout to highlight presentation more than authenticity. The exhibits are divided between the 17th-century **Stables Gallery**, which displays finds from Keiller's excavations, the child-friendly **Barn Gallery**, where you find interactive exhibits about the history of Avebury, and an activity area where kids can dress up in Bronze Age clothes. You can also visit the **Manor House**, where Keiller lived, and its surrounding gardens. The Tudor-era building received several subsequent (Queen Anne, Regency, and art deco) additions, and the rooms have been filled with acquired or commissioned period-appropriate furniture to illustrate how previous occupants lived. ⊠ *High St.* ⊕ *Off A4361* ☎ *01672/539250* ⊕ *www. nationaltrust.org.uk* ⛯ *Museum £4.40; manor house and gardens £9* ⊘ *Manor House closed Jan.–mid-Feb. and Mon.–Wed. in Nov. and Dec.; gardens closed Nov.–late Mar.*

Fodor's Choice
★ **Avebury Stone Circles.** Surrounding part of Avebury village, the Avebury Stone Circles, the largest in the world, are one of England's most evocative prehistoric monuments—not as famous as Stonehenge, but all the more powerful for their lack of commercial exploitation. The stones were erected around 2600 BC, about the same time as the better-known monument. As with Stonehenge, the purpose of this stone circle has never been ascertained, although it most likely was used for similar ritual purposes. Unlike Stonehenge, however, there are no certain astronomical alignments at Avebury, at least none that have survived. The main site consists of a wide, circular ditch and bank, about 1,400 feet across and more than half a mile around. Entrances break the perimeter at roughly the four points of the compass, and inside stand the remains of three stone circles. The largest one originally had 98 stones, although only 27 remain. Many stones on the site were destroyed centuries ago, especially in the 14th century when they were buried for unclear reasons, possibly religious fanaticism. Others were later pillaged in the

18th century to build the thatched cottages you see flanking the fields. You can walk around the circles, a World Heritage Site, at any time; early morning and early evening are recommended. As with Stonehenge, the summer solstice tends to draw the crowds. ✉ *Avebury* ✣ *1 mile north of A4* ☎ *01672/539–250* 🌐 *www.english-heritage.org.uk* 🎫 *Free.*

Fodor's Choice ★ **West Kennet Long Barrow.** One of the largest Neolithic chambered tombs in Britain, West Kennet Long Barrow was built around 3400 BC. You can explore all around the site and also enter the tomb, which was used for more than 1,000 years before the main passage was blocked and the entrance closed, around 2000 BC. More than 300 feet long, it has an elevated position with a great view of Silbury Hill and the surrounding countryside. It's about 1 mile east of Avebury. ✉ *Avebury* ✣ *¾ mile southwest of West Kennett, along footpath off A4* ☎ *01672/539250* 🌐 *www.english-heritage.org.uk* 🎫 *Free.*

WHERE TO EAT

$ BRITISH 🍴 **Waggon and Horses.** A 17th-century thatched-roof building with foundations made from sarsen stones, this traditional inn and pub is a two-minute drive from the Avebury stone circles. With a beer garden that has views of Silbury Hill, it's something of a tourist hub in high season, but lunches and dinners are still excellent. **Known for:** cozy atmosphere with open fire; homemade food using locally sourced ingredients; crowds in high season. [$] *Average main: £12* ✉ *Beckhampton* ✣ *A4, 300 feet east of junction with A361* ☎ *01672/539418* 🌐 *www.waggonandhorsesbeckhampton.co.uk.*

WHERE TO STAY

$$$ B&B/INN 🏨 **The Lodge.** With their eclectic design, rare prints, and antique furnishings, the two spacious guest rooms of this charming B&B are full of character. **Pros:** unique location and views; comfortable rooms; friendly host. **Cons:** can book up; expensive; early 10 am checkout. [$] *Rooms from: £195* ✉ *Rawlings Park* ✣ *Off A4361* ☎ *01672/539023* 🌐 *www.aveburylodge.co.uk* 🛏 *2 rooms* 🍽 *Free Breakfast.*

LONGLEAT HOUSE

31 miles southwest of Avebury, 6 miles north of Stourhead, 19 miles south of Bath, 27 miles northwest of Salisbury.

With its popular safari park and a richly decorated High Elizabethan house to explore, Longleat can provide a day of diversions.

GETTING HERE AND AROUND

Longleat House is off A36 between Bath and Salisbury. The nearest train station is Warminster, about 5 miles away. Your best option is to take a taxi from there.

ESSENTIALS

Visitor Information Warminster Community Hub. ✉ *Central car park, off Station Rd., Warminster* ☎ *01985/218548* 🌐 *www.warminstercommunityhub.co.uk.*

EXPLORING

FAMILY Fodor's Choice ★ **Longleat House.** Home of the Marquess of Bath, Longleat House is one of southern England's most famous stately homes, and possibly the most ambitiously, even eccentrically, commercialized, as evidenced by the presence of a drive-through safari park (open since 1966) with giraffes, zebras, gorillas, monkeys, rhinos, and lions. The house, considered to be one of the finest remaining examples of High Elizabethan, was largely completed in 1580 for more than £8,000, an astronomical sum at the time. It contains outstanding tapestries, paintings, porcelain, furniture, and one of the largest private collections of books in England (more than 40,000 volumes housed in seven libraries). Notable period features include Victorian kitchens, an Elizabethan minstrels' gallery, painted ceilings, and a great hall with massive wooden beams. In addition to 900 acres of parkland designed by Capability Brown, plus formal and pleasure gardens and the safari park, the property has a miniature railway, a petting zoo, an extensive (and fairly fiendish) hedge maze, and an "adventure castle," all of which make it extremely popular, particularly in summer and during school vacations. A first-come, first-served safari bus service is available (£5) for those arriving without their own transport. ✉ *Warminster* ✣ *Off A362* ☎ *01985/844400* 🌐 *www.longleat.co.uk* 🎟 *£34.95; house and grounds only £18.95.*

WHERE TO STAY

$$ HOTEL 🏨 **Bishopstrow House.** This ivy-covered Regency manor house set in 27 acres has been converted into a relaxed country-house hotel that combines well-chosen antiques with modern amenities. **Pros:** country-house ambience; impressive suites; friendly staff. **Cons:** expensive extras; lackluster spa; some tired decor. [$] *Rooms from: £135* ✉ *Boreham Rd., Warminster* ☎ *01985/212312* 🌐 *www.bishopstrow.co.uk* 🛏 *32 rooms* 🍴 *Free Breakfast.*

STOURHEAD

9 miles southwest of Longleat, 15 miles northeast of Sherborne, 30 miles west of Salisbury.

England has many memorable gardens, but Stourhead is one of the most glorious. Its centerpiece is a magnificent artificial lake surrounded by neoclassical temples, atmospheric grottos, and rare trees. The Palladian stately home is also worth a look.

GETTING HERE AND AROUND

By car, you can reach Stourhead via B3092. It's signposted off the main road. From London, board a train to Gillingham and take a five-minute cab ride to Stourton.

EXPLORING

Fodor's Choice ★ **Stourhead.** Close to the village of Stourton lies one of Wiltshire's most breathtaking sights—Stourhead, a country-house-and-garden combination that has few parallels for beauty anywhere in Europe. Most of Stourhead was built between 1721 and 1725 by the wealthy banker Henry Hoare, more colorfully known as Henry the Magnificent. A fire gutted the center of the house in 1902, but it was reconstructed with only a few differences. Many rooms in the Palladian mansion contain Chinese and French porcelain, and some have furniture by Chippendale. The elegant Regency library and picture gallery were built for the cultural enrichment of this cultivated family. Still, the house takes second place to the adjacent gardens designed by Henry Hoare II, which are the most celebrated example of the English 18th-century taste for "natural" landscaping. Temples, grottoes, follies, and bridges have been placed among shrubs, trees, and flowers to make the grounds look like a three-dimensional oil painting. A walk around the artificial lake (1½ miles) reveals changing vistas that conjure up the 17th-century landscapes of Claude Lorrain and Nicolas Poussin; walk counterclockwise for the best views. ■ **TIP→ The best time to visit is early summer, when the massive banks of rhododendrons are in full bloom, or mid-October for autumn color, but the gardens are beautiful at any time of year.** You can get a fine view of the surrounding area from King Alfred's Tower, a 1772 folly (a structure built for picturesque effect). ✉ *Stourton* ✢ *Off B3092, near Mere* ☎ *01747/841152* 🌐 *www.nationaltrust.org.uk* 🎟 *House £13.70; gardens £8.30; King Alfred's Tower £3.40* ⏲ *House closed Jan.–mid-Mar. and mid–late Nov.; King Alfred's Tower closed late Oct.–mid-Mar.*

WHERE TO STAY

$$ B&B/INN 🏨 **The Spread Eagle.** You can't stay at Stourhead, but you can stay at this popular inn built at the beginning of the 19th century just inside the main entrance. **Pros:** period character; lovely rooms; free access to Stourhead. **Cons:** needs some modernization; food can be disappointing; handheld shower attachments as opposed to real showers. [$] *Rooms from: £130* ✉ *Church Lawn, near Warminster, Stourton* ☎ *01747/840587* 🌐 *www.spreadeagleinn.com* 🛏 *5 rooms* 🍴 *Free Breakfast.*

NEW FOREST, DORSET, AND THE SOUTH COAST

The New Forest, a woodland southeast of Salisbury, was once a hunting preserve of William the Conqueror, so he could pursue his favorite sport close to the royal seat at Winchester. Thus protected from the worst of the deforestation that has befallen most of southern England's other forests, this relatively undeveloped, scenic national park has great possibilities for walking, riding, and biking. West of here stretches the largely unspoiled county of Dorset, which encompasses the beaches, coves, rolling hills, and lush fields that were the setting for most of Thomas Hardy's books, including *Far from the Madding Crowd*, and other classic Victorian-era novels. "I am convinced that it is better for a writer to know a little bit of the world remarkably well than to know a great part of the world remarkably little," Hardy wrote, and the bit he chose to know was the towns, villages, and countryside of this rural area, not least the county capital, Dorchester, an ancient agricultural center. North of here is the picturesque market town of Sherborne, with its impressive abbey. Other places of historic interest, such as Maiden Castle, are close to bustling seaside resorts. You may find Lyme Regis (associated with 20th-century novelist John Fowles) and the villages along the route closer to your ideal of coastal England. Fossil enthusiasts should head for the Jurassic Coast.

LYNDHURST

26 miles southeast of Stonehenge, 18 miles southeast of Salisbury, 9 miles west of Southampton.

Lyndhurst is famous as the capital of the New Forest. Although some popular spots can get crowded in summer, there are ample parking lots, picnic areas, and campgrounds. Miles of trails crisscross the region.

GETTING HERE AND AROUND

From Salisbury, follow A36, B3079, and continue along A337 another 4 miles or so. To explore the New Forest, take A35 out of Lyndhurst (the road continues southwest to Bournemouth) or A337 south. The New Forest Tour is a hop-on, hop-off open-top bus. Regular bus services are operated by Bluestar and Wilts & Dorset. Many parts of the New Forest are readily accessible by train from London via the centrally located Brockenhurst Station.

EXPLORING

FAMILY

Fodor'sChoice

★

New Forest. This national park, still largely owned by the Crown, consists of 150 square miles of woodland, heaths, grassland, bogs, and the remains of coppices and timber plantations established in the 17th to 19th century. Residents have had grazing rights since the 12th century, and you can still encounter free-roaming cattle, and, most famously, the hardy New Forest ponies. An extensive network of trails makes it a wonderful place for biking, walking, and horseback riding. ⊠ *Lyndhurst* ⊕ *www.thenewforest.co.uk* ⊠ *Free.*

FAMILY

New Forest Information Centre. This visitor complex with a gallery, museum, and reference library devoted to the New Forest contains displays and activities related to the area's geology, history, wildlife, and culture. The museum is packed with quizzes and other interactive elements that keep children engaged. ⊠ *Main car park, High St.* ☎ *023/8028–3444* ⊕ *www.newforestcentre.org.uk* ⊠ *Free.*

WHERE TO EAT

$$$

MODERN BRITISH

Fodor'sChoice

★

✕ **The Pig.** Funkier sister of glamorous Lime Wood, this New Forest "restaurant with rooms" puts the emphasis on localism and seasonality and is a local favorite. Lunch and dinner are served in a large Victorian greenhouse overlooking lawns, and the frequently changing menu may include dishes like pork belly with oyster mushrooms and a basil-and-sunflower-seed salsa verde, or poached silver mullet with fennel, Dorset olives, and samphire. **Known for:** nearly all ingredients come from their own garden or other sources within 25 miles; porcine dishes, as the name suggests; foraging expeditions with the staff. $ *Average main: £20* ⊠ *Beaulieu Rd., Brockenhurst* ☎ *01590/622354* ⊕ *www.thepighotel.com.*

New Forest, Dorset,
and the South Coast

WHERE TO STAY

$$$$
HOTEL

🛏 **Chewton Glen Hotel and Spa.** This grand early-19th-century country-house hotel and spa on extensive manicured grounds ranks among Britain's most acclaimed—and most expensive—lodgings. **Pros:** classic English luxury; top-notch leisure facilities; high staff-to-guest ratio. **Cons:** expensive rates; can be noisy during school holidays; service not always up to five-star expectations. $ *Rooms from: £325* ✉ *Christchurch Rd., New Milton* ☎ *01425/275341, 800/344–5087 in U.S.* ⊕ *www.chewtonglen.com* ➟ *70 rooms* ⦿ *Some meals.*

$$$$
HOTEL
Fodor's Choice
★

🛏 **Lime Wood.** If you're looking for a discreet, luxurious hideaway in a woodland setting with uninterrupted views and an excellent spa, this hugely relaxing country-house hotel is hard to beat. **Pros:** great location; stylish yet comfortable design; friendly staff. **Cons:** hard to reach without a car; breakfast not included; pricey. $ *Rooms from: £330* ✉ *Beaulieu Rd.* ☎ *023/8028–7177* ⊕ *www.limewoodhotel.co.uk* ➟ *29 rooms* ⦿ *No meals.*

SPORTS AND THE OUTDOORS

Largely unspoiled and undeveloped, yet accessible even to those not normally given to long walks or bike rides, the New Forest provides numerous opportunities to explore the outdoors. Bike rental and horseback riding are widely available. Numerous trails lead through thickly wooded country, across open heaths, and through the occasional bog. With very few hills, it's fairly easy terrain, and rich with wildlife. You're almost guaranteed to see wild ponies and deer, and occasionally free-roaming cattle and pigs.

BIKING

Cycle Experience. Bike rentals from £17.50 per day allow you to explore a range of trails weaving through the New Forest, one of Britain's best terrains for off-road biking. ✉ *2 Brookley Rd., Brockenhurst* ☎ *01590/624808* ⊕ *www.newforestcyclehire.co.uk.*

HORSEBACK RIDING

FAMILY **Brockenhurst Riding Stables.** There are rides for all levels at Burley Manor Riding Stables. Hour-long rides are £35. ✉ *Warren Farm, Balmer Lawn Rd., Brockenhurst* ☎ *01590/624747* ⊕ *www.brockenhurstridingstables.co.uk.*

BEAULIEU

7 miles southeast of Lyndhurst.

The unspoiled village of Beaulieu (pronounced *byoo*-lee) has three major attractions in one at Beaulieu Abbey and is near the museum village of Buckler's Hard.

GETTING HERE AND AROUND

Beaulieu is best reached by car on B3056 from Lyndhurst or B3054 from Lymington. It's signposted off A326 from Southampton. Bus 112 has a limited service (three times daily on Tuesday and Thursday) between Beaulieu and Lymington and Hythe, except during August, when it becomes the "Beach Bus" and runs daily. During the summer, the New Forest Tour bus extends to Beaulieu.

EXPLORING

FAMILY **Beaulieu.** With a ruined 13th-century abbey, a stately home, and an automobile museum, Beaulieu appeals to several different interests. **Beaulieu Abbey** was founded in 1204 by Cistercian monks on land given to them by King John (the name means "beautiful place" in French.) You can still see the ruins of the cloister and the herb garden, as well as two remaining buildings, one containing an exhibition re-creating daily life in the monastery. **Palace House and Gardens** incorporates the abbey's original 14th-century gatehouse and has been the home of the Montagu family since they purchased it in 1538, after the dissolution of the monasteries, when the abbey was badly damaged. You can explore the drawing rooms, dining halls, fine family portraits, and the beautiful grounds. The present Lord Montagu established the **National Motor Museum,** which traces the history of British motoring. The collection contains more than 250 classic cars and motorcycles, from late-19th-century vehicles to futuristic F1 racing cars, plus famous film cars like the flying Ford Anglia from *Harry Potter and the Chamber of Secrets.* Other museum attractions include interactive experiences, audiovisual displays, a World of *Top Gear* attraction devoted to the popular British TV show (complete with test track), and rides in vehicles ranging from a monorail to a 1912 London bus. ✉ *Beaulieu* ✛ *Off B3056* ☎ *01590/612345* ⊕ *www.beaulieu.co.uk* ✉ *Abbey, Palace House, World of Top Gear, and Motor Museum £24.75 (£19.50 in advance).*

CORFE CASTLE

25 miles south of Wimborne Minster, 15 miles south of Poole, 5 miles southeast of Wareham.

The village of Corfe Castle is best known for the ancient, ruined castle that overlooks it.

ESSENTIALS

Visitor Information Discover Purbeck Information Centre. ⊠ *Wareham Library, South St.* ☎ *01929/552740* ⊕ *www.visit-dorset.com.*

EXPLORING

Corfe Castle. One of the most dramatic ruins in Britain, Corfe Castle overlooks the picturesque gray limestone village of the same name. The present ruins are of the castle built in 1086, when the great central keep was erected by William the Conqueror to guard the principal route through the surrounding Purbeck Hills. The outer walls and towers were added in the 1270s. Cromwell's soldiers blew up the castle in 1646 during the Civil War, after a long siege during which its Royalist chatelaine, Lady Bankes, led its defense. ⊠ *A351* ✛ *Off A351, in Corfe Castle* ☎ *01929/481294* ⊕ *www.nationaltrust.org.uk* ☏ *£10.40 Apr.– Oct. weekends and bank holidays; £9.50 all other times.*

FAMILY **Swanage Railway.** Train enthusiasts love this largely volunteer-run railroad that makes 25-minute, 6-mile scenic trips, with steam (and some diesel) locomotives pulling vintage train carriages across the Isle of Purbeck— actually a peninsula. Trips begin from Norden in the center and go to the seaside town of Swanage via Corfe Castle. Small, pretty stations with flower baskets, painted signs, and water bowls for dogs add to the excursion's charm. Trains leave approximately every 80 minutes in low season, and every 40 minutes in high season. ⊠ *Station House, Springfield Rd., Swanage* ☎ *01929/425800* ⊕ *www.swanagerailway.co.uk* ☏ *£2.70–£13* ⊙ *Closed Jan. and weekdays in Nov., Dec., Feb., and Mar.*

WHERE TO STAY

$$$ ▒ **The Pig at the Beach.** The latest outpost of the Hampshire luxury mini-
HOTEL chain is in a Victorian Gothic former private residence in an unspoiled
Fodor'sChoice village on the scenic, peaceful Studland Peninsula. **Pros:** beautiful loca-
★ tion; comfortable bedrooms and welcoming public rooms; excellent restaurant. **Cons:** not many activities for bad weather; breakfast not included; ubiquitous piped music not for everyone. ⓢ *Rooms from: £165* ⊠ *Manor House, Manor Rd., Swanage* ☎ *01929/450288* ⊕ *www. thepighotel.com/on-the-beach* ⌁ *23 rooms, 2 cottages, 1 hut* ꙰*No meals.*

DORCHESTER

21 miles west of Corfe, 30 miles west of Bournemouth, 43 miles south-west of Salisbury.

The traditional market town of Dorchester was immortalized as Casterbridge by Thomas Hardy in his 19th-century novel *The Mayor of Casterbridge.* In fact, the whole area around here, including a number of villages tucked away in the rolling hills of Dorset, has become known as "Hardy country" because of its connection with the author. Hardy was born in a cottage in the hamlet of Higher Bockhampton, about 3 miles northeast of the town, and his bronze statue looks westward from a bank on Colliton Walk. Two important historical sites, as well as the author's birthplace and a former residence, are a short drive from Dorchester.

Dorchester has many reminders of its Roman heritage. A stroll along Bowling Alley Walk, West Walk, and Colliton Walk follows the approximate line of the original Roman town walls, part of a city plan laid out around AD 70. On the north side of Colliton Park is an excavated Roman villa with a marvelously preserved mosaic floor. While the high street in the center of town can be busy with vehicular traffic, the tourist office has walking itineraries that cover the main points of interest along quieter routes and help you appreciate the character of Dorchester today.

GETTING HERE AND AROUND

Dorchester can be reached from Corfe Castle via A351 and A352. From Salisbury take A354. Park wherever you can (pay parking lots are scattered around the center) and explore the town on foot.

ESSENTIALS

Visitor Information Dorchester Tourist Information Centre. ⊠ *Dorchester Library and Learning Centre, Charles St.* ☎ *01305/267992* ⊕ *www.visit-dorset.com.*

EXPLORING

Athelhampton House and Gardens. This outstandingly well-preserved example of 15th-century domestic Tudor architecture (with 16th- and 20th-century additions) turns up as Athelhall in some of Thomas Hardy's writings (Hardy was a frequent visitor and his father, a stonemason, worked on the house). Don't miss the Great Hall, built in 1485, still with its original linenfold paneling, heraldic stained glass, and vaulted timber roof. The paneled Library contains more than 3,000 books. Outside, 20 acres of grounds include eight formal walled gardens created in the 19th century and 12 yew pyramids, each 30 feet high. ⊠ *Dorchester* ✛ *A35, 5 miles east of Dorchester* ☎ *01305/848363* ⊕ *www.athelhampton.co.uk* ▨ *House and garden: £13.50; garden only: £9.50* ⊙ *Closed Fri. and Sat. year-round and weekdays Nov.–Feb.*

Dorset County Museum. This labyrinthine museum contains eclectic collections devoted to nearby Roman and Celtic archaeological finds, Jurassic Coast geology, social history (especially rural crafts and agriculture), decorative arts, regional costumes, and local literary luminaries, primarily Hardy but also T.E. Lawrence and others. ⊠ *High West St.* ☎ *01305/262735* ⊕ *www.dorsetcountymuseum.org* ▨ *£6.35* ⊙ *Closed Sun. Apr.-late July and mid-Sept.–Mar.*

Hardy's Cottage. Thomas Hardy's grandfather built this small thatch-and-cob cottage, where the writer was born in 1840, and little has changed since the family left. Here Hardy grew up and wrote many of his early works, including *Far from the Madding Crowd*, at a desk you can still see. Access is by foot only, via a walk through woodland or down a country lane from the parking lot. There's a visitor center with information about the surrounding landscape and trails that let you follow in Hardy's footsteps. ✉ *Brockhampton La., Higher Bockhampton* ✥ *½ mile south of Blandford Rd.* ☎ *01305/262366* 🌐 *www.nationaltrust.org.uk* 🎟 *£7* ⏲ *Closed Nov.–Feb. and Mon.–Wed.*

Maiden Castle. Although called a castle, this is actually one of the most important pre-Roman archaeological sites in England and the largest, most complex Iron Age hill fort in Europe, made of stone and earth with ramparts that enclose about 45 acres. England's Neolithic inhabitants built the fort some 4,000 years ago, and many centuries later it was a Celtic stronghold. In AD 43 invading Romans, under the general (later emperor) Vespasian, stormed the fort. Finds from the site are on display in the Dorset County Museum in Dorchester. To experience an uncanny silence and sense of mystery, climb Maiden Castle early in the day. Leave your car in the lot at the end of Maiden Castle Way, a 1½-mile lane. ✉ *Winterborne Monkton* ✥ *Off A354, 2 miles southwest of Dorchester* ☎ *0370/333–1181* 🌐 *www.english-heritage.org.uk.*

WHERE TO EAT

$$$$ MODERN FRENCH

🍴 **Yalbury Cottage.** Oak-beamed ceilings, exposed stone walls, and inglenook fireplaces add to the charm of this restaurant in a 300-year-old cottage. It specializes in superior modern French cooking using locally sourced produce, with dishes like seared Lyme Regis scallops, roast breast of West Country duck, and panfried Dorset Coast sea bass. **Known for:** French cuisine with an English twist; good-value fixed-price two- or three-course dinner menus; reservations that book up quickly. [$] *Average main: £26* ✉ *Bockhampton La., Lower Bockhampton* ☎ *01305/262382* 🌐 *www.yalburycottage.com* ⏲ *Closed Sun. No dinner Mon.*

WHERE TO STAY

$$ B&B/INN

🏨 **The Casterbridge.** Small but full of character, this family-owned inn in a Georgian building dating from 1790 is elegantly decorated with period antiques. **Pros:** central location; period setting; good breakfasts. **Cons:** traffic noise in front rooms; annex rooms are small and lack character; Wi-Fi not in all bedrooms. [$] *Rooms from: £115* ✉ *49 High East St.* ☎ *01305/264043* 🌐 *www.thecasterbridge.co.uk* 🛏 *11 rooms* 🍽 *Free Breakfast.*

SPORTS AND THE OUTDOORS

Thomas Hardy Society. From April through October, the Thomas Hardy Society organizes guided walks to sites that inspired locations in Hardy's novels. Readings and discussions accompany the walks, which range from a couple of hours to most of a day. ✉ *Dorset County Museum, 66 High West St.* ☎ *01305/251501* 🌐 *www.hardysociety.org.*

SHERBORNE

20 miles north of Dorchester, 15 miles west of Shaftesbury, 40 miles west of Wilton, 43 miles west of Salisbury.

Originally the capital of Wessex (the actual Saxon kingdom, not Hardy's retro conceit), this unspoiled market town is populated with medieval buildings built using the local honey-colored stone. The focal point of the winding streets is Sherborne Abbey, where King Alfred's older brothers are buried. Also worth visiting are the ruins of Sherborne Castle, a Tudor mansion originally built by Sir Walter Raleigh, and its Capability Brown–designed gardens.

GETTING HERE AND AROUND

Hourly trains from Salisbury take 45 minutes to reach Sherborne. The station is at the bottom of Digby Road, near the abbey. Drivers should take A30, passing through Shaftesbury.

ESSENTIALS

Visitor Information Sherborne Tourist Information Centre. ✉ *3 Tilton Ct., Digby Rd.* ☎ *01935/815341* 🌐 *www.visit-dorset.com.*

EXPLORING

Shaftesbury. The model for the town of Shaston in Thomas Hardy's *Jude the Obscure* is still a small market town. It sits on a ridge overlooking Blackmore Vale—you can catch a sweeping view of the surrounding countryside from the top of Gold Hill, a steep street lined with cottages so picturesque it was used in an iconic TV commercial to evoke the quintessential British village of yore. Shaftesbury is 20 miles west of Salisbury and 15 miles east of Sherborne. ✉ *Sherborne* ✣ *Intersection of A30 and A350* 🌐 *www.shaftesburytourism.co.uk.*

Sherborne Abbey. As much as the golden hamstone exterior, majestic tower, and fine flying buttresses impress, the glory of Sherborne Abbey is the delicate 15th-century fan vaulting that extends the length of the soaring nave and choir. Some features from the original 8th-century cathedral, like a Saxon doorway in the northwest corner, still remain. If you're lucky, you might hear "Great Tom," one of the heaviest bells in the world, pealing out from the bell tower. Guided tours are run from April through September on Tuesday (10:30) and Friday (2:30), or by prior arrangement. ✉ *3 Abbey Close* ☎ *01935/812452* 🌐 *www.sherborneabbey.com.*

Fodor's Choice ★ **Sherborne Castle.** Built by Sir Walter Raleigh in 1594, this castle remained his home for 10 years before it passed to the custodianship of the Digby family. The castle has interiors from a variety of periods, including Tudor, Jacobean, and Georgian. The Victorian Gothic rooms are notable for their splendid plaster moldings on the ceiling. After admiring the extensive collections of Meissen and Asian porcelain, stroll around the lake and 45 acres of landscaped grounds (a designated English Heritage Grade I site), the work of Capability Brown. The house is less than a mile southeast of town. ✉ *New Rd.* ☎ *01935/812072* 🌐 *www.sherbornecastle.com* 🎟 *Castle and gardens, £12; gardens only £6.50* 🕒 *Closed Nov.–Mar., Mon., and Fri. except bank holidays.*

WHERE TO STAY

$ B&B/INN 🏨 **The Alders.** This homey B&B, a secluded stone house set in an old walled garden opposite a 13th-century church, is in a quiet, unspoiled village 3 miles north of Sherborne. **Pros:** peaceful setting; hospitable owners; excellent breakfasts. **Cons:** a bit remote; unlit walk to dinner; small towels. [$] *Rooms from: £80* ✉ *Sandford Orcas* ✣ *Off B3145* ☎ *01963/220666* 🌐 *www.thealdersbb.com* 🛏 *3 rooms* 🍴 *Free Breakfast.*

WEYMOUTH

8 miles south of Dorchester, 28 miles south of Sherborne.

West Dorset's main coastal resort, Weymouth, is known for its sandy and pebble beaches and its royal connections. King George III began seawater bathing here for his health in 1789, setting a trend among the wealthy and fashionable of the day. The legacy of this popularity is Weymouth's many fine buildings, including the Georgian row houses lining the Esplanade. Striking historical details command attention: a wall on Maiden Street holds a cannonball that was embedded in it during the English Civil War, while a nearby column commemorates the embarkation of U.S. forces from Weymouth on D-Day.

Weymouth and its lively harbor provide the full bucket-and-spade seaside experience: donkey rides, sand castles, and plenty of fish-and-chips. Weymouth and Portland hosted the 2012 Olympic sailing events.

GETTING HERE AND AROUND

You can reach Weymouth on frequent local buses and trains from Dorchester, or on less frequent services from Bournemouth. The bus and train stations are close to each other near King's Statue, on the Esplanade. If you're driving, take A354 from Dorchester and park on or near the Esplanade—an easy walk from the center—or in a lot near the harbor.

EXPLORING

Fodor's Choice ★ **Chesil Beach.** The unique geological curiosity known as Chesil Beach (official slogan: "18 miles and 180 billion pebbles") is in fact not a beach but a tombolo, a thin strip of sand and shingle that joins two bits of land together. Part of the Jurassic Coast World Heritage Site, Chesil, 18 miles long, is remarkable for its pebbles that decrease in size from east to west. It's also known as the setting for Ian McEwan's novel and its 2018 movie *On Chesil Beach*. You can access the eastern section leading to the Isle of Portland (a peninsula) and the western section beyond Abbotsbury year-round. However, access to the central section is restricted, with its environmentally sensitive eastern side facing the shallow saltwater Fleet Lagoon entirely off-limits and its western side closed April to August to protect nesting birds. The entire beach is better suited to walking and fossil hunting than sunbathing and swimming since powerful undertows makes the water dangerous (plus it's cold). There are walking and cycle trails along the rugged coastline. **Amenities:** parking (at five access points, £6–£8 per day); toilets (at five access points). **Best for:** walking; windsurfing. ✉ *Portland Beach Rd., Portland* ☎ *01305/206191* 🌐 *www.chesilbeach.org.*

WHERE TO EAT

$ BISTRO 🍴 **Pascal's Brasserie.** Tucked away from the busy harbor, this French-owned local favorite serves classic Gallic dishes such as onion soup, eggs Benedict, and croque monsieur. If you're looking for an afternoon pit stop, try the substantial, and very English, cream tea selection and other superlative baked goods. **Known for:** delicious homemade cakes and scones; gluten-free options; excellent breakfasts. [$] *Average main: £9* ✉ *8 Cove St.* ☎ *01305/777500* 💳 *No credit cards* 🕒 *No dinner.*

LYME REGIS

19 miles west of Abbotsbury.

Fodor's Choice ★ "A very strange stranger it must be, who does not see the charms of the immediate environs of Lyme, to make him wish to know it better," wrote Jane Austen in *Persuasion*. Judging from the summer crowds, many people agree with her. The scenic seaside town of Lyme Regis and the so-called Jurassic Coast are highlights of southwest Dorset. The crumbling Channel-facing cliffs in this area are especially fossil rich.

GETTING HERE AND AROUND

Lyme Regis is off the A35, extending west from Bournemouth and Dorchester. Drivers should park as soon as possible—there are lots at the top of town—and explore the town on foot. First buses run here from Dorchester and Axminster, 6 miles northwest; the latter town is on the main rail route from London Waterloo and Salisbury, as is Exeter, from which you can take the X53 bus.

ESSENTIALS

Visitor Information Lyme Regis Tourist Information Centre. ✉ *Guildhall Cottage, Church St.* ☎ *01297/442138* ⊕ *www.visit-dorset.com.*

EXPLORING

The Cobb. Lyme Regis is famous for its curving stone harbor breakwater, the Cobb, built by King Edward I in the 13th century to improve the harbor. The Duke of Monmouth landed here in 1685 during his ill-fated attempt to overthrow his uncle James II, and the Cobb figured prominently in the movie of John Fowles's novel *The French Lieutenant's Woman*, as well as in the film version of Jane Austen's *Persuasion*. There's a sweeping coastal view to Chesil Beach to the east. ✉ *Lyme Regis.*

FAMILY **Dinosaurland Fossil Museum.** Located in a former church, this compact private museum run by a paleontologist has an excellent collection of local fossils with more than 12,000 specimens dating back 200 million years. It also provides information on regional geology, how fossils develop, and guided fossil-hunting walks. There are more fossils for sale in the shop on the ground floor along with minerals. ✉ *Coombe St.* ☎ *01297/443541* ⊕ *www.dinosaurland.co.uk* 🎟 *£5* ☼ *Closed weekdays mid-Oct.–mid-Feb.*

Lyme Regis Museum. A gabled and turreted Edwardian building on the site of fossilist Mary Anning's former home, this lively museum is devoted to the town's maritime and domestic history, geology, local artists, writers (John Fowles was an honorary curator for a decade), and, of course, fossils. The museum also leads fossil-hunting and local history walks throughout the year. ✉ *Bridge St.* ☎ *01297/443370* ⊕ *www.lymeregis-museum.co.uk* 🎟 *£4.95* ☼ *Closed Mon. and Tues. Oct.–mid-Dec. and early Jan.–Easter.*

WHERE TO EAT

$ ✕ **The Bell Cliff Restaurant and Tea Rooms.** This cozy, child-and-dog-friendly
BRITISH restaurant in a 17th-century building at the bottom of Lyme Regis's main street makes a great spot for a light lunch or a cream tea with views over the bay. Apart from hot drinks and sandwiches, you can

order more substantial dishes like gammon steak (a thick slice of cured ham), vegetarian lasagna, or fresh seafood such as salmon and hollandaise. **Known for:** large portions; fresh seafood; noisy and cramped ambience. $ *Average main: £11* ✉ *5–6 Broad St.* ☎ *01297/442459* ⊘ *No dinner Nov.–Mar.*

$$
SEAFOOD
Fodor'sChoice
★

✕ **Hix Oyster & Fish House.** This coastal outpost of one of London's trendiest restaurants combines stunning views overlooking the Cobb with the celebrity-chef's trademark high standards and originality. Simply cooked and beautifully presented seafood rules here, including fillet of hake with Poole cockles and sea vegetables or Portland crab served whole in the shell. **Known for:** expertly prepared locally sourced seafood; great views of the coast; extensive dessert menu. $ *Average main: £16* ✉ *Cobb Rd.* ☎ *01297/446910* ⊕ *www.hixoysterandfishhouse. co.uk* ⊘ *Closed Mon. and Tues. Nov.–late Mar.*

WHERE TO STAY

$
B&B/INN

🛏 **Coombe House.** In a stone house tucked away on one of the oldest (14th century) lanes in Lyme, and one minute from the seafront, this uncluttered, stylish B&B has genial hosts and airy, modern guest rooms decorated in maritime blue and white. **Pros:** friendly owners; pleasant rooms; central location. **Cons:** books up fast; simple amenities; relaxed atmosphere not for everyone. $ *Rooms from: £72* ✉ *41 Coombe St.* ☎ *01297/443849* ⊕ *www.coombe-house.co.uk* ⊷ *2 rooms, 1 self-contained apartment* ⫿❍⫿ *Free Breakfast.*

SPORTS AND THE OUTDOORS

Dorset Coast Path. This 95-mile path—a section of the 630-mile-long South West Coast Path National Trail—runs east from Lyme Regis to Old Harry Rocks near Studland, bypassing Weymouth and taking in the quiet bays, shingle beaches, and low chalk cliffs of the coast. Some highlights are Golden Cap, the highest point on the South Coast; the Swannery at Abbotsbury; Chesil Beach; Durdle Door; and Lulworth Cove (between Weymouth and Corfe Castle). Villages and isolated pubs dot the route, as do many rural B&Bs. ✉ *Lyme Regis* ☎ *01392/383560* ⊕ *www.southwestcoastpath.com.*

CORNWALL AND THE WEST COUNTRY

WELCOME TO CORNWALL AND THE WEST COUNTRY

TOP REASONS TO GO

★ **Coastal walks:** For high, dramatic cliff scenery, choose the Exmoor coast around Lynmouth or the coast around Tintagel. The South West Coast Path is 630 miles long.

★ **Riding or hiking on Dartmoor:** Escape to southern England's greatest wilderness—a treeless expanse dotted with rocky outcrops; there are many organized walks and pony-trekking operations.

★ **Tate St. Ives Gallery:** There's nowhere better to absorb the local arts scene than this offshoot of London's Tate Museum in the pretty seaside town of St. Ives. A rooftop café claims views over Porthmeor Beach.

★ **A visit to Eden:** It's worth the journey west for Cornwall's Eden Project alone—a wonderland of plant life in a former clay pit. Two gigantic geodesic "biomes" are filled with flora.

★ **Wells Cathedral:** A perfect example of medieval craftsmanship, the building is a stunning spectacle.

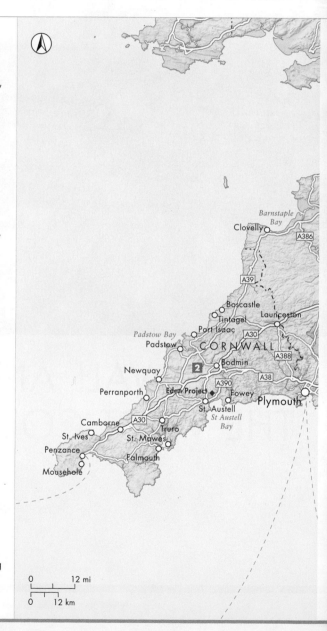

1 **Bristol, Wells, and North Devon.** Bristol is filled with remnants of its long history while small towns like Wells and Glastonbury showcase the full flavor of the region.

2 **Cornwall.** You're never more than 20 miles from the sea in this western outpost of Britain, and the maritime flavor imbues such port towns as Padstow and Falmouth. A string of good beaches and resort towns such as St. Ives pull in the summer crowds.

3 **Plymouth and Dartmoor.** Though modern in appearance, Plymouth has some important historical sights. To the northeast, the open heath and wild moorland of Dartmoor National Park invite walking and horseback riding.

4 **Exeter and South Devon.** Exeter's sturdy cathedral dominates the historic city. South of Exeter are relaxed Totnes and bustling Dartmouth.

5

Updated
by Robert
Andrews

England's West Country is a land of granite promontories, windswept moors, hideaway hamlets, and—above all—the sea. Leafy, narrow country roads lead through miles of buttercup meadows and cider-apple orchards to heathery heights and mellow villages. With their secluded beaches and dreamy backwaters, Somerset, Devon, and Cornwall can be some of England's most relaxing regions to visit.

The counties of the West Country each have their own distinct flavor, and each comes with a regionalism that borders on patriotism. Somerset is noted for its rolling green countryside; Devon's wild and dramatic moors—bare, boggy, upland heath dominated by heathers and gorse—contrast with the restfulness of its many sandy beaches and coves; and Cornwall has managed to retain a touch of its old insularity, despite the annual invasion of thousands of people lured by the Atlantic waves or the ripples of the English Channel.

The historic port of Bristol is where you come across the first unmistakable burrs of the western brogue. Its Georgian architecture and a dramatic gorge create a backdrop to what has become one of Britain's most dynamic cities. To the south lie the cathedral city of Wells and Glastonbury, with its ruined abbey and Arthurian associations. Abutting the north coast is heather-covered Exmoor National Park.

There's more wild moorland in Devon, where Dartmoor is famed for its ponies roaming amid an assortment of strange tors (rocky outcroppings eroded into weird shapes). Devon's coastal towns are as interesting for their cultural and historical appeal—many were smuggler havens—as for their scenic beauty. Parts of south Devon resemble some balmy Mediterranean shore—hence its soubriquet, the English Riviera.

Cornwall, England's westernmost county, has always regarded itself as separate from the rest of Britain, and the Arthurian legends really took root here, not least at Tintagel Castle, the legendary birthplace of Arthur. The south coast is filled with sandy beaches, delightful coves, and popular resorts.

PLANNER

WHEN TO GO

In July and August, traffic chokes the roads leading into the West Country. Somehow the region squeezes in all the "grockles," or tourists, and the chances of finding a remote oasis of peace and quiet are severely curtailed. The beaches and resort towns are either bubbling with zest or unbearably tacky, depending on your point of view. In summer your best option is to find a secluded hotel and make brief excursions from there. Avoid traveling on Saturday, when weekly rentals start and finish and the roads are jammed. Most properties that don't accept business year-round open for Easter and close in late September or October. Those that remain open have reduced hours. Winter has its own appeal: the Atlantic waves crash dramatically against the coast, and the austere Cornish cliffs are at their most spectacular.

FESTIVALS

Glastonbury Festival. Held in Pilton (a few miles from the town of Glastonbury), the Glastonbury Festival is England's biggest and perhaps best annual rock festival. For five days over the last weekend in June, it hosts hundreds of bands—established and up-and-coming—on three main stages and myriad smaller venues. Tickets are steeply priced—around £250—and sell out months in advance; they include entertainment, a camping area, and service facilities. ⊠ *Pilton* ⊕ *www. glastonburyfestivals.co.uk.*

PLANNING YOUR TIME

The elongated shape of Britain's southwestern peninsula means that you may well spend more time traveling than seeing the sights. The key is to base yourself in one or two places and make day trips to the surrounding region. The cities of Bristol, Exeter, and Plymouth make handy bases from which to explore the region, but they can also swallow up a lot of time, at the expense of smaller, less demanding places. The same is true of the resorts of Torquay, Newquay, and Falmouth, which can get very busy. Choose instead towns and villages such as Wells, Lynmouth, Port Isaac, St. Mawes, and Fowey to soak up local atmosphere. If you stick to just a few towns in Somerset and Devon (Bristol, Wells, and Exeter) you could get a taste of the area in four or five days. If you intend to cover Cornwall, at the end of the peninsula, you'll need at least a week. Allow time for aimless rambling—the best way to explore the moors and the coast—and leave enough free time for doing nothing at all.

GETTING HERE AND AROUND

AIR TRAVEL

Bristol International Airport, a few miles southwest of the city, has frequent flights from London, as well as from Dublin, Amsterdam, and other international cities. Exeter International Airport, 5 miles east of the city, and Newquay Cornwall Airport, 5 miles northeast of town, both have daily flights to London.

Airport Information Bristol International Airport. ⊠ *A38, Lulsgate Bottom* ☎ *0871/334–4444* ⊕ *www.bristolairport.co.uk.* **Exeter International Airport.**

A30, Clyst Honiton ☎ *01392/367433* ⊕ *www.exeter-airport.co.uk.* **Newquay Cornwall Airport.** ⊠ *Off A3059, St. Mawgan* ☎ *01637/860600* ⊕ *www. newquaycornwallairport.com.*

BUS TRAVEL

National Express buses leave London's Victoria Coach Station for Bristol (2½ hours), Exeter (4–5 hours), Plymouth (5–6 hours), and Penzance (8–10 hours). Megabus (book online to avoid premium-line costs) offers cheap service to Bristol, Exeter, Plymouth, Newquay, Bodmin, and Falmouth. There's also a good network of regional bus services. First buses serve Somerset, Devon, and Cornwall, and Stagecoach South West covers mainly south Devon and the north Devon coast. Dartline Coaches has a small network in Devon, and Plymouth Citybus operate around Plymouth and north and east Cornwall. First and Stagecoach South West offer money-saving one- or seven-day passes good for unlimited bus travel. Traveline can help you plan your trip.

Bus Contacts Dartline Coaches. ☎ *01392/872900* ⊕ *www.dartline-coaches. co.uk.* **First.** ☎ *0345/602–0121* ⊕ *www.firstgroup.com.* **Megabus.** ☎ *0900/160– 0900 for booking, 0141/352–4444 for general inquiries* ⊕ *www.megabus.com.* **National Express.** ☎ *0871/781–8181* ⊕ *www.nationalexpress.com.* **Plymouth Citybus.** ☎ *01752/662271* ⊕ *www.plymouthbus.co.uk.* **Stagecoach South West.** ☎ *01392/427711* ⊕ *www.stagecoachbus.com.* **Traveline.** ☎ *0871/200– 2233* ⊕ *www.travelinesw.com.*

CAR TRAVEL

Unless you confine yourself to a few towns—for example, Exeter, Penzance, and Plymouth—you'll be at a huge disadvantage without your own transportation. The region has a few main arteries, but you should take minor roads whenever possible, if only to see the real West Country at a leisurely pace.

The fastest route from London to the West Country is via the M4 and M5 motorways. Allow at least two hours to drive to Bristol, three to Exeter. The main roads heading west are the A30 (burrowing through the center of Devon and Cornwall all the way to the tip of Cornwall), the A39 (near the northern shore), and the A38 (near the southern shore, south of Dartmoor and taking in Plymouth).

TRAIN TRAVEL

Rail travelers can make use of a fast service connecting Exeter, Plymouth, and Penzance. Great Western Railway and South Western Railway serve the region from London's Paddington and Waterloo stations. Average travel time to Exeter is 2½ hours, to Plymouth 3¼ hours, and to Penzance about 5½ hours. Once you've arrived, however, you'll find trains to be of limited use in the West Country, as only a few branch lines leave the main line between Exeter and Penzance.

Freedom of the South West tickets provide 3 days of unlimited travel throughout the West Country in any 7-day period, or 8 days in any 15-day period; localized Ranger passes cover Devon or Cornwall.

Train Contacts National Rail Enquiries. ☎ *0345/748–4950* ⊕ *www.national-rail.co.uk.*

RESTAURANTS

The last several years have seen a food renaissance in England's West Country. In the top restaurants the accent is firmly on local and seasonal products. Seafood is the number one choice along the coasts, from Atlantic pollock to Helford River oysters, and it's available in places from haute restaurants to harborside fish shacks. Celebrity chefs have marked their pitch all over the region, including Michael Caines outside Exeter, Rick Stein in Padstow and Falmouth, Mitch Tonks in Dartmouth, and Jamie Oliver in Newquay. Better-known establishments are often completely booked on Friday or Saturday, so reserve well in advance. *Restaurant reviews have been shortened. For full information, visit Fodors.com.*

HOTELS

Accommodations include national hotel chains, represented in all of the region's principal centers, as well as ancient inns and ubiquitous bed-and-breakfast places. Availability can be limited on the coasts during August and during the weekend everywhere, so book well ahead. Many farmhouses also rent out rooms—offering tranquil rural surroundings—but these lodgings are often difficult to reach without a car. If you have a car, though, renting a house or cottage with a kitchen may be ideal. It's worth finding out about weekend and winter deals that many hotels offer. *Hotel reviews have been shortened. For full information, visit Fodors.com.*

WHAT IT COSTS IN POUNDS				
	$	$$	$$$	$$$$
Restaurants	under £15	£15–£19	£20–£25	over £25
Hotels	under £100	£100–£160	£161–£220	over £220

Restaurant prices are the average cost of a main course at dinner, or if dinner is not served, at lunch. Hotel prices are the lowest cost of a standard double room in high season, including 20% V.A.T.

Visitor Information Contacts Visit Cornwall. ⊠ *The Old Bakery Studios, Blewett's Wharf, Malpas Rd., Truro* ☎ *01872/261735* ⊕ *www.visitcornwall.com.* **Visit Devon.** ⊕ *www.visitdevon.co.uk.* **Visit Somerset.** ⊕ *www.visitsomerset. co.uk.*

BRISTOL, WELLS, AND NORTH DEVON

On the eastern side of this region is the vibrant city of Bristol. From here you might head south to the pretty cathedral city of Wells and continue on via Glastonbury, which just might be the Avalon of Arthurian legend. Proceed west along the Somerset coast into Devon, skirting the moorlands of Exmoor and tracing the northern shore via Clovelly.

BRISTOL

120 miles west of London, 46 miles south of Birmingham, 45 miles east of Cardiff, 13 miles northwest of Bath.

The West Country's biggest city (population 430,000), Bristol has in recent years become one of the country's most vibrant centers, with a thriving cultural scene encompassing some of the best contemporary art, theater, and music. Buzzing bars, cafés, and restaurants, and a largely youthful population make it an attractive place to spend time.

Now that the city's industries no longer rely on the docks, the historic harbor along the River Avon has been given over to recreation. Arts and entertainment complexes, museums, and galleries fill the quayside. The pubs and clubs here draw the under-25 set and make the area fairly boisterous (and best avoided) on Friday and Saturday night.

Bristol also trails a great deal of history in its wake. It can be called the "birthplace of America" with some confidence, for John Cabot and his son Sebastian sailed from the old city docks in 1497 to touch down on the North American mainland, which he claimed for the English crown. The city had been a major center since medieval times, but in the 17th and 18th centuries it became the foremost port for trade with North America, and played a leading role in the Caribbean slave trade. Bristol was the home of William Penn, developer of Pennsylvania, and a haven for John Wesley, whose Methodist movement played an important role in colonial Georgia.

GETTING HERE AND AROUND

Bristol has good connections by bus and train to most cities in the country. From London, calculate about 2½ hours by bus or 1¾ hours by train. From Cardiff it's about 50 minutes by bus or train. By train, make sure you get tickets for Bristol Temple Meads Station (not Bristol Parkway), which is a short bus, taxi, or river-bus ride from the center. The bus station is more central, near the Broadmead shopping center. Most sights can be visited on foot, though a bus or a taxi is necessary to reach the Clifton neighborhood.

ESSENTIALS

Visitor Information Bristol Tourist Information Centre. ⊠ *E Shed, Canon's Rd.* ☎ *0906/711–2191* ⊕ *www.visitbristol.co.uk.*

EXPLORING

Church of St. Mary Redcliffe. Built by Bristol merchants who wanted a place in which to pray for the safe (and profitable) voyages of their ships, the rib-vaulted, 14th-century church was called "the fairest in England" by Queen Elizabeth I. High up on the nave wall hang the arms and armor of Sir William Penn, father of the founder of Pennsylvania. The church is a five-minute walk from Temple Meads train station toward the docks. ⊠ *Redcliffe Way* ☎ *0117/931–0060* ⊕ *www. stmaryredcliffe.co.uk* ⊑ *Free.*

FAMILY   **Clifton Suspension Bridge.** A monument to Victorian engineering, this 702-foot-long bridge spans the Avon Gorge. Work began on Isambard Kingdom Brunel's design in 1831, but the bridge wasn't completed until 1864. Free hour-long guided tours usually take place at 3 on weekends

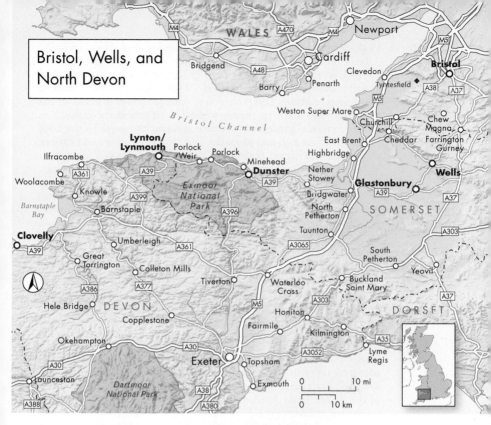

Bristol, Wells, and
North Devon

between Easter and October, departing from the tollbooth at the Clifton end of the bridge. At the far end of the bridge, the **Clifton Suspension Bridge Visitor Centre** has a small exhibition on the bridge and its construction, including a range of videos and hands-on experiences. Near the bridge lies **Clifton Village,** studded with boutiques, antiques shops, and smart crafts shops in its lanes and squares. Bus No. 8 from Bristol Temple Meads Station and the city center stops in Clifton Village. ✉ *Bridge Rd., Leigh Woods* ☎ *0117/974–4664* ⊕ *www.cliftonbridge. org.uk* ✉ *Free.*

FAMILY
Fodor's Choice
★

M Shed. In a refurbished transit shed on the harborside, this museum is dedicated to the city's history. The collection comprises three main galleries—Bristol People, Bristol Places, and Bristol Life—that focus on everything from the slave trade to scientific inventions to recent cultural innovations associated with the city. Check out the artifacts, photos, and sound and video recordings of and by Bristolians, all jazzed up with the latest interactive technology. Don't forget to take in the magnificent harbor views from the top-floor terrace. ✉ *Princes Wharf, Wapping Rd.* ☎ *0117/352–6600* ⊕ *www.mshed.org* ✉ *Free* ⊘ *Closed Mon., except bank holidays.*

Fodor's Choice   **SS _Great Britain_.** On view in the harbor is the first iron ship to cross the
★   Atlantic. Built by the great English engineer Isambard Kingdom Brunel
in 1843, it remained in service until 1970, first as a transatlantic liner
and ultimately as a coal storage hulk. Everything from the bakery to
the officers' quarters comes complete with sounds and smells of the
time, and there are even shadowy glimpses of rats in the galley. You
can try on typical garments of the time, descend into the ship's dry dock
for a view of the hull and propeller, and, between Easter and October,
climb the ship's rigging (£10). Your ticket also admits you to engross-
ing exhibits on the ship's history and on the life of Isambard Brunel.
A short walk east along the harborside from here will bring you to a
replica of the _Matthew,_ the tiny craft that carried John Cabot to North
America in 1497, moored here when it is not sailing on the high seas.
⊠ _Great Western Dockyard, Gas Ferry Rd._ ☎ _0117/926–0680_ ⊕ _www._
ssgreatbritain.org 🎫 _£16.50._

Fodor's Choice   **Tyntesfield.** This extravagant, 35-bedroom Victorian–Gothic Revival
★   mansion has been magnificently restored to reveal a showcase of the
decorative arts where every ornate detail compels attention. Besides
magnificent woodwork, stained glass, tiles, and original furniture and
fabrics, the house contains the modern conveniences of the 1860s,
such as a heated billiards table; the servants' quarters are equally
absorbing. There's a restaurant and family play area, too. You can
see the house, garden, and chapel at your own pace, or join a free
garden tour. ∎TIP➔ **Arrive early in the day to avoid the crowds com-**
peting for timed tickets—Monday and Tuesday are the quietest days. A
food-and-craft market takes place in the grounds on the first Sunday
of the month from April through November. Tyntesfield is 7 miles
southwest of Bristol; the daily bus service X6 is the most convenient
public transport from the city (present your ticket for a 20% discount
on admission charges). The house is a 15-minute walk from the bus
stop. ⊠ _B3128, Wraxall_ ☎ _01275/461900_ ⊕ _www.nationaltrust.org._
_uk_ 🎫 _£15.60; gardens only £9.60._

FAMILY   **We The Curious.** One of the country's top family-friendly science centers,
Fodor's Choice   this multimedia attraction provides a "hands-on, minds-on" explora-
★   tion of science and technology in more than 300 interactive exhibits
and displays. "All About Us" is dedicated to the inner workings of the
human body. Another section allows you to create your own animations. A 3-D planetarium in a gleaming stainless-steel sphere takes
you on a 30-minute voyage through the galaxy. There are up to 10
shows a day, bookable when you buy your ticket. A popular exhibit
lets kids test their skills at creating animations. Allow at least three
hours to see it all. ⊠ _Anchor Rd., Harbourside_ ☎ _0845/345–1235_
⊕ _www.wethecurious.org_ 🎫 _£13.90._

WHERE TO EAT

$$ ✕ **Bell's Diner & Bar Rooms.** A local institution, this bistro in a former
MEDITERRANEAN   grocery shop concentrates on delectable Mediterranean-style tapas
using locally sourced ingredients. Choices include fennel-and-pome-
granate salad with buffalo mozzarella, seared mackerel fillet, and
charcoal-grilled pigeon breast; many of the dishes are available in
small or main-course sizes. **Known for:** cozy neighborhood feel; shared

small dishes; busy bohemian ambience. $) *Average main: £16* ⊠ *1 York Rd., Montpelier* ☎ *0117/924–0357* ⊕ *www.bellsdiner.com* ۞ *No lunch Mon.–Thurs. No dinner Sun.*

$$

MODERN BRITISH

Fodor'sChoice

★

✕ **Riverstation.** Occupying a former police station, this modern, clean-lined restaurant affords serene views over the passing swans and boats. Upstairs, the more formal restaurant serves delicately cooked dishes like grilled Iberico pork with *morcilla* (Spanish blood sausage) and panfried sea bass, while the bar has a more rough-and-ready menu that includes warm savory tarts and rump steak. **Known for:** warm, friendly environment; soothing river views; good fixed-price menus. $) *Average main: £18* ⊠ *The Grove, Harbourside* ☎ *0117/914–4434* ⊕ *www.riverstation. co.uk* ۞ *No dinner Sun.*

WHERE TO STAY

$$

HOTEL

Fodor'sChoice

★

▥ **Hotel du Vin.** This hip chain has brought high-tech flair to six former sugar-refining warehouses, built in 1728 when the River Frome ran outside the front door. **Pros:** tastefully restored old building; great bathrooms; excellent bar and bistro. **Cons:** traffic-dominated location; dim lighting in rooms; limited parking. $) *Rooms from: £129* ⊠ *The Sugar House, Narrow Lewins Mead* ☎ *0330/016–0390* ⊕ *www.hotelduvin. com* ⮑ *40 rooms* ▢ *No meals.*

$$$

HOTEL

Fodor'sChoice

★

▥ **Thornbury Castle.** An impressive lodging, Thornbury has everything a genuine 16th-century Tudor castle needs: huge fireplaces, moody paintings, mullioned windows, and a large garden. **Pros:** grand medieval surroundings; sumptuous rooms; doting service. **Cons:** many steps to climb; some rooms are relatively small; unexciting location. $) *Rooms from: £195* ⊠ *Castle St., off A38, Thornbury* ☎ *01454/281182* ⊕ *www. thornburycastle.co.uk* ⮑ *28 rooms* ▢ *Free Breakfast.*

NIGHTLIFE AND PERFORMING ARTS

Arnolfini. In a converted warehouse on the harbor, the Arnolfini is one of the country's most prestigious contemporary-art venues, known for uncovering innovative yet accessible art. There are galleries, a cinema, a bookshop, and a lively café-bar. ⊠ *16 Narrow Quay* ☎ *0117/917–2300* ⊕ *www.arnolfini.org.uk.*

WELLS

22 miles south of Bristol, 132 miles west of London.

England's smallest cathedral city, with a population of 10,000, lies at the foot of the Mendip Hills. Although set in what feels like a quiet country town, the great cathedral is a masterpiece of Gothic architecture—the first to be built in the Early English style. The city's name refers to the underground streams that bubble up into St. Andrew's Well within the grounds of the Bishop's Palace. Spring water has run through High Street since the 15th century. Seventeenth-century buildings surround the ancient marketplace, which hosts market days on Wednesday and Saturday.

Harmonious and stately, Wells Cathedral is the oldest surviving English Gothic church in the world.

GETTING HERE AND AROUND

Regular First buses from Bristol take one hour to reach Wells; the bus station is a few minutes south of the cathedral. Drivers should take A37, and park outside the compact and eminently walkable center.

ESSENTIALS

Visitor Information Wells Visitor Information Service. ⊠ *Wells Museum, 8 Cathedral Green* ☎ *01749/671770* ⊕ *www.wellssomerset.com.*

EXPLORING

Bishop's Palace. The Bishop's Eye gate leading from Market Place takes you to the magnificent, moat-ringed Bishop's Palace, which retains parts of the original 13th-century residence. The peaceful grounds command the most attention, including the gatehouse, the ramparts, and the impressive remains of a late-13th-century great hall which fell into ruin after the lead in its roof was sold in the 16th century. Most rooms of the palace are closed to the public, but you can see the undercroft, the private chapel, and the sumptuously decorated Long Gallery. Ticket holders can join a free tour of the palace at 11 am in winter or 2 pm in summer, and one of the grounds at noon in winter or 3 pm in summer. ⊠ *Market Pl.* ☎ *01749/988111* ⊕ *www.bishopspalace.org.uk* 🎫 *£8.95.*

Wells Cathedral. The great west towers of the Cathedral Church of St. Andrew, the oldest surviving English Gothic church, can be seen for miles. Dating from the 12th century, Wells Cathedral (as it's more commonly known) derives its beauty from the perfect harmony of all of its parts, the glowing colors of its original stained-glass windows, and its peaceful setting among stately trees and majestic lawns. To appreciate the elaborate west-front facade, approach the building from the cathedral green, accessible from Market Place through a great medieval gate called "penniless porch" (named after the beggars who once waited here to collect alms from worshippers). The cathedral's west front is twice as wide as it is high, and some 300 statues of kings and saints adorn it. Inside, vast inverted arches—known as scissor arches—were added in 1338 to stop the central tower from sinking to one side.

The cathedral has a rare and beautiful medieval clock, the second-oldest working clock in the world, consisting of the seated figure of a man called Jack Blandifer, who strikes a bell on the quarter hour while mounted knights circle in a joust. Near the clock is the entrance to the Chapter House—a small wooden door opening onto a great sweep of stairs worn down on one side by the tread of pilgrims over the centuries. Free guided tours lasting approximately one hour begin at the back of the cathedral. A cloister restaurant serves snacks and teas. ✉ *Cathedral Green* ☎ *01749/674483* 🌐 *www.wellscathedral.org.uk* 🎟 *£6 suggested donation.*

5

WHERE TO EAT

$ MODERN BRITISH 🍴 **The Fountain Inn.** Slightly off the tourist track but only a few minutes from the cathedral, this classic gastro-pub offers a winning combination of traditional decor lightened with tasteful modern touches and great, locally sourced food. The eclectic menu includes such standout dishes as Madras chicken curry, grilled halloumi, and beer-battered haddock. **Known for:** warm, intimate atmosphere; extensive menu with some good English classics; great range of beers, including local ales. [$] *Average main: £14* ✉ *1 St. Thomas St.* ☎ *01749/672317* 🌐 *www.fountaininn.co.uk* 🕒 *No lunch Mon. No dinner Sun.*

WHERE TO STAY

$$ HOTEL 🏨 **Swan Hotel.** A former coaching inn built in the 15th century, the Swan has an ideal spot facing the cathedral. **Pros:** professional service; some great views; good restaurant. **Cons:** standard rooms in the main building are small; occasional noise issues; parking lot tricky to navigate. [$] *Rooms from: £148* ✉ *11 Sadler St.* ☎ *01749/836300* 🌐 *www.swanhotelwells.co.uk* 🛏 *55 rooms* 🍽 *Free Breakfast.*

GLASTONBURY

5 miles southwest of Wells, 27 miles south of Bristol, 27 miles southwest of Bath.

Fodor's Choice ★ A town steeped in history, myth, and legend, Glastonbury lies in the lea of Glastonbury Tor, a grassy hill rising 520 feet above the drained marshes known as the Somerset Levels. The Tor is supposedly the site of crossing ley lines (hypothetical alignments of significant places), and, in legend, Glastonbury is identified with Avalon, the paradise into which King Arthur was reborn after his death.

Partly because of these associations but also because of its world-class rock-music festival, the town has acquired renown as a New Age center, mixing crystal gazers with druids, yogis, and hippies, variously in search of Arthur, Merlin, Jesus—and even Elvis. **TIP→ Between April and September, a shuttle bus runs every half hour between all of Glastonbury's major sights. Tickets are £3, and are valid all day.**

GETTING HERE AND AROUND

Frequent buses link Glastonbury to Wells and Bristol, pulling in close to the abbey. Drivers should take the A39. You can walk to all the sights or take the shuttle bus, though you'll need a stock of energy for ascending the Tor.

ESSENTIALS

Visitor Information Glastonbury Tourist Information Centre. ✉ *The Tribunal, 9 High St.* ☎ *01458/832954* 🌐 *www.glastonburytic.co.uk.*

EXPLORING

Glastonbury Abbey. The ruins of this great abbey, in the center of town, are on the site where, according to legend, Joseph of Arimathea built a church in the 1st century. A monastery had certainly been erected here by the 9th century, and the site drew many pilgrims. The ruins are those of the abbey completed in 1524 and destroyed in 1539, during Henry VIII's dissolution of the monasteries. A sign south of the Lady Chapel marks the sites where Arthur and Guinevere were supposedly buried. Between April and October, guides in period costumes are on hand to point out some of the abbey's most interesting features. The visitor center has a scale model of the abbey as well as carvings and decorations salvaged from the ruins. ✉ *Magdalene St.* ☎ *01458/832267* 🌐 *www.glastonburyabbey.com* 🎫 *£7.50.*

FAMILY Fodor's Choice ★ **Somerset Rural Life Museum.** Occupying a Victorian farmhouse and a 14th-century abbey tithe barn, this museum tells the story of life in Somerset throughout the ages. Exhibits in the six galleries illustrate farming practices and daily life in 19th century using sound recordings and projections as well as an array of tools and domestic objects. The barn, more than 90 feet in length, once stored the one-tenth portion of the town's produce that was owed to the church and now holds exhibitions. Soups and crusty sandwiches are available at the Grain Store Café, which has tables in the yard. There's also an apple cider orchard nearby. For a good walk, take the scenic footpath from the museum that leads up to the Tor, a half mile east. ✉ *Chilkwell St.* ☎ *01458/831197* 🌐 *www.swheritage.org.uk/rural-life-museum* 🎫 *£5.45* ⏲ *Closed Mon. year-round and Sun. Nov.–Easter.*

WHERE TO EAT

$ BRITISH 🍴 **Who'd a Thought It.** As an antidote to the natural-food cafés of Glastonbury's High Street, try this traditional backstreet inn for some more down-to-earth fare that doesn't compromise on quality. Bar classics such as fish pie and Somerset sausages appear alongside chicken curry, vegetable risotto, and sizzling steaks. **Known for:** fast and friendly service; quirky interior crammed with memorabilia; traditional dishes served alongside local beers and ciders. [$] *Average main: £13* ✉ *17 Northload St.* ☎ *01458/834460* 🌐 *www.whodathoughtit.co.uk.*

WHERE TO STAY

$ B&B/INN Fodor's Choice ★ 🏨 **Melrose House.** Superbly situated at the base of Glastonbury Tor, this elegant B&B on the edge of town is surrounded by lush gardens with far-reaching views over the Vale of Avalon. **Pros:** tranquil setting; easy access to Glastonbury Tor; superb breakfasts. **Cons:** not very central; one-night stays not always possible; does not accept credit cards.

[$] *Rooms from: £85* ✉ *Coursing Batch* ☎ *01458/834706* 🌐 *www.melrose-bandb.co.uk* 🛏 *4 rooms* 🍴 *Free Breakfast* 💳 *No credit cards.*

DUNSTER

35 miles west of Glastonbury, 43 miles north of Exeter.

Lying between the Somerset coast and the edge of Exmoor National Park, Dunster is a picture-book village with a broad main street. The eight-sided yarn-market building on High Street dates from 1589.

GETTING HERE AND AROUND

To reach Dunster by car, follow the A39. By bus, there are frequent departures from nearby Minehead and Taunton. Dunster Castle is a brief walk from the village center. In the village is the Exmoor National Park Visitor Centre, which can give you plenty of information about local activities.

ESSENTIALS

Visitor Information Exmoor National Park Visitor Centre. ✉ *Dunster Steep* ☎ *01643/821835* 🌐 *www.exmoor-nationalpark.gov.uk.*

EXPLORING

Fodor's Choice ★ **Dunster Castle.** A 13th-century fortress remodeled in 1868, Dunster Castle dominates the village from its site on a hill. Parkland and unusual gardens with subtropical plants surround the building, which has fine plaster ceilings, stacks of family portraits (including one by Joshua Reynolds), 17th-century Dutch leather hangings, and a magnificent 17th-century oak staircase. The climb to the castle from the parking lot is steep. ✉ *Off A39* ☎ *01643/821314* 🌐 *www.nationaltrust.org.uk* 🎟 *£11.60; gardens only, £6.80* 🕒 *Closed late Oct.–mid-Dec.*

WHERE TO STAY

$$ B&B/INN 🏨 **Luttrell Arms.** In style and atmosphere, this classic inn harmonizes perfectly with Dunster village and castle; it was used as a guesthouse by the abbots of Cleeve in the 14th century. **Pros:** central location; historic trappings; good dining options. **Cons:** some standard rooms are small and viewless; no parking; heavy presence of dogs in the bar not great for allergy sufferers. [$] *Rooms from: £140* ✉ *High St.* ☎ *01643/821555* 🌐 *www.luttrellarms.co.uk* 🛏 *28 rooms* 🍴 *Free Breakfast.*

LYNTON AND LYNMOUTH

13 miles west of Porlock, 60 miles northwest of Exeter.

A steep hill separates this pretty pair of Devonshire villages, which are linked by a Victorian cliff railway you can still ride. Lynmouth, a fishing village at the bottom of the hill, crouches below 1,000-foot-high cliffs at the mouths of the East and West Lyn rivers; Lynton is higher up. The poet Percy Bysshe Shelley visited Lynmouth in 1812, in the company of his 16-year-old bride, Harriet Westbrook. During their nine-week sojourn, the poet found time to write his polemical *Queen Mab*. The grand landscape of Exmoor lies all about, with walks to local beauty spots: Watersmeet, the Valley of Rocks, or Hollerday Hill, where rare feral goats graze.

GETTING HERE AND AROUND

These towns are best reached via the A39. Lynton is a stop on Quantock Heritage Bus 300, which runs Monday through Saturday from Minehead. It's a steep and winding ascent to Lynton from Lynmouth; take the cliff railway to travel between them.

ESSENTIALS

Visitor Information Lynton and Lymouth Tourist Information Centre. ⊠ *Lee Rd., Lynton* ☎ *0845/458–3775* ⊕ *www.lynton-lynmouth-tourism.co.uk.*

EXPLORING

Coleridge Way. The 51-mile Coleridge Way runs between Nether Stowey (site of Coleridge's home) and Lynmouth, passing through the northern fringes of the Quantock Hills, the isolated villages of the Brendon Hills, and along the Exmoor coast. ⊠ *Lynmouth* ⊕ *www.visit-exmoor.co.uk/coleridge-way.*

Lynton and Lynmouth Cliff Railway. Water and a cable system power the 862-foot cliff railway that connects these two towns. As it ascends a rocky cliff, you are treated to fine views over the harbor. Inaugurated in 1890, it was the gift of publisher George Newnes, who also donated Lynton's imposing town hall, near the top station on Lee Road. ⊠ *The Esplanade, Lynmouth* ☎ *01598/753908* ⊕ *www.cliffrailwaylynton. co.uk* ⊠ *£3.90 round-trip* ☉ *Closed mid-Nov.–early Feb.*

WHERE TO EAT

$$

MODERN BRITISH

✕ **Rising Sun.** A 14th-century inn and a row of thatched cottages make up this pub-restaurant with great views over the Bristol Channel. The kitchen specializes in local cuisine with European influences, so expect dishes like confit chicken with wild mushrooms and foie gras terrine. **Known for:** traditional pub decor and ambience; good range of local ales; delicious seafood including fish stew and crab risotto. $ *Average main: £19* ⊠ *Riverside Rd., Lynmouth* ☎ *01598/753223* ⊕ *www. risingsunlynmouth.co.uk.*

WHERE TO STAY

$$

B&B/INN

🏨 **Highcliffe House.** As the name suggests, this luxury Victorian B&B in Lynton occupies a lofty position with spectacular vistas over the Bristol Channel. **Pros:** romantic ambience; inspiring views; generous and wide-ranging breakfasts. **Cons:** design not for everyone; unsightly car park directly below; relatively high room rates. $ *Rooms from: £120* ⊠ *Sinai Hill, Lynton* ☎ *01598/752235* ⊕ *www.highcliffehouse.co.uk* 🛏 *6 rooms* ⏝⏝ *Free Breakfast* ⚑ *No guests under 18 allowed.*

SPORTS AND THE OUTDOORS

West of Lynton, the Atlantic-facing beaches of Saunton Sands, Croyde Bay, and Woolacombe Bay are much beloved by surfers, with plenty of outlets renting equipment and offering lessons. Croyde Bay and Woolacombe Bay are more family-friendly.

Clovelly may have it all: cobbled streets, quaint houses, and the endless blue sea.

CLOVELLY

40 miles southwest of Lynton, 60 miles northwest of Exeter.

Fodor's Choice
★

Lovely Clovelly always seems to have the sun shining on its flower-lined cottages and stepped and cobbled streets. Alas, its beauty is well known, and day-trippers can overrun the village in summer. Perched precariously among cliffs, a steep, cobbled road—tumbling down at such an angle that it's closed to cars—leads to the toylike harbor with its 14th-century quay. Allow about two hours (more if you stop for a drink or a meal) to take in the village. Hobby Drive, a 3-mile cliff-top carriageway laid out in 1829 through thick woods, gives scintillating views over the village and coast.

GETTING HERE AND AROUND

To get to Clovelly by bus, take Stagecoach service 319 from Barnstaple or Bideford. If you're driving, take the A39 and park at the Clovelly Visitor Centre for £7.50. The center of town is steep and cobbled. The climb from the harbor to the parking lot can be exhausting, but from April through early November a reasonably priced shuttle service brings you back.

EXPLORING

Clovelly Visitor Centre. Here you'll see a 20-minute film that puts Clovelly into context. In the village you can visit a 1930s-style fisherman's cottage and an exhibition about Victorian writer Charles Kingsley, who lived here as a child. The admission fee includes parking. To avoid the worst crowds, arrive early or late in the day. ⊠ *Off A39* ☎ *01237/431781* ⊕ *www.clovelly.co.uk* ✉ *£7.50.*

WHERE TO STAY

$$ HOTEL 🏨 **Red Lion Hotel.** You can soak up the tranquility of Clovelly after the day-trippers have gone at the 18th-century Red Lion, located right on the harbor in this coastal village. **Pros:** superb location; clean and comfortable; friendly staff. **Cons:** some rooms and bathrooms are small; restaurant menu is limited; steep walk to get anywhere. [$] *Rooms from: £160* ✉ *The Quay* ☎ *01237/431237* 🌐 *www.clovelly.co.uk* 🛏 *17 rooms* 🍴 *Free Breakfast.*

CORNWALL

Cornwall stretches west into the sea, with plenty of magnificent coastline to explore, along with tranquil towns and some bustling resorts. One way to discover it all is to travel southwest from the cliff-top ruins of Tintagel Castle, the legendary birthplace of Arthur, along the north Cornish coast to Land's End. This predominantly cliff-lined coast, interspersed with broad expanses of sand, has many tempting places to stop, including Padstow (for a seafood feast), Newquay (a surfing and tourist center), or St. Ives (a delightful artists' colony).

From Land's End, the westernmost tip of Britain, known for its savage land- and seascapes and panoramic views, return to the popular seaside resort of Penzance, the harbor town of Falmouth, and the river port of Fowey. The Channel coast is less rugged than the northern coast, with more sheltered beaches. Leave time to visit the excellent Eden Project, with its surrealistic-looking conservatories in an abandoned clay pit.

TINTAGEL

3 miles southwest of Boscastle.

The romance of Arthurian legend thrives around Tintagel's ruined castle on the coast. Ever since the somewhat unreliable 12th-century chronicler Geoffrey of Monmouth identified Tintagel as the home of Arthur, son of Uther Pendragon and Ygrayne, devotees of the legend cycle have revered the site. In the 19th century Alfred, Lord Tennyson described Tintagel's Arthurian connection in *The Idylls of the King*. Today the village has its share of tourist junk—including Excaliburgers—but the headland around Tintagel is still splendidly scenic.

GETTING HERE AND AROUND

To drive to Tintagel, take the A39 to the B3263. Numerous parking lots are found in the village center. There's a bus stop near the tourist office for First Kernow buses from Wadebridge, which has connections from Bodmin Parkway, the nearest train station. Between April and October, a shuttle service brings mobility-impaired passengers to the castle.

ESSENTIALS

Visitor Information Tintagel Visitor Centre. ✉ *Bossiney Rd.* ☎ *01840/779084* 🌐 *www.tintagelparishcouncil.gov.uk.*

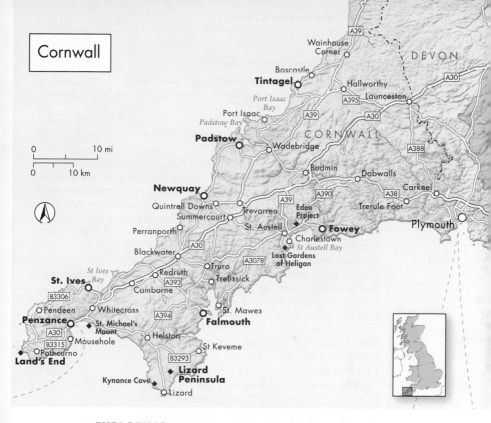

EXPLORING

Fodor's Choice
★

Tintagel Castle. Although all that remains of the ruined cliff-top Tintagel Castle, legendary birthplace of King Arthur, is the outline of its walls, moats, and towers, it requires only a bit of imagination to conjure up a picture of Sir Lancelot and Sir Galahad riding out in search of the Holy Grail over the narrow causeway above the seething breakers. Archaeological evidence, however, suggests that the castle dates from much later—about 1150, when it was the stronghold of the earls of Cornwall. Long before that, Romans may have occupied the site. The earliest identified remains here are of Celtic (AD 5th century) origin, and these may have some connection with the legendary Arthur. Legends aside, nothing can detract from the castle ruins, dramatically set off by the wild, windswept Cornish coast, on an island joined to the mainland by a narrow isthmus. Paths lead down to the pebble beach and a cavern known as **Merlin's Cave.** Exploring Tintagel Castle involves some arduous climbing on steep steps, but even on a summer's day, when people swarm over the battlements and a westerly Atlantic wind sweeps through Tintagel, you can feel the proximity of the distant past. ⊠ *Castle Rd., ½ mile west of the village* ☎ *01840/770328* ⊕ *www. english-heritage.org.uk* ⊡ *£9.50* ☉ *Closed Mon. and Tues. in Mar. and weekdays Nov.–Feb.*

PADSTOW

10 miles southwest of Port Isaac.

A small fishing port at the mouth of the River Camel, Padstow attracts attention and visitors as a center of culinary excellence, largely because of the presence here since 1975 of pioneering seafood chef Rick Stein. Stein's empire includes two restaurants, a café, a fish-and-chips joint, a delicatessen, a patisserie, and a cooking school where classes fill up months in advance.

Even if seafood isn't your favorite fare, Padstow is worth visiting. The cries of seagulls fill its lively harbor, a string of fine beaches lies within a short ride—including some choice strands highly prized by surfers—and two scenic walking routes await: the Saints Way across the peninsula to Fowey, and the Camel Trail, a footpath and cycling path that follows the river as far as Bodmin Moor. If you can avoid peak visiting times—summer weekends—so much the better.

GETTING HERE AND AROUND

Regular buses connect Padstow with Bodmin, the main transportation hub hereabouts, and on the main Plymouth–Penzance train line. To get here from Port Isaac, change buses at Wadebridge. Alternatively, take the bus to Rock and the passenger ferry across the river. There are numerous direct buses on the Newquay–Padstow route. Drivers should take A39/A389 and park in the waterside parking lot before reaching the harbor.

ESSENTIALS

Ferry Contacts Padstow Rock Ferry. ☎ *01841/532239 Harbour Office, 0777/308–1574 Ferry Office* 🌐 *www.padstow-harbour.co.uk.*

Visitor Information Padstow Tourist Information Centre. ✉ *North Quay* ☎ *01841/533449* 🌐 *www.padstowlive.com.*

WHERE TO EAT

$$$$ MODERN BRITISH Fodor's Choice ★

🍴 **Paul Ainsworth at Number 6.** There is more to Padstow's culinary scene than Rick Stein, as this intimate bistro persuasively demonstrates. Diners seated in a series of small, stylish rooms can feast on ingeniously concocted dishes that make the most of local and seasonal produce. **Known for:** exciting, creative cuisine like Tamworth pig fritters and Cornish lamb; affordable set-price lunches; vivacious atmosphere. [$] *Average main: £34* ✉ *6 Middle St.* ☎ *01841/532093* 🌐 *www.paul-ainsworth.co.uk* ⏲ *Closed Sun., Mon., and mid-Jan.–early Feb.*

$$$$ SEAFOOD Fodor's Choice ★

🍴 **The Seafood Restaurant.** Just across from where the lobster boats and trawlers unload their catches, Rick Stein's flagship restaurant has built its reputation on the freshest fish and the highest culinary artistry. The exclusively fish and shellfish menu includes everything from grilled Padstow lobster with herbs to stir-fried Singapore chili crab. **Known for:** top-quality, eclectic seafood dishes creatively prepared; famous regional chef; attentive service. [$] *Average main: £30* ✉ *Riverside* ☎ *01841/532700* 🌐 *www.rickstein.com.*

WHERE TO STAY

$$$$ B&B/INN 🏨 **St. Edmund's House.** The most luxurious Rick Stein venture (the Seafood Restaurant) also offers this lodging with a sophisticated minimalist style. **Pros:** stylish bedrooms; top-notch service; central but secluded. **Cons:** short walk to breakfast; extravagant prices; not all rooms have a sea view. [$] *Rooms from: £315* ✉ *St. Edmund's La.* ☎ *01841/532700* 🌐 *www.rickstein.com* 🛏 *6 rooms* 🍴 *Free Breakfast.*

SPORTS AND THE OUTDOORS

SURFING

Harlyn Surf School. This school can arrange two-hour to four-day surfing courses at its base in Harlyn Bay, 3 miles west of Padstow. ✉ *Harlyn Bay Beach* ☎ *01841/533076* 🌐 *www.harlynsurfschool.co.uk.*

WALKING

Saints Way. This 30-mile inland path takes you between Padstow and the Camel Estuary on Cornwall's north coast to Fowey on the south coast. It follows a Bronze Age trading route, later used by Celtic pilgrims to cross the peninsula. Several relics of such times can be seen along the way. ✉ *Padstow.*

5

NEWQUAY

14 miles southwest of Padstow, 30 miles southwest of Tintagel.

The biggest, most developed resort on the north Cornwall coast is a fairly large town established in 1439. It was once the center of the trade in pilchards (a small herringlike fish), and on the headland you can still see a white hut where a lookout known as a "huer" watched for pilchard schools and directed the boats to the fishing grounds. Newquay has become Britain's surfing capital, and in summer young California-dreamin' devotees often pack the wide, cliff-backed beaches.

GETTING HERE AND AROUND

A branch line links Newquay with the main Plymouth–Penzance train line at Par, and there are regular buses from Padstow, Bodmin, and St. Austell. Train and bus stations are both in the center of town. Newquay has good road connections with the rest of the peninsula via the A30 and A39. The best beaches are a long walk or a short bus ride from the center.

ESSENTIALS

Visitor Information Newquay Tourist Information Centre. ✉ *Marcus Hill* ☎ *01637/838516* 🌐 *www.visitnewquay.org.*

WHERE TO EAT

$$$$ ITALIAN FAMILY Fodor's Choice ★ 🍴 **Jamie Oliver's Fifteen Cornwall.** Bright and capacious, this modern Italian restaurant has won plaudits both for its fabulous food and for its fine location overlooking magnificent Watergate Bay, a broad beach much beloved of water-sports enthusiasts. One of Britain's culinary heroes, Cockney chef Jamie Oliver, helped to set up the enterprise, which has the aim of training local young people for careers in catering. **Known for:** wraparound views at stupendous beach location; boundary-pushing flavor combinations; five-course tasting menu that frequently changes. [$] *Average main: £26* ✉ *Watergate Rd., Watergate Bay* ☎ *01637/861000* 🌐 *www.fifteencornwall.co.uk.*

SPORTS AND THE OUTDOORS

Surfing is Newquay's raison d'être for many of the enthusiasts who flock here throughout the year. Great Western and Tolcarne beaches are most suitable for beginners, while Fistral Beach is better for those with more experience. There are dozens of surf schools around town, many offering accommodation packages, and rental outlets are also ubiquitous.

SURFING

Extreme Academy. One of the West Country's water-sports specialists, Extreme Academy based at Watergate Bay offers courses in wave skiing, kite surfing, kite buggying, paddle surfing, and just plain old surfing, as well as equipment for hire. ⊠ *Trevarrian Hill, Watergate Bay* ☎ *01637/860840* ⊕ *www.extremeacademy.co.uk.*

ST. IVES

25 miles southwest of Newquay, 10 miles north of Penzance.

Fodor's Choice ★ James McNeill Whistler came here to paint his landscapes, Barbara Hepworth to fashion her modernist sculptures, and Virginia Woolf to write her novels. Today sand, sun, and superb art continue to attract thousands of vacationers to the fishing village of St. Ives, named after Saint Ia, a 5th-century female Irish missionary said to have arrived on a floating leaf. Many come to St. Ives for the sheltered beaches; the best are Porthmeor, on the northern side of town, and, facing east, Porthminster—the choice for those seeking more space to spread out.

GETTING HERE AND AROUND

St. Ives has good bus and train connections with Bristol, Exeter, and Penzance. Train journeys usually involve a change at St. Erth (the brief St. Erth–St. Ives stretch is one of the West Country's most scenic train routes). The adjacent bus and train stations are within a few minutes' walk of the center. Drivers should avoid the center—parking lots are well marked in the higher parts of town.

ESSENTIALS

Visitor Information Visit St. Ives Information Centre. ⊠ *The Guildhall, Street-an-Pol* ☎ *01736/796297* ⊕ *www.stives-cornwall.co.uk.*

EXPLORING

Barbara Hepworth Museum and Sculpture Garden. The studio and garden of Dame Barbara Hepworth (1903–75), who pioneered abstract sculpture in England, are now a museum and sculpture garden, managed by Tate St. Ives. The artist lived here for 26 years. ⊠ *Trewyn Studio, Barnoon Hill* ☎ *01736/796226* ⊕ *www.tate.org.uk* 🎟 *£7, £13 combined ticket with Tate St. Ives* ⊗ *Closed Mon. Nov.–Feb.*

Fodor's Choice ★ **Tate St. Ives.** The spectacular sister of the renowned London gallery displays the work of artists who lived and worked in St. Ives, mostly from 1925 to 1975. The collection occupies a modernist building— a fantasia of seaside art deco–period architecture with panoramic views of the rippling ocean. Works of other international artists who influenced the St. Ives school—Picasso, Braque, and Mondrian among them—are exhibited alongside the local figures, and there are frequent exhibitions of contemporary art connected to

West Cornwall. A four-story extension has significantly increased the exhibition space, and the rooftop café provides excellent food and views. ✉ *Porthmeor Beach* ☎ *01736/796226* 🌐 *www.tate.org.uk* 🎟 *£9.50, £13 combined ticket with Barbara Hepworth Museum and Sculpture Garden* 🕓 *Closed Mon. Nov.–Feb.*

WHERE TO EAT

$$ MODERN BRITISH Fodor's Choice ★

🍴 **Gurnard's Head.** This pub with bright, homey furnishings and a relaxed ambience looks past green fields to the ocean beyond. The frequently changing menu features fresh, inventively prepared meat and seafood dishes; look for lamb breast with merguez sausage, cucumber, yogurt, and chickpeas, or red gurnard with creamed leeks and pancetta—and leave room for some stupendous desserts. **Known for:** unusual dishes alongside old English favorites; welcoming atmosphere; good set-price deals. [$] *Average main: £19* ✉ *B3306, near Zennor, Treen* ☎ *01736/796928* 🌐 *www.gurnardshead.co.uk.*

$$$ SEAFOOD

🍴 **Porthminster Café.** Unbeatable for its location alone—on the broad, golden sands of Porthminster Beach—this sleek, modern eatery prepares imaginative breakfasts, lunches, teas, and evening meals that you can savor while you take in the marvelous vista across the bay. The accent is on Mediterranean and Asian flavors, and typical choices include pan-roasted halibut fillet with crispy ham, monkfish curry, and roasted duck breast with celeriac. **Known for:** beachside location; consistently high quality of food; famous monkfish curry. [$] *Average main: £22* ✉ *Porthminster Beach* ☎ *01736/795352* 🌐 *www.porthminstercafe.co.uk* 🕓 *Closed Mon. Nov.–Easter. No dinner Sun., Tues., and Wed. Nov.–Easter.*

WHERE TO STAY

$ B&B/INN Fodor's Choice ★

🏨 **Cornerways.** Everything in St. Ives seems squeezed into the tiniest of spaces, and this cottage B&B in the quiet Downalong quarter is no exception. **Pros:** friendly owners; tasteful decor; excellent breakfast choices. **Cons:** rooms are mostly small; narrow stairways to climb; very limited parking. [$] *Rooms from: £95* ✉ *1 Bethesda Pl.* ☎ *01736/796706* 🌐 *www.cornerwaysstives.com* 💳 *No credit cards* 🛏 *6 rooms* 🍽 *Free Breakfast.*

LAND'S END

17 miles southwest of St. Ives, 9 miles southwest of Penzance.

The coastal road, B3306, ends at the western tip of Britain at what is, quite literally, Land's End.

GETTING HERE AND AROUND

Frequent buses serve Land's End from Penzance (around one hour). There is no direct service from St. Ives in winter, but in summer an open-top double-decker tracks the coast between St. Ives and Penzance, taking in Land's End en route.

EXPLORING

Land's End. The sea crashes against the rocks at Land's End and lashes ships battling their way around the point. ■ **TIP→ Approach from one of the coastal footpaths for the best panoramic view.** Over the years, sightseers have caused some erosion of the paths, but new ones are constantly being built, and Cornish "hedges" (granite walls covered with turf) have been planted to prevent erosion. The scenic grandeur of Land's End remains undiminished. The Land's End Hotel here is undistinguished, though the restaurant has good views. ⊠ *Sennen.*

SPORTS AND THE OUTDOORS

Sennen Cove. Located in the aptly named Whitesand Bay, Sennen Cove is a gorgeous expanse of creamy soft sand on the western tip of Cornwall. When the tide is coming in, the waves attract legions of surfers. When the tide's out, kids paddle in the tidal pools and the sand stretches as far as you can see. Cafés are nearby, and surfing equipment is for rent on the beach. Sennen is off A30 less than 2 miles north of Land's End, and can be reached on foot on the South West Coast Path. **Amenities:** food and drink; lifeguards; parking (fee); toilets; water sports. **Best for:** sunset; surfing; swimming; walking. ⊠ *Off A30, Whitesand Bay.*

PENZANCE

3 miles north of Mousehole, 1½ miles north of Newlyn, 10 miles south of St. Ives.

Superb views over Mount's Bay are one lure of this popular, unpretentious seaside resort. Even though it does get very crowded in summer, Penzance makes a good base for exploring the area. The town's isolated position has always made it vulnerable to attacks from the sea. During the 16th century, Spanish raiders destroyed most of the original town, and the majority of old buildings date from as late as the 18th century. The main street is Market Jew Street, a folk mistranslation of the Cornish expression Marghas Yow, which means "Thursday Market." Where Market Jew Street meets Causeway Head is Market House, an impressive, domed granite building constructed in 1837, with a statue of locally born chemist Humphry Davy in front.

In contrast to artsy St. Ives, Penzance is a no-nonsense working town. Though lacking the traffic-free lanes and quaint cottages of St. Ives, Penzance preserves pockets of handsome Georgian architecture.

GETTING HERE AND AROUND

The main train line from Plymouth terminates at Penzance, which is also served by National Express buses. Bus and train stations are next to each other at the east end of town. A car is an encumbrance here, so use one of the parking lots near the tourist office or the bus and train stations.

ESSENTIALS

Visitor Information Penzance Welcome Centre. ⊠ *Station Approach* ☎ *01736/335530* ⊕ *www.lovepenzance.co.uk.*

EXPLORING

St. Michael's Mount. Rising out of Mount's Bay just off the coast, this spectacular granite-and-slate island is one of Cornwall's greatest natural attractions. The 14th-century castle perched at the highest point—200 feet above the sea—was built on the site of a Benedictine chapel founded by Edward the Confessor. In its time, the island has served as a church

(Brittany's island abbey of Mont St. Michel was an inspiration), a fortress, and a private residence. The castle rooms you can tour include the Chevy Chase Room—a name probably associated with the Cheviot Hills or the French word *chevaux* (horses), after the hunting frieze that decorates the walls of this former monks' refectory. Family portraits include works by Reynolds and Gainsborough. Don't miss the wonderful views from the castle battlements. Around the base of the rock are buildings from medieval to Victorian times, but they appear harmonious. Fascinating gardens surround the Mount, and many kinds of plants flourish in its microclimate.

To get to the island, walk the cobbled causeway from the village of Marazion or, when the tide is in during summer, take the £2 ferry. There are pubs and restaurants in the village, but the island also has a café and restaurant. ■ **TIP**➔ **Wear stout shoes for your visit, which requires a steep climb.** Visits may be canceled in severe weather. ⊠ *A394, Marazion ✛ 3 miles east of Penzance* ☎ *01736/710507* ⊕ *www.stmichaelsmount.co.uk* ✉ *£15; castle only £10; garden only £8* ⊘ *Closed late Oct.–mid-Mar.*

NIGHTLIFE AND PERFORMING ARTS

Minack Theatre. The open-air Minack Theatre perches high above a beach 3 miles southeast of Land's End and about 6 miles southwest of Penzance. The slope of the cliff forms a natural amphitheater, with bench seats on the terraces and the sea as a magnificent backdrop. Different companies present everything from classic dramas to modern comedies, as well as operas and concerts, on afternoons and evenings between Easter and late September. An exhibition center tells the story of the theater's creation. Note that this center is closed afternoons when matinee performances are scheduled. ⊠ *Off B3315, Porthcurno* ☎ *01736/810181* ⊕ *www.minack.com* ✉ *Exhibition center £5, performances £10–£14.*

LIZARD PENINSULA

23 miles southeast of Penzance.

Fodor's Choice ★ The southernmost point on mainland Britain, this peninsula is a government-designated Area of Outstanding Natural Beauty, named so for the rocky, dramatic coast rather than the flat and boring interior. The huge, eerily rotating dish antennae of the Goonhilly Satellite Earth Station are visible from the road as it crosses Goonhilly Downs, the backbone of the peninsula. There's no coast road, unlike Land's End, but the coastal path offers marvelous opportunities to explore on foot—and is often the only way to reach the best beaches. With no large town (Helston at the northern end is the biggest, but isn't a tourist center), it's far less busy than the Land's End peninsula.

GETTING HERE AND AROUND

If you're driving, take A394 to reach Helston, gateway town to the Lizard Peninsula. From Helston, A3083 heads straight down to Lizard Point. Helston is the main public transport hub, but bus service to the villages is infrequent.

EXPLORING

Kynance Cove. A path close to the tip of the peninsula plunges down 200-foot cliffs to this tiny cove dotted with a handful of pint-size islands. The sands here are reachable only during the 2½ hours before and after low tide. The peninsula's cliffs are made of greenish serpentine rock, interspersed with granite; souvenirs of the area are carved out of the stone. ⊠ *Lizard.*

FALMOUTH

8 miles northeast of Lizard Peninsula.

The bustle of this resort town's fishing harbor, yachting center, and commercial port only adds to its charm. In the 18th century Falmouth was the main mail-boat port for North America, and in Flushing, a village across the inlet, you can see the slate-covered houses built by prosperous mail-boat captains. A ferry service now links the two towns. On Custom House Quay, off Arwenack Street, is the King's Pipe, an oven in which seized contraband was burned.

GETTING HERE AND AROUND

Falmouth can be reached from Truro on a branch rail line or by frequent bus service, and is also served by local and National Express buses from other towns. Running parallel to the seafront, the long, partly pedestrianized main drag links the town's main sights. Visitors to Pendennis Castle traveling by train should use Falmouth Docks Station, from which it's a short walk. Alternatively, drive or take a local bus to the castle to save legwork.

ESSENTIALS

Visitor Information Fal River Visitor Information Centre. ⊠ *Prince of Wales Pier, 11 Market Strand* ☎ *01326/741194* ⊕ *www.falmouth.co.uk.*

EXPLORING

FAMILY **National Maritime Museum Cornwall.** The granite-and-oak-clad structure by the harbor is an excellent place to come to grips with Cornish maritime heritage, weather lore, and navigational science. You can view approximately 30 of the collection of 140 or so boats, examine the tools associated with Cornish boatbuilders, and gaze down from the lighthouselike lookout, which is equipped with maps, telescopes, and binoculars. In the glass-fronted Tidal Zone below sea level, you come face-to-face with the sea itself. ⊠ *Discovery Quay* ☎ *01326/313388* ⊕ *www.nmmc.co.uk* ⊠ *£13.50.*

FAMILY **Pendennis Castle.** At the end of its own peninsula stands this formidable
Fodor's Choice castle, built by Henry VIII in the 1540s and improved by his daughter
★ Elizabeth I. You can explore the defenses developed over the centuries. In the Royal Artillery Barracks, the Pendennis Unlocked exhibit explores the castle's history and its connection to Cornwall and England. The castle has sweeping views over the English Channel and across to St. Mawes Castle, designed as a companion fortress to guard the roads. There are free tours of the Half Moon Battery and regular performances, historical reenactments, and shows for kids. ⊠ *Pendennis Head*

☎ *01326/316594* 🌐 *www.english-heritage.org.uk* 🎫 *£10.50* 🕓 *Closed Mon. and Tues. in Mar. and weekdays Nov.–Feb.*

WHERE TO EAT

$$ SEAFOOD 🍴 **Rick Stein's Fish.** Celebrity-chef Rick Stein has expanded his seafood empire to Falmouth, where this no-frills takeaway and restaurant opposite the National Maritime Museum makes a welcome addition to the local dining scene. The hake, plaice, and haddock are grilled, fried to a golden hue, or charcoal roasted and served with salad. **Known for:** celebrity-chef status; down-to-earth ambience; perfect seafood including classic fish-and-chips. [$] *Average main: £15* ✉ *Discovery Quay* ☎ *01841/532700* 🌐 *www.rickstein.com* 🕓 *No dinner Sun. and Mon. Oct.–Easter.*

WHERE TO STAY

$$$ HOTEL 🏨 **St. Michael's Hotel.** A cool, contemporary ambience pervades this seaside hotel overlooking Falmouth Bay and fronted by a lush, subtropical garden. **Pros:** excellent facilities; good restaurant; attentive and amiable staff. **Cons:** spa facilities can be busy; cheapest rooms are small and viewless; some rooms are noisy. [$] *Rooms from: £204* ✉ *Gyllyngvase Beach* ☎ *01326/312707* 🌐 *www.stmichaelshotel.co.uk* 🛏 *61 rooms* 🍽 *Free Breakfast.*

FOWEY

25 miles northeast of St. Mawes.

Fodor's Choice ★ Nestled in the mouth of a wooded estuary, Fowey (pronounced Foy) is still very much a working china-clay port as well as a focal point for the sailing fraternity. Increasingly, it's also a favored home of the rich and famous. Good and varied dining and lodging options abound; these are most in demand during Regatta Week in mid- to late August and the annual Fowey Festival of Words and Music in mid-May. The Bodinnick and Polruan ferries take cars as well as foot passengers across the river for the coast road on to Looe.

A few miles west of Fowey are a pair of very different gardens: the Eden Project, a futuristic display of plants from around the world, and the Lost Gardens of Heligan, a revitalized reminder of the Victorian age.

GETTING HERE AND AROUND

Fowey isn't on any train line, but the town is served by frequent buses from St. Austell. Don't attempt to drive into the steep and narrow-lane town center, which is ideal for strolling around. Parking lots are signposted on the approach roads.

ESSENTIALS

Visitor Information Fowey Tourist Information Centre. ✉ *Daphne du Maurier Literary Centre, 5 South St.* ☎ *0905/151–0262* 🌐 *www.fowey.co.uk.*

EXPLORING

FAMILY Fodor's Choice ★ **Eden Project.** Spectacularly set in a former china-clay pit, this garden presents the world's major plant systems in microcosm. The crater contains more than 70,000 plants—many of them rare or endangered species—from three climate zones. Plants from the temperate zone are outdoors, and those from other zones are housed in hexagonally paneled geodesic domes. In the Mediterranean Biome, olive and citrus groves mix with cacti and other plants indigenous to warmer climates. The Rainforest Biome steams with heat, resounds to the gushing of a waterfall, and blooms with exotic flora; the elevated Canopy Walkway enables you to experience a monkey's-eye view of all of it. The emphasis is on conservation and ecology, but is free of any editorializing. A free shuttle helps the footsore, and well-informed guides provide information. An entertaining exhibition in the visitor center gives you the lowdown on the project, and the Core, an education center, provides amusement and instruction for children—if you can drag them away from the zipwire and giant swing. There are open-air concerts in summer and an ice-skating rink in winter. The Eden Project is 3 miles northeast of Charleston and 5 miles northwest of Fowey. There's frequent bus service from Fowey to St. Austell, and from St. Austell train station to Eden. ✉ *Bodelva Rd., off A30, A390, and A391, St. Austell* ☎ *01726/811911* 🌐 *www.edenproject.com* 🎫 *£27.50, £23.50 if arriving by bike, on foot, or on public transport, £38 combined ticket with Lost Gardens of Heligan* 🕓 *Usually closed Mon. and Tues. Jan.*

Lost Gardens of Heligan. These sprawling grounds have something for all garden lovers, as well as an intriguing history. Begun by the Tremayne family in the late 18th century, they were rediscovered and spruced up in the early 1990s by former rock music producer Tim Smit (the force behind the Eden Project). In Victorian times the gardens displayed plants from around the British Empire. The Jungle area contains surviving plants from this era, including a lone Monterey pine, as well as giant redwood and clumps of bamboo. The Italian Garden and walled Flower Gardens are delightful, but don't overlook the fruit and vegetable gardens or Flora's Green, bordered by a ravine. It's easy to spend half a day here. Guided tours can be arranged for groups. **■ TIP → Travel via St. Austell to avoid confusing country lanes, then follow signs to Mevagissey.** ✉ *B3273, Pentewan* ☎ *01726/845100* 🌐 *www.heligan.com* 🎫 *£14.50, £38 combined ticket with Eden Project.*

WHERE TO EAT

$ AMERICAN FAMILY

🍴 **Sam's.** This small and buzzing bistro has a rock-and-roll flavor, thanks to the walls adorned with posters of music icons. Diners squeeze onto benches and into booths to savor dishes made with local seafood, including a majestic bouillabaisse, or just a simple "Samburger." You may have to wait for a table, but there's a slinky lounge-bar upstairs for a preprandial drink. **Known for:** convivial atmosphere; best burgers in Cornwall; long waits for a table. [$] *Average main: £12* ✉ *20 Fore St.* ☎ *01726/832273* 🌐 *www.samscornwall.co.uk.*

WHERE TO STAY

$$$ HOTEL

🏨 **St. Michael's Hotel.** A cool, contemporary ambience pervades this seaside hotel overlooking Falmouth Bay and fronted by a lush, subtropical garden. **Pros:** excellent facilities; good restaurant; attentive and amiable staff. **Cons:** spa facilities can be busy; cheapest rooms are small and viewless; some rooms are noisy. $ *Rooms from: £204* ✉ *Gyllyngvase Beach, Falmouth* ☎ *01326/312707* ⊕ *www.stmichaelshotel.co.uk* ⮌ *61 rooms* ❍❙ *Free Breakfast.*

PLYMOUTH AND DARTMOOR

Just over the border from Cornwall is Plymouth, an unprepossessing city but one with a historic old core and splendid harbor that recall a rich maritime heritage. North of Plymouth, you can explore the vast, boggy reaches of hilly Dartmoor, the setting for the Sherlock Holmes classic *The Hound of the Baskervilles.* This national park is a great place to hike or go horseback riding away from the crowds.

PLYMOUTH

48 miles southwest of Exeter, 124 miles southwest of Bristol, 240 miles southwest of London.

Devon's largest city has long been linked with England's commercial and maritime history. The Pilgrims sailed from here to the New World in the *Mayflower* in 1620. Although much of the city center was destroyed by air raids in World War II and has been rebuilt in an uninspiring style, there are worthwhile sights. A harbor tour is also a good way to see the city.

GETTING HERE AND AROUND

Frequent trains arrive from Bodmin, Penzance, and Exeter. From London Paddington, trains take three to four hours; Megabus and National Express buses from London's Victoria Coach Station take five or six hours. The train station is 1 mile north of the seafront, connected by frequent buses. Long-distance buses stop at the centrally located bus station off Royal Parade. Drivers can leave their cars in one of the numerous parking lots, including a couple right by the harbor. The seafront and central city areas are best explored on foot.

ESSENTIALS

Visitor Information Plymouth Tourism Information Centre. ✉ *Plymouth Mayflower, 3–5 The Barbican* ☎ *01752/306330* ⊕ *www.visitplymouth.co.uk.*

EXPLORING

Black Friars Distillery. At the Black Friars Distillery, Plymouth's most famous export, gin, has been distilled since 1793. You can purchase bottles of sloe gin, damson liqueur, fruit cup, or the fiery "Navy Strength" gin that traditionally was issued to the Royal Navy. Learn the full story on walking tours around the distillery, ending with a sampling in the wood-paneled Refectory Bar. The building originally housed a friary and was where the Pilgrims spent their last night on English soil in 1620. ✉ *60 Southside St.* ☎ *01752/665292* ⊕ *www.plymouthdistillery.com.*

FAMILY **Plymouth *Mayflower* Exhibition.** On three floors, this interactive exhibition narrates the story of Plymouth, from its beginnings as a fishing and trading port to the modern industrial city it is today. Along the way, you'll take in the stories of various expeditions that embarked from here to the New World, including the *Mayflower* itself. The city's tourist office

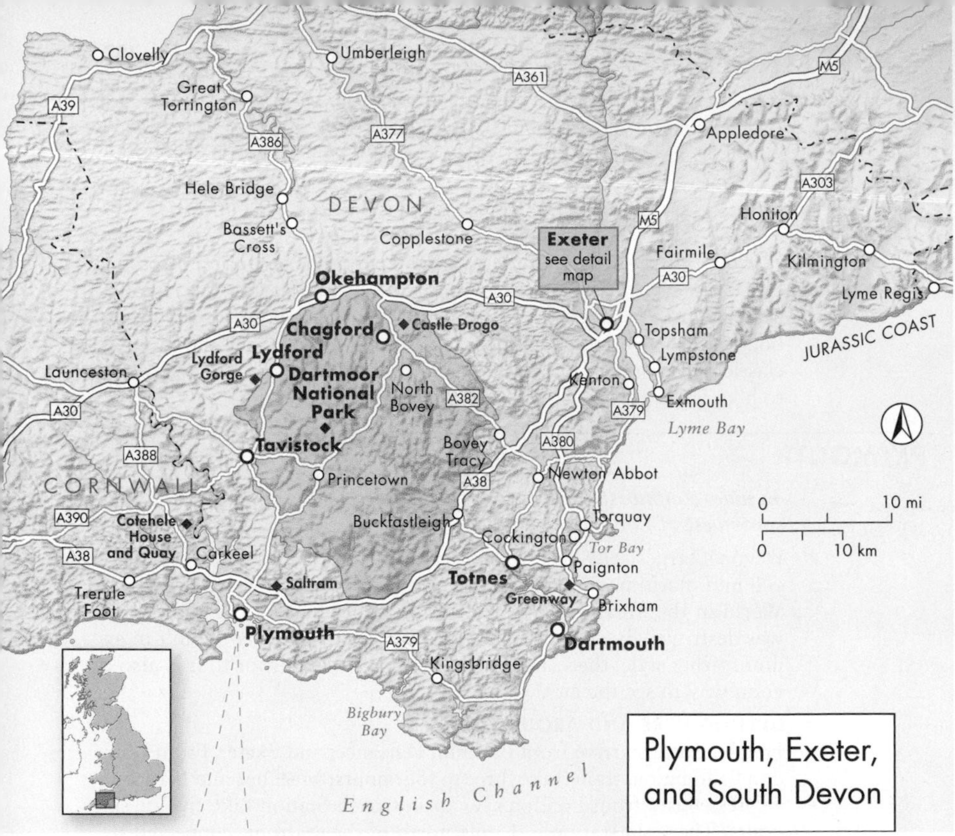

Plymouth, Exeter, and South Devon

is also in this building. ✉ *3–5 The Barbican* ☎ *01752/306330* 🌐 *www.visitplymouth.co.uk* 🎟 *£3* 🕐 *Closed Sun. Nov.–Mar.*

Saltram. An exquisite 18th-century home with many of its original furnishings, Saltram was built around the remains of a late-Tudor mansion. Its jewel is one of Britain's grandest neoclassical rooms—a vast, double-cube salon designed by Robert Adam and hung with paintings by Sir Joshua Reynolds, first president of the Royal Academy of Arts, who was born nearby in 1723. Fine plasterwork adorns many rooms and three have original Chinese wallpaper. The outstanding garden includes rare trees and shrubs, and there's a restaurant and a cafeteria. Saltram is 3½ miles east of Plymouth city center. ✉ *South of A38, Plympton* ☎ *01752/333500* 🌐 *www.nationaltrust.org.uk* 🎟 *Mar.–Oct. £11.60, Nov.–Feb. £8.40.*

WHERE TO EAT

$$ MODERN BRITISH

🍴 **Quay 33.** Fresh seafood landed at the nearby quays, such as sea bass and cod, features high on the menu at this Barbican eatery, but you will also find pastas, risottos, steaks, and slow-cooked duck-leg confit. Exmouth mussels or grilled scallops make an ideal light lunch, while desserts include crème brûlée and homemade cheesecake. **Known for:** first-class service; creative and delicious food; tasty desserts. [$] *Average main: £15* ✉ *33 Southside St.* ☎ *01752/229345* 🌐 *www.quay33.co.uk* 🕐 *Closed Sun.*

WHERE TO STAY

$$ HOTEL **Langdon Court Hotel.** Situated in peaceful grounds 8 miles outside Plymouth, this venerable country-house hotel was once the property of Catherine Parr—last wife of Henry VIII—and later hosted such distinguished guests as the future Edward VII and his mistress Lilie Langtry. **Pros:** tranquil rural setting; attentive staff; great food. **Cons:** few leisure facilities; some rooms are small; poor soundproofing in some rooms. [$] *Rooms from: £149* ✉ *Adam's La., Wembury* ☎ *01752/862358* 🌐 *www.langdoncourt.com* 🛏 *17 rooms* 🍴 *Free Breakfast.*

DARTMOOR NATIONAL PARK

10 miles north of Plymouth, 13 miles west of Exeter.

Devon presents no greater contrast to the country's quaint and picturesque image than the bleak, deserted expanses of Dartmoor. Southern England's greatest natural wilderness is largely a treeless landscape of sometimes alarming emptiness, though it also harbors surprises in the form of hidden lakes, abandoned quarries, and the dramatically wind-sculpted tors, or craggy peaks, that puncture the horizon in every direction. Sudden mists and above-average rainfall levels add to the simultaneously inhospitable and alluring scene.

GETTING HERE AND AROUND

Public transport services are extremely sparse on Dartmoor, making a car indispensable for anywhere off the beaten track. The peripheral towns of Okehampton and Tavistock are well served by bus from Exeter and Plymouth, and Chagford also has direct connections to Exeter, but central Princetown has only sporadic links with the outside world.

ESSENTIALS

Visitor Information National Park Visitor Centre. ✉ *Tavistock Rd., Princetown* ☎ *01822/890414* 🌐 *www.dartmoor.gov.uk.*

EXPLORING

Dartmoor National Park. Even on a summer's day, the brooding hills of this sprawling wilderness appear a likely haunt for such monsters as the hound of the Baskervilles, and it seems entirely fitting that Sir Arthur Conan Doyle set his Sherlock Holmes thriller in this landscape. Sometimes the wet, peaty wasteland of Dartmoor National Park vanishes in rain and mist, although in clear weather you can see north to Exmoor, south over the English Channel, and west far into Cornwall. Much of Dartmoor consists of open heath and moorland, unspoiled by roads—wonderful walking and horseback-riding territory but an easy place to lose your bearings. Dartmoor's earliest inhabitants left behind stone monuments and burial mounds that help you envision prehistoric man roaming these pastures. Ponies, sheep, and birds are the main animals to be seen.

Several villages scattered along the borders of this 368-square-mile reserve—one-third of which is owned by Prince Charles—make useful bases for hiking excursions. Accommodations include simple inns and some elegant havens. **Okehampton** is a main gateway, and **Chagford** is a good base for exploring north Dartmoor. Other scenic spots include

Buckland-in-the-Moor, a hamlet with thatch-roof cottages; **Widecombe-in-the-Moor,** whose church is known as the Cathedral of the Moor; and **Grimspound,** the Bronze Age site featured in Conan Doyle's most famous tale. Transmoor Link buses connect many of Dartmoor's towns and villages. The **National Park Visitor Centre** in Princetown is a good place to start your trip, as are centers in Postbridge and Haytor. You can also pick up information in Ivybridge, Okehampton, Moretonhampstead, Tavistock, and Buckfastleigh. ✉ *National Park Visitor Centre, Tavistock Rd., Princetown* ☎ *01822/890414* ⊕ *www.dartmoor.gov.uk.*

SPORTS AND THE OUTDOORS

Hiking is extremely popular in Dartmoor National Park. The areas around Widgery Cross, Becky Falls, and the Bovey Valley, as well as the short but dramatic walk along Lydford Gorge, have wide appeal, as do the many valleys around the southern edge of the moors. Guided hikes, typically costing £3 to £8, are available through the park's visitor information centers. Reservations are usually not necessary. Longer hikes in the bleak, less-populated regions—for example, the tors south of Okehampton—are appropriate only for most experienced walkers. Dartmoor is a great area for horseback riding; many towns have stables for guided rides.

TAVISTOCK AND AROUND

13 miles north of Plymouth.

On the River Tavy, the ancient town of Tavistock historically owed its importance to its Benedictine abbey (dissolved by Henry VIII in the 16th century) and to its status as a stannary town, where tin was weighed, stamped, and assessed. Today the town of 11,000 preserves a prosperous, predominantly Victorian appearance, especially at the bustling indoor Pannier Market off central Bedford Square. Tavistock makes a useful base for exploring a scattering of nearby sights—Buckland Abbey, Cotehele House, and Morwellham Quay—and for touring Dartmoor's western reaches.

GETTING HERE AND AROUND

Tavistock, on A386 and A390, is easily accessed via the frequent buses from Plymouth, which take about an hour. You'll need your own transportation to visit the attractions scattered around it, however.

EXPLORING

Cotehele House and Quay. About 4 miles west of Buckland Abbey and 9 miles southwest of Tavistock, Cotehele House and Quay was formerly a busy port on the River Tamar, but it is now usually visited for the well-preserved, atmospheric late-medieval manor, home of the Edgcumbe family for centuries. The house has original furniture, tapestries, embroideries, and armor, and you can also visit the impressive gardens, a quay museum, and a restored mill (usually in operation on Sunday and Thursday—call for other days). A limited number of visitors are allowed per day, so arrive early and be prepared to wait during busy periods. Choose a bright day, because the rooms have no electric light. Shops, crafts studios, a gallery, and a restaurant provide other diversions. ■ **TIP→ Take advantage of the shuttle bus that runs every half hour between the house, quay, and mill.** ✉ *Off A390, St. Dominick* ☎ *01579/351346* 🌐 *www.nationaltrust.org.uk* 🎟 *£11.60* 🕓 *Closed Jan.–early Mar.*

WHERE TO EAT

$$$$ MODERN BRITISH Fodor's Choice ★

🍴 **The Horn of Plenty.** The restaurant within this Georgian house has magnificent views across the wooded, rhododendron-filled Tamar Valley and a sophisticated menu favoring local and seasonal ingredients. A typical starter and main course might be seared scallops with cauliflower and cumin followed by Creedy Carver duck with baby leeks and Jerusalem artichokes, while desserts include pear and white chocolate mousse with kiwi, lime, and lychee. **Known for:** extravagant and exceptional fine dining; stunning views; affordable potluck set-menu on Monday nights. [$] *Average main: £50* ✉ *A390, Gulworthy* ☎ *01822/832528* 🌐 *www.thehornofplenty.co.uk.*

WHERE TO STAY

$$$$ HOTEL Fodor's Choice ★

🏨 **Hotel Endsleigh.** Under the auspices of hotelier Olga Polizzi, the Endsleigh has risen to be one of the country's best-loved hotels, nestled in a fold of the Tamar Valley with the river itself rolling serenely by at the bottom of the garden. **Pros:** elegant without being pompous; discreet but ever-present staff; beautiful rural setting. **Cons:** few leisure facilities; some noise intrusion; remote location. [$] *Rooms from: £285* ✉ *Milton Abbot* ☎ *01822/870000* 🌐 *www.hotelendsleigh.com* 🛏 *18 rooms* 🍴 *Free Breakfast.*

LYDFORD

7 miles north of Tavistock, 24 miles north of Plymouth.

The sequestered hamlet of Lydford packs a lot into a small area: there's the dramatic scenery of the gorge just outside the village, the remains of a medieval castle, and some attractive options for eating and sleeping. The Granite Way cycle track, much of it running along a disused railway route, connects Lydford with Okehampton.

GETTING HERE AND AROUND

The gorge is easily accessed on Stagecoach South West buses from Plymouth to Tavistock, then Dartline Coaches to Lydford, and on Dartline Coaches from Okehampton (connected to Exeter). By car, take A386 between Tavistock and Okehampton.

EXPLORING

Fodor's Choice ★

Lydford Gorge. The River Lyd carved a spectacular 1½-mile-long chasm through the rock at Lydford Gorge, outside the pretty village of Lydford, midway between Okehampton and Tavistock. Two paths follow the gorge past gurgling whirlpools and waterfalls with evocative names such as the Devil's Cauldron and the White Lady Waterfall. ■ **TIP→ Sturdy footwear is recommended.** Although the walk can be quite challenging, the paths can still get congested during busy periods. Two tearooms are open early March through late December. In winter, access is restricted to the waterfall and the top of the gorge. ✉ *Off A386, Lydford* ☎ *01822/820320* 🌐 *www.nationaltrust.org.uk* 🎟 *£9.40; £4.50 in winter.*

WHERE TO EAT

$$ MODERN BRITISH 🍴 **Dartmoor Inn.** Locals and visitors alike make a beeline for this gastro-pub in a 16th-century building with a number of small dining spaces done in spare, contemporary country style. The elegantly presented dishes may include roasted rump of lamb, panfried hake with scallop and lobster curry, or peppered wild venison with squash, beetroots, and muscat cherries. **Known for:** cozy ambience; fresh, locally sourced food; affordable bar menu. [$] *Average main: £18* ✉ *Moorside, on A386, Lydford* ☎ *01822/820221* 🌐 *www.dartmoorinn.com* 🕓 *Closed Mon. Sept.–July.*

WHERE TO STAY

$ B&B/INN 🏨 **Castle Inn.** In the heart of Lydford village, this 16th-century inn sits next to Lydford Castle. **Pros:** antique character; tasty pub food; peaceful rural setting. **Cons:** shabby in places; some small rooms; occasionally sloping floors and low ceilings. [$] *Rooms from: £70* ✉ *School Rd., off A386, Lydford* ☎ *01822/820242* 🌐 *www.castleinnlydford.com* 🛏 *8 rooms* 🍽 *Free Breakfast.*

$$$ HOTEL Fodor's Choice ★ 🏨 **Lewtrenchard Manor.** Paneled rooms, stone fireplaces, leaded-glass windows, and handsome gardens outfit this spacious 1620 manor house on the northwestern edge of Dartmoor. **Pros:** beautiful Jacobean setting; conscientious service; outstanding food. **Cons:** creaking doors and floors in main building; rooms in outbuildings have less atmosphere; not very child-friendly. [$] *Rooms from: £189* ✉ *Off A30, Lewdown* ☎ *01566/783222* 🌐 *www.lewtrenchard.co.uk* 🛏 *14 rooms* 🍽 *Free Breakfast.*

CHAGFORD

9 miles southeast of Okehampton, 30 miles northeast of Plymouth.

Once a tin-weighing station, Chagford was an area of fierce fighting between the Roundheads and the Cavaliers during the English Civil War. Although officially a "town" since 1305, Chagford is more of a village, with taverns grouped around a seasoned old church and a curious "pepper-pot" market house on the site of the old Stannary Court. With a handful of cafés and shops to browse around, it makes a convenient base from which to explore north Dartmoor.

GETTING HERE AND AROUND

Infrequent local buses connect Chagford with Okehampton and Exeter (except on Sunday, when there's no service). The village is off A382; a car or bicycle is the best way to see its far-flung sights.

EXPLORING

Castle Drogo. Northeast of Chagford, this castle looks like a stout medieval fortress, complete with battlements, but construction actually took place between 1910 and 1930. Designed by noted architect Sir Edwin Lutyens for Julius Drewe, a wealthy grocer, the castle is only half finished (funds ran out). Inside, medieval grandeur is combined with early-20th-century comforts, and there are awesome views over Dartmoor's Teign Valley. The grounds are well worth a prolonged wander, with paths leading down to the river at Fingle Bridge.

⚠ **Major renovation work will be ongoing until the end of 2018, which means that many parts of the castle are hidden behind scaffolding and some rooms are closed to visitors.** Turn off the A30 Exeter–Okehampton road at Whiddon Down to reach the castle. ✉ *Off A30 and A382, Drewsteignton* ☎ *01647/433306* 🌐 *www.nationaltrust.org.uk* 🎟 *£11.60* 🕒 *Castle closed early Nov.–early Mar.*

Devon Guild of Craftsmen. One of the Southwest's most important contemporary Arts and Crafts centers, the Devon Guild is in a converted 19th-century coach house in the village of Bovey Tracey, 10 miles southeast of Chagford and 14 miles southwest of Exeter. The center has excellent exhibitions of local, national, and international crafts, as well as a shop and café. ✉ *Riverside Mill, Fore St., Bovey Tracey* ☎ *01626/832223* 🌐 *www.crafts.org.uk* 🎟 *Free.*

WHERE TO EAT

$$$$ MODERN BRITISH Fodor's Choice ★

🍴 **Gidleigh Park.** One of England's foremost country-house hotels, Gidleigh Park occupies an enclave of landscaped gardens and streams, reached via a lengthy, winding country lane and private drive at the edge of Dartmoor. The extremely pricey contemporary restaurant, directed by chef Michael Wignall, has been showered with culinary awards. **Known for:** top-notch dining experience; prix-fixe menus with multi-course options; excellent wine menu. [$] *Average main: £125* ✉ *Gidleigh Park* ☎ *01647/432367* 🌐 *www.gidleigh.co.uk.*

WHERE TO STAY

$$$ HOTEL FAMILY Fodor's Choice ★

🏨 **Bovey Castle.** With the grandeur of a country estate and the amenities of a modern hotel, Bovey Castle, built in 1906 for Viscount Hambledon, has it all. **Pros:** baronial splendor; range of activities; good for families. **Cons:** brasserie can be hit-and-miss; overpriced drinks and extras; remote location. [$] *Rooms from: £176* ✉ *Off B3212, North Bovey* ☎ *01647/445000* 🌐 *www.boveycastle.com* 🛏 *60 rooms* 🍽 *No meals.*

EXETER AND SOUTH DEVON

The ancient city of Exeter, Devon's county seat, has preserved some of its historical character despite wartime bombing. To the south, on the banks of the River Dart, is the pretty market town of Totnes, while the well-to-do yachting center of Dartmouth lies south of Torbay (a coastal resort) at the river's estuary.

EXETER

18 miles east of Chagford, 48 miles northeast of Plymouth, 85 miles southwest of Bristol, 205 miles southwest of London.

Exeter has been the capital of the region since the Romans established a fortress here 2,000 years ago, and evidence of the Roman occupation remains in the city walls. Although it was heavily bombed in 1942, Exeter retains much of its medieval character, as well as examples of the gracious architecture of the 18th and 19th centuries. It's convenient to both Torquay and Dartmoor.

GETTING HERE AND AROUND

Once- or twice-hourly train service from London Paddington takes about two hours and 15 minutes; the less frequent service from London Waterloo via Salisbury takes around three hours and 25 minutes. From London's Victoria Coach Station, National Express buses leave every 2 hours and Megabus has four daily departures, all taking between 4½ and 5¼ hours. Exeter is a major transportation hub for Devon. Trains from Bristol, Salisbury, and Plymouth stop at Exeter St. David's, and connect to the center by frequent buses. Some trains also stop at the more useful Exeter Central. The bus station is off Paris Street near the tourist office. Cars are unnecessary in town, so park yours as soon as possible—all the sights are within an easy walk.

ESSENTIALS

Visitor Information Exeter Visitor Information and Tickets. ⊠ *Dix's Field* ☎ *01392/665700* ⊕ *www.visitexeter.com.*

EXPLORING

Fodor'sChoice
★

Cathedral of St. Peter. At the heart of Exeter, the great Gothic cathedral was begun in 1275 and completed almost a century later. Its twin towers are even older survivors of an earlier Norman cathedral. Rising from a forest of ribbed columns, the nave's 300-foot stretch of unbroken Gothic vaulting is the longest in the world. Myriad statues, tombs, and memorial plaques adorn the interior. In the minstrels' gallery, high up on the left of the nave, stands a group of carved figures singing and playing musical instruments, including bagpipes. Guided tours (up to four a day), roof tours (Tuesdays and Saturdays in July through September), and audio tours are available. Outside in Cathedral Close, don't miss the 400-year-old door to No. 10, the bishop of Crediton's house, ornately carved with angels' and lions' heads. ⊠ *Cathedral Close* ☎ *01392/285983* ⊕ *www.exeter-cathedral.org.uk* ⊡ *£7.50.*

Guildhall. On the city's main shopping street, this is said to be the oldest municipal building in the country still in use. The current hall, with its Renaissance portico, dates from 1330, although a guildhall has occupied this site since at least 1160. The walls are adorned with imposing portraits of royal figures and noteworthy locals, and its timber-braced roof, one of the earliest in England, dates from about 1460. ⊠ *High St.* ☎ *01392/665500* ⊕ *www.exeter.gov.uk* ⊡ *Free* ☉ *Closed Sun. and during government functions.*

FAMILY
Fodor'sChoice
★

Royal Albert Memorial Museum. This family-friendly museum is housed in a recently refurbished Victorian building. The centerpiece is the extensive Making History gallery, a giddy mix of objects imaginatively illustrating the city's history and covering everything from Roman pottery to memorabilia from World War II. The geology section is thrillingly enhanced by the latest video technology, and there are also excellent ethnography and archaeological collections, natural-history displays, and works by West Country artists. ⊠ *Queen St.* ☎ *01392/265858* ⊕ *www.rammuseum.org.uk* ⊡ *Free* ☉ *Closed Mon.*

FAMILY
Underground Passages. Exeter's Underground Passages, which once served as conduits for fresh water, are the only medieval vaulted passages open to the public in Britain. They date to the mid-14th century,

Cathedral of St. Peter **1**
Guildhall **2**
Royal Albert Memorial Museum **3**
Underground Passages **4**

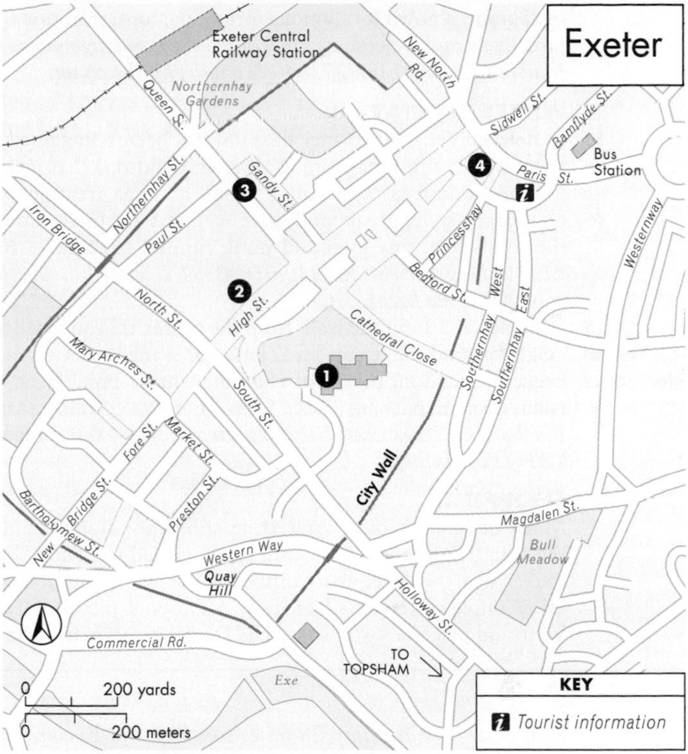

although some were enlarged by the Victorians. An exhibition and video precede the 25-minute guided tour. Many of the passages are narrow and low: be prepared to stoop. The tours often sell out during school vacations, so come early. Children under five are not permitted in the tunnels. ✉ *2 Paris St.* ☎ *01392/665887* 🌐 *www.exeter.gov.uk* 🎟 *£6* ⏲ *Closed Mon. Oct.–May.*

WHERE TO EAT

$$$$ MODERN BRITISH

🍴 **Lympstone Manor.** Exeter-born master chef Michael Caines has breathed new life into this elegant Georgian mansion overlooking the Exe estuary 5 miles south of Exeter, where he has installed three separate dining rooms to showcase his highly original recipes. The wow-factor starts from the moment you arrive, with unforgettable estuary views forming a fitting prelude to the gastronomic feast to follow. **Known for:** fabulous location; stylishly presented and eclectic gourmet cuisine; frequently changing fix-priced menus and multicourse tasting menus. [$] *Average main: £115* ✉ *Courtlands La., Exmouth* ☎ *01395/202040* 🌐 *www.lympstonemanor.co.uk.*

$ BRITISH

🍴 **Ship Inn.** Here you can lift a tankard of stout in the very rooms where Sir Francis Drake and Sir Walter Raleigh enjoyed their ale. The pub dishes out casual bar fare, from sandwiches to grills and beefsteak and ale pie, either in the bar or in the beamed and paneled upstairs restaurant. **Known for:** famous former patrons; traditional English pub fare; lively and welcoming environment. $ *Average main: £8* ⊠ *1–3 St. Martin's La.* ☎ *01392/272040* ⊕ *www.gkpubs.co.uk.*

WHERE TO STAY

$$
HOTEL
Fodor'sChoice
★

⊡ **Hotel du Vin.** This former hospital has been reimagined as a modish hotel with a zippy, happening vibe, and add-ons that include a heated indoor-outdoor pool, a fitness room, and spa treatments. **Pros:** contemporary style; great food; nice wellness facilities. **Cons:** rooms on the small side; tiny gym and pool; limited parking. $ *Rooms from: £131* ⊠ *Magdalen St.* ☎ *0330/016–0391* ⊕ *www.hotelduvin.com* ⇌ *59 rooms* ⦿⦿ *Free Breakfast.*

$
B&B/INN
Fodor'sChoice
★

⊡ **Raffles.** A 10-minute walk from the center, this quirky B&B in a quiet neighborhood makes an ideal base for a night or two in town. **Pros:** peaceful location; plenty of character; great breakfasts. **Cons:** single room is small; parking costs £5; no elevator. $ *Rooms from: £85* ⊠ *11 Blackall Rd.* ☎ *01392/270200* ⊕ *www.raffles-exeter.co.uk* ⇌ *6 rooms* ⦿⦿ *Free Breakfast.*

SHOPPING

Many of Exeter's most interesting shops are along Gandy Street, off the main High Street drag, with several good food and clothes outlets. Exeter was the silver-assay office for the West Country, and the earliest example of Exeter silver (now a museum piece) dates from 1218; Victorian pieces are still sold. The Exeter assay mark is three castles.

TOTNES

8 miles west of Torquay, 28 miles southwest of Exeter.

This busy market town on the banks of the River Dart preserves plenty of its medieval past, and on summer Tuesdays vendors dress in period costume for the Elizabethan Market. Market days are Friday and Saturday, when the town's status as a center of alternative medicine and culture becomes especially clear, and on the third Sunday of the month, when there's a local produce market on Civic Square. The historic buildings include a guildhall and St. Mary's Church.

GETTING HERE AND AROUND

Totnes is on a regular fast bus route between Plymouth and Torbay, and is a stop for main-line trains between Plymouth and Exeter. Buses pull into the center, and the train station is a few minutes' walk north of the center. Drivers should take A38 and A385 from Plymouth or A385 from Torbay.

ESSENTIALS

Visitor Information Visit Totnes. ☎ *01803/863168* ⊕ *www.visittotnes.co.uk.*

EXPLORING

Brixham. At the southern point of Tor Bay, Brixham has kept much of its original charm, partly because it still has an active fishing harbor. Much of the catch goes straight to restaurants as far away as London. Sample fish-and-chips on the quayside, where there's a (surprisingly petite) full-scale reproduction of the vessel on which Sir Francis Drake circumnavigated the world. The village is 10 miles southeast of Totnes by A385 and A3022. ⊠ *Brixham.*

FAMILY **South Devon Railway.** Steam trains of this railway run through 7 miles of the wooded Dart Valley between Totnes and Buckfastleigh, on the edge of Dartmoor. Call about special trips around Christmas. ⊠ *Dart Bridge Rd., Buckfastleigh* ☎ *01364/644370* ⊕ *www.southdevonrailway.co.uk* ⊠ *£15 round-trip.*

WHERE TO STAY

$$ ⛯ **Royal Seven Stars Hotel.** Conveniently located at the bottom of the
HOTEL main street, this centuries-old coaching inn has counted Daniel Defoe
Fodor'sChoice and Edward VII among its former guests. **Pros:** central location; friendly
★ staff; spotless rooms. **Cons:** standard accommodations and bathrooms are small; rooms over bars can be noisy; busy public areas. $ *Rooms from: £130* ⊠ *The Plains* ☎ *01803/862125* ⊕ *www.royalsevenstars. co.uk* ⇨ *21 rooms* ⧖ *Free Breakfast.*

DARTMOUTH

13 miles southeast of Totnes, 35 miles east of Plymouth, 35 miles south of Exeter, 5 miles southwest of Brixham.

An important port in the Middle Ages, Dartmouth is today a favorite haunt of yacht owners. Traces of its past include the old houses in Bayard's Cove at the bottom of Lower Street, where the *Mayflower* made a stop in 1620, the 16th-century covered Butterwalk, and the two castles guarding the entrance to the River Dart. The Royal Naval College, built in 1905, dominates the heights above the town. A few miles south of Dartmouth on Start Bay there are a number of pretty beaches including Blackpool Sands, popular with families.

GETTING HERE AND AROUND

Frequent buses connect Dartmouth with Plymouth and Totnes. Drivers coming from the west should follow A381 and A3122. Approaching from the Torbay area via A3022 and A379, you can save mileage by using the passenger and car ferries crossing the Dart. Travelers on foot can take advantage of a vintage steam train service operating between Paignton and Kingswear, where there are ferry connections with Dartmouth. River ferries also link Dartmouth with Totnes.

ESSENTIALS

Visitor Information Dartmouth Tourist Information Centre. ⊠ *The Engine House, Mayors Ave.* ☎ *01803/834224* ⊕ *www.discoverdartmouth.com.*

EXPLORING

Greenway. A rewarding way to experience the River Dart is to join a cruise from Dartmouth's quay to visit Greenway, the 16th-century riverside home of the Gilbert family (Sir Humphrey Gilbert claimed Newfoundland on behalf of Elizabeth I), more famous today for its association with the crime writer Agatha Christie. Mrs. Mallowan (Christie's married name) made it her holiday home beginning in 1938, and the house displays collections of archaeological finds, china, and silver. The gorgeous gardens are thickly planted with magnolias, camellias, and rare shrubs, and richly endowed with panoramic views. Beware, however, that the grounds are steeply laid out, and those arriving by boat face a daunting uphill climb. Allow three hours to see everything; timed tickets for the house are given on arrival. Parking spaces here are restricted and must be booked in advance. Alternatively, ask at the tourist office about walking and cycling routes to reach the house, as well as about the bus service from Greenway Halt (a stop on the Dartmouth Steam Railway). A round-trip ticket between Dartmouth and Greenway costs £8.50 on the Greenway Ferry (🌐 *www.greenway-ferry.co.uk*). ✉ *Greenway Rd., Galmpton* ☎ *01803/842382* 🌐 *www.nationaltrust.org.uk* 🎟 *£11.60* 🕒 *Closed Jan.–early Feb., and weekdays early Nov.–Dec.*

WHERE TO EAT

$$$$ SEAFOOD 🍴 **The Seahorse.** In a prime riverside location, this seafood restaurant epitomizes the region's ongoing food revolution. The knowledgeable staff will guide you through the Italian-inspired menu, which primarily depends on the day's catch: look for scallops with garlic and white port, grilled Dover sole with seaweed butter, or bream *al cartoccio* (baked in paper with Vermentino wine, rosemary, and garlic). **Known for:** relaxed and convivial atmosphere; good set-price menus; attractive riverside location. [$] *Average main: £26* ✉ *5 S. Embankment* ☎ *01803/835147* 🌐 *www.seahorserestaurant.co.uk* 🕒 *Closed Sun. and Mon.*

WHERE TO STAY

$$$ HOTEL Fodor's Choice ★ 🏨 **Royal Castle Hotel.** Part of Dartmouth's historic waterfront (and consequently a hub of activity), this hotel has truly earned the name "Royal"—several monarchs have slept here. **Pros:** historical resonance; superb central location; professional staff. **Cons:** some cheaper rooms are nondescript; no elevator; noise intrusion in some rooms. [$] *Rooms from: £180* ✉ *11 The Quay* ☎ *01803/833033* 🌐 *www.royalcastle.co.uk* 🛏 *25 rooms* 🍽 *Free Breakfast.*

6

OXFORD AND THE
THAMES VALLEY

Visit Fodors.com for advice, updates, and bookings

WELCOME TO OXFORD AND THE THAMES VALLEY

TOP REASONS TO GO

★ **Oxford:** While scholars' noses are buried in their books, you get to sightsee among Oxford University's ancient stone buildings and memorable museums.

★ **Windsor Castle:** The mystique of eight successive royal houses of the British monarchy permeates Windsor and its famous castle, where a fraction of the current Queen's vast wealth is displayed.

★ **Blenheim Palace:** The only British historic home to be named a World Heritage Site has magnificent baroque architecture, stunning parkland, and remembrances of Winston Churchill.

★ **Boating on the Thames:** Life is slower on the river, and renting a boat or taking a cruise is an ideal way to see verdant riverside pastures and villages. Windsor, Marlow, Henley, and Oxford are good options.

★ **Mapledurham House:** This is the house that inspired Toad Hall from *The Wind in the Willows*; you can picnic here on the grounds and admire the views.

An ideal place to begin any exploration of the Thames Valley is the town of Windsor, about an hour's drive west of central London. From there you can follow the river to Marlow and to Henley-on-Thames, site of the famous regatta. To the north is Oxford, with its pubs, colleges, and museums; it can make a good base for exploring some of the area's charming towns and notable stately homes.

1 **Windsor, Marlow, and Nearby.** Gorgeous Windsor has its imposing and battlemented castle, stone cottages, and tea shops, and nearby Eton is also charming. The meadows and villages around Marlow and Henley are lovely in summer when the flowers are in bloom. Mapledurham House near Henley-on-Thames is an idyllic stop; you can take a boat here.

2 **Oxford.** Wonderfully walkable, this university town has handsome, golden-stone buildings and museum after museum to explore. Take a punt on the local waterways for a break. Oxford's good bars, pubs, and restaurants keep you going late at night as well.

3 **Oxfordshire.** Around the Thames Valley are many intriguing stops, including several grand manor houses. Blenheim (birthplace of Winston Churchill) is a vast, ornate, extraordinary place that takes the better part of a day to see.

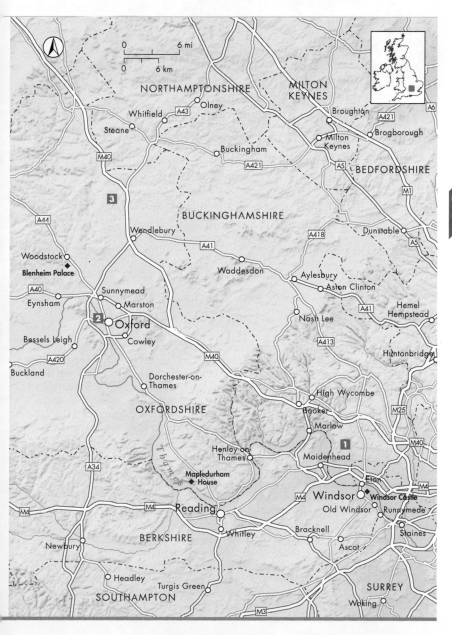

Updated by
Jack Jewers

Easy proximity to London has made the Thames Valley a favored hangout for the wealthy, just as it has been for centuries. The rich and powerful of centuries past built the lavish country estates and castles, including Windsor, that today form the area's most popular tourist attractions. Many of these are easy day trips from London, as is Oxford and its famed university. Consider exploring this stretch of the River Thames by boat, either jumping aboard a cruiser or getting behind the oars. Windsor, Henley, and Marlow all make good starting points.

Once an aquatic highway connecting London to the rest of England and the world, the Thames was critical to the power of the city when the sun never set on the British Empire. By the 18th century the Thames was one of the world's busiest water systems, declining in commercial importance only when the 20th century brought other means of transportation to the forefront. Traditionally, the area west of London is known as the Thames Valley, and the area to the east is called the Thames Gateway.

Anyone who wants to understand the mystique of the British monarchy should visit Windsor, home to the medieval and massive Windsor Castle. Farther upstream, the green quadrangles and graceful spires of Oxford are the hallmarks of one of the world's most famous universities. Within 10 miles of Oxford the storybook village of Woodstock and gracious Blenheim Palace, one of the grandest houses in England, are both well worth your time.

The railroads and motorways carrying traffic to and from London have turned much of this area into commuter territory, but you can still find timeless villages and miles of relaxing countryside. The stretches of the Thames near Marlow and Henley-on-Thames are lovely, with rowing clubs, piers, and sturdy waterside cottages and villas. It all conspires to make the Thames Valley a wonderful find, even for experienced travelers.

PLANNER

WHEN TO GO

High summer is lovely, but droves of visitors have the same effect on some travelers as bad weather. Consider visiting in late spring or early fall, when the weather isn't too bad and the crowds have headed home. Book tickets and accommodations well in advance for Henley's Royal Regatta at the cusp of June and July and Ascot's Royal Meeting in mid-June. Visiting Eton and the Oxford colleges is much more restricted during term time (generally September to late March and late April to mid-July). Most stately homes are open March through September or October only—call in advance. Avoid any driving in the London area during morning and afternoon rush hours.

FESTIVALS

Fodor's Choice ★ **Oxford Literary Festival.** The festival takes place during the last week of March at Christ Church College, the Sheldonian, and other university venues. Leading authors come to give lectures and interviews, and there's plenty to entertain children. ⊠ *Christ Church College, St. Aldate's, Oxford* ☎ *07444/318986* ⊕ *www.oxfordliteraryfestival.org.*

PLANNING YOUR TIME

The major towns of the Thames Valley are easy to visit on a day trip from London. A train to Windsor, for example, takes about an hour, and you can fully explore Windsor and its environs in a day. Base yourself in Oxford for a couple of days, though, if you want to make a thorough exploration of the town and the surrounding countryside. To visit the great houses and the rural castles you need to either rent a car or join an organized tour. Blenheim Palace and Waddesdon Manor require at least half a day to do them justice, as do Stowe Landscape Gardens and Woburn Abbey.

GETTING HERE AND AROUND

BUS TRAVEL

Oxford and the area's main towns are convenient by bus from London, as is Windsor (although trains are faster), but St. Albans is best reached by train.

You can travel between the major towns by local bus, but it's complicated and can require changing more than once. For information, contact Traveline. If you want to see more than one town in this area in a day, it's best to rent a car or join a tour.

Contacts Arriva. ⊕ *www.arrivabus.co.uk.* **First.** ☎ *01224/650100* ⊕ *www. firstgroup.com.* **Megabus.** ☎ *0900/160–0900 booking line, calls cost £0.60 per min* ⊕ *www.megabus.co.uk.* **Oxford Bus Company.** ☎ *01865/785400* ⊕ *www. oxfordbus.co.uk.* **Reading Buses.** ☎ *0118/959–4000* ⊕ *www.reading-buses. co.uk.* **Stagecoach Oxford Tube.** ☎ *01865/772250* ⊕ *www.oxfordtube.com.* **Traveline.** ☎ *0871/200–2233* ⊕ *www.traveline.info.*

CAR TRAVEL

Most towns in this area are within a one- or two-hour drive of central London—except during rush hour, of course. Although the roads are good, this wealthy section of the commuter belt has heavy traffic, even on the secondary roads. Parking in towns can be a problem, so take advantage of public parking lots near the outskirts of town centers.

TRAIN TRAVEL

Trains to Oxford (one hour) and the region depart from London's Paddington Station. Trains bound for Ascot (50 minutes) leave from Waterloo every 30 minutes. Trains to St. Albans (20 minutes) leave from St. Pancras Station. A number of lines, including Chiltern and First Great Western, serve the area; National Rail Enquiries has information.

Contacts National Rail Enquiries. ☎ *0845/748–4950* ⊕ *www.nationalrail.co.uk.*

RESTAURANTS

Londoners weekend here, and where they go, stellar restaurants follow. Bray (near Windsor), Marlow, and Great Milton (near Oxford) claim some excellent tables; you need to book months ahead for these. Simple pub food, as well as classic French cuisine, can be enjoyed in waterside settings at many restaurants beside the Thames. Even in towns away from the river, well-heeled commuters and Oxford professors support top-flight establishments. Reservations are often not required but are strongly recommended, especially on weekends. *Restaurant reviews have been shortened. For full information, visit Fodors.com.*

HOTELS

From converted country houses to refurbished Elizabethan inns, the region's accommodations are rich in history and distinctive in appeal. Many hotels cultivate traditional gardens and retain a sense of the past with impressive collections of antiques. Book ahead, particularly in summer; you're competing for rooms with many Londoners in search of a getaway. *Hotel reviews have been shortened. For full information, visit Fodors.com.*

WHAT IT COSTS IN POUNDS			
$	$$	$$$	$$$$
Restaurants	under £15	£15–£19	£20–£25	over £25
Hotels	under £100	£100–£160	£161–£220	over £220

Restaurant prices are the average cost of a main course at dinner, or if dinner is not served, at lunch. Hotel prices are the lowest cost of a standard double room in high season, including 20% V.A.T.

VISITOR INFORMATION

Contacts Tourism Southeast. ☎ *02380/625400* ⊕ *www.visitsoutheastengland. com.* **Visit Thames.** ⊕ *www.visitthames.co.uk.*

WINDSOR, MARLOW, AND NEARBY

Windsor Castle is one of the jewels of the area known as Royal Windsor, but a journey around this section of the Thames has other pleasures. The town of Eton holds the eponymous private school, Ascot has its famous racecourse, and Cliveden is a stately home turned into a grand hotel.

The stretch of the Thames Valley from Marlow to Henley-on-Thames is enchanting. Walking through its fields and along its waterways, it's easy to see how it inspired Kenneth Grahame's classic 1908 children's book *The Wind in the Willows*. Whether by boat or on foot, you can discover some of the region's most delightful scenery. On each bank are fine wooded hills with spacious homes, greenhouses, flower gardens, and neat lawns that stretch to the water's edge. Grahame wrote his book in Pangbourne, and his illustrator, E. H. Shepard, used the great house at Mapledurham as the model for Toad Hall. It all still has the power to inspire.

WINDSOR

6

21 miles west of London.

Only a small part of old Windsor—the settlement that grew up around the town's famous castle in the Middle Ages—has survived. The town isn't what it was in the time of Sir John Falstaff and the *Merry Wives of Windsor*, when it was famous for its convivial inns—in 1650, it had about 70 of them. Only a handful remain today, with the others replaced, it seems, by endless cafés. Windsor can feel overrun by tourists in summer, but even so, romantics appreciate cobbled Church Lane and noble Queen Charlotte Street, opposite the castle entrance.

GETTING HERE AND AROUND

Fast Green Line buses leave from the Colonnades opposite London's Victoria Coach Station every half hour for the 70-minute trip to Windsor. First Group has frequent services from Heathrow Airport's Terminal 5; the journey takes less than an hour. First Group also runs regional bus services to small towns and villages near Windsor.

Trains travel from London Waterloo every 30 minutes, or you can catch a more frequent train from Paddington and change at Slough. The trip takes less than an hour from Waterloo and around 30 minutes from Paddington. If you're driving, the M4 from London takes around an hour. Park in one of the public lots near the edge of the town center.

TOURS

City Sightseeing. Hop-on, hop-off tours of Windsor and Eton are offered by City Sightseeing, though it's easy to explore the compact Windsor on foot. ☎ 020/444102 ⊕ *www.city-sightseeing.com* ✉ *From £12.*

ESSENTIALS

Bus Contacts First Group. ☎ *0175/352-4144* ⊕ *www.firstgroup.com.* **Green Line.** ☎ *0344/801-7261* ⊕ *www.greenline.co.uk.*

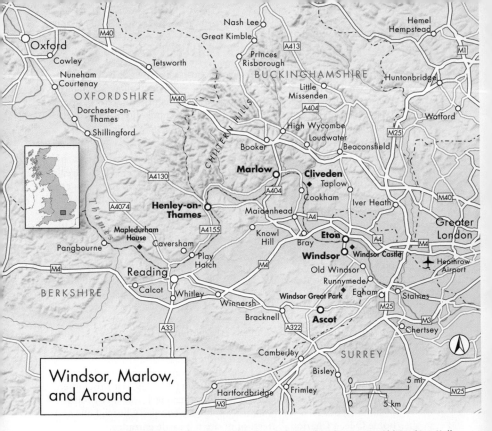

Windsor, Marlow, and Around

Visitor Information Royal Windsor Information Centre. ✉ *Old Booking Hall, Windsor Royal Station, Thames St.* ☎ *01753/743900, 01753/743907 for accommodations* 🌐 *www.windsor.gov.uk.*

EXPLORING

Savill Garden. The main horticultural delight of Windsor Great Park, the exquisite Savill Garden is about 4 miles from Windsor Castle. The 35 acres of ornamental gardens contain an impressive display of 2,500 rosebushes and a tremendous diversity of trees and shrubs. The Savill Building, easily recognizable by its undulating roof in the shape of a leaf, holds a visitor center, restaurant, and terrace where you can dine overlooking the garden, as well as a large shopping area with plenty of gifts, cards, and original artwork. ✉ *Wick Rd., Egham* ☎ *01753/860222* 🌐 *www.windsorgreatpark.co.uk* 💷 *£9.75 Mar.–Nov., free Dec.–Feb.; parking charge.*

Fodor's Choice
★

Windsor Castle. From William the Conqueror to Queen Victoria, the kings and queens of England have added towers and wings to this brooding, imposing castle, visible for miles and now the largest inhabited castle in the world. Most of England's kings and queens have demonstrated their undying attachment to the castle, the only royal residence in continuous use by the Royal Family since the Middle Ages. The State Apartments are open to the public most days and contain priceless furniture and works of art; high points of the tour include the Throne Room, the Waterloo Chamber, and the speculator collection of arms and armor. A visit between October and March also includes the Semi-State rooms, the private apartments of George IV. You can also wander the expansive grounds. **■ TIP→ Entrance lines can be long in season, and you're likely to spend at least half a day here, so come early.** ✉ *Castle Hill* ☎ *0303/123–7304 for tickets* 🌐 *www.royalcollection.org.uk* 🎫 *£22 for Precincts, State Apartments, Gallery, St. George's Chapel, and Queen Mary's Dolls' House; £12.10 when State Apartments are closed.*

Fodor's Choice ★ **Windsor Great Park.** The remains of an ancient royal hunting forest, this park stretches for some 5,000 acres south of Windsor Castle. Much of it is open to the public and can be explored by car or on foot. Its chief attractions are clustered around the southeastern section, known (or at least marketed) as the **Royal Landscape**. These include **Virginia Water,** a 2-mile-long lake that forms the park's main geographical focal point. More than anything, however, the Royal Landscape is defined by its two beautiful gardens. **Valley Gardens**, located on the north shore of Virginia Water, is particularly vibrant in April and May, when the dazzling multicolored azaleas are in full bloom. If you're feeling fit, the romantic **Long Walk** is one of England's most photographed footpaths—the 3-mile-long route, designed by Charles II, starts in the Great Park and leads all the way to Windsor Castle.

Divided from the Great Park by the busy A308 highway, the smaller **Windsor Home Park**, on the eastern side of Windsor Castle, is the private property of the Royal Family. It contains **Frogmore House**, a lavish royal residence. Completed in 1684, Frogmore was bought by George III as a gift for his wife, Queen Charlotte. The sprawling white mansion later became a beloved retreat of Queen Victoria. Today it's mainly used for official functions, but you can visit by guided tour (£10) on a handful of days in June; see 🌐 *www.royalcollection.org.uk*, or call ☎ *0303/123–7321* for more information. ✉ *Entrances on A329, A332, B383, and Wick La.* ☎ *01753/860222* 🌐 *www.windsorgreatpark.co.uk* 🎫 *Free; Savill Garden £12 (free Jan. and Feb.).*

WHERE TO EAT

$$ MODERN BRITISH 🍴 **Bel and the Dragon.** Sit street side and watch as village life streams by, or cozy up in the oak-beamed bar of this historic inn dating from the 11th century. Rotisserie-cooked beef, pork, and chicken are specialties, and they do an exceptionally fine fish pie. **Known for:** excellent dishes right off the grill; perfect fish pie; hip and friendly staff. [$] *Average main: £18* ✉ *Thames St.* ☎ *01753/866056* 🌐 *www.belandthedragon-windsor.co.uk.*

$$$$ MODERN BRITISH Fodor's Choice ★ 🍴 **Fat Duck.** One of the top restaurants in the country, and ranked by many food writers among the best in the world, this extraordinary place packs in fans of hypercreative, hyperexpensive cuisine, who enjoy it for the theater as much as for the food. Culinary alchemist Heston Blumenthal is famed for the so-called molecular gastronomy he creates in his laboratory-like kitchen and his name has become synonymous with weird and funky taste combinations. **Known for:** creative and immersive dining experience; strict booking process and long waiting

CLOSE UP

Boating on the Thames

Whether you're drifting lazily along in your own boat or taking a sightseeing cruise past crucial points of English history, you'll see the River Thames from a new and delightful vantage point out on the water. It's hard to beat gliding peacefully on the river, water meadows on either side of you, and then tying up for a picnic or lunch at a riverside pub. You can just putter about in a rowboat for an hour or so, or hire a boat and organize your own itinerary for a few days. If this doesn't appeal, go on a romantic lunch cruise or take one of the many organized trips. There are 125 miles of navigable water to explore, quieter nearer the source of the Thames in the Cotswolds, perhaps most picturesque between Pangbourne and Marlow, and busiest nearer London. Wherever you go, your pace of life will slow right down: boats aren't allowed to travel above 5 mph.

CHOOSING A BOAT

Most boats rented by the hour accommodate four people. Motorboats are noisy, but you can opt for electric canoes or launches that have the benefit of canopies. Punts (flat-bottom wooden boats) require a strong arm so you can maneuver the long wooden pole and push the boat along. Narrow boats carried freight on canals but are now well equipped for pleasure trips.

RENTING BOATS

The main hubs for hiring self-drive boats on the Thames are at Windsor, Henley-on-Thames, Oxford, and Lechlade. The cost varies from £15 an hour for a rowboat, £25 for an electric boat, £60 for half a day with a punt, to £175 a day for a motor cruiser. A short trip for four on a narrow boat from Oxfordshire Narrowboats ranges from around £160 to £1,000.

Hobbs of Henley. ⊠ *Station Rd., Henley on Thames* ☏ *01491/572035* ⊕ *www.hobbsofhenley.com.*

Oxford River Cruises. ⊠ *Folly Bridge, Oxford* ☏ *01865/987147, 0845/226–9396* ⊕ *www.oxfordrivercruises.com.*

Oxfordshire Narrowboats. ⊠ *Heyford Wharf, Station Rd., Lower Heyford* ☏ *01869/340348* ⊕ *www. oxfordshire-narrowboats.co.uk.*

HIRING BOATS

Hire a private boat with its own skipper to take you on a leisurely cruise. Compleat Angler in Marlow will take you on 1- or 2½-hour-long cruises down the river, as far as Cliveden or even Windsor. The shortest trips available take about one hour.

Compleat Angler. ⊠ *Marlow Bridge, Bisham Rd., Marlow* ☏ *0344/879–9210* ⊕ *www.macdonaldhotels.co.uk/ compleatangler.*

CRUISES

Windsor Castle, Runnymede, Henley (where you can stop for the River and Rowing Museum), and Mapledurham all lie on the banks of the Thames. Salter's Steamers runs short round-trips out of Windsor, Henley, Oxford, and Marlow, and French Brothers runs round-trips from Windsor.

French Brothers. ⊠ *The Promenade, Barry Ave.* ☏ *01753/851900* ⊕ *www. frenchbrothers.co.uk.*

Salter's Steamers. ⊠ *Folly Bridge, Oxford* ☏ *01865/243421* ⊕ *www. salterssteamers.co.uk.*

list for reservations; famed strange dishes like bacon-and-egg ice cream. [$] *Average main: £300* ✉ *High St., Bray* ☎ *01628/580333* 🌐 *www.thefatduck.co.uk* 🕒 *Closed Sun. and Mon.*

$$ BRITISH 🍴 **Two Brewers.** Locals congregate in a pair of low-ceiling rooms at this tiny 17th-century establishment by the gates of Windsor Great Park. Those under 18 aren't allowed inside the pub (although they can be served at a few outdoor tables), but adults will find a suitable collection of wine, espresso, and local beer, plus an excellent menu with dishes like roasted cod with butter sauce and samphire, or steak frites with brandy and peppercorn. **Known for:** classic, adults-only British pub; traditional lunchtime roast on Sundays; historic setting. [$] *Average main: £16* ✉ *34 Park St.* ☎ *01753/855426* 🌐 *www.twobrewerswindsor.co.uk.*

WHERE TO STAY

$$ B&B/INN FAMILY 🏨 **Langton House.** A former residence for representatives of the crown, this Victorian mansion on a quiet, leafy road is a 10-minute walk from Windsor Castle. **Pros:** soothing decor; family-friendly environment; friendly hosts. **Cons:** may hear some airplane noise; a little out of town; cheaper rooms have shared bathrooms. [$] *Rooms from: £100* ✉ *46 Alma Rd.* ☎ *01753/858299* 🌐 *www.langtonhouse.co.uk* 🛏 *5 rooms* 🍽 *Free Breakfast.*

$$$$ HOTEL 🏨 **MGallery Windsor Castle Hotel.** You're treated to an exceptional view of Windsor Castle's Changing the Guard ceremony from this former coaching inn, parts of which date back to the 16th century. **Pros:** excellent location; wonderful afternoon tea; great view of the castle. **Cons:** older rooms are small; furniture is faux antique; a bit pricey. [$] *Rooms from: £350* ✉ *18 High St.* ☎ *01753/252800* 🌐 *www.sofitel.com/gb/hotel-6618-castle-hotel-windsor-mgallery-by-sofitel/index.shtml* 🛏 *112 rooms* 🍽 *Free Breakfast.*

$$$$ HOTEL Fodor's Choice ★ 🏨 **Stoke Park.** On a 350-acre estate, Stoke Park's neoclassical grandeur can make Windsor Castle, visible in the distance, seem almost humble in comparison. **Pros:** luxurious rooms; sweeping grounds; great spa. **Cons:** not for those lukewarm about golf; old-school atmosphere not for everyone; very pricey, even for what you get. [$] *Rooms from: £350* ✉ *Park Rd., Stoke Poges* ☎ *01753/717171* 🌐 *www.stokeparkclub.com* 🛏 *77 rooms* 🍽 *Free Breakfast.*

SHOPPING

Windsor Royal Station. Set within a handsome building that was once a Victorian-era train station, Windsor Royal Station is home to fashion outlets like Mint Velvet, Jigsaw, Whistles, and Vanilla. ✉ *5 Goswell Hill* ☎ *01753/797070* 🌐 *www.windsorroyalshopping.co.uk.*

ETON

23 miles west of London.

Some observers may find it symbolic that almost opposite Windsor Castle—which embodies the continuity of the royal tradition—stands Eton, a school that for centuries has educated many leaders of the country. With High Street, its single main street, leading from the river to the famous school, the old-fashioned town of Eton is much quieter than Windsor.

6

GETTING HERE AND AROUND

Eton is linked to Windsor by a footbridge across the Thames. Most visitors barely notice passing from one to the other.

EXPLORING

Fodor's Choice ★ **Eton College.** Signs warn drivers of "Boys Crossing" as you approach the splendid Tudor-style buildings of Eton College, the distinguished boarding school for boys ages 13–18 founded in 1440 by King Henry VI. It's all terrifically photogenic—during the college semester students still dress in pinstripe trousers, swallowtail coats, and stiff collars. Rivaling St. George's at Windsor in terms of size, the Gothic **Chapel** contains superb 15th-century grisaille wall paintings juxtaposed with modern stained glass by John Piper. Beyond the cloisters are the school's playing fields where, according to the Duke of Wellington, the Battle of Waterloo was really won, since so many of his officers had learned discipline and strategy during their school days. The most recent of the country's many prime ministers to have been educated here is David Cameron, who held the office from 2010 to 2016. The **Museum of Eton Life** has displays on the school's history and vignettes of school life. The school gives public tours on Friday afternoons from early May through early September, bookable online. ⊠ *Brewhouse Yard* ☎ *01753/370100* ⊕ *www.etoncollege.com* 🎟 *£10* ⊘ *Closed mid-Sept.–early May.*

WHERE TO EAT AND STAY

$$ MODERN BRITISH ✗ **Gilbey's Eton.** Just over the bridge from Windsor, this restaurant at the center of Eton's Antiques Row serves a changing menu of imaginative fare, from potted ham hock and rhubarb with sweet onion and mustard seed to crayfish and dill hot-smoked trout fish cakes. Well-priced wines, both French and from the restaurant's own English vineyard, are a specialty, as are the savories—meat, fish, and vegetarian pâtés. **Known for:** traditional English food; old-school charm; bargain fixed-price lunches. $ *Average main: £19* ⊠ *82–83 High St.* ☎ *01753/854921* ⊕ *www.gilbeygroup.com/restaurants/gilbeys-eton.*

$$ HOTEL 🛏 **Christopher Hotel.** This former coaching inn on the village's main shopping street has spacious rooms in the handsome main building as well as in the courtyard mews. **Pros:** a nice mix of modern and historic; good restaurant. **Cons:** steep stairs; courtyard rooms can be noisy. $ *Rooms from: £140* ⊠ *110 High St.* ☎ *01753/852359* ⊕ *www.thechristopher. co.uk* 🛏 *34 rooms* ⦿ *No meals.*

ASCOT

8 miles southwest of Windsor, 28 miles southwest of London.

The posh town of Ascot (pronounced *as*-cut) has for centuries been famous for horse racing and for style. Queen Anne chose to have a racecourse here, and the first race meeting took place in 1711. The impressive show of millinery for which the Royal Meeting (or Royal Ascot, as it is also known) is famed was immortalized in *My Fair Lady,* in which a hat with osprey feathers and black-and-white silk roses transformed Eliza Doolittle into a grand lady. Betting on the races at England's most prestigious course is as important as dressing up; it's all part of the fun.

The horses at Royal Ascot are beautiful and so is the formal attire of the memorably dressed spectators.

GETTING HERE AND AROUND

If you're driving, leave M4 at Junction 6 and take A332. Trains from London leave Waterloo Station every half hour, and the journey takes 50 minutes. The racecourse is a seven-minute walk from the train station.

EXPLORING

Ascot Racecourse. The races run regularly throughout the year, and Royal Ascot takes place annually in mid-June. ■ **TIP→ Tickets for Royal Ascot generally go on sale in November, so buy them well in advance.** Prices range from £15 for standing room on the heath to around £80 for seats in the stands. Car parking costs £25. ⊠ *A329* ☎ *0844/346–3000* ⊕ *www.ascot.co.uk.*

WHERE TO STAY

$$$$
HOTEL
FAMILY
Fodor's Choice
★

🛏 **Coworth Park.** Much imagination and thoughtful renovation has transformed this 18th-century mansion, set in 240 acres of parkland, into a playful and contemporary lodging. **Pros:** country-house atmosphere; attentive and friendly service; free activities for kids. **Cons:** not for traditionalists; eye-wateringly expensive; some bedrooms are small. ⓈRooms from: £318 ⊠ Blacknest Rd. ☎ 01344/876600 ⊕ www.dorchestercollection.com/en/ascot/coworth-park ⇱ 70 rooms ¶◯¶ Free Breakfast.

CLIVEDEN

8 miles northwest of Windsor, 16 miles north of Ascot, 26 miles west of London.

This grand stately home, designed by Charles Barry, the architect of the Houses of Parliament, and the setting of the notorious Profumo affair in the 1960s, has spectacular gardens and sweeping views to the Thames.

GETTING HERE AND AROUND

If you're driving, take the M4 to the A4, where brown signs lead you to the entrance off the A4094.

EXPLORING

Cliveden. Described by Queen Victoria as a "bijou of taste," Cliveden (pronounced *Cliv*-dn) is a magnificent country mansion that for more than 300 years has lived up to its Georgian heritage as a bastion of aesthetic delights. The house, set in 376 acres of gardens and parkland above the River Thames, was rebuilt in 1851; but it was the rich and powerful Astor family, who purchased it in 1893, that made Cliveden famous. In the 1920s and 1930s this was the meeting place for the influential salon known as the "Cliveden Set"—a group of strongly conservative thinkers who many accused of being Nazi sympathizers. Its doyenne was Nancy Astor, an American by birth, who became the first woman to sit in the British Parliament. The ground-floor rooms of the house are open, as well as the Octagon Chapel, with its beautiful gilt-painted ceiling and wall panels. You can wander the beautiful grounds, which include a water garden, miles of woodland and riverbank paths, a kids' play area, and a yew-tree maze. Book your timed ticket for the house beforehand or early on the day. Boat hire and trips are available daily in July and August. Note that opening times of the house can be unpredictable, even at the busiest times of the year; always call before setting out. ✉ *Cliveden Rd., Taplow* ✥ *Near Maidenhead* ☎ *01628/605069* 🌐 *www.nationaltrust.org.uk/cliveden* 🎫 *Garden and woodland £13, house £2.*

WHERE TO STAY

$$$$ HOTEL Fodor's Choice ★ 🏨 **Cliveden House.** If you've ever wondered what it would feel like to be an Edwardian grandee, then sweep up the drive to this stately home, one of Britain's grandest hotels. **Pros:** like stepping back in time; outstanding sense of luxury; beautiful grounds. **Cons:** airplanes fly overhead; two-night minimum on weekends; you'll need deep pockets. [$] *Rooms from: £445* ✉ *Cliveden Rd., Taplow* ☎ *01628/668561* 🌐 *www.clivedenhouse.co.uk* 🛏 *38 rooms, 1 cottage* 🍴 *Free Breakfast.*

MARLOW

7 miles west of Cliveden, 15 miles northwest of Windsor.

Just inside the Buckinghamshire border, Marlow and the surrounding area overflow with Thames-side prettiness. The unusual suspension bridge was built in the 1830s by William Tierney Clark, architect of the bridge in Hungary linking Buda and Pest. Marlow has a number of striking old buildings, particularly the privately owned Georgian houses along Peter and West streets. In 1817 the Romantic poet Percy Bysshe

Shelley stayed with friends at 67 West Street and then bought **Albion House** on the same street. His second wife, Mary, completed her Gothic novel *Frankenstein* here. Ornate **Marlow Place**, on Station Road, dating from 1721, is reputedly the finest building in town.

Marlow hosts its own one-day regatta in mid-June. The town is a good base from which to join the **Thames Path** to Henley-on-Thames. On summer weekends tourism can often overwhelm the town.

GETTING HERE AND AROUND

Trains leave London from Paddington every half hour and involve a change at Maidenhead; the journey takes an hour. By car, leave M4 at Junction 8/9, following A404 and then A4155. From M40, join A404 at Junction 4.

EXPLORING

Swan-Upping. This traditional event, which dates back 800 years, takes place in Marlow during the third week of July. By bizarre ancient laws, the Queen owns every single one of the country's swans, so each year swan-markers in skiffs start from Sunbury-on-Thames, catching the new cygnets and marking their beaks to establish ownership. The Queen's Swan Marker, dressed in scarlet livery, presides over this colorful ceremony. ✉ *Marlow* ☎ *01628/523030* ⊕ *www.royal.gov.uk.*

WHERE TO EAT AND STAY

$$$$ ✕ **Vanilla Pod.** Discreet and intimate, this restaurant is a showcase for
FRENCH the French-inspired cuisine of chef Michael Macdonald, who, as the restaurant's name implies, holds vanilla in high esteem. The fixed-price menu borrows the flavor of a French bistro and shakes it up a bit, so you might have filet mignon with polenta, or something more adventurous, such as fennel escabeche with mackerel and vanilla. **Known for:** French-inspired cooking; a flair for vanilla; great value set lunch. $ *Average main: £45* ✉ *31 West St.* ☎ *01628/898101* ⊕ *www.thevanillapod.co.uk* ⊘ *Closed Sun. and Mon.*

$$ ☐ **Macdonald Compleat Angler.** Although fishing aficionados consider
HOTEL this luxurious 17th-century Thames-side inn the ideal place to stay, the place is stylish enough to attract those with no interest in casting a line. **Pros:** gorgeous rooms; great views of the Thames; legendary fishing spot. **Cons:** river views cost more, except Rooms 9 and 10; need a car to get around; rooms could use some updating. $ *Rooms from: £117* ✉ *Marlow Bridge, Bisham Rd.* ☎ *0844/879-9128, 01628/484444 international* ⊕ *www.macdonaldhotels.co.uk/compleatangler* ⟿ *64 rooms* ⦿| *Free Breakfast.*

HENLEY-ON-THAMES

7 miles southwest of Marlow, 8 miles north of Reading, 36 miles west of central London.

Fodor's Choice Henley's fame is based on one thing: rowing. The Henley Royal Regatta,
★ held at the cusp of June and July on a long, straight stretch of the River Thames, has made the little riverside town famous throughout the world. Townspeople launched the Henley Regatta in 1839, initiating the Grand Challenge Cup, the most famous of its many trophies.

The best amateur oarsmen from around the globe compete in crews of eight, four, or two, or as single scullers. For many spectators, the event is on par with Royal Ascot and Wimbledon.

The town is set in a broad valley between gentle hillsides. Henley's historic buildings, including half-timber Georgian cottages and inns (as well as one of Britain's oldest theaters, the Kenton), are all within a few minutes' walk. The river near Henley is alive with boats of every shape and size, from luxury cabin cruisers to tiny rowboats.

GETTING HERE AND AROUND

Frequent First Great Western trains depart for Henley from London Paddington; the journey time is around an hour. If you're driving from London or from the west, leave M4 at Junction 8/9 and follow A404(M) and then A4130 to Henley Bridge. From Marlow, Henley is a 7-mile drive southwest on A4155.

ESSENTIALS

Visitor Information Henley Visitor Information Centre. ⊠ *Henley Town Hall, Market Pl., Henley* ☏ *01491/578034* ⊕ *www.henleytowncouncil.gov.uk/information-centre-including-tourism.aspx.*

EXPLORING

Mapledurham House. This section of the Thames inspired Kenneth Grahame's 1908 *The Wind in the Willows*, which began as a bedtime story for Grahame's son Alastair while the family lived at Pangbourne. Some of E.F. Shepard's illustrations are of specific sites along the river—none more fabled than this redbrick Elizabethan mansion, bristling with tall chimneys, mullioned windows, and battlements. It became the inspiration for Shepard's vision of Toad Hall. Family portraits, magnificent oak staircases, wood paneling, and plasterwork ceilings abound. Look out for the life-size deer guarding the fireplace in the entrance hall. There's also a 15th-century working grain mill on the river. The house is 10 miles southwest of Henley-on-Thames. ⊠ *Off A074, Mapledurham* ☏ *0118/972–3350* ⊕ *www.mapledurham.co.uk* ⊠ *£9.50.*

FAMILY **River & Rowing Museum.** Focusing on the history and sport of rowing, this absorbing museum built on stilts includes exhibits devoted to actual vessels, from a Saxon log boat to an elegant Victorian steam launch to Olympic boats. One gallery tells the story of the Thames as it flows from its source to the ocean, while another explores the history of the town and its famed regatta. A charming *Wind in the Willows* walk-through exhibit evokes the settings of the famous children's book. ⊠ *Mill Meadows, Henley* ☏ *01491/415600* ⊕ *www.rrm.co.uk* ⊠ *£12.50.*

St. Mary's Church. With a 16th-century "checkerboard" tower, St. Mary's is a stone's throw from the bridge over the Thames. The adjacent, yellow-washed **Chantry House**, built in 1420, is one of England's few remaining merchant houses from the period. It's an unspoiled example of the rare timber-frame design, with upper floors jutting out. You can enjoy tea here on Sunday afternoons in summer. ⊠ *Hart St., Henley* ☏ *01491/577340* ⊕ *www.stmaryshenley.org.uk* ⊠ *Free.*

WHERE TO EAT AND STAY

$$
MODERN BRITISH

✕ **The Three Tuns.** Walk past the cozy bar in this traditional 17th-century pub to eat in the snug dining room with the clutch of locals who come nightly for the traditional British comfort food. Plates such as beer-battered fish-and-chips or local butcher's sausages and mashed potatoes are easy crowd-pleasers. **Known for:** excellent traditional savory pies; lovely old pub atmosphere; delicious desserts. $ *Average main: £16* ⊠ *5 Market Pl., Henley on Thames* ☎ *01491/410138* ⊕ *www.threetunshenley.co.uk* ⊗ *Closed Mon.*

$
B&B/INN

🏠 **The Row Barge.** This historic, 15th-century pub certainly looks the part, with low-beamed ceilings and a fire crackling in the grate. **Pros:** historic inn with lots of character; friendly owners; good food. **Cons:** entrance to guest rooms through bar and up a staircase with very low ceiling; room No. 1 has no door to the bathroom; quirks of historic building not for everyone. $ *Rooms from: £95* ⊠ *West St.* ☎ *01491/572649* ⊕ *www.therowbarge.com* 🍴 *5 rooms* ⦿ *Free Breakfast.*

SPORTS AND THE OUTDOORS

Henley Royal Regatta. A series of rowing competitions attracting participants from many countries, the annual Henley Royal Regatta takes place over five days in late June and early July. Large tents are erected along both sides of a straight stretch of the river known as Henley Reach, and every surrounding field becomes a parking lot. There's plenty of space on the public towpath from which to watch the early stages of the races. ■TIP➔ **If you want to attend, book a room months in advance. After all, 500,000 people turn out for the event.** ⊠ *Henley* ☎ *01491/571900 for ticket line, 01491/572153 for inquiries* ⊕ *www. hrr.co.uk.*

OXFORD

Fodor's Choice
★

With arguably the most famous university in the world, Oxford has been a center of learning since 1167, with only the Sorbonne preceding it. It doesn't take more than a day or two to explore its winding medieval streets, photograph its ivy-covered stone buildings and ancient churches and libraries, and even take a punt down one of its placid waterways. The town center is compact and walkable, and at its heart is Oxford University. Alumni of this prestigious institution include 48 Nobel Prize winners, 26 British prime ministers (including David Cameron), and 28 foreign presidents (including Bill Clinton), along with poets, authors, and artists such as Percy Bysshe Shelley, Oscar Wilde, and W. H. Auden.

Oxford is 55 miles northwest of London, at the junction of the rivers Thames and Cherwell. The city is more interesting and more cosmopolitan than Cambridge, and although it's also bigger, its suburbs aren't remotely interesting to visitors. The charm is all at the center, where the old town curls around the grand stone buildings, good restaurants, and historic pubs. Victorian writer Matthew Arnold described Oxford's "dreaming spires," a phrase that has become famous. Students rush past you on the sidewalks on the way to their exams, clad with marvelous antiquarian style in their requisite mortar caps, flowing dark gowns, stiff collars, and crisp white bow ties. ■TIP➜ Watch your back when crossing roads, as bikes are everywhere.

GETTING HERE AND AROUND

Megabus, Oxford Bus Company, and Stagecoach Oxford Tube all have buses traveling from London 24 hours a day; the trip takes between one hour 40 minutes and two hours. In London, Megabus departs from Victoria Coach Station, while Oxford Bus Company and Stagecoach Oxford Tube have pickup points on Buckingham Palace Road, Victoria; Oxford Tube also picks up from the Marble Arch Underground station. Oxford Bus Company runs round-trip shuttle service from Gatwick (£37) every hour and Heathrow (£29) every half hour. Most of the companies have multiple stops in Oxford, with Gloucester Green, the final stop, being the most convenient for travelers. You can easily traverse the town center on foot, but the Oxford Bus Company has a one-day ticket (£4) for unlimited travel in and around Oxford.

Trains to Oxford depart from London's Paddington Station for the one-hour trip. Oxford Station is at the western edge of the historic town center on Botley Road.

To drive, take the M40 northwest from London. It's an hour's drive, except during rush hour, when it can take twice as long. In-town parking is notoriously difficult, so use one of the five free park-and-ride lots and pay for the bus to the city. The Thornhill Park and Ride and the St. Clement's parking lot before the roundabout that leads to Magdalen Bridge are convenient for the M40.

ESSENTIALS

Bus Contacts Megabus. ☎ 0871/266–3333 for inquiries, 0900/160–0900 booking line ⊕ www.megabus.com. **Oxford Bus Company.** ☎ 01865/785400 ⊕ www.oxfordbus.co.uk. **Stagecoach Oxford Tube.** ☎ 01865/772250 ⊕ www.oxfordtube.com.

VISITOR AND TOUR INFORMATION

Oxford Visitor Information Centre. You can find information here on the many guided walks of the city. The best way of gaining access to the collegiate buildings is to take the two-hour university and city tour, which leaves the Tourist Information Centre at 10:45 am and 1 and 2 pm daily from March through October. You can book in advance online. ✉ 15–16 Broad St. ☎ 01865/686430 ⊕ www.experienceoxfordshire. org ➤ From £14.

EXPLORING

Oxford University isn't one easily identifiable campus, but a sprawling mixture of 38 colleges scattered around the city center, each with its own distinctive identity and focus. Oxford students live and study at their own college, and also use the centralized resources of the overarching university. The individual colleges are deeply competitive. Most of the grounds and magnificent dining halls and chapels are open to visitors, though the opening times (displayed at the entrance gates) vary greatly.

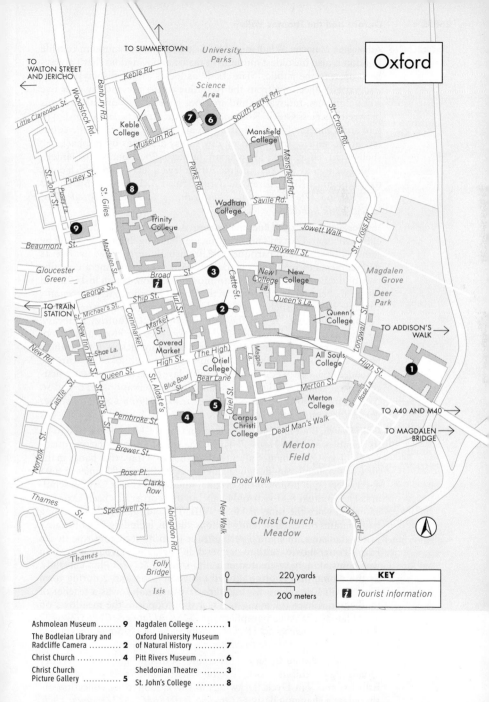

Oxford

TO SUMMERTOWN
TO WALTON STREET AND JERICHO
University Parks
Science Area
Keble Rd.
Museum Rd.
Keble College
Little Clarendon St.
Woodstock Rd.
Banbury Rd.
St. John St.
Pusey St.
Pusey La.
St. Giles
Magdalen St.
Beaumont St.
Gloucester Green
George St.
TO TRAIN STATION
St. Michael's St.
Cornmarket
New Inn Hall St.
Ship St.
Broad St.
Turl St.
Market St.
Covered Market
High St.
Shoe La.
Queen St.
Castle St.
St. Ebbe's St.
New Rd.
Norfolk St.
Pembroke St.
Brewer St.
Rose Pl.
Clarks Row
Speedwell St.
Thames St.
Abingdon Rd.
Folly Bridge
Isis
Thames

Parks Rd.
South Parks Rd.
Mansfield Rd.
St. Cross Rd.
Mansfield College
Savile Rd.
Jowett Walk
Holywell St.
Wadham College
Trinity College
Catte St.
New College La.
New College
Queen's La.
Queen's College
Magdalen Grove
Deer Park
TO ADDISON'S WALK
All Souls College
Oriel College
Bear Lane
Blue Boar St.
Oriel St.
Magpie La.
Merton St.
Corpus Christi College
Merton College
Dead Man's Walk
Longwall St.
Rose La.
High St.
TO A40 AND M40
TO MAGDALEN BRIDGE
Merton Field
Broad Walk
New Walk
Christ Church Meadow
Cherwell

0 — 220 yards
0 — 200 meters

KEY
ℹ Tourist information

Ashmolean Museum 9
The Bodleian Library and Radcliffe Camera 2
Christ Church 4
Christ Church Picture Gallery 5
Magdalen College 1
Oxford University Museum of Natural History 7
Pitt Rivers Museum 6
Sheldonian Theatre 3
St. John's College 8

Ashmolean Museum. What might be Britain's greatest museum outside London is also the oldest museum in the United Kingdom that's always been open to the public. "The Ash," as locals call is, displays its rich and varied collections from the Neolithic to the present day over five stunning floors. Innovative and spacious galleries explore connections between priceless Greek, Roman, and Indian artifacts, as well as Egyptian and Chinese objects, all of which are among the best in the country. In the superb art collection, don't miss drawings by Raphael, the shell-encrusted mantle of Powhatan (father of Pocahontas), the lantern belonging to Guy Fawkes, and the Alfred Jewel, set in gold, which dates to the reign of King Alfred the Great (ruled 871–899). ⊠ *Beaumont St.* ☎ *01865/278000* ⊕ *www.ashmolean.org* ⌑ *Free* ☉ *Closed Mon. except bank holidays.*

The Bodleian Library and Radcliffe Camera. A vast library, the domed Radcliffe Camera is Oxford's most spectacular building, built in 1737–49 by James Gibbs in Italian baroque style. It's usually surrounded by tourists with cameras trained at its golden-stone walls. The Camera contains part of the Bodleian Library's enormous collection, begun in 1602 and one of six "copyright libraries" in the United Kingdom. It also contains valuable treasures such as a Gutenberg Bible and a Shakespeare First Folio. Guided tours reveal the magnificent Duke Humfrey's Library, which was completed in 1488, and the spots used for Hogwarts School in the Harry Potter films. Arrive early to secure tickets for the three to six daily tours. The standard tours can be prebooked, as can the extended tours on Wednesday and Saturday; otherwise, tours are first-come, first-served. Audio tours don't require reservations. ⊠ *Broad St.* ☎ *01865/287400* ⊕ *www.bodleian.ox.ac.uk* ⌑ *From £6* ☉ *Sometimes closed for events; call to confirm.*

Christ Church. Built in 1546, the college of Christ Church is referred to by its members as "The House." This is the site of Oxford's largest quadrangle, Tom Quad, named after the huge bell (6¼ tons) that hangs in the Sir Christopher Wren–designed gate tower and rings 101 times at 9:05 every evening in honor of the original number of Christ Church scholars. The vaulted, 800-year-old chapel in one corner has been Oxford's cathedral since the time of Henry VIII. The college's medieval dining hall contains portraits of many famous alumni, including 13 of Britain's prime ministers, but you'll recognize it from its recurring role in the Harry Potter movies (although they didn't actually film here, the room was painstakingly re-created in a film studio). ■TIP➜ Plan carefully, as the dining hall is often closed between noon and 2 during term time. Lewis Carroll, author of *Alice in Wonderland,* was a teacher of mathematics here for many years; a shop opposite the meadows on St. Aldate's sells Alice paraphernalia. ⊠ *St. Aldate's* ☎ *01865/276492* ⊕ *www.chch.ox.ac.uk* ⌑ *£8 (£10 in July and Aug.)* ☉ *Sometimes closed for events; check website to confirm.*

Christ Church Picture Gallery. This connoisseur's delight in Canterbury Quadrangle exhibits works by the Italian masters as well as Hals, Rubens, and Van Dyck. Drawings in the 2,000-strong collection are shown on a changing basis. ⊠ *Oriel Sq.* ☎ *01865/276172* ⊕ *www.chch. ox.ac.uk/gallery* ⌑ *£4.*

Fodor's Choice ★ **Magdalen College.** Founded in 1458, with a handsome main quadrangle and a supremely monastic air, Magdalen (pronounced *maud*-lin) is one of the most impressive of Oxford's colleges and attracts its most artistic students. Alumni include such diverse people as P. G. Wodehouse, Oscar Wilde, and John Betjeman. The school's large, square tower is a famous local landmark. ■ TIP➜ To enhance your visit, take a stroll around the Deer Park and along Addison's Walk; then have tea in the Old Kitchen, which overlooks the river. ⊠ *High St.* ☎ *01865/276000* ⊕ *www.magd. ox.ac.uk* ⊠ *£6* ⊘ *Closed mornings Oct.–June.*

FAMILY **Oxford University Museum of Natural History.** This highly decorative Victorian Gothic creation of cast iron and glass, more a cathedral than a museum, is worth a visit for its architecture alone. Among the eclectic collections of entomology, geology, mineralogy, and zoology are the towering skeleton of a *Tyrannosaurus rex* and casts of a dodo's foot and head. There's plenty for children to explore and touch. ⊠ *Parks Rd.* ☎ *01865/272950* ⊕ *www.oum.ox.ac.uk* ⊠ *Free.*

FAMILY
Fodor's Choice ★ **Pitt Rivers Museum.** More than half a million intriguing archaeological and anthropological items from around the globe, based on the collection bequeathed by Lieutenant-General Augustus Henry Lane Fox Pitt Rivers in 1884, are crammed into a multitude of glass cases and drawers. In an eccentric touch that's surprisingly thought-provoking, labels are handwritten, and items are organized thematically rather than geographically—a novel way to gain perspective. Give yourself plenty of time to wander through the displays of shrunken heads, Hawaiian feather cloaks, and fearsome masks. ⊠ *S. Parks Rd.* ☎ *01865/270927* ⊕ *www.prm.ox.ac.uk* ⊠ *Free (donations welcome).*

Sheldonian Theatre. This fabulously ornate theater is where Oxford's impressive graduation ceremonies are held, conducted almost entirely in Latin. Dating to 1663, it was the first building designed by Sir Christopher Wren when he served as professor of astronomy. The D-shaped auditorium has pillars, balconies, and an elaborately painted ceiling. The stone pillars outside are topped by 18 massive stone heads. Climb the stairs to the cupola for the best view of the city's "dreaming spires." Guided tours take place a few times per week between late April and early October; call or email tours@sheldon.ox.ac.uk to book a place in advance (or you can buy a ticket from the box office on the day if there's space). ⊠ *Broad St.* ☎ *01865/277299* ⊕ *www.sheldon.ox.ac.uk* ⊠ *£3.50; tours £8.*

St. John's College. One of Oxford's most attractive campuses, St. John's has seven quiet quadrangles surrounded by elaborately carved buildings. You enter the first through a low wooden door. This college dates to 1555, when Sir Thomas White, a merchant, founded it. His heart is buried in the chapel (it's a tradition for students to curse as they walk over it). The Canterbury Quad represented the first example of Italian Renaissance architecture in Oxford, and the Front Quad includes the buildings of the old St. Bernard's Monastery. ⊠ *St. Giles* ☎ *01865/277300* ⊕ *www.sjc.ox.ac.uk* ⊠ *Free.*

6

WHERE TO EAT

$$ FRENCH
🍴 **Brasserie Blanc.** Raymond Blanc's sophisticated brasserie in the Jericho neighborhood is the more affordable chain restaurant cousin of Le Manoir aux Quat'Saisons in Great Milton. The changing menu always lists a good selection of steaks and innovative adaptations of bourgeois French fare, sometimes with Mediterranean or Asian influences. **Known for:** French classics like bouillabaisse; affordable prix-fixe lunch menu; good wine selection. [$] *Average main: £17* ✉ *71–72 Walton St.* ☎ *01865/510999* 🌐 *www.brasserieblanc.com.*

$ SEAFOOD
🍴 **CuttleFish.** The clue's in the name here—this popular local restaurant specializes in fresh, upmarket seafood. Dishes are prepared with a European touch and frequently come with butter, cream, and other sauces, such as sardines served with lemon and parsley butter. **Known for:** excellent seafood; nautical surroundings; good-value lunches. [$] *Average main: £14* ✉ *36–37 St. Clement's St.* ☎ *01865/243003* 🌐 *www.cuttlefishoxford.co.uk.*

$$ MODERN BRITISH
🍴 **Gee's.** With its glass-and-steel framework, this former florist's shop just north of the town center makes a charming conservatory dining room, full of plants and twinkling with lights in the evening. The menu concentrates on the best of Oxfordshire produce. **Known for:** sophisticated British dishes with local produce; prune-and-sherry ice cream for dessert; affordable lunch and early dinner menus. [$] *Average main: £16* ✉ *61 Banbury Rd.* ☎ *01865/553540* 🌐 *www.gees-restaurant.co.uk.*

$$$$ FRENCH
Fodor's Choice ★
🍴 **Le Manoir aux Quat'Saisons.** One of the original gastronomy-focused hotels, Le Manoir was opened in 1984 by chef Raymond Blanc, whose culinary talents have earned the hotel's restaurant two Michelin stars—now held for an incredible 29 years and running. Decide from among such innovative French creations as spiced cauliflower velouté with langoustines, beef fillet with braised Jacob's ladder, or Dover sole with brown butter and rosemary. **Known for:** one of the top restaurants in the country; flawless French-style fine dining; beautiful surroundings. [$] *Average main: £170* ✉ *Church Rd., Great Milton* ☎ *01844/278881* 🌐 *www.manoir.com.*

WHERE TO STAY

$$$$ HOTEL
FAMILY
Fodor's Choice ★
🏨 **Le Manoir aux Quat'Saisons.** Standards are high at this 15th-century stone manor house, the ultimate place for a gourmet getaway, where master-chef Raymond Blanc's epicurean touch shows at every turn, including one of the country's finest kitchens. **Pros:** design is plush, but not stuffy; perfect for romance, but also accommodates kids; famous on-site cooking school and amazing food. **Cons:** every room is different, so if you have specific requirements, let them know when booking; all the food is tough on the waistline; price is even tougher on the wallet. [$] *Rooms from: £450* ✉ *Church Rd., Great Milton* ☎ *01844/278881* 🌐 *www.manoir.com* 🛏 *48 rooms* 🍽 *Free Breakfast.*

$$$ HOTEL
🏨 **Malmaison Oxford Castle.** Housed in what was a 19th-century prison, this high-concept boutique hotel remains true to its unusual history by showing off the original metal doors and exposed-brick walls. **Pros:** modern luxury in a beautifully converted building; unique setting; great bar and restaurant. **Cons:** no matter how comfortable they make it, the prison ambience can still be weird; expensive parking; no

elevator and lots of stairs. $ *Rooms from: £200* ⊠ *3 Oxford Castle* ☎ *01865/689944* ⊕ *www.malmaison.com/locations/oxford* ⟿ *95 rooms* ⭢ *Free Breakfast.*

$$
B&B/INN

⛨ **Newton House.** This handsome Victorian mansion, a five-minute walk from all of Oxford's action, is a sprawling, friendly place on three floors. **Pros:** great breakfasts; handy parking lot; excellent value for the location. **Cons:** on a main road; no elevator; some may be disappointed with the contemporary look. $ *Rooms from: £122* ⊠ *82 Abingdon Rd.* ☎ *01865/240561* ⊕ *www.newtonhouseoxford.co.uk* ⟿ *14 rooms* ⭢ *Free Breakfast.*

$
HOTEL

⛨ **Old Bank Hotel.** From the impressive collection of modern artwork throughout the hotel to the sleek furnishings in the guest rooms, this stately converted bank building displays contemporary style in a city that favors the traditional. **Pros:** excellent location; interesting artwork at every turn; good restaurant. **Cons:** standard rooms can be small; breakfast costs extra; location a bit noisy. $ *Rooms from: £95* ⊠ *91–94 High St.* ☎ *01865/799599* ⊕ *www.oldbank-hotel.co.uk* ⟿ *42 rooms* ⭢ *Free Breakfast.*

$$$$
HOTEL

⛨ **Old Parsonage.** A 17th-century gabled stone house in a small garden next to St. Giles Church, the Old Parsonage is a dignified retreat. **Pros:** beautiful vine-covered building; complimentary walking tours; free parking. **Cons:** pricey; some guest rooms are small; cool, contemporary look favored over period charm. $ *Rooms from: £390* ⊠ *1 Banbury Rd.* ☎ *01865/310210* ⊕ *www.oldparsonage-hotel.co.uk* ⟿ *35 rooms* ⭢ *Free Breakfast.*

6

NIGHTLIFE

Head of the River. Near Folly Bridge, the terrace at the Head of the River is the perfect place to watch life on the water. It gets very crowded on sunny afternoons, but there's a great, quintessentially Oxford atmosphere. ⊠ *St. Aldate's* ☎ *01865/721600* ⊕ *www.headoftheriveroxford.co.uk.*

Fodor's Choice
★

Raoul's. This hip cocktail bar was named one of the 100 best cocktail bars in the world by the *Times* of London, and the bartenders can prove it with their encyclopedic knowledge of mixology and creative flair. The crowd is generally as bright and young as you'd expect. ⊠ *32 Walton St.* ☎ *01865/553732* ⊕ *www.raoulsbar.com.*

Turf Tavern. Off Holywell Street, the Turf Tavern has a higgledy-piggledy collection of little rooms and outdoor spaces where you can enjoy a quiet drink and inexpensive pub food. ⊠ *Bath Pl.* ☎ *01865/243235* ⊕ *www.turftavern-oxford.co.uk.*

White Horse. This cozy pub, dating from at least 1823, serves real ales and traditional food all day. ⊠ *52 Broad St.* ☎ *01865/204801* ⊕ *www. whitehorseoxford.co.uk.*

SHOPPING

Blackwell's. Family owned and run since 1879, Blackwell's stocks an excellent selection of books. Inquire about the literary and historic walking tours that run from late April through October. ⊠ *48–51 Broad St.* ☎ *01865/792792* ⊕ *bookshop.blackwell.co.uk/stores/oxford-bookshop.*

Fodor's Choice **Covered Market.** This is a fine place for a cheap sandwich and a lei-
★ surely browse; the smell of pastries and coffee follows you from
cake shop to jeweler to cheesemonger. ⊠ *High St.* ⊕ *www.oxford-
coveredmarket.co.uk.*

Scriptum. Cards, stationery, handmade paper, and leather-bound journals
can be purchased here, alongside marvelously arcane stuff you didn't
know you needed—like quills, sealing wax, and even Venetian masks.
⊠ *3 Turl St.* ☎ *01865/200042* ⊕ *www.scriptum.co.uk.*

University of Oxford Shop. Run by the university, the University of Oxford
Shop sells authorized clothing, ceramics, and tea towels, all embla-
zoned with university crests. ⊠ *106 High St.* ☎ *01865/247414* ⊕ *www.
oushop.com.*

SPORTS AND THE OUTDOORS
PUNTING
Fodor's Choice You may choose, like many an Oxford student, to spend a summer
★ afternoon punting, while dangling your champagne bottle in the water
to keep it cool. Punts—shallow-bottom boats that are poled slowly up
the river—can be rented in several places, including at the foot of the
Magdalen Bridge.

Cherwell Boathouse. From mid-March through mid-October, Cherwell
Boathouse rents boats, and if you call ahead, someone to punt it. Rentals cost £17 per hour weekdays (£19 weekends), or £85 (£95 on weekends) per day and should be booked ahead. The facility, a mile north
of the heart of Oxford, also includes a stylish restaurant. ⊠ *Bardwell
Rd.* ☎ *01865/515978* ⊕ *www.cherwellboathouse.co.uk.*

Salter's Steamers. At the St. Aldates Road end of Folly Bridge, Salter's
Steamers rents out punts and skiffs (rowboats) for £20 per hour, £60
per half day, and £100 per day. Chauffeured punts are £60 per hour,
booked in advance. Day cruises are also run from Christ Church meadows to nearby Abingdon. ⊠ *Folly Bridge* ☎ *01865/243421* ⊕ *www.
salterssteamers.co.uk.*

SPECTATOR SPORTS
Eights Week. At the end of May, during Oxford's Eights Week (also
known as Summer Eights), men and women from the university's colleges compete to be "Head of the River." This is a particularly fun race
to watch because the shape of the river provides an added element of
excitement. It's too narrow for the eight-member teams to race side by
side, so the boats set off one behind another. Each boat tries to catch
and bump the one in front. ⊠ *Oxford* ⊕ *www.ourcs.org.uk.*

OXFORDSHIRE

The River Thames takes on a new graciousness as it flows along the
borders of Oxfordshire for 71 miles; with each league it increases in size
and importance. Three tributaries swell the river as it passes through
the landscape: the Windrush, the Evenlode, and the Cherwell. Tucked
among the hills and dales are one of England's impressive stately homes,
an Edenic little town, and a former Rothschild estate.

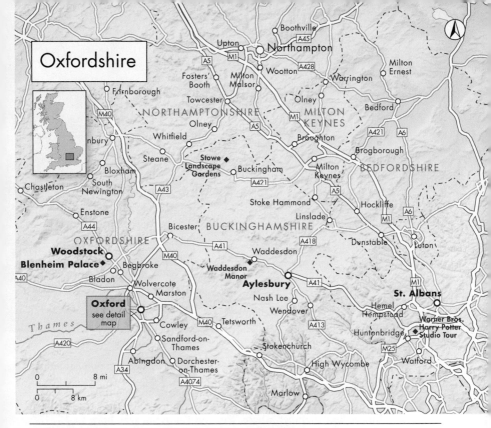

WOODSTOCK AND BLENHEIM PALACE

8 miles northwest of Oxford on A44.

Handsome 17th- and 18th-century houses line the trim streets of Woodstock, at the eastern edge of the Cotswolds. It's best known for nearby Blenheim Palace, and in summer tour buses clog the village's ancient streets. On a quiet fall or spring afternoon, however, Woodstock is a sublime experience: a mellowed 18th-century church and town hall mark the central square, and along its backstreets, you can find flower-bedecked houses and quiet lanes right out of a 19th-century etching.

GETTING HERE AND AROUND

The public bus service S3 runs (usually every half hour) between Oxford and Woodstock and costs £3.40 one way. It can drop you at the gates of Blenheim Palace.

EXPLORING

Fodor's Choice ★ **Blenheim Palace.** This magnificent palace has been called England's Versailles, and with good reason—it's still the only historic house in Britain to be named a World Heritage Site. Designed by Sir John Vanbrugh in the early 1700s in collaboration with Nicholas Hawksmoor, Blenheim was given by Queen Anne and the nation to General John Churchill, first duke of Marlborough. The exterior is nothing short

Fountains and formal Italian gardens set off the monumental baroque pile that is Blenheim Palace.

of sumptuous. Inside, lavishness continues in extremes: you can join a free guided tour or simply walk through on your own. Book a tour of the current duke's private apartments for a more intimate view of ducal life. For some visitors, the most memorable room is the small, low-ceiling chamber where Winston Churchill was born in 1874. He's buried in nearby Bladon. Its 2,000 acres of grounds, the work of Capability Brown, 18th-century England's best-known landscape gardener, are arguably the best example of the "cunningly natural" park in the country. The Pleasure Gardens, reached by a miniature train that stops outside the palace's main entrance, contain a butterfly house, a hedge maze, and a giant chess set. ⊠ *Off A4095, Woodstock* ☎ *01993/810530* ⊕ *www.blenheimpalace.com* ✉ *Palace, park, and gardens £26; park and gardens £16.*

AYLESBURY

22 miles east of Oxford, 46 miles northwest of London.

Aylesbury makes a good base for exploring the surrounding countryside, including stately homes and gardens. It's a pretty, historic place with a 13th-century church surrounded by small Tudor lanes and cottages. This market town has been associated with the Aylesbury duck since the 18th century, when flocks were walked 40 miles to the London markets. Kids appreciate a visit to the Roald Dahl's Children's Gallery, which is open all year.

GETTING HERE AND AROUND

From London, Chiltern Railways runs frequent trains from Marylebone Station (one hour). The town is easily accessible from Oxford by Arriva Bus 280, which runs every 30 minutes; travel time is 80 minutes. If you're driving from Oxford, take A40 and A418. From London, follow M1 and A41 and allow 90 minutes.

EXPLORING

Fodor'sChoice ★ **Stowe Landscape Gardens.** This exquisite example of a Georgian garden was created for the Temple family by the most famous gardeners of the 18th century. Capability Brown, Charles Bridgeman, and William Kent all worked on the land to create 980 acres of trees, valleys, and meadows. More than 40 striking monuments, follies, and temples dot the landscape of lakes, rivers, and pleasant vistas; this is a historically important place, but it's not for those who want primarily a flower garden. Allow at least half a day to explore the grounds. Stowe House, at the center, is now a fancy school with some magnificently restored rooms; it's open for tours most afternoons, but the actual schedule is notoriously changeable, so do call ahead or check ⊕ *www.stowe. co.uk* for more information. The gardens are about 3 miles northwest of Buckingham, which is 14 miles northwest of Aylesbury. You enter the gardens through the New Inn visitor center, where there are period parlor rooms to explore. ⊠ *New Inn Farm, off A422, Stowe* ☎ *01280/817156, 01280/818002 for tours* ⊕ *www.nationaltrust.org. uk/stowegardens* ☒ *£18.50; house only £6.50.*

Fodor'sChoice ★ **Waddesdon Manor.** Many of the regal residences created by the Rothschild family throughout Europe are gone now, but this one is still a vision of the 19th century at its most sumptuous. G.H. Destailleur built the house in the 1880s for Baron Ferdinand de Rothschild in the style of a 16th-century French château, with perfectly balanced turrets and towers and walls of creamy stone. Although intended only for summer weekend house parties, it was lovingly furnished over 35 years with Savonnerie carpets, Sèvres porcelain, furniture made by Riesener for Marie Antoinette, and paintings by Guardi, Gainsborough, and Reynolds. The collection is brought into the 21st century by an extraordinary broken porcelain chandelier, by artist Ingo Maurer, located in the Blue Dining Room. The gardens are equally extraordinary, with an aviary, colorful plants, and winding trails that provide panoramic views. In the restaurant you can dine on English or French fare and order excellent Rothschild wines. Admission is by timed ticket; arrive early or book in advance. ⊠ *Silk St., Waddesdon* ✢ *On A41 west of Aylesbury* ☎ *01296/820414* ⊕ *www.waddesdon.org.uk* ☒ *House and gardens £22; gardens only £10.*

ST. ALBANS

25 miles east of Aylesbury, 20 miles northwest of London.

A lively town on the outskirts of London, St. Albans is known for its historic cathedral, and it also holds reminders of a long history. From AD 50 to 440, the town, then known as Verulamium, was one of the largest communities in Roman Britain. You can explore this past in the

Verulamium Museum and splendid Roman sites around the area. For activities more focused on the present, every Wednesday and Saturday the Market Place on St. Peter's Street bustles with traders from all over England selling everything from fish and farm produce to clothing. A 20-minute drive away from St. Albans is Warner Bros. Harry Potter Studio Tour, which has sets and props from the successful films.

GETTING HERE AND AROUND

About 20 miles northwest of London, St. Albans is off the M1 and M25 highways, about an hour's drive from the center of the capital. Thameslink has frequent trains from London's St. Pancras Station, arriving at St. Albans City Station in 30 minutes. The main train station is on Victoria Street, in the town center. A second station on the south side of town, St. Albans Abbey Station, serves smaller towns in the surrounding area. Trains on this line are operated by London Midland. Bus service is slow and not direct. Central St. Albans is small and walkable. There's a local bus service, but you're unlikely to need it. Taxis usually line up outside the train stations.

ESSENTIALS

Train Contacts London Midland. ☎ 0344/8110133 ⊕ www.londonmidland. com.

Visitor Information St. Albans Tourist and Information Centre. ✉ Town Hall, Market Pl. ☎ 01727/864511 ⊕ www.enjoystalbans.com.

EXPLORING

FAMILY
Fodor's Choice
★

Warner Bros. Harry Potter Studio Tour. Attention all Muggles: this spectacular attraction just outside Watford immerses you in the magical world of Harry Potter for hours. From the Great Hall of Hogwarts—faithfully re-created, down to the finest detail—to magical props beautifully displayed in the vast studio space, each section of this attraction showcases the real sets, props, and special effects used in the eight movies. Visitors enter the Great Hall, a fitting stage for costumes from each Hogwarts house. You can admire the intricacies of the huge Hogwarts Castle model, ride a broomstick, try butterbeer, explore the Forbidden Forest, and gaze through the shop windows of Diagon Alley. The Hogwarts Express section—at a faithfully reproduced Platform 9¾—allows you to walk through a carriage of the actual steam train and see what it's like to ride with Harry and the gang. Tickets, pegged to a 30-minute arrival time slot, must be prebooked online. The studio tour is a 20-minute drive from St. Albans. You can also get here by taking a 20-minute train ride from London's Euston Station to Watford Junction (then a 15-minute shuttle-bus ride). Via car from London, use M1 and M25—parking is free. ✉ Studio Tour Dr., Leavesden Green ☎ 0345/084–0900 ⊕ www. wbstudiotour.co.uk ☎ £41.

BATH, THE COTSWOLDS, AND STRATFORD-UPON-AVON

WELCOME TO BATH, THE COTSWOLDS, AND STRATFORD-UPON-AVON

TOP REASONS TO GO

★ **Architecture:** Bath is perhaps the most perfectly preserved and harmonious English city. Close up, the elegance and finesse of the Georgian buildings is a perpetual delight.

★ **Roman Baths:** Take a break from Bath's Georgian elegance and return to its Roman days on a tour around this ancient bath complex.

★ **Shakespeare in Stratford:** To see a play by Shakespeare in the town where he was born—and perhaps after you've visited his birthplace or other sites—is a magical experience.

★ **Hidcote Manor Gardens:** In a region rich with imaginative garden displays, Hidcote lays good claim to eminence.

★ **Perfect villages:** With their stone cottages, Cotswold villages tend to be improbably picturesque; the hamlets of Upper and Lower Slaughter are among the most charming.

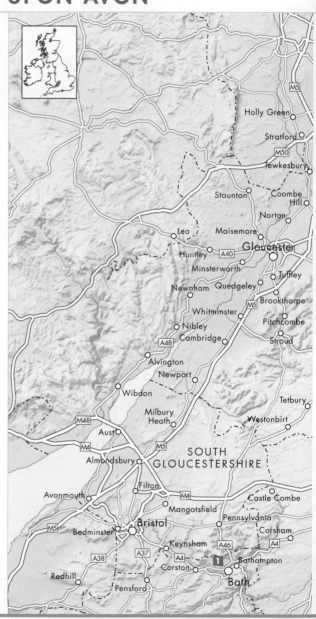

1 Bath and Nearby. With the Roman baths—renovated and embellished in the 18th century—and the late-medieval Bath Abbey at its heart, Bath is one of the country's loveliest towns. You can also soak up its thriving cultural scene and many shops.

2 The Cotswolds. With a scattering of picture-postcard towns and villages separated by sequestered valleys and woods, the Cotswolds are rural England at its best. Nearby Cheltenham, a larger town, with busy cafés and shops, provides a lively counterpoint.

3 Stratford-upon-Avon and Around. Birthplace of Shakespeare, the bustling historic town of Stratford-upon-Avon is liberally dotted with 16th-century buildings the playwright would recognize. Nearby Warwick Castle is well worth a stop.

7

Updated by
Rachael Rowe
and Sally
Coffey

The rolling uplands of the Cotswolds represent all the beauty and charm rural England has to offer, as immortalized in countless books, paintings, and films. In eloquently named settlements from Bourton-on-the-Water to Stow-on-the-Wold, you can taste the glories of the old English village—its stone slate roofs, low-ceiling rooms, and gardens; the atmosphere is as thick as honey, and equally as sweet. On the edge of the Cotswolds is Bath, among the most alluring small cities in Europe, and nothing evokes the England of the imagination more vividly than Stratford-upon-Avon, birthplace of perhaps the nation's most famous son, William Shakespeare.

Bath rightly boasts of being the best-planned town in England. Although the Romans founded the city when they discovered here the only true hot springs in England, its popularity during the 17th and 18th centuries luckily coincided with one of Britain's most creative architectural eras. Today people come to walk in the footsteps of Jane Austen, visit Bath Abbey and the excavated Roman baths, shop in an elegant setting, or have a modern spa experience at the stunning Thermae spa.

North of Bath are the Cotswolds—a region that more than one writer has called the very soul of England. This idyllic region, which from medieval times grew prosperous on the wool trade, remains a vision of rural England. Here are time-defying churches, sleepy hamlets, sequestered ancient farmsteads, and such fabled abodes as Sudeley Castle. The Cotswolds can hardly claim to be undiscovered, but the area's poetic appeal has survived the tour buses and gift shops.

Visits to Strartford-upon-Avon, William Shakespeare's birthplace, and the surrounding areas yield insights into the great playwright's life and inspirations. The sculpted, rolling farmland of Warwickshire may look nothing like the forested countryside of the 16th century, but plenty of sturdy Tudor buildings that Shakespeare knew survive to this day (including his birthplace). There's beauty in this—but also the possibility of tourist overkill. Stratford itself, with its Shakespeare sites and the theaters of the Royal Shakespeare Company, sometimes can get to feel like "Shakespeare World." And while Shakespeare himself would recognize plenty of the ancient, timber-framed buildings that line the main shopping streets, the same cannot be said of the bland, cookie-cutter chain stores that occupy most of these buildings today. Still, there's much more to see—magnificent castles, pastoral churches, and gentle countryside—in this famously lovely part of England. Stop in at Charlecote Park, a grand Elizabethan manor house, and moated Baddesley Clinton, a superb example of late-medieval domestic architecture. The huge fortresses of Warwick Castle and Kenilworth Castle provide glimpses into the past.

PLANNER

WHEN TO GO

This area contains some of England's most popular destinations, and it's best to avoid weekends in the busier areas of the Cotswolds. During the week, even in summer, you may hardly see a soul in the more remote spots. Bath is particularly congested in summer, when students flock to its language schools. On the other hand, Cheltenham is a relatively workaday place that can absorb many tour buses comfortably. The Shakespeare sights get very crowded on weekends and school vacations; Warwick Castle usually brims with visitors, so arrive early in the day.

Book your room well ahead if you visit during the two weeks in May and June when the Bath Festival hits town, or if you visit Cheltenham during the National Hunt Festival (horse racing) in mid-March. Note that the private properties of Hidcote Manor, Snowshill Manor, and Sudeley Castle close in winter; Hidcote Manor Garden is at its best in spring and fall.

FESTIVALS

Fodor's Choice
★ **Bath Festival.** Held over 17 days in May, the Bath Festival is a multi-arts celebration of literature and music in and around the city. Events include classical, jazz, and world-music concerts, dance performances, literary talks, and exhibitions, many in the Assembly Rooms and Bath Abbey. ⊠ *Bath Box Office, 2 Terrace Walk, Bath* ☎ *01225/463362* ⊕ *www.bathfestivals.org.uk.*

Jane Austen Festival. Celebrating the great writer with films, plays, walks, and talks over nine days in mid-September, the Jane Austen Festival is a feast for Janeites. ⊠ *Bath* ☎ *01225/443000* ⊕ *www.janeaustenfestivalbath.co.uk.*

Fodor's Choice
★ **Shakespeare Birthday Celebrations.** These festivities have taken place on and around the weekend closest to April 23, the Bard's birthday, since 1824. Over several days, the streets are filled with performers, impromptu concerts, and pageantry, and special events are held at various venues. The celebrations culminate with a spectacular procession. ⊠ *Stratford-upon-Avon* ☎ *01789/269332* ⊕ *www.shakespearescelebrations.com.*

PLANNING YOUR TIME

You can get a taste of Bath and the Cotswolds in three hurried days; a weeklong visit gives you plenty of time for the slow wandering this small region deserves. Near Bath, it's an easy drive to Lacock and Castle Combe, two stately villages on the southern edge of the Cotswolds, and Winchcombe makes a good entry into the area from Cheltenham. At the heart of the Cotswolds, Stow-on-the-Wold, Bourton-on-the-Water, and Broadway should on no account be missed. Within a short distance of these, Chipping Campden and Moreton-in-Marsh are less showy, with a more relaxed feel. Northleach is fairly low-key but boasts a fine example of a Cotswold wool church, while Bibury and Upper and Lower Slaughter are tiny settlements that can easily be appreciated on a brief passage. On the southern fringes of the area, Burford, Tetbury, and Cirencester have antiques and tea shops galore while avoiding the worst of the crowds.

Stratford-upon-Avon is ideal for day visits from London or as a base for exploring nearby, but even ardent Shakespeare lovers probably won't need more than a day or two here. Warwick can be explored in an hour or two, but allow half a day to tackle the many lines at busy Warwick Castle. A drive through the area's country lanes is a pleasant way to spend a day; a stop at any stately home will take a few hours. You're also near the northern Cotswolds if you want to explore the countryside further.

GETTING HERE AND AROUND

AIR TRAVEL

Bristol and Birmingham have the closest regional airports.

Contacts Birmingham International Airport. ⊠ *A45, off M42, Birmingham* ☎ *0871/222–0072* ⊕ *www.birminghamairport.co.uk.*

BUS TRAVEL

National Express buses head to the region from London's Victoria Coach Station. Megabus, a budget bus company best booked online, also serves Cheltenham and Bath from London. Bus service between some towns can be extremely limited. The First company covers the area around Bath. Stagecoach, Johnson's Coaches, Cotswold Green, Swanbrook, Marchants, and Pulham's Coaches operate in the Cotswolds region. Stagecoach serves local routes throughout the Stratford area. Traveline has comprehensive information about all public transportation.

Contacts Cotswold Green. ☎ *01453/835153* ⊕ *www.bustimes.org.uk/operators/cotswold-green.* **First.** ☎ *0871/200–2233* ⊕ *www.firstgroup.com.* **Johnson's Coaches.** ☎ *01564/797000* ⊕ *www.johnsonscoaches.co.uk.* **Marchants.** ☎ *01242/257714* ⊕ *www.marchants-coaches.com.* **Megabus.** ☎ *141/352–4444 for general inquiries, 0900/160–0900 for bookings* ⊕ *www.megabus.com.* **National Express.** ☎ *0871/781–8181* ⊕ *www.nationalexpress.com.* **Pulham's Coaches.** ☎ *01451/820369* ⊕ *www.pulhamscoaches.com.* **Stagecoach.** ☎ *0871/200–2233* ⊕ *www.stagecoachbus.com.* **Swanbrook.** ☎ *01452/712386* ⊕ *www.swanbrook.co.uk.* **Traveline.** ☎ *0871/200–2233* ⊕ *www.traveline.info.*

CAR TRAVEL

A car is the best way to make a thorough tour of the area, given the limitations of public transportation. M4 is the main route west from London to Bath and southern Gloucestershire; expect about a two-hour drive. From London you can also take M40 and A40 to the Cotswolds, where a network of minor roads links the villages. The M40 serves Stratford and Warwick as well.

TRAIN TRAVEL

First Great Western trains serve the region from London's Paddington Station; First Great Western and CrossCountry trains connect Cheltenham and Birmingham. Travel time from Paddington to Bath is about 90 minutes. Most trains to Cheltenham (two hours and 20 minutes) involve a change at Swindon or Bristol Parkway. Train service within the Cotswold area is extremely limited, with Kemble (near Cirencester) and Moreton-in-Marsh being the most useful stops, both serviced by regular trains from London Paddington. A three-day or seven-day Heart of England Rover pass is valid for unlimited travel within the region. National Rail Enquiries can help with schedules and other information.

Stratford has good train connections and can be seen as a day trip from London if your time is limited (a matinee is your best bet if you want to squeeze in a play). Chiltern Railways trains leave from London Marylebone Station and take 2 hours direct, or 2½–3 hours with transfers. They also go to Warwick. West Midlands serves the area from Birmingham (about 40 miles from Stratford). From London, Virgin and West Midlands trains leave from Euston while Chiltern Railways trains leave from Marylebone. Trains from Euston tend to be quicker (around 1½ hours). Travel times from Paddington to Hereford and Ludlow are about 3 hours (most change at Newport); Euston to Shrewsbury, with a change at Crewe or Birmingham, is 2½ hours; and to Chester, direct or with a change at Crewe, takes 2 hours.

Contacts Chiltern Railways. ☎ *03456/005165* ⊕ *www.chilternrailways.co.uk.* **National Rail Enquiries.** ☎ *03457/484950* ⊕ *www.nationalrail.co.uk.* **West Midlands Rail.** ☎ *0344/811–0133* ⊕ *www.westmidlandsrail.com.*

RESTAURANTS

Good restaurants dot the region, thanks to a steady flow of fine chefs seeking to cater to wealthy locals and waves of demanding visitors. The country's food revolution is in full evidence here. Restaurants have never had a problem with a fresh food supply: excellent regional produce, salmon from the rivers Severn and Wye, local lamb and pork, venison from the Forest of Dean, and pheasant, partridge, quail, and grouse in season. Also look for Gloucestershire Old Spot pork, bacon (try a delicious Old Spot bacon sandwich), and sausage on area menus. Stratford has many reasonably priced bistros and unpretentious eateries offering a broad choice of international fare; Warwick and Kenilworth both have good restaurant options. *Restaurant reviews have been shortened. For full information, visit Fodors.com.*

HOTELS

The hotels of this region are among Britain's most highly rated—from bed-and-breakfasts in village homes and farmhouses to luxurious country-house hotels. Many hotels present themselves as deeply traditional rural retreats, but some have opted for a sleeker, fresher style, with boldly contemporary or minimalist furnishings. Spas are becoming increasingly popular at these hotels. Book ahead whenever possible and brace yourself for some high prices. B&Bs are a cheaper alternative to the fancier hotels, and most places offer two- and three-day packages. Note that the majority of lodgings in Bath and many in the Cotswolds require a two-night minimum stay on weekends and holidays; rates are often higher on weekends. Stratford and Warwick have accommodations to suit every price range. Because Stratford is so popular with theatergoers, you need to book well ahead. Most hotels offer discounted two- and three-day packages. *Hotel reviews have been shortened. For full information, visit Fodors.com.*

WHAT IT COSTS IN POUNDS			
	$	$$	$$$	$$$$
Restaurants	under £15	£15–£19	£20–£25	over £25
Hotels	under £100	£100–£160	£161–£220	over £220

Restaurant prices are the average cost of a main course at dinner or, if dinner is not served, at lunch. Hotel prices are the lowest cost of a standard double room in high season, including 20% V.A.T.

VISITOR INFORMATION

The South West Tourism website has information about the entire region; the Cotswolds site is a government one that has a useful section on tourism. The major towns have Tourist Information Centres that provide advice and help with accommodations. Shakespeare's England offers the Explorer Pass, available for one, two, or three days (£49, £65, and £75 respectively), which allows entry to 19 attractions, including the five Shakespeare family homes. Local tourist offices can recommend day or half-day tours of the region and will have the names of registered Blue Badge guides—a mark of prestige among tour companies.

Contacts The Cotswolds. ⊕ *www.cotswolds.com.* **Shakespeare's England.** ☎ *01789/260677* ⊕ *www.shakespeares-england.co.uk.* **South West Tourism.** ⊕ *www.visitsouthwest.co.uk.*

BATH AND NEARBY

On the eastern edge of the county of Somerset, the city of Bath has strong links with the Cotswolds stretching north, the source of the wool that for centuries underpinned its economy. The stone mansions and cottages of that region are recalled in Bath's Georgian architecture and in the mellow stone that it shares with two of the villages across the Wiltshire border, Lacock and Castle Combe.

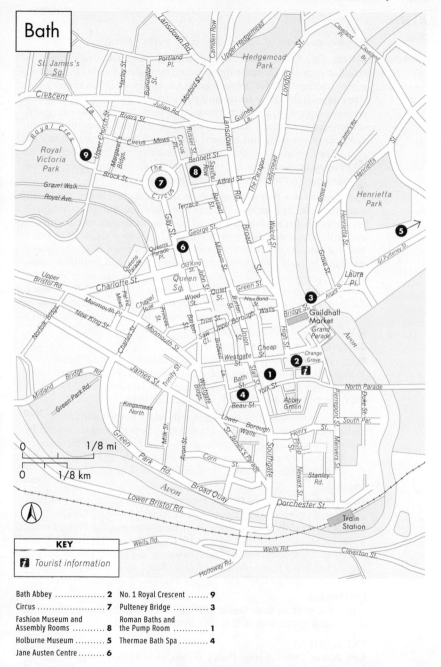

Bath

KEY

🛈 *Tourist information*

BATH

13 miles southeast of Bristol, 115 miles west of London.

Fodor'sChoice
★

In Bath, a UNESCO World Heritage Site, you're surrounded by magnificent 18th-century architecture, a lasting reminder of a vanished world often described by the likes of Jane Austen. In the 19th century the city lost its fashionable luster and slid into a refined gentility that still remains. Bath is no museum, though: it's lively, with good dining and shopping, excellent art galleries and museums, the remarkable excavated Roman baths, and theater, music, and other performances all year. Many people rush through Bath in a day, but there's enough to do to merit an overnight stay—or more. In summer, the sheer volume of sightseers may hamper your progress.

The Romans put Bath on the map in the 1st century when they built a temple here, in honor of the goddess Minerva, and a sophisticated network of baths to make full use of the mineral springs that gush from the earth at a constant temperature of 116°F (46.5°C). ■**TIP→** Don't miss the remains of the baths, one of the city's glories. Visits by Queen Anne in 1702 and 1703 brought attention to the town, and soon 18th-century "people of quality" took it to heart. Assembly rooms, theaters, and pleasure gardens were built to entertain the rich and titled when they weren't busy attending the parties of Beau Nash (the city's master of ceremonies and chief social organizer, who helped increase Bath's popularity) and having their portraits painted by Gainsborough.

GETTING HERE AND AROUND

Frequent trains from Paddington and National Express buses from Victoria connect Bath with London. The bus and train stations are close to each other south of the center. By car from London, take M4 to Exit 18, from which A46 leads 10 miles south to Bath.

Drivers should note that parking is extremely limited within the city, and any car illegally parked will be ticketed. Fees for towed cars can be hundreds of pounds. Public parking lots in the historic area fill up early, but the park-and-ride lots on the outskirts provide inexpensive shuttle service into the center, which is pleasant to stroll around.

TOURS

Mayor of Bath's Honorary Guides. Free two-hour walking tours of Bath are offered year-round by the Mayor of Bath's Honorary Guides. Individuals can just show up outside the main entrance to the Pump Room. Tours are Sunday through Friday at 10:30 and 2, Saturday at 10:30, and there's an additional tour at 7 pm Tuesday and Thursday from May to September. Note that unlike many other free tours, these guides don't accept tips. ☎ *01225/477411* ⊕ *www.bathguides.org.uk.*

ESSENTIALS

Visitor Information Bath Tourist Information Centre. ⊠ *Bridgwater House, 2 Terrace Walk* ☎ *01225/614420,* ⊕ *www.visitbath.co.uk.*

EXPLORING

Bath Abbey. Dominating Bath's center, this 15th-century edifice of golden, glowing stone has a splendid west front, with carved figures of angels ascending ladders on either side. Notice, too, the miter, olive tree,

The remains of the Roman baths evoke the days when the Romans gathered here to socialize and bathe.

and crown motif, a play on the name of the building's founder, Bishop Oliver King. More than 50 stained-glass windows fill about 80% of the building's wall space, giving the interior an impression of lightness. The abbey was built in the Perpendicular (English late-Gothic) style on the site of a Saxon abbey, and the nave and side aisles contain superb fan-vaulted ceilings. Look for the 21st-century expressively carved angels on the choir screens. The building's heating comes from the adjacent Roman baths. There are five services on Sunday, including choral even-song at 3:30. **Tower tours** (45 minutes; daily except Sunday) allow close-up views of the massive bells and panoramic cityscapes from the roof; the 212 dizzying steps demand a level of fitness. ⊠ *Abbey Church-yard* ☎ *01225/422462* ⊕ *www.bathabbey.org* ✉ *Abbey £4 suggested donation, tower tours £6* ⊗ *No tower tours Sun.*

Circus. John Wood designed the masterful Circus, a circle of curving, perfectly proportioned Georgian houses interrupted just three times for intersecting streets. Wood died shortly after work began; his son, the younger John Wood, completed the project. Notice the carved acorns atop the houses: Wood nurtured the myth that Prince Bladud founded Bath, ostensibly with the help of an errant pig rooting for acorns (this is one of a number of variations of Bladud's story). A garden with large plane trees fills the center of the Circus. The painter Thomas Gainsborough (1727–88) lived at No. 17 from 1760 to 1774. ⊠ *Intersection of Bennett, Brock, and Gay Sts.*

Fodor's Choice
★

Fashion Museum and Assembly Rooms. In its role as the **Assembly Rooms**, this neoclassical building was one of the leading centers for social life in 18th-century Bath. Jane Austen came here often, and it's in the Ballroom that Catherine Morland has her first, disappointing encounter with Bath's beau monde in *Northanger Abbey*; the Octagon Room is the setting for an important encounter between Anne Elliot and Captain Wentworth in *Persuasion*. Built by John Wood the Younger in 1771, the building was badly damaged by wartime bombing in 1942 but was faithfully restored. Its stunning chandeliers are the 18th-century originals. Throughout the year, classical concerts are given here, just as they were in bygone days. The Assembly Rooms are also known today for the entertaining **Fashion Museum**, displaying apparel from Jacobean times up to the present. You can see examples of what would have been worn in the heydays here, as well as glamorous frocks from the 20th century—a dress of the year is an annual addition. Besides admiring the changing exhibits, you can have fun trying on corsets and crinolines. An audio guide and daily guided tours at noon and 3:30 are included in the admission. ⊠ *Bennett St.* ☎ *01225/477789* ⊕ *www.fashionmuseum.co.uk* ⊡ *£2.50 for Assembly Rooms; £9 for Assembly Rooms and Fashion Museum; £22.50 combined ticket includes Roman baths.*

Fodor's Choice **Holburne Museum.** One of Bath's gems, this elegant 18th-century building
★ and its modern extension house a superb collection of 17th- and 18th-century decorative arts, ceramics, and silverware. Highlights include paintings by Gainsborough (*The Byam Family*, on indefinite loan) and George Stubbs (*Reverend Carter Thelwall and Family*), and a hilarious collection of caricatures of the Georgian city's fashionable elite. In its original incarnation as the Sydney Hotel, the house was one of the pivots of Bath's high society, which came to perambulate in the pleasure gardens (Sydney Gardens) that still lie behind it. One visitor was Jane Austen, whose main Bath residence was No. 4 Sydney Place, a brief stroll from the museum. There's also an excellent café and tea garden on-site. ⊠ *Great Pulteney St.* ☎ *01225/388569* ⊕ *www.holburne.org* ⊡ *Free; suggested donation £3.*

Jane Austen Centre. The one place in Bath that gives Austen any space provides a briefly diverting exhibition about the influence of Bath on her writings; *Northanger Abbey* and *Persuasion* are both set primarily in the city. The center is brought to life by characters in costume, and displays and a short film give a pictorial overview of life in Bath around 1800. Immerse yourself further by dressing up in costume; assistants are on hand to take your photo. The cozy Georgian house, a few doors up from where the writer lived in 1805 (one of several addresses she had in Bath), also includes the Austen-themed Regency Tea Rooms, open to the public. ⊠ *40 Gay St.* ☎ *01225/443000* ⊕ *www.janeausten.co.uk* ⊡ *£12.*

Fodor's Choice **Number 1 Royal Crescent.** The majestic arc of the Royal Crescent, much
★ used as a film location, is the crowning glory of Palladian architecture in Bath. The work of John Wood the Younger, these 30 houses fronted by 114 columns were laid out between 1767 and 1774. The first house to be built, on the corner of Brock Street and the Royal Crescent, was Number 1 Royal Crescent. The museum now crystallizes a view of the English class system in the 18th century—the status, wealth, and elegance of the upstairs in contrast with the extensive servants' quarters and kitchen downstairs. You can witness the predilections of the first resident, Henry Sandford, in the cabinet of curiosities and the

electrical machine, as well as a Georgian love of display in the sumptuous dessert table arrangement in the dining room. Several varieties of historic mousetraps make their appearance downstairs. Everything is presented with elegant attention to authenticity and detail. ⊠ *Royal Crescent* ☎ *01225/428126* ⊕ *no1royalcrescent.org.uk* 🎫 *£10.30; joint ticket with Museum of Bath Architecture and Herschel Museum £16.80* ⊙ *Closed mid-Dec.–Jan.*

Pulteney Bridge. Florence's Ponte Vecchio inspired this 18th-century span, one of the most famous landmarks in the city and the only work of Robert Adam in Bath. It's unique in Great Britain because shops line both sides of the bridge. ⊠ *Between Bridge St. and Argyle St.*

Fodor'sChoice
★

Roman Baths and the Pump Room. The hot springs have drawn people here since prehistoric times, so it's quite appropriate to begin an exploration of Bath at this excellent museum on the site of the ancient city's primary "watering hole." Roman patricians would gather to immerse themselves, drink the mineral waters, and socialize. With the departure of the Romans, the baths fell into disuse. When bathing again became fashionable at the end of the 18th century, this magnificent Georgian building was erected.

Almost the entire Roman bath complex was excavated in the 19th century, and the museum displays relics that include a memorable mustachioed, Celtic-influenced Gorgon's head, fragments of colorful curses invoked by the Romans against their neighbors, and information about Roman bathing practices. The **Great Bath** is now roofless, and the statuary and pillars belong to the 19th century, but much remains from the original complex (the Roman characters strutting around, however, are 21st century) and the steaming, somewhat murky waters are undeniably evocative. Tours take place hourly for no additional charge, and you can visit after 6:30 pm in July and August to experience the baths lighted by torches. Wear sensible shoes as the ancient stones are uneven and can be slippery.

Adjacent to the Roman bath complex is the famed **Pump Room**, built in 1792–96, a rendezvous for members of 18th- and 19th-century Bath society. Here Catherine Morland and Mrs. Allen "paraded up and down for an hour, looking at everybody and speaking to no one," to quote from Jane Austen's *Northanger Abbey*. Today you can take in the elegant space—or you can simply, for a small fee, taste the fairly vile mineral water. Charles Dickens described it as tasting like warm flatirons. ⊠ *Abbey Churchyard* ☎ *01225/477785* ⊕ *www.romanbaths. co.uk* 🎫 *Roman baths £16.50; £22.50 combined ticket includes the Fashion Museum and Assembly Rooms.*

Thermae Bath Spa. One of the few places in Britain where you can bathe in natural hot-spring water, and in an open-air rooftop location as well, this striking complex designed by Nicholas Grimshaw consists of a Bath-stone building surrounded by a glass curtain wall. The only difficulty is in deciding where to spend more time—in the sleekly luxurious, light-filled Minerva Bath, with its curves and gentle currents, or in the smaller, open-air rooftop pool for the unique sensation of bathing with views of Bath's operatic skyline (twilight is particularly atmospheric

7

here). Two 18th-century thermal baths, the Cross Bath and the Hot Bath, are back in use, too (the latter for treatments only). End your session in the crisp third-floor café and restaurant. ■ **TIP→ It's essential to book spa treatments ahead of time.** Towels, robes, and slippers are available for rent. Note that changing rooms are co-ed. Weekdays are the quietest time to visit. You must be 16 to bathe here and 18 to book a spa treatment. A separate, free **Visitor Centre** (April through October, Monday through Saturday 10–5, Sunday 11–4) opposite the entrance gives an overview of the project and provides audio guides (£2) for a brief tour of the exterior. ✉ *Hot Bath St.* ☎ *01225/331234* 🌐 *www.thermaebathspa.com* 🎟 *£36 for 2 hrs (£40 on weekends) and £10 for each additional hr.*

WHERE TO EAT

$ INDIAN
🍴 **Eastern Eye.** Delicious Indian dishes are the main draw, but the three magnificent glass domes of the large Georgian interior and the arresting South Asian murals mean that a meal here becomes an event. Specialties of the house include *mughlai* chicken (flavored with egg, ginger, and garlic and fried in a sauce of yogurt, coconut, and poppy seeds) and salmon *bhaja* (panfried with Bengali spices and served with diced potatoes). **Known for:** classic Indian and Bengali cuisine; elaborate setting; long menu with lots to choose from. [$] *Average main: £13* ✉ *8a Quiet St.* ☎ *01225/422323* 🌐 *www.easterneye.com.*

$$$$ MODERN BRITISH
🍴 **Menu Gordon Jones.** Step away from the center of town to sample the ingenious cuisine that Michelin-trained chef Gordon Jones conjures up in his open kitchen. There is no set menu, but each course is carefully explained before it's served; there might be smoked eel with maple syrup and purple potatoes, a crisp haggis, roasted turbot with giant raisins and caper dressing, and blackberry sorbet with marinated cucumber. **Known for:** imaginative cuisine served with style; tasting menus that change every single day (so it's always a surprise); reservations required far in advance. [$] *Average main: £55* ✉ *2 Wellsway* ☎ *01225/480871* 🌐 *www.menugordonjones.co.uk* ⏲ *Closed Mon.*

$$ MODERN BRITISH
Fodor's Choice ★
🍴 **The Pig Near Bath.** The Bath outpost of the growing Pig empire is a funky but chic "restaurant with rooms" in a converted country house in the Mendip Hills. It's all about the local and seasonal here (everything comes from within a 25-mile radius): kale, arugula, and other leaves and veggies are sourced from the Pig's kitchen garden; apples, pears, and apricots come from its orchard; and pork, chicken, quail, and venison are provided by animals raised on the property. **Known for:** salmon, bacon, and pancetta smoked on-site; relaxed atmosphere in a quaint deer park setting; alfresco dining in summer. [$] *Average main: £18* ✉ *Hunstrete House, Pensford* ☎ *01761/49049* 🌐 *www.thepighotel.com.*

$ BRITISH
🍴 **Pump Room.** The 18th-century Pump Room, with views over the Roman baths, serves morning coffee, lunches, and afternoon tea, to music by a pianist or string trio who play every day. The stately setting is the selling point rather than the food, but do sample the West Country cheese board and the homemade cakes and pastries. **Known for:** gorgeous setting from a bygone era; classic afternoon tea, coffee, and cakes; long waits during the day and reservations required for dinner.

$ *Average main: £14* ✉ *Abbey Churchyard* ☎ *01225/444477* ⊕ *www. romanbathssearcys.co.uk* ⊗ *No dinner Jan.–June and Sept.–Nov.*

$$
ITALIAN
✕ **Rustico.** Serving old-fashioned Italian country fare along with a dash of dolce vita, this delightful restaurant has a cozy, intimate atmosphere. The welcoming staff gladly serves you homemade pastas like grandma used to make, quantities of seafood casserole, handsome steaks, and pork in sage and white wine sauce, for instance. **Known for:** traditional Italian home-cooking; the area's best tiramisu; cozy outdoor seating. $ *Average main: £15* ✉ *2 Margaret's Bldgs.* ☎ *01225/310064* ⊕ *www. rusticobistroitaliano.co.uk* ⊗ *Closed Mon.*

$
BRITISH
✕ **Sally Lunn's.** Small and slightly twee, this tourist magnet near Bath Abbey occupies the oldest house in Bath, dating to 1482. It's famous for the Sally Lunn bun, a semisweet bread served here since 1680. **Known for:** famed Sally Lunn buns with sweet and savory toppings; lots of tourists; tiny but interesting on-site museum. $ *Average main: £12* ✉ *4 N. Parade Passage* ☎ *01225/461634* ⊕ *www.sallylunns.co.uk.*

WHERE TO STAY

$
B&B/INN
🛏 **Albany Guest House.** Homey and friendly, this Edwardian house close to the Royal Crescent has simply furnished rooms decorated with neutral shades of beige and cream. **Pros:** spotless rooms; convenient location; excellent breakfasts. **Cons:** some rooms are very small; limited parking; on a main road so can get noisy. $ *Rooms from: £85* ✉ *24 Crescent Gardens* ☎ *01225/313339* ⊕ *www.albanybath.co.uk* ⇆ *6 rooms* ❢❂❢ *Free Breakfast.*

$$
B&B/INN
🛏 **Marlborough House.** A warm, informal welcome greets all who stay at this Victorian establishment not too far from the Royal Crescent, where each room charms with period furniture, fresh flowers, and antique beds. **Pros:** obliging and helpful hosts; immaculate rooms; parking available. **Cons:** walk to the center is along a busy road; minimum two-night stay on weekends; gets booked up quickly at peak times. $ *Rooms from: £145* ✉ *1 Marlborough La.* ☎ *01225/318175* ⊕ *www. marlborough-house.net* ⇆ *6 rooms* ❢❂❢ *Free Breakfast.*

$$
HOTEL
🛏 **Queensberry Hotel.** Intimate and elegant, this boutique hotel on a residential street near the Circus occupies three 1772 town houses built by John Wood the Younger for the Marquis of Queensberry; it's a perfect marriage of chic sophistication, homey comforts, and attentive service. **Pros:** efficient service; tranquil ambience; valet parking. **Cons:** occasional street noise; no tea/coffee-making facilities in rooms; slight uphill walk from the city center. $ *Rooms from: £160* ✉ *7 Russel St.* ☎ *01225/447928* ⊕ *www.thequeensberry.co.uk* ⇆ *29 rooms* ❢❂❢ *Free Breakfast.*

$$$$
HOTEL
🛏 **The Royal Crescent.** You can't get a more prestigious address in Bath than the Royal Crescent, and this hotel, discreetly plumb center, overlooks parkland and the town. **Pros:** historic building; total comfort; great location. **Cons:** most bedrooms are very modern in feel; some rooms have no views; some bathrooms are small. $ *Rooms from: £300* ✉ *16 Royal Crescent* ☎ *01225/823333* ⊕ *www.royalcrescent.co.uk* ⇆ *45 rooms* ❢❂❢ *Free Breakfast.*

7

NIGHTLIFE

The Bell. Owned by a co-op, and a favorite among locals, the Bell has live music—jazz, blues, and folk—on Monday, Wednesday, and Sunday, as well as a selection of real ales, good food, computer access, and even self-service laundry. ⊠ *103 Walcot St.* ☎ *01225/460426* ⊕ *www. thebellinnbath.co.uk.*

Circo. This buzzing circular bar whips up a sassy cocktail or glass of champagne in this popular venue. There are movie nights on Wednesday, Cuban Thursdays, and even a gin high tea. Circo also serves tapas-style food. ⊠ *15-18 George St.* ☎ *01225/585100* ⊕ *www.circobar.co.uk.*

Raven. Pub aficionados will relish the friendly, unspoiled ambience of the Raven, a great spot for a pie and a pint. There are regular arts, science, and storytelling nights upstairs. ⊠ *Queen St.* ☎ *01225/425045* ⊕ *www. theravenofbath.co.uk.*

SHOPPING

Bath Christmas Market. For 18 days in late November and early December, the outdoor Bath Christmas Market sells gift items and regional specialties—from handcrafted toys to candles, cards, and edible delights—in over 200 chalet-style stalls concentrated in the area just south of the Abbey. ⊠ *York St.* ☎ *0844/847–5256* ⊕ *www.bathchristmasmarket.co.uk.*

Bath Sweet Shop. The city's oldest candy store, Bath Sweet Shop boasts of stocking some 350 different varieties, including traditional licorice torpedoes, pear drops, and aniseed balls. Sugar-free treats are available. ⊠ *8 N. Parade Passage* ☎ *01225/428040.*

Beaux Arts Bath. This gallery, close by the Abbey, carries the work of prominent artists, potters, sculptors, painters, and printmakers. ⊠ *12–13 York St.* ☎ *01225/464850* ⊕ *www.beauxartsbath.co.uk.*

Guildhall Market. The covered Guildhall Market, open Monday through Saturday 9–5, is the place for everything from jewelry and gifts to delicatessen food, secondhand books, bags, and batteries. There's a café, too. ⊠ *Entrances on High St. and Grand Parade* ⊕ *www.bathguildhallmarket.co.uk.*

CASTLE COMBE

12 miles northeast of Bath, 5 miles northwest of Chippenham.

Fodor's Choice ★ This Wiltshire village lived a sleepy existence until 1962, when it was voted the "prettiest village" in England—without any of its inhabitants knowing that it had even been a contender. The village's magic is that it's so delightfully toylike, you can see almost the whole town at one glance from any one position. Castle Combe consists of little more than a brook, a pack bridge, a street (which is called the Street) of simple stone cottages, a market cross from the 13th century, and the Perpendicular-style church of St. Andrew. The grandest house in the village (on its outskirts) is the Upper Manor House, which was built in the 15th century by Sir John Fastolf and is now the Manor House Hotel. If you're coming by car, use the village car park at the top of the hill and walk down.

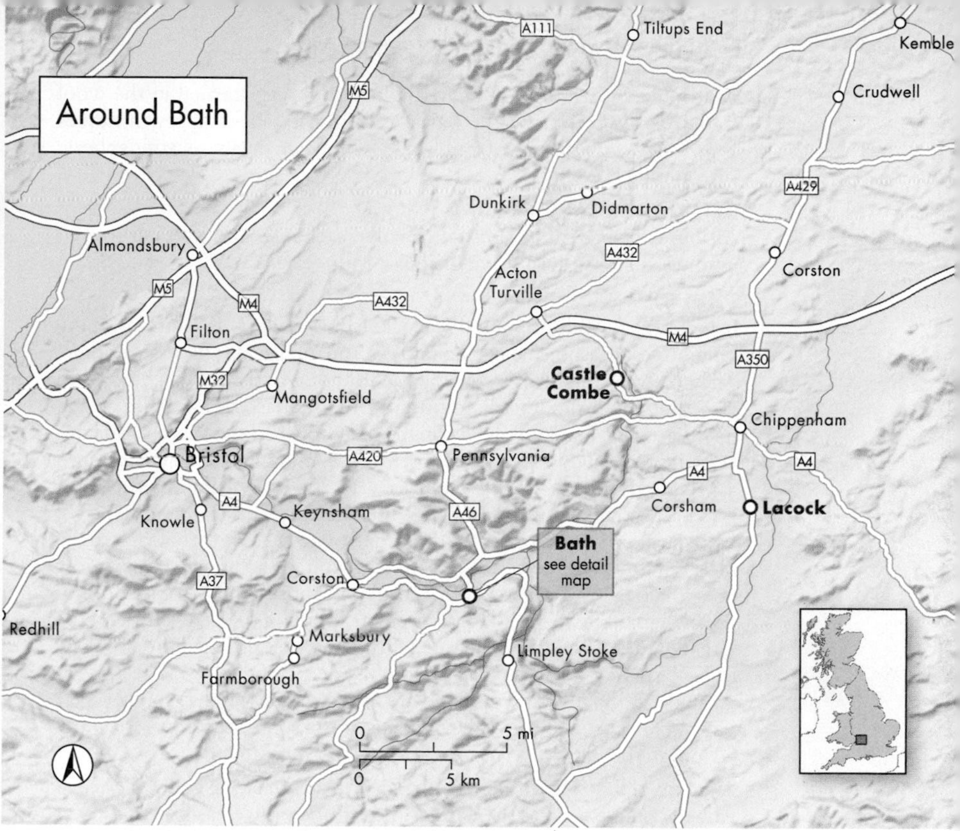

GETTING HERE AND AROUND

Regular buses and trains go to Chippenham, where you can pick up a bus for Castle Combe, but it's easier to drive or join a tour.

WHERE TO STAY

$$$$ HOTEL Fodor's Choice ★ 🏨 **Manor House Hotel.** Secluded in a 23-acre park on the edge of the village, this partly 14th-century manor house has guest rooms—some in mews cottages—that brim with antique character. **Pros:** romantic getaway; rich historical setting; good golf course. **Cons:** some rooms not in main house; not for those who dislike sound of constant running water; might be too stuffy for some. [$] *Rooms from: £260* ✉ *Castle Combe* ☎ *01249/782206* 🌐 *www.exclusive.co.uk/the-manor-house* 🛏 *48 rooms* 🍴 *Free Breakfast.*

LACOCK

8 miles southeast of Castle Combe, 12 miles east of Bath.

Fodor's Choice ★ Owned by the National Trust, this lovely Wiltshire village is the victim of its own charm, its unspoiled gabled and stone-tile cottages drawing tour buses aplenty. Off-season, however, Lacock slips back into its profound slumber, the mellow stone and brick buildings little changed in 500 years and well worth a wander. Besides Lacock Abbey, there's the handsome church of St. Cyriac (built with money earned in the wool trade), a 14th-century tithe barn, and, in the village, a few antiques shops and a scattering of pubs that serve bar meals in atmospheric surroundings.

GETTING HERE AND AROUND

All buses from Bath to Lacock involve a change and take 60 to 110 minutes, so it's best to drive or join a tour.

EXPLORING

Lacock Abbey. Well-preserved Lacock Abbey reflects the fate of many religious establishments in England—a spiritual center became a home. The abbey, at the town's center, was founded in the 13th century and closed down during the dissolution of the monasteries in 1539, when its new owner, Sir William Sharington, demolished the church and converted the cloisters, sacristy, chapter house, and monastic quarters into a private dwelling. The house passed to the Talbot family, the most notable descendant of whom was William Henry Fox Talbot (1800–77), who developed the world's first photographic negative. You can see the oriel window, the subject of this photograph in the upper rooms of the abbey, along with a rare 16th-century purpose-built strong room in the octagonal tower. Look for the sugar lump on the goat's nose in the Great Hall. The last descendant, Matilda Talbot, donated the property as well as Lacock itself to the National Trust in the 1940s. The abbey's grounds and Victorian woodland are also worth a wander. Harry Potter fans, take note: Lacock Abbey was used for some scenes at Hogwarts School in the film *Harry Potter and the Sorcerer's Stone*.

The **Fox Talbot Museum,** in a 16th-century barn at the gates of Lacock Abbey, commemorates the work of Fox Talbot as well as other pioneers and contemporary artists in this field. ⊠ *High St.* ☎ *01249/730459* ⊕ *www.nationaltrust.org.uk* 🖾 *£11.60; excluding Abbey rooms £9.40.*

THE COTSWOLDS

A gently undulating area of limestone uplands, the Cotswolds are among England's best-preserved rural districts, and the quiet but lovely grays and ambers of the stone buildings here are truly unsurpassed. Much has been written about the area's age-mellowed towns, but the architecture of the villages actually differs little from that of villages elsewhere in England. Their distinction lies in their surroundings: the valleys are lush and rolling, and cozy hamlets appear covered in foliage from church tower to garden gate. Beyond the town limits, you can explore, on foot or by car, the "high wild hills and rough uneven ways" that Shakespeare wrote about.

Over the centuries, quarries of honey-color stone have yielded building blocks for many Cotswold houses and churches and have transformed little towns into realms of gold. Make Chipping Campden, Moreton-in-Marsh, or Stow-on-the-Wold your headquarters and wander for a few days. Then ask yourself what the area is all about. Its secret seems shared by two things—sheep and stone. These were once the great sheep-rearing areas of England, and during the peak of prosperity in the Middle Ages, Cotswold wool was in demand the world over. This made the local merchants rich, but many gave back to the Cotswolds by restoring old churches (the famous "wool churches" of the region) or building rows of limestone almshouses now seasoned to a glorious golden-gray. These days the wool merchants have gone but the wealth remains—the region includes some of the most exclusive real estate in the country.

One possible route is to begin with Cheltenham—the largest town in the area and a gateway to the Cotswolds, but slightly outside the boundaries and more of a small city in atmosphere—then move on to the beauty spots in and around Winchcombe. Next are Sudeley Castle, Stanway House, and Snowshill Manor, among the most impressive houses of the region; the oversold village of Broadway; Chipping Campden—the Cotswold cognoscenti's favorite; and Hidcote Manor, one of the most spectacular gardens in England. Then circle back south, down through Moreton-in-Marsh, Stow-on-the-Wold, Upper Slaughter, Lower Slaughter, and Bourton-on-the-Water, and end with Bibury and Tetbury. This is definitely a region where it pays to go off the beaten track to take a look at that village among the trees.

CHELTENHAM

50 miles north of Bath, 13 miles east of Gloucester, 99 miles west of London.

Although Cheltenham has acquired a reputation as snooty—the population (around 110,000) is generally well-heeled and conservative—it's also cosmopolitan. The town has excellent restaurants and bars, fashionable stores, and a thriving cultural life. Its primary claim to renown, however, is its architecture, rivaling Bath's in its Georgian elegance, with wide, tree-lined streets, crescents, and terraces with row houses, balconies, and iron railings.

Like Bath, Cheltenham owes part of its fame to mineral springs. By 1740 the first spa was built, and after a visit from George III and Queen Charlotte in 1788, the town dedicated itself to idleness and enjoyment. "A polka, parson-worshipping place"—in the words of resident Lord Tennyson—Cheltenham gained its reputation for snobbishness when stiff-collared Raj majordomos returned from India to find that the springs—the only purely natural alkaline waters in England—were the most effective cure for their "tropical ailments."

Great Regency architectural set pieces—Lansdown Crescent, Pittville Spa, and the Lower Assembly Rooms, among them—were built solely to adorn the town. The Rotunda building (1826) at the top of Montpellier Walk—now a bank—contains the spa's original "pump room," in which the mineral waters were on tap. More than 30 statues adorn the storefronts of Montpellier Walk. Wander past Imperial Square, with its ironwork balconies, past the ornate Neptune's Fountain, and along the Promenade. In spring and summer lush flower gardens enhance the town's buildings, attracting many visitors.

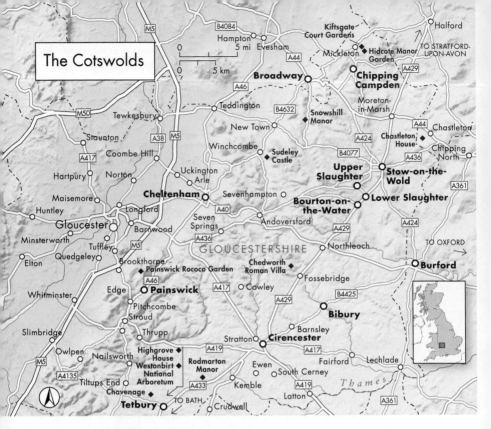

The Cotswolds

GETTING HERE AND AROUND

Trains from London Paddington and buses from London Victoria head to Cheltenham. The train station is west of the center, and the bus station is centrally located off Royal Well Road. Drivers should leave their vehicles in one of the numerous parking lots. The town center is easily negotiable on foot.

EXPLORING

Fodor's Choice
★
Sudeley Castle. One of the grand showpieces of the Cotswolds, Sudeley Castle was the home and burial place of Catherine Parr (1512–48), Henry VIII's sixth and last wife, who outlived him by one year. Here Catherine undertook, in her later years, the education of the ill-fated Lady Jane Grey and the future queen, Princess Elizabeth. Sudeley, for good reason, has been called a woman's castle. The term "castle" is misleading, though, for it looks more like a Tudor-era palace, with a peaceful air that belies its turbulent history. In the 17th century Charles I took refuge here, causing Oliver Cromwell's army to besiege the castle. It remained in ruins until the Dent-Brocklehurst family stepped in with a 19th-century renovation.

The 14 acres of gardens, which include the roses of the Queen's Garden (best seen in June) and a Tudor knot garden, are the setting for Tudor fun days in summer. Inside the castle, visitors see the West Wing, with the Long Room where exhibitions illustrate the castle's history, and the East Wing which contains the private apartments of Lord and Lady Ashcombe, where you can see paintings by Van Dyck, Rubens, Turner, and Reynolds. Art tours can also be booked in advance. Rare and exotically colored birds strut in the pheasantry. The 11 cottages and apartments on the grounds are booked for a minimum of three-night stays. The castle is a mile southeast of Winchcombe. ✉ *Off B4632, Winchcombe* ☎ *01242/602308, 01242/609481 cottages* 🌐 *www.sudeleycastle.co.uk* 🎫 *£16.50* 🕒 *Closed Nov.–mid-Mar.*

Fodor's Choice ★ **The Wilson, Cheltenham Art Gallery and Museum.** From the 1880s onward, Cheltenham was at the forefront of the Arts and Crafts movement and this is still demonstrated by the fine displays of William Morris textiles, furniture by Charles Voysey, and wood and metal pieces by Ernest Gimson at this museum and art gallery. Decorative arts, such as Chinese ceramics, are also well represented, and British artists, including Stanley Spencer, Vanessa Bell, and Jake and Dinos Chapman, make their mark. The Summerfield Galleries demonstrate life through the ages in easily digestible chunks. Exhibits on Cheltenham's history complete the picture; one is devoted to Edward Wilson, who traveled with Robert Scott to the Antarctic on Scott's ill-fated 1912 expedition. ✉ *Clarence St.* ☎ *01242/237431* 🌐 *www.thewilson.org.uk* 🎫 *Free.*

WHERE TO EAT

$ BRITISH 🍴 **The Coffee Dispensary.** Located in a former pharmacy, the Coffee Dispensary is a small independent café that sources its beans from single estates, aiming to bring the best flavors to the people of Cheltenham. It also serves cakes and savory snacks. **Known for:** the best coffee in Cheltenham; friendly vibe; sourcing from single-estate coffee producers. [$] *Average main: £3* ✉ *18 Regent St.* ☎ *01242/260597* 🌐 *www.the-coffee-dispensary.co.uk.*

$$ MODERN BRITISH 🍴 **The Daffodil.** Housed in a former art deco cinema, The Daffodil is themed along 1920s lines with a touch of glamour and an enticing menu. The menu features dishes like twice-baked Double Gloucester soufflé, calves' liver with mustard mash, and curry spiced chicken breast. **Known for:** 1920s decor and style; great cocktail menu; live jazz on Monday nights and Saturday afternoons. [$] *Average main: £17* ✉ *18–20 Suffolk Parade* ☎ *01242/700055* 🌐 *www.thedaffodil.com* 🕒 *Closed Sun.*

WHERE TO STAY

$ B&B/INN 🏨 **The Bradley.** The thoughtful and hospitable owners take great pride in this town house, near the town center, that has been in the same family for more than 100 years. **Pros:** good value; attentive hosts; well-designed rooms. **Cons:** lots of stairs to top rooms; no private parking; some bathrooms are very small. [$] *Rooms from: £88* ✉ *19 Bayshill Rd.* ☎ *01242/519077* 🌐 *www.thebradleyhotel.co.uk* 🛏 *10 rooms* 🍽 *Free Breakfast* ☞ *No children under 11 are allowed.*

$$ HOTEL 🏨 **Malmaison Cheltenham.** Just around the corner from the calming Montpelier Gardens, the Malmaison's classic white building blends with the local architecture. **Pros:** quiet, beautiful rooms; short walk to Montpellier and the Suffolks; very relaxed atmosphere. **Cons:** limited

As enchanting as the house, the gardens at Sudeley Castle provide a perfect spot for summer meanderings.

parking; restaurant is sometimes closed for private functions; gets booked quickly at peak times. $ *Rooms from: £110* ✉ *Bayshill Rd.* ☎ *01242/370–655* ⊕ *www.malmaison.com/locations/cheltenham* ➦ *60 rooms* ⦿ *Free Breakfast.*

SHOPPING

Cavendish House. The town's oldest department store, now run by House of Fraser, stocks designer fashions. ✉ *32–48 The Promenade* ☎ *01242/521300* ⊕ *www.houseoffraser.co.uk/store/cheltenham/0724.*

Martin. This shop carries a good stock of classic and modern jewelry. ✉ *19 The Promenade* ☎ *01242/522821.*

Q and C Militaria. A treasure trove for military buffs, Q and C Militaria offers badges and medals, breastplates, helmets, coats of arms, and books. It's run by ex-soldiers. ✉ *22 Suffolk Rd.* ☎ *01242/519815* ⊕ *www.qcmilitaria.com.*

BROADWAY

8 miles north of Winchcombe, 17 miles northeast of Cheltenham.

The Cotswold town to end all Cotswold towns, Broadway has become a favorite of day-trippers. William Morris first discovered the delights of this village, and J. M. Barrie, Vaughan Williams, and Edward Elgar soon followed. Today you may want to avoid Broadway in summer, when it's clogged with cars and buses. Named for its handsome, wide main street (well worth a stroll), the village includes numerous antiques shops, tea parlors, and boutiques. Step into Broadway's back-roads and alleys and you can discover any number of honey-color houses and colorful gardens.

GETTING HERE AND AROUND

Broadway can be reached by car via A44; park in one of the parking lots signposted from the main street. Johnson's Coaches connects the town with Stratford-upon-Avon, Chipping Campden, and Moreton-in-Marsh; Marchants connects Broadway with Winchcombe and Cheltenham. No buses run on Sunday. You'll need a car to reach Broadway Tower, Stanway House, and Snowshill Manor.

ESSENTIALS

Visitor Information Broadway Tourist Information Centre. ⊠ *Russell Sq.* ☎ *01386/852937* ⊕ *www.broadway-cotswolds.co.uk/tourist-information-centre.*

EXPLORING

FAMILY **Snowshill Manor.** Three miles south of Broadway and 13 miles northeast
Fodor'sChoice of Cheltenham, Snowshill is one of the most unspoiled of all Cotswold
★ villages. Snuggled beneath Oat Hill, with little room for expansion, the hamlet is centered on an old burial ground, the 19th-century St. Barnabas Church, and Snowshill Manor, a splendid 17th-century house that brims with the collections of Charles Paget Wade, gathered between 1919 and 1956. Over the door of the house is Wade's family motto, *Nequid pereat* ("Let nothing perish"). The rooms are bursting with Tibetan scrolls, spinners' tools, ship models, Persian lamps, and bric-a-brac; the Green Room displays 26 suits of Japanese samurai armor. Outside, an imaginative terraced garden provides an exquisite frame for the house. ■**TIP**➜ **Admission is by timed tickets issued on a first-come, first-served basis, so arrive early in peak season.** ⊠ *Off A44, Snowshill* ☎ *01386/852410* ⊕ *www.nationaltrust.org.uk* ⌨*£11.60; garden only £6.80* ⊘ *Closed Nov.–mid-Mar.*

WHERE TO EAT

$$$ ✕ **Russell's.** With a courtyard at the back and a patio at the front, this
MODERN BRITISH chic "restaurant with rooms" is perfect for a light lunch at midday or a full meal in the evening. Menus concentrate on Modern British dishes and change seasonally, with such temptations as Bibury trout or local lamb often available. **Known for:** good-value fixed-price menu; fresh local produce; stylish setting. ⓢ *Average main: £21* ⊠ *20 High St.* ☎ *01386/853555* ⊕ *www.russellsofbroadway.co.uk* ⊘ *No dinner Sun.*

WHERE TO STAY

$$$ ☷ **Mill Hay House.** If the rose garden, trout-filled pond, and sheep on the
B&B/INN hill at this 18th-century Queen Anne house aren't appealing enough, then the stone-flagged floors, leather sofas, and grandfather clocks should satisfy. **Pros:** delightful owners; beautifully landscaped gardens; gourmet breakfasts. **Cons:** books up quickly; no young children admitted; entrance can be hard to find. ⓢ *Rooms from: £185* ⊠ *Snowshill Rd.* ☎ *01386/852498* ⊕ *www.millhay.co.uk* ⤳ *3 rooms* ❂*| Free Breakfast.*

CHIPPING CAMPDEN

4 miles east of Broadway, 18 miles northeast of Cheltenham.

Fodor'sChoice Undoubtedly one of the most beautiful towns in the area, Chipping
★ Campden, with its population of about 2,500, is the Cotswolds in a microcosm. It has St. James, the region's most impressive church;

frozen-in-time streets; a silk mill that was once the center of the Guild of Handicraft; and pleasant, untouristy shops. One of the area's most seductive settings unfolds before you as you travel on B4081 through sublime English countryside and happen upon the town, tucked in a slight valley. North of town is lovely Hidcote Manor Garden. ■ TIP→ Chipping Campden can easily be reached on foot along a level section of the Cotswold Way from Broadway Tower, outside Broadway; the walk takes about 75 minutes.

GETTING HERE AND AROUND

By car, Chipping Campden can be reached on minor roads from A44 or A429. There's a small car park in the center and spaces on the outskirts of the village. By bus, take Johnson's Coaches from Stratford-upon-Avon, Broadway, and Moreton-in-Marsh, or Pulham's Coaches from Bourton-on-the-Water and Cheltenham, changing at Moreton-in-Marsh (no Sunday service).

ESSENTIALS

Visitor Information Chipping Campden Tourism Information Centre. ⊠ *The Old Police Station, High St.* ☎ *01386/841206* ⊕ *www.chippingcampdenonline.org.*

EXPLORING

Fodor's Choice
★

Hidcote Manor Garden. Laid out around a Cotswold manor house, Hidcote Manor Garden is arguably the most interesting and attractive large garden in Britain. Crowds are large at the height of the season, but it's worthwhile anytime. A horticulturist from the United States, Major Lawrence Johnston, created the garden in 1907 in the Arts and Crafts style. Johnston was an imaginative gardener and avid traveler who brought back specimens from all over the world. The formal part of the garden is arranged in "rooms" separated by hedges and often with fine topiary work and walls. Besides the variety of plants, what's impressive are the different effects created, from calm open spaces to areas packed with flowers. ■ TIP→ Look for one of Johnston's earliest schemes, the red borders of dahlias, poppies, fuchsias, lobelias, and roses; the tall hornbeam hedges; and the Bathing Pool garden, where the pool is so wide there's scarcely space to walk. The White Garden was probably the forerunner of the popular white gardens at Sissinghurst and Glyndebourne. If you have time, explore the tiny village of Hidcote Bartrim with its thatched stone houses; it borders the garden and fills a storybook dell. The garden is 4 miles northeast of Chipping Campden. ⊠ *Off B4081* ☎ *01386/438333* ⊕ *www.nationaltrust. uk/hidcote* 🎟 *£12.70* ⊗ *Closed mid-Dec.–mid-Feb. and weekdays mid-Feb.–late Feb. and early Nov.–mid-Dec.*

Kiftsgate Court Gardens. While not so spectacular as Hidcote Manor Garden, this intimate, privately owned garden, just a five-minute stroll away, still captivates. It's skipped by the majority of visitors to Hidcote, so you won't be jostled by the crowds. The interconnecting flower beds present harmonious arrays of color, and the contemporary formal water garden adds an elegant contrast. Don't miss the prized Kiftsgate rose, supposed to be the largest in England, flowering gloriously in mid-July. ⊠ *Off B4081, Mickleton* ☎ *01386/438777* ⊕ *www.kiftsgate.co.uk* 🎟 *£8.50* ⊗ *Closed Oct.–Mar., Thurs. and Fri. year-round, and Sat. and Tues. Apr. and Sept.*

St. James. The soaring pinnacled tower of St. James, a prime example of a Cotswold wool church (it was rebuilt in the 15th century with money from wool merchants), announces Chipping Campden from a distance; it's worth stepping inside to see the lofty, light-filled nave. The church recalls the old saying, which became popular because of the vast numbers of houses of worship in the Cotswolds, "As sure as God's in Gloucestershire." ⊠ *Church St.* ☎ *01386/841927* ⊕ *www. stjameschurchcampden.co.uk* ✉ *£3 donation suggested.*

WHERE TO EAT

$ ✕ **Eight Bells.** Close to St. James Church, this traditional tavern has low
BRITISH   beams, a flagstone floor, and a small courtyard. The long menu includes daily specials, local ales, and enticing dishes like confit duck and deep-fried fish-and-chips. **Known for:** historic pub with lots of character; affordable ciabatta sandwich lunches; local beers. $ *Average main: £14* ⊠ *Church St.* ☎ *01386/840371* ⊕ *www.eightbellsinn.co.uk.*

WHERE TO STAY

$$$ 🏨 **Cotswold House Hotel and Spa.** This luxury hotel in the heart of Chip-
HOTEL   ping Campden injects contemporary design into a stately 18th-century manor house, and from the swirling staircase in the entrance to the individually designed guest rooms studded with contemporary art, it's a winning formula. **Pros:** plenty of pampering; pleasant garden; personalized service. **Cons:** some bathrooms are small; additional charge to use spa; no swimming pool. $ *Rooms from: £185* ⊠ *The Square* ☎ *01386/840330* ⊕ *www.bespokehotels.com/cotswoldhouse* ⊅ *28 rooms* ⦾*| Free Breakfast.*

$$ 🏨 **Noel Arms Hotel.** Dating to the 14th century, Chipping Campden's
HOTEL   oldest inn was built to accommodate foreign wool traders, and even though it's been enlarged, the building retains its exposed beams and stonework. **Pros:** traditional character; friendly staff; excellent curries at restaurant. **Cons:** rooms can be noisy and overheated; annex overlooks car park; some rooms are small. $ *Rooms from: £120* ⊠ *High St.* ☎ *01386/840317* ⊕ *www.noelarmshotel.com* ⊅ *28 rooms* ⦾*| Free Breakfast.*

SHOPPING

Hart. Descendants of an original member of the Guild of Handicraft specialize in fashioning lovely items from silver at this shop. ⊠ *Guild of Handicraft, Sheep St.* ☎ *01386/841100* ⊕ *www.hartsilversmiths.co.uk.*

Stuart House Antiques. Three bay windows filled with silverware and copperware, porcelain, Doulton figurines, and Staffordshire figures show you only a fraction of what's available here over two floors overflowing with antiques. ⊠ *High St.* ☎ *01386/840995* ⊕ *www.antiques-atlas.com/ stuarthouseantiques.*

STOW-ON-THE-WOLD

5 miles south of Moreton-in-Marsh, 15 miles east of Cheltenham.

At an elevation of 800 feet, Stow is the highest town in the Cotswolds—"Stow-on-the-Wold, where the wind blows cold" is the age-old saying. Built around a wide square, Stow's imposing golden stone houses have been discreetly converted into high-quality antiques stores, shops, and tea parlors. The Square, as it's known, has a fascinating history. In the 18th century Daniel Defoe wrote that more than 20,000 sheep could be sold here on a busy day; such was the press of livestock that sheep runs, known as "tures," were used to control the sheep, and these narrow streets still run off the main square. Today pubs and antiques shops fill the area.

Also here are St. Edward's Church and the Kings Arms Old Posting House, its wide entrance still seeming to wait for the stagecoaches that used to stop here on their way to Cheltenham.

GETTING HERE AND AROUND

Stow-on-the-Wold is well connected by road (A429, A424, and A436) and bus (from Moreton-in-Marsh, Bourton-on-the-Water, Northleach, Cirencester, and Cheltenham). There are car parks off Sheep Street and Fosseway (A429). Chastleton House is reachable only by car.

EXPLORING

Chastleton House. One of the most complete Jacobean properties in Britain opts for a beguilingly lived-in appearance, taking advantage of almost 400 years' worth of furniture and trappings accumulated by many generations of the single family that owned it until 1991. The house was built between 1605 and 1612 for William Jones, a wealthy wool merchant, and has an appealing authenticity: bric-a-brac is strewn around, wood and pewter are unpolished, upholstery is uncleaned. The top floor is a glorious, barrel-vaulted long gallery, and throughout the house you can see exquisite plasterwork, paneling, and tapestries. The gardens include rotund topiaries and the first croquet lawn (the rules of croquet were codified here in 1865). During busy periods, admission is by timed ticket on a first-come, first-served basis. Note that there is no tearoom or shop here, but the church next door sells tea and snacks when the house is open. Chastleton is 6 miles northeast of Stow, signposted off A436 between Stow and A44. ✉ *Off A436, Stow on the Wold* ☎ *01608/674981 info line* 🌐 *www.nationaltrust.org.uk* 🎟 *£10.50; garden only £5* 🕒 *Closed Nov.–Feb., Mon., and Tues.*

WHERE TO EAT AND STAY

$ BRITISH 🍴 **Queen's Head.** A convivial stopping-off spot for lunch or dinner, this pub has a courtyard out back that's a quiet retreat on a summer day. Besides standard pub grub like sandwiches, baguettes, and sausage and mash, there are daily specials such as steak-and-kidney pie, suet pudding, and a burger of the week. **Known for:** great ale menu; traditional country pub food; lots of locals. [$] *Average main: £10* ✉ *The Square, Stow on the Wold* ☎ *01451/830563* 🌐 *www.queensheadstowonthewold.com.*

$ B&B/INN 🏨 **Number Nine.** Beyond the traditional Cotswold stone exterior of this former coaching inn—now a bed-and-breakfast—are unfussy, spacious bedrooms done in soothing white and pale colors. **Pros:** helpful and amiable hosts; close to pubs and restaurants; delicious breakfasts. **Cons:** two bathrooms have tubs, not showers; low ceilings; steps to climb. [$] *Rooms from: £85* ✉ *9 Park St., Stow on the Wold* ☎ *01451/870333* 🌐 *www.number-nine.info* 🛏 *3 rooms* 🍽 *Free Breakfast.*

$$ HOTEL **Stow Lodge.** A former rectory, this stately, family-run hotel couldn't be better placed, separated from Stow's main square by a tidy garden. **Pros:** central location; hospitable service; good breakfasts. **Cons:** chiming church clock can be disturbing; steep steps to top-floor rooms; minimum stay on weekends. $ *Rooms from: £150* ✉ *The Square, Stow on the Wold* ☎ *01451/830485* 🌐 *www.stowlodge.co.uk* 🛏 *20 rooms* 🍴 *Free Breakfast* ☞ *No children under 5.*

SHOPPING

Stow-on-the-Wold is the leading center for antiques stores in the Cotswolds, with dealers centered on the Square, Sheep Street, and Church Street.

Baggott Church St. Limited. This shop displays fine old furniture, portraits and landscape paintings, silver, and toys, with their price tags tied on with ribbon. ✉ *Church St., Stow on the Wold* ☎ *01451/830370* 🌐 *www.baggottantiques.com.*

Durham House Antiques. Showcases of jewelry, silver items, and ceramics, along with antiquarian books and period furniture, are on display over two floors. ✉ *48 Sheep St., Stow on the Wold* ☎ *01451/870404* 🌐 *www.durhamhousegb.com.*

Tudor House. Three floors of showcases contain the finds of 20 antiques dealers presenting anything from tiny mother-of-pearl pieces and beaded bags to wooden dressers full of plates and jugs. ✉ *40 Sheep St., Stow on the Wold* ☎ *01451/830021* 🌐 *www.tudor-house-antiques.com.*

7

BOURTON-ON-THE-WATER

4 miles southwest of Stow-on-the-Wold, 12 miles northeast of Cheltenham.

Off A429 on the eastern edge of the Cotswolds, Bourton-on-the-Water is deservedly famous as a classic Cotswold village. Like many others, it became wealthy in the Middle Ages because of wool. The little River Windrush runs through Bourton, crossed by low stone bridges; it's as pretty as it sounds. This village makes a good touring base and has a collection of quirky small museums, but in summer it can be overcrowded. A stroll through Bourton takes you past stone cottages, many converted to small stores and fish-and-chips and tea shops.

GETTING HERE AND AROUND

Bourton-on-the-Water is served by Pulham's Coaches from Stow-on-the-Wold, Moreton-in-Marsh, Cirencester, and Cheltenham. By car, take A40 and A436 from Cheltenham. You may find parking in the center, but if not use the lot outside the village.

ESSENTIALS

Visitor Information Bourton-on-the-Water Visitor Information Centre. ✉ *Victoria St.* ☎ *01451/820211* 🌐 *www.bourtoninfo.com.*

EXPLORING

FAMILY **Cotswold Motoring Museum and Toy Collection.** Housed in an old mill and marked by a topiary vintage Mini car, this museum has seven rooms crammed to the rafters with more than 30 shiny vintage and classic cars, delightful caravans from the 1920s and 1960s, ancient motorbikes and bicycles, road signs from past times, and a shepherd's hut on wheels. If this and the assortment of motoring memorabilia is not enough, there are also children's toys, pedal cars, models, and board games. ✉ *The Old Mill, Sherborne St.* ☎ *01451/821255* 🌐 *www.boundless.co.uk/save-more/boundless-cotswold-motoring-museum* 🎟 *£5.75* 🕒 *Closed mid-Dec.–mid-Feb.*

FAMILY **Model Village.** Built in 1937, this knee-high model of Bourton-on-the-Water took five years to complete. As you walk down its tiny lanes, you'll see how little has changed over the past decades. The small exhibition at Miniature World shows miniature scenes and rooms; some you can make come to life. ✉ *Old New Inn, High St.* ☎ *01451/820467* 🌐 *www.themodelvillage.com* 🎟 *£3.60; Miniature World £1.*

WHERE TO EAT AND STAY

$ BRITISH 🍴 **Rose Tree.** Plain wooden tables and understated decor are the setting for the wholesome British dishes served in this traditional restaurant beautifully sited on the banks of the Windrush with a large outdoor area. Sip a cocktail on the riverside terrace while you wait for your order. **Known for:** beautiful riverside setting; classic ploughman's lunches; locally sourced food. [$] *Average main: £14* ✉ *Victoria St.* ☎ *01451/820635* 🌐 *www.therosetreeinbourton.co.uk* 🕒 *Closed Mon. No dinner Sun.*

$$ HOTEL 🏨 **Chester House Hotel.** Just steps from the River Windrush, this traditional stone building has been tastefully adapted with contemporary fittings and style. **Pros:** friendly staff; stylish rooms; ideal location for exploring the area. **Cons:** busy on weekends; coach-house rooms overlook car park; limited parking. [$] *Rooms from: £110* ✉ *Victoria St.* ☎ *01451/820286* 🌐 *www.chesterhousehotel.com* 🛏 *22 rooms* 🍽 *Free Breakfast.*

SHOPPING

Cotswold Perfumery. This popular shop carries many perfumes that are manufactured on the premises by hand, and also stocks perfume bottles, diffusers, and essential oils, as well as jewelry. Classes are also available onsite for those who want to learn to mix their own perfume. ✉ *Victoria St.* ☎ *01451/820698* 🌐 *www.cotswold-perfumery.co.uk* 🎟 *Factory tour £5.*

LOWER SLAUGHTER AND UPPER SLAUGHTER

2 miles north of Bourton-on-the-Water, 15 miles east of Cheltenham.

Fodor's Choice ★ To see the quieter, more typical Cotswold villages, seek out the evocatively named Lower Slaughter and Upper Slaughter (the names have nothing to do with mass murder, but come from the Saxon word *sloh,* which means "a marshy place"). Lower Slaughter is one of the "water villages," with Slaughter Brook running down the center road of the town. Little stone footbridges cross the brook, and the town's resident gaggle of geese can often be seen paddling through the sparkling water. Nearby, Lower and Upper Swell are two other quiet towns to explore.

GETTING HERE AND AROUND

The Slaughters are best explored by car.

EXPLORING

Warden's Way. Connecting the two Slaughters is the Warden's Way, a mile-long pathway that begins in Upper Slaughter at the town-center parking lot and passes stone houses, green meadows, ancient trees, and a 19th-century corn mill with a waterwheel and brick chimney. The Warden's Way continues south to Bourton-on-the-Water; the full walk from Winchcombe to Bourton is 14 miles. You can pick up maps from local tourist offices. ✉ *Lower Slaughter.*

WHERE TO STAY

$$$$ HOTEL

🏨 **Lords of the Manor Hotel.** You'll find refinement and a warm welcome in this rambling 17th-century manor house with Victorian additions, tucked away in a quintessential Cotswold village. **Pros:** heavenly setting; understated elegance; outstanding food. **Cons:** some rooms on the small side; limited Wi-Fi; packages book up quickly. [$] *Rooms from: £225* ✉ *Off A429, Upper Slaughter* ☎ *01451/820243* 🌐 *www.lordsofthemanor.com* 🛏 *26 rooms* 🍴 *Free Breakfast.*

BURFORD

9 miles east of Northleach, 18 miles north of Swindon, 18 miles west of Oxford.

Burford's broad main street leads steeply down to a narrow bridge across the River Windrush. The village served as a stagecoach stop for centuries and has many historic inns; it's now a popular stop for tour buses and seekers of antiques.

GETTING HERE AND AROUND

Burford can be easily reached by bus from Oxford and Northleach. Once here, it's easy to stroll around. Drivers should park as soon as possible; there are possibilities on and off High Street.

ESSENTIALS

Visitor Information Burford Visitor Information Centre. ✉ *33A High St.* ☎ *01993/823558* 🌐 *www.oxfordshirecotswolds.org.*

EXPLORING

St. John the Baptist. Hidden away at the end of a lane at the bottom of High Street is the splendid parish church of St. John the Baptist, its interior a warren of arches, chapels, and shrines. The church was remodeled in the 15th century from Norman beginnings. Among the monuments is one dedicated to Henry VIII's barber, Edmund Harman, that depicts four Amazonian Indians; it's said to be the first depiction of native people from the Americas in Britain. Also look for the elaborate Tanfield monument and the grave of Christopher Kempster, master mason to Christopher Wren during the rebuilding of St. Paul's Cathedral in London. ✉ *Lawrence La.* ☎ *01993/823788* 🌐 *www.burfordchurch.org* 🎟 *Suggested donation £2.*

WHERE TO EAT AND STAY

$$ MODERN BRITISH

🍴 **The Angel at Burford.** At this informal eatery in a 16th-century coaching inn, the farmhouse-style tables are filled with traditional dishes with locally sourced ingredients. The secluded garden is the perfect place to enjoy lunchtime baguettes or sandwiches in nice weather.

Blue skies, stone buildings, a peaceful brook: villages such as Upper Slaughter demonstrate the enduring appeal of the Cotswolds.

Known for: fantastic steaks and other meats; relaxed and informal atmosphere; beautiful garden. [$] *Average main: £16* ✉ *14 Witney St.* ☎ *01993/822714* 🌐 *www.theangelatburford.co.uk*.

$$$ HOTEL 🏨 **The Lamb Inn.** Step through the door of this ancient coaching inn and be greeted by huge flagstones, gateleg tables, armchairs, and a roaring fire, then wind your way along the tartan carpet through creaking passages and stairways to the immaculate and cozy bedrooms. **Pros:** idyllic location; attentive service; historical building. **Cons:** some rooms are small; some street parking; very pet-friendly, so not for non-dog lovers. [$] *Rooms from: £165* ✉ *Sheep St.* ☎ *01993/823155* 🌐 *www.cotswold-inns-hotels.co.uk* 🛏 *17 rooms* 🍴 *Free Breakfast.*

BIBURY

10 miles southwest of Burford, 6 miles northeast of Cirencester, 15 miles north of Swindon.

The tiny town of Bibury, with a population of less than 1,000, sits idyllically beside the little River Coln on B4425; it was famed Arts and Crafts designer William Morris's choice for Britain's most beautiful village. Fine old cottages, a river meadow, and the church of St. Mary's are some of the delights here.

GETTING HERE AND AROUND

There are a few buses to Bibury operated on weekdays only by Pulham's Coaches from Cirencester which continue on to Bourton-on-the-Water. You'll need a car to reach Chedworth Roman Villa.

EXPLORING

Arlington Row. The town has a famously pretty and much-photographed group of 17th-century weavers' cottages made of stone. ✉ *Bibury.*

FAMILY **Chedworth Roman Villa.** The remains of a mile of walls are what's left of one of the largest Roman villas in England, beautifully set in a wooded valley on the eastern fringe of the Cotswolds. Thirty-two rooms, including two complete bath suites, have been identified, and covered walkways take you over the colorful mosaics, some of the most complete in England. Audio guides are available, and there's a small museum. Look out for the rare large snails, fattened on milk and herbs during Roman times, in the grounds; they come out on warm, wet days. There's a café here, but it's also an ideal place for a picnic. ■ **TIP→ Look carefully for the signs for the villa: from Bibury, go across A429 to Yanworth and Chedworth. The villa is also signposted from A40. Roads are narrow.** The site is 6 miles northwest of Bibury and 10 miles southeast of Cheltenham. ✉ *Off A429, Yanworth* ☎ *01242/890256* 🌐 *www.nationaltrust.org.uk* 🎫 *£9* 🕓 *Closed Nov.–mid-Feb.*

WHERE TO STAY

$$$ HOTEL 🏨 **Swan Hotel.** Few inns can boast of a more idyllic setting than this mid-17th-century coaching inn, originally a row of cottages on the banks of the gently flowing River Coln. **Pros:** idyllic spot; helpful staff; tasty local food. **Cons:** busy with day-trippers, and wedding parties on weekends; most standard rooms lack views; not enough electrical plugs in rooms. [$] *Rooms from: £190* ✉ *B4425* ☎ *01285/740695* 🌐 *www.cotswold-inns-hotels.co.uk* 🛏 *22 rooms* 🍴 *Free Breakfast.*

CIRENCESTER

6 miles southwest of Bibury, 9 miles south of Chedworth, 14 miles southeast of Cheltenham.

A hub of the Cotswolds since Roman times, when it was called Corinium, Cirencester (pronounced *siren*-sester) was second only to London in importance. Today this old market town is the area's largest, with a population of 19,000. It sits at the intersection of two major Roman roads, the Fosse Way and Ermin Street (now A429 and A417). In the Middle Ages Cirencester grew rich on wool, which funded its 15th-century parish church. It preserves many mellow stone buildings dating mainly from the 17th and 18th centuries and bow-fronted shops that still have one foot in the past.

GETTING HERE AND AROUND

Cirencester has hourly bus service from Cheltenham and less frequent service from Moreton-in-Marsh, Tetbury, and Kemble (for rail links). By road, the town can be accessed on A417, A419, and A429. Its compact center is easily walkable.

ESSENTIALS

Visitor Information Cirencester Visitor Information Centre. ✉ *Corinium Museum, Park St.* ☎ *01285/654180* 🌐 *www.cirencester.gov.uk.*

EXPLORING

FAMILY
Fodor's Choice
★
Corinium Museum. Not much of the Roman town remains visible, but the museum displays an outstanding collection of Roman artifacts, including jewelry and coins, as well as mosaic pavements and full-scale reconstructions of local Roman interiors. Spacious and light-filled galleries that explore the town's history in Roman and Anglo-Saxon times and in the 18th century include plenty of hands-on exhibits for kids. ✉ *Park St.* ☎ *01285/655611* 🌐 *www.coriniummuseum.org* 🎫 *£5.40.*

St. John the Baptist. At the top of Market Place is this magnificent Gothic parish church, known as the cathedral of the "woolgothic" style. Its gleaming, elaborate, three-tier, three-bay south porch is the largest in England and once served as the town hall. The chantry chapels and many coats of arms bear witness to the importance of the wool merchants as benefactors of the church. A rare example of a delicate 15th-century wineglass pulpit sits in the nave. ✉ *Market Pl.* ☎ *01285/659317* 🌐 *www.cirenparish.co.uk* 🎫 *£3 donation suggested.*

WHERE TO EAT AND STAY

$$
BRITISH
🍴 **The Fleece.** This 17th-century inn retains its historic past while serving fabulous modern food, real ales, and gin cocktails. Choose from a wide range of dishes including venison, steak, and seafood, or the varied selections on the daily specials board. **Known for:** lots of locals; real ales on tap; cool history with plenty of famous guests. [$] *Average main: £16* ✉ *Market Pl.* ☎ *01285/ 658507* 🌐 *www.thwaites.co.uk/hotels-and-inns/inns/fleece-at-cirencester.*

$$$
HOTEL
🏨 **Barnsley House.** A honey-and-cream Georgian mansion, the former home of garden designer Rosemary Verey has been discreetly modernized and converted into a luxurious retreat without sacrificing its essential charm. **Pros:** romantic setting; great attention to detail; beautiful gardens. **Cons:** some rooms at the top of three flights of stairs; no kids under 14; farm next door not for everyone. [$] *Rooms from: £219* ✉ *B4425, Barnsley* ☎ *01285/740000* 🌐 *www.barnsleyhouse.com* 🛏 *18 rooms* 🍽 *Free Breakfast.*

$
B&B/INN
🏨 **Ivy House.** Delicious breakfasts, hospitable owners, and reasonable rates enhance a stay at this stone Victorian house, close to the center of town. **Pros:** homemade granola at breakfast; child-friendly atmosphere; easy 10-minute walk to town center. **Cons:** on a main road; rooms can be the small side; some ground-floor rooms can be viewed by passing pedestrians. [$] *Rooms from: £95* ✉ *2 Victoria Rd.* ☎ *01285/656626* 🌐 *www.ivyhousecotswolds.com* 🛏 *4 rooms* 🍽 *Free Breakfast.*

SHOPPING

Corn Hall. This is the venue for a home, garden, and fashion market Monday through Thursday, an antiques market on Friday, and a crafts market on Saturday. ✉ *Market Pl.* 🌐 *www.cornhallcirencester.com.*

Makers and Designers Emporium. Better known as MADE, this shop is a cornucopia of unusual designer items, including stationery, textiles, housewares, toys, and jewelry. ✉ *9 Silver St.* ☎ *01285/658225* 🌐 *www.made-gallery.com.*

Market Place. Every Monday and Friday, Cirencester's central Market Place is packed with stalls selling a motley assortment of goods, mainly household items but some local produce and crafts, too. A farmers' market takes place here every second and fourth Saturday of the month. ✉ *Cirencester.*

PAINSWICK

16 miles northwest of Cirencester, 8 miles southwest of Cheltenham, 5 miles south of Gloucester.

Fodor's Choice ★ An old Cotswold wool town of around 2,000 inhabitants, Painswick has become a chocolate-box picture of quaintness, attracting day-trippers and tour buses. But come during the week and you can discover the place in relative tranquility. The huddled gray-stone houses and inns date from as early as the 14th century and include a notable group from the Georgian era. It's worth a stroll through the churchyard of St. Mary's, renowned for its table tombs and monuments and its 100 yew trees planted in 1792. The Cotswold Way passes near the center of the village, making it easy to take a pleasant walk in the countryside.

GETTING HERE AND AROUND

Painswick is on A46 between Stroud and Cheltenham. Stagecoach runs hourly bus connections with Stroud (15 minutes) and Cheltenham (35 minutes), with reduced service on Sunday.

ESSENTIALS

Visitor Information Painswick Visitor Information Centre. ✉ *Grave Diggers Hut, St. Mary's Church* ☎ *01452/812478* 🌐 *www.painswicktouristinfo.co.uk.*

EXPLORING

Painswick Rococo Garden. Half a mile north of town, this delightful garden is a rare survivor from the exuberant rococo period of English garden design (1720–60). After 50 years in its original form, the 6-acre garden became overgrown. Fortunately, the rediscovery of a 1748 painting of the garden by local artist Thomas Robins sparked a full-scale restoration in the 1980s. Now you can view the original structures—such as the pretty Gothic Eagle House and curved Exedra—take in the asymmetrical vistas, and try the modern maze, which, unusually, has three centers you can discover. It's also famous for the snowdrops that bloom in January and February. There's a restaurant and a shop, too. ✉ *B4073* ☎ *01452/813204* 🌐 *www.rococogarden.org.uk* 🎟 *£7.50* 🕒 *Closed Oct.–mid-Jan.*

WHERE TO EAT AND STAY

$$ BRITISH 🍴 **Falcon Inn.** With views of the church of St. Mary's, this historic pub dating from 1554 offers a reassuringly traditional and charming milieu for food and refreshment. Light meals are available at lunchtime, teas in the afternoon, and for the evening meal you might start with deep-fried calamari and whitebait with caper sauce, then try the rump of lamb with minted mashed potato for your main course. **Known for:** traditional British food; beautiful views; plenty of history. [$] *Average main: £15* ✉ *New St.* ☎ *01452/814222* 🌐 *www.falconpainswick.co.uk.*

7

$ HOTEL **Cardynham House.** In the heart of the village, this 15th- to 16th-century former wool merchant's house, which retains its beamed ceilings, Jacobean staircase, and Elizabethan fireplace, has four-poster beds in almost all of its rooms. **Pros:** romantic and quirky; great food in restaurant; tasty breakfasts. **Cons:** some low ceilings; mainly small bathrooms; no Wi-Fi in rooms. [$] *Rooms from: £90* ✉ *The Cross, Tibbiwell St.* ☎ *01452/814006, 01452/810030 restaurant* 🌐 *www.cardynham.co.uk* *9 rooms* 🍴 *Free Breakfast.*

TETBURY

12 miles south of Painswick, 8 miles southwest of Cirencester.

With about 5,300 inhabitants, Tetbury claims royal connections. Indeed, the soaring spire of the church that presides over this Elizabethan market town is within sight of Highgrove House, the Prince of Wales's abode. The house isn't open to the public, but you can book well in advance for a tour of the gardens. Tetbury is known as one of the area's antiques centers.

GETTING HERE AND AROUND

Tetbury is connected to Cirencester by buses operated by Cotswold Green. There are no Sunday services. It's easy to stroll around the compact town.

ESSENTIALS

Visitor Information Tetbury Tourist Information Centre. ✉ *33 Church St.* ☎ *01666/503552* 🌐 *www.visittetbury.co.uk.*

EXPLORING

Chavenage. Tall gate piers and spreading trees frame the family-owned Chavenage, a gray Cotswold-stone Elizabethan manor house. The tour includes a room with fine tapestries, where Cromwell lodged during the Civil War, and a main hall with minstrels' gallery and spy holes. The house is 2 miles northwest of Tetbury. It has recently been used as a filming location for the popular television show *Poldark.* ✉ *Between B4104 and A4135* ☎ *01666/502329* 🌐 *www.chavenage.com* 🎟 *£10* ⏲ *Closed Oct.–Apr., Mon.–Wed., and Sat.*

Fodor's Choice ★ **Highgrove House.** Highgrove House is the much-loved country home of Prince Charles and Camilla, Duchess of Cornwall. Here the prince has been making the 37-acre estate his personal showcase for traditional and organic growing methods and conservation of native plants and animals since 1980. Joining a tour of 26 people, you can appreciate the amazing industry on the part of the royal gardeners who have created the orchards, kitchen garden, and woodland garden almost from nothing. Look for the stumpery, the immaculate and quirky topiaries, and the national collection of hostas. You can sample the estate's produce in the restaurant and shop, or from its retail outlet in Tetbury. Tickets go on sale in February and sell out quickly, though extra dates are released through the year via a mailing list. Be sure to book well ahead. Allow three to four hours for a visit to the garden, which is 1½ miles southwest of Tetbury. Those under 12 aren't permitted. ✉ *Off A433*

☎ *0300/123–7310 tours* 🌐 *www.highgrovegardens.com* 🎟 *£27.50, pre-booked only* 🕓 *Closed late Oct.–early Apr.*

Rodmarton Manor. One of the last English country houses constructed using traditional methods and materials, Rodmarton Manor (built 1909–29) is furnished with specially commissioned pieces in the Arts and Crafts style. Ernest Barnsley, a follower of William Morris, worked on the house and gardens. The notable gardens—wild, winter, sunken, and white—are divided into "rooms" bounded by hedges of holly, beech, and yew. The manor is 5 miles northeast of Tetbury. ✉ *Off A433, Rodmarton* ☎ *01285/841442* 🌐 *www.rodmarton-manor.co.uk* 🎟 *£8; garden only £5* 🕓 *Closed Oct.–Mar., Sun.–Tues., Thurs., and Fri.*

FAMILY **Westonbirt National Arboretum.** Spread over 600 acres and with 17 miles of paths, this arboretum contains one of the most extensive collections of trees and shrubs in Europe. A lovely place to spend an hour or two, it's 3 miles southwest of Tetbury and 10 miles north of Bath. The best times to come for color are in late spring, when the rhododendrons, azaleas, and magnolias are blooming, and in fall, when the maples come into their own. Open-air concerts take place in summer, and there are exhibitions throughout the year. A gift shop, café, and restaurant are on the grounds. ✉ *Off A433* ☎ *0300/067–4890* 🌐 *www.forestry.gov.uk/westonbirt* 🎟 *£10 Mar.–Nov.; £7 Dec.–Feb.*

WHERE TO EAT AND STAY

$ MODERN BRITISH 🍴 **The Royal Oak.** This mellow-stone gabled pub, located in the snug village of Leighterton just 5 miles west of Tetbury, likes to satisfy the good crowd that assembles here with the best local fare in the area. Draw up a stool at the bar or take a kitchen chair at one of the many wooden tables to try the squid, chorizo, and tomato stew, or cauliflower, squash, and chickpea tagine. **Known for:** traditional English country pub; huge desserts; walled garden for summer dining. [$] *Average main: £14* ✉ *1 The Street, Leighterton* ☎ *0166/890250* 🌐 *www.royaloakleighterton.co.uk* 🕓 *No dinner Sun.*

$$$$ HOTEL FAMILY Fodor's Choice ★ 🏨 **Calcot Manor.** In an ideal world everyone would sojourn in this oasis of opulence at least once; however, the luxury never gets in the way of the overall air of relaxation, a tribute to the warmth and efficiency of the staff. **Pros:** delightful rural setting; excellent spa facilities; children love it. **Cons:** all but 12 rooms are separate from main building; some traffic noise; steep prices. [$] *Rooms from: £250* ✉ *A4135* ☎ *01666/890391* 🌐 *www.calcotmanor.co.uk* 🛏 *35 rooms* 🍽 *Free Breakfast.*

SHOPPING

Highgrove Shop. This pleasant, though pricey, shop sells organic products and gifts inspired by Prince Charles's gardens. ✉ *10 Long St.* ☎ *0333/222–4555* 🌐 *www.highgrovegardens.com/shop.html.*

House of Cheese. Farm-produced cheeses, all wonderfully fresh and flavorsome, are on offer at the House of Cheese. Pâtés, preserves, and olive-wood cheese boards are other goodies at this tiny shop. ✉ *13 Church St.* ☎ *01666/502865* 🌐 *www.houseofcheese.co.uk.*

Long Street Antiques. This spacious and elegant shop in a Georgian building offers everything from jewelry and kitchenalia to oak and mahogany furniture. ⊠ *14 Long St.* ☎ *01666/500850* ⊕ *www.longstreetantiques.com.*

STRATFORD-UPON-AVON AND AROUND

The countryside around Stratford is marked by gentle hills, green fields, slow-moving rivers, quiet villages, and time-burnished halls, churches, and castles (Warwick and Kenilworth are the best examples and well worth visiting). Historic houses such as moated Baddesley Clinton and Packwood House Court are another reason to explore. All the sights are close enough to Stratford-upon-Avon that you can easily use the town as a base if you wish.

STRATFORD-UPON-AVON

Even under the weight of busloads of visitors, Stratford, on the banks of the slow-flowing River Avon, has somehow hung on to much of its ancient character and, on a good day, can still feel like an English market town. It doesn't take long to figure out who's the center of attention here. Born in a half-timber, early-16th-century building in the center of Stratford on April 23, 1564, William Shakespeare died on April 23, 1616, his 52nd birthday, in a more imposing house at New Place, also in the center of Stratford. Although he spent much of his life in London, the world still associates him with his hometown, so much so that the town's river is sometimes referred to as "Shakespeare's Avon."

Here, in the years between his birth and 1587, he played as a young lad, attended grammar school, and married Anne Hathaway; and here he returned as a prosperous man. You can see Shakespeare's whole life here: his birthplace on Henley Street; his burial place in Holy Trinity Church; the home of his wife, Anne Hathaway's Cottage; the home of his mother, Mary Arden's Farm, at Wilmcote; New Place; and Hall's Croft, the home of Shakespeare's daughter Susanna, her husband, Dr. John Hall, and their daughter Elizabeth.

By the 16th century, Stratford was a prosperous market town with thriving guilds and industries. Half-timber houses from this era have been preserved, and they're set off by later architecture, such as the elegant Georgian storefronts on Bridge Street, with their 18th-century porticoes and arched doorways.

Most sights cluster around Henley Street (off the roundabout as you come in on the A3400 Birmingham road), the High Street, and Waterside, which skirts the public gardens through which the River Avon flows. Bridge Street and the parallel Sheep Street are Stratford's main thoroughfares and where you will find mostly banks, shops, and eateries. Bridgefoot, between the canal and the river, is next to Clopton Bridge, built in the 15th century by Sir Hugh Clopton, once lord mayor of London and one of Stratford's richest and most philanthropic residents.

GETTING HERE AND AROUND

Stratford lies about 100 miles northwest of London; take the M40 to Junction 15. The town is 35 miles southeast of Birmingham by the A38, M6, M42 ,and M40 (Junction 16).

Chiltern Railways serves the area from London's Marylebone Station and takes on average two hours; some are direct but most have one change. West Midlands trains operates direct routes from Birmingham's Snow Hill Station (journey time under an hour). Stratford has two stations, Stratford-upon-Avon Parkway, northwest of the center at Bishopston, and Stratford-upon-Avon at the edge of the town center on Alcester Road, from where it is a short walk into town.

TOURS

Fodor's Choice ★ **City Sightseeing.** These double-decker tour buses offer two options: a hop-on, hop-off bus tour that allows you to create your own itinerary around 11 landmarks in and around the town, and a six-hour marathon that takes in all five of the Shakespeare family homes. ☎ *01789/299123* ⊕ *www.city-sightseeing.com/en/100/stratford-upon-avon* ⌦ *From £14.*

Fodor's Choice ★ **Shakespeare Birthplace Trust.** The main places of Shakespearean interest (Anne Hathaway's Cottage, Hall's Croft, Mary Arden's House, Shakespeare's New Place, and Shakespeare's Birthplace) are run by the Shakespeare Birthplace Trust, an independent charity that aims to preserve and promote the properties. By far the most economical way to visit the properties is to get a Full Story ticket (£20.25), which gives unlimited access to all five houses for a year. ☎ *01789/204016* ⊕ *www.shakespeare.org.uk.*

ESSENTIALS

Visitor Information Stratford-upon-Avon Tourist Information Centre. ⊠ *Bridgefoot* ☎ *01789/264293* ⊕ *www.visitstratforduponavon.co.uk.*

EXPLORING

Fodor's Choice ★ **Anne Hathaway's Cottage.** The most picturesque of the Shakespeare Birthplace Trust properties, this thatched cottage on the western outskirts of Stratford is the family home of the woman Shakespeare married in 1582. The "cottage," actually a substantial Tudor farmhouse with latticed windows, is astonishingly beautiful. Inside it is surprisingly cozy with lots of period furniture, including the settle where Shakespeare reputedly conducted his courtship, and a rare carved Elizabethan bed. The cottage garden is planted in lush Edwardian style with herbs and flowers. Wildflowers are currently being grown in the adjacent orchard (a nod to what was grown in the garden in the Hathaways' time), and the neighboring arboretum has trees, shrubs, and roses mentioned in Shakespeare's works. ■ TIP➔ The best way to get here is on foot, especially in late spring when the apple trees are in blossom. The signed path runs from Evesham Place (an extension of Grove Road) opposite Chestnut Walk. Pick up a leaflet with a map from the tourist office; the walk takes 25–30 minutes. ⊠ *Cottage La.* ☎ *01789/338532* ⊕ *www.shakespeare.org.uk* ⌦ *£11.25; Full Story ticket £20.25, includes entry to Hall's Croft, Mary Arden's Farm, Shakespeare's New Place, and Shakespeare's Birthplace.*

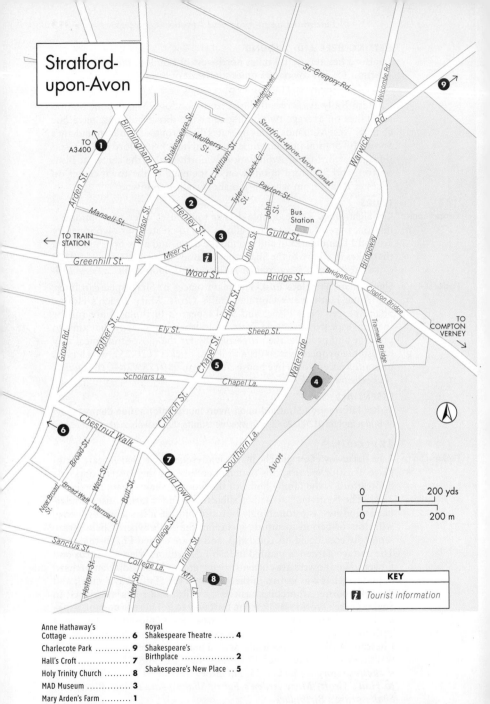

Stratford-upon-Avon

TO A3400 ❶

Birmingham Rd.

Arden St.

Mansell St.

TO TRAIN STATION ←

Greenhill St.

Grove Rd.

Windsor St.

Shakespeare St.

Mulberry St.

Gt. William St.

Tyler St.

Lock Ct.

Meadenhead Rd.

St. Gregory Rd.

Welcombe Rd.

❾ ↗

Warwick Rd.

Stratford-upon-Avon Canal

Payton St.

John St.

Bus Station

Henley St.

❷

❸ MAD Museum

Meer St.

🛈

Union St.

Guild St.

Wood St.

Bridge St.

Bridgefoot

Bridgeway

Clopton Bridge

TO COMPTON VERNEY ↘

High St.

Rother St.

Ely St.

Sheep St.

Chapel St.

Waterside

Tramway Bridge

❺

Scholars La.

Chapel La.

❹

Church St.

Chestnut Walk

❻ ←

Broad St.

Meer St.

Bull St.

Southern La.

Avon

❼

New Broad St.

Broad Walk

Narrow La.

Old Town

0 ─── 200 yds
0 ─── 200 m

Sanctus St.

College St.

Hollom

New St.

College La.

Trinity St.

Mill La.

❽

KEY
🛈 Tourist information

Charlecote Park. A celebrated house in the village of Hampton Lucy just outside Stratford, Charlecote Park is a Prodigy house, built in 1558 by Sir Thomas Lucy to impress Queen Elizabeth I (the house is even shaped like the letter 'E' in her honor). Shakespeare knew the house—he was supposedly even caught poaching deer here. Overlooking the River Avon, the redbrick manor is striking and sprawling. It was renovated in neo-Elizabethan style by the Lucy family, represented here by numerous portraits, during the mid-19th century; a carved ebony bed is one of many spectacular pieces of furniture. The Tudor gatehouse is unchanged since Shakespeare's day, and a collection of carriages, a Victorian kitchen, and a small brewery occupy the outbuildings. Indulge in a game of croquet near the quirky, thatched, Victorian-era summer hut, or explore the deer park landscaped by Lancelot "Capability" Brown. Interesting themed tours and walks take place in summer—call in advance to find out what's on offer. The house is 5 miles northeast of Stratford; by car it is reached via the B4086. ⊠ *Wellesbourne, Warwick* ☎ *01789/470277* ⊕ *www.nationaltrust.org.uk* 🎫 *£12.60; winter admission to grounds and outbuildings £8.40* ☉ *House closed mid-Dec.–mid-Feb.*

Hall's Croft. One of the finest surviving Jacobean (early 17th century) town houses in England, this impressive residence (one of the best preserved of the Shakespeare family homes) has a delightful walled garden and was once the home of Shakespeare's eldest daughter, Susanna, and her husband, Dr. John Hall. John Hall was a wealthy physician who, by prescribing an herbal cure for scurvy, was well ahead of his time. One room is furnished as a medical dispensary of the period, and throughout the building are fine examples of heavy oak Jacobean furniture, including a child's high chair and some 17th-century portraits. The café serves light lunches and afternoon teas. ⊠ *Old Town* ☎ *01789/338533* ⊕ *www.shakespeare.org.uk* 🎫 *£7.65; Full Story ticket £20.25 includes Anne Hathaway's Cottage and Gardens, Shakespeare's Birthplace, Shakespeare's New Place, and Mary Arden's Farm.*

Holy Trinity Church. This 13th-century church on the banks of the River Avon is the final resting place of William Shakespeare. He was buried here not because he was a famed poet but because he was a lay rector of Stratford, owning a portion of the township tithes. On the north wall of the sanctuary, over the altar steps, is the famous marble bust created by Gerard Jansen in 1623 and thought to be a true likeness of Shakespeare. The bust offers a more human, even humorous, perspective when viewed from the side. Also in the chancel are the graves of Shakespeare's wife, Anne; his daughter, Susanna; his son-in-law, John Hall; and his granddaughter's first husband, Thomas Nash. Also here is the christening font in which Shakespeare was baptized. ⊠ *Old Town* ☎ *01789/266316* ⊕ *www.stratford-upon-avon.org* 🎫 *£3 donation requested.*

FAMILY **MAD Museum.** Push buttons and pedals to your heart's content to make the exhibits in the Mechanical Art & Design Museum come alive. Witty, beautiful, and intricate automata and examples of kinetic art will clank, whir, and rattle away. Marbles and Ping-Pong balls thread and bounce through looping runs, a typewriter plays tunes on glasses and bottles, and two trains chuff around high up on the walls. Kids will love constructing their own marble run, and grown-ups will marvel at the Kitchenator display. There's also a shop full of weird and wonderful things to buy. ✉ *4–5 Henley St.* 🕾 *01789/269356* 🌐 *www. themadmuseum.co.uk* 🎫 *£7.80.*

FAMILY
Fodor'sChoice
★
Mary Arden's Farm. This charming working farm was the childhood home of Shakespeare's mother, Mary Arden, and offers great insight into the farming methods employed in Tudor England. The rural heritage attraction, just 3 miles outside Stratford, is great for kids, who can try their hand at basket weaving and gardening, listen as the farmers explain their work in the fields, watch the cooks prepare food in the Tudor farmhouse kitchen, or play in the amazing timber-framed adventure playground. There are also daily falconry and archery displays and opportunities to meet the farm animals, as well as a good café. ✉ *Station Rd., Wilmcote* 🕾 *01789/338535* 🌐 *www.shakespeare.org. uk* 🎫 *£14; Full Story ticket £20.25, includes Anne Hathaway's Cottage and Gardens, Hall's Croft, Shakespeare's New Place, and Shakespeare's Birthplace* ⊘ *Closed Nov.–mid-Mar.*

FAMILY
Fodor'sChoice
★
Royal Shakespeare Theatre. Overlooking Bancroft Gardens and with views along the River Avon, the Stratford home of the world-renowned Royal Shakespeare Company is undoubtedly one of the best places in the world to watch a Shakespearean play. The company has existed since 1879 and today boasts three Stratford venues: the Royal Shakespeare Theatre, the Swan Theatre (on the site of the original Shakespeare Memorial Theatre), and The Other Place. There's a great rooftop restaurant at the Royal Shakespeare Theatre, plus a popular Behind the Scenes tour. You can also ascend to the theater's tower, for a panoramic view of Stratford. ✉ *Waterside* 🕾 *01789/403493* 🌐 *www.rsc. org.uk* 🎫 *Behind the Scenes tour £8.50; tower £2.50.*

Fodor'sChoice
★
Shakespeare's Birthplace. A half-timber house typical of its time, the playwright's birthplace is a much-visited shrine that has been altered and restored since Shakespeare lived here. Passing through the modern visitor center, you are immersed in the world of Shakespeare through a state-of-the-art exhibition that includes evocative audio and visuals from contemporary stagings of his plays. The house itself is across the garden from the visitor center. Colorful wall decorations and furnishings reflect comfortable, middle-class Elizabethan domestic life; you can view his father's workshop and you can see the very room where Shakespeare was born. Mark Twain and Charles Dickens were both pilgrims here, and you can see the signatures of Thomas Carlyle and Walter Scott scratched into the windowpanes. In the garden, actors present excerpts from his plays. There's also a café and bookshop on the grounds. ✉ *Henley St.* 🕾 *01789/204016* 🌐 *www.shakespeare.org.uk* 🎫 *£15.75; Full Story ticket £20.25, includes Anne Hathaway's Cottage and Gardens, Hall's Croft, Shakespeare's New Place, and Mary Arden's Farm.*

Fodor'sChoice
★
Shakespeare's New Place. This is the spot where Shakespeare lived for the last 19 years of his life and where he wrote many of his plays, including *The Tempest.* Though the actual 15th-century building he inhabited was torn down in the 18th century, the site was imaginatively reinterpreted in 2016 as an outdoor space where the footprint of the original

house can be traced. Each of his 38 plays is represented by a pennant in the Golden Garden, and his sonnets are engraved into the stone paving. Highlights include a mulberry tree that some believe was given to Shakespeare by King James I and a restored Elizabethan knot garden. A permanent exhibition inside the neighboring Nash's House tells the story of the New House and Shakespeare's family life within it; there's also a roof terrace, which provides views of the gardens. Nash's House was once home to Thomas Nash, the husband of Shakespeare's granddaughter Elizabeth Hall. ✉ *22 Chapel St.* ☎ *01789/338536* 🌐 *www.shakespeare.org.uk* 🎫 *£11.25; Full Story ticket £20.25, includes Anne Hathaway's Cottage and Gardens, Shakespeare's Birthplace, Hall's Croft, and Mary Arden's Farm.*

WHERE TO EAT

$ BRITISH Fodor's Choice ★

🍴 **The Black Swan/The Dirty Duck.** The only pub in Britain to be licensed under two names (the more informal one came courtesy of American GIs who were stationed here during World War II), this is one of Stratford's most celebrated and consistently rated pubs, attracting actors since the 18th-century days of thespian David Garrick. Along with your pint of bitter, you can choose from the extensive menu of baked potatoes, steaks, burgers, and grills; there are also good-value light bites. **Known for:** classic English pub atmosphere; reservations-only for dinner; veranda overlooking the river. [$] *Average main: £12* ✉ *Waterside* ☎ *01789/297312* 🌐 *www.oldenglishinns.co.uk/our-locations/the-dirty-duck-stratford-upon-avon.*

$ INDIAN

🍴 **Hussain's.** The luxuriant marigolds in the window might draw you in, but locals will tell you it's the Indian dishes that are the real appeal here. The extensive menu lists plenty of balti and rogan josh choices; for a little less heat, try the tandoori chicken with mild spices, cream, ground almonds, and mixed fruits, or increase the heat a bit with *jhinga bhuna* (king-size prawns in a spicy tomato sauce with onions, green peppers, and coriander). **Known for:** range of tandoori specialties; local curry-house atmosphere; prompt, friendly service. [$] *Average main: £12* ✉ *6A Chapel St.* ☎ *01789/267506* 🌐 *www.hussains-restaurant.com* 🕒 *No lunch Mon.–Wed.*

$$ SOUTHERN ITALIAN Fodor's Choice ★

🍴 **Il Moro.** Chef Massimilliano Melis takes pride in serving up Italian dishes with a Sardinian emphasis in this slick, family-run restaurant. You could start with an aperitivo on the roof terrace (in summer), followed by fresh-pea-and- *fregola* (pasta made with semolina) soup, and then move on to pork with pecorino cheese, pancetta, and arugula salad. **Known for:** aperitivos on the roof terrace in summer only; Sardinian-style Italian food; location close to Shakespeare's Birthplace. [$] *Average main: £18* ✉ *27 Henley St., at Windsor St.* ☎ *01789/415770* 🌐 *www.ilmoro.co.uk* 🕒 *Closed Sun.*

$$ BRITISH Fodor's Choice ★

🍴 **Lambs of Sheep Street.** Sit downstairs to appreciate the hardwood floors and oak beams of this local epicurean favorite; upstairs, the look is a bit more contemporary. The updates of tried-and-true dishes include free-range pork belly with braised pig cheeks, and panfried calf's liver with creamed potato, wilted spinach, pancetta, and crisp shallot. **Known for:** good-value set meals; one of the oldest buildings in Stratford;

With its thatched roof, half-timbering, and countryside setting, Anne Hathaway's Cottage is a vision from the past.

modern twists on British classics. $ *Average main: £17* ⊠ *12 Sheep St.* ☎ *01789/292554* ⊕ *www.lambsrestaurant.co.uk* ⊘ *No lunch Mon.*

$$
MODERN BRITISH
Fodor's Choice
★

✕ **The Townhouse.** Theatergoers tucking into an early supper to the strains of the piano in the bar, grandmothers enjoying afternoon tea, and couples lingering over candlelit suppers can all happily be found at this restaurant with rooms on Church Street, which is part of the Brakspear Brewery. Chefs source the best ingredients locally where possible, and serve up dishes such as oven-roasted duck breast and whole grilled plaice. **Known for:** good-value pretheater menus; chic decor; Sunday roast with all the trimmings. $ *Average main: £16* ⊠ *16 Church St.* ☎ *01789/262222* ⊕ *www.stratfordtownhouse.co.uk.*

$
BISTRO

✕ **The Vintner.** The imaginative, bistro-inspired menu varies each day at this café and wine bar set in a 15th-century building. Tempting British and European-style dishes include confit leg of duck bigarade with dauphinoise potatoes, and seared beef fillet Stroganoff. **Known for:** inventive pretheater menu; historic setting; excellent wine list. $ *Average main: £14* ⊠ *4 and 5 Sheep St.* ☎ *01789/297259* ⊕ *www.thevintner.co.uk.*

WHERE TO STAY

$$
HOTEL
Fodor's Choice
★

🏨 **Arden Hotel.** Bedrooms are spacious and discreet with splashes of green, violet, and dark crimson in this redbrick boutique hotel across the road from the Royal Shakespeare Theatre. **Pros:** convenient for theatergoers; crisp and modern style; gorgeous guest areas. **Cons:** gets booked up quickly; may be too noisy for some; can be popular with business travelers. $ *Rooms from: £150* ⊠ *Waterside* ☎ *01789/298682* ⊕ *www.theardenhotelstratford.com* ⇄ *45 rooms* ⊙❘ *Free Breakfast.*

$$ 🖭 **Arden House.** This luxury guesthouse, sister property to the nearby
B&B/INN Arden Hotel, offers a first-class stay, with a help-yourself pantry, books
Fodor'sChoice to borrow, afternoon tea, and a daily gin o'clock. **Pros:** welcoming
★ atmosphere; free afternoon tea and gin; amazing breakfast selection.
Cons: hosts can seem overeager to please; no tea- and coffee-making
facilities in rooms; you may feel obliged to chat with other guests.
Ⓢ *Rooms from: £145* ✉ *58–59 Rother St.* ☎ *01789/298682* ⊕ *www.
theardenhotelstratford.com* ➫ *5 rooms* ⦿ *Some meals.*

$$ 🖭 **The Bell Alderminster.** Just a few miles south of Stratford, this "pub
B&B/INN with rooms" oozes imagination and individuality. **Pros:** rural setting,
close to the Cotswolds; excellent food; homemade biscuits and fresh
milk in the rooms. **Cons:** on a loud main road; bar can get busy; a
bit inconvenient for the Shakespeare attractions. Ⓢ *Rooms from: £125*
✉ *Shipston Rd., Alderminster* ☎ *01789/450414* ⊕ *www.thebellald.
co.uk* ➫ *9 rooms* ⦿ *Free Breakfast.*

$$$ 🖭 **Ettington Park Hotel.** This Victorian Gothic mansion, featuring arched
HOTEL windows and romantic turrets, is approached along a private avenue
and is a soothing retreat for theatergoers who want to escape Stratford's
crowds. **Pros:** gorgeous building; spacious rooms; relaxing lounge.
Cons: a bit too formal for some; well outside Stratford; a lot of wedding
guests on weekends. Ⓢ *Rooms from: £170* ✉ *Off A3400, Alderminster*
☎ *0845/072–7454* ⊕ *www.handpickedhotels.co.uk/hotels/ettington-
park-hotel* ➫ *48 rooms* ⦿ *Free Breakfast.*

$$$ 🖭 **Macdonald Alveston Manor.** This redbrick Elizabethan manor house
HOTEL across the River Avon has plenty of historic features, as well as a mod-
ern spa with a long list of treatments. **Pros:** a nice mix of the modern and
historic; award-winning restaurant; interesting theatrical history. **Cons:**
a lack of charm; no elevator and lots of stairs; fee for parking. Ⓢ *Rooms
from: £174* ✉ *Clopton Bridge* ☎ *0344/879–9138* ⊕ *www.macdonald-
hotels.co.uk/our-hotels/alveston* ➫ *113 rooms* ⦿ *Free Breakfast.*

$ 🖭 **Mercure Stratford-Upon-Avon Shakespeare Hotel.** Built in the 1400s, this
HOTEL Elizabethan town house in the heart of Stratford is a vision right out of
The Merry Wives of Windsor, with its nine gables and long, stunning,
black-and-white half-timber facade. **Pros:** historic building; relaxing
lounge; great food. **Cons:** some very small bedrooms; fee for parking; a
bit dated in places. Ⓢ *Rooms from: £95* ✉ *Chapel St.* ☎ *01789/294997*
⊕ *www.mercure.com* ➫ *78 rooms* ⦿ *No meals.*

$$ 🖭 **White Swan.** None of the character of this black-and-white timbered
HOTEL hotel, in one of Stratford's most historic buildings, has been lost in
its swanky but sympathetic update. **Pros:** great sense of history; large
bathrooms; friendly service. **Cons:** fee for parking, which is not on-
site; striped carpet can cause dizziness; Shakespeare motif can feel a bit
overdone. Ⓢ *Rooms from: £107* ✉ *Rother St.* ☎ *01789/297022* ⊕ *www.
white-swan-stratford.co.uk* ➫ *41 rooms* ⦿ *Free Breakfast.*

NIGHTLIFE AND PERFORMING ARTS
THEATER

Fodor'sChoice **Royal Shakespeare Company.** One of the finest repertory troupes in the
★ world and long the backbone of England's theatrical life, the Royal
Shakespeare Company (RSC) performs plays year-round in Stratford
and at venues across Britain. The stunning Royal Shakespeare Theatre,

7

home of the RSC, has a thrust stage based on the original Globe Theater in London. The Swan Theatre, part of the theater complex and also built in the style of Shakespeare's Globe, stages plays by Shakespeare and his contemporaries such as Christopher Marlowe and Ben Jonson, and contemporary works are staged at The Other Place nearby. Prices start from £5 for rehearsals and previews. ■ TIP➔ Seats book up fast, but day-of-performance and returned tickets are sometimes available. ⊠ *Waterside* ☎ *01789/403493* ⊕ *www.rsc.org.uk* ⊠ *From £10.*

SHOPPING

Antiques Centre. This building set in a Tudor courtyard contains around 50 stalls displaying jewelry, silver, linens, porcelain, and memorabilia. There's also a lovely tearoom next door. ⊠ *59–60 Ely St.*

B&W Thornton. Above Shakespeare's Birthplace, B&W Thornton stocks Moorcroft pottery and glass. ⊠ *23 Henley St.* ☎ *01789/269405* ⊕ *www. bwthornton.co.uk.*

Fodor'sChoice ★ **Chaucer Head Bookshop.** This is the best of Stratford's many secondhand bookshops and a great place to pick up books on British history and travel. ⊠ *21 Chapel St.* ☎ *01789/415691* ⊕ *www.chaucerhead.com.*

Fodor'sChoice ★ **Shakespeare Bookshop.** Run by the Shakespeare Birthplace, the Shakespeare Bookshop carries Elizabethan plays, Shakespeare studies, children's books, and general paraphernalia. ⊠ *Shakespeare's Birthplace, Henley St.* ☎ *01789/292176* ⊕ *www.shakespeare.org.uk/explore-shakespeare/bookshop.html.*

HENLEY-IN-ARDEN

8 miles northwest of Stratford.

A brief drive out of Stratford will take you under the Stratford-upon-Avon Canal aqueduct to pretty Henley-in-Arden, whose wide main street is an architectural pageant of many periods. This area was once the Forest of Arden, where Shakespeare set one of his greatest comedies, *As You Like It.* Among the buildings to look for are the former Guild Hall, dating from the 15th century, and the White Swan pub, built in the early 1600s. Near Henley-in-Arden are two stately homes worth a stop, Packwood House and Baddesley Clinton.

GETTING HERE AND AROUND

The town is on the A3400. West Midlands trains for Henley-in-Arden depart every hour from Stratford; the journey takes about 15 minutes. Train service from Birmingham Moor Street takes about 35 minutes, and trains leave every hour. The town heritage center is open from April through October.

ESSENTIALS

Visitor Information Henley-in-Arden Heritage Centre. ⊠ *Joseph Hardy House, 150 High St., Henley in Arden* ☎ *01564/795919* ⊕ *www.heritagehenley. org.uk.*

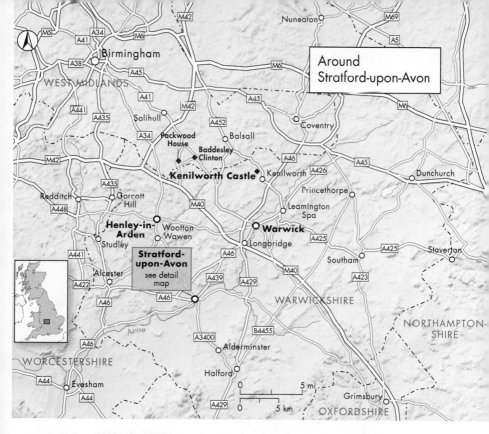

EXPLORING

Fodor'sChoice **Baddesley Clinton.** The eminent architectural historian Sir Nikolaus Pevs-
★ ner described this as "the perfect late medieval manor house" and it's
hard to argue with that assessment. The Tudor mansion, with its elegant
Queen Anne brick bridge reaching over the moat, is like something out
of a period drama. Set off a winding back-road, this grand manor dating
from the 15th century retains its great fireplaces, 17th-century paneling,
and three priest holes (secret chambers for Roman Catholic priests, who
were hidden by sympathizers when Catholicism was banned in the 16th
and 17th centuries). Admission to the house is by timed ticket; Baddesley Clinton is 2 miles east of Packwood House and 15 miles north
of Stratford-upon-Avon. ⊠ *Rising La., Knowle, Henley in Arden ✛ Off
A4141 near Chadwick End* ☎ *01564/783294* ⊕ *www.nationaltrust.org.
uk/baddesley-clinton* ⊠ *£11.45.*

Packwood House. Garden enthusiasts are drawn to Packwood's re-created 17th-century gardens, highlighted by an ambitious topiary Tudor
garden in which yew trees represent Jesus's Sermon on the Mount.
With tall chimneys, the house combines redbrick and half-timbering.
Exquisite collections of 16th-century furniture and tapestries in the
interior's 20th-century version of Tudor architecture make this one of
the area's finest historic houses open to the public. It's 5 miles north of

Henley-in-Arden and 12 miles north of Stratford-upon-Avon. ⊠ *Pack-wood La., Lapworth, Henley in Arden ⊹ Off B4439, 2 miles east of Hockley Heath* ☎ *01564/782024* ⊕ *www.nationaltrust.org.uk/pack-wood-house* ▨ *£11.45; £7.60 in winter.*

WARWICK

8 miles east of Henley-in-Arden, 4 miles south of Kenilworth, 9 miles northeast of Stratford-upon-Avon.

Most famous for Warwick Castle—that vision out of the feudal ages—the town of Warwick (pronounced *war*-ick) is an interesting architectural mix of Georgian redbrick and Elizabethan half-timbered buildings.

GETTING HERE AND AROUND
Frequent trains to Warwick leave London's Marylebone Station; travel time is about 90 minutes. The journey between Stratford-upon-Avon and Warwick takes around 40 minutes by train or bus. Stagecoach Bus X18 is more frequent, running every half hour.

ESSENTIALS
Visitor Information Warwick Tourist Information Centre. ⊠ *Court House, Jury St.* ☎ *01926/492212* ⊕ *www.visitwarwick.co.uk.*

EXPLORING
Collegiate Church of St. Mary. Crowded with gilded, carved, and painted tombs, the Beauchamp Chantry within this church is considered one of the finest medieval chapels in England. Despite the wealth of late-medieval and Tudor chivalry, the chapel was built in the 15th century in honor of the somewhat-less-than-chivalrous Richard de Beauchamp, who consigned Joan of Arc to burn at the stake. Alongside his impressive effigy in gilded bronze lie the fine tombs of Robert Dudley, Earl of Leicester, adviser and favorite of Queen Elizabeth I, and Dudley's brother Ambrose. The church's chancel, distinguished by its flying ribs, houses the alabaster table tomb of Thomas Beauchamp, one of the first knights of the Order of the Garter, and his wife.

In the Norman crypt, look for the rare ducking stool (a chair in which people were tied for public punishment). You can also climb St. Mary's Tower for views of Warwick Castle, just a five-minute walk away. ⊠ *Old Sq.* ☎ *01926/403940* ⊕ *www.stmaryswarwick.org.uk* ▨ *£2 donation suggested; tower £3.*

FAMILY

Fodor's Choice

★

Warwick Castle. The vast bulk of this medieval castle rests on a cliff overlooking the Avon River and is considered "the fairest monument of ancient and chivalrous splendor which yet remains uninjured by time," to use the words of Sir Walter Scott. Today the company that runs the Madame Tussauds wax museums owns the castle, and it has become more theme park than authentic heritage site, but it is still a lot of fun. Warwick's two soaring towers, bristling with battlements, can be seen for miles: the 147-foot-high Caesar's Tower, built in 1356, and the 128-foot-high Guy's Tower, built in 1380. Warwick Castle's monumental walls enclose an impressive armory of medieval weapons, as well as state rooms with historic furnishings and paintings. Other exhibits explore the castle's history through the ages, display the sights and sounds of a great medieval household as it prepares for an important battle, and tell the story of a princess's fairy-tale wedding. Be prepared both to play your part and be spooked in the gruesome dungeon experience (50 minutes and not recommended for under-10s) as you travel through scenes of torture, poisonings, and death sentences. Elsewhere, a working trebuchet (a kind of catapult), falconry displays, and rat-throwing (stuffed, not live) games add to the atmosphere. Below the castle, strutting peacocks patrol the 60 acres of grounds elegantly landscaped by Capability Brown in the 18th century. **■TIP→ Arrive early to beat the crowds. If you book online, you save 30% on ticket prices.** Lavish medieval banquets take place throughout the year, and plenty of food stalls serve lunch. For the ultimate castle experience, you can "glamp" (glamorously camp) in a medieval tent, stay in a wooden lodge in the Knight's Village, or spend the night in your own luxury suite in the 14th-century Caesar's Tower. ✉ *Castle La. off Mill St.* ☎ *01926/495421* 🌐 *www.warwick-castle.com* 🎟 *Castle £13, castle and dungeon £16.*

WHERE TO EAT AND STAY

$$
MODERN BRITISH
Fodor's Choice ★

🍴 **Rose & Crown.** Plain wood floorboards, comfy sofas, sturdy wooden tables, and solidly good food and drink set the tone at this contemporary gastro-pub with rooms on the town's main square. It's popular with locals, and the owners take pride in offering seasonal food that mixes British and international influences with only the best ingredients. **Known for:** seasonal produce; great pub; warm atmosphere. [$] *Average main: £16* ✉ *30 Market Pl.* ☎ *01926/411117* 🌐 *www.roseandcrown-warwick.co.uk.*

$$$
HOTEL
Fodor's Choice ★

🏨 **Mallory Court Country House Hotel and Spa.** This elegant country-house hotel 4 miles southeast of Warwick makes for a quiet, luxurious getaway; it has 43 rooms but still manages to make you feel like you're visiting friends (albeit very wealthy ones). **Pros:** good for pampering; excellent restaurant; real English country-house experience. **Cons:** outside town; lots of weekend weddings; some traffic noise. [$] *Rooms from: £212* ✉ *Harbury La., Bishops Tachbrook* ☎ *01926/330214* 🌐 *www.mallory.co.uk* 🛏 *43 rooms* 🍽 *Free Breakfast.*

KENILWORTH CASTLE

5 miles north of Warwick.

The sprawling, graceful red ruins of Kenilworth Castle loom over the green fields of Warwickshire, surrounded by the low grassy impression of what was once a lake.

GETTING HERE AND AROUND

The local Stagecoach company offers bus services to and from Stratford and Warwick on the X17 and X68 routes. The castle is 1½ miles from the town center.

ESSENTIALS

Visitor Information Kenilworth Library and Information Centre. ✉ *Kenilworth Library, 11 Smalley Pl., Kenilworth* ☎ *0300/555–8171* 🌐 *www.warwickshire.gov.uk/kenilworthlibrary.*

7

EXPLORING

Fodor's Choice ★ **Kenilworth Castle & Elizabethan Garden.** The romantic ruins of Kenilworth give some sense of the turbulent times the castle has witnessed in its 900-year history. In 1326 King Edward II was imprisoned here and forced to renounce the throne before he was transferred to Berkeley Castle in Gloucestershire and allegedly murdered with a red-hot poker. Here the ambitious Robert Dudley, Earl of Leicester, one of Elizabeth I's favorites, entertained the queen four times, most notably in 1575 with 19 days of revelry. It was for this extended visit that Dudley created the elaborate Elizabethan garden in which to woo the queen; the garden has since been restored to its original splendor with arbors, an aviary, and an 18-foot-high Carrara marble fountain. The top of the keep has commanding views of the countryside, one good indication of why this was such a formidable fortress from 1120 until it was dismantled by Oliver Cromwell after the English Civil War in the mid-17th century. Still intact are its keep, with 20-foot-thick walls; its great hall built by John of Gaunt in the 14th century; and its curtain walls, the low outer walls forming the castle's first line of defense. You can climb the stairs to the viewing platforms for the view that Queen Elizabeth would have had when she stayed and visit the restored gatehouse where an excellent exhibition explores her relationship with Dudley. The fine gift shop sells excellent replicas of tapestries and swords. ✉ *Castle Green, off A452, Kenilworth* ☎ *01926/852078* 🌐 *www.english-heritage.org.uk* 🎟 *£10.70* 🕓 *Closed weekdays Jan.–mid-Feb.*

WHERE TO EAT

$ BRITISH 🍴 **Clarendon Arms.** A location close to Kenilworth Castle and some good hand-pulled ales helps make this pub a nice spot for lunch. You can order home-cooked food, including steaks and grills from the bar, or the ever-classic fish-and-chips. **Known for:** classic pub grub; good kids' menu; closed kitchen from 3 to 5:30 pm on weekdays. [$] *Average main: £11* ✉ *44 Castle Hill, Kenilworth* ☎ *01926/852017* 🌐 *www.clarendonarmspub.co.uk.*

MANCHESTER, LIVERPOOL, AND THE PEAK DISTRICT

WELCOME TO MANCHESTER, LIVERPOOL, AND THE PEAK DISTRICT

TOP REASONS TO GO

★ **Manchester theater and nightlife:** The city's theater scene keeps getting more exciting, while bustling café-bars and pubs, together with ornate Victorian-era beer houses, mean there's plenty of ways to continue your night out in style.

★ **Liverpool culture, old and new:** This once-run-down merchant city, already a must-see for fans of the Fab Four, has reinvented itself as a cultural hub with plenty of dining, lodging, and nightlife hot spots.

★ **Outdoor activities in the Peak District:** Even a short hike in Edale or High Peak reveals the craggy, austere beauty for which the area is famous, but cycling, caving, and other sports make the Peaks a veritable natural playground.

★ **Grand country houses:** The stately Chatsworth House and the Tudor manor Haddon Hall will enchant fans of both *Downton Abbey* and quintessentially English architecture alike.

Manchester lies at the heart of a tangle of motorways in the northwest of England, about a half hour across the Pennines from Yorkshire. It's 70 miles from the southern edge of the Lake District. The city spreads west toward the coast and the mouth of the River Mersey and Liverpool. To see any great natural beauty, you must head east to the Peak District, a national park less than an hour's drive southeast of Manchester. It's also where you'll find two of the grandest and best-preserved historic homes in all of Britain: Chatsworth and Haddon Hall. The southwestern part of the region, bordering Wales, is a gentler landscape; the medieval city of Chester is here, along with Ironbridge and its stunning industrial heritage museums.

1 Manchester. This vibrant city mixes a compelling industrial heritage with cutting-edge urban design and thriving music and club scenes. Great museums and art galleries justify its blossoming status as the United Kingdom's second city of culture.

2 Liverpool. The imposing waterfront, the pair of cathedrals, and the grand architecture make it clear that this city—now undergoing a postindustrial rebirth—is more than just the Beatles. Even so, the many museums don't leave out the city's place in rock-and-roll history.

3 The Peak District. Britain's first national park is studded with an array of stately homes, but the real stars of the show are its dramatic moors, sylvan dales, atmospheric limestone caverns, and superb walking trails.

4 Chester, Ludlow, and Around. The southern part of the region, studded with its characteristic half-timber buildings, encompasses the World Heritage Site of Ironbridge Gorge, the ancient city of Chester, and medieval Ludlow with its top-class restaurants.

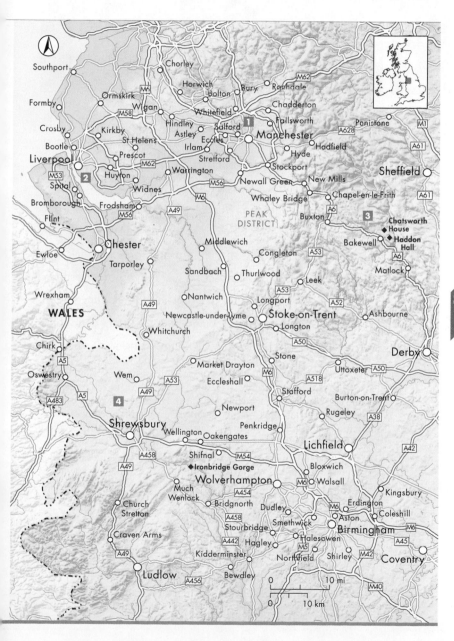

Updated by
Rhonda
Carrier and
Sally Coffey

For those looking for picture-postcard England, the northwest region of the country might not appear at the top of many sightseeing lists, but it has plenty more to offer. Manchester, Britain's third-largest city by size and second by cultural significance, bustles with redevelopment, and Liverpool is undergoing similar revitalization. Yes, the 200 years of smokestack industry that abated only in the 1980s have taken a toll on the landscape, yet the region does have some lovely scenery inland, in Derbyshire (pronounced *Dar-be-sha*)—notably the spectacular Peak District, a national park at the southern end of the Pennine range.

Manchester and Liverpool, the economic engines that propelled Britain in the 18th and 19th centuries, have sloughed off their mid-20th-century decline and celebrate their rich industrial and maritime heritage through some excellent museums—either in converted Victorian edifices, strikingly modern buildings, or, in the case of the Manchester Art Gallery and Whitworth Art Gallery, a stunning combination of the two.

The cities, each with a population of about 500,000, have reestablished themselves as centers of sporting and musical excellence, as well as hot spots for culture and nightlife. Since 1962 the Manchester United, Everton, and Liverpool football (soccer in the United States) clubs have between them won everything worth winning in Britain and Europe. The Beatles launched the Mersey sound of the '60s; contemporary Manchester groups still punch above their weight on both sides of the Atlantic. On the classical side of music, Manchester is also the home of Britain's oldest leading orchestra, the Hallé (founded in 1857)—just one legacy of 19th-century industrialists' investments in culture.

As you head inland to the Peak District, nature comes to the forefront in the form of crags that rear violently out of the plains. The Pennines, a line of hills that begins in the Peak District and runs as far north as Scotland, are sometimes called the "backbone of England." In this landscape of rocky outcrops and undulating meadowland you'll see nothing for miles but sheep, drystone walls (built without mortar), and farms, interrupted—spectacularly—by 19th-century villages and stately homes. In and around this area are Victorian-era spas such as Buxton, pretty towns such as Bakewell, and magnificent houses such as Chatsworth and Haddon Hall. The delight of the Peak District is being able to ramble for days in rugged countryside but still enjoy the pleasures of civilization.

To the west, some of England's prettiest countryside lies along the 160-mile border with Wales in the counties of Herefordshire, Worcestershire, and Shropshire. The Welsh borders are remote and tranquil, dotted with small villages and market towns full of 13th- and 14th-century black-and-white half-timber buildings, the legacy of a forested countryside. The Victorians were responsible for the more recent fashion of painting these structures black and white. The more elaborately decorated half-timber buildings in market towns such as Shrewsbury and Chester are monuments to wealth, dating mostly from the early 17th century. More half-timbered structures are found in Ludlow, now a culinary center nestled in the lee of its majestic ruined castle.

PLANNER

WHEN TO GO

Manchester has a reputation as one of the wettest cities in Britain, and visiting in summer won't guarantee dry weather. Nevertheless, the damp or cold shouldn't spoil a visit because of the many indoor sights and cultural activities here and in Liverpool. Summer is the optimal time to see the Peak District, especially because traditional festivities take place in many villages. The only time to see the great houses of Derbyshire's Wye Valley is from spring through fall.

PLANNING YOUR TIME

It's possible to see the main sights of Manchester or Liverpool in two days, but you'd have to take the museums at a real gallop. In Manchester, the Museum of Science and Industry and the Imperial War Museum North could easily absorb a day by themselves, as could the Albert Dock and waterfront area of Liverpool, where the Beatles Story's main venue, the Tate Liverpool, and the Merseyside Maritime and International Slavery museums, as well as the neighboring Museum of Liverpool, all vie for your attention. In Liverpool, an additional half day is needed to see the homes of John Lennon and Paul McCartney. The excellent nightlife of each city demands at least an overnight stay at each. You can explore the Peak District on a day trip from Manchester in a pinch, but allow longer to visit the stately homes or to hike. In the south of the region, Ironbridge Gorge demands a full day. You could do Ludlow and Chester in a half day each, though it would be a shame to leave Ludlow without sampling its fine dining.

8

FESTIVALS

Fodor's Choice
★ **Manchester International Festival.** This biennial multi-arts festival has played a major role in Manchester's cultural development since it launched in 2007. With international artists like Björk and Marina Abramović making appearances, it often premiers events that go on to tour nationally or globally. Events take place in some of the city's most popular performing arts spaces, as well as obscure locations such as disused buildings. ⊠ *Manchester* ⊕ *www.mif.co.uk.*

GETTING HERE AND AROUND

AIR TRAVEL

Both Manchester and Liverpool are well served by their international airports. Manchester, the third-largest airport in the country (and the busiest outside London), has the greater number of flights, including some from the United States. East Midlands Airport southwest of Derby also provides an alternative international air route into the region.

Airports East Midlands Airport. ⊠ *Castle Donington* ☎ *0871/919–9000* ⊕ *www.eastmidlandsairport.com.* **Liverpool John Lennon Airport.** ⊠ *Hale Rd., Liverpool* ☎ *0871/521–8484* ⊕ *www.liverpoolairport.com.* **Manchester Airport.** ☎ *0800/042–0213* ⊕ *www.manchesterairport.co.uk.*

BUS TRAVEL

National Express buses serve the region from London's Victoria Coach Station. Average travel time to Manchester or Liverpool is five hours. To reach Matlock, Bakewell, and Buxton you can take a bus from London to Derby and change to the TransPeak bus service, though you might find it more convenient to travel first to Manchester.

Bus Contacts National Express. ☎ *0871/781–8181* ⊕ *www.nationalexpress. com.* **TransPeak.** ☎ *0116/410–5050* ⊕ *www.highpeakbuses.com.*

CAR TRAVEL

If you're traveling by road, expect heavy traffic out of London on weekends. Travel time to Manchester or Liverpool from London via the M6 is 3 to 3½ hours. Although a car may not be an asset in touring the centers of Manchester and Liverpool, it's helpful in getting around the Peak District. The bus service there is quite good, but a car allows the most flexibility.

Roads within the region are generally very good, but the deeper you get into the countryside, the more likely you are to encounter narrow, one-lane farm roads once you turn off the main routes. In summer, Peak District traffic is very heavy; watch out for speeding motorbikes, especially on the A6. In winter, know the weather forecast, as moorland roads can quickly become impassable. To reach Ludlow and Chester from London, take M40.

TRAIN TRAVEL

Virgin Trains serves the region from London's Euston Station. Direct services to Manchester and Liverpool take between 2 and 2½ hours. There are trains between Manchester's Piccadilly Station and Liverpool's Lime Street roughly four times an hour during the day; the trip takes 50 minutes. (Trains also go less frequently from Manchester's

Victoria and Oxford Road stations.) Get schedules and other information through National Rail Enquiries.

To reach Buxton in the Peak District from London, take the train to Manchester that stops at Stockport and change there; to Buxton it's another 45-minute ride. The local service—one train an hour (more at peak times)—from Manchester Piccadilly to Buxton takes one hour.

Train Contacts National Rail Enquiries. ☎ *03457/484950* ⊕ *www.national-rail.co.uk.*

TRANSPORTATION DISCOUNTS AND DEALS

A Wayfarer ticket (£13; £26 for groups of up to two adults and two children) covers a day's travel on all forms of transport in Manchester, Lancashire, Cheshire, Staffordshire, Derbyshire, and the Peak District. See ⊕ *www.tfgm.com* or call ☎ *0871/200–2233* for information.

RESTAURANTS

Dining options in Manchester and Liverpool vary from smart cafés offering Modern British, Continental, or global fare to world-class international restaurants for all budgets. Manchester has one of Britain's biggest Chinatowns, and locals also favor the 40-odd Bangladeshi, Pakistani, and Indian restaurants along Wilmslow Road in Rusholme, a mile south of the city center, known as Curry Mile.

One local dish that has survived is Bakewell pudding (*never* called "tart" in these areas, as its imitations are elsewhere in England). Served with custard or cream, the pudding—a pastry covered with jam and a thin layer of almond-flavor filling—is a real joy of visiting Bakewell. *Restaurant reviews have been shortened. For full information, visit Fodors.com.*

HOTELS

Because the larger city-center hotels in Manchester and Liverpool rely on business travelers during the week, they may markedly reduce their rates on weekends. Smaller hotels and guesthouses abound, often in nearby suburbs, many just a short bus ride from downtown. The Manchester and Liverpool visitor information centers operate room-booking services. Also worth investigating are serviced apartments, which are becoming more popular in the cities. The Peak District has inns, bed-and-breakfasts, and hotels, as well as a network of youth hostels and campsites. Local tourist offices have details; reserve well in advance for Easter and summer. *Hotel reviews have been shortened. For full information, visit Fodors.com.*

WHAT IT COSTS IN POUNDS			
$	**$$**	**$$$**	**$$$$**
Restaurants	under £15	£15–£19	£20–£25	over £25
Hotels	under £100	£100–£160	£161–£220	over £220

Restaurant prices are the average cost of a main course at dinner, or if dinner is not served, at lunch. Hotel prices are the lowest cost of a standard double room in high season, including 20% V.A.T.

MANCHESTER

Central Manchester is alive with the vibe of cutting-edge popular music and a swank, often fancy café, cocktail bar, and restaurant culture. The city's once-grim industrial landscape, redeveloped since the late 1980s, includes tidied-up canals, cotton mills transformed into loft apartments, and stylish contemporary architecture that has pushed the skyline ever higher. Beetham Tower, the 11th-tallest building in Britain (the tallest outside London), stands proud and prominent above it all. Bridgewater Hall and the Lowry, as well as the Imperial War Museum North, are among the outstanding cultural facilities. Manchester's imposing Town Hall is closed for six years starting in 2018, but you can still admire its 280-foot-tall clock tower from the outside. Talking about outside—it does rain *a lot* here, but even the rain-soaked streets can be part of the city's charm, in a bleak, northern kind of way.

The now-defunct Haçienda Club marketed the 1980s rock band New Order to the world, and Manchester became the clubbing capital of England. Other Manchester-based bands like Joy Division, the Smiths, Stone Roses, Happy Mondays, and Oasis also rose to the top of the charts throughout the '70s, '80s, and '90s. The extraordinary success of the Manchester United football club (which now faces a stiff challenge from its newly rich neighbor, Manchester City, owing to a stupendous injection of cash from its oil-rich Middle Eastern owner) has kept the eyes of sports fans around the world fixed firmly on Manchester.

GETTING HERE AND AROUND

Manchester Airport has many international flights, so you might not even have to travel through London. There are frequent trains from the airport to Piccadilly Railway Station (15–20 minutes), Metrolink trams to the city center (50 minutes), and buses to Piccadilly Gardens Bus Station (70-80 minutes). A taxi from the airport to Manchester city center costs around £30. For details about public transportation in Manchester, see ⊕ *www.tfgm.com* or call ☎ *0871/200–2233*.

Driving to Manchester from London (3 to 3½ hours), take the M1 north to the M6, then the M62 east, which becomes the M602 as it enters Greater Manchester.

Trains from London's Euston Station drop passengers at the centrally located Piccadilly railway station. The journey takes just over two hours. Manchester Central Coach Station, a five-minute walk west of Piccadilly railway station, is the main bus station for regional and long-distance buses.

Most local buses leave from Piccadilly Gardens bus station, the hub of the urban bus network. Metroshuttle operates three free circular routes around the city center; service runs every 10 minutes Monday to Friday from 7 to 7, every 10 minutes Saturday from 8:30 to 6:30, and every 12 minutes Sunday and public holidays from 9:30 to 5:55.

The ever-expanding Metrolink electric tram service runs through the city center and out to the suburbs and the airport. The Eccles extension has a stop for the Lowry (Harbour City) and the Altrincham line a stop for Manchester United Stadium (Old Trafford). Buy a ticket from the platform machine before you board.

SystemOne Travelcards are priced according to the times of day, number of days, and modes of transport you want to include (for example, unlimited buses and trams after 9:30 am cost £6.70 with a Daysaver); buy from the driver (buses only) or a ticket machine.

TOURS

City Centre Cruises. Take a two- to three-hour round-trip cruise on a barge to the Manchester Ship Canal; some include a traditional Sunday lunch or afternoon tea. Another includes entry to the Manchester United football stadium tour. Times vary; call or go online for departure schedule. ☎ *0161/902–0222* ⊕ *www.citycentrecruises.com* ☜ *From £25.*

Manchester Guided Tours. Group tours run by this tourism board–recommended firm include daily Discover Manchester walks. ☎ *07505/685942* ⊕ *www.manchesterguidedtours.com.*

ESSENTIALS

Transportation Contacts Metrolink. ☎ *0161/205–2000* ⊕ *www.metrolink. co.uk.* **Transport for Greater Manchester.** ☎ *0161/244–1000* ⊕ *www.tfgm.com.*

Visitor Information Manchester Visitor Information Centre. ⊠ *1 Piccadilly Gardens, City Centre* ☎ *0871/222–8223* ⊕ *www.visitmanchester.com.*

EXPLORING

FAMILY **Castlefield Urban Heritage Park.** Site of an early Roman fort, the district of Castlefield was later the center of the city's industrial boom, which resulted in the building of Britain's first modern canal in 1764 and the world's first railway station in 1830. It has been beautifully restored into an urban park with canal-side walks, landscaped open spaces, and refurbished warehouses. The 7-acre site contains the reconstructed gate to the Roman fort of Mamucium, the buildings of the **Museum of Science and Industry,** and several bars and restaurants, many with outdoor terraces. You can easily spend a day here. ⊠ *Liverpool Rd., Castlefield.*

FAMILY **IWM North.** The thought-provoking exhibits in this striking, aluminum-
Fodor's Choice clad building, which architect Daniel Libeskind described as represent-
★ ing three shards of an exploded globe, present the reasons for war and show its effects on society. Hourly Big Picture audiovisual shows envelop you in the sights and sounds of conflicts while a time line from 1914 to the present examines objects and personal stories from veterans showing how war changes lives. The Air Shard, a 100-foot viewing platform, gives a bird's-eye view of the surrounds. Excellent special exhibitions cover everything from life in Britain during the Blitz to artistic responses to conflict. The museum is on the banks of the Manchester Ship Canal in The Quays, across the footbridge from the Lowry. It's a five-minute walk from the MediaCityUK stop of the Metrolink tram. ⊠ *Trafford Wharf Rd.* ☎ *0161/836–4000* ⊕ *www. iwm.org.uk/visits/iwm-north.*

8

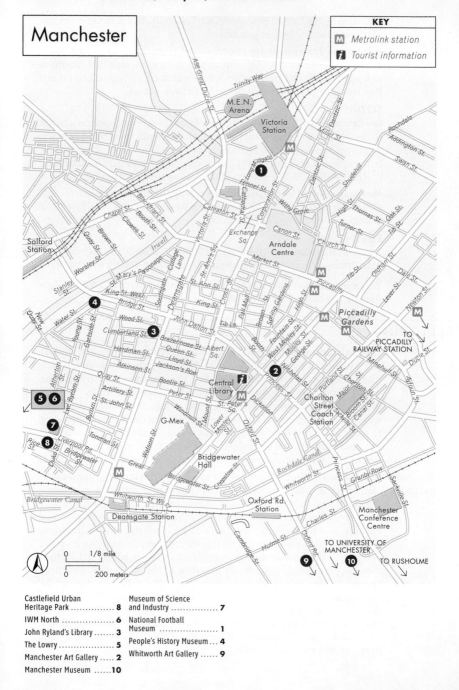

Manchester

KEY

🅼 *Metrolink station*

🛈 *Tourist information*

FAMILY **The Lowry.** Clad in perforated steel and glass, this arts center is one of the highlights of the Salford Quays waterways. L. S. Lowry (1887–1976) was a local artist, and one of the few who painted the industrial landscape; galleries here showcase his work alongside that of contemporary artists. The theater, Britain's largest outside London, has three spaces showcasing everything from West End musicals and new works by up-and-coming theater companies to some of the U.K.'s most popular stand-up comedians. The nearest Metrolink tram stop is Harbour City, a 10-minute walk away. ☒ *Pier 8, Salford* ☎ *0843/208–6000* ⊕ *www. thelowry.com* ☒ *Galleries free, performances vary.*

FAMILY **Manchester Art Gallery.** Behind an impressive classical portico, this splendid museum and its sparkling modern atrium houses an outstanding collection of paintings by the Pre-Raphaelites and their circle, notably Ford Madox Brown's masterpiece *Work*, Holman Hunt's *The Hireling Shepherd*, and Dante Gabriel Rossetti's *Astarte Syriaca*. British artworks from the 18th and the 20th centuries are also well represented. The second-floor Craft and Design Gallery shows off the best of the decorative arts in ceramics, glass, metalwork, and furniture. The Clore Art Studio is a creative space for families. ☒ *Mosley St., City Centre* ☎ *0161/235–8888* ⊕ *www.manchesterartgallery.org* ☒ *Free.*

FAMILY **Manchester Museum.** Run by the University of Manchester, this museum
Fodor's Choice and its superb Gothic Revival building embraces anthropology, natural
★ history, and archaeology. It features one of the U.K.'s largest ancient Egyptian collections as part of its extensive Ancient Worlds galleries; there's also a beautiful Living Worlds gallery designed to raise questions about our attitude towards nature; a vivarium complete with live frogs and other amphibians and reptiles; and a Nature Discovery gallery for children under five. A lively events program for all ages helps lure in repeat visitors. ☒ *Oxford Rd., University Quarter* ☎ *0161/275–2648* ⊕ *www.museum.manchester.ac.uk.*

FAMILY **Museum of Science and Industry.** The venue's five buildings, one of which
Fodor's Choice is the world's oldest passenger rail station (1830), hold marvelous
★ collections relating to the city's industrial past and present. You can walk through a reconstructed Victorian sewer, be blasted by the heat and noise of working steam engines, see cotton looms whirring in action, and watch a planetarium show. The Air and Space Gallery fills a graceful cast-iron-and-glass building, constructed as a market hall in 1877. ■TIP➔ Allow at least half a day to get the most out of all the sites, temporary exhibitions, talks, and events. ☒ *Castlefield Urban Heritage Park, Liverpool Rd., main entrance on Lower Byrom St., Castlefield* ☎ *0161/832–2244* ⊕ *www.mosi.org.uk* ☒ *Free, charges vary for special exhibits.*

FAMILY **National Football Museum.** This striking, glass-skinned triangle of a building includes a galaxy of footballing (soccer) memorabilia, from historic trophies, souvenirs, and shirts (many of them match-worn and signed by legends of the sport) to such near-sacred items as the ball from the 1966 World Cup—the last time England won the sport's ultimate prize. Other exhibits explore football's role in English popular culture. In the interactive Football Plus+ zone you can pick up a microphone and develop

8

Manchester was an industrial powerhouse; learn all about this history at the engaging Museum of Science and Industry.

your commentary style or test your ball skills in a range of activities, including a tense penalty shoot-out; these require paid tickets. ⊠ *Urbis Bldg., Cathedral Gardens, City Centre* ☎ *0161/605–8200* ⊕ *www.nationalfootballmuseum.com* ⊠ *Free; charge for activities.*

People's History Museum. Not everyone in 19th-century Manchester owned a cotton mill or made a fortune on the trading floor. This museum recounts powerfully the struggles of working people in the city and in the United Kingdom as a whole since the Industrial Revolution. Displays include the story of the 1819 Peterloo Massacre—when the army attacked a crowd of civil rights protesters in Manchester's St. Peter's Square, killing 15 and almost sparking revolution—together with an unrivaled collection of trade-union banners, tools, toys, utensils, and photographs, all illustrating the working lives and pastimes of the city's people. ⊠ *Left Bank, City Centre* ☎ *0161/838–9190* ⊕ *www.phm.org.uk* ⊠ *Free.*

FAMILY
Fodor's Choice
★

Whitworth Art Gallery. This University of Manchester–owned art museum is beautifully—and uniquely—integrated into the surrounding parkland through its art garden, sculpture terrace, orchard garden, and landscape gallery. Some of the free events and activities take you into the park itself, including children's outdoor art clubs. The renowned collections inside the gallery embrace British watercolors, Old Master drawings, postimpressionist works, wallpapers, and an outstanding textile gallery befitting a city built on textile manufacturing. There's also a learning studio for families and a "café in the trees" with floor-to-ceiling windows and a seasonal British menu. ⊠ *University of Manchester, Oxford Rd., University Quarter* ☎ *0161/275–7450* ⊕ *www.whitworth.manchester.ac.uk* ⊠ *Free.*

WHERE TO EAT

$
INDIAN

✕ **Bundobost.** Tasty Gujurat-inspired vegetarian street food lures the budget conscious to this colorful and vivacious canteen-style restaurant tucked away in a basement on Piccadilly Gardens. Order from the bar and watch chefs get busy in a semi-open kitchen on Indian dishes both classic and modern. **Known for:** sociable Indian sharing dishes; local and global craft beers; inventive cocktails. Ⓢ *Average main: £6* ✉ *61 Piccadilly, City Centre* ☎ *0161/359–6757* ⊕ *www. bundobust.com.*

$$
MODERN
EUROPEAN
Fodor'sChoice
★

✕ **Hispi.** Part of a small group of famously crowd-funded (yup, people liked this place so much they raised money to bring a locale to their 'hood) restaurants found across northwest England, this neighborhood bistro offers ambitious dining at remarkably fair prices. In pared-back surroundings, expect the likes of mackerel, sea trout, duck hearts, and goat loin, plus wonderful accompaniments including hard-to-find vegetables. **Known for:** great-value early dinners; exceptional kids' menu; Sunday lunch. Ⓢ *Average main: £17.50* ✉ *1C School La., Didsbury* ☎ *0161/445–3996* ⊕ *www.hispi.net.*

$
INTERNATIONAL

✕ **Mackie Mayor.** Located in a 19th-century market building, this food court brings together several casual dining experiences under one stunningly restored roof. Choose from sourdough pizza, rotisserie chicken, fish-and-chips, rare cuts of beef, and Chinese bao, all ordered from the counters and delivered to long shared tables. **Known for:** convivial atmosphere; local artisanal produce; fabulous breakfasts and brunches. Ⓢ *Average main: £7* ✉ *1 Eagle St., Northern Quarter* ⊕ *www.mackiemayor.co.uk* ☾ *Closed Mon. No dinner Sun.*

$$$
MODERN BRITISH

✕ **Masons Manchester Hall.** The first restaurant (more are planned) to open in Manchester's 1920s Freemason's Hall references the building's history with its original features (the reception desk is an old organ) and art deco touches. But the dining is the focal point, as all the ingredients—from Connemara salmon to Gressingham duck breast—are from the British Isles, but are often given a global spin once they're on the plate. **Known for:** gorgeous presentation; fantastic service; historic setting. Ⓢ *Average main: £22* ✉ *36 Bridge St.* ☎ *0161/359–6952* ⊕ *www. masonsrestaurantbar.co.uk* ☾ *Closed Mon.*

$
INTERNATIONAL
Fodor'sChoice
★

✕ **The Refuge by Volta.** This glamorous spot serves eclectic global food amidst the original features of a stunning Victorian Gothic building that's been given new life as the Principal Hotel. Expect dishes from Spanish salt cod croquettes and South American ceviches to Middle Eastern *mutabal* (an eggplant dish similar to baba ganoush) or lamb shawarma. **Known for:** Sunday lunches; local ingredients; buzzy atmosphere. Ⓢ *Average main: £9* ✉ *The Principal Hotel, Oxford St., City Centre* ☎ *0161/233–5151* ⊕ *www.refugemcr.co.uk.*

$$$
BRITISH
Fodor'sChoice
★

✕ **20 Stories.** The latest venture by Aiden Byrne, formerly of the acclaimed Manchester House, this restaurant is perched high above the city and offers panoramic views from floor-to-ceiling windows (beware the selfie-takers). The views are accompanied by a tempting menu that draws on ingredients sourced within 50 miles of Manchester, whether it be in innovative Modern British dishes or classics such as cod cheeks and chips. **Known for:** the best views in Manchester;

8

relaxed take on fine dining; great cocktail and craft beer menu. $ *Average main: £25* ⊠ *1 Spinningfields, 1 Hardman Sq.* ☎ *0161/204–3333* ⊕ *www.20stories.co.uk.*

$$$$ ✕ **Where the Light Gets In.** Food critics were unanimous in their praise of
MODERN BRITISH   this "New Northern" restaurant when it opened in 2017 in a former coffee warehouse. The no-choice tasting menu (£75) depends on "the day's catch, harvest, and slaughter," but regular ingredients include Macclesfield trout, cured Middle White pork, and salt-baked beets in delicious combinations. **Known for:** immense creativity; excellent wine flights; a hip atmosphere. $ *Average main: £75* ⊠ *7 Rostron Brow* ✛ *7 miles southeast of central Manchester in Stockport* ☎ *0161/477–5744* ⊕ *www.wtlgi.co* ⊗ *Closed Sun.–Tues. No lunch.*

WHERE TO STAY

$ ⊞ **Abel Heywood.** In a city with so many chain hotels, the arrival of this
HOTEL   well-priced boutique hotel and bar in the funky Northern Quarter came as a relief. **Pros:** in-room visitor guide to the Northern Quarter and Manchester; free Wi-Fi. **Cons:** rooms are small; some rooms have noise from the kitchen. $ *Rooms from: £70* ⊠ *38 Turner St., Northern Quarter* ☎ *0161/819–1441* ⊕ *www.abelheywood.co.uk* ⊅ *15 rooms* ¶○¶ *No meals.*

$$$ ⊞ **City Suites.** Across the river from Manchester's city center, most of
RENTAL   these chic studio-, one-, and two-bedroom apartments have great views
FAMILY   towards Manchester Cathedral. **Pros:** full kitchens; a very short walk
Fodor'sChoice   from Manchester city center; lovely pool and hot tub. **Cons:** minimum
★   four-night stay; no restaurant (one is in the works); views of railroad tracks from some suites. $ *Rooms from: £218* ⊠ *16 Chapel St., Salford* ☎ *0161/302–0202* ⊕ *citysuites.com* ⊅ *237 rooms* ¶○¶ *No meals.*

$$ ⊞ **The Lowry Hotel.** In a striking curved glass building overlooking the River
HOTEL   Irwell and Santiago Calatrava's Trinity Bridge, this elegant property is a
FAMILY   magnet for footballers, rock stars, and other celebrities visiting the city. **Pros:** a quiet location within an easy stroll of the center; spacious rooms; fantastic dining. **Cons:** views from rooms facing Chapel Street are a bit bleak; cheapest rates don't include breakfast; no swimming pool in the spa. $ *Rooms from: £139* ⊠ *50 Dearman's Pl., City Centre* ☎ *0161/827–4000* ⊕ *www.thelowryhotel.com* ⊅ *164 rooms* ¶○¶ *No meals.*

$$ ⊞ **Oddfellows On The Park.** This boutique hotel has a unique location
HOTEL   in a Victorian Gothic mansion in a vast public park complete with gardens, woods, and ponds, plus a playground and sports amenities. **Pros:** great facilities on the very doorstep; lovely summer terrace; handy location for Manchester airport but good soundproofing against aircraft. **Cons:** gardens can be overrun by kids playing; not well served by public transport; quirky decorative touches won't be to everyone's taste. $ *Rooms from: £155* ⊠ *Bruntwood Hall, Bruntwood Park , Cheadle* ☎ *0161/697–3066* ⊕ *www.oddfellowsonthepark.com* ⊅ *23 rooms* ¶○¶ *Free Breakfast.*

$$ ⊞ **Roomzzz Aparthotel Manchester Corn Exchange.** All spruced up and fresh
RENTAL   from an early-2018 opening, the newest incarnation of the Roomzzz
Fodor'sChoice   Aparthotel group sits within the iconic and historic restaurant hub
★   known as the Manchester Corn Exchange. **Pros:** free grab-and-go breakfasts and 24-hour coffee; on-site gym; round-the-clock essentials

shop. **Cons:** specific rooms can be requested but not booked; not all rooms have bathtubs; water pressure not reliably powerful. $ *Rooms from: £109* ⊠ *Corn Exchange, Exchange Sq., City Centre* ☎ *0203/504–5555* ⊕ *www.roomzzz.com* ⇨ *114 apartments* ⑩ *Free Breakfast.*

$ ⊞ **Staycity Aparthotels.** If you're looking for style on a budget, these
RENTAL colorful, contemporary, one- to three-bedroom apartments are just the
Fodor'sChoice ticket. **Pros:** just a few steps from Piccadilly train station; great sound-
★ proofing; 24-hour café. **Cons:** hot water supply can be inadequate when hotel is full; gym is very small; breakfast choice is limited. $ *Rooms from: £86* ⊠ *Gateway House, Piccadilly, City Centre* ☎ *0161/236–7330* ⊕ *www.staycity.com* ⇨ *182 rooms* ⑩ *No meals.*

NIGHTLIFE AND PERFORMING ARTS

Manchester vies with London as Britain's capital of youth culture, but has vibrant nightlife and entertainment options for all ages. Spending time at a bar, pub, or club is an essential part of any trip. For event listings, check out the free *Manchester Evening News*, widely available throughout the city or as a website or app. Other helpful websites include ⊕ *www.manchesterconfidential.co.uk*, ⊕ *www.manchesterwire. co.uk*, and ⊕ *creativetourist.com*.

NIGHTLIFE

BARS

Cloud 23. This dressy champagne and cocktail bar in the city's tallest building has stunning 360-degree views. Some of its inventive concoctions make a playful nod to local culture, including Bee on Time referencing the city's symbol. You can also get afternoon tea or dine from a small British menu. ⊠ *Hilton Manchester Deansgate, Beetham Tower, 303 Deansgate, City Centre* ☎ *0161/870–1670* ⊕ *www.cloud23bar.com.*

Folk. Bars and restaurants come and go on trendy, ever-evolving Burton Road, but this bar and café has stood the test of time thanks to its heated terrace (complete with palm trees), eclectic tunes by live DJs, chic interiors, and good food. ⊠ *169 Burton Rd., West Didsbury* ☎ *0161/445–2912* ⊕ *www.folkcafebar.co.uk.*

Kosmonaut. With stripped-down decor of exposed brick walls, old tiles, and leather benches, this bar exudes a hipster vibe. There's a Ping-Pong table and changing art exhibitions, as well as a wine list and beer selection, although it's the inventive cocktails that draw the crowds. ⊠ *10 Tariff St., Northern Quarter* ☎ *07496/977443* ⊕ *www.kosmonaut.co.*

The Liars Club. This self-described "tiki dive bar" serves up generously sized cocktails in its kitschy Polynesian beach–style bar. Order a Zombie if you like your drinks set on fire. They also serve a hundred types of rum. ⊠ *19A Back Bridge St., City Centre* ☎ *0161/834–5111* ⊕ *www. theliarsclub.co.uk.*

PUBS

The Angel. You won't find any televisions in this atmospheric real ale pub that serves beers from small independent breweries. British comfort food (sometimes with a modern twist like Lancashire cheese croquettes)

8

is also offered in both the bar and its cozy restaurant that comes with a log fire and grand piano. ✉ *6 Angel St., Northern Quarter* ☎ *0161/833–4786* ⊕ *www.theangelmanchester.com.*

The Briton's Protection. You can sample more than 230 whiskies and bourbons at this gorgeous pub with stained-glass windows, cozy back rooms, a spacious beer garden, and a mural of the Peterloo Massacre. ✉ *50 Great Bridgewater St.* ☎ *0161/236–5895.*

The Oast House. This unique pub occupies a 16th-century oasthouse (where brewers roasted hops) that was brought here, brick by brick, from Kent. Surrounded by a large terrace, the emphasis here is on craft beers and ales, accompanied by food like hanging kebabs and grilled meats. ✉ *The Avenue Courtyard, Crown Sq.* ☎ *0161/829–3830* ⊕ *www.theoasthouse.uk.com.*

DANCE CLUBS

Fodor's Choice ★ **FAC251 – Factory Manchester.** This club and occasional live music venue brings the old offices of the legendary Factory Records to life with sounds ranging from drum 'n' bass to indie. ✉ *118 Princess St., City Centre* ☎ *0161/637–2570* ⊕ *www.factorymanchester.com.*

42's. Off Deansgate, this venue plays retro, indie, sing-along anthems, and classic rock, with Manchester's proud musical heritage at the fore. ✉ *2 Bootle St., City Centre* ☎ *0161/831–7108* ⊕ *www.42s.co.uk.*

Gorilla. Nestled under old railway arches, Gorilla is a live-music venue and gin parlor with an intimate vibe. ✉ *54–56 Whitworth St., University Quarter* ☎ *0161/826–2998* ⊕ *www.thisisgorilla.com.*

LIVE MUSIC

Fodor's Choice ★ **Albert Hall.** One of the city's most exciting venues, this former Wesleyan chapel was abandoned and forgotten about for over four decades; it's now a superb indie music hall and clubbing venue retaining many of the site's original features, including an organ and stained-glass windows. ✉ *27 Peter St., City Centre* ☎ *0161/817–3490* ⊕ *www.alberthallmanchester.com.*

Fodor's Choice ★ **The Deaf Institute.** Good acoustics characterize the intimate domed music hall of this landmark building (a onetime institute for those with hearing and speech impairments) that regularly hosts cutting-edge indie acts. There are also club nights, open mics, and quiz nights. ✉ *135 Grosvenor St., University Quarter* ☎ *0161/276–9350* ⊕ *www.thedeafinstitute.co.uk.*

Manchester Arena. Europe's largest indoor arena hosts shows by major rock and pop stars, as well as large-scale sporting events. ✉ *21 Hunts Bank* ☎ *0845/337–0717 box office* ⊕ *www.manchester-arena.com.*

PERFORMING ARTS

Fodor's Choice ★ **HOME.** This cutting-edge contemporary arts venue houses a main 450-seat theater, a studio theater space, a gallery, five cinema screens, and digital production and broadcast facilities, as well a bar, a café, and a bookshop. ✉ *2 Tony Wilson Pl., University Quarter* ☎ *0161/228–7621* ⊕ *homemcr.org.*

SHOPPING

Afflecks. With a collection that ranges from top hats to punk skinny jeans and skate wear, this emporium has been purveying indie fashion and lifestyle paraphernalia to its many fans for decades. ⊠ *52 Church St., Northern Quarter* ☎ *0161/839–0718* ⊕ *www.afflecks.com.*

Barton Arcade. This charming Victorian arcade houses various specialty stores including fashion and shoes, as well as bars and restaurants. ⊠ *51–63 Deansgate, City Centre* ⊕ *www.barton-arcade.co.uk.*

Fodor's Choice
★
Manchester Craft and Design Centre. This vibrant, airy space in a onetime Victorian fish-market building houses 18 studios for resident artists and craft makers selling to the public. Crafts workshops are hosted too, and there's a wonderful café. ⊠ *17 Oak St., Northern Quarter* ☎ *0161/832–4274* ⊕ *www.craftanddesign.com.*

SPORTS AND THE OUTDOORS

FOOTBALL

Football (soccer in the United States) is *the* reigning passion in Manchester. Locals tend to be torn between Manchester City and Manchester United, the two local clubs. Matches for both clubs are usually sold out months in advance; stadium tours can be a good alternative if you can't snag match tickets.

Manchester City Etihad Stadium. This is the place to see Manchester City in action and also to inspect club memorabilia, visit the changing rooms, and explore the pitch. There are also daily tours, including on match days. ⊠ *Etihad Campus, Rowsley St., Sportcity* ☎ *0161/444–1894* ⊕ *www.mancity.com* ⊠ *£17.50.*

Old Trafford. Matches at Manchester United's home stadium attract fans of one of the biggest names in soccer from near and far. The museum and tour take you behind the scenes into the changing rooms and players' lounge, and down the tunnel. ⊠ *Sir Matt Busby Way, Trafford Park* ☎ *0161/868–8000* ⊕ *www.manutd.com* ⊠ *£21.50.*

LIVERPOOL

A city lined with one of the most famous waterfronts in England, celebrated around the world as the birthplace of the Beatles, and still the place to catch that "Ferry 'Cross the Mersey," Liverpool reversed a downturn in its fortunes with developments in the late 1980s, such as the impressively refurbished Albert Dock area. In 2004, UNESCO named six historic areas in the city center together as one World Heritage Site, in recognition of the city's maritime and mercantile achievements during the height of Britain's global influence. The city's heritage, together with famous attractions and a legacy of cultural vibrancy that includes an ever-growing events program, draws in an increasing number of visitors each year—in turn impacting its growing hotel and dining scenes.

8

The 1960s produced Liverpool's most famous export: the Beatles. The group was one of hundreds influenced by the rock and roll they heard from visiting American GIs and merchant seamen in the late 1950s, and one of many that played local venues such as the Cavern (demolished but rebuilt nearby). All four Beatles were born in Liverpool, but the group's success dates from the time they left for London. Nevertheless, the city has milked the group's Liverpool connections for all they're worth, with a multitude of local attractions such as Paul McCartney's and John Lennon's childhood homes.

GETTING HERE AND AROUND

Liverpool John Lennon Airport, about 5 miles southeast of the city, receives mostly domestic and European flights. The Arriva 500 bus service runs to the city center up to every 30 minutes; other buses to the center are the 80A, 82A, and 86A (24 hours a day). A taxi to the center of Liverpool costs around £25.

Long-distance National Express buses, including a service from London, use the Liverpool One bus station, as do some local buses. Other local bus terminals are Sir Thomas Street and Queen Square. Train service on Virgin Trains from London's Euston Station takes 2½ hours.

If you're walking (easier than driving), you'll find the downtown sights well signposted. Take care when crossing the busy inner ring road separating the Albert Dock from the rest of the city.

TOURS

Magical Mystery Tours. This ever-popular tour departs daily from the Albert Dock visitor center. The bus—decked out in full psychedelic colors—takes you around all the Beatles-related high points, including Penny Lane and Strawberry Fields, in two hours. The ticket price includes entry to the Cavern Club on the evening of your tour day. The firm also offers private tours. ⊠ *City Centre* ☎ *0151/703–9100* ⊕ *www. cavernclub.org/the-magical-mystery-tour* ⊡ *£18.95*.

Mersey Guides. This is your point of contact for dozens of different tours of the city, bringing together professional local guides with in-depth knowledge on topics as diverse as Manchester's maritime or wartime histories. ☎ *07940/933073* ⊕ *www.showmeliverpool.com*.

ESSENTIALS

Bus Contacts Merseytravel. ☎ *0151/330–1000* ⊕ *www.merseytravel.gov.uk.*

Visitor Information Visit Liverpool. ⊠ *Liverpool John Lennon Airport* ☎ *0151/707–0729* ⊕ *www.visitliverpool.com* ⊠ *Anchor Courtyard, Albert Dock, Waterfront.*

EXPLORING

Albert Dock. To understand the city's prosperous maritime past, head for these 7 acres of restored waterfront warehouses built in 1846. Named after Queen Victoria's consort, Prince Albert, the dock provided storage for silk, tea, and tobacco from the Far East until it was closed in 1972. Today the fine colonnaded brick buildings contain the **Merseyside Maritime Museum**, the **International Slavery Museum, Tate Liverpool,**

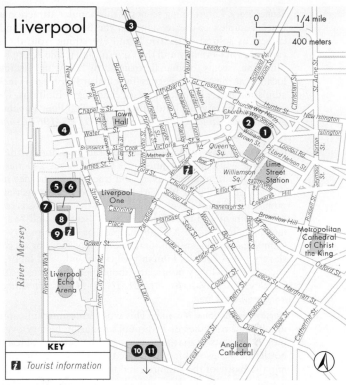

and the main venue of the **Beatles Story.** When weather allows, you can sit at an outdoor café overlooking the dock; there are also bars, restaurants, and even hotels on the site. For a bird's-eye view of the Albert Dock area, take the rotating Liverpool Wheel—a 60-meter-tall version of the London Eye. ■TIP➜ Much of the pedestrian area of the Albert Dock and waterfront area is cobblestone, so wear comfortable shoes. ✉ *Unit 34B, Anchor Courtyard, Off Strand St. (A5036), Waterfront* ☎ *0151/707–0729 visitor center* ⊕ *www.albertdock.com.*

Fodor'sChoice
★ **The Beatles' Childhood Homes.** A must-see for Beatles pilgrims, this tour takes you to Mendips, the 1930s middle-class, semidetached house that was the home of John Lennon from 1946 to 1963, and 20 Forthlin Road, Paul McCartney's childhood home. After his parents separated, John joined his aunt Mimi at Mendips; she gave him his first guitar but banished him to the porch, saying, "The guitar's all very well, John, but you'll never make a living out of it." Meanwhile, Forthlin Road is a modest 1950s council house where a number of the Beatles' songs were written. The tour leaves from Jury's Inn hotel next to Albert Dock (mornings) or Speke Hall (afternoons). ■TIP➜ Advanced bookings are essential—places are strictly limited to 15. ✉ *City Centre* ☎ *0844/800–4791* ⊕ *www.nationaltrust.org.uk/beatles-childhood-homes* 💷 *£23* ☾ *Closed Nov.–Mar.*

Fodor's Choice ★ **Beatles Story.** Entertaining scenes at this popular attraction in the Albert Dock complex re-create stages in the Beatles' story (and their later careers as solo artists). You'll find everything from the enthusiastic early days in Germany and the Cavern Club to the White Room, where "Imagine" seems to emanate from softly billowing curtains. A second location at the Mersey Ferries Terminal at Pier Head is included in the admission price; here you can see changing exhibitions. On-site shops sell every conceivable kind of souvenir a Fab Four fan could wish for. ✉ *Britannia Vaults, Albert Dock* ☎ *0151/709–1963* ⊕ *www.beatlesstory.com* ✉ *£15.*

International Slavery Museum. In the same building as the Merseyside Maritime Museum, this museum's four dynamic galleries recount the history of transatlantic slavery and trace its significance in contemporary society. "Life in West Africa" reproduces a Nigerian Igbo compound; life aboard slave ships bound for the Americas is revealed in the "Enslavement and the Middle Passage" section; and "Legacy" examines the effect of the African diaspora on contemporary society. The Campaign Zone hosts temporary exhibitions focusing on contemporary slavery issues such as human trafficking and child labor; visitors are encouraged to lobby politicians about these injustices. ✉ *Albert Dock, Hartley Quay, Waterfront* ☎ *0151/478–4499* ⊕ *www.liverpoolmuseums.org.uk* ✉ *Free.*

FAMILY **Fodor's Choice** ★ **Merseyside Maritime Museum.** This wonderful museum captures the triumphs and tragedies of Liverpool's seafaring history over five floors. Besides exhibits of maritime paintings, models, ceramics, and ships in bottles, it brings to life the ill-fated stories of the *Titanic* and *Lusitania;* the Battle of the Atlantic; and the city's role during World War II. Seized, the gallery for the Border Force National Museum, explores the heroes and villains of the world of smuggling, together with the story of mass emigration from the port in the 19th century. ■TIP➜ Kids get free activities and events, and there's the Sea Urchins play area. ✉ *Albert Dock, Hartley Quay, Waterfront* ☎ *0151/478–4499* ⊕ *www. liverpoolmuseums.org.uk* ✉ *Free.*

Royal Liver Building. The 322-foot-tall Royal Liver (pronounced *lie-ver*) Building with its twin towers is topped by two 18-foot-high copper birds representing the mythical Liver Birds, the town symbol; local legend has it that if they fly away, Liverpool will cease to exist. For decades Liverpudlians looked to the Royal Liver Society for assistance—it was originally a burial club to which families paid contributions to ensure a decent send-off. ■TIP➜ The building, now offices, can best be seen from one of the Mersey ferries. ✉ *Water St., Waterfront.*

FAMILY **Fodor's Choice** ★ **Tate Liverpool.** This offshoot of the London-based art galleries of the same name occupies a handsome conversion of Albert Dock warehouses by the late James Stirling, one of Britain's leading 20th-century architects. There is no permanent collection; challenging exhibitions of modern and contemporary art change every couple of months. There are children's activities, an excellent gift shop, and a dockside café-restaurant. ✉ *Albert Dock, Waterfront* ☎ *0151/702–7400* ⊕ *www.tate. org.uk* ✉ *Free; charges for certain special exhibitions vary.*

Once a major shipping center and now transformed with museums, restaurants, and shops, the Albert Dock has views of the green dome of the Royal Liver Building.

FAMILY
Fodor's Choice
★

Walker Art Gallery. With a superb display of British art and some outstanding Italian and Flemish works, this is one of the best British art collections outside London. Don't miss the unrivaled collection of paintings by 18th-century Liverpudlian equestrian artist George Stubbs, or works by J.M.W. Turner, Claude Monet, Frederic Lord Leighton, and the Pre-Raphaelites. Modern artists are included, too; on display is one of David Hockney's typically Californian pool scenes. Other excellent exhibits showcase classical Greek and Roman sculptures as well as china, silver, and furniture that once adorned the mansions of Liverpool's industrial barons. There are temporary exhibitions and a dedicated children's art space. The café holds center stage in the airy museum lobby. ⊠ *William Brown St., City Centre* ☎ *0151/478–4199* ⊕ *www.liverpoolmuseums.org.uk* ☒ *Free.*

FAMILY

World Museum Liverpool. Travel from the prehistoric to the space age through the stunning displays in these state-of-the-art galleries. Ethnology, the natural and physical sciences, and archaeology all get their due over five floors; highlights include a collection of Egyptian mummies and a beautiful assemblage of Japanese arms and armory in the World Cultures Gallery. There's plenty to keep kids amused, from fish and other sea creatures in the Aquarium and monster bugs in the Bug House to life-size casts of prehistoric monsters in the Dinosaurs Gallery, plus a busy program of events and activities. ⊠ *William Brown St., City Centre* ☎ *0151/478–4393* ⊕ *www.liverpoolmuseums.org.uk* ☒ *Free.*

WHERE TO EAT

$ **✕ Bakchich.** Those who like good food at great prices head to Bakchich,
LEBANESE a Lebanese street-food joint featuring a large communal table with
FAMILY smaller tables dotted around it. On offer are delicious hot and cold meze,
Fodor's Choice *meshawi* charcoal grills (chicken, lamb, and seafood), wraps, salads, and
★ a small but tasty kids' menu. **Known for:** Middle Eastern breakfasts; fresh
juices and mocktails; huge portions. $ *Average main: £7* ⊠ *54 Bold St.,
City Centre* ☎ *0151/707–1255* ⊕ *www.bakchich.co.uk.*

$ **✕ Lunya.** An 18th-century warehouse on the edge of the Liverpool One
CATALAN shopping district houses this impressive Catalan fusion restaurant and
FAMILY deli, where you can feast on classic and creative tapas dishes. An exten-
Fodor's Choice sive breakfast menu makes this a great place to start your day, while
★ the children's menu tempts those with junior foodies. **Known for:** tastings and skills master classes; Catalan breakfasts; deli platters to share.
$ *Average main: £9* ⊠ *55 Hanover St., City Centre* ☎ *0151/706–9770*
⊕ *www.lunya.co.uk.*

$ **✕ Maray.** Tapping into Liverpool's love affair with the sharing experi-
INTERNATIONAL ence, this tiny bistro serves eclectic and inventive dishes with global
inspirations, ranging from the Middle East and the southern United
States to Scandinavia. The place—all bare bricks, upcycled furniture,
and edgy artwork—takes its name from the Marais district of Paris,
though it's actually inspired more by the falafel joints of the French capital's less scenic Bastille district. **Known for:** falafel (homemade daily);
meat-free Mondays; luscious after-dinner cocktails. $ *Average main:
£7* ⊠ *91 Bold St., City Centre* ☎ *0151/709–5820* ⊕ *www.maray.co.uk.*

$ **✕ Mowgli.** Indian street food is the draw at this fun and colorful spot
INDIAN that has lights fashioned from old birdcages and a bar created from
FAMILY former railway sleepers. Many of the vibrant dishes, such as the hugely
Fodor's Choice popular yogurt chat bombs (crispy, filled bread puffs), are served in
★ tiffin boxes (traditional Indian lunch containers) to charming effect.
Known for: innovative cocktails; enthusiastic, informative staff; hand-
made ice-cream cones. $ *Average main: £7* ⊠ *69 Bold St., City Centre*
☎ *0151/708–9356* ⊕ *www.mowglistreetfood.com.*

$$$ **✕ Panoramic 34.** For some, the waterfront and city views through the
MODERN floor-to-ceiling windows of this 34th-floor restaurant might outdo the
EUROPEAN food, but there's no denying the ambitiousness and wonderful sense of
playfulness behind the Modern European menu. You can also just come
here to soak up that vista over afternoon tea or a cocktail. **Known for:**
best views in town; fantastic tasting menus (one vegetarian); dressed-up
atmosphere. $ *Average main: £22* ⊠ *West Tower, Brook St., 34th fl.,
Waterfront* ☎ *0151/236–5534* ⊕ *www.panoramic34.com* ⦷ *Closed Mon.*

$$ **✕ Wreckfish.** Part of the same crowd-funded group as Manchester's
MODERN BRITISH Hispi, this hip bistro serves up seriously good modern global cuisine
Fodor's Choice from an open kitchen in a once derelict building in the Ropewalks dis-
★ trict. As with Hispi, think excellent local ingredients—lamb's tongue
or beef Featherblade—taken to the next level through the use of luxurious ingredients such as truffle butter, aged feta cheese, or pomegranate
molasses. **Known for:** great-value early dinners; fantastic service; choice
of communal and private tables. $ *Average main: £18* ⊠ *Slater St., City
Centre* ☎ *0151/707–1960* ⊕ *www.wreckfish.co.*

WHERE TO STAY

$$ HOTEL **Hope Street Hotel.** In Liverpool's Georgian Quarter, this quite chic hotel blends old (an 1890s building inspired by Venetian palazzos) and new (a contemporary steel-and-glass facade fitted over part of the frontage) with rooms that come in all shapes and sizes and have minimalist, Scandinavian-esque decor. **Pros:** in-room treatments including shiatsu; frequent upgrades; very good deals in off-season. **Cons:** reception can be overly busy; the on-site Carriageworks restaurant is less impressive than the rooms; rooms can be noisy due to the wooden floors. [$] *Rooms from: £115* ✉ *40 Hope St., City Centre* ☎ *0151/709–3000* 🌐 *www.hopestreethotel.co.uk* 🛏 *89 rooms* 🍴 *No meals.*

$ HOTEL FAMILY Fodor's Choice ★ **The Nadler Liverpool.** The Nadler succeeds in its aim to bring affordable luxury to central Liverpool with its stylish rooms with mini-kitchens (with fridge, microwave, and sink) in an impressive 1850s industrial building. **Pros:** every room has an HDTV with free music, games, and an interactive directory; great value; interesting building. **Cons:** some doubles have twin beds; no dining on-site; some rooms very small. [$] *Rooms from: £87* ✉ *29 Seel St., City Centre* ☎ *0151/705–2626* 🌐 *www.thenadler.com/liverpool.shtml* 🛏 *106 rooms* 🍴 *No meals* 💳 *No credit cards.*

$$ HOTEL **Pullman Liverpool.** The only Pullman hotel in the United Kingdom outside London, this sleek contemporary affair is located in a prime waterfront setting near the Arena concert venue. **Pros:** great views; clean modern feel; enthusiastic staff. **Cons:** gym is small; slightly corporate feel; windows don't open. [$] *Rooms from: £135* ✉ *Kings Dock, Monarchs Quay, Waterfront* ☎ *0151/945–1000* 🌐 *www.pullmanhotels.com* 🛏 *216 rooms* 🍴 *No meals.*

$ RENTAL **Staybridge Suites.** This well-thought-out apartment-hotel close to the Liverpool Echo Arena makes for a great stay on the waterfront. **Pros:** sociable atmosphere; cozy, homey decor; handy kitchenettes. **Cons:** limited parking; some rooms suffer noise from nearby restaurant extractor fans; showers aren't very powerful. [$] *Rooms from: £95* ✉ *21 Keel Wharf, Waterfront* ☎ *0151/703–9700* 🌐 *www.staybridge.com* 🛏 *132 apartments* 🍴 *Free Breakfast.*

$$ B&B/INN Fodor's Choice ★ **2 Blackburne Terrace.** On a cobbled lane in Liverpool's charming Georgian Quarter, this boutique town house B&B is the best place in town for a personalized welcome; its four homey yet stylish rooms come with thoughtful, luxurious touches such as fluffy slippers and marble showers. **Pros:** free parking; complimentary in-room treats; personal coffee machines. **Cons:** no restaurant; hilltop setting; not wheelchair accessible. [$] *Rooms from: £150* ✉ *2 Blackburne Terr., City Centre* ☎ *0151/708–5474* 🌐 *2blackburneterrace.com* 🛏 *4 rooms* 🍴 *Free Breakfast.*

$ HOTEL Fodor's Choice ★ **Z Liverpool.** Modern urban style on a budget and a supercentral location make the Z a superb option; rooms are all clean and simple, with bespoke beds, crisp linen, flat-screen TVs, and free Wi-Fi. **Pros:** thoughtful design features; free wine and cheese in the evening; great views from some rooms. **Cons:** street noise from some rooms; not all rooms have windows; glassed-in shower rooms and toilets don't feel private enough for some guests. [$] *Rooms from: £58* ✉ *2 N. John St., City Centre* ☎ *0151/556–1770* 🌐 *www.thezhotels.com* 🛏 *92 rooms* 🍴 *Free Breakfast.*

NIGHTLIFE AND PERFORMING ARTS

NIGHTLIFE

Alma de Cuba. A church transformed into a luxurious bar, Alma de Cuba has a huge mirrored altar and hundreds of dripping candles. They also serve a popular Sunday brunch with a live gospel choir. ⊠ *St. Peter's Church, Seel St., City Centre* ☎ *0151/305–3744* ⊕ *www. alma-de-cuba.com.*

Berry and Rye. Hidden away behind an unassuming and umarked facade, Berry and Rye is a Prohibition-era speakeasy that brings together expertly mixed cocktails and cakes in a stylish candlelit space. ⊠ *48 Berry St., City Centre* ☎ *0151/345–7271.*

Camp and Furnace. This huge bar, live music venue, and restaurant complex in a former Edwardian foundry and blade-making factory retains a suitably industrial vibe. ⊠ *67 Greenland St., City Centre* ☎ *0151/708– 2890* ⊕ *www.campandfurnace.com.*

Cavern Club. While not the original venue—that was demolished years ago—this is still a top music spot, drawing in rock-and-roll fans with its live acts including Beatles tribute bands. ⊠ *10 Mathew St., City Centre* ☎ *0151/236–9091* ⊕ *www.cavernclub.org.*

Fodor'sChoice ★ **LEAF on Bold Street.** Tea shop meets bar and live music venue (and club nights) at this bohemian spot in a former art deco cinema. ⊠ *65–67 Bold St., City Centre* ☎ *0151/707–7747* ⊕ *www.thisisleaf.co.uk.*

The Shipping Forecast. Big-name acts mean this intimate venue often gets packed to the rafters, but that only adds to the clubby vibe. There are also club nights that range from hip-hop to indie, vintage fairs, plus a menu of well-executed American comfort food classics. ⊠ *15 Slater St., City Centre* ☎ *0151/709–6901* ⊕ *www.theshippingforecastliverpool.com.*

PERFORMING ARTS

Fodor'sChoice ★ **Bluecoat.** The city center's oldest building is now a creative hub encompassing contemporary visual arts, live art, literature, music, and dance, along with a café and bistro. ⊠ *School La., City Centre* ☎ *0151/702– 5324* ⊕ *www.thebluecoat.org.uk.*

SHOPPING

The Beatles Shop. All the mop-top knickknacks of your dreams are available at this hugely popular, official Beatles souvenir shop. ⊠ *31 Mathew St., City Centre* ☎ *0151/236–8066* ⊕ *www.thebeatleshop.co.uk.*

Fodor'sChoice ★ **Liverpool One.** The city's largest shopping complex comprises four districts (Peter's Lane, South John Street, Paradise Street, and Hanover Street) totaling more than 160 stores, from small independent shops to international chains, plus restaurants and leisure amenities. ⊠ *Paradise St., City Centre* ☎ *0151/232–3100* ⊕ *www.liverpool-one.com.*

Metquarter. This luxury shopping district is the place for upmarket boutiques, designer names, and cutting-edge fashions. ⊠ *35 Whitechapel, City Centre* ☎ *0151/224–2390* ⊕ *www.metquarter.com.*

SPORTS AND THE OUTDOORS

FOOTBALL

Football matches are played on weekends and, increasingly, some weekdays. Tickets for Liverpool sell out months in advance; you should have more luck with Everton.

Anfield Stadium. If you can't get tickets to a match at the stadium of Liverpool FC, one of England's top teams, take a trip into the dressing rooms and down the tunnel of Anfield Football Stadium as part of a tour; you can also visit the interactive museum. ⊠ *Anfield Rd., Anfield* ☎ *0151/260–6677* ⊕ *www.liverpoolfc.com* ☑ *£20 (tour).*

Goodison Park. Home to Everton, one of Liverpool's two great football teams, this 40,000-capacity stadium now also hosts tours. ⊠ *Goodison Rd.* ☎ *0151/556–1878* ⊕ *www.evertonfc.com* ☑ *£15 (tours).*

THE PEAK DISTRICT

Heading southeast, away from the urban congestion of Manchester and Liverpool, it's not far to the southernmost contortions of the Pennine Hills. Here, about an hour southeast of Manchester, sheltered in a great natural bowl, is the spa town of Buxton: at an elevation of more than 1,000 feet, it's the second-highest town in England. Buxton makes a convenient base for exploring the 540 square miles of the Peak District, Britain's oldest—and, its fans say, most beautiful—national park. About 38,000 people live in the towns throughout the park.

"Peak" is perhaps misleading; despite being a hilly area, it contains only gentle rises that don't reach much higher than 2,000 feet. Yet a trip around destinations such as Bakewell, Matlock, Castleton, and Edale, as well as around the grand estates of Chatsworth House and Haddon Hall, involves negotiating fairly perilous country roads, each of which repays the effort with enchanting views. Outdoor activities are popular in the Peaks, particularly caving (or "potholing"), walking, and hiking. Bring all-weather clothing and waterproof shoes.

BUXTON

25 miles southeast of Manchester.

Just outside the national park yet almost entirely surrounded by it, Buxton makes a good base for Peak District excursions but it has its own attractions as well. The town's spa days left a notable legacy of 18th- and 19th-century buildings, parks, and open spaces that give the town an air of faded grandeur. The Romans arrived in AD 79 and named Buxton Aquae Arnemetiae, loosely translated as "Waters of the Goddess of the Grove." The mineral springs, which emerge from 3,500 to 5,000 feet belowground at a constant 82°F, were believed to cure assorted ailments; in the 18th century the town became established as a popular spa, a minor rival to Bath. You can still drink water from the ancient St. Ann's Well, and it's also sold throughout Britain. Look out for the long-awaited opening of the Buxton Crescent Hotel & Thermal Spa, a move that will put Buxton back on the global map as

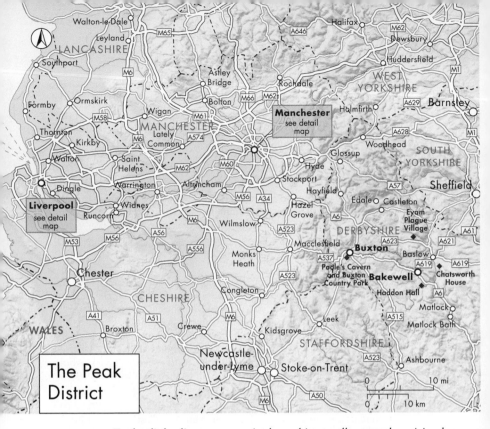

England's leading spa town, in the architecturally revered semicircular 18th-century Crescent.

GETTING HERE AND AROUND

Some National Express bus services to London and all TransPeak bus services to Derby from Manchester stop at Buxton, departing from Manchester's Central Coach Station. If you're driving from Manchester, take the A6 southeast to Buxton. The journey takes one hour. The hourly train from Manchester to Buxton also takes an hour.

ESSENTIALS

Visitor Information **Buxton Tourist Information Centre.** ⊠ *Pavilion Gardens, Water St.* ☎ *01298/25106* ⊕ *www.visitpeakdistrict.com.*

EXPLORING

Buxton Museum and Art Gallery. Reopened in 2017 after large-scale redevelopment, this venue is now focused on its "Wonders of the Peak" gallery with its displays on Derbyshire's geology, archaeology, history, and art. It's a good place to see Blue John, a colorful, semiprecious mineral found only in the Peak District (the name comes from *bleu jaune*—literally "blue yellow"—a term supposedly coined by visiting French mine workers). ⊠ *Terrace Rd.* ☎ *01629/533540* ⊕ *www.derbyshire.gov.uk/ leisure/buxton_museum* ⊠ *Free* ⊙ *Closed Mon.*

Buxton Opera House. Built in 1903, this lovely Edwardian edifice is one of England's best examples of Frank Matcham theater design, with its marble columns, carved cherubs, and gold leaf. A varied performance program includes classical music, opera, dance, drama, and comedy, and it's also host to the Buxton Festival. ✉ *Water St.* ☎ *01298/72190* ⊕ *www.buxtonoperahouse.org.uk.*

Pavilion Gardens. These 25 acres are home to a miniature train and play area and the 1870s Pavilion building. With its ornate iron-and-glass roof, the pavilion was originally a concert hall and ballroom, but it's now the setting for an arts center, three cafés, and a gift boutique. ✉ *St. John's Rd.* ☎ *01298/23114* ⊕ *www.paviliongardens.co.uk.*

FAMILY

Fodor's Choice

★

Poole's Cavern and Buxton Country Park. The Peak District's extraordinary geology can be seen up close in this large limestone cave far beneath the 100 acres of Buxton Country Park. Inhabited in prehistoric times, the cave contains, in addition to the standard stalactites and stalagmites, the source of the River Wye, which flows through Buxton. The Country Park paths take you up to Grin Low, home to the Victorian fortified hill marker Solomon's Tower, the remains of several Bronze Age burial chambers, and views of Mam Tor and Kinder Scout; there's also a fun Go Ape! treetop adventure course on-site. Admission to the cave includes a guided tour lasting nearly an hour. ✉ *Green La.* ☎ *01298/26978* ⊕ *www.poolescavern.co.uk* ✉ *£9.75.*

WHERE TO EAT AND STAY

$$

MODERN BRITISH

Fodor's Choice

★

✕ **Columbine.** The husband-and-wife team behind Columbine are known for their fine use of local ingredients, including High Peak lamb and beef, in their inventive cuisine. The cozy venue, with upstairs and downstairs cellar seating, is an excellent spot for pre- and posttheater meals. **Known for:** produce from small local producers; pre- and posttheater menus (advance booking needed outside festival and Christmas seasons); proximity to Opera House. $ *Average main: £16* ✉ *7 Hall Bank* ☎ *01298/78752* ⊕ *www.columbinerestaurant.co.uk* ⊘ *Closed Tues. No lunch Sun. and late Dec.–mid-Jan.*

$

B&B/INN

FAMILY

🏨 **Old Hall.** In a refurbished 16th-century building claiming to be England's oldest hotel and rumored to have once accommodated Mary, Queen of Scots, this hotel overlooks the ornate Buxton Opera House. **Pros:** family-friendly, with toys for kids; good food in the restaurant; historic ambience. **Cons:** no private parking; some rooms are a bit plain; bathrooms are uninspiring. $ *Rooms from: £79* ✉ *The Square* ☎ *01298/22841* ⊕ *www.oldhallhotelbuxton.co.uk* ⟿ *38 rooms* ⦵ *Free Breakfast.*

$

B&B/INN

🏨 **Roseleigh Guesthouse.** This prize-winning B&B overlooking Pavilion Gardens has comfortable, classic rooms that chime well with the Victorian atmosphere. **Pros:** adventurous hosts who can advise on local activities; some rooms with lake views; private parking. **Cons:** no family rooms; two rooms have private but not ensuite bathrooms; some of the quirkier decorative elements might not be to everyone's taste. $ *Rooms from: £70* ✉ *19 Broad Walk* ☎ *01298/24904* ⊕ *www.roseleighhotel. co.uk* ⊘ *Closed Dec.–mid Jan.* ⟿ *14 rooms* ⦵ *Free Breakfast.*

8

SHOPPING

Buxton has a wide variety of stores, especially around Spring Gardens, the main shopping street.

Cavendish Arcade. Stores in this beautifully tiled building, located on the site of the old thermal baths, sell handmade chocolates, fashion, housewares, gifts, and natural beauty products. ⊠ *The Crescent* ⊕ *www.cavendisharcade.co.uk.*

BAKEWELL

12 miles southeast of Buxton.

In Bakewell, a medieval bridge crosses the winding River Wye in five graceful arches; a 9th-century Saxon cross that stands outside the parish church reveals the town's great age. Narrow streets and houses built out of the local gray-brown stone also make the town extremely appealing. Ceaseless traffic through the streets can take the shine off—though there's respite down on the quiet riverside paths.

This market town is the commercial hub of the Peak District, for locals and visitors. The crowds are really substantial on market day (Monday), attended by area farmers. For a self-guided hour-long stroll, pick up a map at the tourist office, where the town trail begins. A small photography exhibition upstairs explores the landscape of the Peak District.

GETTING HERE AND AROUND

TransPeak buses to Derby from Manchester's Central Coach Station stop at Bakewell, as do some National Express buses to London. By car, Bakewell is a 1½-hour drive southeast on the A6 from Manchester.

ESSENTIALS

Visitor Information Bakewell Visitor Centre. ⊠ *Old Market Hall, Bridge St.* ☏ *01629/816558* ⊕ *www.peakdistrict.gov.uk.*

EXPLORING

FAMILY

Fodor's Choice

★

Chatsworth House. One of England's greatest country houses, the "Palace of the Peak" is the ancestral home of the dukes of Devonshire and stands in vast parkland grazed by deer and sheep. Originally an Elizabethan house, it was altered over several generations starting in 1686 and now has a hodgepodge look, though the Palladian facade remains untouched. It's surrounded by woods, elaborate gardens, greenhouses, rock gardens, and a beautiful water cascade—all designed by Capability Brown in the 18th century and, in the 19th, Joseph Paxton, an engineer as well as a brilliant gardener. ■TIP➔ Plan on at least a half day to explore the grounds; avoid Sunday if you can as it gets very crowded. Inside are intricate carvings, superb furniture, Van Dyck portraits, Sir Joshua Reynolds's *Georgiana, Duchess of Devonshire and Her Baby,* John Singer Sargent's enormous *Acheson Sisters,* and fabulous rooms, including the Sculpture Gallery, the library, and the Painted Hall. Chatsworth is 4 miles northeast of Bakewell. On the estate there's a working farm with milking demonstrations, an adventure playground, cafés, restaurants, a tea shop, and a farm shop; you can even stay in several cottages scattered throughout the grounds. ⊠ *Off B6012* ☏ *01246/565300* ⊕ *www.chatsworth.org* ▣ *House,* *gardens, farm, and adventure playground £22.90 (depending on time of year); house and gardens £20.90; gardens only £12.90; farmyard and adventure playground £6; parking £3 (free with online tickets)* ⏲ *Closed 2nd wk of Jan.–late Mar.*

Eyam Plague Village. After a local tailor died of the plague in this tiny, idyllic, gray-stone village in 1665, locals isolated themselves from the outside world rather than risk the spread of Black Death (the area had hitherto been spared). They succeeded in containing the disease, but at huge cost; by the time it had run its course, most of the residents were dead. Their heroism is commemorated in florid memorials in the village churchyard. The small **Eyam Museum** puts everything into context, while **Eyam Hall and Craft Centre**, run by the National Trust, hosts history walks on the topic. ✉ *Hawkhill Rd., Eyam* ✥ *6 miles north of Bakewell off A623* ☎ *01433/631371 museum* 🌐 *www.eyam-museum.org.uk* 🎟 *Museum £2.50* ⏲ *Museum closed Mon. and Nov.–late Mar.*

Fodor's Choice ★ **Haddon Hall.** One of England's finest stately homes, and perhaps the most authentically Tudor of all the great houses, Haddon Hall bristles with intricate period detail. Built between 1180 and 1565, the house passed into the ownership of the dukes of Rutland and remained largely untouched until the early 20th century, when the ninth duke undertook a superlative restoration that revealed a series of early decorative 15th-century frescoes in the chapel. The finest of the intricate plasterwork and wooden paneling is best seen in the superb Long Gallery on the first floor. A popular filming location, Haddon's starring roles include *The Princess Bride* (1985), *Pride and Prejudice* (2005), and *The Other Boleyn Girl* (2008). ✉ *A6* ☎ *01629/812855* 🌐 *www.haddonhall.co.uk* 🎟 *£14.50, parking £3* ⏲ *Closed Oct., Nov., and late Dec.–early Apr.*

8

WHERE TO EAT AND STAY

$$$$ MODERN BRITISH Fodor's Choice ★

🍴 **Fischer's Baslow Hall.** This stately Edwardian manor on the edge of the Chatsworth Estate houses an intimate, fairly formal restaurant along with 11 elegant bedrooms (from £230). All evening meals and most lunches are fixed price; dishes rely heavily on high-quality British ingredients—wild venison, John Dory, and Cornish Dover sole—used with imagination and aplomb. **Known for:** cozy atmosphere; lovely grounds with a kitchen garden; chef's table experience. [$] *Average main: £55* ✉ *Baslow Hall, Calver Rd., Baslow* ✥ *4 miles north of Bakewell* ☎ *01246/583259* 🌐 *www.fischers-baslowhall.co.uk.*

$ BRITISH

🍴 **The Old Original Bakewell Pudding Shop.** Given the plethora of local rivals, it takes a bold establishment to claim its Bakewell puddings as "original," but those served here are among the best. The "pudding" in question is actually a dense, sugary pie with a jam and almond filling and a puff pastry crust, eaten cold or hot with custard or cream. **Known for:** breakfast sandwiches; afternoon teas ("All Things Bakewell" includes both pudding and tart); on-site deli counter. [$] *Average main: £10* ✉ *The Square* ☎ *01629/812193* 🌐 *www.bakewellpuddingshop.co.uk* ⏲ *No dinner.*

$ **Bagshaw Hall.** This characterful 17th-century property offers upmar-
HOTEL ket suites with kitchenettes or full kitchens as well as luxury touches
including bathrobes and slippers. **Pros:** a short stroll from the center of
Bakewell; self-catering facilities; attractive grounds. **Cons:** no restaurant (breakfast can be brought to rooms); no reception (need to call on
arrival); early checkout (10 am). $ *Rooms from: £90 ⊠ Bagshaw Hill*
☎ *01629/810333 ⊕ www.bagshawhall.com ⇌ 12 rooms* ⊖ *No meals.*

CHESTER, LUDLOW, AND AROUND

Rural Shropshire, one of the least populated English counties, is far
removed from most people's preconceptions of the industrial Midlands. Within its spread are towns long famed for their beauty, such
as Ludlow. Chester, one of the region's most important cities, is
renowned for its medieval heritage and wealth of half-timber buildings. The 6-mile stretch of the Ironbridge Gorge, however, gives you
the chance to experience the cradle of the Industrial Revolution with
none of the reeking smoke that gave this region west of Birmingham its
name—the Black Country—during the mid-19th century. Now taken
over by the Ironbridge Gorge Museum Trust, the bridge, the first in
the world to be built of iron and opened in 1781, is the centerpiece
of this vast museum complex.

CHESTER

75 miles north of Ludlow, 46 miles north of Shrewsbury.

Cheshire's thriving center is Chester, a city similar in some ways to
Shrewsbury, though it has many more black-and-white half-timber
buildings (some built in Georgian and Victorian times), and its medieval walls still stand. History seems more tangible in Chester than in
many other ancient cities, as modern buildings haven't been allowed to
intrude on the center. A negative result of this perfection is that Chester
has become a favorite tour bus destination, with gift shops, noise, and
crowds aplenty.

Chester has been a prominent city since the late 1st century, when
the Roman Empire expanded north to the banks of the River Dee.
The original Roman town plan is still evident: the principal streets,
Eastgate, Northgate, Watergate, and Bridge Street, lead out from the
Cross—the site of the central area of the Roman fortress—to the four
city gates. The partly excavated remains of what is thought to have been
the country's largest Roman amphitheater lie to the south of Chester's
medieval castle.

GETTING HERE AND AROUND

There's a free shuttle bus to the center if you arrive by train, and buses
pull up at Vicar's Lane in the center (Monday to Saturday). Chester
is 180 miles from London and about two hours by train; some trains
change at Crewe. If you're driving and here for a day only, use the
city's Park and Ride lots, as central parking lots fill quickly, especially
in summer.

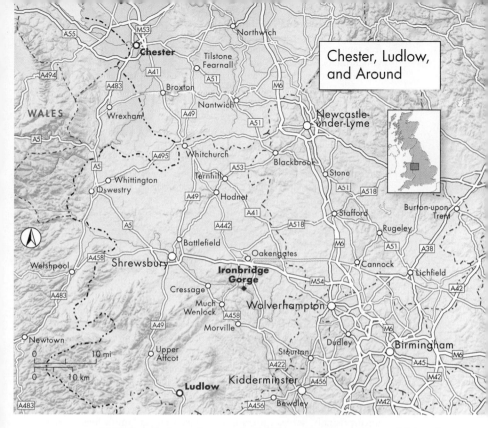

Chester, Ludlow, and Around

Guided walks leave the town hall daily at 10:30 am with an additional tour at 2 pm from Easter to October (£6). In summer the 10:30 am tour ends with a proclamation from the Town Crier, who is dressed in traditional attire.

ESSENTIALS

Visitor and Tour Information Chester Tourist Information Centre. ⊠ *Town Hall, Northgate St.* ☎ *01244/405340* ⊕ *www.visitchester.com/plan-your-visit/visitor-information-centre.* **City Sightseeing.** ☎ *01244/347452* ⊕ *www.city-sightseeing.com/en/89/chester.*

EXPLORING

Fodor's Choice ★ **Chester Cathedral.** Tradition has it that in Roman times a church of some sort stood on the site of what is now Chester Cathedral, but records indicate construction around AD 900. The earliest work traceable today, mainly in the north transept, is that of the 11th-century Benedictine abbey. After Henry VIII dissolved the monasteries in the 16th century, the abbey church became the cathedral church of the new diocese of Chester. The misericords in the choir stalls reveal carved figures of people and animals, both real and mythical, and above is a gilded and colorful vaulted ceiling. Cathedral at Height tours (£8) take you to parts of the building usually off-limits to visitors, including the roof—from which you can see two countries (England and Wales) and five separate counties. You can also take the Cathedral and Cruise tour, which includes a tower visit, entrance to the Cathedral Falconry and Nature Gardens, and a river cruise for just £13.50; reservations are essential. ✉ *St. Werburgh St., off Market Sq.* ☎ *01244/500959* 🌐 *www.chestercathedral.com* 🕒 *No tours Sun.*

Chester Rows. Chester's unique Rows, which originated in the 12th and 13th centuries, are essentially double rows of stores, one at street level and the other on the second floor with galleries overlooking the street. The Rows line the junction of the four streets in the old town. They have medieval crypts below them, and some reveal Roman foundations. **■ TIP→ You can view some of these Roman foundations in the basement of fast-food restaurant Spudulike at 39 Bridge Street.** ✉ *Chester* 🌐 *www.visitchester.com/things-to-do/chester-rows-p22731.*

City walls. Accessible from several points, the city walls provide splendid views of Chester and its surroundings. The whole circuit is 2 miles, but if your time is short, climb the steps at Newgate and walk along toward Eastgate to see the great ornamental **Eastgate Clock,** erected to commemorate Queen Victoria's Diamond Jubilee in 1897. Lots of small shops near this part of the walls sell old books, old postcards, antiques, and jewelry. Where the **Bridge of Sighs** (named after the enclosed bridge in Venice that it closely resembles) crosses the canal, descend to street level and walk up Northgate Street into Market Square. ✉ *Chester.*

WHERE TO EAT

$ BRITISH 🍴 **Albion.** You feel as if you're stepping back in time at this Victorian pub; the posters, advertisements, flags, and curios tell you the idiosyncratic landlord keeps it as it would have been during World War I. The candlelit restaurant forms one of the three snug rooms and, unsurprisingly, serves up traditional fare such as lamb's liver, corned beef hash, and gammon (thick-sliced ham) with pease pudding. **Known for:** old-fashioned British food; historic, old-school ambience. [$] *Average main: £10* ✉ *Park St.* ☎ *01244/340345* 🌐 *www.albioninnchester.co.uk* 🕒 *No dinner Sun.*

$$ BISTRO 🍴 **Chez Jules.** Once a fire station, this bustling bistro is now unashamedly French and rustic, with red-and-white-check tablecloths and a menu chalked up on the blackboard. Start perhaps with some *moules marinières* (mussels cooked in a white-wine-and-onion sauce) or French onion soup, followed by grilled sea bass or a classic rib-eye steak with Café du Paris butter. **Known for:** rural French cooking; dishes that change daily; good value set menus. [$] *Average main: £17* ✉ *71 Northgate St.* ☎ *01244/400014* 🌐 *www.chezjules.com.*

$$$$ FRENCH 🍴 **Simon Radley at the Chester Grosvenor.** Named for its noted chef, this Michelin-starred restaurant has a sophisticated panache and prices to match. Expect the seasonal but not the usual: the Two Hens features black-leg chicken alongside lobster, while the wild halibut comes with shaved octopus and seaweed dumplings. **Known for:** unexpected flavor combinations; smart dress code and no children under 12; reservations needed for weekend. [$] *Average main: £45* ✉ *Chester Grosvenor Hotel, Eastgate St.* ☎ *01244/324024* 🌐 *www.chestergrosvenor.com/simon-radley-restaurant* 🕒 *Closed Sun. and Mon.* 👔 *Jacket required.*

WHERE TO STAY

$$$ HOTEL Fodor'sChoice ★ **Chester Grosvenor Hotel.** Handmade Italian furniture and swaths of French silk fill this deluxe downtown hotel in a Tudor-style building, which was established in 1865. **Pros:** pampered luxury; superb food; excellent service and facilities. **Cons:** no private parking; spa is small; extra for cooked breakfast. [$] *Rooms from: £175* ✉ *Eastgate* ☎ *01244/324024* 🌐 *www.chestergrosvenor.com* 🛏 *80 rooms* 🍴 *Free Breakfast.*

$ B&B/INN **Grove Villa.** This family-run B&B is housed in a charming Victorian building with antique furnishings on the banks of the River Dee. **Pros:** beautiful river location; breakfast around a communal table; friendly and welcoming hosts. **Cons:** no credit cards; no Internet connection; 15 minutes to town center. [$] *Rooms from: £79* ✉ *18 The Groves* ☎ *01244/349713* 🌐 *www.grovevillachester.com* 💳 *No credit cards* 🛏 *3 rooms* 🍴 *Free Breakfast.*

SHOPPING

Chester Market. This indoor market, near the Town Hall, has more than 50 stalls, including Chester's only fishmonger. It's open Monday through Saturday from 8 am until 5 pm (except for bank holidays). ✉ *6 Princess St.* 🌐 *www.chester.market.*

IRONBRIDGE GORGE

4 miles east of Much Wenlock, 15 miles east of Shrewsbury, 28 miles northwest of Birmingham.

Fodor'sChoice ★ The River Severn and its tree-cloaked banks make an attractive backdrop to this cluster of villages; within a mile of the graceful span of the world's first iron bridge are fascinating museums exploring the area's industrial past and the reasons why it's been described as the "cradle of the Industrial Revolution."

8

GETTING HERE AND AROUND

To drive here from Shrewsbury, take the A5 east, A442 south, and then A4169 west before following the brown signs for Ironbridge. On weekends and bank holidays from Easter to late October, the Gorge Connect Bus shuttles passengers between Ironbridge's museums every 30 minutes; it's just £1 to museum passport holders.

ESSENTIALS

Visitor Information Ironbridge Visitor Information Centre. ✉ *The Museum of the Gorge, The Wharfage, Telford* ☎ *01952/433424* 🌐 *www.ironbridge.org.uk.*

EXPLORING

FAMILY Fodor'sChoice ★ **Ironbridge Gorge Museum.** The 10 sites that make up the Ironbridge Gorge Museum—a World Heritage Site spread over 6 square miles—preserve the area's fascinating industrial history in spectacular fashion. The best starting point is the **Museum of the Gorge,** which has a good selection of literature and an audiovisual show on the history of the area. In nearby Coalbrookdale, the **Museum of Iron** explains the production of iron and steel. You can see the blast furnace built by Abraham Darby, who developed the original coke process in 1709. The adjacent **Enginuity** exhibition is a hands-on, feet-on interactive exploration of engineering that's good for kids. From here, drive the few miles along the river until the arches of the **Iron Bridge** come into view. Designed by T.F. Pritchard, smelted by Darby, and erected between 1777 and 1779, this graceful arch spanning the River Severn can best be seen—and photographed—from the towpath, a riverside walk edged with wildflowers and shrubs. The tolhouse on the far side houses an exhibition on the bridge's history and restoration.

A mile farther along the river is the **Jackfield Tile Museum,** a repository of decorative tiles from the 19th and 20th centuries. Another half mile brings you to the **Coalport China Museum.** Exhibits show some of the factory's most beautiful wares, and craftspeople give demonstrations; visit the restrooms for the unique communal washbasins. A short walk from Coalport is the **Tar Tunnel**, part of a 1787 tar mine; note the black bitumen still seeping through the walls. Nearby is Ironbridge's star attraction: **Blists Hill Victorian Town,** where you can see old mines, furnaces, and a wrought-iron works. The main draw is the re-creation of the "town" itself, with its doctor's office, bakery, grocer's, candle maker's, sawmill, printing shop, and candy store. At the entrance you can change some money for specially minted pennies and make purchases from the shops. Shopkeepers, the bank manager, and the doctor's wife are on hand to give you advice. If you don't fancy the refreshments at the Fried Fish Dealers, you could drop into the **New Inn** pub (in Blists Hill) for a traditional ale or ginger beer, and join one of the sing-alongs around the piano that take place a couple of times every afternoon; or, for something more formal, try the **Club Room** restaurant next door. Allow at least a full day to appreciate all the major sights, and perhaps to take a stroll around the famous Iron Bridge or hunt for Coalport china in the stores clustered near it. On weekends and national holidays from April through October, a shuttle bus takes you between sites. ✉ *B4380, Telford* ☎ *01952/433424* 🌐 *www.ironbridge.org.uk* 🎟 *Passport ticket (all attractions, valid 1 year) £25. Individual sites: Blists Hill £16.25; Enginuity, Coalport China Museum, Jackfield Tile Museum, and Museum of Iron £8.85 each; Museum of the Gorge £4.50; Tar Tunnel £3.40.*

WHERE TO EAT AND STAY

$$$$ MODERN BRITISH

🍴 **Restaurant Severn.** At this discreet restaurant set back from the main road in the center of Ironbridge, the concept is simple: locally sourced produce and modern techniques are combined to serve up a twist of British classics and European favorites. Start with a Scotch egg with brown sauce and pancetta before moving on to pork belly stuffed with black pudding, kale, and spiced red cabbage. **Known for:** British classics with a modern slant; personal service; fabulous wines. [$] *Average main: £28* ✉ *33 High St., Ironbridge* ☎ *01952/432233* 🌐 *www.restaurantsevern.co.uk* 🕒 *Closed Mon. and Tues.*

$$ B&B/INN Fodor's Choice ★

🏨 **Library House.** Built in 1740 and at one time the village's library, this small guesthouse sits on the hillside near the Ironbridge museums and just a few steps from the bridge. **Pros:** welcoming hosts; good location; elegant bedrooms. **Cons:** no restaurant; books up quickly; might be too personable for some. [$] *Rooms from: £100* ✉ *11 Severn Bank, Telford* ☎ *01952/432299* 🌐 *www.libraryhouse.com* 🛏 *3 rooms* 🍽 *Free Breakfast.*

LUDLOW

25 miles south of Ironbridge Gorge, 27 miles south of Shrewsbury, 24 miles north of Hereford.

Fodor's Choice ★ Medieval, Georgian, and Victorian buildings jostle for attention in pretty Ludlow, which has a finer display of black-and-white half-timber buildings than even Shrewsbury. Dominating the center is the Church of St. Laurence, its extravagant size a testimony to the town's prosperous medieval wool trade. Cross the River Teme and climb Whitcliffe Common for a spectacular view of the church and the Norman castle.

Several outstanding restaurants have given the town of just 11,000 a reputation as a culinary hot spot (many are also popular hotels or B&Bs). Ludlow is a proponent of the Slow Food movement, which focuses on food traditions and responsible production with the aim of protecting forgotten foods, such as the Shropshire prune, from being lost forever.

GETTING HERE AND AROUND

From London Paddington, the journey time by train is 3½ hours (changing at Newport in southern Wales), from Shrewsbury 30 minutes, and from Birmingham just under 2 hours with a change in Shrewsbury. From the train station, it's less than a 10-minute walk to the city center. Driving from London, take the M40, M42, and A448 to Kidderminster, then the A456 and A4117 to Ludlow. The town has good parking and is easily walkable.

ESSENTIALS

Visitor Information Ludlow Visitor Information Centre. ✉ *Ludlow Assembly Rooms, 1 Mill St.* ☎ *01584/875053* 🌐 *www.ludlow.org.uk.*

8

EXPLORING

FAMILY Fodor's Choice ★ **Ludlow Castle.** The "very perfection of decay," according to author Daniel Defoe, the ruins of this red sandstone castle date from 1085. No wonder the massive structure dwarfs the town: it served as a vital stronghold for centuries and was the seat of the Marcher Lords who ruled "the Marches," the local name for the border region. The two sons of Edward IV—the little princes of the Tower of London—spent time here before being dispatched to London and before their death in 1483. Follow the terraced walk around the castle for a lovely view of the countryside. ✉ *Castle Sq.* ☎ *01584/873355* 🌐 *www.ludlowcastle.com* 🎫 *£5* 🕒 *Closed weekdays early Jan.–early Feb.*

WHERE TO STAY

$ HOTEL 🏨 **The Cliffe at Dinham.** Built in the 1850s, this friendly, redbrick inn near Ludlow Castle has comfortable bedrooms with plenty of natural light, which are simply decorated with heavy pine furniture. **Pros:** lovely staff; great view of the castle; free Wi-Fi. **Cons:** not all rooms have good views; bar area a little bland; rooms aren't very exciting. [$] *Rooms from: £85* ✉ *Dinham* ☎ *01584/872063* 🌐 *www.thecliffehotel.co.uk* 🛏 *12 rooms* 🍴 *Free Breakfast.*

$$$ HOTEL **The Feathers.** Even if you're not staying here, take time to admire the extravagant half-timber facade of this hotel, built in the early 17th century and described by the historian Jan Morris in the *New York Times* as "the most handsome inn in the world." **Pros:** ornate plasterwork; unpretentious feel; some four-poster beds. **Cons:** most guest rooms lack traditional feel; can be very tourist heavy; it's an old building and sometimes this shows. [$] *Rooms from: £195* ✉ *21 Bullring* ☎ *01584/875261* 🌐 *www.feathersatludlow.co.uk* 🛏 *40 rooms* 🍴 *Free Breakfast.*

$ HOTEL Fodor's Choice ★ **Fishmore Hall.** Saved from dereliction in the late 2000s, Fishmore Hall has been beautifully converted from a crumbling old mansion into a relaxing, contemporary lodge. **Pros:** lovely location; well-designed rooms; serene, luxurious spa. **Cons:** restaurant is pricey; a little out of town; outdoor hot tub is not to everyone's liking. [$] *Rooms from: £99* ✉ *Fishmore Rd.* ☎ *01584/875148* 🌐 *www.fishmorehall.co.uk* 🛏 *15 rooms* 🍴 *Free Breakfast.*

$$ B&B/INN FAMILY Fodor's Choice ★ **Timberstone.** The Read family has turned a rambling stone cottage in the Clee Hills into a welcoming haven with rooms furnished in neutral tones in a soothing, contemporary style. **Pros:** relaxing and hospitable; geared to families; great food. **Cons:** far from the center of Ludlow; rustic living may not appeal to everyone; dinner menu is limited. [$] *Rooms from: £100* ✉ *B4363, Cleestanton* ☎ *01584/823519* 🌐 *www.timberstoneludlow.co.uk* 🛏 *4 rooms* 🍴 *Free Breakfast.*

9

THE LAKE DISTRICT

Visit Fodors.com for advice, updates, and bookings

WELCOME TO THE LAKE DISTRICT

TOP REASONS TO GO

★ **Hiking:** Whether it's a demanding trek or a gentle stroll, walking is the way to see the Lake District at its best.

★ **Boating:** There's nowhere better for renting a small boat or taking a cruise. The Coniston Boating Centre and Derwent Water Marina near Keswick are possible places to start.

★ **Literary landscapes:** The Lake District has a rich literary history, in the children's books of Beatrix Potter, in the writings of John Ruskin, and in the poems of William Wordsworth. Stop at any of the writers' homes to enrich your experience.

★ **Pints and pubs:** A pint of real ale in one of the region's inns, such as the Drunken Duck near Hawkshead, may never taste as good as after a day of walking.

★ **Sunrise at Castlerigg:** The stone circle at Castlerigg, in a hollow ringed by peaks, is a reminder of the region's ancient history.

The Lake District is in northwest England, some 70 miles north of the industrial belt which stretches from Liverpool to Manchester, and south of Scotland. The major gateway from the south is Kendal, and from the north, Penrith. Both are on the M6 motorway. Main-line trains stop at Oxenholme, near Kendal, with a branch linking Oxenholme to Kendal and Windermere. Windermere, in the south, is the most obvious starting point and has museums, cafés, and gift shops. But the farther (and higher) you can get from the southern towns, the more you'll appreciate the area's spectacular landscapes. Lake District National Park breaks into two reasonably distinct sections: the gentler, rolling south and the craggier, wilder north.

1 The Southern Lakes. The southern lakes and valleys contain the park's most popular destinations, and thus those most overcrowded in summer. The region incorporates the largest body of water, Windermere, as well as most of the quintessential Lakeland towns and villages: Bowness, Ambleside, Grasmere, Elterwater, Coniston, and Hawkshead. To the east and west of this cluster of habitation, the valleys and fells climb to some beautiful upland country.

2 Penrith and the Northern Lakes. In the north, the landscape opens out across the bleaker fells to reveal challenging, spectacular walking country. Here, in the northern lakes, south of Keswick, you have the best chance to get away from the crowds. This region's northwestern reaches are largely unexplored.

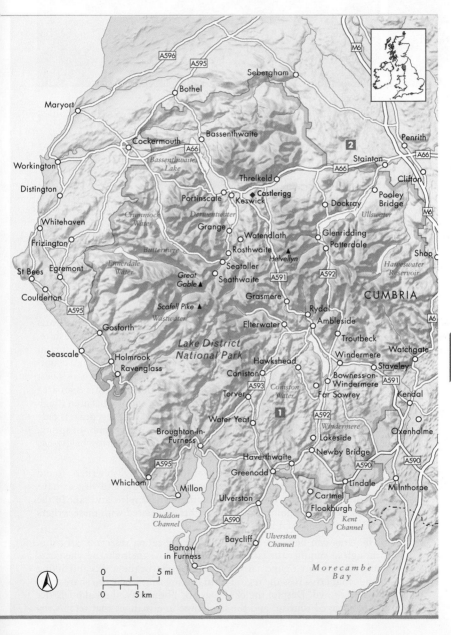

Maryort

Workington

Distington

Whitehaven

Frizington

St Bees

Egremont

Coulderton

Gosforth

Seascale

Holmrook
Ravenglass

Broughton-in-Furness

Whicham

Millon

A596

A595

Bothel

Sebergham

Cockermouth

Bassenthwaite

A66

*Bassenthwaite
Lake*

Threlkeld

Portinscale   ◆ **Castlerigg**
              Keswick

*Crummock
Water*

Derwentwater

Grange

Watendlath

Rosthwaite

Seatoller

Buttermere

*Ennerdale
Water*

Seathwaite

Great
Gable ▲

Scafell Pike ▲

Wastwater

Grasmere

Elterwater

Lake District
National Park

Hawkshead

Coniston

A593   *Coniston
        Water*

Torver

Water Yeat

2

Penrith

Stainton   A66

A66

Clifton

Dockray   Pooley
           Bridge

Ullswater

M6

Glenridding
Patterdale

Helvellyn ▲

A591   A592

Shap

*Haweswater
Reservoir*

CUMBRIA

A6

Rydal
Ambleside

Troutbeck

Windermere

Bowness-on-
Windermere

Far Sawrey

Watchgate

Staveley

A591

Kendal

9

A592

Windermere

Oxenholme

Lakeside

Newby Bridge

Haverthwaite

Greenodd

Ulverston

Baycliff

*Duddon
Channel*

A595

A590

Lindale

Cartmel

Flookburgh

Milnthorpe

A590

*Ulverston
Channel*

*Kent
Channel*

Barrow
in Furness

*M o r e c a m b e
B a y*

0   5 mi

0   5 km

M6

Updated
by Sophie
Ibbotson

"Let nature be your teacher." Wordsworth's ideal comes true in this popular national park of jagged mountains, waterfalls, wooded valleys, and stone-built villages. No mountains in Britain give a greater impression of majesty; deeper and bluer lakes can be found, but none that fit so readily into the surrounding scene. Outdoors enthusiasts flock to this region for boating or hiking, while literary types visit the homes of Beatrix Potter, William Wordsworth, and other classic writers.

In 1951 the Lake District National Park was created here from parts of the old counties of Cumberland, Westmorland, and Lancashire. The Lake District is a contour map come to life, covering an area of approximately 885 square miles and holding 16 major lakes and countless smaller stretches of water. The scenery is key to all the park's best activities: you can cross it by car in about an hour, but this is an area meant to be walked or boated or climbed. The mountains aren't high by international standards—Scafell Pike, England's highest peak, is only 3,210 feet above sea level—but they can be tricky to climb. In spring, many summits remain snowcapped long after the weather below has turned mild.

The poets Wordsworth and Coleridge, and other English writers, found the Lake District an inspiring setting for their work, and visitors have followed ever since, to walk, go boating, or just relax and take in the views. Seeing the homes and other sights associated with these writers can occupy part of a trip.

This area can be one of Britain's most appealing reservoirs of calm, though in summer the lakeside towns can lose their charm when cars and tour buses clog the narrow streets. Similarly, the walks and hiking trails that crisscross the region seem less inviting when you share them with a crowd. Despite the challenges of popularity, the Lake District has managed tourism and the landscape in a manner that retains the character of the villages and the natural environment. Explore beyond Windermere and Keswick to discover little farming communities eking out a living despite the occasionally harsh conditions.

Today, too, a new generation of hotel and restaurant owners is making more creative use of the local foods and other assets of the Lakeland fells, and chic modern or foodie-oriented establishments are springing up next to traditional tearooms and chintz-filled inns.

Off-season visits can be a real treat. All those inns and bed-and-breakfasts that turn away crowds in summer are eager for business the rest of the year (and their rates drop accordingly). It's not an easy task to find a succession of sunny days in the Lake District—some malicious statisticians allot to it about 250 rainy days a year—but when the sun breaks through and brightens the surfaces of the lakes, it's an away-from-it-all place to remember.

PLANNER

WHEN TO GO

The Lake District is one of the rainiest areas in Britain, but June, July, and August hold the best hope of fine weather, and summer is the time for all the major festivals. You will, however, be sharing the lakes with thousands of other people. If you travel at this time, turn up early at popular museums and attractions and expect to work to find parking. April and May, as well as September and October, are good alternatives. Later and earlier in the year there'll be even more space and freedom, but many attractions close, and from December to March, snow and ice can sometimes block high passes and may preclude serious hill walking without heavy-duty equipment.

PLANNING YOUR TIME

You could spend months tramping the hills, valleys, and fells of the Lake District, or, in three days you could drive through the major towns and villages. The key is not to do too much in too short a time. If you're traveling by public transportation, many places will be off-limits. As a base, Windermere has the best transport links, but it can be crowded and it has less character than some of the smaller towns like Ambleside and Keswick, which also have plenty of sleeping and eating options. For a more intimate version of village life, try Coniston, Hawkshead, or Grasmere. Keep in mind that the northern and western lakes have the most dramatic scenery and offer the best opportunity to escape the summertime hordes.

The Lake District may be compact, but it's not a place to hurry. Allow plenty of time for walking: paths can be steep and rocky, and in any case you'll want to stop frequently to look at the great views. A good day's walking with a picnic can be done from nearly anywhere. Driving brings its own speed inhibitors, from sheep on the roads to slow tractors.

You're likely to be based down near lake level, but try to experience the hills, too. If you're short of time, a drive over one of the high passes such as Honister will give you a glimpse of the enormity of the landscape.

GETTING HERE AND AROUND

AIR TRAVEL

Manchester Airport has its own rail station with direct service to Carlisle, Windermere, and Barrow-in-Furness. Manchester is 70 miles from the southern part of the Lake District.

Contact Manchester Airport. ✉ *M56, Near Junctions 5 and 6* ☎ *0808/169–7030* ⊕ *www.manchesterairport.co.uk.*

BOAT TRAVEL

Whether you rent a boat or take a ride on a modern launch or vintage vessel, getting out on the water is a fun (and often useful) way to see the Lake District. Windermere, Coniston Water, and Derwentwater all have boat rental facilities.

BUS TRAVEL

National Express serves the region from London's Victoria Coach Station and from Manchester's Chorlton Street Station. Average travel time to Kendal is just over 7 hours from London; to Windermere, 7½ hours; and to Keswick, 8¼ hours. From Manchester there's one bus a day to Windermere via Ambleside, Grasmere, and Keswick. There's direct bus service to the Lake District from Carlisle, Lancaster, and York.

Stagecoach in Cumbria provides local service between Lakeland towns and through the valleys and high passes. Bus service between main tourist centers is fairly frequent on weekdays, but much reduced on weekends and bank holidays. Don't count on reaching the more remote parts of the area by bus. Off-the-beaten-track touring requires a car or strong legs. A one-week Cumbria Megarider ticket (£28), available on the bus, is valid on all routes. Dayrider tickets (£6–£8) are valid for a day; the price varies depending on how far you wish to travel. Contact Traveline for up-to-date timetables.

Contacts National Express. ☎ *0871/781–8181* ⊕ *www.nationalexpress.com.* **Stagecoach.** ☎ *01228/589222* ⊕ *www.stagecoachbus.com.* **Traveline.** ☎ *0871/200–2233* ⊕ *www.traveline.info.*

CAR TRAVEL

A car is almost essential in the Lake District; bus service is limited and trains can get you to the edge of the national park but no farther. You can rent cars in Penrith and Kendal. Roads within the region are generally good, although minor routes and mountain passes can be steep and narrow. Warning signs are often posted if snow or ice has made a road impassable; check local weather forecasts in winter before heading out. In July and August and during the long public holiday weekends, expect heavy traffic. The Lake District has plenty of parking lots; use them to avoid blocking narrow lanes.

To reach the Lake District by car from London, take M1 north to M6, getting off either at Junction 36 and joining A590/A591 west (around the Kendal bypass to Windermere) or at Junction 40, joining A66 direct to Keswick and the northern lakes region. Travel time to Kendal is about four to five hours, to Keswick five to six hours. Expect heavy traffic out of London on weekends.

TRAIN TRAVEL

There are direct trains from Manchester and Manchester airport to Windermere. For schedule information, call National Rail Enquiries. Two train companies serve the region from London's Euston Station: take a Virgin or Northern Rail train bound for Carlisle, Edinburgh, or Glasgow and change at Oxenholme for the branch line service to Kendal and Windermere. Average travel time from London to Windermere (including the change) is 3¼ hours. If you're heading for Keswick, you can either take the train to Windermere and continue from there by Stagecoach bus (Bus 554/555/556; 70 minutes) or stay on the main London–Carlisle train to Penrith Station (4 hours), from which Stagecoach buses (Bus X5) also run to Keswick (45 minutes). Direct trains from Manchester depart for Windermere five times daily (travel time 2 hours). First North Western runs a local service from Windermere and Barrow-in-Furness to Manchester Airport. National Rail can handle all questions about trains.

Train connections are good around the edges of the Lake District, but you must take the bus or drive to reach the central Lakeland region. Trains are sometimes reduced, or nonexistent, on Sunday.

Contacts National Rail Enquiries. ☎ *03457/484950* ⊕ *www.nationalrail. co.uk.* **Northern Rail.** ☎ *0800/200–6060* ⊕ *www.northernrail.org.* **Virgin Trains.** ☎ *0344/556–5650* ⊕ *www.virgintrains.co.uk.*

THE LAKE DISTRICT NATIONAL PARK

The Lake District National Park head office (and main visitor center) is at Brockhole, north of Windermere. Helpful regional national-park information centers sell books and maps, book accommodations, and provide walking advice.

Contacts Bowness Bay Information Centre. ✉ *Glebe Rd., Bowness-on-Windermere* ☎ *0845/901–0845* ⊕ *www.lakedistrict.gov.uk.* **Keswick Information Centre.** ✉ *Moot Hall, Main St., Keswick* ☎ *0845/901–0845* ⊕ *www.keswick. org.* **Lake District Visitor Centre.** ✉ *Brockhole, Ambleside Rd., Windermere* ☎ *015394/46601* ⊕ *www.brockhole.co.uk.* **Ullswater Information Centre.** ✉ *Beckside Car Park, off Greenside Rd., Glenridding* ☎ *0845/901–0845* ⊕ *www. lakedistrict.gov.uk.*

TOURS

Fodor's Choice
★
Head to the Hills. With more than 80 lakes, meres, and tarns, Cumbria is a great place for open-water swimming. Head to the Hills has specialized swimming wet suits and a wealth of knowledge and enthusiasm about the best places to swim. Guided trips range from a couple of hours to weekends with accommodation and food included. As a way to see the lakes, the view and the experience from the water is hard to beat. ✉ *2 Compston Rd., Ambleside* ☎ *015394/33826* ⊕ *www. headtothehills.co.uk.*

RESTAURANTS

Lakeland restaurants increasingly reflect a growing British awareness of good food. Local sourcing and international influences are common, and even old Cumberland favorites are being creatively reinvented. Pub dining in the Lake District can be excellent—the hearty fare often makes use of local ingredients such as Herdwick lamb, and real ales are a good accompaniment. If you're going walking, ask your hotel or B&B about making you a packed lunch. Some local delicatessens also offer this service. *Restaurant reviews have been shortened. For full information, visit Fodors.com.*

HOTELS

Your choices include everything from small country inns to grand lakeside hotels; many hotels offer the option of paying a higher price that includes dinner as well as breakfast. The regional mainstay is the bed-and-breakfast, from the house on Main Street to an isolated farmhouse. Most country hotels and B&Bs gladly cater to hikers and can provide on-the-spot information. Wherever you stay, book well in advance for summer visits, especially those in late July and August. In winter many accommodations close for a month or two. On weekends and in summer it may be hard to get a reservation for a single night. Internet access is improving, and an increasing number of hotels and cafés offer Wi-Fi access. *Hotel reviews have been shortened. For full information, visit Fodors.com.*

WHAT IT COSTS IN POUNDS			
$	**$$**	**$$$**	**$$$$**
Restaurants	under £15	£15–£19	£20–£25	over £25
Hotels	under £100	£100–£160	£161–£220	over £220

Restaurant prices are the average cost of a main course at dinner, or if dinner is not served, at lunch. Hotel prices are the lowest cost of a standard double room in high season, including 20% V.A.T.

VISITOR INFORMATION

Contacts Cumbria Tourism. ⊠ *Windermere Rd., Staveley* ☎ *01539/822222* ⊕ *www.golakes.co.uk.*

THE SOUTHERN LAKES

Among the many attractions here are the small resort towns clustered around Windermere, England's largest lake, and the area's hideaway valleys, rugged walking centers, and monuments rich in literary associations. This is the easiest part of the Lake District to reach, with Kendal, the largest town, just a short distance from the M6 motorway. An obvious route from Kendal takes in Windermere, the area's natural touring center, before moving north through Ambleside and Rydal Water to Grasmere. Some of the loveliest Lakeland scenery is to be found by then turning south, through Elterwater, Hawkshead, and Coniston.

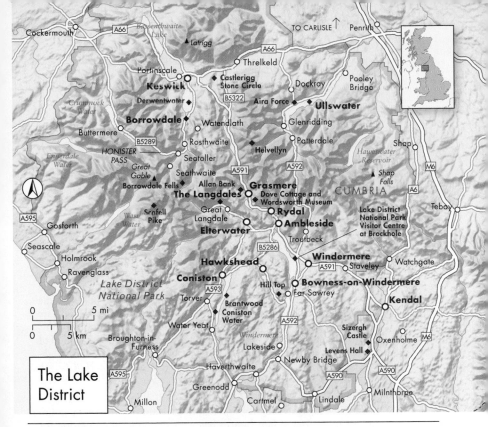

KENDAL

70 miles north of Manchester.

The southern gateway to the Lake District is the "Auld Gray Town" of Kendal, outside the national park and less touristy than the towns to the northwest. You may want to stay closer to the action, but the town has some worthwhile sights. Nearby hills frame Kendal's gray stone houses and provide some delightful walks; you can also explore the ruins of Kendal Castle. ■ TIP➔ Pack a slab of Kendal mint cake, the local peppermint candy that British walkers and climbers swear by. It's for sale around the region.

The town's motto, "Wool Is My Bread," refers to its importance as a textile center in northern England before the Industrial Revolution. It was known for manufacturing woolen cloth, especially Kendal Green, which archers favored. Away from the main road are quiet courtyards and winding medieval streets known as "ginnels." Wool merchants used these for easy access to the River Kent.

GETTING HERE AND AROUND

Kendal is just off the M6, about 70 miles north of Manchester. It has train service via a branch line from Oxenholme, and National Express bus service from London as well. It's the largest town in the area but is still plenty small enough to walk around.

ESSENTIALS

Visitor Information **Kendal Tourist Information Centre.** ✉ *Made in Cumbria, 48 Branthwaite Brow* ☎ *01539/735891* 🌐 *www.exploresouthlakeland.co.uk.*

EXPLORING

Fodor's Choice ★ **Abbot Hall.** The region's finest art gallery, Abbot Hall occupies a Palladian-style Georgian mansion built in 1759. In the permanent collection are works by Victorian artist and critic John Ruskin, who lived near Coniston, and by 18th-century portrait painter George Romney, who worked in Kendal. *The Great Picture*, a grand 17th-century triptych of the life of Lady Ann Clifford, is attributed to Flemish painter Jan Van Belcamp. The gallery also owns some excellent contemporary art, including work by Barbara Hepworth, Ben Nicholson, Winifred Nicholson, and L.S. Lowry, and the always interesting temporary exhibitions showcase the best of British art. There's also an excellent café. Abbot Hall is on the River Kent, next to the parish church. The **Museum of Lakeland Life** (🌐 *www.lakelandmuseum.org.uk*) has exhibits on 1930s photography, blacksmithing, and wheelwrighting as well as a wonderful re-creation of a period pharmacy; it's in the former stable block of the hall. ✉ *Off Highgate* ☎ *01539/722464* 🌐 *www.abbothall.org.uk* 🎫 *Abbot Hall £7.70; Museum of Lakeland Life £5.50; combined ticket £9.90* ⏲ *Closed Sun.*

WHERE TO EAT AND STAY

$$ MODERN BRITISH 🍴 **The Moon Highgate.** Small but sleek, this restaurant with an open fire and artfully battered floorboards has won a good local reputation for high-quality dishes. The vegetarian selections are always worthwhile, and the sometimes adventurous Modern British cooking shows Mediterranean flourishes. **Known for:** imaginative British menu; seasonal ingredients; fixed-price early dinners. [$] *Average main: £17* ✉ *129 Highgate* ☎ *01539/729254* 🌐 *www.themoonhighgate.com* ⏲ *Closed Sun. and Mon.*

$ HOTEL 🏨 **Kendal Hostel.** Right on Kendal's main street, this upscale hostel is located in an attractive building with plenty of character. **Pros:** central location; friendly staff; self-catering facilities. **Cons:** shared bathrooms; can get noisy with large groups; no free parking. [$] *Rooms from: £78* ✉ *118-120 Highgate* ☎ *153/972–4066* 🌐 *www.kendalhostel.com* 🛏 *14 rooms* 🍽 *No meals.*

NIGHTLIFE AND PERFORMING ARTS

Fodor's Choice ★ **Brewery Arts Centre.** A contemporary complex in a converted brewery, the Brewery Arts Centre includes a gallery, theater, cinemas, and workshop spaces. The Grain Store, overlooking lovely gardens, serves lunch and dinner; the Warehouse Café offers tasty toasted sandwiches and occasional live performances; and Vats Bar has good craft beer on tap as well as a nice wine selection. In November the Mountain Film Festival presents productions aimed at climbers and walkers. ✉ *Highgate* ☎ *01539/725133* 🌐 *www.breweryarts.co.uk* 🎫 *Free.*

WINDERMERE AND BOWNESS-ON-WINDERMERE

10 miles northwest of Kendal.

For a natural touring base for the southern half of the Lake District, you don't need to look much farther than Windermere, though it does get crowded in summer. The resort became popular in the Victorian era when the arrival of the railway made the remote and rugged area accessible. Wordsworth and Ruskin opposed the railway, fearing an influx of tourists would ruin the tranquil place. Sure enough, the railway terminus in 1847 brought with it Victorian day-trippers, and the original hamlet of Birthwaite was subsumed by the new town of Windermere, named after the lake.

Windermere has continued to flourish, despite being a mile or so from the water; the development now spreads to envelop the slate-gray lakeside village of Bowness-on-Windermere. Bowness is the more attractive of the two, but they're so close it doesn't matter where you stay.

GETTING HERE AND AROUND

Windermere is easily reached by car, less than a half hour off the M6. There's also a train station at the eastern edge of town; change at Oxenholme for the branch line to Kendal and Windermere.

Bus 599, leaving every 20 minutes in summer (hourly the rest of the year) from outside the Windermere train station, links the town with Bowness.

The Windermere Ferry, which carries cars and pedestrians, crosses from Ferry Nab on the Bowness side of the lake to reach Far Sawrey and the road to Hawkshead. With year-round ferry service between Ambleside, Bowness, Brockhole, and Lakeside, Windermere Lake Cruises is a pleasant way to experience the lake.

ESSENTIALS

Contacts Windermere Ferry. ☎ *01228/227653* ⊕ *www.cumbria.gov.uk.* **Windermere Lake Cruises.** ☎ *015394/43360* ⊕ *www.windermere-lakecruises. co.uk.*

EXPLORING

Fodor'sChoice **Blackwell.** From 1898 to 1900, architect Mackay Hugh Baillie Scott
★ (1865–1945) designed Blackwell, a quintessential Arts and Crafts house with carved paneling, delicate plasterwork, and a startling sense of light and space. Originally a retreat for a Manchester brewery owner, the house is a refined mix of modern style and the local vernacular. Lime-washed walls and sloping slate roofs make it fit elegantly into the landscape above Windermere, and the artful integration of decorative features into stained glass, stonework, friezes, and wrought iron gives the house a sleekly contemporary feel. Accessibility is wonderful here: nothing is roped off and you can even play the piano. There's some Bailie Scott furniture, too, and an exhibition space upstairs. Peruse the shop and try the honey-roast ham in the excellent tearoom. The grounds are also worth a visit; they often host contemporary sculpture installations. ✉ *B5360, Windermere* ☎ *015394/46139* ⊕ *www.black- well.org.uk* ✐ *£8.*

9

FAMILY **Brockhole.** A lakeside 19th-century mansion with 30 acres of terraced gardens sloping down to the water, Brockhole serves as the park's official visitor center and has some exhilarating activities: "treetop trek"—a rope bridge and zipline route high up through oak trees—and the U.K.'s only "treetop nets," allowing everyone over the age of three to climb and bounce around safely among the twigs and leaves more than 25 feet up, supported by elastic ropes. There's also a 30-foot climbing wall. The gardens, designed in the Arts and Crafts style by Thomas Mawson, are at their best in spring, when daffodils punctuate the lawns and azaleas burst into bloom. There's an adventure playground, pony rides, minigolf, and rowboats for rent. The bookstore carries hiking guides and maps, and you can picnic here or eat at the café-restaurant. Bus 555/559 goes to the visitor center from Windermere, and boats from Waterhead stop at a pier. Windermere Lake Cruises has seasonal ferry service to Brockhole from Waterhead in Ambleside. ✉ *Ambleside Rd., Windermere* ☎ *015394/46601* 🌐 *www.brockhole.co.uk* 🎟 *Free; treetop trek £22; treetop nets from £12.50.*

FAMILY Fodor's Choice ★ **Lakes Aquarium.** On the quayside at the southern end of Windermere, this excellent aquarium has wildlife and waterside exhibits. One highlight is an underwater tunnel walk along a re-created lake bed, complete with diving ducks and Asian short-clawed otters. Piranhas, rays, and tropical frogs also have their fans, and there are some unexpected treats such as marmosets. A friendly, knowledgeable staff is eager to talk about the animals. ■ **TIP→ Animal handling takes place daily at 12:45 in the rain-forest areas.** Tickets are cheapest if booked in advance online. ✉ *C5062, Newby Bridge* ☎ *015394/30153* 🌐 *www.lakesaquarium.co.uk* 🎟 *£5.90; £16.25 combined ticket with Bowness–Lakeside cruise.*

FAMILY **Lakeside & Haverthwaite Railway Company.** Vintage steam trains chug along on the 18-minute, 4-mile branch line between Lakeside and Haverthwaite, giving you a great view of the lake's southern tip. You can add on a lake cruise for another perspective on the region's natural beauty. Departures from Lakeside coincide with ferry arrivals from Bowness and Ambleside. See the website for timetables. ✉ *A590, Haverthwaite* ☎ *015395/31594* 🌐 *www.lakesiderailway.co.uk* 🎟 *£6.80 round-trip; £10 unlimited 1-day travel* ⏲ *Closed Nov.–Mar.*

FAMILY **World of Beatrix Potter.** A touristy attraction aimed at kids interprets the author's 23 tales with three-dimensional scenes of Peter Rabbit and more. Skip it if you can and visit Potter's former home at Hill Top and the Beatrix Potter Gallery in Hawkshead. ✉ *The Old Laundry, Crag Brow, Bowness-on-Windermere* ☎ *015394/88444* 🌐 *www.hop-skip-jump.com* 🎟 *£7.50.*

WHERE TO EAT

$ BRITISH 🍴 **Angel Inn.** Up the steep slope from the water's edge in Bowness, this spacious, stylish pub serves good home-cooked fare as well as a fine collection of beers that includes its own Hawkshead brew. Specials, chalked on a board, may include dishes such as roasted cod with bok choy or goat cheese and fig tart. **Known for:** draft beers and ciders; landscaped gardens; local, seasonal food. [$] *Average main: £14* ✉ *Helm Rd., Bowness-on-Windermere* ☎ *015394/44080* 🌐 *www.angelbowness.com.*

$ **✕ Masons Arms.** With fabulous views over the rolling countryside of
BRITISH the Winster Valley to the east of Windermere, the Masons Arms is a
FAMILY slate-floored traditional old inn serving local ales and good pub food.
Old mirrors and tankards decorate the walls, and there's a special
ity gin list as well as a menu showcasing the best local ingredients.
Known for: locally farmed meats; homemade desserts; popular children's menu. $ *Average main: £14* ⊠ *Strawberry Bank, Windermere*
☎ *015395/68486* ⊕ *www.masonsarmsstrawberrybank.co.uk.*

WHERE TO STAY

$$$$ ⊡ **Gilpin Hotel and Lake House.** Hidden among 22 acres of grounds with
HOTEL meandering paths leading to sleek, spacious lodges, this rambling country house provides the ultimate in pampering. **Pros:** plenty of pampering; notable food; a policy of no weddings or conferences. **Cons:** a little
Fodor's Choice
★ out of the way; expensive rates; might be too posh for some. $ *Rooms
from: £225* ⊠ *Crook Rd., Bowness-on-Windermere* ✛ *2 miles east of
Windermere* ☎ *015394/88818* ⊕ *thegilpin.co.uk* ⇝ *20 rooms, 5 lodges*
❄️⃝ *All-inclusive* ☞ *No children under 7.*

$ ⊡ **1 Park Road.** On a quiet corner, this upmarket boutique B&B has
B&B/INN spacious guest rooms with carefully chosen fabrics and wallpaper, comfortable mattresses, and contemporary touches. **Pros:** welcoming and
Fodor's Choice
★ stylish; hosts will pick guests up from the station; good food, wine,
and beer. **Cons:** a 15-minute walk to the lake; limited car parking;
not suitable for wheelchair users. $ *Rooms from: £79* ⊠ *1 Park Rd.,
Windermere* ☎ *015394/42107* ⊕ *www.1parkroad.co.uk* ⇝ *6 rooms*
❄️⃝ *Free Breakfast.*

SHOPPING

Fodor's Choice **More? The Artisan Bakery** Between Kendal and Windermere, this bakery is
★ the place to stop for mouthwatering, award-winning bread, cakes, and
sandwiches, including an unforgettable bright green matcha tea blondie.
It also brews fine coffee. ⊠ *Mill Yard, Staveley* ☎ *01539/822297*
⊕ *www.moreartisan.co.uk.*

Peter Hall & Son. This woodcraft workshop, between Kendal and Windermere, sells bespoke furniture and finely honed boxes and bowls,
among other items. ⊠ *Danes Rd., Staveley* ☎ *01539/821633* ⊕ *www.
peter-hall.co.uk.*

SPORTS AND THE OUTDOORS
BIKING
Country Lanes Cycle Hire. This shop rents a variety of bikes from £21
per day. Helmets are included with the price. ⊠ *Windermere Railway Station, off A591, Windermere* ☎ *015394/44544* ⊕ *www.countrylaneslakedistrict.co.uk.*

BOATING
Windermere Lake Holidays. This company rents a wide range of vessels, from small sailboats to houseboats. They also have a number
of self-catering houses and apartments by the lakeside. ⊠ *Mereside,
Ferry Nab, Bowness-on-Windermere* ☎ *015394/43415* ⊕ *www.
lakewindermere.net.*

9

AMBLESIDE

7 miles northwest of Windermere.

Unlike Kendal and Windermere, Ambleside seems almost part of the hills and fells. Its buildings, mainly of local stone and many built in the traditional style that forgoes the use of mortar in the outer walls, blend perfectly into their setting. The small town sits at the northern end of Windermere along A591, making it a popular center for Lake District excursions. It has recently seen a sharp rise in quality restaurants, and the numerous outdoor shops are handy for walkers. Ambleside does, however, suffer from overcrowding in high season. Wednesday, when the local market takes place, is particularly busy.

GETTING HERE AND AROUND

An easy drive along A591 from Windermere, Ambleside can also be reached by ferry.

ESSENTIALS

Visitor Information Ambleside Tourist Information Centre. ⊠ *The Hub, Central Bldgs., Market Cross, Rydal Rd.* ☎ *0844/225–0544* ⊕ *www.amblesideon-line.co.uk.*

EXPLORING

Armitt Museum. Ambleside's fine local museum is a scholarly place, focusing on influential German artist Kurt Schwitters and Beatrix Potter. Schwitters lived out his final years in Ambleside, and the museum now has a room filled with his art. The museum also shows the less well-known aspects of Beatrix Potter, revealing her work as an important scientific and intellectual figure. Exhibits shed light on her as a naturalist, mycologist, sheep breeder, and conservationist. A large collection of her natural-history watercolors and a huge number of photographic portraits can be viewed by appointment in the excellent library upstairs. ⊠ *Rydal Rd.* ☎ *015394/31212* ⊕ *www.armitt.com* 🎟 *£5.*

Bridge House. This tiny 17th-century stone building, once an apple store, perches on an arched stone bridge spanning Stone Beck. It may have been built here to avoid land tax. This much-photographed building, which is cared for by the National Trust, holds a shop and an information center. ⊠ *Rydal Rd.* ☎ *015394/32617* 🎟 *Free.*

WHERE TO EAT

$ ✕ **Fellinis.** Billing itself as "Vegeterranean" to reflect its Mediterranean

VEGETARIAN   culinary influences, Fellinis is one of Cumbria's finest foodie destina-

Fodor's Choice   tions and a real treat for vegetarians in particular. Upstairs is a plush stu-

★   dio cinema screening art-house releases, while downstairs the restaurant rustles up sumptuous concoctions for a sophisticated crowd. **Known for:** unpretentious fine dining; vegetarian and vegan dishes; romantic dinner-and-a-movie ambience. 💲 *Average main: £14* ⊠ *Church St.* ☎ *015394/32487* ⊕ *www.fellinisambleside.com* ☾ *No lunch.*

$$$$ ✕ **Lake Road Kitchen.** Cuttlefish shells piled in the window and a Nor-

MODERN BRITISH   dic-style wood-paneled interior give a clue as to the culinary style of Lake Road Kitchen, quite possibly the most awarded restaurant in Ambleside. About 80% of everything green on the menu is foraged; the remainder comes from the highest-quality, mainly local suppliers.

Known for: homegrown and foraged produce; mouthwatering set menu with wine pairings; small space so reservations necessary. $ *Average main: £65* ⊠ *Lake Rd.* ☎ *015394/22012* ⊕ *www.lakeroadkitchen.co.uk* ⊘ *Closed Mon. and Tues. No lunch.*

$$$

BRITISH

Fodor'sChoice

★

✕ **Old Stamp House.** The quality of locally sourced and foraged food has been raised to a new level by this startlingly good restaurant, which together with the Lake Road Kitchen has given Ambleside unexpected status on the British gastro map. Chef Ryan Blackburn has created a menu anchored to Cumbrian traditions, but at the same time mouthwateringly creative and contemporary. **Known for:** creative seasonal menu; celebrity chef; excellent wine list. $ *Average main: £22* ⊠ *Church St.* ☎ *015394/32775* ⊕ *www.oldstamphouse.com* ⊘ *Closed Sun. and Mon. No lunch Tues.*

$

VEGETARIAN

✕ **Rattle Gill.** Hidden away up a winding lane past the old mill waterwheel, homey Rattle Gill is a deservedly popular little café serving great homemade cakes, soups, sandwiches, and salads. The tasting plate of cakes is an especially good option. **Known for:** homemade soups; tasting plates of cakes; outdoor seating. $ *Average main: £7* ⊠ *2 Bridge St.* ☎ *07975/912990* ⊕ *www.rattlegill.com* ⊘ *Closed Mon. and Tues. No dinner.*

WHERE TO STAY

$

B&B/INN

🛏 **Rooms at The Apple Pie.** Converted from what were once the offices of Beatrix Potter's solicitor husband, this Ambleside café has branched out into accommodations, with eight simple but stylishly furnished rooms decorated with photos of delights from the café next door. **Pros:** scrumptious breakfasts; central location; stylish rooms. **Cons:** not staffed 24 hours a day; breakfast is extra; limited parking. $ *Rooms from: £53* ⊠ *Rydal Rd., Keswick* ☎ *015394/33679* ⊕ *www.applepieambleside. co.uk* ⊸ *8 rooms* �‖*No meals.*

$$$$

HOTEL

🛏 **The Samling.** On its own sculpture-dotted 67 acres not far from Ambleside and Windermere, this place oozes exclusivity from the moment you enter the long, winding drive. **Pros:** set on gorgeous private estate; superb restaurant; celebrity guest list. **Cons:** exclusivity doesn't come cheap; steep climb up from the lake; outside Ambleside. $ *Rooms from: £470* ⊠ *Ambleside Rd., Windermere* ☎ *015394/31922* ⊕ *www. thesamlinghotel.co.uk* ⊸ *12 rooms* �‖*Breakfast.*

SPORTS AND THE OUTDOORS

The fine walks in the vicinity include routes north to Rydal Mount or southeast over Wansfell to Troutbeck. Each walk will take up to a half day, there and back. Ferries from Bowness-on-Windermere dock at Ambleside's harbor, called Waterhead. ■TIP➜ To escape the crowds, rent a rowboat at the harbor for an hour or two.

GRASMERE

3 miles north of Rydal, 4 miles northwest of Ambleside.

Fodor'sChoice

★

Lovely Grasmere, on a tiny, wood-fringed lake, is made up of crooked lanes in which Westmorland slate–built cottages hold shops and galleries. The village is a focal point for literary and landscape associations because this area was the adopted heartland of the Romantic poets,

9

One of the Lake District's literary landmarks, Dove Cottage near Grasmere was where poet William Wordsworth wrote many famous works.

notably Wordsworth and Coleridge. The Vale of Grasmere has changed over the years, but many features Wordsworth wrote about are still visible. Wordsworth lived on the town's outskirts for almost 50 years and described the area as "the loveliest spot that man hath ever known."

GETTING HERE AND AROUND

On the main A591 between Ambleside and Keswick, Grasmere is easily reached by car.

ESSENTIALS

Visitor Information Grasmere Tourist Information Centre. ⊠ *Church Stile* ☎ *015394/35665* ⊕ *www.nationaltrust.org.uk/allan-bank-and-grasmere.*

EXPLORING

FAMILY

Fodor's Choice

★

Allan Bank. Rope swings on the grounds, picnics in atmospheric old rooms, free tea and coffee, and huge blackboards you can write on: Allan Bank is unlike most other historic houses cared for by the National Trust. On a hill above the lake near Grasmere village, this grand house was once home to poet William Wordsworth as well as to Canon Rawnsley, the founder of the National Trust. Seriously damaged by fire in 2011, it has been partially restored but also left deliberately undecorated. It offers a much less formal experience than other stops on the Wordsworth trail. There are frequent activities for both children and adults: arts and crafts but also music and astronomy. Red squirrels can be seen on the 30-minute woodland walk through the beautiful grounds. ⊠ *Off A591* ☎ *015394/35143* ⊕ *www.nationaltrust.org.uk/ allan-bank-and-grasmere* 🖼 *£6.50* ⊘ *Closed Jan.–mid-Feb.*

Dove Cottage and Wordsworth Museum. William Wordsworth lived in Dove Cottage from 1799 to 1808, a prolific and happy time for the poet. During this time he wrote some of his most famous works, including "Ode: Intimations of Immortality" and *The Prelude*. Built in the early 17th century as an inn, this tiny, dim, and, in some places, dank house is beautifully preserved, with an oak-paneled hall and floors of Westmorland slate. It first opened to the public in 1891 and remains as it was when Wordsworth lived here with his sister, Dorothy, and wife, Mary. Bedrooms and living areas contain much of Wordsworth's furniture and many personal belongings. Coleridge was a frequent visitor, as was Thomas De Quincey, best known for his 1822 autobiographical masterpiece *Confessions of an English Opium-Eater*. De Quincey moved in after the Wordsworths left. You visit the house on a timed guided tour, and the ticket includes admission to the spacious, modern **Wordsworth Museum**, which documents the poet's life and the literary contributions of Wordsworth and the Lake Poets. The museum includes space for major art exhibitions. The **Jerwood Centre,** open to researchers by appointment, houses 50,000 letters, first editions, and manuscripts. Afternoon tea is served at a café next to the car park. ⊠ *A591, south of Grasmere* ☏ *015394/35544* ⊕ *www. wordsworth.org.uk* 🎫 *£8.95* ⊘ *Closed Jan.*

St. Oswald's. William Wordsworth, his wife Mary, his sister Dorothy, and four of his children are buried in the churchyard of this church on the River Rothay. The poet planted eight of the yew trees here. As you leave the churchyard, stop at the Gingerbread Shop, in a tiny cottage, for a special local treat. ⊠ *Stock La.* ⊕ *www.parishmag.willow-bank.net.*

WHERE TO EAT

$$

BRITISH

Fodor's Choice

★

✕ **The Jumble Room.** A small stone building dating to the 18th century, Grasmere's first shop is now a friendly, fashionable, and colorful restaurant, with children's books, bold animal paintings, and hanging lamps. The food is an eclectic mix of international and traditional British; think porcini mushroom arancini, beetroot and pumpkin ravioli, or Lebanese chicken with clementine and fennel. **Known for:** freshly baked bread; lively atmosphere; imaginative menu. Ⓢ *Average main: £15* ⊠ *Langdale Rd.* ☏ *015394/35188* ⊕ *www.thejumbleroom.co.uk* ⊘ *No lunch.*

$$

MODERN BRITISH

Fodor's Choice

★

✕ **Tweedies Bar.** One of the region's best gastro-pubs, Tweedies attracts many locals as well as visitors. Delicious updated British classics include beer-battered Fleetwood haddock, braised ox cheek with lardons, and an 8-ounce burger with roasted shallots. **Known for:** live music; classic British menu including great burgers; awesome local ales. Ⓢ *Average main: £16* ⊠ *Langdale Rd.* ☏ *015394/35300* ⊕ *www. tweediesbargrasmere.co.uk.*

WHERE TO STAY

$

B&B/INN

Fodor's Choice

★

🏨 **Heidi's Grasmere Lodge.** Small but sumptuous, this lodging has a distinctly feminine sensibility, with floral wallpaper, curly steel lamps, and painted woodwork. **Pros:** chic bathrooms with whirlpool tubs; warm welcome; some rooms have mountain views. **Cons:** no children allowed; so pristine you may worry about your muddy boots; rooms vary in size. Ⓢ *Rooms from: £69* ⊠ *Red Lion Sq.* ☏ *015394/35248* ⊕ *www. heidisgrasmerelodge.co.uk* 🛏 *6 rooms* ⊘ *Free Breakfast.*

9

$$ B&B/INN **Moss Grove Organic.** A Victorian building in the heart of Grasmere, the chic and spacious Moss Grove Organic puts an emphasis on its environmental credentials. **Pros:** roaring fire in the evenings; homemade marmalade at breakfast; modern design with a conscience. **Cons:** tight parking; not the place for a big fry-up breakfast; service can be slow. [$] *Rooms from: £114* ✉ *Red Lion Sq.* ☎ *015394/35251* 🌐 *www.mossgrove.com* 🛏 *11 rooms* 🍴 *Free Breakfast.*

SHOPPING

Fodor'sChoice ★ **Grasmere Gingerbread Shop.** The smells wafting across the churchyard draw many people to the Grasmere Gingerbread Shop. Since 1854 Sarah Nelson's gingerbread has been sold from this cramped 17th-century cottage, which was once the village school. The delicious treats, still made from a secret recipe, are sold by costumed ladies and packed into attractive tins for the journey home or to eat right away. ✉ *Church Cottage* ☎ *015394/35428* 🌐 *www.grasmeregingerbread.co.uk.*

SPORTS AND THE OUTDOORS

Loughrigg Terrace. The most panoramic views of lake and village are from the south of Grasmere, from the bare slopes of Loughrigg Terrace, reached along a well-signposted track on the western side of the lake or through the woods from parking lots on the A591 between Grasmere and Rydal Water. It's less than an hour's walk from the village, though your stroll can be extended by continuing around Rydal Water, passing Rydal Mount, detouring onto White Moss Common before returning to Dove Cottage and Grasmere, a 4-mile (three-hour) walk in total. ✉ *Grasmere.*

ELTERWATER AND THE LANGDALES

2½ miles south of Grasmere, 4 miles west of Ambleside.

The delightful village of Elterwater, at the eastern end of the Great Langdale Valley on B5343, is a good stop for hikers. It's barely more than a cluster of houses around a village green, but from here you can choose from a selection of excellent circular walks. Great Langdale winds up past hills known as the Langdale Pikes towards Great End and England's highest hill, Scafell Pike. To the south, Little Langdale is another of Cumbria's most beautiful valleys with walks aplenty. At its head, the high passes of Wrynose and Hardknott lead west across wild fells to Eskdale and one of the most beautiful and remote lakes, Wast Water. Beyond that, at Ravenglass, the national park reaches all the way to the Cumbrian coast. Between the two Langdales are plenty more great walking opportunities over fells and past far-flung beauty spots such as Blea Tarn.

WHERE TO EAT AND STAY

$ BRITISH 🍴 **Britannia Inn.** At this 500-year-old pub, restaurant, and inn in the heart of superb walking country, antiques, comfortable chairs, and prints and oil paintings furnish the cozy, beamed public rooms. The hearty traditional British food—from grilled haggis with homemade plum jam to pan-seared sea bass and wild-mushroom Stroganoff—is popular with locals, as are the many whiskies and ales, including a specially brewed

Britannia Gold beer. **Known for:** speciality beers; traditional oak-beamed interior; annual beer festival in November. [$] *Average main: £13* ✉ *B5343* ☎ *015394/37210* 🌐 *www.thebritanniainn.com.*

$ HOTEL 🏨 **Old Dungeon Ghyll Hotel.** There's no more comforting stop after a day outdoors than the Hiker's Bar of this 300-year-old hotel at the head of the Great Langdale Valley. **Pros:** ideally situated for walking; wonderfully isolated; spectacular views all around. **Cons:** no-nonsense approach not to everyone's taste; busy in summer; remote location. [$] *Rooms from: £80* ✉ *Off B5343, Great Langdale* ☎ *015394/37272* 🌐 *www.odg.co.uk* 🛏 *12 rooms* 🍴 *Some meals.*

SPORTS AND THE OUTDOORS

There are access points to Langdale Fell from several spots along B5343, the main road; look for information boards at local parking places. You can also stroll up the river valley or embark on more energetic hikes to Stickle Tarn or to one of the summits of the Langdale Pikes. Beyond the Old Dungeon Ghyll Hotel, the Great Langdale Valley splits in two around a hill known as the Band—a path up its spine has particularly good views back down over the valley and can be continued to the summit of Scafell Pike.

CONISTON

5 miles south of Elterwater.

This small lake resort and boating center attracts climbers to the steep peak of the **Old Man of Coniston** (2,635 feet), which towers above the slate-roof houses. It also has sites related to John Ruskin. Quieter than Windermere, Coniston is a good introduction to the pastoral and watery charms of the area, though the small town itself can get crowded in summer.

9

GETTING HERE AND AROUND

The Coniston Launch connects Coniston Pier with Ruskin's home at Brantwood and some other stops around the lake, offering hourly service (£11.25 for a daylong, hop-on, hop-off ticket; £18.25 including entry to Brantwood) on its wooden Ruskin and Ransome launches.

ESSENTIALS

Visitor Information Coniston Launch. ☎ *01768/775753* 🌐 *www.conistonlaunch.co.uk.* **Coniston Tourist Information Centre.** ✉ *Ruskin Ave.* ☎ *015394/41533* 🌐 *www.conistontic.org.*

EXPLORING

Fodor's Choice ★ **Brantwood.** On the eastern shore of Coniston Water, Brantwood was the cherished home of John Ruskin (1819–1900), the noted Victorian artist, writer, critic, and social reformer, after 1872. The rambling 18th-century house (with Victorian alterations) is on a 250-acre estate that stretches high above the lake. Here, alongside mementos such as his mahogany desk, are Ruskin's own paintings, drawings, and books. On display is art that this great connoisseur collected, and in cerebral corners such as the Ideas Room visitors are encouraged to think about meaning and change. Ruskin's Rocks explores his fascinations with stones and music with a brilliant bit of modern technology. A video on Ruskin's life shows the lasting influence of his thoughts, and the Severn Studio has rotating art exhibitions. Ruskin himself laid out the extensive grounds; take time to explore the gardens and woodland walks, which include some multilayered significance: Ziggy Zaggy, for example, originally a garden built by Ruskin to reflect Dante's Purgatorial Mount, is now an allegory of the seven deadly sins. Brantwood hosts a series of classical concerts on some Saturdays as well as talks, guided walks, and study days. ⊠ *Off B5285* ☎ *015394/41396* ⊕ *www.brantwood.org.uk* ✎ *£7.70; gardens only £5.35.*

Coniston Boating Centre. The National Trust's restored Victorian steam yacht and the slightly more utilitarian Coniston Launch both leave from the town's spruced-up waterside satellite, a 15-minute stroll from the center. There's a parking lot, a smart café, and various boat- and bike-hire options, too. Originally launched in 1859 and restored in the 1970s, the Steam Yacht (⊕ *www.nationaltrust.org.uk/gondola*) runs between Coniston Pier, Brantwood, and Park-a-Moor at the south end of Coniston Water daily from late March through October (half-lake cruise £11; 10% discount for National Trust members). The Coniston Launch (⊕ *www.conistonlaunch.co.uk*) runs similar routes and is marginally cheaper, though also a little less romantic. Both will get you across the lake to Brantwood, and a stop at Monk Coniston jetty, at the lake's northern tip, connects to the footpaths through the Monk Coniston Estate and the beauty spot of Tarn Hows. ⊠ *Coniston Pier* ☎ *015394/41366* ⊕ *www.conistonboatingcentre.co.uk.*

Coniston Water. The lake came to prominence in the 1930s when Arthur Ransome made it the setting for *Swallows and Amazons,* one of a series of novels about a group of children and their adventures. The lake is about 5 miles long, a tempting stretch that drew Donald Campbell here in 1959 to set a water-speed record of 260 mph. He was killed when trying to beat it in 1967. His body and the wreckage of *Bluebird K7* were retrieved from the lake in 2001. Campbell is buried in St. Andrew's church in Coniston, and a stone memorial on the village green commemorates him. ⊠ *Coniston.*

Ruskin Museum. This repository of fascinating and thought-provoking manuscripts, personal items, and watercolors by John Ruskin illuminates his thinking and influence. There is also a focus on speedboat racer Donald Campbell; his *Bluebird K7,* dragged up from Coniston Water, will eventually rest here once it has been painstakingly put back together. Good local-interest exhibits include copper mining, geology, lace, and more. Upstairs, the Dawson Gallery occasionally hosts high-profile artists. ⊠ *Yewdale Rd.* ☎ *01539/441164* ⊕ *www.ruskinmuseum. com* ✎ *£6* ☉ *Closed Mon. and mid-Nov.–mid-Mar.*

WHERE TO EAT AND STAY

$ ✕ **Black Bull Inn.** Attached to the Coniston Brewing Company, whose ales

BRITISH   are on tap here, the Black Bull is an old-fashioned pub in the heart of the village. It can feel a little dated, but it's a good pick for simple, hearty food such as fried whitebait, homemade leek-and-potato soup, and a tasty steak-and-ale pie. **Known for:** locally sourced ingredients; large range of real ales; old-fashioned decor. $ *Average main: £12* ⊠ *Coppermines Rd.* ☎ *015394/41335* ⊕ *www.blackbullconiston.co.uk.*

$$ ⛆ **Bank Ground Farm.** Used by Arthur Ransome as the setting for *Swal-*
HOTEL *lows and Amazons,* 15th-century Bank Ground is beautifully situated
Fodor'sChoice on the eastern shore of Coniston Water, opposite the village of Coniston
★ on the western shore. **Pros:** stunning lake views; homey atmosphere;
traditional welcome. **Cons:** a fair walk from the village; some rooms
are cramped; low ceilings in the cottage. $ *Rooms from: £100* ⌧ *Off*
B5285 ☎ *015394/41264* ⊕ *www.bankground.com* ☉ *Guesthouse*
closed Nov.–Easter ⇥ *7 rooms, 4 cottages* †◎† *Free Breakfast.*

$ ⛆ **Lakeland House.** In the middle of Coniston, Lakeland House has
B&B/INN smart, modern rooms with bold wallpaper, beamed ceilings, and slate-
floored bathrooms. **Pros:** café downstairs; good value; open fire for cozy
evenings. **Cons:** not as homey as a traditional B&B; on a main road;
attic rooms have low ceilings. $ *Rooms from: £45* ⌧ *Tilberthwaite*
Ave., Keswick ☎ *015394/41303* ⊕ *www.lakelandhouse.co.uk* ⇥ *12*
rooms †◎† *Free Breakfast.*

SPORTS AND THE OUTDOORS
HIKING
Steep tracks lead up from the village to the **Old Man of Coniston.** The trail
starts near the Sun Hotel on Brow Hill and goes past an old copper mine
to the peak, which you can reach in about two hours. It's one of the
Lake District's most satisfying hikes—not too arduous, but high enough
to feel a sense of accomplishment and get fantastic views (west to the
sea, south to Morecambe Bay, and east to Windermere). Experienced
hikers include the peak in a seven-hour circular walk from the village,
also taking in the heights and ridges of Swirl How and Wetherlam.

HAWKSHEAD

3 miles east of Coniston.

In the Vale of Esthwaite, this small market town is a pleasing hodge-
podge of tiny squares, cobbled lanes, and whitewashed houses. There's
a good deal more history here than in most local villages, however. The
Hawkshead Courthouse, just outside town, was built by the monks
of Furness Abbey in the 15th century. Hawkshead later derived much
wealth from the wool trade, which flourished here in the 17th and
18th centuries.

As a thriving market center, Hawkshead could afford to maintain the
Hawkshead Grammar School, at which William Wordsworth was a
pupil from 1779 to 1787; he carved his name on a desk inside, now on
display. In the village, Ann Tyson's House claims the honor of having
provided the young William with lodgings. The twin draws of Word-
sworth and Beatrix Potter—apart from her home, Hill Top, there's
a Potter gallery—conspire to make Hawkshead crowded year-round.

GETTING HERE AND AROUND
Hawkshead is east of Coniston on B5285 and south of Ambleside via
B5286. An alternative route is to cross Windermere via the car ferry
from Ferry Nab, south of Bowness. Local buses link the village to oth-
ers nearby.

9

ESSENTIALS

Visitor Information Hawkshead Tourist Information Centre. ✉ *Main St.* ☎ *015394/36946* 🌐 *www.hawksheadtouristinfo.org.uk.*

EXPLORING

FAMILY Fodor's Choice ★ **Beatrix Potter Gallery.** In the 17th-century solicitor's offices formerly used by Potter's husband, the Beatrix Potter Gallery displays a selection of the artist-writer's original illustrations, watercolors, and drawings. There's also information about her interest in conservation and her early support of the National Trust. The house looks almost as it would have in her day, though with touch screens in wooden frames and a children's play area upstairs. Admission is by timed ticket when the place gets busy. ✉ *Main St.* ☎ *015394/36355* 🌐 *www.nationaltrust.org.uk/beatrix-potter-gallery* 🎫 *£6.50* ⏲ *Closed Jan.–mid-Feb.*

Fodor's Choice ★ **Hill Top.** Children's author and illustrator Beatrix Potter (1866–1943), most famous for her *Peter Rabbit* stories, called this place home. The house looks much the same as when Potter bequeathed it to the National Trust, and fans will recognize details such as the porch and garden gate, old kitchen range, Victorian dollhouse, and four-poster bed, which were depicted in the book illustrations. **■ TIP→ Admission to this often-crowded spot is by timed ticket; book in advance and avoid summer weekends and school vacations.** Hill Top lies 2 miles south of Hawkshead by car or foot, though you can also approach via the car ferry from Bowness-on-Windermere. ✉ *Off B5285, Near Sawrey* ☎ *015394/36269* 🌐 *www.nationaltrust.org.uk/hill-top* 🎫 *£10.90* ⏲ *Closed Jan.–mid Feb. and Mon.–Thurs. in late Oct.–Dec.*

WHERE TO EAT

$ BRITISH Fodor's Choice ★ 🍴 **Tower Bank Arms.** With a porch that appears in a Beatrix Potter story and a location just a rabbit's hop from the author's home, you might expect this pub to be something of a tourist trap, but luckily it's anything but. The meals are tasty and copious, making use of local ingredients; the chicken liver–and–pistachio parfait, Cumbrian beef-and-ale stew, and sticky toffee pudding with honeycomb ice cream are especially good. **Known for:** literary influences; standard pub fare; some of the area's best ales. [$] *Average main: £12* ✉ *Off B5285, Near Sawrey* ☎ *015394/36334* 🌐 *www.towerbankarms.co.uk* ⏲ *Closed Mon. in winter.*

WHERE TO STAY

$$ HOTEL Fodor's Choice ★ 🏨 **Drunken Duck Inn.** After four centuries, this friendly old coaching inn remains an outstanding place for both food and lodging. **Pros:** superchic rural style; excellent dining and drinking; courtyard and garden views. **Cons:** hunting paraphernalia not for everyone; can feel isolated; standard rooms are small. [$] *Rooms from: £125* ✉ *Off B5286, Ambleside* ☎ *015394/36347* 🌐 *www.drunkenduckinn.co.uk* 🛏 *16 rooms* 🍽 *Some meals.*

$ B&B/INN Fodor's Choice ★ 🏨 **Yewfield Vegetarian Guesthouse.** With the laid-back friendliness of a B&B and the sophisticated style of a country house, Yewfield is a very good value—especially if you can score one of the rooms at the front of the house with a great view across the valley. **Pros:** good location to begin walks; pretty garden; apartments are great for weeklong stays. **Cons:** not good for families with young kids; remote; closed in winter. [$] *Rooms from: £90* ✉ *Hawkshead Hill* ☎ *015394/36765* 🌐 *www.yewfield.co.uk* 🕓 *Closed Dec. and Jan.* 🛏 *19 rooms, 2 apartments* 🍴 *Free Breakfast.*

SPORTS AND THE OUTDOORS

Grizedale Forest Park. Stretching southwest from Hawkshead and blanketing the hills between Coniston and Windermere, Grizedale Forest Park has a thick mix of oak, pine, and larch woods crisscrossed with biking and walking paths. Forty permanent outdoor sculptures are scattered beside the trails and more are planned. The **visitor center** has information, maps, a café, and an adventure playground. ✉ *Off B5286* ☎ *0300/0674495* 🌐 *www.forestry.gov.uk/grizedaleforestpark.*

Grizedale Mountain Bikes. If you have the urge to explore the trails of the national park, Grizedale Mountain Bikes rents all the right equipment, with bicycles from £35 per day. They also have a workshop staffed by mechanics if you need to service or repair your own bike. ✉ *Grizedale Forest Park Visitor Centre, off B5286* ☎ *01229/860335* 🌐 *www.grizedalemountainbikes.co.uk.*

THE NORTHERN LAKES

The scenery of the northern lakes is considerably more dramatic—some would say bleaker—than much of the landscape to the south. A 30-mile drive on the A6 takes you through the wild and desolate Shap Fells, which rise to a height of 1,304 feet. This is one of the most notorious moorland crossings in the country: even in summer it's a lonely place to be, and in winter, snow on the road can be dangerous. From Penrith the road leads to Ullswater, possibly the grandest of all the lakes; then there's a winding route west past Keswick, south through the marvelous Borrowdale Valley, and on to Cockermouth. Outside the main towns such as Keswick it can be easier to escape the summer crowds in the northern lakes.

ULLSWATER

6 miles southwest of Penrith.

Hemmed in by towering hills, Ullswater, the region's second-largest lake, is one of the least developed, drawing people for its calm waters and good access to the mountain slopes of Helvellyn. The A592 winds along the lake's pastoral western shore, through the adjacent hamlets of Glenridding and Patterdale at the southern end. Lakeside strolls, great views, tea shops, and rowboat rentals provide the full Lakeland experience.

ESSENTIALS

Visitor Information Ullswater Tourist Information Centre. ✉ *Beckside Car Park, off A592, Glenridding* ☎ *017684/82414* 🌐 *www.lakedistrict.gov.uk.*

EXPLORING

Aira Force. A spectacular 65-foot waterfall pounds under a stone bridge and through a wooded ravine to feed into Ullswater. From the parking lot it's a 10-minute walk to the falls, with more-serious walks on Gowbarrow Fell and to the village of Dockray beyond. A new 1¼-mile footpath allows visitors to leave their cars at Glencoyne Bay, to the south, and walk through a deer park. **TIP→ Bring sturdy shoes, especially in wet or icy weather, when the paths can be treacherous.** Just above Aira Force in the woods of Gowbarrow Park is the spot where, in 1802, William Wordsworth's sister Dorothy observed daffodils that, as she wrote, "tossed and reeled and danced and seemed as if they verily laughed with the wind that blew upon them." Two years later Wordsworth transformed his sister's words into the famous poem "I Wandered Lonely as a Cloud." Two centuries later, national park wardens patrol Gowbarrow Park in season to prevent tourists from picking the few remaining daffodils. ✉ *A592, near A5091* 🌐 *www.nationaltrust.org.uk/aira-force-and-ullswater* 🎟 *Parking £5 for 2 hrs.*

Helvellyn. West of Ullswater's southern end, the brooding presence of Helvellyn (3,118 feet), one of the Lake District's most formidable mountains and England's third highest, recalls the region's fundamental character. It's an arduous climb to the top, especially via the challenging ridge known as Striding Edge, and the ascent shouldn't be attempted in poor weather or by inexperienced hikers. Signposted paths to the peak run from the road between Glenridding and Patterdale and pass by **Red Tarn,** which is the highest small mountain lake in the region at 2,356 feet. ✉ *Glenridding.*

Fodor's Choice ★ **Ullswater Steamers.** These antique vessels, including a 19th-century steamer that is said to be the oldest working passenger ship in the world, run the length of Ullswater between Glenridding in the south and Pooley Bridge in the north, via Howtown on the eastern shore. It's a pleasant tour, especially if you combine it with a lakeside walk. One-way trips start at £6, or you can sail the entire day for £14.20 with the Round the Lake Pass. ✉ *Pier House, off A592, Glenridding* ☎ *017684/82229* 🌐 *www.ullswater-steamers.co.uk.*

WHERE TO STAY

$$$ HOTEL 🏨 **Inn on the Lake.** With some of the best lake views in the Lake District, Inn on the Lake is a large Victorian property right on the edge of Ullswater, with only its own terrace and lawns separating it from the water. **Pros:** right on the lakeshore; beautiful scenery; plenty of parking. **Cons:** very busy in summer; can be noisy if there's a wedding; decor in the rooms is a bit fussy. [$] *Rooms from: £180* ✉ *Ullswater, Glenridding* ☎ *0800/8401245* 🌐 *www.lakedistricthotels.net/innonthelake* 🛏 *47 rooms* 🍴 *Free Breakfast.*

KESWICK

14 miles west of Ullswater.

Fodor's Choice ★ The great mountains of Skiddaw and Blencathra brood over the gray slate houses of Keswick (pronounced *kezz*-ick), on the scenic shores of Derwentwater. The town is a natural base for exploring the rounded, heather-clad Skiddaw range to the north, while the hidden valleys of Borrowdale and Buttermere (the latter reached by stunning Honister Pass) take you into the rugged heart of the Lake District. Nearby, five beautiful lakes are set among the three highest mountain ranges in England. The tourist information center here has regional information and is the place to get fishing permits for Derwentwater.

Keswick's narrow, cobbled streets have a grittier charm compared to the refined Victorian elegance of Grasmere or Ambleside. However, it's the best spot in the Lake District to purchase mountaineering gear and outdoor clothing. There are also many hotels, guesthouses, restaurants, and pubs.

GETTING HERE AND AROUND

Keswick is easily reached along A66 from Penrith, though you can get there more scenically via Grasmere in the south. Buses run from the train station in Penrith to Keswick. The town center is pedestrianized.

■**TIP→** Traffic can be horrendous in summer, so consider leaving your car in Keswick. The open-top Borrowdale bus service between Keswick and Seatoller (to the south) runs frequently, and the Honister Rambler minibus is perfect for walkers aiming for the high fells of the central lakes; it makes stops from Keswick to Buttermere. The Keswick Launch service on Derwentwater links to many walks as well as the Borrowdale bus service.

ESSENTIALS

Visitor Information Keswick Information Centre. ☒ *Moot Hall, Market Sq.* ☎ *017687/72645* ⊕ *www.keswick.org.*

EXPLORING

Fodor's Choice ★ **Castlerigg Stone Circle.** A Neolithic monument about 100 feet in diameter, this stone circle was built around 3,000 years ago on a hill overlooking St. John's Vale. The brooding northern peaks of Skiddaw and Blencathra loom to the north, and there are views of Helvellyn to the south. The 38 stones aren't large, but the site makes them particularly impressive. Wordsworth described them as "a dismal cirque of Druid stones upon a forlorn moor." The site, always open to visitors, is 4 miles east of Keswick. There's usually space for cars to park beside the road that leads along the northern edge of the site: head up Eleventrees off Penrith Road at the eastern edge of Keswick. ☒ *Off A66* ⊕ *www. english-heritage.org.uk* ☜ *Free.*

FAMILY **Derwent Pencil Museum.** Legend has it that shepherds found graphite on Seathwaite Fell after a storm uprooted trees in the 16th century. The Derwent company still makes pencils here, and the museum contains the world's longest colored pencil (it takes 28 men to lift it), a pencil produced for World War II spies that contains a rolled-up map, and displays about graphite mining. There's a café and plenty of opportunities for kids to draw, so it's a good, family-friendly option on a rainy day. ☒ *Southey Works, Carding Mill La.* ☎ *01768/773626* ⊕ *www. pencilmuseum.co.uk* ☜ *£4.95.*

Derwentwater. To understand why Derwentwater is considered one of England's finest lakes, take a short walk from Keswick's town center to the lakeshore and past the jetty, and follow the **Friar's Crag** path, about a 15-minute level walk from the center. This pine-tree-fringed peninsula is a favorite vantage point, with its view of the lake, the ring of mountains, and many tiny islands. Ahead, crags line the **Jaws of Borrowdale** and overhang a mountain ravine—a scene that looks as if it emerged from a Romantic painting. ✉ *Keswick.*

Keswick Launch Company. For the best lake views, take a wooden-launch cruise around Derwentwater. Between late March and November, circular cruises set off every half hour in alternate directions from a dock; there's a more limited (roughly hourly) winter timetable. You can also rent a rowboat here in summer. Buy a hop-on, hop-off Around the Lake ticket (£10.50) and take advantage of the seven landing stages around the lake that provide access to hiking trails, such as the two-hour climb up and down Cat Bells, a celebrated lookout point on the western shore of Derwentwater. ■ **TIP→ Buy slightly discounted tickets at the Moot Hall information office in the center of town.** ✉ *Lake Rd.* ☎ *017687/72263* 🌐 *www.keswick-launch.co.uk* 🎫 *From £2.25* 🕑 *Closed mid-Dec.–early Feb.*

WHERE TO EAT

$ BRITISH Fodor's Choice ★

🍴 **Fellpack.** Created by four friends who have returned home to the Lakes, the menu at Fellpack is designed as a celebration of Cumbria's ingredients and traditional recipes, albeit with a quirky twist. At lunchtime, opt for a hearty fellpot, such as the eight-hour braised beef chili served in a pot made by a local potter. **Known for:** food served in handmade dishes; delicious, hearty cuisine; awesome landscape photography. [$] *Average main: £14* ✉ *Lake Rd.* ☎ *01768/771177* 🌐 *www.fellpack.co.uk* 🕑 *Closed Tues. and Wed. in winter.*

$ CAFÉ

🍴 **Square Orange Café Bar.** Young locals and windblown walkers gather in Keswick's liveliest café for excellent coffee or tea, fruit-flavored cordials, and some serious hot chocolate. The music is laid-back, the staff are undeniably cool, the walls are hung with paintings and photos, and there are homemade pizzas, tapas, and pints of local beer for long rainy days or cold winter nights. **Known for:** decadent chocolate orange cake; ethically sourced tea and coffee; live music on Wednesday evenings. [$] *Average main: £10* ✉ *20 St. John's St.* ☎ *017687/73888* 🌐 *www.thesquareorange.co.uk.*

WHERE TO STAY

$$ B&B/INN Fodor's Choice ★

🏨 **Howe Keld.** In a town that overflows with B&Bs, this comfortable town house stands out because of its contemporary flair and pampering touches. **Pros:** famously filling breakfasts; good ecological practices; one room accessible for people with disabilities. **Cons:** a short distance from the heart of town; backs onto a busy road; some rooms have low ceilings. [$] *Rooms from: £115* ✉ *5–7 The Heads* ☎ *017687/72417* 🌐 *www.howekeld.co.uk* 🕑 *Closed Jan.* 🛏 *14 rooms* 🍽 *Free Breakfast.*

$ B&B/INN

🏨 **The Lookout.** Up the hill from the town center, this friendly and economical B&B lives up to its name, with balconies gazing out onto the high fells. **Pros:** welcoming hosts; stylish rooms; great views. **Cons:** some distance from Keswick's amenities; only one room has a tub; single-night bookings only accepted last minute. [$] *Rooms from: £95*

The setting of the Castlerigg Stone Circle, ringed by stunning mountains, makes this Neolithic monument deeply memorable.

✉ *Chestnut Hill* ☎ *017687/80407* ⊕ *www.thelookoutkeswick.co.uk* ⌁ *3 rooms* ⦿ *Free Breakfast.*

NIGHTLIFE AND PERFORMING ARTS

Theatre by the Lake. In one of Cumbria's most vibrant cultural settings, the company at the Theatre by the Lake presents classic and contemporary productions year-round. The Keswick Music Society season runs from September through January, and the Words by the Water literary festival takes place here in March. ✉ *Lake Rd.* ☎ *017687/74411* ⊕ *www.theatrebythelake.com.*

SHOPPING

George Fisher. The area's largest and best outdoor equipment store, George Fisher sells sportswear, travel books, and maps; staff are faultlessly friendly, helpful, and well informed. Daily weather information is posted in the window, and there's a children's play den. ✉ *2 Borrowdale Rd.* ☎ *017687/72178* ⊕ *www.georgefisher.co.uk.*

Needle Sports. This company stocks all the best equipment for mountaineering and for rock and ice climbing. They also provide information about local climbing and fell running clubs. ✉ *56 Main St.* ☎ *01768/772227* ⊕ *www.needlesports.com.*

Thomasons. A butcher and delicatessen, Thomasons sells some very good meat pies—just the thing for putting in your pocket before you climb a Lakeland fell. The homemade sausages are fantastic if you're planning a barbecue. ✉ *8–10 Station St.* ☎ *017687/80169.*

SPORTS AND THE OUTDOORS

BIKING

Keswick Bikes. This company rents bikes (from £25 per day) and provides information on all the nearby trails. Guided tours can be arranged with advance notice. ⊠ *133 Main St.* ☎ *017687/73355* ⊕ *www.keswickbikes. co.uk.*

WATER SPORTS

Derwent Water Marina. Rental boats in all shapes and sizes and instruction in canoeing, sailing, and windsurfing can be had at Derwent Water Marina. Other water-related activities include ghyll scrambling—the fine art of walking up or down a steep Lakeland stream. A two-day sailing or windsurfing course costs £200. ⊠ *Portinscale* ☎ *017687/72912* ⊕ *www.derwentwatermarina.co.uk.*

BORROWDALE

7 miles south of Keswick.

Fodor'sChoice ★ South of Keswick and its lake lies the valley of Borrowdale, whose varied landscape of green valley floor and surrounding crags has long been considered one of the region's most magnificent treasures. **Rosthwaite,** a tranquil farming village, and **Seatoller,** the southernmost settlement, are the two main centers (both are accessible by bus from Keswick), though they're little more than clusters of aged buildings surrounded by glorious countryside.

GETTING HERE AND AROUND

The valley is south of Keswick on B5289. The Borrowdale bus service between Keswick and Seatoller runs frequently.

EXPLORING

Fodor'sChoice ★ **Borrowdale Fells.** These steep fells rise up dramatically behind Seatoller. Get out and walk whenever inspiration strikes. Trails are well signposted, or you can pick up maps and any gear in Keswick. ⊠ *Seatoller.*

Scafell Pike. England's highest mountain at 3,210 feet, Scafell (pronounced *scar*-fell) Pike is visible from Seatoller. One route up the mountain, for experienced walkers, is from the hamlet of Seathwaite, a mile south of Seatoller. ⊠ *Seatoller.*

WHERE TO STAY

$$ | B&B/INN | Fodor'sChoice ★ | **Hazel Bank Country House.** Though this stately, carefully restored home retains original elements from its days as a grand Victorian country pile, its welcoming owners have invested in handsome local furniture and stripped away some of the chintz, opening up inspiring views across the pristine lawns to the valley and the central Lakeland peaks beyond. **Pros:** serene location; immaculate gardens; attentive staff. **Cons:** not near many amenities; car required to get here; deposit required for bookings. $ *Rooms from: £119* ⊠ *Off B5289, Rosthwaite* ☎ *017687/77248* ⊕ *www.hazelbankhotel.co.uk* ☞ *8 rooms, 1 cottage* ‖○‖ *Breakfast.*

CAMBRIDGE AND
EAST ANGLIA

WELCOME TO CAMBRIDGE AND EAST ANGLIA

TOP REASONS TO GO

★ **Cambridge:** A walk through the colleges is grand, but the best views of the university's buildings and immaculate lawns (and some famous bridges) are from a punt on the river.

★ **Constable Country:** In the area where Constable grew up, you can walk or row downstream from Dedham straight into the setting of one of the English landscape painter's masterpieces at Flatford Mill.

★ **Ely Cathedral:** The highlight of Ely, north of Cambridge, is its beautiful cathedral, known for its octagonal Lantern Tower.

★ **Lavenham:** This old town is the most comely of the tight-knit cluster of places that prospered from the medieval wool trade, with architecture including timber-frame houses gnarled into crookedness by age.

★ **Aldeburgh:** A trip to Suffolk isn't complete without a stop by the seaside. Aldeburgh fills the bill and is also home to the famous Aldeburgh Festival, which includes music and more.

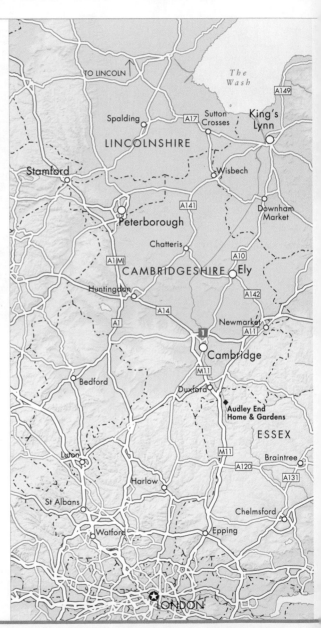

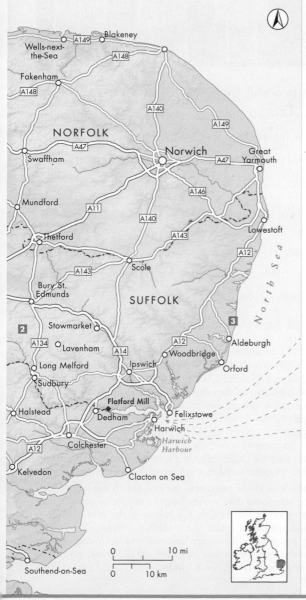

0   10 mi

0   10 km

East Anglia, in south-eastern England, can be divided into distinct areas for sightseeing. The central area surrounds the ancient university city of Cambridge and includes Ely, with its magnificent cathedral rising out of the flatlands, and the towns of inland Suffolk. The Suffolk Heritage Coast is home to historic small towns and villages.

1 Cambridge. The home of the ancient university is East Anglia's liveliest town. The city center is perfect for ambling around the colleges, museums, and King's College Chapel, one of England's greatest monuments.

2 Ely and Central Suffolk. The villages within a short drive of Cambridge remain largely unspoiled. Ely's lofty cathedral dominates the surrounding flatlands, and Long Melford and Lavenham preserve their rich historical flavor.

3 The Suffolk Coast. Idyllic villages such as Dedham and Flatford form the center of what's been dubbed "Constable Country," while the nearby Suffolk Coast includes such atmospheric seaside towns as Aldeburgh.

10

Updated by
Jack Jewers

One of those beautiful English inconsistencies, East Anglia has no spectacular mountains or rivers to disturb the quiet, storied land of rural delights. Occupying an area of southeastern England that pushes out into the North Sea, its counties of Essex, Norfolk, Suffolk, Lincolnshire, and Cambridgeshire feel cut off from the pulse of the country. Among its highlights is Cambridge, a lovely and ancient university city. East Anglia also has four of the country's greatest stately homes: Holkham Hall, Blickling Hall, Houghton Hall, and Sandringham—where the Queen spends Christmas.

In times past, East Anglia was one of the most important centers of power in northern Europe. Towns like Lincoln were major Roman settlements, and the medieval wool trade brought huge prosperity to the higgledy-piggledy streets of tiny Lavenham. Thanks to its relative lack of thoroughfares and canals, however, East Anglia was mercifully untouched by the Industrial Revolution. The area is rich in idyllic, quintessentially English villages: sleepy, sylvan settlements in the midst of otherwise deserted lowlands. Even the towns feel small and manageable; the biggest city, Norwich, has a population of just 130,000. Cambridge, with its ancient university, is the area's most famous draw, along with incomparable cathedrals, at Ely and Lincoln particularly, and one of the finest Gothic buildings in Europe, King's College Chapel.

And yet, despite all of these treasures, the real joy of exploring East Anglia is making your own discoveries. Spend a couple of days exploring the hidden byways of the fens, or just taking in the subtle beauties of the many England-like-it-looks-in-the-movies villages. If you find yourself driving down a small country lane and an old church or mysterious, ivy-covered ruin peeks out from behind the trees, give in to your curiosity and look inside. Such hidden places are East Anglia's best-kept secrets.

PLANNER

WHEN TO GO

Summer and late spring are the best times to visit East Anglia. Late fall and winter can be cold, windy, and rainy, though this is England's driest region and crisp, frosty days here are beautiful. To escape crowds, avoid the popular Norfolk Broads in late July and August. You can't visit most of the Cambridge colleges during exam period (late May to mid-June), and the competition for hotel rooms heats up during graduation week (late June). The Aldeburgh Festival of Music and the Arts, one of the biggest events on the British classical music calendar, takes place in June.

PLANNING YOUR TIME

Cambridge is the region's most interesting city, and ideally you should allow two days to absorb its various sights. (In a pinch you could do it as a day trip from London, but only with an early start and a good pair of walking shoes.) You could easily use the city as a base for exploring Ely, Lavenham, and Long Melford, although accommodations are available in these towns as well. The Suffolk Coast has enticing overnight stops in such small towns as Dedham and Aldeburgh.

FESTIVALS

Fodor's Choice
★

Aldeburgh Festival. East Anglia's most important arts festival, and one of the best known in Britain, is the Aldeburgh Festival. It's held for two weeks in June in the small village of Snape, 5 miles west of Aldeburgh. Founded by Benjamin Britten, the festival concentrates on music but includes exhibitions, poetry readings, and lectures. A handful of events are aimed specifically at children. ⊠ *Snape* ☎ *01728/687100 for inquiries, 01728/687110 for box office* ⊕ *www.snapemaltings.co.uk/season/aldeburgh-festival.*

GETTING HERE AND AROUND

AIR TRAVEL

Norwich International Airport serves a limited number of domestic and international destinations, though not the United States. London Stansted Airport, 30 miles south of Cambridge, is used mainly for European flights. The vast majority of travelers to the region arrive by train, car, or bus.

Airports London Stansted Airport. ⊠ *Bassingbourn Rd., Bishop's Stortford* ☎ *0808/169–7031* ⊕ *www.stanstedairport.com.* **Norwich International Airport.** ⊠ *Amsterdam Way, off A140, Norwich* ☎ *01603/411923* ⊕ *www.norwichairport.co.uk.*

BUS TRAVEL

National Express buses serve the region from London's Victoria Coach Station. Average travel times are three hours to Cambridge.

Long-distance buses are useful for reaching the region and traveling between its major centers, but for smaller hops, local buses are best. First and Stagecoach buses cover the Cambridge area. Traveline can answer public transportation questions.

10

Bus Contacts Stagecoach. 🖀 *01223/433250* ⊕ *www.stagecoachbus.com/ cambridge.* **Traveline.** 🖀 *0871/200–2233, 84268 text "Traveline" from mobile phone for link to bus finder* ⊕ *www.traveline.info.*

CAR TRAVEL

If you're driving from London, Cambridge (54 miles) is off M11. A12 from London goes through east Suffolk via Ipswich. Once off the A roads, traveling within the region often means taking country lanes that have many twists and turns. Going even just a few miles can take much longer than you think.

TRAIN TRAVEL

The entire region is well served by trains from London's Liverpool Street and King's Cross stations. The quality and convenience of these services varies enormously, however. Cambridge trains leave from King's Cross and Liverpool Street, take about 45 minutes to an hour, and cost about £26. A good way to save money on local trains in East Anglia is to buy an Anglia Plus Ranger Pass. It costs £18.50 for one day or £37 for three days, and allows unlimited rail travel in Norfolk, Suffolk, and part of Cambridgeshire. You can add up to four kids for an extra £2 each.

Train Contacts Abellio Greater Anglia. 🖀 *0345/600–7245* ⊕ *www. abelliogreateranglia.co.uk.* **East Midlands Trains.** 🖀 *03457/125678* ⊕ *www. eastmidlandstrains.co.uk.* **Great Northern Rail.** 🖀 *0345/026–4700* ⊕ *www. greatnorthernrail.com.* **National Rail Enquiries.** 🖀 *03457/484950* ⊕ *www. nationalrail.co.uk.*

RESTAURANTS

In summer the coast gets so packed with people that reservations are essential at restaurants. Getting something to eat at other than regular mealtime hours isn't always possible in small towns; head to cafés if you want a mid-morning or after-lunch snack. Look for area specialties, such as crab, lobster, duckling, Norfolk black turkey, hare, and partridge, on menus around the region. *Restaurant reviews have been shortened. For full information, visit Fodors.com.*

HOTELS

The region is full of centuries-old, half-timber inns with rooms full of roaring fires and cozy bars. Bed-and-breakfasts are a good option in pricey Cambridge. It's always busy in Cambridge and along the coast in summer, so reserve well in advance. *Hotel reviews have been shortened. For full information, visit Fodors.com.*

WHAT IT COSTS IN POUNDS			
	$	**$$**	**$$$**	**$$$$**
Restaurants	under £15	£15–£19	£20–£25	over £25
Hotels	under £100	£100–£160	£161–£220	over £220

Restaurant prices are the average cost of a main course at dinner, or if dinner is not served, at lunch. Hotel prices are the lowest cost of a standard double room in high season, including 20% V.A.T.

VISITOR INFORMATION
Contacts **East of England Tourism.** ✉ *Dettingen House, Dettingen Way, Bury St. Edmunds* ☎ *0333/320–4202* ⊕ *www.visiteastofengland.com.*

CAMBRIDGE

Fodor's Choice
★

With the spires of its university buildings framed by towering trees and expansive meadows, and its medieval streets and passages enhanced by gardens and riverbanks, the city of Cambridge is among the loveliest in England. The city predates the Roman occupation of Britain, but there's confusion over exactly how and when the university was founded. The most widely accepted story is that it was established in 1209 by a pair of scholars from Oxford, who left their university in protest over the wrongful execution of a colleague for murder.

Keep in mind there's no recognizable campus: the scattered colleges *are* the university. The town reveals itself only slowly, filled with tiny gardens, ancient courtyards, imposing classic buildings, alleyways that lead past medieval churches, and wisteria-hung facades. Perhaps the best views are from the Backs, the green parkland that extends along the River Cam behind several colleges. This sweeping openness, a result of the larger size of the colleges and lack of industrialization in the city center, is what distinguishes Cambridge from Oxford.

This university town may be beautiful, but it's no museum. Well-preserved medieval buildings sit cheek by jowl with the latest in modern architecture (for example, the William Gates Building, which houses Cambridge University's computer laboratory) in this growing city dominated culturally and architecturally by its famous university (students make up around one-fifth of the city's 109,000 inhabitants), and beautified by parks, gardens, and the quietly flowing River Cam.

GETTING HERE AND AROUND

Good bus (three hours) and train (one hour) services connect London and Cambridge. The long-distance bus terminal is on Drummer Street, very close to Emmanuel and Christ's colleges. Several local buses connect the station with central Cambridge, including the frequent Citi 7 and 8 services, although any bus listing City Centre or Emmanuel Street among its stops will do. The journey takes just under 10 minutes. If you're driving, don't attempt to venture very far into the center—parking is scarce and pricey. The center is amenable to explorations on foot, or you could join the throng by renting a bicycle.

Stagecoach sells Dayrider (£4.30) tickets for all-day bus travel within Cambridge, and Megarider tickets (£13) for seven days of travel within the city. You can extend these to cover the whole county of Cambridgeshire (£6.70 and £25, respectively), or even an extension to a week as far as Oxford (£40.50). Buy any of them from the driver.

TOURS

Visit Cambridge. Walking tours are led by official Blue or Green Badge guides. The 1½- or 2-hour tours leave from the tourist information center at Peas Hill. Hours vary according to the tour, with the earliest

10

leaving at 11 am and the latest at 1 or 2 pm. ⊠ *The Guildhall, Peas Hill* ☎ *01223/791501* ⊕ *www.visitcambridge.org/official-tours* 🖾 *From £15.*

ESSENTIALS

Visitor Information Cambridge Visitor Information Centre. ⊠ *The Guildhall, Peas Hill* ☎ *01223/791500* ⊕ *www.visitcambridge.org.*

EXPLORING

Exploring the city means, in large part, exploring the university. Each of the 25 oldest colleges is built around a series of courts, or quadrangles, framing manicured, velvety lawns. Because students and fellows (faculty) live and work in these courts, access is sometimes restricted, and you're asked not to picnic in the quadrangles at any time.

Visitors aren't normally allowed into college buildings other than chapels, dining halls, and some libraries; some colleges charge admission for certain buildings. Public visiting hours vary from college to college, depending on the time of year, and it's best to call or to check with the city tourist office. Colleges close to visitors during the main exam time, late May to mid-June. Term time (when classes are in session) means roughly October to December, January to March, and April to June; summer term, or vacation, runs from July to September. ■TIP→ Bring a pair of binoculars, as some college buildings have highly intricate details, such as the spectacular ceiling at King's College Chapel. When the colleges are open, the best way to gain access is to join a walking tour led by an official Blue Badge guide—many areas are off-limits unless you do. The 90-minute and two-hour tours (£10 to £18) leave up to four times daily from the city tourist office. The other traditional view of the colleges is gained from a punt—the boats propelled by pole on the River Cam.

OFF THE BEATEN PATH

Audley End House and Gardens. A famous example of early-17th-century architecture, Audley End was once owned by Charles II, who bought it as a convenient place to break his journey on the way to the Newmarket races. Although the palatial building was remodeled in the 18th and 19th centuries, the Jacobean style is still on display in the magnificent Great Hall. You can walk in the park, landscaped by Capability Brown in the 18th century, and the fine Victorian gardens. Exhibitions focus on the lives of domestic servants in the late 19th century. A recent renovation opened up the Nursery Suite, bedecked in the style of the 1830s, and the Coal Gallery, which once provided hot water for the family upstairs (though not the servants). The Service Wing lets you look "below stairs" at the kitchen, scullery (where fish were descaled and chickens plucked), and game larder (where pheasants, partridges, and rabbits were hung), while the Stable Yard gives kids the chance to see old saddles and tack and don Victorian riding costumes. The house is in Saffron Waldon, 14 miles south of Cambridge. ⊠ *Off London Rd., Saffron Walden* ☎ *01799/522842* ⊕ *www.english-heritage.org.uk/ visit/places/audley-end-house-and-gardens* 🖾 *£18.10 Apr.–Oct., £11.80 Nov.–Mar.* ☉ *House closed Nov.–Mar.*

Cricket, anyone? Audley End, a 17th-century house, serves as an idyllic backdrop for a cricket match.

Christ's College. To see the way a college has grown over the centuries you could not do better than a visit here. The main gateway bears the enormous coat of arms of its patroness, Lady Margaret Beaufort, mother of Henry VII, who established the institution in 1505. It leads into a fine courtyard, with the chapel framed by an ancient magnolia. In the dining hall hang portraits of John Milton and Charles Darwin, two of the college's most famous students. Next, walk past a fellows' building credited to Inigo Jones, who transformed English architecture in the early 17th century, to the spacious garden (once a favorite haunt of Milton's), and finally to a modern zigguratlike confection from the 1960s. ⊠ *St. Andrew's St.* ☎ *01223/334900* ⊕ *www.christs.cam.ac.uk* ✉ *Free* ☉ *Gardens closed weekends. Closed during exam periods.*

Emmanuel College. The master hand of architect Sir Christopher Wren (1632–1723) is evident throughout much of Cambridge, particularly at Emmanuel, built on the site of a Dominican friary, where he designed the chapel and colonnade. A stained-glass window in the chapel has a likeness of John Harvard, founder of Harvard University, who studied here. The college, founded in 1584, was an early center of Puritan learning; a number of the Pilgrims were Emmanuel alumni, and they remembered their alma mater in naming Cambridge, Massachusetts. ⊠ *St. Andrew's St.* ☎ *01223/334200* ⊕ *www.emma.cam.ac.uk* ✉ *Free* ☉ *Closed during exam periods.*

Fodor's Choice
★ **Fitzwilliam Museum.** In a Classical Revival building renowned for its grand Corinthian portico, "The Fitz," founded by the 7th Viscount Fitzwilliam of Merrion in 1816, has one of Britain's most outstanding collections of art and antiquities. Highlights include two large Titians,

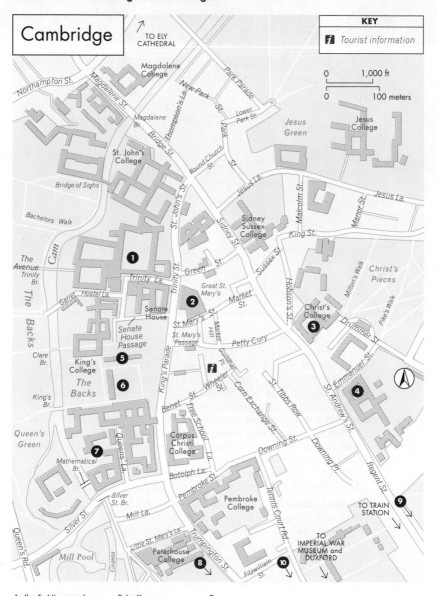

Cambridge

TO ELY
CATHEDRAL

0   1,000 ft

0   100 meters

an extensive collection of French impressionist paintings, and many works by Matisse and Picasso. The opulent interior displays these treasures to marvelous effect, from Egyptian pieces like inch-high figurines and painted coffins to sculptures from the Chinese Han dynasty of the 3rd century BC. Other collections of note here include a fine collection of flower paintings, an assortment of medieval illuminated manuscripts, and a fascinating room full of armor and muskets. ☒ *Trumpington St.* ☎ *01223/332900* ⊕ *www.fitzmuseum.cam.ac.uk* ☒ *Free* ☉ *Closed Mon. except bank holidays.*

Great St. Mary's. Known as the "university church," Great St. Mary's has its origins in the 11th century, although the current building dates from 1478. The main reason to visit is to climb the 113-foot tower, which has a superb view over the colleges and marketplace (though it may be closed in bad weather). Also here is the Michaelhouse Centre, a small café, gallery, and performing arts venue with frequent free lunchtime concerts. Tours must be booked in advance. ☒ *Market Hill, King's Parade* ☎ *01223/747273* ⊕ *www.gsm.cam.ac.uk* ☒ *Free; tower £4; guided tours £10.*

King's College. Founded in 1441 by Henry VI, King's College has a magnificent late-15th-century chapel that is its most famous landmark. Other notable architecture includes the neo-Gothic Porters' Lodge, facing King's Parade, which was a comparatively recent addition in the 1830s, and the classical Gibbs building. ■TIP➔ Head down to the river, from where the panorama of college and chapel is one of the university's most photographed views. Past students of King's College include the novelist E.M. Forster, the economist John Maynard Keynes, and the World War I poet Rupert Brooke. ☒ *King's Parade* ☎ *01223/331100* ⊕ *www.kings.cam.ac.uk* ☒ *£9, includes chapel.*

Fodor'sChoice **King's College Chapel.** Based on Sainte-Chapelle, the 13th-century royal ★ chapel in Paris, this house of worship is perhaps the most glorious flowering of Perpendicular Gothic in Britain. Henry VI, the king after whom the college is named, oversaw the work. From the outside, the most prominent features are the massive flying buttresses and the fingerlike spires that line the length of the building. Inside, the most obvious impression is of great space—the chapel was once described as "the noblest barn in Europe"—and of light flooding in from its huge windows. The brilliantly colored bosses (carved panels at the intersections of the roof ribs) are particularly intense, although hard to see without binoculars. An exhibition in the chantries, or side chapels, explains more about the chapel's construction. Behind the altar is *The Adoration of the Magi,* an enormous painting by Peter Paul Rubens. ■TIP➔ The chapel, unlike the rest of King's College, stays open during exam periods. Every Christmas Eve, a festival of carols is sung by the chapel's famous choir. It's broadcast on national television and considered a quintessential part of the traditional English Christmas. To compete for the small number of tickets available, join the line at the college's main entrance early—doors open at 7 am. ☒ *King's Parade* ☎ *01223/331–212* ⊕ *www.kings.cam.ac.uk* ☒ *£9, includes college and grounds* ☉ *Sometimes closed for events; check ahead to confirm.*

10

Fodor's Choice ★ **Polar Museum.** Beautifully designed, this museum at Cambridge University's Scott Polar Research Institute chronicles the history of polar exploration. There's a particular emphasis on the British expeditions of the 20th century, including the ill-fated attempt by Robert Falcon Scott to be the first to reach the South Pole in 1912. Norwegian explorer Roald Amundsen reached the pole first; Scott and his men perished on the return journey, but their story became legendary. There are also collections devoted to the science of modern polar exploration; the indigenous people of northern Canada, Greenland, and Alaska; and frequently changing art installations. ✉ *Scott Polar Research Institute, Lensfield Rd.* ☎ *01223/336540* 🌐 *www.spri.cam.ac.uk/museum* 🎫 *Free* 🕒 *Closed Sun. and Mon. except bank holidays.*

Queens' College. One of the most eye-catching colleges, with a secluded "cloister court" look, Queens' is named after Margaret, wife of Henry VI, and Elizabeth, wife of Edward IV. Founded in 1448 and completed in the 1540s, the college is tucked away on Queens' Lane, next to the wide lawns that lead down from King's College to the Backs. The college's most iconic piece of architecture is the wooden lattice Mathematical Bridge, first built in 1749. The original version is said to have been built without any fastenings, though the current bridge (reconstructed in 1902) is securely bolted. ✉ *Queens' La.* ☎ *01223/335511* 🌐 *www.quns.cam.ac.uk* 🎫 *£3* 🕒 *Closed weekends Jan. and Feb. and during exam periods, certain wks Apr.–July; call to confirm.*

Trinity College. Founded in 1546 by Henry VIII, Trinity replaced a 14th-century educational foundation and is the largest college in either Cambridge or Oxford, with nearly 1,000 undergraduates. In the 17th-century great court, with its massive gatehouse, is **Great Tom,** a giant clock that strikes each hour with high and low notes. The college's true masterpiece is Sir Christopher Wren's **library,** colonnaded and seemingly constructed with as much light as stone. Among the things you can see here is A. A. Milne's handwritten manuscript of *The House at Pooh Corner.* Trinity alumni include Sir Isaac Newton, William Thackeray, Lord Byron, Lord Tennyson, and 31 Nobel Prize winners. ✉ *St. John's St.* ☎ *01223/338400* 🌐 *www.trin.cam.ac.uk* 🎫 *£3* 🕒 *College and chapel closed exam period and event days; Wren library closed Sun.*

WHERE TO EAT

$ ITALIAN 🍴 **Jamie's Italian.** Run by celebrity chef Jamie Oliver, this is one of the busiest restaurants in Cambridge, but the atmosphere is relaxed and casual, and the prices are lower than you'd expect. In truth, the long queues on weekend nights have more to do with Oliver's star power and the no-reservations policy; however, the food—a combination of authentic Italian flavors and modern variations on the classics—deserves some praise. **Known for:** casual dining; authentic Italian flavors; first-come, first-served booking policy. [$] *Average main: £13* ✉ *Old Library, Wheeler St.* ☎ *01223/654094* 🌐 *www.jamieoliver.com/italian.*

$$ SEAFOOD 🍴 **Loch Fyne.** Part of a Scottish chain that harvests its own oysters, this airy, casual place across from the Fitzwilliam Museum is deservedly popular. The seafood is fresh and well prepared, served in a traditional

setting with a modern ambience. **Known for:** Bradan Rost smoked salmon; Scottish oysters; great Scotch whisky menu. $ *Average main: £17* ✉ *37 Trumpington St.* ☎ *01223/362433* ⊕ *www.lochfyneseafoodandgrill.co.uk.*

$$$$
FRENCH
Fodor's Choice
★

✕ **Midsummer House.** Beside the River Cam on the edge of Midsummer Common, this gray-brick 19th-century villa holds a two–Michelin star restaurant set in a comfortable conservatory. Fixed-price menus for lunch and dinner (with five to eight courses) present innovative French and Mediterranean-influenced dishes that often include apples from the trees in the garden. **Known for:** great river views; beautiful historic setting; special-occasion dining. $ *Average main: £145* ✉ *Midsummer Common* ☎ *01223/369299* ⊕ *www.midsummerhouse.co.uk* ⊗ *Closed Sun. and Mon. No lunch Tues.*

$$
BRITISH

✕ **The Oak.** This charming, intimate restaurant is a local favorite. It's near an uncompromisingly busy intersection, but the friendliness of the staff and classic bistro food more than make up for it. **Known for:** bistro-style menus; excellent steaks; delicious, regional seafood. $ *Average main: £18* ✉ *6 Lensfield Rd.* ☎ *01223/323361* ⊕ *www.theoakbistro.co.uk* ⊗ *Closed Sun.*

$$$$
BRITISH

✕ **Restaurant 22.** Pretty stained-glass windows separate this sophisticated little restaurant from bustling Chesterton Road. The setting, in a terrace of houses, is low-key, but the food is creative and eye-catching. **Known for:** low-key setting; creative approach to classics; delicious desserts. $ *Average main: £37* ✉ *22 Chesterton Rd.* ☎ *01223/351880* ⊕ *www.restaurant22.co.uk* ⊗ *Closed Sun. and Mon. No lunch.*

$$$
MODERN BRITISH

✕ **River Bar Steakhouse & Grill.** Across the river from Magdalene College, this popular waterfront bar and grill serves delicious steak burgers and pies, plus specialties such as lobster mac and cheese, and salmon steak with molasses and spices. There's an extensive evening cocktail menu as well. **Known for:** classic British mains; rooftop terrace dining; huge cocktail menu. $ *Average main: £20* ✉ *Quayside, Thompsons La., off Bridge St.* ☎ *01223/307030* ⊕ *www.riverbarsteakhouse.com.*

$$
MEDITERRANEAN

✕ **Three Horseshoes.** This early-19th-century pub and restaurant in a thatched cottage has an elegant dining space in the conservatory and more casual tables in the airy bar. Sourcing of ingredients is taken seriously here—the menu lists not only the suppliers, but specific reasons for choosing them—and this is all put to good use in Modern British dishes with hints of the Mediterranean. **Known for:** local ingredients; seafood board; excellent wine. $ *Average main: £19* ✉ *High St., Madingley* ☎ *01954/210221* ⊕ *www.threehorseshoesmadingley.co.uk.*

WHERE TO STAY

$$
B&B/INN
Fodor's Choice
★

⌂ **Duke House.** This beautifully converted town house (home of the Duke of Gloucester when he was a student) is forever cropping up in British newspaper articles about the best B&Bs in the country. **Pros:** beautiful house; great location; suites are quite spacious. **Cons:** books up fast; two-night minimum on weekends; cheaper rooms are small. $ *Rooms from: £150* ✉ *1 Victoria St.* ☎ *01223/314773* ⊕ *www.dukehousecambridge.co.uk* ⇄ *5 rooms* ⦿ *Free Breakfast.*

10

$ B&B/INN **Finches Bed and Breakfast.** Although it's in a rather inauspicious building, the diminutive Finches is a well-run B&B with prices that make it an excellent value. **Pros:** cheerful staff; quiet location; good level of service. **Cons:** away from the action; no tubs in bathrooms; no credit cards. [$] *Rooms from: £70* ✉ *144 Thornton Rd.* ☎ *01223/276653* 💳 *No credit cards* 🛏 *3 rooms* 🍴 *Free Breakfast.*

$$ B&B/INN **5 Chapel Street.** This sweet Georgian town house and B&B in the northeastern corner of the city is a beautiful 20-minute walk along the river from central Cambridge. **Pros:** quiet location; wonderful host; excellent breakfast. **Cons:** some rooms are small; suburban location; 20-minute walk to the center. [$] *Rooms from: £110* ✉ *5 Chapel St., Chesterton* ☎ *01223/514856* 🌐 *www.5chapelstreet.com* 🛏 *3 rooms* 🍴 *Free Breakfast.*

$$ HOTEL **Regent Hotel.** A rare small hotel in central Cambridge, this handsome Georgian town house has wooden sash windows that look out over a tree-lined park called Parker's Piece. **Pros:** good view from top rooms; close to bars and restaurants; cozy atmosphere. **Cons:** no parking; a tad scruffy; disappointing breakfasts. [$] *Rooms from: £125* ✉ *41 Regent St.* ☎ *01223/351470* 🌐 *www.regenthotel.co.uk* 🛏 *22 rooms* 🍴 *Free Breakfast.*

$$$$ HOTEL Fodor's Choice ★ **The Varsity.** This stylish boutique hotel with an adjoining spa has wide windows that flood the place with light. **Pros:** beautiful location; gorgeous views; stylish design. **Cons:** not such great views in the less expensive rooms; prices are a bit high (particularly on weekdays); not much choice at breakfast. [$] *Rooms from: £225* ✉ *Thompson's La., off Bridge St.* ☎ *01223/306030* 🌐 *www.thevarsityhotel.co.uk* 🛏 *48 rooms* 🍴 *No meals.*

$ B&B/INN **Warkworth House.** The location of this B&B could hardly be better, as the Fitzwilliam Museum and several of Cambridge's colleges are within a 15-minute walk. **Pros:** excellent location; lovely hosts; family rooms are great value. **Cons:** few frills; no restaurant on-site; some free parking but not enough for everyone. [$] *Rooms from: £95* ✉ *Warkworth Terr.* ☎ *01223/363682* 🌐 *www.warkworthhouse.co.uk* 🛏 *14 rooms* 🍴 *Free Breakfast.*

NIGHTLIFE AND PERFORMING ARTS

NIGHTLIFE

The Eagle. This 16th-century coaching inn with a cobbled courtyard has lost none of its old-time character. It also played a walk-on part in scientific history when, on February 28, 1953, a pair of excited Cambridge scientists announced to a roomful of rather surprised lunchtime patrons that they'd just discovered the secret of life: DNA. (Unfortunately they forgot to mention their third colleague, Rosalind Franklin, who has been largely erased from the history of their discovery). A plaque outside commemorates the event. ✉ *8 Benet St.* ☎ *01223/505020* 🌐 *www.greeneking-pubs.co.uk/pubs/cambridgeshire/eagle.*

Fort St. George. Overlooking the university boathouses, this lovely old pub gets honors for its riverside views. ⊠ *Midsummer Common* ☎ *01223/354327* ⊕ *https://www.greeneking-pubs.co.uk/pubs/cambridgeshire/fort-st-george.*

Free Press. A favorite of student rowers, this small pub has an excellent selection of traditional ales. ⊠ *7 Prospect Row* ☎ *01223/368337* ⊕ *www.freepresskitchen.co.uk.*

PERFORMING ARTS

King's College Chapel. During regular terms, King's College Chapel has evensong services Monday through Saturday at 5:30, Sunday at 3:30. ■ **TIP→** Your best chance of seeing the full choir is Thursday to Sunday. ⊠ *King's Parade* ☎ *01223/331212* ⊕ *www.kings.cam.ac.uk.*

SHOPPING

Head to the specialty shops in the center of town, especially in and around Rose Crescent and King's Parade. Bookshops, including antiquarian stores, are Cambridge's pride and joy.

BOOKS

Cambridge University Press Bookshop. In business since at least 1581, the Cambridge University Press runs this store on Trinity Street. ⊠ *1 Trinity St.* ☎ *01223/333333* ⊕ *www.cambridge.org/about-us/visit-bookshop.*

David's. Near the Arts Theatre, G. David (known locally as just David's) sells antiquarian books. ⊠ *16 St. Edward's Passage* ☎ *01223/354619* ⊕ *www.davidsbookshop.co.uk.*

Haunted Bookshop. This shop carries a great selection of old, illustrated books and British classics. And (the clue's in the name) apparently it has a ghost, too. ⊠ *9 St. Edward's Passage* ☎ *01223/312913* ⊕ *www.sarahkeybooks.co.uk.*

Heffer's. Filled with rare and imported books, Heffer's boasts a particularly fine arts section. ⊠ *20 Trinity St.* ☎ *01223/463200* ⊕ *blackwells.co.uk/bookshop/shops.*

CLOTHING

Ryder & Amies. Need a straw boater? This shop is the official outlet for Cambridge University products, from hoodies to ties to cuff links. ⊠ *22 King's Parade* ☎ *01223/350371* ⊕ *www.ryderamies.co.uk.*

MARKETS

All Saints Garden Art & Craft Market. This market displays the wares of local artists outdoors on Saturday. It's also open Fridays in July and August and some weekends in December (weather permitting). ⊠ *Trinity St.* ⊕ *www.cambridge-art-craft.co.uk.*

10

Punting on the Cam

To punt is to maneuver a flat-bottom, wooden, gondolalike boat—in this case, through the shallow River Cam along the verdant Backs behind the colleges of Cambridge. One benefit of this popular activity is that you get a better view of the ivy-covered walls from the water. Mastery of the sport lies in your ability to control a 15-foot pole, used to propel the punt. With a bottle of wine, some food, and a few friends, you may find yourself saying things such as, "It doesn't get any better than this." One piece of advice: if your pole gets stuck, let go. You can use the smaller paddle to go back and retrieve it. Hang on to a stuck punt for too long and you'll probably fall in with it.

The lazier-at-heart may prefer chauffeured punting, with food supplied. Students from Cambridge often do the work, and you get a fairly informative spiel on the colleges. For a romantic evening trip, there are illuminated punts.

One university punting society once published a useful "Bluffer's Guide to Punting" featuring detailed instructions and tips on how to master the art. It has been archived online at ⊕ *duramecho.com/Misc/HowToPunt. html.*

SPORTS AND THE OUTDOORS

BIKING

City Cycle Hire. This shop charges supercheap rates of £7 per half day, £10 per day, and £20 for a week. All bikes are mountain or hybrid bikes. Advance reservations are essential in July and August. ✉ *61 Newnham Rd.* ☎ *01223/365629* ⊕ *www.citycyclehire.com.*

PUNTING

You can rent punts at several places, notably at Silver Street Bridge–Mill Lane, at Magdalene Bridge, and from outside the Rat and Parrot pub on Thompson's Lane on Jesus Green. Hourly rental costs around £10 to £25. Chauffeured punting, usually by a Cambridge student, is also popular. It costs upwards of £15 to £20 per person.

Scudamore's Punting Co. This company rents chauffeured and self-drive punts. Daily, 45-minute tours start at around £20 per person (less if booked online). Scudamore's also runs various special tours—for afternoon tea or Halloween, for example. Private tours and punting lessons are also available. High-stakes romantics can even arrange a "Proposal Tour," which includes champagne and roses if your beloved says yes. ✉ *Granta Place, Mill La.* ☎ *01223/359750* ⊕ *www.scudamores.com.*

ELY AND CENTRAL SUFFOLK

This central area of towns and villages within easy reach of Cambridge is testament to the amazing changeability of the English landscape. The town of Ely is set in an eerie, flat, and apparently endless marsh, or fenland. (A medieval term, "the fens," is still used informally to describe the surrounding region.) Only a few miles south and east into Suffolk, however, all this changes to pastoral landscapes of gently undulating hills and clusters of villages including pretty Long Medford and Lavenham.

ELY

16 miles north of Cambridge.

Known for its magnificent cathedral, Ely is the "capital" of the fens, the center of what used to be a separate county called the Isle of Ely (literally "island of eels"). Until the land was drained in the 17th century, Ely was surrounded by treacherous marshland, which inhabitants crossed wearing stilts. Today Wicken Fen, a nature reserve 9 miles southeast of town (off A1123), preserves the sole remaining example of fenland in an undrained state.

Enveloped by fields of wheat, sugar beets, and carrots, Ely is a small, dense town that somewhat fails to live up to the high expectations created by its big attraction, its magnificent cathedral. The shopping area and market square lie to the north and lead down to the riverside, and the medieval buildings of the cathedral grounds and the King's School (which trains cathedral choristers) spread out to the south and west. Ely's most famous resident was Oliver Cromwell, whose house is now a museum.

GETTING HERE AND AROUND

The 9 and 12 buses leave twice an hour from the Drummer Street bus station in Cambridge. The journey to Ely takes around an hour. To drive there from Cambridge, simply take the A10 road going north out of the city. Ely is quite small, so find somewhere to park and walk to the center. Trains from Cambridge to Ely leave three times an hour and take 15 minutes.

ESSENTIALS

Visitor Information Visit Ely. ✉ *Oliver Cromwell's House, 29 St. Mary's St.* ☏ *01353/662062* ⊕ *www.visitely.org.uk.*

EXPLORING

10

Fodor's Choice **Ely Cathedral.** Known affectionately as the Ship of the Fens, Ely Cathe-
★ dral can be seen for miles, towering above the flat landscape on one of the few ridges in the fens. In 1083 the Normans began work on the cathedral, which stands on the site of a Benedictine monastery founded by the Anglo-Saxon princess Etheldreda in 673. In the center of the cathedral you see a marvel of medieval construction—the unique octagonal **Lantern Tower,** a sort of stained-glass skylight of colossal proportions, built to replace the central tower that collapsed in 1322. The cathedral's **West Tower** is even taller; the view from the top (if you can manage the 288 steps) is spectacular. Tours of both towers run daily. The cathedral is also notable for its 248-foot-long **nave,** with its simple Norman arches and Victorian painted ceiling. Much of the decorative carving of the 14th-century **Lady Chapel** was defaced during the Reformation (mostly by knocking off the heads of the statuary), but enough traces remain to show its original beauty.

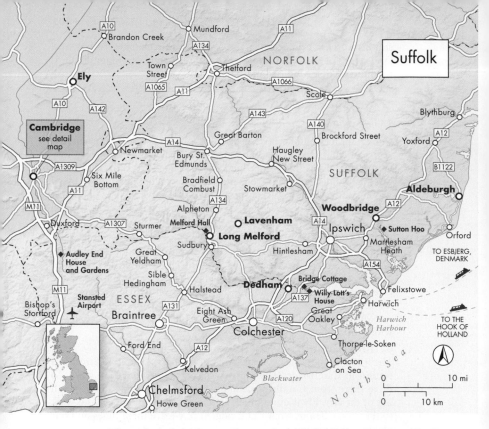

The cathedral also houses the wonderful **Stained Glass Museum** (⊕ *www.stainedglassmuseum.com*). Exhibits trace the history of stained glass from medieval to modern times, including some stunning contemporary pieces. Ely Cathedral is a popular filming location; it doubled for Westminster Abbey in *The King's Speech* (2010) and *The Crown* (2015).

■**TIP**➔ There are guided tours of the cathedral from Monday to Saturday (and Sunday in summer); generally they start at 10:45, noon, and 2, with extra tours in the summer, but times vary so it's a good idea to call ahead. ⊠ *The Gallery* ☎ *01353/667735* ⊕ *www.elycathedral.org* ✉ *£8–£18.*

LONG MELFORD

2 miles north of Sudbury, 14 miles south of Bury St. Edmunds.

It's easy to see how this village got its name, especially if you walk the full length of its 2-mile-long main street, which gradually broadens to include green squares and trees, and finally opens into a large triangular green on the hill. Long Melford grew rich on its wool trade in the 15th century, and the town's buildings are an appealing mix, mostly Tudor half-timber or Georgian. Many house antiques shops. Away from the main road, Long Melford returns to its resolutely late-medieval roots.

GETTING HERE AND AROUND

Long Melford is just off the main A134. If you're driving from Sudbury, take the smaller B1064; it's much quicker than it looks on the map. There are several bus connections with Sudbury, Bury St. Edmunds, and Ipswich.

EXPLORING

Holy Trinity Church. This largely 15th-century church, founded by the rich clothiers of Long Melford, stands on a hill at the north end of the village. Close up, the delicate flint flush-work (shaped flints set into a pattern) and huge Perpendicular Gothic windows that take up most of the church's walls have great impact, especially because the nave is 150 feet long. The Clopton Chapel, with an ornate (and incredibly rare) painted medieval ceiling, predates the rest of the church by 150 years. The beautiful Lady Chapel has an unusual cloister; the stone on the wall in the corner is an ancient multiplication table, used when the chapel served as a school in the 17th and 18th centuries. **■TIP→ Tours can be arranged in advance; email alisonewbankis@gmail.com for more details and to make reservations.** ✉ *Main St.* ☎ *01787/310845* 🌐 *www.longmelfordchurch.com* 🎫 *Free.*

Melford Hall. Distinguished from the outside by its turrets and topiaries, Melford Hall is an Elizabethan house with its original banqueting room, a fair number of 18th-century additions, and pleasant gardens. Much of the porcelain and other fine pieces here come from the *Santisima Trinidad,* a ship loaded with gifts from the emperor of China and bound for Spain that was captured in the 18th century. Children's writer Beatrix Potter, related to the owners, visited often; there's a small collection of Potter memorabilia. ✉ *Off A134* ☎ *01787/379228* 🌐 *www.nationaltrust.org.uk/melfordhall* 🎫 *£8.20* 🕒 *Closed Nov.–Feb.*

WHERE TO STAY

$ HOTEL 🏨 **The Bull.** This half-timber Elizabethan building reveals its long history with stone-flagged floors, bowed and twisted oak beams, and heavy antique furniture. **Pros:** historic atmosphere; comfortable bedrooms; friendly staff. **Cons:** minimum stay on summer weekends; popular with wedding parties; small bathrooms. [$] *Rooms from: £90* ✉ *Hall St.* ☎ *0345/6086040* 🌐 *www.oldenglishinns.co.uk/our-locations/the-bull-hotel-long-melford* 🛏 *25 rooms* 🍴 *Some meals.*

LAVENHAM

4 miles northeast of Long Melford, 10 miles southeast of Bury St. Edmunds.

Fodor's Choice ★ Virtually unchanged since the height of its wealth in the 15th and 16th centuries, Lavenham is one of the most perfectly preserved examples of a Tudor village in England. The weavers' and wool merchants' houses occupy not just one show street but most of the town. The houses are timber-frame in black oak, the main posts looking as if they could last another 400 years, although their walls are often no longer entirely perpendicular to the ground. The town has many examples of so-called "Suffolk pink" buildings—actually a catch-all term for brightly painted colors, including rose, yellow, and apricot; many of these house small galleries selling paintings and crafts.

GETTING HERE AND AROUND

Lavenham is on the A1141 and B1071. Take the latter if possible, as it's a prettier drive. There are hourly buses from Sudbury and Bury St. Edmunds and slightly less frequent buses from Ipswich.

ESSENTIALS

Visitor Information Lavenham Tourist Information Centre. ✉ *Lady St.* ☎ *01787/248207* 🌐 *www.visitsuffolk.com.*

EXPLORING

Church of St. Peter and St. Paul. Set apart from the village on a hill, this grand 15th-century church was built between 1480 and 1520 by cloth merchant Thomas Spring. The height of its tower (141 feet) was meant to surpass those of the neighboring churches—and perhaps to impress rival towns. The rest of the church is perfectly proportioned, with intricately carved wood. ✉ *Church St.* ☎ *01787/247244* 🌐 *www.lavenhamchurch.onesuffolk.net* 🎟 *Free.*

Lavenham Guildhall. Also known as the Guildhall of Corpus Christi, this higgledy-piggledy timber-framed building dating from 1529 dominates Market Place, an almost flawlessly preserved medieval square. Upstairs is a rather dull exhibition on local agriculture and the wool trade, although looking around the building itself is worth the admission charge. ✉ *Market Pl.* ☎ *01787/247646* 🌐 *www.nationaltrust.org.uk/lavenham-guildhall* 🎟 *£7* 🕒 *Closed weekdays Jan. and Feb., and Mon.–Wed. early Nov.–late Dec.*

Little Hall. This timber-frame wool merchant's house (brightly painted on the outside, in the local custom) contains a display showing the building's progress from its creation in the 14th century to its subsequent "modernization" in the 17th century. It also has a beautiful garden at the back. ✉ *Market Pl.* ☎ *01787/247019* 🌐 *www.littlehall.org.uk* 🎟 *£4* 🕒 *Closed Fri. and Mon. except holidays, and Nov.–Mar.*

WHERE TO EAT

$$$ FRENCH Fodor's Choice ★

🍴 **Great House.** This excellent "restaurant with rooms" on the medieval Market Square takes deeply traditional flavors of the British countryside and updates them with a slight French twist in dishes like grilled salmon with spinach fondue, or lamb with onion and thyme pie. Served in an elegant, whitewashed dining room, the three-course, fixed-price menus use a reassuring amount of local and regional ingredients. **Known for:** elegant, refined menus; local ingredients; a French touch. [$] *Average main: £23* ✉ *Market Pl.* ☎ *01787/247431* 🌐 *www.greathouse.co.uk* 🕒 *Closed Mon. and Jan. No dinner Sun. No lunch Tues.*

$ INDIAN Fodor's Choice ★

🍴 **Memsaab.** In a town ready to burst with cream teas, it's a bit of a surprise to find an Indian restaurant, let alone such an exceptional one. Among the classics one would expect from a curry house—from mild kormas to spicy *madrases* and *jalfrezies* (traditional curries made with chili and tomato)—are some finely executed specialties, including Nizami chicken (a fiery dish prepared with yogurt and fresh ginger) and king prawn *bhuna* (with ginger, garlic, and spring onion). **Known for:**

Colorful and ancient, the timbered houses in pretty towns such as Lavenham recall the days when these buildings housed weavers and wool merchants.

top-notch Indian food; more than the usual choices; lively atmosphere. $ *Average main: £11* ✉ *2 Church St.* ☎ *01787/249431* ⊕ *www.memsaaboflavenham.co.uk.*

WHERE TO STAY

$$$
RENTAL
🛏 **Lavenham Priory.** You can immerse yourself in Lavenham's Tudor heritage at this sprawling house, one of the most widely photographed in the village. **Pros:** historic building; charming rooms; lovely garden. **Cons:** minimum two-night stay; no amenities; traffic noise in side rooms. $ *Rooms from: £365 (2 nights)* ✉ *Water St.* ☎ *01787/247404* ⊕ *www.lavenhampriory.co.uk* 🛏 *2 rooms* ⦿| *No meals.*

$$$$
HOTEL
🛏 **Swan Hotel.** This half-timber 14th-century lodging has rambling public rooms, roaring fireplaces, and corridors so low that cushions are strategically placed on beams. **Pros:** lovely old building; atmospheric rooms; beautiful spa. **Cons:** creaky floors; lots of steps to climb; popular wedding venue. $ *Rooms from: £235* ✉ *High St.* ☎ *01787/247477* ⊕ *www.theswanatlavenham.co.uk* 🛏 *49 rooms* ⦿| *Some meals.*

THE SUFFOLK COAST

The 40-mile Suffolk Heritage Coast, which wanders northward from Felixstowe up to Kessingland, is one of the most unspoiled shorelines in the country. The lower part of the coast is the most impressive; however, some of the loveliest towns and villages, such as Dedham and the older part of Flatford, are inland. The best way to experience the countryside around here is to be willing to get lost along its tiny, ancient back roads.

DEDHAM

62 miles southeast of Cambridge, 15 miles southeast of Bury St. Edmunds.

Fodor's Choice
★
Dedham is the heart of Constable Country. Here gentle hills and the cornfields of Dedham Vale, set under the district's delicate, pale skies, inspired John Constable (1776–1837) to paint some of his most celebrated canvases. He went to school in Dedham, a picture-book village that did well from the wool trade in the 15th and 16th centuries and has retained a prosperous air ever since. The 15th-century church looms large over handsomely sturdy, pastel-color houses.

Nearby towns have several other sites of interest to Constable fans. About 2 miles from Dedham is Flatford, where you can see Flatford Mill, one of the two water mills owned by Constable's father. Northeast of Dedham, off A12, the Constable trail continues in East Bergholt, where Constable was born in 1776. Although the town is mostly modern, the older part has some atmospheric buildings like the church of St. Mary-the-Virgin.

GETTING HERE AND AROUND

From the main A12 road, Dedham is easily reached by car via B1029. Public transportation is extremely limited; there's no nearby train station.

EXPLORING

Bridge Cottage. On the north bank of the Stour, this 16th-century home in East Bergholt has a shop, an exhibition about Constable's life, and a pleasant tearoom overlooking the river. You can also rent rowboats here. ⊠ *Off B1070, East Bergholt* ☎ *01206/298260* ⊕ *www.national-trust.org.uk/flatford* ☲ *Free* ⊘ *Closed mid-Dec.–late-Dec. and weekdays Jan., Feb., and Nov.–mid-Dec.*

Fodor's Choice
★
St. Mary-the-Virgin. One of the most remarkable churches in the region, St. Mary-the-Virgin was started just before the Reformation. The doors underneath the ruined archways outside (remnants of a much older church) contain a series of mysterious symbols—actually a coded message left by Catholic sympathizers of the time. The striking interior contains a mini-museum of treasures, including an ancient wall painting of the Virgin Mary in one of the rear chapels, a 14th-century chest, and an extraordinary series of florid memorial stones on the nave wall opposite the main entrance. A unique feature of the church is that its bells are rung from a cage in the graveyard; this was erected as a temporary measure, pending the construction of a tower in 1531 that was never completed. ⊠ *Flatford Rd., East Bergholt* ☎ *01206/392646* ☲ *Free.*

Willy Lott's House. A five-minute stroll down the path from Bridge Cottage brings you to this 16th-century structure that is instantly recognizable from Constable's painting *The Hay Wain* (1821). Although the house is not usually open to the public, the road is a public thoroughfare, so you can just walk right on up to see the famous—and completely unchanged—view for yourself. Just stand across from the two trees on the far bank, with the mill on your right, and look upstream. On the outside wall of the mill is a handy reproduction of the painting to help you compose your own photo. ⊠ *Flatford Rd., off B1070, East Bergholt.*

WHERE TO EAT AND STAY

$$$$ BRITISH Fodor's Choice ★ 🍴 **Le Talbooth.** This sophisticated restaurant serving excellent British-French fare is set in a Tudor house beside the idyllic River Stour. Outside, there are lighted terraces where food and drinks are served on warm evenings and jazz and steel bands play on Sunday evenings in summer; inside, original beams, leaded-glass windows, and a brick fireplace add to the sense of history. **Known for:** superb British-French cooking; excellent service; summer barbecues. [$] *Average main: £28* ✉ *Gun Hill* ☎ *01206/323150* 🌐 *www.milsomhotels.com/letalbooth* 🕒 *No dinner Sun. mid-Sept.–early June.*

$ BRITISH 🍴 **Marlborough Head.** This friendly, 300-year-old pub across from Constable's school in Dedham serves traditional English pub food. Dishes such as bangers and mash (sausages and mashed potato) and roast chicken share the menu with fish-and-chips and burgers. **Known for:** traditional pub food; proper village "local" feel; good old-school comfort eating. [$] *Average main: £11* ✉ *Mill La.* ☎ *01206/323250* 🕒 *No dinner Sun.*

$$$$ HOTEL Fodor's Choice ★ 🏨 **Maison Talbooth.** Constable painted the rich meadowlands in which this luxurious Victorian country-house hotel is set. **Pros:** good food; lovely views over Dedham Vale; some private hot tubs. **Cons:** restaurant books up fast; prices are high; need a car to get here. [$] *Rooms from: £300* ✉ *Stratford Rd.* ☎ *01206/322367* 🌐 *www.milsomhotels.com/le-talbooth/restaurant* 🛏 *10 rooms* 🍽 *Free Breakfast.*

SPORTS AND THE OUTDOORS

Boathouse Restaurant. From Dedham, on the banks of the River Stour, you can rent a rowboat from the Boathouse Restaurant. They're available daily during July and August, and on weekends from April through June and September to October (plus occasional weekdays during local school holiday periods). The cost is £14 per hour, although you can rent for half an hour for £7 if you only want a brief sojourn in the water. ✉ *Mill La.* ☎ *01206/323153* 🌐 *www.dedhamboathouse.com.*

WOODBRIDGE

18 miles northeast of Dedham.

One of the first good ports of call on the Suffolk Heritage Coast, Woodbridge is a town whose upper reaches center on a fine old market square, site of the 16th-century Shire Hall. Woodbridge is at its best around its old quayside, where boatbuilding has been carried out since the 16th century. The most prominent building is a white-clapboard mill, which dates from the 18th century and is powered by the tides.

GETTING HERE AND AROUND

Woodbridge is on A12. There are a few local buses, but they mostly serve commuters. By train, Woodbridge is 1½ hours from London and just under 2 hours from Cambridge (with connections).

ESSENTIALS

Visitor Information Woodbridge Tourist Information Centre. ✉ *Station Building, Station Rd.* ☎ *01394/382240* 🌐 *choosewoodbridge.co.uk/listings/tourist-information-centre.*

EXPLORING

Fodor's Choice ★ **Sutton Hoo.** The visitor center at Sutton Hoo tells the story of one of Britain's most significant Anglo-Saxon archaeological sites. In 1938 a local archaeologist excavated a series of earth mounds and discovered a 7th-century burial ship, probably that of King Raedwald of East Anglia. A complete replica of the 90-foot-long ship stands in the visitor center, which has artifacts and displays about Anglo-Saxon society. Nothing can quite make up for the fact that the best finds have been moved to the British Museum in London, but it is, nonetheless, all quite fascinating. Trails around the 245-acre site explore the area along the River Deben. ✉ *Off B1083* ☎ *01394/389700* 🌐 *www.nationaltrust.org.uk/suttonhoo* 🎟 *£8.90.*

WHERE TO EAT AND STAY

$ SEAFOOD Fodor's Choice ★ 🍴 **Butley Orford Oysterage.** What started as a little café that sold oysters and cups of tea is now a bustling restaurant, with a nationwide reputation. It has no pretenses of grandeur but serves some of the best smoked fish you're likely to taste anywhere. **Known for:** legendary fish pie; traditional, local flavors; great, simple seafood. [$] *Average main: £13* ✉ *Market Hill, Orford* ☎ *01394/450277* 🌐 *www.pinneysoforford.co.uk* 🕒 *No dinner Sun.–Tues. Apr.–July, Sept., and Oct., and Sun.–Thurs. Nov.–Mar.*

$$ B&B/INN Fodor's Choice ★ 🏨 **Crown and Castle.** Artsy, laid-back, and genuinely friendly, this little gem occupies an 18th-century building in the village of Orford, 10 miles east of Woodbridge. **Pros:** warm service; relaxed atmosphere; good restaurant. **Cons:** need a car to get around; not great for families; not close to major sights. [$] *Rooms from: £160* ✉ *Market Hill, Orford* ☎ *01394/450205* 🌐 *www.crownandcastle.co.uk* 🛏 *19 rooms* 🍽 *Free Breakfast.*

$$ HOTEL Fodor's Choice ★ 🏨 **Seckford Hall.** The sense of history at this delightfully old-school hotel comes from more than just the magnificent Tudor architecture; several pieces of furniture are castoffs from Buckingham Palace, and one of the beds was supposedly slept in by Elizabeth I. **Pros:** antique charm; lovely setting; great atmosphere. **Cons:** no elevator; antique beds are creaky; minimum stay on weekends. [$] *Rooms from: £130* ✉ *Off A12* ☎ *01394/385678* 🌐 *www.seckford.co.uk* 🛏 *32 rooms* 🍽 *Free Breakfast.*

ALDEBURGH

15 miles northeast of Woodbridge.

Aldeburgh (pronounced *orl*-bruh) is a quiet seaside resort, except in June, when the town fills with people attending the noted Aldeburgh Festival. Its beach is backed by a promenade lined with candy-color dwellings. The 20th-century composer Benjamin Britten lived here for some time. He was interested in the story of Aldeburgh's native son, poet George Crabbe (1754–1832), and turned his life story into *Peter Grimes,* a celebrated opera that perfectly captures the atmosphere of the Suffolk Coast.

GETTING HERE AND AROUND

You have little choice but to drive to Aldeburgh; turn off A12 near Farnham and follow signs. There's no train station and no bus service.

ESSENTIALS

Visitor Information Aldeburgh Tourist Information Centre. ✉ *48 High St.* ☎ *01728/453637* 🌐 *www.visit-suffolkcoast.co.uk.*

EXPLORING

Aldeburgh Beach Lookout. This tiny, disused lookout tower is in the middle of the main beachfront in Aldeburgh and has been converted into a bijou space for contemporary art and performances. Artists take up weekly residences here, welcoming the public on Saturdays to observe what they've created during the week. This isn't just a space for local talent, however; some big names in the British arts world have taken part in recent years, including the poet Michael Horovitz and painter Eileen Cooper, the first female head of the Royal Academy. They also sometimes show art films projected on the side of the building—an arresting sight against a backdrop of dark seas lapping on the nighttime shore. ✉ *31 Crag Path* ☎ *01728/452754* 🌐 *www.aldeburghbeachlookout.com* 🎟 *Free* 🕒 *Closed Sun.–Fri. Sometimes closed in winter.*

Moot Hall and Aldeburgh Museum. Moot Hall was the place where local elders met to debate and make decisions about the locality. Built of flint and timber, the 16th-century building once stood in the center of a thriving town; the fact that it's now just a few steps from the beach is testament to the erosive powers of the North Sea. Today it contains the Aldeburgh Museum, a low-key collection that includes finds from an Anglo-Saxon ship burial. ✉ *Market Cross Pl.* ☎ *01728/454666* 🌐 *www.aldeburghmuseumonline.co.uk* 🎟 *£2* 🕒 *Closed Nov.–Mar.*

WHERE TO EAT AND STAY

$ BRITISH Fodor's Choice ★

🍴 **Aldeburgh Fish and Chip Shop.** A frequent (and deserving) entry on "best fish-n-chips in Britain" lists, Aldeburgh's most celebrated eatery always has a long line of eager customers come frying time. The fish is fresh and local, the batter melts in your mouth, and the chips (from locally grown potatoes) are satisfyingly chunky. **Known for:** one of the most famous fish-and-chips shops in Britain; perfect house-special batter; long queues. [$] *Average main: £6* ✉ *226 High St.* ☎ *01728/452250* 🌐 *www.aldeburghfishandchips.co.uk* 🕒 *Closed Mon. No dinner Sun., Tues., and Wed.*

$$$ HOTEL

🏨 **Brudenell.** With its good food, modest but comfortable rooms, and sweeping views of the sea, Brudenell is the very definition of an English seaside hotel. **Pros:** laid-back atmosphere; the beach is literally a stone's throw away; pleasant and quiet bedrooms. **Cons:** rooms are small for the price; car park is tiny; beach bar gets full early. [$] *Rooms from: £200* ✉ *The Parade* ☎ *01728/452071* 🌐 *www.brudenellhotel.co.uk* 🛏 *42 rooms* 🍽 *Free Breakfast.*

10

NIGHTLIFE AND PERFORMING ARTS

Fodor's Choice ★   **Snape Maltings.** It's worth a stop to take in the peaceful River Alde location of this cultural center. It includes nine art galleries and crafts shops in distinctive large brick buildings once used to malt barley, plus a café and tearoom. There's a farmers' market on the first Saturday of the month, a major food festival in September, and a Benjamin Britten festival in October. Leisurely 45-minute river cruises (£7.50) leave from the quayside in spring and summer. From the Maltings you can stroll out along an elevated trail through some reed marshes for beautiful views—just watch for uneven ground. ⊠ *Off B1069, Snape* ☎ *01728/688303* ⊕ *www.snapemaltings.co.uk.*

YORKSHIRE AND THE NORTHEAST

WELCOME TO YORKSHIRE AND THE NORTHEAST

TOP REASONS TO GO

★ **York Minster:** The largest Gothic cathedral in northern Europe helps make York one of the country's most visited cities. An interactive exhibit in the undercroft explores the site's history from Roman times onward.

★ **Haworth:** Looking as if it were carved from stone, this picture-perfect hillside town where the Brontë sisters lived is a lovely place to learn about them.

★ **Hadrian's Wall:** The ancient Roman wall is a wonder for the wild countryside around it as well as its stones and forts, such as Housesteads and Vindolanda.

★ **Castles:** Fought over by the Scots and the English, and prey to Viking raiders, the northeast was heavily fortified. Durham, Alnwick, and Dunstanburgh castles are spectacular remnants of this history.

★ **Medieval Durham:** A splendid Norman cathedral that dates back to the 11th century is just one of the city's charms. Take a stroll on its ancient winding streets.

Yorkshire is the largest of England's historic counties. At its heart is the ancient city of York, with its Gothic cathedral and medieval city walls. To the west is the bustling city of Leeds, while a few miles away are the unspoiled hills that form what the tourist office calls Brontë Country—Haworth, where the Brontë family lived, and the valleys and villages of the Yorkshire Dales. The historic cathedral city of Durham, one of the region's top attractions, sits to the east of the wooded foothills of the Pennines mountain range, in the southern part of the region. Farther north, busy Newcastle straddles the region's main river, the muddy Tyne. West of Newcastle, the remains of Hadrian's Wall snake through rugged scenery.

1 York. Still enclosed within its medieval city walls, this beautifully preserved city makes the perfect introduction to Yorkshire. Its towering Minster and narrow streets are alive with history.

2 Around York. Heading away from the city, you'll find the elegant Georgian and Victorian spa town of Harrogate as well as the baroque masterpiece, Castle Howard.

3 Brontë Country. Rocky and bleak, this windswept stretch of country provides an appropriate setting for the dark, dramatic narratives penned by the Brontë sisters in Haworth.

4 Durham. The historic city of Durham, set on a rocky spur, has a stunning castle and cathedral. South and west are scenic towns with castles and industrial heritage sites.

5 Hadrian's Wall Country. England's wildest countryside is traversed by the remains of the wall that marked the northern border of the Roman Empire. Hexham is a useful base, and Housesteads Roman Fort is a key site. It's stunning country for walking or biking.

6 The Far Northeast Coast. In this dramatic landscape rocky hillsides plunge into the sea. Alnwick, inland, has spectacular gardens.

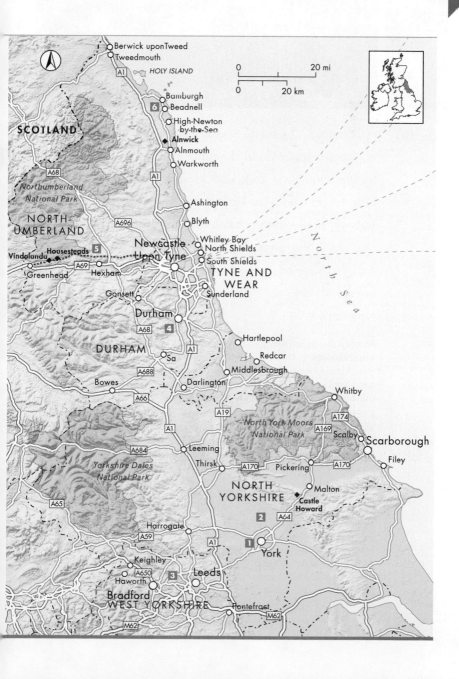

SCOTLAND

Berwick uponTweed
Tweedmouth
A1 HOLY ISLAND

Bamburgh
6 Beadnell
High-Newton
by-the-Sea
◆ **Alnwick**
Alnmouth
Warkworth

A68

Northumberland
National Park

A1

NORTH-
UMBERLAND

A696

Ashington

Blyth

Vindolanda Housesteads **5**
Greenhead Hexham A69
Newcastle
Upon Tyne
Whitley Bay
North Shields
South Shields
TYNE AND
WEAR
Sunderland

Consett
Durham
A68 **4**

DURHAM
A1
Sa
A688
Bowes
A66 Darlington

Hartlepool
Redcar
Middlesbrough

Whitby

A19

A1

A174
North York Moors
National Park A169 Scalby
Scarborough
A684
Leeming
Thirsk
A170 Pickering A170 Filey

Yorkshire Dales
National Park

A65

Harrogate
A59
A1

Keighley
A650 **3**
Haworth
Bradford
WEST YORKSHIRE Pontefract

M62

M62

NORTH
YORKSHIRE ◆ Malton
**Castle
Howard**
2 A64

1
York

Leeds

North Sea

0   20 mi
0   20 km

Updated by
Ellin Stein and
Jack Jewers

A hauntingly beautiful region, Yorkshire is known for its wide-open spaces and dramatic landscapes. Period architecture abounds in York, with its narrow medieval streets, or historic spa towns like Harrogate, while ancient cathedrals, abbeys, and castles provide majestic backdrops to day-to-day life in the area. England's Northeast, a more remote and less-traveled area, has its own appeal, including the cathedral city of Durham and the Roman remains of Hadrian's Wall.

Some of the region's biggest attractions are the result of human endeavor: York's towering Gothic cathedral, created by unknown master craftsmen; Castle Howard, Vanbrugh and Hawksmoor's baroque masterpiece near York; and the Georgian parsonage (now a museum), in the small hilltop village of Haworth, where the Brontë sisters changed literature.

For many Britons, the words "the Northeast" provoke a vision of near-Siberian isolation. But although there are wind-hammered, wide-open spaces and empty roads threading the wild high moorland, the Northeast also has simple fishing towns, small villages of remarkable charm, and historic abbeys and castles that are all the more romantic for their often-ruinous state. This is also where you'll find two of England's most iconic sights: the medieval city of Durham and the stark remains of Hadrian's Wall.

Mainly composed of the two large counties of Durham and Northumberland, the Northeast includes English villages adjacent to the Scottish border area, renowned in ballads and romantic literature for feuds, raids, and battles. Fittingly, Durham Cathedral, the seat of bishops for nearly 800 years, was once described as "half church of God, half castle 'gainst the Scot." Hadrian's Wall, which marked the northern limit of the Roman Empire, stretches across prehistoric remains and moorland.

PLANNER

WHEN TO GO

To see the Yorkshire heather at its most vibrant, visit in summer (but despite the season, be prepared for some chilly days). It's also the best time to see the coast, as colorful regattas and arts festivals are underway. York Minster makes a splendidly atmospheric focal point for the prestigious York Early Music Festival in early July. Spring and fall bring their own rewards: far fewer crowds and crisp, clear days, although there's an increased risk of rain and fog. The harsh winter is tricky: while the moors and dales are beautiful covered in snow and the coast sparkles on a clear, bright day, storms and blizzards can set in quickly, making the moorland roads impassable and villages at risk of being cut off entirely. In winter, stick to York and the main towns.

The best time to see the Northeast is in summer. This ensures that the museums—and the roads—will be open, and you can take advantage of the countryside walks that are one of the region's greatest pleasures. Rough seas and inclement weather make it dangerous to swim at any of the beaches except in July and August; even then, don't expect warm water. Winter here isn't for the fainthearted. The weather is terrible, but there are few places in England so beautiful and remote.

FESTIVALS

FAMILY **Viking Festival.** Held every February in York, this weeklong commemoration of the conquest of England by the Great Viking Army in 866 (only the British would hold a festival celebrating a losing battle) has more than 60 events, including a longship regatta and workshops for kids ranging from Viking-era crafts to fighting skills like archery and swordplay, as well as historical lectures. It ends with the Jorvik Viking Centre combat reenactment, where the invading Norsemen confront the Anglo-Saxon defenders. ⊠ *Jorvik Viking Centre, Coppergate, York* ☎ *01904/615505* ⊕ *www.jorvikvikingfestival.co.uk.*

PLANNING YOUR TIME

Yorkshire is a vast region and difficult to explore in a short amount of time. If you're in a hurry, you could see the highlights of York as a day trip from London; the fastest trains take just two hours. But it's an awful lot to pack into one day, and you're bound to leave out places you'll probably regret missing. Proper exploration—especially of the countryside—requires time and effort. If you're interested in exploring Hadrian's Wall and the Roman ruins, you'll probably want to base yourself at a guesthouse in or around Hexham. From there you can easily take in Housesteads and the other local landmarks. Anywhere in this area is within easy reach of Durham, with its lovely ancient buildings.

GETTING HERE AND AROUND

AIR TRAVEL

Leeds Bradford Airport, 11 miles northwest of Leeds, has frequent flights from other cities in England and Europe. Look for cheap fares on British Airways, flybe, Jet2, or Ryanair. Another good choice for this region is Manchester Airport, about 40 miles southwest of Leeds. This larger airport is well served by domestic and international carriers.

Airports Leeds Bradford International Airport. ✥ *Off A658* ☎ *0871/288–2288* ⊕ *www.leedsbradfordairport.co.uk.* **Manchester Airport.** ✉ *M56, near Junctions 5 and 6, Manchester* ☎ *0800/042–0213* ⊕ *www.manchesterairport.co.uk.*

BUS TRAVEL

National Express and Megabus have numerous daily departures from London's Victoria Coach Station to major cities in Yorkshire and to Durham. Once you're in the region, local bus companies take over the routes. There are Metro buses from Leeds and Bradford into the more remote parts of the Yorkshire Dales. Other companies are Harrogate Bus Company and Keighley Bus Company for services to Harrogate and Haworth, and Coastliner for Castle Howard. In York the main local bus operator is Transdev. Traveline has route information. The Explorer Northeast Pass (£10 [£20 for families of up to five]) allows unlimited one-day travel on most local bus and Metro train services in the region and is available from the bus driver or local bus or Metro stations.

Bus Contacts Coastliner. ☎ *01653/692556* ⊕ *www.yorkbus.co.uk.* **Explorer Northeast Pass.** ☎ *0191/276–3706* ⊕ *www.networkonetickets.co.uk.* **The Harrogate Bus Company.** ☎ *01423/566061* ⊕ *www.harrogatebus.co.uk.* **Keighley Bus Company.** ☎ *01535/603284* ⊕ *www.keighleybus.co.uk.* **Megabus.** ☎ *0141/352–4444* ⊕ *uk.megabus.com.* **Metro.** ☎ *0113/245–7676* ⊕ *www.wymetro.com.* **National Express.** ☎ *0871/581–8181* ⊕ *www.nationalexpress.com.* **Traveline.** ☎ *0871/200–2233* ⊕ *www.traveline.info.*

CAR TRAVEL

If you're driving, the M1 is the principal route north from London. This major highway gets you to Leeds in about four hours. For York (215 miles), stay on M1 to Leeds (197 miles), and then take A64. For the Yorkshire Dales, take M1 to Leeds, then A65 north and west to Skipton. The trans-Pennine motorway, the M62 between Liverpool and Hull, crosses the bottom of this region. North of Leeds, the A1 is the major north–south road, although narrow stretches, roadworks, and heavy traffic make this route slow going at times.

Some of the steep, narrow roads in the countryside off the main routes are difficult drives and can be perilous (or closed altogether) in winter. Main roads often closed by snowdrifts are the moorland A169 and the coast-and-moor A171. If you plan to drive in the dales or moors in winter, check the weather forecast in advance.

If you're headed to small villages in the Northeast, remote castles, or Hadrian's Wall, traveling by car is the best alternative. The A1 highway links London and Newcastle (five to six hours). The scenic route is the A697, which branches west off A1 north of Morpeth. For the coast, leave the A1 at Alnwick and follow the minor B1340 and B1339 for Craster, Seahouses, and Bamburgh.

TRAIN TRAVEL

Virgin Trains East Coast travel to York, Leeds, and the Northeast from London's King's Cross Station. Grand Central trains head to York, Bradford, and Thirsk. Average travel times from King's Cross are two hours to York and three hours to Durham. Northern Rail trains also operate throughout the region. Contact National Rail for train times, and to find out if any discounted Rover tickets are available for your journey.

Train Contacts Grand Central Trains. ☏ *0345/603–4852* ⊕ *www.grandcentralrail.com.* **National Rail Enquiries.** ☏ *0345/748–4950* ⊕ *www.nationalrail. co.uk.* **Northern Rail.** ☏ *0800/200–6060* ⊕ *www.northernrailway.co.uk.* **Virgin Trains East Coast.** ☏ *0345/722–5333* ⊕ *www.virgintrainseastcoast.com.*

RESTAURANTS

Yorkshire is known for hearty food, though bacon-based breakfasts and lunches of pork pies do tend to get old fairly quickly. Indian restaurants (often called curry houses) can be very good in northern cities. Out in the countryside, pubs are your best bet for dining. Many serve excellent home-cooked food and locally reared meat (especially lamb) and vegetables. Roast beef dinners generally come with Yorkshire pudding, the tasty, puffy, oven-baked dish made from egg batter known as a popover in the United States. It's generally served with lots of gravy. Be sure to sample local cheeses, especially Wensleydale, which has a delicate flavor and honey aftertaste.

In the Northeast, make sure to sample fine local meats and produce. Look for restaurants that serve game from the Kielder Forest, local lamb from the hillsides, salmon and trout from the rivers, and shellfish, crab, and oysters from the coast. Outside the cities, the region lags somewhat behind other parts of England in terms of good places to eat, although there are special spots to be found. Aside from the ubiquitous chains, the best bets are often small country pubs that serve the traditional, hearty fare associated with the region. Don't wait until 9 pm to have dinner, though, or you may have a hard time finding a place that's still serving. *Restaurant reviews have been shortened. For full information, visit Fodors.com.*

HOTELS

Traditional hotels are limited primarily to major towns and cities; those in the country tend to be guesthouses, inns, bed-and-breakfasts, or pubs with rooms, plus the occasional luxurious country-house hotel. Many of the better guesthouses are at the edge of town, but some proprietors will pick you up at the main station if you're relying on public transportation—verify before booking. Rooms fill quickly at seaside resorts in July and August, and some places close in winter. Always call ahead to make sure a hotel is open and has space available. *Hotel reviews have been shortened. For full information, visit Fodors.com.*

WHAT IT COSTS IN POUNDS			
	$	**$$**	**$$$**	**$$$$**
Restaurants	under £15	£15–£19	£20–£25	over £25
Hotels	under £100	£100–£160	£161–£220	over £220

Restaurant prices are the average cost of a main course at dinner or, if dinner is not served, at lunch. Hotel prices are the lowest cost of a standard double room in high season, including 20% V.A.T.

VISITOR INFORMATION

Contact **Durham Visitor Contact Center.** ☎ *03000/262626* ⊕ *www.thisisdurham.com.* **Hadrian's Wall Country.** ☎ *0191/440–5720* ⊕ *www.visithadrianswall.co.uk.* **Welcome to Yorkshire.** ☎ *0113/322–3500* ⊕ *www.yorkshire.com.*

YORK

Fodor's Choice
★

For many people, the first stop in Yorkshire is the historic cathedral city of York. Much of the city's medieval and 18th-century architecture has survived, making it a delight to explore. It's one of the most popular short-stay destinations in Britain and only two hours by train from London's King's Cross Station.

Named "Eboracum" by the Romans, York was the military capital of Roman Britain, and traces of garrison buildings survive throughout the city. After the Roman Empire collapsed in the 5th century, the Saxons built "Eoforwic" on the ruins of a fort, but were soon defeated by Vikings, who called the town "Jorvik" and used it as a base from which to subjugate the countryside. The Normans came in the 11th century and emulated the Vikings by using the town as a military base. They also established the foundations of York Minster, the largest Gothic cathedral in northern Europe. The 19th century saw large houses built on the outskirts of the city center.

GETTING HERE AND AROUND

If you're driving, take the M1 north from London. Stay on it to Leeds, and then take the A64 northeast for 25 miles to York. The journey should take around four to five hours. Megabus coaches leave from St. Pancras International Station 8 times a day (six hours), and National Express buses depart from London's Victoria Coach Station approximately 12 times a day (seven hours). Grand Central and Virgin Trains East Coast run from London's King's Cross Station every 10–30 minutes during the week (two hours). York Station, just outside the city walls, has a line of taxis out front to take you to your hotel. If you don't have bags, the walk to town takes eight minutes.

York's city center is mostly closed to traffic and very walkable. The old center is a compact, dense web of narrow streets and tiny medieval alleys called "snickelways." These provide shortcuts across the city center, but they're not on maps, so you never quite know where you'll end up, which in York is often a pleasant surprise.

TOURS

FAMILY **Association of Voluntary Guides to the City of York.** Established more than 60 years ago, this organization arranges short walking tours around the city, taking in two medieval gateways, a walk along the ancient walls, and a visit to a medieval church, in addition to well-known sights. The tours are free, but tips are appreciated. Tours happen three times a day in June through August, and two times a day the rest of the year. ✉ *1 Museum St.* ☎ *01904/550098* ⊕ *www.avgyork.co.uk* ✉ *Free.*

FAMILY **Ghost Trail of York.** Still going strong after 21 years, the Ghost Trail of York has guides well versed in local lore, combining traditional spooky

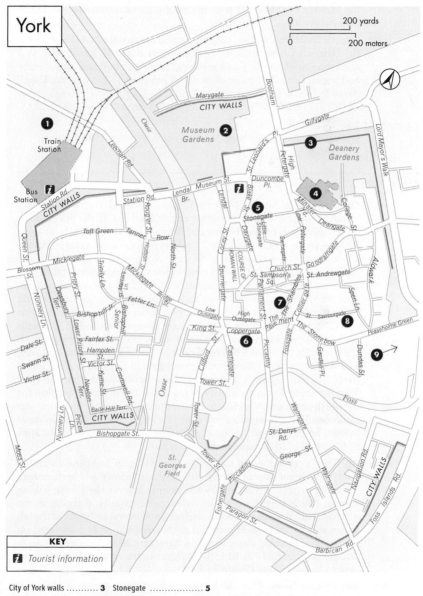

York

0 ____ 200 yards
0 ____ 200 meters

Train Station

Bus Station

i Tourist information

CITY WALLS

Marygate

Museum Gardens

Deanery Gardens

Lord Mayor's Walk

Gillygate

Bootham

St. Leonard's Pl.

High Petergate

College St.

Duncombe Pl.

Minster Yd.

Low Petergate

Deangate

Aldwark

Spen La.

Station Rd.

Lendal Museum St.

Lendal Br.

Leeman Rd.

Ouse

Blake St.

Stonegate

Little Stonegate

Davygate

Swinegate

Goodramgate

St. Andrewgate

Saviourgate

Peasholme Green

Church St.

St. Sampson's Sq.

Parliament St.

The Shambles

The Pavement

The Stonebow

Colliergate

Fossgate

Garden Pl.

Dundas St.

Toft Green

Tanner Row

North St.

Micklegate

Hudson St.

Bridge St.

Mickelgate

Century St.

Fetter Ln.

Low Ousegate

High Ousegate

King St.

Coppergate

Clifford St.

Castlegate

Piccadilly

Tower St.

Foss

Queen St.

Blossom St.

Nunnery Ln.

Priory St.

Trinity Ln.

Bishophill Jr.

Bishophill Senior

Lower Priory St.

Dewsbury Terr.

Dale St.

Swann St.

Victor St.

Fairfax St.

Hampden St.

Victor St.

Kyme St.

Cromwell Rd.

Newton Terr.

Baile Hill Terr.

Prices Ln.

Bishopgate St.

Nunnery Ln.

Moss St.

Ouse

Tower St.

St. Georges Field

Navigation Rd.

Foss Islands Rd.

St. Denys Rd.

George St.

Walmgate

Fishergate

Paragon St.

Piccadilly

Barbican Rd.

CITY WALLS

COURSE OF ROMAN WALL

Station Rd.

Rougier St.

Spurriergate

Micklegate

KEY

i *Tourist information*

tales, Victorian tragedies, and more recent reports of modern ghostly phenomena. The 70-minute tours start at 7:30 pm at the west doors of the Minster. ⊠ *York* ✛ *By west doors of the Minster* ☏ *01904/633276* ⊕ *www.ghosttrail.co.uk* ⊡ *£4.*

FAMILY **Original Ghost Walk of York.** Claiming to be the world's first Ghost Walk, the Original Ghost Walk of York presents the city's ghost tales as a combination of "history and mystery," with an emphasis on accuracy and authenticity. The tours depart at 8 pm from in front of the King's Arms Pub near Ouse Bridge. ⊠ *Kings St.* ✛ *In front of King's Arms Pub* ☏ *01759/373090* ⊕ *www.theoriginalghostwalkofyork.co.uk* ⊡ *£5.*

ESSENTIALS

Visitor Information Visit York. ⊠ *1 Museum St.* ☏ *01904/550099* ⊕ *www. visityork.org.*

EXPLORING

City of York Walls. Almost 3 miles of original medieval town walls remain around York, more than any other city in England. In the 9th century, invading Vikings buried the original Roman defensive walls, built some 1900 years ago, under earthen ramparts topped with wooden stakes. These in turn were replaced by the current stone walls in the 13th and 14th centuries. In the mid-19th century the walls, which had fallen into disrepair, were restored and maintained for public access, and you can now walk along a narrow paved path at the top and enjoy outstanding views (the whole circuit takes about two hours). In spring, the remains of the Viking embankment at the base are alive with daffodils. The walls are crossed periodically by York's distinctive "bars," or fortified gates: the portcullis on Monk's Bar on Goodramgate is still in working order, and Walmgate Bar in the east is the only gate in England with an intact barbican, although one scarred by the cannonballs during the Civil War. Bootham Bar in Exhibition Square was the defensive bastion for the north road, and Micklegate Bar, in the city's southwest corner, was traditionally the monarch's entrance. To access the path and lookout towers, find a staircase at one of the many breaks in the walls. ⊠ *York* ☏ *01904/551550* ⊕ *www.yorkwalls.org.uk.*

FAMILY **Dig.** This reproduction of an archaeological dig in and beneath an old church is a great way to inspire an interest in history and archaeology in young people. A venture by the people behind the Jorvik Viking Centre, Dig is supervised by knowledgeable experts. Kids dig in the dirt to "find" Roman or Viking artifacts, and everyone heads to the lab afterwards to learn what previous archaeological finds discovered on the site have revealed about former inhabitants. ⊠ *St. Saviour's Church, St. Saviourgate* ☏ *01904/615505* ⊕ *digyork.com* ⊡ *£6.50; joint admission to Jorvik Viking Centre £15.50.*

FAMILY **Jorvik Viking Centre.** This kid-focused exhibition re-creates a 10th-century Viking village, with everything from the blind storyteller to the slaughter yard awash in offal based on extensive research. The olfactory element is especially popular with children (even the open sewer), as is the Disneyesque "travel through time" machine that propels you

The Shambles, a narrow medieval street in York, once held butchers' shops, but now has stores that serve the city's many shoppers and visitors.

above straw huts and mannequins clad in Viking garb. Commentary is provided in six languages. Kids get a lot out of it, but adults are unlikely to learn anything new. A small collection of Viking-era artifacts is on display at the end of the ride. ⊠ *Coppergate* ☎ *01904/615505* ⊕ *www. jorvikvikingcentre.co.uk* ✉ *£11; joint admission to Dig £15.50.*

FAMILY **National Railway Museum.** A must for train lovers, Britain's biggest railway museum houses part of the national collection of rail vehicles. Don't miss such gleaming giants of the steam era as the *Mallard*, holder of the world speed record for a steam engine (126 mph), and a replica of the prototype steam engine, the *Rocket*. Passenger cars used by Queen Victoria are on display, as is the only Japanese bullet train to be seen outside Japan, along with railway-related art, posters, and memorabilia. You can climb aboard some of the trains and occasionally take a short trip on one. There's also a little tourist train that makes the short journey to York Minster (£3). ⊠ *Leeman Rd.* ☎ *08448/153139* ⊕ *www.nrm.org.uk.*

The Shambles. York's best-preserved medieval street has shops and residences in half-timbered buildings with overhangs so massive you could almost reach across the narrow gap from one second-floor window to another. Once a hub of butchers (meat hooks are still fastened outside some of the doors), today it's mostly filled with independent shops and remains highly atmospheric. ⊠ *York ✛ Off The Stonebow* ⊕ *www. insideyork.co.uk.*

Stonegate. This narrow, pedestrian-only street lined with Tudor and 18th-century storefronts retains considerable charm. It's been in daily use for almost 2,000 years and was first paved during Roman times.

Today it's a vibrant shopping strip lined with upscale boutiques, jewelers, and quirky one-offs. A passage just off Stonegate, at 52A leads to the remains of a 12th-century Norman stone house attached to a more recent structure. You can still see the old Norman wall and window. ■ TIP➔ Look out for the little red "printer's devil" at No. 33, a medieval symbol of a printer's premises. At the intersection of Stonegate and High Petergate, Minerva reclines on a stack of books, indicating they were once sold inside. ✉ *Stonegate between Petergate and Davygate.*

Fodor's Choice   **York Minster.** The focal point of the city, this vast cathedral is the largest
★ Gothic building north of the Alps and attracts almost as many visitors as London's Westminster Abbey. Inside, the effect created by its soaring pillars and lofty vaulted ceilings is almost overpowering. Come with binoculars if you wish to study the loftier of the 128 dazzling stained-glass windows. While mere statistics can't convey the scale of the building, the central towers are 200 feet high, and the Minster itself is 519 feet long, 249 feet across its transepts, and 90 feet from floor to roof. Especially notable contributions to the spacious, uplifting splendor is the ornamentation of the 14th-century nave: the east window, one of the greatest pieces of medieval glazing in the world; the north transept's Five Sisters windows, five tall lancets of gray-tinged 13th-century glass; the enormous choir screen depicting stylized images of every king of England from William the Conqueror to Henry VI; and the masterful tracery of the Rose Window, with elements commemorating the marriage of Henry VII and Elizabeth of York in 1486, which ended the Wars of the Roses and began the Tudor dynasty. Don't miss the exquisite 13th-century **Chapter House,** with its superb medieval ribbed wooden roof and fine traceried stained-glass windows; the **Treasury;** the **Crypt;** and the interactive Revealing York Minster exhibition in the **undercroft,** which displays Roman plasterwork, the Norman foundation, stained glass, and the 10th-century Horn of Ulf, carved from an elephant tusk and donated by a Viking nobleman. After exploring the cathedral at ground level, climb the 275 winding steps to the roof of the great **Central Tower,** where close-up views of the cathedral's detailed carvings mingle with panoramic ones of the city. Allow 45 minutes for the Tower tour, which is by timed admission only. Don't miss the newly restored great east window, the largest expanse of medieval stained glass in the country, with 311 stained-glass panels dating back to the 15th century. ■ TIP➔ To experience the cathedral at its most atmospheric, attend one of the evensong services with organ and choir. ✉ *Minster Yard* 🕾 *01904/557200* ⊕ *www.yorkminster.org* 🖃 *Minster £10, Minster and Tower £15.*

FAMILY   **Yorkshire Air Museum.** Located on 22 acres of parkland, this is the country's largest World War II airbase that's open to the public. The independent museum showcases more than 60 historic vehicles and aircraft, many of which are still in working condition and are certain to delight aviation enthusiasts. Planes range from early-20th-century biplanes and gliders, such as the Eastchurch Kitten (the only surviving one in the world), to Spitfires, other World War II–era planes, and contemporary fighter jets. There are also exhibits devoted to military vehicles, aircraft weaponry, and Royal Air Force uniforms. The museum is home

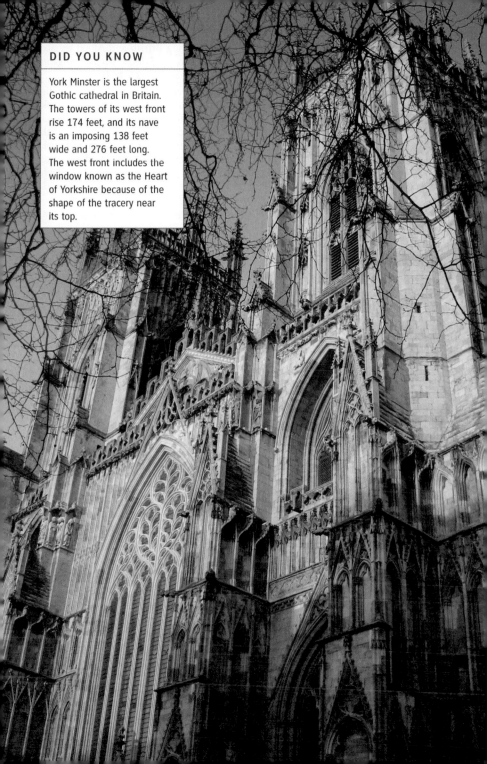

DID YOU KNOW

York Minster is the largest Gothic cathedral in Britain. The towers of its west front rise 174 feet, and its nave is an imposing 138 feet wide and 276 feet long. The west front includes the window known as the Heart of Yorkshire because of the shape of the tracery near its top.

to a memorial and gardens commemorating British and Allied service members who lost their lives in conflict. ⌂ *Halifax Way, Elvington* ☎ *01904/608595* ⊕ *www.yorkshireairmuseum.org* ☜ *£10.*

Yorkshire Museum. The ecological and archaeological history of the county is the focus of this museum in an early-19th-century Greek Revival–style building with massive Doric columns. Themed galleries focus mostly on Roman, Anglian, Viking, and medieval periods, with nearly 1 million objects, including the 15th-century Middleham Jewel, a pendant gleaming with a large sapphire; a Paleolithic hand axe; and an extremely rare Copperplate Helmet, a 1,200-year-old Viking artifact. Another exhibition documents Yorkshire during the Jurassic period. ⌂ *St. Mary's Lodge, Museum Gardens* ☎ *01904/687687* ⊕ *www.yorkshiremuseum.org.uk* ☜ *Museum £6.81; gardens and observatory free.*

WHERE TO EAT

$$
MODERN BRITISH
Fodor'sChoice
★

✕ **Blue Bicycle.** One of York's best restaurants is in a building that once served as a brothel, a past reflected in its murals featuring undraped women. The menu changes with the seasons and concentrates on local seafood. **Known for:** inventive, frequently changing menu; quirky atmosphere; impressive wine list. $ *Average main: £19* ⌂ *34 Fossgate* ☎ *01904/673990* ⊕ *www.thebluebicycle.com.*

$$
BRITISH

✕ **Café Concerto.** Wallpaper made from sheet music reveals the musical theme at this relaxed, intimate bistro in sight of York Minster. The kitchen serves simple rustic classics with an emphasis on local ingredients. **Known for:** hearty portions; vegan and gluten-free options; friendly atmosphere. $ *Average main: £15* ⌂ *21 High Petergate* ☎ *01904/610478* ⊕ *www.cafeconcerto.biz.*

$$$$
MODERN BRITISH

✕ **Melton's.** This former Victorian shop, now restaurant, uses locally sourced Yorkshire produce to create a seasonal, highly imaginative take on Modern British cuisine. Selections include butternut squash with curried granola; venison with chocolate oil; and cod and mussels with smoked cream, apples, dates, and raisins. **Known for:** informal atmosphere despite Michelin star; friendly, involved owners; lots of extras like amuse-bouches and palate cleansers. $ *Average main: £30* ⌂ *7 Scarcroft Rd.* ☎ *01904/634341* ⊕ *www.meltonsrestaurant.co.uk* ⊘ *Closed Sun., Mon., and 3 wks at Christmas.*

$
CAFÉ

✕ **Spurriergate Centre.** Churches aren't just for services, as this 15th-century house of worship proves. Resurrected as a cafeteria (there's also a café on the upper floor) using fresh local ingredients, Spurriergate is a favorite spot for both tourists and locals to refuel spiritually (you can request use of the prayer room upstairs) as well as physically. **Known for:** reasonably priced, wholesome food; family-friendly atmosphere with children's play area; impressive building. $ *Average main: £8* ⌂ *Spurriergate* ☎ *01904/629393* ⊕ *www.thespurriergatecentre.com* ⊟ *No credit cards* ⊘ *Closed Sun. No dinner.*

WHERE TO STAY

$$ B&B/INN 🏨 **Dairy Guest House.** Victorian stained glass, fine woodwork, and intricate plaster cornices are original features of this former dairy near the city walls. **Pros:** nice period details; comfortable rooms; good breakfast. **Cons:** small bathrooms; two-night minimum stay; few amenities. [$] *Rooms from: £130* ✉ *3 Scarcroft Rd.* ☎ *01904/639367* 🌐 *www.dairyguesthouse.co.uk* 🛏 *6 rooms* 🍴 *Free Breakfast.*

$$$ HOTEL 🏨 **The Grand Hotel and Spa.** This handsome, comfortable hotel near the train station—not surprising, considering it was formerly the headquarters of the regional railroad—was built in 1906 and retains many original features, such as solid mahogany doors, beautiful tilework on the stairwells, and art nouveau ironwork. **Pros:** beautiful building; spacious rooms; good location. **Cons:** continental breakfast is average; occasional lapses in service; can be noisy. [$] *Rooms from: £177* ✉ *Station Rise* ☎ *01904/380038* 🌐 *www.thegrandyork.co.uk* 🛏 *120 rooms* 🍴 *Free Breakfast.*

$$ HOTEL 🏨 **Grange Hotel.** Built in the early 19th century as the home for two wealthy members of the York clergy, this luxurious boutique hotel decorated with racing memorabilia is reminiscent of a grand country house. **Pros:** spacious rooms; lovely design; good food. **Cons:** decor worn in places; restaurant service uneven; on busy road. [$] *Rooms from: £126* ✉ *1 Clifton* ☎ *01904/644744* 🌐 *www.grangehotel.co.uk* 🛏 *36 rooms* 🍴 *Free Breakfast.*

$$$ HOTEL 🏨 **Gray's Court Hotel.** With an unbeatable location between York Minster and its own half-acre garden, Gray's Court is an oasis of country-house peacefulness in the city center. **Pros:** peaceful but convenient location; attentive staff; lovely period decor. **Cons:** expensive parking; skimpy breakfast buffet. [$] *Rooms from: £190* ✉ *Chapter House St.* ☎ *01904/612613* 🌐 *www.grayscourtyork.com* 🛏 *11 rooms* 🍴 *Free Breakfast.*

$$ HOTEL 🏨 **Hotel du Vin.** A 19th-century orphanage, this historic building has been converted into a swanky hotel that preserves the original exposed brick walls and arched doorways. **Pros:** makes great use of the space; friendly staff; comfortable beds. **Cons:** high parking charges; low bathroom lighting; on outskirts of city. [$] *Rooms from: £129* ✉ *89 The Mount* ☎ *0844/748–9268* 🌐 *www.hotelduvin.com* 🛏 *44 rooms* 🍴 *Free Breakfast.*

$$$ HOTEL 🏨 **Middlethorpe Hall & Spa.** Aimed at those who prize period details like oak-paneled walls, four-poster beds, carved wood bannisters, and window seats, and whose idea of luxury is a bowl of fresh daffodils, this splendidly restored Queen Anne building with mid-18th-century additions feels less like a country-house hotel than an actual country house. **Pros:** period luxury; gorgeous grounds; attentive staff. **Cons:** poor water pressure; outside city center; might be too old-fashioned for some. [$] *Rooms from: £205* ✉ *Bishopthorpe Rd.* ☎ *01904/641241* 🌐 *www.middlethorpe.com* 🛏 *29 rooms* 🍴 *Free Breakfast.*

NIGHTLIFE

Black Swan. In a 15th-century timber-framed building (a pub since the 16th century), complete with flagstone floors and mullioned windows, this pub serves home-cooked bar food and hosts a roster of local folk musicians as well as comedy nights. ⊠ *Peasholme Green* ☎ *01904/679131* ⊕ *www.blackswanyork.com.*

Old White Swan. Spreading across five half-timbered, 16th-century buildings on busy Goodramgate, the Old White Swan is known for good its pub lunches and ghosts—it claims to have more than the equally venerable Black Swan. ⊠ *80 Goodramgate* ☎ *01904/540911* ⊕ *www. nicholsonspubs.co.uk.*

Snickleway Inn. Built in the 15th century, the Snickleway Inn's wood paneling and open brick fireplaces provide a real sense of stepping back in time. During the English Civil War, it was used by Royalists to store ammunition and explosives. ⊠ *47 Goodramgate* ☎ *01904/656138.*

SHOPPING

The Antiques Centre York. With five showrooms spread over three floors in a Georgian town house, the center sells antiques, collectables, and vintage items—Roman, Georgian, Victorian, Edwardian, and art deco—from more than 100 dealers, who display their wares in "cabinets." ⊠ *41 Stonegate* ☎ *01904/635888* ⊕ *www.theantiquescentreyork.co.uk.*

Minster Gate Bookshop. This bookshop in a Georgian town house has been in the trade since 1580 and sells secondhand and antiquarian books as well as new children's books, illustrated editions, old maps, and prints, largely of Yorkshire in general and York in particular. ⊠ *8 Minster Gate* ☎ *01904/621812* ⊕ *www.minstergatebooks.co.uk.*

AROUND YORK

West and north of York a number of sights make easy, appealing day trips from the city: the spa town of Harrogate, the ruins of Fountain Abbey, and Castle Howard, a magnificent stately home.

HARROGATE

21 miles west of York, 11 miles south of Ripon, 16 miles north of Leeds.

During the Regency and early Victorian periods, it became fashionable for the aristocratic and wealthy to "take the waters" at British spa towns, combining the alleged health benefits with socializing. In Yorkshire the most elegant spa destination was Harrogate, where today its mainly Victorian buildings, parks, and spas still provide a relaxing getaway.

GETTING HERE AND AROUND

Trains from York leave every hour or so, and the journey takes about 40 minutes. There's at least one direct train daily from London. National Express buses leave from York every 30 minutes most days; the journey takes about three hours (due to a long layover in Leeds). By car,

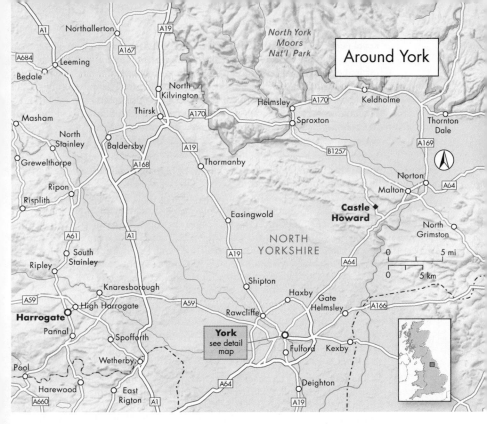

Harrogate is off A59 and well marked. It's a walkable town, so you can park in one of its central parking lots and explore on foot.

Within and around Harrogate, the Harrogate & District bus company provides area services, and taxis are plentiful.

ESSENTIALS

Visitor Information **Harrogate Tourist Information Centre.** ✉ *Royal Baths, Crescent Rd.* ☎ *01423/537300* ⊕ *www.visitharrogate.co.uk.*

EXPLORING

Harrogate Turkish Baths and Health Spa. Dating from 1897, these exotic and fully restored Turkish baths are as enjoyable now as they were for the many Victorians who came to Harrogate to visit them. After changing into your bathing suit, relax on luxurious lounge chairs in the stunning mosaic-tile warming room. Move on to increasingly hot sauna rooms, and then soak up eucalyptus mist in the steam room before braving the icy plunge pool. You can also book a massage or facial. Open hours are divided into women-only and mixed sessions, so book in advance. ✉ *Royal Baths, Parliament St.* ☎ *01423/556746* ⊕ *www.turkishbathsharrogate.co.uk* 🎟 *£18–£29.50 per session; guided tour, £3.75.*

Royal Pump Room Museum. This octagonal structure was built in 1842 over the original sulfur well that brought great prosperity to the town (at its height, the Pump Room sold 1,500 glasses of water each morning). You can still sniff the pungent spa waters here. The museum has displays of bygone spa treatment paraphernalia, alongside a somewhat eccentric collection of 19th-century clothes, fine china, and bicycles. ⊠ *Crown Pl.* 🕾 *01423/556188* ⊕ *www.harrogate.gov.uk* 🖼 *£4.*

The Stray. Wrapping around the town center, this 200-acre grassy parkland is a riot of color in spring. Many of the mineral springs that first made Harrogate famous bubble below. ⊠ *Harrogate* 🕾 *01423/841097* ⊕ *www.harrogate.gov.uk.*

FAMILY **Valley Gardens.** Southwest of the town center, these 17 acres of formal gardens include a children's boating lake, tennis courts, skate park, adventure playground, paddling pool, and little café. ⊠ *Valley Dr.* ✛ *Junction with Cornwall Rd. and Royal Parade* 🕾 *01423/500600* ⊕ *www.harrogate.gov.uk.*

WHERE TO EAT

$ ✕ **Betty's Cafe Tea Rooms.** This celebrated Yorkshire tearoom began life
CAFÉ in Harrogate in 1919, when a Swiss restaurateur brought his Alpine
Fodor's Choice pastries and chocolates to England. The welcoming interior has changed
★ little since it first opened, and the extensive array of teas not at all. **Known for:** classic English afternoon tea; traditional cakes, pastries, and sandwiches; nightly live piano music. 🟊 *Average main: £13* ⊠ *1 Parliament St.* 🕾 *01423/814070* ⊕ *www.bettys.co.uk.*

$$$$ ✕ **The Yorke Arms.** The peaceful rural location of this "restaurant with
INTERNATIONAL rooms" in the scenic Nidderdale Valley belies the sophistication of its
Fodor's Choice distinctive cooking, which has been consistently rated as one of the top
★ five dining spots not only in Yorkshire, but in the United Kingdom. It won its Michelin star with an emphasis on seasonal ingredients, creative combinations of flavors, and elegant presentations. **Known for:** daily changing menu of high-quality English dishes; fabulous dessert selection; historic building in a peaceful setting. 🟊 *Average main: £35* ⊠ *Ramsgill-in-Nidderdale, Pateley Bridge* 🕾 *01423/755243* ⊕ *www. yorke-arms.co.uk* ⊗ *Closed Sun. and Mon.*

WHERE TO STAY

$$ 🛏 **Hotel du Vin.** This hip hotel sprawls through eight Georgian houses,
HOTEL with stripped-wood floors, clubby leather armchairs, and a purple billiard table setting the tone. **Pros:** tasty food; wonderful wine list; modern vibe. **Cons:** some rooms dark; no free breakfast; the bar can take over the lounge. 🟊 *Rooms from: £124* ⊠ *Prospect Pl.* 🕾 *01423/608121* ⊕ *www.hotelduvin.com* ⤴ *52 rooms* 🍴 *No meals.*

CASTLE HOWARD

15 miles northeast of York.

The baroque grandeur of Castle Howard is without equal in northern England. The grounds, enhanced by groves of trees, a twinkling lake, and a perfect lawn, add to the splendor.

11

GETTING HERE AND AROUND

There's daily scheduled bus service between Malton and Castle Howard, which is well outside any town and several miles off any public road. The nearest train stop is Malton, and you can take a taxi from there. By car, follow signs off A64 from York.

EXPLORING

Fodor's Choice **Castle Howard.** Standing in the Howardian Hills to the west of Malton, ★ Castle Howard is an outstanding example of English baroque architecture, with a distinctive roofline punctuated by a magnificent central dome. It served as Brideshead, the home of the fictional Flyte family in *Brideshead Revisited*, Evelyn Waugh's tale of aristocratic woe, in both its 1981 TV and 2008 film adaptations. The house was the first commission for playwright-turned-architect Sir John Vanbrugh, who, assisted by Nicholas Hawksmoor, designed it for the third Earl of Carlisle, a member of the Howard family. Started in 1701, the central portion took 25 years to complete, with a Palladian wing added subsequently, but the end result was a stately home of audacious grandeur.

A spectacular central hallway with soaring columns supports a hand-painted ceiling that dwarfs all visitors, and there's no shortage of splendor elsewhere: vast family portraits, intricate marble fireplaces, immense tapestries, Victorian silver on polished tables, and a great many marble busts. Outside, the neoclassical landscape of carefully arranged woods, lakes, and lawns led 18th-century bon vivant Horace Walpole to comment that a pheasant at Castle Howard lived better than a duke elsewhere. Hidden throughout the 1,000 acres of formal and woodland gardens are temples, statues, fountains, and a grand mausoleum—even a fanciful children's playground. Hourly tours of the grounds, included in the admission price, fill you in on more background and history. ⊠ *Castle Howard, Malton ✦ A64 past York, then B1257* ☎ *01653/648333* ⊕ *www.castlehoward.co.uk* ✉ *House and gardens £18.95; gardens only £9.95* ☉ *House closed early Jan.–late Mar.*

BRONTË COUNTRY

From the busy city of Leeds, you can strike out for the traditional wool towns, such as Saltaire, a UNESCO-protected gem. But the main thrust of many visits to West Yorkshire is to the west of Leeds, where the stark hills north of the Calder Valley and south of the River Aire form the landscape immortalized in the equally unsparing novels of the Brontë sisters. The gray-stone village of Haworth might have faded into obscurity were it not for the enduring fame of the literary sisters. Every summer, thousands toil up the steep main street to visit their former home, but to truly appreciate the setting that inspired their books you need to go farther afield to the ruined farm of Top Withens, which in popular mythology, if not in fact, was the model for Wuthering Heights.

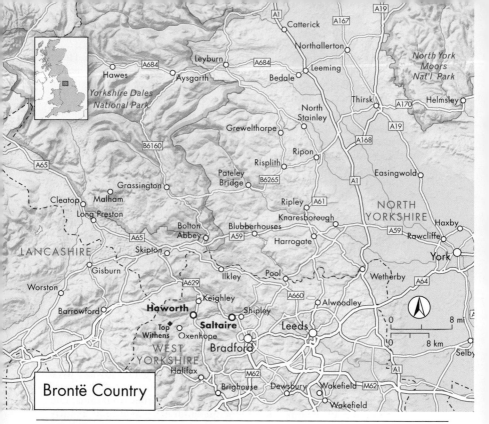

Brontë Country

SALTAIRE

12 miles east of Leeds, 8 miles east of Haworth.

This planned community, built by a philanthropic Victorian industrialist in the wool trade to house his workers, perfectly preserves the architecture—both residential and industrial—of the period.

GETTING HERE AND AROUND

Saltaire has regular bus and train services from the nearby town of Bradford. Drivers should take A650 from Bradford and follow the signs.

ESSENTIALS

Visitor Information Saltaire Visitor Information Centre. ⊠ *Salt's Mill, Victoria Rd., Shipley* ☎ *01274/437942* ⊕ *www.saltairevillage.info.*

EXPLORING

Hockney 1853 Gallery. This gallery, housed in a historic mill building that dates back to 1853, is devoted to a remarkable exhibition of over 300 works by Bradford-born artist David Hockney. There are two restaurants on-site. ⊠ *Salt's Mill, Victoria Rd., Shipley* ☎ *01274/531163* ⊕ *www.saltsmill.org.uk.*

Saltaire. A UNESCO World Heritage Site, Saltaire was built as a model village in the mid-19th century by textile magnate Sir Titus Salt. When he decided to relocate his factories from the dark mills of Bradford to the countryside, he hoped to create an ideal industrial community. The Italianate village is remarkably well preserved, its former mills and houses now turned into shops, restaurants, and galleries, as well as private homes. Part of Salt's Mill, the main building, resembles a palazzo. The largest factory in the world when it was built in 1853, today it contains an art gallery, along with crafts and furniture shops. One-hour guided tours (£4) of the village depart weekends and some bank holidays at 2 pm from the tourist information center. ⊠ *Saltaire Rd., Shipley* ☎ *01274/599887* ⊕ *www.saltairevillage.info.*

HAWORTH

8 miles west of Saltaire.

Whatever Haworth might have been in the past, today it's Brontë Country. This old stone-built textile village on the edge of the Yorkshire Moors long ago gave up its own personality and allowed itself to be taken over by the literary sisters, their powerful novels, and legions of fans. In 1820, when Anne, Emily, and Charlotte were very young, their father relocated them and their other three siblings away from their old home in Bradford to Haworth. The sisters—Emily (author of *Wuthering Heights,* 1847), Charlotte (*Jane Eyre,* 1847), and Anne (*The Tenant of Wildfell Hall,* 1848) were all influenced by the stark, dramatic landscape.

These days, it seems that every building they ever glanced at has been turned into a memorial, shop, or museum. The Haworth Visitor Center has good information about accommodations, maps, books on the Brontës, and inexpensive leaflets to help you find your way to such outlying *Wuthering Heights* sites as Ponden Hall (Thrushcross Grange) and Ponden Kirk (Penistone Crag).

GETTING HERE AND AROUND

To reach Haworth by bus or train, buy a Metro Day Rover for bus and rail (£8.40) and take the Metro train from Leeds train station to Keighley and walk to the bus stop, where you change to a Keighley & District bus to Haworth. On weekends and bank holidays you can opt to take the old-school steam-engined Keighley and Worth Valley Railway to continue on to Haworth.

By car, Haworth is an easy 25-mile drive on A629 from Leeds; it's well signposted, and there's plenty of cheap parking in town.

ESSENTIALS

Visitor Information Haworth Visitor Information Centre. ⊠ *2–4 West La., Haworth* ☎ *01535/642329* ⊕ *www.visitbradford.com.*

EXPLORING

Fodor's Choice
★

Brontë Parsonage Museum. The best of Haworth's Brontë sights is this somber Georgian (1778) house where the sisters grew up. It displays original furniture (some bought by Charlotte after the success of *Jane Eyre*), portraits, and books. The Brontës moved here when the Reverend Patrick Brontë was appointed to the local church, but tragedy soon struck—his wife, Maria, and their two eldest children died within five

The streets and houses of Haworth look much as they did when the Brontë sisters lived and wrote their famous novels in this village near the moors.

years. The museum explores the family's tragic story, bringing it to life with a strong collection of enchanting mementos of the four children. These include tiny books they made when they were still very young; Charlotte's wedding bonnet; and the sisters' spidery, youthful graffiti on the nursery wall. Branwell, the Brontës' only brother, painted several of the portraits on display. ⊠ *Church St., Haworth* ☎ *01535/642323* ⊕ *www.bronte.org.uk* ✉ *£8.50.*

Brontë Waterfall. If you have the time, pack a lunch and walk for 2¾ miles or so from Haworth along a field path, lane, and moorland track to the lovely, isolated waterfall that has, inevitably, been renamed in honor of the sisters. It was one of their favorite haunts, which they wrote about in poems and letters. ⊠ *Haworth* ✛ *From Haworth Church on Main St., follow signs* ⊕ *www.haworth-village.org.uk.*

FAMILY **Keighley and Worth Valley Railway.** Haworth is one stop along the route of this scenic 5-mile heritage railway between Keighley and Oxenhope through the picturesque Worth Valley, as seen in numerous film and television shows including *Peaky Blinders*. Many of the trains are pulled by handsome steam engines. Frequent themed special events add to the fun. ⊠ *Haworth Station, Station Rd., Haworth* ☎ *01535/645214* ⊕ *www.kwvr.co.uk* ✉ *£12 round-trip, £18 Day Rover ticket* ⊗ *Closed Jan.; Mon., Tues., Thurs., and Fri. in Feb.; mid-Apr.–May; mid-Sept.–mid-Oct.; and Mon.–Thurs. in Nov.–late Dec.*

Main Street. Haworth's steep, cobbled high street has changed little in outward appearance since the early 19th century, but it now acts as a funnel for crowds heading for points of interest: the **Black Bull** pub, where the reprobate Branwell Brontë drank himself into an early grave (his stool is kept in mint condition); the former **post office** (now a bookshop) from which Charlotte, Emily, and Anne sent their manuscripts to their London publishers; and the **church,** with its atmospheric graveyard (Charlotte and Emily are buried in the family vault inside the church; Anne is buried in Scarborough). ✉ *Haworth.*

Top Withens. A ruined, gloomy mansion on a bleak hilltop farm 3 miles from Haworth, Top Withens is often taken to be the inspiration for the fictional Wuthering Heights. Brontë scholars say it probably isn't; even in its heyday, the house never fit the book's description of Heathcliff's domain. Still, it's an inspirational walk across the moors. There and back from Haworth is a 3½-hour walk along a well-marked footpath that goes past the Brontë waterfall. If you've read *Wuthering Heights,* you don't need to be reminded to wear sturdy shoes and protective clothing. ✉ *Haworth* 🌐 *www.haworth-village.org.uk.*

WHERE TO EAT

$ BRITISH

🍴 **Haworth Old Hall.** This 16th-century building with two magnificent stone fireplaces is now a welcoming gastro-pub, and the friendly and efficient service gets high marks. The menu is hearty British food, with mains like pan-roast chicken with pumpkin ravioli; venison and wild boar sausages with mashed potatoes and black pudding fritters; and a beetroot-and-squash Wellington. **Known for:** good beer selection; filling portions of classic British dishes; atmospheric setting. [$] *Average main: £13* ✉ *Sun St., Haworth* ☎ *01535/642709* 🌐 *www.hawortholdhall.co.uk.*

WHERE TO STAY

$ B&B/INN

🏨 **The Apothecary Guest House.** Built in 1640, this family-run B&B is located at the top of the cobbled main street, opposite the Brontë church. **Pros:** scenic views; town center location; helpful hosts. **Cons:** rooms at front may have noise from pub; limited time to order breakfast; decor may be too simple for some. [$] *Rooms from: £60* ✉ *86 Main St., Haworth* ☎ *01535/643642* 🌐 *www.theapothecaryguesthouse.co.uk* 🛏 *7 rooms* 🍽 *Free Breakfast.*

DURHAM

250 miles north of London, 15 miles south of Newcastle.

The great medieval city of Durham, seat of County Durham, stands dramatically on a rocky spur, overlooking the countryside. Its cathedral and castle, a World Heritage Site, rise together on a wooded peninsula almost entirely encircled by the River Wear (rhymes with "beer"). For centuries these two ancient structures have dominated Durham—a thriving university town, the Northeast's equivalent of Oxford or Cambridge. Steep, narrow streets overlooked by perilously angled medieval houses and 18th-century town houses make for fun exploring. In the most attractive part of the city, near the Palace Green and along the river, people go boating, anglers cast their lines, and strollers walk along the shaded paths. For great views, take a short stroll along the River Wear and cross the 17th-century Prebends Footbridge. You can return to town via the 12th-century Framwellgate Bridge.

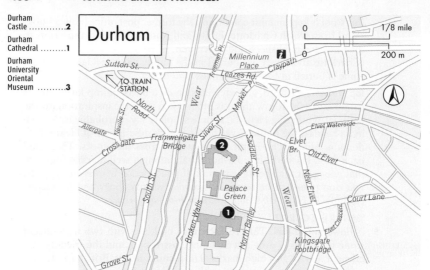

Despite the military advantages of its location, Durham was founded surprisingly late, probably in about the year 1000, growing up around a small Saxon church erected to house the remains of St. Cuthbert. It was the Normans, under William the Conqueror, who put Durham on the map, building the first defensive castle and beginning work on the cathedral. From here Durham's prince-bishops, granted almost dictatorial local powers by William in 1072, kept a tight rein on the county, coining their own money and maintaining their own laws and courts; not until 1836 were these rights finally restored to the English Crown.

GETTING HERE AND AROUND

East Coast trains from London's King's Cross Station arrive at the centrally located Durham Station once an hour during the day. The journey takes about three hours. Trains from York arrive three to four times an hour; that journey takes roughly 50 minutes. A handful of National Express and Megabus buses make the seven-hour trip from London daily. The Durham Cathedral Bus (Route 40) links parking lots and the train and bus stations with the cathedral, castle, and university. Between 10 and 4 Monday through Saturday, cars are charged £2 (on top of parking charges) to enter the Palace Green area. You pay the charge at an automatic tollbooth on exiting. ■TIP→ If you don't have change for the tollbooth, press the button and an attendant will take down your information. Pay later, in person or over the phone, at the Parking Shop. But don't forget to pay by 6 pm the next day (excluding Sunday) or you'll be fined £30.

ESSENTIALS

Visitor Information Durham Visitor Contact Centre. ⊠ *Claypath* ☎ *0300/026–2626* ⊕ *www.thisisdurham.com.* **Parking Shop.** ⊠ *Forster House, Finchdale Rd.* ☎ *0191/384–6633* ⊕ *www.durham.gov.uk.*

EXPLORING

Durham Castle. Facing the cathedral across Palace Green, Durham's stately, manorlike castle commands a strategic position above the River Wear. For almost 800 years the castle was the home of the enormously powerful prince-bishops; from here they ruled large tracts of the countryside and acted as the main line of defense against Scottish raiders from the north. Henry VIII was the first to curtail the bishops' autonomy, although it wasn't until the 19th century that they finally had their powers annulled. The castle was given over to University College, part of the University of Durham (founded 1832), the oldest in England after Oxford and Cambridge. The castle interior can only be seen on a 45-minute guided tour. Times can vary, especially on summer afternoons, when the building can be hired out for private events, so it's best to call ahead. ■TIP→ During university vacation times, the castle also offers bed-and-breakfast accommodations in the state rooms for around £200 per night; call or check the website for details. ⊠ *Palace Green* ☎ *0191/334–2932* ⊕ *www.dur.ac.uk/durham.castle* ⊒ *£5.*

Fodor'sChoice
★
Durham Cathedral. A Norman masterpiece in the heart of the city, Durham Cathedral is a vision of strength and fortitude, a far cry from the airy lightness of later Gothic cathedrals. Construction began about 1090, and the main body was finished about 1150. The round arches of the nave and the deep zigzag patterns carved into them typify the heavy, gaunt style of Norman, or Romanesque, building. The technology of Durham, however, was revolutionary; this was the first European cathedral to be given a stone, rather than a wooden, roof.

Note the enormous bronze **Sanctuary Knocker,** shaped like the head of a ferocious mythological beast, mounted on the massive northwestern door. By grasping the ring clenched in the animal's mouth, medieval felons could claim sanctuary; cathedral records show that 331 criminals sought this protection between 1464 and 1524. An unobtrusive tomb at the western end of the cathedral, in the Moorish-influenced **Galilee Chapel,** is the final resting place of the Venerable Bede, an 8th-century Northumbrian monk whose contemporary account of the English people made him the country's first reliable historian. In good weather you can climb the tower, which has spectacular views of Durham. Guided tours of the cathedral are offered two or three times daily except Sunday.

The brand-new, £10 million **Open Treasure** exhibition displays priceless artifacts from the cathedral's own collection. The exhibition also allows visitors to see parts of the cathedral that were previously closed to the public, including the **Monks Dormitory** and the **Great Kitchen,** with its breathtaking octagonal roof. Treasures on display include Anglo-Saxon art, gold and garnet crosses, elaborate vestments, illuminated manuscripts, and the original coffin of St. Cuthbert. Together it represents one of the most significant single collections of Anglo-Saxon artifacts in the world.

■ TIP→ Guided tours of the cathedral (75 minutes) are available Monday–Saturday; call ahead for times. A choral evensong service takes place Tuesday to Saturday at 5:15 and Sunday at 3:30. ⊠ *Palace Green* ☎ *0191/386–4266* ⊕ *www.durhamcathedral.co.uk* ▣ *Free (requested donation £5); Open Treasure £7.50; tower £5; guided tours £5; combined tour and Open Treasure £10* ⊘ *No tours Sun.*

Durham University Oriental Museum. A 15-minute walk from the cathedral, this museum displays fine art and craftwork from all parts of Asia and the Middle East. Galleries are ordered by culture, including Ancient Egypt, Japan, China, and Korea. Among the highlights are some exquisite Qing dynasty jade and lacquer ornaments, ancient tapestries and embroideries from the Himalayas, and a collection of Japanese woodblock prints from the Edo period. ⊠ *Elvet Hill, off South Rd.* ☎ *0191/334–5694* ⊕ *www.dur.ac.uk/oriental.museum* ▣ *£1.50.*

WHERE TO EAT

$ ✕ **Cafedral.** Ignore the dad-joke pun—this is a really good, modern,
CAFÉ vegetarian- and celiac-friendly café. Mismatched, shabby-chic furniture
FAMILY fills the cozy dining room, where you can enjoy delicious, fresh scones, cakes, gluten-free desserts, and tasty paninis and wraps. **Known for:** fantastic gluten-free treats; vegetarian food; good coffee. Ⓢ *Average main: £6* ⊠ *Owengate House, 1st fl., Owengate.*

$$$ ✕ **Finbarr's.** Excellent seafood and indulgent desserts are the specialties
EUROPEAN at this popular bistro, but there are steaks and a few veggie options on the menu as well. If the fish cakes with buttered spinach or grilled jumbo shrimp (have them cooked Tandoori style, with a hint of Indian spice) are available, you must order them, and save room for the Knickerbocker Glory, an old-fashioned concoction of ice cream, sponge cake, fruit, and chocolate, served in a tall glass. **Known for:** intimate atmosphere; great seafood; heavenly desserts. Ⓢ *Average main: £22* ⊠ *Aykley Heads House, Aykley Heads* ⊹ *About a mile north of the city center* ☎ *0191/307–7033* ⊕ *www.finbarrsrestaurant.co.uk.*

WHERE TO STAY

$ ▤ **Georgian Town House.** At the top of a cobbled street overlooking the
B&B/INN cathedral and castle, this family-run guesthouse has small, snug bedrooms with pleasant city views. **Pros:** great location; jovial owners; free Wi-Fi. **Cons:** most rooms are small; decor won't please everyone; some noise from nearby pubs. Ⓢ *Rooms from: £95* ⊠ *11 Crossgate* ☎ *0191/386–8070* ⊕ *www.thegeorgiantownhousedurham.co.uk* ⊘ *Closed last wk of Dec.* ⇝ *8 rooms* ⦿ *Free Breakfast.*

$
HOTEL
Fodor'sChoice
★

⊞ Lumley Castle Hotel. This is a real Norman castle, right down to the dungeons and maze of dark flagstone corridors—one room even has a bathroom hidden behind a bookcase. **Pros:** great for antiques lovers; festive meals; good value for such a historic place. **Cons:** it's easy to get lost down the winding corridors; original castle rooms pricier; verily, ye banquet is way cheesy. $ *Rooms from: £95* ⊠ *B1284, Chester-le-Street* ☎ *0191/389–1111* ⊕ *www.lumleycastle.com* ⇆ *59 rooms* ℟ *Some meals.*

NIGHTLIFE

Half Moon. This handsome old pub is popular for its excellent range of traditional ales, as well as for its old-school atmosphere that reminds you that pubs like this are a dying breed. ⊠ *New Elvet* ☎ *0191/374–1918* ⊕ *www.thehalfmooninndurham.co.uk.*

Market Tavern. Fans of real ales are drawn to the Market Tavern, which has been in business since the late 18th century. They also serve decent pub food. ⊠ *27 Market Pl.* ☎ *0191/386–2069* ⊕ *www.taylor-walker.co.uk.*

SHOPPING

Bramwells Jewellers. The specialty here is a pendant copy of the gold-and-silver cross of St. Cuthbert. ⊠ *24 Elvet Bridge* ☎ *0191/386–8006.*

Durham Indoor Market. The food and bric-a-brac stalls in Durham Indoor Market, a Victorian arcade, are open Monday through Saturday 9–5. An excellent farmers' market is held in Market Place on the third Thursday of every month. ⊠ *Market Pl.* ☎ *0191/384–6153* ⊕ *www.durham-markets.co.uk.*

HADRIAN'S WALL COUNTRY

A formidable line of Roman fortifications, Hadrian's Wall was the Romans' most ambitious construction in Britain. The land through which the old wall wanders is wild and inhospitable in places, but that seems only to add to the powerful sense of history it evokes. Museums and information centers along the wall make it possible to learn as much as you want about the Roman era.

HADRIAN'S WALL

73 miles from Wallsend, north of Newcastle, to Bowness-on-Solway, beyond Carlisle.

The most important Roman relic in Britain extends across the countryside and can be accessed in many ways. In Northumberland National Park, about half a mile north of Vindolanda, the Once Brewed National Park Visitor Centre has informative displays about Hadrian's Wall and can advise about local walks.

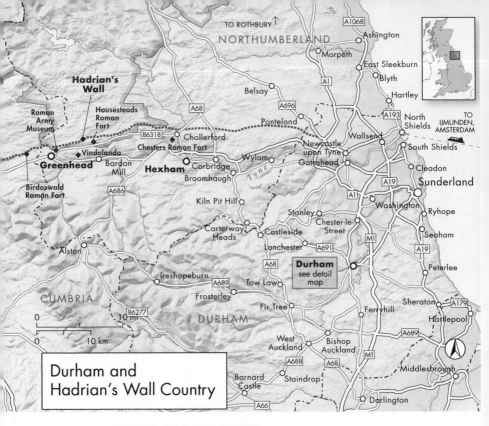

Durham and
Hadrian's Wall Country

GETTING HERE AND AROUND

The A69 roughly follows Hadrian's Wall, although sometimes it's a few miles in either direction. The best sections of the wall are near the narrower B6318, including Vindolanda, Housesteads Roman Fort, and Chesters Roman Fort. There's a small railway station at Hexham, with frequent trains from Newcastle.

The aptly named AD122 public bus runs between Newcastle and Carlisle during the summer months, stopping near all the major destinations along the way. A special Hadrian's Wall Bus offers "rover ticket" passes that give you unlimited travel on the route for one (£12) or three (£24) days. You can extend the tickets to cover any bus operating on the same route for a few extra pounds. Several other local buses depart from Newcastle and other towns in the region to various parts of the wall.

ESSENTIALS

Visitor Information Hadrian's Wall Country Bus. ☎ 0191/4205050 ⊕ www. gonortheast.co.uk/timesfares/ad122.

EXPLORING

Fodor's Choice   **Hadrian's Wall.** Dedicated to the Roman god Terminus, the massive span
★   of Hadrian's Wall once marked the northern frontier of the Roman Empire. Today, remnants of the wall wander across pastures and hills, stretching 73 miles from Wallsend in the east to Bowness-on-Solway

in the west. The wall is a World Heritage Site, and excavating, interpreting, repairing, and generally managing it remains a Northumbrian growth industry. ■ TIP→ Chesters, Housesteads, Vindolanda, and the Roman Army Museum near Greenhead give you a good introduction to the life led by Roman soldiers. In summer there are talks, plays, and festivals; local tourist offices have details.

At Emperor Hadrian's command, three legions of soldiers began building the wall in AD 122 and finished it in four years. It was constructed by soldiers and masons after repeated invasions by troublesome Pictish tribes from what is now Scotland. During the Roman era it was the most heavily fortified wall in the world, with walls 15 feet high and 9 feet thick; behind it lay the vallum, a ditch about 20 feet wide and 10 feet deep. Spaced at 5-mile intervals along the wall were massive forts (such as those at Housesteads and Chesters), which could house up to 1,000 soldiers. Every mile was marked by a thick-walled milecastle (a fort that housed about 30 soldiers), and between each milecastle were two turrets, each lodging four men who kept watch. For more than 250 years the Roman army used the wall to control travel and trade and to fortify Roman Britain against the barbarians to the north.

During the Jacobite Rebellion of 1745, the English army dismantled much of the Roman wall and used the stones to pave what is now the B6318 highway. The most substantial stretches of the remaining wall are between Housesteads and Birdoswald (west of Greenhead). Running through the southern edge of Northumberland National Park and along the sheer escarpment of Whin Sill, this section is also an area of dramatic natural beauty. The ancient ruins, rugged cliffs, dramatic vistas, and spreading pastures make it a great area for hiking. ⊕ *www. visithadrianswall.co.uk.*

SPORTS AND THE OUTDOORS
BIKING
The Bike Place. Mountain bike rentals start at £25 per day. ■ TIP→ Make reservations if your trip coincides with busy holiday periods. ⊠ *1 King St., Bellingham* ☎ *01434/220210* ⊕ *www.thebikeplace.co.uk.*

Hadrian's Cycleway. Between Tynemouth and Whitehaven, Hadrian's Cycleway follows the River Tyne from the east coast until Newcastle, where it traces the entire length of Hadrian's Wall. It then continues west to the Irish Sea. Maps and guides are available at the Tourist Information Centre in Newcastle. ⊕ *www.cyclenorthumberland.org. uk/listing/hadrians-cycleway.*

HIKING
Hadrian's Wall Path. One of Britain's national trails, Hadrian's Wall Path runs the entire 73-mile length of the wall. If you don't have time for it all, take one of the less-challenging circular routes. One of the most scenic but also most difficult sections is the 12-mile western stretch between Sewingshields and Greenhead. ⊕ *www.nationaltrail.co.uk/ hadrianswall.*

HEXHAM

22 miles west of Newcastle, 31 miles northwest of Durham.

The area around the busy market town of Hexham is a popular base for visiting Hadrian's Wall. Just a few miles from the most significant remains, it's a bustling working town, but it has enough historic buildings and winding medieval streets to warrant a stop in its own right. First settled in the 7th century, around a Benedictine monastery, Hexham later became a byword for monastic learning, famous for its book painting, sculpture, and singing.

GETTING HERE AND AROUND

The A1 highway links London and the region (five to six hours). No major bus companies travel here, but the AD122 tourist bus from Newcastle and Carlisle does. East Coast trains take about three hours to travel from London's King's Cross to Newcastle. From there, catch a local train.

Hexham is a small, walkable town. It has infrequent local bus service, but you're unlikely to need it. If you're driving, park in the lot by the tourism office and walk into town. The tourism office has free maps and will point you in the right direction.

ESSENTIALS

Visitor Information Hexham Tourism Information Centre. ⊠ *Wentworth Car Park, Wentworth Pl.* ☎ *01670/620450* ⊕ *www.visitnorthumberland.com.*

EXPLORING

Birdoswald Roman Fort. Beside the longest unbroken stretch of Hadrian's Wall, Birdoswald Roman Fort reveals the remains of gatehouses, a granary, and a parade ground. You can also see the line of the original turf wall, later rebuilt in stone. Birdoswald has a unique historical footnote: unlike other Roman forts along the wall, it was maintained by local tribes long after being abandoned by the Romans. The small visitor center has artifacts discovered at the site, a full-scale model of the wall, and a good café. ⊠ *Wallace Dr., Ravenglass* ☎ *01697/747602* ⊕ *www. hadrianswallcountry.co.uk/visit/birdoswald-roman-fort* ⊠ *£5.70.*

Fodor's Choice   **Chesters Roman Fort.** In a wooded valley on the banks of the North
★   Tyne River, this cavalry fort was known as Cilurnum in Roman times, when it protected the point where Hadrian's Wall crossed the river. Although the setting is not as dramatic as the nearby Housesteads Roman Fort, this mazelike layout of surviving fortifications is said to be Britain's most complete Roman cavalry fort; the military bathhouse by the river is supposedly the best-preserved Roman structure of its kind in the British Isles. The Museum of Roman Finds includes a fascinating array of artifacts including statues of river and water gods and Roman jewelry. ⊠ *B6318, Chollerford* ✦ *4 miles north of Hexham* ☎ *01434/681379* ⊕ *www.english-heritage.org.uk* ⊠ *£6.60* ⊙ *Closed weekdays in Nov.–Mar.*

Fodor's Choice   **Hexham Abbey.** A site of Christian worship for more than 1,300 years,
★   ancient Hexham Abbey forms one side of the town's main square. Inside, you can climb the 35 worn stone "night stairs," which once led from the main part of the abbey to the canon's dormitory, to overlook the whole

ensemble. Most of the current building dates from the 12th and 13th centuries, and much of the stone, including that of the Anglo-Saxon crypt, was taken from the Roman fort at Corbridge. Note the portraits on the 16th-century wooden rood screen and the four panels from a 15th-century *Dance of Death* in the sanctuary. In September, the abbey hosts the renowned Festival of Music and the Arts, which brings classical musicians from around the world. ✉ *Beaumont St.* ☎ *01434/602031* 🌐 *www.hexhamabbey.org.uk* 🎫 *Free; requested donation £3.*

FAMILY **Old Gaol.** Dating from 1330, Hexham's Old Gaol houses fascinating exhibits about the history of the borderlands, including tales of the terrifying "reavers" and their bloodthirsty raids into Northumberland from Scotland during the 16th and 17th centuries. Photographs, weapons, and a reconstructed house interior give a full account of what the region was like in medieval times. A glass elevator takes you to four floors, including the dungeon. ✉ *Hallgate* ☎ *01670/624523* 🌐 *www.hexhamoldgaol.org.uk* 🎫 *£5.*

WHERE TO EAT

$$$$ BRITISH Fodor's Choice ★ 🍴 **Langley Castle.** This lavish 14th-century castle with turrets and battlements offers an elegant fine-dining experience. Choose from an excellent five-course prix-fixe menu of traditional English dishes with hints of Asian influence—perhaps the mutton served with miso broth and lobster wonton, or the halibut with samphire and razor clams. **Known for:** romantic, historic setting; lavish afternoon tea; affordable snack menu. [$] *Average main: £45* ✉ *A686, Langley* ☎ *01434/688888* 🌐 *www.langleycastle.com.*

WHERE TO STAY

$ B&B/INN 🏨 **Dene House.** This peaceful stone farmhouse on 9 acres of lovely countryside has beamed ceilings and homey rooms with pine furniture and colorful quilts. **Pros:** tasty breakfasts; warm atmosphere; reasonable rates. **Cons:** no restaurant; decor a bit worn. [$] *Rooms from: £70* ✉ *B6303* ☎ *01434/673413* 🌐 *www.denehouse-guesthouse.co.uk* 💳 *No credit cards* 🛏 *3 rooms, 1 with bath* 🍽 *Free Breakfast.*

SPORTS AND THE OUTDOORS

The Bike Place. This shop in Kielder is the nearest cycle-hire shop to Hexham (outside Newcastle upon Tyne itself). Prices start at £25 per day, and they can arrange delivery and collection for an extra fee. ✉ *Station Garage, Kielder* ✣ *30 miles north of Hexham; take A6079 from the main A69 road. The shop is clearly signposted on the main road through the village* ☎ *01434/250457* 🌐 *www.thebikeplace.co.uk.*

GREENHEAD

18 miles west of Hexham, 49 miles northwest of Durham.

In and around tiny Greenhead you'll find a wealth of historical sites related to Hadrian's Wall, including the fascinating Housesteads Roman Fort, the Roman Army Museum, and the archaeologically rich Vindolanda. In Northumberland National Park, about half a mile north of Vindolanda, the Once Brewed National Park Visitor Centre has informative displays about Hadrian's Wall and can advise about local walks.

GETTING HERE AND AROUND

Greenhead is on the A69 and B6318. The nearest train station is 3 miles east, in Haltwhistle.

ESSENTIALS

Visitor Information *Once* Brewed National Park Visitor Centre. ⊠ *Northumberland National Park, Military Rd., Bardon Mill* ☎ *01434/344396* ⊕ *www.northumberlandnationalpark.org.uk*

EXPLORING

Fodor's Choice
★

Housesteads Roman Fort. If you have time to visit only one Hadrian's Wall site, Housesteads Roman Fort, Britain's most complete example of a Roman fort, is your best bet. It includes long sections of the wall, an excavated fort, and a new visitor center with a collection of artifacts discovered at the site and computer-generated images of what the fort originally looked like. The fort itself is a 10-minute walk uphill from the parking lot (not for those with mobility problems), but the effort is worth it to see the surprisingly extensive ruins, dating from around AD 125. Excavations have revealed the remains of granaries, gateways, barracks, a hospital, and the commandant's house. ■ TIP→ The northern tip of the fort, at the crest of the hill, has one of the best views of Hadrian's Wall, passing beside you before disappearing over hills and crags in the distance. ⊠ *B6318, Haydon Bridge* ☎ *01434/344363* ⊕ *www.english-heritage.org.uk* ⊠ *£8.30.*

FAMILY
Fodor's Choice
★

Roman Army Museum. At the garrison fort of Carvoran, this museum makes an excellent introduction to Hadrian's Wall. Full-size models and excavations bring this remote outpost of the empire to life; authentic Roman graffiti adorns the walls of an excavated barracks. There's a well-designed museum with Roman artifacts and a flashy 3-D film that puts it all into historical context. Opposite the museum, at Walltown Crags on the Pennine Way (one of Britain's long-distance national hiking trails), are 400 yards of the best-preserved section of the wall. The museum is 1 mile northeast of Greenhead. ⊠ *Off B6318* ☎ *01697/747485* ⊕ *www.vindolanda.com* ⊠ *£6.60; £11.60 with admission to Vindolanda.*

Fodor's Choice
★

Vindolanda. About 8 miles east of Greenhead, this archaeological site holds the remains of eight successive Roman forts and civilian settlements, providing an intriguing look into the daily life of a military compound. Most of the visible remains date from the 2nd and 3rd centuries, and new excavations are constantly under way. A reconstructed Roman temple, house, and shop provide context, and the museum displays rare artifacts, such as a handful of extraordinary wooden tablets with messages about everything from household chores to military movements. A full-size reproduction of a section of the wall gives a sense of its massiveness. The site is sometimes closed in bad weather. ⊠ *Off B6318, Bardon Mill* ☎ *01434/344277* ⊕ *www.vindolanda.com* ⊠ *£7.90; £11.60 includes admission to Roman Army Museum.*

WHERE TO EAT

$
BRITISH

✕ **Milecastle Inn.** The snug bar and restaurant of this remote, peaceful 17th-century pub make an excellent place to dine. Fine local meat goes into its famous pies; take your pick from wild boar and ducklin pie, or maybe a plate of Whitby scampi with chips. **Known for:** tasty house specialty meat pies; traditional pub food; 17th-century building. $ *Average main: £12* ✉ *Military Rd., Haltwhistle* ☎ *01434/321372.*

WHERE TO STAY

$ | 🏨 **Holmhead Guest House.** Talk about a feel for history—this former
B&B/INN | farmhouse in open countryside, graced with stone arches and exposed beams, is not only built *on* Hadrian's Wall but also partly *from* it. **Pros:** full of atmosphere; close to Hadrian's Wall; reasonable rates. **Cons:** rooms are a bit of a squeeze; won't suit those who don't like isolation; you need a car to get around. $ *Rooms from: £72* ✉ *Off A69* ☎ *01697/747402* ⊕ *www.bandbhadrianswall.com* ▭ *No credit cards* ⇨ *4 rooms, 8 beds, 1 apartment* ⦿ *Free Breakfast.*

THE FAR NORTHEAST COAST

Extraordinary medieval fortresses and monasteries line the final 40 miles of the Northeast coast before England gives way to Scotland. Castles abound, including the spectacularly sited Bamburgh. The region also has some magnificent beaches, though because of the cold water and rough seas they're far better for walking than swimming.

ALNWICK

30 miles north of Newcastle, 46 miles north of Durham.

Dominated by a grand castle, the little market town of Alnwick (pronounced *ahn*-ick) is the best base from which to explore the dramatic coast and countryside of northern Northumberland.

GETTING HERE AND AROUND

If you're driving, Alnwick is just off the A1. Buses X15 and X18 connect Alnwick with Newcastle, Berwick, and Morpeth. The nearest train station is 4 miles away in Alnmouth (pronounced *alun*-mowth); trains travel between here and Newcastle roughly every hour and take 30 minutes.

ESSENTIALS

Visitor Information Visit Alnwick. ✉ *2 The Shambles* ☎ *01670/622152* ⊕ *www.visitalnwick.org.uk.*

EXPLORING

FAMILY | **Alnwick Castle.** Sometimes called the "Windsor of the North," the impos-
Fodor's Choice | ing Alnwick Castle will more likely provoke cries of "Hogwarts!" from
★ | younger visitors as it comes into view over the hill. (The grounds appear as the exterior of the famous School of Witchcraft and Wizardry in the Harry Potter movies.) The castle is still home to the dukes of Northumberland, whose family, the Percys, dominated in the northeast for centuries. Family photos and other knickknacks are scattered around the lavish staterooms, a subtle but pointed reminder that this is a family home rather than a museum. Highlights include the extraordinary gun room, lined with hundreds of antique pistols arranged in swirling patterns; the formal dining room, its table set as if guests are due at any

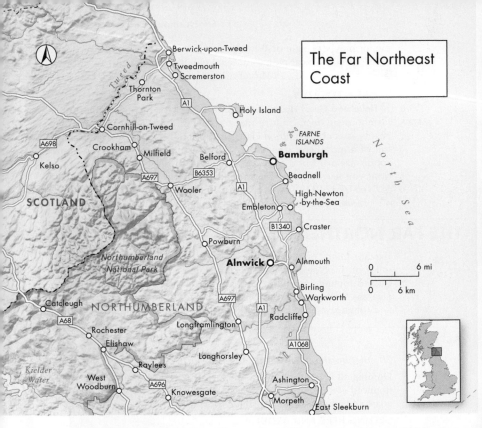

minute; and the magnificent galleried library, containing 14,000 books in floor-to-ceiling cases.

There's plenty here for younger visitors: **Knights' Quest** lets kids dress up and complete interactive challenges; **Dragon's Quest** is a labyrinth designed to teach a bit of medieval history; and for the very young, there are Harry Potter–style events on certain dates, including **Broomstick Lessons** on the exact spot used in the movie (check website for schedule). Spooky ghost stories are told by costumed actors in the **Lost Cellars**. In addition, the staff hides a toy owl somewhere in each room of the castle, and kids get a certificate if they spot them all. Tickets are valid for one year, so you can come back if you don't see everything in a day. ✉ *Narrowgate* ☎ *01665/511100* ⊕ *www.alnwickcastle.com* 🎫 *£14.40; combined ticket with Alnwick Gardens £23.55.*

FAMILY
Fodor'sChoice
★

Alnwick Garden. A marvelous flight of fancy, Alnwick Garden was designed by Capability Brown in 1750. Centering on modern terraced fountains by Belgian designers Jacques and Peter Wirtz, the gardens include traditional features (shaded woodland walks, a rose garden) and funkier, kid-appealing elements such as a Poison Garden and a labyrinth of towering bamboo. ■TIP→ **You can buy clippings of the unique varieties of roses in the shop.** Opening and closing times are subject to change due to season and weather, so call ahead. This is also the location of one of the area's most unique restaurants, the Treehouse. ✉ *Denwick La.* ☎ *01665/511350* 🌐 *www.alnwickgarden.com* 🎟 *£8; combined ticket with Alnwick Castle £23.55.*

WHERE TO EAT

$$$$ MODERN BRITISH Fodor's Choice ★

🍴 **The Treehouse.** The treetop location may sound gimmicky, but the effect at this extraordinary restaurant is quite magical, especially when the place is lit up at night. The Modern British fare is excellent—seared turbot with coriander (cilantro) and hazelnuts, for instance, or duck breast with honey and sesame. **Known for:** unique setting; Northumbrian flavors for a twist; romantic vibe. [$] *Average main: £28.50* ✉ *Alnwick Garden, Denwick La.* ☎ *01665/511852* 🌐 *www.alnwickgarden.com* 🕓 *No dinner Mon.–Wed.*

WHERE TO STAY

$ B&B/INN Fodor's Choice ★

🏨 **Redfoot Lea.** This cozy farmhouse B&B, a couple of miles from Alnwick Castle, is an oasis of contemporary style and homespun charm. **Pros:** beautifully restored farmhouse; truly welcoming hosts; great breakfasts. **Cons:** one room has twin beds; 2-mile walk into town; bedrooms so pretty and white you might feel bad bringing your muddy boots inside. [$] *Rooms from: £90* ✉ *Greensfield Moor Farm, off A1* ☎ *01665/510700, 07870/586214* 🌐 *www.redfootlea.co.uk* 🛏 *2 rooms* 🍽 *Free Breakfast.*

BAMBURGH

14 miles north of Alnwick.

Tiny Bamburgh has a splendid castle, and several beaches are a few minutes' walk away.

GETTING HERE AND AROUND

Bamburgh can be reached by car on B3140, B3141, or B3142. Buses X18 and 418 run from Alnwick to Bamburgh a few times per day. The nearest train station is in Chathill, about 7 miles away.

EXPLORING

Fodor's Choice ★

Bamburgh Castle. You'll see Bamburgh Castle long before you reach it: a solid, weather-beaten, cliff-top fortress that dominates the coastal view for miles around. A fortification of some kind has stood here since the 6th century, but the Norman castle was damaged during the 15th century and the central tower is all that remains intact. Much of the structure—the home of the Armstrong family since 1894—was restored during the 18th and 19th centuries. The interior is mostly late Victorian (most impressively, the Great Hall), although a few rooms, such as the small but alarmingly well-stocked armory, have a more authentically medieval feel. The breathtaking view across the North Sea is worth the trip; bring a picnic if the weather's good (or order to-go sandwiches at the café). ✉ *Off B1340* ☎ *01668/214515* 🌐 *www.bamburghcastle.com* 🎟 *£10.85.*

WHERE TO EAT

$$
BRITISH
Fodor's Choice
★

✕ **Gray's Restaurant.** Located on a quiet bay between Bamburgh and Holy Island, 6 acres of woodland surround the elegant Waren House Hotel, which is home to this crisply elegant restaurant. Three-course fixed-price dinners might include monkfish and mussel tart, or slow-cooked local lamb with rosemary and Madeira sauce. **Known for:** picturesque surroundings; elegant, traditional menus; fine dining. $ *Average main: £19* ✉ *B1342* ☎ *01668/214581* ⊕ *www.warenhousehotel.co.uk.*

WHERE TO STAY

$$
HOTEL

⚏ **Lord Crewe Hotel.** This cozy, stone-walled inn with oak beams sits in the heart of the village, close to Bamburgh Castle. **Pros:** in the center of the village; good restaurant; close to Bamburgh Castle. **Cons:** pub can get quite crowded; rather uninspiring decor in the bedrooms; very dog-friendly bar—great for dog lovers, but not for allergy sufferers. $ *Rooms from: £135* ✉ *Front St.* ☎ *01668/214243* ⊕ *www.lord-crewe. co.uk* ⤴ *18 rooms* ⎶ *Free Breakfast.*

WALES

WELCOME TO WALES

TOP REASONS TO GO

★ **Castle country:** Wales doesn't quite have a castle in each town, but there is a greater concentration than almost anywhere else in Europe—more than 600 in all.

★ **The Gower Peninsula:** This stretch of coastland near Swansea includes some of the region's prettiest beaches, as well as spectacular coastal views and ancient sites.

★ **Snowdonia:** The biggest of the country's three national parks contains its highest mountain, Snowdon, as well as picture-perfect villages.

★ **Brecon Beacons:** Moorlands, mountains, and valleys make up this rough and wild stretch of the Welsh midlands, as popular with hikers as it is with those who are just happy to take in the stunning views from the road.

★ **Hay-on-Wye:** This pretty village on the Welsh-English border has become world famous as a book lover's paradise; every street is lined with secondhand bookstores.

Wales has three main regions: South, Mid-, and North. South Wales is the most varied, and in just a few miles you can travel from Wales's bustling and cosmopolitan capital city, Cardiff, to the most enchanting old villages and historical sights. Mid-Wales is almost entirely rural (its largest town has a population of just 16,000), and it's fringed on its western shores by the arc of Cardigan Bay. Here you'll find mountain lakes, quiet roads, hillside sheep farms, and traditional market towns. North Wales is a mixture of mountains, popular sandy beaches, and coastal hideaways. Although dominated by rocky Snowdonia National Park, the north has a gentler, greener side along the border with England.

1 **South Wales.** Cardiff, the lively young capital city, is here, as are two very different national parks: the green, swooping hills of the Brecon Beacons and, in the far west, the sea cliffs, beaches, and estuaries of the Pembrokeshire Coast. Both are excellent for outdoor activities such as walking and mountain biking. Swansea and Laugharne are essential stops for fans of poet Dylan Thomas.

2 **Mid-Wales.** The quietest part of Wales is home to scenic countryside, from rolling hills to more rugged mountains. Aberystwyth is a Victorian resort town on the coast, and Hay-on-Wye is a magnet for lovers of antiquarian bookstores.

3 **North Wales.** Wales's most famous castles are in its northern region. The cream of the crop is Caernarfon, a medieval palace dominating the waterfront on the Menai Strait. Conwy (castle and town) is popular, too. Snowdonia's mountains are a major draw, as is the quirky, faux-Italian village of Portmeirion.

12

ISLE·OF ANGLESEY

Holyhead
Beaumaris
Llandudno
Prestatyn
Pensarn
Conwy
Conwy Bay
Dee
M53
A5
A55
A55

Caernarfon
Betws-y-Coed
A5
A494
A483
Llanberis
A496
Blaenau Ffestiniog
A5
Llangollen
Pant Glas
Tyn-y-cefn
Portmeirion
Bala
Chirk
Porthmadog
Snowdonia National Park
Oswestry
Pwllheli
A470
A494
A5

Hells Mouth
Dolgellau
A458
Welshpool
BARDSEY ISLAND
Barmouth
Mallwyd
Irish Sea
Cardigan Bay
Machynlleth
Cemmaes Road
A483
A487
2
Caersws
Newtown
Aberystwyth
A44
ENGLAND
Llangurig
Llanrhystud
Rhayader
Hay-on-Wye
Aberaeron
A470
Crossgates
A487
Synod Inn
Builth Wells
Mynydd Preseli
A483
Cardigan
Fishguard
Llandovery
Llyswen
Pembrokeshire Coast
Brecon
St. David's
National
A40
A40
St. Brides Bay
Park
Llandeilo
Crickhowell
A487
Carmarthen
Brecon Beacons National Park
Abergavenny
Haverfordwest
A40
Milford Haven
Laugharne
A465
Merthyr Tydfil
Pembroke
Llanelli
Llandovery
A470
Tenby
A40
Carmarthen Bay
M4
Newport
M4
Gower Peninsula
Swansea
Pontypridd
Swansea Bay
M4

Bristol Cannel
Barry
CARDIFF
1

0   10 mi
0   10 km

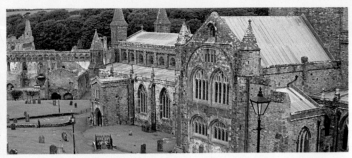

Updated by
Victoria Trott

Wales is a land of dramatic national parks, plunging, unspoiled coastlines, and awe-inspiring medieval castles. Its ancient history and deep-rooted Celtic culture make Wales similar in many ways to its more famous neighbors, Scotland and Ireland; and yet it doesn't attract the same hordes of visitors, which is a big part of the appeal.

Vast swaths of Wales were untouched by the industrial boom of the 19th century. Although pockets of the country were given over to industries such as coal mining and manufacturing (both of which have all but disappeared), most of Wales remained unspoiled. The country is largely rural, and there are more than 10 million sheep—but only 3 million people. It has a Britain-as-it-used-to-be feel that can be hugely appealing.

The country has been politically autonomous since 1997 and Welsh culture is flourishing. Cardiff has the most successful creative economy in the U.K. outside of London, with a burgeoning television and film industry, as well as thriving art scenes in most towns and cities. Welsh produce is constantly being celebrated and championed by a passionate new generation of chefs and artisan foodies. And of course, national rugby matches still bond the nation together. Simply put, Wales loves being Wales, and that enthusiasm is infectious to visitors. It also means that the tourism industry has grown by leaps and bounds, including some truly unique and special places to stay.

Although Wales is a small country—on average, about 60 miles wide and 170 miles north to south—looking at it on a map is deceptive. It's quite a difficult place to get around, with a distinctly old-fashioned road network and poor public transportation connections. To see it properly, you really need a car. The good news is that along the way you'll experience some beautiful drives. There are rewards to be found in the gentle folds of its valleys and in the shadow of its mountains.

Were some of the more remote attractions in Wales in, say, the west of Ireland, they'd be world famous and overrun with millions of visitors. Here, if you're lucky, you can almost have them to yourself.

PLANNER

12

WHEN TO GO

The weather in Wales, as in the rest of Britain, is a lottery. It can be hot in summer or never stop raining. Generally it's cool and wet in spring and autumn, but could also be surprisingly warm and sunny. The only surefire rule is that you should be prepared for the unexpected.

Generally speaking, southwest Wales tends to enjoy a milder climate than elsewhere in Britain, thanks in part to the moderating effects of the Gulf Stream. In contrast, mountainous areas like Snowdonia and the Brecon Beacons can be chilly at any time of the year. Book far ahead for major festivals such as the literary Hay Festival, Brecon Jazz, Llangollen International Musical Eisteddfod, and the Abergavenny Food Festival.

FESTIVALS

FAMILY
Fodor's Choice
★

Abergavenny Food Festival. Held on the third weekend in September, the Abergavenny Food Festival is a celebration for foodies and a symbol of the growing interest in Welsh cuisine, regularly attracting leading figures from the British food scene. There are demonstrations, lectures, special events, and, of course, a huge indoor and outdoor food market. Be sure to sample the delicious local cheese called Y Fenni, flavored with a piquant combination of mustard seeds and ale. ⊠ *Abergavenny* ☎ *01873/851643* ⊕ *www.abergavennyfoodfestival.com.*

FAMILY
Fodor's Choice
★

International Musical Eisteddfod. The six-day International Musical Eisteddfod, held in early July, brings together amateur choirs and dancers—more than 12,000 participants in all—from all corners of the globe for a colorful folk festival. The tradition of the eisteddfod, held throughout Wales, goes back to the 12th century. Originally gatherings of bards, the *eisteddfodau* of today are more like national festivals. ⊠ *Llangollen* ☎ *01978/862001* ⊕ *www.international-eisteddfod.co.uk.*

FAMILY
Fodor's Choice
★

Victorian Festival. For a week in late August, the Victorian Festival takes over Llandrindod Wells. Everyone from shopkeepers to hotel clerks dresses up in period costume for events from tea dances to street parades. ⊠ *Llandrindod Wells* ☎ *01597/829498* ⊕ *www.victorian-festival.co.uk* ⊠ *Free; special events £8–£25.*

PLANNING YOUR TIME

First-time visitors often try to cover too much ground in too little time. It's not hard to spend half your time traveling between points that look close on the map but take the better part of a day to reach. From Cardiff, it's easy to visit the Wye Valley, Brecon Beacons, and the Gower Peninsula. Along the North Wales coast, Llandudno and Lake Vyrnwy make good bases for Snowdonia National Park.

The location of Wales lends itself to a border-hopping trip—in both directions. Well-known locations like Bath (near South Wales) and Chester (near North Wales) are no more than an hour from the Welsh border, and you can even take a ferry to Ireland if you want to go farther afield.

GETTING HERE AND AROUND
AIR TRAVEL

If you're arriving from the United States, London's Heathrow and Gatwick airports are generally the best options because of their large number of international flights. Heathrow (2 hours) is slightly closer than Gatwick (2½ hours), but both have excellent motorway links with South Wales. For North Wales, the quickest access is via Manchester Airport, with a travel time of less than an hour to the Welsh border.

Cardiff International Airport, 12 miles from downtown Cardiff, is the only airport in Wales with international flights, but these are mostly from Europe. The T9 bus service runs from the airport to Cardiff's central train station.

Airports Cardiff International Airport. ✉ *A4226, Rhoose* ☎ *01446/711111* ⊕ *www.cardiff-airport.com.*

BUS TRAVEL

Most parts of Wales are accessible by bus, but long-distance bus travel takes a long time. National Express travels to all parts of Wales from London's Victoria Coach Station and also direct from London's Heathrow and Gatwick airports. The company also has routes into Wales from many major towns and cities in England and Scotland. Average travel times from London are 3½ hours to Cardiff, 4 hours to Swansea, 7 hours to Aberystwyth, and 4½ hours to Llandudno.

Many of Wales's national parks run summer bus services. In the North, the excellent Snowdon Sherpa runs into and around Snowdonia and links with main rail and bus services. The Pembrokeshire Coastal Bus Service operates in Pembrokeshire Coast National Park.

Bus Contacts National Express. ☎ *0871/781-8181* ⊕ *www.nationalexpress. com.* **Pembrokeshire Coastal Bus.** ☎ *0800/464-0000 Traveline* ⊕ *www. pembrokeshirecoast.wales.* **Snowdon Sherpa.** ☎ *0800/464-0000 Traveline* ⊕ *www.gwynedd.llyw.cymru/en.*

CAR TRAVEL

To explore the Welsh heartland properly, you really need a car. Be prepared to take the scenic route: there are no major highways north of Swansea (which means virtually all of Wales). For the most part it's all back-roads, all the way. There are some stunning routes to savor: the A487 road runs along or near most of the coastline, while the A44 and A470 both wind through mountain scenery with magnificent views.

FERRY TRAVEL

Three ferry ports that connect Britain with Ireland are in Wales. Regular daily ferries with Stena Line and Irish Ferries sail from Fishguard and Pembroke, in the southwest, and Holyhead, in the northwest.

Ferry Contacts Irish Ferries. ☎ *08717/300400* ⊕ *www.irishferries.com.* **Stena Line.** ☎ *0844/770-7070* ⊕ *www.stenaline.co.uk.*

TRAIN TRAVEL

Travel time on the Great Western Railway service from London's Paddington Station is about two hours to Cardiff and three hours to Swansea. Trains connect London's Euston Station with Mid-Wales and North

Wales, often involving changes in cities such as Birmingham. Travel times average between three and five hours. Regional train service covers much of South and North Wales but, frustratingly, there are virtually no direct connections between these regions. For example, to make the 73-mile trip between Cardiff and Aberystwyth you have to make a connection in Shrewsbury, doubling the trip to 147 miles. North Wales has a cluster of steam railways, but these are tourist attractions rather than a practical way of getting around. The mainline long-distance routes can be very scenic indeed, such as the Cambrian Coast Railway, running between Machynlleth and Pwllheli, and the Heart of Wales Line, linking Swansea with Shrewsbury on the Welsh-English border.

Train Contacts National Rail Enquiries. ☎ *0345/748–4950* ⊕ *www.nationalrail.co.uk.*

DISCOUNTS AND DEALS

For travel within Wales, ask about money-saving unlimited-travel tickets (such as the Explore Wales Pass, the North and Mid-Wales Pass, and the South Wales Flexi Pass), which include the use of bus services. A discount card offering a 20% reduction on each of the steam-driven Great Little Trains of Wales is also available. It costs £10, is valid for 12 months, and can be purchased online.

The Cadw/Welsh Historic Monuments Explorer Pass is good for unlimited admission to most of Wales's historic sites. The seven-day pass costs £32 per person, £51 per couple, or £62 per family; the three-day pass costs £21, £33, and £44, respectively. Passes are available at any site covered by the Cadw program. All national museums and galleries in Wales are free.

Discount Information Cadw/Welsh Historic Monuments. ✉ *Plas Carew, Unit 5–7 Cefn Coed, Nantgarw* ☎ *0300/025–6000* ⊕ *cadw.gov.wales.* **Explore Wales Pass Information.** ☎ *03457/484950* ⊕ *www.nationalrail.co.uk.* **Great Little Trains of Wales.** ☎ *0800/464–0000 Traveline* ⊕ *www.greatlittletrainsofwales.co.uk.*

TOURS

In summer there are all-day and half-day tour-bus excursions to most parts of the country. In major resorts and cities, ask for details at a tourist information center or bus station.

Wales Official Tourist Guide Association. The country's official guide organization will set you up only with guides recognized by VisitWales. You can book a driver-guide or someone to accompany you as you drive, or a tailor-made tour. ☎ ⊕ *www.wotga.com.*

RESTAURANTS

Wales has developed a thriving restaurant scene over the last 20 years or so, and not just in major towns. Some truly outstanding food can be found in rural pubs and hotel restaurants. More and more restaurants are creating dishes using fresh local ingredients—Welsh lamb, Welsh Black beef, Welsh cheeses, and seafood from the Welsh coast—that show off the best of the region's cuisine. *Restaurant reviews have been shortened. For full information, visit Fodors.com.*

HOTELS

A 19th-century dictum, "I sleeps where I dines," still holds true in Wales, where good hotels and good restaurants often go together. Castles, country mansions, and even disused railway stations are being transformed into interesting hotels and restaurants. Traditional inns with low, beamed ceilings, wood paneling, and fireplaces are often the most appealing places to stay. The best ones tend to be off the beaten track. Cardiff and Swansea have some large chain hotels, and, for luxury, some excellent spas have cropped up in the countryside. An added bonus is that prices are generally lower than they are for equivalent properties in the Cotswolds, Scotland, or southeast England. *Hotel reviews have been shortened. For full information, visit Fodors.com.*

WHAT IT COSTS IN POUNDS			
	$	$$	$$$	$$$$
Restaurants	under £15	£15–£19	£20–£25	over £25
Hotels	under £100	£100–£160	£161–£220	over £220

Restaurant prices are the average cost of a main course at dinner, or if dinner is not served, at lunch. Hotels prices are the lowest cost of a standard double room in high season, including 20% V.A.T.

VISITOR INFORMATION

Contacts Visit Wales. ☎ *0333/006–3001* ⊕ *www.visitwales.com.* **Wales in Style.** ⊕ *www.walesinstyle.com.*

SOUTH WALES

The most diverse of Wales's three regions, the south covers the area around Cardiff that stretches southwest as far as the rugged coastline of Pembrokeshire. It's the most accessible part of the country, as the roads are relatively good and the rail network is more extensive than it is elsewhere in Wales. Pleasant seaside towns such as Tenby are within a four- to five-hour drive of London; from Cardiff and Swansea you're never more than a half hour away from some gorgeous small villages.

Cardiff, the capital, and Swansea, the country's second largest city, have enjoyed a certain success in reinventing themselves as cultured, modern areas, but other smaller towns like Newport have struggled to find their place in this postindustrial region. With a few exceptions, it's better to stick to the countryside in South Wales. The heart-stopping Gower Peninsula stretches along 16 miles of sapphire-blue bays and rough-hewn sea cliffs, and Brecon Beacons National Park is an area of grassy mountains and craggy limestone gorges.

Castell Coch looks medieval, but don't be fooled: it's a delightful Victorian-Gothic fantasy.

CARDIFF CAERDYDD

30 miles southwest of the Second Severn Bridge.

With a population of around 360,000, Cardiff is the largest and most important city in Wales. It's also one of the youngest capitals in Europe: although a settlement has existed here since Roman times, Cardiff wasn't declared a city until 1905, and didn't become the capital until 50 years later. This is an energetic, youthful place, keen to show its newfound cosmopolitanism to the world. Cardiff has experienced something of a cultural renaissance since the opening of the Wales Millennium Centre in Cardiff Bay.

For all its urban optimism, however, Cardiff is still a rather workaday town, with little to detain you for more than a couple of days. See Cardiff Castle and the National Museum, wander Cardiff Bay, and maybe catch a show. Otherwise, it's a convenient base for exploring the nearby countryside.

GETTING HERE AND AROUND

The capital is a major transportation hub with good connections to other parts of South Wales and with England. Getting to Mid-Wales and North Wales is more difficult, as there's no direct north–south train route (you'll have to connect in Bristol or Shrewsbury) and north–south buses are painfully slow. From London, trains from Paddington to Cardiff Central take about two hours; National Express coaches take about three hours. Cardiff is easily accessible by the M4 motorway. You must pay a £5.60 toll to cross the Severn Bridge between England and Wales (though crossing back is free).

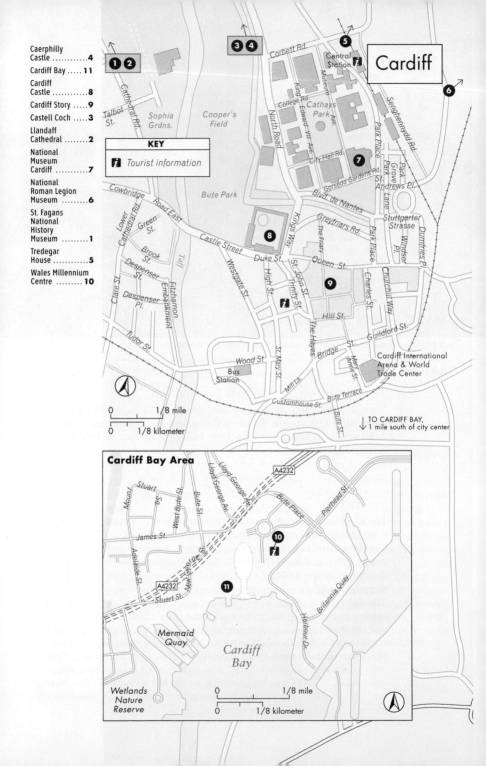

Cardiff

KEY

🛈 *Tourist information*

Corbett Rd.

Central Station 🛈

Senghennydd Rd.

Cathedral St.

Talbot St.

Sophia Grdns.

Cooper's Field

College Rd.

King Edward VII Ave.

Museum Ave.

North Road

Cathays Park

Park Place

Park Grove

Park Lane

St. Andrews Pl.

City Hall Rd.

Gorsedd Gardens Rd.

Blvd. de Nantes

Stuttgarter Strasse

Dumfries Pl.

Windsor Pl.

Cowbridge Road East

Lower Cathedral Rd.

Green St.

Brook St.

Despenser St.

Clare St.

Despenser Pl.

Tudor St.

Bute Park

Kings Way

Castle Street

Greyfriars Rd.

The Friary

Duke St.

Queen St.

Charles St.

Churchill Way

Fitzhammon Embankment

Westgate St.

High St.

St. John St.

Trinity St.

Taff

St. Mary St.

Hill St.

Guildford St.

Wood St.

Bus Station

Mill La.

Bridge St.

Mary Ann St.

Cardiff International Arena & World Trade Center

Customhouse St.

Bute Terrace

Bute St.

0   1/8 mile

0   1/8 kilometer

↓ TO CARDIFF BAY,
↓ 1 mile south of city center

Cardiff Bay Area

A4232

Mount Stuart Sq.

West Bute St.

Bute St.

Lloyd George Av.

Bute Place

Pierhead St.

James St.

Adelaide St.

A4232

Stuart St.

Lloyd George Av.

🛈

Britannia Quay

Harbour Dr.

Mermaid Quay

Cardiff Bay

Wetlands Nature Reserve

0   1/8 mile

0   1/8 kilometer

12

ESSENTIALS

Visitor and Tour Information Cardiff Bay Visitor Centre. ✉ *Wales Millennium Centre, Bute Pl.* ☎ *029/2087–3573* ⊕ *www.visitcardiff.com.* **Cardiff City Centre Visitor Centre.** ✉ *The Old Library, The Hayes* ☎ *029/2087–3573* ⊕ *www. visitcardiff.com.*

EXPLORING

FAMILY

Fodor's Choice

★

Caerphilly Castle. The largest and most impressive fortress in Wales, and one of the few still to be surrounded by its original moat, Caerphilly must have been awe-inspiring at the time of its construction in the 13th century. Built by an Anglo-Norman lord, the concentric fortification contained powerful inner and outer defenses. It was badly damaged during the English Civil War (check out the leaning tower), although extensive 20th-century renovations have restored much of its former glory. The original Great Hall is still intact, and near the edge of the inner courtyard there's a replica of a trebuchet—a giant catapult used to launch rocks and other projectiles at the enemy. Additionally, an interesting collection of modern interpretive sculptures has been placed around the castle, both inside and outside. To celebrate the town's famous cheese, a free festival, The Big Cheese, is held here every year at the end of July. Caerphilly is 7 miles north of Cardiff. ✉ *Castle St., Caerphilly* ☎ *029/2088–3143* ⊕ *cadw.gov.wales* ✍ *£7.95.*

Cardiff Bay. Perhaps the most potent symbol of Cardiff's 21st-century rebirth, this regenerated district is a 15-minute bus ride from St. Mary Street. It's the location of Y Senedd, the National Assembly building, and Wales Millennium Centre, as well as a good selection of restaurants and bars. Don't miss the Norwegian Church Arts Centre, where children's author Roald Dahl was baptized; you can also take a boat trip around the bay. It was from Roath Dock in 1910 that Captain Robert Falcon Scott and his crew left aboard the SS *Terra Nova* for their ill-fated British Antarctic Expedition. ✉ *Between Stuart St. and Harbour Dr.* ⊕ *www.visitcardiffbay.info.*

FAMILY

Fodor's Choice

★

Cardiff Castle. A mishmash of styles, from austere Norman keep to over-the-top Victorian mansion, Cardiff Castle is an odd but beguiling place, located right in the middle of the city. Take the tour of the Victorian portion to discover the castle's exuberant side. William Burges (1827–81), an architect obsessed by the Gothic period, transformed the castle into an extravaganza of medieval color for the third marquess of Bute. The result was the Moorish-style ceiling in the Arab Room, the intricately carved shelves lining the Library, and gold leaf murals everywhere. Look for the painting of the Invisible Prince in the Day Nursery; on first glance it's just a tree, but stare long enough and a man takes shape in the branches. Note the not-so-subtle rejection of Darwin's theory of evolution, represented by monkeys tearing up his book around the library's doorway. Fans of military history shouldn't miss "Firing Line," an exhibition tracing the history of Welsh regiments. The vast castle grounds, which include beautiful rhododendron gardens and a habitat for owls and falcons, are sometimes the setting for jousting matches in summer. Tours, including of the clock tower and evening ghost tours, are held on certain dates year-round; call or check the website for schedule and booking information. ⊠ *Castle St.* 🕿 *029/2087–8100* ⊕ *www.cardiffcastle.com* 🎟 *£12.50.*

FAMILY **Cardiff Story.** This well-executed museum tells the story of Cardiff and its people from the city's medieval origins to the present day. There's a particularly interesting exhibit on the old docks (now Cardiff Bay), one of the biggest ports in the world in the early 1900s. It's also worth a visit to see the building itself, formerly the Cardiff Free Library, which was built in the 1880s and is now a recognized historic building; note the lovely green ceramic tiles. On the ground floor is the Cardiff City Centre Visitor Centre and also a shop, Bodlon, selling tasteful Welsh gifts and souvenirs. ⊠ *The Old Library, The Hayes* 🕿 *029/2034–6214* ⊕ *www.cardiffstory.com* 🎟 *Free.*

FAMILY **Castell Coch.** Perched on a hillside is this fairy-tale castle. The turreted
Fodor's Choice Red Castle was built on the site of a medieval stronghold in the 1870s,
★ about the time that the "Fairy-Tale King" Ludwig II of Bavaria was creating his castles in the mountains of Germany. This Victorian fantasy wouldn't look out of place among them. The castle was another collaboration of the third marquess of Bute and William Burges, who transformed Cardiff Castle. Burges created everything, including the whimsical furnishings and murals, in a remarkable exercise of Victorian-Gothic whimsy. ⊠ *A470, 4 miles north of Cardiff, Tongwynlais* 🕿 *029/2081–0101* ⊕ *cadw.gov.wales* 🎟 *£6.50.*

Llandaff Cathedral. In a suburb that retains its village feeling, you can visit this cathedral, which was repaired after serious bomb damage in World War II. The cathedral includes the work of a number of Pre-Raphaelites as well as *Christ in Majesty,* a 15-foot-tall aluminum figure by sculptor Jacob Epstein (1880–1959). From Cardiff, cross the River Taff and follow Cathedral Road for about 2 miles. Buses 25 and 63 from Westgate Street stop in Llandaff. ⊠ *Cathedral Close, Llandaff* 🕿 *029/2056–4554* ⊕ *www.llandaffcathedral.org.uk* 🎟 *Free.*

FAMILY **National Museum Cardiff.** This splendid neoclassical museum in Cardiff's
Fodor's Choice civic center houses the National Museum of Art and the National
★ Museum of Natural History. It is renowned for its exquisite collection of impressionist and modern art, featuring many of the art world's major players as well as one of the world's best collections of British silverware. This is also the main venue of the biannual Artes Mundi, the United Kingdom's largest arts prize. The Evolution of Wales gallery, showing the country's history from the Big Bang onward, uses inventive robotics and audiovisual effects. Kids, however, will be more interested in the dinosaurs and the enormous, 9-meter (29-foot) skeleton of a humpback whale that washed ashore near Cardiff in 1982. ⊠ *Cathays Park* 🕿 *029/2057–3000* ⊕ *www.museum.wales* 🎟 *Free* ⊘ *Closed Mon.*

FAMILY **National Roman Legion Museum.** Located within the remains of one of only three permanent Roman fortresses in Britain (built AD 75), this fascinating museum looks at all aspects of Roman life, and includes an exquisite collection of gemstones and a coffin complete with male remains. Of particular note are the ruins of the amphitheater, the baths, and the only Roman barracks on view in Europe. On Saturdays, families can meet with costumed Roman soldiers and dress up themselves; there are also occasionally reenactments of battles. The reconstructed Roman garden is particularly attractive. Caerleon is 4 miles northeast of Newport. ⊠ *High St., Newport* ☎ *0300/111–2333* ⊕ *www.museum.wales* 🎟 *Free.*

FAMILY

Fodor's Choice

★

St. Fagans National Museum of History. On 100 acres of gardens, this excellent open-air museum celebrates the region's architectural history with a collection of farmhouses, cottages, shops, chapels, a school, and a 16th-century manor house. All but two of the structures were brought here from around Wales. Of special note are the string of ironworkers' cottages, each reflecting a different era from 1805, 1855, 1925, 1955, and 1985, from the decor to the technology to the gardens. Craftspeople work at the museum using traditional methods; most of the work is for sale. Galleries display clothing and other articles from daily life, and special events highlight local customs. The native animal breeds are popular with kids. ⊠ *Off A4232, St. Fagans* ☎ *0300/111–2333* ⊕ *www. museum.wales* 🎟 *Free; parking £5.*

Tredegar House. Bought by the National Trust in 2011, Tredegar House is one of the grandest stately homes in Wales. Highlights of the self-guided tour include the grand baroque Jacobean New Hall and the enormous Victorian kitchens, both restored to their former glory. Don't miss the lavish Victorian Side Hall, lined with portraits of the Morgan family, which owned Tredegar until the 1950s. The grounds include immaculately laid-out formal gardens and an orangery. Tredegar is just outside Newport, 12 miles northwest of Cardiff. ⊠ *Tredegar House Dr., off A48, Newport* ☎ *01633/815880* ⊕ *www.nationaltrust.org.uk/ tredegar-house* 🎟 *£10.40; gardens free.*

Wales Millennium Centre. Inviting comparisons to Bilbao's Guggenheim, Cardiff's main arts complex (known locally as "The Armadillo" for its coppery, shingled exterior) is an extraordinary building, inside and out. The materials used in the construction are intended to represent "Welsh-ness." (Slate is for the rocky coastline, for example, while wood is for its ancient forests.) The massive words carved into the curving facade read "In These Stones Horizons Sing" in English and Welsh. Inside there's a maritime feel, from the curving wooden stairs to balconies evoking the bow of a ship. A broad range of cultural programs take place on the various stages, from ballet and opera to major touring shows. You might be lucky enough to catch a production by the innovative National Theatre Wales. There are often free daily musical performances in the foyer along with cafés, a restaurant, and a shop selling Welsh gifts. ⊠ *Bute Pl., Cardiff Bay* ☎ *029/2063–6464* ⊕ *www.wmc.org.uk* 🎟 *Free (event tickets vary).*

WHERE TO EAT

$$

MODERN

EUROPEAN

✕ **The Classroom.** On the top floor of Cardiff and Vale College's City Centre Campus, this smart restaurant is run by catering and hospitality students with panoramic views from the floor-to-ceiling windows. The menus, which change monthly, reflect the seasons and are overseen by some of the top Welsh chefs working in the U.K. **Known for:** panoramic views; first-class cuisine; creative use of Welsh produce. $ *Average main: £18* ⊠ *CAVC City Centre Campus, Dumballs Rd.* ☎ *029/2025–0377* ⊕ *www.theclassroom.wales* ۞ *Closed Sun. No dinner Mon.*

$$
BRITISH
Fodor's Choice
★

✕ **The Clink.** Well, this is unusual: a trendy restaurant in which all the food is prepared by prisoners; the idea behind The Clink (British slang for jail) is that those serving time for minor crimes are given the chance to turn their lives around by gaining experience as gourmet chefs. The restaurant (just outside the prison grounds) is a bright, modern space, and the Modern British food, made with local, seasonal produce, is genuinely delicious. **Known for:** unique atmosphere and concept; local, seasonal produce; no-alcohol policy. $ *Average main: £16* ✉ *Knox Rd., in front of Cardiff Prison* ☎ *029/2092–3130* ⊕ *www.theclinkcharity. org/the-clink-restaurants/cardiff-wales* ⊗ *No dinner Sun.–Tues.*

$
EUROPEAN

✕ **Madame Fromage.** In one of Cardiff's most atmospheric Victorian arcades, this café-deli has a Welsh-French menu, where cheese features heavily. The daily specials usually include salads, quiches, and soups—all with a Welsh-Continental feel. **Known for:** Welsh and French cheeses; famed cawl (lamb stew); delicious cakes. $ *Average main: £8* ✉ *21-25 Castle Arcade* ☎ *029/206–4888* ⊕ *www.madamefromage. co.uk* ⊗ *Closed Sun. No dinner.*

$$$$
FRENCH
Fodor's Choice
★

✕ **Park House.** In a building designed by William Burges (the same architect who helped design Cardiff Castle and Castell Coch), this upscale restaurant with a Welsh-French menu is one of the city's top eateries. Its grand surroundings make it a popular venue for afternoon tea, and there's also a simple bar menu featuring cheese and charcuterie. **Known for:** one of the best wine lists in the United Kingdom; charming building; local produce. $ *Average main: £28* ✉ *20 Park Pl.* ☎ *029/2022–4343* ⊕ *www.parkhouserestaurant.co.uk* ⊗ *Closed Mon. No dinner Sun.*

$$$
BRITISH

✕ **The Potted Pig.** Vaulted ceilings and exposed brick walls provide a dramatic backdrop to this restaurant down the block from Cardiff Castle. Formerly a bank vault, today the Potted Pig turns out superb Welsh dishes. **Known for:** pork in various forms; extensive gin menu; romantic dining room. $ *Average main: £21* ✉ *27 High St.* ☎ *029/2022–4817* ⊕ *www.thepottedpig.com* ⊗ *No dinner Sun.*

WHERE TO STAY

$
HOTEL

⊞ **The Exchange Hotel.** Formerly the Coal Exchange, where it is said the world's first £1 million deal was struck in 1901, this building has now been turned into luxury lodging. **Pros:** historic building; beautiful public areas; fashionable bar. **Cons:** no parking; a 10-minute drive from the city center; restoration ongoing. $ *Rooms from: £89* ✉ *The Exchange Bldg., Mount Stuart Sq.* ☎ *029/2010–7050* ⊕ *www.exchangehotelcardiff.co.uk* ⟿ *60 rooms* ⊖ *No meals.*

$
HOTEL
Fodor's Choice
★

⊞ **Hotel Indigo.** Housed in an art deco shopping arcade on one of the city's main shopping streets, Hotel Indigo is the stylish hotel Cardiff has been waiting for. **Pros:** stylish decor; city center location; excellent roof terrace. **Cons:** rooms are spread between two buildings; no parking on-site; can feel a bit impersonal. $ *Rooms from: £86* ✉ *Dominions Arcade, Queen St.* ☎ *029/2010–2710* ⊕ *www.hotelindigo.com/cardiff* ⟿ *122 rooms* ⊖ *No meals.*

$
B&B/INN

⊞ **Jolyons Boutique Hotel.** This town house, a hop and a skip from the Wales Millennium Centre in Cardiff Bay, bucks the trend in a city where big, modern hotels are usually a safer bet than boutique lodgings. **Pros:** loads of character; eco-friendly toiletries; cozy lounge.

Cons: 10-minute drive from the city center; no elevator; no parking. [$] *Rooms from: £89* ✉ *5 Bute Crescent* ☎ *029/2048–8775* 🌐 *www.jolyons.co.uk* 🛏 *7 rooms* 🍴 *Free Breakfast.*

$ B&B/INN 🏨 **Lincoln House Private Hotel.** Perhaps the best of the many B&Bs on Cathedral Road—a handsome enclave of Victorian houses—this place close to the city center is a great find. **Pros:** good service; handy location; free parking. **Cons:** attractive road is spoiled by traffic; no restaurant; no elevator. [$] *Rooms from: £85* ✉ *118 Cathedral Rd.* ☎ *029/2039–5558* 🌐 *www.lincolnhotel.co.uk* 🛏 *24 rooms* 🍴 *Free Breakfast.*

NIGHTLIFE AND PERFORMING ARTS

NIGHTLIFE

Café Jazz. With live jazz or blues six nights a week, Café Jazz has video monitors in the bar and restaurant so you can enjoy the on-stage action. ✉ *21 St. Mary St.* ☎ *029/2038–7026* 🌐 *www.cafejazzcardiff.com.*

Clwb Ifor Bach. This hot spot, whose name means "Little Ivor's Club" in Welsh, has three floors of eclectic music from funk to folk to rock. They also regularly host gigs for hip, young bands. ✉ *11 Womanby St.* ☎ *029/2023–2199* 🌐 *www.clwb.net.*

PERFORMING ARTS

Fodor's Choice ★ **Chapter Arts Centre.** In the suburb of Canton, a 10-minute cab ride from Cardiff's center, Chapter is the hippest place in town to hang out. There's a cinema showing art-house and independent films; an auditorium for theater and comedy; a contemporary art gallery; and a bar serving food and Welsh craft beer. ✉ *Market Rd.* ☎ *029/2030–4400* 🌐 *www.chapter.org.*

SHOPPING

Cardiff Antiques Centre. In an 1858 arcade, the Cardiff Antiques Centre is a good place to buy vintage jewelry and accessories. ✉ *Royal Arcade* ☎ *029/2039–8891.*

Cardiff Market. The traditional Cardiff Market sells tempting fresh foods beneath its Victorian glass canopy. Be sure to try the Welshcakes at Cardiff Bakestones. ✉ *St. Mary St.* ☎ *029/2087–1214* 🌐 *www.cardiffcouncilproperty.com/cardiff-market.*

Fodor's Choice ★ **Craft in the Bay.** Located opposite Wales Millennium Centre, this shop stocks tasteful arts and crafts from makers around Wales. ✉ *The Flourish, Lloyd George Ave.* ☎ *029/2048–4611* 🌐 *www.makersguildinwales.org.uk.*

Spillers Records. The world's oldest record store stocks vinyl and CDs in every genre and occasionally hosts live gigs on the tiny premises. Established in 1894, it originally sold phonographs and shellac. ✉ 27 *Morgan Arcade* ☎ *029/2022–4905* 🌐 *www.spillersrecords.co.uk.*

12

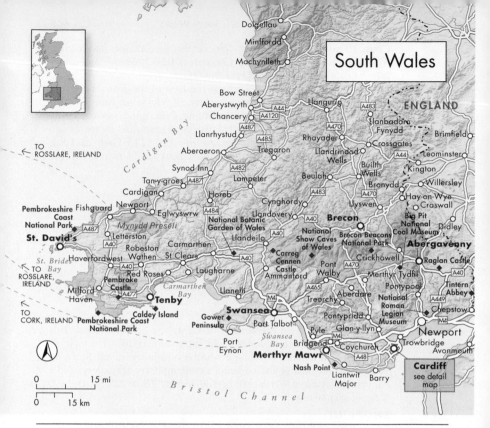

ABERGAVENNY Y FENNI

32 miles northeast of Cardiff.

The market town of Abergavenny, just outside Brecon Beacons National Park, is a popular base for walkers and hikers. It has a ruined castle and is near the industrial history sites at Blaenavon. It's also a foodie hot spot.

GETTING HERE AND AROUND

Abergavenny is on the A40 road, about an hour's drive from Cardiff. Direct trains connect with Cardiff about every half hour and take around 40 minutes.

ESSENTIALS

Visitor Information Abergavenny Tourist Information Centre. ⊠ *Tithe Barn, Monk St.* ☎ *01873/853254* ⊕ *www.visitabergavenny.co.uk.*

EXPLORING

FAMILY **Abergavenny Castle and Museum.** Built early in the 11th century, this castle witnessed a tragic event on Christmas Day, 1176: the Norman knight William de Braose invited the neighboring Welsh chieftains to a feast, and in a crude attempt to gain control of the area, had them all slaughtered as they sat to dine. The Welsh retaliated and virtually demolished the castle. Most of what now remains dates from the 13th and 14th centuries. The castle's 19th-century hunting lodge houses an excellent museum of regional history. There's a re-created saddler's shop and a World War II air-raid shelter, but the Victorian Welsh farmhouse kitchen, with its old utensils and butter molds, is perhaps the most diverting exhibit. ⊠ *Castle St.* ☎ *01873/854282* ⊕ *www.abergavenny-museum.co.uk* ☒ *Free.*

FAMILY
Fodor's Choice
★ **Big Pit National Coal Museum.** For hundreds of years, South Wales has been famous for its mining industry. Decades of decline—particularly during the 1980s—left only a handful of mines in business. The mines around Blaenavon, a small town 7 miles northeast of Abergavenny, have been designated a UNESCO World Heritage Site, and this fascinating museum is the centerpiece. Ex-miners lead you 300 feet underground into a coal mine. You spend just under an hour examining the old stables, machine rooms, and exposed coalfaces. Afterward you can look around an exhibition housed in the old Pithead Baths, including an extraordinary section on child labor in British mines. ■TIP➔ **Children under 3½ feet tall are not allowed on the underground portion of the tour.** ⊠ *Off A4043, Blaenavon* ☎ *029/2057–3650* ⊕ *www.museum. wales* ☒ *Free; £3 parking.*

Blaenavon Ironworks. A UNESCO World Heritage Site, the 1789 Blaenavon Ironworks traces the entire process of iron production in the late 18th century. Well-preserved blast furnaces, a water-balance lift used to transport materials to higher ground, and a terraced row of workers' cottages show how the business operated. ⊠ *A4043, Blaenavon* ☎ *01495/792615* ⊕ *cadw.gov.wales* ☒ *Free* ☉ *Closed Sun.–Wed. in Nov.–Mar.*

FAMILY **Raglan Castle.** Impressively complete from the front, majestically ruined within, Raglan was built in the 15th century and was the childhood home of Henry Tudor (1457–1509), who seized the throne of England in 1485 and became Henry VII. Raglan's heyday was relatively short-lived. The castle was attacked by Parliamentary forces in 1645, during the English Civil War, and has lain in ruins ever since. The hexagonal Great Tower survives in reasonably good condition (you can climb to the top), as do a handful of rooms on the ground floor. ⊠ *A40, Raglan* ☎ *01291/690228* ⊕ *cadw.gov.wales* ☒ *£6.90.*

OFF THE BEATEN PATH **Tintern Abbey.** Literally a stone's throw from the English border, Tintern is one of the region's most romantic monastic ruins. Founded in 1131 by the Cistercians and dissolved by Henry VIII in 1536, it has inspired its fair share of poets and painters over the years—most famously J.M.W. Turner, who painted the transept covered in moss and ivy, and William Wordsworth, who idolized the setting in his poem "Lines Composed a Few Miles Above Tintern Abbey." Come early or late to avoid the crowds. The abbey, 5 miles north of Chepstow and 19 miles southeast of Abergavenny, is on the banks of the River Wye. ⊠ *A466, Tintern* ☎ *01291/689251* ⊕ *cadw.gov.wales* ☒ *£6.90.*

WHERE TO EAT AND STAY

$$$
MODERN BRITISH
Fodor's Choice
★ ✕ **The Walnut Tree.** Regarded as one of the best chefs in the United Kingdom, Shaun Hill has been at the helm of this rustic-chic restaurant 3 miles northeast of Abergavenny since 2008. The focus here is on local, seasonal produce with international influences; lunch is an accessible

£25 for two courses. **Known for:** superb cooking; attractive dining room; peaceful location. [$] *Average main: £25* ✉ *Llanddewi Skirrid* ✥ *Along the B4521 northeast of Abergavenny* ☎ *01873/852797* 🌐 *www.thewalnuttreeinn.com* ⏲ *Closed Sun. and Mon.*

$ HOTEL Fodor's Choice ★ **Angel Hotel.** This country-chic hotel in the town center is renowned for its excellent food, especially the afternoon tea. **Pros:** stylish decor; delicious afternoon tea; friendly, professional staff. **Cons:** not all rooms are in the main building; limited, pricey parking; very busy on weekends. [$] *Rooms from: £95* ✉ *15 Cross St.* ☎ *01873/857121* 🌐 *www.angelabergavenny.com* 🛏 *35 rooms* 🍴 *No meals* [M] *NP7 5EN.*

$$ HOTEL Fodor's Choice ★ **Llansantffraed Court Hotel.** Dating from 1400, this grand country house 4 miles southeast of Abergavenny is set on 20 acres of well-tended grounds with lovely views of the Brecon Beacons. **Pros:** excellent food; peaceful setting; plenty of history. **Cons:** out-of-the-way location; popular wedding venue; haunted history not for anyone afraid of ghosts. [$] *Rooms from: £139* ✉ *Old Raglan Rd., Monmouth* ☎ *01873/840678* 🌐 *www.llch.co.uk* 🛏 *21 rooms* 🍴 *Free Breakfast.*

BRECON ABERHONDDU

19 miles northwest of Abergavenny, 41 miles north of Cardiff.

The historic market town of Brecon is known for its Georgian buildings, narrow passageways, and pleasant riverside walks. It's also the gateway to Brecon Beacons National Park. The town is particularly appealing on the second Saturday of each month, when the farmers' market takes place. A smaller market is also held every Tuesday and Friday. Brecon is also renowned for its jazz festival in August.

GETTING HERE AND AROUND

Brecon is easily accessible from Swansea and Cardiff, as well as many other towns, by direct buses. The nearest railway stations are at Merthyr Tydfil and Abergavenny (both about 19 miles away). Brecon is a handsome town to explore on foot—especially the riverside walk along the Promenade.

EXPLORING

FAMILY Fodor's Choice ★ **Brecon Beacons National Park.** About 5 miles southwest of Brecon you encounter mountains and wild, windswept uplands that are tipped by shafts of golden light when the weather's fine, or fingers of ghostly mist when it's not. This 519-square-mile park is one of Wales's most breathtaking areas, perfect for a hike or scenic drive; it's also one of the world's few accredited International Dark Sky Reserves, which means it's an excellent location for star-gazing. Start at the visitor center on Mynydd Illtyd, a grassy stretch of upland west of the A470. Also known as the Mountain Centre, it's an excellent source of information about the park, including maps and advice on the best routes (guided or self-guided). There's also an excellent tearoom where you can fuel up for the journey or reward yourself with an indulgent slice of cake afterward. If you want to see it all from your car, any road that crosses the Beacons will offer you with beautiful views, but the most spectacular is the high and undulating A4069, between Brynamman and Llangadog in the park's western end. ■ **TIP→ To explore the moorlands on foot, come prepared. Mist and rain descend quickly, and the summits are exposed to high**

One of three national parks in Wales, Brecon Beacons offers some panoramic mountain views, whether you're on foot or in a car.

winds. ⊠ *Off A470, Brecon Beacons National Park* ☎ *01874/623366* ⊕ *www.breconbeacons.org* ✉ *Free; parking £1 for 2 hrs, £2.50 all-day.*

FAMILY
Fodor's Choice
★

Carreg Cennen Castle. On the edge of Brecon Beacons National Park, about 30 miles west of Brecon, this decaying cliff-top fortress was built in the 12th century, and remains of earlier defenses have been found dating back to the Iron Age. The castle, though a ruin, has a partially intact barbican (fortified outer section) and some inner chambers hewn dramatically from the bedrock. The climb to get there is somewhat punishing—you have to trudge up a steep, grassy hill—but the views of the valley, with its patchwork of green fields framed by the peaks of the Black Mountains, are enough to take away whatever breath you have left. Thankfully, there's a tearoom in the farm below the castle to take a breather after the climb. ⊠ *Off Derwydd Rd., Llandeilo* ☎ *01558/822291* ⊕ *www.cadw.wales.gov.uk* ✉ *£5.50.*

FAMILY

National Show Caves of Wales. This underground cave system was discovered by two local men in 1912—make that rediscovered, as one of the caves contained 42 human skeletons that had lain undisturbed for around 7,000 years. The main cave system, Dan Yr Ogof (Welsh for "beneath the cave"), is an impressive natural wonder, particularly the Cathedral Cave with natural stone archways and a dramatic waterfall. The whole thing is pitched at kids, with "dramatic" piped music to "enhance" the atmosphere, and a park featuring 200 life-size models of dinosaurs and other prehistoric creatures. There's also a playground, petting zoo, shire horse center, and Victorian farm. The caves are 17 miles southwest of Brecon. ⊠ *Off A48 or B4310, Abercraf* ☎ *01639/730284* ⊕ *www.show-caves.co.uk* ✉ *£15* ☉ *Closed Nov.–mid-Mar.*

CLOSE UP

Hiking and Biking in Wales

The Wales Coast Path is an 870-mile walking path that snakes along the entire coastline. Linking existing routes like the Pembrokeshire Coast Path in southeast Wales with newer sections, it passes as close to the coastline as possible. Managed by the Welsh government, the route can be pretty wild in places and there isn't always a guardrail, so keep a close eye on small children. Work is currently underway to link it up with other popular routes, which should create an unbroken system of walking trails extending for more than 1,000 miles within a few years.

Other long-distance paths include north–south Offa's Dyke Path, based on the border between England and Wales established by King Offa in the 8th century, and the Glyndr Way, a 128-mile-long highland route that traverses Mid-Wales from the border town of Knighton via Machynlleth to Welshpool. Signposted footpaths in Wales's forested areas are short and easy to follow. Dedicated enthusiasts might prefer the wide-open spaces of Brecon Beacons National Park or the mountains of Snowdonia.

Wales's reputation as both an on-road and off-road cycling mecca is well established. There's an amazing choice of scenic routes and terrain from challenging off-road tracks (🌐 *www.mbwales.com* is for the serious cyclist) to long-distance road rides and gentle family trails; VisitWales has information to get you started.

WHERE TO EAT AND STAY

$$ MODERN BRITISH Fodor's Choice ★ 🍴 **Felin Fach Griffin.** This excellent "restaurant with rooms" is renowned for its creative use of local products and the rustic-chic vibe. Fruit and vegetables come from the Griffin's own organic kitchen garden, while meat is sourced from surrounding estates such as the Welsh Venison Centre. **Known for:** great Sunday lunch; delicious local produce and meat; cozy atmosphere. [$] *Average main: £19* ✉ *A470, Felin Fach* ☎ *01874/620111* 🌐 *www.eatdrinksleep.ltd.uk.*

$ B&B/INN 🏨 **Coach House.** This former coach house in the center of Brecon has been converted into a luxurious place to stay, and the friendly hosts—a wealth of information about the local area—can arrange transport to and from the best walking paths in the Beacons. **Pros:** lovely staff; central location; private parking. **Cons:** on a main road; minimum two-night stay most weekends; supper must be booked in advance. [$] *Rooms from: £89* ✉ *12 Orchard St.* ☎ *01874/620043* 🌐 *www.coachhousebrecon.com* 🛏 *7 rooms* 🍽 *Free Breakfast.*

$ B&B/INN 🏨 **Felin Glais.** In the 17th century Felin Glais was a barn; today it provides spacious and comfortable accommodations but still hasn't lost its ancient character. **Pros:** beautiful building; spacious rooms; good food. **Cons:** dog-friendly environment won't please everyone; cash or check only; cancellations within 72 hours are charged in full. [$] *Rooms from: £95* ✉ *Abersycir* ☎ *01874/623107* 🌐 *www.felinglais.co.uk* 💳 *No credit cards* 🛏 *4 rooms* 🍽 *Free Breakfast.*

12

NIGHTLIFE AND PERFORMING ARTS

Theatr Brycheiniog. On the canal, Theatr Brycheiniog is the town's main venue for plays, live music, and comedy shows. It also has a café (lunch only) and a bar. ✉ *Canal Wharf* ☎ *01874/611622* ⊕ *www. brycheiniog.co.uk.*

SPORTS AND THE OUTDOORS

Biped Cycles. The Brecon Beacons contain some of the best cycling routes in Britain. Biped Cycles will rent you the right bike and equipment. ✉ *10 Ship St.* ☎ *01874/622296* ⊕ *www.bipedcycles.co.uk.*

SHOPPING

Fodor'sChoice **The Hours.** This lovely little building on the main shopping street sells
★ a good selection of books by Welsh writers as well as guides to the area. It also has a very nice café serving sandwiches and salads made with local ingredients. Local artwork adorns the walls. ✉ *15 Ship St.* ☎ *01874/622800* ⊕ *www.the-hours.co.uk.*

MERTHYR MAWR

45 miles south of Brecon, 22 miles west of Cardiff.

Fodor'sChoice As you cross over an ancient stone bridge into Merthyr Mawr, you feel
★ as if you've entered another world. From stone cottages with beehive-shape thatched roofs to the Victorian-era Church of St. Teilo, with the pieces of its long-gone 5th-century predecessor lined up in its churchyard, it's an idyllic place to wander around. The picturesque ruin of Ogmore Castle is just off the B4524, but the most memorable way to reach it is via the walking path that starts in the car park at the very southern tip of the village. The mile-long route goes through a farm and past a Shetland pony stable.

GETTING HERE AND AROUND

Merthyr Mawr is signposted from the A48 and B4524, 7 miles southwest of junction 35 on the M4. The nearest train station is in Bridgend. There's no bus service to the village, but you can take bus 303 from Bridgend to Ogmore, just south of the river.

EXPLORING

Fodor'sChoice **Nash Point.** Just a few miles south of Merthyr Mawr is this stunning
★ promontory overlooking the Bristol Channel. Twin lighthouses stand guard against the elements; one is still operational, but the other is open for tours. This is also a popular picnic spot, and a small snack kiosk is open during summer months. Nothing beats this place at sunset, when the evening sky ignites in a riot of color. It's one of the most romantic spots in South Wales. ⚠ **There's no guardrail on the cliff, so keep a close eye on children.** ✉ *Marcross* ☎ *07850/047721* ⊕ *www.nashpoint.co.uk* ▨ *Free; lighthouse £4* ⊗ *Closed weekdays and Nov.–Feb.*

Ogmore Castle. Just south of the village are these atmospheric ruins, nestled by a river that can only be crossed via stepping-stones. A number of legends are associated with the castle, one concerning a ghost that supposedly forces passersby to embrace a large rock known as the "Goblin Stone." When you try to draw back, so the story goes, you find that your hands and feet have become part of the rock. ✉ *Ogmore Rd.* ▨ *Free.*

Stretching west of Swansea, the Gower Peninsula has some stunning beaches, including Rhossili.

WHERE TO EAT

$ BRITISH FAMILY 🍴 **The Plough and Harrow.** A short drive from Nash Point is this friendly local pub, on the edge of the tiny cliff-top village of Monknash. The food is delicious and unfussy; the menu changes regularly, but features tasty pub classics like burgers and fish-and-chips. **Known for:** craft beer and cider; delicious pies; lively atmosphere. [$] *Average main: £10* ✉ *Off Heol Las, Monknash* ☎ *01656/890209.*

SWANSEA ABERTAWE

22 miles northwest of Merthyr Mawr, 40 miles west of Cardiff.

The birthplace of poet Dylan Thomas (1914–53), Swansea adores its native son. Every year the poet is honored with his own day: May 14th, the anniversary of when *Under Milk Wood* was first read onstage. For many years, Swansea wasn't a place that inspired much poetry; heavily bombed in World War II, it was clumsily rebuilt. However, now times are changing and a cultural renaissance is taking place, with a thriving arts-and-music scene developing in recent years. There are also several good museums. In the surrounding area, the National Botanic Gardens and Laugharne make for interesting diversions, and the stunning Gower Peninsula contains some of the country's best beaches.

GETTING HERE AND AROUND

There's an hourly rail service from London's Paddington Station. The city has direct National Express bus connections to other parts of Wales, as well as to London and other cities.

ESSENTIALS
Visitor Information Swansea Tourist Information. ⊕ *www.visitswanseabay. com.*

EXPLORING

Dylan Thomas Centre. Situated on the banks of the Tawe in the Maritime Quarter, the Dylan Thomas Centre celebrates the life of the writer with an excellent permanent exhibition as well as literary events and activities. In summer, guided tours showcasing Dylan's Swansea start from here. There's also a cozy little café serving locally sourced products. Fans of the poet can buy a booklet here that outlines the Dylan Thomas Trail around South Wales. It includes the Boathouse (now a museum) in Laugharne, where the poet lived and wrote for the last four years of his life. ⊠ *Somerset Pl.* ☎ *01792/463980* ⊕ *www. dylanthomas.com* ⊡ *Free.*

5 Cwmdonkin Drive. Dylan Thomas was born in this suburban Edwardian house, which remains a place of pilgrimage for the poet's devotees. You can wander the house with no restrictions (they're proud of the fact that nothing is roped off), or prebook tours that are tailored according to how much time you want to spend here. You can also arrange tours of other Thomas-related sites in Swansea and farther afield in the region. The house can be rented as self-catering accommodation for around £150 per night. You can also book lunch, afternoon tea, or, for 4r to 10 diners, dinner. ⊠ *5 Cwmdonkin Dr.* ☎ *01792/472555* ⊕ *www. dylanthomasbirthplace.com* ⊡ *£8.*

FAMILY
Fodor'sChoice
★

Glynn Vivian Art Gallery. Founded in 1911 by a bequest from Richard Glynn Vivian (1835–1910), an art collector and philanthropist whose family were prominent industrialists in the city, the public gallery is one of Swansea's highlights. Exhibits include an internationally important collection of Swansea china as well as works by acclaimed local artists. There is usually a busy calendar of events, including regular temporary exhibitions; check the website for more details. ⊠ *Alexandra Rd.* ☎ *01792/516900* ⊕ *www.swansea.gov.uk/glynnvivian* ⊡ *Free* ⊙ *Closed Mon.*

FAMILY
Fodor'sChoice
★

Gower Peninsula. This peninsula, which stretches westward from Swansea, was the first part of Britain to be designated an Area of Outstanding Natural Beauty. Its shores are a succession of sheltered sandy bays and awesome headlands. The seaside resort of Mumbles, on the outskirts of Swansea, is the most famous town along the route. It's a pleasant place to wander on a sunny afternoon, with a Norman castle, an amusement pier, and a seaside promenade, as well as a variety of independent cafés and boutiques. Farther along the peninsula, the secluded Pwlldu Bay can only be reached on foot from nearby villages like Southgate. A few miles westward is the more accessible (and very popular) Three Cliffs Bay, with its sweeping views and wide, sandy beach. At the far western tip of the peninsula, Rhossili has perhaps the best beach of all. Its unusual, snaking causeway—known locally as the Worm's Head—is inaccessible at high tide. Gower is a popular destination with surfers and you'll find many other water sports offered here. ⊠ *Swansea* ⊕ *www.explore-gower.co.uk.*

12

Laugharne. According to Dylan Thomas, this attractive estuary town 39 miles west of Swansea was the "strangest town in Wales"; nonetheless, he spent the last four years of his adult life here and is buried in the graveyard at St. Martin's Church. Visitors should first head to the Boathouse, where Dylan lived with his family from 1949 to 1953 and where he wrote *Do Not Go Gentle* and *Under Milk Wood*. Then head for a drink at The Brown's, his local pub. Be sure to also check out the ruined castle, browse the secondhand bookshop, and enjoy a coastal walk. Laugharne buzzes in April when the arts festival, Laugharne Weekend, takes place. 🌐 *www.laugharnelines.co.uk*.

FAMILY Fodor's Choice ★ **National Botanic Garden of Wales.** This 568-acre, 18th-century estate is dotted with lakes, fountains, and a Japanese garden. The centerpiece is the Norman Foster–designed Great Glass House, the largest single-span greenhouse in the world, which blends into the curving landforms of the Tywi Valley. The greenhouse's interior landscape includes a 40-foot-deep ravine and thousands of plants from all over the world. The Ghost Forest is a stunning art installation, made from the carved stumps of 10 giant hardwood trees—a powerful statement on how rapidly the world's forests are being destroyed. The grounds have lovely views across the Carmarthenshire countryside, especially from the Paxton's View lookout point. It's marked by Paxton's Tower, a Gothic folly built to honor Horatio Nelson, now owned by the National Trust (it's free to wander, though there's nothing to see inside). The garden, 20 miles northwest of Swansea, is signposted off the main road between Swansea and Carmarthen. ✉ *Off A48 or B4310, Llanarthne* ☎ *01558/667149* 🌐 *www.gardenofwales.org.uk* 🎟 *£10.50*.

Swansea Market. Swansea's covered market, part of the Quadrant Shopping Centre, is one of the best fresh-foods markets in Wales. You can buy cockles from the Penclawdd beds on the nearby Gower Peninsula, and laverbread, that unique Welsh delicacy made from seaweed, which is usually served with bacon and eggs. ✉ *Oxford St.* ☎ *01792/654296* 🌐 *www.swanseaindoormarket.co.uk* 🕑 *Closed Sun.*

FAMILY **Swansea Museum.** Founded in 1841, this museum contains a quirky and eclectic collection that includes an Egyptian mummy, local archaeological exhibits, and the intriguing Cabinet of Curiosity, which holds artifacts from Swansea's past. In 2016, a forgotten Flemish masterpiece by Jacob Jordaens (1593–1678) was discovered in the museum's storeroom and is now on show. ✉ *Victoria Rd.* ☎ *01792/653763* 🌐 *www.swanseamuseum.co.uk* 🎟 *Free* 🕑 *Closed Mon.*

WHERE TO EAT AND STAY

$$$ MODERN BRITISH 🍴 **Beach House.** On the beach at Oxwich, this stylish eatery is considered one of the best in all of Wales. The beautifully presented dishes are made using the best local ingredients, particularly seafood. **Known for:** beachside location; creative fish dishes; interesting wine list. [$] *Average main: £25* ✉ *Oxwich Beach* ☎ *01792/390965* 🌐 *www.beachhouseoxwich.co.uk* 🕑 *Closed Mon. and Tues.*

$$ BRITISH 🍴 **The Cliff.** After a bracing walk around Three Cliffs Bay, head to this restaurant on the top floor of Three Cliffs Coffee Shop. The emphasis here is on showcasing local produce, including cured meats

and salt-marsh lamb. **Known for:** dishes with local produce; delicious cakes and other desserts; coastal location. [$] *Average main: £15* ✉ *68 Southgate Rd.* ☎ *01792/399030* 🌐 *www.the-cliff.co.uk* 🕒 *No dinner Sun.–Tues.*

$$ MODERN BRITISH Fodor's Choice ★ 🍴 **Hanson at the Chelsea.** Tucked down a lane off Wind Street, the town's main nightlife area, this cozy restaurant is the most consistently reliable for good food in the city center. The London Ritz–trained chef deftly turns out delicious dishes made with the best local ingredients. **Known for:** one of the city's best restaurants; delicious fish dishes; affordable two-course lunch menu. [$] *Average main: £18* ✉ *17 St. Mary St.* ☎ *01792/464068* 🌐 *www.hansonatthechelsea.co.uk* 🕒 *Closed Sun.*

$ HOTEL FAMILY Fodor's Choice ★ 🏨 **Morgans.** Now a hotel, the Victorian-era Port Authority building in the Maritime Quarter has lost none of its period features: moldings, pillars, stained glass, and wood floors. **Pros:** near the marina; short walk to shops; historic building. **Cons:** no room service in Townhouse; on the busy main road into Swansea; bar gets crowded. [$] *Rooms from: £85* ✉ *Somerset Pl.* ☎ *01792/484848* 🌐 *www.morganshotel.co.uk* 🛏 *42 rooms* 🍽 *Free Breakfast.*

$$$$ RENTAL FAMILY 🏨 **Scamper Holidays.** At the far end of Gower, a local couple rents out luxury shepherd huts in an idyllic, bucolic location near Rhossili Beach. **Pros:** quirky accommodations; location by the beach; welcoming hosts. **Cons:** minimum two-night stay; outside bathroom facilities; maximum of five people per hut. [$] *Rooms from: £250* ✉ *Pitton Cross Caravan & Camping Park* ☎ *01792/202325* 🌐 *www.scamperholidays.co.uk* 🕒 *Closed Oct.–Mar.* 🛏 *18 huts* 🍽 *No meals.*

TENBY DINBYCH-Y-PYSGOD

53 miles west of Swansea.

Fodor's Choice ★ Pastel-color Georgian houses cluster around a harbor in this seaside town, which became a fashionable resort in the 19th century and is still popular. Two golden sandy beaches stretch below the hotel-lined cliff top. Medieval Tenby's ancient town walls still stand, enclosing narrow streets and passageways full of shops, inns, and places to eat. From the harbor you can take a short boat trip to Caldey Island, with its active Cistercian community.

GETTING HERE AND AROUND

Tenby is on the southwest Wales rail route from London's Paddington Station. You have to change trains at Swansea or Newport. The center of Tenby, a maze of narrow medieval streets, has parking restrictions. In summer, downtown is closed to traffic, so park in one of the lots and take the shuttle buses.

ESSENTIALS

Visitor Information Tenby Tourist Information Centre. ✉ *Upper Park Rd.* ☎ *01437/775603* 🌐 *www.visitpembrokeshire.com.*

EXPLORING

FAMILY **Caldey Island.** This beautiful little island off the coast at Tenby has whitewashed stone buildings that lend it a Mediterranean feel. The island is best known for its Cistercian order, whose black-and-white-robed monks make a famous perfume from the local plants. You can visit tiny St. Illtyd's Church to see the Caldey Stone, an early Christian artifact from circa AD 600, engraved in Latin and ancient Celtic. St. David's Church, on a hill above the village, is a simple Norman chapel noted for its art-deco stained glass. The monastery itself isn't open to the public, but its church has a public viewing gallery if you want to observe a service. Boats to Caldey Island leave from Tenby's harbor every 20 minutes or so between Easter and October. ✉ *Caldey Island* ☎ *01834/844453* 🌐 *www.caldeyislandwales.com* 🎟 *Free; boats £13 round-trip* 🕓 *Closed Sun.*

FAMILY **Pembroke Castle.** About 10 miles east of Tenby is this remarkably complete Norman fortress dating from 1199, and where Henry VII was born in 1457. Its walls remain stout, its gatehouse mighty, and the enormous cylindrical keep proved so impregnable to cannon fire in the Civil War that Cromwell's men had to starve out its Royalist defenders. Climb the towers and walk the walls for fine views. A well-stocked gift shop sells faux-medieval knickknacks. ✉ *Westgate Hill, Pembroke* ☎ *01646/681510* 🌐 *www.pembroke-castle.co.uk* 🎟 *£6.60.*

FAMILY **Tenby Museum and Art Gallery.** Close to the castle, this small but informative museum recalls the town's maritime history and its growth as a fashionable resort. Kids will appreciate the section on Tenby's role in the golden age of piracy. Two art galleries feature works by local artists. ✉ *Castle Hill* ☎ *01834/842809* 🌐 *www.tenbymuseum.org.uk* 🎟 *£4.95* 🕓 *Closed Sun. and Mon.*

FAMILY **Tudor Merchant's House.** This late-15th-century home shows how a prosperous trader would have lived in Tudor times. Kids can try on Tudor-style costumes. The gift shop sells handmade pottery based on unique, original designs found at the house. ✉ *Quay Hill* ☎ *01834/842279* 🌐 *www.nationaltrust.org.uk/tudor-merchants-house* 🎟 *£5.25* 🕓 *Closed Tues.*

WHERE TO EAT AND STAY

$$ MODERN BRITISH 🍴 **The Lighthouse Kitchen.** On Tenby's main street, this informal, contemporary café-restaurant emphasizes local produce with a menu that changes with the seasons. Burgers, made with beef from the area, are a popular option for lunch or dinner; the skinny fries are also delicious. **Known for:** good-value lunch dishes; bright, contemporary dining room; great local beer. [$] *Average main: £16* ✉ *Vernon House, St. Julian's St.* ☎ *01834/844555* 🌐 *www.thelighthousetenby.com.*

$$$ BRITISH Fodor's Choice ★ 🍴 **Plantagenet House.** Flickering candles, open fireplaces, exposed stone walls, and top-notch locally sourced food are hallmarks of this popular restaurant and bar. The menu contains a selection of Welsh-reared steaks and other meat dishes, but outstanding seafood is the real specialty. **Known for:** romantic setting; extensive menu with local produce; great seafood dishes. [$] *Average main: £23* ✉ *Quay Hill* ☎ *01834/842350* 🌐 *www.plantagenettenby.co.uk* 🕓 *Closed Jan.–mid-Feb.*

$$ HOTEL Fodor's Choice ★ 🏨 **Penally Abbey.** Built on the site of a 6th-century abbey in 5 acres of lush forest overlooking Camarthen Bay, this dignified 18th-century house is awash with period details. **Pros:** informal luxury; great views; friendly hosts. **Cons:** cheaper rooms are in the Coach House; seven-day

cancellation rule; no elevator. Ⓢ *Rooms from: £145* ✉ *Off A4139, 2 miles west of Tenby, Penally* ☎ *01834/843033* ⊕ *www.penally-abbey. com* ◷ *Closed Jan.* ⇴ *11 rooms* ⦿❘ *Free Breakfast.*

$$$
HOTEL
Fodor's Choice
★

⌖ **St. Brides Spa Hotel.** Between Amroth and Tenby, this luxury hotel has a breathtaking location perched above Carmarthen Bay; most of the superbly appointed rooms have stunning sea views. **Pros:** amazing views; wonderful spa; good restaurant. **Cons:** steep walk from the beach; minimum stay on weekends; pricey for the area. Ⓢ *Rooms from: £195* ✉ *St. Brides Hill, Saundersfoot* ☎ *01834/812304* ⊕ *www. stbridesspahotel.com* ⇴ *34 rooms* ⦿❘ *Free Breakfast.*

SPORTS AND THE OUTDOORS

The town's beaches are hugely popular in summertime. North Beach is the busiest, with shops and a little café along the promenade. The adjoining Harbour Beach is prettier and more secluded. Castle Beach is in a little cove where you can walk out to a small island at low tide. Past that is South Beach, which stretches for more than a mile.

ST. DAVIDS TYDDEWI

35 miles northwest of Tenby.

Despite its minuscule size, this community of fewer than 1,800 people isn't a village or a town—it's actually Britain's smallest city. Historically, little St. Davids has punched above its weight due to the presence of St. Davids Cathedral, the resting place of the patron saint of Wales and once a major destination for pilgrims. These days, visitors with time on their hands might want to consider approaching the city via the Wales Coast Path, around the St. Davids headland from St. Justinian to Caerfai Bay. You might also consider a wildlife-watching boat trip or an afternoon surfing at Whitesands Beach. In May and June the town's hedgerows and coastal paths are ablaze with wildflowers. The Pembrokeshire Coast National Park Visitor Centre is also here and features an exhibition of works by Pembrokeshire artists, notably Graham Sutherland.

GETTING HERE AND AROUND

St. Davids is on the A487. The nearest train station is 14 miles southeast in Haverfordwest. Bus 411 travels from Haverfordwest to St. Davids every hour or so.

ESSENTIALS

Visitor Information Oriel y Parc Gallery and Visitor Centre. ✉ *The Grove, St. Davids* ☎ *01437/720392* ⊕ *www.pembrokeshirecoast.wales.*

EXPLORING

OFF THE BEATEN PATH

Last Invasion Tapestry. The 100-foot-long Last Invasion Tapestry, on display in the Town Hall in Fishguard, is modeled on the famous Bayeux Tapestry depicting the Norman invasion of 1066. This modern version marks a lesser known and certainly less successful assault on the country. In 1797, a unit of French soldiers, led by an Irish-American general, landed in Fishguard Harbour. They were defeated by a hastily assembled local militia, which included many women. The impressive tapestry, commissioned to mark the event's 200th anniversary, took

70 local women more than 40,000 hours to complete. Fishguard is 16 miles northeast of St. Davids off the A487. ✉ *Fishguard Town Hall, Market Sq., Fishguard* ☎ *01437/776638* 🌐 *www.lastinvasiontapestry.co.uk* 🎟 *Free* 🕒 *Closed Sun.*

Fodor's Choice ★ **Pembrokeshire Coast National Park.** By far the smallest of the country's three national parks, Pembrokeshire Coast is no less strikingly beautiful than the other two. The park has several Blue Flag beaches and a host of spectacular cliff-top drives and walks, including some of the most popular stretches of the Wales Coast Path. The park has a smattering of historic sites, including the impossibly picturesque St. Davids Cathedral, built in a Viking-proof nook by the Irish Sea. The information center in St. Davids is a good place to start. ✉ *Oriel Y Parc Gallery and Visitor Centre, The Grove, St. Davids* ☎ *01437/720392* 🌐 *www.pembrokeshirecoast.wales* 🎟 *Free.*

Fodor's Choice ★ **St. Davids Cathedral.** The idyllic valley location of this cathedral helped protect the church from Viking raiders by hiding it from the view of invaders who came by sea. Originally founded by St. David himself around AD 600, the current building dates from the 12th century, although it has been added to at various times since. You must climb down 39 steps (known locally as the Thirty-Nine Articles) to enter the grounds; then start at the Gatehouse, with its exhibition on the history of the building. In the cathedral itself, the 15th-century choir stalls still have their original floor tiles, while the Holy Trinity Chapel contains an intricate fan-vaulted ceiling and a casket said to contain the patron saint's bones. ■ **TIP→ Don't miss the Treasury and its illuminated gospels, silver chalices, and 700-year-old golden bishop's crosier.** At the rear of the grounds of St. Davids Cathedral are the ruins of the 13th-century Bishop's Palace, particularly beautiful at dusk. In August, guided tours costing £5 begin Monday at 11:30 and Friday at 2:30, and on other days by arrangement. The cathedral has a good café. ✉ *The Close, St. Davids* ☎ *01437/720202* 🌐 *www.stdavidscathedral.org.uk* 🎟 *Free; £3 donation requested.*

WHERE TO STAY

$$$ HOTEL 🏨 **Twr-Y-Felin Hotel.** This luxury hotel on the southeast edge of the city features spacious, contemporary rooms, a restaurant with delicious Welsh produce, and a strong contemporary art collection. **Pros:** contemporary luxury; good restaurant; excellent art collection. **Cons:** brown decor might not appeal to some; limited facilities; on the pricier side. [$] *Rooms from: £180* ✉ *Ffordd Caerfai, St. Davids* ☎ *01437/725555* 🌐 *www.twryfelinhotel.com* 🛏 *21 rooms* 🍴 *Free Breakfast* ☞ *No children under 12.*

MID-WALES

Traditional market towns and country villages, small seaside resorts, quiet roads, and rolling landscapes filled with sheep farms, forests, and lakes make up Mid-Wales, the country's green and rural heart. There are no cities here—the area's largest town is barely more than a big village. Outside of one or two towns, such as Aberystwyth and Llandrindod

Wells, accommodations are mainly country inns, small hotels, and rural farmhouses. This area also has some splendid country-house hotels.

There are no motorways through Mid-Wales, and the steam railways that once linked this area with Cardiff are long gone. Getting around requires a bit of advance planning, but it's worth the trouble. The bibliophilic charms of Hay-on-Wye have made the town world famous, while the countryside around Aberystwyth is peppered with peaceful sandy beaches and dramatic beauty spots.

12

HAY-ON-WYE Y GELLI GANDRYLL

57 miles north of Cardiff, 25 miles north of Abergavenny.

Fodor'sChoice
★
With its crumbling old castle and low-slung buildings framed by lolloping green hills, Hay-on-Wye is a beautiful little place. In 1961 Richard Booth established a small secondhand bookshop here. Other booksellers soon got in on the act, and now there are dozens of shops. It's now the largest secondhand bookselling center in the world, and priceless 14th-century manuscripts rub spines with "job lots" selling for a few pounds.

For 10 days every May and June, Hay-on-Wye is taken over by its Literary Festival, a celebration of literature that attracts famous writers from all over the world. (Bill Clinton, himself an attendee, once called it "the Woodstock of the mind.") Plan ahead if you want to attend, as hotels get booked several months in advance.

GETTING HERE AND AROUND
You'll need a car to get to Hay. Use one of the public lots on the outskirts of town and walk—the whole town is accessible on foot. The nearest train stations are Builth Wells in Wales (19 miles) and Hereford in England (22 miles).

ESSENTIALS
Visitor Information Hay-on-Wye Tourist Information Bureau. ⊠ *Chapel Cottage, Oxford Rd., Hay-on-wye* ☎ *01497/820144* ⊕ *www.hay-on-wye.co.uk/ tourism.*

EXPLORING
FAMILY **Gospel Pass.** About 5 miles south of Hay on the B4350 is the highest mountain pass in Wales (1,801 feet). Park your car at the top, and take a walk along part of Offa's Dyke. ⊠ *Hay-on-wye* 🕁 *Free.*

Hay Castle. On a hilltop are the handsome remains of a 12th-century castle keep, jutting out from behind a 16th-century manor house. The castle is in a dilapidated state and closed to the public. However, a restoration project is due to begin in 2018 with the eventual goal of turning it into an arts center. ⊠ *Castle St., Hay-on-wye* ⊕ *www.haycastletrust.org.*

WHERE TO EAT AND STAY
$$
BRITISH
✕ **Old Black Lion.** This 17th-century coaching inn close to Hay's center is ideal for a lunch break after you're done ransacking the nearby bookshops. The restaurant's sophisticated cooking emphasizes local meats and produce—in, for example, a pork, apple, and sage burger, or roast salmon in a white-wine-and-cheese sauce. **Known**

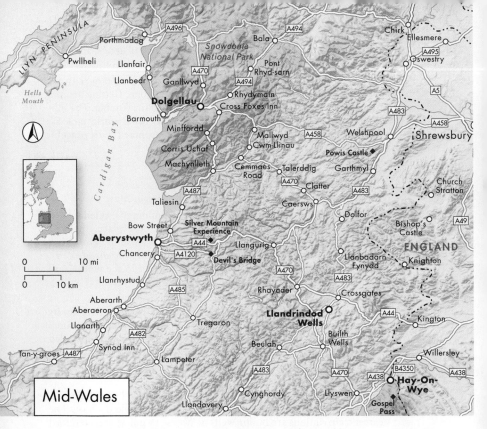

Mid-Wales

for: charming building; craft beer and local cider; great breakfasts. **$** *Average main: £15* ✉ *Lion St., Hay-on-wye* ☎ *01497/820841* ⊕ *www.oldblacklion.co.uk.*

$$$ 🏨 **Llangoed Hall.** This magnificent Jacobean mansion on the banks of
HOTEL the River Wye, about 7 miles west of Hay-on-Wye, has beautiful fab-
Fodor's Choice rics and furnishings, open fireplaces, a sweeping carved staircase, and
★ a paneled library dating back to 1632. **Pros:** secluded setting by River
Wye; wonderful art collection; regular special events and offers. **Cons:**
often filled with wedding parties; minimum stay sometimes required;
no attractions within walking distance. **$** *Rooms from: £175* ✉ *A470,
Llyswen* ☎ *01874/754525* ⊕ *www.llangoedhall.co.uk* ⬎ *23 rooms*
🍽 *Free Breakfast.*

$$ 🏨 **The Swan.** Once a coaching inn, this sophisticated lodging on the
HOTEL edge of town retains its sense of history. **Pros:** gorgeous building;
popular bar; good food. **Cons:** wedding parties dominate in summer;
some rooms are small; narrow, steep staircases. **$** *Rooms from: £105*
✉ *Church St., Hay-on-wye* ☎ *01497/821188* ⊕ *www.swanathay.co.uk*
⬎ *19 rooms* 🍽 *No meals.*

SHOPPING

The Thursday Market takes over much of the town center every Thursday
morning. Traders sell everything from antiques to home-baked cakes.

Boz Books. The kind of dusty old bookshop you see in movies, Boz Books has an impressive range of 19th-century first editions, including many by Dickens. ✉ *13A Castle St., Hay-on-wye* ☎ *01497/821277* ⊕ *www. bozbooks.co.uk.*

Murder and Mayhem. True to its name, this shop specializes in crime and horror. Head upstairs for a cheaper and more eclectic selection, including old pulp novellas. ✉ *5 Lion St., Hay-on-wye* ☎ *01497/821613.*

Fodor's Choice
★ **Richard Booth Books.** Shopkeeper Richard Booth once tried to declare Hay an independent kingdom—with himself as king. His bookstore has a huge collection from all over the world, piled haphazardly across two labyrinthine floors. There's also a tiny cinema (around the corner on Brook Street) and a café along with regular events. ✉ *44 Lion St., Hay-on-wye* ☎ *01497/820322* ⊕ *www.boothbooks.co.uk.*

FAMILY **Rose's Books.** Easy to spot for its fuchsia-pink front, Rose's Books is devoted entirely to children's books, including rare first editions. ✉ *14 Broad St., Hay-on-wye* ☎ *01497/820013* ⊕ *www.rosesbooks.com.*

LLANDRINDOD WELLS LLANDRINDOD

27 miles north of Hay-on-Wye, 67 miles north of Cardiff.

Also known as Llandod, the old spa town of Llandrindod Wells preserves its Victorian look with turrets, cupolas, loggias, and balustrades everywhere. Cross over to South Crescent, passing the Glen Usk Hotel with its wrought-iron balustrade and the Victorian bandstand in the gardens opposite, and you reach Middleton Street, a Victorian thoroughfare. From there, head to Rock Park and the path that leads to the Pump Room. This historic building is now an alternative health center, but visitors can freely "take the waters."

GETTING HERE AND AROUND
There are about half a dozen trains daily from Cardiff Central Station, and the journey takes around three to four hours. Direct trains from Swansea and Shrewsbury also stop here, but they're less frequent.

ESSENTIALS
Visitor Information Llandrindod Wells Tourist information Centre. ✉ *The Old Town Hall, Temple St.* ☎ *01597/822600* ⊕ *www.llandrindod.co.uk.*

EXPLORING
OFF THE BEATEN PATH
Powis Castle. Continuously occupied since the 13th century, Powis Castle rises above the town of Welshpool. One of the most elegant residential castles in Britain, Powis is equally renowned for its magnificent terraced gardens. The interior contains an outstanding art collection, from Greek vases to paintings by Thomas Gainsborough and Joshua Reynolds. The **Clive of India Museum** contains perhaps the most extensive private collection of antique Indian art in Britain. Powis Castle is north of Llandrindod Wells on the A483. ✉ *A483, Welshpool* ☎ *01938/551944* ⊕ *www.nationaltrust.org.uk/powis-castle-and-garden* 🎫 *£14.30.*

Radnorshire Museum. In Memorial Gardens, this museum tells the story of the town's development from prehistory onwards and includes a small collection of Roman and medieval artifacts. The largest and

Hay-on-Wye's claims to fame are its many secondhand bookstores and the annual Literary Festival.

most interesting section is devoted to the town's Victorian heyday, with some of the "cures" at the spa explained in detail. ✉ *Temple St.* ☎ *01597/824513* 🌐 *customer.powys.gov.uk/article/1703/radnorshire-museum* 🎟 *£1* 🕒 *Closed Sun.*

WHERE TO EAT AND STAY

$ MEDITERRANEAN 🍴 **Sugar and Spice.** This sweet and friendly little bistro looks unassuming from the outside, but its pan-Mediterranean fare has won over legions of local fans. Choose from the selection of tapas (Spanish with a hint of Greek), fresh pasta or pizza, a Mediterranean salad, or just a tasty hamburger. **Known for:** good selection of tapas; creative cocktails; Mediterranean flavors. [$] *Average main: £14* ✉ *Park Crescent* ☎ *01597/824442* 🌐 *www.sugarandspicebistro.co.uk* 🕒 *No dinner Sun.–Thurs.*

$$$ HOTEL 🏨 **Lake Country House Hotel & Spa.** The place to go for total Victorian country elegance, Lake Country and its 50 acres of sloping lawns contain a trout-filled lake bordered by an impressive spa. **Pros:** superb grounds; good food; luxurious spa. **Cons:** remote location; dress code in evenings; dinner is a bit pricey. [$] *Rooms from: £205* ✉ *Off B4519, Llangammarch Wells* ☎ *01591/620202* 🌐 *www.lakecountryhouse.co.uk* 🛏 *30 rooms* 🍽 *Free Breakfast.*

$$ HOTEL 🏨 **The Metropole Hotel & Spa.** This grand-looking hotel from 1896 is surprisingly contemporary on the inside, with modern furnishings that complement the original architectural flourishes. **Pros:** very central; good service; inexpensive spa. **Cons:** lacks character; can be taken over by conferences; popular meeting place for vintage car and motorbike owners. [$] *Rooms from: £121* ✉ *Temple St.* ☎ *01597/823700* 🌐 *www.metropole.co.uk* 🛏 *120 rooms* 🍽 *Free Breakfast.*

ABERYSTWYTH

41 miles northwest of Llandrindod Wells via A44, 118 miles northwest of Cardiff.

A pleasingly eccentric combination of faded Victorian seaside resort and artsy college town, Aberystwyth is the largest community in Mid-Wales, with a population of barely 16,000. When the weather's fine, the beaches along the bay fill up with sunbathers; when it's not, waves crash so ferociously against the seawall that even the hotels across the street get soaked. To the east of the town are the Cambrian Mountains and the Veil of Rheidol, which can be visited by steam train.

GETTING HERE AND AROUND

All journeys from South Wales are routed through Shrewsbury and take four to five hours. From London, the trip here takes five to six hours. Long-distance buses are infrequent and painfully slow, though the local bus system is good. There are two roads to Aberystwyth, both of them among the most scenic in Wales: the coastal A487 and the mountainous A44.

ESSENTIALS

Visitor Information Aberystwyth Tourist Information Centre. ⊠ *Ceredigion Museum, Terrace Rd.* ☎ *01970/612125* ⊕ *www.visitmidwales.co.uk.*

EXPLORING

Aberystwyth Castle. The British writer Caitlin Moran once wrote fondly of Aberystwyth's "Glitter-glue sea and smashed-cake castle," and these crumbling ruins at the southern end of the bay do have an endearing quality. Built in 1277, the castle was one of the key strongholds captured in the early 15th century by Owain Glyndwr, a Welsh prince who led the country's last serious bid for independence from England. Today it's a romantic, windswept ruin, rather incongruously used as a cut-through walking path by locals for whom it's nothing out of the ordinary at all. To find the ruins, just walk along the bay, away from the town center; they are located just after the small pier. ⊠ *New Promenade* ☜ *Free.*

FAMILY **Aberystwyth Cliff Railway.** The Victorian-era Aberystwyth Cliff Railway deposits you at the top of Constitution Hill. Opened in 1896, it's the longest electric cliff railway in Britain. ⊠ *Cliff Terr.* ☎ *01970/617642* ⊕ *www.aberystwythcliffrailway.co.uk* ☜ *£5 round-trip* ⊘ *Closed Nov.–Easter.*

Ceredigion Museum. Housed on the upper floor of a flamboyant 1905 Edwardian theater, the Ceredigion Museum has collections related to folk history and the building's own music hall past. Highlights include a reconstructed mud-walled cottage from 1850 and items illustrating the region's seafaring, lead-mining, and farming history. There's a nice café here selling local products, and the tourist information center is downstairs. ⊠ *Terrace Rd.* ☎ *01970/633088* ⊕ *www.ceredigionmuseum.wales* ☜ *Free* ⊘ *Closed Sun.*

FAMILY **Constitution Hill.** At the northern end of the beach promenade, Constitution Hill dominates the skyline. From the top you can see much of the Welsh coastline (and, on *exceptionally* clear days, Ireland). There's a small café at the top and plenty of space for a picnic. If you're feeling hale and hearty, there's a long footpath that zigzags up to the 430-foot summit. From there, a 5-mile-long coastal path stretches to the village of Borth, a smaller, sleepier resort north of Aberystwyth where the remains of a 3,000-year-old petrified forest may be seen on the beach at low tide. ✉ *Aberystwyth.*

FAMILY **Great Aberystwyth Camera Obscura.** A modern version of a Victorian amusement, Great Aberystwyth Camera Obscura is a massive 14-inch lens that gives you a bird's-eye view of Cardigan Bay and 26 Welsh mountain peaks. It's reached via the Aberystwyth Cliff Railway. ✉ *Cliff Terr.* ☎ *01970/617642* 🌐 *www.aberystwythcliffrailway.co.uk* 🎟 *Free* 🕒 *Closed Nov.–Easter.*

FAMILY **Silver Mountain Experience.** Outside the village of Ponterwyd, 10 miles east of Aberystwyth, this 200-year-old silver-lead mine is now a museum where you can tour reproductions of mining buildings and some original machinery, including working waterwheels. Kids over the age of eight can also enjoy a few harmless scares on the Black Chasm ghost tour, though very young ones will be better off sticking to the Woo Hoo Woods adventure playground. ■ **TIP→ It's cold in the mine, even on hot days, so bring a jacket or sweater.** Times can vary; call to check, especially in off-season. ✉ *Off A44, Pont-erwyd* ☎ *01970/890620* 🌐 *www.silvermountainexperience.co.uk* 🎟 *£12.95* 🕒 *Closed Nov.–Easter.*

FAMILY **Vale of Rheidol Railway.** At Aberystwyth Station you can hop on the steam-powered Vale of Rheidol Railway for an hour-long ride to the **Devil's Bridge** (*Pont y Gwr Drwg*, or, literally, "the Bridge of the Evil One"), where the rivers Rheidol and Mynach meet in a series of spectacular falls. Clamped between two rocky cliffs where a torrent of water pours unceasingly, there are actually three bridges, one built on top of the other. The oldest bridge is about 800 years old. ✉ *Park Ave.* ☎ *01970/625819* 🌐 *www.rheidolrailway.co.uk* 🎟 *£24.20 round-trip* 🕒 *Closed Nov.–mid-Feb.*

WHERE TO EAT

$$ SEAFOOD Fodor's Choice ★ 🍴 **Pysgoty.** This small café-bar overlooking the sea is run by the town's only independent fishmongers. The seafood, such as the Cardigan Bay lobster served with chunky chips, is mostly locally caught. **Known for:** great seafood and local beer; seaside location; lovely outside terrace. [$] *Average main: £17* ✉ *The Harbour, South Promenade* ☎ *01970/624611* 🌐 *www.pysgoty.co.uk* 🕒 *Closed Sun. and Mon. No dinner Tues.*

$ SPANISH 🍴 **Ultracomida.** This lively, modern Spanish eatery brings a splash of Mediterranean color to the Mid-Wales coastline. The lunch menu is served tapas-style: hake with lentils and Serrano ham, squid fried in garlic with salsa verde, or maybe just some fresh hummus and toast. **Known for:** delicious tapas; Spanish wine list; convivial atmosphere. [$] *Average main: £12* ✉ *31 Pier St.* ☎ *01970/630686* 🌐 *www.ultracomida.co.uk* 🕒 *No dinner Sun. and Mon.*

$$$$ ✕ **Ynyshir Restaurant and Rooms.** This Michelin-starred restaurant, housed
MODERN BRITISH in a Georgian mansion set among parkland, is one of the best eateries
Fodor's Choice in Wales thanks to its wonderful dishes featuring local meats. The res-
★ taurant has just five tables next to the open kitchen; a series of tasting
menus are offered. **Known for:** tasting menus featuring creative meat
dishes; award-winning wine list; stylish dining room. $ *Average main:*
£110 ☒ Eglwys Fach, Eglwys-fach ☎ 01654/781209 ⊕ www.ynyshir.
co.uk ⊗ Closed Sun. and Mon. No lunch Tues.

WHERE TO STAY

$ ⛩ **Glandyfi Castle.** This fanciful 19th-century folly 12 miles north of
B&B/INN Aberystwyth was built to look like the epitome of a fairy-tale castle,
complete with battlements and turrets, and the playful pastiche carries
through the luxurious, contemporary guest rooms, which incorporate
features such as four-poster beds into the otherwise modern design.
Pros: charming and fanciful building; unique setting; incredible views.
Cons: style may be a bit twee for some; limited dining options; cheaper
rooms inevitably miss out on the views. $ *Rooms from: £90 ☒ A487,*
Glandyfi, Machynlleth ☎ 01654/781238 ⊕ www.glandyficastle.co.uk
↩ 8 rooms ⦿ Free Breakfast.

$ ⛩ **Gwesty Cymru.** Converted into one of Aberystwyth's more stylish
HOTEL lodgings, this seafront Edwardian town house has public areas deco-
Fodor's Choice rated with original paintings and illuminated Welsh poetry, and most of
★ the comfortable guest rooms have gorgeous views across the bay. **Pros:**
contemporary design; beautiful location; delicious breakfast. **Cons:**
seafront can be noisy at night; limited parking; no elevator. $ *Rooms*
from: £90 ☒ 19 Marine Terr. ☎ 01970/612252 ⊕ www.gwestycymru.
com ↩ 8 rooms ⦿ Free Breakfast.

$$ ⛩ **Harbourmaster Hotel.** A drive south on the coast road from Aberyst-
HOTEL wyth brings you to this early 19th-century Georgian-style, bright blue
Fodor's Choice building right on the harbor, among many other colorfully painted
★ structures. **Pros:** good food; stunning harbor location; friendly hosts.
Cons: difficult parking; often booked up; minimum stay on weekends.
$ *Rooms from: £145 ☒ Pen Cei, 15 miles south of Aberystwyth,*
Aberaeron ☎ 01545/570755 ⊕ www.harbour-master.com ↩ 13 rooms
⦿ Free Breakfast.

NIGHTLIFE AND PERFORMING ARTS

Aberystwyth Arts Centre. In addition to a cinema, the lively Aberyst-
wyth Arts Centre has a theater, a gallery, shops, and a good café and
bar. The list of movies is varied, including an international horror
movie festival every fall (the rather brilliantly named "Abertoir").
☒ *Aberystwyth University, Penglais Rd. ☎ 01970/623232 ⊕ www.*
aberystwythartscentre.co.uk.

DOLGELLAU

34 miles northeast of Aberystwyth.

A solidly Welsh town with dark stone buildings and old coaching inns made of the local gray dolerite and slate, Dolgellau (pronounced dol-*geth*-lie) thrived with the wool trade until the mid-19th century. Prosperity left striking architecture with buildings of different eras side by side on crooked streets that are a legacy from Norman times.

Dolgellau has long been a popular base for people eager to walk the surrounding countryside, which forms the southern tip of Snowdonia National Park. To the south of Dolgellau rises the menacing bulk of 2,927-foot Cadair Idris. The name means "the Chair of Idris," a reference to a giant from ancient Celtic mythology.

GETTING HERE AND AROUND

Dolgellau's nearest railway station is at the town of Barmouth, about 10 miles away. The town is small and full of interesting nooks and crannies easily explored on foot. To discover the surrounding area you'll need a car.

EXPLORING

FAMILY **Ty Siamas.** The National Centre for Welsh Folk Music is in the converted Victorian Market Hall and Assembly Rooms. It has a fascinating interactive folk music exhibition, performance auditorium, and café and bar. ⊠ *Neuadd Idris, Eldon Sq.* ☎ *01341/421800* ⊕ *www.tysiamas. com* ✉ *Free.*

NORTH WALES

Wales masses its most dramatic splendor and fierce beauty in the north. Dominating the area is Snowdon, at 3,560 feet the highest peak in England and Wales. The peak gives its name to 823-square-mile Snowdonia National Park, which extends southward all the way to Machynlleth in Mid-Wales. As in other British national parks, much of the land is privately owned, so inside the park are towns, villages, and farms, in addition to some spectacular mountain scenery.

The mock-Italianate village of Portmeirion is an extraordinary architectural flight of fancy, and the seaside resort of Llandudno is as popular today as it was during its Victorian heyday. And scattered across the countryside are a ring of mighty medieval castles, built by King Edward I (1239–1307) at the end of a bloody war to bring the population under English rule.

Although North Wales is more popular with travelers than Mid-Wales, the road network is even more tortuous. In fact, you haven't really experienced North Wales until you've spent a maddening hour snaking along a narrow mountain road, all the while with your destination in plain view.

WELSH: A SHORT PRIMER

The native language of Wales, Welsh (or *Cymraeg*, as it's properly called) is spoken fluently by around 19% of the country's population (most Welsh people do know a little of the language, however). Not legally recognized in Britain until the 1960s, it was suppressed beginning in the time of Henry VIII and blamed for poor literacy during the reign of Queen Victoria. Today Welsh children under 17 are required to take classes to learn the language.

Welsh may look daunting, with its complicated words and confusing double consonants, but it's a phonetic language, so pronunciation is actually quite easy once the alphabet is learned. A quick primer to get you started: "dd" is sounded like "th" in they, "f" sounds like "v" in save, and "ff" is the equivalent of the English "f" in forest. The "ll" sound has no English equivalent; the closest match is the "cl" sound in "close."

Terms that crop up frequently in Welsh are *bach* or *fach* (small; also a common term of endearment similar to "dear"), *craig* or *graig* (rock), *cwm* (valley; pronounced coom), *dyffryn* (valley), *eglwys* (church), *glyn* (glen), *llyn* (lake), *mawr* or *fawr* (great, big), *pentre* (village, homestead), *plas* (hall, mansion), and *pont* or *bont* (bridge).

12

LLANGOLLEN

23 miles southwest of Chester, 60 miles southwest of Manchester.

Llangollen's setting in a deep valley carved by the River Dee gives it a typically Welsh appearance. The bridge over the Dee, a 14th-century stone structure, is named in a traditional Welsh folk song as one of the "Seven Wonders of Wales." In July the very popular International Musical Eisteddfod brings crowds to town.

For a particularly scenic drive in this area, head for the Horseshoe Pass. For other views, follow the marked footpath from the north end of the canal bridge up a steep hill to see Castell Dinas Bran, the ruins of a 13th-century castle built by a native Welsh ruler. The views of the town and the Vale of Llangollen are worth the 45-minute (one-way) walk.

GETTING HERE AND AROUND

You'll need a car to get here, but once you arrive you can take a trip on the Llangollen Railway. Along the Llangollen Canal longboat tours head both west and east. The town itself is easy to explore on foot.

ESSENTIALS

Visitor Information Llangollen Tourist Information Centre. ✉ *Y Capel, Castle St.* ☎ *01978/860828* ⊕ *www.llangollen.org.uk.*

EXPLORING

Castell Dinas Brân. This romantic hilltop ruin looks out over a breathtaking patchwork of green fields and mountains. The fortress was built in the 1260s on the site of an earlier castle, which was an Iron Age fort before that. Its heyday was incredibly short lived; by the end of the 13th century it had been captured and abandoned by English forces after which it gradually fell into ruin. The castle is located on top of

For a touch of whimsy, visit the mock-Italianate village of Portmeirion, set on the coast.

a hill just north of Llangollen town center. There are no roads to the summit; the best walking path starts at Canal Bridge in Llangollen and zigzags up the side of the hill. The rather punishing hike is a little over a mile long. ⊠ *Llangollen* 🎫 *Free.*

Fodor'sChoice **Chirk Castle.** This impressive medieval fortress has evolved from its ★ 14th-century origins into a grand home complete with an 18th-century servants' hall and interiors furnished in 16th- to 19th-century styles. However, it still looks satisfyingly medieval from the outside—and also belowground, where you tour the original dungeons. Surrounding the castle are beautiful formal gardens and parkland. Chirk Castle is 5 miles southeast of Llangollen. ⊠ *Off B4500, Chirk* 🕿 *01691/777701* ⊕ *www. nationaltrust.org.uk/chirk-castle* 🎫 *£14.*

FAMILY **Llangollen Railway.** This restored standard-gauge steam line runs for 10 miles along the scenic Dee Valley. The terminus is near the town's bridge. ⊠ *Abbey Rd.* 🕿 *01978/860979* ⊕ *www.llangollen-railway.co.uk* 🎫 *£16 round-trip.*

Fodor'sChoice **Plas Newydd.** From 1778 to 1828 Plas Newydd (not to be confused ★ with the similarly named Isle of Anglesey estate) was the home of Lady Eleanor Butler and Sarah Ponsonby, the eccentric Ladies of Llangollen, who set up a then-scandalous single-sex household, collected curios and magnificent carvings, and made it into a tourist attraction even during their lifetimes. You can take tea there, as did Wordsworth and the Duke of Wellington, and stroll in the attractively terraced gardens. ⊠ *Hill St.* 🕿 *01978/862834* ⊕ *www.plasnewyddllangollen.co.uk* 🎫 *£6* ⊗ *Closed Oct.–Mar.*

12

FAMILY
Fodor's Choice
★

Pontcysyllte. From the Llangollen Canal Wharf you can take a 45-minute or two-hour trip on a horse-drawn boat or a narrow boat (a slender barge) along the canal to the world's longest and highest navigable cast-iron aqueduct: Pontcysyllte (Welsh for "the bridge that connects"), a UNESCO World Heritage Site. The aqueduct is more than 1,000 feet long. Pontcysyllte is 3 miles east of Llangollen. ⊠ *Llangollen Canal Wharf, Wharf Hill* ☎ *01978/860702 Llangollen Wharf* ⊕ *www.horse-drawnboats.co.uk* ⊠ *£14 (2 hrs).*

Vale of Ceiriog. Near Llangollen is this verdant valley, known locally as "Little Switzerland." The B4500 road, running between Chirk and the village of Glyn Ceiriog, at the foothills of the Berwyn Mountains, is one of the region's great drives. It's just remote enough that you can often have the road to yourself. ⊠ *Llangollen.*

Fodor's Choice
★

Valle Crucis Abbey. The last abbey of the Cistercian order to be founded in Wales, Valle Crucis was built in 1201 and abandoned in 1537—a victim of Henry VIII's violent dissolution of the monasteries. Today it's a highly picturesque ruin beside a glassy lake. Surprisingly large sections survive relatively intact—particularly the sacristy and more or less complete chapter house, with its intricate vaulted ceiling. In its day Valle Crucis was one of the richest and most powerful abbeys in Wales; despite half a millennium of decay, this is still an impressive site to wander. ⊠ *Off A542* ☎ *01639/651931* ⊕ *cadw.gov.wales* ⊠ *£4; free Nov.–Mar.*

WHERE TO EAT AND STAY

$
BRITISH

✕ **The Corn Mill.** In a converted mill on the River Dee, this pub and restaurant has an old waterwheel that turns behind the bar. Dine on the open-air deck or in the cozy dining room, sampling stylishly updated pub fare, such as Isle of Anglesey sea bass with crab croquettes. **Known for:** attractive riverside location; good pub food, including a Welsh cheese board; ales from Welsh microbreweries. $ *Average main: £13* ⊠ *Dee La.* ☎ *01978/869555* ⊕ *www.brunningandprice.co.uk/cornmill.*

$$
B&B/INN

⌂ **Cornerstones Guesthouse.** Made up of three 16th-century cottages with views over the River Dee, this little B&B mixes period charm with modern comfort. **Pros:** spacious bedrooms; free passes for town parking lots; charming building. **Cons:** directly on the street; £10 for secure parking; rooms could use updating. $ *Rooms from: £120* ⊠ *15 Bridge St.* ☎ *01978/861569* ⊕ *www.cornerstones-guesthouse.co.uk* ⟿ *3 rooms* ⦿*| Free Breakfast.*

$$
B&B/INN

⌂ **Townhaus.** Most of the stylish, contemporary rooms in this Victorian town house have their own lounge, but the real highlight here is the rooftop hot tub with panoramic views. **Pros:** stylish decor; great views, especially from the rooftop; self-catering cottage available. **Cons:** reached via steps; no elevator; off-site parking. $ *Rooms from: £100* ⊠ *Hill St.* ☎ *01978/860775* ⊕ *www.manorhaus.com* ⟿ *8 rooms* ⦿*| Free Breakfast.*

EN
ROUTE

Pistyll Rhaeadr. The peat-brown water of Pistyll Rhaeadr, the highest waterfall in Wales, thunders down a 240-foot double cascade. When you're driving on the B4500 between Llangollen and Llanwddyn, take the road leading northwest from the town of Llanrhaeadr ym Mochnant in the peaceful Tanat Valley. There's also a pretty 18th-century restaurant and tearoom on-site. It was near here that, in 1588, the Bible was

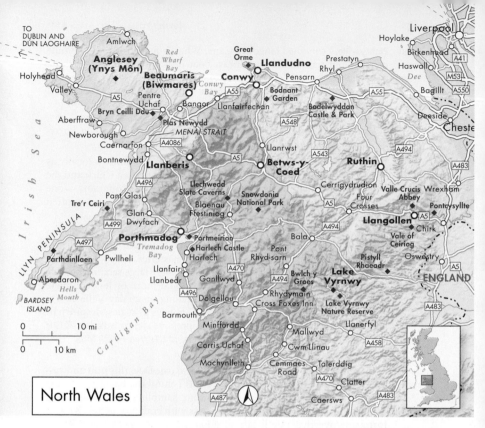

TO DUBLIN AND DUN LAOGHAIRE

translated into Welsh—one of the key moments that helped to ensure the survival of the language. ✉ *Llanrhaeadr-ym-Mochnant* ☎ *01691/780392* ⊕ *www.pistyllrhaeadr.co.uk* ✉ *Parking £4; £3 in winter.*

LAKE VYRNWY LLYN EFYRNWY

27 miles southwest of Llangollen.

This beautiful lake has a sense of tranquillity that doesn't entirely befit its history. Lake Vyrnwy was created in the 1880s to provide water for the people of Liverpool, 80 miles north. Unfortunately, this meant forcibly evicting the residents of a small town—an act that's still controversial in Wales. Today it's a peaceful spot surrounded by a thriving nature reserve. The closest settlement is tiny Llanwddyn, and a bit farther away is Bala, a pretty town with an almost-as-lovely natural lake of its own.

GETTING HERE AND AROUND

Rural bus service is infrequent, so you need a car to explore the area. The B4393 circles Lake Vyrnwy itself; from here, Bala is a 14-mile drive over hair-raising Bwlch y Groes pass or a circuitous drive along the B4391. Llangollen is 27 miles northeast of Lake Vyrnwy on the B4396.

EXPLORING

FAMILY **Bala Lake Railway.** The steam-powered train runs along the southern shores of Bala Lake (Llyn Tegid, or "Lake of Beauty"), a large natural reservoir just northeast of Lake Vyrnwy. Bala Lake is also popular for kayaking and other water sports. Look on the website for departure times. ✉ *Off B4403, Llanuwchllyn* ☎ *01678/540666* 🌐 *www.bala-lake-railway.co.uk* 🎟 *£11 round-trip* 🕒 *Closed Nov.–Jan.*

Bwlch y Groes. One of the great drives of North Wales, the sweeping, vertiginous panoramas of Bwlch y Groes (Pass of the Cross) form the second-highest mountain pass in the country at 1,788 feet. From Lake Vyrnwy, drive for a mile on B4393 before heading west on the mountain road. ✉ *Bwlch y Groes.*

FAMILY
Fodor's Choice ★ **Lake Vyrnwy Nature Reserve.** Bordered by lush forest and emerald green hills, Lake Vyrnwy is a haven for wildlife. It's rich in rare bird species, from falcons to siskins and curlews. Stretching out along the shores of the lake near the visitor center, the Lake Vyrnwy Sculpture Park is a collection of pieces by talented local artist Andy Hancock. Arranged along a paved walking trail, many of the wooden sculptures resemble oversize versions of the lake's wildlife, including a 15-foot-long dragonfly. It's an extremely popular cycling route, and there's a bike shop and coffee shop near the visitor center. ✉ *Visitor Centre, Off B4393 via southwest side, Llanwddyn* ☎ *01691/870278* 🌐 *www.lake-vyrnwy.com* 🎟 *Free.*

WHERE TO STAY

$$ HOTEL
Fodor's Choice ★ 🏨 **Lake Vyrnwy Hotel & Spa.** Awesome views of mountain-ringed Lake Vyrnwy are just one asset of this country mansion on a 24,000-acre estate. **Pros:** perfect for outdoor pursuits; luxurious spa; excellent package deals. **Cons:** too remote for some; minimum stay on some summer weekends; decor could use updating. [$] *Rooms from: £136* ✉ *Off B4393, Llanwddyn* ☎ *01691/870692* 🌐 *www.lakevyrnwy.com* 🛏 *52 rooms* 🍴 *Free Breakfast.*

PORTHMADOG

35 miles southeast of Lake Vyrnwy, 16 miles southeast of Caernarfon.

The little seaside town of Porthmadog, built as a harbor to export slate from nearby Blaenau Ffestiniog, stands at the gateway to the Llŷn Peninsula (pronounced like "lean," with your tongue touching your palate), with its virtually unspoiled coastline and undulating wildflower-covered hills. It's also near the town of Harlech, which contains one of the great castles of Wales, and the weird and wonderful Portmeirion.

GETTING HERE AND AROUND

The picturesque Cambrian Coast Railway runs from Machynlleth, near Aberystwyth, up the coast to Porthmadog. When you arrive you can take a scenic trip on the town's "little railways." Porthmadog is a stop on the excellent Snowdon Sherpa bus service. The town itself is totally walkable and has good access to coastal trails.

EXPLORING

FAMILY **Ffestiniog Railway.** Founded in the early 19th century to carry slate, the Ffestiniog Railway starts at the quayside and climbs up 700 feet through a wooded vale, past a waterfall, and across the mountains. The northern terminus is in Blaenau Ffestiniog, where you can visit an old slate mine. The Ffestiniog Railway is perhaps the best of several small steam lines in this part of the country. Porthmadog gets very crowded in summer, and parking is limited, so you might want to make this journey from Blaenau Ffestiniog to Porthmadog instead. Check the website for the daily timetable. ⊠ *Harbour Station, High St.* ☎ *01766/516024* ⊕ *www. festrail.co.uk* 🖾 *£25 round-trip* ۞ *Closed Nov.–Jan.*

FAMILY
Fodor'sChoice
★
Harlech Castle. A wealth of legend, poetry, and song is conjured up by the 13th-century Harlech Castle, built by Edward I to help subdue the Welsh. Its mighty ruins, visible for miles, are as dramatic as its history (though you have to imagine the sea, which used to crash against the rocks below but receded in the 19th century). Harlech was occupied by the Welsh Prince Owain Glyndwr from 1404 to 1408 during his revolt against the English. The music of the traditional folk song "Men of Harlech" refers to the heroic defense of this castle in 1468 by Dafydd ap Eynion, who, summoned to surrender, is alleged to have replied: "I held a castle in France until every old woman in Wales heard of it, and I will hold a castle in Wales until every old woman in France hears of it." On a clear day you can climb the battlements for a spectacular view of the surrounding countryside. A helpful visitor center explains the castle's history; you can also arrange to stay overnight in the castle in one of five luxury apartments. The castle dominates the coastal town of Harlech, 12 miles south of Porthmadog. ⊠ *Off B4573, Harlech* ☎ *01766/780552* ⊕ *www.cadw.wales.gov.uk* 🖾 *£6.90.*

FAMILY
Fodor'sChoice
★
Llechwedd Slate Caverns. At these caverns you can descend 500 feet on Britain's deepest underground railway to a mine where you walk by an eerie underground lake. Here Victorian working conditions have been re-created, and the tour gives a good idea of the difficult lives the miners had to endure. Above are a re-created Victorian village and slate-splitting demonstrations. Thrill-seekers will enjoy the hair-raising 5-mile zipline, where you can reach speeds of up to 70 mph; visit ⊕ *www.zipworld.co.uk* for more information. There's also a fun underground trampoline playground for children and adults. Zipworld also operates the world's fastest (and Europe's longest) zipwire at Penrhyn Quarry in nearby Bethesda (see website for details). Wear sturdy footwear when visiting the mine—during busy times you may have to climb 70 steps as part of the tour. ⊠ *Off A470, Blaenau-Ffestiniog* ☎ *01766/830306* ⊕ *www.llechwedd-slate-caverns.co.uk* 🖾 *£20; zipline £50; trampoline £25.*

Porthdinllaen. On the very tip of a thumb-shape bay jutting out into the Irish Sea, this miniscule but gorgeous little harbor community is 20 miles from Porthmadog. There's a wide, sheltered beach where the sand is so fine that it squeaks underfoot, and whitewashed cottages line the curving seafront. Park at the nearby visitor center, one mile from the beach. ⊠ *Porthdinllaen* ⊕ *www.nationaltrust.org.uk/porthdinllaen.*

Fodor's Choice ★ **Portmeirion.** One of the true highlights of North Wales is Portmeirion, a tiny fantasy-Italianate village on a private peninsula surrounded by hills; it's said to be loosely modeled after Portofino in Italy. Designed in the 1920s by architect Clough Williams-Ellis (1883–1978), the village has a hotel and restaurant among its multicolored buildings, and gift shops sell a distinctive local pottery. On the edge of town is a peaceful woodland trail punctuated here and there by such flourishes as a red iron bridge and a miniature pagoda. Williams-Ellis called it his "light-opera approach to architecture," and the result is magical, though distinctly un-Welsh. The village hosts a hip art festival, Festival Number 6, on the first weekend in September. Portmeirion is about 2 miles east of Porthmadog. ✉ *Off A487, Portmeirion* ☎ *01766/772409* 🌐 *www.portmeirion-village.com* 🎫 *£11.*

Fodor's Choice ★ **Tre'r Ceiri.** Remote, atmospheric, and astoundingly little-known, Tre'r Ceiri is one of the most impressive ancient monuments in Wales. Today parts of the 4th-century fort's outer walls are still intact (rising more than 18 feet in places), and within are the ruins of 150 stone huts. They were inhabited by a Celtic tribe known as the Ordovices, and may have survived as a settlement for up to 700 years. From Porthmadog, take the A497 west, then turn left onto the A499 just before Pwllheli. At the village of Llanaelhaearn, turn left onto the B4417. Less than a mile down this road is an unmarked footpath on the right leading straight up a hill to Tre'r Ceiri. ✉ *B4417, Llanaelhaearn* 🎫 *Free.*

WHERE TO EAT AND STAY

$$$$ BRITISH Fodor's Choice ★ 🍴 **Castle Cottage.** Close to Harlech's mighty castle, this friendly "restaurant with rooms" is a wonderful find. Chef-proprietor Glyn Roberts uses locally sourced ingredients from lobster to lamb to create imaginative, beautifully presented contemporary dishes. **Known for:** excellent Welsh menu featuring local produce; good wine list; historic building. [$] *Average main: £39* ✉ *Y Llech, Harlech* ☎ *01766/780479* 🌐 *www.castlecottageharlech.co.uk* ⏲ *No lunch.*

$ BRITISH 🍴 **Ty Coch Inn.** In a seafront building in picture-postcard Porthdinllaen, this pub has what is undoubtedly one of the best locations in Wales. The lunches are honest and unpretentious: pies, sandwiches, or perhaps a plate of local mussels in garlic butter. **Known for:** stunning beach location; local craft beers; laid-back vibe. [$] *Average main: £8* ✉ *Off B4417, Porthdinllaen* ☎ *01758/720498* 🌐 *www.tycoch.co.uk* ⏲ *No dinner.*

$$$ HOTEL Fodor's Choice ★ 🏨 **Hotel Portmeirion.** One of the most elegant and unusual places to stay in Wales, this waterfront mansion is located at the heart of Portmeirion. **Pros:** unique location; beautiful building; woodland walks. **Cons:** gets crowded with day-trippers; minimum stay on weekends; expensive food. [$] *Rooms from: £209* ✉ *Off A487, Portmeirion* ☎ *01766/772440* 🌐 *www.portmeirion-village.com* 🛏 *42 rooms* 🍽 *Free Breakfast.*

$ B&B/INN 🏨 **Y Branwen Hotel.** A pleasant, no-frills lodging just down the hill from Harlech Castle, Y Branwen is a popular local pub and a friendly place for an overnight stay. **Pros:** pleasant and comfortable; close to Harlech Castle; good food. **Cons:** some rooms are small; inevitable noise from the bar; on the main road. [$] *Rooms from: £95* ✉ *Fford Newydd, Harlech* ☎ *01766/780477* 🌐 *www.branwenhotel.co.uk* 🛏 *8 rooms* 🍽 *Free Breakfast.*

BETWS-Y-COED

25 miles northeast of Porthmadog, 19 miles south of Llandudno.

The rivers Llugwy and Conwy meet at Betws-y-Coed, a popular village surrounded by woodland with excellent views of Snowdonia. It can be used as a base to explore the national park, although its diminutive size means that it can get overcrowded in summer. The most famous landmark in the village is the ornate iron Waterloo Bridge over the River Conwy, designed in 1815 by Thomas Telford.

GETTING HERE AND AROUND

The town is easy to reach on the Conwy Valley Railway that runs from Llandudno to Blaenau Ffestiniog. Betws-y-Coed is also a hub for the excellent Snowdon Sherpa bus service that covers most of Snowdonia's beauty spots, so it's feasible to explore this part of Wales without a car.

ESSENTIALS

Visitor Information Snowdonia National Park Visitor Centre. ⊠ *Royal Oak Stables, Station Rd.* ☎ *01690/710426* ⊕ *www.betws-y-coed.co.uk.*

EXPLORING

Gwydyr Forest and Swallow Falls. Betws-y-Coed is bordered by Gwydyr Forest, which has several well-marked walking trails. The forest also contains a half dozen or so mines, the last of which was abandoned in the 1940s. On the western approach to the village you'll find Swallow Falls, where the River Llugwy tumbles down through a wooded chasm. ■ TIP→ Be careful on the footpath: there's no guardrail. ⊠ *Off A5.*

FAMILY
Fodor$Choice
★

Snowdonia National Park. Stretching from the Welsh midlands almost to its northern coast, Snowdonia National Park covers a vast swath of North Wales. The park consists of 840 square miles of rocky mountains, valleys clothed in oak woods, moorlands, lakes, and rivers, all guaranteeing natural beauty and, to a varying extent, solitude. Its most famous attraction, by far, is the towering peak of Mt. Snowdon. The view from the top is jaw-dropping: to the northwest you can see the Menai Strait and Anglesey; to the south, Harlech Castle and the Cadair Idris mountain range. To the southwest, on an exceedingly clear day, you can make out the distant peaks of Ireland's Wicklow Mountains. There are six different walking paths to the top, but a far less punishing way is via the Snowdon Mountain Railway in nearby Llanberis.

Perched at the top of Snowdon is Hafod Eryri, an eco-friendly replacement for the previous visitor center (once described by Prince Charles as "the highest slum in Wales"). The granite-roof building, which blends beautifully into the rocky landscape, has a café and exhibitions about the mountain, its ecology, and its history. If you're planning to make the ascent, the visitor center in Betws-y-Coed is the best place to stop for information. ⊠ *Royal Oak Stables, Station Rd.* ☎ *01690/710426* ⊕ *www.eryri-npa.gov.uk/home.*

WHERE TO EAT AND STAY

$
BRITISH

✕ **Ty Gwyn.** This coaching inn, built in 1636, is one of the best places to eat in Snowdonia. The food is traditional Welsh fare, beautifully prepared with local ingredients. **Known for:** charming, historic building in a beautiful setting; South Wales lamb with local produce; nice

The Llanberis Path is one route to the top of Snowdon, the highest peak in Wales, in Snowdonia National Park.

options for vegetarians. $ *Average main: £14* ✉ *A5* ☎ *01690/710383* ⊕ *www.tygwynhotel.co.uk.*

$
B&B/INN

Aberconwy House. This luxurious Victorian house has panoramic views over Betws-y-Coed. **Pros:** breathtaking countryside views; great breakfasts; charge for kids under three only £5 per night. **Cons:** no bar or evening meal; climbing stairs required; minimum stay in high season. $ *Rooms from: £85* ✉ *Lôn Muriau, off A470* ☎ *01690/710202* ⊕ *www.aberconwy-house.co.uk* ➘ *8 rooms* ⦿ *Free Breakfast.*

$
B&B/INN
Fodor's Choice
★

Pengwern Country House. Hosts Ian and Gwawr Mowatt are charmingly adept at making their guests feel at home in this former Victorian artists' colony. **Pros:** woodland location; wealth of Victorian details; lovely hosts. **Cons:** close to main road; car is essential; minimum two-night stay on weekends and in high season. $ *Rooms from: £84* ✉ *A5* ☎ *01690/710480* ⊕ *www.snowdoniaaccommodation.co.uk* ➘ *3 rooms* ⦿ *Free Breakfast.*

$$
B&B/INN

Tan-y-Foel Country House. Hidden away on a wooded hillside outside Betws-y-Coed, this quiet, contemporary hideaway has views over the Conwy Valley. **Pros:** bold decor; complimentary bottle of prosecco if you book directly; lovely location. **Cons:** no restaurant; too far to walk into town; decor style not for everyone. $ *Rooms from: £100* ✉ *Off A5, Capel Garmon* ☎ *01690/710507* ⊕ *www.tanyfoelcountryhouse.co.uk* ➘ *6 rooms* ⦿ *Free Breakfast* ⌖ *No children under 12.*

LLANBERIS

17 miles west of Betws-y-Coed.

Like Betws-y-Coed, Llanberis is a focal point for people visiting Snowdonia National Park.

GETTING HERE AND AROUND

Llanberis is accessible by bus. The most convenient service, targeted at visitors, is the Snowdon Sherpa bus route.

ESSENTIALS

Visitor Information Llanberis Tourist Information. ⊠ *Electric Mountain, Off A4086* ☎ *01286/870500* ⊕ *www.visitsnowdonia.info.*

EXPLORING

Fodor's Choice **Caernarfon Castle.** The grim, majestic mass of Caernarfon Castle, a
★ UNESCO World Heritage Site, looms over the waters of the River Seiont. Numerous bloody encounters were witnessed by these sullen walls, erected by Edward I in 1283 as a symbol of his determination to subdue the Welsh. The castle's towers, unlike those of Edward I's other castles, are polygonal and patterned with bands of different-color stone. In 1284 the monarch thought of a scheme to steal the Welsh throne. Knowing that the Welsh chieftains would accept no foreign prince, Edward promised to designate a ruler who could speak no word of English. Edward presented his infant son to the assembled chieftains as their prince "who spoke no English, had been born on Welsh soil, and whose first words would be spoken in Welsh." The ruse worked, and on that day was created the first prince of Wales of English lineage. In the Queen's Tower, a museum charts the history of the local regiment, the Royal Welch Fusiliers. The castle is in the town of Caernarfon, 7 miles west of Llanberis. ⊠ *Castle Hill, Caernarfon* ☎ *01286/677617* ⊕ *cadw.gov.wales* ⊡ *£9.50.*

National Slate Museum. In Padarn Country Park, this museum in the old Dinorwig Slate Quarry is dedicated to what was once an important industry for the area. The museum has quarry workshops and slate-splitting demonstrations, as well as restored worker housing, all of which convey the development of the industry and the challenges faced by those who worked in it. The narrow-gauge Llanberis Lake Railway departs from here. ⊠ *Padarn Country Park, A4086* ☎ *0300/111–2333* ⊕ *www.museum.wales/slate* ⊡ *Free* ☉ *Closed Sat. Nov.–Easter.*

FAMILY **Snowdon Mountain Railway.** One of the region's most famous attractions
Fodor's Choice is the rack-and-pinion Snowdon Mountain Railway, with some of its
★ track at a thrillingly steep grade. The 3,560-foot-high Snowdon—*Yr Wyddfa* in Welsh—is the highest peak south of Scotland and lies within the 840-square-mile national park. Weather permitting, trains go all the way to the summit; on a clear day you can see as far as the Wicklow Mountains in Ireland, about 90 miles away. You can take two types of train: a modern diesel-driven version, or "heritage" version, complete with restored carriages and working steam engine. From mid-March to May, or in times of high winds, the journey is truncated so you don't get all the way up to the summit; if so, tickets are a few pounds cheaper. ■TIP→ Tickets can sell out early on busy days, so try to book

in advance. ⊠ *A4086* ☎ *01286/870223* ⊕ *www.snowdonrailway.co.uk* 🖭 *Diesel service, £29 round-trip; heritage service, £37 round-trip* ⊙ *Closed Nov.–mid-Mar.*

12

FAMILY **Welsh Highland Railway.** You can take a trip on a coal-fired steam locomotive at this narrow-gauge line that operates on the scenic route of a 25-mile abandoned railway line from Caernarfon to Porthmadog, linking with the Ffestiniog Railway. First-class afternoon tea trips for two are a fun way to spend a special occasion (£155 per couple). ⊠ *St. Helens Rd., Caernarfon* ☎ *01766/516024* ⊕ *www.festrail.co.uk* 🖭 *£39.80 round-trip* ⊙ *Closed Jan.*

WHERE TO EAT AND STAY

$ ✕ **Gallt y Glyn.** This laid-back restaurant is popular with locals, drawn by
PIZZA the delicious, fresh pizza made entirely to order. They also serve salads,
FAMILY steaks, and other comfort food. **Known for:** delicious pizza; craft beer (including one free pint with each main course); lively atmosphere. 🏷 *Average main: £11* ⊠ *A4086* ☎ *01286/870370* ⊕ *www.galltyglyn. com* ⊙ *Closed Sun.–Tues. No lunch.*

$ 🏠 **Dolafon Guest House.** This cozy, traditional B&B in the center of Llan-
B&B/INN beris makes no pretense to contemporary style, and that's precisely the appeal. **Pros:** characterful house; charming owner; central location. **Cons:** style may be a bit fussy for some; one room has a bathroom down the hall; full cooked breakfast (as opposed to Continental-style) is £7.99 extra. 🏷 *Rooms from: £65* ⊠ *High St.* ☎ *01286/870993* ⊕ *www. dolafon.com* 🛏 *7 rooms* 🍽 *Free Breakfast.*

BEAUMARIS (BIWMARES) AND ANGLESEY (YNYS MÔN)

14 miles north of Llanberis.

Elegant Beaumaris is on the Isle of Anglesey, the largest island directly off the shore of Wales. It's linked to the mainland by the Britannia road and rail bridge and by Thomas Telford's remarkable chain suspension bridge, built in 1826 over the Menai Strait. Though its name means "beautiful marsh," Beaumaris has become a town of pretty cottages, Georgian houses, and bright shops; it also has Plas Newydd, one of the grandest stately homes in Wales.

Around 70% of Anglesey's 70,000 or so inhabitants speak Welsh, so you'll probably hear it more than English.

GETTING HERE AND AROUND

Anglesey is linked to the mainland by the A55 and A5. The roads on the island are in good condition, and there's a relatively extensive bus network. Ferries and catamarans to Ireland leave from Holyhead, on the island's western side.

EXPLORING

FAMILY **Beaumaris Castle.** The town of Beaumaris dates from 1295, when
Fodor's Choice Edward I commenced work on this impressive castle, the last and larg-
★ est link in an "iron ring" of fortifications around North Wales built to contain the Welsh. Guarding the western approach to the Menai Strait, the unfinished castle (a World Heritage Site) is solid and symmetrical, with concentric lines of fortification, arrow slits, and a moat: a

superb example of medieval defensive planning. ✉ *Castle St., Beaumaris* ☎ *01248/810361* 🌐 *cadw.gov.wales* 🎟 *£6.50.*

Fodor's Choice ★ **Bryn Celli Ddu.** Dating from around 3000 BC, this megalithic passage tomb is the most complete site of its kind in Wales. You enter via a narrow opening built into a burial mound. The passage extends for around 25 feet before opening out into a wider burial chamber. The far wall, made of quartz, is illuminated at dawn on the summer solstice. Bring a flashlight, as the tomb has no artificial lighting. Next to the entrance is a replica of a stone pillar carved with Celtic spirals, found here in 1928. The original is in the National Museum in Cardiff. The site is 7 miles southwest of Beaumaris. ✉ *Off A4080, Llanddaniel Fab* 🌐 *www.cadw.gov.wales* 🎟 *Free.*

Fodor's Choice ★ **Plas Newydd.** Some historians consider Plas Newydd to be the finest mansion in Wales. Remodeled in the 18th century by James Wyatt (1747–1813) for the marquesses of Anglesey (whose descendants still live here), it stands on the Menai Strait about 7 miles southwest of Beaumaris. The interior has some fine 18th-century Gothic Revival decorations. Between 1936 and 1940 the society artist Rex Whistler (1905–44) painted the mural in the dining room. A museum commemorates the Battle of Waterloo, where the first marquess led the cavalry. The woodland walk and rhododendron gardens are worth exploring, and it's sometimes possible to take boat trips on the strait. Plas Newydd is not to be confused with the Gothic mansion of the same name in Llangollen. ✉ *Off A4080, southwest of Britannia Bridge, Llanfairpwllgwyngyll* ☎ *01248/714795* 🌐 *www.nationaltrust.org.uk/plas-newydd-country-house-and-gardens* 🎟 *House and garden £12.76; garden only £10.12.*

WHERE TO STAY

$$ HOTEL 🏨 **Ye Olde Bull's Head and Townhouse.** These twin hotels, a stone's throw away from each other, could hardly be more different: one is a restored 15th-century coaching inn, the other a contemporary lodging. **Pros:** lovely blend of historic and contemporary; good food; luxury bedding. **Cons:** Bull's Head has low ceilings; no on-site parking; breakfast portions are small for some. [$] *Rooms from: £100* ✉ *Castle St., Beaumaris* ☎ *01248/810329* 🌐 *www.bullsheadinn.co.uk* 🛏 *13 rooms* 🍴 *No meals.*

SPORTS AND THE OUTDOORS

Isle of Anglesey Coastal Path. Extending 130 miles around the island, this path leads past cliffs, sandy coves, and plenty of scenic variety. Pick up information at any of the regional tourist offices and choose a section; the west coast has the most dramatic scenery. ✉ *Beaumaris* 🌐 *www.visitanglesey.co.uk.*

CONWY

23 miles east of Beaumaris, 48 miles northwest of Chester.

The still-authentic medieval town of Conwy grew up around its castle on the west bank of the River Conwy. A ring of ancient but well-preserved walls, built in the 13th century to protect the English merchants who lived here, enclose the old town and add to the pervading sense of history. Sections of the walls, with their 21 towers, can still be walked. The impressive views from the top take in the castle and the estuary, with mountains in the distance.

GETTING HERE AND AROUND

The A55 expressway links Conwy into the central U.K. motorway system via the M56. The town is also on the North Wales coast rail route, which ends at Holyhead on Anglesey. The town itself—surrounded by its wonderfully preserved walls—is perfect for pedestrians.

ESSENTIALS

Visitor Information Conwy Tourist Information Centre. ⊠ *Muriau Bldgs., Rosehill St.* ☎ *01492/577566* ⊕ *www.visitconwytown.co.uk.*

EXPLORING

Aberconwy House. Thought to be the oldest complete medieval house in Wales, Aberconwy House's rooms have been restored to reflect three distinct periods in its history: medieval, Jacobean, and Victorian. It's a diverting and atmospheric little place, which also holds the distinction of (supposedly) being one of the most haunted buildings in North Wales. ⊠ *Castle St.* ☎ *01492/592246* ⊕ *www.nationaltrust.org.uk/ aberconwy-house* ☑ *£4.60.*

Fodor's Choice
★

Bodnant Garden. Undoubtedly one of the best gardens in Wales, Bodnant Garden is something of a pilgrimage spot for horticulturists from around the world. Laid out in 1875, the 87 acres are particularly famed for rhododendrons, camellias, and magnolias. ■**TIP**➔ **Visit in late May to see the laburnum arch that forms a huge tunnel of golden blooms.** The mountains of Snowdonia form a magnificent backdrop to the Italianate terraces, rock and rose gardens, and pinetum. The gardens are about 5 miles south of Conwy. ⊠ *Off A470, Tal-y-Cafn* ☎ *01492/650460* ⊕ *www.nationaltrust.org.uk/bodnant-garden* ☑ *£14.60.*

Fodor's Choice
★

Conwy Castle. Of all Edward I's Welsh strongholds, it is perhaps Conwy Castle that best preserves a sheer sense of power and dominance. The eight large round towers and tall curtain wall, set on a rocky promontory, provide sweeping views of the area and the town walls. Although the castle is roofless (and floorless in places), the signage does a pretty good job of helping you visualize how rooms such as the Great Hall must once have looked. Conwy Castle can be approached on foot by a dramatic suspension bridge completed in 1828; engineer Thomas Telford designed the bridge with turrets to blend in with the fortress's presence. ⊠ *Rose Hill St.* ☎ *01492/592358* ⊕ *cadw.gov.wales* ☑ *£9.50.*

Plas Mawr. Dating from 1576, Plas Mawr is one of the best-preserved Elizabethan town houses in Britain. Richly decorated with ornamental plasterwork, it gives a unique insight into the lives of the Tudor gentry and their servants. ⊠ *High St.* ☎ *01492/580167* ⊕ *cadw.gov.wales* ☑ *£6.90* ⊙ *Closed Nov.–Mar.*

Smallest House in Great Britain. What is said to be Britain's smallest house is furnished in mid-Victorian Welsh style. The house, which is 6 feet wide and 10 feet high, was reputedly last occupied in 1900 by a fisherman who was more than 6 feet tall. ✉ *Lower Gate St.* ☎ *01492/573965* 🌐 *www.thesmallesthouse.co.uk* 🎫 *£1* 🕒 *Closed Nov.–Mar.*

WHERE TO EAT

$$$ BRITISH Fodor's Choice ★ 🍴 **Bodnant Welsh Food Centre.** Wales has undergone something of a culinary renaissance in the last decade and a half, and this fantastic center is a great place to explore why. Traditional cheeses, homemade ice creams, and other artisanal food products are for sale in the farm shop and deli; there's also a bakery, a full-service restaurant, and a wineshop where you can pick up Welsh malt whisky. **Known for:** one-stop farm shop for all things Welsh; delicious cuisine made with local produce; cooking classes. [$] *Average main: £20* ✉ *Furnace Farm, Tal-y-Cafn* ☎ *01492/651100* 🌐 *www.bodnant-welshfood.co.uk* 🕒 *Closed Mon. and Tues.*

$ MODERN BRITISH 🍴 **Groes Inn.** Beamed ceilings, log fires, and rambling rooms abound at this old inn dating back to the 15th century. The menu consists of pub classics done well—think Welsh beef burger with local Bodnant cheese, or sea bass with potato and asparagus salad. **Known for:** charming, historic building; lovely garden; traditional Welsh pub cuisine. [$] *Average main: £14* ✉ *B5106* ☎ *01492/650545* 🌐 *www.groesinn.com.*

$$ BRITISH 🍴 **Watson's Bistro.** This popular bistro in central Conwy combines traditional Welsh flavors with accents of the Mediterranean. In the rustic dining room, try the crab fritters to start followed by slow-roast shoulder of lamb with minted port wine jus and potato gratin. **Known for:** local produce with a Mediterranean twist; delicious desserts; affordable lunch menu. [$] *Average main: £17* ✉ *Chapel St.* ☎ *01492/596326* 🌐 *www.watsonsbistroconwy.co.uk* 🕒 *Closed Mon. No lunch Tues.–Thurs.*

WHERE TO STAY

$$ HOTEL 🏨 **Castle Hotel.** Nestled within Conwy's medieval walls, this former coaching inn has wood beams, stone fireplaces, and plenty of antiques. **Pros:** plenty of history; in the heart of Conwy; good food. **Cons:** small rooms; noisy seagulls; allegedly one of the most haunted buildings in Wales. [$] *Rooms from: £150* ✉ *High St.* ☎ *01492/582800* 🌐 *www.castlewales.co.uk* 🛏 *27 rooms* 🍽 *Free Breakfast.*

$$ HOTEL 🏨 **Sychnant Pass House.** On a peaceful wooded hillside 2 miles west of Conwy, this country-house hotel has a laid-back atmosphere. **Pros:** great indoor pool and hot tub; beautiful grounds; unforced hospitality. **Cons:** far outside Conwy; some rooms pricey; beds can be a bit hard. [$] *Rooms from: £145* ✉ *Sychnant Pass Rd.* ☎ *01492/596868* 🌐 *www.sychnant-pass-house.co.uk* 🛏 *12 rooms* 🍽 *Free Breakfast.*

LLANDUDNO

3 miles north of Conwy, 50 miles northwest of Chester.

This engagingly old-fashioned North Wales seaside resort has a wealth of well-preserved Victorian architecture and an ornate amusement pier with entertainments, shops, and places to eat. Grand-looking small hotels line the wide promenade with a view of the deep-blue waters of the bay. The shopping district beyond retains its original canopied walkways.

GETTING HERE AND AROUND

Llandudno is on the North Wales railway line with fast access from London and other major cities. By road, it's connected to the motorway system via the A55 expressway. The scenic Conwy Valley rail line runs to Blaenau Ffestiniog, and the town is also on the network covered by the Snowdon Sherpa bus service.

ESSENTIALS

Visitor Information Llandudno Tourist Information Centre. ✉ *Victoria Centre, Mostyn St.* ☎ *01492/577577* 🌐 *www.visitllandudno.org.uk.*

EXPLORING

OFF THE BEATEN PATH **Bodelwyddan Castle & Park.** Between Abergele and St. Asaph, this medieval castle, which was rebuilt in the 19th century, was used as a hospital during World War I. Inside, you can see an exhibition of portraits from the era, as well as a fine collection of Welsh art. The castle grounds contain a fascinating, if somber, historical footnote: a network of overgrown World War I trenches, used by the army to train new recruits. A replica of the trenches brings the history to life. Also on the grounds are a maze, an aviary, and pretty woodland walks. The castle is 16 miles east of Llandudno. ✉ *Off A55, Bodelwyddan* ☎ *01745/584060* 🌐 *www.bodelwyddan-castle.co.uk* 🎫 *£8.25* 🕒 *Closed Mon.*

FAMILY **Great Orme.** Named for the Norse word meaning "sea monster," the 679-foot headland called Great Orme towers over Llandudno, affording extraordinary views over the bay. The Llandudno Cable Car (North Parade) zips you one mile to the top of Great Orme. At the summit there's a visitor center (Easter through October only), an artificial ski slope, and a toboggan run. The most picturesque way to reach the summit is the Great Orme Tramway (Victoria Station, Church Walks). Trips depart about every 20 minutes. The summit is a sylvan spot, with open grassland, fields of wildflowers, and rare butterflies. Also look out for a wild herd of Kashmir goats. ✉ *Llandudno* ☎ *01492/877205 cable car, 01492/577877 tramway, 01492/874151 visitor center* 🌐 *www.greatormetramway.co.uk* 🎫 *Cable car £10 round-trip; tramway £8.10 round-trip* 🕒 *Closed Nov.–Easter.*

FAMILY **Great Orme Mines.** Discovered in 1987, these mines date back 4,000 years to when copper was first mined in the area. You can take a tour and learn about the technology that ancient people used to dig the tunnels, which are thought to be the largest surviving prehistoric mines in the world. ✉ *Pyllau Rd.* ☎ *01492/870447* 🌐 *www.greatormemines.info* 🎫 *£7* 🕒 *Closed Nov.–Easter.*

Mostyn Art Gallery. Housed in a restored Edwardian building, this is the leading contemporary art gallery in Wales. Six spaces host temporary exhibitions along with a shop and café. ✉ *12 Vaughan St.* ☎ *01492/879201* 🌐 *www.mostyn.org* 🎫 *Free* 🕒 *Closed Mon.*

WHERE TO STAY

$$$ HOTEL Fodor's Choice ★ 🏨 **Bodysgallen Hall.** Tasteful antiques, polished wood, and comfortable chairs by cheery fires distinguish one of Wales's most luxurious country-house hotels. **Pros:** superb spa and pool; rare 17th-century knot garden; elegant dining and afternoon tea. **Cons:** too formal for some; hard to get to without a car; lots of steps and stairs. [$] *Rooms*

from: £190 ✉ *Off A470* ☎ *01492/584466* 🌐 *www.bodysgallen.com* 🛏 *31 rooms* 🍴 *Free Breakfast.*

$ HOTEL 🏨 **Bryn Derwen Hotel.** This immaculate, impeccably run Victorian hotel is traditional in style, but has a contemporary edge. **Pros:** historic building; charming decor; close to the beach. **Cons:** no sea views; one-night nonrefundable deposit required; breakfast not free. [$] *Rooms from: £88* ✉ *34 Abbey Rd.* ☎ *01492/876804* 🌐 *www.bryn-derwen.co.uk* 🛏 *9 rooms* 🍴 *No meals* ☞ *No children under 12.*

$ HOTEL 🏨 **St. Tudno Hotel.** Perfectly situated on the seafront promenade overlooking the beach and pier, this hotel has been run by the same family for nearly 40 years. **Pros:** ocean views; free on-site parking; good food. **Cons:** some rooms are snug; overly fussy decor; popular wedding venue. [$] *Rooms from: £90* ✉ *Promenade* ☎ *01492/874411* 🌐 *www.st-tudno.co.uk* 🛏 *18 rooms* 🍴 *Free Breakfast.*

RUTHIN RHUTHUN

33 miles southeast of Llandudno, 23 miles southwest of Chester.

Once a stronghold of the rebel Welsh prince Owain Glyndwr (c. 1354–1416), Ruthin is a delightful market town with elegant shops, good inns, and a fascinating architectural mix of medieval, Tudor, and Georgian buildings. The town also has a crafts complex with displays of the artisans' creations.

GETTING HERE AND AROUND

Ruthin is on the A494 and A525 roads. The nearest railway stations are Rhyl and Wrexham, both about 20 miles away. Local bus connections are reasonably good; most useful bus connections go through Rhyl.

EXPLORING

Nantclwyd y Dre. Dating from 1435, the oldest known timbered house in Wales offers visitors the opportunity to see how its inhabitants lived throughout the centuries; there's a useful interactive display, too. A colony of Lesser Horseshoe bats lives in the attic and you can watch them via a bat cam. Outside, the original medieval garden has been restored. ✉ *Castle St.* ☎ *01824/706868* 🎟 *£5* 🕒 *Closed Oct.–Mar.*

FAMILY **Ruthin Gaol.** You can tour the local jail, where from 1654 to 1916 thousands of prisoners were incarcerated, and learn about prison conditions in Victorian times. ✉ *Clwyd St.* ☎ *01824/708281* 🌐 *www.ruthingaol.co.uk* 🎟 *£5* 🕒 *Closed Tues.*

WHERE TO STAY

$$ B&B/INN 🏨 **manorhaus.** A Georgian town house in the heart of Ruthin has been converted into a gorgeous boutique hotel. **Pros:** cutting-edge design; local art in each room; trendy bistro. **Cons:** small rooms; limited parking; two-night minimum on some dates. [$] *Rooms from: £100* ✉ *Well St.* ☎ *01824/704830* 🌐 *www.manorhaus.com* 🛏 *8 rooms* 🍴 *Free Breakfast.*

SHOPPING

Ruthin Craft Centre. Along with exhibitions and artist residencies, this Center for the Applied Arts sells works by leading artists and craftspeople from around Wales. There's also a nice café. ✉ *Park Rd.* ☎ *01824/704774* 🌐 *www.ruthincraftcentre.org.uk.*

EDINBURGH

WELCOME TO EDINBURGH

TOP REASONS TO GO

★ **The Royal Mile:** History plays out before your eyes along the centuries-old Royal Mile. Edinburgh Castle and the Palace of Holyroodhouse were the locations for some of the most important struggles between Scotland and England.

★ **Architecture:** From the Old Town's labyrinthine medieval streets to the neoclassical orderliness of the New Town to imaginative modern developments like the Scottish Parliament, the architecture of Auld Reekie spans the ages.

★ **Food:** Edinburgh has an ever-expanding restaurant scene that attracts chefs serving up dishes from around the world. Perhaps the most exotic, however, is genuine Scottish cuisine, with its classic dishes like *Cullen skink* and haggis with neeps and tatties.

★ **Shopping:** Scotland has a strong tradition of distinctive furniture makers, silversmiths, and artists. Look to places like Leith for exclusive designer clothing, edgy knitwear, and other high-end items.

For all its steep roads and hidden alleyways, Edinburgh is not a difficult place to navigate. Most newcomers gravitate to two areas, the Old Town and the New Town. The former funnels down from the castle on either side of the High Street, better known as the Royal Mile. Princes Street Gardens and Waverly Station separate the oldest part of the city from the stately New Town, known for its neoclassical architecture and verdant gardens. To the north, the city sweeps down to the Firth of Forth. It is here you will find the port of Leith with its trendy pubs and fine-dining restaurants. The southern and western neighborhoods are mainly residential, but are home to a few attractions such as Edinburgh Zoo.

1 Old Town. The focal point of Edinburgh for centuries, the Old Town is a picturesque jumble of medieval tenements. Here are prime attractions such as Edinburgh Castle and the newer symbol of power, the Scottish Parliament. Amid the historic buildings you will find everything from buzzing bars and nightclubs to ghostly alleyways and vaults.

2 New Town. Built in the 18th and 19th centuries to prevent the wealthier residents of overcrowded Old Town from decamping to London, the neoclassical sweep of the New Town is a masterpiece of city planning. Significant sights include the National Gallery of Scotland and Calton Hill, which offers some of the best views of the city from its summit. The

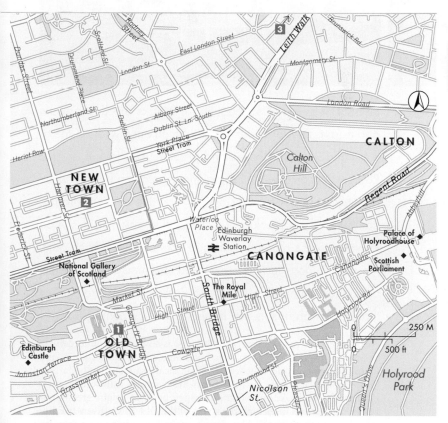

city's main shopping thoroughfares, Princes Street and George Street, are also found here.

3 Leith. On the southern shore of the Firth of Forth, Edinburgh's port of Leith is where you'll find the now-retired Royal Yacht *Britannia*, along with some of the city's smartest restaurants and bars.

4 The Lothians. Known collectively as the Lothians, the areas of green countryside and seafront villages around Edinburgh are replete with historic houses, castles, towns, and museums. They are quick and easy to reach by car, bus, or train, making them welcome day-trip escapes from the summer festival crush.

Updated by
Joseph Reaney

Edinburgh is a city so beautiful it breaks the heart again and again, as Alexander McCall Smith once wrote. One of the world's stateliest cities and proudest capitals, it is—like Rome—built on seven hills, making it a striking backdrop for the ancient pageant of history. In a skyline of sheer drama, Edinburgh Castle looks out over the city, frowning down on Princes Street's glamour and glitz. But despite its rich past, the city's famous festivals, excellent museums and galleries, as well as the modernist Scottish Parliament, are reminders that Edinburgh has its feet firmly in the 21st century.

Nearly everywhere in Edinburgh (the *burgh* is always pronounced *burra* in Scotland) there are spectacular buildings, whose Doric, Ionic, and Corinthian pillars add touches of neoclassical grandeur to the largely Presbyterian backdrop. Large gardens are a strong feature of central Edinburgh, while Arthur's Seat, a craggy peak of bright green-and-yellow furze, rears up behind the spires of the Old Town. Even as Edinburgh moves through the 21st century, its tall guardian castle remains the focal point of the city and its venerable history.

Modern Edinburgh has become a cultural capital, staging the Edinburgh International Festival and the Festival Fringe in every possible venue each August. The stunning National Museum of Scotland complements the city's wealth of galleries and artsy hangouts. Add Edinburgh's growing reputation for food and nightlife and you have one of the world's most beguiling cities.

Today, Edinburgh is the second-most-important financial center in the United Kingdom, and is widely renowned for its exceptional (and ever-expanding) dining and nightlife scenes—some of the reasons it regularly ranks near the top of quality-of-life surveys.

Take time to explore the city's streets—peopled by the spirits of Mary, Queen of Scots, Sir Walter Scott, and Robert Louis Stevenson—and enjoy candlelit restaurants or a folk ceilidh (pronounced *kay-lee,* a traditional Gaelic dance with music). But remember: you haven't earned your porridge until you've climbed Arthur's Seat. Should you wander around a corner, say, on George Street, you might see not an endless cityscape, but blue sea and a patchwork of fields. This is the county of Fife, beyond the inlet of the North Sea called the Firth of Forth—a reminder, like the mountains to the northwest that can be glimpsed from Edinburgh's highest points, that the rest of Scotland lies within easy reach.

13

PLANNER

WHEN TO GO

Scotland's reliably variable weather means that you could visit at the height of summer and be forced to wear a scarf. Conversely, conditions can be balmy in early spring and late autumn. You may choose to avoid the crowds (and hotel price hikes) of July and August, but you'd also miss some of the greatest festivals on Earth. May, June, and September are probably the most hassle-free months in which to visit, while still offering hope of good weather. Short days and grim conditions make winter less appealing, though there are few better New Year's Eve celebrations than Edinburgh's Hogmanay.

FESTIVALS

FAMILY
Fodor'sChoice
★

Edinburgh Festival Fringe. During the world's largest arts festival in August, most of the city center becomes one huge performance area, with fire eaters, sword swallowers, unicyclists, jugglers, string quartets, jazz groups, stand-up comedians, and magicians all thronging into High Street and Princes Street. Every available performance space—church halls, community centers, parks, sports fields, putting greens, and nightclubs—is utilized for every kind of event, with something for all tastes. There are even family-friendly shows. Many events are free; others start at a few pounds and rise to £15 or £20. There's so much happening in the three weeks of the festival that it's possible to arrange your own entertainment program from early morning to midnight. ■TIP➜ Be aware that hotels get booked up months in advance during the Fringe and bargains are virtually impossible to come by, so plan your trip as far in advance as possible. ⊠ *Edinburgh Festival Fringe Office, 180 High St., Old Town* ☎ *0131/226–0026* ⊕ *www.edfringe.com.*

FAMILY
Edinburgh International Book Festival. This two-week-long event held every August pulls together a heady mix of authors from around the world, from Nobel laureates to best-selling fiction writers, and gets them talking about their work in a magnificent tent village. There are more than 750 events in total, with the workshops for would-be writers and children proving hugely popular. ⊠ *Edinburgh International Book Festival Admin Office, Charlotte Sq. Gardens, New Town* ☎ *0131/718–5666* ⊕ *www.edbookfest.co.uk.*

FAMILY
Edinburgh International Festival. Running throughout August, this flagship traditional arts festival attracts international performers and audiences to a celebration of music, dance, theater, opera, and art. Programs,

tickets, and reservations are available from the Hub, set within the impressive Victorian-Gothic Tolbooth Kirk. Tickets for the festival go on sale in April, and the big events sell out within the month. However, you'll still be able to purchase tickets for some events during the festival; prices range from around £4 to £60. ⊠ *The Hub, Castlehill, Old Town* ☎ *0131/473–2015* ⊕ *www.eif.co.uk.*

Edinburgh International Film Festival. One of Europe's foremost film festivals, promoting the best of global independent cinema since 1947, this event takes place from mid-June to early July each year. It's a great place for a first screening of a new film—movies from *Billy Elliot* to *Little Miss Sunshine* to the *Hurt Locker* have premiered here. ⊠ *Edinburgh Film Festival Office, 88 Lothian Rd., West End* ☎ *0131/228–4051* ⊕ *www.edfilmfest.org.uk.*

Fodor's Choice **Edinburgh's Hogmanay.** Nowadays, most capital cities put on decent
★ New Year's celebrations, but Edinburgh's three-day-long Hogmanay festivities are on a whole other level. There's a reason this city is famous around the world as the best place to see in the New Year. Yes, it's winter and yes, it's chilly, but joining a crowd of 80,000 people in a monster street party, complete with big-name rock concerts, torchlight processions, ceilidh dancing, and incredible fireworks, is something you won't forget in a hurry. The headline city center events are ticketed (and can be pricey), but there are free parties happening all over the city. ⊠ *Princes St., Old Town* ⊕ *www.edinburghshogmanay.com* 🎫 *£25.*

PLANNING YOUR TIME

One of Edinburgh's greatest virtues is its compact size, which means that it is possible to pack a fair bit into even the briefest of visits. The two main areas of interest are the Old Town and the New Town, where you'll find Edinburgh Castle, the Scottish Parliament, Princes Street Gardens, and the National Gallery of Scotland. You can cover the major attractions in one day, but to give the major sights their due, you should allow at least two. You can also choose between the Palace of Holyroodhouse and the important museums of Edinburgh, or explore the Royal Botanic Garden and Holyrood Park. Head down to leafy, villagelike Stockbridge, then immerse yourself in the greenery along the Water of Leith, visiting the Gallery of Modern Art along the way.

Getting out of town is also an option for longer stays. Hop on a bus out to Midlothian to see the magnificent Rosslyn Chapel (it's of interest to more than just *The Da Vinci Code* fans), and visit Crichton Castle, parts of which date back to the 14th century. Consider spending another half day traveling out to South Queensferry to admire the three Forth bridges (including the iconic red railway bridge); then visit palatial Hopetoun House, with its wealth of portraits and fine furniture.

GETTING HERE AND AROUND
AIR TRAVEL
Edinburgh Airport is 7 miles west of the city center. Flights bound for Edinburgh depart virtually every hour from London's Gatwick, Heathrow, and City airports.

There are no rail links to the city center, so the most efficient way to do the journey on public transport is by tram; the service runs every 8 to 12 minutes and takes about half an hour. Tickets cost £5.50. By bus or car you can usually make it to Edinburgh in a half hour, unless you hit the morning (7:30 to 9) or evening (4 to 6) rush hours. Lothian Buses runs an Airlink express service to Waverley railway station via Haymarket that usually takes around half an hour, depending on traffic. Buses run every 10 minutes (every 30 minutes throughout the night); tickets cost £4.50 one way or £7.50 round-trip and are available from the booth beside the bus. Local buses also run between Edinburgh Airport and the city center every 15 minutes or so from 9 to 5, and roughly every hour during off-peak hours; they are far cheaper—just £1.50 one way—but can take twice as long.

13

You can arrange for a chauffeur-driven limousine to meet your flight at Edinburgh Airport through Transvercia Chaffeur Drive, Little's, or W L Sleigh Ltd., for upwards of £50.

Taxis are readily available outside the terminal. The trip takes 20 to 30 minutes to the city center, 15 minutes longer during rush hour. The fare is roughly £25. Note that airport taxis picking up fares from the terminal are any color, not the typical black cabs.

Airport Contacts Edinburgh Airport. ⊠ *Glasgow Rd., Ingliston* ☎ *0844/448– 8833* ⊕ *www.edinburghairport.com.* **Little's.** ⊠ *1282 Paisley Rd. W, Glasgow* ☎ *0141/883–2111* ⊕ *www.littles.co.uk.* **Transvercia Chaffeur Drive.** ⊠ *The Harland Bldg., Unit 6, Suite 19, Pilrig Heights, Leith* ☎ *0131/555–0459* ⊕ *www. transvercia.co.uk.* **W L Sleigh.** ⊠ *Unit 11A West Craigs, Turnhouse Rd., Edinburgh* ☎ *0131/339–9607* ⊕ *sleigh.co.uk.*

BUS TRAVEL

National Express provides a coach service to and from London and other major towns and cities. The main terminal, Edinburgh Bus Station, is a short walk north of Waverley Station, immediately east of St. Andrew Square. Long-distance coaches must be booked in advance online, by phone, or at the terminal. Edinburgh is approximately eight hours by bus from London.

Lothian Buses provides most of the services between Edinburgh and the Lothians and conducts day tours around and beyond the city. First runs additional buses out of Edinburgh into the surrounding area. Megabus offers dirt-cheap fares to selected cities across Scotland.

Lothian Buses is the main operator within Edinburgh. You can buy tickets from the driver on the bus, though you will need the exact fare. Alternatively, you can buy tickets in advance at a Lothian Buses store or on your phone through the *Lothian Buses M-Tickets* app. It's £1.60 for a single ticket or £4 for a *DAYticket,* which allows unlimited one-day travel on the city's buses. A single NIGHTticket costs £3, or you can get unlimited travel from 6 pm to 4:30 am with a DAY&NIGHT ticket (£3.50). The Ridacard (for which you'll need a photo) is valid on all buses for seven days (Sunday through Saturday night) and costs £17; the four-week Rider costs £51. ■ TIP➔ **Buses can be packed on Friday and Saturday nights, so you may want to consider a taxi.**

Bus Contacts First. ☎ *0871/200–2233* ⊕ *www.firstgroup.com.* **Lothian Buses.** ☎ *0131/554–4494* ⊕ *www.lothianbuses.com.* **Megabus.** ☎ *0900/160–0900* ⊕ *www. megabus.com.* **National Express.** ☎ *0871/781–8181* ⊕ *www.nationalexpress.co.uk.*

CAR TRAVEL

It's not necessary to have a car in Edinburgh as the city is quite walkable and well linked by an efficient bus system. Driving in Edinburgh has its quirks and pitfalls—particularly at the height of festival season. Metered parking in the city center is scarce and expensive, and the local traffic wardens are a feisty, alert bunch. Note that illegally parked cars are routinely towed away, and getting your car back will be expensive. After 6 pm the parking situation improves considerably, and you may manage to find a space quite near your hotel, even downtown. If you park on a yellow line or in a resident's parking bay, be prepared to move your car by 8 the following morning, when the rush hour gets under way. Parking lots are clearly signposted; overnight parking is expensive and not always permitted.

TAXI TRAVEL

Taxi stands can be found throughout the city, mostly in the New Town. The following are the most convenient: the west end of Princes Street; South St. David Street and North St. Andrew Street (both just off St. Andrew Square); Waverley Mall; Waterloo Place; and Lauriston Place. Alternatively, hail any taxi displaying an illuminated "for hire" sign.

TRAIN TRAVEL

Edinburgh's main train hub, Waverley Station, is downtown, below Waverley Bridge and around the corner from the unmistakable spire of the Scott Monument. Travel time from Edinburgh to London by train is as little as 4½ hours for the fastest service.

Edinburgh's other main station is Haymarket, about four minutes (by rail) west of Waverley. Most Glasgow and other western and northern services stop here.

Train Contacts National Rail Enquiries. ☎ 08457/484950 ⊕ www.nationalrail. co.uk. **ScotRail.** ☎ 0344/811–0141 ⊕ www.scotrail.co.uk.

TRAM TRAVEL

Absent since 1956, trams returned to the streets of Edinburgh in 2014. The 8½-mile stretch of track runs between Edinburgh Airport in the west to York Place in the east. Useful stops for travelers include Haymarket, Princes Street, and St. Andrew Square (for Waverley Station). Tickets are £1.60 for a single journey in the "City Zone" (which is every stop excluding the airport), or £5.50 to get to or from the airport. Day tickets, allowing unlimited travel, cost £4 in the City Zone and £9 including the airport.

Tram Contact Edinburgh Trams. ☎ 0131/555–6363 ⊕ www.edinburghtrams. co.uk.

TOURS

The Cadies and Witchery Tours. Spooky tours tracing Edinburgh's ghouls, gore, and mysteries commence outside the Witchery Restaurant. The Cadies and Witchery Tours, a member of the Scottish Tourist Guides Association, has built a reputation for combining entertainment and historical accuracy in its lively and enthusiastic Murder and Mystery and (in summer only) Ghosts and Gore tours. Both take you through the narrow Old Town alleyways and closes, with costumed guides and other theatrical characters popping up along the route. ✉ *The Witchery, 352 Castlehill, Old Town* ☎ *0131/225–6745* ⊕ *www.witcherytours.com* ✉ *From £10.*

Edinburgh Bus Tours. Explore every corner of Edinburgh with this company's range of bus tours. The most popular are the Edinburgh Tour, which mainly covers Old Town sights including Edinburgh Castle, the Royal Mile, and the Palace of Holyroodhouse; and the Majestic Tour, which explores the New Town and farther corners of the city, including the Royal Yacht *Britannia* at Leith and the Royal Botanic Garden. Buses depart from Waverley Bridge, with each tour lasting an hour. ■ TIP→ If you plan more than one bus tour during a weekend, buy a money-saving Grand 48 ticket. ✉ *Waverley Bridge, New Town* ☎ *0131/220–0770* ⊕ *www.edinburghtour.com* ✉ *From £15.*

The Edinburgh Literary Pub Tour. Professional actors invoke local literary characters while taking you around some of the city's most hallowed watering holes on these lively and informative tours. The experience is led by "Clart and McBrain"—one a bohemian, the other an intellectual—who regale you with tales of the literary past of Edinburgh's Old and New towns. The experience is so witty and fun that you might just forget you're learning something along the way. Tours run daily from May to September, Thursday to Sunday in April and October, Friday and Sunday from January to March, and Friday only in November and December. Tours meet outside the Beehive Inn. ✉ *The Beehive Inn, 18–20 Grassmarket, Edinburgh* ☎ *0800/169–7410* ⊕ *www.edinburghliterarypubtour.co.uk* ✉ *£14.*

VISITOR INFORMATION

The VisitScotland Edinburgh iCentre, located next to Waverley Station (follow the signs in the station), offers an accommodation-booking service, along with regular tourist information services. There's also a VisitScotland Edinburgh Airport iCentre, for any questions you have upon arrival in the city.

Visitor Information VisitScotland Edinburgh Airport iCentre. ✉ *East Terminal, Edinburgh International Airport, Edinburgh* ☎ *0131/473-3690* ⊕ *www. visitscotland.com.*

EXPLORING

Edinburgh's Old Town, which bears a great symbolic weight as the "heart of Scotland's capital," is a boon for lovers of atmosphere and history. In contrast, if you appreciate the unique architectural heritage of the city's Enlightenment, then the New Town's for you. If you belong to both categories, don't worry—the Old and New towns are only yards apart. Princes Street runs east–west along the north edge of the Princes Street Gardens. Explore the main thoroughfares, but don't forget to get lost among the tiny *wynds* and *closes*: old medieval alleys that connect the winding streets.

Like most cities, Edinburgh incorporates small communities within its boundaries, and many of these are as rewarding to explore as Old Town and New Town. Dean Village, for instance, even though it's close to the New Town, has a character all its own. Duddingston, just southeast of Arthur's Seat, has all the feel of a country village. Then there's Corstorphine, to the west of the city center, famous for being the site of Murrayfield, Scotland's international rugby stadium. Edinburgh's port, Leith, sits on the shore of the Firth of Forth, and throbs with smart bars and restaurants.

OLD TOWN

East of Edinburgh Castle, the historic castle esplanade becomes the street known as the Royal Mile, leading from the castle down through Old Town to the Palace of Holyroodhouse. The Mile, as it's called, is actually made up of one thoroughfare that bears, in consecutive sequence, different names—Castlehill, Lawnmarket, Parliament Square, High Street, and Canongate. This thoroughfare, and the streets and passages that wind off it on both sides, really *were* Edinburgh until the 18th century saw expansions to the south and north. Everybody lived here: the richer folk on the lower floors of houses; the less well-to-do families on the middle floors; and the poor highest up.

Time and progress (of a sort) have swept away some of the narrow closes and tall tenements of the Old Town, but enough survive for you to be able to imagine the original profile of Scotland's capital. There are many guided tours of the area, or you can simply stroll around at your leisure. The latter is often a better choice in summer, when tourists pack the area and large guided groups have trouble making their way through the crowds.

Arthur's Seat. The high point of 640-acre Holyrood Park is this famously spectacular viewpoint. You'll have seen it before—countless photos have been snapped from this very spot. The "seat" in question is actually the 822-foot-high plateau of a small mountain. A ruined church—the 15th-century Chapel of St. Anthony—adds to its impossible picturesqueness. There are various starting points for the walk, but one of the most pleasant begins at the Scottish Parliament building. Cross the road from Parliament, skirt around the parking lot, cross a second road, and join the gently rising path to the left (rather than the steeper fork to the right). At a moderate pace, this climb takes around 45 minutes up and 30 minutes down, and is easy so long as you're reasonably fit. Even if you aren't, there are plenty of places to stop for a rest and to admire the views along the way. A faster—though less beautiful—way to reach the summit is to drive to the small parking area at Dunsapie Loch, on Queen's Road, then follow the footpath up the hill; this walk takes about 20 minutes. ⊠ *Queen's Dr., Old Town.*

Canongate Tolbooth and People's Story Museum. Nearly every city and town in Scotland once had a tolbooth. Originally a customhouse, where tolls were gathered, it soon came to mean town hall and later prison, as there were detention cells in the cellar. The building where Canongate's town council once met now has a museum, the **People's Story Museum,** which focuses on the lives of everyday folk from the 18th century to today. Exhibits describe how Canongate once bustled with the activities of the tradespeople needed to supply life's essentials. There are also displays on the politics, health care, and leisure time (such as it was) in days of yore. Other exhibits leap forward in time to show, for example, a typical 1940s kitchen. ⊠ *163 Canongate, Old Town* ☎ *0131/529–4057* ⊕ *www.edinburghmuseums.org.uk* ⊘ *Closed Mon. and Tues.*

FAMILY **Dynamic Earth.** Using state-of-the-art technology, the 11 theme galleries at this interactive science museum educate and entertain as they explore the wonders of the planet, from polar regions to tropical rain forests. Geological history, from the big bang to the unknown future, is also examined, all topped off with a 360-degree-dome movie-theater experience. Book tickets online for a 10% discount. ⊠ *112–116 Holyrood Rd., Old Town* ☎ *0131/550–7800* ⊕ *www.dynamicearth.co.uk* ⊠ *£15 at door; £13.50 online* ⊘ *Closed Mon. and Tues. in Nov.–Mar.*

Fruitmarket Gallery. This contemporary gallery behind Waverley Station showcases cutting-edge art, mostly from Europe and the United States, including world-renowned artists like Louise Bourgeois, Eva Hesse, and Dieter Roth. Turner Prize–winning artist Martin Creed was also commissioned by the gallery to create a piece of public art nearby—walk up or down the Scotsman Steps to see his colorful marble creation. ■ TIP→ **Free, hour-long tasting tours happen every Saturday at 2.** ⊠ *45 Market St., Old Town* ☎ *0131/225–2383* ⊕ *www.fruitmarket.co.uk.*

FAMILY
Fodor's Choice
★
Edinburgh Castle. The crowning glory of the Scottish capital, Edinburgh Castle is popular not only for its pivotal role in Scottish history, but also because of the spectacular views from its battlements: on a clear day the vistas stretch all the way to the "kingdom" of Fife. You need at least three hours to see everything it has to offer (especially if you're a military history buff), though if you're in a rush, its main highlights can be squeezed into an hour and a half. You enter across the Esplanade, the huge forecourt built in the 18th century as a parade ground, then proceed to the curvy ramparts of the Half-Moon Battery, which give Edinburgh Castle its distinctive silhouette. Highlights include the tiny 11th-century St. Margaret's Chapel, the oldest part of the castle; the Crown Room, which contains the crown, scepter, and sword that once graced the Scottish monarch—and the Stone of Scone, where Scottish monarchs once sat to be crowned; and the famous 15th-century Belgian-made cannon Mons Meg. ⊠ *Castle Esplanade and Castlehill, Old Town* ☎ *0131/225–9846 Edinburgh Castle, 0131/225–9846* ⊕ *www. edinburghcastle.gov.uk* ⊠ *£17.*

George IV Bridge. Here's a curiosity—a bridge that most of its users don't ever realize is a bridge. With buildings closely packed on both sides, George IV Bridge can feel to many like a regular Edinburgh street, but for those forewarned, the truth is plain to see. At the corner of the bridge stands one of the most photographed sculptures in Scotland, *Greyfriars Bobby*. This statue pays tribute to the legendarily loyal Skye terrier who kept vigil beside his master's grave for 14 years after he died in 1858. The 1961 Walt Disney film *Greyfriars Bobby* tells a version of the heartrending tale. ⊠ *Bank St. and Lawnmarket, Old Town.*

Gladstone's Land. This narrow, six-story tenement, situated next to the Assembly Hall, is one of the oldest buildings on the Royal Mile. It's a

13

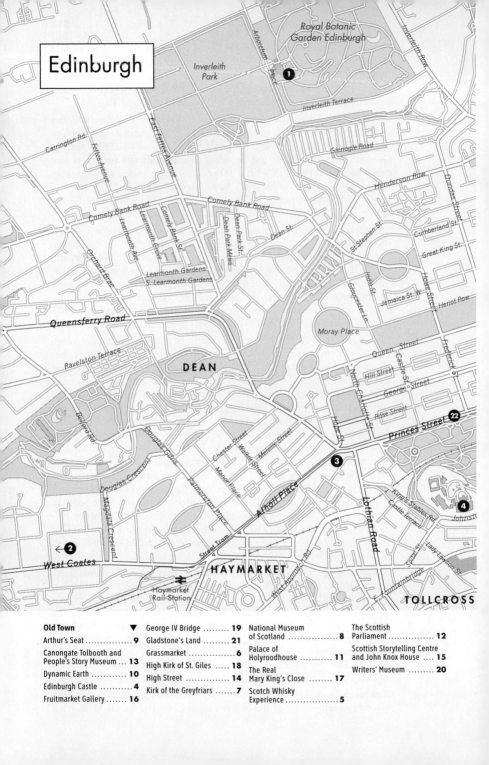

Edinburgh

Royal Botanic Garden Edinburgh

Inverleith Park

Inverleith Terrace

Arboretum Place

Inverleith Row

Carrington Rd.

Fettes Avenue

East Fettes Avenue

Glenogle Road

Henderson Row

Dundas Street

Comely Bank Road

Comely Bank Road

Comely Bank Road

Comely Bank St.

Learmonth Ave.

Learmonth Grove

Dean Park St.

Dean Park Mews

Dean St.

St Stephen St.

Cumberland St.

Great King St.

Orchard Brae

Learmonth Gardens

S. Learmonth Gardens

St Stephen's St.

Gloucester Ln.

India St.

Jamaica St. W.

Heriot Row

Queensferry Road

Moray Place

Queen Street

Frederick Street

Hill Street

Castle St.

Ravelston Terrace

DEAN

George Street

Belford Rd.

Rose Street

North Charlotte St.

Princes Street **22**

Douglas Gdns.

Chester Street

Walker Street

Melville Street

3

Douglas Crescent

Manor Place

Palmerston Place

Atholl Place

Lothian Road

King's Stables Rd.

Castle Terrace

4

Johnst

Magdala Crescent

2

West Coates

Street Tram

Spittal St.

Lady Lawson St.

HAYMARKET

West Approach Rd.

Fountainbridge

TOLLCROSS

Haymarket Rail Station

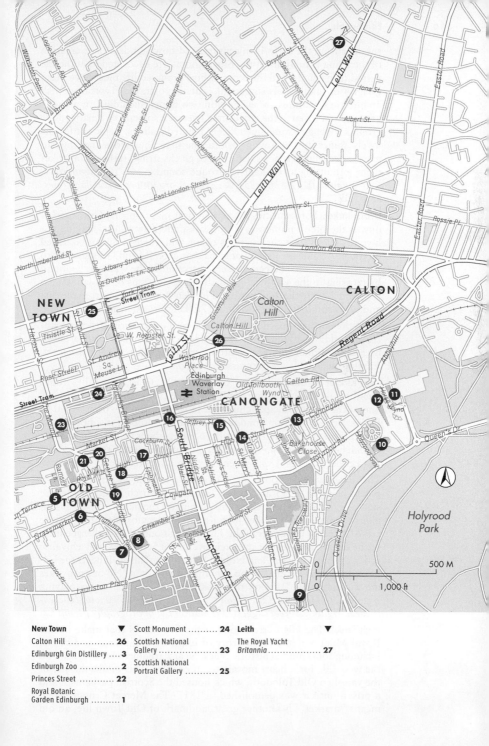

survivor from the early 17th century, and now stands as a re-creation of the living conditions of the time. Rooms are decorated in authentic period furnishings, and the sense of how cramped life must have been, even for the moderately successful, is deftly portrayed. Typical Scottish architectural features are evident on two floors, including an arcaded ground floor (even in the city center, livestock sometimes inhabited the ground floor) and some magnificent painted ceilings. Look out for the lovely spinet in the drawing room; the ingeniously designed instrument, resembling a space-saving piano, plucks strings rather than strikes them, producing a resonantly baroque sound. ⊠ *477B Lawnmarket, Old Town* ☎ *0131/226–5856* ⊕ *www.nts.org.uk/property/gladstones-land* ⊡ *£7.*

Grassmarket. For centuries an agricultural marketplace, Grassmarket now is the site of numerous shops, bars, and restaurants, making it a hive of activity at night. Sections of the Old Town wall can be traced on the north side by a series of steps that ascend from Grassmarket to Johnston Terrace. The best-preserved section of the wall can be found by crossing to the south side and climbing the steps of the lane called the Vennel. Here the 16th-century **Flodden Wall** comes in from the east and turns south at Telfer's Wall, a 17th-century extension.

From the northeast corner of the Grassmarket, **Victoria Street,** a 19th-century addition to the Old Town, leads to the George IV Bridge. Shops here sell antiques, designer clothing, and souvenirs. ⊠ *Grassmarket, Edinburgh* ⊕ *www.greatergrassmarket.co.uk.*

High Kirk of St. Giles (*St Giles' Cathedral*). St. Giles, which lies about one-third of the way along the Royal Mile from Edinburgh Castle, is one of the city's principal churches. However, don't expect a rival to Paris's Notre Dame or London's Westminster Abbey; it's more like a large parish church than a great European cathedral. There has been a church here since AD 854, although most of the present structure dates from either 1120 or 1829, when the church was restored.

The tower, with its stone crown 161 feet above the ground, was completed between 1495 and 1500. Inside the church stands a life-size statue of the Scot whose spirit still dominates the place—the great religious reformer and preacher John Knox. But the most elaborate feature is the **Chapel of the Order of the Thistle,** built onto the southeast corner of the church in 1911 for the exclusive use of Scotland's only chivalric order, the Most Ancient and Noble Order of the Thistle. It bears the belligerent national motto "nemo me impune lacessit" ("No one provokes me with impunity"). Look out for the carved wooden angel playing bagpipes. ⊠ *High St., Old Town* ☎ *0131/225–9442* ⊕ *www.stgilescathedral.org.uk* ⊡ *Free; suggested donation £3; photography permit £2.*

High Street. The High Street (one of the five streets that make up the Royal Mile) is home to an array of impressive buildings and sights, including some hidden historic relics. Near Parliament Square, look on the west side for a **heart** mosaic set in cobbles. This marks the site of the vanished Old Tolbooth, which housed the Scottish parliament and a prison until it was demolished in 1817. The Mercat Cross (*mercat* means "market") is another great landmark of Old Town life, an old mercantile center, where royal proclamations were—and are still—read. Across High Street from the High Kirk of St. Giles stands the City Chambers, built by John Fergus and now the seat of local government; note how the building drops 11 stories to Cockburn Street on its north side. Finally, the Tron Kirk (named after a salt tron, or weight beam, that used to stand nearby) was built after 1633, when St. Giles's became an Episcopal cathedral for a brief time. ☒ *Between Lawnmarket and Canongate, Old Town.*

Fodor's Choice
★

Kirk of the Greyfriars. Greyfriars Church, built on the site of a medieval monastery, was where the National Covenant was signed in 1638. The covenant, which declared the Presbyterian Church in Scotland independent of the monarch, plunged Scotland into decades of civil war—informative panels here tell the full story.

However, the real attraction here is the sprawling, hillside graveyard, surely one of the most evocative in Europe. Its old, tottering tombstones mark the graves of some of Scotland's most respected heroes and despised villains. Some of the larger tombs are arranged in avenues; a few are closed off, but others you can wander. It's a hugely atmospheric place to explore, especially at twilight. Look out for two rare surviving *mortsafes*: iron cages erected around graves in the early 1800s to prevent the theft of corpses for sale to medical schools. Nearby, at the corner of George IV Bridge and Candlemaker Row, stands one of Scotland's most photographed sites: the statue of Greyfriars Bobby, a Skye terrier who supposedly spent 14 years guarding the grave of his departed owner. ☒ *Greyfriars Pl., Old Town* ☏ *0131/225–1900* ⊕ *www.greyfriarskirk.com* ☒ *Free.*

FAMILY
Fodor's Choice
★

National Museum of Scotland. This museum traces the country's fascinating story from the oldest fossils to the most recent popular culture, making it a must-see for first-time visitors to Scotland. Two of the most famous treasures are the Lewis Chessmen, 11 intricately carved 12th-century ivory chess pieces found on one of Scotland's Western Isles, and Dolly the sheep, the world's first cloned mammal and biggest ovine celebrity. A dramatic, cryptlike entrance gives way to the light-filled, birdcage wonders of the Victorian grand hall and the upper galleries. Other exhibition highlights include the hanging hippo and sea creatures of the Wildlife Panorama, beautiful Viking brooches, Pictish stones, and Queen Mary's *clarsach* (harp). Take the elevator to the lovely rooftop terrace for spectacular views of Edinburgh Castle and the city below. ☒ *Chambers St., Old Town* ☏ *0300/123–6789* ⊕ *www. nms.ac.uk* ☒ *Free.*

Fodor's Choice
★

Palace of Holyroodhouse. Onetime haunt of Mary, Queen of Scots, with a long history of gruesome murder, destructive fire, and power-hungry personalities, the Palace of Holyroodhouse is now Queen Elizabeth's official residence in Scotland. A doughty, impressive palace standing at the foot of the Royal Mile, it's built around a graceful, lawned central court at the end of Canongate. And when royals are not in residence, you can take a tour. There's plenty to see here, so make sure you have at least two hours to tour the palace, gardens, and the ruins of the 12th-century abbey; pick up the free audio guide for the full experience.

13

The Palace of Holyroodhouse, now the Queen's official residence in Scotland, contains the rooms of Mary, Queen of Scots.

The **King James Tower** is the oldest surviving section of the palace, containing Mary's rooms on the second floor, and Lord Darnley's rooms below. The 150-foot-long **Great Picture Gallery,** on the north side, displays the portraits of 110 Scottish monarchs. ✉ *Canongate, Old Town* ☎ *0131/123–7306* ⊕ *www.royalcollection.org.uk* ✉ *£12.50; £17.50 includes Queen's Gallery; £21.50 includes garden history tour.*

FAMILY **The Real Mary King's Close.** Buried beneath the City Chambers, this narrow, cobbled close, or lane, provides a glimpse into a very different Edinburgh. It was once a busy open-air thoroughfare with hundreds of residents and a lively market, but in 1753 it was sealed off when the Royal Exchange (now the City Chambers) was built on top. Today, costumed guides take you around the claustrophobic remains of the shops and houses, describing life here for the residents from plague and quarantine to rivers of sewage, as well as the odd murder mystery and ghost story. But for all the (somewhat over-the-top) theatricality, the real highlights here are historical; the sealed-in street is a truly fascinating insight into 17th-century Edinburgh. ✉ *2 Warriston's Cl., Old Town* ☎ *0131/225–0672* ⊕ *www.realmarykingsclose.com* ✉ *£14.75.*

Scotch Whisky Experience. Transforming malted barley and spring water into one of Scotland's most important exports—that's the subject of this popular Royal Mile attraction. An imaginative approach to the subject has guests riding in low-speed barrel cars and exploring Scotland's diverse whisky regions and their distinct flavors. Sniff the various aromas and decide whether you like fruity, sweet, or smoky, and afterward experts will help you select your perfect dram. Your guide will then take you into a vault containing the world's largest collection of Scotch whiskies. Opt for one of the premium tours (from £26 to £70) for extras ranging from additional tastings to a Scottish dining experience. ⊠ *354 Castlehill, Old Town* ☎ *0131/220–0441* ⊕ *www. scotchwhiskyexperience.co.uk* 🔖 *From £15.*

The Scottish Parliament. Scotland's now-iconic Parliament building is starkly modernist, with irregular curves and angles that mirror the twisting shapes of the surrounding landscape. Stylistically, it is about as far removed from Westminster as can be. Originally conceived by the late Catalan architect Enric Miralles, and completed by his widow, Benedetta Tagliabue, the structure's artistry is most apparent when you step inside, where the gentle slopes, forest's worth of oak, polished concrete and granite, and walls of glass create an understated magnificence. Take a free guided tour to see the main hall and debating chamber, a committee room, and other areas of the building, or choose a specialist subject for your tour, from history to literature to art. All tour reservations must be made online. Call well in advance to get a free ticket to view Parliament in action. ⊠ *Horse Wynd, Old Town* ☎ *0131/348–5000* ⊕ *www.scottish.parliament.uk* ☉ *Closed Sun.*

Fodor's Choice
★ **Scottish Storytelling Centre and John Knox House.** The stripped-down, low-fi, traditional art of storytelling has had something of a resurgence in Britain over the last decade or so, and there are few places better than this to experience a master storyteller in full flow. Housed in a modern building that manages to blend seamlessly with the historic structures on either side, the center hosts a year-round program of storytelling, theater, music, and literary events. A café serves lunch, tea, and home-baked cakes.

The center's storytellers also hold tours of John Knox House next door. It isn't certain that the religious reformer ever lived here, but there's evidence he died here in 1572. Mementos of his life are on view inside, and the distinctive dwelling gives you a glimpse of what Old Town life was like in the 16th century—projecting upper floors were once commonplace along the Royal Mile. ⊠ *43-45 High St., Old Town* ☎ *0131/556–9579* ⊕ *www.tracscotland.org/scottish-storytelling-centre* 🔖 *Storytelling Centre: free; John Knox House: £5* ☉ *Closed Sun. in Sept.–June.*

Writers' Museum. Situated down a narrow close off Lawnmarket is the 1662 Lady Stair's House, a fine example of 17th-century urban architecture. Inside, the Writers' Museum evokes Scotland's literary past with such exhibits as the letters, possessions, and original manuscripts of Sir Walter Scott, Robert Burns, and Robert Louis Stevenson. ⊠ *Lady Stair's Close, Old Town* ☎ *0131/529–4901* ⊕ *www.edinburghmuseums.org. uk* ☉ *Closed Mon. and Tues.*

NEW TOWN

It was not until the Scottish Enlightenment, a civilizing time of expansion in the 1700s, that the city's elite decided to break away from the Royal Mile's craggy slope and narrow closes to create a new neighborhood below the castle. This was to become the New Town, with elegant squares, classical facades, wide streets, and harmonious proportions.

In the Old Town, shops and restaurants keep the Grassmarket lively day and night, especially during Edinburgh's August festivals.

Clearly, change had to come. At the dawn of the 18th century, Edinburgh's unsanitary conditions—primarily a result of overcrowded living quarters—were becoming notorious. The well-known Scottish fiddle tune "The Flooers (flowers) of Edinburgh" was only one of many ironic references to the capital's unpleasant environment.

To help remedy this sorry state of affairs, in 1767 James Drummond, the city's lord provost (the Scottish term for mayor), urged the town council to hold a competition to design a new district for Edinburgh. The winner was an unknown young architect named James Craig (1744–95). His plan called for a grid of three main east–west streets, balanced at either end by two grand squares. These streets survive today, though some of the buildings that line them have been altered by later development. Princes Street is the southernmost, with Queen Street to the north and George Street as the axis, punctuated by St. Andrew and Charlotte squares. A look at the map will reveal a geometric symmetry unusual in Britain. Even the Princes Street Gardens are balanced by the Queen Street Gardens, to the north. Princes Street was conceived as an exclusive residential address, with an open vista facing the castle. It has since been altered by the demands of business and shopping, but the vista remains.

The New Town was expanded several times after Craig's death and now covers an area about three times larger than Craig envisioned. Indeed, some of the most elegant facades came later and can be found by strolling north of the Queen Street Gardens.

Calton Hill. Robert Louis Stevenson's favorite view of his beloved city was from the top of this hill, and it's easy to see why. Located in the heart of the city, Calton Hill offers stunning vistas of the Old and New towns and out to the Firth of Forth, making it a popular setting for picnicking and watching festival fireworks. Great views aside, the hill is also home to a number of impressive monuments. The most notable is the so-called **National Monument,** also known as "Scotland's Disgrace," which was commissioned in 1822 and intended to mimic Athens's Parthenon. However, after 12 columns the money ran out, leaving the facade as a monument to high aspirations and poor fund-raising. Nearby, the 100-foot-high **Nelson Monument,** completed in 1815 in honor of Britain's greatest naval hero, is topped with a "time ball" that is dropped at 1 pm every day. Other monuments include the circular Corinthian **Burns Monument** and **Dugald Stewart Monument,** named for the Scottish philosopher.

The hill is also home to the **City Observatory,** divided into the domed Playfair House and the old Gothic Tower. ⊠ *Bounded by Leith St. to the west and Regent Rd. to the south, New Town* ☎ *0131/529–7061* ⊕ *www.edinburgh.gov.uk* ⊠ *Nelson Monument £5* ⊗ *Nelson Monument closed Sun. in Oct.–Mar.*

13

Fodor'sChoice
★

Edinburgh Gin Distillery. Whisky may be Scotland's most famous spirit, but gin also has a long and storied history here—and it's making a comeback. Edinburgh Gin is a small distillery and visitor center just off Princes Street, offering tours and tastings that give a fascinating insight into craft gin production. Two copper stills, Flora and Caledonia, produce a variety of gins, from the navy-strength Cannonball Gin to the coastal botanical-infused Seaside Gin. Take a discovery tour (£10) or a connoisseur tour (£25), then head into the Heads and Tales bar to sample a good selection of Scottish gins and gin cocktails. ⊠ *1a Rutland Pl., West End* ☎ *0131/656–2810* ⊕ *www.edinburghgin.com* ⊠ *£10.*

OFF THE BEATEN PATH

Edinburgh Zoo. Home to star attractions Tian Tian and Yang Gaung, the United Kingdom's only two giant pandas, Edinburgh's Zoo hosts more than 1,000 animals over 80 acres. Don't miss the famous Penguin Parade, which takes place every afternoon (as long as the penguins are willing), or the ever-popular Koala Territory, where you can get up close to the zoo's four koalas—including Yoonarah, born in 2014, the first-ever British-born koala. Discounted tickets are available online. ■**TIP→ Free 15-minute panda-viewing sessions must be booked in advance.** ⊠ *134 Corstorphine Rd., Corstorphine* ☎ *0131/334–9171* ⊕ *www.edinburghzoo.org.uk* ⊠ *£19.*

Princes Street. The south side of this dominant New Town street is occupied by the well-kept Princes Street Gardens, which act as a wide green moat to the castle on its rock. The north side is now one long sequence of chain stores with mostly unappealing modern fronts, with one or two exceptions: most notably the handsome Victorian facade that is home to Jenners department store. ⊠ *Waterloo Pl. to Lothian Rd., New Town.*

Fodor'sChoice
★

Scottish National Gallery. Opened to the public in 1859, the Scottish National Gallery presents a wide selection of paintings from the Renaissance to the postimpressionist period within a grand neoclassical building. Most famous are the Old Master paintings bequeathed by the Duke of Sutherland, including Titian's *Three Ages of Man.* Many masters are here: works by Velázquez, El Greco, Rembrandt, Goya, Poussin, Turner, Degas, Monet, and Van Gogh, among others, complement a fine collection of Scottish art, including Sir Henry Raeburn's *Reverend Robert Walker Skating on Duddingston Loch* and other works by Ramsay, Raeburn, and Wilkie. The gallery also has an information center, gift shop, and the excellent Scottish Cafe and Restaurant.

You can also hop on a free bus (£1 donation requested) from here to the Scottish National Gallery of Modern Art, which has paintings and sculptures by Pablo Picasso, Georges Braque, Henri Matisse, and André Derain, among others. ⊠ *The Mound, New Town* ☎ *0131/624–6200* ⊕ *www.nationalgalleries.org.*

Scott Monument. What appears to be a Gothic cathedral spire that's been chopped off and planted on Princes Street is in fact Scotland's tribute to one of its most famous sons, Sir Walter Scott. Built in 1844 and soaring to 200 feet, it remains the largest monument to a writer anywhere in the world. Climb the 287 steps to the top for a stunning view of the city and the hills and coast beyond. ⊠ *Princes St., New Town* ☎ *0131/529–4068* ⊕ *www.edinburghmuseums.org.uk* 🎫 *£5; cash only.*

OFF THE BEATEN PATH

Royal Botanic Garden Edinburgh. Explore Britain's largest rhododendron and azalea gardens at this beautiful 70-acre botanical garden. Founded in 1670 as a physic garden, it now has a range of natural highlights such as soaring palms in the glass-domed Temperate House and the steamy Tropical Palm House, an extensive Chinese garden, and a pretty rock garden and stream. There's a visitor center with exhibits on biodiversity, a fabulous gift shop selling plants, books, and gifts, and two cafeterias. There's also the handsome 18th-century Inverleith House, which hosts art exhibitions. Guided walks of the gardens cost £7 and take place daily from April to October, or you can book a private tour including afternoon tea (£45 for two) at any time. It takes 20 minutes to walk to the garden from Princes Street, or you can take a bus. ⊠ *Arboretum Pl., Inverleith* ☎ *0131/248–2909* ⊕ *www.rbge.org.uk* 🎫 *Free; Glasshouses £6.50.*

Scottish National Portrait Gallery. Set within a magnificent red-sandstone Gothic building from 1889, this gallery is an Edinburgh must-see. Conceived as a gift to the people of Scotland, it divides into five broad themes, from Reformation to Modernity, with special galleries for photography and contemporary art—all centered around the stunning Great Hall. It also plays host to regular temporary exhibitions, including the annual BP Portrait Award. ⊠ *1 Queen St., New Town* ☎ *0131/624–6200* ⊕ *www.nationalgalleries.org.*

LEITH

Just north of the city is Edinburgh's port, a place brimming with seafaring history and undergoing a slow revival after years of postwar neglect. It may not be as pristine as much of modern-day Edinburgh, but there are plenty of cobbled streets, dockside buildings, and bobbing boats to capture your imagination. Here along the lowest reaches of the Water of Leith (the river that flows through town), you'll find an ever-growing array of modish shops, pubs, and restaurants. Leith's major attraction is the Royal Yacht *Britannia,* moored outside the huge Ocean Terminal shopping mall. You can reach Leith from the center by walking down Leith Walk from the east end of Princes Street (20 to 30 minutes)—or, better yet, walk along the beautiful Water of Leith (a great way to forget you're in a capital city). Alternatively, take Lothian Bus 22.

FAMILY **The Royal Yacht *Britannia.*** Moored on the waterfront at Leith is the Royal Yacht *Britannia*—launched in Scotland in 1953, retired in 1997, and now returned to her home country. A favorite of Queen Elizabeth II (she is reported to have shed a tear at its decommissioning ceremony), it is now open for the public to explore, from the royal apartments on the upper floors to the more functional engine room, bridge, galleys, and captain's cabin. The visitor center, based within the hulking, on-shore Ocean Terminal shopping mall, has a variety of fascinating exhibits and photographs relating to the yacht's history. ⊠ *Ocean Dr., Leith* ☏ *0131/555–5566* ⊕ *www.royalyachtbritannia.co.uk* ☏ *£15.50.*

WHERE TO EAT

Edinburgh's eclectic restaurant scene has attracted a brigade of well-known chefs, including the award-winning trio of Martin Wishart, Tom Kitchin, and Paul Kitching. They and dozens of others have abandoned the tried-and-true recipes for more adventurous cuisine. Of course, you can always find traditional fare, which usually means the Scottish-French style that harks back to the historical "Auld Alliance" of the 13th century. The Scottish element is the preference for fresh and local foodstuffs; the French supply the sauces. In Edinburgh, you can sample anything from Malaysian *rendang* (a thick, coconut-milk stew) to Kurdish kebabs, while the long-established French, Italian, Chinese, Pakistani, and Indian communities ensure that the majority of the globe's most treasured cuisines are well represented.

PRICES AND HOURS

It's possible to eat well in Edinburgh without spending a fortune. Multi-course prix-fixe options are common, and almost always less expensive than ordering à la carte. Even at restaurants in the highest price category, you can easily spend less than £35 per person. People tend to eat later in Scotland than in England—around 8 pm on average—and then drink on in leisurely Scottish fashion. *Restaurant reviews have been shortened. For full information, visit Fodors.com. Use the coordinate (✛ B2) at the end of each listing to locate a site on the corresponding map.*

WHAT IT COSTS IN POUNDS			
$	**$$**	**$$$**	**$$$$**
Restaurants	under £15	£15–£19	£20–£25	over £25

Restaurant prices are the average cost of a main course at dinner or, if dinner is not served, at lunch.

OLD TOWN

$ INTERNATIONAL 🍴 **Checkpoint.** Originally run as a pop-up during the Festival Fringe, this supercool café-bar became a permanent part of the Edinburgh dining scene in 2015. The coffee is sensational, but the comfort food is just as much of a draw. **Known for:** excellent coffee; delicious light lunches; hip hangout in the evening. [$] *Average main: £6* ✉ *3 Bristo Pl., Old Town* ☎ *0131/225–9352* 🌐 *www.checkpointedinburgh.com* ✣ *F5.*

$$ ITALIAN Fodor's Choice ★ 🍴 **Contini Cannonball.** The name refers to one of the most delightful quirks of Edinburgh's Old Town—the cannonball embedded in the wall outside, said to have been fired at the castle while Bonnie Prince Charlie was in residence (not true, but a good story). The atmosphere in this three-story restaurant and whisky bar is casual and relaxed, despite the gorgeous art deco dining room with views of the castle esplanade. **Known for:** scrumptious Italian-Scottish cuisine; great views of the castle; bread-crumbed haggis cannonballs. [$] *Average main: £15* ✉ *356 Castlehill, Old Town* ☎ *0131/225–1550* 🌐 *www.contini.com/contini-cannonball* ✣ *E5.*

$ VEGETARIAN 🍴 **David Bann.** This hip eatery, situated just off the Royal Mile, serves exclusively vegetarian and vegan favorites, and its inventive dishes and modern interior make it a popular place with young locals. The menu changes constantly, but the invariably creative, flavorful dishes often leave carnivores forgetting they're eating vegetarian. **Known for:** superb vegetarian and vegan cuisine; very affordable. [$] *Average main: £13* ✉ *56–58 St. Mary's St., Old Town* ☎ *0131/556–5888* 🌐 *www.davidbann.com* ✣ *G4.*

$$ MIDDLE EASTERN 🍴 **Hanam's.** Kurdish food may not be as well known as other Middle Eastern cuisines, but dishes like *bayengaan surocrau* (marinated slow-roasted eggplant) and lamb *tashreeb* (a flavorful casserole) are worth checking out. Hanam's proudly cooks up Kurdish cuisine, but also serves more familiar Middle Eastern fare, from shish kebabs to falafel. **Known for:** traditional Kurdish cooking; BYOB; hookah on heated terrace. [$] *Average main: £15* ✉ *3 Johnston Terr., Old Town* ☎ *0131/225–1329* 🌐 *www.hanams.com* ✣ *E5.*

$ BRITISH 🍴 **Howies.** The Victoria Street branch of this bistro chain is a good choice for contemporary Scottish fare, with lots of fresh local produce. Alongside the daily specials and quality Scottish steaks and salmon, there are some nicely inventive vegetarian options. **Known for:** quality Scottish menu; good value set-price lunch. [$] *Average main: £8* ✉ *10–14 Victoria St., Old Town* ☎ *0131/225–1721* 🌐 *www.howies.uk.com* ✣ *E5.*

$$$ FRENCH 🍴 **La Garrigue.** Edinburgh is blessed with several excellent French bistros, and this is one of the best. Although the modern decor evokes Paris, the food has the rustic flavor of the southern Languedoc region. **Known for:** rustic French cuisine; attentive service. [$] *Average main: £21* ✉ *31 Jeffrey St., Old Town* ☎ *0131/557–3032* 🌐 *www.lagarrigue.co.uk* ✣ *G4.*

$$ BISTRO 🍴 **La Petite Mort.** This exceptionally fine bistro treats its seasonal, regional Scottish flavors with Continental reverence, and the crowds that pack the place to the rafters every night are testament to its success. With its superb flavors, its extensive wine list, and its wallet-friendly prices, we'll forgive them the indulgence of the name: La Petite Mort is French for, let's say... climax. **Known for:** beautiful velouté sauces; inventive cocktails;

charming environs. $ Average main: £16 ⊠ 32 Valleyfield St., Old Town ☎ 0131/229–3693 ⊕ www.lapetitemortedinburgh.co.uk ✛ D6.

$ ✕ **Lovecrumbs.** A bakery-café with an inordinately sweet tooth, Lovecrumbs joyously, deliciously, and unashamedly focuses on what really matters in life: cake. It serves wonderful cakes of all kinds, from pistachio and chocolate to heavenly peanut-butter brownies to mouthwatering tarts. **Known for:** extraordinary cakes galore; junk-shop-esque interior decor; hit-or-miss service. $ Average main: £4 ⊠ 155 W. Port, Old Town ☎ 0131/629–0626 ⊕ www.lovecrumbs.co.uk ✛ D5.

CAFÉ

Fodor's Choice ★

$$ ✕ **Michael Neave Kitchen and Whisky Bar.** Young chef Michael Neave delivers exceptional cuisine at affordable prices in his restaurant just off the Royal Mile. With a mission to "explore the best of Scotland's larder," quality Scottish produce is the star here. **Known for:** superb Scottish cuisine; inventive sauces; great value fixed-price menus. $ Average main: £18 ⊠ 21 Old Fishmarket Cl., Old Town ☎ 0131/226–4747 ⊕ www. michaelneave.co.uk ☾ Closed Sun. and Mon. ✛ F4.

MODERN BRITISH

$ ✕ **Oink.** For a quick, cheap bite while wandering the Royal Mile, you can't beat Oink—possibly the best hog roast (pulled pork) in Edinburgh. Located at the bottom of the Royal Mile (there are two other outlets, but this one is the best), it was founded by two farmers in 2008, and their high-quality, hand-reared pork has proved a huge hit ever since. **Known for:** unbelievable pulled pork; extra crackling on request; great value lunch. $ Average main: £5 ⊠ 82 Canongate, Old Town ☎ 07584/637416 ⊕ www.oinkhogroast.co.uk ✛ H4.

BRITISH

Fodor's Choice ★

$$$ ✕ **Ondine.** This fabulous seafood restaurant just off the Royal Mile has been making waves since 2009 with its expertly prepared dishes from sustainable fishing sources. A wall of windows shines bountiful amounts of sunlight on an attractive monochromatic dining room and an art deco oyster bar. **Known for:** spectacular seafood; lavish decor; snappy service. $ Average main: £25 ⊠ 2 George IV Bridge, Old Town ☎ 0131/226–1888 ⊕ www.ondinerestaurant.co.uk ☾ Closed Sun. ✛ E5.

SEAFOOD

$ ✕ **Timberyard.** There are few restaurants that feel so wonderfully, well, Edinburgh as this one. The freshest seasonal ingredients, mostly sourced from small local producers, go into creating delicious, inventive fare. **Known for:** exciting dishes; hip interior; pricey multicourse menus. $ Average main: £13 ⊠ 10 Lady Lawson St., Old Town ☎ 0131/221–1222 ⊕ www.timberyard.co ☾ Closed Sun. and Mon. ✛ D5.

BRITISH

Fodor's Choice ★

$$$ ✕ **Wedgwood the Restaurant.** Rejecting the idea that fine dining should be a stuffy affair, owners Paul Wedgwood and Lisa Channon opened this Royal Mile gem in 2007. Local produce and some unusual foraged fronds enliven the taste buds, as Scottish and Asian influences are creatively fused together throughout the menu, including desserts. **Known for:** unfussy fine dining; Asian-influenced menu; unintrusive service. $ Average main: £20 ⊠ 267 Canongate, Old Town ☎ 0131/558–8737 ⊕ www.wedgwoodtherestaurant.co.uk ✛ G4.

MODERN BRITISH

Fodor's Choice ★

13

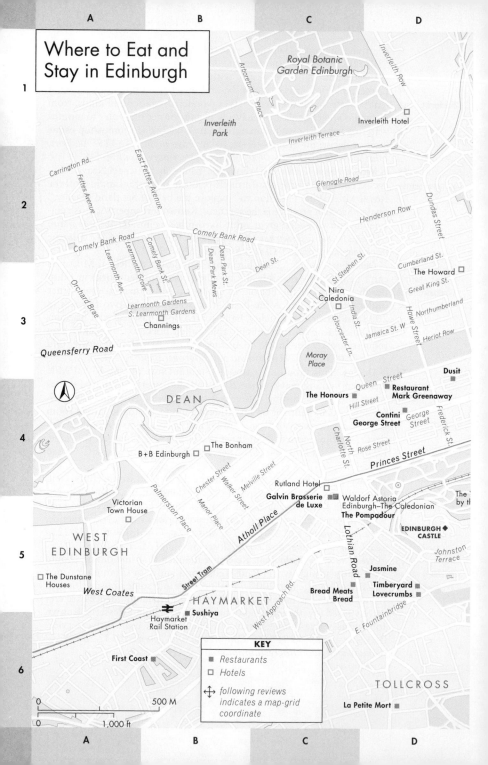

Where to Eat and Stay in Edinburgh

A **B** **C** **D**

1

Royal Botanic
Garden Edinburgh

Inverleith Row

Arboretum Place

Inverleith Park

Inverleith Hotel □

Inverleith Terrace

2

Carrington Rd.

Fettes Avenue

East Fettes Avenue

Glenogle Road

Henderson Row

Dundas Street

Comely Bank Road

Comely Bank Road

Cumberland St.

The Howard □

Comely Bank Road

Learmonth Grove

Comely Bank St.

Dean Park Mews

Dean Park St.

Dean St.

St Stephen St.

Great King St.

3

Orchard Brae

Learmonth Ave.

Learmonth Gardens
S. Learmonth Gardens

Channings □

Nira
Caledonia ■

India St.

Gloucester Ln.

Jamaica St. W

Howe Street

Northumberland

Heriot Row

Queensferry Road

Moray
Place

Queen Street

Dusit ■

The Honours ■

Hill Street

**Restaurant
Mark Greenaway** ■

DEAN

**Contini
George Street** ■

George
Street

Frederick St.

4

North
Charlotte St.

Rose Street

Princes Street

B + B Edinburgh □   □ The Bonham

Chester Street

Walker Street

Melville Street

Manor Place

Rutland Hotel □

**Galvin Brasserie
de Luxe** ■■

Waldorf Astoria
Edinburgh–The Caledonian

The Pompadour ■

Victorian
Town House □

Palmerston Place

Atholl Place

Lothian Road

**EDINBURGH ◆
CASTLE**

Johnston
Terrace

The
by th

**WEST
EDINBURGH**

5

□ The Dunstane
Houses

West Coates

Street Tram

HAYMARKET

West Approach Rd.

Jasmine ■

Timberyard ■

**Bread Meats
Bread** ■

Lovecrumbs ■

E. Fountainbridge

✈
Haymarket
Rail Station ■ **Sushiya**

First Coast ■

6

KEY

■ Restaurants
□ Hotels
✦ following reviews
indicates a map-grid
coordinate

TOLLCROSS

La Petite Mort ■

0 _____ 500 M

0 _____ 1,000 ft

A **B** **C** **D**

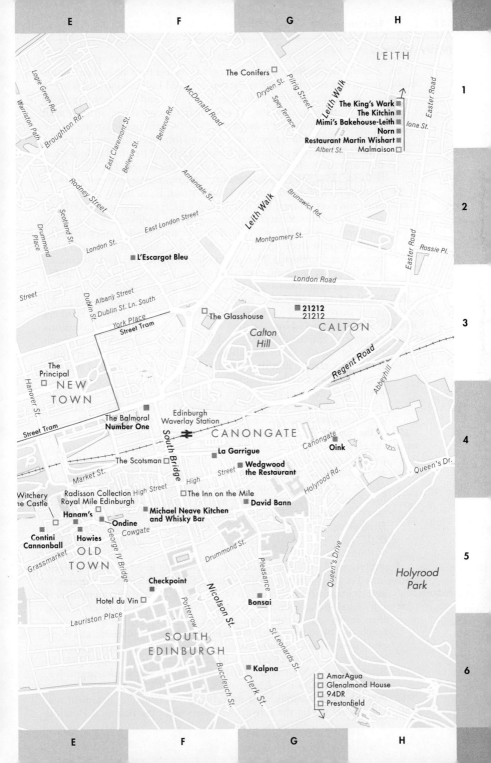

LEITH

The Conifers

Dryden St.
Pilrig Street
Spey Terrace

Leith Walk
The King's Wark
The Kitchin
Mimi's Bakehouse-Leith
Norn
Restaurant Martin Wishart
Albert St.   Malmaison

Iona St.
Easter Road

McDonald Road
Bellevue Rd.
East Claremont St.
Bellevue St.
Annandale St.

Logie Green Rd.
Warriston Path
Broughton Rd.
Rodney Street
Scotland St.

Brunswick Rd.

East London Street
London St.
Leith Walk

Montgomery St.

Easter Road
Rossie Pl.

Drummond Place

Street
Dublin St.
Albany Street
Dublin St. Ln. South

London Road

York Place
Street Tram

The Glasshouse

21212
21212

CALTON

Calton Hill

The Principal

NEW TOWN

Hanover St.

Regent Road
Abbeyhill

The Balmoral
Number One

Street Tram

Edinburgh Waverlay Station

CANONGATE

Canongate
Oink

Market St.
The Scotsman

La Garrigue

Street
High

Wedgwood the Restaurant

Holyrood Rd.

Queen's Dr.

Witchery
the Castle

Radisson Collection
Royal Mile Edinburgh   High Street

The Inn on the Mile

David Bann

Hanam's
Ondine

Michael Neave Kitchen
and Whisky Bar

Contini
Cannonball   Howies

Cowgate

OLD TOWN

George IV Bridge

Drummond St.

Pleasance

Queen's Drive

Holyrood Park

Grassmarket

Checkpoint

Hotel du Vin

Lauriston Place

Nicolson St.

Bonsai

St Leonards St.

Potterrow

SOUTH EDINBURGH

Kalpna

AmarAgua
Glenalmond House
94DR
Prestonfield

Buccleuch St.
Clerk St.

E F G H

1 2 3 4 5 6

NEW TOWN

$$
ITALIAN
✕ **Contini George Street.** Set within a grand former banking hall on George Street, this superb restaurant serves inspired Italian food and wine in a relaxing, airy setting. Refurbished in 2017, and now complete with grand Corinthian columns, an open marble-topped bar, intricate wall hangings, and soft gray banquettes, it offers light but satisfying Italian favorites divided into *primi, secondi,* and *formaggi.* **Known for:** lovely, light Italian cuisine; grand but relaxing setting; free Italian lessons in the bathrooms. $ *Average main: £18* ✉ *103 George St., New Town* ☎ *0131/225–1550* ⊕ *www.contini.com/contini-george-street* ✛ *D4.*

$$
THAI
Fodor'sChoice
★
✕ **Dusit.** Tucked down narrow Thistle Street, Dusit doesn't register on most travelers' radars, but it has been a local favorite since 2002. An authentic, contemporary Thai restaurant run by Bangkok-born Pom, the menu here delights with deliciously creamy curries, spicy stir-fries, and fragrant seafood specialties, all of which use a mix of fresh local produce and imported Thai vegetables. **Known for:** award-winning Thai food; locals' haunt; expensive mains. $ *Average main: £16* ✉ *49a Thistle St., New Town* ☎ *0131/220–6846* ⊕ *www.dusit.co.uk* ✛ *D3.*

$$$
BRASSERIE
FAMILY
Fodor'sChoice
★
✕ **Galvin Brasserie de Luxe.** This Parisian-style brasserie combines handsome surroundings with first-class cuisine from London brothers Chris and Jeff Galvin. Dapper waiters glide around the cavernous dining area with its central bar, while the menu marries classic French dishes alongside Scottish staples, so you should expect everything from steak tartare and duck terrine to smoked salmon and peppery haggis. **Known for:** delicious French-Scottish cuisine; superb service; a family favorite. $ *Average main: £22* ✉ *Waldorf Astoria Edinburgh— The Caledonian, Rutland St., New Town* ☎ *0131/222–8988* ⊕ *www. galvinbrasseriedeluxe.com* ✛ *C4.*

$$$
BISTRO
Fodor'sChoice
★
✕ **The Honours.** Run by Edinburgh restaurant grandee Martin Wishart, the Honours is a more relaxed (though almost as pricey) alternative to his eponymous flagship in Leith. Inside its gorgeous black-and-white, art deco interior, diners can enjoy a range of excellent Scottish seafood dishes; but those in the know order the meat, with extraordinary rare-breed sirloin and fillet steaks as well as more unusual cuts like hanger steak and ox cheek. **Known for:** incredible meat dishes; beautiful Art Deco decor. $ *Average main: £24* ✉ *58a North Castle St., New Town* ☎ *0131/220–2513* ⊕ *www.thehonours.co.uk* ☻ *Closed Sun. and Mon.* Ⓜ *Princes St.* ✛ *C4.*

$
FRENCH
Fodor'sChoice
★
✕ **L'Escargot Bleu.** When it comes to quality at a good value, this pretty little French bistro, situated on one of Edinburgh's trendiest streets, is almost impossible to beat. You're warmly welcomed into an upmarket but casual space of stripped wooden floors and period French posters, then shown a menu that seems to have a typo: £12.90 for a two-course lunch, or £14.90 for dinner of fine French cuisine as authentic as a withering stare on the Champs-Élysées. **Known for:** authentic French fare; hard-to-believe low prices; friendly service. $ *Average main: £13* ✉ *56 Broughton St., New Town* ☎ *0131/557–1600* ⊕ *www.lescargotbleu. co.uk* ☻ *Closed Sun.* ✛ *F2.*

$$$$
BRITISH
✕ **Number One.** Clublike but unstuffy, this outstanding basement restaurant, set within the Edwardian splendor of the Balmoral Hotel, is

made for intimate dining. The food is extraordinary, with a menu that highlights the best of Scottish seafood and meat in inventive fashion, but the prices make this a place for serious special occasions; the regular 3-course prix-fixe is £80 per person, while the 10-course tasting menu is £120, drinks not included. **Known for:** wonderfully intimate setting; inventive dishes; very expensive. $ *Average main: £80* ✉ *Balmoral Hotel, 1 Princes St., New Town* ☎ *0131/557–6727* ⊕ *www.roccoforte-hotels.com* ☾ *No lunch* Ⓜ *Princes St.* ✛ *F4.*

$$$$
FRENCH FUSION

✕ **The Pompadour.** Sophisticated surroundings and sumptuous cuisine make this restaurant, originally opened in 1925, one of Edinburgh's best spots for fine dining. London chef–restaurateur brothers Jeff and Chris Galvin impart their expertise in the classic French-inspired cuisine and impressive wine list. **Known for:** beautiful dining room; subtly sumptuous flavors; gorgeous presentation. $ *Average main: £65* ✉ *Waldorf Astoria Edinburgh–The Caledonian, Princes St., New Town* ☎ *0131/222–8975* ⊕ *www.thepompadourbygalvin.com* ☾ *Closed Sun. and Mon. No lunch Tues.–Fri.* ✛ *C4.*

13

$$$$
MODERN BRITISH

✕ **Restaurant Mark Greenaway.** Fine dining with a real sense of fun is what makes Restaurant Mark Greenaway stand out from the crowd. Inventive dishes and serving styles populate the menu at this cozy but high-end eatery, from an amuse bouche served in a cardboard egg box to a broth that's boiled in a beaker at your table. **Known for:** fun and inventive food; attentive service; occasional style over substance. $ *Average main: £28* ✉ *69 N. Castle St., New Town* ☎ *0131/226–1155* ⊕ *www.markgreenaway.com* ☾ *Closed Sun. and Mon.* ✛ *D3.*

$$$$
MODERN FRENCH
Fodor'sChoice
★

✕ **21212.** Paul Kitching is one of Britain's most innovative chefs, and the theatrical dining experience at 21212 delivers surprises galore. Set within a Georgian town house, the Michelin-starred restaurant is sumptuously appointed; the Belle Époque decor and quirky crockery make this a perfect destination for couples (who should ask for a romantic alcove window table). **Known for:** contemporary Franco-Anglo-Scottish cuisine; romantic; friendly and informed staff. $ *Average main: £85* ✉ *3 Royal Terr., New Town* ☎ *0131/523–1030* ⊕ *www.21212restaurant. co.uk* ☾ *Closed Sun. and Mon.* ✛ *G3.*

HAYMARKET

$$
INTERNATIONAL

✕ **First Coast.** This laid-back bistro, just a few minutes from Haymarket Station, has a loyal following—and for good reason. Its multicultural menu has everything from Thai mango salads to Brazilian seafood stews to Korean rice cakes, as well as an unusually good selection of vegetarian options. **Known for:** great international fare; big on flavor; relaxing interior. $ *Average main: £15* ✉ *99–101 Dalry Rd., Haymarket* ☎ *0131/313–4404* ⊕ *www.first-coast.co.uk* ☾ *Closed Sun.* ✛ *B6.*

$
JAPANESE
Fodor'sChoice
★

✕ **Sushiya.** It may look underwhelming from the outside, but step inside for amazing, atmospheric, and authentic Japanese dining. It's a tiny place, with just 22 seats facing an open counter, but the array of sushi and sashimi assembled by the resident chef is magical. **Known for:** delicious sushi and sashimi; very affordable lunch. $ *Average main: £9* ✉ *19 Dalry Rd., Haymarket* ☎ *0131/313–3222* ⊕ *www.sushiya.co.uk* ☾ *Closed Sun. and Mon.* ✛ *B5.*

WEST END

$ BURGER Fodor's Choice ★ 🍴 **Bread Meats Bread.** This family-run burger joint, first opened in Glasgow in 2012 and expanded to Edinburgh in 2016, has already gained a nationwide reputation for its over-the-top add-ons like bone-marrow butter, kimchi, 'Nduja (spicy salami spread), and pomegranate molasses. Take a seat inside the chic, reclaimed-wood interior and choose from a menu packed with amped-up burgers, as well as chicken, veggie, and halal options. **Known for:** Lothian Wolf burger; some of the best burgers in United Kingdom; large portions; smart, modern interior. [$] *Average main: £13* ✉ *92 Lothian Rd., West End* ☎ *0131/225–3000* 🌐 *www.breadmeatsbread.com* ✢ *D5.*

$ CHINESE FAMILY 🍴 **Jasmine.** Fresh seafood and meat matched with just the right spices is the main attraction of this small, friendly Cantonese restaurant. The standout dishes here include steamed whole sea bass with ginger and spring onions and crispy almond chicken with orange sauce. **Known for:** delicious Cantonese cuisine; friendly service; a little cramped. [$] *Average main: £14* ✉ *32–34 Grindlay St., West End* ☎ *0131/229–5757* 🌐 *www.jasminechinese.co.uk* ✢ *D5.*

SOUTH SIDE

$ JAPANESE 🍴 **Bonsai.** The owners of Bonsai regularly visit Tokyo to research the casual dining scene, and their expertise is setting a high standard for Japanese cuisine in Edinburgh. The succulent *gyoza* (steamed dumplings) are pliant and tasty, while the wide variety of noodle, teriyaki, and sushi dishes balance sweet and sour deliciously. **Known for:** authentic sushi; dragon gaijin-zushi (inside-out roll). [$] *Average main: £8* ✉ *46 W. Richmond St., South Side* ☎ *0131/668–3847* 🌐 *www.bonsaibarbistro.co.uk* ✢ *G5.*

$ INDIAN Fodor's Choice ★ 🍴 **Kalpna.** Amid an ordinary row of shops, the facade of this vegetarian Indian restaurant may be unremarkable, but the food is exceptional, and a great value, too. You'll find south- and west-Indian specialties, including *dam aloo kashmiri (*a medium-spicy potato dish with a sauce made from honey, pistachios, and almonds) and *bangan achari* (super-spicy marinated eggplants). **Known for:** authentic veggie Indian fare; lively interior with exotic mosaics; great value. [$] *Average main: £9* ✉ *2–3 St. Patrick Sq., South Side* ☎ *0131/667–9890* 🌐 *www.kalpnarestaurant.com* ⏲ *No lunch Sun.* ✢ *G6.*

LEITH

$$ BRITISH 🍴 **The King's Wark.** This gastro-pub at The Shore in Leith combines a beautiful historic setting with great quality food and a wide selection of Scottish gins. At lunchtime, the dark-wood bar does a roaring trade in simple fare such as gourmet burgers, fish cakes, and haggis (traditional or vegetarian), but in the evening, the kitchen ups the ante with a chalkboard menu of locally caught seafood specialties, from hake to monkfish. **Known for:** affordable quality cuisine; atmospheric setting. [$] *Average main: £16* ✉ *The Shore, 36 The Shore, Leith* ☎ *0131/554–9260* 🌐 *kingswark.co.uk/* ✢ *H1.*

$$$$ FRENCH

🍴 **The Kitchin.** A perennially popular high-end dining option, Tom Kitchin's Michelin-starred venture packs in the crowds. Kitchin, who trained in France, runs a tight ship, and his passion for using seasonal and locally sourced produce to his own creative ends shows no sign of waning. **Known for:** nose-to-tail philosophy; lovely setting; affordable prix-fixe lunch. [$] *Average main: £33* ✉ *78 Commercial Quay, Leith* ☎ *0131/555–1755* 🌐 *thekitchin.com* 🕒 *Closed Sun. and Mon.* ✣ *H1.*

$ BAKERY FAMILY Fodor's Choice ★

🍴 **Mimi's Bakehouse - Leith.** Despite its large interior with acres of seating, this bakery-café still regularly has lines out the door. The reason is simple: it does the best cakes in Edinburgh, using everything from Oreos to Reese's Pieces to strawberries and cream. **Known for:** delicious and creative cakes; to-die-for breakfasts; fun and cheeky decor. [$] *Average main: £10* ✉ *63 The Shore, Leith* ☎ *0131/555–5908* 🌐 *www.mimisbakehouse.com* 🕒 *No dinner* ✣ *H1.*

$$$$ SCANDINAVIAN Fodor's Choice ★

🍴 **Norn.** Opened in summer 2016, Norn is a relative newcomer to Leith's upmarket dining scene, but the signs are it's here to stay. Owner and chef Scott Smith serves up seasonal, Scandinavian-inspired fare with rare Scottish island ingredients, from beremeal (an ancient form of barley) bread to black potato. **Known for:** sublime and sustainable cuisine; unusual ingredients and tastes; four-course £40 prix fixe is a steal. [$] *Average main: £40* ✉ *50–54 Henderson St., Leith* ☎ *0131/629–2525* 🌐 *www.nornrestaurant.com* 🕒 *Closed Sun. and Mon.* ✣ *H1.*

$$$$ FRENCH Fodor's Choice ★

🍴 **Restaurant Martin Wishart.** Leith's premier dining experience, this high-end restaurant combines imaginative cuisine, luxuriously understated decor, and a lovely waterfront location. Renowned Michelin-starred chef Martin Wishart woos diners with his inspired menu of artistically presented, French-influenced dishes. **Known for:** impeccable cuisine; exceptional and flexible service; beautiful location; weekend reservations essential. [$] *Average main: £85* ✉ *54 The Shore, Leith* ☎ *0131/553–3557* 🌐 *www.restaurantmartinwishart.co.uk* 🕒 *Closed Sun. and Mon.* ✣ *H1.*

WHERE TO STAY

From stylish boutique hotels to homey B&Bs, Edinburgh has a world-class array of accommodation options to suit every taste. Its status as one of Britain's most attractive and fascinating cities ensures a steady influx of visitors, but the wealth of overnight options means there's no need to compromise on where you stay. Grand old hotels are rightly renowned for their regal bearing and old-world charm, but if your tastes are a little more contemporary, the city's burgeoning contingent of chic-design hotels offers an equally alluring alternative. For those on a tighter budget, the town's B&Bs are the most likely choice. If you've previously found B&Bs to be restrictive, keep in mind that Scots are trusting people—many proprietors provide front-door keys and very few impose curfews.

Rooms are harder to find in August and September, when the Edinburgh International Festival and the Festival Fringe take place, so reserve at least three months in advance. B&Bs may prove trickier to find in the winter months (with the exception of Christmas and New Year), as this is when many proprietors choose to close up shop and go on vacation themselves.

PRICES

To save money and see how local residents live, stay in a B&B in one of the areas away from the city center, such as Pilrig to the north, Murrayfield to the west, or Sciennes to the south. Public buses can whisk you to the city center in 10 to 15 minutes. *Hotel reviews have been shortened. For full information, visit Fodors.com. Use the coordinate (✥ B2) at the end of each listing to locate a site on the corresponding map.*

	WHAT IT COSTS IN POUNDS			
	$	$$	$$$	$$$$
Hotels	under £100	£100–£160	£161–£220	Over £220

Hotel prices are the lowest cost of a standard double room in high season, including 20% V.A.T.

OLD TOWN

$$$ HOTEL Fodor's Choice ★ 🏨 **Hotel du Vin.** Leave it to one of the United Kingdom's most forward-thinking hotel chains to convert a Victorian-era asylum into this understated luxury property, which combines a real sense of history with contemporary decor and trappings. **Pros:** unique and historic building; trendy design; lively on-site dining and drinking. **Cons:** quarter-mile walk to nearest parking; neighborhood can be noisy. [$] *Rooms from: £195* ✉ *11 Bristo Pl., Old Town* ☎ *0131/285–1479* 🌐 *www.hotelduvin.com* 🛏 *47 rooms* 🍴 *Free Breakfast* ✥ *F5.*

$$$ B&B/INN 🏨 **The Inn on the Mile.** This chic and welcoming boutique inn could hardly be more central—some rooms even overlook the Royal Mile. **Pros:** views of the Royal Mile; lovely staff; great design. **Cons:** lots of steps and no elevator; sometimes noisy; nearest parking at a public lot (three-minute walk). [$] *Rooms from: £195* ✉ *82 High St., Old Town* ☎ *0131/556–9940* 🌐 *www.theinnonthemile.co.uk* 🛏 *9 rooms* 🍴 *Free Breakfast* ✥ *F4.*

$$$$ HOTEL Fodor's Choice ★ 🏨 **Radisson Collection Royal Mile Edinburgh.** The bright primary colors, striking stenciled wallpapers, and bold, eclectic furnishings inside this übertrendy design hotel contrast with the Gothic surroundings of the Royal Mile—and yet, somehow, it works. **Pros:** perfect location in the heart of the city; bold and fashionable decor; inventive cocktails. **Cons:** decor is a little Austin Powers in places. [$] *Rooms from: £260* ✉ *1 George IV Bridge, Old Town* ☎ *0131/220–6666* 🌐 *www.radissoncollection.com/en/royalmile-hotel-edinburgh* 🛏 *136 rooms* 🍴 *Free Breakfast* ✥ *E5.*

$$$$ HOTEL 🏨 **The Scotsman.** This magnificent turn-of-the-20th-century building, with its grand marble staircase and its fascinating history—it was once the headquarters of the *Scotsman* newspaper—now houses this modern luxury hotel. **Pros:** gorgeous surroundings; personalized service. **Cons:** no air-conditioning; spa can be noisy; could do with some renovation. [$] *Rooms from: £270* ✉ *20 N. Bridge, Old Town* ☎ *0131/556–5565* 🌐 *scotsmanhotel.co.uk* 🛏 *69 rooms* 🍴 *Free Breakfast* ✥ *F4.*

$$$$ HOTEL **The Witchery by the Castle.** This lavishly theatrical lodging promises a night to remember. **Pros:** Gothic drama and intriguing antiques; a truly romantic retreat; sumptuous dining. **Cons:** can be noisy at night; decor not for everybody; pricey. [$] *Rooms from: £345* ✉ *352 Castlehill, Old Town* ☎ *0131/225–5613* 🌐 *www.thewitchery.com* ⇒ *9 suites* 🍴 *Free Breakfast* ✣ *E5.*

NEW TOWN

Calton Hill, which offers some of the best views of the city from its summit, is just one of the reasons to base yourself in the New Town, filled with gorgeous 18th- and 19th-century architecture.

$$$$ HOTEL Fodor's Choice ★ **The Balmoral.** The attention to detail in the elegant rooms—colors were picked to echo the country's heathers and moors—and the sheer Edwardian splendor of this grand, former railroad hotel, make staying at the Balmoral a special introduction to Edinburgh. **Pros:** big and beautiful Edwardian building; top-hatted doorman; top-notch spa. **Cons:** small pool; spa books up fast. [$] *Rooms from: £325* ✉ *1 Princes St., New Town* ☎ *0131/556–2414* 🌐 *www.roccofortehotels.com* ⇒ *188 rooms* 🍴 *Free Breakfast* ✣ *F4.*

$$$ HOTEL **The Glasshouse.** Glass walls extend from the 19th-century facade of a former church, foreshadowing the daring, modern interior of one of the city's original boutique hotels. **Pros:** near all the attractions; very modern and stylish; good dining in the brasseries. **Cons:** a little sterile for some; noise from the street sometimes a problem. [$] *Rooms from: £195* ✉ *2 Greenside La., New Town* ☎ *0131/525–8200* 🌐 *www.theglasshousehotel.co.uk* ⇒ *98 rooms* 🍴 *Free Breakfast* ✣ *F3.*

$$$ HOTEL **The Howard.** This intimate New Town boutique hotel is set within a classic Georgian town house, elegantly proportioned and superbly outfitted, and has the decor, service, and views to match its five-star status. **Pros:** small but grand building; friendly staff; very special afternoon tea. **Cons:** decor a little tired; noisy neighborhood. [$] *Rooms from: £205* ✉ *34 Great King St., New Town* ☎ *0131/557–3500* 🌐 *www.thehoward.com* ⇒ *19 rooms* 🍴 *Free Breakfast* ✣ *D3.*

$ B&B/INN **Inverleith Hotel.** Across from the Royal Botanic Gardens, this renovated Victorian town house has cozy, well-lit rooms with velour bedspreads, dark-wood furniture, and pale-gold curtains—at an incredible value. **Pros:** quiet surroundings; knowledgeable staff; cheap parking nearby (free on weekends). **Cons:** some rooms are small; uphill walk to the city center. [$] *Rooms from: £80* ✉ *5 Inverleith Terr., New Town* ☎ *0131/556–2745* 🌐 *www.inverleithhotel.co.uk* ⇒ *15 rooms* 🍴 *Free Breakfast* ✣ *D1.*

$$$$ HOTEL **Nira Caledonia.** A modern and worldly boutique hotel on the edge of the New Town, Nira Caledonia defiantly casts aside old Edinburgh luxury in favor of contemporary comfort and style. **Pros:** refreshingly modern luxury; individually designed rooms; comfy king beds. **Cons:** a little out of the center. [$] *Rooms from: £270* ✉ *6–10 Gloucester Pl., Stockbridge* ☎ *0131/225–2720* 🌐 *www.niracaledonia.com* ⇒ *28 rooms* 🍴 *Some meals* ✣ *C3.*

$$$$ HOTEL Fodor'sChoice ★ **The Principal.** Built in 1775 for Edinburgh's elite, this row of five Georgian town houses in the heart of the New Town now hosts a luxury hotel. **Pros:** excellent central location; stylish and comfortable rooms; fast Wi-Fi throughout. **Cons:** regular wedding parties in reception. [$] *Rooms from: £235* ✉ *19–21 George St., New Town* ☎ *0131/225–1251* 🌐 *www.phcompany.com/principal/edinburgh-george-street* 🛏 *240 rooms* 🍴 *Free Breakfast* ⊕ *E3.*

$$$$ HOTEL **Waldorf Astoria Edinburgh—The Caledonian.** An imposing and ornate red sandstone building situated at the west end of Princes Street Gardens, "The Caley" has dramatic Victorian decor, beautifully restored interiors, and the best hotel dining in Edinburgh. **Pros:** impeccable service; not as pricey as some other grande dame hotels; outstanding restaurants. **Cons:** expensive parking (£20 per night); no wow factor for some. [$] *Rooms from: £245* ✉ *Princes St., New Town* ☎ *0131/222–8888* 🌐 *www.thecaledonian.waldorfastoria.com* 🛏 *241 rooms* 🍴 *Free Breakfast* ⊕ *C4.*

HAYMARKET

$$$$ HOTEL Fodor'sChoice ★ **The Dunstane Houses.** Set within two Victorian town houses that sit across the road from one another, this hotel is one of Edinburgh's most luxurious boutique options. **Pros:** beautifully appointed town-house buildings; excellent food and service; quiet, residential area. **Cons:** no elevator (and stairs to climb); a 20-minute walk to Princes Street. [$] *Rooms from: £235* ✉ *4 W. Coates and 5 Hampton Terr., Haymarket* ☎ *0131/337–6169* 🌐 *www.thedunstane.com* 🛏 *35 rooms* 🍴 *Free Breakfast* ⊕ *A5.*

$$ B&B/INN **Victorian Town House.** This handsome B&B, situated in a quiet, leafy crescent but within walking distance of Princes Street, offers bright and spacious rooms with a quirky mix of Edwardian and modern furnishings. **Pros:** serene surroundings; gracious staff; beautiful Water of Leith at your doorstep. **Cons:** no parking nearby; a little way from the Old Town. [$] *Rooms from: £120* ✉ *14 Eglinton Terr., Haymarket* ☎ *0131/337–7088* 🌐 *www.thevictoriantownhouse.co.uk* 🛏 *3 rooms* 🍴 *Free Breakfast* ⊕ *A5.*

WEST END

$$ B&B/INN FAMILY **B+B Edinburgh.** Standing out along an elegant and tranquil West End terrace, this excellent B&B is the first Scottish outpost of supertrendy B+B Belgravia of London. **Pros:** fascinating building in tranquil area; superb views; newly refurbished rooms. **Cons:** no night porter; hint of previous institutional use. [$] *Rooms from: £135* ✉ *3 Rothesay Terr., West End* ☎ *0131/225–5084* 🌐 *www.bb-edinburgh.com* 🛏 *27 rooms* 🍴 *Free Breakfast* ⊕ *B4.*

$$$ HOTEL **The Bonham.** There's a clubby atmosphere throughout this hotel, where the typical high-ceilinged town-house rooms have gorgeous late-19th-century architectural features mixed with boldly colored furnishings, vibrant fabrics, and contemporary Scottish art. **Pros:** thorough yet unobtrusive service; excellent restaurant; pleasant location. **Cons:** few common areas; needs upgrading in places. [$] *Rooms from: £175*

✉ 35 Drumsheugh Gardens, West End ☎ 0131/226–6050 🌐 www.thebonham.com 🛏 49 rooms 🍴 Some meals ⊕ B4.

$$ HOTEL 🏨 **Channings.** Five Edwardian terraced town houses make up this intimate, elegant hotel, with a clubby, oak-paneled lobby lounge and quiet guest rooms complete with well-chosen antiques and marble baths. **Pros:** near Stockbridge shops and eateries; inventive color schemes; good discounts available online. **Cons:** not all rooms equally nice; breakfast could be better. [$] *Rooms from: £125 ✉ 12–16 S. Learmonth Gardens, West End ☎ 0131/315–2226 🌐 www.channings.co.uk 🛏 42 rooms 🍴 Free Breakfast ⊕ B3.*

$$ HOTEL Fodor's Choice ★ 🏨 **Rutland Hotel.** Nominated for several style awards, this chic boutique hotel at the west end of Princes Street offers 12 luxury guest rooms with flamboyant fabrics and classic furnishings, as well as nine stylish serviced apartments, a flexible option for a family or two couples traveling together. **Pros:** friendly staff; unpretentious; great bar and restaurant. **Cons:** decor too loud and busy for some. [$] *Rooms from: £150 ✉ 1–3 Rutland St., West End ☎ 0131/229–3402 🌐 www.therutlandhotel.com 🛏 26 rooms 🍴 Free Breakfast [M] West End-Princes St. ⊕ C4.*

13

SOUTH SIDE

$$ B&B/INN 🏨 **AmarAgua.** Four-poster beds, a tranquil location, and bountiful breakfasts set this Victorian town-house B&B apart. **Pros:** quiet setting; snug rooms; wonderful and varied breakfasts. **Cons:** far from the city center; minimum two-night stay. [$] *Rooms from: £105 ✉ 10 Kilmaurs Terr., Newington ☎ 0131/667–6775 🌐 www.amaragua.co.uk ⏲ Closed Jan. 🛏 5 rooms 🍴 Free Breakfast ⊕ G6.*

$$ B&B/INN 🏨 **Glenalmond House.** Elegantly furnished rooms, a friendly atmosphere, and a hearty breakfast are three big factors that make this town-house B&B a popular budget stay. **Pros:** knowledgeable owners; elegant furnishings; amazing sausages at breakfast. **Cons:** a 30-minute walk to the Royal Mile. [$] *Rooms from: £100 ✉ 25 Mayfield Gardens, South Side ☎ 0131/668–2392 🌐 www.glenalmondhouse.com 🛏 9 rooms 🍴 Free Breakfast ⊕ G6.*

$$ B&B/INN 🏨 **94DR.** Like the infectiously optimistic owners, Paul and John, 94DR reaches for the stars with its stylish decor and contemporary trappings, while maintaining a comfortable, homey feel. **Pros:** warm welcome; gay-friendly vibe; smashing breakfast; free bikes to help get into the center. **Cons:** 25-minute walk to the city center. [$] *Rooms from: £160 ✉ 94 Dalkeith Rd., South Side ☎ 0131/662–9265 🌐 www.94dr.com 🛏 7 rooms 🍴 Free Breakfast ⊕ G6.*

$$$$ HOTEL Fodor's Choice ★ 🏨 **Prestonfield.** The Highland "coos" (cows), peacocks, and grouse wandering around this hotel's 20-acre grounds transport you to a whole new world; one that's only five minutes by car from the Royal Mile. **Pros:** baroque grandeur; comfortable beds; extensive grounds. **Cons:** underwhelming showers; brooding decor can look gloomy. [$] *Rooms from: £235 ✉ Priestfield Rd., Prestonfield ☎ 0131/225–7800 🌐 www.prestonfield.com 🛏 23 rooms 🍴 Some meals ⊕ G6.*

LEITH

$$ B&B/INN 🏨 **The Conifers.** This small family-run guesthouse in a red sandstone town house offers simple, traditionally decorated rooms and warm hospitality. **Pros:** nice mix of old and new; many original fittings; hearty breakfasts. **Cons:** a long walk to the city center; one bathroom not en suite. [$] *Rooms from: £100* ✉ *56 Pilrig St., Leith* ☎ *0131/554–5162* 🌐 *www.conifersguesthouse.com* 🛏 *4 rooms* 🍴 *Free Breakfast* ✥ *G1.*

$$ HOTEL 🏨 **Malmaison.** Once a seamen's hostel, this French-inspired boutique hotel, which is part of a pioneering U.K.-wide chain, draws a refined clientele to its superchic shorefront rooms. **Pros:** impressive building; elegant interiors; great waterfront location. **Cons:** price fluctuates wildly; bar sometimes rowdy at night; a long way from the center of town. [$] *Rooms from: £135* ✉ *1 Tower Pl., Leith* ☎ *0131/285–1478* 🌐 *www.malmaison-edinburgh.com* 🛏 *100 rooms* 🍴 *Free Breakfast* ✥ *H1.*

NIGHTLIFE AND PERFORMING ARTS

NIGHTLIFE

The nightlife scene in Edinburgh is vibrant—whatever you're looking for, you'll find it here. There are traditional pubs, chic modern bars, and cutting-edge clubs. Live music pours out of many watering holes on weekends, particularly folk, blues, and jazz, while well-known artists perform at some of the larger venues.

Edinburgh's 400-odd pubs are a study in themselves. In the eastern and northern districts of the city, you can find some grim, inhospitable-looking places that proclaim that drinking is no laughing matter. But throughout Edinburgh, many pubs have deliberately traded in their old spit-and-sawdust vibe for atmospheric revivals of the warm, oak-paneled, leather-chaired *howffs* (meeting places). Most pubs and bars are open weekdays, while on weekends they're open from about 11 am to midnight (some until 2 am on Saturday).

The List and *The Skinny* carry the most up-to-date details about cultural events. *The List* is available at newsstands throughout the city, while *The Skinny* is free and can be picked up at a number of pubs, clubs, and shops around town. The *Herald* and *The Scotsman* newspapers are good for reviews and notices of upcoming events throughout the city and beyond.

OLD TOWN

BARS AND PUBS

Fodor's Choice ★ **The Holyrood 9A.** Billed as "great beers, great burgers," this wood-paneled hipster hangout has a fine array of craft beers on tap, as well as an impressive whisky collection. The gourmet burgers are worthy of their billing, too. ✉ *9A Holyrood Rd., Old Town* ☎ *0131/556–5044* 🌐 *www.theholyrood.co.uk.*

The Last Drop. There's plenty of atmosphere (and plenty of tourists) amid the nooks and crannies at the Last Drop. The name has a grim double meaning, as it was once the site of public hangings. ✉ *74–78*

Grassmarket, Old Town ☎ *0131/225–4851* ⊕ *www.nicholsonspubs. co.uk.*

The Three Sisters. This pub is a hive of activity during festival season, when the courtyard transforms into a beer garden with food stalls, and is packed wall-to-wall with revelers until the wee hours. Outside of the summer months, it remains a lively local favorite, and the best place to watch live sport in Edinburgh. ⊠ *139 Cowgate, Old Town* ☎ *0131/622–6802* ⊕ *www.thethreesistersbar.co.uk.*

Under the Stairs. As the name suggests, this shabby-chic cocktail bar-cum–bistro is secreted below street level. A cozy, low-ceilinged place, full of quirky furniture and hip art exhibits, Under the Stairs serves specialty, seasonal cocktails, as well as superb bar food, to a mostly young crowd. ⊠ *3A Merchant St., Old Town* ☎ *0131/466–8550* ⊕ *www. underthestairs.org.*

FOLK AND JAZZ CLUBS

Fodor'sChoice **The Jazz Bar.** This basement music venue delivers exactly what the name
★ promises: jazz, in all its many weird and wonderful forms. Blues, funk, acoustic, electric—there's something new to discover every night of the week. There's usually a small cover charge (cash only), but this all goes to musicians, not the venue. ⊠ *1A Chambers St., Old Town* ☎ *0131/220–4298* ⊕ *www.thejazzbar.co.uk.*

NIGHTCLUBS

Cabaret Voltaire. The vaulted ceilings of this subterranean club reverberate with dance music most nights, with an ever-changing lineup of cutting-edge DJs on the decks. The club also hosts regular live gigs and, during the Fringe, stand-up comedy shows. ⊠ *36–38 Blair St., Old Town* ☎ *0131/247–4704* ⊕ *www.thecabaretvoltaire.com.*

NEW TOWN

BARS AND PUBS

Bramble Bar. This easily walked-by basement bar on Queen Street—take the stairs down to a clothing-alteration shop and you'll see a small sign—is one of Edinburgh's great hidden gems. Expect superb cocktails, eclectic music (DJs spin most nights), young crowds, and lots of nooks and crannies. ⊠ *16A Queen St., New Town* ☎ *0131/226–6343* ⊕ *www. bramblebar.co.uk.*

Fodor'sChoice **Café Royal Circle Bar.** Famed for its atmospheric Victorian interiors—
★ think ornate stucco, etched mirrors, tiled murals, stained glass, and leather booths—the Café Royal Circle Bar has been drawing a cast of Edinburgh characters since it opened in 1863. Regulars and newcomers alike pack in for the drinks (a host of real ales and malt whiskies) and tasty bar food—everything from yummy sandwiches and small plates to elaborate seafood platters. ⊠ *19 W. Register St., New Town* ☎ *0131/556–1884* ⊕ *www.caferoyaledinburgh.co.uk.*

Cask and Barrel. A spacious, traditional pub on trendy Broughton Street, the Cask and Barrel serves hand-pulled ales from a horseshoe-shaped bar, ringed by a collection of brewery mirrors. ⊠ *115 Broughton St., New Town* ☎ *0131/556–3132.*

FAMILY
Fodor's Choice
★

Joseph Pearce's. One of six Swedish bars and restaurants in Edinburgh owned by the Boda group, Joseph Pearce's has a distinctly northern European feel, despite its solidly Edwardian origins. Scandi-themed cocktails are popular here, as are the meatballs, open sandwiches, and other Swedish dishes. There's a children's corner with toys to keep the little ones occupied, and a sunny outdoor space in summer. ⊠ *23 Elm Row, New Town* ☎ *0131/556–4140* ⊕ *www.bodabar.com/joseph-pearces.*

Fodor's Choice
★

Juniper. Situated right opposite Waverley Station, Juniper cultivates an air of glamorous fun, helped by its postcard-worthy views of the city and the castle. The wine list is good (if a little pricey), but it's the wildly imaginative cocktails that really make this place. A longstanding favorite is Strawberries and Steam, a strawberry-infused gin cocktail served in a teapot that's bubbling over with dry ice. You can soak up your drinks with nibbles from the modern Scottish "street food" menu. ⊠ *20 Princes St., New Town* ☎ *0131/652–7370* ⊕ *www.juniperedinburgh.co.uk.*

Kay's Bar. Housed in a former Georgian coach house, this diminutive but friendly spot serves 50 single-malt whiskies, a range of guest ales, and decent bottled beers. Check out the cute little wood-paneled library room, with its tiny fireplace and shelves full of books. ⊠ *39 Jamaica St., New Town* ☎ *0131/225–1858* ⊕ *www.kaysbar.co.uk.*

Starbar. Well worth seeking out, the tucked-away Starbar has a beer garden, table soccer, and—a rarity—a very good jukebox. It is also rumored to be haunted—get the owners to regale you with scary stories, including a specific clause in their lease that prevents them from removing a human skull from the building. ⊠ *1 Northumberland Pl., New Town* ☎ *0131/539–8070.*

GAY AND LESBIAN

CC Blooms. Modern and colorful, CC Blooms is a club spread over two levels, playing a mix of musical styles and with regular cabaret nights. Open nightly, it's been a mainstay on the gay scene since the early '90s, and can now count several other gay-friendly bars and clubs as neighbors. ⊠ *23–24 Greenside Pl., New Town* ☎ *0131/556–9331* ⊕ *www.ccbloomsedinburgh.com.*

Regent. Billing itself as "the best real ale gay pub in Edinburgh," this popular drinking hole is warm, homey, and welcoming—and it's dog-friendly too. As advertised, the real ales selection is great. ⊠ *2 Montrose Terr., Abbeyhill* ☎ *0131/661–8198* ⊕ *www.theregentbar.co.uk.*

NIGHTCLUBS

Liquid Room. Top indie bands and an eclectic mix of club nights (techno, hip-hop, and alternative, to name a few) have made the Liquid Room a favorite after-dark venue since 1997. ⊠ *9C Victoria St., New Town* ☎ *0131/225–2564* ⊕ *www.liquidroom.com.*

Opal Lounge. This casual but stylish nightspot with a glam VIP lounge was favored by Prince William when he was a student at St. Andrew's University. ⊠ *51A George St., New Town* ☎ *0131/226–2275* ⊕ *www.opallounge.co.uk.*

COMEDY CLUBS

The Stand. Laugh until your sides split at The Stand, a legendary basement comedy club that hosts both famous names and up-and-coming acts all throughout the year, though it's particularly popular during the Fringe. There's a free improv show every Sunday lunchtime. ⊠ *5 York Pl., East End* ☏ *0131/558–7272* ⊕ *www.thestand.co.uk.*

LEITH

BARS AND PUBS

Fodor'sChoice
★ **King's Wark.** Set within a charming 15th-century building, the popular King's Wark is renowned for its superb yet sensibly priced food, from the legendary breakfasts to the lip-smacking Sunday roasts to the sublime Scottish cheese boards. The specials board here often features freshly caught seafood and traditional Scottish fare. In warm weather you can snag a table on the sidewalk. ⊠ *36 The Shore, Leith* ☏ *0131/554–9260* ⊕ *kingswark.co.uk.*

Malt & Hops. First opening its doors in 1749, Malt & Hops has a fine waterfront location and serves microbrewery cask ales—with a selection good enough to be endorsed by CAMRA (the Campaign for Real Ale). It also has a resident ghost. ⊠ *45 The Shore, Leith* ☏ *0131/555–0083* ⊕ *www.barcalisa.com.*

Fodor'sChoice
★ **Teuchter's Landing.** Tucked away down a side street near The Shore, Teuchter's Landing is a perennially popular pub for its wide range of whiskies and beers, its excellent pub food (try the nachos with cheddar and haggis), and its pontoon for sunny days. It's also a great place for watching live sports. If you're feeling lucky, try the "Hoop of Destiny" game, for your chance to land a vintage dram for a fraction of its usual price. ⊠ *1c Dock Pl., Leith* ☏ *0131/554–7427* ⊕ *www.aroomin.co.uk/ teuchters-landing-bar-edinburgh.*

PERFORMING ARTS

Think Edinburgh's arts scene consists of just the elegiac wail of a bagpipe and the twang of a fiddle? Think again. Edinburgh is one of the world's great performing-arts cities. The jewels in the crown are the famed Edinburgh Festival Fringe and Edinburgh International Festival, which attract the best in music, dance, theater, circus, stand-up comedy, poetry, painting, and sculpture from all over the globe in August. The *Scotsman* and *Herald,* Scotland's leading daily newspapers, carry listings and reviews in their arts pages every day, with special editions during the festival. Tickets are generally sold in advance; in some cases they're also available from certain designated travel agents or at the door, although concerts by national orchestras often sell out long before the day of the performance.

FILM

Fodor'sChoice
★ **Filmhouse.** Widely considered to be among the best independent cinemas in Britain, the excellent three-screen Filmhouse is the go-to venue for modern, foreign-language, offbeat, and any other less-commercial films. It also holds frequent live events and mini-festivals for the discerning cinephile, and is the main hub for the International Film Festival each

summer. The café and bar here are open late on weekends. ⊠ *88 Lothian Rd., West End* ☎ *0131/228–2688* ⊕ *www.filmhousecinema.com.*

MUSIC

Festival Theatre. This theater hosts regular concerts, as well as musical theater and Scottish Opera productions. ⊠ *13–29 Nicolson St., Old Town* ☎ *0131/529–6000* ⊕ *www.edtheatres.com.*

Usher Hall. Edinburgh's grandest concert venue, Usher Hall hosts a wide range of national and international performers, from Kraftwerk and Ryan Adams to the Royal Scottish National Orchestra. ⊠ *Lothian Rd., West End* ☎ *0131/228–1155* ⊕ *www.usherhall.co.uk.*

THEATER

Church Hill Theatre. The intimate, 335-seat Church Hill Theatre, managed by the city council, hosts high-quality productions by local amateur dramatic societies. ⊠ *33 Morningside Rd., Morningside* ☎ *0131/220–4348* ⊕ *www.assemblyroomsedinburgh.co.uk.*

Edinburgh Playhouse. Big-ticket concerts and musicals, along with the occasional ballet and opera production, are staged at the popular Playhouse, with its enormous 3,000-seat auditorium. ⊠ *18-22 Greenside La., East End* ☎ *0844/871–3014* ⊕ *www.atgtickets.com.*

King's Theatre. Built in 1906 and adorned with vibrant murals by artist John Byrne, the art nouveau King's Theatre has a great program of contemporary dramatic works. ⊠ *2 Leven St., Tollcross* ☎ *0131/529–6000* ⊕ *www.edtheatres.com/kings.*

The Lyceum. Traditional plays and contemporary works, including previews or tours of London West End productions, are presented here. ⊠ *Grindlay St., West End* ☎ *0131/248–4848* ⊕ *www.lyceum.org.uk.*

Traverse Theatre. With its specially designed space, the Traverse Theatre has developed a solid reputation for new, stimulating plays by Scottish dramatists, as well as innovative dance performances. ⊠ *10 Cambridge St., West End* ☎ *0131/228–1404* ⊕ *www.traverse.co.uk.*

SHOPPING

Despite its renown as a shopping street, **Princes Street** in the New Town may disappoint some visitors with its dull modern architecture, average chain stores, and fast-food outlets. One block north of Princes Street, **Rose Street** has many smaller specialty shops; part of the street is a pedestrian zone, so it's a pleasant place to browse. The shops on **George Street** in New Town tend to be fairly upscale. London names, such as Laura Ashley and Penhaligons, are prominent, though some of the older independent stores continue to do good business.

The streets crossing George Street—Hanover, Frederick, and Castle— are also worth exploring. **Dundas Street,** the northern extension of Hanover Street, beyond Queen Street Gardens, has several antiques shops. **Thistle Street,** originally George Street's "back lane," or service area, has several boutiques and more antiques shops.

As may be expected, many shops along the **Royal Mile** in Old Town sell what may be politely or euphemistically described as "touristware"—whiskies, tartans, and tweeds. Careful exploration, however, will reveal some worthwhile establishments, including shops that cater to highly specialized interests and hobbies. A street below the Royal Mile, East Market Street, close to the castle end of the Royal Mile, just off George IV Bridge, is **Victoria Street**, with specialty shops grouped in a small area. Follow the tiny West Bow to **Grassmarket** for more specialty stores.

Stafford and William streets form a small, upscale shopping area in a Georgian setting. Walk to the west end of Princes Street and then along its continuation, Shandwick Place, then turn right onto Stafford Street. William Street crosses Stafford halfway down.

North of Princes Street, on the way to the Royal Botanic Garden Edinburgh, is **Stockbridge**, an oddball shopping area of some charm, particularly on St. Stephen Street. To get here, walk north down Frederick Street and Howe Street, away from Princes Street, then turn left onto North West Circus Place.

Edinburgh's newest (and hippest) shopping area is **The Arches**, which has a number of glass-fronted independent stores set within Victorian-era archways. You'll find it on East Market Street, to the east of Waverley train station and below the Royal Mile. And coming in 2020 is the refurbished **Edinburgh St. James**, a vast, state-of-the-art shopping complex being built between Princes Street and Leith Walk.

OLD TOWN

BOOKS, PAPER, MAPS, AND GAMES

Armchair Books. Just a two-minute walk from Grassmarket, Armchair Books is a chaotic but characterful bookshop heaving with secondhand and antiquarian books. ⊠ *72–74 W. Port, Old Town* ☎ *0131/229–5927* ⊕ *www.armchairbooks.co.uk.*

Carson Clark Gallery. This gallery specializes in antique maps, sea charts, and prints. ⊠ *34 Northumberland St., Old Town* ☎ *0131/556–4710* ⊕ *www.carsonclarkgallery.co.uk.*

Main Point Books. This bibliophile's haven is stacked high with obscure first editions and bargain tomes. It also hosts regular literary events. ⊠ *77 Bread St., Old Town* ☎ *0131/228–4837* ⊕ *www.mainpointbooks. co.uk.*

CLOTHING BOUTIQUES

Bill Baber. One of the more imaginative Scottish knitwear designers, Bill Baber's creative and colorful pieces are a long way from the conservative pastel woolies sold at some of the large mill shops. ⊠ *66 Grassmarket, Old Town* ☎ *0131/225–3249* ⊕ *www.billbaber.com.*

JEWELRY

Clarksons. A family firm, Clarksons handcrafts a unique collection of jewelry, from Celtic to contemporary styles. The pieces here are made with silver, gold, platinum, and precious gems, with a particular emphasis on diamonds. ⊠ *87 West Bow, Old Town* ☎ *0131/225–8141* ⊕ *www.clarksonsedinburgh.co.uk.*

SCOTTISH SPECIALTIES

Fodor's Choice **Cranachan & Crowdie.** This lovely gourmet shop on the Royal Mile is
★ brimming with the finest Scottish food and drink, from crunchy oatcakes to melt-in-the-mouth shortbread. There's even a chocolate counter for those with a particularly sweet tooth. Staff are happy to put
together hampers of food for any occasion—including an impromptu
picnic back in your room. They also sell tweeds, handmade candles,
and other gift-worthy knickknacks. ✉ *263 Canongate, Old Town*
📞 *0131/556–7194* ⊕ *www.cranachanandcrowdie.com.*

Geoffrey (Tailor) Highland Crafts. This shop can clothe you in full Highland
dress, with high-quality kilts made in its own workshops. ✉ *57–59 High
St., Old Town* 📞 *0131/557–0256* ⊕ *www.geoffreykilts.co.uk.*

NEW TOWN

ANTIQUES

Fodor's Choice **Unicorn Antiques.** This Victorian basement is crammed with fascinating
★ antiques, including artworks, ornaments, silverware, and other such
curios. ✉ *65 Dundas St., New Town* 📞 *0131/556–7176* ⊕ *www.uni-
cornantiques.co.uk.*

CLOTHING BOUTIQUES

Elaine's Vintage Clothing. This wee boutique in trendy Stockbridge is
crammed full of vintage threads for women and men. The finds span
the 20th century, but most are from the '40s to the '70s. The friendly
owner is happy to share her knowledge of the many elegant and quirky
outfits on her rails. ✉ *55 St. Stephen St., New Town* 📞 *0131/225–5783.*

DEPARTMENT STORES

Fodor's Choice **Jenners.** Jenners, a long-standing Edinburgh landmark that is now part
★ of the U.K.-wide House of Fraser chain, specializes in traditional china
and glassware, as well as Scottish tweeds and tartans—though you'll
find everything else you'd expect from a large department store, too. Its
famous food hall, run by Valvona & Crolla, stocks traditional culinary
delights including shortbread, marmalade, and honey. ✉ *48 Princes St.,
New Town* 📞 *0344/800–3725* ⊕ *www.houseoffraser.co.uk.*

John Lewis. John Lewis specializes in furnishings and household goods,
but also stocks designer clothes. It's part of the Edinburgh St. James
shopping complex, which is currently closed for extensive redevelopment (due to finish in 2020), but John Lewis remains open as usual
with access from Leith Street. ✉ *Edinburgh St. James, Leith St., New
Town* 📞 *0131/556–9121* ⊕ *www.johnlewis.com/our-shops/edinburgh.*

HOME FURNISHINGS

Hannah Zakari. Quirky handmade pieces, including embroidered cushions, are a specialty at Hannah Zakari. Keep an eye out for unusual
jewelry, artwork, and accessories, too. ✉ *43 Candlemaker Row, New
Town* 📞 *0131/226–5433* ⊕ *www.hannahzakari.co.uk.*

JEWELRY

Hamilton and Inches. Established in 1866, this jeweler is worth visiting
not only for its gold and silver pieces, but also for its late-Georgian
interior. Designed by David Bryce in 1834, it's all columns and elaborate

plasterwork. ⊠ *87 George St., New Town* ☎ *0131/225–4898* ⊕ *www. hamiltonandinches.com.*

Joseph Bonnar. Tucked behind George Street, Joseph Bonnar stocks Scotland's largest collection of antique jewelry, including 19th-century agate jewels. ⊠ *72 Thistle St., New Town* ☎ *0131/226–2811* ⊕ *www. josephbonnar.com.*

Fodor's Choice **Sheila Fleet.** As much art gallery as jewelry shop, designer Sheila Fleet's
★ store in Stockbridge displays a variety of stunning jewelry inspired by her native Orkney, from wind and waves to Celtic spirals to island wildlife. ⊠ *18 St. Stephen St., Stockbridge* ☎ *0131/225–5939* ⊕ *www. sheilafleet.com.*

LEITH

ARCADES AND SHOPPING CENTERS

Ocean Terminal. As well as being home to the Royal Yacht *Britannia,* this on-the-water mall also has an impressive range of big-name brand stores and independent craft shops, as well as bars, restaurants, and a cinema. ⊠ *Ocean Dr., Leith* ☎ *0131/555–8888* ⊕ *www.oceanterminal.com.*

OUTDOOR SPORTS GEAR

Tiso Edinburgh Outdoor Experience. This sizable store stocks outdoor clothing, boots, and jackets ideal for hiking in the Highlands. It also sells tents and camping accessories, for the truly hardy. There's a café inside, too. ⊠ *41 Commercial St., Leith* ☎ *0131/554–0804* ⊕ *www. tiso.com.*

SPORTS AND THE OUTDOORS

FOOTBALL

Heart of Midlothian Football Club. Better known simply as "Hearts," the Heart of Midlothian Football Club plays in maroon and white and is based at Tynecastle. The club's crest is based on the Heart of Midlothian mosaic on the Royal Mile. ⊠ *Tynecastle Stadium, McLeod St., Edinburgh* ☎ *0333/043–1874* ⊕ *www.heartsfc.co.uk.*

Hibernian Football Club. Known as the Hibs, the green-and-white-bedecked Hibernian Club was founded in 1875—one year after Hearts—and plays its home matches at Easter Road Stadium in Leith. ⊠ *Easter Road Stadium, 12 Albion Pl., Leith* ☎ *0131/661–2159* ⊕ *www.hiberninfc.co.uk.*

GOLF

Edinburgh is widely considered to be the birthplace of modern golf, as its first official rules were developed at Leith Links. Naturally, there are a number of great courses in the city. For more information, the VisitScotland website has an extensive, searchable guide to Scottish courses.

Braid Hills. Known to locals and many others as Braids, this course is beautifully laid out over a rugged range of small hills in the southern

suburbs of Edinburgh. The views in each direction—the Pentland Hills in the south; the city skyline and Firth of Forth to the north—are worth a visit in themselves. The city built this course at the turn of the 20th century after urban development forced golfers out of the city center. There's also a 9-hole "Wee Braids" course for beginners and younger players. Reservations are recommended for weekend play. ⊠ *27 Braids Hill Approach, Edinburgh* ☎ *0131/447–6666* ⊕ *www.edinburghleisure.co.uk/venues/braid-hills-golf-course* ☒ *Braids, £25 weekdays, £27 weekends; Wee Braids, £14 weekdays, £16 weekends* ⅄ *Braids: 18 holes, 5865 yards, par 71; Wee Braids: 9 holes, 2232 yards, par 31.*

Royal Burgess Golfing Society. Edinburgh's other Victorian courses are newcomers when compared to Royal Burgess—it opened in 1735, making it one of the world's oldest golf clubs. Its members originally played on Bruntsfield Links; now they and their guests play on elegantly manicured parkland in the city's northwestern suburbs. It's a challenging course with fine, beautifully maintained greens. There's a fairly conservative dress code—no denim or T-shirts allowed, and you must wear a jacket and tie in the clubhouse. ⊠ *181 Whitehouse Rd., Barnton* ☎ *0131/339–2075* ⊕ *www.royalburgess.co.uk* ☒ *£100* ⅄ *18 holes, 6511 yards, par 71* ⚘ *Reservations essential.*

RUGBY

Fodor's Choice **Murrayfield Stadium.** Home of the Scottish Rugby Union, Murrayfield
★   Stadium hosts rugby matches in early spring and fall, including internationals. Crowds of good-humored rugby fans from all over the world add greatly to the sense of excitement in the streets of Edinburgh. Stick around after the game as there's often live music, food, and drinks to enjoy in the stadium grounds. Outside of the rugby season, you can still see Murrayfield with a stadium tour; tickets are £10 for adults. ⊠ *Roseburn St., Murrayfield* ☎ *0131/346–5250* ⊕ *www.scottishrugby.org.*

THE LOTHIANS

The Lothians is the collective name given to the swath of countryside south of the Firth of Forth and surrounding Edinburgh. Many courtly and aristocratic families lived here, and the region still has the castles and mansions to prove it. And with the rich came deer parks, gardens in the French style, and Lothian's fame as a seed plot for Lowland gentility.

You can explore a number of historic houses and castles of West Lothian and the Forth Valley, and territory north of the River Forth, in a day or two, or you can just pick one excursion. Stretching east to the sea and south to the Lowlands from Edinburgh, Midlothian is no more than one hour from Edinburgh: Rosslyn Chapel is a highlight.

GETTING HERE AND AROUND

First Bus and Lothian Buses link most of this area. If you're planning to see more than one sight in the region by bus, it's worth planning an itinerary in advance. Dalmeny (for South Queensferry), Linlithgow, and Dunfermline all have rail stations and can be reached from Edinburgh stations.

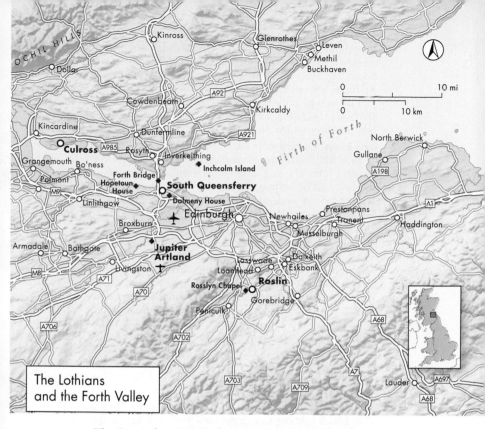

The Lothians
and the Forth Valley

The Queensferry Road, also known as the A90, is the main thoroughfare running through this region. After crossing the Forth Bridge, it joins
the M90 heading north, with branches off to Culross (on the A985),
Dunfermline (on the A823), and the Ochil Hills (on the A91).

SOUTH QUEENSFERRY

7 miles west of Edinburgh.

This pleasant little waterside community, a former ferry port, is completely dominated by the Forth Bridges, three dramatic structures of
contrasting architecture (dating from the 19th, 20th, and 21st centuries)
that span the Firth of Forth at this historic crossing point. It's near a
number of historic and other sights.

GETTING HERE AND AROUND

The Queensferry Road, also known as the A90, is the main artery west
from Edinburgh toward the Forth Bridge, Hopetoun House, the House
of the Binns, and Blackness Castle.

EXPLORING

Dalmeny House. The first of the stately houses clustered on the western
edge of Edinburgh, Dalmeny House is the home of the Earl and Count-
ess of Rosebery. This 1815 Tudor Gothic mansion displays among its

sumptuous interiors the best of the family's famous collection of 18th-century French furniture. Highlights include the library, the Napoléon Room, the Vincennes and Sevres porcelain collections, and the drawing room, with its tapestries and intricately wrought French furniture. Admission is by guided tour in June and July only. ⊠ *South Queensferry* ☎ *0131/331–1888* ⊕ *dalmeny.co.uk* ☑ *£10* ⊘ *Closed Thurs.–Sat., in June and July; closed Aug.–May.*

Forth Bridge. Opened in 1890, when it was hailed as the eighth wonder of the world, this iconic red cantilevered rail bridge is a UNESCO World Heritage Site. The extraordinary, 1½-mile-long crossing expands by another yard or so on a hot summer's day. The famous 19th-century bridge has since been joined by two neighbors; the 20th-century Forth Road Bridge (opened 1964) and the 21st-century Queensferry Crossing (opened 2017). ⊠ *South Queensferry.*

Hopetoun House. The palatial premises of Hopetoun House are among Scotland's grandest courtly seats, and are now home to the Marquesses of Linlithgow. The enormous property was started in 1699 to the original plans of Sir William Bruce, then enlarged between 1721 and 1754 by William Adam and his sons Robert and John. The house has decorative work of the highest order and a notable painting collection, plus all the trappings to keep you entertained: a nature trail, a restaurant in the former stables, a farm shop, and a museum. The estate also specializes in clay pigeon shooting; groups of six or more can book an expert-led introductory session, with prices starting at £45 per person. ⊠ *Lime Ave.* ☎ *0131/331–2451* ⊕ *www.hopetoun.co.uk* ☑ *£9.85; grounds only £4.65* ⊘ *Closed Oct.–mid-Apr.*

Fodor's Choice ★ **Inchcolm Island.** Accessible by boat tour from South Queensferry, Inchcolm Island is home to a beautifully preserved 12th-century abbey, a First World War fortress, green cliffs, sandy beaches, and an abundance of wildlife, from playful gray seals to brightly colored puffins. Prepare to be dive-bombed by seagulls if you visit during nesting season. The island is run by Historic Scotland, which levies an entry fee of £6, but boat tours (run by Maid of the Forth and Forth Boat Tours) include this in the price of their tickets. ⊠ *Inchcolm Island* ☎ *01383/823332* ⊕ *www.historicenvironment.scot* ☑ *£20 (boat tour and island entry).*

WHERE TO EAT

$$
MODERN BRITISH ✕ **The Boat House.** Scotland's natural larder is on display at this romantic restaurant on the banks of the Forth. Seafood is the star of the show, and chef Paul Steward is the man behind the imaginative yet unfussy recipes. **Known for:** delicious seafood; spectacular views from the patio. Ⓢ *Average main: £18* ⊠ *22 High St.* ☎ *0131/331–5429* ⊕ *www.theboathouse-sq.co.uk.*

JUPITER ARTLAND

10 miles west of Edinburgh.

For anyone drawn to interesting art and beautiful open spaces, a visit to this open-air collection of sculptures by world-renowned artists is a must.

GETTING HERE AND AROUND

To reach Jupiter Artland from Edinburgh, take the A71 southwest toward Kilmarnock. Just after Wilkieston, turn right onto the B7015. It's also easy to reach by bus: the X27 departs from Princes Street, while Bus 27 leaves from Dalry Road near Haymarket.

EXPLORING

Fodor'sChoice **Jupiter Artland.** The beautiful grounds of a Jacobean manor house have
★ been transformed by an art-loving couple, Robert and Nicky Wilson, into an impressive sculpture park. With the aid of a map you can explore the magical landscapes and encounter works by renowned artists including Andy Goldsworthy, Anya Gallaccio, Jim Lambie, Nathan Coley, Ian Hamilton Finlay, and Anish Kapoor, among many others. A highlight is walking around Charles Jencks's *Cells of Life,* a series of shapely, grass-covered mounds. ⊠ *Bonnington House Steadings, Wilkieston, Edinburgh* ☎ *01506/889900* ⊕ *www.jupiterartland.org* ⌑ *£8.50* ⊙ *Closed Oct.–Apr. and Mon.–Wed. in May, June, and Sept.*

CULROSS

17 miles northwest of Edinburgh.

The town is a fascinating open-air museum that gives you a feel for life in Scotland in the 17th and 18th centuries.

GETTING HERE AND AROUND

To get here by car, head north of the Forth Bridge on the A90, then westward on the A985. You can get here by bus (No. 8) from Dunfermline, which in turn is easily reached by train from Edinburgh.

EXPLORING

Fodor'sChoice **Culross.** With its mercat cross, cobbled streets, tolbooth, and narrow
★ wynds (alleys), seaside Culross is a picturesque little town. It's also a living museum of 17th-century Scottish life, with preserved historic properties open to the public. Culross once had a thriving industry and export trade in coal and salt (the coal was used in the salt-panning process), but as local coal became exhausted, the impetus of the Industrial Revolution passed Culross by, while other parts of the Forth Valley prospered. Culross became a backwater town, and the merchants' houses of the 17th and 18th centuries were never replaced by Victorian developments or modern architecture. In the 1930s, the National Trust for Scotland started to buy up the decaying properties with a view to preservation. Today, ordinary citizens live in many of these properties, but others—namely the palace, study, and town house—are available to explore. Town walking tours are also available for a small fee. ⊠ *Culross Palace* ☎ *01383/880359* ⊕ *www.nts.org.uk* ⌑ *Palace: £10.50; town tour: £3* ⊙ *Palace closed Nov.–mid-Apr.; Sun. in mid-Apr.–May, Sept., and Oct.; Tues. in June.*

13

ROSLIN

7 miles south of Edinburgh.

It may be best known for its extraordinary chapel, but Roslin itself is a pleasant place to while away some time. There are some lovely walks from the village along the North River Esk.

GETTING HERE AND AROUND

By car, take the A701 south from Edinburgh, turning off onto the B7006 just north of the town. Lothian Buses also shuttle passengers from Edinburgh: Bus 37 from North Bridge is the most direct way.

EXPLORING

Fodor's Choice **Rosslyn Chapel.** This chapel has always beckoned curious visitors
★ intrigued by the various legends surrounding its magnificent carvings, but today it pulses with tourists as never before. Much of this can be attributed to Dan Brown's best-selling novel *The Da Vinci Code*, which featured the chapel heavily, claiming it has a secret sign that can lead you to the Holy Grail. Whether you're a fan of the book or not, this Episcopal chapel (services continue to be held here) remains an imperative stop on any traveler's itinerary. Originally conceived by Sir William Sinclair (circa 1404–80) and dedicated to St. Matthew in 1446, the chapel is outstanding for the quality and variety of the carving inside. Covering almost every square inch of stonework are human figures, animals, and plants. The meaning of these remains subject to many theories; some depict symbols from the medieval order of the Knights Templar and from Freemasonry. The chapel's design called for a cruciform structure, but only the choir and parts of the east transept walls were fully completed. Free talks about the building's history are held daily. ⊠ *Chapel Loan* ☎ *0131/440–2159* ⊕ *www.rosslynchapel. com* ⊠ *£9.*

WHERE TO EAT

$ ✕ **The Original Rosslyn Inn.** This atmospheric inn, on the crossroads in the
BRITISH center of Roslin village, serves tasty, hearty pub grub, including fish-and-chips, burgers, and pies, plus good veggie options. The inn is very close to Rosslyn Chapel; walk past the car park for a few minutes and you'll see it on the other side of the main road. **Known for:** great steak-and-ale pie; convenient location. Ⓢ *Average main: £9* ⊠ *2–4 Main St., Roslin, Edinburgh* ☎ *0131/440–2384* ⊕ *www.theoriginalrosslyninn. co.uk.*

GLASGOW

WELCOME TO GLASGOW

TOP REASONS TO GO

★ **Architecture:** The Victorians left a legacy of striking architecture, and Glasgow's buildings manifest the city's love of grand artistic statements—just remember to look up. The Arts and Crafts buildings by Charles Rennie Mackintosh are reason alone to visit.

★ **Art:** Some of Britain's best art galleries are in Glasgow. Check out Hunterian Art Gallery, the Kelvingrove Art Gallery and Museum, and the Gallery of Modern Art.

★ **Parks and gardens:** From Kelvingrove Park to the Glasgow Botanic Gardens, the city has more parks per square mile than any other in Europe. Stop by the botanic garden for outdoor theatrical productions in summer, or Bellahouston Park for the annual piping festival.

★ **Pubs and cafés:** Whether you fancy a Guinness in a traditional old-man's pub like the Scotia or a Pinot Noir in a fashionable wine bar, there's a place to quench all thirsts. Locals also love their cafés and tearooms.

1 City Centre. From Buchanan Street west to Hope Street and beyond, look up to see wonderful Victorian buildings expressing the confidence of an industrial capital. George Square's City Chambers are worth a visit before you trawl the shops, duck into one of the trendy eateries, or explore the bars and music venues

2 Merchant City. In the Middle Ages, the city grew up around Glasgow Cathedral. As the city expanded along with the growing transatlantic trade, wealthy tobacco and cotton traders built palatial houses here. They were laid to rest in the glorious tombs of the Necropolis, which overlooks the city. Today the area is busy with high-end restaurants, clubs, and shops, many of them occupying converted mansions.

3 West End. In the quieter, slightly hillier western part of the city is Glasgow University and the more bohemian side of Glasgow. The West End's treasures include the Glasgow Botanic Gardens, Kelvingrove Park, and the Kelvingrove Art Gallery and Museum. Its social life focuses around the university, where there are well-priced restaurants and lively bars. Byres Road is at its

heart, especially when it fills with weekend revelers.

4 Finnieston. Once lined with shipyards, the River Clyde has been reborn as a relaxing destination that entrances visitors and locals. The Glasgow Science Centre and the Museum of Transport face each other across the water, while the Scottish Exhibition Centre and the new SSE Hydro are major

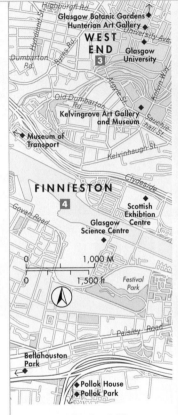

14

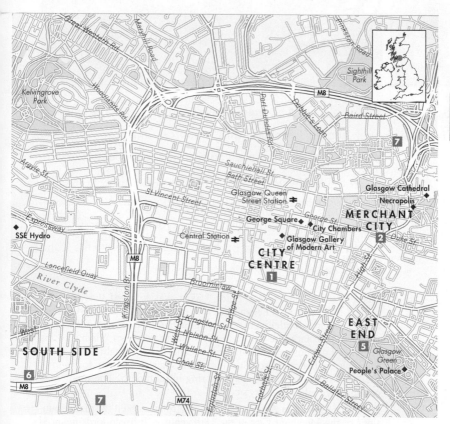

event venues. Argyle Street, once a slightly faded area near Kelvingrove Park, has been transformed into a fashionable strip of restaurants and bars now almost as crowded as the West End.

5 East End. What was once a neglected corner of Glasgow is being treated to a major face-lift. Glasgow Green's wonderful People's Palace draws visitors throughout the year, and on weekends the nearby Barras market is a reminder of the area's past.

6 South Side. Often overlooked, this less-visited side of the city includes beautiful Pollok Park as well as Pollok House, with Its art collection and its elegant gardens. A couple of architectural gems are here, too.

Updated by Mike Gonzalez

Trendy stores, a booming cultural life, fascinating architecture, and stylish restaurants reinforce Glasgow's claim to being Scotland's most exciting city. After decades of decline, it has experienced an urban renaissance uniquely its own. The city's grand architecture reflects a prosperous past built on trade and shipbuilding. Today buildings by Charles Rennie Mackintosh hold pride of place along with the Zaha Hadid–designed Riverside Museum.

Glasgow (the "dear green place," as it was known) was founded some 1,500 years ago. Legend has it that the king of Strathclyde, irate about his wife's infidelity, threw a ring he had given her into the River Clyde. (Apparently she had passed it on to an admirer.) When the king demanded to know where the ring had gone, the distraught queen asked the advice of her confessor, St. Mungo. He suggested fishing for it—and the first salmon to emerge had the ring in its mouth. The moment is commemorated on the city's coat of arms.

The vast profits from American cotton and tobacco built the grand mansions of the Merchant City in the 18th century. Tobacco lords financed the building of wooden ships, and by the 19th century the River Clyde had become the center of a vibrant shipbuilding industry, fed by the city's iron and steel works. The city grew again, but its internal divisions grew at the same time. The West End harbored the elegant homes of the newly rich shipyard owners. Down by the river, areas like the infamous Gorbals, with its crowded slums, or Govan, sheltered the laborers who built the ships. They came from the Highlands, expelled to make way for sheep, or from Ireland, where the potato famines drove thousands from their homes.

During the 19th century the city's population grew from 80,000 to more than a million. The new prosperity gave Glasgow its grand neoclassical buildings, such as those built by Alexander "Greek" Thomson, as well as the adventurous visionary buildings designed by Charles Rennie Mackintosh and others who produced Glasgow's Arts and Crafts movement.

The decline of shipbuilding and the closure of the factories in the later 20th century led to much speculation as to what direction the city would take now. The curious thing is that, at least in part, the past gave the city its new lease on life. It was as if people looked at their city and saw Glasgow's beauty for the first time: its extraordinarily rich architectural heritage, its leafy parks, its artistic heritage, and its complex social history. Today Glasgow is a dynamic cultural center and a commercial hub, as well as a launching pad from which to explore the rest of Scotland, which, as it turns out, is not so far away. In fact, it takes only 40 minutes to reach Loch Lomond, where the other Scotland begins.

PLANNER

14

WHEN TO GO

The best times to visit Glasgow are spring and summer and into early fall. Although you may encounter crowds, the weather is more likely to be warm and dry. In summer the days can be long and pleasant—if the rain holds off—and festivals and outdoor events are abundant. Fall can be nice, although cold weather begins to set in after mid-September and the days grow shorter. From November to February it is cold, wet, and dark. Although thousands of people flock to Glasgow for New Year's celebrations, the winter months are relatively quiet in terms of crowds.

FESTIVALS

Aye Write. This highly successful literary festival brings together writers from Scotland and the world to discuss their work and exchange ideas. It is held in the Mitchell Library and other venues over one week in spring. ⊠ *Mitchell Library, North St., West End* ☎ *0141/287–2999* ⊕ *www.ayewrite.com* Ⓜ *St. George's Cross.*

Fodor's Choice **Celtic Connections.** Continually expanding, this music festival is held
★ throughout the second half of January in venues across the city. Musicians from Scotland, Ireland, and other countries celebrate Celtic music, both traditional and contemporary. There are a series of hands-on workshops and a popular late-night club at the Royal Concert Hall. ⊠ *Glasgow* ☎ *0141/353–8000* ⊕ *www.celticconnections.com.*

Glasgow Jazz Festival. For five days in late June or early July, Glasgow hosts jazz musicians from around the world in venues throughout the city, though mainly in the City Centre. ⊠ *City Centre* ☎ *0141/552–3552* ⊕ *www.jazzfest.co.uk* ☞ *Tickets from Scottish Music Centre* Ⓜ *Buchanan St.*

PLANNING YOUR TIME

You could quite easily spend five comfortable days here, although in a pinch, two would do and three would be pleasant. The best strategy for seeing the city is to start at High Street on the east side of Merchant City and work your way west. On the first day explore the city's medieval heritage, taking in Glasgow Cathedral, the Museum of Religious Life, and Provand's Lordship, as well as the Necropolis with its fascinating crumbling monuments. The gentle walk west from here to the Merchant City is also a walk through time, to 17th- and 18th-century Glasgow, and George Square, around which spread the active and crowded shopping areas. For those interested in architect Charles Rennie Mackintosh, the Mackintosh Trail connects the many buildings designed by this outstanding Glasgow designer and architect. Full information on all his buildings can be found online at ⊕ *www.crmsociety. com*, where you can also purchase tickets, or at the individual sites. Another day could be well spent between the Kelvingrove Art Gallery (you can lunch here and listen to the daily concert on its organ) and the nearby Hunterian Museum and Gallery in the university. From here it's only minutes to lively Byres Road and its shops, pubs, and cafés. The redevelopment of the riverside offers another route—to the Transport Museum and the Science Centre.

If you have a few extra days, head out to Robert Burns Country and the extraordinary Burns Birthplace Museum in Ayrshire. It's a scenic 45-minute drive from Glasgow. Most destinations on the Clyde Coast are easily accessible from Glasgow. Direct trains from Central Station take you to Paisley, Irvine, and Lanark in less than an hour. These small towns need no more than a day to explore. To get a flavor of island life, take the hour-long train ride to Wemyss Bay and then the ferry to the Isle of Bute.

GETTING HERE AND AROUND
AIR TRAVEL
Glasgow Airport (GLA) is about 7 miles west of the City Centre on the M8 to Greenock. The airport serves international and domestic flights, and most major European carriers have frequent and convenient connections to many cities on the continent; it closes overnight. There's a frequent shuttle service from London, as well as regular flights from Birmingham, Bristol, East Midlands, Leeds/Bradford, Manchester, Southampton, Isle of Man, and Jersey. There are also flights from Wales (Cardiff) and Ireland (Belfast, Dublin, and Londonderry). Local Scottish connections can be made to Aberdeen, Barra, Benbecula, Campbeltown, Inverness, Islay, Kirkwall, Shetland (Sumburgh), Stornoway, and Tiree.

Prestwick Airport (PIK), on the Ayrshire coast about 30 miles southwest of Glasgow, is known mainly as an airport for budget airlines like Ryanair and Vueling.

Airport Contacts Glasgow Airport. ⊠ *Caledonia Way, Paisley* ☎ *0844/481– 5555* ⊕ *www.glasgowairport.com.* **Prestwick Airport.** ⊠ *A79, Prestwick* ☎ *0871/223–0700* ⊕ *www.glasgowprestwick.com.*

TRANSFERS   Although there's a railway station about 2 miles from Glasgow Airport (Paisley Gilmour Street), it is not very accessible. Transport to the City Centre is by bus or taxi and takes about 20 minutes. Metered taxis cost around £22. Express buses depart every 15 minutes from Glasgow Airport to Central and Queen Street stations and to the Buchanan Street bus station. The fare is £7.50 one way, £10 open round-trip per person.

The drive from Glasgow Airport into the City Centre via the M8 motorway (Junction 29) is normally quite easy. Most companies that provide chauffeur-driven cars and tours will also do limousine airport transfers. TBR Global Chauffeuring is a worldwide organization offering chauffeur-driven transport in Glasgow and across the United Kingdom.

There's a rapid half-hourly train service (hourly on Sunday) direct from Prestwick Airport's terminal to Glasgow Central. Strathclyde Passenger Transport and ScotRail offer a discount ticket that allows you to travel for half the standard fare; just show a valid airline ticket for a flight to or from Prestwick Airport. An hourly coach service makes the same trip but takes much longer than the train. Travelers arriving after 11 pm can take a late bus (X99); book this online with Dodds of Troon.

By car, the City Centre is reached from Prestwick via the fast M77 in about 40 minutes. Metered taxis are available at the airport. The fare to Glasgow is about £40.

Airport Transfer Contacts Dodds of Troon. ☎ *01292/288100* ⊕ *www. doddsoftroon.com.* **Little's Chauffeur Drive.** ☎ *0141/883–2111* ⊕ *www. littles.co.uk.* **Strathclyde Passenger Transport Travel Centre.** ✉ *Buchanan Street Bus Station, Killermont St., City Centre* ☎ *0141/332–6811* ⊕ *www.spt. co.uk* Ⓜ *Buchanan St.* **TBR Global Chauffeuring.** ☎ *0141/280–4800* ⊕ *www. tbrglobal.com.*

BIKE TRAVEL

Increasingly cycle-friendly, Glasgow has networks of off-road cycle paths. The city has a public bike-rental scheme run by nextbike; ranks of blue cycles at over 30 stations around the city are available for rent. You provide a credit card number and a £10 deposit on the smartphone app, over the phone, or on the on-bike computer, and give the cycle number. You'll be given the number for the combination lock and off you go. It's a great way to see the city, and you can return the bike at any station. Bikes cost £1 per 30 minutes up to 5 hours or £10 for 5–24 hours. The Glasgow Cycle Map available at information centers provides comprehensive route information, or see ⊕ *www.glasgow.gov. uk/cycling.*

Bike Contacts nextbike. ☎ *0208/166–9851* ⊕ *www.nextbike.co.uk.*

BUS TRAVEL

The main intercity operators are National Express, Scottish Citylink, and Megabus, which serve numerous towns and cities in Scotland, Wales, and England, including London and Edinburgh. Glasgow's bus station is on Buchanan Street, not far from Queen Street Station.

When traveling from the City Centre to either the West End or the South Side, it's easy to use the city's integrated network of buses, subways, and trains. Service is reliable and connections are convenient from buses to trains and the subway. Many buses require exact fare, which is usually around £1.75.

Traveline Scotland provides information on schedules, fares, and route planning, as does the Strathclyde Passenger Transport Travel Centre, which has an information center.

Bus Contacts Buchanan Street Bus Station. ✉ *Killermont St., City Centre* ☎ *0141/333–3708* ⊕ *www.spt.co.uk* Ⓜ *Buchanan St.* **Megabus.** ☎ *0141/352–4444* ⊕ *uk.megabus.com.* **National Express.** ☎ *0871/781–8181* ⊕ *www. nationalexpress.com.* **Scottish Citylink.** ☎ *0871/266–3333* ⊕ *www.citylink.co.uk.* **Traveline Scotland.** ☎ *0871/200–2233* ⊕ *www.travelinescotland.com.*

14

CAR TRAVEL

If you're driving to Glasgow from England and the south of Scotland, you'll approach the city via the M6, M74, and A74. From Edinburgh, the M8 leads to the City Centre. From the north, the A82 from Fort William and the A82/M80 from Stirling join the M8 in the City Centre.

You don't need a car in Glasgow, and you're probably better off without one. In the City Centre meters are expensive, running about £2.40 per hour during the day. In the West End they cost 80 pence per hour. Don't park illegally, as fines are upward of £30. Multistory garages are open 24 hours a day at Anderston Centre, George Street, Waterloo Place, Mitchell Street, Cambridge Street, and Concert Square. Rates run between £1 and £2 per hour. More convenient are the park-and-ride operations at some subway stations (Kelvinbridge, Bridge Street, and Shields Road).

SUBWAY TRAVEL

Glasgow's small subway system—it has 15 stations—is useful for reaching all the City Centre and West End attractions. Stations are signposted by a prominent letter "S." You can choose between a flat fare (£1.40) and a one-day pass (£4) that can be used after 9 am on weekdays and all day on weekends. A Smart Card, which you can buy free online or at stations for £3, will give you reduced fares. A Roundabout ticket costs £6.50 a day and covers subway and trains. A Day Tripper ticket is well worth it for families, covering bus, subway, rail, and some ferries. It costs £11.95 for one adult and up to two children or £21 for two adults and up to four kids. The distance between many central stops is no more than a 10-minute walk. More information is available from Strathclyde Passenger Transport Travel Centre or its website, including transportation maps.

TAXI TRAVEL

Taxis are a fast and cost-effective way to get around. You'll find metered taxis (usually black and of the London sedan type) at stands all over the City Centre. Most have radio dispatch. Some have also been adapted to take wheelchairs. You can hail a cab on the street if its "for hire" sign is illuminated. A typical ride from the City Centre to the West End or the South Side costs around £6. Uber is also available in Glasgow.

Taxi Contact Glasgow Taxis. ☎ 0141/429–7070 ⊕ www.glasgowtaxis.co.uk.

TRAIN TRAVEL

Glasgow has two main rail stations: Central and Queen Street. Central serves Virgin trains from London's Euston Station (five hours). Trains for Ayr and to the south of Glasgow also depart from Central. East Coast trains run from London's Kings Cross (via Edinburgh) to Glasgow's Queen Street Station. For details, contact National Rail. All routes heading north from Glasgow depart from Queen Street.

A regular bus service links the Queen Street and Central stations (although you can easily walk if you aren't too encumbered). Queen Street is near the Buchanan Street subway station, and Central is close to St. Enoch. Taxis are available at both stations.

The Glasgow area has an extensive network of suburban railway services. Locals still call them the Blue Trains, even though most are now painted maroon and cream. For more information and a free map, contact the Strathclyde Passenger Transport Travel Centre or National Rail.

Train Contacts National Rail. ☎ *08457/484950* ⊕ *www.nationalrail.co.uk.*

TOURS

City Sightseeing. Daily hop-on, hop-off bus tours of Glasgow in open-topped double-decker buses are offered by City Sightseeing. The full tour lasts just under two hours, with an English-speaking guide aboard and a multilingual commentary. Tours begin at George Square. ✉ *153 Queen St., City Centre* ☎ *0141/204–0444* ⊕ *www.citysightseeingglasgow.co.uk* ✆ *From £17.*

Glasgow Historic Walks. These themed walks will introduce you to the history and heritage of the city, from its architecture to local history associated with individuals such as St. Patrick and Mary, Queen of Scots. ☎ *No phone* ⊕ *www.glasgowhistoricwalks.com* ✆ *From £8.*

14

Scottish Tourist Guides Association. The association provides qualified and accredited Blue Badge Guides with specific areas of expertise; guides also speak a range of languages. Tours start at half a day, and driver guides are available. Book online in advance. ✉ *Glasgow* ☎ *01786/451953* ⊕ *www.stga.co.uk* ✆ *From £140 for half-day tours.*

FAMILY **Waverley Excursions.** The last seagoing paddle steamer, the wonder-
Fodor's Choice ful *Waverley* has retired several times, but the city refuses to let this
★ Glasgow institution fade away. It sails from Glasgow to the Clyde estuary (Glaswegians call it "doon the watter") and the islands of the west coast. The riotous evening jazz cruises remain very popular. The *Waverley* is permanently based at Lancefield Quay, beside the science museum. ✉ *36 Lancefield Quay, Clyde* ☎ *0845/130–4647* ⊕ *www. waverleyexcursions.co.uk* ✆ *From £29* ⊘ *Closed Nov.–Apr.*

VISITOR INFORMATION

The Glasgow Tourist Information Centre provides information about different types of tours and has an accommodations-booking service. Books, maps, and souvenirs are also available. There's a branch at Glasgow Airport, too.

Contact Glasgow Tourist Information Centre. ✉ *Gallery of Modern Art, Royal Exchange Sq., City Centre* ☎ *0141/566–4083* ⊕ *www.peoplemakeglasgow.com.*

EXPLORING

As cities go, Glasgow is contained and compact. It's set up on a grid system, so it's easy to navigate and explore, and the best way to tackle it is on foot. In the eastern part of the city, start by exploring Glasgow Cathedral and other highlights of the oldest section of the city, then wander through the rest of the Merchant City. From there you can just continue into the City Centre with its designer shops, art galleries, and eateries. From here you can either walk (it takes a good 45 minutes) or take the subway to the West End. If you walk, head up Sauchiehall Street. Once in the West End, visit the Glasgow Botanic Gardens, Glasgow University, and the Kelvingrove Art Gallery and Museum. A walk through Kelvingrove Park will being you to the Finnieston area. You can take a taxi to the South

Side to experience Pollok House. For Glasgow's East End, walk down High Street from the cathedral to the Tron Cross; from there you can walk to the Barras market and Glasgow Green.

CITY CENTRE

Some of the city's most important historical buildings are found in the City Centre close to George Square, many of them converted to very different purposes now. Along the streets of this neighborhood are some of the best examples of the architectural confidence and vitality that so characterized the burgeoning Glasgow of the turn of the 20th century. There are also plenty of shops, trendy eateries, and pubs.

GETTING HERE

Every form of public transportation can bring you here, from bus to train to subway. Head to George Square and walk from there.

Fodor's Choice
★ **City Chambers.** Dominating the east side of George Square, this exuberant expression of Victorian confidence, built by William Young in Italian Renaissance style, was opened by Queen Victoria in 1888. Among the interior's outstanding features are the entrance hall's vaulted ceiling, sustained by granite columns topped with marble, the marble-and-alabaster staircases, and Venetian mosaics. The enormous banqueting hall has murals illustrating Glasgow's history. Free guided tours lasting about an hour depart weekdays at 10:30 and 2:30; tours are very popular so pick up a ticket beforehand from the reception desk. The building is closed to visitors during civic functions. ⊠ *80 George Sq., City Centre* ☎ *0141/287–2000* ⊕ *www.glasgow.gov.uk* ✎ *Free* ☉ *Closed weekends* Ⓜ *Buchanan St.*

Fodor's Choice
★ **Glasgow School of Art.** Scotland's only public art school's main claim to fame used to be the iconic architecture of its main building, designed by architect Charles Rennie Mackintosh; sadly, the building was badly damaged by fires in 2014 and 2018. The 2018 fire completely gutted the building, but plans to rebuild it are already in the works. Fortunately, there are other wonderful Mackintosh buildings in and around the city. Stephen Holl's new **Reid Building**, directly opposite the original, is a spectacular modern homage to it; daily walking tours of Mackintosh's Glasgow continue to be organized from the art school shop there. ⊠ *164 Renfrew St., City Centre* ☎ *0141/353–4526* ⊕ *www.gsa.ac.uk/tours* ✎ *Tours from £7* Ⓜ *Cowcaddens.*

The Lighthouse. Charles Rennie Mackintosh designed these former offices of the *Glasgow Herald* newspaper, with the emblematic Mackintosh Tower, in 1893. On the third floor, the **Mackintosh Interpretation Centre** is a great place to start exploring this groundbreaking architect's work, which is illustrated in a glass wall with alcoves containing models of his buildings. From here you can climb the more than 130 steps up the tower and, once you have caught your breath, look out over Glasgow. (Alternatively, a viewing platform on the sixth floor can be reached by elevator.) Today the Lighthouse serves as Scotland's **Centre for Architecture, Design and the City,** celebrating all facets of architecture and design. The fifth-floor Doocot Cafe is a great place to take a break from sightseeing. ⊠ *11 Mitchell La., City Centre* ☎ *0141/271–5365* ⊕ *www.thelighthouse.co.uk* ✎ *Free* Ⓜ *St. Enoch.*

Fodor's Choice **Tenement House.** This ordinary first-floor apartment is anything but ordi-
★ nary inside: it was occupied from 1937 to 1982 by Agnes Toward (and
before that by her mother), both of whom seem never to have thrown
anything away. Agnes was a dressmaker, and her legacy is this fascinating time capsule, painstakingly preserved with her everyday furniture
and belongings. A small museum explores the life and times of its careful occupant. The red-sandstone building dates from 1892 and is in the
Garnethill area near the Glasgow School of Art. ⊠ *145 Buccleuch St.,
City Centre* ☎ *0141/333–0183* ⊕ *www.nts.org.uk* ✍ *£6.50* ☉ *Closed
Nov.–Mar.* Ⓜ *Cowcaddens.*

MERCHANT CITY

14

Near the remnants of medieval Glasgow is the Merchant City, with
some of the city's most important 18th-century buildings. Many of
them, like the great mansions along Ingram Street, were built by tobacco
merchants with profits from the tobacco trade. Today those palatial
homes hold restaurants and designer stores; one especially grand
example houses the Gallery of Modern Art. Many of Glasgow's young
and upwardly mobile have made their home here, in converted buildings ranging from warehouses to the old Sheriff's Court. Shopping is
expensive, but the area is worth visiting if you're seeking the youthful
Glasgow style.

GETTING HERE

Buchanan Street is the handiest subway station when you want to
explore the Merchant City, as it puts you directly on George Square.
You can also easily walk from Central Station or the St. Enoch subway station.

Gallery of Modern Art (*GoMA*). One of Glasgow's boldest, most innovative galleries occupies the neoclassical former Royal Exchange building.
The modern art, craft, and design collections include works by Scottish
conceptual artists such as David Mach, and also paintings and sculptures from around the world, including Papua New Guinea, Ethiopia,
and Mexico. Each floor of the gallery reflects one of the elements—air,
fire, earth, and water—which creates some unexpected juxtapositions
and also allows for various interactive exhibits. In the basement is a
café, a tourist information center, and an extensive library. The building, designed by David Hamilton (1768–1843) and finished in 1829,
was a meeting place for merchants and traders; later it became Stirling's
Library. It incorporates the mansion built in 1780 by William Cunning-
hame, one of the wealthiest tobacco lords. ⊠ *Queen St., Merchant City*
☎ *0141/287-3050* ⊕ *www.glasgowlife.org.uk* ✍ *Free* Ⓜ *Buchanan St.*

George Square. The focal point of Glasgow is lined with an impressive
collection of statues of worthies: Queen Victoria; Scotland's national
poet, Robert Burns (1759–96); the inventor and developer of the steam
engine, James Watt (1736–1819); Prime Minister William Gladstone
(1809–98); and, towering above them all atop a column, Scotland's
great historical novelist, Sir Walter Scott (1771–1832). The column
was intended for George III (1738–1820), after whom the square is
named, but when he was found to be insane toward the end of his

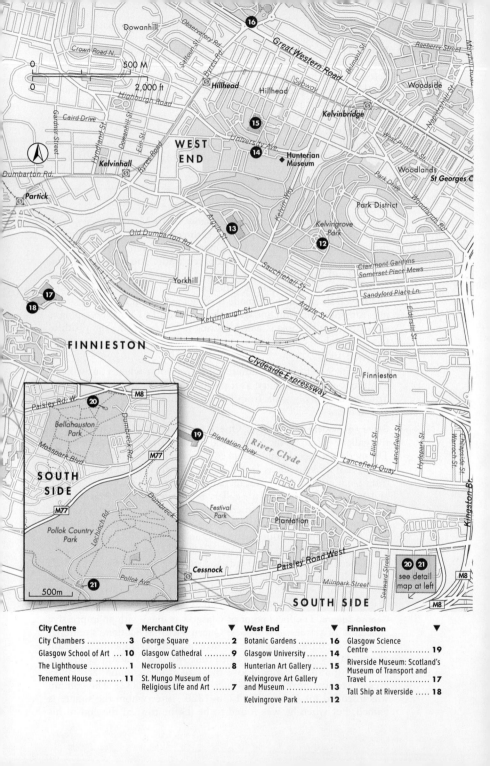

Glasgow

reign, a statue of him was never erected. On the square's east side stands the magnificent Italian Renaissance–style **City Chambers**; the handsome **Merchants' House** fills the corner of West George Street, crowned by a globe and a sailing ship. The fine old Post Office building, now converted into flats, occupies the northern side. There are plenty of benches in the center of the square where you can pause and contemplate. ⊠ *Merchant City* ⊡ *Free* Ⓜ *Buchanan St.*

Fodor's Choice
★
Glasgow Cathedral. The most complete of Scotland's cathedrals (it would have been more complete had 19th-century vandals not pulled down its two rugged towers), this is an unusual double church, one above the other, dedicated to Glasgow's patron saint, St. Mungo. Consecrated in 1136 and completed about 300 years later, it was spared the ravages of the Reformation—which destroyed so many of Scotland's medieval churches—mainly because Glasgow's trade guilds defended it. A late-medieval open-timber roof in the nave and lovely 20th-century stained glass are notable features.

In the lower church is the splendid crypt of St. Mungo, who was originally known as St. Kentigern (*kentigern* means "chief word"), but who was nicknamed St. Mungo (meaning "dear one") by his early followers. The site of the tomb has been revered since the 6th century, when St. Mungo founded a church here. Mungo features prominently in local legends; one such legend is about a pet bird that he nursed back to life, and another tells of a bush or tree, the branches of which he used to miraculously relight a fire. The bird, the tree, and the salmon with a ring in its mouth (from another story) are all found on the city's coat of arms, together with a bell that Mungo brought from Rome. ⊠ *Cathedral St., Merchant City* ☎ *0141/552–6891* ⊕ *www.glasgow-cathedral. com* ⊡ *Free* Ⓜ *Buchanan St.*

Fodor's Choice
★
Necropolis. A burial ground since the beginning of recorded history, the large Necropolis, modeled on the famous Père-Lachaise Cemetery in Paris, contains some extraordinarily elaborate Victorian tombs. A great place to take it all in is from the monument of John Knox (1514–72), the leader of Scotland's Reformation, which stands at the top of the hill at the heart of the Necropolis. Around it are grand tombs that resemble classical palaces, Egyptian tombs, or even the Chapel of the Templars in Jerusalem. You'll also find a smattering of urns and broken columns, the Roman symbol of a great life cut short. The Necropolis was designed as a place for meditation, which is why it is much more than just a graveyard. The main gates are behind the St. Mungo Museum of Religious Life and Art. ■**TIP→** Call ahead for free guided tours. ⊠ *70 Cathedral Sq., Merchant City* ☎ *0141/287–3961* ⊕ *www.glasgownecropolis.org* ⊡ *Free* Ⓜ *Buchanan St.*

St. Mungo Museum of Religious Life and Art. An outstanding collection of artifacts, including Celtic crosses and statuettes of Hindu gods, reflects the many religious groups that have settled throughout the centuries in Glasgow and the west of Scotland. A Zen garden creates a peaceful setting for rest and contemplation, and elsewhere stained-glass windows include a depiction of St. Mungo himself. Pause to look at the beautiful Chilkat Blanketwofven, made from cedar bark and wool by

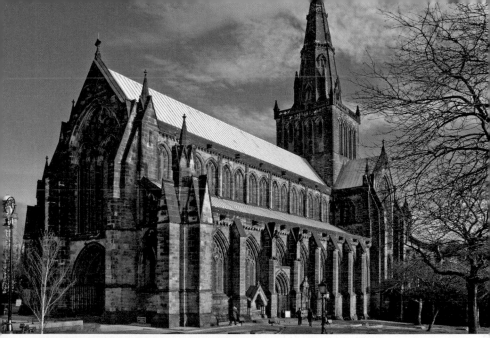

Medieval Glasgow Cathedral has the crypt of St. Mungo and a magnificent open-timber roof in the nave.

the Tlingit people of North America. ⊠ *2 Castle St., Merchant City* ☎ *0141/276–1625* ⊕ *www.glasgowlife.org.uk* ⊠ *Free* ⊘ *Closed Mon.* Ⓜ *Buchanan St.*

WEST END

Glasgow University dominates the West End, creating a vibrant neighborhood. Founded in 1451, the university is the third oldest in Scotland, after St. Andrews and Aberdeen. The industrialists and merchants who built their grand homes on Great Western Road and adjacent streets endowed museums and art galleries and commissioned artists to decorate and design their homes, as a stroll will quickly reveal. In summer the Glasgow Botanic Gardens, with the iconic glasshouse that is the Kibble Palace, becomes a stage for new and unusual versions of Shakespeare's plays. A fun way to save money is to picnic in the park; you can buy sandwiches, salads, and other portable items at shops on Byres Road. Alternatively, stroll past the university and down Gibson Street and Woodlands Road with their cafés and pubs.

GETTING HERE

The best way to get to the West End from the City Centre is by subway; get off at the Hillhead Station. A taxi is another option.

FAMILY
Fodor's Choice
★

Botanic Gardens. It is a minor Glasgow miracle how as soon as the sun appears, the Botanics (as they're known to locals) fill with people. Beautiful flower displays and extensive lawns create the feeling that this is a large back garden for the inhabitants of the West End's mainly apartment homes. At the heart of the gardens is the spectacular circular greenhouse, the **Kibble Palace,** a favorite haunt of Glaswegian families. Originally built in 1873, it was the conservatory of a Victorian eccentric. Kibble Palace and the other greenhouses contain tree ferns, palm trees, and the Tropicarium, where you can experience the lushness of a rain forest or see its world-famous collection of orchids. There is a tearoom, and in June and July the gardens host presentations of Shakespeare's plays (⊕ *www.bardinthebotanics.co.uk*). ⊠ *730 Great Western Rd., West End* ☎ *0141/276–1614* ⊕ *www.glasgowbotanicgardens.com* 🎟 *Free* ☉ *Closed dusk–7 am* Ⓜ *Hillhead.*

Glasgow University. Gorgeous grounds and great views of the city are among the many reasons to visit this university. The Gilbert Scott Building, the university's main edifice, is a lovely example of the Gothic Revival style. **Glasgow University Visitor Centre,** near the main gate on University Avenue, has exhibits on the university and a small coffee bar; one-hour guided walking tours of the campus (Thursday–Sunday at 2) start here. A self-guided tour starts at the visitor center and takes in the east and west quadrangles, the cloisters, Professor's Square, Pearce Lodge, and the not-to-be-missed University Chapel. The university's Hunterian Museum is also well worth a visit. ⊠ *University Ave., West End* ☎ *0141/330–2000* ⊕ *www.glasgow.ac.uk* 🎟 *Free* Ⓜ *Hillhead.*

Hunterian Art Gallery. Opposite Glasgow University's main gate, this gallery houses William Hunter's (1718–83) collection of paintings. You'll also find prints, drawings, and sculptures by Tintoretto, Rembrandt, and Auguste Rodin, as well as a major collection of paintings by James McNeill Whistler, who had a great affection for the city that bought one of his earliest paintings. Also in the gallery is a replica of **Charles Rennie Mackintosh's town house,** which once stood nearby and where Mackintosh and his artist wife, Margaret, lived between 1906 and 1914. These stunning rooms, faithfully rebuilt here, contain Mackintosh's distinctive art nouveau chairs, tables, beds, and cupboards, and the walls are decorated in the equally distinctive style devised by him and his wife. Free guided tours are available. ⊠ *Hillhead St., West End* ☎ *0141/330–5431* ⊕ *www.gla.ac.uk/hunterian* 🎟 *Free; Mackintosh House £5* ☉ *Closed Mon.* Ⓜ *Hillhead.*

FAMILY
Fodor'sChoice
★
Kelvingrove Art Gallery and Museum. Worthy of its world-class reputation, the Kelvingrove Art Gallery and Museum attracts local families as well as international visitors. This combination of cathedral and castle was designed in the Renaissance style and built between 1891 and 1901. The stunning red-sandstone edifice is an appropriate home for works by Botticelli, Rembrandt, Monet, and others, not to mention the collection of arms and armor. The Glasgow Room houses extraordinary works by local artists. Whether the subject is Scottish culture, design, or storytelling, every room begs you to look deeper; labels are thought-provoking and sometimes witty. You could spend a weekend here, but in a pinch three hours would do one level justice—there are three. Leave time to visit the gift shop and the attractive basement restaurant. Daily free recitals on the massive organ (usually at 1) are well worth the trip. ⊠ *Argyle St., West End* ☎ *0141/276–9599* ⊕ *www.glasgowlife.org.uk* 🎟 *Free (some special exhibitions require admission)* Ⓜ *Kelvinhall.*

FAMILY **Kelvingrove Park.** Both a peaceful retreat and a well-used playground, the park was purchased by the city in 1852. The River Kelvin flows through its green spaces. The park's numerous statues of prominent Glaswegians include one of Lord Kelvin (1824–1907), the Scottish mathematician and physicist remembered for his pioneering work in electricity. The shady park has a massive fountain commemorating a lord provost of Glasgow from the 1870s, a duck pond, two children's playgrounds, and a skateboard park. The An Clachan café beside the children's play area is an excellent daytime eatery and a boon to parents looking for a refuge. Public bowling greens are free, as are the tennis courts. The Bandstand, a 2,300-seat open-air theater, hosts major concerts in summer. ⊠ *Bounded by Sauchiehall St., Woodlands Rd., and Kelvin Way, West End* ⊕ *www.glasgowlife.org.uk* ⊠ *Free* Ⓜ *Kelvinhall.*

14

FINNIESTON

The River Clyde has long been the city's main artery, bearing Clyde-built ships, from warships to ocean liners, to the sea. Few of the yards remain open, and the Finnieston Crane, which once moved locomotives on to ships, is no longer active. But the area around it, bounded by the river on one side and Sauchiehall Street on the other, has undergone a great transformation since the 1990s. The riverside has been reborn, with Zaha Hadid's Transport Museum and the Tall Ship, as well as the Scottish Event Campus (SEC) occupying pride of place on the Finnieston bank and the Science Museum on the opposite side. The SSE Hydro, an ultramodern concert arena, has generated a new fashionable strip of bars and restaurants along Argyle Street.

GETTING HERE
From the Partick subway station it's a 10-minute walk to the Riverside Museum. From that museum it's a short stroll along the river (and across a bridge) to the Glasgow Science Centre. Argyle Street is a short walk from Kelvin Hall subway station or across Kelvingrove Park from Glasgow University.

FAMILY **Glasgow Science Centre.** Fun and engaging, this museum for children has three floors packed with games, experiments, and hands-on machines from pendulums to small-scale whirlpools, soundscapes to optical illusions. Its space-age home on the south side of the Clyde has a whole wall of glass looking out on to the river. The *BodyWorks* exhibition explores every aspect of our physical selves—try and reconstruct a brain. There are daily events and science shows, a lovely play area for under-sevens, a planetarium, an IMAX theater, and the spectacular Glasgow Tower, 400 feet high, from which to survey the whole city from the river to the surrounding hills. Always inquire whether the tower is open—even moderate winds will close it down. ■TIP➔ Admission is expensive, but the tower and planetarium cost less if you buy all the tickets at the same time. ⊠ *50 Pacific Quay, Finnieston* ✛ *Across the footbridge by the SEC Centre* ☎ *0141/420–5000* ⊕ *www.glasgowsciencecentre.org* ⊠ *£10.50, planetarium extra £2.50, tower extra £3.50; tower only £6.50* ☉ *Closed Mon., Tues., and Thurs. Nov.–Mar.* Ⓜ *Cessnock.*

The outstanding Kelvingrove Art Gallery and Museum presents engaging displays focusing on Scottish art, design, and culture.

FAMILY **Riverside Museum: Scotland's Museum of Transport and Travel.** Designed by
Fodor's Choice   Zaha Hadid to celebrate the area's industrial heritage, this huge metal
★   structure with curving walls echoes the covered yards where ships were
built on the Clyde. Glasgow's shipbuilding history is remembered with a
world-famous collection of ship models. Locomotives built at the nearby
St. Rollox yards are also on display, as are cars from every age and many
countries. You can wander down Main Street, circa 1930, without leaving the building: the pawnbroker, funeral parlor, and Italian restaurant
are all frozen in time. Relax with a coffee in the café, wander out onto
the expansive riverside walk, or board the Tall Ship that is moored permanently behind the museum. Take Bus 100 from the City Centre, or
walk from Partick subway station. ✉ *100 Poundhouse Pl., Finnieston*
☎ *0141/287–2720* ⊕ *www.glasgowlife.org.uk* 🚇 *Free* Ⓜ *Partick.*

FAMILY **Tall Ship at Riverside.** Built in 1896, this fine tall sailing ship now sits on the
River Clyde immediately behind the Riverside Museum. The *Glenlee* once
belonged to the Spanish Navy (under a different name), but carried cargo
all over the world in her day. She returned to Glasgow and the River Clyde
in 1993, and now forms part of the museum. You can wander throughout
this surprisingly large cargo ship with or without an audio guide, peer into
cabins and holds, and stand on the forecastle as you gaze down the river.
Bus 100 from George Square brings you here, or you can walk from the
Partick subway station in 10 minutes. ✉ *150 Pointhouse Pl., Finnieston*
☎ *0141/357–3699* ⊕ *www.thetallship.com* 🚇 *Free* Ⓜ *Partick.*

EAST END

Glasgow Green has always been the heart of Glasgow's East End, a formerly down-at-heel neighborhood that has seen many changes over time. One of the top attractions is the People's Palace, which tells the story of daily life in the city. On Sunday head to the nearby Barras market to hunt for bargains.

GETTING HERE

To get to the East End, take the subway to the St. Enoch Station and walk along Argyle Street to the Tron Cross. From there, London Road takes you to Glasgow Green.

FAMILY **Glasgow Green.** Glasgow's oldest park has a long history as a favorite spot for public recreation and political demonstrations. Note the Nelson Column, erected long before London's; the McLennan Arch, originally part of the facade of the old Assembly Halls in Ingram Street; and the Templeton Business Centre, a former carpet factory built in the late 19th century in the style of the Doge's Palace in Venice. There is an adventure playground for kids and a small cycle track beside it, with children's bikes for rent. Don't miss the **People's Palace** and the Doulton Fountain that faces it. ⊠ *East End* ✛ *North side of River Clyde between Green St. and Saltmarket St.*

FAMILY **Hampden Park.** A mecca for soccer enthusiasts, who come from far and near to tread the famous turf, the home field for the country's national team was the largest stadium in the world when it was built in 1903. There are stadium tours on nonmatch days at 11, 12:30, 2, and 3. You can then visit the Scottish Football Museum, which traces the history of the game; the museum may close on game days. ⊠ *Letherby Dr., East End* ✛ *Nearest rail stations are Mount Florida and Kings Park. Buses from City Centre* ☎ *0141/616–6139* ⊕ *www.hampdenpark.co.uk* 🎫 *Stadium tour £8, museum entrance £8, combined ticket £13.*

FAMILY **People's Palace and Winter Gardens.** The excited conversations among local visitors are a sign that this museum tells the story of everyday lives in Glasgow. There is always something that sparks a memory: a photo, an object, a sound. On display, for example, are the writing desk of John McLean (1879–1923), the famous "Red Clydeside" political activist, and the banana boots worn on stage by Glasgow-born comedian Billy Connolly. On the top floor a sequence of fine murals by Glasgow artist Ken Currie tells the story of the city's working-class citizens. In contrast, the Doulton Fountain opposite the entrance celebrates the British empire. The museum is housed in a Victorian red-sandstone building at the heart of Glasgow Green, and behind it are the restored Winter Gardens (a Victorian conservatory) and a popular café. To get here from the St. Enoch subway station, walk along Argyle Street past Glasgow Cross. ⊠ *Glasgow Green, Monteith Row, East End* ☎ *0141/276–0788* ⊕ *www.glasgowlife.org.uk* 🎫 *Free* ⊙ *Closed Mon.* Ⓜ *St. Enoch.*

14

SOUTH SIDE

Just southwest of the City Centre in the South Side are two of Glasgow's dear green spaces—Bellahouston Park and Pollok Country Park—which have important art collections: Charles Rennie Mackintosh's House for an Art Lover in Bellahouston, and Pollok House in Pollok Country Park. A respite from the buzz of the city can also be found in the parks, where you can have a picnic or ramble through greenery and gardens. The famous Burrell Collection is also in the area, but the museum will be closed until 2019 for a substantial renovation.

GETTING HERE

Both parks are off Pollokshaws Road, about 3 miles southwest of City Centre. You can take a taxi or car, city bus, or a train from Glasgow Central Station to Pollokshaws West Station or Dumbreck.

House for an Art Lover. Within Bellahouston Park is a "new" Mackintosh house, based on a competition entry Charles Rennie Mackintosh submitted to a German magazine in 1901. The house was never built in his lifetime, but took shape between 1989 and 1996. It is home to Glasgow School of Art's postgraduate study center, and displays show designs for the various rooms and decorative pieces by Mackintosh and his wife, Margaret. The main lounge is spectacular. There's also a café and shop filled with art. Buses 9, 53, and 54 from Union Street will get you here. Call ahead, as opening times can vary. ⊠ *Bellahouston Park, 10 Dumbreck Rd., South Side* ☎ *0141/353–4770* ⊕ *www.houseforanartlover.co.uk* 🖾 *£5.50* ⊘ *Closed weekdays Oct.–Mar.* Ⓜ *Ibrox.*

Pollok House. This classic Georgian house, dating from the mid-1700s, sits amid landscaped gardens and avenues of trees that are now part of Pollok Country Park. It still has the tranquil air of a wealthy but unpretentious country house. The Stirling Maxwell Collection includes paintings by Blake and a strong grouping of Spanish works by El Greco, Murillo, and Goya. Lovely examples of 18th- and early-19th-century furniture, silver, glass, and porcelain are also on display. The house has beautiful gardens that overlook the White Cart River. The downstairs servants' quarters include the kitchen, which is now a café-restaurant. The closest train station is Pollokshaws West, from Central Station; or you can take Buses 45, 47, or 57 to the gate of Pollok County Park. ⊠ *Pollok County Park, 2060 Pollokshaws Rd., South Side* ☎ *0141/616–6410* ⊕ *www.nts.org.uk* 🖾 *£6.50.*

WHERE TO EAT

Glasgow's vibrant restaurant culture is constantly renewing itself. Some of Britain's best-known chefs have opened kitchens here, including Jamie Oliver and Yotam Ottolenghi. More recently, the city has responded enthusiastically to the small-plate and sharing-platter trends, but there are still plenty of fine-dining options on the one hand, and steak houses and burger places on the other. The city continues to present the best that Scotland has to offer: grass-fed beef, free-range chicken, wild seafood, venison, duck, and goose, not to mention superb fruits and vegetables. The growing emphasis on organic food is reflected on menus that increasingly provide detailed information about the source of their ingredients. Around the city, an explosion of coffee shops offer artisanal macchiatos and mochas.

You can eat your way around the world in Glasgow. A new generation of Italian restaurants serves updated versions of classic Italian dishes. Chinese, Indian, and Pakistani foods, longtime favorites, are now more varied and sophisticated, and Thai and Japanese restaurants have become popular. Spanish-style tapas are now quite common, and the small-plate trend has extended to every kind of restaurant. Seafood restaurants have moved well beyond the fish-and-chips wrapped in newspaper that were always a Glasgow staple, as langoustines, scallops, and monkfish appear on menus with ever more unusual accompaniments. And Glasgow has an especially good reputation for its vegan and vegetarian restaurants.

Smoking isn't allowed in any enclosed space in Scotland, but more restaurants have placed tables outside under awnings during the warmer summer months, some of which permit smoking. *Restaurant reviews have been shortened. For full information, visit Fodors.com. Use the coordinate (✥ B2) at the end of each listing to locate a site on the corresponding map.*

PRICES

Eating in Glasgow can be casual or lavish. For inexpensive dining, consider the benefit of lunch or pretheater set menus. Beer and spirits cost much the same as they would in a bar, but wine is relatively expensive in restaurants. Increasing numbers of pubs offer food, but their kitchens usually close early. **■TIP→ Some restaurants allow you to bring your own bottle of wine, charging just a small corkage fee. It's worth the effort.**

WHAT IT COSTS IN POUNDS

	$	$$	$$$	$$$$
Restaurants	under £15	£15–£19	£20–£25	over £25

Restaurant prices are the average cost of a main course at dinner or, if dinner is not served, at lunch.

CITY CENTRE

$$$ STEAKHOUSE 🍴 **Anchor Line.** Occupying the former headquarters of the Anchor Line, whose ships sailed from Scotland to America, this bar and restaurant near St. George Square has been impressively refurbished to create the sense of fine dining aboard a luxury ocean liner. The menu reflects the voyage, too, including Scottish seafood and lamb, and a full range of steaks and their sauces to represent America. **Known for:** high-end cocktails; luxurious fine dining; steak of all kinds. [$] *Average main: £20* ✉ *12 St. Vincent Pl., City Centre* ☎ *0141/248–1434* 🌐 *www.theanchorline.co.uk* [M] *Buchanan St.* ✥ *F5.*

$ MODERN EUROPEAN 🍴 **Café Rogano.** Filled with photos of Hollywood greats, the brasserie at Glasgow institution Rogano's is more intimate, more relaxed, and a little more crowded than the famous restaurant upstairs. The mellow atmosphere also reflects the slightly more adventurous and less expensive menu, which often includes Moroccan-style lamb tagine and roast belly of pork. **Known for:** fish soup; chilled seafood platter; portraits of film stars on the wall. [$] *Average main: £14* ✉ *11 Exchange Pl.* ☎ *0141/248–4055* 🌐 *www.roganoglasgow.com* [M] *Buchanan St* ✥ *F5.*

$ THAI Fodor's Choice ★ 🍴 **Chaophraya.** You can experience dining at its most sumptuous and elegant for a good price in the grand surroundings of what was the Glasgow Conservatoire, where golden Buddhas sit comfortably beside busts of great composers. The delicate flavors of Thai cooking are at their finest here in the chef's wonderful signature Massaman lamb (and beef) curry, flavorsome Fisherman's Soup, and fusion dishes like scallops with black pudding. **Known for:** Massaman lamb curry; luxurious surroundings; extensive menu. [$] *Average main: £12* ✉ *The Town House, Nelson Mandela Pl., City Centre* ☎ *0141/332–0041* 🌐 *www.chaophraya.co.uk* [M] *Buchanan St.* ✥ *F4.*

$$ SPANISH 🍴 **Ibérica.** The Spanish small-plates revolution has arrived in Glasgow in this grand former bank, going a step beyond tapas with portions that are larger and encourage sharing and combining flavors at the table. The qualities of each dish are patiently explained: the different kinds of Serrano ham, the flavors of cheese, how aioli (homemade garlic mayonnaise) is made. **Known for:** black-rice dishes; Galician-style octopus; range of Serrano ham. [$] *Average main: £18* ✉ *140 St. Vincent St., City Centre* ☎ *0141/530-7985* 🌐 *www.ibericarestaurants.com* [M] *Buchanan St.* ✥ *F4.*

$ SOUTH AMERICAN 🍴 **Las Iguanas.** The bright interior of this restaurant, part of a popular chain, echoes the Latin American–themed menu in its vibrant colors and decoration. The extensive menu has the familiar Spanish and Mexican classics like tapas and burritos, but less familiar Brazilian dishes, too—and the cocktail list covers everything from tequila to a pisco sour. **Known for:** Xinxim, a Brazilian stew of chicken and crayfish; colorful cocktails; equally colorful decor. [$] *Average main: £14* ✉ *15–20 W. Nile St., City Centre* ☎ *0141/248–5705* 🌐 *www.iguanas.co.uk* [M] *Buchanan St.* ✥ *F5.*

$$ SEAFOOD Fodor's Choice ★ 🍴 **Mussel Inn.** West-coast shellfish farmers own this sleek restaurant and feed their customers incredibly succulent oysters, scallops, and mussels. The pots of mussels, steamed to order and served with any of a number of sauces, are revelatory, and scallops, prawns, and oysters come together in a wonderful seafood pasta. **Known for:** seafood pasta; Queenie oysters; mussels Moroccan style. [$] *Average main: £18* ✉ *157 Hope St., City Centre* ☎ *0141/572–1405* 🌐 *www.mussel-inn.com* [M] *Buchanan St.* ✥ *F4.*

$$ ASIAN 🍴 **Opium.** This eatery has completely rethought Asian cuisine, taking Chinese, Malaysian, and Thai cooking in new directions and using sauces that are fragrant and spicy but never overpowering. Subdued lighting, neutral tones, and dark wood create a calm setting for specialties including superb dim sum and crisp wontons filled with delicious combinations of crab, shrimp, and chicken. **Known for:** Asian-fusion

food; great cocktails; dim sum. $ *Average main: £17* ⊠ *191 Hope St., City Centre* ☎ *0141/332–6668* ⊕ *www.opiumrestaurant.co.uk* Ⓜ *Buchanan St.* ✛ *F4.*

$$$
MODERN BRITISH
Fodor's Choice
★

✕ **Rogano.** It is the surroundings that strike you first in Rogano's beautiful art deco bar, which has all the ambience of a 1930s Clyde-built luxury ocean liner. The restaurant is known for its seafood and has held its own despite the serious competition among fish restaurants that is emerging in the city. **Known for:** art deco bar; Glasgow institution; exquisite cocktails. $ *Average main: £23* ⊠ *11 Exchange Pl., City Centre* ☎ *0141/248–4055* ⊕ *www.roganoglasgow.com* Ⓜ *Buchanan St.* ✛ *F5.*

$
VEGETARIAN

✕ **Stereo.** Down a quiet lane near Central Station, this ultracool eatery dishes up a fantastic range of vegan food, from paella to gnocchi to a colorful platter with hummus, red-pepper pâté, and home-baked flat bread; roasted sweet-potato chips are the perfect side dish. The decor is homey and relaxed, and there always seems to be someone nearby reading or writing. **Known for:** imaginative vegan food; hipster comes to Glasgow; good music. $ *Average main: £10* ⊠ *20–28 Renfield La., City Centre* ☎ *0141/222–2254* ⊕ *www.stereocafebar. com* Ⓜ *Buchanan St.* ✛ *F5.*

$$$
SEAFOOD

✕ **Two Fat Ladies.** From its start in 1989 in a tiny West End space, Two Fat Ladies raised the standards of seafood cuisine in the city, and superb fish still dominates the menu. The restaurant is named after two famous TV cooks (or alternatively after the bingo call for number 88, the street number of the original location); the Blythswood Square branch is somewhat larger and airier, but still intimate. **Known for:** seafood; traditional high tea; intimate milieu. $ *Average main: £20* ⊠ *118A Blythswood St., City Centre* ✛ *Just off Blythswood Sq.* ☎ *0141/847–0088* ⊕ *www.twofatladiesrestaurant.com* Ⓜ *Cowcaddens* ✛ *E4.*

$
CAFÉ

✕ **Where the Monkey Sleeps.** This quirky basement café, in a series of small rooms with brightly colored sofas, serves huge sandwiches with amusing names—the "Wytchfinder" has chorizo sausage and cheese, while the "Serious Operation" contains practically everything on the menu. Enjoy your choice with one of the wonderful smoothies. **Known for:** brilliant sandwiches; secret corners; cheerful service. $ *Average main: £6* ⊠ *182 W. Regent St., City Centre* ☎ *0141/226–3406* ⊕ *www.monkeysleeps.com* ☾ *Closed weekends. No dinner* Ⓜ *Cowcaddens* ✛ *E4.*

$
BRITISH

✕ **Willow Tearooms.** Very Scottish breakfasts, lunches, and an array of cakes and scones baked in-house are served in a tearoom that was once part of a department store designed by Charles Rennie Mackintosh. It retains copies of the designer's trademark furnishings, including high-backed chairs with elegant lines and subtle curves. **Known for:** high tea; Mackintosh furniture; St. Andrew's seafood platter. $ *Average main: £10* ⊠ *97 Buchanan St., City Centre* ☎ *0141/332–0521* ⊕ *www.willowtearooms.co.uk* ☾ *No dinner* Ⓜ *Buchanan St.* ✛ *F5.*

14

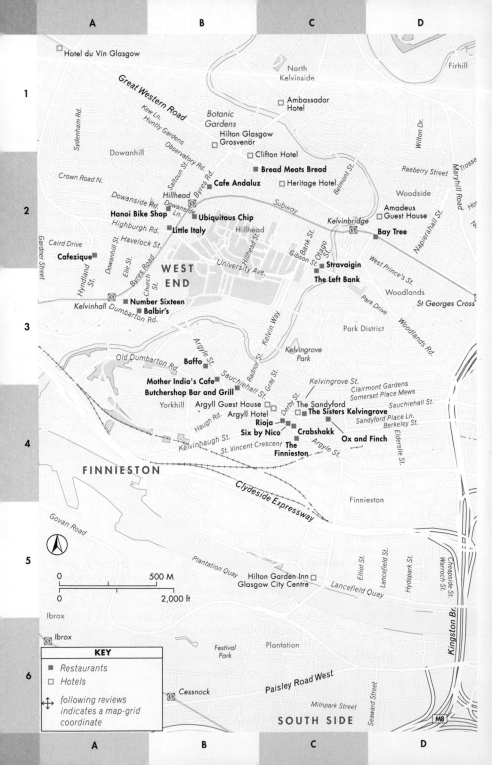

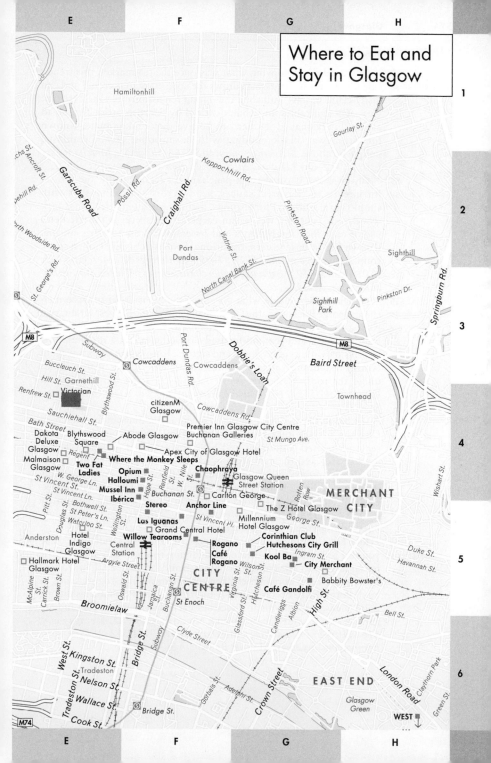

MERCHANT CITY

$$ MODERN BRITISH
🍴 **Café Gandolfi.** Occupying what was once the tea market, this trendy café known for its breakfasts draws the style-conscious crowd and can justly claim to have launched the dining renaissance of the Merchant City. Wooden tables and chairs crafted by Scottish artist Tim Stead are so fluidly shaped it's hard to believe they're inanimate. **Known for:** Stornaway black pudding with mushrooms; great breakfasts; unique furniture. [$] *Average main: £15* ✉ *64 Albion St., Merchant City* ☎ *0141/552–6813* 🌐 *www.cafegandolfi.com* [M] *Buchanan St.* ✥ *G5.*

$$ MODERN BRITISH
🍴 **City Merchant.** If you have a penchant for fresh cuisine and a taste for intense and flavorful sauces, head to this welcoming spot with simple but traditional furnishings, including white tablecloths, dark wood, soft lighting, and tartan carpets. The secret is the kitchen's use of only local ingredients and its emphasis on Scottish cuisine. **Known for:** intense sauces; traditional Scottish cuisine; Cullen skink soup. [$] *Average main: £19* ✉ *97–99 Candleriggs St., Merchant City* ☎ *0141/553–1577* 🌐 *www.citymerchant.co.uk* 🕓 *Closed Sun.* [M] *Buchanan St.* ✥ *G5.*

$$$ MODERN BRITISH
🍴 **Corinthian Club.** Inside what was once the mansion of tobacco merchant George Buchanan, the Corinthian Club includes a restaurant, two bars, a nightclub, and a casino in its maze of rooms. Its main restaurant, the steak-and-seafood-focused Brasserie, makes a dramatic first impression with its glass dome and statues. **Known for:** its extravagant central restaurant; range of menus and spaces; spectacular columns under the roof. [$] *Average main: £20* ✉ *191 Ingram St., Merchant City* ☎ *0141/552–1101* 🌐 *www.thecorinthianclub.co.uk* [M] *Buchanan St.* ✥ *G5.*

$$$ BRITISH
🍴 **Hutchesons City Grill.** One of the most iconic buildings in the Merchant City, the 17th-century Hutchesons Hospital, has become an elegant, seafood-focused restaurant and bar. Downstairs is divided between the bar area and the café section, its dark-wood decor recalling earlier times; upstairs the dining room has tall windows and beautifully decorated ceilings. **Known for:** Sunday roast with Champagne; weekend and lunch deals; subdued elegance in iconic building. [$] *Average main: £20* ✉ *158 Ingram St., Merchant City* ☎ *0141/552–4050* 🌐 *www.hutchesonsglasgow.com* [M] *Buchanan St.* ✥ *G5.*

$$ ASIAN FUSION
🍴 **Kool Ba.** Thick wooden tables, tapestries, and soft candlelight make you feel at home in the comfortable dining room of this atmospheric haven serving an intriguing mix of Indian and Persian fare. It's all about healthy, flavorful cooking: chicken tikka masala in a yogurt sauce or lamb korma with coconut cream and fruit or the Persian shashlik are good picks, and the menu describes each dish. **Known for:** Indian-Persian fusion; wide-ranging menu; attentive service. [$] *Average main: £16* ✉ *109–113 Candleriggs, Merchant City* ☎ *0141/552–2777* 🌐 *www.koolba.com* 🕓 *Closed Mon.* [M] *Buchanan St.* ✥ *G5.*

WEST END

$$$ INDIAN 🍴 **Balbir's.** Don't let the tinted windows discourage you: this place is a temple for pure, healthy Indian food that's impressive in taste and presentation. Twinkling chandeliers, immaculate white tablecloths, and perfectly polished silverware set the stage. **Known for:** fast, attentive service; multiple spice (and heat) combinations; everything on a grand scale. [$] *Average main: £22* ✉ *7 Church St., West End* ☎ *0141/339–7711* 🌐 *www.balbirs.co.uk* 🕓 *No lunch* [M] *Kelvinhall* ✣ *B3.*

$ MIDDLE EASTERN 🍴 **Bay Tree.** This popular small café in the university area is unpretentious and quite cheap. It serves wonderful Middle Eastern food—mostly vegetarian dishes, but there are a few lamb and chicken creations as well. **Known for:** good meze; Turkish and Lebanese dishes; standard café fare, too. [$] *Average main: £11* ✉ *403 Great Western Rd., West End* ☎ *0141/334–5898* 🌐 *www.thebaytreewestend.co.uk* [M] *Kelvinbridge* ✣ *D2.*

14

$ BURGER 🍴 **Bread Meats Bread.** One of a new breed of burger joints that has emerged in the city, this casual spot with long wooden tables, stools, and benches is also a meeting place for coffee or a drink. The many creatively stuffed burgers and sauces are accompanied by different poutines (the basic version of this Canadian dish is fries topped with cheese curds and gravy) and cheese toasties, a variation on the British classic known as rarebit (for reasons unknown). **Known for:** burgers; poutines; rarebits. [$] *Average main: £10* ✉ *701 Great Western Rd., West End* ☎ *0141/648 0399* 🌐 *www.breadmeatsbread.com* [M] *Hillhead* ✣ *B2.*

$$ TAPAS 🍴 **Cafe Andaluz.** With Iberian flair, this lively basement eatery is beautifully decorated using Spanish decorated tiles throughout. The first tapas place to make an impact in Glasgow, it has been followed by others (and has opened a second location in the City Centre) but remains one of the most successful. **Known for:** Spanish wine; lively but intimate; good paellas. [$] *Average main: £15* ✉ *2 Cresswell La., West End* ☎ *0141/339–1111* 🌐 *www.cafeandaluz.com* [M] *Hillhead* ✣ *B2.*

$$ BRITISH 🍴 **Cafezique.** Small but inviting, this bistro-style café has a vibrant, bustling atmosphere while remaining unhurried. Its changing breakfast, lunch, and dinner menus of British fare are always fresh and exciting. **Known for:** wonderful breakfasts; sobreasada (a chorizo spread); nearby bakery. [$] *Average main: £15* ✉ *66 Hyndland St., West End* ☎ *0141/339–7180* 🌐 *www.delizique.com* [M] *Hillhead* ✣ *A2.*

$ VIETNAMESE 🍴 **Hanoi Bike Shop.** Glasgow's first Vietnamese canteen offers a different style of dining, which is apparent from the moment you walk through the door and see the rustic setting, low tables, and stools. This is street food: choices include blood sausage with razor clam salad, hot-and-sour fish soup, and versions of pho, the fragrant Vietnamese soup with noodles and sliced meat. **Known for:** pho; street food in small plates; organic tofu options. [$] *Average main: £14* ✉ *8 Ruthven La., West End* ✣ *Down the alley opposite Hillhead subway station* ☎ *0141/334–7165* 🌐 *hanoibikeshop.co.uk* [M] *Hillhead* ✣ *B2.*

$$ ECLECTIC 🍴 **The Left Bank.** Close to Glasgow University, this popular bar and restaurant attracts a more mature student crowd. It's an airy spot with high ceilings, leather sofas, and wood floors, and the specialty is good, eclectic international food at reasonable prices. **Known for:** small plates;

open early until late; brunch. $ *Average main: £15* ⊠ *33–35 Gibson St., West End* ☎ *0141/339–5969* ⊕ *www.theleftbank.co.uk* Ⓜ *Kelvinbridge* ✛ *C2.*

$	✕ **Little Italy.** This busy, noisy, and extremely friendly Italian café sits
ITALIAN	in the heart of the West End. Its pizzas, made on the premises while
FAMILY	you wait with a coffee or a glass of Italian wine, are probably the best around, and its house-made pastas are consistently good. **Known for:** pizza; Italian wines; house-made pasta. $ *Average main: £14* ⊠ *205 Byres Rd., West End* ☎ *0141/339–6287* ⊕ *littleitalyglasgow.com* Ⓜ *Hillhead* ✛ *B2.*

$$	✕ **Number Sixteen.** This tiny, intimate restaurant serves only the fresh-
BRITISH	est ingredients, superbly prepared, on a constantly changing menu. Halibut is served with choucroute and a passion-fruit dressing—a typically unpredictable meeting of flavors. **Known for:** excellent set menu; surprising flavor combinations; cozy interior. $ *Average main: £17* ⊠ *16 Byres Rd., West End* ☎ *0141/339–2544* ⊕ *www.number16. co.uk* Ⓜ *Kelvin Hall* ✛ *A3.*

$$	✕ **Stravaigin.** For many years Stravaigin has maintained the highest qual-
ECLECTIC	ity of cooking, creating adventurous dishes that often combine Asian
Fodor's Choice	and local flavors and unusual marriages of ingredients. You can try the
★	*piri piri* quail (the seasoning is used in Africa) or the restaurant's famous haggis and neeps (turnips), symbolizing its commitment to local produce. **Known for:** buzzy bar, quieter restaurant downstairs; haggis and neeps; daily-changing curry. $ *Average main: £18* ⊠ *28 Gibson St., West End* ☎ *0141/334–2665* ⊕ *www.stravaigin.co.uk* Ⓜ *Kelvinbridge* ✛ *C2.*

$$$	✕ **Ubiquitous Chip.** Occupying a converted stable behind the Hillhead
MODERN BRITISH	subway station on busy Ashton Lane, this restaurant is a Glasgow insti-tution, with an untarnished reputation for creative Scottish cooking. Its street-level restaurant is a beautiful courtyard protected by a glass roof, and the more informal brasserie upstairs also serves less expensive dishes like haggis with neeps and tatties or a plate of mussels. **Known for:** venison haggis; imaginative fish cookery; lovely courtyard. $ *Average main: £24* ⊠ *12 Ashton La., West End* ☎ *0141/334–5007* ⊕ *www. ubiquitouschip.co.uk* Ⓜ *Hillhead* ✛ *B2.*

FINNIESTON

$$	✕ **Baffo.** There has been something of an explosion of new pizzerias
ITALIAN	in Glasgow, many of them newer chains, but Baffo has made its mark and won approval from a demanding audience. The decor of this busy spot is casual but smart, with exposed brick, white tiles and tables, black chairs, and wood floors. **Known for:** the half-meter pizza; busy in a friendly way; good pasta at good prices. $ *Average main: £15* ⊠ *1377 Argyle St., Finnieston* ✛ *Opposite the Kelvingrove Museum* ☎ *0141/583–0000* ⊕ *www.baffo.co.uk* Ⓜ *Kelvin Hall* ✛ *B3.*

$$	✕ **Butchershop Bar and Grill.** An early arrival in the redeveloping Fin-
STEAKHOUSE	nieston area, Butchershop occupies what was once a pub and overlooks the bowling greens in Kelvingrove Park. Modern, open, and airy, it preserves the sociable atmosphere of its predecessor, though it is now a quality steak house offering a range of cuts from rump to T-bone. **Known for:** steaks of every variety; good offers and fixed-price menus;

publike atmosphere. $ *Average main: £19* ⊠ *1055 Sauchiehall St., Finnieston* ✛ *Opposite Kelvingrove Park* ☏ *0141/339–2999* ⊕ *www. butchershopglasgow.com* Ⓜ *Kelvin Hall* ✛ *B4.*

$$$
SEAFOOD
Fodor's Choice
★

✕ **Crabshakk.** Anything but a shack, this intimate dining room has heavy wooden tables and chairs, an elegantly ornate ceiling, and a bar so shiny and inviting that it seems to almost insist you have a drink. The food comes from the sea—oysters, lobster, and squid—and you can have your choice served iced, grilled, roasted, or battered. **Known for:** great seafood cooking; art deco feel; very intimate. $ *Average main: £20* ⊠ *1114 Argyle St., Finnieston* ☏ *0141/334–6127* ⊕ *www.crabshakk. com* ☺ *Closed Mon.* Ⓜ *Kelvin Hall* ✛ *C4.*

$$
SEAFOOD
Fodor's Choice
★

✕ **The Finnieston.** A 19th-century inn turned into an elegant restaurant, the Finnieston retains the dark wood and narrow cubicles of earlier times, but today it is one of the new high-quality fish restaurants that have transformed the faded Finnieston area into a fashionable district. The menu allows you to choose the fish and how it is prepared, the sauce, and salad or vegetable sides. **Known for:** seafood and fish cuisine; stunning array of cocktails; comfy wooden booths. $ *Average main: £16* ⊠ *1125 Argyle St., Finnieston* ☏ *0141/222–2884* ⊕ *www.thefinniestonbar.com* Ⓜ *Kelvin Hall* ✛ *C4.*

$$
INDIAN

✕ **Mother India's Cafe.** At this progeny of the older Mother India restaurant nearby and early small-plates convert, the style is casual, with an extensive list of very fresh dishes and a no-reservations policy that makes for a (fast-moving) line. What makes this place across from Kelvingrove Art Gallery so popular is the combination of high-quality cooking and an extensive range of tastes that runs from creamy classics, through the vegetarian dal served cold, to spicy ginger chicken. **Known for:** small-plates Indian cuisine; quick service; bring your own wine. $ *Average main: £15* ⊠ *1355 Argyle St., Clyde* ☏ *0141/339–9145* ⊕ *www.motherindiaglasgow.co.uk* Ⓜ *Kelvin Hall* ✛ *B3.*

$$$
ECLECTIC
Fodor's Choice
★

✕ **Ox and Finch.** This immensely popular restaurant shines at every level—service, presentation, and taste. The stripped-back, rustic decor encourages chatter and the sharing of the eclectic small plates that are its specialty. **Known for:** small-plates dining; open kitchen; the buzz of conversation. $ *Average main: £20* ⊠ *920 Sauchiehall St., Finnieston* ☏ *0141/339–8627* ⊕ *www.oxandfinch.com* Ⓜ *Kelvin Hall* ✛ *C4.*

$$
SPANISH

✕ **Rioja.** Rioja belongs to the second generation of tapas restaurants, combining the classics with new and innovative interpretations. At this dark, rustic spot with exposed brick, wood floors and sturdy tables, and dark walls, *patatas riojanas* go a stage beyond *patatas bravas,* adding pork and chorizo, while the spring lamb with almond crust adds new flavors to the tapas range. **Known for:** contemporary take on tapas; good Spanish wines; late-night dining. $ *Average main: £15* ⊠ *1116 Argyle St., Clyde* ☏ *0141/334–0761* ⊕ *www.riojafinnieston. co.uk* Ⓜ *Kelvin Hall* ✛ *C4.*

$$$
BRITISH

✕ **The Sisters Kelvingrove.** Walk up the smooth sandstone steps to this restaurant, which aims to inspire both your palate and your heart with a menu that is locally sourced and always changing: a typical dish is Carluke ham with buttered savoy cabbage and colcannon mash. Douglas Gray tartan pads the pristine room, and polished floorboards reflect

14

the natural light shining in from the long windows around the unusual oval-shape room. **Known for:** fine Scottish cooking carefully sourced; gooseberry fool dessert; being ahead of its time. [$] *Average main: £20* ✉ *36 Kelvingrove St., Finnieston* ☎ *0141/564–1157* 🌐 *www.thesisters.co.uk* [M] *Kelvin Hall* ✣ *C4.*

$$$ BRITISH 🍴 **Six by Nico.** In a street of adventurous eateries, Six by Nico adds a new dimension of fun and wit. The concept at this intimate, modern restaurant with black tile, wood floors and tables, and black chairs is a six-course tasting menu linked to a theme that changes every six weeks, whether it's fish-and-chips or Route 66, with dishes that deconstruct and reconstruct the familiar. **Known for:** highly original approach to tasting menu; imaginative dishes; adventurous dining out. [$] *Average main: £25* ✉ *1132 Argyle St., Finnieston* ☎ *0141/334 5661* 🌐 *www.sixbynico.co.uk* 🕒 *Closed Mon.* [M] *Kelvin Hall* ✣ *C4.*

EAST END

$ GERMAN 🍴 **West.** This microbrewery serves beer brewed "according to German purity laws of 1516"—in other words, no additives to muddy the flavor. The German theme is continued with the slightly cavernous dining space dotted with large wooden tables, and the food, which includes wursts, Wiener schnitzel, and goulash. **Known for:** wurst and potato salad; variety of its own beers; goulash soup. [$] *Average main: £13* ✉ *Templeton Bldg., Templeton St., East End* ☎ *0141/550–0135* 🌐 *www.westbeer.com* [M] *St. Enoch* ✣ *H6.*

WHERE TO STAY

Since new or revamped grand hotels such as the Blythswood Square (2009) and Grand Central (2010) opened, a fresh generation of hotels has appeared around the city, from basic budget options to stylish boutique properties. Glasgow's City Centre never sleeps, so downtown hotels may be noisier than those in the leafy and genteel West End or in fashionable Finnieston. Downtown hotels are within walking distance of all the main sights, while West End lodgings are more convenient for museums and art galleries.

Although big hotels are spread out all around the city, B&Bs are definitely a more popular, personal, and cheaper option. For country-house luxury you should look beyond the city—try Mar Hall, near Paisley. Regardless of the neighborhood, hotels are about the same in price. Some B&Bs as well as the smaller properties may also offer discounts for longer stays. Make your reservations in advance, especially when there's a big concert, sporting event, or holiday (New Year's Eve is popular). Glasgow is busiest in summer, but it can fill up when something special is going on. If you arrive in town without a place to stay, contact the Glasgow Tourist Information Centre.

14

PRICES

It is always worthwhile to inquire about special deals or rates, especially if you book online and in advance. Another money-saving option is to rent an apartment. B&Bs are the best-priced short-term lodging option, and you're sure to get breakfast.

Most smaller hotels and all guesthouses include breakfast in the room rate. Larger hotels usually charge extra for breakfast. Also note that the most expensive hotels often exclude V.A.T. (Value-Added Tax, the sales tax) in the initial price quote but budget places include it. *Hotel reviews have been shortened. For full information, visit Fodors.com. Use the coordinate (⊕ B2) at the end of each listing to locate a site on the corresponding map.*

WHAT IT COSTS IN POUNDS

	$	$$	$$$	$$$$
Hotels	under £100	£100–£160	£161–£220	over £220

Hotel prices are the lowest cost of a standard double room in high season, including 20% V.A.T.

CITY CENTRE

$ HOTEL 🏨 **Abode Glasgow.** Stylish and modern, this boutique hotel in an Edwardian building was once the home of a prime minister, and it retains architectural features like the wrought-iron elevator and walls lined with 2,000 gold-leaf lions. **Pros:** stylish rooms; great location. **Cons:** limited public areas; some front rooms noisy; pricey parking. [$] *Rooms from: £90* ✉ *129 Bath St., City Centre* ☎ *0141/221–6789,* 🌐 *www.abode-glasgow.co.uk* 🛏 *60 rooms* 🍴 *Free Breakfast* [M] *Buchanan St.* ⊕ *E4.*

$$ HOTEL 🏨 **Apex City of Glasgow Hotel.** Its extraordinary projecting floor-to-ceiling windows set this modern chain hotel apart, providing a panoramic view over Glasgow and beyond from the upper floors (sixth and seventh). **Pros:** bright rooms; central location; city views from higher floors. **Cons:** lower-floor rooms overlook other buildings; no parking facility and nearby lot closes at night. [$] *Rooms from: £160* ✉ *110 Bath St., City Centre* ☎ *0141/375-3333* 🌐 *www.apexhotels.co.uk* 🛏 *106 rooms* 🍴 *Free Breakfast* [M] *Buchanan St.* ⊕ *F4.*

$$$ HOTEL Fodor'sChoice ★ 🏨 **Blythswood Square.** History and luxury come together at this smart conversion of the former headquarters of the Royal Automobile Club of Scotland, which occupies a classical building on peaceful Blythswood Square. **Pros:** airy and luxurious; glorious bathrooms; lovely common areas with the original gold-topped columns. **Cons:** room lighting may be too dim for some; some street noise. [$] *Rooms from: £166* ✉ *11 Blythswood Sq., City Centre* ☎ *0141/248–8888* 🌐 *www.blythswood-square.com* 🛏 *117 rooms* 🍴 *Free Breakfast* [M] *Cowcaddens* ⊕ *E4.*

$$ HOTEL 🏨 **Carlton George.** A narrow revolving doorway, a step back from busy West George Street, creates the illusion of a secret passageway leading into this lavish boutique hotel. **Pros:** near City Centre attractions; discounted parking nearby. **Cons:** entrance very small and often crowded;

area sometimes noisy at night. $ *Rooms from: £131* ✉ *44 W. George St., City Centre* ☎ *0141/353–6373* ⊕ *www.carlton.nl/george* ⇆ *64 rooms* ❍❘ *Free Breakfast* Ⓜ *Buchanan St.* ✛ *F4.*

$$ Ⓗ **citizenM Glasgow.** There's no lobby at the futuristic citizenM—no
HOTEL reception area at all, because you can only book online—but there
Fodor's Choice are chic "living rooms" with ultramodern furnishings where guests
★ congregate. **Pros:** wonderful design; all the creature comforts; central location. **Cons:** not for the claustrophobic; breakfast costs more if you don't book it ahead. $ *Rooms from: £119* ✉ *60 Renfrew St., corner of Hope St., City Centre* ☎ *01782/488–3490* ⊕ *www.citizenm.com* ⇆ *198 rooms* ❍❘ *No meals* Ⓜ *Buchanan St.* ✛ *F4.*

$$ Ⓗ **Dakota Deluxe Glasgow.** At this extremely stylish addition to Glasgow's
HOTEL hotel scene, the textured, neutral decor creates a restful, subdued
Fodor's Choice atmosphere. **Pros:** beautiful modern design and details; spacious, well-
★ appointed rooms; lovely bathrooms. **Cons:** unexciting views from hotel; toward edge of City Centre, though near Blythswood Square. $ *Rooms from: £145* ✉ *179 W. Regent St., City Centre* ☎ *0141/404 3680* ⊕ *glasgow.dakotahotels.co.uk* ⇆ *83 rooms* ❍❘ *Free Breakfast* Ⓜ *Cowcaddens* ✛ *E4.*

$$ Ⓗ **Grand Central Hotel.** This late-19th-century hotel next to Central Sta-
HOTEL tion certainly deserves its name, as everything about it, from the mag-
Fodor's Choice nificent marble-floor champagne bar to the ballroom fully restored to
★ its original glory, is grand. **Pros:** a real air of luxury; generally spacious rooms; great champagne bar for lingering. **Cons:** some noise from street; parking a couple of blocks away; some small rooms. $ *Rooms from: £145* ✉ *99 Gordon St., City Centre* ☎ *0141/240–3700* ⊕ *www.grandcentralhotel.com* ⇆ *233 rooms* ❍❘ *Free Breakfast* Ⓜ *Buchanan St.* ✛ *F5.*

$ Ⓗ **Hallmark Hotel Glasgow.** Behind a rather austere exterior built on to
HOTEL what was once a mill, the Hallmark clearly sees itself as a family-ori-
FAMILY ented hotel, with the facilities of a large chain but decor and ambience
that are unpretentious and comfortable. **Pros:** pleasant atmosphere; good spa and leisure center available to guests; close to City Centre. **Cons:** no views; some noise from nearby elevated motorway; hotel vehicle entrance not easy to find. $ *Rooms from: £90* ✉ *27 Washington St., City Centre* ☎ *0141/222–2929* ⊕ *www.hallmarkhotels.co.uk* ⇆ *129 rooms* ❍❘ *Free Breakfast* Ⓜ *St. Enoch* ✛ *E5.*

$$ Ⓗ **Hotel Indigo Glasgow.** In the center of the city, the fashionable Indigo
HOTEL is awash with bold colors and modern designs that emphasize comfort
and calm. **Pros:** well-designed rooms; vivid colors, patterns, and light-
ing; no conference rooms. **Cons:** narrow corridors; only showers in the bathrooms. $ *Rooms from: £118* ✉ *75 Waterloo St., City Centre* ☎ *0141/226–7700* ⊕ *www.hinglasgow.co.uk* ⇆ *94 rooms* ❍❘ *No meals* Ⓜ *St. Enoch* ✛ *E5.*

$$ Ⓗ **Malmaison Glasgow.** Housed in a converted church, this modern
HOTEL boutique hotel prides itself on personal service and outstanding ame-
nities like plasma televisions and high-end stereo systems. **Pros:** stun-
ning lobby; attention to detail; five-minute walk to Sauchiehall Street. **Cons:** bland views; dark hallways; no on-site parking. $ *Rooms from: £135* ✉ *278 W. George St., City Centre* ☎ *0141/572–1000* ⊕ *www.malmaison.com* ⇆ *72 rooms* ❍❘ *Free Breakfast* Ⓜ *Cowcaddens* ✛ *E4.*

$ HOTEL 🏨 **Premier Inn Glasgow City Centre Buchanan Galleries.** It would be easy to miss the big City Centre branch of this popular budget hotel chain, since its entrance on Renfield Street is quite small, but it's worth seeking out for its winning location just around the corner from the pedestrian precinct in Sauchiehall Street. **Pros:** great location; bargain rates; modern rooms. **Cons:** some front rooms a bit noisy; entrance easily missed at street level; no parking facilities. [$] *Rooms from: £70* ✉ *Buchanan Galleries, 141 W. Nile St., City Centre* ☎ *0871/527–9360* 🌐 *www.premierinn.com* 🛏 *220 rooms* 🍴 *No meals* [M] *Buchanan St.* ✣ *F4.*

$ B&B/INN 🏨 **Victorian House.** Compared with the bright-yellow entrance hall, the rooms in this hotel are rather plain, but its location—on a quiet residential street only a block from the Charles Rennie Mackintosh–designed Glasgow School of Art—is prime, and the rates are reasonable. **Pros:** appealing and central location; basement rooms very spacious. **Cons:** a little expensive for what it offers; no elevator; on-street parking sometimes difficult to find. [$] *Rooms from: £90* ✉ *212 Renfrew St., City Centre* ☎ *0141/332–0129* 🌐 *www.thevictorian.co.uk* 🛏 *60 rooms* 🍴 *Free Breakfast* [M] *Cowcaddens* ✣ *E4.*

14

MERCHANT CITY

$ B&B/INN 🏨 **Babbity Bowster's.** This warm and welcoming old merchant's house in the heart of the Merchant City is essentially a pub with rooms—simple, no-frills accommodation on its second floor. **Pros:** couldn't be more central; good food; great atmosphere; parking for guests. **Cons:** a bit noisy; no elevator. [$] *Rooms from: £70* ✉ *16–18 Blackfriars St., Merchant City* ☎ *0141/552–5055* 🌐 *www.babbitybowster.com* 🛏 *6 rooms* 🍴 *Free Breakfast* [M] *Buchanan St.* ✣ *G5.*

$$ HOTEL 🏨 **Millennium Hotel Glasgow.** This huge hotel in an older building, which occupies almost a whole side of George Square and stretches above the rail station next door, has restrained and comfortable rooms with ample bathrooms. **Pros:** couldn't be more central; ample comfortable public areas. **Cons:** very long corridors; views of the square only from some (more expensive) rooms; can feel very anonymous; some areas are looking a bit tired. [$] *Rooms from: £135* ✉ *40 George Sq., City Centre* ☎ *0141/332–6711* 🌐 *www.millenniumhotels.co.uk* 🛏 *116 rooms* 🍴 *Free Breakfast* [M] *Buchanan St.* ✣ *G5.*

$ HOTEL 🏨 **The Z Hotel Glasgow.** Just a few yards from George Square, this good-value modern hotel is one of the newer additions to Merchant City's accommodation options. **Pros:** central location; compact rooms but good beds and bedding; close to Queen Street Station. **Cons:** internal rooms have small (or no) windows; no restaurant; no parking facilities. [$] *Rooms from: £80* ✉ *36 N. Frederick St., Merchant City* ☎ *0141/212-4550* 🌐 *www.thezhotels.com* 🛏 *104 rooms* 🍴 *No meals* ✣ *G4.*

WEST END

$ **Amadeus Guest House.** This attractive Victorian town house has
B&B/INN comfortably furnished rooms that are flooded with plenty of natural
light. **Pros:** near West End attractions; two-minute walk from subway;
kids under six free. **Cons:** some rooms small; finding parking sometimes difficult. $ *Rooms from: £90* ✉ *411 N. Woodside Rd., West
End* ☎ *0141/339–8257* ⊕ *www.amadeusguesthouse.co.uk* ⇨ *9 rooms*
⦿| *Free Breakfast* Ⓜ *Kelvinbridge* ✛ *D2.*

$ **Ambassador Hotel.** Opposite the West End's peaceful Glasgow Botanic
HOTEL Gardens and within minutes of busy Byres Road, the Ambassador is
FAMILY part of a terrace of elegant town houses on the banks of the River Kelvin. **Pros:** views of Botanic Gardens; great for families with kids; five-
minute walk to public transportation and West End amenities. **Cons:**
no elevator; on-street parking difficult after 6 pm. $ *Rooms from: £72*
✉ *7 Kelvin Dr., West End* ☎ *0141/946–1018* ⊕ *www.ambassador-hotel.
net* ⇨ *26 rooms* ⦿| *Free Breakfast* Ⓜ *Hillhead* ✛ *C1.*

$ **Clifton Hotel.** Occupying two of the grand houses along a terrace above
HOTEL Great Western Road, this popular hotel offers wallet-friendly rates and
simply furnished rooms done up in cheerful shades. **Pros:** conveniently
located; attentive staff; good budget option. **Cons:** some rooms overlook the parking lot; no elevator. $ *Rooms from: £52* ✉ *26–27 Buck-
ingham Terr., West End* ☎ *0141/334–8080* ⊕ *www.cliftonhotelglasgow.
co.uk* ⇨ *26 rooms* ⦿| *Free Breakfast* Ⓜ *Hillhead* ✛ *B2.*

$ **Heritage Hotel.** This small, unpretentious, but well-established hotel
HOTEL in a very central West End location has cozy, simply decorated rooms
at very reasonable rates. **Pros:** very good location; friendly and agreeable staff; very reasonable rates. **Cons:** rooms quite small. $ *Rooms
from: £60* ✉ *4/5 Albert Terr., West End* ✛ *Entrance by Hillhead St.*
☎ *0141/339–6955* ⊕ *www.theheritagehotel.net* ⇨ *27 rooms* ⦿| *Free
Breakfast* Ⓜ *Hillhead* ✛ *C2.*

$$ **Hilton Glasgow Grosvenor.** Behind a row of grand terrace houses, this
HOTEL modern hotel overlooks the Glasgow Botanic Gardens. **Pros:** close to
Byres Road; some rooms have good views; tasty eatery. **Cons:** rooms at
the back overlook a parking lot; a rather institutional feel; parking is
extremely limited in the area. $ *Rooms from: £109* ✉ *1–9 Grosvenor
Terr., West End* ☎ *0141/339–8811* ⊕ *www3.hilton.com* ⇨ *96 rooms*
⦿| *Free Breakfast* Ⓜ *Hillhead* ✛ *B1.*

$$ **Hotel du Vin Glasgow.** Once the legendary One Devonshire Gardens
HOTEL hotel, frequented by such celebrities as Luciano Pavarotti and Elizabeth
Fodor's Choice Taylor, the Hotel du Vin Glasgow is still a destination for those in .
★ search of luxury. **Pros:** stunning Scottish-style rooms; doting service;
complimentary whisky on arrival. **Cons:** no elevator; on-street parking can be difficult after 6 pm. $ *Rooms from: £140* ✉ *1 Devonshire
Gardens, West End* ☎ *0330/016–0390* ⊕ *www.hotelduvin.com* ⇨ *49
rooms* ⦿| *Free Breakfast* Ⓜ *Hillhead* ✛ *A1.*

FINNIESTON

$ B&B/INN 🏨 **Argyll Guest House.** In this budget-minded annex to the Argyll Hotel, across the road on Sauchiehall Street, the rooms are plainly furnished but scrupulously clean. **Pros:** close to Kelvingrove Park; near public transportation; bargain prices. **Cons:** front rooms noisy on weekends; no elevator; parking on street is metered. [$] *Rooms from: £80* ✉ *966–970 Sauchiehall St., Finnieston* ☎ *0141/357–5155* 🌐 *www.argyllhotelglasgow.co.uk* 🛏 *20 rooms* 🍴 *Free Breakfast* [M] *Kelvin Hall* ✣ *C4.*

$$ HOTEL 🏨 **Argyll Hotel.** The tartan in the reception area reflects the clan theme throughout the hotel; each room is named after a clan, but each is also very different from the next. **Pros:** centrally located; comfortable rooms; reasonable prices. **Cons:** street a little noisy; metered parking on the street; downstairs breakfast area and bar need refurbishing. [$] *Rooms from: £100* ✉ *973 Sauchiehall St., Finnieston* ☎ *0141/337–3313* 🌐 *www.argyllhotelglasgow.co.uk* 🛏 *38 rooms* 🍴 *Free Breakfast* [M] *Kelvin Hall* ✣ *C4.*

$ HOTEL 🏨 **The Sandyford.** The Victorian exterior of this hotel anticipates the colorful decor you'll find inside, where the large windows in the reception area let in lots of light. **Pros:** extremely well located; minutes from several good eateries; very competitive prices. **Cons:** front rooms can get late-night noise; no elevator. [$] *Rooms from: £65* ✉ *904 Sauchiehall St., Finnieston* ☎ *0141/334–0000* 🌐 *www.sandyfordhotelglasgow.com* 🛏 *55 rooms* 🍴 *Free Breakfast* [M] *Kelvin Hall* ✣ *C4.*

NIGHTLIFE AND PERFORMING ARTS

Glasgow's music scene is vibrant and creative, and many successful pop artists began their careers in its pubs and clubs. When it comes to nightlife, the City Centre and the West End are alive with pubs and clubs offering an eclectic mix of everything from bagpipes to salsa to punk. The biweekly magazine *List,* available at newsstands and many cafés and arts centers, is an indispensable guide to Glasgow's bars and clubs.

NIGHTLIFE

Glasgow's busy nightlife scene is impressive and varied. Bars and pubs often close at midnight on weekends, but nightclubs often stay open until 3 or 4 am. Traditional *ceilidh* (a mix of country dancing, music, and song; pronounced *kay*-lee) is not as popular with locals as it used to be (except at weddings), but you can still find it at many more tourist-oriented establishments.

CITY CENTRE

BARS AND PUBS

Baby Grand. One of Glasgow's best-kept secrets, this intimate piano bar is hidden behind the King's Theatre. It serves good food all day (excellent breakfasts), and it manages to be crowded but never overcrowded, even at the busiest times. The pretheater menu is a good value, and tapas are available on weekends. ✉ *3 Elmbank Gardens, City Centre* ☎ *0141/248–4942* 🌐 *www.babygrandglasgow.com* [M] *Cowcaddens.*

14

King Tut's Wah Wah Hut. An intimate venue showcasing up-and-coming independent bands since 1990, King Tut's Wah Wah Hut claims to have been the venue that discovered the U.K. pop band Oasis. Indeed, the list of those who have played here reads like a catalog of indie music history. It's a favorite with students and hosts live music most nights, but the cozy and traditional pub setting draws people of all ages, and the refurbished bar is a pleasant and comfortable place for a drink or a meal. ⊠ *227A St. Vincent St., City Centre* ☎ *0141/221–5279* ⊕ *www. kingtuts.co.uk* Ⓜ *Cowcaddens.*

Fodor'sChoice
★
Sloans. One of Glasgow's oldest and most beautiful pubs, the wood-paneled Sloans is always lively and welcoming; it serves traditional pub food like fish-and-chips throughout the day. The upstairs ballroom is a magnificent mirrored affair, and on the floor above there's a dance floor with a ceilidh—traditional music and dancing—every Friday night (booking essential). The pub has a good selection of beers and spirits, and the outdoor area is always lively when the weather cooperates. ⊠ *108 Argyle St., City Centre* ⊹ *Entrance is in an alley off Argyle St.* ☎ *0141/221–8886* ⊕ *www.sloansglasgow.com* Ⓜ *St. Enoch.*

CLUBS

Stereo. The small downstairs music venue gets crowded quickly when bands play Sunday to Thursday night, but that only adds to the electric atmosphere at Stereo. There's also a hopping nightclub where DJs spin on Friday and Saturday nights until the wee hours of the morning. Upstairs, a café-bar serves tasty vegan food and organic drinks. ⊠ *20–28 Renfield La., City Centre* ☎ *0141/222–2254* ⊕ *www.stereocafebar. com* Ⓜ *Buchanan St.*

Sub Club. This atmospheric underground venue has staged cutting-edge music events since its jazz club days in the '50s. Legendary favorites like Saturday's SubCulture (House) and Sunday's Optimo (a truly eclectic mix for musical hedonists) pack in friendly and sweaty crowds. ⊠ *22 Jamaica St., City Centre* ☎ *0141/248–4600* ⊕ *www.subclub.co.uk* Ⓜ *St. Enoch.*

MERCHANT CITY
BARS AND PUBS

Babbity Bowster's. A busy, friendly spot, Babbity Bowster's serves real ales and excellent, mainly Scottish food, prepared by a French chef who adds his own special touch. The atmosphere is lively and very friendly; there is an outdoor terrace in summer and a fireplace in winter. If you like traditional music, make a point of coming on Saturday and Wednesday afternoon. ⊠ *16–18 Blackfriars St., Merchant City* ☎ *0141/552–5055* ⊕ *www.babbitybowster.com* Ⓜ *Buchanan St.*

Fodor'sChoice
★
Scotia Bar. This longtime bar serves up a taste of an authentic Glasgow pub, with traditional folk music regularly thrown in. Dark wood, a wood-beamed ceiling, and a classic L-shaped bar set the mood. ⊠ *112 Stockwell St., Merchant City* ☎ *0141/552–8681* ⊕ *www.scotiabar-glasgow.co.uk* Ⓜ *St. Enoch.*

CLUBS

Polo Lounge. Oozing with Edwardian style, the Polo Lounge is Glasgow's largest gay club. Upstairs is a bar that resembles an old-fashioned gentlemen's club. On the two dance floors downstairs, the DJs spin something for everyone. ✉ *84 Wilson St., Merchant City* ☎ *0141/553–1221* ⊕ *www.pologlasgow.co.uk* Ⓜ *Buchanan St.*

Swing. Hidden behind a narrow doorway on Hope Street, Swing comes as a surprise. It is an art deco bar that has survived the city's changes, and jazz bands play here three times a week. Blues and soul are heard other nights. Cocktails enhance the atmosphere, so go ahead and ask for a Manhattan. ✉ *183A Hope St., City Centre* ☎ *0141/332–2147* ⊕ *www.swingltd.co.uk* Ⓜ *Buchanan St.*

WEST END

BARS AND PUBS

Dram! With mismatched furnishings and the odd stag's head on the wall, the four large rooms here are decorated in a style that can only be described as "ultra eclectic." It's no place for a quiet, intimate evening, but Dram feels like a traditional bar while being brashly youthful and up-to-the-minute. There's a wide range of beers, and the place takes special pride in the 75 whiskies. On Thursday and Sunday, musicians gather in an informal jam session. Food is served every night until 9. ✉ *232–246 Woodlands Rd., West End* ☎ *0141/332–1622* ⊕ *www. dramglasgow.co.uk* Ⓜ *Kelvinbridge.*

Òran Mór. At the top of Byres Road, Òran Mór is in a massive church that still has its beautiful stained-glass windows as well as an upper hall, once the nave of the church, gloriously decorated by Glasgow artist Alasdair Gray. The bar fills with different crowds at different times of day, but its late license means that it tends to be very full on Friday and Saturday nights. In the basement, the hugely successful lunchtime theater series A Play, a Pie, and a Pint plays to capacity crowds. It also houses a busy bistro, a brasserie, and an evening music venue, as well as a late-night club. The small beer garden fills up quickly in good weather. ✉ *731 Great Western Rd., West End* ☎ *0141/357–6200* ⊕ *www.oran-mor.co.uk* Ⓜ *Hillhead.*

FINNIESTON

BARS AND PUBS

Ben Nevis. A traditional pub still holding its own on the trendy Finnieston strip, this eccentric spot is full of Highland artifacts. There are more than 180 whiskies from which to choose and traditional live music on Wednesday, Thursday, and Sunday. ✉ *1147 Argyle St., Finnieston* ☎ *0141/576–5204* ⊕ *www.thebennevis.co.uk* Ⓜ *Kelvinhall.*

78. Enjoy cozy sofas, a real coal fire, and tasty vegan food throughout the day. There's live music every night, with jazz on Sunday. ✉ *10–14 Kelvinhaugh St., Finnieston* ☎ *0141/576–5018* ⊕ *www.the78cafebar. com* Ⓜ *Kelvinhall.*

PERFORMING ARTS

Because the Royal Scottish Conservatoire is in Glasgow, there is always a pool of impressive young talent that's pressing the city's artistic boundaries in theater, music, and film. The city has a well-deserved reputation for its theater, with everything from cutting-edge plays to over-the-top pantomimes. The Citizens Theatre is one of Europe's leading companies, and the Kings and the Theatre Royal play host to touring productions.

ARTS CENTERS

FAMILY **Tramway.** South of the City Centre, this innovative arts center is well worth seeking out. It hosts regular exhibitions in its two galleries, and plays—often of a very experimental nature—in its flexible theater space. It has a café and a more formal restaurant on the first floor. Don't miss the Hidden Garden, which has transformed an empty lot behind the building into a sculpture park. This is a great place to go with kids. Take the train from Central Station to Pollokshields East (one stop). ✉ *25 Albert Dr., South Side* ☎ *0845/330–3501* ⊕ *www.tramway.org.*

Trongate 103. This vibrant contemporary arts center, housed in a converted Edwardian warehouse, is home base for diverse groups producing film, photography, paintings, and prints. It contains the Russian Cultural Centre and the Sharmanka Kinetic Theatre, as well as the Glasgow Print Studio, a well-established outlet for Glasgow artists; Street Level Photoworks, which aims at making photography more accessible; and the Transmission Gallery, a key exhibition space supporting nonconceptual art in the city. ✉ *103 Trongate, Merchant City* ☎ *0141/276–8380* Ⓜ *St. Enoch.*

CONCERTS

Glasgow Royal Concert Hall. The 2,500-seat Glasgow Royal Concert Hall is the venue for a wide range of concerts, from classical to pop. It also hosts the very popular late-night club during the annual Celtic Connections music festival. ✉ *2 Sauchiehall St., City Centre* ☎ *0141/353–8000* ⊕ *www.glasgowconcerthalls.com* Ⓜ *Buchanan St.*

Old Fruitmarket. A wonderful venue for almost every type of music, this was once the city's fruit and vegetable market. The first-floor balcony, with its intricate iron railings, still carries some of the original merchants' names. It's adjacent to City Halls in the heart of the Merchant City. ✉ *Candleriggs, Merchant City* ☎ *0141/353–8000* ⊕ *www. glasgowconcerthalls.com* Ⓜ *Buchanan St.*

Royal Scottish Conservatoire. An important venue for music and drama, the Royal Scottish Conservatoire hosts regular concerts by well-known performers, as well as by its own students. The lunchtime concert series is popular. ✉ *100 Renfrew St., City Centre* ☎ *0141/332–4101* ⊕ *www. rcs.ac.uk* Ⓜ *Cowcaddens.*

St. Andrew's in the Square. A beautifully restored 18th-century church close to Glasgow Cross, the glorious St. Andrew's in the Square is a popular arts venue. Drop by to see fiddle players on Monday evening or take traditional Scottish dance classes on Wednesday night. Concerts are held here from time to time. The downstairs Cafe Source serves a good range of Scottish food for lunch or dinner. ✉ *1 St. Andrew's in the Square, East End* ☎ *0141/559–5902* ⊕ *www.standrewsinthesquare. com* Ⓜ *St. Enoch.*

THEATER

FodorśChoice
★
Citizens' Theatre. Some of the most exciting theatrical performances take place at the internationally renowned Citizens' Theatre, where productions are often of hair-raising originality. The more experimental work is presented in the smaller studio theater. The theater has always had a strong commitment to working with the community, and tickets for most performances are £15. Behind the theater's striking contemporary glass facade is a glorious red-and-gold Victorian-era auditorium. ✉ *119 Gorbals St., East End* ☎ *0141/429–0022* ⊕ *www.citz.co.uk* Ⓜ *West St.*

King's Theatre. Dramas, variety shows, and musicals are staged at the King's Theatre, open since 1904. Check ticket websites to see what's on. ✉ *297 Bath St., City Centre* ☎ *0141/240–1111* Ⓜ *Cowcaddens.*

FodorśChoice
★
A Play, a Pie, and a Pint. In a former church, Glasgow's hugely successful lunchtime theater series called "A Play, a Pie, and a Pint" (and you do get all three) showcases new writing from Scotland and elsewhere. ■TIP➔ **Performances sell out quickly, particularly late in the week, so book well in advance on the website.** Doors open at 12:15 and shows begin at 1 Monday through Saturday. ✉ *Òran Mór, 731 Great Western Rd., Byres Rd. and Great Western Rd., West End* ☎ *0141/357–6200* ⊕ *www.playpiepint.com* Ⓜ *Hillhead.*

FAMILY
FodorśChoice
★
Sharmanka Kinetic Theatre. A unique spectacle, Sharmanka Kinetic Theatre is the brainchild of Eduard Bersudsky, who came to Glasgow from Russia in 1989 to continue making the mechanical sculptures that are his stock in trade. They are witty and sometimes disturbing, perhaps because they are constructed from scrap materials. They move in a kind of ballet to haunting, specially composed music punctuated by a light show. The shows are 45 or 70 minutes. ✉ *103 Trongate, Merchant City* ☎ *0141/552–7080* ⊕ *www.sharmanka.com* Ⓜ *St. Enoch.*

SHOPPING

You'll find the mark of the fashion industry on Glasgow's hottest shopping streets. In the Merchant City, Ingram Street is lined on either side by high-fashion and designer outlets like Cruise. Buchanan Street, in the City Centre, is home to many chains geared toward younger people, including Diesel, Monsoon, and USC, and malls like the elegant Princes Square and Buchanan Galleries. The adjacent Argyle Street Arcade is filled with jewelry stores. Antiques tend be found on and around West Regent Street in the City Centre. The West End has a number of small shops selling crafts, vintage clothing, and trendier fashions—punctuated by innumerable cafés and restaurants. The university dominates the area around West End, and many shops cater to students.

CITY CENTRE

ANTIQUES AND FINE ART

Compass Gallery. The gallery is something of an institution, having opened in 1969 to provide space for young and unknown artists—a role it continues. It shares space with Cyril Gerber Fine Arts, which specializes in British paintings from 1880 to the present. ⊠ *178 W. Regent St., City Centre* ☎ *0141/221–3095* ⊕ *www.compassgallery. co.uk* Ⓜ *Cowcaddens.*

ARCADES AND SHOPPING CENTERS

Argyll Arcade. An interesting diversion off Argyle Street is the covered Argyll Arcade, the region's largest collection of jewelers under one roof. The L-shape edifice, built in 1827, houses several locally based jewelers and a few shops specializing in antique jewelry. ⊠ *Buchanan St., City Centre* ⊕ *www.argyll-arcade.com* Ⓜ *St. Enoch.*

Buchanan Galleries. Next to the Glasgow Royal Concert Hall, Buchanan Galleries is packed with more than 80 high-quality shops. Its top attraction is the John Lewis department store. ⊠ *220 Buchanan St., City Centre* ☎ *0141/333–9898* ⊕ *www.buchanangalleries.co.uk* Ⓜ *Buchanan St.*

Fodor's Choice **Princes Square.** The city's best shopping center is the art nouveau Princes
★ Square, a lovely space filled with high-quality shops and pleasant cafés and restaurants. A stunning glass dome was fitted over the original building, which dates back to 1841. ⊠ *48 Buchanan St., City Centre* ☎ *0141/221–0324* ⊕ *www.princessquare.co.uk* Ⓜ *St. Enoch.*

St. Enoch's Shopping Centre. Eye-catching if not especially pleasing, this modern glass building resembles an overgrown greenhouse. It has dozens of stores, including the huge Hamley's toy store. ⊠ *55 St. Enoch Sq., City Centre* ☎ *0141/204–3900* ⊕ *www.st-enoch.com* Ⓜ *St. Enoch.*

BOOKS, PAPER, AND MUSIC

Cass Art Store. One of the country's largest suppliers of art and craft materials operates this store near the Glasgow Gallery of Modern Art. There's plenty to inspire your creativity, and good choices for kids as well. ⊠ *63–67 Queen St., City Centre* ☎ *0141/248–5899* ⊕ *www.cassart.co.uk* Ⓜ *Buchanan St.*

Monorail Music. For the latest on the city's ever-thriving music scene try Monorail Music, inside a café-bar called Mono. The shop specializes in indie music and has a large collection of vinyl with everything from rock to jazz. ⊠ *12 Kings Ct., City Centre* ⊹ *Close to the Tron Theatre* ☎ *0141/552–9458* ⊕ *www.monorailmusic.com* Ⓜ *St. Enoch.*

Paperchase. For everything that stationery has to offer—cards, notebooks, books—Paperchase is the place. And there's a café where you can ponder which notebook you want to buy. ⊠ *185–221 Buchanan St., City Centre* ☎ *0141/353–3491* ⊕ *www.paperchase.co.uk* Ⓜ *Buchanan St.*

Waterstones. In an age of online sales, bookstores seem to be becoming scarcer. Waterstones remains as the city's main bookshop, and it has an excellent selection on its four floors. There's also a good basement café. ⊠ *153–57 Sauchiehall St., City Centre* ☎ *0141/248–4814* ⊕ *www.waterstones.com* Ⓜ *Buchanan St.*

CLOTHING

Mr. Ben. A large, funky selection of vintage clothing for men and women is what you'll find at Mr. Ben. ✉ *6 King's Ct., City Centre* ☎ *0141/553–1936* ⊕ *mrbenretroclothing.com* Ⓜ *St. Enoch.*

DEPARTMENT STORES

Debenham's. One of Glasgow's principal department stores, Debenham's has fine china and crystal as well as women's and men's clothing. ✉ *97 Argyle St., City Centre* ☎ *0844/561–6161* ⊕ *www.debenhams.com* Ⓜ *St. Enoch.*

Fodor's Choice ★ **House of Fraser.** A Glasgow institution, the House of Fraser stocks wares that reflect the city's material aspirations, including European designer clothing. There are also more locally produced articles, such as tweeds, tartans, glass, and ceramics. The magnificent interior, set off by the grand staircase rising to various floors and balconies, is itself worth a visit. ✉ *21–45 Buchanan St., City Centre* ☎ *0141/221–3880* ⊕ *www. houseoffraser.co.uk* Ⓜ *St. Enoch.*

John Lewis. This store is a favorite for its stylish mix of clothing, household items, electronics, and practically everything else. John Lewis claims to have "never been knowingly undersold" and prides itself on its customer service. It has a very elegant second-floor balcony café. ✉ *Buchanan Galleries, 220 Buchanan St., City Centre* ☎ *0141/353–6677* ⊕ *www.johnlewis.com/glasgow* Ⓜ *Buchanan St.*

HOME FURNISHINGS AND TEXTILES

Linens Fine. Wonderful embroidered and embellished bed linens and other textiles are the specialty of this shop in the Princes Square shopping center. ✉ *Princes Square, 48 Buchanan St., Unit 6, City Centre* ☎ *0141/248–7082* Ⓜ *St. Enoch.*

SCOTTISH SPECIALTIES

Hector Russell Kiltmakers. Primarily for men, this shop specializes in Highland outfits, wool, and cashmere clothing. ✉ *110 Buchanan St., City Centre* ☎ *0141/221–0217* ⊕ *www.hector-russell.com* Ⓜ *Buchanan St.*

MacDonald MacKay Ltd. The well-regarded MacDonald MacKay Ltd. makes, sells, and exports Highland dress and accessories for men. ✉ *161 Hope St., City Centre* ☎ *0141/204–3930* Ⓜ *Buchanan St.*

SHOPPING DISTRICTS

Argyle Street. On the often-crowded pedestrian area of Argyle Street you'll find chain stores like Debenham's and some of the more popular and less expensive chains like Gap, Next, and Schuh as well as Primark and H&M. ✉ *City Centre* Ⓜ *St. Enoch.*

Buchanan Street. This pedestrian-only street has become increasingly upmarket, with Monsoon, Topshop, Burberry, Jaeger, Pretty Green, and All Saints as well as House of Fraser and other chain stores along its length. Always crowded with shoppers, it has also become a mecca for the growing community of buskers in Glasgow's streets, playing every kind of music. ✉ *City Centre* Ⓜ *Buchanan St.*

590 <   **Glasgow**

MERCHANT CITY

ANTIQUES AND FINE ART

Fodor's Choice **Glasgow Print Studio.** Essentially an artists' cooperative, the Glasgow Print
★ Studio's facilities launched a generation of outstanding painters, printers,
and designers. The work of members past and present can be seen (and
bought) at the Print Studio Gallery on King Street. ⊠ *103 Trongate, Merchant City* ☏ *0141/552–0704* ⊕ *www.gpsart.co.uk* Ⓜ *St. Enoch*.

CLOTHING

Cruise. As one of the first haute couture stores in central Glasgow, Cruise
can claim to have launched a new commercial era in the city. It now
has two stores in the Merchant City, where its high-fashion clothes and
accessories for men and women are beautifully and characteristically
displayed to those who can stretch their budgets to its levels. ⊠ *180
Ingram St., Merchant City* ☏ *0141/332–5797* ⊕ *www.cruisefashion.
com* Ⓜ *Buchanan St.*

Jigsaw. You'll find a wide and ever-changing range of fashion items for
women and men at Jigsaw, well tailored and glamorous but at accessible
prices. A U.K.-based chain, its Glasgow store is especially dramatic,
occupying one of the tobacco lords' mansions on Ingram Street. ⊠ *177
Ingram St., Merchant City* ☏ *0141/552–7639* ⊕ *www.jigsaw-uk.co.uk*
Ⓜ *Buchanan St.*

JEWELRY

Orro. The beautiful and contemporary jewelry here uses modern designs
and new materials in unexpected ways. The shop has a gallery feel,
and you can browse uninterrupted. ⊠ *12 Wilson St., Merchant City*
☏ *0141/552–7888* ⊕ *www.orro.co.uk* Ⓜ *Buchanan St.*

WEST END

BOOKS, PAPER, AND MUSIC

Caledonia Books. This well-organized and well-stocked secondhand
bookstore fills the gap left by the departure of other bookstores. The
owners are knowledgeable and willing to search for even the most
obscure volumes. ⊠ *483 Great Western Rd., West End* ☏ *0141/334–
9663* ⊕ *www.caledoniabooks.co.uk* Ⓜ *Kelvinbridge.*

Fopp. This funky shop is an extravaganza of music, books, and DVDs.
It's a small space, but the selection is huge. The prices are a lot more
reasonable than those at most other chain stores. ⊠ *358 Byres Rd., West
End* ☏ *0141/222–2128* ⊕ *www.fopp.com* Ⓜ *Hillhead.*

CLOTHING

Charles Clinkard. This traditional shoe store—a rare thing these days—
has an impressive range of choices, often unusual lines, principally for
women but for men, too. There are also regular bargains here, and the
staff knows their shoes. ⊠ *149 Byres Rd., West End* ☏ *0345/241–7742*
⊕ *www.charlesclinkard.co.uk* Ⓜ *Hillhead.*

Glasgow Vintage Co. You can find plenty of genuine bargains here for upmarket vintage clothes at down-market prices. There are choices for men, women, and children from the 1950s to the 1980s. ⊠ *453 Great Western Rd., West End* ☎ *0141/338–6633* ⊕ *www. glasgowvintage.co.uk.*

Strawberry Fields. Designer clothing for children is the specialty of Strawberry Fields. ⊠ *517 Great Western Rd., West End* ☎ *0141/339–1121* Ⓜ *Kelvinbridge.*

FOOD
Demijohn. Specializing in infused wines, spirits, oils, and vinegars, Demijohn calls itself a "liquid deli." ⊠ *382 Byres Rd., West End* ☎ *0141/337–3600* ⊕ *www.demijohn.co.uk* Ⓜ *Hillhead.*

Iain Mellis Cheesemonger. This shop has a superb, seemingly endless selection of fine Scottish cheeses, in addition to others from England and across Europe, as well as bread and olives. ⊠ *492 Great Western Rd., West End* ☎ *0141/339–8998* ⊕ *www.mellischeese.net* Ⓜ *Kelvinbridge.*

HOME FURNISHINGS AND TEXTILES
Nancy Smillie. Local to the floorboards, Nancy Smillie is a one-of-a-kind boutique that sells unique glassware, jewelry, and furnishings. It also runs a jewelry boutique at 425 Great Western Road. ⊠ *53 Cresswell St., West End* ☎ *0141/334–0055* ⊕ *www.nancysmillieshop.com* Ⓜ *Hillhead.*

Time and Tide. Loosely described as a household goods store, Time and Tide sells an eclectic mix of lamps and candleholders and cushions and things you never realized you needed until you see them. ⊠ *398 Byres Rd., West End* ☎ *0141/357–4548* ⊕ *www.timeandtidestores. co.uk* Ⓜ *Hillhead.*

EAST END

Fodor's Choice
★

Barras. Scotland's largest indoor market—named for the barrows, or pushcarts, formerly used by the stallholders—prides itself on selling everything "from a needle to an anchor" and is a must-see for anyone addicted to searching through piles of junk for bargains. The century-old institution, open weekends, consists of nine markets. The atmosphere is always good-humored, and you can find just about anything here, in any condition, from dusty model railroads to antique jewelry. Haggling is compulsory. You can reach the Barras by walking along Argyle Street from the St. Enoch subway station. The Barrowland ballroom, which forms part of the market, was once where Glaswegians went to dance; today it is a venue for concerts of every kind. ■TIP→ Across the road is one of Glasgow's oldest pubs, the Saracen's Head; enter with caution—ghosts are said to abound. ⊠ *Gallowgate, East End* ⊕ *www. theglasgowbarras.com.*

SPORTS AND THE OUTDOORS

You can't go far these days in Glasgow without seeing a runner or cyclist; numerous parks provide plenty of opportunities, and the next-bike (⊕ *www.nextbike.co.uk)* public bike-rental program has been a boon to cyclists. It rains a lot in Glasgow, but don't let the weather stop you. It doesn't deter the locals who play soccer, tennis, hike, bike, run, swim, and walk in the rain.

FOOTBALL

The city has been sports mad, especially for football (soccer), for more than 100 years. The historic rivalry between its two main football clubs, Rangers and Celtic, is legendary. Partick Thistle is a less contentious alternative for football fans. Matches are held usually on Saturday or Sunday in winter. Admission prices start at about £20, and don't go looking for a family-day-out atmosphere. Football remains a fiercely contested game attended mainly by males, though the stadiums at Ibrox and Celtic Park are fast becoming family-friendly.

Celtic. This famous football club wears white-and-green stripes and plays in the east at Celtic Park, or Perkhead as it is know locally. Daily stadium tours must be booked ahead, and the Celtic Museum is also in the stadium. To get here, take a taxi from central Glasgow or a train from Central Station to Dalmarnock (10-minute walk from station). ✉ *Celtic Park, 18 Kerrydale St., East End* ☎ *0871/226–1888* ⊕ *www. celticfc.net* ✉ *Stadium tours £12.50.*

Partick Thistle. Soccer in Glasgow isn't just blue or green, nor is it dominated by international players and big money. Partick Thistle Football Club, known as the Jags, wears red and yellow, and its home field is Firhill Park. ✉ *80 Firhill Rd., West End* ☎ *0141/579–1971* ⊕ *www.ptfc. co.uk* Ⓜ *St. George's Cross.*

Rangers. The Rangers wear blue and play at Ibrox, on the south side of the Clyde. Stadium tours are on Friday, Saturday, and Sunday; booking ahead is essential. ✉ *150 Edmiston Dr., South Side* ☎ *0871/702–1972* ⊕ *www.rangers.co.uk* ✉ *Stadium tours £8* Ⓜ *Ibrox.*

SPORTS ARENA

Emirates Arena. Built to host a number of events during the Commonwealth Games of 2014, the arena continues to present sporting events but also contains a gym and spa that are open to the public. It also includes the Sir Chris Hoy Velodrome. The stadium has transformed an East End area that was neglected and abandoned. Trains from Central Station go to Dalmarnock, a 10-minute walk from the stadium. ✉ *1000 London Rd., East End* ☎ *0141/287–7000* ⊕ *www.emiratesarena.co.uk.*

THE BORDERS AND
THE SOUTHWEST

WELCOME TO THE BORDERS AND THE SOUTHWEST

TOP REASONS TO GO

★ **Ancient abbeys:** The great abbeys of the Border regions, and the Whithorn Priory and the wonderful Sweetheart Abbey in the southwest, are mainly in ruins, but they retain an air of their former grandeur.

★ **Outdoor activities:** You can walk, bicycle, or even ride horses across Galloway or through the Borders. Abandoned railway tracks make good paths, and there are forests and moorlands if you prefer wilder country.

★ **Stately homes and castles:** The landed aristocracy still lives in grand mansions like Floors Castle or Traquair House, and most of the homes are open to visitors. Threave, Drumlanrig, and the magical Caerlaverock Castle near Dumfries evoke grander times.

★ **Literary Scotland:** The Borders region has enough monuments dedicated to Sir Walter Scott to make him the focus of a visit, including Abbotsford House, which he built for himself. The poet Robert Burns spent much of his working life in Dumfries.

Once a battleground region separating Scotland and England, today the Borders area is a bridge between the two countries. This is a place of upland moors and hills, farmland, and forested river valleys. Yet it also embraces the rugged coastline between Edinburgh and Berwick. It's rustic and peaceful, with textile mills, abbeys, castles, and gardens. The area is a big draw for hikers and walking enthusiasts, too.

1 The Borders. Borders towns cluster around and between two rivers—the Tweed and its tributary, the Teviot. These are mostly textile towns with plenty of personality, where residents take pride in their local municipalities. The cut-down version of rugby (the Sevens), where teams consist of 7 rather than 15 players, brings the Borders

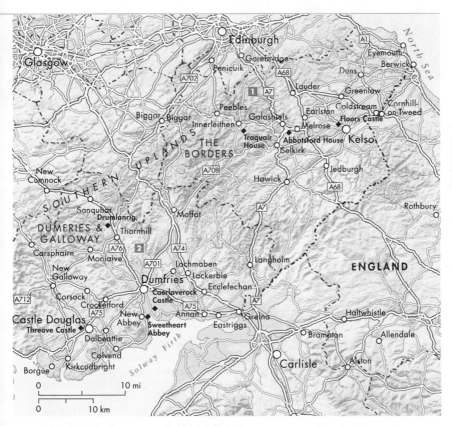

15

towns into fierce (but friendly) rivalry. The area's top attractions include Jedburgh Abbey, Floors Castle in Kelso, and Abbotsford House just outside Melrose.

2 Dumfries and Galloway. Easygoing and peaceful, towns in this southwestern region are usually very attractive, with wide streets and colorful buildings. The Solway Firth is a vast nature preserve, and the climate of the west sustains the surprising tropical plants at the Logan Botanic Gardens and the gardens at Threave Castle.

Updated
by Mike
Gonzalez

In the Borders region, south of Edinburgh, are more stately homes, fortified castles, and medieval abbeys than in any other part of Scotland. This is also Sir Walter Scott territory, including his pseudo-baronial home at Abbotsford. The area embraces the whole 90-mile course of one of Scotland's great rivers, the Tweed. Passing woodlands luxuriant with game birds, the river flows in rushing torrents through this fertile land. To the west of the Borders is Dumfries and Galloway, an area of gentle coasts, forests, and lush hills, ideal country for walkers and cyclists.

For centuries the Borders was a battlefield, where English and Scottish troops remained locked in a struggle for its possession. At different times, parts of the region have been in English hands, just as slices of northern England (Berwick-upon-Tweed, for example) have been under Scottish control. The castles and fortified houses as well as the abbeys across the Borders are the surviving witnesses to those times. After the Union of 1707, fortified houses gradually gave way to the luxurious country mansions that pepper the area. And by the 19th century they had become grand country houses built by fashionable architects.

All the main routes between London and Edinburgh traverse the Borders, whose hinterland of undulating pastures, woods, and valleys is enclosed within three lonely groups of hills: the Cheviots, the Moorfoots, and the Lammermuirs. Hamlets and prosperous country towns dot the land, giving valley slopes a lived-in look, yet the total population is still sparse. The sheep that are the basis of the region's prosperous textile industry outnumber human beings by 14 to 1.

To the west is the region of Dumfries and Galloway, on the shores of the Solway Firth. It might appear to be an extension of the Borders, but the southwest has a history all its own. From its ports ships sailed to the Americas, carrying country dwellers driven from their land to make room for sheep. Inland, the earth rises toward high hills, forest, and bleak but captivating moorland, whereas nearer the coast you can find pretty farmlands, small villages, and unassuming towns. The shoreline is washed by the North Atlantic Drift (Scotland's answer to the Gulf Stream), and first-time visitors are always surprised to see palm trees and exotic plants thriving in gardens and parks along the coast.

At the heart of the region is Dumfries, the "Queen o' the South." Once a major port and commercial center, its glamour is now slightly faded. But the memory of poet Robert Burns, who spent several years living and working here and who is buried in the town, remains very much alive.

PLANNER

WHEN TO GO
Because many lodgings and some sights are privately owned and shut down from early autumn until early April, the area is less suited to off-season touring than some other parts of Scotland. The best time to visit is between Easter and late September. The region does look magnificent in autumn, especially along the wooded river valleys of the Borders. Late spring is the time to see the rhododendrons in the gardens of Dumfries and Galloway.

FESTIVALS
Common Ridings. More than 10 Borders communities have reestablished their identities through the annual summer gatherings known as the Common Ridings. In medieval times it was essential that each town be able to defend its area by "riding the marches," or patrolling the boundaries. The Common Ridings that celebrate this history are more authentic than the Highland Games concocted by the Victorians. Although this is above all a celebration for native Borderers, you will be welcome to share the excitement of clattering hooves and banners proudly displayed. ⊕ *www.returntotheridings.co.uk.*

Rugby Sevens. The Borders invented the fast and furious, cut-down version of rugby in 1883, though it has now spread worldwide. Teams are made up of 7 players rather than 15, and the matches are shorter. Although the population of the Borders is about 100,000, the region boasts a total of 17 clubs and some of Scotland's best players. Each spring, 10 teams compete for the Kings of the Sevens title. ⊕ *www. kingsofthesevens.net.*

PLANNING YOUR TIME
The rail line that began operating in 2015 from Edinburgh's Waverley Station to Tweedbank, in the heart of the Borders, is helping to open up a fascinating region. Its 30-mile journey passes through Galashiels (for connections to Traquair House) and ends at Tweedbank, which is near Melrose and Walter Scott's home at Abbotsford. Beyond the Borders Railway, it is still more convenient to explore by car. If you're driving north along the A1 toward Edinburgh, it's easy to take a tour around the prosperous Borders towns. Turn onto the A698 at Berwick-upon-Tweed, which will take you along the Scottish–English border toward Kelso, Jedburgh, Dryburgh, and Melrose. It's 36 miles from Jedburgh

15

to Peebles, a good place to stay overnight. Another day might begin with a visit to Walter Scott's lovely Abbotsford House, and then some shopping in any of these prosperous towns.

To the west, Dumfries and Galloway beckon. If you're traveling north toward Glasgow on the M6/A74, take the A70 west toward Dumfries. From the A1, on the east coast, travel west on the A708 to Moffat and pick up the A70 there. From Glasgow take the A74 south to Beattock and pick up the A701 there. Two days would give you time to explore Burns sites and more in Dumfries. From Dumfries you can visit Sweetheart Abbey (8 miles away), Caerlaverock Castle (9 miles away), and Threave Gardens (20 miles away). Castle Douglas is a good place to stop for lunch. The A710 and A711 take you along the dramatic coastline of the Solway Firth. Farther west along the A75 are the towns of Newton Stewart and Portpatrick, and on the A714, Glen Trool. The region does not have good rail links but there is good bus service, and by car it is a charming and compact region.

GETTING HERE AND AROUND
AIR TRAVEL
The nearest Scottish airports are at Edinburgh, Glasgow, and Prestwick (outside Glasgow).

BOAT AND FERRY TRAVEL
P&O European Ferries and Stena Line operate from Larne, in Northern Ireland, to Cairnryan, near Stranraer, several times daily. The crossing takes one hour on the Superstar Express, two hours on other ferries.

Boat and Ferry Contacts P&O European Ferries. ☎ *0800/130–0030* ⊕ *www. poferries.com.* **Stena Line.** ☎ *08447/707070* ⊕ *www.stenaline.co.uk.*

BUS TRAVEL
If you're approaching from the south, check with Scottish Citylink, National Express, or First about buses from Edinburgh and Glasgow. In the Borders, Firstborders and Perryman's Buses offer service within the region. Stagecoach Western is the main bus company serving Dumfries and Galloway.

Bus Contacts First Bus. ☎ *01224/650000* ⊕ *www.firstgroup.com.* **Firstborders.** ☎ *01896/754350* ⊕ *www.firstborders.co.uk.* **National Express.** ☎ *0871/781–8181* ⊕ *www.nationalexpress.com.* **Perryman's Buses.** ☎ *01289/308719* ⊕ *www.perrymansbuses.co.uk.* **Scottish Citylink.** ☎ *0871/266–3333* ⊕ *www.citylink.co.uk.* **Stagecoach Western.** ☎ *0141/552– 4961 in Glasgow, 01387/253496 in Dumfries* ⊕ *www.stagecoachbus.com.*

CAR TRAVEL
Traveling by car is the best and easiest way to explore the area, especially if you get off the main, and often crowded, arterial roads and use the little back-roads. The main route into both the Borders and Galloway from the south is the M6, which becomes the M74 at the border. You can then take the scenic and leisurely A7 northwestward through Hawick toward Edinburgh, or the A75 and other parallel routes westward into Dumfries, Galloway, and the former ferry ports of Stranraer (nearby Cairnryan is an active ferry port) and Portpatrick.

There are several other possible routes: starting from the east, the A1 brings you from the English city of Newcastle to the border in about an hour. Moving west, the A697, which leaves the A1 north of Morpeth (in England) and crosses the border at Coldstream, is a leisurely back-road option. The A68 is probably the most scenic route to Scotland: after climbing to Carter Bar, it reveals a view of the Borders hills and windy skies before dropping into the ancient town of Jedburgh.

TRAIN TRAVEL

Apart from the main London–Edinburgh line, the Borders had no train service until 2015, when the rail link from Edinburgh to Tweedbank began service. The Borders Railway website has information about using it to explore the area. In the southwest, trains headed from London's Euston to Glasgow stop at Carlisle, just south of the border, and some also stop at Lockerbie. Trains between Glasgow and Carlisle stop at Gretna Green, Annan, and Dumfries. From Glasgow there is service on the coastal route to Stranraer.

First Bus provides connections between Hawick, Selkirk, and Galashiels and train service at Carlisle, Edinburgh, and Berwick.

Train Contacts Borders Railway. ☏ *0344/811–0141* ⊕ *bordersrailway. co.uk.* **National Rail.** ☏ *03457/484950* ⊕ *www.nationalrail.co.uk.* **ScotRail.** ☏ *0344/811–0141* ⊕ *www.scotrail.co.uk.* **Trainline.** ☏ *0871/244–1545* ⊕ *www. thetrainline.com.*

RESTAURANTS

Most good restaurants in the region used to be located in hotels, but today things are changing. Good independent eateries are popping up in small (and sometimes unlikely) towns and villages, and many new establishments specialize in fresh local ingredients. Seasonal menus are now popular. It is important to remember that restaurants here usually serve dinner until 8:30 only. *Restaurant reviews have been shortened. For full reviews, see Fodors.com.*

HOTELS

From top-quality, full-service hotels to quaint 18th-century drovers' inns to cozy bed-and-breakfasts, the Borders has all manner of lodging options. Choices in Dumfries and Galloway may be a little less expensive than in the Borders (with the same full range of services). These days many establishments are willing to lower their rates depending on availability. *Hotel reviews have been shortened. For full reviews, see Fodors.com.*

WHAT IT COSTS IN POUNDS			
$	**$$**	**$$$**	**$$$$**
Restaurants	under £15	£15–£19	£20–£25	over £25
Hotels	under £100	£100–£160	£161–£220	over £220

Restaurant prices are the average cost of a main course at dinner or, if dinner is not served, at lunch. Hotel prices are the lowest cost of a standard double room in high season, including 20% V.A.T.

VISITOR INFORMATION

Visit Scottish Borders has offices in Jedburgh, Hawick, and Peebles. The Dumfries & Galloway Tourist Board can be found in Dumfries and Stranraer. Seasonal information centers are at Castle Douglas, Eyemouth, Galashiels, Gretna Green, Kelso, Kirkcudbright, Langholm, Moffat, Sanquhar, and Selkirk. Liveborders provides online information on cultural and sporting activities in the Borders.

Contacts Dumfries & Galloway Tourist Board. ⊠ *64 Whitesands, Dumfries* ☎ *01387/253862* ⊕ *www.visitscotland.com.* **Liveborders.** ⊠ *Melrose Rd., Galashiels* ☎ *01896/661166* ⊕ *www.liveborders.org.uk.* **Visit Scottish Borders.** ⊠ *Murray's Green, Jedburgh* ☎ *01835/863170* ⊕ *www.visitscotland.com.*

THE BORDERS

Although the Borders has many attractions, it's most famous for being the home base for Sir Walter Scott (1771–1832), the early-19th-century poet, novelist, and creator of *Ivanhoe*. Scott single-handedly transformed Scotland's image from that of a land of brutal savages to one of romantic and stirring deeds and magnificent landscapes. The novels of Scott are not read much nowadays—frankly, some of them are difficult to wade through—but the mystique that he created, the aura of historical romance, has outlasted his books. The ruined abbeys, historical houses, and grand vistas of the Borders provide a perfect backdrop.

A visit to at least one of the region's four great ruined abbeys makes the quintessential Borders experience. The monks in these powerful, long-abandoned religious communities were the first to work the fleeces of their sheep flocks, thus laying the groundwork for what is still the area's main manufacturing industry.

Borders folk take great pride in the region's fame as Scotland's main woolen-goods manufacturing area. Its main towns—Jedburgh, Hawick, Selkirk, Peebles, Kelso, and Melrose—retain an air of prosperity and confidence with their solid stone houses and elegant town squares. Although many mills have closed since the 1980s, the pride in local identity is still evident in the fiercely contested Melrose Sevens rugby competition in April and the annual Common Ridings—local events commemorating the time when towns needed to patrol their borders—throughout June and July.

JEDBURGH

50 miles south of Edinburgh, 95 miles southeast of Glasgow, 14 miles northeast of Hawick.

The town of Jedburgh (*burgh* is always pronounced *burra* in Scots) was for centuries the first major Scottish target of invading English armies. In more peaceful times it developed textile mills, most of which have since languished. The large landscaped area around the town's tourist information center was once a mill but now provides an encampment for the armies of modern tourists. The past still clings to this little town, however. The ruined abbey dominates the skyline, a reminder of the formerly strong governing role of the Borders abbeys.

GETTING HERE AND AROUND

By car from Edinburgh, you can take the A68 (about 45 minutes) or the A7 (about an hour). From Glasgow take the M8, then the A68 direct to Jedburgh (about two hours).

There are fairly good bus connections from all major Scottish cities to Jedburgh. From Edinburgh, direct routes to Melrose take about two hours. From Glasgow it takes 3½ hours to reach Melrose. From Melrose it's just 20 minutes to Jedburgh.

The Borders Railway runs between Edinburgh and Tweedbank, about 15 miles northwest of Jedburgh.

ESSENTIALS

Visitor Information Jedburgh Visitor Centre. ⊠ *Abbey Pl.* ☎ *01835/863170* ⊕ *www.visitscotland.com.*

15

EXPLORING

FAMILY **Harestanes Countryside Visitor Centre.** Housed in a former farmhouse 4 miles north of Jedburgh, this visitor center portrays life in the Scottish Borders through art exhibitions and natural history displays. Crafts such as woodworking and tile making are taught here, and finished projects are often on display. Outside are meandering paths, quiet roads for bike rides, and the biggest children's play area in the Borders. There's plenty for children, including a fascinating puzzle gallery full of sturdy wooden games. It is also on one of the best-known walking routes in the Borders, the St. Cuthbert's Path. ⊠ *Junction of A68 and B6400, 4 miles north of Jedburgh* ☎ *01835/830306* ⊕ *www.liveborders.org.uk* ⊠ *Free* ⊗ *Closed Nov.–Mar.*

Fodor'sChoice **Jedburgh Abbey.** The most impressive of the Borders abbeys towers ★ above Jedburgh. Built by David I, king of Scots in the 12th century, the abbey was nearly destroyed by the English Earl of Hertford's forces in 1544–45, during the destructive time known as the Rough Wooing. This was English king Henry VIII's (1491–1547) armed attempt to persuade the Scots that it was a good idea to unite the kingdoms by the marriage of his young son to the infant Mary, Queen of Scots (1542–87); the Scots disagreed and sent Mary to France instead. The story is explained in vivid detail at the visitor center, which also has information about the ruins and an audio tour. The arched abbey walls, the nave, and the cloisters still give a sense of the power these buildings represented. ⊠ *High St.* ☎ *01835/863925* ⊕ *www.historicenvironment.scot* ⊠ *£6.*

FAMILY **Jedburgh Castle Jail and Museum.** The site of the Howard Reform Prison was named after 18th-century prison reformer John Howard, who campaigned for improved conditions. Established in 1820, the prison sits where the front of the castle originally stood. Today you can inspect prison cells, rooms with period furnishings, and costumed figures. The audio guide, which recounts the history of the jail and of Jedburgh, is useful. ⊠ *Castlegate* ☎ *01835/864750* ⊕ *www.scotborders.gov.uk/ museums* ⊠ *Free* ⊗ *Closed Nov.–Mar.*

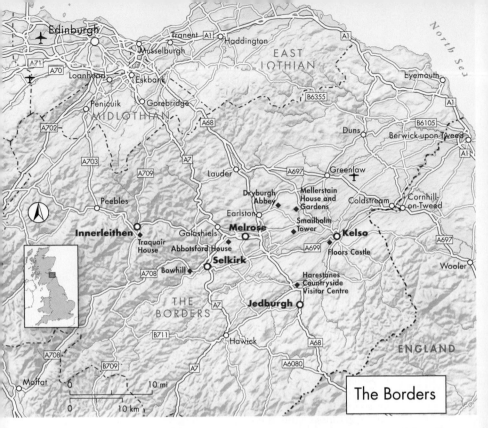

The Borders

Mary, Queen of Scots Visitor Centre. This *bastel* (from the French *bastille*) was the fortified town house in which, as the story goes, Mary stayed before embarking on her famous 20-mile ride to Hermitage Castle to visit her wounded lover, the Earl of Bothwell (circa 1535–78) in 1566. Displays relate the tale and other episodes in her life, including her doubtful choices of lovers and husbands and her own reflections on her life. Still, Mary's death mask suggests that she was serene at the end. There are tapestries and furniture of the period, and the house's ornamental garden has pear trees leading down to the river. ⊠ *Queen St.* ☎ *01835/863331* ⊕ *www.scotborders.gov.uk* 🎫 *Free* ☉ *Closed Dec.–Feb.*

WHERE TO EAT AND STAY

$$
BRITISH

✗ **Ancrum Cross Keys.** The quintessential village inn, this storybook traditional pub on the village green has a river running beyond the beer garden at the back. It serves good, hearty pub food that refreshes classics such as game pies and fish-and-chips. **Known for:** craft beer; traditional bar; village setting. $ *Average main: £15* ⊠ *The Green, Ancrum* ☎ *01835/830242* ⊕ *www.ancrumcrosskeys.com* ☉ *Closed Mon. and Tues. No lunch weekdays.*

$ **Hundalee House.** The richly decorated Victorian-style rooms of this
B&B/INN 18th-century stone manor house have nice touches such as four-poster
FAMILY beds and cozy fireplaces; 15 acres of gardens and woods surround the
B&B. **Pros:** fantastic views of apple orchards; hearty breakfasts; good
children's facilities. **Cons:** farm aromas; far from shops and restau-
rants; small rooms. $ *Rooms from: £70* ⊠ *Off A68* ✢ *1 mile south
of Jedburgh* ☎ *01835/863011* ⊕ *www.accommodation-scotland.org*
☉ *Closed Jan.–Mar.* ⤳ *5 rooms* ⍟ *Free breakfast.*

$ **Meadhon House.** On a row of medieval buildings in the heart of town,
B&B/INN Meadhon House is a charming 17th-century house with a history to
match; rooms are bright and clean, with views onto the street or over
the large and fragrant garden behind the house. **Pros:** central; pleasant rooms; welcoming atmosphere. **Cons:** rooms on the small side.
$ *Rooms from: £75* ⊠ *48 Castlegate* ☎ *01835/862504* ⊕ *www.mead-
hon.co.uk* ▤ *No credit cards* ⤳ *5 rooms* ⍟ *Free breakfast.*

SHOPPING
Edinburgh Woollen Mill. The shelves at this shop burst with sweaters,
kilts, tartan knitwear, and scarves. It's a good place to stock up on
gifts. ⊠ *Bankend North, Edinburgh Rd.* ☎ *01835/863773* ⊕ *www.ewm.
co.uk.*

KELSO

12 miles northeast of Jedburgh.

One of the most charming Borders burghs, Kelso is often described
as having a Continental flavor—some people think its broad, paved
square makes it resemble a Belgian market town. The community has
some fine examples of Georgian and Victorian Scots town architecture.

GETTING HERE AND AROUND
There are direct bus routes from Jedburgh to Kelso. Edinburgh has
direct buses to Jedburgh; buses from Glasgow aren't direct. Your best
option is to travel by car. From Jedburgh to Kelso take the A698, which
is 12 miles, or about 20 minutes. Alternatively, the A699 is a scenic
half-hour drive.

ESSENTIALS
Visitor Information Kelso Tourist Information Centre. ⊠ *Town House, The
Square* ☎ *01573/221119* ⊕ *www.kelso.bordernet.co.uk.*

EXPLORING
Fodor'sChoice **Floors Castle.** The palatial Floors Castle, the largest inhabited castle in
★ Scotland, is an architectural extravagance bristling with pepper-mill
turrets. Not so much a castle as the ancestral seat of a wealthy and
powerful landowning family, the Roxburghes, it stands on the "floors,"
or flat terrain, on the banks of the River Tweed. The enormous home
was built in 1721 by William Adam (1689–1748) and modified by
William Playfair (1789–1857), who added the turrets and towers in
the 1840s. Rooms are crowded with valuable furniture, paintings,
porcelain, and an eerie circular room full of stuffed birds; each has a
knowledgeable guide at the ready. The surrounding 56,000-acre estate
is home to more than 40 farms. ⊠ *A6089* ☎ *01573/223333* ⊕ *www.*

15

Scotland's largest inhabited castle, topped with 19th-century towers, Floors brims with family treasures.

floorscastle.com ✉ *Castle and grounds £11.50* ☉ *Closed Nov.–Mar. and weekdays in Oct.*

Kelso Abbey. The least intact ruin of the four great abbeys, Kelso Abbey is just a bleak fragment of what was once the largest of the group. It was here in 1460 that the nine-year-old James III was crowned king of Scotland. On a main invasion route, the abbey was burned three times in the 1540s alone, on the last occasion by the English Earl of Hertford's forces in 1545, when the 100 men and 12 monks of the garrison were butchered and the structure all but destroyed. ✉ *Bridge St.* ☎ *0131/668–8600* ⊕ *www.historicenvironment.scot* ✉ *Free* ☉ *Closed Thurs. and Fri. Oct.–Mar.*

Mellerstain House and Gardens. One fine example of the Borders area's ornate country homes is Mellerstain House, begun in the 1720s and finished in the 1770s by Robert Adam (1728–92); it is considered one of his finest creations. Sumptuous plasterwork covers almost all interior surfaces, and there are outstanding examples of 18th-century furnishings, porcelain and china, and paintings and embroidery. The beautiful terraced gardens (open an hour before the house itself) are as renowned as the house. ✉ *Off A6089, 7 miles northwest of Kelso, Gordon* ☎ *01573/410636* ⊕ *www.mellerstain.com* ✉ *Gardens £5, house and gardens £8.50* ☉ *Closed Oct.–Apr.*

Fodor's Choice
★ **Smailholm Tower.** Standing uncompromisingly on top of a barren, rocky ridge in the hills south of Mellerstain, this 16th-century peel tower, characteristic of the Borders, was built solely for defense, and its unadorned stones contrast with the luxury of Mellerstain House. If you let your imagination wander at this windy spot, you can almost see the rising

dust of an advancing raiding party. Sir Walter Scott found this spot inspiring, and he visited the tower often during his childhood. Anne Carrick's tableaux in the tower illustrate some of Scott's Border ballads, and the ticket includes an audio tour of the building. ✉ *Off B6404, 4½ miles south of Mellerstain House* ☎ *01573/460365* 🌐 *www.historicenvironment.scot* 🎫 *£5* ⏲ *Closed Oct.–Mar.*

WHERE TO EAT AND STAY

$$ BRITISH 🍴 **The Cobbles.** Just off the town's cobbled square, this well-established pub and restaurant with wooden tables and a bustling, cheerful atmosphere seems to be permanently busy. The extensive menu combines generously sized burgers, steaks, and meat pies with more unusual pub items such as homemade artichoke-and-truffle ravioli in a seafood sauce. **Known for:** homemade desserts; friendly atmosphere; generous portions. [$] *Average main: £16* ✉ *7 Bowmont St.* ☎ *01573/223548* 🌐 *www.thecobbleskelso.co.uk.*

$$$ HOTEL Fodor's Choice ★ 🏨 **Ednam House Hotel.** People return again and again to this stately hotel on the banks of the River Tweed, close to Kelso's grand abbey and sprawling market square. **Pros:** great outdoor activities; atmospheric lobby; impressive restaurant. **Cons:** some rooms need a makeover; popular for weddings and other events so can be crowded; rooms with a river view cost more. [$] *Rooms from: £167* ✉ *Bridge St.* ☎ *01573/224168* 🌐 *www.ednamhouse.com* ⏲ *Closed late Dec.–early Jan.* 🛏 *32 rooms* 🍽 *Free breakfast.*

15

MELROSE

15 miles west of Kelso, 4 miles southeast of Galashiels.

Though it's small, there is nevertheless a bustle about Melrose, the perfect example of a prosperous Scottish market town and one of the loveliest in the Borders. It's set around a square lined with 18th- and 19th-century buildings housing myriad small shops and cafés. Despite its proximity to the much larger Galashiels, Melrose has rejected industrialization. You'll likely hear local residents greet each other by first name in the square.

GETTING HERE AND AROUND

Buses do go to Melrose, and the new Borders Railway ends at Tweedbank, just 2 miles to the northwest. Driving remains the easiest way to get here from the south or east. From Galashiels, take the A6091 (10 minutes).

EXPLORING

Fodor's Choice ★ **Abbotsford House.** In this great house overlooking the Tweed, Sir Walter Scott lived, worked, and received the great and the good in luxurious salons. In 1811, the writer bought a farm on this site named Cartleyhole, which was a euphemism for the real name, Clartyhole (*clarty* is Scots for "muddy" or "dirty"). The romantic Scott renamed the property after a ford in the nearby Tweed used by the abbot of Melrose. Scott eventually had the house entirely rebuilt in the Scottish baronial style. It was an expensive project, and Scott wrote feverishly to keep his creditors at bay. John Ruskin, the art critic, disapproved, calling it an "incongruous pile," but most contemporary visitors find it fascinating, particularly because of its expansive views and delightful gardens.

A free audio tour guides you around the salon, the circular study, and the library with its 9,000 leather-bound volumes. Perhaps more than anyone else, Scott redefined Scotland as a place of mystery and romance, and awoke the English, who read him avidly, to its natural beauty and its past—or at least a heavily dramatized version of it. The visitor center houses displays about Scott's life, a gift shop, and a restaurant serving lunch. To get here, take the A6091 from Melrose and follow the signs for Abbotsford. ■TIP→ You can also stay on the estate, in the Hope Scott Wing (£120). ⊠ *B6360* ✢ *Between Melrose and Tweedbank* ☎ *01896/752043* ⊕ *www.scottsabbotsford.co.uk* ⊠ *House and gardens £9.60; gardens only £5. Last admission 1 hr before closing* ⊙ *House closed Dec.–Feb.*

Dryburgh Abbey. The final resting place of Sir Walter Scott and his wife, and the most peaceful and secluded of the Borders abbeys, the "gentle ruins" of Dryburgh Abbey sit on parkland in a loop of the Tweed. The abbey, founded in 1150, suffered from English raids until, like Melrose, it was abandoned in 1544. The style is transitional, a mingling of rounded Romanesque and pointed early English. The north transept, where the Haig and Scott families lie buried, is lofty and pillared, and once formed part of the abbey church. ⊠ *St. Boswell's, B6404* ☎ *01835/822381* ⊕ *www.historicenvironment.scot* ⊠ *£6.*

FodorsChoice **Melrose Abbey.** Just off Melrose's town square sit the ruins of Melrose
★ Abbey, one of the four Borders abbeys: "If thou would'st view fair Melrose aright, go visit it in the pale moonlight," wrote Scott in *The Lay of the Last Minstrel.* So many of his fans took the advice literally that a custodian begged him to rewrite the lines. Today the abbey is still impressive: a red-sandstone shell with slender windows, delicate tracery, and carved capitals, all carefully maintained. Among the carvings high on the roof is one of a bagpipe-playing pig. An audio tour is included in the admission price. The heart of 14th-century national hero Robert the Bruce is rumored to be buried here. ⊠ *Abbey St.* ☎ *01896/822562* ⊕ *www.historicenvironment.scot* ⊠ *£6.*

Priorwood Garden and Harmony Garden. The National Trust for Scotland's Priorwood Garden, next to Melrose Abbey, specializes in flowers for drying, and dried flowers are on sale in the shop. Next to the gardens is an orchard with some old apple varieties. The walled Harmony Garden, belonging to the lovely Georgian house at its heart, sits nearby opposite the abbey. ⊠ *Abbey St.* ☎ *01896/822493* ⊕ *www.nts.org.uk* ⊠ *Free* ⊙ *Closed Nov.–Mar.*

WHERE TO EAT AND STAY

$$ ✕ **Hergés on the Loch.** At this light and airy place, a wall of windows
ECLECTIC allows you to contemplate swans and ducks as they float serenely across Gunknowe Loch, and, if the weather allows, you can dine on the terrace. The elegant but understated food, well presented and served in generous portions, includes familiar dishes like steak-and-ale pie and oat-and-mustard-crusted loin of venison cooked pink and melt-in-your-mouth tender. **Known for:** restful setting with loch view; reasonable

Of the ruined abbeys in the Borders, Melrose is notable for its red-sandstone architecture and carvings.

prices; familiar food well cooked. *Average main: £15* *Tweedbank Dr., Tweedbank* *01896/759909* *www.hergesontheloch.com.*

$$ HOTEL **Burts Hotel.** Dating from the 18th century, this charming white-washed building in the center of Melrose has individually decorated and different rooms filled with floral pastels. **Pros:** walking distance to restaurants and pubs; good menu in restaurant. **Cons:** some tiny rooms; slightly overpriced for some rooms. *Rooms from: £145* *Market Sq.* *01896/822285* *www.burtshotel.co.uk* *20 rooms* *Free breakfast.*

$$ HOTEL **Dryburgh Abbey Hotel.** Mature woodlands and verdant lawns surround this imposing, 19th-century mansion-turned-hotel, which is adjacent to the ruins of Dryburgh Abbey on a sweeping bend of the River Tweed. **Pros:** beautiful grounds; romantic setting. **Cons:** some rooms need to be freshened up; service can be on the slow side. *Rooms from: £135* *Off B6404, St. Boswells* *01835/822261* *www.dryburgh.co.uk* *38 rooms* *Free breakfast.*

SHOPPING

Abbey Mill. Take a break from sightseeing at Abbey Mill, where you'll find handwoven knitwear as well as homemade jams and fudge. The wee tearoom is also popular. *Annay Rd.* *01896/822138.*

SELKIRK

6 miles south of Galashiels, 11 miles north of Hawick.

Selkirk is a hilly outpost with a smattering of antiques shops and an assortment of bakers selling Selkirk bannock (fruited sweet bread) and other cakes. It is the site of one of Scotland's iconic battles, Flodden Field, commemorated here with a statue in the town. Sir Walter Scott was sheriff (judge) of Selkirkshire from 1800 until his death in 1832, and his statue stands in Market Place. Selkirk is also near Bowhill, a stately home.

The town claims its Common Riding (⊕ *returntotheridings.co.uk*) is the largest mounted gathering anywhere in Europe. More than 400 riders take part in the event in June. It's also the oldest Borders festival, with roots back to the Battle of Flodden in 1513.

GETTING HERE AND AROUND

If you're driving, take the A7 south to Galashiels. The scenic journey is less than 7 miles and takes around 10 minutes. First Edinburgh Bus offers a regular service between Galashiels and Selkirk.

ESSENTIALS

Visitor Information Selkirk Visitor Information Centre. ⊠ *Halliwell's House, Market Pl.* ☎ *01750/20054* ⊕ *www.visitscotland.com.*

EXPLORING

Bowhill. Home of the Duke of Buccleuch, Bowhill dates from the 19th century and houses an outstanding collection of works by Gainsborough, Van Dyck, Canaletto, Reynolds, and Raeburn, as well as porcelain and period furniture. Access is by guided tour on specific days in summer. There is an excellent adventure playground for the kids and a 57-mile country ride for those who prefer horseback riding. A local stable hires out horses. ⊠ *Off A708, 3 miles west of Selkirk* ☎ *01750/22204* ⊕ *www.bowhillhouse.co.uk* ⊠ *Grounds £4.50, house and grounds £10* ☉ *Closed Oct.–Mar. and selected days rest of the year; check website.*

Lochcarron Visitor Centre. You can take an informative guided tour of this world-renowned mill and also purchase some of the best woolen goods on offer, from knitwear to tartans and tweeds. The shop also sells Scottish jewelry. ⊠ *Dinsdale Rd.* ☎ *01750/726100* ⊕ *www.lochcarron. com* ⊠ *£9.50 for tour* ☉ *Closed Sun.*

Sir Walter Scott's Courtroom. The historic courtroom where Sir Walter Scott presided as sheriff from 1804 to 1832 contains a display examining his life, writings, and time on the bench. It uses models to re-create the atmosphere of a 19th-century Scottish court and includes an audiovisual presentation. A statue of the famous writer overlooks the comings and goings outside the court. ⊠ *Market Sq.* ☎ *01750/720761* ⊕ *www. scotborders.gov.uk* ⊠ *Free* ☉ *Closed Nov.–Feb.*

WHERE TO EAT AND STAY

$

ITALIAN

✕ **Buon Gusto Ristorante.** A small, busy, and very popular restaurant in central Selkirk, Buon Gusto claims to be genuinely Italian, and its well-made pastas and pizzas attest to this. The predominantly pasta menu includes imaginative variations on the usual fare: pasta with scallops, for example. **Known for:** all-you-can-eat option; superior pizzas; good dessert menu. $ *Average main: £10* ✉ *73 High St.* ☎ *01750/778174* ⊕ *www.buongustoristorante.co.uk* ⊘ *Closed Mon. and Tues. No lunch.*

$$
HOTEL

Best Western Philipburn House Hotel. West of Selkirk, this alpine-style hotel enjoys a lovely setting among the woods and hills. **Pros:** pleasant rural setting; bright rooms; on-site parking. **Cons:** no elevator; restaurant closes rather early; breakfast is extra. $ *Rooms from: £140* ✉ *Linglie Rd.* ✛ *Opposite Salmon Viewing Centre* ☎ *01750/720747* ⊕ *www.bw-philipburnhousehotel.co.uk* ⇥ *24 rooms* ⦿ *No meals.*

INNERLEITHEN

17 miles northwest of Hawick.

Innerleithen is one of the larger Borders towns; you'll feel that you've entered a hub of activity when you arrive. It's also dramatically beautiful. Surrounded by hills and glens, the town is where the Tweed and Leithen rivers join, then separate. Historically, Innerleithen dates back to pre-Roman times, and there are artifacts all around for you to see. Once a booming industrial town of wool mills, today it's a great destination for outdoor activities including hiking, biking, and fly-fishing.

GETTING HERE AND AROUND

To drive to Innerleithen, take the A7 north from Hawick and then the A707 northwest from Selkirk. There are no trains between the two towns.

EXPLORING

FAMILY **Robert Smail's Printing Works.** Try your hand at printing the way it used to be done: painstakingly setting each letter by hand. Robert Smail's print shop, founded in 1866 to produce materials for nearby factories, boat tickets, theater posters, and the local newspaper, is still a working print shop as well as a museum. Two great waterwheels once powered the presses, and they are still running. The guided tour, which includes making your own bookmark, takes 90 minutes. ✉ *7–9 High St.* ☎ *01896/830206* ⊕ *www.nts.org.uk* ✉ *£6.50* ⊘ *Closed Jan.–Mar.; Apr.–Oct., Tues.–Thurs.; Nov. and Dec., Tues., Wed., and Sun.*

Fodor'sChoice **Traquair House.** Said to be the oldest continually occupied home in Scotland (since 1107), Traquair House has secret stairways and passages, a library with more than 3,000 books, and a bed said to be used by Mary, Queen of Scots, in 1566. You can walk freely through the rooms, and there is an explanatory leaflet in each as well as helpful guides. The top floor of the house is an interesting small museum. Outside is a reasonably scary maze, an adventure playground, and some lovely woodland walks as well as pigs, goats, and chickens. The 18th-century brew house still makes highly recommended ale, and there's a café on the grounds near the beautiful walled garden. The Traquair Fair in August is the nearest you are likely to get to a medieval fair, and well worth the visit. You may even spend the night, if you wish. ✉ *B709* ✛ *From the A70 some 6 miles south of Peebles, take the B709 for 7 miles; the car entrance into the house is in the village* ☎ *01896/830323* ⊕ *www.traquair.co.uk* ✉ *Grounds £4.50, house and grounds £8.80* ⊘ *Closed Dec.–Mar. and weekdays in Nov.*

15

WHERE TO STAY

$$$
B&B/INN
⟨T⟩ **Traquair House.** Staying in one of the guest rooms in the 12th-century wing of Traquair House is to experience a slice of Scottish history. **Pros:** stunning grounds; spacious rooms; great breakfast. **Cons:** nearly 2 miles to restaurants and shops; rooms fill up quickly in summer. ⟨$⟩ *Rooms from: £190* ⊠ *B709* ☎ *01896/830323* ⊕ *www.traquair.co.uk* ➽ *3 rooms* ⎮◯⎮ *Free breakfast.*

$$$
HOTEL
⟨T⟩ **Windlestraw Lodge.** This elegant bed-and-breakfast occupies a grand country home surrounded by extensive gardens. **Pros:** beautifully designed rooms; excellent restaurant. **Cons:** a bit expensive for what you get; not all rooms have Tweed views. ⟨$⟩ *Rooms from: £175* ⊠ *9 Galashiels Rd., Walkerburn* ✛ *On the A72 between Galashiels and Innerleithen* ☎ *01896/870636* ⊕ *www.windlestraw.co.uk* ➽ *6 rooms* ⎮◯⎮ *Free breakfast.*

DUMFRIES AND GALLOWAY

Galloway covers the southwestern portion of Scotland, west of the main town of Dumfries; it's a quiet and less-visited region of Scotland, in general. Here a gentle coastline gives way to farmland and then breezy uplands that gradually merge with coniferous forests. The region now claims two extraordinary public art projects—Charles Jencks's *Crawick Multiverse* and Andy Goldsworthy's *Striding Arches*.

DUMFRIES

24 miles west of Gretna Green, 76 miles south of Glasgow, 81 miles southwest of Edinburgh.

The River Nith meanders through Dumfries, and the pedestrian-only center of this town of 31,000 makes wandering and shopping a pleasure. Author J. M. Barrie (1860–1937) spent his childhood in Dumfries, and the garden of Moat Brae House is said to have inspired his boyish dreams in *Peter Pan*. But the town also has a justified claim to Robert Burns, who lived and worked here for several years. His house and his favorite *howff* (pub), the Globe Inn, are here, too, as is his final resting place in St. Michael's Churchyard.

The Dumfries & Galloway Tourist Board has a lodging service, and also sells golf passes for the region at £70 for three rounds.

GETTING HERE AND AROUND

Public transportation is a good option for reaching Dumfries—there's a good train station here, and most major Scottish cities have regular daily bus routes to the town. If you're driving from Gretna Green, take the A75; it's a 35-minute drive. From Glasgow, take the M74 to the A701. From Edinburgh, take the A701.

ESSENTIALS

Visitor Information Dumfries & Galloway Tourist Board. ⊠ *64 Whitesands* ☎ *01387/253862* ⊕ *www.visitscotland.com.*

Dumfries and Galloway

EXPLORING

Dumfries Museum and Camera Obscura. A camera obscura is essentially a huge reflecting mirror that projects an extraordinarily clear panoramic view of the surrounding countryside onto an internal wall. The one at the Dumfries Museum is housed in the old Windmill Tower, built in 1836. The museum itself covers the culture and daily life of the people living in the Dumfries and Galloway region from the earliest times. ✉ *Rotchell Rd.* ☎ *01387/253374* 🌐 *www.dumgal.gov.uk/artsandmuseums* 🎫 *Museum free; Camera Obscura £2.30* ⏲ *Closed Nov.–Mar.*

Globe Inn. Poet Robert Burns spent quite a lot of time at the Globe Inn, where he frequently fell asleep in the tack room beside the stables; today it's still an active pub where you can eat and drink. Burns later graduated to the upstairs bedroom where he slept with his wife, Jean Armour, and scratched some lines of poetry on the window. The room is preserved (or at least partly re-created), and the bar staff will happily show you around if you ask. ✉ *56 High St.* ☎ *01387/252335* 🌐 *www.globeinndumfries.co.uk* 🎫 *Free.*

Gracefield Arts Centre. With galleries hosting changing exhibits of Scottish art mostly from the 1840s to today, Gracefield Arts Centre also has a well-stocked crafts shop. A café serves lunch and snacks. ✉ *28 Edinburgh Rd.* ☎ *01387/262084* 🌐 *www.exploreart.co.uk* 🎫 *Free.*

Robert Burns Centre. Not surprisingly, Dumfries has its own Robert Burns Centre, housed in a sturdy 18th-century former mill overlooking the River Nith. The center has an audiovisual program and an extensive exhibit about the life of the poet. There's a restaurant upstairs. ✉ *Mill Rd.* ☎ *01387/264808* 🌐 *www.dumgal.gov.uk/artsandmuseums* 🎫 *Free.*

Robert Burns House. Poet Robert Burns (1759–96) lived here, on what was then called Mill Street, for the last three years of his life, when his salary from the customs service allowed him to improve his living standards. Many distinguished writers of the day visited him here, including William Wordsworth. The house contains some of his writings and letters, a few pieces of furniture, and some family memorabilia. ✉ *Burns St.* ☎ *01387/255297* 🌐 *www.dumgal.gov.uk/artsandmuseums* 🎫 *Free.*

St. Michael's Churchyard. When he died in 1796, poet Robert Burns was buried in a modest grave in St. Michael's Churchyard. English poet William Wordsworth, visiting a few years later, was horrified by the small gravestone and raised money to build this much grander monument. ✉ *39 Cardiness St.* ☎ *01387/253849* 🌐 *www.dumgal.gov.uk/artsandmuseums* 🎫 *Free.*

WHERE TO EAT

$ BRITISH

🍴 **Cavens Arms.** This lively, welcoming traditional pub in the center of town has a separate bar and dining area, comfortable seating, and a large selection of beers. It's a magnet for locals at dinnertime and always seems to be busy, a testimony to the quality of its food as well as the large portions. **Known for:** local beers; good food in generous pub portions; vibrant atmosphere. [$] *Average main: £13* ✉ *20 Buccleuch St.* ☎ *01387/252896.*

$$ ✕**Hullabaloo.** Occupying the top floor of the Robert Burns Centre, itself
ECLECTIC an old mill, this restaurant serves a substantial, varied lunch and din-
ner menu. The melts are the highlight of the imaginative, tasty lunch
menu, and the dinner menu is equally ambitious, ranging from roe deer
loin with tomato pesto to king prawns flambéed in vodka. **Known for:**
melts for lunch; creative vegan menu; prawns in vodka. $ *Average
main: £16* ✉ *Robert Burns Centre, Mill Rd.* ☎ *01387/259679* ⊕ *www.
hullabaloorestaurant.co.uk* ⊘ *Closed Sun. No dinner Mon.*

WHERE TO STAY

$$ 🏨 **Cairndale Hotel.** Centrally located, the Cairndale has a Victorian
HOTEL Gothic appearance and spacious and comfortable rooms. **Pros:** cen-
tral location; comfortable rooms; pool, sauna, and gym. **Cons:** a generally old-fashioned feel. $ *Rooms from: £143* ✉ *132–6 English St.*
☎ *01387/354111* ⊕ *www.cairndalehotel.co.uk* 🛏 *91 rooms* ⦿ *Free
breakfast.*

SHOPPING

Fodor'sChoice **Loch Arthur Creamery and Farm Shop.** Known for its high-quality dairy
★ products, this lively and active farm run by the Camphill community
in the charmingly named village of Beeswing has an expansive café and
retail store selling a range of organic products. Much of what you eat or
buy is produced on the farm, where they make their own bread, butcher
their meat, and cook the delicious food served here. The building itself
has large windows opening directly on to the fields beyond. ✉ *A711,
6 miles south of Dumfries on the A711, Beeswing* ☎ *01387/259669*
⊕ *www.locharthur.org.uk.*

NORTH OF DUMFRIES

18 miles northwest of Dumfries.

Travel north along the A70 from Dumfries for a short trip through
time at some very different attractions. Drumlanrig Castle is one of
Scotland's grandest houses, set amid hills, moorland, and forest. In
contrast, the world of lead miners, explored at the Museum of Lead
Mining, was a great deal harsher. A spectacular modern addition to the
area, the land artwork *Crawick Multiverse*, transforms the landscape
into a mirror of the heavens.

GETTING HERE AND AROUND

Trains run from Dumfries to Sanquhar, near *Crawick Multiverse*. You
can get a bus from Dumfries to Drumlanrig and Sanquhar along the
A701. For Ledhills and the mining museum, it's best to drive. The same
is true for *Striding Arches:* Take the A76 from Dumfried to Thornhill,
and then the A702 toward Monaive.

EXPLORING

Fodor'sChoice **Crawick Multiverse.** The extraordinary 2015 land artwork by Charles
★ Jencks, 45 minutes north of Dumfries near the village of Sanquhar,
must surely become a focus for visitors to the region for years to
come. Jencks has transformed a 55-acre site, once an open-pit mine,
into a beautiful and inspiring created landscape, at the heart of which
are two grass spiral mounds that represent the Milky Way and the

15

Andromeda Constellation. But they are simply the heart of a site where woodland, moor, mountain, and desert meet. Local rocks have been lifted to form avenues and labyrinths across the site. As you look across from its highest point, it is as if you were looking in a mirror in which the skies were reflected on the earth. Set aside two or three hours at least for the experience. ⊠ *Crawick, off B740, by Sanquhar* ✢ *Take the A75 toward Kirkconnel from Sanquhar, then turn on to the B740 (signposted Crawfordjohn)* ☎ *01659/50242* ⊕ *www.crawick-multiverse.co.uk* ☒ *£5* ⟳ *Nov.–Feb., pedestrian access only; road to site and parking lot are closed.*

FAMILY

Fodor's Choice

★

Drumlanrig Castle. A spectacular estate, Drumlanrig Castle is as close as Scotland gets to the treasure houses of England—which is not surprising, since it's owned by the dukes of Buccleuch, one of the wealthiest British peerages. Resplendent with romantic turrets, this pink-sandstone palace was constructed between 1679 and 1691 by the first Duke of Queensbury, who, after nearly bankrupting himself building the place, stayed one night and never returned. The Buccleuchs inherited the palace and filled the richly decorated rooms with paintings by Holbein, Rembrandt, and Murillo, among others. Because of the theft of a Leonardo da Vinci painting in 2003, all visits are conducted by guided tour. There's also a playground, a gift shop, and a tearoom. The grounds are varied and good for mountain biking; bikes can be rented at the castle. ⊠ *Off A76, Thornhill* ✢ *18 miles northwest of Dumfries* ☎ *01848/600283* ⊕ *www.drumlanrig.com* ☒ *Park £6, castle and park £10* ☉ *Castle closed Sept.–mid-Apr. Grounds closed Oct.–Mar.*

Museum of Lead Mining. The Lochnell Mine was abandoned in 1861, after 150 years of operation, and the mine and miners' homes now form part of this museum re-creating their lives. The isolated village of Warnlockhead, where the mine was located, has not changed a great deal since then—there was little alternative employment for the miners and their families. The visitor center, housed in the old smithy, exhibits some of the minerals the mine yielded. The nearby Leadhills and Warnlockhead Narrow Gauge Railway runs on weekends throughout the summer and costs £4, with a 10% reduction for a joint ticket with the museum. ⊠ *Off B797, Wanlockhead* ✢ *32 miles north of Dumfries* ☎ *01659/74387* ⊕ *www.leadminingmuseum.co.uk* ☒ *£9.50* ☉ *Closed Oct.–Mar.*

CASTLE DOUGLAS

18 miles southwest of Dumfries, 25 miles west of Caerlaverock Castle, 84 miles south of Glasgow, 90 miles southwest of Edinburgh.

A quaint town that sits beside Carlingwark Loch, Castle Douglas is a popular base for exploring the surrounding countryside. The loch sets off the town perfectly, reflecting its dramatic architecture of sharp spires and soft sandstone arches. Its main thoroughfare, King Street, has unique shops and eateries.

GETTING HERE AND AROUND

There's no train station in Castle Douglas, and buses from Dumfries make several stops along the way. The best way to get here is by car. From Dalbeattie, take the A711/A745 (10 minutes). From Glasgow, take the A713 (just under two hours). From Edinburgh, take the A70 (a little over two hours).

ESSENTIALS

Visitor Information Castle Douglas. ✉ *Market Hill* ☎ *01556/502611* 🌐 *www.visitscotland.com.*

EXPLORING

Fodor's Choice ★ **Threave Castle.** At this early home of the Black Douglases, who were the earls of Nithsdale and lords of Galloway, the imposing towers reflect well the Lord of Galloway who built it, Archibald the Grim, in the 14th century. Not to be confused with the mansion in Threave Gardens, the castle was dismantled in the religious wars of the mid-17th century, though enough of it remained to have housed prisoners from the Napoleonic Wars two centuries later. It's a few minutes from Castle Douglas by car and is signposted from the main road. To get here, leave your car in a farmyard and make your way down to the edge of the river. Ring the bell (loudly) and, rather romantically, a boatman will come to ferry you across to the great stone tower looming from a marshy island in the river. ✉ *A75, 3 miles west of Castle Douglas* ☎ *07711/223101* 🌐 *www.historicenvironment.scot* 🎫 *£5 including ferry; buy tickets online or from the NTS Osprey Centre on the site* ⏲ *Closed Nov.–Mar.*

Threave Garden and Estate. The National Trust for Scotland cares for the gently sloping parkland and gardens around an 1867 mansion built by William Gordon, a Liverpool businessman. The house, fully restored in the 1930s, gives a glimpse into the daily life of a prosperous 19th-century family. The grounds demand an army of gardeners, and today many of them are students at the National Trust's School of Heritage Gardening, which has developed the variety of gardens here. Bats, ospreys, and other birds and animals share the space. Entry to the house is by timed guided tour, and it's wise to book ahead. There's an on-site restaurant. ✉ *South of A75* ✥ *1 mile west of Castle Douglas* ☎ *01556/502575* 🌐 *www.nts.org.uk/Visits* 🎫 *Gardens £7.50, house and gardens £12.50* ⏲ *House closed Nov.–Mar.*

WHERE TO EAT

$ CAFÉ 🍴 **The Café at Designs Gallery.** For a good balance of art and food, look no further than this café at a contemporary art and crafts gallery in the town center. You'll find the freshest ingredients here, from soup to salads, sandwiches to quiches; everything is made on-site, including the bread, and it's all organic. **Known for:** good lunch menu; homemade soups; lovely garden. [$] *Average main: £9* ✉ *179 King St.* ☎ *01556/504552* 🌐 *www.designsgallery.co.uk* ⏲ *Closed Sun. No dinner.*

SHOPPING

By the Book. This well-stocked and (more importantly) well-organized secondhand bookshop on Castle Douglas's main shopping street has large windows that invite you in to browse, which you can do without interruption—there's bound to be something you want, though it may be in a box or under the table. ⊠ *201 King St.* ☎ *01556/503338.*

Galloway Gems and Craft Centre and Outback Yarns. In this glittery shop you can purchase mineral specimens, polished stone slices, and a range of Celtic- and Nordic-inspired jewelry, as well as craft materials of every kind. For fiber artists and sewers, it's a real find. ⊠ *130–132 King St.* ☎ *01556/503254* ⊕ *www.outbackyarns.co.uk.*

KIRKCUDBRIGHT

9 miles southwest of Castle Douglas, 89 miles south of Glasgow, 99 miles southwest of Edinburgh.

Kirkcudbright (pronounced kir -coo-bray) is an 18th-century town of Georgian and Victorian houses, some of them washed in pastel shades and roofed with the blue slate of the district. It sits on an inlet from the Solway Firth. In the early 20th century the town became a haven for artists, and its L-shape main street is full of crafts and antiques shops.

GETTING HERE AND AROUND
Driving is your best and only real option. From Castle Douglas, take the A711 (15 minutes). From Glasgow, take the A713 (about two hours). From Edinburgh, take the A701 (about 2½ hours).

ESSENTIALS
Visitor Information Kirkcudbright Tourist Information Centre. ⊠ *Harbour Sq.* ☎ *01557/330494* ⊕ *www.visitscotland.com.*

EXPLORING
Fodor'sChoice
★
Broughton House. The 18th-century Broughton House was the home of the artist E. A. Hornel from 1901 until his death in 1933 and remains largely as it was in his time. Hornel was a member of the late-19th-century school of painters called the "Glasgow Boys," who were influenced by the Vienna Secession and art nouveau. You can see many of his paintings in the gallery Hornel built onto the house to impress the guests and buyers who came to see his work. His use and love of color is obvious in the beautiful garden, which combines lawns, ponds, and formal and wildflower beds. The knowledgeable guides will gladly provide information about the life and work of the painter. ⊠ *12 High St.* ☎ *01557/330437* ⊕ *www.nts.org.uk* ⊠ *£6.50* ☉ *House closed Nov.–Mar. Garden closed Nov.–Jan.*

MacLellan's Castle. Conspicuous in the center of town are the stone walls of MacLellan's Castle, a once-elaborate castellated mansion dating from the 16th century. You can walk around the interior, still atmospheric even though the rooms are bare. The "Lairds Lug," behind the fireplace, allowed the *laird* (lord) to listen in to what his guests were saying about him. You can also get a glimpse of life below stairs in the kitchen vaults beneath the main staircase. The mansion has lovely views over the town. ⊠ *Off High St.* ☎ *01557/331856* ⊕ *www.historicenvironment. scot* ⊠ *£4* ☉ *Closed Oct.–Mar.*

Tolbooth Arts Centre. In the 17th-century tolbooth (a combination town hall–courthouse–prison), the Tolbooth Arts Centre describes how the town attracted famous artists, among them E. A. Hornel, Jessie King, and Charles Oppenheimer. Some of their paintings are on display, as are works by contemporary artists. ⊠ *High St.* ☎ *01557/331556* ⊕ *www. dumgal.gov.uk* ✉ *Free* ⊙ *Closed Sun. Oct.–May.*

WHERE TO EAT AND STAY

$$ ✕ **Artistas at the Selkirk Arms.** Paintings of Scotland, starched white table-
MODERN BRITISH cloths, and giant windows overlooking the well-kept garden beckon you into this highly praised eatery. Locals love that the food on the bar and regular menus is locally sourced and full of imagination. **Known for:** local produce; both familiar and more exotic dishes; charming location in town. $ *Average main: £16* ⊠ *Selkirk Arms, High St.* ☎ *01557/330402* ⊕ *www.selkirkarmshotel.co.uk.*

$$ ⌃ **Selkirk Arms.** Bursting with charm, this elegant 18th-century hotel has
HOTEL a lot going for it, including spacious guest rooms that are individually decorated with cozy beds, contemporary wood furniture, and soft lighting. **Pros:** attentive service; massive breakfast; lively traditional pub. **Cons:** rooms closest to restaurant can be noisy; bar gets crowded during sporting events. $ *Rooms from: £112* ⊠ *High St.* ☎ *01557/330402* ⊕ *www.selkirkarmshotel.co.uk* ⇗ *16 rooms* ⦿ *Free breakfast.*

15

WHITHORN

17 miles south of Newton Stewart, 94 miles southwest of Glasgow, 121 miles southwest of Edinburgh.

Known for its early-Christian settlement, Whithorn is full of history. The main street is notably wide, with pretty pastel buildings nestled up against each other, their low doorways and small windows creating images of years long past. It's still mainly a farming community, but is fast becoming a popular tourist destination. Several scenes from the original *Wicker Man* (1973) were shot in and around the area. During the summer months, it's a popular place for festivals. The Isle of Whithorn, just beyond the town, is not an island at all but a fishing village of great charm.

GETTING HERE AND AROUND

There's no train station in Whithorn, and most of the buses are local (getting to main Scottish cities from Whithorn takes careful planning and several transfers). To drive from Newton Stewart, take the A714 and then A746. From Glasgow, take the A77 (about 2½ hours). From Edinburgh, take the A702 (about three hours).

EXPLORING

Whithorn Priory and Museum. The road that is now the A746 was a pilgrims' path that led to the royal burgh of Whithorn, where sat Whithorn Priory, one of Scotland's great medieval cathedrals, now an empty shell. It was built in the 12th century and is said to occupy the site of a former stone church, the Candida Casa, built by St. Ninian in the 4th century. As the story goes, the church housed a shrine to Ninian, the earliest of Scotland's saints, and kings and barons tried to visit the shrine at least once in their lives. As you approach the priory, observe the royal arms of pre-1707 Scotland—that is, Scotland before the Union with England— carved and painted above the *pend* (covered walkway). The museum houses restored stonework from the period, including crosses. ✉ *Off A746* 🌐 *www.historicenvironment.scot* 🎟 *£5 (includes the Whithorn Story and Visitor Centre)* ⏲ *Closed Nov.–Mar.*

WHERE TO EAT

$ BRITISH 🍴 **Steam Packet Inn.** Lovely and old-fashioned, this inn is always full, mainly because of its good beer and hearty, well-cooked food including fish-and-chips and lamb shanks. Located directly on the harbor, it has few local rivals, but customers come from far and wide to eat here and walk the headland behind the pub to the rocky shore of the Solway Firth. **Known for:** superior pub food; outstanding desserts; fast and friendly service. [$] *Average main: £14* ✉ *Harbour Row, Isle of Whithorn* ☎ *01988/500334* 🌐 *www.thesteampacketinn.biz.*

STRANRAER

31 miles northwest of Whithorn, 86 miles southwest of Glasgow via A77, 131 miles southwest of Edinburgh.

Stranraer was for more than a century the main ferry port between Scotland and Northern Ireland. Its closure, and the transfer of ferry traffic to nearby Cairnryan, is changing the town now and in the future. The city center has had a major face-lift, and there are plans to redevelop the harbor as a leisure centre and transportation hub. Stranraer has a lovely garden.

GETTING HERE AND AROUND

Stranraer's train station is directly accessible from Glasgow; bus services are also good (with many connections to smaller towns). If you're driving, take the A747 from Whithorn (about 45 minutes). From Glasgow, take the M77/A77 (two hours), and from Edinburgh, take the A77 (three hours).

ESSENTIALS

Visitor Information **Stranraer Visitor Information Centre.** ✉ *28 Harbour St.* ☎ *01776/702595* 🌐 *www.visitscotland.com.*

EXPLORING

Fodor's Choice ★ **Castle Kennedy Gardens.** The lovely Castle Kennedy Gardens surround the shell of the original Castle Kennedy, which burned down in 1716. Parks scattered around the property were built by the second Earl of Stair in 1733. The earl was a field marshal and used his soldiers to help with the heavy work of constructing banks, ponds, and other major landscape features. When the rhododendrons are in bloom (April through July, depending on the variety), the effect is kaleidoscopic. There's also a pleasant tearoom. ✉ *Castle Kennedy* ✣ *3 miles east of Stranraer on the A875* ☎ *01776/702024* 🌐 *www.castlekennedygardens.co.uk* 🎟 *£5.50* ⏲ *Closed Nov.–Jan. and weekdays in Feb. and Mar.*

THE CENTRAL HIGHLANDS, FIFE, AND ANGUS

WELCOME TO THE CENTRAL HIGHLANDS, FIFE, AND ANGUS

TOP REASONS TO GO

★ **Loch Lomond:** You can see the sparkling waters of Scotland's largest loch by car, by boat, or on foot. A popular option is the network of bicycle tracks that creep around Loch Lomond and the Trossachs National Park, offering every conceivable terrain.

★ **Castles:** Among the highlights are Stirling Castle, with its palace built by James V, and Scone Palace, near Perth, with its grand aristocratic acquisitions.

★ **Golf:** If you can't get on the Old Course in St. Andrews by ballot or by any other means, Fife and Angus have fabulous fairways aplenty, including the famous links course at Carnoustie.

★ **Hikes:** The way to experience the Central Highlands is to head out on foot. The fit and well equipped can "bag a Munro" (climb hills over 3,000 feet, named after the mountaineer who listed them). The less demanding woodland paths and gentle rambles of the Trossachs will stir even the least adventurous rambler.

The reference points for your trip are Stirling, an ancient historic town from whose castle you can see central Scotland laid out before you; Perth, 36 miles away, the gateway to the Highlands; the city of Dundee, on the river Tay; and the historic center and home of golf, St. Andrews, in Fife. North from Stirling, you cross the fertile open plain (the Carse of Stirling) dotted with historic cathedral towns. The Trossachs are the Scotland of the Romantic imagination, lochs and woodland glens, drovers' inns and grand country houses. The small towns of the region are bases from which to explore this varied countryside. To the west lies Loch Lomond, along whose banks the road leads from industrial Glasgow to the hills and glens of the Highlands.

1 Stirling. Famous for its castle and vibrant with history, Stirling has a small Old Town on the hill that is worth covering on foot. The town is a good center from which to explore the changing landscape of central Scotland

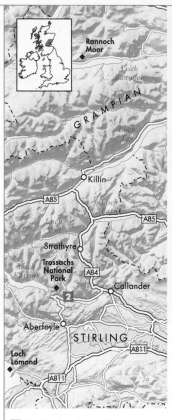

2 The Trossachs and Loch Lomond. This area is small but incredibly varied—from dramatic mountain peaks that attract walkers and climbers, to the gentler slopes and forests that stretch from Perth westward to Aberfoyle and the shores of Loch Lomond.

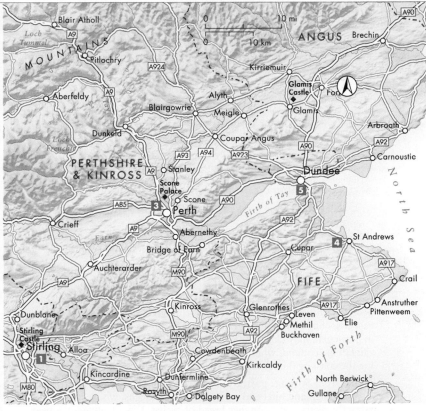

16

3 Perthshire. The prosperous air of Perth, once the capital of Scotland, testifies to its importance as a port exporting wool, salmon, and whisky to the world. The route northward leads across the Highland Boundary and into the changing landscapes beyond Pitlochry to Rannoch Moor.

4 St. Andrews and East Neuk. St. Andrews isn't just a playground for golfers. This religious and academic center is steeped in history and prestige, with grand buildings and a palpable air of prosperity. Beyond St. Andrews the colorful fishing villages of the East Neuk are a day-tripper's (and fish eater's) delight.

5 Dundee and Angus. Dundee has a knockout setting beside Britain's mightiest river, historical sights, and a vibrant social life. The tree-lined country roads of the Angus heartlands roll through strawberry and raspberry fields to busy market towns, wee villages, and Glamis Castle.

Updated by Mike Gonzalez and Nick Bruno

The Central Highlands are home to superb castles, moody mountains, and gorgeous glens that are best explored at a leisurely pace. The waters of Loch Lomond reflect the crags and dark woods that surround it, and attract those in search of a more romantic and nostalgic Scotland enshrined in the verses of the famous song that bears its name. When you finish a day of exploring, celebrate with a glass of one of the region's top-notch whiskies.

East of the Central Highlands, breezy cliff-top walkways, fishing villages, and open beaches characterize Fife and Angus. They sandwich Scotland's fourth-largest city, the rejuvenated city of Dundee. Scotland's east coast has only light rainfall throughout the year; northeastern Fife, in particular, may claim the record for the most sunshine and the least rainfall in Scotland, which all adds to the enjoyment when you're touring the coast or the famous golf center of St. Andrews.

North from Stirling, past Dunblane, are the birch-, oak-, and pine-covered Highland hills and valleys of the Trossachs, whose high peaks attract walkers and a tougher breed of cyclist. From Callander, a neat tourist town, the hills stretch westward to the "bonnie bonnie banks" of Loch Lomond. The Victorians were drawn here by the lyrical descriptions of the area by Romantic poets like Sir Walter Scott (1771–1832), who set his dramatic verse narrative of 1810, "The Lady of the Lake," in the landscape of the Trossachs. From the peaks of the Trossachs, on a good day, you can see Edinburgh Castle to the east and the tower blocks of Glasgow's housing projects to the west.

Farther north is Perth, once Scotland's capital; its wealthy mansions reflect the prosperous agricultural land that surrounds the city, and it is still an important market town today. Overlooking the River Tay, the city can reasonably claim to be the gateway to the Highlands, sitting as it does on the Highland Fault that divides Lowlands from Highlands. From Perth the landscape begins to change on the road to Pitlochry and the high, rough country of Rannoch Moor.

To the east, Fife proudly styles itself as a "kingdom," and its long history—which really began when the Romans went home in the 4th century and the Picts moved in—lends some substance to the boast. From medieval times its earls were first among Scotland's nobility and crowned her kings. For many, however, the most historic event in the region was the birth of golf, in the 15th century, which, legend has it, occurred in St. Andrews, an ancient university town with stone houses and seaside ruins. The Royal & Ancient Golf Club, the ruling body of the game worldwide, still has its headquarters here.

North, across the Firth of Tay, lies the region of Angus, whose charm is its variety: in addition to its seacoast and pleasant Lowland market centers, there's also a hinterland of lonely rounded hills with long glens running into the typical Grampian Highland scenery beyond. One of Angus's interesting features, which it shares with the eastern Lowland edge of Perthshire, is its fruit-growing industry, which includes raspberries. Within it, you'll also find the city of Dundee, once a hub for textile industry based on jute and now seeking a new identity as a city of culture.

16

PLANNER

WHEN TO GO
The Trossachs and Loch Lomond are in some ways a miniature Scotland, from the tranquil east shore of Loch Lomond to the hills and glens of the Trossachs and the mountains to the west—and all within a few hours' drive. In spring and summer, despite the erratic weather, the area is always crowded; this is a good time to go. However, the landscape is notably dramatic when the trees are turning red and brown in autumn, and evening skies are spectacular. Scotland in winter has a different kind of beauty, especially for skiers and climbers.

PLANNING YOUR TIME
Scotland's beautiful interior is excellent touring country, though the cities of Stirling and Perth are worth your time, too; Stirling is a good starting point, and exploring its castle can take a half day. Two (slightly rushed) days would be enough to explore the Trossachs loop, to gaze into the waters of Loch Venachar and Loch Achray. The glens, in some places, run parallel to the lochs, including those along Lochs Earn, Tay, and Rannoch, making for satisfying loops and round-trips. Loch Lomond is easily accessible from either Glasgow or Stirling, and is well worth exploring. Don't miss the opportunity to take a boat trip on a loch, especially on Loch Lomond or on Loch Katrine. St. Andrews, 52 miles from Edinburgh, is not to be missed, for its history and atmosphere as much as for the golf; allot an overnight stop and at least a whole day if you can. The nearby East Neuk of Fife has some of Scotland's finest coastline, now becoming gentrified by the Edinburgh second-home set but still evoking Fife's past. Dundee, with a rich maritime history and a grand museum, is an ideal base for a drive round the small towns of Angus; if you make a three-hour stop at Glamis Castle, this trip will take about a day.

SPORTS AND THE OUTDOORS

Lowland/Highland Trail. The region's big attraction for cyclists is the Lowland/Highland Trail, which stretches more than 60 miles and passes through Drymen, Aberfoyle, the Trossachs, Callander, Lochearnhead, and Killin. This route runs along former railroad-track beds, as well as private and minor roads, to reach well into the Central Highlands. Another almost completely traffic-free option is the roadway around Loch Katrine. Almost every town along the route has cycle-hire shops.

Fodor's Choice **West Highland Way.** The long-distance walkers' route, the West High-
★ land Way, begins in Glasgow, running 96 miles from the Lowlands of central Scotland to the Highlands at Fort William. Nearly 50,000 people discover the glens each year, climbing the hills and listening to birds singing in the tree canopy. This is not a difficult walk, but keep Scotland's ever-changing weather in mind and go properly prepared. From Milngavie, in Glasgow, the route passes along the banks of Loch Lomond before snaking northward into the more demanding hills beyond, crossing Rannoch Moor, and finishing at Fort William. ⊕ *www.west-highland-way.co.uk.*

GETTING HERE AND AROUND

AIR TRAVEL

Perth and Stirling can be reached easily from the Edinburgh, Dundee, and Glasgow airports by train, car, or bus. Dundee Airport is off A85, 2 miles west of city center. If you are traveling to St. Andrews directly from Edinburgh Airport, the St. Andrews Shuttle offers transfers from £19.

BUS TRAVEL

A good network of buses connects with this area via Edinburgh and Glasgow. For more information, contact Scottish Citylink or National Express. The Perth and Kinross Council supplies a map (available in tourist information centers) showing all public transport routes in Perthshire, marked with nearby attractions. Stagecoach connects St. Andrews and Dundee to small towns in the area, while Megabus has a regular service to Dundee from Edinburgh and Glasgow. First, Scottish Citylink, and Stagecoach organize reliable local service on routes throughout the Central Highlands, Fife, and Angus.

Bus Contacts First. ☎ *01224/650100* ⊕ *www.firstgroup.com.* **National Express.** ☎ *08717/818181* ⊕ *www.nationalexpressgroup.com.* **Scottish Citylink.** ☎ *0871/266–3333* ⊕ *www.citylink.co.uk.* **Stagecoach.** ☎ *01292/613502* ⊕ *www.stagecoachbus.com.*

CAR TRAVEL

It's easy to access the area from the central belt of Scotland via the motorway network. The M80 connects Glasgow to Stirling, and then briefly joins the M9 from Edinburgh, which runs within sight of the walls of Stirling Castle. From there the A9 runs from Stirling to Perth, and onward to Pitlochry; it is a good road but a little too fast (so take care). Perth can also be reached via the M90 over the Forth Bridge from Edinburgh. Three signed touring routes are useful: the Perthshire Tourist Route, the Deeside Tourist Route, and the Pitlochry Tourist Route, a beautiful and unexpected trip via Crieff and Loch Tay. Eastern Fife is served by a network of country roads. Local tourist information centers can supply maps of these routes, or you can check online (⊕ *www.vis-itscotland.com*). Once you leave the major motorways, roads become narrower and slower, with many following the contours of the lochs. Be prepared for your journey to take longer than distances might suggest.

TRAIN TRAVEL

The Central Highlands are linked to Edinburgh and Glasgow by rail, with through routes to England (some direct-service routes from London take less than five hours). Several discount ticket options are available, although in some cases on the ScotRail system a discount card must be purchased before your arrival in the United Kingdom. Note that families with children and travelers under 26 or over 60 are eligible for significant discounts. Contact Trainline, Traveline Scotland, National Rail, or ScotRail for details.

The West Highland Line runs through the western portion of the area. Services also run to Stirling, Dunblane, Perth, and Gleneagles; stops on the Inverness–Perth line include Dunkeld, Pitlochry, and Blair Atholl. In the east, ScotRail stops at Kirkcaldy, Leuchars (for St. Andrews), and Dundee.

Train Contacts National Rail Enquiries. ☎ *03457/484950* ⊕ *www. nationalrail.co.uk.* **ScotRail.** ☎ *0344/811–0141* ⊕ *www.scotrail.co.uk.* **Train-line.** ☎ *0871/244–1545* ⊕ *www.thetrainline.com.* **Traveline Scotland.** ☎ *0871/2002233* ⊕ *www.travelinescotland.com.*

16

RESTAURANTS

Regional country delicacies—loch trout, river salmon, lamb, and venison—appear regularly on even modest menus in restaurants across the region. In all the towns and villages in the area, you will find simple pubs, often crowded and noisy, many of them serving substantial food at lunchtime and in the evening until about 9 (eaten balanced on your knee, perhaps, or at a shared table). The more luxurious restaurants tend to be in upscale hotels, with prices to match. It can be difficult to find a place to eat later in the evening, so plan ahead. With an affluent population, St. Andrews supports several stylish hotel restaurants. Because it's a university town and popular tourist destination, there are also many good cafés and bistro-style restaurants. Bar lunches are the rule in large and small hotels throughout the region, and in seaside places the carry- *oot* (to-go) meal of fish-and-chips is an enduring tradition. *Restaurant reviews have been shortened. For full information, visit Fodors.com.*

HOTELS

A wide selection of accommodations is available throughout the region. They range from bed-and-breakfasts to private houses with a small number of rooms to rural accommodation (often on farms). The grand houses of the past—family homes to the landed aristocracy—have for the most part become country-house hotels. Their settings, often on ample grounds, offer an experience of grand living—but the area also has modern hotels, for those who prefer 21st-century amenities. If you're staying in Fife, the obvious choice for a base is St. Andrews, with ample accommodations of all kinds. *Hotel reviews have been shortened. For full information, visit Fodors.com.*

WHAT IT COSTS IN POUNDS			
	$	$$	$$$	$$$$
Restaurants	under £15	£15–£19	£20–£25	over £25
Hotels	under £100	£100–£160	£161–£220	over £220

Restaurant prices are the average cost of a main course at dinner or, if dinner is not served, at lunch, excluding tax. Hotel prices are the lowest cost of a standard double room in high season, including 20% V.A.T.

STIRLING

26 miles northeast of Glasgow, 36 miles northwest of Edinburgh.

Stirling is one of Britain's great historic towns. An impressive proportion of the Old Town walls can be seen from Dumbarton Road, a cobbled street leading to Stirling Castle, built on a steep-sided plug of rock. From its esplanade there is a commanding view of the surrounding Carse of Stirling. The guns on the castle battlements are a reminder of the military advantage to be gained from its position.

GETTING HERE AND AROUND

Stirling's central position in the area makes it ideal for travel to and from Glasgow and Edinburgh (or north to Perth and the Highlands) by rail or bus. The town itself is compact and easily walkable, though a shuttle bus travels to and from the town center up the steep road to Stirling Castle every 20 minutes. You can stroll the Back Walk on a circuit around the base of the castle walls—set aside at least 30 minutes for a leisurely walk. The National Wallace Monument (2 miles away) is on the outskirts of the town and can be reached by taxi or on foot.

ESSENTIALS

Visitor Information Stirling Visitor Information Centre. ⊠ *Old Town Jail, St. John St.* ☎ *01786/465019* ⊕ *www.visitscotland.com/stirling.*

EXPLORING

FAMILY
Fodor's Choice
★

Battle of Bannockburn Visitor Centre. You can almost hear horses' hooves and the zip of arrows in this 21st-century re-creation of the battle that changed the course of Scotland's history in 1314. Robert the Bruce's defeat of the armies of the English king, despite a 2-to1-disadvantage, is the stuff of legend. Using 3-D technology, the battle rages across screens that ring the central hall. Participants on both sides speak directly to you, courtesy of holograms. Later you can play a role in a Bannockburn battle game (reservations essential; age seven and over only). Bruce pursued the Scottish crown, ruthlessly sweeping aside enemies; but his victory here was masterful, as he drew the English horses into marshy land (now the area around the new center) where they sank in the mud. A circular monument commemorates the battlefield. ■ TIP→ Book ahead; tickets are for timed entry. ⊠ *Glasgow Rd., Bannockburn* ☎ *01786/812664* ⊕ *www.battleofbannockburn.com* ☜ *£11.50.*

National Wallace Monument. This Victorian-era shrine to William Wallace (circa 1270–1305), the Scottish freedom fighter reborn as "Braveheart" in Mel Gibson's 1995 film of the same name, was built between 1856 and 1869. It sits on Abbey Craig, from which Wallace watched the English armies struggle across the old Stirling Bridge before attacking them and winning a major victory in 1297. A steep stone spiral staircase leads to the roof gallery, with views of the bridge and the whole Carse of Stirling. A less flamboyant version of Wallace's life is told in an exhibition and audiovisual presentation on the second floor. To reach the monument, follow the Bridge of Allan signs (A9) northward, crossing the River Forth by the New Bridge of 1832, next to the old one. The monument is signposted at the next traffic circle. From the car park a free shuttle will take you to the monument or you can walk (15 minutes). ⊠ *Abbey Craig, Hillfoot Rd.* ☎ *01786/472140* ⊕ *www. nationalwallacemonument.com* ☒ *£9.99.*

FAMILY

Fodor's Choice

★

Stirling Castle. Its magnificent strategic position on a steep-sided crag made Stirling Castle the grandest prize in the Scots Wars of Independence in the late 13th and early 14th centuries. Robert the Bruce's victory at Bannockburn won both the castle and freedom from English subjugation for almost four centuries. Take time to visit the **Castle Exhibition** beyond the lower gate to get an overview of its evolution as a stronghold and palace. ■ TIP➜ It's a good idea to book tickets online before your visit.

16

The daughter of King Robert I (Robert the Bruce), Marjory, married Walter Fitzallan, the high steward of Scotland. Their descendants included the Stewart dynasty of Scottish monarchs (Mary, Queen of Scots, was a Stewart, though she preferred the French spelling, *Stuart*). The Stewarts were responsible for many of the works that survive within the castle walls. They made Stirling Castle their court and power base, creating fine Renaissance-style buildings that were never completely obliterated, despite reconstruction for military purposes.

Enter the castle through its outer defenses, which consist of a great curtained wall and batteries from 1708. From this lower square the most conspicuous feature is the **Palace,** built by King James V (1512–42) between 1538 and 1542. The decorative figures festooning the ornate outer walls show the influence of French masons. An orientation center in the basement, designed especially for children, lets you try out the clothes and musical instruments of the time. Across a terrace are the **Royal Apartments,** which re-create the furnishings and tapestries found here during the reign of James V and his French queen, Mary of Guise. The queen's bedchamber contains copies of the beautiful tapestries in which the hunt for the white unicorn is clearly an allegory for the persecution of Christ. Overlooking the upper courtyard is the **Great Hall,** built by King James IV (1473–1513) in 1503. Before the Union of Parliaments in 1707, when the Scottish aristocracy sold out to England, this building had been used as one of the seats of the Scottish Parliament.

Among the later works built for regiments stationed here, the **Regimental Museum** stands out; it's a 19th-century baronial revival on the site of an earlier building. Nearby, the **Chapel Royal** is unfurnished. The oldest building on the site is the **Mint,** or **Coonzie Hoose,** perhaps dating as far back as the 14th century. Below it is an arched passageway leading to the westernmost ramparts, the **Nether Bailey,** with a view of the *carselands* (valley plain) of the Forth Valley.

To the castle's south lies the hump of the Touch and the Gargunnock Hills, which diverted potential direct routes from Glasgow and the south. For centuries all roads into the Highlands across the narrow waist of Scotland led through Stirling. If you look carefully northward, you can still see the Old Stirling Bridge, the site of William Wallace's most famous victory. ✉ *Castlehill* ☎ *01786/450000* 🌐 *www.stirling-castle.gov.uk* 🎟 *£15, includes Argyll's Lodging.*

WHERE TO EAT

$$ BRITISH 🍴 **Brea.** A fresh, welcome addition to Stirling's restaurant scene, this unpretentious place with wooden tables and chairs has a menu that celebrates Scottish food, though well-made burgers and steaks are also permanent features. The food offers some new takes on traditional favorites such as the rolled haddock with salmon, the Cullen skink soup, and haggis in various guises. **Known for:** burgers; good seafood; house-made desserts. [$] *Average main: £18* ✉ *5 Baker St.* ✣ *Down the hill from Stirling Castle* ☎ *01786/446277* 🌐 *www.brea-stirling.co.uk.*

$$ ECLECTIC FAMILY 🍴 **River House.** Behind Stirling Castle, this friendly, light-filled restaurant built in the style of a Scottish *crannog* (ancient loch dwelling) sits by its own tranquil little loch, with tables on a deck overlooking the water. Local produce dominates a menu that includes seafood pie with Arbroath smokies, rump of lamb, and, naturally, haggis and neeps. **Known for:** burgers and steaks; afternoon tea; lochside dining. [$] *Average main: £16* ✉ *Castle Business Park, B8051* ☎ *01786/465577* 🌐 *www.riverhouse-restaurant.co.uk.*

WHERE TO STAY

$ B&B/INN 🏨 **Castlecroft.** Tucked beneath Stirling Castle, this comfortable modern house with traditionally furnished guest rooms welcomes you with freshly cut flowers and homemade breakfasts. **Pros:** great location; lovely views; hearty breakfasts. **Cons:** a little hard to find if you are not arriving directly from the motorway. [$] *Rooms from: £85* ✉ *Ballengeich Rd.* ☎ *01786/474933* 🌐 *castlecroft-uk.co.uk/* 🛏 *5 rooms* 🍽 *Free breakfast.*

$$ HOTEL 🏨 **Friars Wynd.** At this small boutique hotel in a restored town house in the heart of Stirling, the rooms have been tastefully modernized and feature some exposed brick and a range of interesting paintings. **Pros:** pleasant and relaxing atmosphere; tasteful decor; reasonably priced. **Cons:** Wi-Fi in public areas only; no parking. [$] *Rooms from: £119* ✉ *17 Friars St.* ☎ *01786/447501* 🌐 *www.friarswynd.co.uk* 🛏 *8 rooms* 🍽 *Free breakfast.*

$$ B&B/INN 🏨 **Portcullis Hotel.** This small hotel with a lively traditional pub scores above all on location: it is just outside the walls of Stirling Castle, and the views are spectacular, especially from the upper floors where the guest rooms are located. **Pros:** excellent location close to the castle;

fine views. **Cons:** can get noisy; snug rooms; not cheap in high season. [$] *Rooms from: £125* ✉ *Castle Wynd* ☎ *01786/472290* 🌐 *www.theportcullishotel.com* 🛏 *4 rooms* 🍴 *Free breakfast.*

SHOPPING

CLOTHING

House of Henderson. A Highland outfitter, House of Henderson sells tartans, woolens, and accessories, and offers a made-to-measure kilt service. ✉ *6–8 Friars St.* ☎ *01786/473681* 🌐 *www.houseofhenderson.co.uk.*

Mill Trail. East of Stirling is Mill Trail country, along the foot of the Ochil Hills. A leaflet from any local tourist information center will lead you to the delights of a real textile mill shop and low mill prices—even on cashmere—at Tillicoultry, Alva, and Alloa.

GIFTS

Fotheringham Gallery. The upscale Fotheringham Gallery stocks contemporary Scottish paintings by various artists, as well as striking modern jewelry by Leigh Fortheringham. ✉ *78 Henderson St., Bridge of Allan* ☎ *01786/832861* 🌐 *www.fotheringhamgallery.co.uk.*

Stirling Bagpipes. This small shop sells bagpipes of every type and at every price, including antiques by legendary craftspeople that are displayed in glass cases. In the room behind the shop, the owner lovingly turns the chanters and drones, but he will happily take time to talk you through the history of these instruments. ✉ *8 Broad St.* ☎ *01786/448886* 🌐 *www.stirlingbagpipes.com.*

THE TROSSACHS AND LOCH LOMOND

Immortalized by Wordsworth and Sir Walter Scott, the Trossachs (the name means "bristly country") contains some of Scotland's loveliest forest, hills, and glens, well justifying the area's designation as a national park. The area has a special charm, combining the wildness of the Highlands with the prolific vegetation of an old Lowland forest. Its open ground is a dense mat of bracken and heather, and its woodland is of silver birch, dwarf oak, and hazel—trees that fasten their roots into the crevices of rocks and stop short on the very brink of lochs. There are also many small towns to visit along the way, some with their roots in a medieval world; others sprang up and expanded in the wake of the first tourists who came to Scotland in the late 19th century in search of wild country or healing waters.

The best way to explore this area is by car, by bike, or on foot; the latter two depend, of course, on the weather. Keep in mind that roads in this region of the country are narrow and winding, which can make for dangerous conditions in all types of weather.

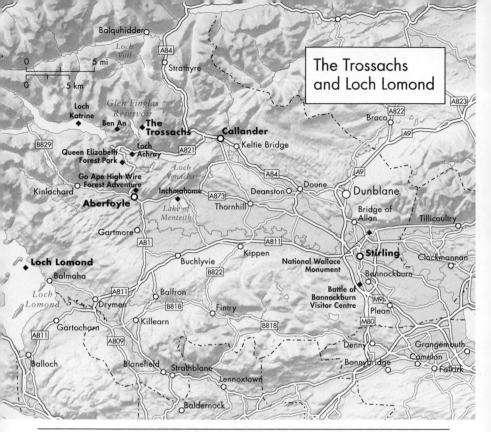

CALLANDER

8 miles northwest of Doune.

A traditional Highland-edge resort, the little town of Callander bustles throughout the year, even during off-peak times, simply because it's a gateway to Highland scenery and Loch Lomond and the Trossachs National Park. As a result, there's plenty of window-shopping here, plus nightlife in pubs and a selection of mainly bed-and-breakfast accommodations.

GETTING HERE AND AROUND

You can access Callander by bus from Stirling, Glasgow, or Edinburgh. If you're traveling by car from Stirling, take the M8 to Dunblane, then the A820 (which becomes the A84) to Callander. If you are coming from Glasgow, take the A81 through Aberfoyle to Callander; an alternative route (longer but more picturesque) is to take the A821 around Loch Venachar, then the A84 east to Callander.

ESSENTIALS

Visitor Information Callander Visitor Information Centre. ⊠ *52–54 Main St.* ☎ *01877/330342* ⊕ *www.visitscotland.com.*

EXPLORING

FAMILY **Hamilton Toy Collection.** One of those eccentric museums born of one person's (or one family's) passionate obsession, this small, crowded house and shop on Callander's main street contains one of the most extensive toy collections in Britain. The rooms throughout the house are filled with everything from Corgi cars and an enormous number of toy soldiers, carefully organized by regiment, to Amanda Jane dolls and Beatles memorabilia. The collection of model railways has extended into tracks in the back garden. The museum is jammed and quirky, but full of reminders of everyone's childhood. ✉ *111 Main St.* ☎ *01877/330004* 🌐 *www.thehamiltontoycollection.co.uk* 🎟 *£3* ⏲ *Closed Nov.–Mar.*

WHERE TO EAT

$$ MODERN BRITISH Fodor's Choice ★ 🍴 **Venachar Lochside.** There is a special pleasure in dining overlooking a loch, and this restaurant's glass wall affords a lovely panorama of the water and surrounding hills—a pleasant surprise given that all you see from the road is what seems to be a large shed. The menu lives up to its surroundings, with an emphasis on fish—mussels, scallops, the excellent smoked-fish selection to start, and the trout with roast chorizo. **Known for:** smoked-fish platter; fine seafood; lochside dining. [$] *Average main: £15* ✉ *Loch Venachar* ✥ *On the A821 about 6 miles from Callander, at Brig o' Turk* ☎ *01877/330011* 🌐 *www.venachar-lochside.co.uk.*

WHERE TO STAY

$$$ HOTEL Fodor's Choice ★ 🏨 **Monachyle MHOR.** Splendidly isolated, this beautiful converted farmhouse with contemporary interiors is set amid forests and moorland, looking out on to Lochs Voil and Doine. **Pros:** stunning scenery; delicious food; complimentary salmon and trout fishing. **Cons:** remote location; rooms are on the small side. [$] *Rooms from: £190* ✉ *Off A84, Balquhidder* ✥ *17 miles (a 40-min drive) northwest of Callander* ☎ *01877/384622* 🌐 *www.mhor.net* 🛏 *14 rooms* 🍽 *Free breakfast.*

$$ B&B/INN Fodor's Choice ★ 🏨 **Roman Camp.** Within a hundred yards of Callander's main street, pass through an unpretentious arch and you'll find this 17th-century hunting lodge surrounded by ornate gardens. **Pros:** beautiful grounds; luxurious rooms; close to everything in town. **Cons:** restaurant is expensive; no Internet in rooms. [$] *Rooms from: £160* ✉ *Off Main St.* ☎ *01877/330003* 🌐 *www.romancamphotel.co.uk* 🛏 *15 rooms* 🍽 *Free breakfast.*

SHOPPING

Trossachs Woollen Mill. The Edinburgh Woollen Mill Group owns this mill shop in Kilmahog, a mile west of Callander. It has a vast selection of woolens on display, including luxurious cashmere and striking tartan throws, and will provide overseas mailing and tax-free shopping. ✉ *Main St., Kilmahog* ☎ *01877/330178* 🌐 *www.ewm.co.uk.*

THE TROSSACHS

10 miles west of Callander.

The Trossachs has been a popular touring region since the late 18th century, at the dawn of the age of the Romantic poets. Influenced by the writings of Sir Walter Scott, early visitors who strayed into the Highlands from the central belt of Scotland admired this as the first "wild" part of Scotland they encountered. Perhaps because the Trossachs represent the very essence of what the Highlands are supposed to be, the whole of this area, including Loch Lomond, is now protected as a national park. Here you can find birch and pine forests, vistas down lochs where the woods creep right to the water's edge, and, in the background, peaks that rise high enough to be called mountains, though they're not as high as those to the north and west.

GETTING HERE AND AROUND

To reach the Trossachs, take the A84 from Callander through the Pass of Leny, then on to Crianlarich on the A85; from here you can continue down the western shore of Loch Lomond or carry on toward Fort William. Alternately, turn onto the A821 outside Callander and travel past Loch Katrine through the Duke's Pass to Aberfoyle.

EXPLORING

Loch Achray. Stretching west of the small community of Brig o' Turk, Loch Achray dutifully fulfills expectations of what a verdant Trossachs loch should be: small, green, reedy meadows backed by dark plantations, rhododendron thickets, and lumpy hills, thickly covered with heather. ⊠ *A821, Brig o'Turk.*

Fodor's Choice ★ **Ben An.** The parking lot by Loch Achray is near the beginning of the path that ascends steep, heathery Ben An, which affords some of the best Trossachs views. The climb requires a couple of hours and good lungs. ⊠ *A821, Aberfoyle.*

FAMILY
Fodor's Choice ★ **Loch Katrine.** This loch was a favorite among Victorian visitors—mysterious and wide and, at times, quite wild. Today it's the source of Glasgow's freshwater. Take a cruise around the loch if time permits, as the shores remain undeveloped and scenic. The steamship *Sir Walter Scott* and the motor launch *Lady of the Lake* sail from the lake's eastern end several times a day in season. You can make the round-trip journey around the loch, or head directly across to Stronachlachar and return by bicycle on the lochside road. There are café facilities and cycle-hire shops at the head of the loch; reservations are required if you're taking a bike on the boat. ⊠ *Trossachs Pier, Aberfoyle* ✛ *Off A821* ☎ *01877/376316* ⊕ *www.lochkatrine.com* ☒ *Sir Walter Scott £16.50 round-trip, £13.50 one way; Lady of the Lake £14.50 round-trip, £11.50 one way* ☉ *Closed Oct.–May.*

ABERFOYLE

11 miles south of Loch Katrine, in the Trossachs.

This small tourist-oriented town has a somewhat faded air, but the surrounding hills (some snowcapped) and the green slopes visible from the town are the reason so many people pause here before continuing up to Duke's Pass or on to Inversnaid on Loch Lomond. Access to nearby Queen Elizabeth Forest Park is another reason to visit.

GETTING HERE AND AROUND
The main route out of Glasgow, the A81, takes you through Aberfoyle and on to Callander and Stirling. There are regular buses from Stirling and Glasgow to Aberfoyle.

ESSENTIALS
Visitor Information Trossachs Discovery Centre. ✉ *Main St.* ☎ *01877/382352* ⊕ *www.visitscotland.com.*

EXPLORING

FAMILY **Go Ape High Wire Forest Adventure.** Near the David Marshall Lodge, this is an exhilarating experience for thrill seekers age 10 and over. After a short orientation course, you can travel 40 feet above the forest via ziplines and rope ladders on a sort of midair assault course. ✉ *Queen Elizabeth Forest Park, A821, 1 mile north of Aberfoyle* ☎ *0845/643–9215* ⊕ *www.goape.com* ✉ *£31 (3 hrs), £25 (2 hrs)* ⊗ *Closed weekdays in Nov., Feb., and Mar.*

Fodor's Choice ★ **Inchmahome.** The 13th-century ruined priory on the tiny island of Inchmahome, on the Lake of Menteith, is a lovely place for a picnic after you explore the building's chapter house and other remains. It was a place of refuge in 1547 for the young Mary, Queen of Scots. In season, a seven-minute ferry takes passengers to the island, now owned by the National Trust for Scotland. The ferry jetty is just past the Port of Menteith (a village). ✉ *Off A81* ✛ *Take the A81 to the B8034; it's 4 miles east of Aberfoyle* ☎ *01786/385294* ⊕ *www.historicenvironment. scot* ✉ *Ferry £7.50* ⊗ *Closed. Nov.–Mar.*

Fodor's Choice ★ **Queen Elizabeth Forest Park.** For exquisite nature, drive north from Aberfoyle on the A821 and turn right at signposts to Queen Elizabeth Forest Park. Along the way you'll be heading toward higher moorland blanketed with conifers. The conifers hem in the views of Ben Ledi and Ben Venue, which can be seen over the spiky green waves of trees as the road snakes around heathery knolls and hummocks. There's another viewing area, and a small parking lot, at the highest point of the road. Soon the road swoops off the Highland edge and leads downhill.

At the heart of the Queen Elizabeth Forest Park, the **Lodge Forest Visitor Centre** leads to four forest walks, a family-friendly bicycle route, and the 7-mile 3 Lochs Forest Drive, open April to October. Or you can sit on the terrace of the Bluebell Cafe and scan the forests and hills of the Trossachs. The visitor center has a wildlife-watch room where you can follow the activities of everything from ospreys to water voles. ✉ *Off A821, 1 mile north of Aberfoyle* ☎ *01877/382383* ⊕ *www.forestry.gov. uk/qefp* ✉ *Free, parking £3.*

16

FAMILY **Scottish Wool Centre.** Besides selling a vast range of woolen garments and knitwear, the Scottish Wool Centre has a small café and some activities. Three times a day from April to September it presents an interactive "gathering" during which dogs herd sheep and ducks in the large amphitheater, with a little help from the public. ✉ *Off Main St.* ☎ *01877/382850* 🌐 *www.ewm.co.uk* 🎟 *Free.*

WHERE TO EAT AND STAY

$ BRITISH 🍴 **Pier Café.** At the historic Stronachlachar Pier, this light-filled coffee shop has a satisfying lunch menu (burgers and sandwiches) and a deck with expansive views over Loch Katrine. Cakes, scones, and soups are made on the premises. **Known for:** home baking; good coffee; loch views. [$] *Average main: £10* ✉ *B829, Stronachlachar* ☎ *01877/386374* 🌐 *www.thepiercafe.com* 🕒 *No dinner Mon.–Wed.*

$$ HOTEL Fodor's Choice ★ 🏨 **Lake of Menteith Hotel.** At this beautifully located hotel overlooking the Lake of Menteith, muted colors and simple but elegant rooms create a restful air, enhanced, perhaps, by the silent hills that ring the hotel and the tranquil lake. **Pros:** elegant, unpretentious bedrooms; beautiful setting. **Cons:** not well signposted; not all rooms have lake views and those that do are more expensive. [$] *Rooms from: £145* ✉ *Off A81* ☎ *01877/385258* 🌐 *www.lake-hotel.com* 🛏 *17 rooms* 🍽 *Free breakfast.*

SPORTS AND THE OUTDOORS

GOLF

Aberfoyle Golf Club. Queen Elizabeth Forest Park provides the backdrop for this hilly course. One of the area's many James Braid–designed parkland courses, it dates back to 1890. There are views of Ben Lomond and Stirling Castle from different points on the course, which is relatively short but varied and challenging even for quite experienced players, with several uphill shots and undulating ground. ✉ *Braeval* ✥ *Off A821* ☎ *01877/382493* 🌐 *www.aberfoylegolf.co.uk* 🎟 *£20 weekdays, £25 weekends* ⛳ *18 holes, 5158 yards, par 66.*

LOCH LOMOND

14 miles west of Aberfoyle.

The waters of Scotland's largest loch, which also happens to be one of its most beautiful, create a perfect reflection of the surrounding hills. You can cruise among its small islands or follow the low road that carries you from Glasgow to the beginning of the Highlands.

GETTING HERE AND AROUND

To reach Loch Lomond from Aberfoyle, take the A81 toward Glasgow, then the A811 to Drymen and then the B837 as far as it will take you. From Glasgow, take the A82 to the Balloch roundabout and either go right through Balloch for Drymen and the eastern shore, or continue along the A82 as it hugs the west bank all the way to Crianlarich.

You can drive, cycle, or walk along the 32 miles of Loch Lomond along its western shores, and watch the changing face of the loch as you go, or look up toward the shifting slopes of Ben Lomond.

ESSENTIALS

Visitor Information Loch Lomond and the Trossachs National Park Headquarters. ⊠ *Carrochan Rd., Balloch* ☎ *01389/722600* ⊕ *www.lochlomond-trossachs.org.*

EXPLORING

Fodor'sChoice
★

Loch Lomond. Known for its "bonnie, bonnie banks," Loch Lomond is Scotland's largest loch in terms of surface area, and its waters reflect the crags that surround it. The song "The Banks of Loch Lomond" is said to have been written by a Jacobite prisoner incarcerated in Carlisle, England.

On the western side of the loch, the A82 follows the shore for 24 miles, continuing a farther 7 miles to Crianlarich, passing picturesque Luss, which has a pier where you can hop aboard boats cruising along the loch, and Tarbert, the starting point for the *Maid of the Loch*. On the eastern side of the loch, take the A81 to Drymen, and from there the B837 signposted toward Balmaha, where you can hire a boat or take the ferry to the island of Inchcailloch. Once you're there, a short walk takes you to the top of the hill and a spectacular view of the loch. Equally spectacular, but not as wet, is the view from Conic Hill behind Balmaha. If you continue along the B837 beyond Rowardennan to where it ends at a car park, you can join the walkers at the beginning of the path up Ben Lomond. Don't underestimate this innocent-looking hill; go equipped for sudden changes in the weather. Hikers can also try part of the 96-mile West Highland Way (⊕ *www.west-highland-way.co.uk*) that runs along the shore of Loch Lomond on its way north.

WHERE TO EAT

$
BRITISH
Fodor'sChoice
★

✕ **Coach House Coffee Shop.** This lively restaurant and café serving Scottish classics fits perfectly into its surroundings with its cheerful, over-the-top Scottishness. Long wooden tables, a large chimney with an open fire in the winter months, and a cabinet full of mouthwatering cakes baked by the owner create the atmosphere. **Known for:** teapots; stovies; Scottish style. ⑤ *Average main: £11* ⊠ *Church Rd., Luss* ✛ *Off A82* ☎ *01436/860341* ⊗ *No dinner.*

$
BRITISH

✕ **Drovers Inn.** Knowing its clientele, this quirky, noisy, friendly inn serves huge, hearty portions that are what you need after a day's walking on the nearby West Highland Way. Scottish staples like sausage and mash, minced beef, and haggis jostle for a place beside occasionally more adventurous dishes. **Known for:** big portions; old stuffed animals; good bar. ⑤ *Average main: £12* ⊠ *A82, Balloch* ✛ *On the A82 toward Crianlarich, north of Ardlui, just north of Loch Lomond* ☎ *01301/704234* ⊕ *www.thedroversinn.co.uk.*

WHERE TO STAY

$
HOTEL

🏨 **Balloch House.** Cute, cozy, and very Scottish, this small hotel offers tasty breakfasts and good, hearty pub meals like fish-and-chips and local smoked salmon for reasonable prices. **Pros:** beautiful building; peat fires; near shopping. **Cons:** noisy pinball machine next to bar; not all rooms have views. ⑤ *Rooms from: £98* ⊠ *Balloch Rd., Balloch* ☎ *01389/752579* ⊕ *www.innkeeperslodge.com/loch-lomond* � *12 rooms* ⎮⚪⎮ *Free breakfast.*

16

$$$$ HOTEL **Cameron House.** There is little that you cannot do at this luxury resort hotel beside Loch Lomond, including taking to the water in a motorboat or riding a seaplane above the trees. **Pros:** beautiful grounds; away-from-it-all feel; good dining. **Cons:** prices are high; slightly difficult access from A82. [$] *Rooms from: £310* ✉ *Loch Lomond, off A82, Alexandria* ☎ *01389/755565* 🌐 *www.cameronhouse.co.uk* 🛏 *103 rooms* 🍴 *Free breakfast.*

SPORTS AND THE OUTDOORS

BOATING

FAMILY **Cruise Loch Lomond.** You can take tours year-round with this company. From April to October boats depart from various ports around the loch, including Tarbet, Luss, Balmaha, and Inversnaid. There is also a Two-Loch Tour taking in Loch Lomond and Loch Katrine. From November to March the boats operate on demand. ✉ *A82, Tarbet* ☎ *01301/702356* 🌐 *www.cruiselochlomond.co.uk* 🎟 *From £10.*

Macfarlane and Son. At this longtime favorite, boats with outboard motors rent for £60 per day. Rowboats rent for £10 per hour or £40 per day. From Balmaha, it is a short trip to the lovely island of Incailloch. Macfarlane's also runs a ferry to the island for £5 per person. ✉ *Balmaha Boatyard, B837, Balmaha* ☎ *01360/870214* 🌐 *www.balmahaboatyard.co.uk* 🎟 *From £40 per day.*

PERTHSHIRE

If Perthshire's castles invoke memories of past conflicts, the grand houses and spa towns here are testimony to the continued presence of a wealthy landed gentry. This is also a place for walking, cycling, and water sports. In some ways Perthshire is a crossing point where Lowlands and Highlands, two Scottish landscapes and two histories, meet. Perthshire itself is rural, agricultural Scotland, fertile and prosperous. Its woodlands, rivers, and glens (and agreeable climate and strategic position) drew the Romans and later the Celtic missionaries. In fact, the motto of the capital city, Perth, is "the perfect center."

PERTH

36 miles northeast of Stirling, 43 miles north of Edinburgh, 61 miles northeast of Glasgow.

For many years Perth was Scotland's capital, and central to its history. One king (James I) was killed here, and the Protestant reformer John Knox preached in St. John's Kirk, where his rhetoric moved crowds to burn down several local monasteries. Perth's local whisky trade and the productive agriculture that surrounds the town have sustained it through the centuries. Its grand buildings, especially on the banks of the River Tay, testify to its continued wealth. The open parkland within the city (the Inches) gives the place a restful air, and shops range from small crafts boutiques to department stores. Impressive Scone Palace is nearby.

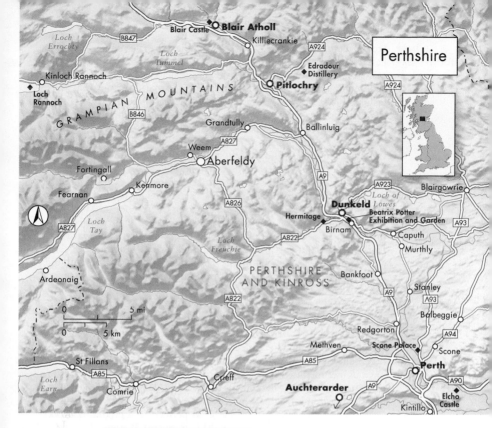

GETTING HERE AND AROUND

Perth is served by the main railway line to Inverness, and regular and frequent buses run here from Glasgow, Edinburgh, and Stirling. The central artery, the A9, passes through the city en route to Pitlochry and Inverness, while a network of roads opens the way to the glens and hills around Glen Lyon, or the road to Loch Lomond (the A85) via Crianlarich.

ESSENTIALS

Visitor Information Perth Visitor Centre. ✉ *45 High St.* ☎ *01738/450600* ⊕ *www.visitscotland.com.*

EXPLORING

Elcho Castle. Built around 1560 by the River Tay, the castle marks a transition period when these structures began to be built as grand houses rather than fortresses, and it's easy to see that Elcho was built for both comfort and defense. The well-preserved but uncluttered rooms let you imagine how life might have been here in the 17th century. The staircases still give access to all floors, and a flashlight is provided for the darker corners. From the battlements of the castle you can see the river stretching east and west. ✉ *Off A912* ✛ *Close to Rhynd* ☎ *01738/639998* ⊕ *www.historicenvironment.scot* 🎫 *£5* ☺ *Closed Oct.–Mar.*

FAMILY
Fodor'sChoice
★

Scone Palace. The current residence of the Earl of Mansfield, Scone Palace (pronounced *skoon*) is much more cheerful than the city's other castles. Although it incorporates various earlier works, the palace today has mainly a 19th-century theme, with mock castellations that were fashionable at the time. There's plenty to see if you're interested in the acquisitions of an aristocratic Scottish family: magnificent porcelain, some sumptuous furniture, a fine collection of ivory, clocks, and 16th-century needlework. Each room has a guide who will happily talk you through its contents and their associations. In one bedroom hangs a portrait of Dido Elizabeth Belle, a young black slave adopted by the family, who became a well-known society beauty in the 1760s. A coffee shop, restaurant, gift shop, and play area are on-site. The palace has its own mausoleum nearby, on the site of a long-gone abbey on **Moot Hill,** the ancient coronation place of the Scottish kings. To be crowned, they sat on the Stone of Scone, which was seized in 1296 by Edward I of England, Scotland's greatest enemy, and placed in the coronation chair at Westminster Abbey, in London. The stone was returned to Scotland in November 1996 and is now on view in Edinburgh Castle. ⊠ *Braemar Rd.* ✛ *2 miles north of Perth* ☎ *01738/552300* ⊕ *www.scone-palace. co.uk* ⊠ *£11.50* ⊙ *House closed Nov.–Mar. Grounds closed Mon.– Thurs. Nov.–Mar.*

WHERE TO EAT AND STAY

$$
BRITISH

✕ **Deans Restaurant.** The varied clientele reflects the broad appeal of noted chef Willie Deans's imaginative and satisfying cuisine, including a dinner menu with starters such as ceviche of sea bream, passion fruit, and lime, and Shetland fish curry and delicious Orkney steak for main courses. Deans is airy and pleasant, merging warm colors and light woods with comfortable sofas perfect for a predinner drink. **Known for:** pretheater menu; good lunch menu; Shetland fish curry. $ *Average main: £19* ⊠ *77–79 Kinnoull St.* ☎ *01738/643377* ⊕ *www. letseatperth.co.uk.*

$$
BRITISH
Fodor'sChoice
★

✕ **63 Tay Street.** Dine looking out on to the River Tay in this elegant but relaxed restaurant with tall windows, gray-and-white walls, and wooden tables. Known for imaginative fare with an emphasis on seasonal and local produce, chef Graeme Pallister produces combinations that are adventurous, such as the "witch sole" with curry and sprouting broccoli or red deer with pear, parsnips, and licorice. **Known for:** imaginative use of seasonal ingredients; excellent tasting menu; wine list. $ *Average main: £19* ⊠ *63 Tay St.* ☎ *01738/441451* ⊕ *www.63taystreet.com.*

$$
HOTEL

🏨 **Huntingtower Hotel.** Less than 5 miles from Perth, this tranquil, traditional country hotel with an air of understated elegance has a spacious garden and trees that make it feel more rural than it really is. **Pros:** restful setting; amply sized rooms. **Cons:** no elevator; perhaps a slight excess of tartan. $ *Rooms from: £110* ⊠ *Crieff Rd.* ☎ *01738/583771* ⊕ *www.huntingtowerhotel.co.uk* ⌁ *34 rooms* ⍾ *Free breakfast.*

$
B&B/INN

🏨 **Sunbank House Hotel.** This handsome early Victorian gray-stone mansion near Perth's Branklyn Gardens overlooks the River Tay and the city of Perth. **Pros:** reasonably priced; friendly staff; delicious local cuisine. **Cons:** some rooms are very small; some traffic noise from the main road. $ *Rooms from: £90* ⊠ *50 Dundee Rd.* ☏ *01738/624882* ⊕ *www. sunbankhouse.com* ⇌ *9 rooms* |◯| *Free breakfast.*

SHOPPING

Cairncross of Perth. The Romans coveted freshwater pearls from the River Tay. If you do, too, then head to Cairncross of Perth, where you can admire a display of some of the more unusual shapes and colors. Some of the delicate settings take their theme from Scottish flowers. ⊠ *18 St. John's St.* ☏ *01738/624367* ⊕ *www.cairncrossofperth.co.uk.*

Timothy Hardie. Stunning antique jewelry and silver, including a few Scottish items, can be found here, as well as modern pieces. ⊠ *25 St. John's St.* ☏ *01738/633127* ⊕ *www.timothyhardie.co.uk.*

Whispers of the Past. This lovely shop has a collection of jewelry, china, and other gift items, some vintage and some new. ⊠ *15 George St.* ☏ *01738/635472* ⊕ *whispers-of-the-past.weebly.com.*

DUNKELD

14 miles north of Perth.

16

The historic town of Dunkeld remains intact and beautifully preserved with its rows of white houses around the town square. The original village was destroyed in 1689 in a ferocious battle during the Jacobite rebellion and was rebuilt after its defeat by the Atholl family. Today it survives as part of the National Trust for Scotland's Little Houses Project, which helps maintain the houses. The town is overlooked by the grand but semi-ruined 12th-century cathedral (still used for services). Atholl Street, leading down to the River Tay, has several crafts shops and a hotel.

The bridge across the River Tay takes you to Birnam Wood, where Shakespeare's Macbeth met the three witches who issued the prophecy about his death. Witty wooden notices lead you to the right tree, a gnarled hollow oak.

GETTING HERE AND AROUND

Dunkeld is on the A9 between Perth and Pitlochry. The town is also on the main train line to Inverness.

ESSENTIALS

Visitor Information Dunkeld and Birnam Tourist Information Centre. ⊠ *The Cross* ☏ *01350/727688* ⊕ *www.visitscotland.com.*

EXPLORING

FAMILY **Beatrix Potter Exhibition and Garden.** The garden and exhibition celebrates the life and work of this much-beloved children's writer who, for many years, spent her family holidays in the area. You're free to walk around the enchanting garden where you can peep into the homes of Peter Rabbit and Mrs. Tiggy-Winkle, her best-known characters. The visitors center has a well-stocked shop, a small café, and an imaginative small exhibition on the writer's life and work. The garden is a mile south of Dunkeld, in Birnam. ⊠ *Birnam Arts Centre, Station Rd., Birnam* ☏ *01350/727674* ⊕ *www.birnamarts.com* ⊒ *£3 exhibition, garden free.*

Hermitage. On the outskirts of Dunkeld, the Hermitage is a 1½-mile woodland walk that follows the River Braan. In the 18th century, the dukes of Atholl constructed two follies (fantasy buildings) here, **Ossian's Cave** and the awesomely decorated **Ossian's Hall**, above a spectacular—and noisy—waterfall. (Ossian was a fictional Celtic poet invented by James MacPherson in the 18th century for an era fascinated by the "primitive" past.) You'll also be in the presence of Britain's tallest tree, a Douglas fir measuring 214 feet. ✉ *Hermitage Car Park, off A9, 2 miles west of Dunkeld* 🌐 *www.nts.org.uk* 🎟 *Free, parking lot £2.*

WHERE TO EAT

$ BRITISH 🍴 **The Taybank.** This lovely spot overlooking the River Tay is a musical meeting place owned by Scottish singer Dougie MacLean. It serves unpretentious but plentiful traditional pub food, like haggis, Cullen skink (fish soup), and stovies (a beef-and-potato dish) in the friendly, rough-and-ready bar; the more elegant dinner menu uses local produce and changes daily. **Known for:** traditional Scottish fare; excellent music; beer garden. [$] *Average main: £13* ✉ *Tay Terr.* ☎ *01350/727340* 🌐 *www.thetaybankdunkeld.com.*

SHOPPING

Jeremy Law of Scotland. Here you can purchase deerskin shoes and moccasins, as well as leather items including jackets, gloves, shoes, and wallets. ✉ *City Hall, Atholl St.* ☎ *0800/146780* 🌐 *www.moccasin.co.uk.*

PITLOCHRY

15 miles north of Dunkeld.

In the late 19th century Pitlochry was an elegant Victorian spa town, famous for its mild microclimate and beautiful setting. Today it is a busy tourist town, with wall-to-wall gift shops, cafés and B&Bs, large hotels, and a huge golf course. The town itself is oddly nondescript, but it's a convenient base from which to explore the surrounding hills and valleys.

GETTING HERE AND AROUND

The main route through central Scotland, the A9, passes through Pitlochry, as does the main railway line from Glasgow/Edinburgh to Inverness. From here the B8019 connects to the B846 west to Rannoch Moor or south to Aberfeldy.

ESSENTIALS

Visitor Information Pitlochry Visitor Information Centre. ✉ *22 Atholl Rd.* ☎ *01796/472215* 🌐 *www.visitscotland.com.*

EXPLORING

Edradour Distillery. If you have a whisky-tasting bent, visit Edradour Distillery, which claims to be the smallest single-malt distillery in Scotland (but then, so do others). There's a fun, informative tour of the distillery where you get to see how the whisky is made; you also get to savor a free dram at the end of the tour. ✉ *Pitlochry* ✥ *Off A924, 2½ miles east of Pitlochry* ☎ *01796/472095* 🌐 *www.edradour.com* 🎟 *Tours £7.50* ⏲ *Closed Sun. and Nov.–Mar.*

Fodor's Choice ★ **Loch Rannoch.** With its shoreline of birch trees framed by dark pines, Loch Rannoch is the quintessential Highland loch, stretching more than 9 miles from west to east. Fans of Robert Louis Stevenson (1850–94), especially of *Kidnapped* (1886), will not want to miss the last, lonely section of road. Stevenson describes the setting: "The mist rose and died away, and showed us that country lying as waste as the sea, only the moorfowl and the peewees crying upon it, and far over to the east a herd of deer, moving like dots." ⊠ *Pitlochry* ✛ *B846, 20 miles west of Pitlochry.*

WHERE TO EAT

$$
BRITISH
× **Moulin Hotel and Brewery.** At this traditional pub, you can eat in the airy, pleasant dining room or at the lively bar, with its dark, wooden interiors and some stuffed animals on the walls. Expect standard Scottish fare in generous quantities, including venison, scallops, and mussels; local produce is favored. **Known for:** Scottish cuisine; ales made on-site; choice of lively or quiet dining. $ *Average main: £15* ⊠ *11–30 Kirkmichael Rd.* ✛ *Between Pitlochry and Edradour* ☎ *01796/472196* ⊕ *www.moulinhotel.co.uk.*

WHERE TO STAY

$$$$
HOTEL
Fodor's Choice ★ **Green Park Hotel.** Set among woods and on the shores of Loch Faskally, Green Park is a genuinely luxurious country house hotel; most guest rooms have views over the loch or the gardens, and the most sought-after are those with a balcony on the second floor. **Pros:** great location; very attentive staff; country house comfort. **Cons:** a slightly conservative feel; very popular so books up early. $ *Rooms from: £236* ⊠ *Clunie Bridge Rd.* ✛ *5 mins north of Pitlochry center on A924* ☎ *01796/473248* ⊕ *www.thegreenpark.co.uk* ➭ *51 rooms* ❑ *Free breakfast.*

16

SPORTS AND THE OUTDOORS
GOLF

Blairgowrie Golf Club. Well known to area golfers looking for a challenge, the Blairgowrie Golf Club's Rosemount Course is laid out on rolling land in the pine, birch, and fir woods, which bring a wild air to the scene. There are, however, wide fairways and at least some large greens. If Rosemount is hosting a tournament, you can play on Lansdowne, another 18-hole course, or Wee, a 9-hole course. ⊠ *Golf Course Rd., Blairgowrie* ☎ *01250/872622* ⊕ *www.theblairgowriegolfclub.co.uk* ☑ *Rosemount, £59.50; Lansdowne, £59.50; Wee, £17.50* ⚑ *Rosemount: 18 holes, 6630 yards, par 72; Lansdowne: 18 holes, 6886 yards, par 72; Wee: 9 holes, 2327 yards, par 32.*

Pitlochry Golf Course. A decent degree of stamina is needed for the first three holes at Pitlochry, where steep climbs are involved. The reward is magnificent Highland scenery. Despite its relatively short length, this beautiful course has more than its fair share of surprises. The course offers golf with food packages. ⊠ *Golf Course Rd.* ☎ *01796/472792* ⊕ *www.pitlochrygolf.co.uk* ☑ *Mar., Apr., Oct., and Nov.: £32 weekdays, £40 weekends; May–Sept.: £40 weekdays, £50 weekends* ⚑ *18 holes, 5681 yards, par 69.*

BLAIR ATHOLL

10 miles north of Pitlochry.

Located where the Tilt and Garry rivers flow together, this small town sits in the middle of the Grampian Mountains. Here you'll find Blair Castle, one of Scotland's grandest grand houses.

GETTING HERE AND AROUND

Popular Blair Castle is just off the A9 Pitlochry-to-Inverness road, beyond the village of Blair Atholl. The village has a railway station that is on the main Inverness line.

EXPLORING

Fodor's Choice ★ **Blair Castle.** Its setting among woodlands and gardens, together with its war-torn past, make Blair Castle one of Scotland's most highly rated sights. The turreted white castle was home to successive dukes of Atholl and their families, the Murrays, one of the most powerful in the land. During the Jacobite rebellion of 1745 the loyalties of the Atholls were divided—a preserved piece of floor shows the marks of red-hot shot fired when the castle was under siege. In the end the supporters of the English king held off the rebels and were well rewarded for it. The dukes were allowed to retain a private army, the Atholl Highlanders. The castle entrance hall presents some of the dukes' collections of weapons, while a rich collection of furniture, china, and paintings occupies the family rooms. The grounds contain a 9-acre walled garden, an 18th-century folly, and a play area for children. ✉ *Off B8079* ☎ *01796/481207* 🌐 *www.blair-castle.co.uk* 🎫 *Castle and gardens £11, grounds only £6* 🕒 *Closed Nov.–Mar.*

AUCHTERARDER

11 miles southeast of Crieff.

Famous for the Gleneagles Hotel (including its restaurant by Andrew Fairlie) and nearby golf courses, Auchterarder also has a flock of tiny antiques shops to amuse Gleneagles's golf widows and widowers.

GETTING HERE AND AROUND

Gleneagles Station is on the main Inverness line, while the A9 gives direct access to Gleneagles and Auchterarder via the A823.

ESSENTIALS

Visitor Information Auchterarder Visitor Information Centre. ✉ *90 High St.* ☎ *01764/663450* 🌐 *www.visitscotland.com.*

WHERE TO STAY

$$$$ HOTEL Fodor's Choice ★ 🏨 **Gleneagles Hotel.** One of Britain's most famous hotels, Gleneagles is the very essence of modern grandeur, a vast palace that stands hidden in breathtaking countryside amid its world-famous golf courses. **Pros:** luxurious rooms; famous Andrew Fairlie restaurant; the three courses are a golfer's paradise. **Cons:** steep price. [$] *Rooms from: £495* ✉ *Off A823* ☎ *01764/662231* 🌐 *www.gleneagles.com* 🛏 *258 rooms* 🍴 *Free breakfast.*

SPORTS AND THE OUTDOORS

GOLF

Fodor's Choice **Gleneagles.** Its superb courses have made Gleneagles a part of golfing
★ history. The 18 holes of the King's Course, designed by James Braid in
1919, have quirky names—many golfers have grappled with the tough
17th hole, known as the Warslin' Lea (Wrestling Ground). The Queen's
Course mixes varied terrain, including woods and moors. Jack Nicklaus
designed the PGA Centenary Course (host of the 2014 Ryder Cup),
which sweeps into the Ochil Hills and has views of the Grampians.
The 9-hole Wee Course provides challenges for beginners and pros.
Gleneagles is also home to the PGA National Academy, a good place to
improve your skills. ✉ *A823* ☏ *01764/662231* ⊕ *www.gleneagles.com*
⚐ *King's, Queen's, and PGA Centenary courses, £195; Wee Course,
£35* ⛳ *King's: 18 holes, 6790 yards, par 71; Queen's: 18 holes, 6790
yards, par 68; PGA Centenary: 18 holes, 6815 yards, par 72; Wee
Course: 9 holes, 1418 yards, par 27.*

ST. ANDREWS AND EAST NEUK

16

In its western parts Fife still bears the scars of heavy industry, especially
coal mining, but these signs are less evident as you move east. Northeastern Fife, around the town of St. Andrews, seems to have played no
part in the Industrial Revolution; instead, its residents earned a living
from the grain fields or from the sea. Fishing has been a major industry,
and in the past a string of Fife ports traded across the North Sea. Today
the legacy of Dutch-influenced architecture, such as crowstep gables (the
stepped effect on the ends of the roofs)—gives these East Neuk villages
a distinctive character.

St. Andrews is unlike any other Scottish town. Once Scotland's most
powerful ecclesiastical center as well as the seat of the country's oldest
university and then, much later, the very symbol and spiritual home
of golf, the town has a comfortable, well-groomed air, sitting almost
smugly apart from the rest of Scotland. Its latest boast, being the town
where Prince William first kissed Kate Middleton, has boosted university applications from around the world.

ST. ANDREWS

52 miles northeast of Edinburgh, 83 miles northeast of Glasgow.

Fodor's Choice It may have a ruined cathedral and a grand university—the oldest in
★ Scotland—but the modern claim to fame for St. Andrews is mainly its
status as the home of golf. Forget that Scottish kings were crowned here,
or that John Knox preached here and that Reformation reformers were
burned at the stake here. Thousands flock to St. Andrews to play at the
Old Course, home of the Royal & Ancient Club, and to follow in the
footsteps of Hagen, Sarazen, Jones, and Hogan.

The layout is pure Middle Ages: its three main streets—North, Market, and South—converge on the city's earliest religious site, near the
cathedral. Like most of the ancient monuments, the cathedral ruins are
impressive in their desolation—but this town is no dusty museum. The

streets are busy, the shops are stylish, the gray houses sparkle in the sun, and the scene is particularly brightened during the academic year by bicycling students in scarlet gowns.

GETTING HERE AND AROUND

If you arrive by car, be prepared for an endless drive round the town as you look for a parking space. The parking lots around Rose Park (behind the bus station and a short walk from the town center) are your best bet. If you arrive by local or national bus, the bus station is a five-minute walk from town. The nearest train station, Leuchars, is 10 minutes away by taxi (£15) or bus (£3), both of which can be found outside the station. St. Andrews can be fully enjoyed on foot without too much exertion.

ESSENTIALS

Visitor Information St. Andrews. ✉ *70 Market St.* ☎ *01334/472021* ⊕ *www. visitstandrews.com.*

EXPLORING

Fodor's Choice
★
Bell Pettigrew Museum of Natural History. Founded by Elsie Bell Pettigrew in memory of her husband James, a former professor of medicine, this fascinating collection of zoological specimens takes you from sea to jungle, mountain to sky. The antiquated manner of their presentation reminds you of their significance in an age when most of these creatures were still unknown to most people. In the handsome 16th-century St. Mary's Quadrangle, home to the St. Andrews University's divinity and psychology departments, it is dominated by a holm oak supposedly planted by Mary, Queen of Scots. ✉ *Bute Medical Bldg., Queens Gardens, off South St.* ☎ *01334/463608* ⊕ *www.st-andrews.ac.uk/museum/bellpettigrew* ✉ *Free.*

British Golf Museum. Just opposite the Royal & Ancient Golf Club, this museum explores the centuries-old relationship between St. Andrews and golf and displays golf memorabilia from the 18th century to the 21st century. ✉ *Bruce Embankment* ☎ *01334/460046* ⊕ *www.british-golfmuseum.co.uk* ✉ *£8.*

St. Andrews Castle. On the shore north of the cathedral stands ruined St. Andrews Castle, begun at the end of the 13th century. The remains include a rare example of a cold and gruesome bottle-shape dungeon, in which many prisoners spent their last hours. Even more atmospheric is the castle's mine and countermine. The former was a tunnel dug by besieging forces in the 16th century; the latter, a tunnel dug by castle defenders in order to meet and wage battle belowground. You can stoop and crawl into this narrow passageway—an eerie experience, despite the addition of electric light. The visitor center has a good audiovisual presentation on the castle's history. In the summer, the beach below is popular with sunbathers and tide-pool investigators, weather permitting. ✉ *N. Castle St.* ☎ *01334/477196* ⊕ *www.historicenvironment.scot* ✉ *£6, £9 with St. Andrews Cathedral and St. Rule's Tower.*

St. Andrews Cathedral. These are the poignant remains of what was once the largest and most magnificent church in Scotland. Work on it began in 1160, and after several delays it was finally consecrated in 1318. The church was subsequently damaged by fire and repaired, but fell

St. Andrews is famous for golf, but its ruined castle by the sea and other sights are well worth a look.

into decay during the Reformation. Only ruined gables, parts of the nave's south wall, and other fragments survive. The on-site museum helps you interpret the remains and gives a sense of what the cathedral must once have been like. ✉ *Off Pends Rd.* ☎ *01334/472563* ⊕ *www. historicenvironment.scot* ✉ *£5, includes St. Rule's Tower; £9 includes St. Andrews Castle.*

St. Rule's Tower. Local legend has it that St. Andrews was founded by St. Regulus, or Rule, who, acting under divine guidance, carried relics of St. Andrew by sea from Patras in Greece. He was shipwrecked on this Fife headland and founded a church. The holy man's name survives in the cylindrical tower, consecrated in 1126 and the oldest surviving building in St. Andrews. Enjoy dizzying views of town from the top of the tower, reached via a steep staircase. ✉ *Off Pends Rd.* ☎ *01334/472563* ⊕ *www.historicenvironment.scot* ✉ *£5, includes St. Andrews Cathedral; £9 includes St. Andrews Castle.*

University of St. Andrews. Scotland's oldest university is the alma mater of John Knox (Protestant reformer), King James II of Scotland, the Duke and Duchess of Cambridge (William and Kate), and Chris Hoy, Scotland's Olympic cyclist. Founded in 1411, the university's buildings pepper the town. For the quintessential University of St. Andrews experience, **St. Salvator's Quadrangle** reveals the magnificence of this historic institution. Looking out onto this impressive college green is the striking St. Salvator's Chapel, founded in 1450. It bears the marks of a turbulent past: the initials PH, carved into the paving stones under the bell tower, are those of Patrick Hamilton, who was burned alive outside the chapel for his Protestant beliefs. ✉ *St. Mary's Pl.*

WHERE TO EAT

$$$$ CONTEMPORARY Fodor's Choice ★ 🍴 **The Grange Inn.** Fife foodies flock to this beautifully converted 17th-century farmhouse surrounded by verdant fields just 10 minutes outside town. The atmospheric, dark-beamed, stone-walled interior has the warmth of an open fire and stunning views over the green landscape and St. Andrews. **Known for:** stunning location; great lunch deals; quality Scots produce. [$] *Average main: £30* ✉ *Grange Rd.* ☎ *01334/472670* 🌐 *www.thegrangeinn.com* 🕒 *Closed Mon. No dinner Sun.*

$ SEAFOOD 🍴 **Tailend Restaurant.** The line of customers outside might be a bit off-putting, but just focus on the sweet smell of fish-and-chips from St. Andrews's best chipper. There's a light-filled dining room and modish seating area, or you can carry out and eat on the university grounds (though be wary of the dive-bombing gulls). **Known for:** the best fish-and-chips in St. Andrews; Arbroath smokies. [$] *Average main: £13* ✉ *130 Market St.* ☎ *01334/474070* 🌐 *www.thetailend.co.uk.*

$ MODERN BRITISH FAMILY 🍴 **West Port Bar & Kitchen.** It's easy to forget that St. Andrews is a university town when the students are on summer break, but this modern bar and eatery remains vibrant and youthful year-round. The reasonably priced menu offers decent modern pub grub—everything from gourmet burgers to smoked haddock fishcakes to pork T-bone—making this a satisfying stop for lunch or dinner. **Known for:** lively beer garden; decent pub grub. [$] *Average main: £14* ✉ *170 South St.* ☎ *01334/473186* 🌐 *www.thewestport.co.uk.*

WHERE TO STAY

$$$$ HOTEL 🏨 **Fairmont St Andrews.** Two miles from St. Andrews, this modern hotel has spectacular views of the bay and two superb golf courses. **Pros:** spacious feel; excellent spa; golf at your doorstep. **Cons:** the huge atrium feels like a shopping center; paintings made to match the decor. [$] *Rooms from: £288* ✉ *A917* ☎ *01334/837000* 🌐 *www.fairmont.com/standrews* 🛏 *209 rooms* 🍽 *Free breakfast.*

$$ HOTEL 🏨 **Macdonald Rusacks.** The grand Victorian hotel building with grandstand views of the Old Course's 18th hole and West Sands offers affordable luxury and an unstuffy atmosphere. **Pros:** fabulous views; affordable food options; golf enthusiasts' heaven. **Cons:** service can fall short; bathrooms and bedroom decor lacks the wow factor. [$] *Rooms from: £150* ✉ *Pilmour, The Links* ☎ *0344/879–9136* 🌐 *www.macdonaldhotels.co.uk* 🛏 *70 rooms* 🍽 *Free breakfast.*

$$$$ HOTEL Fodor's Choice ★ 🏨 **Old Course Hotel.** Regularly hosting international golf stars and jet-setters, the Old Course Hotel has undergone a renaissance in the last five years—the guest rooms and public spaces have been reinvigorated, and the service has warmed up. **Pros:** fabulous location and lovely views; unpretentious service; golfer's heaven. **Cons:** all the golf talk might bore nongolfers; spa is on the small side; expensive. [$] *Rooms from: £399* ✉ *Old Station Rd.* ☎ *01334/474371* 🌐 *www.oldcoursehotel.co.uk* 🛏 *179 rooms* 🍽 *Free breakfast.*

$$$$ HOTEL 🏨 **Rufflets Country House Hotel.** Ten acres of formal and informal gardens surround this vine-covered country house just outside St. Andrews. **Pros:** attractive gardens; cozy drawing room; popular restaurant. **Cons:** too far to walk to St. Andrews; it's a venue for those celebrating. [$] *Rooms*

from: £230 ⊠ *Strathkinness Low Rd.* ☎ *01334/472594* ⊕ *www.rufflets. co.uk* ⮠ *23 rooms* ⎮○⎮ *Free breakfast.*

NIGHTLIFE AND PERFORMING ARTS

Central Bar. There are still some old-fashioned pubs to be found among the cocktail bars of St. Andrews, and this wood-and-leather-furnished haunt is a good bet for a friendly mingle with a pint in hand. You'll find a good range of beers (bottled and on tap) and decent pub food. ⊠ *77 Market St.* ☎ *01334/478296.*

SHOPPING

Artery. This well-curated shop sells work by local, Scottish, and British artists, including jewelry, ceramics, paintings, and intriguing handmade clocks. ⊠ *183 South St.* ☎ *01334/473153* ⊕ *arterygifts.com.*

Balgove Larder. Here you'll discover a huge selection of Scottish items, from spurtles (for stirring your porridge) to tablet (sugary toffee) to big, thick sausages made in its butchery. Foodies should check out the monthly Night Market, while carnivores can follow their noses to the Steak Barn, where platters piled with huge hunks of beef and sausages are combined with twice-fried chips and onion rings. ⊠ *A91* ☎ *01334/898145* ⊕ *www.balgove.com.*

Mellis. This place is truly a cheese-lover's mecca. Look for a soft, crumbly local cheese called Anster. ⊠ *149 South St.* ☎ *01334/471410* ⊕ *www. mellischeese.net.*

Topping and Company Booksellers. This is a bibliophile's dream haunt, with high ceilings and alcoves lined with over 45,000 titles, knowledge-able staff, and frequent readings and literary events. ⊠ *7 Greyfriars Garden* ☎ *01334/585 111* ⊕ *www.toppingbooks.co.uk.*

GOLF

Eden Course. The aptly named Eden Course, designed in 1914 by Harry S. Colt, winds through inland fields bordered with lovely foliage. It's a bit more forgiving compared to other St. Andrews courses. ⊠ *West Sands Rd.* ⊕ *www.standrews.com* ▦ *£22–£45* ⛳ *18 holes, 6250 yards, par 70.*

Jubilee Course. This windswept course offers quite a challenge even for experienced golfers. When it opened in 1897 it was intended for beginners, but the popularity of its seaside location encouraged the powers that be to convert it into a championship course. Many golfers say the 15th hole is one of the best in the sport. ⊠ *West Sands Rd.* ⊕ *www. standrews.com* ▦ *£37–£75* ⛳ *18 holes, 6742 yards, par 72.*

Fodor'sChoice **Old Course.** Believed to be the oldest golf course in the world, the Old ★ Course was first played in the 15th century. Each year, more than 44,000 rounds are teed off, and no doubt most get stuck in one of its 112 bunkers. A handicap certificate and some very early morning waits for a possible tee off are required. ⊠ *West Sands Rd.* ⊕ *www.standrews. com* ▦ *£88–£175* ⛳ *18 holes, 6721 yards, par 72.*

16

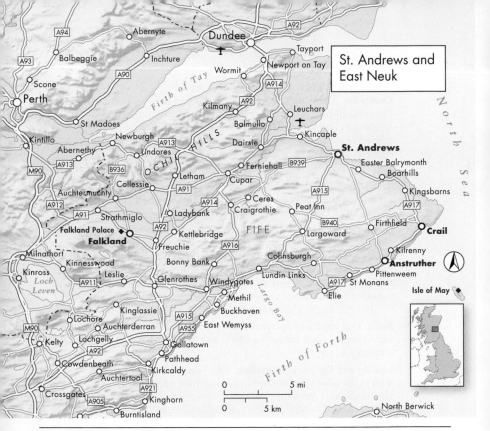

CRAIL

10 miles south of St. Andrews.

Fodor's Choice The oldest and most aristocratic of East Neuk burghs, pretty Crail is
★ where many fish merchants retired and built cottages. The town landmark is a picturesque Dutch-influenced town house, or *tolbooth*, which
contains the oldest bell in Fife, cast in Holland in 1520. Crail may now
be full of artists, but it remains a working harbor; take time to walk
the streets and beaches and to sample fish by the harbor. ■ TIP→ **As you
head into East Neuk from this tiny port, look about for market crosses,
merchant houses, and little doocots (dovecotes, where pigeons were
kept)—typical picturesque touches of this region.**

GETTING HERE AND AROUND
Stagecoach bus No. 95 operates between Crail and St. Andrews. This
service also takes you on to Anstruther, Pittenweem St. Monans, and
Lower Largo. Crail is about 15 minutes from St. Andrews by
car via A917.

EXPLORING
Crail Museum and Heritage Centre. The story of this trading and fishing
town can be found in the delightfully crammed Crail Museum and
Heritage Centre, entirely run by local volunteers. There is a small

tourist information desk within the center. ✉ *62–64 Marketgate* ☎ *01333/450869* 🌐 *www.crailmuseum.org.uk* 🎟 *Free* ⏲ *Closed Oct.–Mar. Limited hrs Apr. and May.*

WHERE TO EAT AND STAY

$$ SEAFOOD 🍴 **Lobster Hut.** This hut on the pier, a hidden gem, sells beautifully cooked lobsters for £12–£20 each (depending on size) and other items at times, including lobster rolls and dressed crab. They'll crack the lobster for you to allow for easy eating on a nearby bench; there is no seating, but the lobster is wonderful. **Known for:** freshest seafood; alfresco eating. [$] *Average main: £15* ✉ *34 Shoregate* ☎ *01333/450476* ⏲ *No dinner* 💳 *No credit cards.*

$ B&B/INN 🏨 **Hazelton.** Beautifully polished wood, exquisitely restored period features, and gentle hues put the Hazelton head and shoulders above the typical seaside B&B. **Pros:** handsome building; excellent location. **Cons:** a couple of rooms on the small side; unreliable communication via email. [$] *Rooms from: £85* ✉ *29 Marketgate N* ☎ *01333/450250* 🌐 *www.thehazelton.co.uk* ⏲ *Closed Jan.* 🛏 *5 rooms* 🍽 *Free breakfast.*

ANSTRUTHER

16

4 miles southwest of Crail.

Anstruther, locally called Ainster, has a lovely waterfront with a few shops brightly festooned with children's pails and shovels, a gesture to summer vacationers.

GETTING HERE AND AROUND

Stagecoach bus No. 95 operates between St. Andrews, Crail, Anstruther, Pittenweem, St. Monans, and Lower Largo. Anstruther is 5 to 10 minutes from Crail by car via A917.

EXPLORING

FAMILY **Isle of May Boat Trip.** Take to the waves on the compact *May Princess* for a round-trip to the Isle of May, a rocky bird reserve near the mouth of the Forth. Measuring just under a mile long and a third of a mile wide, it harbors 14 species of breeding birds including arctic terns, guillemots, and puffins. The round-trip takes five hours, with three hours on shore to explore the island's history, monastery remains, and the breathtaking sights, sounds, and smells of the avian multitudes. ✉ *Middle Pier, Anstruther Harbour* ☎ *07957/585200* 🌐 *www.isleofmayferry.com* 🎟 *£26.*

FAMILY Fodor's Choice ★ **Scottish Fisheries Museum.** Facing Anstruther Harbor, the Scottish Fisheries Museum is inside a colorful cluster of buildings, the earliest of which dates from the 16th century. A charming trail around the various buildings and odd spaces illustrates the life of Scottish fisherfolk: you can spend a couple of hours examining the many documents, artifacts, model ships, paintings, and displays (complete with the reek of tarred rope and net). There are floating exhibits at the quayside and a window onto a working boatyard. ✉ *Harbourhead* ☎ *01333/310628* 🌐 *www.scotfishmuseum.org* 🎟 *£9.*

WHERE TO EAT

$

SEAFOOD

Fodor's Choice

★

✕ **Anstruther Fish Bar and Restaurant.** Next door to the Scottish Fisheries Museum, this popular fish-and-chips shop has a functional space to eat, but most people order takeout. Try local specialties including Pittenweem prawns in batter or the catch of the day, which could be mackerel (line caught by the owners), hake, or local crab. **Known for:** best fish-and-chips in the East Neuk; friendly fryers. $ *Average main: £10* ✉ *42–44 Shore St.* ☎ *01333/310518* ⊕ *www.anstrutherfishbar.co.uk.*

$$$$

EUROPEAN

✕ **The Cellar.** Entered through a cobbled courtyard, this unpretentious, atmospheric restaurant has been run since 2014 by talented head chef Billy Boyter and family. The three-course prix-fixe meals feature locally sourced seafood and meat such as crab, hake, mussels, beef, lamb, and quail. **Known for:** elegant yet informal dining; exquisite produce; friendly service. $ *Average main: £60* ✉ *24 E. Green* ☎ *01333/310378* ⊕ *www.thecellaranstruther.co.uk* ⊘ *Closed Mon. and Tues. No lunch Wed.*

NIGHTLIFE AND PERFORMING ARTS

Dreel Tavern. A 16th-century coaching inn, the Dreel Tavern was resurrected and refurbished in 2017 by two sisters who have built on the characterful stone building and added some tasteful improvements. Alongside decent draft beers, there's now an excellent modern menu showcasing local produce such as lobster and smoked fish. The low-ceilinged wood-beamed bar makes for a lively atmosphere, especially during the low-key musical gigs that happen here. It's a fab beer garden for sunshine supping. ✉ *16 High St.* ☎ *01333/279238* ⊕ *www. dreeltavern.co.uk.*

FALKLAND

24 miles northwest of Pittenweem, 15 miles northwest of Elie.

Fodor's Choice

★

One of the loveliest communities in Scotland, Falkland is a royal burgh of twisting streets and crooked stone houses.

GETTING HERE AND AROUND

Stagecoach bus No. 64 is the only direct service connecting Falkland to St. Andrews as well as Cupar and Ladybank (both of which are train stations on the Edinburgh to Dundee line). Falkland is about 15 minutes from Cupar and a half hour from St. Andrews by car via A91 and A912, or A91 to A914 to A912.

EXPLORING

Falkland Palace. A former hunting lodge of the Stuart monarchs, Falkland Palace dominates the town. The castle is one of the country's earliest examples of the French Renaissance style. Overlooking the main street is the palace's most impressive feature, the walls and chambers on its south side, all rich with buttresses and stone medallions, built by French masons in the 1530s for King James V (1512–42). He died here, and the palace was a favorite resort of his daughter, Mary, Queen of Scots (1542–87). The beautiful gardens behind Falkland Palace contain a rare survivor: a royal tennis court, built in 1539. In the gardens, overlooked by the palace turret windows, you may easily imagine yourself back at the solemn hour when James on his deathbed pronounced the doom of the house of Stuart: "It cam' wi' a lass and it'll gang wi a lass." ✉ *Main St.* ☎ *01337/857397* 🌐 *www.nts.org.uk* 🎟 *£12.50* 🕒 *Closed Nov.–Feb.*

WHERE TO EAT

$ VEGETARIAN FAMILY Fodor's Choice ★ 🍴 **Pillars of Hercules.** Head down a country lane to this organic farm and café-bistro for a tasty vegetarian meal made of produce grown in the wonderful gardens. On a sunny day take your crepe or heaped salad to a bench outside by the nursery, or grab some take-away deli foods from the shop. **Known for:** organic food; inventive dishes; beautiful grounds. [$] *Average main: £7* ✉ *A912* ✛ *1 mile northwest of Falkland* ☎ *01337/857749* 🌐 *www.pillars.co.uk* 🕒 *No dinner.*

DUNDEE AND ANGUS

The small, friendly city of Dundee sits near the mouth of the River Tay surrounded by the farms and glens of rural Angus and the coastal grassy banks and golf courses of northeastern Fife. A vibrant, industrious, and cultural city, it's undergoing a postindustrial renaissance of sorts, with the V&A Museum as the centerpiece of the emerging waterfront regeneration. The first outpost of London's world-famous Victoria and Albert Museum, a repository of the decorative arts and design, is housed in a sculptural building jutting into Britain's most powerful river. Dundee is the United Kingdom's sole UNESCO City of Design, with a large student population, a lively arts and nightlife scene, and several historical and nautical sights.

Angus combines coastal agriculture on rich, red soils with dramatic inland glens that pierce their way into the foothills of the Grampian mountain range to the northwest. ■ **TIP→ The main road from Dundee to Aberdeen—the A90—requires special care with its mix of fast cars and unexpectedly slow farm traffic.**

16

DUNDEE

14 miles northwest of St. Andrews, 58 miles north of Edinburgh, 79 miles northeast of Glasgow.

Dundee makes an excellent base for a cultural stay and Fife and Angus exploration at any time of year. The Dundee Contemporary Arts center gave the city a much-needed boost in 1999; today artsy and foodie hangouts and a vibrant mix of student and creative life make it a beguiling stop. As you explore the streets and new waterfront, including the green expanse of Slessor Gardens, you may glimpse contrasting bold lines of the 2018 V&A Museum of Design, 1966 Tay Road Bridge, and 1888 Tay Rail Bridge. Those ever-changing views of the Tay led actor and wordsmith Stephen Fry to describe Dundee's setting as "ludicrously ideal." Heading southwest down cobbled Roseangle you reach Magdalen Green, where landscape artist James McIntosh Patrick (1907–98) found inspiration from the river and skyscapes. Dundonians' deadpan humor was distilled in the popular comic strips *The Beano* and *The Dandy,* first published here in the 1930s; statues by Scottish sculptors

Tony and Susie Morrow depicting characters Desperate Dan, Dawg, and a catapult-wielding Minnie the Minx are in City Square.

GETTING HERE AND AROUND

The East Coast train line runs through the city, linking it to Edinburgh (and beyond, to London), Glasgow (and the West Coast of England), and Aberdeen, with trains to all every hour or half hour at peak times. Cheaper bus service is available to all these locations, as well as St. Andrews and several other towns in Fife and Angus.

If you're traveling by car, the A92 will take you north from Fife to Abroath and the Angus coast towns. The A90, from Perth, heads north to Aberdeen.

Most of the sights in Dundee are clustered together, so you can easily walk around the city. If the weather is bad or your legs are heavy, hail one of the many cabs on the easy-to-find taxi ranks for little more than a few pounds.

ESSENTIALS

Visitor Information Angus and Dundee Tourist Board. ⊠ *16 City Sq.* ☎ *01382/527527* ⊕ *www.dundee.com, www.visitangus.com, www.visitscotland.com.*

EXPLORING

FAMILY **Dundee Botanic Garden.** This renowned botanical garden contains an extensive collection of native and exotic plants outdoors and in tropical and temperate greenhouses. There are some beautiful areas for picnicking, as well as a visitor center, an art gallery, and a coffee shop. ⊠ *Riverside Dr.* ☎ *01382/381190* ⊕ *www.dundee.ac.uk/botanic* ☑ *£3.90.*

FAMILY **Dundee Contemporary Arts.** Between a 17th-century mansion and a
Fodor's Choice cathedral, this strikingly modern building houses one of Britain's most
★ exciting artistic venues. The two galleries house five shows a year by internationally acclaimed contemporary artists. There are children's and adult's workshops, special events, and meet-the-artist events throughout the year. Two movie theaters screen mainly independent, revival, and children's films. There's also a craft shop and a buzzing café-bar that's open until midnight. ⊠ *152 Nethergate* ☎ *01382/909900* ⊕ *www.dca. org.uk* ☑ *Free.*

Fodor's Choice **McManus Galleries.** Dundee's principal museum and art gallery, housed
★ in a striking Gothic Revival–style building, has an engaging collection of artifacts that document the city's history and the working, social, and cultural lives of Dundonians throughout the Victorian period and the 20th century. Its varied fine art collection includes paintings by Rossetti, Raeburn, and Peploe as well as thought-provoking yet accessible contemporary works and visiting exhibitions, often in connection with London's Victoria and Albert Museum. ⊠ *Albert Sq.* ☎ *01382/432350* ⊕ *www.mcmanus.co.uk* ☑ *Free.*

FAMILY **RRS Discovery.** Dundee's urban-renewal program—the city is determined
Fodor's Choice to celebrate its industrial past—was motivated in part by the arrival of
★ the RRS (Royal Research Ship) *Discovery,* the vessel used by Captain Robert F. Scott (1868–1912) on his polar explorations. The steamer was originally built and launched in Dundee; now it's a permanent resident. At Discovery Point, under the handsome cupola, the story of the ship

and its famous expedition unfold; you can even feel the Antarctic chill as if you were there. The ship, berthed outside, is the star: wander the deck, then explore the quarters to see the daily existence endured by the ship's crew and captain. ✉ *Discovery Quay, Riverside Dr.* ☎ *01382/309060* 🌐 *www.rrsdiscovery.com* 🎟 *£9.25, £16 includes Verdant Works.*

Fodor's Choice ★ **V&A Museum of Design.** Scheduled to open in late 2018, the first outpost of the Victoria and Albert Museum of London is housed in an arresting riverside building by Japanese architect Kengo Kuma. Scotland's first-ever design museum contains seminal works and inspiring displays by Scots and international designers. The Scottish Design Galleries present the past, present, and future through the V&A collections and loans from around the world. Among the many highlights is Charles Rennie Mackintosh's Oak Room, unveiled for the first time in 50 years. Stellar shows, exclusively created for the new V&A galleries, spark inspiration among young and old. This "living room for the city," as Kuma described his design, is worth a visit for the building and setting alone: the vistas in and around its sea-cliff-like edges and perches provide places to linger, mingle, and reflect. ✉ *Discovery Quay* 🌐 *www.vandadundee.org* 🎟 *Free.*

16

FAMILY **Verdant Works.** In a former jute mill, Verdant Works houses a multifaceted exhibit on the story of jute and the town's involvement in the jute trade. Restored machinery, audiovisual displays, and tableaux all bring to life the hard, noisy life of the jute worker. A light and airy café serves lovely little cakes. ✉ *W. Hendersons Wynd* ☎ *01382/309060* 🌐 *www.verdantworks.com* 🎟 *£9.25, £16 includes RRS* Discovery 🕒 *Closed Mon. and Tues. Nov.–Mar.*

WHERE TO EAT

$$ FRENCH 🍴 **Cafe Montmartre.** A friendly and experienced culinary couple serve delicious French and Mediterranean dishes at this relaxed yet sophisticated eatery, bringing Parisian ganache and panache to the Perth Road. A refined but hearty menu has prix-fixe and à la carte options; baked and grilled fish and meat creations dominate, with classics like duck confit, escargot, and *moules marinière* mainstay favorites. **Known for:** relaxed yet professional service; reliable quality and value; need to book in advance. [$] *Average main: £15* ✉ *91 Perth Rd.* ☎ *01382/204417* 🌐 *www.cafemontmartre.co.uk* 🕒 *Closed Sun. and Mon.*

$$ BRITISH Fodor's Choice ★ 🍴 **Jute.** Downstairs at Dundee Contemporary Arts, this lively eatery serves breakfast at the bar, cocktails and snacks on the terrace in fine weather, or dinner in the open-plan dining area with huge windows that offer views of artists at work in the printmakers studio. There are plenty of handsomely presented dishes, featuring quality Scots meat, fish, and vegetables. **Known for:** open-plan dining in artsy atmosphere; great set-menu deals; busy bar on weekends. [$] *Average main: £15* ✉ *152 Nethergate* ☎ *01382/909246* 🌐 *www.jutecafebar.co.uk.*

$$$ TAPAS Fodor's Choice ★ 🍴 **Sol y Sombra Tapas Bar.** It looks like an old Scottish pub, and it is, but the tapas and sangria are so authentic they'll make you feel as if you're in España. There's no menu (you are asked if there is anything you don't like) and for £10 lunch or £23 dinner per head you'll be served a steady stream of cracking little dishes. **Known for:** boisterous atmosphere;

revelatory tapas. $ *Average main: £23* ⊠ *27 Gray St., Broughty Ferry* ☎ *01382/776941* ⊕ *solysombra.co.*

WHERE TO STAY

$$
B&B/INN

⛲ **Duntrune House.** Set among acres of tidy lawns and rustling trees, this mansion is a genteel contrast to the city. **Pros:** owners are keen genealogists and can offer advice to ancestor-seekers; the house and gardens are full of interest; tasty meals. **Cons:** might be too cluttered for some tastes; minimum two-night stay. $ *Rooms from: £110* ⊠ *Off A90, Duntrune* ✛ *5 miles northeast of Dundee* ☎ *01382/350239* ⊕ *www.duntrune-house.co.uk* ☉ *Closed Nov.–Feb.* ➣ *3 rooms* ⦿ *Free breakfast.*

$
HOTEL
Fodor's Choice
★

⛲ **Shaftesbury Lodge.** Just off the Perth Road, this Victorian-era villa set among well-tended shrubs is a find for those who like smaller, more intimate hotels. **Pros:** first-rate service; fresh, well-maintained rooms; close, but not too close, to the city. **Cons:** some bathrooms are small. $ *Rooms from: £90* ⊠ *1 Hyndford St.* ☎ *01382/669216* ⊕ *www.shaftesburylodge.co.uk* ➣ *12 rooms* ⦿ *Free breakfast.*

NIGHTLIFE AND PERFORMING ARTS

BARS AND PUBS

Dundee's pub scene, centered in the West End–Perth Road area, is one of the liveliest in Scotland.

Draffens. Secreted down a wynd (alley), this small speakeasy has stylish, exposed-brick interiors, with decorative nods to the defunct Draffens department store and muckle (a lot in Scots) cocktail shaking going on. ⊠ *Couttie's Wynd, Nethergate.*

Jute Cafe Bar. Better known as the bar at Dundee Contemporary Arts, this places attracts film fans (the art-house cinema's entrance is next door), students, and the well-heeled for European beers, wine, cocktails, or coffee. It serves tasty bar snacks every night until 9:30. ⊠ *152 Nethergate* ☎ *01382/909246* ⊕ *www.jutecafebar.co.uk.*

Fodor's Choice
★

Speedwell Bar. Called Mennie's by locals, the Speedwell Bar is in a mahogany-paneled building brimming with Dundonian characters and architectural features. It's renowned for its superb cask beers, choice of malts, and Edwardian interior. ⊠ *165–168 Perth Rd.* ☎ *01382/667783* ⊕ *www.speedwell-bar.co.uk.*

Fodor's Choice
★

Clarks on Lindsay Street. This busy bar hosts live music until the early hours. Get in early to avoid the lines. ⊠ *80 N. Lindsay St.* ☎ *01382/224925* ⊕ *www.clarksonlindsaystreet.com.*

THEATER

Fodor's Choice
★

Dundee Repertory Theatre. This is home to the award-winning Dundee Rep Ensemble and to Scotland's preeminent contemporary-dance group, Scottish Dance Theatre. Popular with locals, the restaurant and bar welcome late-night comedy shows and jazz bands. ⊠ *Tay Sq.* ☎ *01382/223530* ⊕ *www.dundeerep.co.uk.*

SHOPPING

COFFEE AND TEA

J. Allan Braithwaite. Established in 1868 and in its current home since 1932, this enticingly aromatic emporium has large old vats of many freshly roasted coffee blends and tea that you can pop into one of the quaint teapots you'll find here. ⊠ *6 Castle St.* ☎ *01382/322693.*

MUSIC

Fodor'sChoice **Groucho's Record Store.** Music lovers, film buffs, and the curious drop by
★ for some crate digging in this store founded by music and jukebox collector Alistair "Breeks" Brodie in 1976. The Victorian interior spins you right around with a dizzying display of rare vinyl, CDs, DVDs, books, T-shirts, and vintage audio supplies. It's also a great place to pick up info, flyers, and tickets for gigs and to chat about the local scene. ⊠ *132 Nethergate* ☎ *01382/228496* ⊕ *www.grouchos.co.uk.*

SPORTS AND THE OUTDOORS

GOLF

Camperdown Golf Course. For an alternative to the wild and windy east-coast links, try this magnificent municipal parkland course on the outskirts of Dundee. You can enjoy a game amid tree-lined fairways near the imposing Camperdown House. ■TIP→ On a fine night in June or July, try the Twilight Session. ⊠ *Camperdown Park, Coupar Angus Rd.* ☎ *01382/431820* ⊕ *www.golfdundee.com/camperdown-golf-course* ⌨ *£19–£27* ⅃. *18 holes, 6548 yards, par 71.*

Fodor'sChoice **Carnoustie Golf Links.** The venue for the British Open in 1999, 2007,
★ and 2018, the coastal links around Carnoustie have challenged golfers since at least 1527. Winners here have included many of the sport's biggest names: Armour, Hogan, Cotton, Player, and Watson. There are three courses, the most famous of which is the breathtaking Championship Course, ranked among the very best in the world. The choice Burnside course is full of historical interest and local color, as well as being tough and interesting. The Buddon course, designed by Peter Allis and Dave Thomas, is recommended for links novices. ⊠ *20 Links Parade, Carnoustie* ☎ *01241/802270* ⊕ *www.carnoustiegolflinks.co.uk* ⌨ *Championship, £175; Buddon, £46; Burnside, £46* ⅃. *Championship Course: 18 holes, 6948 yards, par 72; Buddon Course: 18 holes, 5921 yards, par 68; Burnside Course: 18 holes, 6028 yards, par 68* ⌂ *Reservations essential.*

THE ANGUS GLENS

25 miles northwest of Brechin.

You can rejoin the hurly-burly of the A90 for the return journey south from Montrose or Brechin; the more pleasant route, however, leads southwesterly on minor roads (there are several options) that travel along the face of the Grampians, following the fault line that separates Highland and Lowland. The **Angus Glens** extend north from points on A90. Known individually as the glens of Isla, Prosen, Clova, and Esk, these long valleys run into the high hills of the Grampians and some clearly marked walking routes. Those in Glen Clova are especially appealing.

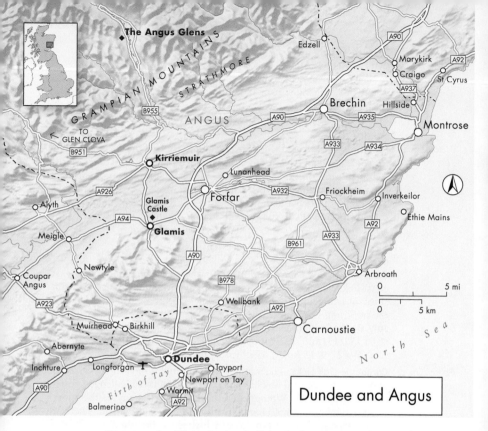

Dundee and Angus

Be aware that Thursday is a half day in Angus; many shops and attractions close at lunch.

GETTING HERE AND AROUND

You really need a car to reach the Angus Glens and enjoy the gentle (and not so gentle) inclines here. Glamis and Kirriemuir are both on the A928 (just off the A90), and the B955—which loops round at Glen Clova—is one of the loveliest Scottish roads to drive along, especially when the heather is blooming in late summer.

WHERE TO STAY

$$
HOTEL

Glen Clova Hotel. Since the 1850s, the hospitality of this hotel has lifted the spirits of many a bone-tired hill walker, and refurbishment and extension in 2016 have enhanced the comfort. **Pros:** stunning location; great base for outdoor pursuits; spacious accommodations. **Cons:** lack of decent public transportation; bar and live-music nights may be noisy. $ *Rooms from: £110* ✉ *B955, Glen Clova* ☎ *01575/550350* ⊕ *www. clova.com* ⇄ *10 rooms* ⦿ *Free breakfast.*

KIRRIEMUIR

15 miles southwest of Brechin.

Kirriemuir stands at the heart of Angus's red-sandstone countryside and was the birthplace of the writer J.M. Barrie (1860–1937), best known abroad as the author of *Peter Pan* (a statue of whom you can see in the town's square). *Kirrie,* as it's known here, salutes favorite son Bon Scott (1946–80)—the rasping AC/DC vocalist—in a bronze-and-Caithness-rock memorial statue at Bellies Brae. Metal pilgrims gather each springtime for Bonfest.

GETTING HERE AND AROUND

A number of roads lead to Kirriemuir, but A928 (off A90), which also passes Glamis Castle, is one of the loveliest. Stagecoach Strathtay runs buses to this area; Nos. 20 and 22 from Dundee are the most regular.

EXPLORING

FAMILY **Camera Obscura.** J. M. Barrie donated the Camera Obscura to the town. The device—a dark room with a small hole in one wall that projects an image of the outside world onto the opposite wall—is one of only four in the country. In a cricket pavilion, it affords magnificent views of the surrounding area on bright days. ⊠ *Kirrie Hill* ☎ *01575/575885* ⊕ *www.kirriemuircameraobscura.com* 🎫 *Free (donations welcome)* ⊘ *Closed Nov.–Mar., and weekdays in Apr.–June, Sept., and Oct.*

J.M. Barrie's Birthplace. At J. M. Barrie's Birthplace, the National Trust pays tribute to the man who sought to preserve the magic of childhood more than any other writer of his age. The house's upper floors are furnished as they might have been in Barrie's time, complete with domestic necessities, while downstairs is his study, replete with manuscripts and personal mementos. The outside washhouse is said to have served as Barrie's first theater. ⊠ *9 Brechin Rd.* ☎ *01575/572646* ⊕ *www.nts. org.uk/Property/J-M-Barries-Birthplace/* 🎫 *£6.50* ⊘ *Closed Oct.–Mar., Tues.–Fri. in Apr.–June and Sept., and Tues. and Wed. in July and Aug.*

Kirriemuir Gateway to the Glens Museum. As is the style in Angus, the local museum doubles as the visitor center, meaning you can get all the information you need and admire a few stuffed birds and artifacts at the same time. Rock fans will appreciate the exhibit celebrating local lad made good (or rather bad), the late Bon Scott, original lead singer of the rock band AC/DC. ⊠ *32 High St.* ☎ *01575/575479* ⊕ *archive. angus.gov.uk* 🎫 *Free* ⊘ *Closed Sun. and Mon.*

WHERE TO EAT

$ ✕ **88 Espresso.** If you're not in a rush (service can be slow), take time
CAFÉ to savor excellent coffee, inventive sandwiches, pizzettes, cakes, and
FAMILY handmade chocolates at this appealing café and shop selling quality fare. **Known for:** home baking including sourdough; handmade chocolates and truffles. 🅢 *Average main: £7* ⊠ *17 High St.* ☎ *07449/345089* ⊘ *Closed Mon. and Tues. No dinner* ▭ *No credit cards.*

16

GLAMIS

5 miles southwest of Forfar, 6 miles south of Kirriemuir.

Set in rolling countryside is the little village of Glamis (pronounced *glahms*), the highlight of which is nearby famous Glamis Castle.

GETTING HERE AND AROUND

The drive to Glamis Castle, along beech- and yew-lined roads, is as majestic as the castle itself. Take the A90 north from Dundee, then off onto the A928. The village of Glamis can be reached by the Stagecoach Strathtay No. 22, but service is rather infrequent.

EXPLORING

Fodor's Choice   **Glamis Castle.** One of Scotland's best known and most beautiful castles, ★ Glamis Castle connects Britain's royalty through 10 centuries, from Macbeth (Thane of Glamis) to the late Queen Mother and her daughter, the late Princess Margaret, born here in 1930 (the first royal princess born in Scotland in 300 years). The property of the earls of Strathmore and Kinghorne since 1372, the castle was largely reconstructed in the late 17th century; the original keep, which is much older, is still intact. One of the most famous rooms in the castle is Duncan's Hall, the legendary setting for Shakespeare's *Macbeth*. Guided tours allow you to see fine collections of china, tapestries, and furniture. Within the castle is the delightful Castle Kitchen restaurant; the grounds contain a huge gift shop, a shop selling local produce, and a pleasant picnic area. ■TIP➔ If you are looking to hear the pipes and see some Highland dancing and games of strength, the Strathmore Highland Games are held here around the second weekend of June. See www.strathmorehighlandgames.co.uk for more information. ✉ *A94* ✚ *1 mile north of Glamis* ☎ *01307/840393* ⊕ *www.glamis-castle.co.uk* ✑ *£12.50* ⊘ *Closed Nov.–Mar.*

ABERDEEN AND
THE NORTHEAST

WELCOME TO ABERDEEN AND THE NORTHEAST

TOP REASONS TO GO

★ **Castles:** With more than 75 castles, some Victorian and others dating back to the 13th century, this area has everything from ravaged ruins like Dunnottar to opulent Fyvie Castle.

★ **Distilleries:** The valley of the River Spey is famous for its single-malt distilleries, including those connected by the signposted Malt Whisky Trail. You can choose from bigger operations such as Glenfiddich to the iconic Strathisla, where Chivas Regal is blended.

★ **Seaside cities and towns:** The fishing industry may be in decline, but the big-city port of Aberdeen and the colorful smaller fishing towns of Stonehaven and Cullen in the northeast are great (and very different) places to soak up the seagoing atmosphere—and some seafood.

★ **Walking:** There are all types of walking for all kinds of walkers, from the bracing but spectacular inclines of the Grampian Hills to the wooded gardens and grounds of Balmoral and Haddo House.

Aberdeen, on the North Sea in the eastern part of the region, is Scotland's third-largest city; many people start a trip here. Once you have spent time in the city, you may be inclined to venture west into rural Deeside, with its royal connections and looming mountain backdrop. To the north of Deeside is Castle Country, with many ancient fortresses. Speyside and the Whisky Trail lie at the western edge of the region and are equally accessible from Inverness. From Speyside you might travel back east along the pristine coastline at Scotland's northeastern tip.

1 Aberdeen. Family connections or Royal Deeside often take travelers to this part of Scotland, but many are surprised by how grand and rich in history Aberdeen is. The august granite-turreted buildings and rose-lined roads make this a surprisingly pleasant city to explore; don't miss Old Aberdeen in particular.

2 Royal Deeside and Castle Country. Prince Albert designed Balmoral Castle for Queen Victoria, and so began the royal family's love affair with Deeside—and Deeside's love affair with it. However, this area has long been the retreat or the fortress of distinguished families, as the clutter of castles throughout the region shows. The

majesty of the countryside also guarantees a superlative stop for everyone interested in history and romance.

3 The Northeast and the Malt Whisky Trail. For lovers of whisky, this is a favored part of Scotland to visit. Unique in their architecture, their ingredients, and the end product, the distilleries of Speyside are keen to share with you their passion for "the water of life." This region also has rolling hills and, to the north, the beautiful, wild coastline of the North Sea.

17

Updated by
Robin Gauldie

Here, in this granite shoulder of Grampian, are some of Scotland's most enduring travel icons: Royal Deeside, the countryside that Queen Victoria made her own; the Castle Country route, where fortresses stand hard against the hills; and the Malt Whisky Trail, where peaty streams embrace the country's greatest concentration of distilleries. The region's gateway is the city of Aberdeen. Once a prosperous merchant port, it became a boomtown in the 1970s with the discovery of oil beneath the North Sea, but as oil and gas reserves dwindle the city is looking in new directions for its wealth.

More than 125 miles north of the central belt of Glasgow and Edinburgh, Aberdeen has historically been a fairly autonomous place. Even now it's perceived by many U.K. inhabitants as lying almost out of reach in the northeast. In reality, it's a 90-minute flight from London or a little more than two hours by car from Edinburgh. Its 18th- and early-19th-century city center amply rewards exploration. Yet even if this popular base for travelers vanished from the map, an extensive portion of the northeast would still remain at the top of many travelers' wish lists.

Balmoral, the Scottish baronial–style house built for Queen Victoria as a retreat, is merely the most famous castle in the area, and certainly not the oldest. There are so many others that in one part of the region a Castle Trail has been established. In later structures, such as Castle Fraser, you can trace the changing styles and tastes of each of their owners over the centuries. Grand mansions such as 18th-century Haddo House, with its symmetrical facade and elegant interior, surrender any defensive role entirely.

A trail leading to a more ephemeral kind of pleasure can be found south of Elgin and Banff, where the glens embrace Scotland's greatest concentration of malt-whisky distilleries. With so many in Morayshire, where the distilling is centered on the valley of the River Spey and its tributaries, there's now a Malt Whisky Trail. Follow it, and visit other distilleries as well, to experience a surprising wealth of flavors.

The northeast's chief topographical attraction lies in the gradual transition from high mountain plateau—by a series of gentle steps through hill, forest, and farmland—to the Moray Firth and North Sea coast, where the word "unadulterated" is redefined. Here you'll find some of the United Kingdom's most perfect wild shorelines, both sandy and sheer cliff, and breezy fishing villages like Cullen on the Banffshire coast and Stonehaven, south of Aberdeen. The Grampian Mountains, to the west, contain some of the highest ground in the nation, in the area of the Cairngorms. In recognition of this area's special nature, Cairngorms National Park was created in 2003.

PLANNER

WHEN TO GO
May and June are probably the loveliest times to visit, but many travelers arrive from late spring to early fall. The National Trust for Scotland tends to close its properties in winter, so many of the northeast's castles are not open for off-season travel, though you can always see them from the outside. The distilleries are open much of the year, but some close during winter months, so check before visiting.

PLANNING YOUR TIME
How you allocate your time may depend on your special interests—castles or whisky, for example. But even if you can manage only a morning or an afternoon, do not miss a walk around the granite streets of Old Aberdeen, and take in St. Nicholas Kirk and a pint in the Prince of Wales pub. A trip southward to the fishing town of Stonehaven and the breathtaking cliff-top fortress of Dunnottar makes a rewarding afternoon. Royal Deeside, with a good sprinkling of castles and grandeur, needs a good two days; even this might be tight for those who want to lap up every moment of majesty at Balmoral, Crathes, Fraser, and Fyvie, the best of the bunch. A visit to malt-whisky country should include tours of Glenfiddich, Glenfarclas, Glenlivet, and Glen Grant distilleries, and although it's not technically a maker of malt whisky, Strathisla. Real enthusiasts should allot two days for the distilleries, and they shouldn't pass up a visit to Speyside Cooperage, one of the few remaining cooperages in Scotland. Cullen and Duff House gallery in Banff, on the coast, can be done in a day before returning to Aberdeen.

GETTING HERE AND AROUND
AIR TRAVEL
The city is easy to reach from other parts of the United Kingdom as well as Europe. British Airways, bmi, Eastern Airways, EasyJet, Flybe, Loganair, and Ryanair are some of the airlines with service to other parts of Britain. Aberdeen Airport—serving both international and domestic flights—is in Dyce, 7 miles west of the city center on the A96 (Inverness). The drive to the center of Aberdeen is easy via the A96 (which can be busy during rush hour).

17

Airport Contact Aberdeen Airport. ⊠ *Dyce Dr., Dyce* ☏ *0844/481–6666* ⊕ *www.aberdeenairport.com.*

BOAT AND FERRY TRAVEL

Northlink Ferries has service between Aberdeen, Lerwick (Shetland), and Kirkwall (Orkney).

Boat and Ferry Contact Northlink Ferries. ⊠ *Jamieson's Quay, Aberdeen* ☏ *0845/600–0449* ⊕ *www.northlinkferries.co.uk.*

BUS TRAVEL

Long-distance buses run to Aberdeen from most parts of Scotland, England, and Wales. Contact Megabus, National Express, and Scottish Citylink for bus connections with English and Scottish towns. There's a network of local buses throughout the northeast run by Stagecoach, but they can take a long time and connections are not always well timed.

Bus Contacts Megabus. ☏ *0900/160–0900* ⊕ *uk.megabus.com.* **National Express.** ☏ *08717/818178* ⊕ *www.nationalexpress.com.* **Scottish Citylink.** ☏ *0871/266–3333* ⊕ *www.citylink.co.uk.* **Traveline.** ☏ *0871/200–2233* ⊕ *www. travelinescotland.com.*

CAR TRAVEL

A car is the best way to see the northeast. If you are coming from the south, take the A90, continuing on from the M90 (from Edinburgh) or the M9/A9 (from Glasgow), which both stop at Perth. The coastal route, the A92, is a more leisurely alternative, with its interesting resorts and fishing villages. The most scenic route, however, is the A93 from Perth, north to Blairgowrie and into Glen Shee. The A93 then goes over the Cairnwell Pass, the highest main road in the United Kingdom. This route isn't recommended in winter, when snow can make driving difficult.

Around the northeast roads can be busy, with speeding and erratic driving a problem on the main A roads.

TRAIN TRAVEL

You can reach Aberdeen directly from Edinburgh (2½ hours), Inverness (2½ hours), and Glasgow (3 hours). ScotRail timetables have full details. There are also London–Aberdeen routes that go through Edinburgh and the east-coast main line connecting Aberdeen to all corners of the United Kingdom. The Caledonian Sleeper, a luxury overnight train, runs nightly between London and Aberdeen, taking just over 10 hours.

Train Contact Caledonian Sleeper. ⊠ *Aberdeen railway station, Guild St., Aberdeen* ☏ *0330/060–0500* ⊕ *www.sleeper.scot.* **ScotRail.** ⊠ *Aberdeen railway station, Guild St., Aberdeen* ☏ *0344/811–0141* ⊕ *www.scotrail.co.uk.*

RESTAURANTS

As in much of the rest of Scotland, Aberdeen and the northeast have rediscovered the quality and versatility of the local produce. Juicy Aberdeen Angus steaks, lean lamb, and humanely reared pork appear on local menus, and there's a great choice of locally sourced seafood, from old-school fish-and-chips to dishes that fuse Mediterranean, Asian, and Latin influence. Traditional favorites like *Cullen skink* (a creamy smoked-fish soup) are on many menus. *Restaurant reviews have been shortened. For full information, visit Fodors.com.*

HOTELS

The northeast has some splendid country hotels with log fires and old Victorian furnishings, where you can also be sure of eating well. Many hotels in Aberdeen are in older buildings that have a baronial feel. The trend for serviced apartments has caught on here, with some extremely modish and good-value options for those who want a bit more privacy. This trend is now extending into Deeside, where it's been notoriously difficult to find good accommodations beyond some country-house hotels, even though it's a popular tourist spot. *Hotel reviews have been shortened. For full information, visit Fodors.com.*

WHAT IT COSTS IN POUNDS			
	$	**$$**	**$$$**	**$$$$**
Restaurants	under £15	£15–£19	£20–£25	over £25
Hotels	under £100	£100–£160	£161–£220	over £220

Restaurant prices are the average cost of a main course at dinner or, if dinner is not served, at lunch. Hotel prices are the lowest cost of a standard double room in high season, including 20% V.A.T.

VISITOR INFORMATION

The tourist information center in Aberdeen supplies information on all of Scotland's northeast. There are also year-round tourist information offices in Braemar and Elgin. In summer, also look for tourist information centers in Alford, Ballater, Banchory, Braemar, Elgin, and Stonehaven.

Contact Aberdeen Visitor Information Centre. ⊠ *23 Union St., Aberdeen* ☎ *01224/269180* ⊕ *www.visitscotland.com, www.visitabdn.com.*

17

ABERDEEN

As a gateway to Royal Deeside and the Malt Whisky Trail, Aberdeen attracts visitors, though many are eager to get out into the countryside. Today, though, the city's unique history is finally being recognized as more impressive than many Scots had previously realized, and Aberdeen is being rediscovered. Distinctive architecture, some fine museums, universities, and good restaurants, nightlife, and shopping add to the appeal of Scotland's third-largest city (population 217,000). Union Street is the heart of the city, but take time to explore the university and the pretty streets of Old Aberdeen.

In the 18th century local granite quarrying produced a durable silver stone that would be used boldly in the glittering blocks, spires, columns, and parapets of Victorian-era Aberdonian structures. The city remains one of the United Kingdom's most distinctive, although some would say it depends on the weather and the brightness of the day. The mica chips embedded in the rock look like a million mirrors in the sunshine. In rain (and there is a fair amount of driving rain from the North Sea) and heavy clouds, however, their sparkle is snuffed out.

The city lies between the Dee and Don rivers, with a working harbor that has access to the sea; it has been a major fishing port and is the main commercial port in northern Scotland. The North Sea has always been important to Aberdeen. In the 1850s the city was famed for its sleek, fast clippers that sailed to India for cargoes of tea. In the 1970s, exploitation of newly discovered offshore oil and gas turned Aberdeen into a world energy capital. As reserves dwindle and the oil industry winds down, the city is seeking new ways to diversify its economy.

GETTING HERE AND AROUND

AIR TRAVEL

Stagecoach Bluebird Jet Service 727 and First Aberdeen Bus 16 operate between the airport terminal and Union Square in the center of Aberdeen. Buses (£3.20 and £2.50 respectively) run frequently at peak times, less often at midday and in the evening; the journey time is approximately 40 minutes.

Dyce is on ScotRail's Inverness–Aberdeen route. The rail station is a short taxi ride from the terminal building (£10). Alternatively, the Jet Connect Service 80 operates between 6:06 am and 6:27 pm (£1.75). The ride takes 12 minutes, and trains run approximately every two hours.

BUS TRAVEL

First Aberdeen has easy and reliable service within the city of Aberdeen. Timetables are available from the tourist information center in Union Street.

Contact First Aberdeen. ☎ *01224/650000* ⊕ *www.firstgroup.com.*

CAR TRAVEL

Aberdeen is a compact city with good signage. Its center is Union Street, the main east–west thoroughfare, which tends to get crowded with traffic. Anderson Drive is an efficient ring road on the city's west side; be extra careful on its many traffic circles. It's best to leave your car in one of the parking garages (arrive early to get a space) and walk around, or use the convenient park-and-ride stop at the Bridge of Don, north of the city. Street maps are available from the tourist information center, newsstands, and booksellers.

TAXI TRAVEL

You can find taxi stands throughout the center of Aberdeen: at the railway station and at Back Wynd, Chapel Street, Dee Street, and Hadden Street. The taxis have yellow plates, meters, and might be saloon cars (sedans) or black cabs. They are great ways to travel between neighborhoods.

TRAIN TRAVEL

Aberdeen has good ScotRail service.

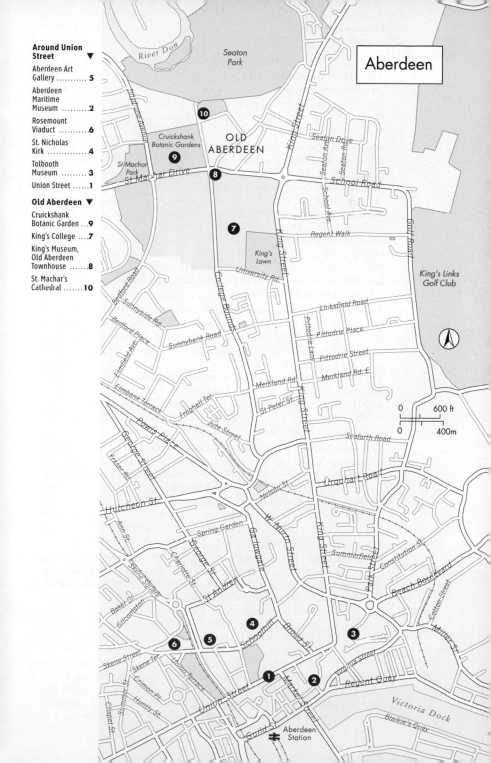

Aberdeen

EXPLORING

AROUND UNION STREET

Aberdeen centers on Union Street, with its many fine survivors of the Victorian and Edwardian streetscape. Marischal College, dating from the late 16th century, is a city-center landmark, and has many grand buildings that are worth exploring.

Aberdeen Art Gallery. The museum contains excellent paintings, prints, drawings, sculpture, porcelain, costumes, and much else—from 18th-century art to major contemporary British works by Lucien Freud and Henry Moore. Scottish artists are well represented in the permanent collection and special exhibits. Local stone has been used in interior walls, pillars, and the central fountain, designed by the acclaimed British sculptor Barbara Hepworth. Look for the unique collection of Aberdeen silver on the ground floor. The museum also has a cake-filled café and well-stocked gift shop. ■TIP→ Until the museum's reopening, some of the most important works in its collection can be seen at Drum Castle and in the Aberdeen Maritime Museum. ⊠ *Schoolhill* ☎ *01224/523700* ⊕ *www.aagm.co.uk* ✑ *Free.*

FAMILY
Fodor'sChoice
★

Aberdeen Maritime Museum. This excellent museum, which incorporates the 1593 Provost Ross's House, tells the story of the city's relationship with the sea, from early inshore fisheries to tea clippers and the North Sea oil boom. The information-rich exhibits include the bridge of a fishing boat and the cabins of a clipper, in addition to models, paintings, and equipment associated with the fishing, shipbuilding, and oil and gas industries. The Gateway to the North gallery on the top floor, installed in 2016, is a lively introduction to the archaeology of the region, with exhibits spanning the years 1136–1660. ⊠ *Ship Row* ☎ *01224/337700* ⊕ *www.aagm.co.uk* ✑ *Free* ⊙ *Closed Mon.*

Rosemount Viaduct. Three silvery, handsome buildings on this bridge are collectively known by all Aberdonians as Education, Salvation, and Damnation. The **Central Library** and **St. Mark's Church** date from the last decade of the 19th century, and **His Majesty's Theatre** (1904–08) has been restored inside to its full Edwardian splendor. If you're taking photographs, you can choose an angle that includes the statue of Scotland's first freedom fighter, Sir William Wallace (1270–1305), in the foreground pointing majestically to Damnation. ⊠ *Aberdeen.*

St. Nicholas Kirk. The original burgh church, the Mither Kirk, as this edifice is known, is not within the bounds of the early town settlement; that was to the east, near the end of present-day Union Street. During the 12th century the port of Aberdeen flourished, and there wasn't room for the church within the settlement. Its earliest features are its pillars—supporting a tower built much later—and its clerestory windows: both date from the 12th century. The East Kirk is closed for renovation work, which has been extended due to the discovery of numerous skeletons, mainly children, that date back to the 12th century; the post-excavation work can be viewed from a large window in the Drum's Aisle. In the chapel, look for Shona McInnes's stained-glass window commemorating the victims of the 1989 Piper Alpha oil-rig disaster and a glass case containing two books. One lists the names of all those who've lost their lives in the pursuit of oil exploration in the North Sea; the second is empty, a testament to the many "unknown" workers whose deaths were never officially recorded. ⊠ *Union St.* ☎ *01224/643494* ⊕ *www. kirk-of-st-nicholas.org.uk* ⊠ *Free, but donations welcome.*

FAMILY **Tolbooth Museum.** The city was governed from this 17th-century building, which was also the burgh court and jail, for 200 years. Now a museum of crime and punishment, highly entertaining tour guides take you around its cells and dungeons and bring life and death to the various instruments of torture—including the "Maiden," a decapitating machine—making it a must-see for older kids. ⊠ *Castle St.* ☎ *01224/621167* ⊕ *www.aagm.co.uk* ⊠ *Free.*

Union Street. This great thoroughfare is to Aberdeen what Princes Street is to Edinburgh: the central pivot of the city plan and the product of a wave of enthusiasm to rebuild the city in a contemporary style in the early 19th century. ⊠ *Aberdeen.*

OLD ABERDEEN

Very much a separate area of the city, Old Aberdeen is north of the modern center, clustered around St. Machar's Cathedral and the many fine buildings of the University of Aberdeen. Take a stroll on College Bounds; handsome 18th- and 19th-century houses line this cobbled street in the oldest part of the city.

Cruickshank Botanic Garden. Built on land bequeathed by Miss Anne Cruickshank in memory of her beloved brother Alexander, the 11-acre Cruickshank Botanic Garden at the heart of Old Aberdeen has a peaceful water garden and lush greens ideal for lounging—when the weather allows—and beautifully tended subtropical and alpine collections. Botanical tours are available. ⊠ *St. Machar Dr., at the Chanonry* ☎ *01224/272704* ⊕ *www.abdn.ac.uk/botanic-garden* ⊠ *Free.*

King's College. Founded in 1494, King's College is now part of the University of Aberdeen. Its **chapel,** built around 1500, has an unmistakable flying (or crown) spire. That it has survived at all was because of the zeal of the principal, who defended his church against the destructive fanaticism that swept through Scotland during the Reformation, when the building was less than a century old. Today the renovated chapel plays an important role in university life. Don't miss the tall oak screen that separates the nave from the choir, the ribbed wooden ceiling, and the stalls, as these constitute the finest medieval wood carvings found anywhere in Scotland. ⊠ *25 High St.* ☎ *01224/272137* ⊕ *www.abdn. ac.uk* ⊗ *Closed weekends.*

King's Museum, Old Aberdeen Townhouse. Across from the archway leading to King's College Chapel, this plain but handsome Georgian building was the center of all trading activity in the city before it became a grammar school, a Masonic lodge, and then a library. Now housing the university's museum, it hosts constantly changing exhibitions. It presents some impressive and often strange curiosities from the university's collection, from prehistoric flints to a tiger's penis. ⊠ *17 High St.* ☎ *01224/274300* ⊕ *www.abdn.ac.uk/kingsmuseum* ⊠ *Free* ⊗ *Closed Sun. and Mon.*

17

Fodor's Choice
★

St. Machar's Cathedral. It's said that St. Machar was sent by St. Columba to build a church on a grassy platform near the sea, where a river flowed in the shape of a shepherd's crook. This beautiful spot, now the still-beating heart of Old Aberdeen, fits the bill. Although the cathedral was founded in AD 580, most of the existing building dates from the 15th and 16th centuries. Built as a fortified kirk, its twin towers and thick walls give it a sturdy standing. The former can be seen up close by climbing the spiral staircases to the upper floors, which also affords an admirable view of the "body of the kirk" inside and graveyard outside. It lost its status as a cathedral during the Reformation and has since been part of the Church of Scotland. The stained-glass windows depicting the martyrdom of the saints and handsome heraldic ceiling are worth noting. ⊠ *Chanonry* ☎ *01224/485988* ⊕ *www. stmachar.com.*

WHERE TO EAT

$
BRITISH
FAMILY

✗ **Ashvale.** Ask anyone about this long-established place and the response will probably be overwhelmingly positive. Fish-and-chips is the specialty, and the secret-recipe batter is now the stuff of legend. **Known for:** perfectly crunchy battered cod; gluten-free options. $ *Average main: £12* ⊠ *42–48 Great Western Rd.* ☎ *01224/575842* ⊕ *theashvale.co.uk.*

$
BRITISH
FAMILY

✗ **Foodstory.** A friendly, homespun café-eatery, Foodstory pulls in a loyal crowd to graze on its healthy, freshly made breakfasts, lunches, and wonderful cakes. Expect organic breakfast and brunch choices such as superfood porridge, scones, Aberdeenshire bacon rolls, and Ellon pork sausage. **Known for:** oatmeal enriched with nuts, fruit, and berries; sinfully delicous bacon and sausage rolls. $ *Average main: £7* ⊠ *13–15 Thistle St.* ☎ *01224/611717* ⊕ *www.foodstorycafe.co.uk.*

$$$
SEAFOOD
Fodor's Choice
★

✗ **Silver Darling.** Huge windows overlook the harbor and beach at this quayside favorite in a former customshouse, long one of Aberdeen's most acclaimed restaurants. The French-inspired menu focuses on fish: try the crab bisque with samphire to start, then move on to a lavish seafood platter of scallops, mussels, langoustes, prawns, and cockles. **Known for:** classic seafood, sensitively prepared; French-inspired entrées. $ *Average main: £25* ⊠ *North Pier, Pocra Quay* ☎ *01224/576229* ⊕ *thesilverdarling.co.uk* ☾ *Closed Sun. No lunch Sat.*

WHERE TO STAY

$$
HOTEL

🏨 **Atholl Hotel.** With its many turrets and gables, this granite hotel recalls a bygone era but has modern amenities. **Pros:** family-run establishment; tasty restaurant; very pleasant staff. **Cons:** some rooms are a little generic; some bathrooms need updating. $ *Rooms from: £145* ⊠ *54 Kings Gate* ☎ *01224/323505* ⊕ *www.atholl-aberdeen.com* ⇨ *34 rooms* ⏁❘ *Free breakfast.*

$
B&B/INN

🏨 **The Jays Guest House.** Alice Jennings or her husband, George, will greet you at the front door of this granite house, a homey bed-and-breakfast they've run for more than 30 years. **Pros:** immaculate rooms; expert advice on city's sites; near Old Aberdeen and the university. **Cons:** no public areas; popular so book ahead. $ *Rooms from: £52* ✉ *422 King St.* ☎ *01224/612771* ⊕ *www.jaysguesthouse. co.uk* ⬅ *10 rooms* ⦿ *Free breakfast.*

$
HOTEL
Fodor'sChoice
★

◻ **Malmaison.** Part of a British minichain, this boutique hotel with fabulously comfy rooms and suites—some with terraces from which you can watch the sunset—sets the standard by which all rivals in Aberdeen are judged. **Pros:** stylish rooms; excellent restaurant; delightful staff; spa and minigym. **Cons:** not very central. $ *Rooms from: £89* ✉ *45–93 Queen's Rd.* ☎ *01224/507097* ⊕ *www.malmaison.com/locations/aberdeen* ⬅ *77 rooms* ⦿ *All-inclusive.*

NIGHTLIFE AND PERFORMING ARTS

Aberdeen has a fairly lively nightlife scene revolving around pubs and clubs. Theaters, concert halls, arts centers, and cinemas are also well represented. The principal newspapers—the *Press and Journal* and the *Evening Express*—and *Aberdeen Leopard* magazine can fill you in on what's going on anywhere in the northeast. Aberdeen's tourist information center has a monthly publication with an events calendar.

NIGHTLIFE

BARS AND PUBS

BrewDog. Aberdeen's pioneering craft brewery turned global brand runs its flagship bar with suitable gusto and no lack of style. A bare-brick warehouse interior with lots of steel means there's lots of noise and chatter flying around the cavernous space, oiled by a choice of over 100 craft beers. ✉ *17 Gallowgate* ☎ *01224/631223* ⊕ *www.brewdog.com.*

Cellar 35. This intimate bar and club space (capacity 80) is known for its almost nightly live music, DJ sets, and comedy. ✉ *35 Rosemount Viaduct* ☎ *01224/640483* ⊕ *www.thenooseandmonkey.com.*

Old Blackfriars. With a nice location near the end of Union Street, Old Blackfriars has dim lighting and a big fireplace to warm things up on a chilly evening, although it can get crowded as the night goes on. This cask-ale pub has a great selection—Belhaven St. Andrews Ale and Caledonian 80 top the list. ✉ *52 Castle St.* ☎ *01224/581922* ⊕ *www. oldblackfriars-aberdeen.co.uk.*

The Prince of Wales. Dating from 1850, the Prince of Wales has retained its paneled walls and wooden tables. Still regarded as Aberdeen's most traditional pub, it's hardly regal, but good-quality food and reasonable prices draw the regulars back. ✉ *7 St. Nicholas La.* ☎ *01224/640597* ⊕ *www.princeofwales-aberdeen.co.uk.*

SHOPPING

Fodor'sChoice
★

Aitkens. You can't leave Aberdeen without trying one of its famous *rowies* (or *butteries*), the fortifying morning roll. Aitkens Bakery is considered the finest purveyor of this local speciality. ✉ *14–16 Menzies Rd.* ☎ *01224/899124* ⊕ *www.aitkens-bakery.co.uk/the-bakery.*

17

Alex Scott & Co. For Scottish kilts, tartans, crests, and other traditionally Scottish clothes (including a stunning "Scotland" hoodie), a good place to start is Alex Scott & Co. ⊠ *43 Schoolhill* 🕾 *01224/674874* ⊕ *www. kiltmakers.co.uk.*

Books and Beans. This independent bookshop has its own Internet café (one of the few surviving such places in the city center) and sells a good range of flavored coffees. You're welcome to browse, sip, and surf the Web at the same time. ⊠ *22 Belmont St.* 🕾 *01224/646438* ⊕ *www. booksandbeans.co.uk.*

Candle Close Gallery. This shop has some strange and wonderful mirrors, clocks, ceramics, and jewelry that you're unlikely to see elsewhere. ⊠ *123 Gallowgate* 🕾 *01224/624940* ⊕ *www.candleclose-gallery.co.uk.*

Peapod. Check out vintage and retro clothing and housewares: think Bakelite, chichi cups and saucers, and 1920s cocktail dresses. ⊠ *144 Rosemount Pl.* 🕾 *01224/874087.*

Fodor's Choice ★ **Teasel & Tweed.** If you are in need of a Harris tweed iPod cover, this is your place. All manner of housewares and accessories made by Scottish designers and craftspeople are on offer. Downstairs Ti (formerly Yvi's House of Tea) serves delicious waffles and connoisseur teas. ⊠ *85 Rosemount Viaduct* 🕾 *01224/652352.*

SPORTS AND THE OUTDOORS

GOLF

Murcar Links Golf Club. Sea views and a variety of rugged terrain—from sand dunes to tinkling burns—are the highlights of this course, founded in 1909. It's most famous for breathtaking vistas at the 7th hole, appropriately called the Serpentine. Designer Archibald Simpson considered this course to be one of his finest. ⊠ *Bridge of Don* 🕾 *01224/704354* ⊕ *www.murcarlinks.com* ⬚ *£105 weekdays, £130 weekends* 🏌 *18 holes, 6314 yards, par 73.*

Fodor's Choice ★ **Royal Aberdeen Golf Club.** This venerable club, founded in 1780, is the archetypal Scottish links course: tumbling over uneven ground, with the frequently added hazard of sea breezes. Prickly gorse is inclined to close in and form an additional hurdle. The two courses are tucked behind the rough, grassy sand dunes, and there are surprisingly few views of the sea. One historical note: in 1783 this club originated the five-minute-search rule for a lost ball. A handicap certificate and letter of introduction are required. Visitors are only allowed on weekdays. ⊠ *Links Rd., Bridge of Don* 🕾 *01224/702571* ⊕ *www.royalaberdeen-golf.com* ⬚ *Balgownie, £172; Silverburn, £70* 🏌 *Balgownie: 18 holes, 6900 yards, par 71; Silverburn: 18 holes, 4021 yards, par 64* ⌁ *Reservations essential.*

ROYAL DEESIDE AND CASTLE COUNTRY

Deeside, the valley running west from Aberdeen down which the River Dee flows, earned its "royal" appellation when discovered by Queen Victoria. To this day, where royalty goes, lesser aristocracy and freshly minted millionaires follow. Many still aspire to own a grand shooting estate in Deeside, and you may appreciate this yearning when you see the piney hills, purple moors, and blue river intermingling. As you travel deeper into the Grampian Mountains, Royal Deeside's gradual scenic change adds a growing sense of excitement.

There are castles along the Dee as well as to the north in Castle Country, another region that illustrates the gradual geological change in the northeast: uplands lapped by a tide of farms. All the Donside and Deeside castles are picturesquely sited, with most fitted out with tall, slender turrets, winding stairs, and crooked chambers that epitomize Scottish baronial style. All have tales of ghosts and bloodshed, siege and torture. Many were tidied up and "domesticated" during the 19th century. Although best toured by car, much of this area is accessible either by public transportation or on tours from Aberdeen.

STONEHAVEN

15 miles south of Aberdeen.

Stonehaven's golden sands made this historic town near spectacular Dunnottar Castle a popular holiday destination, until Scots began vacationing in sunnier climates. The surrounding red-clay fields were made famous by Lewis Grassic Gibbon (real name James Leslie Mitchell), who attended school in the town and wrote the seminal Scottish trilogy *A Scots Quair,* about the people, the land, and the impact of World War I. Stonehaven is now famous for its Hogmanay (New Year's Eve) celebrations, where local men swing huge balls of fire on chains before tossing them into the harbor, and as the birthplace of a quirky Scots delicacy, the deep-fried Mars bar.

GETTING HERE AND AROUND

Most trains heading south from Aberdeen stop at Stonehaven; there's at least one per hour making the 15-minute trip. Stagecoach Bluebird runs bus services between Stonehaven and Aberdeen; the fastest, the X70, takes around 40 minutes. Drivers should take A90 south and turn off at A957.

ESSENTIALS

Visitor Information Stonehaven Visitor Information Centre. ⊠ *66 Allardyce St.* ☎ *01569/762806* ⊕ *www.visitscotland.com.*

EXPLORING

Fodor'sChoice **Dunnottar Castle.** It's hard to beat the cinematic majesty of the magnificent cliff-top ruins of Dunnottar Castle, with its panoramic views of the
★ North Sea. Building began in the 14th century, when Sir William Keith, Marischal of Scotland, decided to build a tower house to demonstrate his power. Subsequent generations added to the structure, and important visitors included Mary, Queen of Scots. The castle is most famous

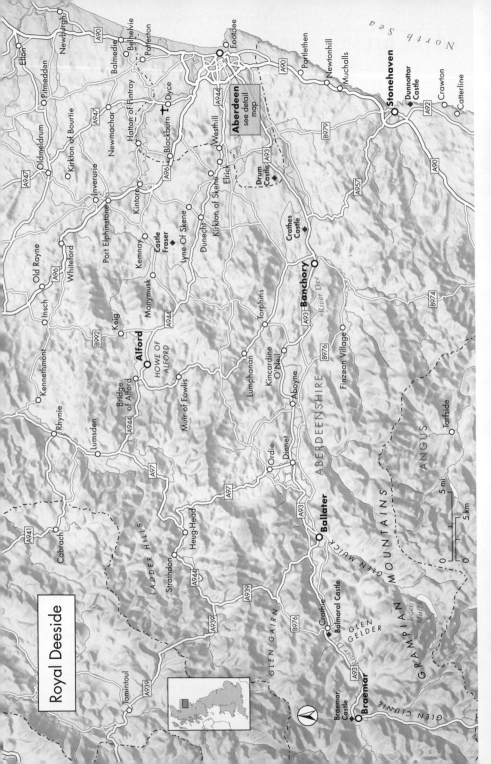

for holding out for eight months against Oliver Cromwell's army in 1651 and 1652, thereby saving the Scottish crown jewels, which had been stored here for safekeeping. Reach the castle via the A90; take the Stonehaven turnoff and follow the signs. Wear sensible shoes, and allow about two hours. ✉ *Off A92* ☎ *01569/762173* 🌐 *www.dunnottarcastle.co.uk* 🎫 *£7.*

FAMILY **Stonehaven Open-Air Swimming Pool.** A vintage art deco gem, Stonehaven Open-Air Swimming Pool is the only remaining outdoor heated pool in Scotland. Seawater is pumped in and warmed up to a balmy 29°C (82°F). Run by a local trust, this place is perfect for families. Wednesday's midnight swims (£7.10) let you float under the stars. ✉ *Queen Elizabeth Park, off A90* ☎ *01569/762134* 🌐 *www.stonehavenopenairpool.co.uk* 🎫 *£5.40* 🕒 *Closed Oct.–May.*

WHERE TO EAT AND STAY

$$ SEAFOOD 🍴 **The Ship Inn.** This former coaching inn is exactly where you want to take nourishment after a bracing walk from Dunnottar Castle. Refurbishment has taken away much of the history, but wood paneling and rattan chairs make it comfortable, and huge new windows provide views of the harbor. **Known for:** knowledgeably prepared harbor-fresh seafood; tempting Scottish desserts. [$] *Average main: £16* ✉ *5 Shore Head* ☎ *01569/762617* 🌐 *www.shipinnstonehaven.com.*

$$ B&B/INN 🏨 **Bayview B&B.** This contemporary bed-and-breakfast couldn't be in a more convenient location or have better views. **Pros:** spic-and-span rooms; right on the beach; fresh, modern design. **Cons:** standard rooms are smallish. [$] *Rooms from: £125* ✉ *Beachgate La.* ✥ *On the beach, down the lane from the town square* ☎ *07791/224227* 🌐 *www.bayviewbandb.co.uk* 🛏 *4 rooms* 🍽 *Free breakfast.*

SHOPPING

FAMILY **Aunty Betty's.** Even if the weather is lousy, this coffee, sweets, and ice-cream shop confirms you are on your summer holidays. Grown-ups will love the gin-and-tonic or champagne sorbets, kids the complimentary sprinkles. ✉ *The Promenade* ☎ *01569/763656.*

BANCHORY

15 miles west of Stonehaven, 19 miles west of Aberdeen.

Banchory is an immaculate town filled with pinkish granite buildings. It's usually bustling with ice-cream-eating strollers, out on a day trip from Aberdeen. Nearby are Crathes and Drum castles.

GETTING HERE AND AROUND

A car is by far the best way to get around the area; A93 is one of the main roads connecting the towns.

For those reliant on public transport, Stagecoach buses operate a number of services for towns along or just off A93 (Drum Castle, Banchory, Kincardine, Aboyne, Ballater, Balmoral, and Braemar).

ESSENTIALS

Visitor Information **Banchory Visitor Information Centre.** ✉ *Bridge St.* ☎ *01330/822000* 🌐 *www.visitbanchory.com.*

17

A cliff-top setting by the North Sea gives ruined Dunnottar Castle spectacular views.

EXPLORING

FAMILY

Fodor'sChoice

★

Crathes Castle. About 16 miles west of Aberdeen, Crathes Castle was once the home of the Burnett family and is one of the best-preserved castles in Britain. Keepers of the Forest of Drum for generations, the family acquired lands here by marriage and later built a castle, completed in 1596. The National Trust for Scotland cares for the castle, which is furnished with many original pieces and family portraits. Outside are grand yet lovingly tended gardens with calculated symmetry and flower-rich beds. Make sure you browse the Horsemill bookshop and sample the tasty baked goods in the tearoom. There's an adventure park for kids, and the staff organizes activities that are fun and educational. ⊠ Off A93 ☎ 01330/844525 ⊕ www.nts.org.uk 🖃 £12.50 ⊗ Closed weekdays Nov.–Mar.

Fodor'sChoice

★

Drum Castle. This foursquare tower has an evocative medieval chapel that dates from the 13th century; like many other castles, it also has later additions up to Victorian times. Note the tower's rounded corners, said to make battering-ram attacks more difficult. Nearby, fragments of the ancient Forest of Drum still stand, dating from the days when Scotland was covered by great stands of oak and pine. The Garden of Historic Roses, open from April to October, lays claim to some old-fashioned roses not commonly seen today. ⊠ Drumoak, by Banchory ✛ Off the A93, 8 miles east of Banchory and 11 miles west of Aberdeen ☎ 01330/700334 ⊕ www.nts.org.uk 🖃 £12.50 ⊗ Closed weekdays Oct.–Mar.; closed Tues. and Wed. in Apr.–June and Sept.

WHERE TO STAY

$ **Banchory Lodge.** Right on the River Dee, this Georgian lodge offers the
HOTEL   lovely touches you expect at a luxury hotel, but at a moderate cost. **Pros:**
Fodor's Choice   a warm welcome; great bar; excellent food and afternoon teas. **Cons:**
★   popular for weddings. $ *Rooms from: £69* ✉ *Dee St.* ☎ *01330/822625*
⊕ *www.banchorylodge.com* ⇄ *28 rooms* ❍❘ *Free breakfast.*

BALLATER

25 miles west of Banchory, 43 miles west of Aberdeen.

The handsome holiday resort of Ballater, once noted for the curative
properties of its waters, has profited from the proximity of the royals,
nearby at Balmoral Castle. You might be amused by the array of "by
royal appointment" signs proudly hanging from many of its various
shops (even monarchs need bakers and butchers).

The locals have long taken the town's royal connection in stride. To this
day, the hundreds who line the road when the Queen and her family
arrive for services at the family's parish church at Crathie are invariably
visitors to Deeside—one of Balmoral's attractions for the monarch has
always been the villagers' respect for royal privacy.

GETTING HERE AND AROUND

There's good train service to Aberdeen, but you'll need to catch a bus
to get to this and other towns near A93. Stagecoach Bluebird Buses
201 and 202 operate hourly to all the main towns, including Ballater.
Otherwise, it's an easy car trip.

ESSENTIALS

Visitor Information Ballater Visitor Information Centre. ✉ *Albert Memorial
Hall, Station Sq.* ☎ *01339/755306* ⊕ *www.visitscotland.com.*

EXPLORING

Fodor's Choice   **Balmoral Castle.** The British royal family's favorite vacation spot is a
★   fabulous fake-baronial pile, with emphasis on the "fake." Compared
with Scotland's most authentic castles, Balmoral is a right royal upstart,
designed in the 19th century by Queen Victoria's German-born consort,
Prince Albert. That doesn't stop it being one of Scotland's most visited
castles, though only the formal gardens, the ballroom, and the carriage
hall, with their exhibitions of royal artifacts, commemorative china, and
stuffed native wildlife, are on view.

When members of the royal family are in residence, usually from mid-
August to the end of September, Balmoral is closed to visitors, including
the grounds. You can take a guided tour in November and December;
if the weather is crisp and bright, the estate is at its most dramatic and
romantic. You're only allowed a peek inside, but the Royal Cottage is
where Queen Victoria spent much of her time. You can see the table
where she took breakfast and wrote her correspondence.

Around and about Balmoral are some notable spots—Cairn O'Mount,
Cambus O'May, and the Cairngorms from the Linn of Dee—that are
home to golden eagles, red squirrels, red deer, black and red grouse,
snow bunting, and the United Kingdom's only free-roaming reindeer,
some of which may be seen on the quintessentially queenlike Land

17

Rover Safari Tour. Tempted by the setting? Balmoral Castle has a number of cottages (some very large) for rent by the week at certain times. These are atmospheric but can be basic (which, believe it or not, is how the royal family likes its holidays to be—though the late Diana, Princess of Wales, who vacationed here before the breakup of her marriage to Prince Charles, hated Balmoral's lack of luxury). ✉ *A93* ✣ *7 miles west of Ballater* ☎ *01339/742534* 🌐 *www.balmoralcastle.com* 🎟 *£11.50* ⏲ *Closed when royals are in residence.*

WHERE TO EAT

$ ECLECTIC 🍴 **Rocksalt & Snails.** This cheeky little contemporary café-bar, with its fancy metalwork interiors and solid wooden tables, has an interesting take on local produce, serving Heidi (goat meat) and Deerstalker (venison) pies and the abundant Rocksalt & Snails platter (with all kinds of salmon and trout). For sweetness try huge scones or cakes with very good coffee or loose-leaf tea. **Known for:** game pies; trout and salmon; cakes and pastries. [$] *Average main: £10* ✉ *2 Bridge St.* ☎ *07834/452583.*

WHERE TO STAY

$$ HOTEL FAMILY Fodor's Choice ★ 🏨 **Hilton Grand Vacations at Craigendarroch Suites.** This grand mansion has been turned into a resort with a luxury spa and country club, combining Victorian style with modern comforts. **Pros:** a great pool and decent gym facilities; good amenities for kids; rooms and suites have kitchenettes. **Cons:** if there's a conference, nonattending guests can feel lost among the crowds. [$] *Rooms from: £136* ✉ *Braemar Rd.* ☎ *01339/755558* 🌐 *www.hiltongrandvacations.com/scotland/hgvc-craigendarroch-suites/* 🛏 *51 rooms* 🍽 *Free breakfast.*

SHOPPING

Atholl Countrywear. At either location of Countrywear, men (and women) can find everything that's necessary for Highland country living, including fishing tackle, natty tweeds, and that flexible garment popular in Scotland between seasons: the body warmer. ✉ *13 Bridge St.* ☎ *01339/755453* 🌐 *www.athollcountrywear.com* ⏲ *Closed Sun.–Tues.*

McEwan Gallery. A mile west of Ballater, the McEwan Gallery displays fine paintings, watercolors, prints, and books (many with a Scottish or golf theme) in an unusual house built by the Swiss artist Rudolphe Christen in 1902. ✉ *A939* ☎ *01339/755429* 🌐 *www.mcewangallery.com* ⏲ *Closed Mon.*

BRAEMAR

17 miles west of Ballater, 60 miles west of Aberdeen, 51 miles north of Perth via A93.

Synonymous with the British monarchy, due to its closeness to Balmoral, and with the famous Highland Games, this village is popular year-round as a base for walkers and climbers enjoying the Grampian Mountains.

GETTING HERE AND AROUND

The town is on A93; there's bus service here, as to other towns on the road.

ESSENTIALS

Visitor Information Braemar Visitor Information Centre. ✉ *The Mews, Mar Rd.* ☎ *01339/741600* 🌐 *braemarscotland.co.uk, www.visitscotland.com.*

EXPLORING

Braemar Castle. On the northern outskirts of town, Braemar Castle dates from the 17th century, although its defensive walls, in the shape of a pointed star, came later. At Braemar (the *braes,* or slopes, of the district of Mar), the standard, or rebel flag, was first raised at the start of the unsuccessful Jacobite rebellion of 1715. About 30 years later, during the last Jacobite rebellion, Braemar Castle was strengthened and garrisoned by government troops. From the early 1800s the castle was the clan seat of the Farquharsons, who hold their clan reunion here every summer.

Thanks to the commitment of local volunteers, a remarkable 2008 renovation restored Braemar to the home it would have been in the early 20th century, complete with all the necessary comforts and family memorabilia. A dozen rooms are on view, including the laird's day room with a plush daybed and the kitchen. ✉ *Off A93* ☎ *01339/741219* 🌐 *www.braemarcastle.co.uk* 🎟 *£8* 🕒 *Closed Nov.–Easter. Closed Mon. and Tues. in Apr.–June, Sept., and Oct.*

FAMILY **Braemar Highland Gathering.** The village of Braemar is associated with the Braemar Highland Gathering, held the first Saturday in September. Although there are many such gatherings celebrated throughout Scotland, this one is distinguished by the presence of the royal family. Competitions and events include hammer throwing, caber tossing, and bagpipe playing. If you plan to attend, book your accommodations months in advance and be sure to buy tickets and, if necessary, your car parking ticket about six months in advance, as they do sell out. ✉ *Princess Royal and Duke of Fife Memorial Park, Broombank Terr.* 🌐 *www.braemargathering.org.*

WHERE TO EAT AND STAY

$ CAFÉ 🍴 **Taste.** Tasty and fresh soups and sandwiches made with local ingredients like venison pâté and Cambus O' May artisanal cheeses adorn the menu at this chalet-style café. You can order moist cakes and tasty lattes here, too. **Known for:** homemade soups; fresh-baked bread. [$] *Average main: £6* ✉ *Auchendryne Sq.* ☎ *01339/741425* 🌐 *www.taste-braemar.co.uk* 🕒 *Closed Sun.*

$ B&B/INN 🏨 **Ivy Cottage.** Everything at this 19th-century inn, from the silky bedding to the bright bathroom fittings, is of the highest standard and done with good taste. **Pros:** relaxing rooms; owners who go out of their way to make you feel at home; facilities for walkers and cyclists. **Cons:** next to the church, so expect bells on Sunday morning. [$] *Rooms from: £75* ✉ *Cluniebank Rd.* ☎ *01339/741642* 🌐 *www.ivycottagebraemar.co.uk* 🛏 *5 rooms* 🍽 *Free breakfast.*

GOLF

Braemar Golf Course. It's worth playing the tricky 18-hole Braemar Golf Course if only to say you've played the highest 18-hole course in Scotland. Founded in 1902, it is laden with foaming water hazards. ✉ *Cluny Bank Rd.* ☎ *01339/741618* 🌐 *www.braemargolfclub.co.uk* 🎟 *£25 weekdays, £30 weekends* ⛳ *18 holes, 4935 yards, par 65.*

CLOSE UP

Language and the Scots

Until quite recently, many Scots were made to feel uncomfortable—even within Scotland—about using their native regional dialects. After the Union of England and Scotland in 1707, Scotland's professional middle class, including its politicians, adopted an only mildly accented form of "standard English." Even today, the voices of the Scottish aristocracy—usually educated in elite English schools—are almost indistinguishable from those of their English counterparts. Liz Lochhead, Scotland's Makar (poet laureate) from 2011 to 2016 and a champion of spoken and written Scots, put it like this in her poem *Kidspoem/Bairnsang*: "Oh saying it was one thing / but when it came to writing it / in black and white / the way it had to be said / was as if you were posh, grown-up, male, English and dead." But in recent generations, Scots urban accents and rural dialects have become accepted once again. The creation of the post of Makar (first held by Edwin Morgan from 2004 to 2010 and now by Jackie Kay) signaled that Scots is once again to be taken seriously. Taking up the mantle of Robert Burns, whose poems drew on the *Lallans* (Lowlands) of his native southwest, contemporary authors such as Irvine Welsh and William McIlvanney and others write in the voices of working-class Scots city dwellers.

LOWLAND SCOTS

The Scots language (that is, Lowland Scots, not Gaelic), a northern form of Middle English influenced by Norse, Gaelic, French, and Dutch, was used in the court and in literature until the late 16th century. After the Scottish court moved to London in 1603 it declined as a literary or official language. But Scots survives in various forms, some of which—like the broadest urban accents of Dundee and Glasgow—are almost impenetrable to an ear used to "standard" English.

Some Scottish words are used and understood across the entire country (and world), such as *wee* (small), *aye* (yes), *lassie* (girl), and *bonny* (pretty). You may even find yourself exporting a few useful words, such as *dreich* (gloomy), *glaikit* (acting and looking foolish), or *dinna fash* (don't worry), all of which are much more expressive than their English equivalents. Doric, the regional dialect of Aberdeenshire, is the purest direct descendant of the old Scots tongue. It's loaded with borrowings from Norse, such as *quine* (a young woman) and *loon* (a young man), while "what" becomes "fit," "who" becomes "faa," and "which" becomes "fitna." The local version of "How do you do?" is "Fit like?" A country dweller might refer to an urban Aberdonian as a *toonser*; his city cousin might call him a *teuchter*. Neither term is entirely complimentary.

GAELIC

Scottish Gaelic—an entirely different language—is not, despite what many still think, Scotland's national tongue. This Celtic language is incomprehensible to 99% of Scots and spoken by fewer than 60,000 people. Most live in the Western Isles (*Eilean Siar* in Gaelic), with a handful in the Highlands and Argyll. All speak English as well as their mother tongue. Gaelic was frowned upon after the failure of the 1745 Jacobite rebellions, and numbers of Gaelic speakers have declined ever since, though the decline has slowed in recent years.

ALFORD

28 miles west of Aberdeen, 41 miles northeast of Braemar.

A plain and sturdy settlement in the Howe (Hollow) of Alford, this town gives those who have grown somewhat weary of castle-hopping a break: it has a museum instead. Craigievar Castle and Castle Fraser are nearby, though.

GETTING HERE AND AROUND
The town is on A944.

EXPLORING

Fodor'sChoice ★ **Castle Fraser.** The massive Castle Fraser is the ancestral home of the Frasers and one of the largest of the castles of Mar; it's certainly a contender as one of the grandest castles in the northeast. Although the well-furnished building shows a variety of styles reflecting the taste of its owners from the 15th through the 19th century, its design is typical of the cavalcade of castles in the region, and for good reason. This—along with many others, including Midmar, Craigievar, Crathes, and Glenbuchat—was designed by a family of master masons called Bell. There are plenty of family items, but don't miss the two Turret Rooms—one of which is the trophy room—and Major Smiley's Room. He married into the family but is famous for having been one of the escapees from Colditz (a high-security prisoner-of-war camp) during World War II. The walled garden includes a 19th-century knot garden, with colorful flower beds, box hedging, gravel paths, and splendid herbaceous borders. Have lunch in the tearoom or the picnic area. ⊠ *Off A944 ✚ 8 miles southeast of Alford* ☎ *01330/833463* ⊕ *www.nts.org. uk* ⊠ *£10.50* ⊗ *Closed Nov.–Mar.*

FAMILY **Grampian Transport Museum.** The entertaining and enthusiastically run Grampian Transport Museum specializes in road-based means of locomotion, backed up by archives and a library. Its collection of buses and trams is second to none, but the Craigievar Express, a steam-driven creation invented by the local postman to deliver mail more efficiently, is the most unusual. Look out for the Hillman Imp: if Scotland has a national car, this is it. There's a small café that offers tea, baked goods, and ice cream. ⊠ *Montgarrie Rd.* ☎ *01975/562292* ⊕ *www.gtm.org.uk* ⊠ *£10 (includes 2 children)* ⊗ *Closed Oct.–Mar.*

17

THE NORTHEAST AND THE MALT WHISKY TRAIL

North of Deeside another popular area of this region lies inland, toward Speyside—the valley, or strath, of the River Spey—famed for its whisky distilleries, some of which it promotes in another signposted trail. Distilling Scotch is not an intrinsically spectacular process. It involves pure water, malted barley, and sometimes peat smoke, then a lot of bubbling and fermentation, all of which cause a number of odd smells. The result is a prestigious product with a fascinating range of flavors that you may either enjoy immensely or not at all.

Instead of closely following the Malt Whisky Trail, dip into it and blend visits to distilleries with some other aspects of the county of Moray, particularly its coastline. Whisky notwithstanding, Moray's scenic qualities, low rainfall, and other reassuring weather statistics are worth remembering. You can also sample the northeastern seaboard, including some of the best but least-known coastal scenery in Scotland.

DUFFTOWN

54 miles west of Aberdeen.

On one of the Spey tributaries, Dufftown was planned in 1817 by the Earl of Fife. Its simple cross layout with a square and a large clock tower (originally from Banff and now the site of the visitor center) is typical of a small Scottish town built in the 19th century. Its simplicity is made all the more stark by the brooding, heather-clad hills that rise around it. Dufftown is convenient to a number of distilleries.

GETTING HERE AND AROUND

To get here from Aberdeen, drive west on A96 and A920; then turn west at Huntly. It's not easy or quick, but you can take the train to Elgin or Keith and then the bus to Dufftown.

EXPLORING

Balvenie Distillery. As soon as you step into the old manager's office at Balvenie Distillery—now gently restored and fitted with knotted-elm furniture—you realize Balvenie wants to make sure that all visitors get to see, smell, and feel the magic of the making of this malt. Balvenie is unusual because it has its own cooperage with six coopers hard at work turning the barrels. Tours show the mashing, fermentation, and distillation process and end with a tasting. ■ TIP→ **Visitors must be 18 or older.** ⊠ *Balvenie St.* ☎ *01340/822210* ⊕ *www.thebalvenie.com* ☞ *£40* ⊘ *Closed weekends.*

Fodor's Choice   **Glenfiddich Distillery.** Many make Glenfiddich Distillery their first stop
★   on the Malt Whisky Trail. The independent company of William Grant and Sons Limited was the first to realize the tourist potential of the distilling process. The company began offering tours around the typical pagoda-roof malting buildings and subsequently built an entertaining visitor center. Besides a free 20-minute tour of the distillery there are various tours for more discerning visitors that include nosing and tasting sessions. Check out the Malt Barn Bar, serving a limited but tasty menu, and look out for viewings of the current Glenfiddich Distillery Artists in Residence's work. ⊠ *A941* ⊹ *½ mile north of Dufftown* ☎ *01340/820373* ⊕ *www.glenfiddich.com* ☞ *Tours from £10.*

Strathisla Distillery. Whisky lovers should take the B9014 11 miles northeast from Dufftown—or alternatively, ride the Keith Dufftown Railway—to see one of Scotland's most iconic distilleries, the Strathisla Distillery, with its cobblestone courtyard and famous double pagoda roofs. Stretching over the picturesque River Isla, the Strathisla Distillery was built in 1786 and now produces the main component of the Chivas Regal blend. Guided tours, for those 18 and over only, take you to the mash house, tun room, and still house—all pretty much the same as

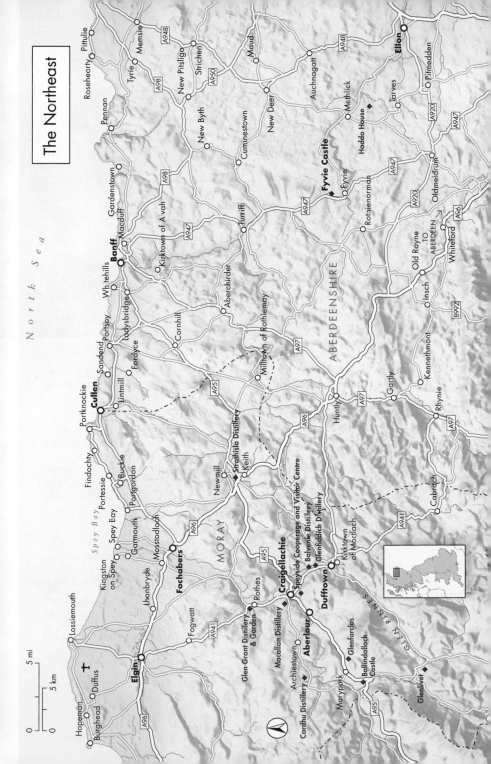

Tours at Glenfiddich Distillery include older buildings and a modern visitor center—plus a wee dram.

they were when production began. The tour ends with a tasting session. ✉ *Seafield Ave., Keith* ☎ *01542/783044* 🌐 *www.maltwhiskydistilleries.com* 🎟 *£7.50* 🕒 *Closed weekends mid-Nov.–mid.-Mar.*

WHERE TO STAY

$ B&B/INN 🏨 **The Fife Arms Hotel.** This 18th-century coaching inn offers a whiff of atmosphere and acceptable accommodations for a one-night stay in motel-style rooms attached to an old-school pub popular with locals. **Pros:** full Scottish breakfast; off-street parking; very central. **Cons:** some noise from adjoining pub. [$] *Rooms from: £70* ✉ *2 The Square* ☎ *01340/820220* 🌐 *www.fifearmsdufftown.co.uk* 🛏 *6 rooms* 🍴 *Free breakfast.*

SHOPPING

Collector's Cabin. Two adjoining shops—one with Scottish silver, fossils, and book illustrations, the other with kilts, ceramics, and other curiosities—are filled with conversation starters. This is truly a trove worth delving into. ✉ *22 and 24 Balvenie St.* ☎ *01340/821393* 🕒 *Closed Wed.*

Dufftown Glassworks. This light and airy gallery sells interesting fused and painted glass, as well as prints and crafts by local makers. The adjoining café sells the best coffee in Dufftown, leaf tea, and a good selection of cakes from scones to lemon drizzle to gooey chocolate. ✉ *16 Conval St.* ☎ *01340/821534* 🌐 *dufftownglassworks.com.*

CRAIGELLACHIE

4 miles northwest of Dufftown via A941.

Renowned as an angling resort, Craigellachie, like so many settlements on the River Spey, is sometimes enveloped in the malty reek of the local industry. Glen Grant is one of the distilleries nearby. The Spey itself is crossed by a handsome suspension bridge, designed by noted engineer Thomas Telford (1757–1834) in 1814 and now bypassed by the modern road.

GETTING HERE AND AROUND

The town is on A491; it's best to drive here, as public transportation is infrequent and complicated.

EXPLORING

Fodor's Choice
★

Glen Grant Distillery & Garden. James Grant founded this distillery in 1840 when he was only 25, and it was the first in the country to be electrically powered. This place will come as a welcome relief to companions of dedicated Malt Whisky Trail followers, because in addition to the distillery there's a large and beautiful garden. It's planted and tended as Grant envisioned, with orchards and woodland walks, log bridges over waterfalls, a magnificent lily pond, and azaleas and rhododendrons in profusion. Using peculiarly tall stills and special purifiers that follow a design introduced over a century ago, Glen Grant produces a distinctive pale-gold whisky with an almost floral or fruity finish. The tour is excellent value, with perhaps the friendliest guides and certainly the most generous tastings. There's a coffee shop, too, selling huge scones. ⊠ *A941, Rothes* ✛ *North of town, left at junction of A941 and B9015* ☎ *01340/832118* ⊕ *www.glengrant.com* ☞ *£5.*

Macallan Distillery. On the sprawling Easter Elchies Estate, Macallan Distillery offers unique whisky matured in sherry casks and, more recently, in oak bourbon casks. The tour lasts an hour and 45 minutes and, aiming to give you a full understanding of the six pillars of whisky making, it takes you from the still house to the warehouse where maturation takes place, finishing off with a nosing and tasting session. Booking is essential. ⊠ *Easter Elchies* ✛ *About 1 mile west of Craigellachie, off B9102* ☎ *01304/872280* ⊕ *www.themacallan.com* ☞ *£15* ⊘ *Closed Sun. Easter–Sept. and weekends Oct.–Easter.*

Speyside Cooperage and Visitor Centre. A major stop on the Malt Whisky Trail, the huge Speyside Cooperage and Visitor Centre is a must for all whisky fans. Retired coopers will talk you through the making of the casks, a surprisingly physical and dramatic process that uses the same tools and skills employed for hundreds of years. Inside you can watch highly skilled craftspeople make and repair oak barrels used in the local whisky industry. The Acorn to Cask exhibit tells all about the ancient craft of coopering. There's a cottage café with huge cakes and sandwiches for those in need of sustenance. ⊠ *Dufftown Rd.* ☎ *01340/871108* ⊕ *www.speysidecooperage.co.uk* ☞ *£3.50* ⊘ *Closed weekends.*

17

WHERE TO EAT AND STAY

$$
BRITISH
✕ **Copper Dog.** With its reclaimed woodwork and mismatched wooden chairs, rows of malt whisky bottles, decorative oak barrel-ends, and walls hung with prints, the Craigellachie Hotel's bar-restaurant is an edgy blend of cozy and shabby chic. The menu is equally relaxed, with dishes such as locally produced gourmet sausages, rumbledethumps (a casserole of baked potato, cabbage, and onions), and an outstanding platter of Scottish cheeses with homemade chutney, all of which can be matched with regional craft beers. **Known for:** local produce; malt whiskies; craft beers. $ *Average main: £15* ✉ *Craigellachie Hotel, Victoria St.* ☎ *01340/881204* ⊕ *www.craigellachiehotel.co.uk.*

$
B&B/INN
⛏ **Highlander Inn.** Don't be fooled by the rather alpine exterior: this very Scottish hotel prides itself on its whisky bar and its friendly welcome. **Pros:** simple accommodations; warm atmosphere; great bar. **Cons:** dated decor; could be rather too lively for some. $ *Rooms from: £90* ✉ *Victoria St.* ☎ *01340/881446* ⊕ *www.whiskyinn.com* ↝ *8 rooms* ⊙*❙ Free breakfast.*

ABERLOUR

2 miles southwest of Craigellachie.

Aberlour, often listed as Charlestown of Aberlour on maps, is a handsome little burgh, essentially Victorian in style, though actually founded in 1812 by the local landowner. The names of the noted local whisky stills are Cragganmore, Aberlour, and Glenfarclas; Glenlivet and Cardhu are also nearby. Also in Aberlour is Walkers, famous for producing shortbread, tins of buttery, crumbly goodness, since 1898.

GETTING HERE AND AROUND

Aberlour is on A95; public transportation here is infrequent.

EXPLORING

Ballindalloch Castle. The family home of the Macpherson-Grants since 1546, Ballindalloch Castle is every visitor's idea of what a Scots laird's lair should look like. You can wander around the beautifully kept rooms and meticulously tended gardens at your leisure; you may even bump into the lord and lady of the manor, who live here all year. There's also a splendid tea shop offering large slices of cake. ✉ *Off A95* ✛ *8 miles southwest of Craigellachie* ☎ *01807/500205* ⊕ *www.ballindallochcastle.co.uk* ▤ *£11.50* ⊙ *Closed Sept.–Easter.*

Cardhu Distillery. The striking outline of Cardhu Distillery, whose main product lies at the heart of Johnnie Walker blends, is set among the heather-clad Mannoch Hills. Established by John and Helen Cumming in 1811, it was officially founded in 1824 after distilling was made legal by the Excise Act of 1823. Guides take you to the mashing, fermenting, and distilling halls, and they explain the malting process, which now takes place on the coast at Burghead. ✉ *B1902, Knockando* ✛ *10 miles north of Glenlivet and 7 miles west of Aberlour* ☎ *01340/875635* ⊕ *www.discovering-distilleries.com/cardhu/find-us/* ▤ *£5* ⊙ *Closed weekends Oct.–Mar.*

Glenfarclas. Glenfarclas is one of Scotland's few remaining family-owned distilleries, passed down from father to son since 1865. That link to the past is most visible among its low buildings, where the retired still sits outside: if you didn't know what it was, you could mistake it for part of a submarine. The tours end with tastings in the superlative Ship Room, the intact lounge of an ocean liner called the *Empress of Australia.* ✉ *Off A95, Ballindalloch* ☎ *01807/500345* 🌐 *www.glenfarclas.co.uk* 🎟 *£7.50* ⏰ *Closed weekends Oct.–June and Sun. in July–Sept.* ☞ *In-depth tasting tours from £100.*

Glenlivet. The famous Glenlivet was the first licensed distillery in the Highlands, founded in 1824 by George Smith. Today it produces one of the best-known 12-year-old single malts in the world. The 75-minute Classic Tour offers an introduction to malt whisky making, explains the distillery's history, and includes a free dram; more in-depth tours are available. There's a coffee shop with baked goods and, of course, a whisky shop. Visitors must be 18 or over. ✉ *Off B9008, Ballindalloch* ✥ *10 miles southwest of Aberlour via A95 and B9008.* ☎ *01340/821720* 🌐 *www.glenlivet.com* 🎟 *£10* ⏰ *Closed mid-Nov.–mid-Mar.*

WHERE TO STAY

$$ B&B/INN 🏨 **Mash Tun.** Curvy yet sturdy, this former station hotel, now a smart B&B with a popular restaurant, is the social hub of the village. **Pros:** superb accommodations; tasty meals; great atmosphere in the restaurant and bar. **Cons:** book well ahead in summer. [$] *Rooms from: £115* ✉ *8 Broomfield Sq.* ☎ *01340/881771* 🌐 *www.mashtun-aberlour.com* 🛏 *5 rooms* 🍴 *Free breakfast.*

FOCHABERS

9 miles east of Elgin.

With its hanging baskets of fuchsia in summer and its perfectly mowed village square, Fochabers has a cared-for charm that makes you want to stop here, even just to stretch your legs. Lying just to the south of the River Spey, the former market town was founded in 1776 by the Duke of Gordon. The duke moved the village from its original site because it was too close to Gordon Castle. Famous today for being home to the Baxters brand of soups and jams, Fochabers is near some of the best berry fields: come and pick your own in the summer months.

GETTING HERE AND AROUND

Fochabers is not on the Inverness-to-Aberdeen train line, but there is an hourly bus service (Stagecoach Bluebird No. 10) from Fochabers to Elgin. It's near the junction of A98 and A96.

EXPLORING

Baxters Highland Village. Legendary Scottish food brand Baxters of Fochabers makes gourmet products here on the banks of the River Spey for worldwide export. From Tokyo to New York, upmarket stores stock the company's soups, jams, and chutneys. Watch cooking demonstrations, have a look at a re-creation of the Baxters' first grocery shop, or browse around the Best of Scotland, specializing in all kinds of Scottish products. A restaurant serves up an assortment of delectables. ✉ *A96* ☎ *01343/820666* 🌐 *www.baxters.com.*

FAMILY **Fochabers Folk Museum & Heritage Centre.** Once over the Spey Bridge and past the cricket ground (a very unusual sight in Scotland), you can find the symmetrical, 18th-century Fochabers village square. The old Pringle Church is now the home of the Fochabers Folk Museum, which boasts a fine collection of items relating to past life of all types of residents in the village and surrounding area. Exhibits include carts and carriages, farm implements, domestic labor-saving devices, and an exquisite collection of Victorian toys. ✉ *High St.* ☎ *01343/821204* 🌐 *www.fochabers-heritage.org.uk* 🕓 *Closed Oct.–mid-May.*

WHERE TO EAT

$$ BRITISH 🍴 **Gordon Castle Walled Garden Cafe.** With light streaming through the large windows onto the wooden tables and rattan chairs, there is an airiness and freshness to this eatery. Fish landed just a few miles away on the Moray coast is a good bet, as are the long-aged steaks. **Known for:** local steak and seafood; fresh summer fruit desserts. [$] *Average main: £15* ✉ *Fochabers* ✣ *Just off A96, Fochabers Bypass Rd.* ☎ *01343/612317* 🌐 *www.gordoncastlescotland.com.*

SHOPPING

Watt's Antiques. This shop has small collectibles, jewelry, ornaments, and china. ✉ *45 High St.* ☎ *01343/820077* 🌐 *www.wattsantiques.com.*

CULLEN

21 miles east of Elgin, 13 miles east of Fochabers.

Fodor's Choice ★ Look for some wonderfully painted homes at Cullen, in the old fishing town below the railway viaduct. The real attractions of this charming little seaside resort, however, are its white-sand beach (the water is quite cold, though) and the fine view west toward the aptly named Bowfiddle Rock. In summer Cullen bustles with families carrying buckets and spades and eating ice cream and chips.

A stroll past the small but once busy harbor reveals numerous fishers' cottages, huddled together with small yards where they dried their nets. Beyond these, the vast stretch of beach curves gently round the bay. Above are the disused Victorian viaduct—formerly the Peterhead train line—and the 18th-century town.

GETTING HERE AND AROUND

Cullen is on A98, on Cullen Bay.

EXPLORING

Seafield Street. The town has a fine *mercat* (market) cross and one main street—Seafield Street—that splits the town. It holds numerous specialty shops—antiques and gift stores, an ironmonger, a baker, a pharmacy, and a locally famous ice-cream shop among them—as well as several cafés. ✉ *Cullen.*

WHERE TO EAT AND STAY

$ SEAFOOD FAMILY 🍴 **Linda's Fish & Chips.** This casual place serves the freshest fish, caught in nearby Buckie and cooked to crispy perfection (gluten-free batter is available, too). There's a seating area inside, but it's best for takeout. **Known for:** fish battered to perfection; crispy fries. [$] *Average main: £10* ✉ *54 Seafield St.* ☎ *01542/840202.*

$ B&B/INN 🏨 **Academy House.** In the picturesque village of Fordyce, this luxurious bed-and-breakfast in a handsomely preserved Victorian house was once the headmaster's house for a famous local secondary school. **Pros:** good home cooking; delightful setting; helpful owners eager to help you find your way around. **Cons:** rooms book up fast. [$] *Rooms from: £90* ✉ *School Rd., Fordyce* ☎ *01261/842743* 🌐 *www.fordyceaccommodation.com* 🛏 *2 rooms* 🍽 *Free breakfast* ☞ *Dinner on request.*

BANFF

36 miles east of Elgin, 47 miles north of Aberdeen.

Midway along the northeast coast, overlooking Moray Firth and the estuary of the River Deveron, Banff is a dour fishing town, huddled around a small harbor, with a bleak but sometimes lovely coastline of crags, cliffs, and sandy coves to either side. Sixteenth-century houses huddle around the harbor, while surprisingly grand Georgian streets are reminders of its glory years as a hub of the fishing industry.

17

GETTING HERE AND AROUND

Banff is on the A98 coastal road and at the end of the tree-lined A947 to Aberdeen. If you are relying on public transportation, Bus 325 from Aberdeen bus station takes two hours and gets you into Low Street, just five minutes from Duff House.

ESSENTIALS

Visitor Information Banff Visitor Information Centre. ✉ *Collie Lodge, Low St.* ☎ *01261/812419* 🌐 *www.visitscotland.com.*

EXPLORING

Fodor's Choice ★ **Duff House.** The jewel in Banff's crown is the grand mansion of Duff House, a splendid William Adam–designed (1689–1748) Georgian mansion. It's now an annex of the National Galleries, housing works by El Greco, Sir Henry Raeburn, and Thomas Gainsborough. A good tearoom and a gift shop are on the ground floor. ✉ *Off A98* ☎ *01261/818181* 🌐 *www.duffhouse.org.uk* 🎟 *£7.50* 🕒 *Closed Nov.–Mar.*

FYVIE CASTLE

18 miles south of Banff.

This castle mixes ancient construction with Edwardian splendor and includes excellent art. The grounds are also worth exploring.

GETTING HERE AND AROUND

If you're driving from Banff, take the A947 south for 20 minutes or so until you see the turnoff.

EXPLORING

Fyvie Castle. In an area rich with castles, Fyvie Castle stands out as the most complex. Five great towers built by five successive powerful families turned a 13th-century foursquare castle into an opulent Edwardian statement of wealth. Some superb paintings are on view, including 12 works by Sir Henry Raeburn. There are myriad sumptuous interiors—the circular stone staircase is considered one of the best examples in the country—and delightfully laid-out gardens. A former lady of the house, Lillia Drummond, was apparently starved to death by her husband, who entombed her body inside the walls of a secret room. In the 1920s, when the bones were disrupted during renovations, a string of such terrible misfortunes followed that they were quickly returned and the room sealed off. Her name is carved into the windowsill of the Drummond Room. ☒ *Off A947, Turriff* ☎ *01651/819226* ⊕ *www.nts. org.uk* 🎫 *£12.50* ☉ *Closed Oct.–Mar.*

ELLON

32 miles southeast of Banff, 14 miles north of Aberdeen.

Formerly a market center on what was then the lowest bridging point of the River Ythan, Ellon, a bedroom suburb of Aberdeen, is a small town at the center of a rural hinterland. It's also well placed for visiting Fyvie Castle and Haddo House.

GETTING HERE AND AROUND

To get to Ellon, take the A947 from Banff or the A90 from Aberdeen; both routes take half an hour.

EXPLORING

Haddo House. Built in 1732, this elegant mansion has a light and graceful Georgian design, with curving wings on either side of a harmonious, symmetrical facade. The interior is late-Victorian ornate, filled with magnificent paintings (including works by Pompeo Batoni and Sir Thomas Lawrence) and plenty of objets d'art. Pre-Raphaelite stained-glass windows by Sir Edward Burne-Jones grace the chapel. Outside is a terrace garden with a fountain, and a few yards farther is Haddo Country Park, which has walking trails leading to memorials about the Gordon family. ■TIP➜ Visits to the house are by prebooked tour only, which are held at 11 and 2. ☒ *Off B999* ✛ *8 miles northwest of Ellon* ☎ *01651/851440* ⊕ *www.nts.org.uk* 🎫 *£10.50* ☉ *Closed Nov.–Mar.*

SPORTS AND THE OUTDOORS

GOLF

Cruden Bay Golf Club. This historic golf course, sheltered among extensive sand dunes, offers a quintessential Scottish golf experience. Narrow channels and deep valleys on challenging fairways ensure plenty of excitement, making Cruden Bay one of the northeast's most outstanding courses. ☒ *Aulton Rd., Cruden Bay* ☎ *01779/812285* ⊕ *www.cruden-baygolfclub.co.uk* 🎫 *Championship, £110; St. Olaf, weekdays £25, weekends £35* 🏌 *Championship: 18 holes, 6287 yards, par 70; St. Olaf: 9 holes, 2463 yards, par 32* ⚠ *Reservations essential* ☞ *Book months in advance for a round on weekends.*

ARGYLL AND THE ISLES

WELCOME TO ARGYLL AND THE ISLES

TOP REASONS TO GO

★ **Whisky:** With 14 distilleries—9 on Islay, 1 each on Jura and Mull, and just 3 on the mainland—the region has been nicknamed Scotland's whisky coast.

★ **Iona and its abbey:** Maybe it's the remoteness that creates the almost mystical sense of history on Iona. From this early center of Scottish Christianity, evangelists traveled throughout Europe from the 6th century onward. It was also the burial place of Scottish kings, including Macbeth.

★ **The great outdoors:** Salmon and trout fill the lochs and rivers, while even bigger trophy fish await farther out to sea. Golfers have more than two dozen courses to choose from, and cyclists and walkers will find every kind of terrain at hand.

★ **Castles:** Often poised on cliffs overlooking the sea, the region's castles tell the story of eight centuries of occupations, sieges, and conflicts between warring clan chiefs and nobles.

With long sea lochs carved into its hilly, wooded interior, Argyll is a beguiling interweaving of water and land. The Mull of Kintyre, a narrow finger of land, points south towards nearby Ireland, separating the Firth of Clyde and its islands from the Atlantic and the isles of the Inner Hebrides. Arran, largest of the Clyde isles, looms near the mouth of the Clyde, separated from Kintyre by Kilbrannan Sound.

1 Argyll. The linked peninsulas of Knapdale and Kintyre—separated by the Crinan Canal at Tarbert—are areas of moorland and forest dotted with small lochs. From Inveraray at the head of Loch Fyne, you can take in Auchindrain's re-created fishing village on the way to the Arran ferry. Or turn west toward Crinan and the prehistoric sites around Kilmartin, then travel northward toward Loch Awe and its island ruins. A short drive away is Oban, an active ferry and fishing port.

2 Arran. Touring this island will give you a glimpse in a day or two of the whole of Scotland in miniature. In the north, the forbidding Goatfell is a challenge that draws walkers and climbers. The island's wilder west coast attracts bird-watchers and naturalists, while the fertile south of the island contains nine lovely golf courses, leisurely walks, and Brodick Castle.

3 Islay and Jura. The smell of peat that hangs in the air on Islay is bottled in its famous whiskies. The whitewashed cottages along the coast of Islay line clean and beautiful beaches, many of them visited by a variety of wildlife. Jura is wilder and more dramatic, its twin mountains (the Paps) dominating its infertile moorland.

4 Isle of Mull and Iona. The pretty harbor of Tobermory, with its painted houses, is a relaxing base from which to explore the varied and beautiful island of Mull. Along Mull's west coast, spectacular cliffs and rocky beaches look out on to the Atlantic. From Craignure, the road crosses the sweeping green valleys of the Ross of Mull to Fionnphort and the ferry to the meditative island of Iona.

18

Updated by
Robin Gauldie

Argyll's rocky seaboard looks out onto islands that were once part of a single prehistoric landmass. Its narrow roads slow travel but give time to admire its lochs and woods, and the ruins that recall the region's dramatic past. Here, too, are grand houses like Brodick and Inveraray castles and elegant gardens such as Crarae. This is whisky country, too: the peaty aroma of Islay's malts is unmistakable. Yet all this is within three hours of Glasgow.

Western Scotland has a complicated, splintered coastline where you'll observe the interplay of sea, loch, and rugged green peninsula. The islands are breathtakingly beautiful, though they often catch the extremely wet weather arriving here from the Atlantic. It is common to experience four seasons in a day, as cliffs and woods suddenly and dramatically disappear in sea mists then reappear just as suddenly.

Ancient castles like Dunstaffnage and the ruined towers on the islands of Loch Awe testify to the region's past importance. Prehistoric peoples left their mark here in the stone circles, carved stones, and Bronze and Iron Age burial mounds around Kilmartin and on Islay and Arran. The gardens of Inveraray and Brodick castles, nourished by the temperate west-coast climate, are the pride of Argyll while the paths of Crarae's, south of Inveraray, wind through plantings of magnolias and azaleas.

The working people of Glasgow traditionally spent their family holidays on the Clyde estuary, taking day trips by steamer down the Firth, or making longer journeys to Rothesay on the Isle of Bute or to Arran and the Ayrshire coast. From Ardrossan, farther down the coast, ferries cruise to the prosperous and varied Isle of Arran.

Western Scotland's small islands have jagged cliffs or tongues of rock, long white-sand beaches, fertile pastures where sheep and cattle graze, fortresses, and shared memories of clan wars and mysterious beasts. Their cliff paths and lochside byways are a paradise for walkers and cyclists, and their whisky the ideal reward after a long day outside.

While the islands' western coasts are dramatic, their more sheltered eastern seaboards are the location for pretty harbor towns like brightly painted Tobermory on Mull, or Port Ellen on Islay, with its neat rows of low whitewashed houses.

PLANNER

WHEN TO GO

This part of the mainland is close enough to Glasgow to make it accessible year-round. Oban is just over two hours from the city by car (three hours by bus), but getting to the isles via ferries takes longer, and the crossings are less frequent out of season. You can take advantage of quiet roads and plentiful accommodations in early spring and late autumn. The summer months of July and August can get very busy indeed; book accommodations and restaurants in advance during high season. In winter, short daylight hours and winds can make island stays rather bleak, but add allure to the prospect of sipping malt whisky by a log fire. Birding enthusiasts can observe vast flocks of migrant Arctic wildfowl arriving and leaving Islay in autumn and spring. At any time, come prepared with adequate clothing for fast-changing weather.

PLANNING YOUR TIME

You could easily spend a week exploring the islands alone, so consider spending at least a few nights in this region. Argyll and some island excursions make pleasant and easy side trips from Glasgow and Loch Lomond. Driving anywhere here takes a little longer than you'd think, so allow ample travel time. A leisurely day will take you to Inveraray, its castle, and the surrounding gardens (don't miss the folk museum at Auchindrain) before driving on to Kennacraig to take the ferry for Islay and Jura. Two or three days here will give you a sense of the history and varied landscapes of these stunning islands—and time for a distillery or two. If you have time to visit just one island, sail from Oban to Mull, returning the same day or the next to take in the Scottish Sea Life Sanctuary. If you can, drive around beautiful Loch Awe on your way back to Glasgow. If time is really tight, consider flying from Glasgow to Islay or Tiree.

18

Plan ahead: car ferries fill up in the summer months (there is usually no problem for foot passengers), and some of the smaller islands are served only once or twice a week. Bear in mind that it is not easy to find places to eat after 9 pm at any time of year—though you can usually find a place that will sell you a whisky until much later.

GETTING HERE AND AROUND
AIR TRAVEL

Flybe operates flights from Glasgow to Campbeltown, Islay, Tiree, and Mull. Hebridean Air Services flies from Oban to Islay, Coll, Colonsay, and Tiree.

Air Travel Contacts Flybe. ☎ *0371/700–2000* ⊕ *www.flybe.com.* **Hebridean Air Services.** ☎ *0845/805–7465* ⊕ *www.hebrideanair.co.uk.*

BOAT AND FERRY TRAVEL

Caledonian MacBrayne (CalMac) operates car-ferry and passenger services to and from the main islands. It is important to plan ahead when traveling to the islands in order to coordinate the connecting ferries; CalMac can advise you on this. Multiple-island tickets are available and can significantly reduce the cost of island-hopping.

CalMac ferries run from Oban to Mull, Lismore, Coll, and Tiree; from Kennacraig to Islay, Jura, and Gigha; from Ardrossan to Arran; and from Port Askaig on Islay to Feolin on Jura; as well as a number of shorter routes. Western Ferries operate between Dunoon, in Argyll, and Gourock, west of Glasgow. The ferry passage between Dunoon and Gourock is one frequented by locals; it saves a lot of time, and you can take your car across as well. Jura Passenger Ferry operates between Tayvallich (on the mainland) and Craighouse on Jura.

Ferry reservations are needed if you have a car; passengers traveling by foot do not need to make reservations.

Boat and Ferry Travel Contacts Caledonian MacBrayne (*CalMac*). ☎ *0800/066–5000* ⊕ *www.calmac.co.uk.* **Jura Passenger Ferry.** ☎ *07768/450000* ⊕ *www.jurapassengerferry.com.* **Western Ferries.** ☎ *01369/704452* ⊕ *www.western-ferries.co.uk.*

BUS TRAVEL

You can travel throughout the region by bus, but service here tends to be less frequent than elsewhere in Scotland. Scottish Citylink runs daily service from Glasgow's Buchanan Street Station to the mid-Argyll region and Kintyre; the trip to Oban takes about three hours. Several other companies provide local services within the region.

Bus Contacts Garelochhead Coaches. ☎ *01436/810200* ⊕ *www.garelochheadcoaches.co.uk.* **Islay Coaches.** ☎ *01496/840273* ⊕ *www.bmundell.co.uk.* **Scottish Citylink.** ☎ *0871/266–3333* ⊕ *www.citylink.co.uk.* **Stagecoach West Scotland.** ☎ *01770/302000* ⊕ *www.stagecoachbus.com.* **West Coast Motors.** ☎ *01586/552319* ⊕ *www.westcoastmotors.co.uk.*

CAR TRAVEL

Negotiating this area is easy except in July and August, when the roads around Oban may be congested. There are a number of single-lane roads, especially on the east side of the Kintyre Peninsula and on the islands, which require special care. Remember that white triangles indicate places where you can pass. You'll probably have to board a ferry at some point during your trip; nearly all ferries take cars as well as pedestrians.

From Glasgow, take the A82 and the A85 to Oban, the main ferry terminal for Mull and the islands (about 2½ hours by car). From the A82, take the A83 at Arrochar; it rounds Loch Fyne to Inveraray. From there you can take the A819 from Inveraray around Loch Awe and rejoin the Glasgow–Oban road. Alternatively, you can stay on the A83 and head down Kintyre to Kennacraig, the ferry terminal for Islay. Farther down the A83 is Tayinloan, the ferry port for Gigha. You can reach Brodick on Arran by ferry from Ardrossan, on the Clyde coast (M8/A78 from

Glasgow); in summer you can travel to Lochranza from Claonaig on the Kintyre Peninsula, but there are very few crossings.

TRAIN TRAVEL

Oban and Ardrossan are the main rail stations; it's a three-hour trip from Glasgow to Oban. For information call ScotRail. All trains connect with ferries.

Train Contact ScotRail. ☎ 0344/811–0141 ⊕ www.scotrail.co.uk.

RESTAURANTS

Argyll and the Isles have earned a reputation for excellent gastro-pubs and restaurants (many of which also offer accommodations) that use superb locally sourced produce, including luscious seafood, lamb, wild and farmed venison, and game of many kinds. Most hotels and many guesthouses offer evening meals, and it may often be your best option to look to hotel restaurants, though the quality can vary. Most restaurants and pubs stop serving food by 9 pm; lunch usually ends at 2:30. *Restaurant reviews have been shortened. For full information, visit Fodors.com*

HOTELS

Accommodations in Argyll and on the Isles range from country-house hotels to private homes offering a bed and breakfast. Most small, traditional, provincial hotels in coastal resorts have been updated and modernized, while still retaining personalized service. And though hotels often have a restaurant offering evening meals, the norm is to offer breakfast only. *Hotel reviews have been shortened. For full information, visit Fodors.com*

WHAT IT COSTS IN POUNDS				
	$	**$$**	**$$$**	**$$$$**
Restaurants	under £15	£15–£19	£20–£25	over £25
Hotels	under £100	£100–£160	£161–£220	over £220

Restaurant prices are the average cost of a main course at dinner or, if dinner is not served, at lunch. Hotel prices are the lowest cost of a standard double room in high season, including 20% V.A.T.

TOURS

FAMILY **Sea Life Surveys.** Dolphins, seals, porpoises, and (if you're fortunate) Fodor'sChoice minke whales and basking sharks are among the stars of the show on ★ a Sea Life Surveys cruise from pretty Tobermory. Seabirds abound, too, and you may spot huge white-tailed eagles, once extinct here but reintroduced to this part of Scotland in recent years. Several cruises are offered: if time is short, choose the two-hour Ecocruz. ✉ A848, Tobermory ✢ Cruises leave from floating pontoons opposite Mull Aquarium ☎ 01688/302916 ⊕ www.sealifesurveys.com ✆ From £25.

FAMILY **Staffa Tours.** This company organizes a number of tours to the smaller islands, with the emphasis on wildlife. Tours run from Mull, Ardnamurchan on the mainland, or from Iona. The three-hour trip to uninhabited Staffa includes Fingal's Cave, commemorated by Mendelssohn in his famous overture. With luck you may encounter dolphins on the way. Staffa also runs tours to the Treshnish islands, famous for the puffin colonies on Lunga. ⊠ *The Boat Shed, Iona, Iona* ☎ *07732/912370* ⊕ *www.staffatours.com* ⊠ *From £30.*

West Coast Tours. A range of bus tours in and around Oban and on Mull are available through West Coast Tours. The company can also arrange combined bus and boat tours. ⊠ *1 Queenspark Pl., Oban* ☎ *01631/566809* ⊕ *www.westcoasttours.co.uk* ⊠ *From £7.*

VISITOR INFORMATION
The tourist offices in Tarbert and Tobermory (Mull) are open April through October only; other offices are open year-round.

ARGYLL

Topographical grandeur and rocky shores are what make Argyll special. Try to take to the water at least once, even if your time is limited. The sea and the sea lochs have played a vital role in the history of western Scotland since the time of the war galleys of the clans. Oban is the major ferry gateway and transport hub, with a main road leading south into the Kintyre Peninsula.

OBAN

96 miles northwest of Glasgow, 125 miles northwest of Edinburgh, 50 miles south of Fort William, 118 miles southwest of Inverness.

It's almost impossible to avoid Oban when touring the west. Its waterfront has some character, but the town's main role is as a launch point for excursions into Argyll and for ferries to the islands. A traditional Scottish resort town, Oban has many music festivals, *ceilidhs* with Highland dancing, as well as all the usual tartan kitsch and late-night revelry in pubs and hotel bars. The Oban Distillery offers tours and a shop. Still, there are more exciting destinations just over the horizon, on the islands and down into Kintyre.

GETTING HERE AND AROUND
From Glasgow, the A82 along Loch Lomond meets the A85 at Crianlarich. Turn left and continue to Oban. In summer the center of Oban can become gridlocked with ferry traffic, so leave yourself time for the wait. Alternatively, the A816 from Lochgilphead enters Oban from the less crowded south. Train services run from Glasgow to Oban (ScotRail); Scottish Citylink runs buses from Glasgow to Oban several times a day.

ESSENTIALS
Visitor Information Oban Tourist Information Centre. ⊠ *3 North Pier* ☎ *01631/563122* ⊕ *www.oban.org.uk.*

EXPLORING
Dunstaffnage Castle. Standing high atop volcanic rock, Dunstaffnage commands the hills and lochs that surround it. That is why this 13th-century castle was so strategic and contested by those battling for control of Argyll and the Isles. From the walk along the walls you have

outstanding views across the **Sound of Mull** and the **Firth of Lorne.** A small well-illustrated guidebook (£2.50) lets you take your own guided tour, but there are storyboards throughout the building that give you a sense of how it was used across the ages. In the woods is the ruined chapel of St. Cuthbert, built by the Macdougall clan at the same time as the castle. ⊠ *Off A85* ☎ *01631/562465* ⊕ *www.historicenvironment. scot* ⊠ *£6* ⊗ *Closed Oct.–Apr.*

Oban Distillery. One of Scotland's oldest and smallest distilleries was founded in 1794, several years before the town where it now stands. It produces a well-known 14-year-old malt which, according to those who know, has a taste somewhere between the smoky Islay whiskies and the softer, sweeter Highland varieties—a distinctive West Highland flavor. ⊠ *Stafford St.* ✛ *Opposite North Pier* ☎ *01631/572004* ⊕ *www.discovering-distilleries.com/oban* ⊠ *Basic tour £8* ⊗ *Closed weekends in Dec.*

FAMILY **Ocean Explorer Centre.** On the Firth of Lorn, this imaginative venture lets you get a look under the sea. Hands-on exhibits include microscopes where you can observe tiny algae and a live undersea camera where you can see what's happening below the waves. Part of a scientific research center, it's educational, but also accessible and fun. There is a bright little café and a shop with books on marine science and other topics. It's 2 miles from Oban—follow the signs for nearby Dunstaffnage Castle. ⊠ *Kirk Rd.* ☎ *01631/559123* ⊕ *www.oceanexplorercentre.org* ⊠ *Free* ⊗ *Closed weekends.*

FAMILY **Scottish Sea Life Sanctuary.** On the shores of Loch Creran, this marine sanctuary is part aquarium, where you can get an up-close look at everything from sharks to stingrays, and part animal-rescue facility. Adorable otters and seals receive rehabilitation here before being released back into the wild. Kids will appreciate the adventure playground. The restaurant serves morning coffee, a full lunch menu, and afternoon tea. To get here, drive 10 miles north from Oban on the A828; West Coast Motors also provides regular bus service. ■TIP→ **Book online for significantly cheaper tickets.** ⊠ *Barcaldine, off A828, Connel* ☎ *01631/720386* ⊕ *www.visitsealife.co.uk/oban* ⊠ *£13.40* ⊗ *Closed Tues.–Thurs. Nov.–Mar.*

WHERE TO EAT

$$$ ✕ **Ee-usk.** This clean-lined restaurant's name means "fish" in Gaelic, and
SEAFOOD   it has earned quite a reputation for serving excellent dishes made with
Fodor'sChoice   the freshest fish and shellfish delivered directly from Oban's harbor. The
★   signature creations use appealingly simple sauces; try oven-baked wild halibut with creamed leeks or the full-scale seafood platter. **Known for:** lobster and crab; Mull scallops; Loch Linnhe oysters and langoustines. Ⓢ *Average main: £20* ⊠ *North Pier* ☎ *01631/565666* ⊕ *www.eeusk. com* ⊗ *Closed Sun.*

$ ✕ **Oban Seafood Hut.** Serving arguably the best-value seafood in Oban,
SEAFOOD   ex-fisherman John Ogden's quayside fish shack is a local legend. Look for a green-painted shed on the pier, then join the line of cognoscenti waiting for simply sautéed scallops, grilled langoustine and lobster, oysters, and mussels. **Known for:** superbly fresh shellfish,

langoustine, crab, and lobster; simple, sublime preparations. $ *Average main: £8* ✉ *CalMac Pier* ☎ *07881/418565* ☉ *Closed Nov.–Apr.* ▭ *No credit cards.*

WHERE TO STAY

$
B&B/INN
🏨 **Kilchrenan House.** Just a few minutes from the town center, this Victorian-era stone house has been transformed into a lovely bed-and-breakfast. **Pros:** great sea views; tasteful attention to detail. **Cons:** some bedrooms may be too colorfully decorated for some tastes; attic rooms have a slanting roof; credit cards not accepted for one-night stays. $ *Rooms from: £75* ✉ *Corran Esplanade* ☎ *01631/562663* ⊕ *www.kilchrenanhouse.co.uk* ☉ *Closed Dec. and Jan.* ⤳ *13 rooms* ⏺ *Free breakfast.*

$$$
HOTEL
Fodor'sChoice
★
🏨 **Manor House Hotel.** On the coast near Oban, this 1780 stone house—once the home of the Duke of Argyll—has sea views and a convenient location. **Pros:** excellent restaurant; near all necessary amenities; nice garden overlooking the bay. **Cons:** smallish bedrooms; no children under 12. $ *Rooms from: £185* ✉ *Gallanach Rd.* ☎ *01631/562087* ⊕ *www.manorhouseoban.com* ⤳ *11 rooms* ⏺ *Free breakfast.*

APPIN

17 miles north of Oban.

GETTING HERE AND AROUND

From Oban, follow the A828 around Loch Creran and take the left turn to Port Appin just beyond Tynribbie. Continue for just over 2 miles to the old pier. From the port, the passenger ferry runs to the island of Lismore throughout the year. Steamers once plied the waters of Loch Linnhe, but today the largest boats here are those taking workers to the quarries of Kingairloch.

18

WHERE TO EAT AND STAY

$$$
SEAFOOD
Fodor'sChoice
★
✕ **Pierhouse Hotel and Restaurant.** The round towers of the old pier mark the entrance to this restaurant, appealingly situated on the water's edge. The restaurant serves the freshest seafood; try its signature platter of lobster, scallops, mussels, and langoustine. **Known for:** ultrafresh lobster; lively atmosphere. $ *Average main: £25* ✉ *Port Appin* ☎ *01631/730302* ⊕ *www.pierhousehotel.co.uk.*

$$$$
HOTEL
FAMILY
Fodor'sChoice
★
🏨 **Isle of Eriska.** On one of Scotland's few private islands, this sybaritic enclave conceals luxury facilities like a spa, pool, gym, golf course, and a Michelin-starred restaurant behind a severe baronial facade. **Pros:** exceptional food; good service; superb leisure facilities; families actively welcomed. **Cons:** remote; dining out not an easy option. $ *Rooms from: £340* ✉ *Off A828, Benderloch* ⊕ *Island signposted from Benderloch village and connected to mainland by short bridge* ☎ *01631/720371* ⊕ *www.eriska-hotel.co.uk* ⤳ *27 rooms* ⏺ *Free breakfast.*

LOCH AWE

18 miles east of Oban.

Measuring more than 25 miles long, Loch Awe is Scotland's longest stretch of freshwater. Its northwest shore is quiet; forest walks crisscross the Inverliever Forest here. At the loch's northern end tiny islands, many with ruins, pepper the water. One, Inishail, is home to a 13th-century chapel.

GETTING HERE AND AROUND

From Oban the A85 will bring you to the head of Loch Awe and the small village of the same name. Turn onto the B845 at Taynuilt to reach the loch's northern shore, or continue through the forbidding Pass of Brander and turn onto the A819 to get to the southern shore. From here you can continue on to Inveraray, or drive along the loch on the B840.

EXPLORING

FAMILY
Fodor's Choice
★

Bonawe Iron Furnace. Seemingly out of place in this near-wilderness setting, Bonawe is a fascinating relic from the dawn of Britain's Industrial Revolution. In the mid-18th century, Argyll's virgin forests attracted ironmasters from England, where such valuable fuel sources were harder to find. Business boomed when wars with France boosted demand for pig iron and cannonballs, and in its heyday Bonawe employed up to 600 unskilled local wood gatherers and skilled southern foundrymen. ⊠ *Off B845, Bonawe* ☎ *01866/822432* ⊕ *www.historicenvironment. scot* ⊠ *£5* ⊘ *Closed Oct.–Mar.*

FAMILY
Cruachan. Like the lair of a classic James Bond villain, this triumph of 20th-century British technology lurks deep within a vast man-made cavern. Hidden 3,000 feet beneath the slopes of Ben Cruachan, the colossal water-driven turbines of this subterranean power station, completed in 1965, supply clean energy to much of Scotland. The ½-mile bus ride from the surface to the generating hall is a surreal experience, made all the more so by the subtropical plants that thrive under artificial light in the warm, humid atmosphere. ⊠ *A85, Dalmally* ☎ *01866/822618* ⊕ *www.visitcruachan.co.uk* ⊠ *£7* ⊘ *Closed weekends Nov.–Mar.*

WHERE TO STAY

$
HOTEL
Fodor's Choice
★

Taychreggan Hotel. Peace and quiet are the big selling points of this lovely country-house hotel beside Loch Awe. Once a drovers' inn, the whitewashed building is surrounded by lawns and wooded gardens. **Pros:** lovely setting; activities including fishing and kayaking; wonderful meals. **Cons:** off the beaten track. $ *Rooms from: £99* ⊠ *Off B845, Kilchrenan* ☎ *01866/833211* ⊕ *www.taychregganhotel.co.uk* ⇆ *18 rooms* ♭⊙♭ *Free breakfast.*

INVERARAY

21 miles south of Loch Awe, 61 miles north of Glasgow, 29 miles west of Loch Lomond.

Fodor's Choice
★

Inveraray's star attraction is the grandiose seat of the Campbell Dukes of Argyll, for centuries the most powerful magnates of the Highlands. It's a trim little township, planned and built in the mid-18th century at the behest of the third duke. There are fine views of Loch Fyne, and there are gardens and museums to see nearby.

GETTING HERE AND AROUND

Driving from Oban, take the A85 and the A819 beyond Loch Awe (the village). From Glasgow, take the A82, turn on to the A83 at Arrochar, and make the long drive around Loch Fyne.

ESSENTIALS

Visitor Information Inveraray Tourist Information Centre. ✉ *Front St.* ☎ *01499/302063* ⊕ *www.visitscotland.com.*

EXPLORING

Ardkinglas Woodland Garden. Rambling over 12,000 acres, one of Britain's finest collections of conifers is set off by rhododendron blossoms in early summer. You can find the garden around the head of Loch Fyne, about 10 miles east of Inveraray. There's a wild woodland walk beyond the garden; both are open all year. The house, regarded as architect Sir Robert Lorimer's masterpiece, is only open to visitors on Fridays between April and October. ✉ *Ardkinglas Estate, Cairndow* ☎ *01499/600261* ⊕ *www.ardkinglas.com* ✄ *£5.*

FAMILY
Fodor's Choice
★
Auchindrain Museum. Step a few centuries back in time at this open-air museum, a rare surviving example of an 18th-century communal-tenancy farm. About 250 years ago, there were several thousand working communities like Auchindrain. Auchindrain was the last of them, its final tenant leaving in 1963. Today the bracken-thatch and iron-roof buildings, about 20 in all, give you a feel for early farming life in the Highland communities. Several houses are furnished and tell the story of their occupants. A tearoom is open morning to afternoon. ✉ *Auchindrain* ✢ *Off A83 about 6 miles south of Inveraray* ☎ *01499/500235* ⊕ *auchindrain.org.uk* ✄ *£7.50* ☉ *Closed Nov.–Mar.*

Crarae Garden. Exotic Himalayan plants flourish in the gentle microclimate of this 100-acre garden, where the Crarae Burn, a small stream, cascades through a rocky gorge. Rhododendrons, azaleas, and magnolias lend color, and native flowers and trees attract birds and butterflies. ✉ *A83* ✢ *10 miles southwest of Inveraray* ☎ *01546/886614* ⊕ *www.nts.org.uk* ✄ *£6.50* ☉ *Closed Nov.–Mar.*

Inveraray Castle. The current seat of the Chief of the Clan Campbell is a smart, grayish-green turreted stone house with a self-satisfied air. Set among well-tended grounds, it contains displays of luxurious furnishings and interesting art, as well as a huge armory. Built between 1743 and 1789, the castle has spires on the four corner turrets that give it a vaguely French look. Tours of the castle follow the history of the powerful Campbell family and how it acquired its considerable wealth. There is a tearoom for snacks and light lunches. You can hike around the extensive estate grounds, but wear sturdy footwear. ✉ *Off A83* ☎ *01499/302203* ⊕ *www.inveraray-castle.com* ✄ *£11* ☉ *Closed Nov.–Mar.*

18

WHERE TO EAT AND STAY

$$ SEAFOOD Fodor's Choice ★ 🍴 **Loch Fyne Oyster Bar and Restaurant.** The legendary flagship of a chain of seafood restaurants that now stretches across the United Kingdom, this restaurant continues to please with its emphasis on ultrafresh, locally sourced seafood, simply prepared. Oysters, are, of course, a keynote, but the menu also features mussels, lobster, prawns, salmon, and much more from the sea, accompanied by perfect crunchy green vegetables such as peas, beans, and asparagus. **Known for:** plump oysters perfectly prepared; meltingly tender smoked salmon. [$] *Average main: £19* ✉ *Clachan Farm, A83, Cairndow* ☎ *01499/600482* 🌐 *www.lochfyne.com.*

$ HOTEL Fodor's Choice ★ 🏨 **The George Hotel.** The George has been Inveraray's social hub since the 18th century, when it was a coaching inn, and it still exudes history. **Pros:** excellent restaurant; atmospheric bars. **Cons:** too much tartan for some; unattractive reception area. [$] *Rooms from: £85* ✉ *Main St. E* ☎ *01499/302111* 🌐 *www.thegeorgehotel.co.uk* 🛏 *25 rooms* 🍽 *Free breakfast.*

KINTYRE PENINSULA

57 miles south of Crinan (to Campbeltown).

Rivers and streams crisscross this long, narrow strip of green pasturelands and hills stretching south from Lochgilphead.

GETTING HERE AND AROUND

Continue south on the A83 (the road to Campbeltown) to Tarbert. Some 4 miles farther along the A83 is Kennacraig, where you catch the ferry to Islay. Beyond that is the pier at Tayinloan; CalMac ferries run from here to the Isle of Gigha.

Flybe operates flights from Glasgow to Campbeltown.

ESSENTIALS

Air Travel Contact Campbeltown Airport. ✉ *Off A83, Campbeltown* ✣ *At Machrihanish, 3 miles west of Campbeltown* ☎ *01586/553797* 🌐 *www.hial.co.uk.*

Visitor Information Campbeltown Information Centre. ✉ *Mackinnon House, The Pier, Campbeltown* ☎ *01586/556162* 🌐 *www.visitscotland.com.* **Tarbert Information Centre.** ✉ *Harbour St.* ☎ *01880/820429* 🌐 *www.tarbertlochfyne.com.*

EXPLORING

Isle of Gigha. Barely 7 miles long, this sheltered island between Kintyre and Islay has sandy beaches and rich wildlife. Ferries make the 20-minute trip from Tayinloan on the mainland. ✉ *Isle of Gigha* ☎ *01583/505390* 🌐 *www.gigha.org.uk.*

GOLF

Machrihanish Golf Club. For many Scots golfers (and they should know) Machrihanish's out-of-the-way location makes it a place of pilgrimage. Laid out in 1876, it's an intimidatingly memorable links course by a sandy bay. There is also a 9-hole course, The Pans. ✉ *Off B843, Machrihanish* ☎ *01586/810213* 🌐 *www.machgolf.com* 🎫 *£65 Apr.–Oct., £30 Nov.–Mar.* ⛳ *Championship Course: 18 holes, 6235 yards, par 70; The Pans: 9 holes (out), 2376 yards, par 34* ✍ *Reservations essential.*

ARRAN

Approaching Arran by sea, you'll first see forbidding Goatfell (2,868 feet) in the north, then the green fields of the south. These varied landscapes earn the island its sobriquet: "Scotland in Miniature." A temperate microclimate attracted ancient settlers whose stone circles still stand on the island. This weather also explains why it has long been a favorite getaway for Glaswegians, who come here to walk, climb Goatfell, or play golf.

GETTING HERE AND AROUND

Caledonian MacBrayne runs regular car and passenger ferries that cross the Firth of Clyde from Ardrossan (near Saltcoats) to Brodick throughout the year; crossing takes just under an hour. There is also a small ferry from Claonaig on the Kintyre Peninsula to Lochranza during the summer months.

Connecting trains run to the ferry at Ardrossan from Glasgow's Queen Street Station. Stagecoach runs regular local bus services around the island. Exploring the island by car is easy, as the A841 road circles it.

BRODICK

1 hour by ferry from Ardrossan.

Arran's largest village, Brodick, has a main street that is set back from the promenade and the lovely bay. Beyond that, it is really little more than a gateway to the rest of the island.

GETTING HERE AND AROUND

You can reach Brodick from Ardrossan by ferry. From Brodick the A841 circles the island; head south to reach Lamlash, north to reach Lochranza. The String Road crosses the island between Brodick and Machrie.

ESSENTIALS

The information center, opposite the landing point for the Ardrossan Ferry, has an accommodation desk as well as tourist information.

Visitor Information Brodick Information Centre. ⊠ *The Pier* ☎ *01770/303774* ⊕ *www.visitscotland.com.*

EXPLORING

Brodick Castle and Country Park. On the north side of Brodick Bay, this red sandstone mansion with typical Scottish-baronial features was built in the 16th century and was the seat of the dukes of Hamilton, who added to it extensively during the 19th century. ■ **TIP→ The castle is closed for repairs until 2019, but you can explore the expansive gardens, which are open all year.** In summer they are ablaze with azaleas and rhododendrons.

The country park that surrounds the castle embraces Arran's most striking scenery, rising to the 2,867-foot summit of Goatfell, the island's highest peak. The beautiful upland landscape is more challenging to explore than it seems, so it's important to go prepared with sturdy footwear and waterproof clothing. From the summit there is a stunning panoramic view of the Firth, Kintyre, and the Ayrshire coast, and on a

18

clear day you can just see Ireland. ✉ *Off A841, 1 mile north of Brodick Pier* ☎ *0844/493–2152* 🌐 *www.nts.org.uk* ⏲ *Castle closed until 2019.*

Isle of Arran Heritage Museum. A typical Arran cottage, a re-created 1940s schoolroom, and farm buildings filled with antiquated implements that were in use within living memory make this lively little museum a must-see for anyone interested in the island's social history. ✉ *Rosaburn, A841* ☎ *01770/302636* 🌐 *www.arranmuseum.co.uk* 🎟 *£4* ⏲ *Closed Nov.–Mar.*

WHERE TO EAT AND STAY

$$ BRITISH 🍴 **Brodick Bar and Brasserie.** This lively bar and restaurant serves fixed-price lunch and dinner menus featuring popular if unadventurous seafood favorites such as monkfish, halibut, and scallops, and adds spice to the mix with an array of Asian-influenced dishes. Like many places in the west of Scotland, hours are restricted so it is well worth booking ahead. **Known for:** perfect grilled scallops; surprising seafood curries. [$] *Average main: £16* ✉ *Alma Rd.* ☎ *01770/302169* 🌐 *www.brodickbar.co.uk.*

$$$$ RESORT FAMILY Fodor's Choice ★ 🏨 **Auchrannie Resort.** With outstanding indoor and outdoor leisure facilities (including two pools and a spa), well-designed modern rooms, and three restaurants and bars, Auchrannie is by far the best place to stay on Arran. **Pros:** choice of restaurants; good for families; excellent outdoor activities. **Cons:** could be anywhere. [$] *Rooms from: £269* ✉ *Auchrannie Rd.* ☎ *01770/30234* 🌐 *www.auchrannie.co.uk* 🛏 *115 rooms* 🍽 *Free breakfast.*

SHOPPING

Arran Aromatics. This is one of Scotland's best-known suppliers of scents, soaps, and perfumes of every kind. The shop is filled with pleasant smells, and between May and September a tour of the soap factory is available every Thursday evening. ✉ *Home Farm, A841* ☎ *01770/302595* 🌐 *www.arranaromatics.com.*

Isle of Arran Cheese Company. Arran is famous for its cheeses, especially its cheddar and its Arran blue; stop here to sample and buy handmade Scottish cheeses. ✉ *The Home Farm, A841* ☎ *01770/302788* 🌐 *www.arranscheeseshop.co.uk.*

MACHRIE

10 miles west of Brodick, 11 miles north of Lagg.

The area surrounding Machrie, home to a popular beach, is littered with prehistoric sites: chambered cairns, hut circles, and standing stones dating from the Bronze Age.

GETTING HERE AND AROUND

The quick route to Machrie is via the String Road (B880) from Brodick; turn off onto the Machrie Road 5 miles outside Brodick. A much longer but stunning journey will take you from Brodick, north to Lochranza, around the island to Machrie, and down the island's dramatic west coast, a distance of some 28 miles.

EXPLORING
Machrie Moor Stone Circles. Six ancient circles of boulders and head-high sandstone pillars are scattered across Machrie Moor. These relics of a prehistoric culture are as old as Egypt's pyramids, if not quite as impressive, and the site evokes a dim and distant past. ⊹ *1½ miles north of Machrie* ⊕ *www.historicenvironment.scot.*

WHERE TO EAT
$

TURKISH

✕ **Cafe Thyme.** This bright and pleasant restaurant offers a combination of Scottish and Turkish flavors (an expression of the owners' backgrounds) as well as fine views out to sea. Look for meze as well as *pides* (Turkish pizza)—try the haggis-and-cheese or crayfish-and-olive combinations. **Known for:** Turkish-style meze; unusual East-West fusion dishes. **$** *Average main: £12* ✉ *Machrie* ⊹ *Next to Old Byre Visitor Centre* ☎ *01770/840608* ⊕ *www.oldbyre.co.uk/cafethyme.irs* ⊗ *No dinner Oct.–Apr. and Sun. in May–Sept.*

LOCHRANZA

13 miles north of Machrie, 14 miles north of Brodick.

Lochranza shows Arran's wilder northern side, with rocky seashores and sweeping slopes leading to the stark granite peaks of Goatfell and Caisteal Abahail (2,735 feet), which dominate the skyline.

Arran's only distillery, the sparkling Isle of Arran Distillery, nestles in the hills overlooking Lochranza Bay.

GETTING HERE AND AROUND
Lochranza is north of Brodick via the A841.

EXPLORING
Fodor's Choice

★

Isle of Arran Distillery. The open aspect and closeness to the sea explains the taste of Arran's well-respected single malt, light and airy and with the scent of sea and fields. The round white building housing the distillery sits comfortably among fields and hills in the northernmost part of the island. The tours take the visitor through the process of creating whisky, with a small or slightly larger tasting depending on the level. The basic tour ends with a dram. The CASKS café-restaurant is a comfortable place for a long lunch. ✉ *Distillery Visitor Centre* ☎ *01770/830264* ⊕ *www.arranwhisky.com* ☜ *Tours from £8.*

Fodor's Choice

★

Lochranza Castle. Perched above the bay, Lochranza is Arran's most picturesque ruin and occupies a special place in Scotland's history. It was here that Robert the Bruce, after years of dithering, returned from exile to commit himself to the war for Scotland's independence. ✉ *Off A841* ☎ *0131/668–8800* ⊕ *www.historicenvironment.scot* ⊗ *Closed Oct.–Mar.*

WHERE TO STAY
$

B&B/INN

🛏 **Butt Lodge.** Set in 2 acres of private woods and gardens overlooking Kilbrannan Sound, this onetime Victorian shooting lodge offers a personalized welcome from owners who really make guests feel at home with hearty (but healthy) Scottish breakfasts and complimentary afternoon tea, served in a cozy lounge. **Pros:** peace and quiet; luxurious rooms and suites; great views. **Cons:** a little hard to find, up a farm

18

track; no bar. $ *Rooms from: £95* ✉ *off Newton Rd.* ✛ *½ mile east of Lochranza* ☎ *01770/830333* ⊕ *www.buttlodge.co.uk* ⮐ *6 rooms* ⦿ *Free breakfast.*

ISLAY AND JURA

Islay is an island of rolling fields and pastures, heather-covered uplands where red deer roam and rutting stags clash antlers in spring, and white-sand beaches that on a summer day can look as enticing as any Caribbean strand. Huge flocks of Arctic wildfowl migrate to Islay in fall, leaving again in spring, when their wings literally darken the sunset sky. This was the long-ago seat of the Macdonald Lords of the Isles, a mongrel Celtic-Norse dynasty that held sway over the southern Hebrides for almost three centuries. Some of their heritage can still be seen. But it's a different inheritance that draws many visitors, namely the smoky, peaty malt whisky produced here by eight world-famous distilleries. In sharp contrast to Islay's gaggle of villages set among rolling moorland and fertile pastures, thinly populated Jura is ruggedly beautiful, with a hilly landscape dominated by twin summits, the Paps of Jura, so named because of their silhouette, reminiscent of shapely bosoms.

BOWMORE

On Islay: 11 miles north of Port Ellen.

Bowmore, Islay's capital, is a good base for touring because it's central to Islay's main routes. A tidy town, its grid pattern was laid out in 1768 by local landowner Daniel Campbell, of Shawfield. Main Street stretches from the pier head to the commanding parish church, built in 1767 in an unusual circular design—so the devil could not hide in a corner.

GETTING HERE AND AROUND

Flybe flights from Glasgow to Islay Airport take 40 minutes; the airport is 5 miles north of Port Ellen. The trip by CalMac ferry from Kennacraig to Port Ellen takes about 2½ hours; ferries also travel less frequently to Port Askaig. From Port Ellen it is 10 miles on the A846 to reach Bowmore; drivers should use caution during the first mile out of Port Ellen, as the road is filled with sharp turns. The rest of the route is straight but bumpy, because the road is laid across peat bog.

Bus service is available on the island through Islay Coaches; comprehensive timetables are available from the tourist information center.

ESSENTIALS

Air Travel Contact Islay Airport. ✉ *A846, Glenegedale* ☎ *01496/302022* ⊕ *www.hial.co.uk.*

Visitor Information Bowmore Visitor Information Centre. ✉ *The Square* ☎ *01496/305165* ⊕ *www.visitscotland.com.*

EXPLORING

Fodor's Choice ★ **Bowmore Distillery.** Bowmore is the grand old lady of Islay's distilleries, and a tour is a must for any visitor. In business since 1779, the distillery, like all Islay whisky makers, stands by the sea. Standard tours include a walk around the malting areas and the stills, and connoisseurs can opt for in-depth tours that include tutored tastings. ✉ *School St.* ☎ *01496/810441* 🌐 *www.bowmore.com* 🎟 *From £7* 🕓 *Closed Sun. Nov.–Mar.*

Islay Woollen Mill. Gorgeous tweed, plaid, and tartan clothing, wraps, and throws—woven at this historic mill and dyed in subtle, traditional tones—are sold here. ✉ *A846* ✣ *4 miles outside Bowmore on the A846* ☎ *01496/810563* 🌐 *www.islaywoollenmill.co.uk* 🎟 *Free* 🕓 *Closed Sun.*

WHERE TO EAT

$$ SEAFOOD Fodor's Choice ★ 🍴 **Harbour Inn.** An adjunct of the Bowmore distillery, the Harbour Inn has a bar frequented by locals and a more upscale restaurant with a menu that emphasizes oysters, langoustines, mussels, and other local seafood. The elegant dining room looks out onto the water. **Known for:** imaginative seafood combinations; North African–influenced vegetarian dishes. [$] *Average main: £18* ✉ *The Square* ☎ *01496/810330* 🌐 *www.bowmore.com/harbour-inn.*

SHOPPING

Islay Whisky Shop. If you don't have time to visit all of Islay's distilleries, let alone those elsewhere, you can do worse than visit this shop with its enormous collection of whiskies. ✉ *Shore St.* ☎ *01496/810684* 🌐 *www.islaywhiskyshop.com.*

PORT CHARLOTTE

On Islay: 11 miles west of Bowmore.

Planned by a benevolent 19th-century laird (and named after his mom), Port Charlotte is an unusually (for Scotland) pretty village, with wild landscapes and sandy beaches nearby. South of the village, the A847 road leads to **Portnahaven** and **Port Wemyss**, where pleasing white cottages stand in a crescent around the headland.

GETTING HERE AND AROUND

To reach Port Charlotte from Bowmore, take the A846 via Bridgend and then the A847, Portnahaven Road. Islay Coaches and Royal Mail buses also travel here from Bowmore.

EXPLORING

Museum of Islay Life. A converted church is home to this local museum, a haphazard collection of local artifacts, photographs, and memorabilia. There is also a local history archive. ✉ *A847* ☎ *01496/850358* 🌐 *www.islaymuseum.org* 🎟 *£3.50* 🕓 *Closed weekends and Nov.–Mar.*

WHERE TO STAY

$$$$ HOTEL Fodor's Choice ★ 🏨 **Port Charlotte Hotel.** Once a row of fishermen's cottages and with views over a sandy beach, this whitewashed Victorian hotel has been lovingly restored. **Pros:** beautiful location; lovely restaurant; views over the water. **Cons:** can be a little noisy from the bar; rooms are quite small.

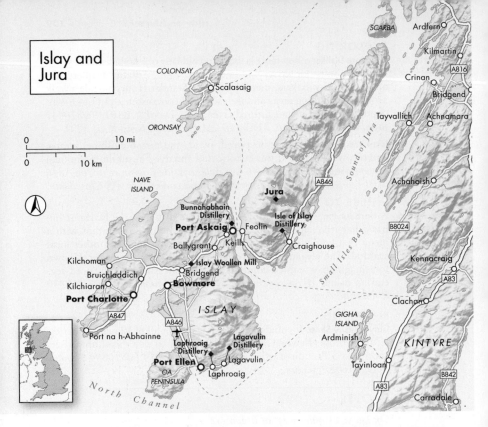

$ Rooms from: £230 ⊠ Main St. ☎ 01496/850360 ⊕ www.portcharlot-tehotel.co.uk ⇆ 10 rooms ⦿ Free breakfast.

PORT ELLEN

On Islay: 11 miles south of Bowmore.

Islay's sturdy community of Port Ellen was founded in the 1820s, and much of its architecture dates from the following decades. It has a harbor (ferries stop here), a few shops, and a handful of inns. The road traveling east from Port Ellen (the A846 to Ardbeg) passes three top distilleries and makes a pleasant afternoon's "whisky walk." All three distilleries offer tours, but you should call ahead for an appointment; there may be no tours on weekends at times. The last week in May, large numbers of whisky lovers descend on the island for the Islay Festival of Music and Malt, the heart of which is Port Ellen.

GETTING HERE AND AROUND

It is likely that Port Ellen will be your port of arrival on Islay. From here you can travel north to Bowmore, along the A846 before turning northwest towards Bridgend and Port Askaig.

EXPLORING

Lagavulin Distillery. Many malt whisky connoisseurs say the Lagavulin is the strongest nosed of all Islay's peaty malt whiskies. You can find out why, and how, with a distillery tour and tasting here. ✉ *A846* ☎ *01496/302400* 🌐 *www.discovering-distilleries.com* 🎫 *From £6.*

Laphroaig Distillery. Laphroiag (say la- *froig*) is Islay's most distinctive malt, redolent of peat, seaweed, and iodine. You can take a tour of the distillery, then settle in for a spell of sipping at the new whisky bar, which opened in 2017. ✉ *A846* ☎ *01496/302418* 🌐 *www.laphroaig.com* 🎫 *From £10* 🕒 *No tours weekends Jan.–Mar.*

WHERE TO STAY

$$$ HOTEL 🏨 **The Islay Hotel.** This charming hotel overlooking Port Ellen's harbor has large, bright rooms decorated in muted contemporary colors. **Pros:** central location; bright, welcoming interior; friendly staff. **Cons:** can get crowded. [$] *Rooms from: £190* ✉ *Charlotte St.* ☎ *01496/300109* 🌐 *www.theislayhotel.com* 🔑 *13 rooms* 🍴 *Free breakfast.*

PORT ASKAIG

On Islay: 11 miles northeast of Bowmore.

Serving as the ferry port for Jura and receiving ferries from Kennacraig, Port Askaig is a mere cluster of cottages. Uphill, just outside the village, a side road travels along the coast, giving impressive views of Jura on the way. There are distilleries near here, too; make appointments for tours.

GETTING HERE AND AROUND

Traveling from Bowmore, you can reach Port Askaig (where the road ends) via A846. The village is also served by local buses.

EXPLORING

Fodor's Choice ★ **Bunnahabhain Distillery.** Established in 1881, the Bunnahabhain (pronounced *Boon*-a- *ha*-bin) Distillery sits on the shore, with dramatic views across to the Paps of Jura. This is one of Scotland's most picturesque and evocative malt whisky distilleries, redolent of a preindustrialized era. ✉ *A846* ☎ *01496/840646* 🌐 *www.bunnahabhain.com* 🎫 *From £7* 🕒 *Closed Nov.–Mar. and Sun. in Apr.*

WHERE TO STAY

$$ B&B/INN 🏨 **Kilmeny Country House.** This luxurious bed-and-breakfast is on a 300-acre farm, but the rooms are so elegantly furnished that the place feels more like a hotel. **Pros:** elegant and quiet; great breakfast. **Cons:** easy to miss. [$] *Rooms from: £140* ✉ *A846, Ballygrant* ✥ *Signposted off the A846 to Port Askaig just before the village of Ballygrant* ☎ *01496/840668* 🌐 *www.kilmeny.co.uk* 🔑 *5 rooms* 🍴 *Free breakfast.*

JURA

5 minutes by ferry from Port Askaig.

The rugged, mountainous landscape of the island of Jura—home to only about 200 people—looms immediately east of Port Askaig, across the Sound of Islay: a perfect landscape for walkers. Jura has only one single-track road (the A846), which begins at Feolin, the ferry pier. It climbs across moorland, providing scenic views of the island's most striking feature, the Paps of Jura, three breast-shaped rounded peaks. The ruined Claig Castle, on an island just offshore, was built by the Lords of the Isles to control the sound. The island has no cash machines, so plan ahead.

GETTING HERE AND AROUND

The Port Askaig–Feolin car ferry takes five minutes to cross the Sound of Islay, and there is a passenger-only ferry during the summer from Tayvallich on Argyll to Craighouse. Bus service is also available from Craighouse and Inverlussa.

EXPLORING

Isle of Jura Distillery. The community of Craighouse has the island's only distillery, producing malt whisky since 1810. Tours must be booked in advance by phone or online. ✉ *Craighouse* ☎ *01496/820385* 🌐 *www.jurawhisky.com* 🎫 *Tours from £6* 🕒 *Closed mid-July–mid-Aug., weekends in Nov.–Mar., and Sun. in Apr.–Oct.*

WHERE TO STAY

$$ HOTEL 🏨 **Jura Hotel.** Jura's only hotel, next to the island's renowned distillery, has simple but cozy no-frills rooms, and its pleasant gardens are attractive on a summer day. **Pros:** convenient location; good, unpretentious restaurant; lively bar. **Cons:** some shared bathrooms. [$] *Rooms from: £100* ✉ *A846, Craighouse* ☎ *01496/820243* 🌐 *www.jurahotel.co.uk* 🛏 *17 rooms* 🍴 *Free breakfast.*

ISLE OF MULL AND IONA

Mull is one of the most beguiling of Scotland's isles, and happily it's also one of the easiest to get to. The island's landscapes range from the pretty harbor of Tobermory to dramatic Atlantic beaches on the west. In the south, the long road past the sweeping green slopes of the Ross of Mull leads to Iona, Scotland's holy island and a year-round attraction.

GETTING HERE AND AROUND

Ferries to Mull are run by the ubiquitous Caledonian MacBrayne. Its most frequent car-ferry route to Mull is from Oban to Craignure (45 minutes). Two shorter routes are from Lochaline on the Morvern Peninsula to Fishnish (15 minutes), or Kilchoan (on the Adrnamurchan Peninsula) to Tobermory (15 minutes). The Kilchoan-Lochaline ferry is not bookable. West Coast Tours serves the east coast, running between Tobermory, Craignure, and Fionnphort (for the ferry to Iona).

CRAIGNURE

On Mull: 40-minute ferry crossing from Oban, 15-minute ferry crossing to Fishnish (5 miles northwest of Craignure) from Lochaline.

Craignure, little more than a pier and some houses, is close to the well-known Duart Castle. Reservations for the year-round ferries that travel from Oban to Craignure are advisable in summer. The ferry from Lochaline to Fishnish, just northwest of Craignure, does not accept reservations and does not run on Sunday.

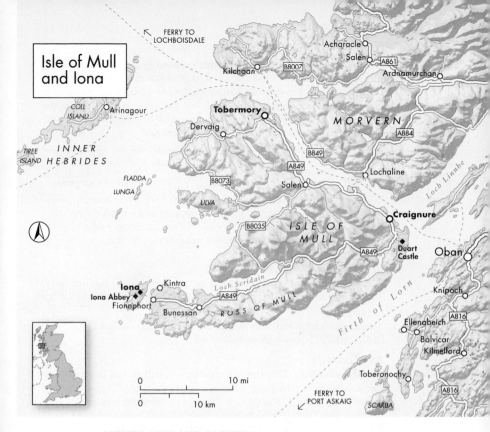

Isle of Mull and Iona

FERRY TO LOCHBOISDALE

Acharacle
Salen
A861
Kilchoan
B8007
Ardnamurchan

COLL ISLAND Arinagour
Tobermory
Dervaig
MORVERN
A884

TIREE ISLAND INNER HEBRIDES
B849
A849
Lochaline

FLADDA
B8073
Salen
LUNGA
ULVA

B8035
ISLE OF MULL
Craignure

A849
Duart Castle
Oban

Iona
Kintra
Loch Scridain
Knipoch

Iona Abbey
A849
Fionnphort
Bunessan
ROSS OF MULL
Firth of Lorn

Ellenabeich
Balvicar
Kilmelford

Toberonochy
A816

0   10 mi
0   10 km

FERRY TO PORT ASKAIG
SCARBA

GETTING HERE AND AROUND

The arrival point for the 40-minute ferry crossing from Oban, Craignure is the starting point for further travel on Mull northwest toward Salen and Tobermory, or toward Fionnphort and the Iona ferry to the southwest.

ESSENTIALS

Visitor Information Craignure Information Centre. ⊠ *The Pierhead* ☎ *01680/812377* ⊕ *www.visitscotland.com.*

EXPLORING

Fodor'sChoice ★ **Duart Castle.** The 13th-century Duart Castle stands dramatically atop a cliff overlooking the Sound of Mull. The ancient seat of the Macleans, it was ruined by the Campbells, their archenemies, in 1691 but restored by Sir Fitzroy Maclean in 1911. Inside you can visit the dungeons and state rooms, then climb the keep for a view of the waterfront. Nearby stands the **Millennium Wood,** planted in 2000 with indigenous trees. To reach Duart by car, take the A849 and turn left around the shore of Duart Bay. From Craignure's ferry port, there is a direct bus that takes you to the castle in about 10 minutes. ⊠ *A849, 3 miles southeast of Craignure* ☎ *01680/812309* ⊕ *www.duartcastle.com* ⊠ *£6.50* ⊗ *Closed Nov.–Mar.*

WHERE TO STAY

$ B&B/INN **Craignure Inn.** Snug bedrooms with exposed beams, polished wood furniture, and views of the Sound of Mull make this 18th-century inn very appealing. **Pros:** lively bar scene; hearty local food; expansive views. **Cons:** live music can get loud; bar can get very busy. [$] *Rooms from: £82* ✉ *A849, near the ferry pier* ☎ *01680/812305* 🌐 *www.craignure-inn.co.uk* 🛏 *3 rooms* 🍴 *Free breakfast.*

TOBERMORY

On Mull: 5 miles northeast of Dervaig, 21 miles north of Craignure.

Fodor's Choice ★ With its rainbow crescent of brightly painted harborside houses, Tobermory is the most photogenic village in the Isles and among the prettiest in all Scotland. Unsurprisingly, it's a lively tourist center and a popular base for exploring Mull, its smaller neighbors, and the sea-life-filled surrounding waters.

GETTING HERE AND AROUND

The most frequent service to Mull is via the Oban-Craignure ferry. Tobermory is 21 miles from Craignure along the A849/848 (via Salen).

ESSENTIALS

Visitor Information Mull Information Centre. ✉ *Ledaig Car Park* ☎ *01683/302875* 🌐 *www.isle-of-mull.net.*

EXPLORING

Fodor's Choice ★ **Tobermory Distillery.** Tobermory's cute little distillery has been making distinctive malts (the peaty Ledaig and the unpeated, lighter-tasting Tobermory) since 1798, though there have been intervening decades when it was "silent" and produced no whisky. It was relaunched in 1993, and a tour here is a more personal experience than is offered by some bigger, better-known distilleries. ✉ *Bad-Daraich House, Ledaig* ✣ *Off Main St. on south side of harbor* ☎ *01688/302647* 🌐 *www.tobermorydistillery.com* 🎫 *Tours from £8.*

Fodor's Choice ★ **Whale Watch With Us.** High-speed boats carrying 12 passengers leave from Tobermory's harbor on scenic cruises, wildlife sea safaris, and whale-watching trips lasting up to four hours. You'll have a good chance of spotting dolphins, porpoises, and minke whales. If you're lucky, basking sharks and some of the sound's orcas may also put in an appearance. ✉ *Raraig House, Raeric Rd.* ✣ *Ledaig pontoons, opposite car park and Tobermory Harbor Authority on Tobermory waterfront* ☎ *01688/302875* 🌐 *whalewatchwithus.com* 🎫 *From £30.*

WHERE TO EAT AND STAY

$$ SEAFOOD Fodor's Choice ★ 🍴 **Café Fish.** This restaurant's location has certainly contributed to its success—it's perched on the pier at the end of Tobermory. The owners pride themselves on the freshness of their fish; they have their own boat and bring in their own seafood each day. **Known for:** hand-dived scallops; very fresh lobster. [$] *Average main: £18* ✉ *The Pier* ☎ *01688/301253* 🌐 *www.thecafefish.com* ⏲ *Closed Jan.–mid-Mar.*

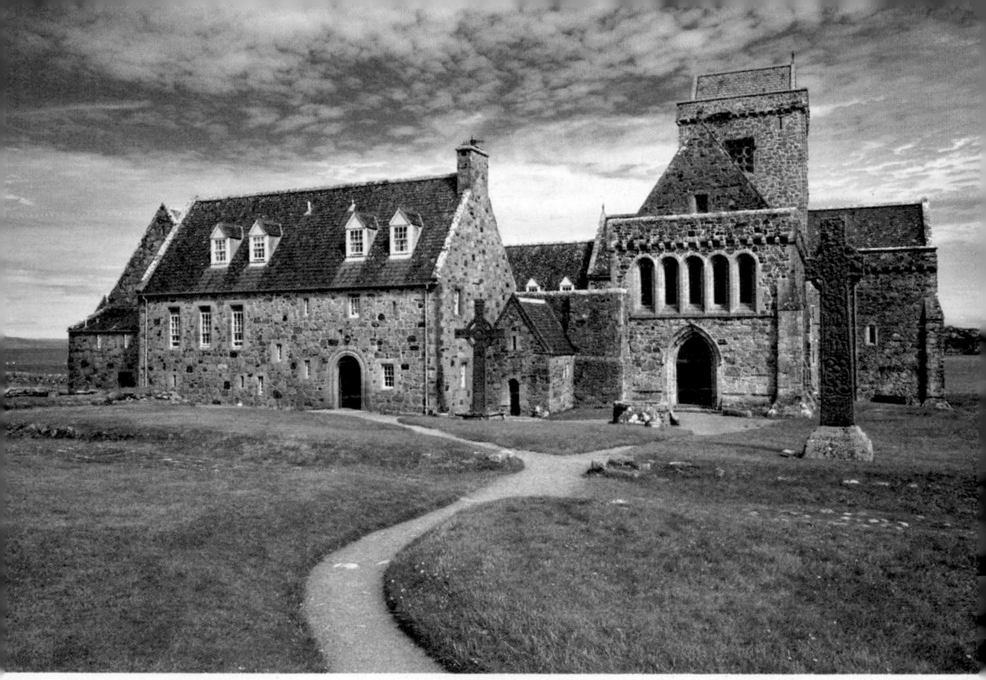

Once a key center of Christianity in Scotland, Iona Abbey still serves an ecumenical religious community.

$$ **HOTEL** 🏨 **Western Isles Hotel.** This grand hotel from the Victorian era looks down on Tobermory from its idyllic location overlooking the Sound of Mull. **Pros:** the view is brilliant; spacious public rooms; great food. **Cons:** some rooms look onto the car park; rooms vary in size. [$] *Rooms from: £130* ✉ *Off B882* ☎ *01688/302012* 🌐 *www.westernisleshotel.co.uk* 🛏 *26 rooms* 🍴 *Free breakfast.*

IONA

5 minutes by ferry from Fionnphort (Mull), which is 36 miles west of Craignure.

The ruined abbey on Iona gives little hint that this was once one of the most important Christian religious centers in the land. The priceless *Book of Kells* (now in Dublin) was illustrated here, and it was the monks of Iona who spread Christian ideas across Scotland and the north. The abbey was founded in the year 563 by the fiery and argumentative Columba (circa 521–97) after his expulsion from Ireland. Until the 11th century, many of Scotland's kings and rulers were buried here, their tombstones still visible inside the abbey. While few visitors venture beyond the pier and the abbey, there are several tranquil paths around the island.

GETTING HERE AND AROUND

Caledonian MacBrayne's ferry from Fionnphort departs at regular intervals throughout the year (£4.50 round-trip). Timetables are available on the Caledonian MacBrayne website. Note that cars are not permitted; there's a parking lot by the ferry at Fionnphort.

EXPLORING

Fodor's Choice ★ **Iona Abbey.** Overseen by St. Columba, who traveled here from Ireland, Iona was the birthplace of Christianity in Scotland in the 6th century. It survived repeated Norse sackings before falling into disuse around the time of the Reformation. Restoration work began at the beginning of the 20th century. Today the restored buildings serve as a spiritual center under the jurisdiction of the Church of Scotland. Guided tours by the Iona Community, an ecumenical religious group, begin every half hour in summer and on demand in winter. ✉ *Iona* ☎ *01681/700512* 🌐 *www.iona.org.uk* 🎟 *£7.50.*

WHERE TO STAY

$$ HOTEL 🏨 **St. Columba Hotel.** As befits a religious retreat, rooms in this 1846 minister's home are simple to the point of being spartan, but those in the front make up for it with glorious views across the Sound of Iona to Mull. **Pros:** impressive views; nice log fires; Wi-Fi throughout the hotel. **Cons:** no TVs; basic decor. [$] *Rooms from: £135* ✉ *Next to cathedral* ✥ *About ¼ mile from the ferry pier* ☎ *01681/700304* 🌐 *www.stcolumba-hotel.co.uk* ⏲ *Closed Nov.–Mar.* 🛏 *27 rooms* 🍴 *Free breakfast.*

SHOPPING

Iona Community Shop. The shop carries Celtic-inspired gift items, as well as sheet music, songbooks, and CDs. It also sells local crafts and the Wild Goose publications of the Iona Community. ✉ *Across from Iona Abbey* ☎ *01681/700404* 🌐 *www.iona.org.uk.*

Low Door. This shop attached to the St. Columba Hotel sells locally produced jams, chutneys, and other artifacts as well as cookbooks. ■ **TIP→ The store is only open April to October.** ✉ *Beside St. Columba Hotel* ☎ *01681/700483* 🌐 *www.stcolumba-hotel.co.uk.*

INVERNESS, SKYE, AND THE NORTHERN HIGHLANDS

Visit Fodors.com for advice, updates, and bookings

WELCOME TO INVERNESS, SKYE, AND THE NORTHERN HIGHLANDS

TOP REASONS TO GO

★ **History:** Hear stories of the Highland people and famous figures like Bonnie Prince Charlie, and absorb the atmosphere of castles and battlefields, at Culloden Moor, Cawdor and Dunvegan castles, Fort George, and Glencoe.

★ **The outdoors:** The Great Glen is renowned for its hill walking. Some of the best routes are around Glen Nevis, Glencoe, and on Ben Nevis, the highest mountain in Britain. The landscapes of Skye and the Northern Highlands are stunning.

★ **Whisky:** The two western-most distilleries on the Malt Whisky Trail are in Forres. Benromach is the smallest distillery in Moray and has excellent tours; Dallas Dhu is preserved as a museum.

★ **Skye:** Scotland in miniature, the landscape of Skye ranges from the lush, undulating hills and coastal tracks of Sleat to the deep glens and sawtooth peaks of the Cuillin Mountains.

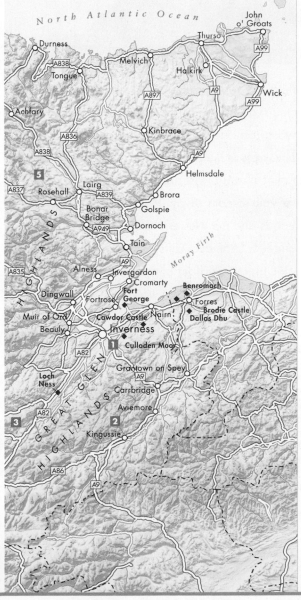

1 Inverness and Nearby. From the small city of Inverness, just about anywhere in the Great Glen is a day trip. Spend your days exploring Culloden Moor, Brodie Castle, or Cawdor Castle.

2 Speyside and the Cairngorms. Speyside is best known for Its whisky distilleries while in and around the Cairngorms there are mountains, lochs, rivers, and dozens of cycling and walking paths.

3 Loch Ness, Fort William, and Nearby. Have a go trying to spot Nessie from the banks of Loch Ness. For something wilder, base yourself at Fort William and take in the spectacular scenery of Glencoe and Glen Nevis or climb Britain's highest peak, Ben Nevis.

4 Isle of Skye. Scotland's most famous island is home to the 11 peaks of the Cuillin Mountains, the quiet gardens of Sleat, and the dramatic peninsulas of Waternish and Trotternish.

5 The Northern Highlands. Northwest Scotland is known for its dramatic coastlines and craggy hills.

19

Updated by Eilidh McCabe and Joseph Reaney

Defined by its striking topography, the Great Glen brings together mountains and myths, history and wild nature— then lets you wash it all down with a dram of the world's finest whisky. Inverness is the gateway to an area in which the views from almost every twist and bend in the circuitous roads may take your breath away. Wild and remote, the Northern Highlands and the Western Isles of Scotland have a timeless grandeur. Dramatic cliffs, long beaches, and craggy mountains that rise up out of moorland like islands in a sea heighten the romance and mystery.

The Great Glen Fault runs diagonally through the Highlands of Scotland and was formed when two tectonic plates collided, shoving masses of the crust southwest toward the Atlantic Ocean. Over time the rift broadened into a glen, and a thin line of lochs now lies along its seam. The most famous of these is deep, murky Loch Ness, home to the elusive Loch Ness monster.

The city of Inverness has a growing reputation for excellent restaurants, and from here nearly everything in the Great Glen is an easy day trip. Just south of the city the 13th-century ruined Urquhart Castle sits on the shores of Loch Ness. In Fort Augustus, the Caledonian Canal joins Inverness to Fort William via a series of 29 locks. At the western end of the canal, Ben Nevis, Britain's highest mountain, rises sharply. The Nevis Range, like Cairngorms National Park to the east, is ideal for walking, climbing, and mountain biking through the hills and glens.

Impressive long, sandy beaches stretch out along the coast from the towns of Nairn and Findhorn. Finally, the Malt Whisky Trail begins in Forres and follows the wide, fast River Spey south until it butts against the Cairngorm Mountains and the old Caledonian forests, with their diverse and rare wildlife.

The Northern Highlands is a region where roads hug the coast, dipping down toward beaches and back up for stunning views over the clear ocean, across to the dramatic mountains, or along stunning heather moorland. These twisted, undulating roads—many of them single-track—demand that you shift down a gear, pause to let others pass, and take the time to do less and experience more of the rough-hewn beauty. If you're lucky, you may see a puffin fishing below the cliffs, an eagle swooping for a hare, or perhaps even a pod of dolphins or whales swimming off the coast. Adorable Highland *coos* (cows) are sure to make an appearance, too.

Sutherland was once the southern land belonging to the Vikings, and some names reflect this. Cape Wrath got its name from the Viking word *hvarth*, meaning "turning point," and Suilven translates as "pillar." The Isle of Skye and the Outer Hebrides are referred to as the Western Isles, and remain the stronghold of the Gaelic language. Skye is often called Scotland in miniature because the terrain shifts from lush valleys in the south, to the rugged girdle of the Cuillin Mountains, and then to the steep cliffs that define the northern coast. A short ferry journey away, the moody island of Lewis and Harris lays claim to the brilliant golden sands of Luskentyre and incredible prehistoric sites, from the lunar-aligned Calanais Standing Stones to the Iron Age Doune Broch.

PLANNER

WHEN TO GO

Late spring to early autumn is the best time to visit this region. If you catch good weather in summer, the days can be glorious. Unfortunately summer is also when you will encounter midges (tiny biting insects: keep walking, as they can't move very fast). The earlier in the spring or later in the fall you go, the greater the chances of your encountering the elements in their extreme form, and the fewer attractions and accommodations you will find open (even Skye closes down almost completely by the end of October.) Then again, you'll also find fewer tourists. Winter is best avoided altogether, although many Scots value the open fires and the warming whisky that make the off-season so appealing

PLANNING YOUR TIME

The Great Glen is an enormous area that can easily be broken into two separate trips. The first would be based in or near Inverness, allowing an exploration of Speyside, the Cairngorms, Cawdor and Brodie castles, and perhaps a few whisky-distillery tours. The second moves through the cloud-laden Glencoe and down through the moody Rannoch Moor, or toward the Road to the Isles; you could stay near Glencoe or in Fort William. To do the area justice you probably need at least three days.

The rough landscape of the Highlands and islands, as this region is sometimes called, means this isn't a place you can rush through. It could take eight busy days to do a coastal loop and also see some islands. Single-lane roadways, undulating landscapes, and eye-popping views will slow you down. You can base yourself in a town like Ullapool or Portree, or choose a B&B or hotel (of which there are many) tucked into the hills or sitting at the edge of a sea loch. If you have only a couple of days, head directly to the Isle of Skye and the other islands off the coast. They attract hordes of tourists, and for good reason, yet you don't have to walk far to find yourself in wild places, often in solitude. Sunday is a day of minimal activity here; restaurants, bars, and shops are closed, as are many sites.

GETTING HERE AND AROUND

AIR TRAVEL
Inverness Airport has flights from London, Edinburgh, and Glasgow. Domestic flights covering the Highlands and islands are operated by easyJet and Flybe. Fort William has bus and train connections with Glasgow, so Glasgow Airport can be a good access point.

Airport Contact Inverness Airport. ☎ 01667/464000 ⊕ www.invernessairport. co.uk.

BOAT AND FERRY TRAVEL
Ferry services are generally reliable, weather permitting. Car and passenger ferries run from Ullapool to Stornoway (Lewis and Harris), from Oban to Castlebay (Barra), from Mallaig to Lochboisdale (South Uist), and from Uig (Skye) to Tarbert (Lewis and Harris) and Lochmaddy (North Uist). The Hopscotch planned-route ticket by Caledonian MacBrayne (known locally as CalMac) gives considerable reductions on interisland ferry fares; it is worth calling ahead and asking for the best route plan.

Boat and Ferry Contact Caledonian MacBrayne (*CalMac*). ☎ 0800/066–5000 ⊕ www.calmac.co.uk.

BUS TRAVEL
A long-distance Scottish Citylink service connects Glasgow and Fort William. Inverness is also well served from the central belt of Scotland. Discount carrier Megabus (book online to avoid phone charges) has service to Inverness from various cities. Traveling around the Great Glen area without a car is challenging if not impossible, especially in the more rural areas. Stagecoach Highlands serves the Great Glen and around Fort William. A handful of postbus services (run by the postal service) can help get you to a few of the more remote corners of the area, although just a few seats are available on each bus.

Scottish Citylink runs two main routes in the Northern Highlands; one heading west to Ullapool and the other up the east coast to Scrabster (via Dornoch, Wick, and Thurso). It also has a route across the Isle of Skye to Uig, as does National Express. These buses can be a good way to see the region, but they don't run frequently. Once you're in the Northern Highlands, Stagecoach has some routes up the east coast of the mainland to Brora. It also has regular services on Skye.

Bus Contacts Megabus. ☎ 0900/160–0900 ⊕ www.megabus.com. **National Express.** ☎ 0871/781–8181 ⊕ www.nationalexpress.com. **Royal Mail Post Buses.** ☎ 0345/774–0740 ⊕ www.royalmail.com. **Scottish Citylink.** ☎ 0871/266–3333 ⊕ www.citylink.co.uk. **Stagecoach Highlands.** ☎ 01463/233371 ⊕ www.stagecoachbus.com.

CAR TRAVEL

As in all areas of rural Scotland, a car is a great asset for exploring this region, especially because the best of the area is away from the main roads. The winding single-lane roads in the Northern Highlands demand a degree of driving dexterity, however. On good days, single-track driving can be relaxing, with a lovely pace of stopping, waving, moving on. Note that in this sparsely populated area distances between gas stations can be considerable, so it is wise to fill your tank when you see one. You can reach Inverness in 3½ hours from Edinburgh or Glasgow; it's around 4½ hours to Skye. You can use the main A82 from Inverness to Fort William, or use the smaller B862/B852 roads to explore the much quieter east side of Loch Ness. Mallaig, west of Fort William, is reached via a new road, but there are still a few narrow and winding single-lane roads, which require slower speeds and concentration.

TRAIN TRAVEL

ScotRail has connections from London to Inverness and Fort William (including overnight sleeper service), as well as reliable links from Glasgow and Edinburgh. There's train service between Glasgow (Queen Street) and Inverness, via Aviemore, which gives access to the heart of Speyside.

Although there's no rail connection among towns within the Great Glen, this area has the West Highland Line, which links Fort William to Mallaig. This train, run by ScotRail, remains the most enjoyable way to experience the rugged hills and loch scenery between these two places. The Jacobite Steam Train is an exciting summer (mid-May to mid-October) option on the same route.

Train Contacts Jacobite Steam Train. ☎ *0844/850–4685* ⊕ *www.westcoastrailways.co.uk.* **ScotRail.** ☎ *0344/811–0141* ⊕ *www.scotrail.co.uk.*

RESTAURANTS

Northern Scotland has many fine restaurants, where talented chefs use locally grown produce. Inverness, Aviemore, and Fort William have plenty of cafés and restaurants in all price ranges. Inverness has particularly diverse dining options. Outside the towns there are many country-house hotels serving superb meals. The Isle of Skye has the most, and the most expensive, restaurants, many of them quite good. But you can find tasty meals almost everywhere, though in more remote regions you may have to drive some distance to find them. Remember that locals eat early, so most restaurants stop serving dinner at 9. *Restaurant reviews have been shortened. For full information, visit Fodors.com.*

HOTELS

In the countryside, towns have accommodations ranging from cozy inns to expansive hotels; in more remote areas your choice will usually be limited to smaller establishments. Book as far in advance as you can; the areas are very busy in the peak season and the best places fill up early. In Inverness, you may find it more appealing to stay outside the city center or in the pretty countryside nearby. In the more remote parts of Scotland your best lodging option may be to rent a cottage or house. Besides allowing you to make your own meals and to come and go as you please, it can also be less expensive. VisitScotland (⊕ *www. visitscotland.com*), the official tourism agency, lists many cottages and even rates them with stars, just like hotels. *Hotel reviews have been shortened. For full information, visit Fodors.com.*

WHAT IT COSTS IN POUNDS			
$	$$	$$$	$$$$
Restaurants	under £15	£15–£19	£20–£25	over £25
Hotels	under £100	£100–£160	£161–£220	over £220

Restaurant prices are the average cost of a main course at dinner or, if dinner is not served, at lunch. Hotel prices are the lowest cost of a standard double room in high season, including 20% V.A.T.

TOURS

Inverness Tours. This outfitter runs the occasional boat cruise, but it's mainly known for very good tours around the Highlands in well-equipped vehicles, led by expert guides and heritage enthusiasts. However, the price is per minibus, not per person, so while it's quite a bargain for parties of six or seven, it's less appealing for small groups. It may be possible to get single tickets if another group will sell its unused space. ☎ *01667/455699* ⊕ *www.invernesstours.com* ✉ *From £150.*

Rabbie's. This popular tour operator organizes tours throughout the Highlands, starting from Edinburgh, Glasgow, or Inverness. In small, comfortable, 16-seater minibuses, tours range from 1 to 17 days. ☎ *0131/226–3133* ⊕ *www.rabbies.com* ✉ *From £34.*

Scotland Tours. Choose from a wide range of bus tours for a wide range of budgets, taking anything from one to eight days. The company is Highland-owned, and the guides know their region well. ☎ *0131/226–1414* ⊕ *www.scotlandtours.com* ✉ *From £42.*

INVERNESS AND NEARBY

At the center of this region is Inverness, a small but appealing city that makes a useful gateway to the Great Glen. It has an increasingly strong range of restaurants and accommodations, but its cultural offerings remain more or less limited to what is happening at the Eden Court Theatre and the live music at a few good pubs.

East of Inverness, the infamous Culloden Moor still looks desolate on most days, and you can easily imagine the fierce, brief, and bloody battle that took place here in 1746 that ended in final, catastrophic defeat for the Jacobites and their quest to restore the exiled Stewarts to the British throne. Because Jacobite tales are interwoven with landmarks throughout this entire area, you will get much more out of this storied landscape if you first learn something about this thorny but colorful period of Scottish history. The Morayshire coast boasts many long beaches and some refined castles (Cawdor and Brodie) that are definitely worth a visit. Moving east along the inner Moray Firth, you might be tempted by Benromach distillery in Forres, a taste of what you can find farther south if you follow the Malt Whisky Trail.

INVERNESS

176 miles north of Glasgow, 109 miles northwest of Aberdeen, 161 miles northwest of Edinburgh.

It's not the prettiest or the most charming Scottish city, but with a few attractions and some reliably good hotels and restaurants, Inverness makes a practical base for exploring a region that has a lot to offer. From here you can fan out in almost any direction for interesting day trips: east to Moray and the distilleries near Forres, southeast to the Cairngorms, and south to Loch Ness. Throughout its past the town was burned and ravaged by Highland clans competing for dominance.

GETTING HERE AND AROUND

You can easily fly into Inverness Airport, as there are daily flights from London, Bristol, Birmingham, Manchester, and Belfast. However, there are also easy train and bus connections from Glasgow Airport. Scottish Citylink has service here, and Megabus has long-distance bus service from Edinburgh and Glasgow. ScotRail runs trains here from London, Edinburgh, Glasgow, and other cities.

Once you're here, you can explore much of the city on foot. A rental car makes exploring the surrounding area much easier. But if you don't have a car, there are bus and boat tours from the city center to a number of places in the Great Glen.

An unusual option from Inverness is a day trip to Orkney. John O'Groats Ferries runs day tours from Inverness to Orkney, daily from June through August. They cost £37 round-trip.

ESSENTIALS

Boat Contact John O'Groats Ferries. ☎ *01955/611353* ⊕ *www.jogferry.co.uk.*

Bus Contact Inverness Bus Station. ⊠ *Margaret St.* ☎ *01463/233371.*

Visitor Information Inverness. ⊠ *Castle Wynd* ☎ *01463/252401* ⊕ *www. inverness-scotland.com.*

EXPLORING

Fort George. After the fateful battle at Culloden, the nervous government in London ordered the construction of a large fort on a promontory reaching into the Moray Firth. Fort George was started in 1748 and completed some 20 years later. It's one of the best-preserved 18th-century military fortifications in Europe. At its height it housed 1,600 men and around 30,000 pounds of gunpowder. The on-site Highlanders Museum gives you a glimpse of the fort's history. The fort is 14 miles northeast of Inverness. ⊠ *Old Military Rd., Ardersier* ☎ *01667/460232* ⊕ *www.historicenvironment.scot* ⊠ *£9.*

Inverness Castle. One of Inverness's few historic landmarks is reddish sandstone Inverness Castle (now the local Sheriff Court), nestled above the river off Castle Road on Castle Hill. The current structure is Victorian, built after a former fort was blown up by the Jacobites in the

19

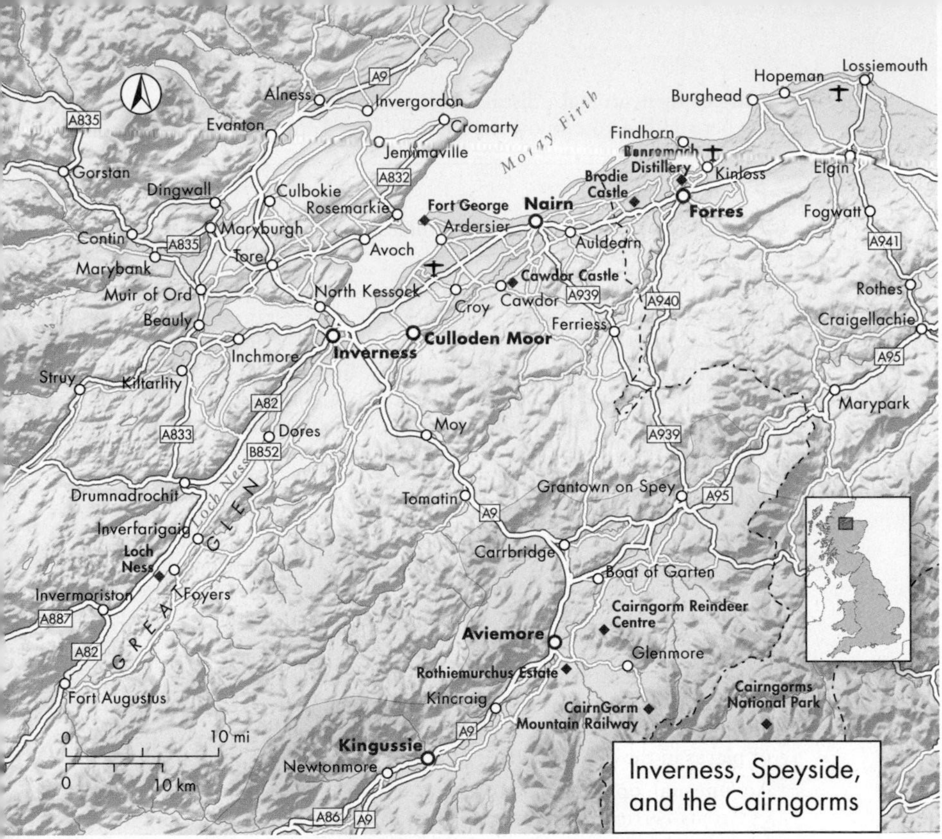
Inverness, Speyside, and the Cairngorms
A9
A835
Alness
Invergordon
Cromarty
Evanton
Moray Firth
Hopeman
Lossiemouth
Burghead
Findhorn
Benromach Distillery
Kinloss
Elgin
Brodie Castle
Forres
Jemimaville
A832
Gorstan
Dingwall
Culbokie
Rosemarkie
Fort George
Nairn
Ardersier
Fogwatt
Contin
A835
Maryburgh
Avoch
Auldearn
A941
Marybank
Tore
Cawdor Castle
Rothes
Muir of Ord
North Kessock
Croy
Cawdor
A939
A940
Beauly
Ferriess
Craigellachie
Inchmore
Inverness
Culloden Moor
A95
Struy
Kiltarlity
Marypark
A82
Moy
A833
Dores
B852
A939
Loch Ness
Drumnadrochit
Grantown on Spey
A95
Tomatin
A9
Inverfarigaig
Loch Ness
Carrbridge
Boat of Garten
Invermoriston
Foyers
A887
GREAT GLEN
Cairngorm Reindeer Centre
Aviemore
A82
Glenmore
Rothiemurchus Estate
Fort Augustus
Kincraig
Cairngorms National Park
CairnGorm Mountain Railway
0
10 mi
A9
Kingussie
0
10 km
Newtonmore
A86
A9

1745 campaign. The castle isn't open to the public, but you are free to wander the grounds. ✉ *41 Castle St.*

Inverness Cathedral. This handsome Victorian cathedral, dating from 1869, has two unique claims to fame; in addition to being the northernmost cathedral in the British Isles, it was, more significantly, the first cathedral to be built in Britain after the Reformation. The twin-turreted exterior of the building is made from characteristically reddish local Tarradale stone. Inside it follows a medieval layout, with the addition of an unusual patterned wooden floor. Check out the beautiful white marble font, carved in the shape of a seated angel. ✉ *Ardross St.* ☎ *01463/233535* 🌐 *www.morayepiscopalchurch.scot/inverness-cathedral* 🎟 *Free.*

WHERE TO EAT

$$
MODERN BRITISH
Fodor's Choice ★

🍴 **Cafe 1.** Consistently recommended by locals as one of the best restaurants in the area, Cafe 1 really practices what it preaches in terms of sustainable, local produce. Taking inspiration from such big names as Blue Hill in New York, the restaurant rears its own herds to provide the Hebridean lamb and Highland beef on the menu, maybe served with a simple order of chips (thick-cut fries) and rich garlic butter. **Known for:** castle views; melt-in-your-mouth lamb; ethically sourced ingredients. [$] *Average main: £18* ✉ *75 Castle St.* ☎ *01463/226200* 🌐 *www.cafe1.net* ⏲ *Closed Sun.*

$$$ MODERN BRITISH Fodor's Choice ★ 🍴 **Chez Roux.** The menu is as sleek as the service at this restaurant in the Rocpool Reserve Hotel, with clean modern design throughout (think monochrome walls, straight lines, and a whole lot of upholstery in tasteful accent colors). Expect indulgent yet creative dishes, such as Loch Duart salmon set off with Keta caviar, and a lavish signature soufflé that is far more filling than a lighter-than-air starter ought to be. **Known for:** exceptional service; inventive dishes; beautiful presentation. [$] *Average main: £22* ✉ *Rocpool Reserve Hotel, Culduthel Rd.* ☎ *01463/240089* 🌐 *www.rocpool.com/dining.*

$$$ SEAFOOD 🍴 **River House.** Head chef and owner Alfie Little draws heavily on local inspiration to shape the menu at this tiny riverside seafood restaurant, which has an interior as stylish as its appealing gray and white exterior. Start with mussels or oysters from the Scottish islands, then take your pick from mains based on native fish such as Shetland halibut and Scrabster hake, and wash it all down with a local beer. **Known for:** intimate atmosphere; fresh, sustainable local seafood. [$] *Average main: £22* ✉ *1 Greig St.* ☎ *01463/222033* 🌐 *www.riverhouseinverness.co.uk* 🕒 *Closed Sun. and Mon. No lunch.*

$$$ BRASSERIE Fodor's Choice ★ 🍴 **Rocpool Restaurant.** Another perennial, the Rocpool has a frequently changing menu of modern bistro classics, with a few international twists. Local seafood is a specialty, and the wine list is excellent. **Known for:** outstanding wine selection; contemporary twists on traditional dishes; quality meat and seafood. [$] *Average main: £20* ✉ *1 Ness Walk* ☎ *01463/717274* 🌐 *www.rocpoolrestaurant.com* 🕒 *Closed Sun.*

WHERE TO STAY

$ B&B/INN 🏨 **Bluebell House.** Each room at Bluebell House has sturdy oak furnishings, including a downstairs bedroom with a full-curtained four-poster bed and a curved chaise lounge. **Pros:** large rooms; decadent furnishing; great hosts. **Cons:** smallish bathrooms; no windows in bathrooms. [$] *Rooms from: £95* ✉ *31 Kenneth St.* ☎ *01463/238201* 🌐 *www.bluebell-house.com* 🛏 *4 rooms* 🍽 *Free breakfast.*

$$$$ HOTEL 🏨 **Bunchrew House Hotel.** This 17th-century baronial mansion, its turrets reflected in a glassy lake, looks like something from a Scottish fairy tale. **Pros:** beautiful setting; atmospheric building; good restaurant. **Cons:** some rooms could do with refurbishment; quite expensive. [$] *Rooms from: £345* ✉ *Off A862* ✥ *About 3 miles west of Inverness* ☎ *01463/234917* 🌐 *www.bunchrew-inverness.co.uk* 🛏 *16 rooms* 🍽 *Free breakfast.*

$ B&B/INN 🏨 **Moyness House.** On a quiet residential street with well-trimmed hedges a few minutes from downtown Inverness, this lovely Victorian villa was once the home of Scottish author Neil M. Gunn (1891–1973), known for short stories and novels that evoke images of the Highlands, such as *Morning Tide, Highland River,* and *Butcher's Broom*. **Pros:** beautiful building; lovely garden; great location near the river. **Cons:** public rooms a bit fussy for some; books up quickly; harsh cancellation policy. [$] *Rooms from: £92* ✉ *6 Bruce Gardens* ☎ *01463/233836* 🌐 *www.moyness.co.uk* 🛏 *6 rooms* 🍽 *Free breakfast.*

$$ B&B/INN 🏨 **Strathness House.** Standing on the banks of the River Ness, this 12-room guesthouse is a quick walk from the well-regarded Eden Court Theatre and the rest of the attractions of the city center. **Pros:** overlooks the river; close to the city center; free Wi-Fi. **Cons:** parking can

be difficult. [$] *Rooms from: £107* ✉ *4 Ardross Terr.* ☎ *01463/232765* 🌐 *www.strathnesshouse.com* 🛏 *12 rooms* 🍴 *Free breakfast.*

$$ B&B/INN 🏨 **Trafford Bank.** A 15-minute walk from downtown Inverness, this delightful little B&B makes for a practical but stylish base. **Pros:** welcoming atmosphere; stylish rooms; relaxing vibe. **Cons:** rooms on the small side. [$] *Rooms from: £130* ✉ *96 Fairfield Rd.* ☎ *01463/241414* 🌐 *www.traffordbankguesthouse.co.uk* 🛏 *5 rooms* 🍴 *Free breakfast.*

NIGHTLIFE AND PERFORMING ARTS

Hootananny. An odd combination of Scottish pub, concert hall, and Thai restaurant, Hootananny is one of the best places in the region to hear live music. The excellent pub has a warm atmosphere and serves food that comes highly recommended by locals. Several bands play each Saturday evening and a few during the week, too—check the website for listings. ✉ *67 Church St.* ☎ *01463/233651* 🌐 *www.hootanannyinverness.co.uk.*

SHOPPING

Castle Gallery. The excellent Castle Gallery sells contemporary paintings, sculpture, prints, and crafts. It also hosts frequently changing exhibitions by up-and-coming artists. ✉ *43 Castle St.* ☎ *01463/729512* 🌐 *www.castlegallery.co.uk.*

Duncan Chisholm. This shop specializes in Highland dress and tartans. Mail-order and made-to-measure services are available. ✉ *47–51 Castle St.* ☎ *01463/234599* 🌐 *www.kilts.co.uk.*

Inverness Coffee Roasting Co. An ideal place to pick up a gift, this beautifully presented little coffee shop stocks a good selection of locally roasted beans to enjoy on the premises or take away with you. Indulgent handmade treats made in Inverness by luxury chocolatiers The Chocolate Place are also available here. ✉ *15 Chapel St.* ☎ *01463/242555* 🌐 *www.invernesscoffeeroasting.co.uk.*

Leakey's Secondhand Bookshop. This shop claims to be the biggest secondhand bookstore in Scotland. When you get tired of leafing through the 100,000 or so titles, climb to the mezzanine café and study the cavernous church interior. Antique prints and maps are housed on the balcony. ✉ *Greyfriars Hall, Church St.* ☎ *01463/239947.*

Victorian Market. Don't miss the colorful Victorian Market, built in 1870. The atmospheric indoor space houses more than 40 privately owned specialty shops. ✉ *Academy St.* ☎ *01463/724273.*

SPORTS AND THE OUTDOORS

Fodor's Choice ★ **Castle Stuart Golf Links.** Opened in 2009, this course overlooking the Moray Firth is already considered one of Scotland's finest, hosting the Scottish Open in 2011. Expect undulating fairways and extensive bunkers that test your mettle. The 210-yard 17th hole provides perilous cliff-top play; the wind can defeat the canniest player. The art deco–inspired clubhouse offers stunning views of the water. ✉ *B9039* ☎ *01463/796111* 🌐 *www.castlestuartgolf.com* 🎟 *£195 May–Oct., £140 Apr. and Nov.* ⛳ *18 holes, 6553 yards, par 72* ☞ *Closed mid-Nov.–Mar.*

Inverness Golf Club. Established in 1883, and partly designed by famous British Open champion and course designer James Braid, Inverness Golf Club welcomes visitors to its parkland course 1 mile from downtown.

The tree-lined course overlooking the Beauly Firth presents some unique challenges to keep even experienced golfers on their toes. ⊠ *Culcabock Rd.* ☎ *01463/239882* ⊕ *www.invernessgolfclub.co.uk* ☜ *£38 Apr., £50 May–Sept., £28 Oct., £20 Nov.–Mar.* ⚑ *18 holes, 6102 yards, par 69.*

CULLODEN MOOR

8 miles east of Inverness.

Culloden Moor was the scene of the last battle fought on British soil—and to this day its name is enough to invoke raw and tragic feelings in Scotland. Austere and windswept, it's also a place of outstanding natural beauty.

GETTING HERE AND AROUND

Driving along the B9006 from Inverness is the easiest way to Culloden Moor, and there's a large car park to handle many visitors. Local buses also run from Inverness to the battlefield.

EXPLORING

Fodor'sChoice **Culloden Moor.** Here, on a cold April day in 1746, the hopelessly out-
★ gunned Jacobite forces of Bonnie Prince Charlie were destroyed by King George II's army. The victorious commander, the Duke of Cumberland (George II's son), earned the name of the "Butcher" of Cumberland for the bloody reprisals carried out by his men on Highland families, Jacobite or not, caught in the vicinity. In the battle itself, the duke's army—greatly outnumbering the Jacobites—killed up to 2,000 soldiers. (The victors, by contrast, lost just 50). It was the last battle to be fought on British soil. The National Trust for Scotland has re-created a slightly eerie version of the battlefield as it looked in 1746 that you can explore with a guided audio tour. An innovative visitor center enables you to get closer to the sights and sounds of the battle and to interact with the characters involved. A viewing platform helps (literally) put things into perspective from on high. Academic research and technology have helped re-create the Gaelic dialect, song, and music of the time. There's also a good on-site café. ⊠ *B9006, Culloden* ☎ *0844/493–2159* ⊕ *www. nts.org.uk/Culloden* ☜ *£11* ☻ *Visitor center closed late Dec.–Feb.*

19

NAIRN

12 miles east of Culloden Moor, 17 miles east of Inverness, 92 miles west of Aberdeen.

This once-prosperous fishing village is now more likely to lure golfers than sailors. Nearby is Cawdor Castle, loaded with history. East of Nairn pier is a long beach, great for a stroll.

GETTING HERE AND AROUND

A car gives you the most flexibility, but Nairn is close to Inverness (via A96), and regular local buses serve the town.

EXPLORING

FAMILY **Cawdor Castle.** Shakespeare's Macbeth was the Thane of Cawdor (a local
Fodor'sChoice officer of the crown), but the sense of history that exists within the turreted
★ walls of Cawdor Castle is certainly more than fictional. Cawdor is a lived-in castle, not an abandoned, decaying structure. The earliest part is the

14th-century central tower; the rooms contain family portraits, tapestries, fine furniture, and paraphernalia reflecting 600 years of history. Outside the walls are sheltered gardens and woodland walks. Children will have a ball exploring the lush and mysterious Big Wood, with its wildflowers and varied wildlife. There are lots of creepy stories and fantastic tales amid the dank dungeons and drawbridges. If the castle sounds appealing, keep in mind that the estate has cottages to rent. ✉ *B9090, Cawdor* ✥ *5 miles southwest of Nairn* ☎ *01667/404401* 🌐 *www.cawdorcastle.com* 🎫 *Castle £11.20; grounds only £6.50* 🕒 *Closed mid-Oct.–Apr.*

Phoenix Boat Trips. With one-hour and two-hour trips by boat from Nairn Harbour into the Moray Firth, Phoenix Boat Trips offers you the chance to see dolphins in their breeding areas. The daily departure times for the modern, ex-naval SWIFT vessels vary depending on the tides and the weather. Evening trips are offered on certain dates in summer. ✉ *Nairn Harbour* ☎ *0770/316–8097* 🌐 *www.dolphin-trips-nairn.co.uk* 🎫 *Tours from £18.*

WHERE TO STAY

$$$$ B&B/INN Fodor's Choice ★ 🏨 **Boath House.** Built in the 1820s, this stunning Regency manor house is surrounded by 20 acres of lovingly nurtured gardens. **Pros:** excellent dining; beautiful 20-acre grounds; relaxed atmosphere. **Cons:** some airplane noise; pricey. [$] *Rooms from: £325* ✉ *Off A96, Auldearn* ☎ *01667/454896* 🌐 *www.boath-house.com* 🛏 *8 rooms* 🍴 *Free breakfast.*

SHOPPING

Auldearn Antiques. It's easy to spend an hour wandering around an old church filled with furniture, fireplaces, architectural antiques, and linens. The converted farmsteads have tempting antique (or just old) chinaware and textiles. ✉ *Dalmore Manse, Lethen Rd., Auldearn* ✥ *3 miles east of Nairn* ☎ *01667/453087* 🌐 *www.auldearnantiques.co.uk.*

Brodie Countryfare. Visit Brodie Countryfare only if you're feeling flush: you may covet the unusual knitwear, quality designer clothing and shoes, gifts, and toys, but they are *not* cheap. The excellent restaurant, on the other hand, is quite inexpensive. ✉ *On A96, Brodie, Forres* ☎ *01309/641555* 🌐 *www.brodiecountryfare.com.*

SPORTS AND THE OUTDOORS

Nairn Golf Club. Well regarded in golfing circles, the Nairn Golf Club dates from 1887 and is the regular home of Scotland's Northern Open. Huge greens, aggressive gorse, a beach hazard for five of the holes, a steady prevailing wind, and distracting views across the Moray Firth make play on the Championship Course unforgettable. The adjoining 9-hole Cameron Course is ideal for a warm-up or a fun round for the family. ✉ *Seabank Rd.* ☎ *01667/453208* 🌐 *www.nairngolfclub.co.uk* 🎫 *Championship Course, £135 (£85 off-peak) Apr.–Oct., £50 Nov.–Mar.; Cameron Course, £20* 🏌 *Championship Course: 18 holes, 6774 yards, par 72; Cameron Course: 9 holes, 1634 yards, par 29* ✍ *Reservations essential.*

FORRES

10 miles east of Nairn.

The burgh of Forres is everything a Scottish medieval town should be, with a handsome tolbooth (the former courthouse and prison) and impressive gardens as its centerpiece. It's remarkable how well the old buildings have adapted to their modern retail uses. With two distilleries—one still operating, the other preserved as a museum—Forres is a key point on the Malt Whisky Trail. Brodie Castle is also nearby. Just 6 miles north you'll find Findhorn Ecovillage, and a sandy beach stretches along the edge of the semi-enclosed Findhorn Bay, which is excellent bird-watching territory.

GETTING HERE AND AROUND

Forres is easy to reach by car or bus from Inverness on the A96. Daily ScotRail trains run here from Inverness and Aberdeen.

EXPLORING

Benromach Distillery. The smallest distillery in Moray, Benromach was founded in 1898. It's now owned by whisky specialist Gordon and MacPhail, and it stocks a vast range of malts. An informative hourly tour ends with a tutored nosing and tasting. ✉ *Invererne Rd.* ☎ *01309/675968* 🌐 *www.benromach.com* 🎟 *£6* ⏲ *Closed late Dec.–early Jan.*

Brodie Castle. This medieval castle was rebuilt and extended in the 17th and 19th centuries. Fine examples of late-17th-century plasterwork are preserved in the Dining Room and Blue Sitting Room; an impressive library and a superb collection of pictures extend into the 20th century. The castle is about 24 miles east of Inverness, making it a good day trip. ✉ *Off A96, Brodie* ☎ *01309/641371* 🌐 *www.nts.org.uk* 🎟 *Castle £10.50, grounds free* ⏲ *Castle closed mid-Oct.–Mar. Grounds open all year.*

Dallas Dhu Historic Distillery. The final port of call on the Malt Whisky Trail, the Dallas Dhu Historic Distillery was the last distillery built in the 19th century and was still in operation until the 1980s. Today it holds a small museum that tells the story of Scotland's national drink. ✉ *Mannachie Rd.* ☎ *01309/676548* 🌐 *www.historicenvironment.scot* 🎟 *£6* ⏲ *Closed Thurs. and Fri. Oct.–Mar.*

WHERE TO STAY

$$ HOTEL 🏨 **Cluny Bank Hotel.** Take one look at any of this pretty Victorian hotel's unique bedrooms, filled with personal touches, and you could easily guess that this is a family-run venture. **Pros:** lovely hosts; tranquil residential area. **Cons:** some bathrooms a bit small. [$] *Rooms from: £130* ✉ *69 St Leonard's Rd.* ☎ *01309/674304* 🌐 *www.clunybankhotel.co.uk* 🛏 *7 rooms* 🍴 *Free breakfast.*

SPEYSIDE AND THE CAIRNGORMS

The Spey is a long river, running from Fort Augustus to the Moray Firth, and its fast-moving waters make for excellent fishing at many points along the way. They also give Speyside malt whiskies a softer flavor than those made with peaty island water. The area's native and planted pine

19

forests draw many birds each spring and summer, and people come for miles to see the capercaillies and ospreys.

Defining the eastern edge of the Great Glen, Cairngorms National Park provides sporty types with all the adventure they could ask for, including walking, kayaking, rock climbing, and even skiing, if the winter is cold enough. The park has everything but the sea: craggy mountains, calm lochs, and swift rivers. While the unremarkable town of Aviemore may put off some travelers, the Cairngorms are truly stunning.

AVIEMORE

6 miles southwest of Boat of Garten, 30 miles south of Inverness.

At the foot of the Cairngorms, once-quiet Aviemore now has all the brashness and boxiness of a year-round holiday resort. In the summer months it's filled with walkers, cyclists, and rock climbers, so it's a convenient place for stocking up on supplies. However, many of the smaller villages nearby are quieter places to stay. ■TIP➔ Be forewarned: this region can get very cold above 3,000 feet, and weather conditions can change rapidly, even in the middle of summer.

GETTING HERE AND AROUND

The A9, Scotland's major north–south artery, runs past Aviemore. From Boat of Garten, take the A95. The town is serviced by regular trains and buses from Inverness, Edinburgh, and Glasgow.

ESSENTIALS

Visitor Information Aviemore Visitor Information Centre. ⊠ *7 Grampian Rd.* ☏ *01479/810930* ⊕ *visitcairngorms.com.*

EXPLORING

Fodor'sChoice ★ **CairnGorm Mountain Railway.** A funicular railway to the top of Cairn Gorm (the mountain that gives its name to the region), the CairnGorm Mountain Railway operates daily, year-round, and affords sweeping views across the Cairngorms and the broad valley of the Spey. At the top is a visitor center and restaurant. The round-trip journey takes about half an hour. Reservations are recommended. ⊠ *B970* ☏ *01479/861261* ⊕ *www.cairngormmountain.co.uk* ☏ *£13.50.*

FAMILY **Cairngorm Reindeer Centre.** On the high slopes of the Cairngorms, you may see the reindeer herd that was introduced here in the 1950s. The reindeer are docile creatures that seem to enjoy human company. Ranger-led visits to the herd are offered at least once a day from February to December, weather permitting. From June to August you can also accompany rangers on gentle half-day treks through the mountains. From April through December a small herd of young reindeer are cared for at a paddock near the visitor center; you can visit (and pet them) for a small fee. Bring waterproof gear, as conditions can be wet and muddy. ⊠ *Glenmore Forest Park, B970* ✛ *6 miles east of Aviemore* ☏ *01479/861228* ⊕ *www.cairngormreindeer.co.uk* ☏ *£14; paddock £3.50* ☉ *Closed Jan.–early Feb.*

Fodor'sChoice ★ **Cairngorms National Park.** A rugged wilderness of mountains, moorlands, glens, and lochs, the sprawling Cairngorms National Park, established in 2003, takes in more than 1,700 square miles. Past Loch Morlich, at the high parking lot on the exposed shoulders of the Cairngorm Mountains, are dozens of trails for hiking and cycling. This is a massive park, encompassing small towns as well as countryside, but a good place to start exploring is the main visitor center in Aviemore. The staff can dispense maps, expert advice on the best trails, and also information on guided walks and other activities. (There are additional Cairngorms visitor centers in Braemar, Glenmore, Ballater, Tomintoul, Newtonmore, and Grantown-on-Spey.) Because much of the best scenery in the park is off-road—including ancient pine forests and open moorland—a particularly good way to cover ground in the park is on a pony trek. The **Rothiemurchus Estate** leads guided hacks for riders of all ability levels. The park is a haven for rare wildlife: a full 25% of Britain's endangered species have habitats in the park. Birding enthusiasts come here to look (and listen) for the Scottish crossbill—the only bird completely unique to Britain. Weather conditions in the park change abruptly, so be sure to bring cold-weather gear, particularly if you plan on hiking long distance. ✉ *Visitor Information Centre, 7 The Parade, Grampian Rd.* ☎ *01479/810930* 🌐 *cairngorms.co.uk*.

FAMILY Fodor's Choice ★ **Rothiemurchus Estate.** This excellent activity center is among the best in the Cairngorms. It offers a host of organized outdoor diversions, including guided pony rides, mountain biking, fishing, gorge swimming, and white-water rafting. It also offers ranger-guided safaris to see the park's rare and endangered wildlife, including red squirrels and "hairy heilan coos" (Highland slang for Highland cattle—docile, yaklike creatures). The Rothiemurchus Centre is the best place to get oriented and book activities; it also has a handy restaurant and a well-stocked shop selling plenty of fresh produce from the estate. One of the most beautiful parts of the estate is a nature reserve called **Loch an Eilein**. There are great low-level paths around the tree-rimmed loch—perfect for bikes—or longer trails to Glen Einich. A converted cottage beside Loch an Eilein serves as a visitor center, art gallery, and craft store. ✉ *Rothiemurchus Centre, on B970, Inverdruie* ☎ *01479/812345* 🌐 *www.rothiemurchus.net* 🎟 *Free* 🕓 *Gallery closed Oct.–Easter.*

19

WHERE TO EAT

$ CAFÉ 🍴 **Mountain Café.** On the main street in Aviemore, the Mountain Café is a useful pit stop for a hearty lunch or afternoon snack. Crowned Best Café in Scotland at the 2017 Scottish Food Awards, this small place has a big reputation that means it's rarely empty. **Known for:** lively atmosphere (be prepared to wait); award-winning baked goods. [$] *Average main: £10* ✉ *111 Grampian Rd.* ☎ *01479/812473* 🌐 *mountaincafe-aviemore.co.uk* 🕓 *No dinner.*

$ CAFÉ Fodor's Choice ★ 🍴 **The Potting Shed.** Seasonal fruits and smooth cream top many of the delectable desserts at this cake shop in a scenic garden south of Aviemore. Taught by his Norwegian mother, John Borrowman makes light sponges that contain no butter or fat (although you can't say the same thing about the rich cream they're topped with). **Known for:** outrageously tasty cakes; beautiful garden setting. [$] *Average main: £5* ✉ *Inshriach Nursery, B970* ☎ *01540/651287* 🌐 *www.inshriachnursery.co.uk* 🕓 *Closed Mon., Tues., and Nov.–Feb.*

WHERE TO STAY

$$ **Cairngorm Hotel.** Walk past the suit of armor standing guard at the
HOTEL entrance and you should already have a good idea of what awaits
within this grand old house, the first building you'll see on exiting the
train station. **Pros:** practical location; simple, traditional rooms; family rooms offered. **Cons:** not scenic; interior needs a refresh. $ *Rooms
from: £104* ✉ *77 Grampian Rd.* ☎ *01479/810233* ⊕ *www.cairngorm.
com* ➴ *31 rooms* ⏐⊙⏐ *Free breakfast.*

SPORTS AND THE OUTDOORS

Glenmore Lodge. In Cairngorms National Park, this is a good center for
day and residential courses on rock and ice climbing, hiking, kayaking, ski touring, mountain biking, and more. Some classes are aimed at
under-18s. There are superb facilities, such as an indoor climbing wall.
✉ *Signposted on B970, Glenmore* ✛ *About 9 miles east of Aviemore*
☎ *01479/861256* ⊕ *www.glenmorelodge.org.uk.*

G2 Outdoor. The wide range of adventures at G2 Outdoor includes
white-water rafting, gorge walking, and rock climbing. The company
offers a family float trip on the River Spey in summer, and in winter
runs ski courses. ✉ *The Hatchery, Alvie Estate, off A9* ☎ *01540/651784*
⊕ *www.g2outdoor.co.uk.*

KINGUSSIE

13 miles southwest of Aviemore.

Set in a wide glen, Kingussie is a pretty town east of the Monadhliath
Mountains. With great distant views of the Cairngorms, it's perfect for
those who would prefer to avoid the far more hectic town of Aviemore.

GETTING HERE AND AROUND

From Aviemore, Kingussie is easy to reach by car via the A9 and the
A86. There are also good bus and train services between the two towns.

EXPLORING

FAMILY **Highland Folk Museum.** Explore reconstructed Highland buildings, including a Victorian-era schoolhouse, and watch tailors, clock makers, and
Fodor's Choice
★ joiners demonstrating their trades at this museum. Walking paths (or
old-fashioned buses) take you to the 18th-century township that was a
setting for the hit TV show *Outlander* and includes a peat house, made
of turf, and a weaver's house. Throughout the museum there are hands-on exhibits like a working quern stone for grinding grain. ✉ *Kingussie
Rd., Newtonmore* ☎ *01540/673551* ⊕ *www.highlandfolk.com* 🖾 *Free*
⊙ *Closed Nov.–late Mar.*

Ruthven Barracks. Looking like a ruined castle on a mound, Ruthven
Barracks is redolent with tales of "the '45" (as the last Jacobite rebellion is often called). The defeated Jacobite forces rallied here after the
battle at Culloden, but then abandoned and blew up the government
outpost they had earlier captured. You'll see its crumbling, yet imposing, stone outline as you approach. ✉ *B970* ✛ *½ mile south of Kingussie*
☎ *01667/460232* ⊕ *www.historic-scotland.gov.uk* 🖾 *Free.*

WHERE TO EAT AND STAY

$$$$ BRITISH Fodor's Choice ★ 🍴 **The Cross at Kingussie.** This former tweed mill, with a narrow river running alongside its stone walls, is set in 4 acres of woodlands. With stone walls painted a creamy white, the intimate dining room is warmed by a crackling fireplace. **Known for:** perfectly curated set menus; stunning location; effortlessly beautiful interior. [$] *Average main: £55* ✉ *Tweed Mill Brae, Ardbroilach Rd.* ☎ *01540/661166* 🌐 *www.thecross.co.uk* 🕒 *Closed Jan. No dinner Sun. and Mon.*

$ B&B/INN 🏨 **Coig Na Shee.** This century-old Highland lodge has a warm and cozy atmosphere, and each of its spacious bedrooms is unique, with well-chosen furnishings and soothing color schemes. **Pros:** quiet location; great walks from house; kids aged 8–16 can share with parents for £20 (including breakfast). **Cons:** tricky to get to without a car; no children under eight. [$] *Rooms from: £75* ✉ *Laggan Rd., Newtonmore* ☎ *01540/670109* 🌐 *www.coignashee.co.uk* 🛏 *5 rooms* 🍽 *Free breakfast.*

$$ B&B/INN Fodor's Choice ★ 🏨 **Sutherlands Guest House.** Finding that sweet spot where contemporary meets cozy is no mean feat, but the husband-and-wife team behind this welcoming guesthouse make it look simple. **Pros:** lovely rooms; great value. **Cons:** hilltop location best accessed by car. [$] *Rooms from: £105* ✉ *Old Distillery Rd.* ☎ *01540/661155* 🌐 *www.sutherlandskingussie.co.uk* 🛏 *5 rooms* 🍽 *Free breakfast.*

LOCH NESS, FORT WILLIAM, AND NEARBY

Compared with other lochs, Loch Ness is by no means known for its beauty, but it draws attention for its famous monster. Heading south from Inverness, you can travel along the loch's quiet east side or the more touristy west side. A pleasant morning can be spent at Urquhart Castle, in the tiny town of Drumnadrochit, or a bit farther south in the pretty town of Fort Augustus, where the Caledonian Canal meets Loch Ness. As you travel south and west, the landscape opens up and the Nevis Range comes into view.

19

From Fort William you can visit the dark, cloud-laden mountains of Glencoe and the desolate stretch of moors and lochans at Rannoch Moor. Travelers drive through this region to experience the landscape, which changes at nearly every turn. It's a brooding, haunting area that's worth a visit in any season.

The Road to the Isles, less romantically known as the A830, leads from Fort William to the coastal towns of Arisaig, Morar, and Mallaig, with access to the Small Isles of Rum, Eigg, Canna, and Muck. From here you can also visit the Isle of Skye via the ferry at Mallaig.

DRUMNADROCHIT

14 miles south of Inverness.

A tourist hub at the curve of the road, Drumnadrochit is not known for its style or culture, but it attracts plenty of people interested in searching for mythical monsters. There aren't many good restaurants, but there are some decent-enough hotels.

GETTING HERE AND AROUND

It's easy to get here from Fort Augustus or Inverness via the A82, either by car or by local bus. However, a more leisurely alternative is driving the B862 south from Inverness and along the east bank of Loch Ness. Take the opportunity to view the waterfalls at Foyers and the peaceful, reedy Loch Tarff. Descend through forests and moorland until the road runs around the southern tip of Loch Ness. The half-hidden track beside the road is a remnant of the military road built by General Wade.

EXPLORING

Fort Augustus. The best place to see the Caledonian Canal's 29 locks in action is at Fort Augustus, at the southern tip of Loch Ness and around a half-hour drive from Drumnadrochit. At the visitor center in this scenic village you can learn all about this historic marvel of engineering, and set off on a picturesque walk that takes in the stunning vistas along the canal: mountains, lochs, and glens, and to the south, the profile of Ben Nevis. Fort Augustus itself was captured by the Jacobite clans during the 1745 rebellion. Later the fort was rebuilt as a Benedictine abbey, but the monks no longer live here. ⊠ *Fort Augustus.*

Loch Ness. From the A82 you get many views of the formidable and famous Loch Ness, which has a greater volume of water than any other Scottish loch, a maximum depth of more than 800 feet, and—perhaps you've already heard?—a monster. Early travelers who passed this way included English lexicographer Dr. Samuel Johnson (1709–84) and his guide and biographer, James Boswell (1740–95), who were on their way to the Hebrides in 1783. They remarked at the time about the poor condition of the population and the squalor of their homes. Another early travel writer and naturalist, Thomas Pennant (1726–98), noted that the loch kept the locality frost-free in winter. Even General Wade—remembered for destroying much of Hadrian's Wall in England—came here, his troops blasting and digging a road up much of the eastern shore. None of these observant early travelers ever made mention of a monster. Clearly, they had not read the local guidebooks. ⊠ *Drumnadrochit.*

FAMILY **Loch Ness Centre & Exhibition.** If you're in search of the infamous monster, the Loch Ness Centre & Exhibition documents the fuzzy photographs, the unexplained sonar readings, and the sincere testimony of eyewitnesses. It's said that the loch's huge volume of water has a warming effect on the local weather, making the loch conducive to mirages in still, warm conditions—but you'll have to make up your own mind. From Easter to October you can also take hourly cruises of the loch (£14). The cruises leave from the little craft store at the Loch Ness Lodge Hotel in Drumnadrochit; no prebooking allowed. ⊠ *On A82* ☎ *01456/450573* ⊕ *www.lochness.com* ✉ *£7.95.*

Urquhart Castle. About 2 miles southeast of Drumnadrochit, this castle is a favorite Loch Ness monster–watching spot. This romantically broken-down fortress stands on a promontory overlooking the loch, as it has since the Middle Ages. Because of its central and strategic position in the Great Glen line of communication, the castle has a complex history involving military offense and defense, as well as its own destruction and renovation. The castle was begun in the 13th century and was

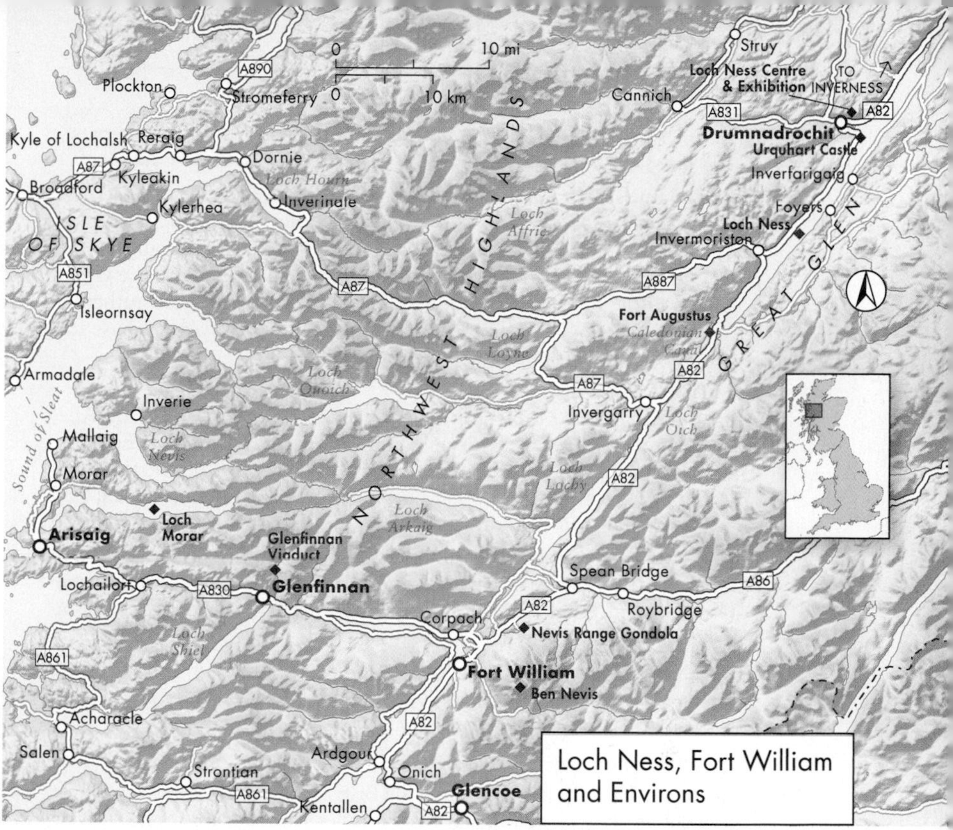

Loch Ness, Fort William and Environs

destroyed before the end of the 17th century to prevent its use by the Jacobites. A visitor center gives an idea of what life was like here in medieval times. ✉ *A82* ☎ *01456/450551* 🌐 *www.historic-scotland.gov.uk/places* 🎟 *£9.*

WHERE TO STAY

$$ HOTEL Fodor's Choice ★ 🏨 **Glengarry Castle Hotel.** Tucked away in Invergarry, this rambling baronial mansion is just south of Loch Ness and within easy reach of the Great Glen's most popular sights. **Pros:** atmospheric building and gardens; good-value take-out lunches; family rooms available. **Cons:** no elevator. [$] *Rooms from: £145* ✉ *Off A82, Invergarry* ✥ *26 miles south of Drumnadrochit* ☎ *01809/501254* 🌐 *www.glengarry.net* 🕓 *Closed mid-Nov.–mid-Mar.* 🛏 *26 rooms* 🍴 *Free breakfast.*

$$$ B&B/INN Fodor's Choice ★ 🏨 **Loch Ness Lodge.** Run by siblings Scott and Iona Sutherland, Loch Ness Lodge is an exquisite place: opulent, classy, and welcoming. **Pros:** excellent staff; superb views; lovely rooms. **Cons:** near a busy road; no restaurant; don't confuse it with a (lesser) hotel of the same name in Drumnadrochit. [$] *Rooms from: £210* ✉ *A82, Brachla* ☎ *01456/459469* 🌐 *www.loch-ness-lodge.com* 🛏 *7 rooms* 🍴 *Free breakfast.*

FORT WILLIAM

32 miles southwest of Fort Augustus, 69 miles southwest of Inverness, 108 miles northwest of Glasgow, 138 miles northwest of Edinburgh.

As its name suggests, Fort William originated as a military outpost, first established by Oliver Cromwell's General Monk in 1655 and refortified by George I (1660–1727) in 1715 to help combat an uprising by the turbulent Jacobite clans. It remains the southern gateway to the Great Glen and the far west. It's not Scotland's most charming or authentic town, but it's got several good hotels and makes a convenient base for exploring the surrounding countryside.

GETTING HERE AND AROUND

From Glasgow (to the south) and Inverness (to the north), the A82 takes you the entire way. From Edinburgh, take the M9 to the A84. This empties into the A85, which connects to the A82 that takes you to Fort William. Roads around Fort William are well maintained, but mostly one lane in each direction. They can be very busy in summer.

A long-distance Scottish Citylink bus connects Glasgow and Fort William. ScotRail has trains from London, as well as connections from Glasgow and Edinburgh. It also operates a train service three times a day between Fort William and Mallaig.

ESSENTIALS

Visitor Information Fort William Tourist Information Centre. ⊠ *15 High St.* ☎ *01397/701801* ⊕ *www.visitfortwilliam.co.uk, www.visitscotland.com.*

EXPLORING

Ben Nevis. The tallest mountain in the British Isles, 4,406-foot Ben Nevis looms over Fort William, less than 4 miles from Loch Linnhe. A trek to its summit is a rewarding experience, but you should be fit and well prepared—food and water, map and compass, first-aid kit, whistle, hat, gloves, and warm clothing (yes, even in summer) for starters—as the unpredictable weather can make it a hazardous hike. Ask for advice at the local tourist office before you begin.

FAMILY   **Jacobite Steam Train.** The most relaxing way to take in the landscape of
Fodor's Choice   birch- and bracken-covered wild slopes is by rail. The best ride is on
★   the Jacobite Steam Train, a spectacularly scenic 84-mile round-trip that runs between Fort William and Mallaig. You'll see mountains, lochs, beaches, and islands along the way. There are two trips a day (weekdays only outside high season). ⊠ *Station Sq.* ☎ *0844/850–4685* ⊕ *www. westcoastrailways.co.uk* ☒ *£35* ⊘ *Closed late Dec.–late Apr.*

Nevis Range Gondola. Those who want to climb a mountain, without the need for hiking boots and an iron will, will prefer to make the journey in a gondola. These cable cars rise nearly 2,000 feet to the summit of Aonach Mor, part of the Nevis range. The journey takes about 15 minutes, and needless to say the views of the Great Glen are incredible—but definitely not for those without a head for heights. Call ahead for times, especially in winter—the published opening hours are a little confusing. ⊠ *A82* ☎ *01397/705825* ⊕ *www.nevisrange.co.uk* ☒ *£14* ⊘ *Closed mid-Nov.–mid-Dec.*

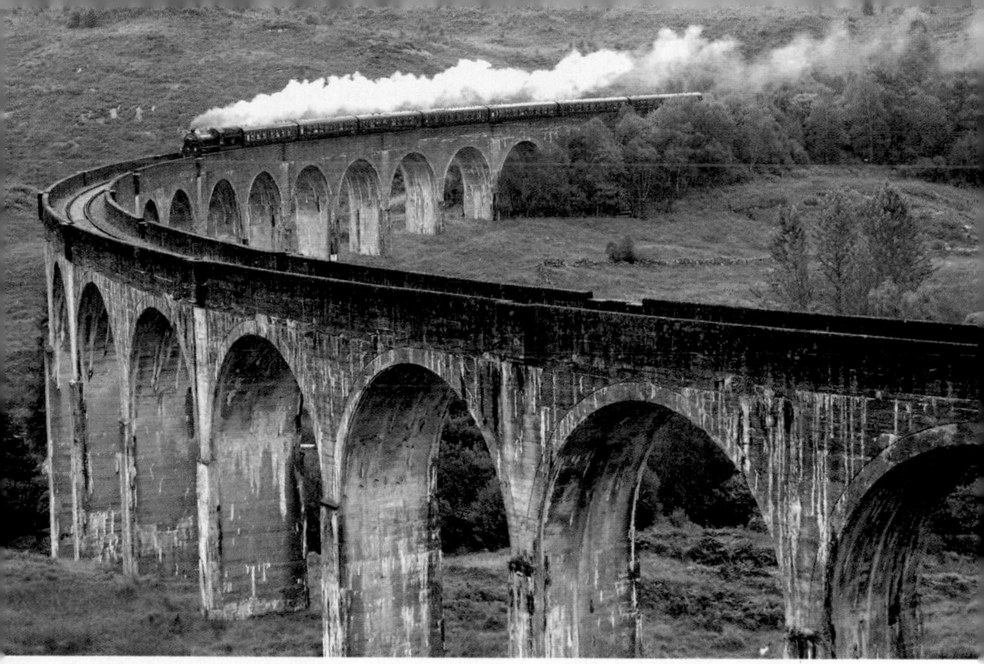
The scenic Jacobite Steam Train from Fort William provides a ride over the 21 arches of the Glenfinnan Viaduct.

Fodor's Choice ★ **West Highland Museum.** In the town center, the small but fascinating West Highland Museum explores the history of Prince Charles Edward Stuart and the 1745 rebellion. Included in the museum's folk exhibits are a costume and tartan display and an excellent collection of Jacobite relics. One of the most intriguing objects here is a tray decorated with a distorted image of Bonnie Prince Charlie that only becomes visible when reflected in a wine glass or goblet. This elaborate ruse enabled clandestine supporters among the nobility to raise a (treasonous) toast without fear of discovery. ✉ *Cameron Sq.* ☎ *01397/702169* 🌐 *www.westhighlandmuseum.org.uk* 🎫 *Free* ⏲ *Closed Sun. in Sept.–June, and Mon.–Sat. in July and Aug.*

WHERE TO EAT

$$ SEAFOOD Fodor's Choice ★ 🍴 **Crannog Seafood Restaurant.** With a reputation for quality and simplicity, this restaurant on the town pier serves outstanding seafood. Fishing boats draw up on the shores of Loch Linnhe and deliver their catch straight to the kitchen. **Known for:** small but well-curated menu; idyllic lochside location. [$] *Average main: £19* ✉ *The Pier* ☎ *01397/705589* 🌐 *www.crannog.net.*

WHERE TO STAY

$$ B&B/INN Fodor's Choice ★ 🏨 **Crolinnhe.** An elegant Victorian house with colorful gardens, this exceptionally comfortable B&B overlooks Loch Linnhe, yet is only a 10-minute walk from town. **Pros:** stunning loch views; great breakfasts; comfortable rooms. **Cons:** final payment only by cash or check. [$] *Rooms from: £140* ✉ *Grange Rd.* ☎ *01397/702709* 🌐 *www.crolinnhe.co.uk* 💳 *No credit cards* ⏲ *Closed Nov.–Easter* 🛏 *3 rooms* 🍽 *Free breakfast.*

$$$ B&B/INN Fodor's Choice ★ **The Grange.** This meticulously renovated Victorian villa stands in pretty gardens a 10-minute walk from downtown. **Pros:** amazing location; great attention to detail; elegant lounge with plenty of books. **Cons:** no restaurant; not suitable for families with younger children. [$] *Rooms from: £180* ✉ *Grange Rd.* ☎ *01397/705516* 🌐 *www.grangefortwilliam.com* 🕓 *Closed Oct.–Mar.* 🛏 *2 rooms* 🍴 *Free breakfast.*

SPORTS AND THE OUTDOORS

This area—especially around Glen Nevis, Glencoe, and Ben Nevis—is popular with hikers; however, routes are not well marked, so contact the Fort William tourist information center before you go. The center will provide you with expert advice based on your interests, level of fitness, and hiking experience.

Fodor's Choice ★ **Glen Nevis.** For a walk in Glen Nevis, drive north from Fort William on the A82 toward Fort Augustus. On the outskirts of town, just before the bridge over the River Nevis, turn right up the road signposted Glen Nevis. About 8 miles along this road is a parking lot where a footpath leads to waterfalls and a steel-cable bridge (1 mile), and then to Steall, a ruined croft beside a boulder-strewn stream (a good picnic place). You can continue up the glen for some distance without danger of becoming lost, so long as you stay on the path and keep the river to your right. Watch your step going through the tree-lined gorge. The return route is back the way you came.

GLENCOE

16 miles south of Fort William, 92 miles north of Glasgow, 44 miles northwest of Edinburgh.

Fodor's Choice ★ Glencoe is both a small town and a region of stunning grandeur, with high peaks and secluded glens. Dramatic scenery is the main attraction here; it's as awesomely beautiful for a drive as it is for a hike. The A82—the main route through Glencoe—can get surprisingly crowded in high season, but it's one of the great scenic drives in Scotland. This area, where wild, craggy buttresses loom darkly over the road, has a special place in the folk memory of Scotland: the glen was the site of an infamous massacre in 1692, still remembered in the Highlands for the treachery with which soldiers of the Campbell clan, acting as a government militia, treated their hosts, the MacDonalds. According to Highland code, in his own home a clansman should give shelter even to his sworn enemy. In the face of bitter weather, the Campbells were accepted as guests by the MacDonalds. Apparently acting on orders from the British crown, the Campbells turned on their hosts and murdered them. The Massacre of Glencoe has gained an unlikely resurgence of fame in recent years, since it was revealed to be the historical basis for the so-called "Red Wedding" in George R.R. Martin's popular books (and HBO series) *Game of Thrones*.

GETTING HERE AND AROUND

Glencoe is easily accessed by car via the A82. ScotRail trains and regional buses arrive from most of Scotland's major cities.

EXPLORING

Visitor Center at Glencoe. The National Trust for Scotland's Visitor Center at Glencoe tells the story of the MacDonald massacre and has excellent displays about this area of outstanding natural beauty. You can also get expert advice about hiking trails. ✉ *Off A82* ⊕ *1 mile south of Glencoe Village* ☎ *01855/811307* 🌐 *www.glencoe-nts.org.uk* 🎫 *Exhibition £6.50* ⏲ *Closed Mon.–Wed. Nov.–late Mar.*

WHERE TO STAY

$$$$ B&B/INN Fodor's Choice ★ 🏨 **Glencoe House.** Peaceful surroundings, arresting views, and the friendliest of welcomes await you at this former Victorian hunting lodge. **Pros:** beautiful landscape; superb restoration; lovely hosts. **Cons:** expensive; few facilities. [$] *Rooms from: £340* ✉ *Glencoe Lochan* ☎ *01855/811179* 🌐 *www.glencoe-house.com* 🛏 *13 rooms* 🍴 *No meals.*

SPORTS AND THE OUTDOORS

FAMILY **Glencoe Activities.** This popular outdoor center west of Ballachulish offers a long list of high-energy activities, from rock climbing to white-water rafting, and even hair-raising vertical canyon explorations complete with 500-foot descents. However, there's a welcome twist here—it also caters to those with more limited mobility (or less adventurous souls). Guided Segway tours (£35) last 50 minutes and take you through some spectacular scenery, with stunning mountain views and even a trail along a stretch of Loch Leven. ✉ *Dragon's Tooth Golf Course, off A828* ⊕ *4 miles west of Glencoe* ☎ *01855/811695* 🌐 *www.glencoeactivities.com.*

GLENFINNAN

10 miles west of Fort William, 33 miles northwest of Glencoe.

Perhaps the most visitor-oriented stop on the route between Fort William and Mallaig, Glenfinnan has much to offer if you're interested in Scottish history. Here the National Trust for Scotland has capitalized on the romance surrounding the story of the Jacobites and their attempts to return a Stewart monarch and the Roman Catholic religion to a country that had become staunchly Protestant. It was at Glenfinnan that the rash adventurer Bonnie Prince Charlie gathered his meager forces for the final Jacobite rebellion of 1745–46.

GETTING HERE AND AROUND

If you're driving from Fort William, travel via the A830. For great views, take a ride on the Jacobite Steam Train, which you can catch in Fort William.

EXPLORING

Glenfinnan Monument. One of the most striking monuments in Britain, the Glenfinnan Monument commemorates the place where Bonnie Prince Charlie raised his standard. The tower, which was built in 1815, overlooks Loch Shiel; note, however, that the figure on the top is a Highlander, not the prince himself. The story of his ill-fated campaign is told in the nearby visitor center. You have to pay a small access fee, which includes a tour, when the center is open, but in truth the monument is just as picturesque when seen from the car park. ■ **TIP→ The view**

down Loch Shiel from the Glenfinnan Monument is one of the most photographed in Scotland. ✉ *A830* ☎ *01397/722250* 🌐 *www.nts.org.uk* 🎫 *Exhibition free; guided tour £3.50* 🕒 *Visitor center closed Nov.–Mar.*

Glenfinnan Viaduct. The 1,248-foot-long Glenfinnan Viaduct was a genuine wonder when it was built in 1897, and remains so today. The railway's contractor, Robert MacAlpine (known among locals as "Concrete Bob") pioneered the use of concrete for bridges when his company built the Mallaig extension, which opened in 1901. In more recent times the viaduct became famous for its appearance in the Harry Potter films. The viaduct can be seen on foot; about half a mile west of the railway station in Glenfinnan, on the A380 road, is a small parking lot. Take the footpath from here; you'll reach the viaduct in about ½ mile. ✉ *A380.*

WHERE TO STAY

$$ HOTEL 🏨 **Glenfinnan House.** This handsome hotel on the shores of Loch Shiel was built in the 18th century as the home of Alexander MacDonald VII of Glenaladale, who was wounded fighting for Bonnie Prince Charlie; it was transformed into an even grander mansion in the 19th century. **Pros:** fabulous setting; atmospheric dining experience. **Cons:** some shared bathrooms. [$] *Rooms from: £140* ✉ *A830* ☎ *01397/722235* 🌐 *www.glenfinnanhouse.com* 🕒 *Closed mid-Nov.–mid-Mar.* 🛏 *14 rooms* 🍴 *Free breakfast.*

ARISAIG

15 miles west of Glenfinnan.

Considering its small size, Arisaig, gateway to the **Small Isles,** offers a surprising choice of high-quality options for dining and lodging. To the north of Arisaig the road cuts across a headland to reach a stretch of coastline where silver sands glitter with the mica in the local rock; clear water, blue sky, and white sand lend a tropical flavor to the beaches—when the sun is shining.

From Arisaig try to visit a couple of the Small Isles: **Rum, Eigg, Muck,** and **Canna,** each tiny and with few or no inhabitants. Rum serves as a wildlife reserve, while Eigg has the world's first solely wind-, wave-, and solar-powered electricity grid.

GETTING HERE AND AROUND

From Glenfinnan, you reach Arisaig on the A830, the only road leading west. The Fort William–Mallaig train also stops here.

EXPLORING

Arisaig Marine. Along with whale-, seal-, and bird-watching excursions, Arisaig Marine runs a boat service from the harbor at Arisaig to the islands from May to September. There's also a handy gift shop and café. ✉ *Arisaig Harbour* ☎ *01687/450224* 🌐 *www.arisaig.co.uk* 🎫 *Round-trip fares from £18.*

Loch Morar. A small, unnamed side road just south of Mallaig leads east to an even smaller road that will bring you to Loch Morar, the deepest of all the Scottish lochs (more than 1,000 feet). The next deepest point is miles out into the Atlantic, beyond the continental shelf. The loch is said to have a resident monster, Morag, which undoubtedly gets less recognition than its famous cousin Nessie. Whether that means you have more chance of getting her to appear for a photograph, we can't say. ✉ *Loch Morar, Mallaig.*

WHERE TO EAT AND STAY

$$
FRENCH

✕ **Old Library.** On the waterfront, this 1722 barn has been converted into a fine, reasonably priced restaurant. Expect fairly simple, but tasty plates of local fish and meats, prepared in a French-bistro style—lamb shank, sirloin, or perhaps a fillet of buttery hake, served with seasonal veggies. **Known for:** hearty meals; ultrafresh produce; local character. $ *Average main: £17* ✉ *B8008* ☎ *01687/450651* ⊕ *www.oldlibrary.co.uk.*

$$$
HOTEL
Fodor's Choice
★

▦ **Arisaig House.** An open-arms welcome and stunning views of the Isle of Skye await you at this wonderful mansion. **Pros:** beautiful views; lovely hosts; outstanding food. **Cons:** a bit isolated. $ *Rooms from: £175* ✉ *Beasdale* ☎ *01687/450730* ⊕ *www.arisaighouse.co.uk* ⇌ *12 rooms* ⫯⊘⫯ *Free breakfast.*

ISLE OF SKYE

The misty Isle of Skye is awash with romance and myth, lush green gardens, and steep, magnetic mountains. Its extraordinary natural beauty and royal connections see it rank highly on most visitors' must-see lists, while its proximity to the mainland makes it one of Scotland's most easily accessible islands.

Skye has a dramatic, mysterious, and mountainous landscape, where sunsets linger brilliantly until late at night and otherworldly mists roll gently through the valleys. Much photographed are the old crofts, one or two of which are still inhabited today. It also has an impressive range of accommodation, and restaurants that showcase the best of the island's produce and culinary talent.

To reach Skye, cross over the bridge spanning the narrow channel of Kyleakin, between Kyle of Lochalsh and Kyleakin. Or, if you're visiting in the summer, take a romantic boat trip between Mallaig and Armadale or between Glenelg and Kylerhea. You can tour comfortably around the island in two or three days, but a bit longer will allow extra time for hiking or sea kayaking.

Orientation is easy: in the north, follow the roads that loop around the peninsulas of Waternish and Trotternish; in the south, enjoy the road running the length of the Sleat Peninsula. There are some stretches of single-lane road, but for careful drivers these shouldn't pose a problem.

19

KYLE OF LOCHALSH

55 miles west of Inverness, 120 miles northwest of Glasgow.

This little town is the mainland gateway to Skye. Opened in 1995, the bridge transformed not only travel to Skye but the very seascape itself. The most noticeable attraction, though (in fact, almost a cliché), is not in Kyle at all, but 8 miles farther east at Dornie—Eilean Donan Castle.

GETTING HERE AND AROUND

From the north, you reach Kyle of Lochalsh via the A890; from the south, take the A87. There are four direct trains a day from Inverness.

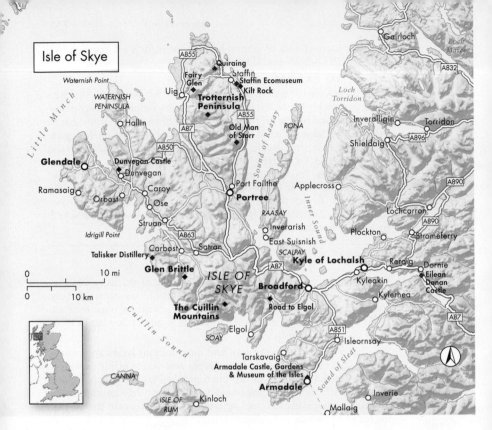

EXPLORING

Fodor'sChoice **Eilean Donan Castle.** Guarding the confluence of lochs Long, Alsh, and
★ Duich stands the most picturesque of all Scottish castles. Eilean Donan
Castle, perched on an islet connected to the mainland by a stone-arched
bridge, dates from the 14th century and has all the dramatic stone walls,
timber ceilings, and winding stairs you could possibly desire. Empty and
neglected for years after being bombarded by frigates of the Royal Navy
during an abortive Spanish-Jacobite landing in 1719, this romantic Scottish icon was almost entirely rebuilt from a ruin in the early 20th century.
The kitchen re-creates the busy scene before a grand banquet, and the
upper floors show how the castle was transformed into a grand house.
The picturesque cover of a thousand travel brochures, Eilean Donan has
also appeared in a number of Hollywood movies and TV shows, from
The Wicker Man to *Highlander*. There's a shop and a coffeehouse for
the many visitors. ⊠ *A87, Dornie* ☎ *01599/555202* ⊕ *www.eileandonan-
castle.com* ☜ *£7.50* ⊗ *Closed Jan.*

WHERE TO STAY

$$ ⬛ **Glenelg Inn.** Looking out over the Sound of Sleat, the Glenelg Inn's
B&B/INN pleasant, contemporary rooms are furnished in wood and cane and are
bright and clean. **Pros:** lively atmosphere; pretty views; excellent local
seafood. **Cons:** no sea views in some rooms; out-of-the-way location.

$ *Rooms from: £110* ✉ *Kirkton* ☎ *01599/522273* ⊕ *www.glenelg-inn. com* ⇥ *7 rooms* ⦿| *Free breakfast.*

BROADFORD

8 miles west of Kyle of Lochalsh via Skye Bridge.

One of the larger of Skye's settlements, Broadford lies along the shore of Broadford Bay, which has been known to welcome whales to its sheltered waters.

GETTING HERE AND AROUND

Broadford is on the A87, the main road crossing the Isle of Skye.

ESSENTIALS

Visitor Information Broadford Visitor Information Centre. ✉ *The car park, off A87* ☎ *01471/822361* ⊕ *www.visitscotland.com.*

EXPLORING

FAMILY
Fodor's Choice
★

Misty Isle Boat Trips. For fantastic views of the Cuillin Mountains and the Inner Hebrides, book a place on one of the Misty Isle Boat Trips. The expansive scenery around Loch Coruisk is some of the most spectacular in Scotland. Round-trip journeys depart from the town of Elgol, and booking ahead is essential. Prices vary, but a cruise to a seal colony costs £17.50. Private charters are available. ✉ *Elgol jetty, Sealladh na Mara, Elgol* ☎ *01471/866288* ⊕ *www.mistyisleboattrips.co.uk* ✉ *From £12.50* ☉ *Closed Nov.–Mar. and Sun.*

▌OFF THE
BEATEN
PATH

Road to Elgol. The B8083 leads from Broadford to one of the finest vistas anywhere in Scotland. This road passes by **Strath Suardal** and little **Loch Cill Chriosd** (Kilchrist), and also takes in breathtaking views of the mountain **Bla Bheinn** en route. As the A881 continues to Elgol, see a gathering of traditional crofts that descends to a pier, then admire the heart-stopping profile of the Cuillin peaks from the shore. Seek out the path, around halfway down the hill, that leads across rough grasslands into the mountains. ✉ *Elgol.*

19

WHERE TO EAT AND STAY

$$
SEAFOOD
Fodor's Choice
★

✕ **Creelers of Skye.** Don't be fooled by its humble appearance; Creelers is a celebrated French seafood restaurant. From its pan-roasted sea bass to its seafood gumbo, it is a compulsory stop for all passing gourmands. **Known for:** excellent bouillabaisse; sea views. $ *Average main: £18* ✉ *Lower Harrapool* ☎ *01471/822281* ⊕ *www.skye-seafood-restaurant. co.uk* ☉ *Closed Sun.*

$$$
HOTEL

⌂ **Broadford Hotel.** Watch over Broadford Bay in comfort and style with a stay at this well-appointed hotel, which takes pride in being the place where Drambuie was invented. **Pros:** quintessentially Scottish; convenient location; free Wi-Fi. **Cons:** no elevator; poorly lit public areas. $ *Rooms from: £164* ✉ *Torrin Rd.* ☎ *01471/822204* ⊕ *www.broad- fordhotel.co.uk* ⇥ *11 rooms* ⦿| *Free breakfast.*

ARMADALE

17 miles south of Broadford, 43 miles south of Portree, 5 miles (ferry crossing) west of Mallaig.

Rolling moorlands, scattered with rivers and lochans, give way to enchanting hidden coves and scattered waterside communities. Welcome to **Sleat**, Skye's southernmost peninsula.

GETTING HERE AND AROUND

The Mallaig-Armadale ferry arrives here. There's a short (and beautiful) road to the southwest, while the main road heads east following the stunning coast.

EXPLORING

Armadale Castle, Gardens & Museum of the Isles. As the name suggests, this attraction has three distinct strings to its bow: a romantic, ruined castle; a lush, flower-filled estate; and a fascinating museum of local history. The castle is a windswept 17th-century mansion house built by the influential Clan Donald, while the extensive gardens cover 40 acres, offering magnificent views across the Sound of Sleat to Knoydart and the Mallaig Peninsula. The highlight, however, is the fascinating museum, which tells the story of the clan and their proud title, the Lords of the Isles, with the help of an excellent audiovisual presentation. There's a gift shop, restaurant, library, and center for genealogy research. Also on the grounds are high-quality accommodations in the form of seven cottages, complete with kitchen facilities. Access is from Armadale Pier, where signs indicate the different forest walks that are available. ✉ *Off A851* ✥ *½ mile north of Armadale Pier* ☎ *01471/844305* 🌐 *www.clandonald.com* 🎟 *Gardens free, museum £8.50* ⏲ *Closed Nov.–Mar.*

WHERE TO STAY

$$$$ HOTEL Fodor's Choice ★ 🏨 **Hotel Eilean Iarmain.** Built on a small peninsula dotted by a quiet lighthouse, this hotel has an unforgettable location and an enchanting collection of wood paneling, chintz fabrics, and country-style antiques. **Pros:** spectacular waterfront location; plenty of sporting activities; excellent wine list. **Cons:** temperamental Wi-Fi. [$] *Rooms from: £235* ✉ *Off A851, Isleornsay* ☎ *01471/833332* 🌐 *www.eileaniarmain.co.uk* 🛏 *16 rooms* 🍴 *Free breakfast.*

SHOPPING

Fodor's Choice ★ **Ragamuffin.** This well-stocked shop specializes in designer knitwear and has some of the nicest staff you could hope to meet. On cold winter days, they might make you coffee while you browse, then mail your purchases back home for you. ✉ *Armadale Pier, off A851* ☎ *01471/844217* 🌐 *www.ragamuffinloves.blogspot.co.uk.*

PORTREE

42 miles northwest of Armadale.

Portree, the population center of the island, is a pleasant place clustered around a small and sheltered bay. Although not overburdened by historical features, it's a fine touring base with a number of good shops and an excellent bakery.

GETTING HERE AND AROUND

The biggest town on Skye, Portree is well served by local buses and by a well-maintained road, the A87.

ESSENTIALS

Visitor Information VisitScotland Portree iCentre. ✉ *Bayfield House, Bayfield Rd.* ☎ *01478/612992* 🌐 *www.visitscotland.com.*

EXPLORING

Aros. On the outskirts of town, Aros is a community center that screens films, exhibits artworks, and hosts live music, dance, and theater productions. It's the cultural hub of the Isle of Skye. ✉ *Viewfield Rd.* ☎ *01478/613649* 🌐 *www.aros.co.uk* 🎟 *Free.*

WHERE TO EAT

$ BRITISH 🍴 **Café Arriba.** Up a steep flight of stairs, the laid-back café has window seats with great views over Portree Harbour. Using only local produce (whatever is "fresh, local, and available"), this is a good option for no-frills eating. **Known for:** delicious homemade cakes; mildly treacherous stairs. [$] *Average main: £8* ✉ *Quay Brae, Quay St.* ☎ *01478/611830* 🌐 *www.cafearriba.co.uk.*

$$$ BRITISH 🍴 **Scorrybreac Restaurant.** It may be tiny, but this 20-seater restaurant has made big waves since opening in 2013. The vibe is relaxed and informal, while the cooking is imaginative and varied, creating unexpected marriages such as coffee-crusted venison or coconut and hake. **Known for:** intimate dining; inventive dishes. [$] *Average main: £20* ✉ *7 Bosville Terr.* ☎ *01478/612069* 🌐 *www.scorrybreac.com* 🕒 *Closed Mon. No lunch.*

WHERE TO STAY

$$$ HOTEL 🏨 **Cuillin Hills Hotel.** This Victorian-era hunting lodge looks down on Portree and the brightly painted houses around the harbor. **Pros:** a short stroll from Portree; good breakfast menu; attentive service. **Cons:** rooms at back overpriced; restaurant can be full; no elevator. [$] *Rooms from: £215* ✉ *Off A855* ☎ *01478/612003* 🌐 *www.cuillinhills-hotel-skye.co.uk* 🛏 *29 rooms* 🍽 *Free breakfast.*

$$$ B&B/INN 🏨 **Peinmore House.** A former manse (the minister's residence), Peinmore House has panoramic views to die for: to the north, Portree Bay (on a clear day, all the way to the Old Man of Storr); to the south, the moody Cuillin Mountains. **Pros:** tranquil location; great breakfast; impeccable rooms. **Cons:** rather pricey; car required to get here. [$] *Rooms from: £165* ✉ *Off B883, 2 miles south of Portree* ☎ *01478/612574* 🌐 *www.peinmorehouse.co.uk* 🛏 *4 rooms* 🍽 *Free breakfast.*

SHOPPING

Isle of Skye Soap Company. This charming little shop handcrafts its own soaps, aromatherapy oils, candles, and other pleasingly fragranced gifts. Founder (and soap-maker in chief) Fiona is an aromatherapist. ✉ *Somerled Sq.* ☎ *01478/611350* 🌐 *www.skye-soap.co.uk.*

TROTTERNISH PENINSULA

16 miles north of Portree.

Travel north from Portree on the A855 and you'll see cliffs rising to the left. These are the closest edge of an ancient lava flow, set back from the road and running the length of the peninsula. Fossilized dinosaur bones have been uncovered at the base of these cliffs, while overhead, you might just spot a sea eagle, identifiable by the flash of its white tail.

GETTING HERE AND AROUND

From Portree, take the twisting, undulating A855 as it follows the coast.

EXPLORING

Fodor's Choice ★ **Fairy Glen.** Out of the way and little visited, Fairy Glen is a magical place—an enchanting, otherworldly valley of strange green hillocks, eerily still pools, crumbling cottages, and roaming sheep. To get here, take a small road just south of Uig signed "Sheader and Balnaknock" and drive for about a mile. ✣ *11 miles southwest of Staffin* 🎫 *Free.*

Kilt Rock. No drive between Portree and Staffin is complete without a sojourn at Skye's most famous sea cliff. Named for the shape of its sheer rock face, which is ridged like a pleated kilt and swoops out to sea at the "hem," soaring Kilt Rock (and its gushing waterfall) can be seen from a specially built viewing platform. ✉ *Staffin* ✣ *1½ miles south of Staffin.*

Old Man of Storr. Along the dramatic road around the Trotternish Peninsula, a gate beside a car park marks the beginning of the climb to the Old Man of Storr, one of Skye's most iconic landmarks. At 2,000 feet, this volcanic pinnacle is the highest point on the peninsula, so give yourself at least three hours to explore and enjoy the spectacular views from the top. ⚠ **The weather here changes very quickly, so be prepared.**

Fodor's Choice ★ **Quiraing.** A spectacular geological formation of rocky crags and towering stacks, Quiraing dominates the horizon of the Trotternish Peninsula. It is situated about 5 miles beyond Kilt Rock, so for a closer look, make a left onto a small road at Brogaig by Staffin Bay. There's a parking lot near the point where this road breaches the ever-present cliff line. The road is very narrow and rough, so drive cautiously. The rambler's trail is on uneven, stony ground, and it's a steep scramble up to the rock formations. In ages past, stolen cattle were hidden deep within the Quiraing's rocky jaws.

FAMILY **Staffin Ecomuseum.** Billed as "a museum without walls," the Staffin Ecomuseum is a collection of 13 open-air geological and social exhibits dotted along the landscape of the peninsula. Follow the map along the coastal route and you will discover dinosaur footprints, a healing well, a deserted village, and more. This is not to be confused with Staffin Museum, Dugald Ross's nearby exhibition. ✉ *Staffin Community Trust, 3 Ellishadder, Staffin* 🌐 *www.skyecomuseum.co.uk.*

WHERE TO EAT AND STAY

$ BRITISH 🍴 **Skye Pie Café at Glenview.** For a gourmet pie made using locally sourced, organic ingredients, look no further than this sweet café. Housed in a renovated, whitewashed croft building, complete with wooden floors and cheerfully painted walls. the café serves every style of pie imaginable, from savory meat or fish to sweet apple or toffee. **Known for:** delicious pies; specialty sausage rolls; comfortable rooms. [$] *Average*

The Old Man of Storr, a volcanic pinnacle, is part of the dramatic scenery on Skye's Trotternish Peninsula.

main: £5 ✉ *A855, Culnacnoc, Staffin* ☎ *01470/562248* 🌐 *skyepiecafe.co.uk* ⏲ *Closed Nov.–Easter and weekends. No dinner.*

$ B&B/INN **Corran House.** Set back off the A87 near Kingsburgh, this cozy B&B is a convenient, good-value stay at the base of the Trotternish Peninsula, 7 miles northwest of Portree. **Pros:** great location between sights; splendid views; good value. **Cons:** not close to any one particular attraction. [$] *Rooms from: £80* ✉ *1 Eyre, Portree* ✣ *Set back from the road; look out for the small white sign* ☎ *01470/532699* 🌐 *www.corranhouseskye.co.uk* 🛏 *6 rooms* 🍴 *Free breakfast.*

$$$ HOTEL **The Flodigarry Hotel.** With spectacular coastal views and antique furnishings throughout, the Flodigarry Hotel retains the feel of a grand country manor. **Pros:** spectacular views; a good base for walking; free Wi-Fi. **Cons:** steep road down; expensive rooms. [$] *Rooms from: £210* ✉ *A855, Staffin* ☎ *01470/552203* 🌐 *www.hotelintheskye.co.uk* 🛏 *18 rooms* 🍴 *Free breakfast.*

GLENDALE

14 miles southwest of Waternish.

Glendale is a region rich in flora and fauna: otters, seals, and dolphins can be spotted off its rocky coast, while white-tailed sea eagles soar overhead. Dunvegan Castle is just at the region's eastern edge.

GETTING HERE AND AROUND

Traveling south from Dunvegan, the B884 road twists and curves along the coast. It can feel rather isolated in bad weather or after dark.

EXPLORING

Fodor's Choice ★ **Dunvegan Castle.** In a commanding position looming over a sea loch, Dunvegan Castle has been the seat of the chiefs of Clan MacLeod for more than 700 years. Though the structure has been greatly changed over the centuries, a gloomy ambience prevails, and there's plenty of family history on display; most notable is the Fairy Flag—a silk banner, thought to be originally from Rhodes or Syria, which is credited with protecting the clan from danger. Enthusiastic guides take you through several rooms, and an interesting collection of photos hangs in the lower corridors. Make time to visit the gardens, with their water garden and falls, fern house, walled garden, and various viewing points. There's a café beside the car park. Boat trips from the castle to the nearby seal colony run mid-April through September. ✉ *Junction of A850 and A863, Dunvegan* ☎ *01470/521206* 🌐 *www.dunvegancastle.com* 🎟 *Castle and gardens £13; gardens only £11; seal trips £7.50.*

WHERE TO EAT AND STAY

$$$$ MODERN BRITISH Fodor's Choice ★ 🍴 **Three Chimneys.** Perhaps the Isle of Skye's biggest culinary draw, this old stone-walled restaurant on the banks of Loch Dunvegan serves consistently daring, well-crafted food. The chef's belief in quality Scottish ingredients is evident in every dish, from the locally sourced game to the sublime Scottish seafood, and when aligned with the simple but chic interior—all crisp white walls and exposed brickwork—it makes for a luxury dining experience you won't soon forget. ■ **TIP→ Reservations are essential.** **Known for:** inventive seafood dishes; faultless service. [$] *Average main: £65* ✉ *Colbost House, B884, Colbost* ☎ *01470/511258* 🌐 *www.threechimneys.co.uk* 🕓 *Closed mid-Dec.–mid-Jan.* ☞ *No children under 8 at dinner.*

$ B&B/INN 🏨 **Roskhill House.** A 19th-century croft house that once housed the local post office, this pretty Glendale hotel feels like a home away from home. **Pros:** friendly and helpful hosts; cozy lounge with fireplace; free Wi-Fi. **Cons:** very small place; need to reserve far in advance. [$] *Rooms from: £93* ✉ *A863, Roskhill* ✣ *3 miles south of Dunvegan* ☎ *01470/521317* 🌐 *www.roskhillhouse.co.uk* 🛏 *5 rooms* 🍽 *Free breakfast.*

GLEN BRITTLE AND THE CUILLIN MOUNTAINS

28 miles southeast of Glendale.

Fodor's Choice ★ The gentle slopes of this valley are a gateway to the dramatic peaks and ridges of the Cuillin Mountains. Glen Brittle's lower slopes are fine for walkers and weekend climbers, but the higher ridges are strictly for serious mountaineers.

GETTING HERE AND AROUND

Glen Brittle extends off the A863/B8009 on the west side of the island.

EXPLORING

Fodor's Choice ★ **Fairy Pools.** One of the most magical sights in Scotland, the Fairy Pools are a spectacularly beautiful collection of waterfalls and plunge pools in the midst of Glen Brittle. The rocky gray landscape contrasts with the vivid blue-green of the pools, the colorful plant life, and visiting wildlife (including, occasionally, red deer) to give the environment a fairy-tale feel. You can walk to the pools from a parking lot 20 minutes away. Come at sunrise or sunset for a truly enchanting swim—just don't expect the water to be warm. ⌧ *Glenbrittle* ⛶ *Free.*

Glen Brittle. Enjoy spectacular mountain scenery in Glen Brittle, including some unforgettable views of the Cuillin Mountains (these are not for the casual walker, due to steep and dangerous cliff faces). The drive from Carbost along a single-track road is one of the most dramatic in Scotland and draws outdoorsy types from across the globe. At the southern end of the glen is a murky-color beach, a campground, and gentle foothills that were made for strolling. ⌧ *Off A863 and B8009.*

Talisker Distillery. The only distillery on the Isle of Skye is one of the best in Scotland. Talisker produces a sweet, light single malt that has the distinctive peaty aroma of island whiskies, yet with less intensity—making it a great introductory dram for newcomers to Scotch. Robert Louis Stevenson called Talisker "the king of drinks," and the inhabitants of Skye are very proud of it. Classic tours here take about 45 minutes, while tasting tours (available weekdays) take two hours. Book ahead, as tours are very popular. ⌧ *B8009, Carbost* ☎ *01478/614308* ⊕ *www. discovering-distilleries.com/talisker* ⛶ *Tours from £10* ⊘ *Closed mid-Feb.–mid-Mar., Sun. in Apr., May, and Oct., and weekends in Nov.–Mar.*

THE NORTHERN HIGHLANDS

The northernmost part of Scotland, from Inverness all the way up to John O'Groats in the east and Cape Wrath in the west, has some of the most distinctive mountain profiles and coastal stretches in all of Scotland. The rim roads around the wilds of Durness overlook rocky shores, and the long beaches are as dramatic as the awe-inspiring and desolate cross-country routes like Destitution Road in Wester Ross. Follow the North Coast 500 loop from Inverness to see the very best of the region. If you head counterclockwise up the east coast, along the north coast, and down the west coast, the spectacular landscape gets more and more dramatic at every turn. Travel clockwise, and you might find the east coast down from John O'Groats feels a bit anticlimactic.

19

GAIRLOCH

55 miles southwest of Ullapool.

Aside from its restaurants and lodgings, peaceful Gairloch has one further advantage: it often escapes the rain clouds that can cling to the high summits. You can enjoy a round of golf here and perhaps stay dry, even when the nearby Torridon Hills are deluged.

GETTING HERE AND AROUND
From Ullapool, this coastal town can be reached via the winding A832.

EXPLORING
Destitution Road. The road south between **Corrieshalloch Gorge** (a very worthwhile stop) and Gairloch passes through wild woodlands around Dundonnell and Loch Broom, then takes in stunning coastal scenery with views of Gruinard Bay and its white beaches. Look out for the

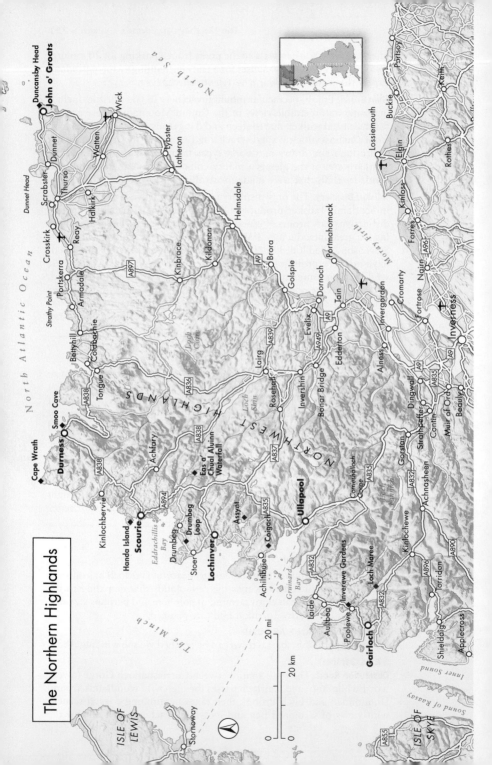

The Northern Highlands

toothed ramparts of the mountain **An Teallach** (pronounced tyel-lack), visible on the horizon for miles. The moorland route you travel is known, rather chillingly, as Destitution Road; a holdover from the terrible potato famines of the 1840s.

Fodor'sChoice ★ **Inverewe Gardens.** A highlight of the area, Inverewe Gardens has lush plantings tucked away behind a dense barrier of trees and shrubs. This is all thanks to the warm North Atlantic Drift, which takes the edge off winter frosts. Inverewe is sometimes described as subtropical, but this inaccuracy irritates the head gardener; do not expect coconuts and palm trees here. Instead, look for rarities like the blue Himalayan poppy. ⊠ *A832, 6 miles northeast of Gairloch, Poolewe* ☎ *01445/781229* ⊕ *www.nts.org.uk/visit/inverewe* ⊠ *£10.50.*

Fodor'sChoice ★ **Loch Maree.** Southeast of Gairloch stretches one of Scotland's most scenic lochs, Loch Maree. Its harmonious setting, with tall Scots pines and the mountain Slioch looming as a backdrop, is regularly visited by red deer, as well as the endangered pine marten (a member of the weasel family)—though they're just as likely to be hanging around the trash cans as in the trees. There are few official parking places along the loch, but these are nestled between the trees with limited views, so be prepared to park and climb to a better vantage point. ⊠ *Gairloch.*

WHERE TO STAY

$$ HOTEL ⌕ **The Dundonnell.** Thirty miles from Gairloch, this lovely family-run hotel, set on the roadside by Little Loch Broom with the mountains of An Leachall rising up behind, couldn't be more picturesque. **Pros:** fabulous scenery; plenty of outdoor activities; good dining options. **Cons:** bland exterior. Ⓢ *Rooms from: £100* ⊠ *A832, 30 miles northeast of Gairloch, Dundonnell* ☎ *01854/633204* ⊕ *www.dundonnellhotel. com* ⌁ *28 rooms* ⎢⎥ *Free breakfast.*

ULLAPOOL

19

35 miles south of Lochinver, 238 miles north of Glasgow, 57 miles northwest of Inverness.

Ullapool is an ideal base for hiking throughout Sutherland and taking wildlife and nature cruises, especially to the Summer Isles. By the shores of salty Loch Broom, the town was founded in 1788 as a fishing station to exploit the local herring stocks. There's still a smattering of fishing vessels, as well as visiting yachts and foreign ships. When their crews fill the pubs, Ullapool has a surprisingly cosmopolitan feel. The harbor area comes to life when the Lewis and Harris ferry arrives and departs.

GETTING HERE AND AROUND

A desolate but well-maintained stretch of the A835 takes you from Inverness to Ullapool, with a connection to Torridon via the A832.

ESSENTIALS

Visitor Information VisitScotland Ullapool iCentre. ⊠ *Argyle St.* ☎ *01854/612486.*

EXPLORING

The Ceilidh Place. Ullapool's cultural focal point is The Ceilidh Place, an excellent venue for concerts and other events all through the year (*ceilidh* is a Scottish social gathering with traditional music and dance). It started out as a small café, but over the years has added space for local performers, an excellent bookshop specializing in Scottish writing, and a handful of comfortable rooms (as well as a basic bunkhouse) for those who want to spend the night. It's a great place for afternoon coffee or a wee dram in the evening. ✉ *12–14 W. Argyle St.* ☎ *01854/612103* 🌐 *www.theceilidhplace.com.*

Coigach and Assynt. North of Ullapool lies a different kind of landscape, one of brooding mountains and languid lochs, where peaks punch their way out of heathered terrain and appear to constantly shift positions. Even their names have a more mysterious air than those of the *bens* (mountain peaks or hills) elsewhere: Cul Mor, Cul Beag, Stac Pollaidh, Canisp, Suilven. Some hark back to Norse rather than to Gaelic—a reminder that Vikings used to sail this northern shore. ■ **TIP→ This vast empty region, within the North West Highlands Geopark, is spectacular from top to bottom, but the highlight is the eerily pretty Loch Assynt, peppered with tiny wooded isles.** ✣ *15 miles north of Ullapool on the A835.*

WHERE TO EAT AND STAY

$ CAFÉ Fodor's Choice ★ 🍴 **The West Coast Delicatessen.** This charming family-run deli serves delicious homemade sandwiches, pies, soups, salads, and hummus to a long line of locals and tourists. It also has great cakes and baked goods. **Known for:** great homemade soups; excellent coffee; an array of artisanal products. [$] *Average main: £8* ✉ *Argyle St.* ☎ *01854/613450* 🌐 *www.westcoastdeli.co.uk* ⏲ *Closed Sun. No dinner.*

$ B&B/INN Fodor's Choice ★ 🏨 **Tanglewood House.** Sitting on a headland above a rocky beach, with spectacular views across Loch Broom toward Ullapool, one of Scotland's most unique and appealing B&Bs feels wonderfully remote while only being a short drive (or even a walk) into town. **Pros:** truly unique property; beautiful setting; fast and reliable Wi-Fi. **Cons:** a steep drive down to the house. [$] *Rooms from: £99* ✉ *Off A835* ☎ *01854/612059* 🌐 *www.tanglewoodhouse.co.uk* 🛏 *3 rooms* 🍽 *Free breakfast.*

LOCHINVER

28 miles south of Scourie.

Lochinver is a very pretty, quiet, shoreside community of whitewashed cottages, with lovely beaches to the north, a harbor used by the west-coast fishing fleet, and a couple of good dining and lodging options. Behind the town the mountain Suilven rises abruptly. Take the cul-de-sac, **Baddidarroch Road,** for a great photo opportunity. Lochinver is a perfect base for exploring Sutherland.

GETTING HERE AND AROUND

To get to Lochinver from Scourie, head south, then turn off the A894 to the A837.

ESSENTIALS

Visitor Information VisitScotland Lochinver iCentre. ✉ *The Mission, Culag Park* ☎ *01571/841073* 🌐 *www.visitscotland.com.*

EXPLORING

Fodor's Choice ★ **Drumbeg Loop.** Bold souls spending time at Lochinver may enjoy the interesting single-track B869 Drumbeg Loop to the north of Lochinver—it has several challenging hairpin turns along with breathtaking views. The junction is on the north side of the River Inver bridge on the outskirts of the village, signposted as "Stoer" and "Clashnessie." Just beyond the scattered community of Stoer, a road leads west to **Stoer Point Lighthouse.** If you're an energetic walker, you can hike across the short turf and heather along the cliff top for fine views west towards the Isle of Skye. There's also a red-sandstone sea stack: the **Old Man of Stoer** (not to be confused with the Old Man of Storr on Skye). This makes a pleasant excursion on a long summer evening.

Eas a' Chual Aluinn Waterfall. With a drop of 685 feet, this is the longest waterfall in the United Kingdom. A rugged hike leads to the falls, which are at the head of Loch Glencoul. Start from the car park off A894, approximately 17 miles east and north from Lochinver. In summer, cruises (£25) from Kylesku Old Ferry Pier offer a less taxing alternative. ✉ *A894, 3 miles southeast of Kylesku Bridge.*

WHERE TO EAT AND STAY

$ BRITISH 🍴 **Lochinver Mission Cafe.** An abandoned fishermen's mission (a place where fishermen stayed while in port), situated at the far end of town near the harbor, now houses this pleasant café serving lunch, soup, sandwiches, and home baking. The specials often include fish freshly delivered from the harbor. **Known for:** delicious homemade soup; great fish-and-chips; friendly staff. [$] *Average main: £9* ✉ *Culag Park* ☎ *01571/844324* 🌐 *www.lochinvermission.org.uk* 💳 *No credit cards* 🕓 *Closed Sun.*

$$$$ HOTEL 🏨 **Inver Lodge Hotel.** In a commanding location on a hillside above Lochinver, this modern luxury hotel has stunning views of the coast, as well as smart guest rooms that are decorated in contemporary colors and traditional mahogany furniture. **Pros:** cozy public room with a fireplace; refreshing sauna; great fishing nearby. **Cons:** slightly drab exterior; not good for families with children. [$] *Rooms from: £275* ✉ *Iolaire Rd.* ☎ *01571/844496* 🌐 *www.inverlodge.com* 🛏 *21 rooms* 🍽 *Free breakfast.*

SHOPPING

Highland Stoneware. The huge sofa and television composed entirely of broken crockery are a witty introduction to the beautiful ceramic works of art made at Highland Stoneware. The potters and decorators busy themselves in a studio behind the shop, and visitors are encouraged to watch as they create pieces incorporating Highland themes. If you miss this one, there's a second Highland Stoneware store in Ullapool. ✉ *Baddidarroch* ☎ *01571/844376* 🌐 *www.highlandstoneware.com.*

SCOURIE

27 miles southwest of Durness.

Scourie is a small coastal settlement catering to visitors—particularly fisherfolk—with a good range of accommodations. The bay-side town makes a good base for a trip to the bird sanctuary on Handa Island.

GETTING HERE AND AROUND

From Durness, head south on the A838, turning onto the A894.

EXPLORING

Fodor's Choice
★

Handa Island. Just off the coast of Scourie is Handa Island, a bird sanctuary that shelters huge seabird colonies, especially impressive at nesting time. You can gaze at more than 200,000 birds nesting on dramatic cliffs here, including guillemots, razorbills, great skuas, kittiwakes, and, of course, crowd-pleasingly colorful puffins. This remarkable reserve, administered by the Scottish Wildlife Trust, is open only in spring and summer, and can be reached by a small open boat from Tarbert; contact the tourist information center in Lochinver or Durness for details. ■TIP→ Note that ferries don't run on Sunday. Sturdy boots, a waterproof jacket, and a degree of fitness are needed to walk the path around the island. ⊕ *scottishwildlifetrust.org.uk* ☉ *Closed Oct.–Mar.*

WHERE TO EAT AND STAY

$$
SEAFOOD
Fodor's Choice
★

✕ **Shorehouse Restaurant.** If you're feeling peckish after a trip to Handa Island, make a stop at this exceptional seafood restaurant overlooking Tarbet Harbor. It serves freshly caught seafood specialties, from hand-dived scallops and hot smoked mackerel to whole lobsters, in a quaint, maritime-theme setting. **Known for:** spectacular seafood; gorgeous views; friendly and attentive service. $ *Average main: £15* ⊠ *Tigh Na Mara, Tarbet* ☎ *01971/502251* ☉ *Closed Sun. and Oct.–Easter.*

$$
B&B/INN
Fodor's Choice
★

🏨 **Eddrachilles Hotel.** With one of the most spectacular vistas of any hotel in Scotland—out toward the picturesque islands of Badcall Bay—Eddrachilles sits on a huge plot of private moorland just south of the Handa Island bird sanctuary. **Pros:** attractive garden; stunning shoreline nearby; close to bird sanctuary. **Cons:** needs a lick of paint. $ *Rooms from: £125* ⊠ *Off A894* ☎ *01971/502080* ⊕ *www.eddrachilles.com* ☉ *Closed Nov.–Mar.* ➴ *10 rooms* ⧖*Free breakfast.*

DURNESS

70 miles west of Thurso.

The sudden patches of green surrounding the village of Durness, on the north coast, are caused by the richer limestone outcrops among the acid moorlands. The town is the jumping-off point for several natural highlights, from a beautiful sandy beach to the country's highest cliff.

GETTING HERE AND AROUND

From Thurso, simply head west along the A836, which will turn into A838 at Tongue.

ESSENTIALS

Visitor Information VisitScotland Durness iCentre. ⊠ *Sango* ☎ *01971/511368* ⊕ *www.visitscotland.com.*

EXPLORING

Cape Wrath. If you've made it this far north, you'll probably want to go all the way to Cape Wrath, a rugged headland at the northwest tip of Scotland. The white-sand beaches, impressive dunes covered in marram grass, and crashing seas of nearby Balnakeil Bay make it an exhilarating place to visit. As this land is owned by the Ministry of Defence (it is listed as an area for air force training), you can't drive your own vehicle. From May through September, a small boat ferries people here from Keoldale, 2 miles outside Durness. En route look out for Clo Mor; at 920 feet, they're the United Kingdom's highest sea cliffs. Once you're across the sea inlet, a minibus will take you to the lighthouse. Call ahead or check departure times on the board at the jetty. ☎ *01971/511284* 🌐 *www.visitcapewrath.com* 🎟 *£12 boat/bus return* 🕒 *No boat Oct.–Apr.*

Fodor's Choice ★ **Smoo Cave.** This atmospheric cavern, hollowed out of the limestone by rushing water, feels like something out of a fantasy novel. The combined sea-and-freshwater cave, complete with gushing waterfall, can be reached via a steep cliff stairway from the Smoo Cave car park. However, don't start your descent before reading the explanatory boards at the top of the stairs, which tell the history of those who lived and used the caves in much earlier times. ✉ *Durness* 🎟 *Free.*

WHERE TO EAT AND STAY

$ CAFÉ **Cocoa Mountain.** A must for those with a sweet tooth, this "chocolate bar" serves up world-class truffles and stunningly rich hot chocolate made in its specialist "chocolate factory," which sources the beans from around the world. There are also sandwiches, cakes, and coffee available, in case the chocolate gets to be too much. **Known for:** sublime chocolate truffles; house-made hot chocolate. [$] *Average main: £9* ✉ *Balnakeil* ☎ *01971/511233* 🌐 *www.cocoamountain.co.uk.*

$$ HOTEL 🏨 **Tongue Hotel.** With open fireplaces, tartan rugs, and floral wallpaper, this traditional Highland hotel is a great base for exploring the northern coast of the Scottish mainland. **Pros:** warm and friendly staff; beautiful location with stunning views; deliciously creamy porridge at breakfast. **Cons:** Wi-Fi only in public areas; TV sets from the '80s. [$] *Rooms from: £105* ✉ *Tongue* ☎ *01847/611206* 🌐 *www.tonguehotel.co.uk* 🛏 *19 rooms* 🍴 *Free breakfast.*

SHOPPING

Balnakeil Craft Village. Artisans sell pottery, leather, weavings, paintings, and more from their studios at Balnakeil Craft Village. It is a rather odd place, housed as it is on an unnamed road running northwest from Durness in a collection of shabby former military buildings framed by dramatic views of Balnakeil Bay. There are galleries, workshops, and a range of crafts for sale. The village is open during the summer, with most shops open daily from 10 to 5. ✉ *Balnakeil* ☎ *01971/511777* 🌐 *www.balnakeilcraftvillage.weebly.com.*

Sculpture Croft. This odd garden of delights provokes a double-take from most drivers traveling along the A838, thanks to its incongruous ceramic-topped gates. Park opposite and take a stroll down into Lotte Glob's pottery wonderland, where ceramic and metal sculptures are scattered across the gardens. Several paths lead down to the coast, and there are hundreds of pieces en route, including a library of ceramic books. Her work reflects and adds to the landscape, using natural shapes and forms and building patterns into the rocks themselves. End your visit with a trip to the studio and pottery shop. ✉ *105 Laid* ☎ *01971/511727* 🌐 *www.lotteglob.co.uk.*

JOHN O'GROATS

15 miles north of Wick.

The windswept little outpost of John O'Groats is usually taken to be the northernmost point on the Scottish mainland, though that is not strictly true, as a short drive to Dunnet Head will reveal. From the harbor, you can take a boat to see the dolphins and seals that live beneath the coastal cliffs—or head farther afield with a ferry to Orkney. The little town has charms of its own, including a row of colorful wooden houses (part of the Inn at John O' Groats) and a crafts center with high-quality shops selling knitwear, candles, and gifts.

GETTING HERE AND AROUND

Traveling north from Wick, take the A99. From the east, take the coast-hugging A836.

EXPLORING

Duncansby Head. Head to Duncansby Head for spectacular views of cliffs and sea stacks by the lighthouse, as well as seabirds like guillemots and (if you're lucky) puffins. It's on the coastal road east of town. ✉ *John O'Groats* 🎫 *Free.*

John O'Groats Ferries. Sailing from John O'Groats Harbor, this company offers 90-minute wildlife cruises past spectacular cliff scenery and birdlife into the Pentland Firth, to Duncansby Stacks, and to the island of Stroma. Trips cost £18 and are available daily at 2:30 between mid-June and August. The company also offers a "Maxi Day" tour of Orkney between May and September. It leaves at 8:45 am and costs £56. ✉ *County Rd., John O'Groats* ☎ *01955/611353* 🌐 *www.jogferry.co.uk* 🎫 *Tours from £18.*

WHERE TO STAY

$$ RENTAL Fodor's Choice ★ 🏨 **Natural Retreats John O'Groats.** A local landmark in their own right, the brightly colored lodges here are the region's best self-catering accommodation—not to mention the most photogenic. **Pros:** very comfy beds; good Wi-Fi (a rarity here); natural light all day long. **Cons:** can feel understaffed. [$] *Rooms from: £125* ✉ *John O'Groats* ✣ *Just west of ferry terminal* ☎ *01625/416430* 🌐 *www.naturalretreats.com* 🛏 *23 rooms* 🍴 *No meals.*

NIGHTLIFE AND PERFORMING ARTS

Lyth Arts Centre. Housed in a Victorian-era school building with a modern interior, the Lyth Arts Centre serves as a cultural hub for the region. From April to November, professional music and theater companies fill the schedule and locals fill the seats. There are also exhibitions of contemporary fine art. Lyth is 11 miles southwest of John O'Groats. ✉ *Lyth* ☎ *01955/641434* 🌐 *www.lytharts.org.uk* 🎫 *By event.*

TRAVEL SMART
GREAT BRITAIN

GETTING HERE AND AROUND

▌ AIR TRAVEL

The least expensive airfares to England are often priced for round-trip travel and must usually be purchased in advance. Airlines generally allow you to change your return date for a fee; most low-fare tickets, however, are nonrefundable.

Flying time to London is about 6¾ hours from New York, 7¾ hours from Chicago, 9¼ hours from Dallas, 10½ hours from Los Angeles, and 20¾ hours from Sydney. From London, flights take an hour to Paris or Amsterdam, 1¼ hours to Luxembourg, 2 hours to cities in Switzerland, and 2¼ hours to Rome.

Scotland's main hubs are Glasgow, Prestwick (near Glasgow), Edinburgh, Inverness, and Aberdeen. Glasgow and Prestwick are the gateways to the west and southwest, Edinburgh the east and southeast, Aberdeen and Inverness the north. All these cities have excellent bus and train transportation services and well-maintained roads that link them with each other and other cities within Scotland. Taxis are also an efficient and reliable option, but they are three to four times the cost of going by public transport.

Flying time to Glasgow and Aberdeen is 6½ hours from New York, 7½ hours from Chicago, 9½ hours from Dallas, 10 hours from Los Angeles, and 21½ hours from Sydney. Flying time to Edinburgh is 7 hours from New York, 8 hours from Chicago, 10 hours from Dallas, 10½ hours from Los Angeles, and 22 hours from Sydney. Not all airlines offer direct flights to Scotland; many go via London. For those flights allow an extra four to five hours of travel (two to three for the layover in London plus an additional hour or two for the duration of the flight).

Airline Security Issues Transportation Security Administration. ☎ *866/289–9673 in U.S.* ⊕ *www.tsa.gov.*

AIRPORTS

England: Most international flights to London arrive at either Heathrow Airport (LHR), 15 miles west of London, or at Gatwick Airport (LGW), 27 miles south of the capital. Most flights from the United States go to Heathrow, with Terminals 3, 4, and 5 handling transatlantic flights (British Airways uses Terminal 5). Gatwick is London's second gateway, serving many U.S. destinations. A third, much smaller airport, Stansted (STN), is 40 miles northeast of the city. It handles mainly European and domestic traffic.

London City Airport (LCY), a small airport inside the city near Canary Wharf, has a daily business-class-only flight to New York on British Airways, as well as flights to European destinations. Luton Airport (LLA), 32 miles north of the city, is also quite small, and serves British and European destinations. Luton is the hub for low-cost easyJet. Manchester (MAN) in northwest England handles some flights from the United States, as does Birmingham (BHX).

Heathrow and Gatwick are enormous and can seem like shopping malls (Heathrow even offers a personal shopping service). Both airports have bars and pubs and dining options. Several hotels are connected to each airport, and both Gatwick and Heathrow are near dozens of hotels that run free shuttles to the airports. Heathrow has a Hotel Hoppa service that runs shuttles between the airport and around 25 nearby hotels for £4.50 (online) or £5 (on bus) each way. A free, subsidized local bus service operates between the Central Bus Station serving Terminals 2 and 3 and nearby hotels. The bus also stops directly outside Terminals 4 and 5. You can find out more at the Central Bus Station or at the Transport for London (TfL) Information Centre in the Underground station serving Terminals 2 and 3. Yotel has budget pod hotels in both Heathrow and Gatwick with cabin-size rooms to be booked in advance in four-hour blocks or overnight. Prices begin at about £39, depending on how long you stay and the time of day.

In comparison, other British airports have much more limited shopping, hotel, and dining options; a delay of a few hours can seem like years.

Airport Information Birmingham Airport (*BHX*). ☎ *0871/222-0072* ⊕ *www.birminghamairport.co.uk*. **Gatwick Airport** (*LGW*). ☎ *0844/892-0322* ⊕ *www.gatwickairport.com*. **Heathrow Airport** (*LHR*). ☎ *0844/335-1801* ⊕ *www.heathrowairport.com*. **London City Airport** (*LCY*). ☎ *0207/646-0000* ⊕ *www.londoncityairport.com*. **Luton Airport** (*LLA*). ☎ *01582/405100* ⊕ *www.london-luton.co.uk*. **Manchester Airport** (*MAN*). ☎ *0800/042-0213* ⊕ *www.manchesterairport.co.uk*. **Stansted Airport** (*STN*). ☎ *0844/355-1803* ⊕ *www.stanstedairport.com*.

Scotland: The major international gateways to Scotland are Glasgow Airport (GLA), about 7 miles outside Glasgow, and Edinburgh Airport (EDI), 7 miles from the city. Both offer connections for dozens of European cities and regular flights to London's Gatwick (LGW) and Heathrow (LHR) airports. Aberdeen Airport (ABZ) has direct flights to most major European cities. Prestwick (PIK) has direct flights to some European cities at discounted rates. Inverness (INV) offers direct flights in and around the United Kingdom.

Airport tax is included in the price of your ticket. Generally the tax for economy tickets within the United Kingdom from European Union countries is £13. For all other flights it is £78. The standard rate for flights from the United Kingdom and European Union is £26; for all other destinations it's £146.

Airport Information Aberdeen Airport. ☎ *0844/481-6666* ⊕ *www.aberdeenairport.com*. **Edinburgh Airport.** ☎ *0844/448-8833* ⊕ *www.edinburghairport.com*. **Glasgow Airport.** ☎ *0844/481-5555* ⊕ *www.*

glasgowairport.com. **Glasgow Prestwick Airport.** ☎ *0871/223-0700* ⊕ *www.glasgowprestwick.com*. **Inverness Airport.** ☎ *01667/464000* ⊕ *www.hial.co.uk/inverness-airport*.

LONDON GROUND TRANSPORTATION
London has excellent bus and train connections between its airports and downtown. Train service can be the fastest, but the downside is that you must get yourself and your luggage to the terminal, often via a series of escalators and connecting trams. Airport buses (generally run by National Express) may be located nearer to the terminals and drop you closer to central hotels, but they're subject to London traffic, which can be horrendous. Taxis can be more convenient than buses, but prices can go through the roof. Minicabs are more economical, but go with recommended companies. Starting summer 2018, the new Crossrail (aka Elizabeth) Underground line will replace the Heathrow Connect train, operating between Heathrow Terminals 2, 3, 4, and 5 and Paddington Station. Starting December 2019, the line will also serve Terminal 5 and several central London destinations also served by the Central Line.

The Transport for London website has helpful information, as does Airport Travel Line. The official sites for Gatwick, Heathrow, and Stansted are useful resources for transportation options.

FROM HEATHROW TO CENTRAL LONDON		
Travel Mode	Time	Cost
Taxi	40–80 minutes	£50–£90
Heathrow Express Train	15 minutes	£25 one way
Underground	50 minutes	£6 one way
National Express Bus	45–80 minutes	£6–£10 one way

Heathrow by Bus: National Express buses take around one hour (longer at peak time) to reach the city center (Victoria

Coach Station) and cost £7.50 one way and £15 round-trip. Buses leave every 5 to 75 minutes from 4:20 am to 10 pm. The National Express Hotel Hoppa service runs from all terminals to around 25 hotels near the airport (£5). Alternatively, nearly every hotel in London is served by the Heathrow Airport Hotel Shuttle service. Fares to central London begin at £21.30. The N9 night bus runs every 15 minutes from 11:35 pm to 4:55 am to Kensington, Hyde Park Corner, Trafalgar Square, and Aldwych; it takes about 75 minutes and costs £1.50. ■TIP➔ Like all London buses, the N9 takes cash, Visitor Oyster cards, Oyster cards, or contactless "tap and go" debit cards only.

Heathrow by Train: The cheap, direct route into London is via the Piccadilly Line of the Underground (London's extensive subway system, or "Tube"). Trains normally run every 3 to 7 minutes from all terminals from around 5 am until just before midnight (a 24-hour service runs every 10 minutes to Terminals 2, 3, and 5 on Friday and Saturday). The 50-minute trip into central London costs £6 (cash), £5.10 (Oyster card peak times) or £3.10 (Oyster card off-peak). The Heathrow Express train is comfortable and very convenient, if costly, speeding into London's Paddington Station in 15 minutes. Standard one-way tickets cost £22 (off-peak), £25 (peak), or £32 for first class. All fares are substantially discounted if booked in advance online. If you arrive without tickets you should purchase them at a kiosk before you board, as they're more expensive on the train. There's daily service from 5:10 am (6:10 am on Sunday) to 11:25 pm, with departures every 15 minutes. The new Crossrail (Elizabeth Line) Tube service runs from Terminals 2, 3, 4, and 5 to Paddington Station, takes about 25 minutes, and costs the same as the other Tube lines.

Gatwick by Bus: Hourly bus service runs from Gatwick's north and south terminals to Victoria Coach Station with 11 stops along the way. The journey takes 70–120

minutes and costs from £8 one way. Make sure you get on a direct bus not requiring a change; otherwise the journey could take much longer. The easyBus service runs a service to West Brompton Underground Station in west London from as little as £2; the later the ticket is booked online, the higher the price (up to £10 on board).

Gatwick by Train: There are three train services to Gatwick. The fast, nonstop Gatwick Express leaves for Victoria Station every 15 minutes 5 am–10:30 pm. The 30-minute trip costs £17.80 one way online. Tickets cost more on board. The Southern rail company's nonexpress services are cheaper. Trains run regularly throughout the day until midnight to London Victoria, London Bridge, and Blackfriars stations; daytime departures are every 10–25 minutes (hourly between 1 am and 5 am), and the journey to London Victoria takes about 40 minutes. Tickets are from £10.70 one way and you can pay by Oyster card. You can also reach Gatwick by Southern trains coming from Brighton in the opposite direction. Thameslink offers a service similar to Southern but terminating at St. Pancras International instead of Victoria. The Thameslink and Southern services are on commuter trains, and during rush hour trains can be crowded, with little room for baggage and seats at a premium.

Stansted by Bus: National Express Airport bus A6 (24 hours a day) to Victoria Coach Station via Waterloo Station and Southwark costs from £12 one way, leaves every 15 minutes (hourly 2:40 am–5 am, then half hourly until 7:50 am), and takes 90–120 minutes. The A7 National Express bus serving west London goes to Portman Square, with stops including Golders Green, Finchley Road, St. John's Wood, Baker Street, Paddington Station, and Marble Arch. It leaves every 30–40 minutes and journey time is 90–180 minutes, with fares from £12. The east London A8 service leaves every 30–40 minutes before 11:50 pm and after 6 am (hourly otherwise), terminating at Bethnal

Green and stopping at Bow Church Street, Mile End, Whitechapel, Liverpool Street Station, and Shoreditch High Street. Fares are from £10 and journey time is 67–77 minutes.

Stansted by Train: The Stansted Express to Liverpool Street Station (with a stop at Tottenham Hale) runs every 15 minutes 5:30 am–12:30 am daily. The 45-minute trip costs £17 each way if booked online. Tickets cost more on board.

Luton by Bus and Train: A free airport shuttle runs from Luton Airport to the nearby Luton Airport Parkway Station every 10 minutes, where you can take a train or bus into London. From there, the Thameslink train service runs to St. Pancras, Farringdon, Blackfriars, and London Bridge. The journey takes 25–50 minutes. Trains leave every 10 minutes or so from 5 am until midnight, hourly at other times. One-way tickets begin at £14.70. The Green Line 757 bus service from Luton to Victoria Station runs every 30 minutes between 7 am and 12:35 am (hourly other times), takes 60 to 100 minutes, and costs from £11, while an easyBus shuttle has tickets starting from £2. National Express runs coaches from Victoria Coach Station to Luton from £5 one way.

Heathrow, Gatwick, Stansted, and Luton by Taxi: This is an expensive and time-consuming option. If your destination is within the city's congestion zone, £11.50 will be added to the bill during charging hours. If you get stuck in traffic, a taxi from the stand will be even more expensive; a cab booked ahead is a set price. A taxi trip from Heathrow to Victoria, for example, can take more than an hour and cost between £48 and £90. Private-hire cars may be the same price or even less—at this writing, the fee to Victoria Station is about £50 from Heathrow and £70 from Gatwick and Stansted, not including the congestion charge. Another option, if you have friends in the London area, is to have them book a reputable minicab firm to pick you up. The cost of a minicab from Heathrow to central London is approximately £47. The Uber fare from Heathrow is currently £28–£37, from Gatwick £60–£75, and from Stansted £55–£71, but as of this writing Uber's continued ability to operate in the London area is the subject of legal proceedings. Your hotel may also be able to recommend a car service.

SCOTLAND GROUND TRANSPORTATION
The best way to get to and from the airport based on speed and convenience is by taxi. All airport taxi stands are just outside the airport's front doors and are well marked with clear signs. Most taxis have a set price when going to and from the airport to the city center but will turn on the meter at your request. Ask the driver to turn on the meter to confirm the flat-rate price.

If you're traveling with a large party, you can request a people carrier to transport everyone, luggage included. Luggage is included in the taxi fare; you should not be charged extra for it.

If you're traveling alone, a more economical transfer option is public transportation. Buses travel between city centers and Glasgow, Edinburgh, Aberdeen, and Inverness airports. Trams travel between Edinburgh Airport and the city center; Edinburgh Gateway station links the airport to the tram and rail network; trains go direct to Glasgow Prestwick Airport. All are fast, inexpensive, and reliable.

▮ BOAT TRAVEL

Ferries and other boats travel regular routes to France, Spain, Ireland, and Scandinavia. P&O runs ferries to Belgium, France, Ireland, and the Netherlands. DFDS Seaways serves France, Denmark, Belgium, and the Netherlands, and Stena Line serves Ireland, Northern Ireland, France, and the Netherlands.

Low-cost airlines and Eurotunnel (which lets you take a car to France on the train) have cut into ferry travel, but companies have responded by cutting fares and upgrading equipment.

Prices vary; booking early ensures cheaper fares, but also ask about special deals. Seaview is a comprehensive online ferry- and cruise-booking portal for Britain and continental Europe. Ferry Cheap is a discount website.

Information DFDS Seaways. ☎ *0871/522–9955, 330/333–0245 in U.S.* ⊕ *www.dfdsseaways.co.uk.* **Ferry Cheap.** ☎ *0844/493–1474* ⊕ *www.ferrycheap.com.* **P&O.** ☎ *0130/444–8888* ⊕ *www.poferries.com.* **Seaview.** ☎ *01442/843050* ⊕ *www.seaviewferries.co.uk.* **Stena Line.** ☎ *0844/770–7070* ⊕ *www.stenaline.co.uk.*

WITHIN SCOTLAND

Because Scotland has so many islands, plus the great Firth of Clyde waterway, ferry services are of paramount importance. Most ferries transport vehicles as well as foot passengers, although a few smaller ones are for passengers only.

It's a good idea to make a reservation ahead of time, although reservations are not absolutely necessary. Most travelers show up on the day of departure and buy their tickets from the stations at the ports. Keep in mind that these are working ferries, not tourist boats. Although journeys are scenic, most people use these ferries as their daily means of public transportation to and from their hometowns.

The main operator is Caledonian MacBrayne, known generally as CalMac. Services extend from the Firth of Clyde in the south, where there's an extensive network, right up to the northwest of Scotland and all the Hebrides. CalMac offers 25 island-hopping itineraries, called Hopscotch, valid for 31 days, which can be combined for tailored exploration. Fares can range from £2 to £6 for a short trip to over £50 for a longer trip with several legs.

The Dunoon–Gourock route on the Clyde is served by Western Ferries (for cars) and Argyll Ferries (for passengers and cycles only).

Northlink Ferries operates a car ferry for Orkney between Scrabster, near Thurso,

and Stromness, on the main island of Orkney; and between Aberdeen and Kirkwall, which is also on the mainland of Orkney. Northlink also runs an efficient ferry to Lerwick, Shetland, and Kirkwall, Orkney. The journey to Lerwick is overnight, but comfortable cabins are available. These ferries can be busy in summer, so book well in advance.

Cash and major credit cards are accepted for payment. *See the Orientation and Planning sections of each chapter for more details about ferry services.*

Information Argyll Ferries. ☎ *0800/066–5000* ⊕ *www.argyllferries.co.uk.* **Caledonian MacBrayne.** ☎ *0800/066–5000* ⊕ *www.calmac.co.uk.* **Northlink Ferries.** ☎ *0845/600–0449* ⊕ *www.northlinkferries.co.uk.* **Western Ferries.** ☎ *01369/704452* ⊕ *www.western-ferries.co.uk.*

TRANSATLANTIC AND OTHER CRUISES

Most cruise ships leave from southern England—particularly Southampton and Portsmouth. Some ships leave from Liverpool and Dover, or from Harwich, near Cambridge.

▌BUS TRAVEL

Britain has a comprehensive bus (short-haul, multistop public transportation) and coach (more direct, plusher long-distance buses) network that offers an inexpensive way of seeing England. National Express is the major coach operator, and Victoria Coach Station, near Victoria Station in central London, is its hub in the region. The company serves more than 1,000 destinations within Britain (and, via Eurolines, 500 more in continental Europe). There are 2,000 ticket agents nationwide, including offices at London's Heathrow and Gatwick airport coach stations.

Green Line is the second-largest national service, serving airports and major tourist towns. A budget option for long-distance travel, Megabus has double-decker buses that serve cities across Britain, with seats that turn into bunk beds on routes to Scotland. In London, Megabus departs from Victoria Coach Station as well as other stops, while Green Line buses also stop at Baker Street and Hyde Park Corner.

Bus tickets can be much less than the price of a train ticket (even lower if you take advantage of special deals). For example, an Oxford Tube bus ticket from London to Oxford is £15, whereas a train ticket may be £26.50. Buses are also just as comfortable as trains. However, buses often take twice as long to reach their destinations. The Oxford Tube has onboard Wi-Fi. All bus services forbid smoking.

Double-decker buses, run by private companies, offer local bus service in cities and regions. Check with the local bus station or tourist information center for routes and schedules. Most companies offer daylong or weeklong unlimited-travel tickets, and those in popular tourist areas operate special scenic tours in summer. The top deck of a double-decker bus is a great place from which to view the countryside.

Long-distance buses usually provide the cheapest way to travel between England and Scotland; fares may be as little as a third of the rail fares for comparable trips and are cheaper if you buy in advance. However, the trip is not as comfortable as by train (no dining cart, smaller bathrooms, less spacious seats), and travel takes longer. Glasgow to London by nonstop bus takes 8 hours, 45 minutes; by train it takes about 5 hours, 30 minutes. Scotland's bus (short-haul) and coach (long-distance) network is extensive. Bus service is comprehensive in cities, less so in country districts. Express service links main cities and towns, connecting, for example, Glasgow and Edinburgh to Inverness, Aberdeen, Perth, Skye, Ayr, Dumfries, and Carlisle; or Inverness with Aberdeen, Wick, Thurso, and Fort William. Express service is very fast, and fares are reasonable. Scottish Citylink, National Express, and Megabus are among the main operators; there are about 20 in all. The Royal Mail Post Bus provides a valuable service—generally twice-daily—in the Highlands, Argyll, and Bute and the Western Isles. All buses are nonsmoking.

DISCOUNTS AND DEALS

National Express's Young Persons' CoachCard for students age 16 to 26 costs £10 annually and gets 10% to 30% discounts off many fares. Most companies also offer a discount for children under 15. A Senior CoachCard for the over-60s cuts many fares by a third. Apex tickets (advance-purchase tickets) save money on standard fares, and traveling midweek is cheaper than over weekends and holidays.

On Scottish Citylink, the Explorer Passes offer complete freedom of travel on all services throughout Scotland. Three permutations give 3 days of travel out of a 5-day period, 5 days of travel out of 10, and 8 days of travel out of 16. They're available from Scottish Citylink offices, and cost £49, £74, and £99 respectively.

FARES AND SCHEDULES

You can find schedules online, pick them up from tourist information offices, or get them by phone from the bus companies. Fares vary based on how close to the time of travel you book—Megabus tickets, for example, are cheaper if ordered in advance online. Contact Traveline Scotland for information on all public transportation and timetables.

RESERVATIONS

Book in advance, as buses on busy routes fill up quickly. With most bus companies (National Express, Megabus, Green Line), advance payment means you receive an email receipt and your name is placed on a list given to the bus driver.

Bus Contacts Green Line. ☎ *0344/801–7261* ⊕ *www.greenline.co.uk.* **Megabus.** ☎ *0141/352-4444* ⊕ *uk.megabus.com.* **National Express.** ☎ *0871/781-8181* ⊕ *www.nationalexpress.com.* **Oxford Tube.** ☎ *01865/772250* ⊕ *www.oxfordtube.com.* **Royal Mail Post Bus.** ☎ *03457/740740* ⊕ *www.royalmail.com.* **Scottish Citylink.** ☎ *0871/266-3333* ⊕ *www.citylink.co.uk.*

Traveline. ☎ 0871/200–2233 ⊕ www.traveline.info. **Traveline Scotland.** ☎ 0871/200–2233 ⊕ www.travelinescotland.com. **Victoria Coach Station.** ✉ 164 Buckingham Palace Rd., London ☎ No phone ⊕ www.tfl.gov.uk.

▌CAR TRAVEL

Britain can be a challenging place for most foreigners to drive, considering that people drive on the left side of the often disconcertingly narrow roads, many rental cars have standard transmissions, and the gearshift is on the "wrong" side entirely.

There's no reason to rent a car for a stay in London because the city and its suburbs are well served by public transportation and traffic is desperately congested. Here and in other major cities it's best to rely on public transportation.

Outside the cities, a car can be very handy. Many sights aren't easily reached without one—castles, for example, are rarely connected to any public transportation system. Small villages might have only one or two buses a day pass through them. If you're comfortable on the road, the experience of driving between the tall hedgerows or on country roads is a truly English experience.

In Great Britain, your own driver's license is acceptable. However, you may choose to get an International Driving Permit (IDP), which can be used only in conjunction with a valid driver's license and which translates your license into 10 languages. Check the Automobile Association of America website for more info as well as for IDPs ($20) themselves. These permits are universally recognized, and having one in your wallet may save you a problem with the local authorities.

GASOLINE

Gasoline is called petrol in Britain and is sold by the liter. The price you see posted at a petrol station is the price of a liter, and there are about 4 liters in a U.S. gallon. Petrol is expensive; it was around £1.24 per liter, or $1.96 per liter, at the time of this writing. Supermarket pumps just outside city centers frequently offer the best prices. Premium and superpremium are the two varieties, and most cars run on premium. Diesel is widely used; be sure not to use it by mistake. Along busy motorways, most large stations are open 24 hours a day, 7 days a week. In rural areas, hours can vary. Most service stations accept major credit cards, and most are self-service.

PARKING

Parking regulations are strictly enforced, and fines are high. If there are no signs on a street, you can park there. Many streets have centralized "pay and display" machines, in which you deposit the required money and get a ticket allowing you to park for a set period of time. In London's City of Westminster (⊕ www.westminster.gov.uk) and some other boroughs, parking machines have been replaced by a pay-by-phone plan, enabling you to pay by cell phone if you've preregistered. In town centers your best bet is to park in a public lot marked with a square blue sign with a white "P" in the center.

If you park on the street, follow these basic rules: Do not park within 15 yards of an intersection. Never park in bus lanes or on double yellow lines, and do not park on single yellow lines when parking meters are in effect. On busy roads with red lines painted on the street you cannot park or stop to let a passenger out of the car.

RENTALS

Rental rates are generally reasonable, and insurance costs are lower than in the United States. If you want the car only for country trips, consider renting outside London. Rates are cheaper, and you avoid traversing London's notoriously complex road system. Rental rates vary widely, beginning at £54 a day and £132 a week for a midsize car, usually with manual transmission. As in the United States, prices rise in summer and during holidays. Car seats for children cost £8 per day, and

GPS is usually around £10 per day. You can also arrange for cell phone hire or a portable Wi-Fi hot spot with your rental.

Major car-rental agencies are much the same in Britain as in the United States: Alamo, Avis, Budget, Enterprise, Hertz, Thrifty, and National all have offices in Britain. Europcar is another large company. Companies may not rent cars to people who are under 23. Some have an upper age limit of 75.

ROAD CONDITIONS

There's a good network of major highways (motorways) and divided highways (dual carriageways) throughout most of Great Britain. Motorways (with the prefix "M"), shown in blue on most maps, are mainly two or three lanes in each direction. Other major roads (with the prefix "A") are shown on maps in green and red. Sections of fast dual carriageways (with black-edged, thick outlines on maps) have both traffic lights and traffic circles. Turn-offs are often marked by highway numbers, rather than place names. An exit is called a junction in Britain.

The vast network of lesser roads, for the most part old coach and turnpike roads, might make your trip twice as long but show you twice as much. Minor roads are drawn in yellow or white on maps, the former prefixed by "B," the latter unlettered and unnumbered. Should you take one of these, be prepared to back up into a passing place if you meet an oncoming car.

Dual carriageways, usually shown on a map as a thick red line (often with a black line in the center) and the prefix "a" followed by a number perhaps with a bracketed "t" (for example, "a304[t]"), are similar to motorways, except that right turns are sometimes permitted, and you'll find both traffic lights and traffic circles along the way. The vast network of other main roads, which typical maps show as either single red *A* roads, or narrower brown *B* roads, also numbered, are for the most part the old roads originally intended for horses and carriages. Travel along these roads is slower than on motorways, and passing is more difficult. On the other hand, you'll see much more of Scotland. The A9, Perth to Inverness, is a particularly dangerous road with the worst road accident record in Scotland because of the stopping and starting on the dual carriageway.

ROADSIDE EMERGENCIES

On major highways emergency roadside telephone booths are positioned at regular intervals. Contact your car-rental company or call the police. You can also call the British Automobile Association (AA) toll-free. You can join and receive assistance from the AA or the RAC on the spot, but the charge is higher than a simple membership fee. If you're a member of the American Automobile Association, check before you travel; reciprocal agreements may give you free roadside aid.

Emergency Services Ambulance, fire, police. ☎ *999 emergency, 101 police nonemergency.* **Automobile Association.** ☎ *0800/887766 emergency service, 0344/209–0754 general calls ⊕ www.theaa. com.* **RAC.** ☎ *0333/200–0999 emergency service, 01922/437–0000 general inquiries ⊕ www.rac.co.uk.*

RULES OF THE ROAD

Driving on the left side of the road might be easier than you expected, as the steering and mirrors on British cars are designed for driving on the left. If you have a standard transmission car, you have to shift gears with your left hand. Give yourself time to adjust before leaving the rental-car lot. Seat belts are obligatory in the front and back seats. It's illegal to talk on a handheld cell phone while driving.

Pick up a copy of the official Highway Code (£2.50) at a service station, newsstand, or bookstore, or check it out online by going to ⊕ *www.gov.uk* and putting "Highway Code" in the search bar. Besides driving rules and illustrations of signs and road markings, this booklet contains information for motorcyclists, cyclists, and pedestrians.

Speed limits are complicated, and there are speed cameras everywhere. The speed limit (shown on circular red signs) is generally 20 or 30 mph in towns and cities, 40 to 60 mph on two-lane highways, and 70 mph on motorways. At traffic circles (called roundabouts), you turn clockwise. As cars enter the circle, they must yield to those already in the circle or entering from the right. If you're taking an exit all the way around the circle, signal right as you enter, stay to the center, and then signal and move left just before your own exit.

Pedestrians have the right-of-way on "zebra" crossings (black-and-white-stripe crosswalks between two orange-flashing globe lights). At other crossings, pedestrians must yield to traffic, but they do have the right-of-way over traffic turning left.

Drunk-driving laws are strictly enforced. The legal limit is 80 milligrams of alcohol per 100 milliliters of blood, which means two units of alcohol—approximately one glass of wine, 1–1½ pints of beer, or two shots of whisky. However, these figures will vary according to the alcohol's strength, your size and weight (so women tend to reach the limit on less), and how much you've eaten that day.

▌ TRAIN TRAVEL

Operated by several different private companies, the train system in Britain is extensive and useful, though less than perfect. Some regional trains are old, and virtually all lines suffer from occasional delays, schedule changes, and periodic repair work that runs over schedule. The pricing structure is complex and prices tend to be high compared to the rest of Europe. All major cities and many small towns are served by trains, and despite the difficulties, rail travel is the most pleasant way to cover long distances.

Train service within Scotland is generally run by ScotRail, one of the most efficient of Britain's service providers. Trains are generally modern, clean, and comfortable. Long-distance services carry buffet and refreshment cars. Scotland's rail network extends all the way to Thurso and Wick, the most northerly stations in the British Isles. Lowland services, most of which originate in Glasgow or Edinburgh, are generally fast and reliable. A shuttle makes the 50-minute trip between Glasgow and Edinburgh every 15 minutes. It's a scenic trip with plenty of rolling fields, livestock, and traditional houses along the way. Rail service throughout the country, especially the Highlands, is limited on Sunday.

CLASSES

Most rail lines have first-class and second-class cars. In virtually all cases, second class is perfectly comfortable. First class is quieter and less crowded, has better furnishings, and marginally larger seats. It also usually costs two to three times the price of second class, but not always, so it's worth comparing prices. Most train operators offer a Weekend First ticket. Available on weekends and holidays, these tickets allow you to upgrade for as little as £5. ▌TIP→ Some train lines only let you buy Weekend First tickets on board.

FARES AND SCHEDULES

National Rail Enquiries is a helpful, comprehensive, and free service that covers all the country's rail lines. National Rail will help you choose the best train, and then connect you with the right ticket office. You can also book tickets online. A similar service is offered by the Trainline, which provides online train information and ticket booking for all rail services. The Man in Seat 61, a website, offers objective information along with booking facilities.

Ticket prices are more expensive during rush hour, so plan accordingly. For long-distance travel, tickets cost more the longer you wait. Book in advance and tickets can be half of what you'd pay on the day of departure. A journey from London to Cardiff costs £12 if you buy a ticket two weeks in advance, but the fare rises to £45 if you wait until the day of your trip.

■ TIP→ Ask the local tourist board about hotel and local transportation packages that include tickets to major events.

Information **The Man in Seat 61.** ⊕ *www. seat61.com.* **National Rail Enquiries.** ☎ *0345/748–4950* ⊕ *www.nationalrail.co.uk.* **ScotRail.** ☎ *0344/811–0141* ⊕ *www.scotrail. co.uk.* **Trainline.** ☎ *033/202–2222* ⊕ *www. thetrainline.com.*

PASSES

National Rail Enquiries has information about rail passes such as All Line Rovers, which offers unlimited travel on National Rail services for a week, with some restrictions, for £772. Children, seniors, and disabled Rovers are one-half to one-third less.

If you plan to travel a lot by train throughout Great Britain, consider purchasing a BritRail Pass, which gives unlimited travel over the entire British rail network and can save you money. If you don't plan to cover many miles, you may come out ahead by buying individual tickets. Buy your BritRail Pass before you leave home, as they are not sold in Britain. The passes are available from most U.S. travel agents or from ACP Rail International, Flight Centre, or VisitBritain. Note that Eurail Passes aren't honored in Britain.

BritRail passes come in two basic varieties: the Consecutive Pass and the England FlexiPass. You can get a Consecutive Pass good for 3, 4, 8, 15, or 22 consecutive days or one month starting at $164 standard and $247 first class for 3 days. The FlexiPass for 3, 4, or 8 days of travel in one month or 15 days in two months costs from $207 standard and $306 first class for 3 days. If you're based in London, the BritRail London Plus pass offers access to southern England destinations such as Oxford, Cambridge, Bath, or Stratford-upon-Avon from $159 for standard class, $223 for first class. Tickets can be used for 3, 4, or 8 days of travel within one month.

Don't assume that a rail pass guarantees you a seat on a particular train. You need to book seats even if you're using a rail pass, especially on trains that may be crowded, particularly in summer on popular routes.

Discount Passes **ACP Rail International.** ☎ *866/938–7245 in U.S., 0207/953–4062 in U.K.* ⊕ *www.acprail.com.* **BritRail.** ☎ *866/938–7245 in U.S.* ⊕ *www.britrail.net.* **Flight Centre.** ☎ *0203/056–7993 in U.K., 877/992–4732 in U.S.* ⊕ *www.flightcentre.co.uk.* **VisitBritain.** ☎ *01271/336110 or free callback after submitting website form* ⊕ *www.visitbritainshop.com.*

RESERVATIONS

Reserving your ticket in advance is recommended. Even a reservation 24 hours in advance can provide a substantial discount. Look into cheap day returns if you plan to travel a round-trip in one day.

CHANNEL TUNNEL

Short of flying, taking the Eurostar through the Channel Tunnel is the fastest way to cross the English Channel (and perhaps faster after factoring in airport travel time and security). Travel time is 2½ hours from London's St. Pancras Station to Paris's Gare du Nord. Trains also travel to Brussels (2 hours), Lille (1½ hours), and Disneyland Paris (2¾ hours), and to Lyon (5¾ hours), Avignon (6½ hours), and Marseille (7¼ hours), Friday, Saturday, and Monday from May through mid-September (plus Sunday in July and August). On Friday (night train) and Saturday (day train) from late December through March, ski trains go to Moûtiers (9 hours) and four other nearby Alpine ski resorts.

Early risers can easily take a day trip to Paris if time is short. Book ahead, as Eurostar ticket prices increase as the departure date approaches. If purchased in advance, round-trip tickets to Paris start at £58 Monday–Thursday, £78 Friday–Sunday. The SnapEurostar site has last-minute tickets from £25 one way, but although you can specify the general time of day, the exact time of departure is potluck.

Channel Tunnel Car Transport Eurotunnel.
☎ *0844/335–3535 in U.K.* ⊕ *www.eurotunnel.
com.*

**Channel Tunnel Passenger Service
Eurostar.** ☎ *0343/218–6186 in U.K.,
1233/617575 from U.S.* ⊕ *www.eurostar.com;
snap.eurostar.com.* **Rail Europe.** ☎ *800/622–
8600 in U.S., 0844/848–5848 in U.K.* ⊕ *www.
raileurope.com.*

FROM ENGLAND TO SCOTLAND

There are two main rail routes to Scotland from the south of England. The first,
the west-coast main line, runs from London Euston to Glasgow Central; it takes
5½ hours to make the 400-mile trip to
central Scotland, and service is frequent
and reliable. Useful for daytime travel to
the Scottish Highlands is the direct train
to Stirling and Aviemore, terminating at
Inverness. For a restful route to the Scottish Highlands, take the overnight sleeper
service, with sleeping carriages. It runs
from London Euston, departing in late
evening, to Perth, Stirling, Aviemore, and
Inverness, where it arrives the following
morning. The new *Caledonian Sleeper*
operator as of 2015, Serco Abellio, has
introduced some improvements to the
long-established service. New trains, carriages, en suite berths, and sleeping pods
are due in 2018.

The east-coast main line from London
King's Cross to Edinburgh provides
the quickest trip to the Scottish capital.
Between 8 am and 6 pm there are usually trains every half hour to Edinburgh;
three of them travel directly to Aberdeen.
Virgin East Coast's limited-stop expresses
like the *Flying Scotsman* make the 393-
mile London-to-Edinburgh journey in
about 4½ hours. Connecting services to
most parts of Scotland—particularly the
Western Highlands—are often better from
Edinburgh than from Glasgow.

Trains from elsewhere in England are
good: regular service connects Birmingham, Manchester, Liverpool, and Bristol with Glasgow and Edinburgh. From
Harwich (the port of call for ships from

Holland, Germany, and Denmark), you
can travel to Glasgow via Manchester.
But it's faster to change at Peterborough
for the east-coast main line to Edinburgh.

SCENIC ROUTES

Although many routes in Scotland run
through extremely attractive countryside,
several stand out: from Glasgow to Oban
via Loch Lomond; to Fort William and
Mallaig via Rannoch (ferry connection to
Skye); from Edinburgh to Inverness via the
Forth Bridge and Perth; from Inverness to
Kyle of Lochalsh and to Wick; and from
Inverness to Aberdeen.

A private train, the *Royal Scotsman*, does
all-inclusive scenic tours, with banquets
en route. This is a luxury experience:
you choose itineraries from two nights
(£2,420) to seven nights (£9,200) per
person.

Special Trains Caledonian Sleeper.
☎ *0330/060–0500, 141/555–0888* ⊕ *www.
sleeper.scot.* **The Royal Scotsman.**
☎ *0845/077–2222 in U.K., 800/524–2420 in
U.S.* ⊕ *www.royalscotsman.com.* **Virgin Trains.**
☎ *03457/225333* ⊕ *www.virgintrainseastcoast.
com.*

ESSENTIALS

■ ACCOMMODATIONS

Hotels, bed-and-breakfasts, rural inns, or luxurious country houses—there's a style and price to suit most travelers. Wherever you stay, make reservations well in advance.

Our local writers vet every hotel to recommend the best overnights in each price category, from budget to expensive. Unless otherwise specified, you can expect private bath, phone, and TV in your room. *For expanded reviews, visit Fodors.com.*

APARTMENT AND HOUSE RENTALS

If you deal directly with local agents, get a recommendation from someone who's used the company. Unlike with hotels, there's no accredited system for apartment-rental standards.

In the country your chances of finding a small house to rent are good; in the city you're more likely to find a flat (apartment) to let (rent). Either way, your best bet for finding these rentals is online. Individuals and large consortiums can own these properties, so it just depends on what you're looking for. Citybase Apartments is a handy resource for finding an apartment, from single studios to large apartments suitable for families and groups. Dreamhouse Apartments has swanky, serviced flats in Edinburgh, Glasgow, and Aberdeen. The National Trust for Scotland has many unique properties, from island cottages to castles, for rent. Knight Residence has 19 well-appointed, modern apartments in the heart of the Old Town, Edinburgh; it has 16 similarly smart apartments in Inverness, many with spectacular terrace views.

BED-AND-BREAKFASTS

B&Bs can be a good budget option, and will also help you meet the locals. Cottages, unlike B&Bs, usually do not provide breakfast.

Reservation Services Bed & Breakfast. com. ☏ 512/322–2710 ⊕ www.bedandbreakfast.com. **The Bed and Breakfast Club.** ☏ 07879/661346 ⊕ www.bedandbreakfasts. co.uk/breakfast-club. **Wolsey Lodges.** ☏ 0208/696–0399 ⊕ www.wolseylodges.com.

COTTAGES

Contacts Classic Cottages. ☏ 01326/555555 ⊕ www.classic.co.uk. **National Trust Cottages.** ☏ 344/335–1287, 0344/800–2070 booking ⊕ www.nationaltrust.org.uk. **Rural Retreats.** ☏ 01386/701177 ⊕ www.ruralretreats.co.uk. **VisitBritain.** ☏ 01271/336110 ⊕ www.visitbritain.com.

FARMHOUSES

A popular option for families with children is a farmhouse holiday, combining the freedom of B&B accommodations with the hospitality of Scottish family life. You'll need a car if you're staying deep in the country, though. Information is available from VisitBritain or VisitScotland, and from the Farm Stay UK.

Contacts Farm & Cottage Holidays UK. ☏ 01237/459888 ⊕ www.holidaycottages. co.uk. **Farm Stay UK.** ☏ 02476/696909 ⊕ www.farmstayuk.co.uk.

HISTORIC BUILDINGS

Contacts Celtic Castles. ☏ 01422/323200 ⊕ www.celticcastles.com. **English Heritage.** ☏ 0370/333–1181 ⊕ www.english-heritage. org.uk. **The Folly Fellowship.** ⊕ follies. org.uk. **Landmark Trust.** ☏ 01628/825925 ⊕ www.landmarktrust.org.uk. **National Trust Cottages.** ☏ 0344/800–2070 ⊕ www. nationaltrustorg.uk. **Portmeirion Cottages.** ☏ 01766/772300 ⊕ www.portmeirion-village. com. **Rural Retreats.** ☏ 01386/701177 ⊕ www.ruralretreats.co.uk. **Unique Home Stays.** ☏ 01637/881183 ⊕ www.uniquehome-stays.com.

HOME EXCHANGES

With a direct home exchange you stay in someone else's home while they stay in yours. Some outfits handle vacation homes, so you're staying in someone's vacant weekend place. Home Exchange. com offers a one-year membership for $100; HomeLink International costs $95 for an annual online membership, which includes a directory listing; and Intervac U.S. offers international membership for $100.

Exchange Clubs Home Exchange.com. ☎ 888/609–4660 in U.S., 330/808–5185 in U.K. ⊕ www.homeexchange.com. **HomeLink International.** ☎ 800/638–3841 in U.S., 01962/886882 in U.K. ⊕ www.homelink-usa. org. **Intervac.** ☎ 866/884–7567 in U.S. ⊕ www.intervac-homeexchange.com.

HOTELS

Most hotels have rooms with "ensuite" bathrooms—as private bathrooms are called—although some B&Bs may have only washbasins; in this case, showers and toilets are usually down the hall. Especially in London, rooms and bathrooms may be smaller than those you find in the United States.

Besides familiar international chains, Britain has some local chains that are worth a look; they provide rooms from the less expensive (the basic but bargain Travelodge and the slightly more upscale Premier Inn are the most widespread, with the latter and Jurys Inns offering good value in city centers) to the trendy (ABode, Hotel du Vin, Malmaison).

Local Chains ABode. ⊕ www.abodehotels. co.uk. **Apex Hotels.** ⊕ www.apexhotels.co.uk. **Hotel du Vin.** ☎ 0330/016–0390 ⊕ www. hotelduvin.com. **Jurys Inn.** ☎ 0870/410–0800 ⊕ www.jurysinn.com. **Malmaison.** ☎ 0330/026–0380 ⊕ www.malmaison.com. **Premier Inn.** ☎ 0871/527–9222 ⊕ www. premierinn.com. **Travelodge.** ☎ 0871/984–8484 ⊕ www.travelodge.co.uk.

HOTEL GRADING SYSTEM

Hotels, guesthouses, inns, and B&Bs in the United Kingdom are all graded from one to five stars by the tourism board, VisitBritain. Basically, the more stars a property has, the more amenities it has, and the facilities will be of a higher standard.

It's a fairly good reflection of lodging from small B&Bs up to palatial hotels. The most luxurious hotels will have five stars; a simple, clean, acceptable hostelry will have one star.

DISCOUNTS AND DEALS

Hotel rates in major cities tend to be cheapest on weekends, whereas rural hotels are cheapest on weeknights. The lowest occupancy is between November and April, so hotels lower their prices substantially during these months.

Lastminute.com offers deals on hotel rooms all over the United Kingdom. VisitLondon.com, London's official website, has some good deals.

Local Resources Lastminute.com. ☎ 0800/083–4000 ⊕ www.lastminute.com.

∎ COMMUNICATIONS

INTERNET

Wi-Fi is usually available in hotels—either included or with a surcharge—and broadband coverage is widespread in cities. You can also buy a dongle or MiFi device from a cell-phone network's retail outlet to create a personal Wi-Fi hot spot. Many London Underground stations now have Wi-Fi (for a fee). Outside big cities, wireless access is relatively rare in cafés and coffee shops, but its popularity there is growing.

Contacts Wi-Fi Freespot. ⊕ www. wififreespot.com.

PHONES

All landline calls (including local calls) made within the United Kingdom are charged according to the time of day. The standard landline rate usually applies weekdays 7 am to 7 pm; a cheaper rate is in effect weekdays 7 pm to 7 am and all day on weekends, when it's even cheaper. Mobile rates tend to be double the landline rate.

A word of warning: 0870 numbers are *not* toll-free numbers in Britain; in fact, numbers beginning with this or the 0871–0873 or 0843–0845 prefixes cost extra to call. The amount varies and is usually relatively small—except for numbers with the premium-rate 090 prefix, which cost an eye-watering £3.60 per minute when dialed from within the country—but can be excessive when dialed from outside Britain.

CALLING BRITAIN

The country code for Great Britain (and thus England) is 44. When dialing an English number from abroad, drop the initial 0 from before the local phone prefix code. For example, let's say you're calling Buckingham Palace—0303/123–7300—from the United States. First, dial 011 (the international access code), then 44 (Great Britain's country code), then 303 (without its initial 0), then the remainder of the number.

CALLING WITHIN BRITAIN

For all calls within Britain, dial the area code (which usually begins with 01, except in London), followed by the telephone number.

There are two types of pay phones: those that make calls to landlines or mobiles and those that also let you send texts or email. Most coin-operated phones take 10p, 20p, 50p, £1 (in newer phones, £2) coins. There are very few of either type left except at air and rail terminals. BT will phase out its public pay phones by 2022, but is now installing smart kiosks, which offer public Wi-Fi, free U.K. phone calls, USB device charging, and a range of other digital services. SIM cards for your own cell phone and inexpensive pay-as-you-go cell phones are widely available from mobile network retailers such as 3, O2, T-Mobile, Vodaphone, and Virgin, as well as the Carphone Warehouse chain.

For pay and other phones, if you hear a repeated single tone after dialing, the line is busy; a continuous tone means the number didn't work.

There are several different directory-assistance providers, all beginning with the prefix 118, such as 118–855 or 118–429;

you'll need to know the town and the street (or at least the neighborhood) of the person you're trying to reach. Charges, which have gone up by more than 25% in the last two years, range from $1.58 (118–811) to $14.24 (118-118) per minute from a landline. Cell-phone networks may charge even more. For the operator, dial 100. For genuine emergencies, dial 999. For nonurgent police matters, dial 101.

CALLING OUTSIDE BRITAIN

For direct overseas dialing from Britain, dial 00, then the country code, area code, and number. For the international operator, credit card, or collect calls, dial 155; for international directory assistance, dial 118505 ($2.14 per minute). The country code for the United States is 1.

CALLING CARDS

You can buy international cards similar to U.S. calling cards for making calls to specific countries from post offices, some supermarkets, cell-phone network retail outlets, or on the Internet. Rates vary, but the USA-Canada Express card charges as little as one cent per minute to call the United States. Where credit cards are taken, slide the card in as indicated.

MOBILE PHONES

Any cell phone can be used in Europe if it's tri-band, quad-band, or GSM. Travelers should ask their cell-phone company if their phone fits in this category and make sure it's activated for international calling before leaving their home country. Roaming fees can be steep, however: $1 a minute is considered reasonable. And overseas you normally pay the toll charges for incoming calls. It's almost always cheaper to send a text message than to make a call, since text messages have a low set fee (often less than 50¢).

If you just want to make local calls, consider buying a new SIM card (your provider may have to unlock your phone for you) and a prepaid local service plan. You'll then have a local number and can make local calls at local rates. You can also rent a cell phone from most major car-rental agencies in England. Some upscale hotels now provide loaner cell phones to their guests. Beware, however, of the per-minute rates charged. Alternatively, you may want to buy a basic pay-as-you-go phone for around £10.

Contacts Carphone Warehouse.
☎ *0800/049–6250* ⊕ *www.carphoneware-house.com.* **Cellular Abroad.** ☎ *800/287–5072* ⊕ *www.cellularabroad.com.* **Mobal.** ☎ *888/888–9162* ⊕ *www.mobal.com.* **Planet Fone.** ☎ *888/988–4777* ⊕ *www.planetfone.com.*

CUSTOMS AND DUTIES

You're always allowed to bring goods of a certain value back home without having to pay any duty or import tax. But there's a limit on the amount of tobacco and liquor you can bring back duty-free, and some countries have separate limits for perfumes; for exact figures, check with your customs department. The values of so-called duty-free goods are included in these amounts. When you shop abroad, save all your receipts, as customs inspectors may ask to see them as well as the items you purchased. If the total value of your goods is more than the duty-free limit, you'll have to pay a tax (most often a flat percentage) on the value of everything beyond that limit.

Fresh meats, plants and vegetables, controlled drugs, and firearms (including replicas) and ammunition may not be brought into the United Kingdom, nor can dairy products from non-EU countries. Pets from the United States with the proper documentation may be brought into the country without quarantine under the U.K. Pet Travel Scheme (PETS). The process takes about four months to complete and involves detailed steps.

You'll face no customs formalities if you enter Scotland or Wales from any other part of the United Kingdom.

EATING OUT

The stereotypical notion of British meals as parades of roast beef, overcooked vegetables, and stodgy desserts has largely been replaced—particularly in London, other major cities, and some country hot spots—with an evolving picture of the country as foodie territory. From trendy gastro-pubs to interesting ethnic-fusion restaurants to see-and-be-seen dining shrines, English food is now known for an innovative take on traditional dishes, with an emphasis on the local and seasonal. In less cosmopolitan areas, though, you're still looking at lots of offerings that are either stodgy, fried, sausages, or Indian.

In general, restaurant prices are high. If you're watching your budget, seek out pubs and ethnic restaurants.

DISCOUNTS AND DEALS

Eating out in Britain's big cities in particular can be expensive, but you can do it cheaply. Try local cafés, more popularly known as "caffs," where heaping plates of British comfort food (bacon sandwiches and stuffed baked potatoes, for example) are served. Britain has plenty of the big names in fast food, as well as smaller places selling sandwiches, fish-and-chips, burgers, falafels, kebabs, and the like. For a local touch, check out Indian restaurants, which are found almost everywhere. Marks & Spencer, Sainsbury's, Morrison's, Tesco, Lidl, Aldi, and Waitrose are chain supermarkets with outlets throughout the country. They're good choices for groceries, premade sandwiches, or picnic fixings.

MEALS AND MEALTIMES

Cafés serving the traditional English breakfast (called a "fry-up") of eggs, bacon, sausage, beans, mushrooms, half a grilled tomato, toast, and strong tea are often the cheapest—and most authentic—places for breakfast. For lighter morning fare (or for real brewed coffee), try the Continental-style sandwich bars and coffee shops—the Pret-a-Manger chain being one of the largest—offering croissants and other pastries. In London, the Leon chain offers healthy alternatives.

At lunch you can grab a sandwich between sights, pop into the local pub, or sit down in a restaurant. Dinner, too, has no set rules, but a three-course meal is standard in most mid-range or high-end restaurants. Pre- or post-theater menus, offering two or three courses for a set price, are usually a good value.

Note that most traditional pubs don't have any waitstaff and you're expected to go to the bar to order a beverage and your meal. Also, in cities many pubs don't serve food after 3 pm, so they're usually a better lunch option than dinner, unless they're gastro-pubs. In rural areas it's not uncommon for pubs to stop serving lunch after 2:30 and dinner after 9 pm.

Breakfast is generally served between 7:30 and 9, lunch between noon and 2, and dinner or supper between 7:30 and 9:30—sometimes earlier and seldom later except in large cities and tourist areas. These days high tea is rarely a proper meal anymore (it was once served between 4:30 and 6), and tearooms are often open all day in touristy areas (they're not found at all in nontouristy places). So you can have a cup and pastry or sandwich whenever you feel you need it. Sunday roasts at pubs last from 11 am or noon to 3 pm.

Smoking is banned in pubs, clubs, and restaurants throughout Britain.

PAYING

Credit cards are widely accepted in restaurants and pubs, though some require a minimum charge of around £10. Be sure that you don't double-pay a service charge. Many restaurants exclude service charges from the printed menu (which the law obliges them to display outside), and then add 10% to 15% to the check. Others will stamp "Service not included" along the bottom of the bill, in which case you should add 10% to 15%. You can also add to the included charge if the service was particularly good. Cash is always appreciated, as it's more likely to go to the specific waiter.

PUBS

A common misconception among visitors to Britain is that pubs are simply bars. Pubs are also community gathering places and even restaurants. In many pubs the social interaction is as important as the alcohol. Pubs are, generally speaking, where people go to meet their friends and catch up on one another's lives. In small towns pubs act almost as town halls. Traditionally pub hours are 11–11, with last orders called about 20 minutes before closing time, but pubs can apply for a license to stay open until midnight or 1 am, or later.

Though to travelers it may appear that there's a pub on almost every corner, in fact pubs are something of an endangered species, closing at a rate of 29 a week (as of 2017), with independent, nonchain pubs in smaller localities at particular risk.

Most pubs tend to be child-friendly, but others have restricted hours for children. If a pub serves food, it'll generally allow children in during the day with adults. Some pubs are stricter than others, though, and won't admit anyone younger than 18. Some will allow children in during the day, but only until 6 pm. Family-friendly pubs tend to be packed with kids, parents, and all of their accoutrements.

RESERVATIONS AND DRESS

Regardless of where you are, it's a good idea to make a reservation if you can. For popular restaurants, book as far ahead as you can (often 30 days), and reconfirm as soon as you arrive. (Large parties should always call ahead to check the reservations policy.) We mention dress only when men are required to wear a jacket or a jacket and tie.

Online reservation services aren't as popular in Britain as in the United States, but Open Table and Square Meal have a fair number of listings in Britain.

Contacts ChariTable. ☎ *0330/055–3747* ⊕ *www.charitablebookings.com*. **Open Table.** ✉ *0207/299–2949* ⊕ *www.opentable.co.uk*. **Square Meal.** ☎ *0207/582–0222* ⊕ *www. squaremeal.co.uk*.

WINES, BEER, AND SPIRITS

Although hundreds of varieties of beer are brewed around the country, the traditional brew is known as bitter and isn't carbonated; it's usually served at room temperature. Fizzy American-style beer is called lager. There are also plenty of other alternatives: stouts like Guinness and Murphy's are thick, pitch-black brews you'll either love or hate; ciders, made from apples, are alcoholic in Britain (Bulmer's and Strongbow are the big names, but look out for local microbrews); shandies are a low-alcohol mix of lager and lemon soda. Real ales, which have a natural second fermentation in the cask, have a shorter shelf life (so many are brewed locally) but special flavor; these are worth seeking out. Craft beers are also taking off, especially in cities. Generally, the selection and quality of cocktails is higher in a wine bar or café than in a pub. The legal drinking age is 18.

You can order Scotland's most famous beverage—whisky (most definitely spelled without an *e*)—at any local pub. All pubs serve single-malt and blended whiskies. It's also possible to tour numerous distilleries, where you can sample a dram and purchase a bottle. Most distilleries are concentrated in Speyside and Islay, but there are notable ones on Orkney and Skye. In recent years a new breed of craft gin producers have opened stills, many producing small batches of botanically infused tipples and offering tours, tastings, and lessons.

▌ ELECTRICITY

The electrical current in Great Britain is 220–240 volts (in line with the rest of Europe), 50 cycles alternating current (AC); wall outlets take three-pin plugs, and shaver sockets take two round, oversize prongs. British bathrooms aren't permitted to have 220–240 volt outlets in them. Consider making a small investment in a universal adapter, which has several types of plugs in one lightweight, compact unit. Most laptops and mobile phone chargers are dual voltage (i.e., they operate equally well on 110 and 220 volts), so require only an adapter. These days the same is true of small appliances such as hair dryers. Always check labels and manufacturer instructions. Don't use 110-volt outlets marked "For shavers only" for high-wattage appliances such as hair dryers.

▌ EMERGENCIES

If you need to report an emergency, dial 999 for police, fire, or ambulance. Be prepared to give the telephone number you're calling from. For nonurgent police calls, such as reporting a stolen car, dial 101. You can get 24-hour treatment in Accident and Emergency at British hospitals, although you may have to wait hours for treatment. Prescriptions are valid only if made out by doctors registered in the United Kingdom.

Although Britain has a subsidized National Health Service, free at the point of service for British residents, foreign visitors are expected to pay for any treatment they receive. Expect to receive a bill after you return home. Check with your health-insurance company to make sure you're covered. Some British hospitals now require a credit card or other payment before they'll offer treatment.

U.S. Embassies American Embassy. ✉ *33 Nine Elms La., London* ☎ *0207/499–9000* ⊕ *uk. usembassy.gov*. **U.S. Passport Unit.** ✉ *33 Nine Elms La., London* ☎ *0207/499–9000* ⊕ *uk. usembassy.gov*.

▌ HEALTH

If you take prescription drugs, keep a supply in your carry-on luggage and make a list of all your prescriptions to keep on file at home while you're abroad. You won't be able to renew a U.S. prescription at a pharmacy in Britain. Prescriptions are accepted only if issued by a U.K.-registered physician.

If you're traveling in the Highlands and islands in summer, pack some midge repellent and antihistamine cream to reduce swelling: the Highland midge is a force to be reckoned with. Check ⊕ *www.smidgeup.com/midge-forecast* for updates on these biting pests.

OVER-THE-COUNTER REMEDIES

Over-the-counter medications in Britain are similar to those in the United States, with a few significant differences. Medications are sold in boxes rather than bottles, and are sold in small amounts—usually no more than 24 pills. There may also be fewer brands. All headache medicine is usually filed under "painkillers." You can buy generic ibuprofen or a popular European brand of ibuprofen, Nurofen. Tylenol isn't sold in the United Kingdom, although its main ingredient, acetaminophen, is found in brands like Panadol.

Among sinus and allergy medicines, Clarityn is the main option here; it's spelled slightly differently but is the same brand sold in the United States. Some medicines are pretty much the same as brands sold in the United States—instead of Nyquil cold medicine, there's Sudafed or Lemsip. The most popular over-the-counter cough medicine is Benylin.

Drugstores are generally called pharmacies, but sometimes referred to as chemists' shops. The biggest drugstore chain in the country is Boots, which has outlets everywhere, except for the smallest towns. If you're in a rural area, look for shops marked with a sign of a green cross.

If you can't find what you want, ask at the counter; many over-the-counter medicines are kept behind the register.

SHOTS AND MEDICATIONS

No special shots are required or suggested for Great Britain.

▌HOURS OF OPERATION

In big cities, most banks are open weekdays from 9 until 4 or 5. Some are open until 7, and many are open Saturday morning until 1 and some until 4. In smaller towns, hours are 9:30 to 3:30. Saturday hours are 10 to 2, if they're open at all. However, bank branches are being replaced by ATMs and are harder to find. Normal office hours for most businesses are weekdays 9 to 5.

The major national museums and galleries are open daily 9–6, including lunchtime, but have shorter hours on Sunday. Regional museums are usually closed Monday and have shorter hours in winter. In London many museums are open late one evening a week.

Independently owned pharmacies are generally open Monday through Saturday 9:30–5:30, although in larger cities some stay open until 10 pm; local newspapers list which pharmacies are open late.

Usual retail business hours are Monday through Saturday 9–5:30 or 10–6:30, Sunday noon–4. In some small villages shops may close at 1 pm once a week, often Wednesday or Thursday. They may also close for lunch and not open on Sunday at all. In large cities—especially London—department stores stay open late (usually until 7:30 or 8) one night a week, usually Thursday. On national holidays most stores are closed, and over the Christmas holidays most restaurants are closed as well.

HOLIDAYS

In England and Wales, holidays are January 1, New Year's Day; Good Friday and Easter Monday; May Day (first Monday in May); spring and summer bank holidays (last Monday in May and August, respectively); December 25, Christmas Day; and December 26, Boxing Day (day after Christmas). If these holidays fall on a weekend, the holiday is observed on the following Monday. During the Christmas holidays many restaurants, as well as museums and other attractions, may close for at least a week—call to verify hours. Book hotels for Christmas travel well in advance, and check whether the hotel restaurant will be open.

The following days are public holidays in Scotland; note that the dates for England and Wales are slightly different. Ne'er Day and a day to recover (January 1–2), Good Friday, May Day (first Monday in May), Spring Bank Holiday (last Monday in May), Summer Bank Holiday (first Monday in August), St. Andrews Day (November 30; for Scots government but optional for businesses), and Christmas (December 25–26).

▌MAIL

Stamps can be bought from post offices (hours vary according to branch, but usual opening hours are weekdays 9–5:30, with some closing early one day a week, especially in smaller towns, and Saturday 9–noon), from stamp machines outside post offices, and from newsagents. Some post offices are located within supermarkets or general stores. Specialized shipping shops like Mail Boxes Etc. also sell stamps. Mailboxes, known as post or letter boxes, are painted bright red. Allow 7 days for a letter to reach the United States and about 10 days to two weeks to Australia or New Zealand. The useful Royal Mail website has information on everything from buying stamps to finding a post office.

As of this writing, airmail letters up to 20 grams (0.75 ounce) to North America cost £1.17. Letters within Britain weighing up to 100 grams (3.5 ounces) are 65p for first class, 56p for second class. Rates for envelopes larger than 353 mm (13.9 inches) long, 250 mm (9.84 inches) wide, and 25 mm (1 inch) deep are higher. You can find prices and print postage on the Royal Mail website.

Contact Royal Mail. ☎ 03457/740740 ⊕ www.royalmail.com.

SHIPPING PACKAGES

Most department stores and retail outlets can ship your goods home. You should check your insurance for coverage of possible damage. Private delivery companies such as Federal Express and DHL offer two-day delivery service to the United States, but you'll pay a considerable amount for the privilege.

Express Services DHL. ☎ 0844/248-0844 ⊕ www.dhl.co.uk. **Federal Express.** ☎ 0345/600-0068 ⊕ www.fedex.com/gb. **Mail Boxes Etc.** ☎ 0800/623123 ⊕ www.mbe.co.uk. **Parcelforce.** ☎ 0344/800-4466 ⊕ www.parcelforce.com. **UPS.** ☎ 0345/787-7877 ⊕ www.ups.com.

▌MONEY

Prices in England can seem high because of the exchange rate. London remains one of the most expensive cities in the world. But for every yin there's a yang, and travelers can get breaks: staying in bed-and-breakfasts or renting a city apartment brings down lodging costs, and national museums are free.

Prices throughout this guide are given for adults. Substantially reduced fees—generally referred to as "concessions" throughout Great Britain—are almost always available for children, students, and senior citizens.

▌**TIP→** Banks have limited amounts of foreign currencies on hand, and it may take as long as a week to order. If you're planning to exchange funds before leaving home, don't wait until the last minute.

ATMS AND BANKS

Make sure before leaving home that your credit and debit cards have been programmed for ATM use abroad—ATMs in England and Wales accept PINs of four or fewer digits only. If you know your PIN as a word, learn the numerical equivalent, since most keypads in England show numbers only, not letters. Most ATMs are on both the Cirrus and Plus networks. ATMs are available at most main-street banks, large supermarkets such as Sainsbury's and Tesco, some Tube stops in London, and many gas and rail stations. Major banks include Barclays, HSBC, and NatWest.

Your own bank will probably charge a fee for using ATMs abroad (unless you use your bank's British partner); the foreign bank you use may also charge a fee. Nevertheless, you'll usually get a better rate of exchange at an ATM than you will at a currency-exchange office or even when changing money in a bank. And extracting funds as you need them is a safer option than carrying around a large amount of cash.

CREDIT CARDS

The Discover card isn't accepted throughout Britain. Other major credit cards, except Diners Club and American Express, are accepted virtually everywhere in Britain; if your card is equipped for contactless "tap and go" payment you can use it in shops and restaurants for purchases under £30. However, if your card doesn't support it or if you're spending over that amount, you'll be expected to know and use your pin number—even for credit cards. So it's a good idea to do some quick memorization for whichever card you intend to use in England.

Inform your credit-card company before you travel, especially if you're going abroad and don't travel internationally very often. Otherwise, the credit-card company might put a hold on your card owing to unusual activity. Record all your credit-card numbers in a safe place. Both MasterCard and Visa have general numbers you can call (collect if you're abroad) if your card is lost, but you're better off calling the number of your issuing bank, since MasterCard and Visa usually just transfer you to your bank; your bank's number is usually printed on your card.

If you plan to use your credit card for cash advances, you'll need to apply for a PIN at least two weeks before your trip. Although it's usually cheaper (and safer) to use a credit card abroad for large purchases (so you can cancel payments or be reimbursed if there's a problem), note that some credit-card companies *and* the banks that issue them add substantial percentages to all foreign transactions, whether they're in a foreign currency or not. Check on these fees before traveling.

CURRENCY AND EXCHANGE

The unit of currency in Great Britain is the pound sterling (£), divided into 100 pence (p). The bills (called notes in Britain) are 50, 20, 10, and 5 pounds. Coins are £2, £1, 50p, 20p, 10p, 5p, 2p, and 1p. If you're traveling beyond England and Wales, note that Scotland and the Channel Islands have their own bills, and the Channel Islands their own coins, too. Scottish bills are accepted (often reluctantly) in the rest of Britain, but you can't use Channel Islands currency outside the islands.

At the time of this writing, the exchange rate was about U.S. $1.41 to £1.

British post offices exchange currency with no fee, and at decent rates.

■TIP→ Even if a currency-exchange booth has a sign promising no commission, rest assured that there's some kind of huge, hidden fee. And as for rates, you're almost always better off getting foreign currency at an ATM or exchanging money at a bank. XE.com, Oanda.com, and Currency have popular conversion apps that are available for both Android and iPhone.

▌PACKING

Britain can be cool, damp, and overcast, even in summer. You'll want a heavy coat for winter and a lightweight coat or warm jacket for summer. There's no time of year when a raincoat or umbrella won't come in handy. For the cities, pack as you would for an American city: coats and ties for expensive restaurants and nightspots, casual clothes elsewhere. If you plan to stay in budget hotels, take your own soap.

It's also a good idea to take a washcloth. Pack insect repellent if you plan to hike.

Some visitors to Scotland appear to think it necessary to adopt Scottish dress. It's not unless you've been invited to a wedding, and even then it's optional. Scots themselves do not wear tartan ties or Balmoral "bunnets" (caps), and only an enthusiastic minority prefers the kilt for everyday wear.

▌ PASSPORTS

U.S. citizens need only a valid passport to enter Great Britain for stays of up to six months. Travelers should be prepared to show sufficient funds to support and accommodate themselves while in Britain (credit cards will usually suffice for this) and to show a return or onward ticket. If you're within six months of your passport's expiration date, renew it before you leave—nearly expired passports aren't strictly banned, but they make immigration officials anxious, and may cause you problems. Health certificates aren't required.

▌ RESTROOMS

Public restrooms are sparse in Britain, although most big cities maintain limited public facilities that are clean and modern. Train stations and department stores have public restrooms that occasionally charge a small fee, usually 30p. Most pubs, restaurants, and even fast-food chains reserve their bathrooms for customers. Hotels and museums are usually a good place to find clean, free facilities. On the road, gas-station facilities are usually clean and free.

▌ SAFETY

Britain has a low incidence of violent crime. However, petty crime, mostly in urban areas, is on the rise, and tourists can be the targets. Use common sense: when in a city center, if you're paying at a shop or a restaurant, never put your wallet down or let your bag out of your hand. When sitting on a chair in a public place, keep your purse on your lap or between your feet. Don't wear expensive jewelry or watches, and don't flash fancy smart phones on the street in London, where there have been snatchings by moped-riding thieves. Store your passport in the hotel safe, and keep a copy with you. Don't leave anything in your car.

Although scams do occur in Britain, they aren't pervasive. If you're getting money out of an ATM, beware of someone bumping into you to distract you. You may want to use ATMs inside banks rather than those outside them. In London scams are most common at ATMs near tourist meccas like Oxford Street and Piccadilly Circus. Watch out for pickpockets, particularly in London. They often work in pairs, one distracting you in some way.

Always take a licensed black taxi or call a car service (sometimes called minicabs) recommended by your hotel. Avoid drivers who approach you on the street, as in most cases they'll overcharge you. As of this writing, Uber is still operating in London while its legal situation is resolved. Always buy theater tickets from a reputable dealer. If you're driving in from a British port, beware of thieves posing as customs officials who try to "confiscate illegal goods."

While traveling, don't leave any bags unattended, as they may be viewed as a security risk and destroyed by the authorities. If you see an unattended bag on the train, bus, or Tube, find a worker and report it. Never hesitate to get off a Tube, train, or bus if you feel unsafe.

▌TIP➜ Distribute your cash, credit cards, IDs, and other valuables between a deep front pocket, an inside jacket or vest pocket, and a hidden money pouch. Don't reach for the money pouch once you're in public.

General Information and Warnings Transportation Security Administration (TSA). ☎ 855/787–2227 ⊕ www.tsa.gov. **U.K. Foreign**

& Commonwealth Office. ☎ *0207/008–1500* ⊕ *www.gov.uk/foreign-travel-advice.* **U.S. Department of State.** ☎ *888/407–4747 traveler hotline, 202/501–4444 from outside the U.S.* ⊕ *www.state.gov/travel.*

■ SIGHTSEEING PASSES

DISCOUNT PASSES

If you plan to visit castles, gardens, and historic houses during your stay in Britain, look into discount passes or memberships that offer significant savings. Just be sure to match what the pass or membership offers against your itinerary to see if it's worthwhile.

The National Trust, English Heritage, and the Historic Houses Association each encompass hundreds of properties. English Heritage's Overseas Visitors Pass costs £31 for a 9-day pass and £37 for a 16-day pass for one adult. You can order it in advance by phone or online, or purchase it at a participating property in England. The National Trust Touring Pass, for overseas visitors, must be purchased in advance, either by phone or online. A 7-day pass is £31; a 14-day pass is £36.

The London Pass gets you into more than 60 attractions and tours in the capital at a considerable saving, and can help you bypass some queues. Packages range from one day (£62.10) to six days (£129.60). There is a similar pass for Yorkshire that gains discounted entrance to 30 attractions and costs from £38 for one day to £65 for three days. Annual membership in the National Trust (through the Royal Oak Foundation, the U.S. affiliate) is $80 a year. English Heritage membership is £54, and the Historic Houses Association is £55. Memberships entitle you to free entry to properties.

The Explorer Pass, available from any staffed Historic Scotland (HS) property and from many tourist information centers, allows visits to HS properties for 3 days in a 5-day period (£31) or 7 days in a 14-day period (£42). The Discover Scotland pass is available for 3 days (£27),

7 days (£32), or 14 days (£37) and allows access to all National Trust for Scotland properties. It's available to overseas visitors only and can be purchased online and by phone, or at properties and some of the main tourist information centers.

Information English Heritage. ☎ *01761/452966 for online shop queries* ⊕ *www.english-heritage.org.uk.* **Historic Houses Association.** ☎ *01462/896688* ⊕ *www.hha.org.uk.* **Historic Scotland.** ☎ *0131/668–8600* ⊕ *www.historicenvironment.scot.* **London Pass.** ☎ *0207/293–0972* ⊕ *www.londonpass.com.* **National Trust.** ☎ *0344/800–2329 touring pass information line* ⊕ *www.nationaltrust.org.uk.* **National Trust for Scotland.** ☎ *0131/458–0303* ⊕ *www.nts.org.uk.* **Royal Oak Foundation.** ☎ *212/480–2889 in U.S* ⊕ *www.royal-oak.org.*

■ SPORTS AND THE OUTDOORS

VisitBritain and local Tourist Information Centres can recommend places to enjoy your favorite sport.

BIKING

The national body promoting cycle touring is the Cycling UK (£45 a year), which can organize cycling vacations. Members get free advice and route information and a magazine. Transport for London publishes maps of recommended routes across the capital, and British Cycling has online route maps of the United Kingdom.

Contacts British Cycling. ☎ *0161/274–2000* ⊕ *www.britishcycling.org.uk.* **Cycling UK.** ☎ *0844/736–8451* ⊕ *www.cyclinguk.org.*

BOATING

Boating—whether on bucolic rivers or industrial canals—can be a leisurely way to explore the English landscape. For boat-rental operators along Britain's several hundred miles of historic canals and waterways, from the Norfolk Broads to the Lake District, contact British Marine Inland Boating or Waterways Holidays. The Canal and River Trust has maps and other information. Waterways Holidays arranges boat accommodations from traditional narrow boats to wide-beam canal boats, motorboats, and sailboats.

Contacts British Marine Inland Boating. ☎ 01784/473377 ⊕ www.britishmarine.co.uk. **Canal and River Trust.** ☎ 0303/040–4040 ⊕ www.canalrivertrust.org.uk. **Waterways Holidays.** ☎ 01252/796400 ⊕ www.waterwaysholidays.com.

WALKING

Walking and hiking, from the slowest ramble to a challenging mountainside climb, are enormously popular in Britain. National Trails, funded by Natural England and the Countryside Counsel for Wales, has great resources online. The Ramblers, a well-known charitable organization promoting walking and care of footpaths, has helpful information, including a list of B&Bs close to selected long-distance footpaths. Some of the best maps for walking are the Explorer Maps, published by the Ordnance Survey.

Contacts National Trails. ⊕ www.nationaltrail.co.uk. **Ordnance Survey.** ⊕ www.ordnancesurvey.co.uk. **The Ramblers.** ☎ 0207/339–8500 ⊕ www.ramblers.org.uk.

▌ TAXES

Air Passenger Duty (APD) is a tax included in the price of your ticket. The U.K.'s APD fees, currently among the highest in the world, are divided into two bands: short-haul destinations under 2,000 miles, £13 per person in economy, £26 in all first and business class, and £78 (private jets with fewer than 19 seats); long-haul destinations over 2,000 miles (including the United States), £78 economy, £156 first and business class (£172 as of April 2019), and £468 (private jets with fewer than 19 seats).

The British sales tax (Value Added Tax, or V.A.T.) is 20%. The tax is almost always included in quoted prices in shops, hotels, and restaurants. The most common exception is at high-end hotels, where prices often exclude V.A.T. Outside of hotels and rental-car agencies, which have specific additional taxes, there's no other sales tax in England.

Refunds apply for V.A.T. only on goods being taken out of Britain. Many large stores provide a voluntary V.A.T.–refund service, but only if you request it. You must ask the store to complete Form V.A.T. 407, to be given to customs at departure along with a V.A.T. Tax Free Shopping scheme invoice. If no customs official is on duty, there will be a customs post box where you can leave your forms. Fill in the form at the shop, have the salesperson sign it, have it stamped by customs when you leave the country, then mail the stamped form to the shop or to a commercial refund company. Alternatively, you may be able to take the form to an airport refund-service counter after you're through passport control for an on-the-spot refund. There is an extra fee for this service, and lines tend to be long. ▌TIP➔ **You can only get V.A.T. refunds on goods bought in the last three months.**

Global Blue is a Europe-wide service with 270,000 affiliated stores. It has refund counters in the United Kingdom at Heathrow and Gatwick, at Harrods, in The City, Victoria, and Bloomsbury, and in the Westfield Shopping Centre. Outside London, counters are in Birmingham, Manchester, Oxford, and at Manchester airport. Its refund form, called a Tax Free Check, is the most common across the European continent. The service issues refunds in the form of cash, check, or credit-card adjustment. The latter is useful for small purchases as the cost of cashing a foreign-currency check may exceed the amount of the refund.

V.A.T. Refunds Global Blue. ☎ 866/706–6090 in U.S., 800/3211–1111 in U.K. ⊕ www.globalblue.com. **HM Revenue and Customs.** ☎ 0300/200–3700 ⊕ www.gov.uk/tax-on-shopping.

∎ TIME

England sets its clocks by Greenwich Mean Time, five hours ahead of the U.S. East Coast. British summer time (GMT plus one hour) generally coincides with American daylight saving time adjustments.

TIPPING GUIDELINES FOR ENGLAND	
Bartender	£1–£2 per round of drinks, depending on the number of drinks, except in pubs, where tipping isn't the custom
Bellhop	£1 per bag, depending on the level of the hotel
Hotel Concierge	£5 or more, if he or she performs a service for you
Hotel Doorman	£1 if he helps you get a cab
Hotel Maid/ Housekeeping	£2 per day
Hotel Room-Service Waiter	Same as a waiter, unless a service charge has been added to the bill
Porter at Airport or Train Station	£1 per bag
Taxi Driver	10p per pound of the fare, then round up to nearest pound
Tour Guide	Tipping optional: £1 or £2 is generous
Waiter	12.5%–15%, with 15% being the norm at high-end London restaurants; nothing additional if a service charge is added to the bill, unless you want to reward particularly good service. Tips in cash preferred
Other	Restroom attendants in more expensive restaurants expect some small change or £1. Tip coat-check personnel £1 unless there's a fee, then nothing. Hairdressers and barbers get 10%–15%

∎ TIPPING

Tipping is done in Britain just as in the United States, but at a lower level than you would back home, generally 12.5% to 15%. You can tip more if service was exceptional. The server is likely to get more if you leave cash (employers can deduct administrative costs if it's left as a service charge or on a credit card.) Don't tip bar staff in pubs—although you can always offer to buy them a drink. There's no need to tip at clubs (it's acceptable at posher establishments, though) unless you're being served at your table. Rounding up to the nearest pound or 50p is appreciated.

∎ TOURS

Visiting London on a fully escorted tour is unnecessary because of its extensive public transport and wide network of taxicabs. Many tour companies offer day tours to the main sights, and getting around is fairly easy.

If you're traveling beyond London, packaged tours can be very useful, particularly if you don't want to rent a car. Because many sights are off the beaten track and not accessible by public transportation—particularly castles, great houses, and small villages—tour groups make the country accessible to all. There are a few downsides to escorted tours: rooms in castles and medieval houses tend to be small and can feel overrun when tour groups roll in. And as on a cruise, your traveling companions are inescapable.

Dozens of companies offer fully guided tours in Britain. Most of these are full packages including lodging, food, and transportation costs in one flat fee. Do a bit of research before booking. You'll want to know about the hotels you'll be staying in, how big your group is likely to be, how your days will be structured, and who the other people are likely to be.

SPECIAL-INTEREST TOURS

CULINARY

Contact Culinary Vacations. ☎ *213/344–4290 in U.S.* ⊕ *www.bookculinaryvacations.com.*

GARDENS

Contacts Adderley Travel Ltd. ☎ *01953/606706* ⊕ *www.adderleytravel.com.* **Coopersmith's.** ☎ *415/669–1914 in U.S.* ⊕ *www.coopersmiths.com.* **Flora Garden Tours.** ☎ *01366/328946* ⊕ *www.flora-garden-tours.co.uk.*

GOLF TOURS

Scotland has fabulous golf courses; a tour can help enthusiasts make the most of their time. VisitScotland has a dedicated golf website with a list of tour companies.

Contacts Golf Scotland. ☎ *866/875–4653* ⊕ *www.golfscotland.com.* **Scotland for Golf.** ☎ *01334/611466* ⊕ *www.scotlandforgolf.co.uk.*

HIKING AND WALKING

Contacts Adventureline. ☎ *01209/820847* ⊕ *www.adventureline.co.uk.* **CW Adventures.** ☎ *800/234–6900 in U.S.* ⊕ *www.cwadventures.com.* **English Lakeland Ramblers.** ☎ *800/724–8801 in U.S.* ⊕ *www.ramblers.com.* **The Wayfarers.** ☎ *800/249–4620 in U.S.* ⊕ *www.thewayfarers.com.*

HISTORY

Contacts Classic England. ☎ *01277/841651 in U.K., 866/464–7389 toll-free in U.S.* ⊕ *www.classic-england.com.*

■ VISITOR INFORMATION

ONLINE TRAVEL TOOLS

GENERAL INFORMATION

All of Britain's regions, along with most major towns and cities, have their own dedicated tourism websites providing information. VisitBritain (⊕ *www.visitbritain.com*), the official visitor website, focuses on information most helpful to England-bound U.S. travelers, from practical information to money-saving deals; you can even find out about movie locations. The London visitor website (⊕ *www.visitlondon.com*) can help you book your accommodations.

SCOTLAND

VisitScotland is Scotland's official website and includes a number of special-interest sites on topics from golf to genealogy.

Historic Scotland cares (which is being renamed Historic Environment Scotland) for the more than 300 historic properties described on its site. The National Trust for Scotland has information about stately homes, gardens, and castles. Both offer sightseeing passes.

Contacts Historic Scotland. ⊕ *www.historicenvironment.scot.* **National Trust for Scotland.** ⊕ *www.nts.org.uk.* **VisitScotland.** ✉ *Princes Mall, 3 Princes St., Edinburgh* ☎ *0131/473–3868* ⊕ *www.visitscotland.com.*

HISTORIC SITES

The Royal Family has an official website with information about visiting royal homes and more. English Heritage, the National Trust, and VisitBritain all offer discount passes.

Contacts English Heritage. ☎ *0370/333–1181* ⊕ *www.english-heritage.org.uk.* **National Trust.** ☎ *0344/800–1895* ⊕ *www.nationaltrust.org.uk.* **The Royal Family.** ☎ *0207/930–4832* ⊕ *www.royal.uk.*

VISITOR INFORMATION OFFICES

In some towns there are local and regional tourist information centers; many have websites. Offices offer services ranging from discounts for local attractions to visitor guides, maps, parking information, and accommodation advice.

In the U.S. VisitBritain. ☎ *212/850–0336 in U.S., 0207/578–1000 in U.K.* ⊕ *www.visitbritain.com.*

INDEX

NOTES

ABOUT OUR WRITERS

Longtime contributor Robert Andrews updated the West Country chapter this edition.

Based in Dundee, Nick Bruno is a travel writer, journalist, and a Fodor's contributor for over a decade. For this edition, he updated Fife and Angus and contributed to Experience and Travel Smart.

Jo Caird is a travel and arts journalist who writes on theater, visual arts, film, literature, and food and drink. For this edition, she updated the Performing Arts section of the London chapter, as well as several neighborhoods.

A leading family travel expert, Manchester-based writer Rhonda Carrier writes for publications such as *National Geographic Traveller*, the *Guardian*, and *Condé Nast Traveller*. She updated Manchester, Liverpool, and the Peak District this edition.

Sally Coffey is a journalist who specializes in British travel and tourism. She updated our Stratford-upon-Avon and select towns in the Heart of England this edition.

Robin Gauldie is a freelance journalist specializing in travel and the tourism industry, and is the author of more than 30 travel guidebooks. Robin updated Aberdeen and the Northeast and Argyll and the Isles.

Mike Gonzalez is emeritus professor of Latin American Studies at Glasgow University and also writes regularly for the *Herald* and other publications on politics and culture. He updated Glasgow, the Borders and the Southwest, and the Central Highlands.

Writer and editor Kate Hughes acquired a liking for the big city when she studied classical literature in Liverpool. She is contributed to the Experience chapter this edition.

Sophie Ibbotson is a writer, entrepreneur, and lover of wild places, which means updating the Lake District chapter was right up her alley.

A Londoner since public transportation was cheap, Jack Jewers has directed films for the BBC and reviewed pubs for *Time Out*. He updated the Southeast, Thames Valley, East Anglia, and Northeast chapters.

Eilidh McCabe is an editor at travel writing agency World Words and is the short fiction editor of the *Glasgow Review of Books*. She updated the Inverness, Skye, and the Northern Highlands chapter for this edition.

James O'Neill loves London and—as his work updating several neighborhood sections for this edition proves—loves rediscovering it, too.

Having studied in London and never left—aside from a brief sojourn in Madrid—Toby Orton has experienced everything in the capital from Hackney to Notting Hill, Highgate to Peckham, and still finds it the most inspiring city in the world. He updated the London hotels this edition.

Joseph Reaney is an experienced travel writer and editor based part-time in Scotland and part-time in the Czech Republic—and regularly writes about both. This edition, he updated Edinburgh and the Northern Highlands and contributed to the Experience chapter.

Rachael Rowe lives and works in southwest England and has written various walking guides to Devon and Wiltshire. For this edition, she updated the Bath and Cotswolds chapter.

Ellin Stein has written for multiple publications on both sides of the Atlantic. For this edition, Ellin updated the South and Yorkshire chapters and contributed to Travel Smart. Her territory also included London shopping and several London neighborhoods.

Victoria Trott is a Wales based writer who updated the Wales chapter this edition.

London restaurant maven Alex Wijeratna is always amazed by the capital's rocket-fueled restaurant scene. Alex updated the Where to Eat and Nightlife sections of London.